THE OXFORD HANDBOOK OF
DIGITAL MEDIA SOCIOLOGY

THE OXFORD HANDBOOK OF

DIGITAL MEDIA SOCIOLOGY

Edited by
DEANA A. ROHLINGER *and* SARAH SOBIERAJ

OXFORD
UNIVERSITY PRESS

Oxford University Press is a department of the University of Oxford. It furthers
the University's objective of excellence in research, scholarship, and education
by publishing worldwide. Oxford is a registered trade mark of Oxford University
Press in the UK and certain other countries.

Published in the United States of America by Oxford University Press
198 Madison Avenue, New York, NY 10016, United States of America.

© Oxford University Press 2022

All rights reserved. No part of this publication may be reproduced, stored in
a retrieval system, or transmitted, in any form or by any means, without the
prior permission in writing of Oxford University Press, or as expressly permitted
by law, by license, or under terms agreed with the appropriate reproduction
rights organization. Inquiries concerning reproduction outside the scope of the
above should be sent to the Rights Department, Oxford University Press, at the
address above.

You must not circulate this work in any other form
and you must impose this same condition on any acquirer.

Library of Congress Control Number: 2022012633

ISBN 978-0-19-751063-6

DOI: 10.1093/oxfordhb/9780197510636.001.0001

1 3 5 7 9 8 6 4 2

Printed by Marquis, Canada

Contents

About the Editors — ix
About the Contributors — xi

When the Extraordinary Becomes Mundane: Digital Media and the Sociological Lens — 1
DEANA A. ROHLINGER AND SARAH SOBIERAJ

PART I. THEORETICAL EXPLORATIONS OF DIGITAL LIFE

1. Technology and Time — 9
   JUDY WAJCMAN

2. Media and the Social Construction of Reality — 27
   NICK COULDRY AND ANDREAS HEPP

3. Theorizing Curation — 40
   JENNY L. DAVIS

4. Affective Publics: Solidarity and Distance — 61
   ZIZI PAPACHARISSI

5. Big Data from the South(s): An Analytical Matrix to Investigate Data at the Margins — 76
   STEFANIA MILAN AND EMILIANO TRERÉ

PART II. DIGITAL MEDIA AND SOCIAL INSTITUTIONS

6. From "Impact" to "Negotiation": Educational Technologies and Inequality — 97
   CASSIDY PUCKETT AND MATTHEW H. RAFALOW

7. Journalism in the Age of Twitter ... 118
   STEPHEN R. BARNARD

8. Families, Relationships, and Technology ... 138
   RAELENE WILDING

9. Digital Religion ... 159
   STEF AUPERS AND LARS DE WILDT

10. Technology, Labor, and the Gig Economy ... 178
    JAMIE WOODCOCK

PART III. DIGITAL MEDIA IN EVERYDAY LIFE

11. The Sociology of Mobile Apps ... 197
    DEBORAH LUPTON

12. Folding and Friction: The Internet of Things and Everyday Life ... 219
    MURRAY GOULDEN

13. Negotiating Intimacy via Dating Websites and Apps: Digital Media in Everyday Life ... 241
    SHANTEL GABRIEAL BUGGS

14. Digital Pornography and Everyday Life ... 269
    JENNIFER A. JOHNSON

15. Use of Information and Communication Technologies among Older Adults: Usage Differences, Health-Related Impacts, and Future Needs ... 291
    ALEXANDER SEIFERT AND SHELIA R. COTTEN

16. The Sociology of Self-Tracking and Embodied Technologies: How Does Technology Engage Gendered, Raced, and Datafied Bodies? ... 316
    ELIZABETH WISSINGER

PART IV. DIGITAL MEDIA, COMMUNITY, AND IDENTITY

17. LGBTQ+ Communities and Digital Media ... 339
    BRADY ROBARDS, PAUL BYRON, AND SAB D'SOUZA

18. Facework on Social Media in China 362
    Xiaoli Tian and Qian Li

19. Video Games and Identity Formation in Contemporary Society 378
    Daniel Muriel

20. Fans and Fan Activism 394
    Thomas V. Maher

21. Trolls and Hacktivists: Political Mobilization from Online Communities 417
    Jessica L. Beyer

22. Networked Street Life 443
    Jeffrey Lane and Will Marler

PART V. SOCIAL INEQUALITIES IN THE DIGITAL LANDSCAPE

23. The Feminization of Social Media Labor 469
    Sophie Bishop and Brooke Erin Duffy

24. Electronic Waste and Environmental Justice 490
    David N. Pellow

25. Digital War: Mediatized Conflicts in Sociological Perspective 511
    Olga Boichak

26. Masculinity, Everyday Racism, and Gaming 528
    Stephanie M. Ortiz

27. Socioeconomic Inequalities and Digital Skills 548
    Matías Dodel

28. The Digital Production Gap in the Algorithmic Era 567
    Jen Schradie and Liam Bekirsky

PART VI. DIGITAL MEDIA, POWER, AND POLITICS

29. Detect, Document, and Debunk: Studying Media Manipulation and Disinformation 589
    Gabrielle Lim and Joan Donovan

30. Gender, Digital Toxicity, and Political Voice Online 614
    SARAH SOBIERAJ

31. Digital Media in Grassroots Anti-Corruption Mobilizations 644
    ALICE MATTONI

32. Digital Youth Politics 663
    JENNIFER EARL, SAM SCOVILL, AND ELLIOT RAMO

33. Transformations in American Political Participation 683
    DEANA A. ROHLINGER

Index 701

About the Editors

Deana A. Rohlinger is a professor of sociology at Florida State University with expertise in political participation, political change, and digital technologies. She is author of *Abortion Politics, Mass Media, and Social Movements in America* (Cambridge University Press, 2015) and *New Media and Society* (New York University Press, 2019) as well as dozens of research articles and book chapters that analyze topics as diverse as the kinds of claims individuals make in the emails they sent Jeb Bush about the Terri Schiavo case to collective identity processes in MoveOn.org and the Tea Party movement. Her most recent articles can be found in *Information, Communication & Society*, *Signs*, *Mobilization*, *New Media & Society*, and *Social Media + Society*. Rohlinger has co-edited three volumes, *Strategy in Action: Movements and Social Change* (University of Minnesota Press, 2012), *Research in Social Movements, Conflicts and Change: Media, Movements, and Political Change* (2012), and *Emerald Studies in Media and Communication: Social Movements and Mass Media* (2017); guest-edited issues of two journals (*Information, Communication & Society* in 2018 and the *American Behavioral Scientist* in 2009); served as the book review editor for the journal *Mobilization* (2012–2018); and was the editor of the section on social movements for *Sociology Compass* (2012–2015). Rohlinger chaired the American Sociological Association's Communication, Information Technologies and Media Sociology section (2018–2019) and is chair-elect for the Collective Behavior, Social Movements section. She has been interviewed on a range of topics including digital politics and controversies involving Planned Parenthood as well as written commentaries for a variety of media outlets including *U.S. News & World Report*, *Fortune*, *The American Prospect*, and *The Conversation*. Her body of research was recently honored with the 2021 William F. Ogburn Mid-Career Achievement Award from the Communications and Information Technologies and Media Sociology section of the American Sociological Association.

Sarah Sobieraj is a professor and chair of The Department of Sociology at Tufts University and a faculty associate with the Berkman Klein Center for Internet & Society at Harvard University. Her most recent book, *Credible Threat: Attacks Against Women Online and the Future of Democracy* (Oxford University Press, 2020), examines the impact of identity-based digital abuse on women's participation in social and political discourse. She is also the author of *The Outrage Industry: Political Opinion Media and the New Incivility* (Oxford University Press, 2014) with Jeff Berry and *Soundbitten: The Perils of Media-Centered Political Activism* (New York University Press, 2011). Sobieraj also edited (with Rob Boatright, Danna Young, and Tim Schaffer)

A Crisis of Civility: Political Discourse and Its Discontents (Routledge, 2019). Her most recent journal articles can be found in *Information, Communication & Society, Social Problems, PS: Political Science & Politics, Poetics, Political Communication,* and *Sociological Theory*. Her work has been featured in venues such as *The New York Times, The Washington Post, The Boston Globe, Politico, Vox, CNN, PBS, NPR, The American Prospect, National Review, The Atlantic, Pacific Standard,* and *Salon*. Sobieraj serves on the advisory board of the Social Science Research Council's Disinformation Research Mapping Initiative and is a member of the National Institute for Civil Discourse Research Network.

About the Contributors

Stef Aupers is a professor of media culture in the Department of Communication Sciences, Institute for Media Studies at KU Leuven. His research deals with the transformation and mediatization of Western culture, and he has published widely in international journals on topics such as digital religion, artificial intelligence in everyday life, online game culture, and conspiracy theories on the internet. His most recent book, edited with Dick Houtman and Rudi Laermans (KU Leuven) is *Science under Siege: Contesting the Secular Religion of Scientism* (Palgrave, 2021).

Stephen R. Barnard is an associate professor and chair of the Department of Sociology and Criminology at Butler University. His work focuses on the roles media and communication technologies play in relations of power, practice, and democracy. He is the author of *Citizens at the Gates: Twitter, Networked Publics, and the Transformation of American Journalism* and co-author of *All Media Are Social: Sociological Perspectives on Mass Media*. His scholarship has been published in *New Media & Society*, *Journalism*, *Cultural Studies ↔ Critical Methodologies*, *Hybrid Pedagogy*, and several edited volumes.

Liam Bekirsky is a doctoral student at the Oxford Internet Institute. His research interests are at the intersection of sociology and social network analysis, education, and knowledge building. Prior to joining the Oxford Internet Institute, Bekirsky completed a dual master's degree at Sciences Po Paris in digital and new technology and public policy and in global affairs at the University of Toronto. He is also trained and certified as a secondary school teacher. Outside of academia, he has worked in education policy at the Organisation for Economic Co-operation and Development's Centre for Educational Research and Innovation and at the Council of Ministers of Education, Canada.

Jessica L. Beyer is a lecturer in the Henry M. Jackson School of International Studies at the University of Washington, where she co-leads the Cybersecurity Initiative. Her research focuses on international cybersecurity politics, online communities, and dis/misinformation. Her past research explored political mobilization emerging from highly populated online communities and focused on actors such as Anonymous and other hacktivists, the Pirate Parties, and digital pirates. Her book *Expect Us: Online Communities and Political Mobilization* was published by Oxford University Press in 2014.

Sophie Bishop is a lecturer in cultural and creative industries at the University of Sheffield. Her research focuses on promotional cultures on social media platforms, through the lens of feminist political economy. Her current projects examine the use of paid targeted advertising by women and nonbinary creative practitioners. Her work has been published in journals such as *Social Media + Society*, *New Media & Society*, and *Feminist Media Studies*. She is the specialist advisor to the UK Parliamentary Inquiry into Influencer Culture.

Olga Boichak is a sociologist of media and culture and lecturer in digital cultures at the University of Sydney, Australia. She holds a master's of public administration and a PhD in social science from Syracuse University, and her research spans networks, narratives, and cultures of activism in the digital age. She is the editor of the *Digital War Journal*, and her work has appeared in *Big Data & Society*, *International Journal of Communication*, *Global Networks*, and *Media, War & Conflict*, among others.

Shantel Gabrieal Buggs is an assistant professor of sociology and African American studies at Florida State University. Her research focuses on race, gender, culture, intimacy, and digital life, employing a Black feminist and critical race theory approach. Her primary research agenda explores multiracial women's online dating experiences and conceptions of interracial relationships. She has published in a variety of academic outlets including: the *Journal of Marriage and Family*, *Sociology of Race and Ethnicity*, *Women's Studies International Forum*, and *Identities*. She also regularly contributes to the online platform for the feminist magazine *Bitch*. You can find her on Twitter at @sgbuggs.

Paul Byron is a postdoctoral researcher at the University of Technology Sydney, working in the discipline of digital and social media within the School of Communication. His current research focuses on LGBTQ+ young people's digital peer support practices in relation to mental health. He is author of *Digital Media, Friendship and Cultures of Care* (Routledge, 2021).

Shelia R. Cotten, a sociologist, is Provost's Distinguished Professor and the associate vice president for research development at Clemson University. Her areas of research focus on technology use across the life course and the health, quality of life, and workforce impacts of technology use. Her recent research has focused on the impacts of COVID-19 on technology access for older adults, autonomous vehicles, wearables, and digital overuse. She is a past chair of the American Sociological Association's Communication, Information Technologies, and Media Sociology section. Her research has been funded by the National Institutes of Health and the National Science Foundation, among others.

Nick Couldry is professor of media communications and social theory at the London School of Economics and Political Science, and since 2017 he has been a faculty associate at Harvard's Berkman Klein Center for Internet and Society. He is the author of more than 150 journal articles and book chapters and the author or editor of 15 books including *The Mediated Construction of Reality* (co-authored with Andreas Hepp; Polity, 2016), *The Costs of Connection* (co-authored with Ulises Mejias; Stanford University Press, 2019), *Media: Why It Matters* (Polity, 2019), and *Media, Voice, Space and Power* (Routledge, 2020).

Sab D'Souza is a research assistant at the University of Technology Sydney and a digital artist working on Gadigal land. Their work documents the emergent social media practices of marginalized users and the materiality of their (web)site-specific intimacies. They consider how users negotiate and challenge normative infrastructures of the internet.

Jenny L. Davis is a sociologist at the Australian National University (ANU). She works at the intersection of critical technology studies and social psychology. She runs the Role-Taking Lab at ANU, is a chief investigator for the Humanising Machine Intelligence project, and recently served as chair of the Communication, Information Technologies & Media Sociology section of the American Sociological Association. Davis is on Twitter @Jenny_L_Davis.

Lars de Wildt is postdoctoral researcher in media studies at KU Leuven, currently as part of the AHRC project "Everything Is Connected: Conspiracy Theories in the Age of the Internet." He has been a visiting scholar at Tampere University (and the Centre of Excellence in Game Culture Studies), the University of Montreal, and Deakin University in Melbourne. He studies how technologies change contemporary culture, including how online platforms changed conspiracy theories in a post-truth age and how video games changed religion in a post-secular age. For more, see larsdewildt.eu.

Matías Dodel (PhD) is an associate professor in the Department of Social Sciences at the Catholic University of Uruguay. He coordinates the Uruguayan chapters of international comparative internet studies such as the World Internet Project, the DiSTO project, and Global Kids Online. He has also for international and local organizations such as the United Nations International Children's Emergency Fund (UNICEF) and the Uruguayan E-government and Information Society Agency. His work can be found in several peer-reviewed journals such as *Computers in Human Behavior*, *Information, Communication & Society*, *Computers & Security*, and *Journal of Children and Media*. His research interests include digital inequalities, social stratification, digital safety, e-government, and cybercrime.

Joan Donovan is the research director for the Harvard Kennedy School's Shorenstein Center on Media, Politics and Public Policy. Dr. Donovan also heads The Technology and Social Change Project. She leads the field in examining internet and technology studies, online extremism, media manipulation, and disinformation campaigns. Her work can be found in multiple academic peer-reviewed journals, in books on data science and social media, and in popular media.

Brooke Erin Duffy, PhD, is an associate professor in the Department of Communication at Cornell University. Her areas of research include the cultures and economies of social media; gender and feminism; media and cultural production; and work, labor, and employment. She is the author of *(Not) Getting Paid to Do What You Love: Gender, Social Media, and Aspirational Work* (Yale University Press, 2017), *Remake, Remodel: Women's Magazines in the Digital Age* (University of Illinois Press, 2013), and *Platforms and Cultural Production*, with Thomas Poell and David Nieborg (Polity, 2022).

Jennifer Earl is a professor of sociology and (by courtesy) government and public policy at the University of Arizona. Her research focuses on social movements, information technologies, and the sociology of law, with research emphases on youth activism, internet activism, social movement repression, and legal change. She is the recipient of a National Science Foundation CAREER Award for research from 2006 to 2011 on web activism, was a member of the MacArthur Research Network on Youth and Participatory Politics, and co-authored, with Katrina Kimport, *Digitally Enabled Social Change* (MIT Press, 2011).

Murray Goulden is an assistant professor of sociology at the University of Nottingham, whose work explores the role of digital technologies in everyday life, particularly in the home and in the workplace. His specific focus is on the everyday mundane and how those practices and relationships are remade by—and how they remake—the technologies that we come into contact with.

Andreas Hepp is professor of media and communications and head of ZeMKI, Centre for Media, Communication and Information Research, University of Bremen, Germany. He has been a visiting researcher and professor at leading institutions such as the London School of Economics and Political Science, Goldsmiths University of London, Université Paris II Panthéon ASSAS, Stanford University, and others. He is the author of 12 monographs including *The Mediated Construction of Reality* (with Nick Couldry; Polity, 2017), *Transcultural Communication* (Wiley Blackwell, 2015), and *Cultures of Mediatization* (Polity, 2013). His latest book is *Deep Mediatization* (Routledge, 2020).

Jennifer A. Johnson is a professor and chair of the Department of Sociology, Virginia Tech. Her principal research interests include the sociology of pornography and digital sexual media, sexual and relationship health, social network analysis, gender and sexuality, and family. Johnson has published articles in *The Social Science Journal*, the *Journal of Sex & Marital Therapy*, and the *Journal of Health Communication*, among other journals.

Jeffrey Lane is an associate professor of communication (PhD Princeton University, sociology) at Rutgers University School of Communication & Information. He co-chairs the Rutgers Digital Ethnography Working Group and is the author of *The Digital Street* (Oxford University Press, 2018). He studies communication and technology as it relates to urban life, criminal justice, and social inequalities.

Qian Li is a PhD candidate in the Department of Sociology at the University of Hong Kong. Her research interests include media and culture, online fandom, and mediated interaction. She is working on her thesis about the online fandom of Chinese mobile game players and wants to explore how players generate meanings and identities through their gaming experiences, their online interaction, and the social–cultural structures in which they are embedded.

Gabrielle Lim is a researcher with the Technology and Social Change Project at Harvard Kennedy School's Shorenstein Center as well as a fellow at the Citizen Lab at the University of Toronto. Her research lies at the intersection of technology and security, with a focus on media manipulation, international relations, and civil society. You can learn more about her at gabriellelim.com.

Deborah Lupton is SHARP Professor in the Faculty of Arts, Design & Architecture, University of New South Wales (UNSW), Sydney, Australia. Her research is interdisciplinary, spanning sociology, communication, and cultural studies. She is located in the Centre for Social Research in Health and the Social Policy Research Centre, leading both the Vitalities Lab and the UNSW Node of the Australian Research Council Centre of Excellence for Automated Decision-Making and Society. She is an elected fellow of the Academy of the Social Sciences in Australia and holds an honorary doctor of social science degree awarded by the University of Copenhagen.

Thomas V. Maher is an assistant professor in the Sociology, Anthropology, and Criminal Justice Department at Clemson University. His research focuses on the intersection between social movements, organizations, and political sociology. He is primarily interested in how social movements and other non-institutional actors create change, who participates in these efforts, and how states and organizations sustain the status quo. He has published work on these issues in outlets such as *Mobilization*, *American Sociological Review*, and the *Journal of Peace Research*.

Will Marler is a postdoctoral research and teaching associate in the Department of Communication and Media Research at the University of Zurich. He is interested in how marginalized communities adapt digital technologies to meet their social and material needs. He has studied homelessness and social isolation among older adults through ethnography and survey studies.

Alice Mattoni is an associate professor in the Department of Political and Social Sciences at the University of Bologna and an adjunct professor at the School of Advanced International Studies of the Johns Hopkins University (Europe Campus). Her research focuses on the intersections between media—digital and otherwise—and social movements. She has published extensively on this topic, focusing on precarious workers' movements, environmental civil society actors, and anti-corruption grassroots initiatives. Since 2019, as principal investigator of the European Research Council–funded project BIT-ACT, she has investigated how movement organizations develop and employ digital media platforms to counter corruption across the world.

Stefania Milan (stefaniamilan.net) is associate professor of new media and digital culture at the University of Amsterdam and faculty associate at the Berkman Klein Center for Internet & Society, Harvard University. Her work explores the interplay between digital technology and data, political participation, and governance, with a focus on infrastructure and agency. Milan leads the project Citizenship and Standard-Setting in Digital Networks (in-sight.it), funded by the Dutch Research Council. She is also co-principal investigator in the Marie Skłodowska-Curie Innovative Training Network's Early Language Development in the Digital Age (e-ladda.eu). Among others, Milan is the author of *Social Movements and Their Technologies: Wiring Social Change*

(Palgrave Macmillan, 2013/2016), co-author of *Media/Society* (Sage, 2011), and co-editor of *COVID-19 from the Margins: Pandemic Invisibilities, Policies and Resistance in the Datafied Society* (Institute of Network Cultures, 2021).

Daniel Muriel holds a PhD in sociology from the University of the Basque Country. Muriel is an expert on identity, video game culture, leisure, digital technology, and cultural heritage. He has worked at universities across Spain, the United Kingdom, and Argentina and, more recently, has collaborated with public and private institutions to create and design art exhibitions and cultural events. He is author of *Identidad Gamer* (Anaitgames, 2021, 2nd ed.; 2018, 1st ed.) and co-author of *Video Games as Culture* (Routledge, 2018) and *Un mes en Tinder siendo mujer gamer* (Applehead, 2021). Website: https://danielmuriel.com/

Stephanie M. Ortiz is a sociologist at the University of Massachusetts at Lowell, where she examines everyday racism and sexism, with a particular focus on online spaces. Her work has been published in *New Media and Society*, *Social Problems*, and *Ethnic and Racial Studies*.

Zizi Papacharissi (PhD, University of Texas Austin, 2000) is professor and head of communication and a professor of political science at the University of Illinois Chicago. Papacharissi is the founding and current editor of the open-access journal *Social Media & Society*. She has published 10 books and over 80 journal articles in her research area of technology, democracy, and society.

David N. Pellow is the Dehlsen Chair and Professor of Environmental Studies and director of the Global Environmental Justice Project at the University of California, Santa Barbara. His teaching, research, and activism focus on environmental justice in the United States and globally. His books include *What Is Critical Environmental Justice?* (Polity, 2017), *The Slums of Aspen: Immigrants vs. the Environment in America's Eden* (with Lisa Sun-Hee Park; New York University Press, 2011), *The Silicon Valley of Dreams: Environmental Injustice, Immigrant Workers, and the High-Tech Global Economy* (with Lisa Sun-Hee Park; New York University Press, 2002), and *Garbage Wars: The Struggle for Environmental Justice in Chicago* (MIT Press, 2002). He has served on the boards of directors of Greenpeace USA and International Rivers.

Cassidy Puckett is an assistant professor of sociology at Emory University. Using a mixed-methods approach, she interrogates the relationship between technological change and inequality in education, occupations, and healthcare. Her first book, *Redefining Geek: Bias and the Five Hidden Habits of Tech-Savvy Teens* (University of Chicago Press, 2022), examines what it means to be tech-savvy in the digital age and how that shapes inequality. Her work appears in *Social Science and Medicine*, *Social Science Computer Review*, *Qualitative Sociology*, *Harvard Educational Review*, and *Teachers College Record*. Her research is funded by the US Department of Education, National Science Foundation, ACLS, and the MacArthur and Mellon Foundations.

Matthew H. Rafalow is a social scientist at Google and a senior researcher at Stanford University. He is author of the award-winning book *Digital Divisions: How Schools Create Inequality in the Tech Era* (University of Chicago Press, 2021) and co-author of *Affinity Online: How Connection and Shared Interests Fuel Learning* (New York University Press, 2018). His work has appeared in journals such as the *American Journal of Sociology*, *Symbolic Interaction*, and *Social Currents*.

Elliot Ramo is a PhD student at the University of Arizona School of Sociology. They study (ethical) artificial intelligence, information and knowledge, law, social control, and various intersections of data and social issues. Ramo is currently working on a project concerning the predictive power of policing technologies and is co-authoring a paper about conspiracy theory. Prior to graduate school, Ramo enjoyed a 7-year career in the business, insurance, and technology sectors. They are a queer, nonbinary, first-generation college student and advocate for disability justice.

Brady Robards is a senior lecturer in sociology at Monash University. Robards is a sociologist of youth and digital cultures, with a focus on how people use and produce social media. Robards has studied social media use among different groups, including young people, LGBTIQ+ people, tourists, and in the context of alcohol consumption. Robards's latest book is *Growing Up on Facebook* (with Sian Lincoln; Peter Lang, 2020). See bradyrobards.com and follow @bradyjay for more information.

Jen Schradie is a sociologist at the Observatoire sociologique du changement at Sciences Po in Paris. She graduated from the Harvard Kennedy School and received her PhD in sociology at the University of California (UC) Berkeley. Her research on digital democracy has been featured on CNN and the BBC and in the *New Yorker*, *Le Monde*, and *WIRED*, among others. She was awarded the UC Berkeley Public Sociology Alumni Prize, and her book *The Revolution That Wasn't: How Digital Activism Favors Conservatives* (Harvard University Press, 2019) won the Charles Tilly Distinguished Scholarship Award from the American Sociological Association. Follow on Twitter @schradie or the book at www.therevolutionthatwasnt.com.

Sam Scovill is a PhD candidate in the School of Sociology at the University of Arizona. Their research centers on young people's political imaginations and political participation. Their dissertation focuses on how young people ages 18–24 define politics, their political identities, how they think about significant political moments in their lives, and ultimately the development of their political imaginations.

Alexander Seifert, PhD in sociology, is senior researcher at the University of Applied Sciences and Arts Northwestern Switzerland. He is also division manager of the Research Department at the Centre of Competence for Gerontology at the University of Zurich (Switzerland). His research interests include social gerontology, technology use, and older adults' lifestyles.

Xiaoli Tian is associate professor in the Department of Sociology at the University of Hong Kong. She received her PhD in sociology from the University of Chicago. Her research interests include how preexisting knowledge paradigms and cultural norms influence the way people respond to unexpected transformations of their everyday routines. Her writings have been published in the *American Journal of Sociology, Sociological Forum, Qualitative Sociology, Modern China, Journal of Contemporary China, Information, Communication and Society, Journal of Contemporary Ethnography, Media, Culture and Society, Symbolic Interaction*, and the *Journal of Social and Personal Relationships*, among others.

Emiliano Treré is senior lecturer in media ecologies and social transformation in the School of Journalism, Media and Culture at Cardiff University, UK. He is a widely cited author in digital activism, social movement, and critical data studies with a special focus on the Global South. Treré has published more than 80 publications in six languages in peer-reviewed publications. He is one of the co-directors of the Data Justice Lab and the co-founder of the Big Data from the South initiative. His book *Hybrid Media Activism* (Routledge, 2019) won the Outstanding Book Award of the International Communication Association's Activism, Communication, and Social Justice Interest Group.

Judy Wajcman is the Anthony Giddens Professor of Sociology at the London School of Economics. She is also the principal investigator on the Women in Data Science and Artificial Intelligence project at the Alan Turing Institute. Her books include *The Social Shaping of Technology* (Open University Press, 1999), *TechnoFeminism* (Polity, 2004), *The Politics of Working Life* (Oxford University Press, 2005), and *Pressed for Time: The Acceleration of Life in Digital Capitalism* (University of Chicago Press, 2015), which was awarded the Fleck Prize by the Society for the Social Studies of Science.

Raelene Wilding is a sociologist at La Trobe University, Melbourne, Australia. Her research uses a variety of qualitative and co-design methods to explore the experiences and practices of young people and older adults from migrant and non-migrant backgrounds in Australia and beyond. Her current projects consider the role of digital media, virtual reality, and communication technologies in sustaining families, relationships, care, and well-being in local communities as well as across national borders and cultural boundaries. Wilding's recent publications include *Families, Intimacy and Globalization* (Palgrave, 2018).

Elizabeth Wissinger is a professor of fashion studies and sociology. She is a City University of New York faculty member in the Master of Arts in Liberal Studies program at the Graduate Center and the Department of Social Sciences at the Borough of Manhattan Community College. She has written, spoken, and published about fashion, technological embodiment, and biodesign, both in the United States and internationally.

Jamie Woodcock is a senior lecturer at the Open University and a researcher based in London. He is the author of *The Fight Against Platform Capitalism* (University of Westminster Press, 2021), *The Gig Economy* (Polity, 2019), *Marx at the Arcade* (Haymarket, 2019), and *Working the Phones* (Pluto, 2017). His research is inspired by workers' inquiry and focuses on labor, work, the gig economy, platforms, resistance, organizing, and video games. He is on the editorial board of *Notes from Below* and *Historical Materialism*.

WHEN THE EXTRAORDINARY BECOMES MUNDANE

Digital Media and the Sociological Lens

DEANA A. ROHLINGER AND SARAH SOBIERAJ

Many disciplines, from communications and cultural studies to computer science, attend carefully to the study of digital media. Considering the infinite ways our social worlds shape (and are shaped by) digital media, sociology as a discipline has been late to the party. While some sociologists, such as Ron Anderson, Ed Brent, Eszter Hargittai, James Katz, Alondra Nelson, Russell Neuman, John Robinson, Judy Wajcman, and Barry Wellman, have been sounding the call since the 1990s, these frontrunners were few and far between.

This is partially attributable to a waning in American media sociology from the late 1980s through the early 2000s that disincentivized conducting related research for graduate students and junior scholars (see, e.g., Katz 2009; Brienza and Revers 2016). During that period, the disciplinary climate remained relatively supportive of inquiries related to expressly political communications such as news or media work undertaken by social movements, but research on popular entertainment media was treated as frivolous and devalued by many. It is of little surprise, then, that even as new internet and communication technologies revealed themselves to be undeniably social, sociologists at the forefront turned outside the discipline to publish and find intellectual community.

Since then, many scholars have demanded and helped create space for sociological approaches to digital media, and for digital sociology more generally. Books devoted to digital sociology written and edited by scholars such as Tressie McMillan Cottom, Jessie Daniels, Karen Gregory, Deborah Lupton, Noortje Marres, Kate Orton-Johnson, Nick Prior, and Neil Selwyn have served as spaces to publish related work for a sociology audience and as inspiration for other researchers. Alongside this groundwork, there has been a marked increase in research on digital media. The volume at hand is an excellent point of entry for those eager to traverse the state of the field. Each chapter takes on a different topic, from digital warfare to dating apps; reviews the sociological work to date; and points to unanswered questions ripe for intervention.

In some ways, sociology's late arrival is well timed for a grand entrance—because digital media have become normal. This was not always true.

For a long time, lay discourse, pop culture narratives, pitches to investors, and advocacy groups constructed new information and communication technologies (ICTs) as exceptional. Whether they were seen as extraordinary because they were believed to be revolutionary, dangerous, rife with opportunity, or otherworldly, these tools and technologies were framed as abnormal. Many early academic characterizations were similarly exceptionalist, tending toward digital dualism, and heavily utopian or dystopian. But digital media are now mundane, thoroughly embedded—and often unquestioned—in everyday life. Smartphones are as important to grandparents as they are to teens, our data trails shape markets and politics, and platform affordances shape everything from pedagogy to the public sphere. Digital ICTs are enmeshed in health and wellness, work and organizations, elections, capital flows, intimate relationships, social movements, and even our own identities. In many ways, we have come to take them for granted.

And although the study of these technologies has always been interdisciplinary—at the crossroads of computer science, cultural studies, science and technology studies, and communications—never has a sociological perspective been more valuable. Sociology excels at helping us re-see the normal. There is still much to learn, and we hope this handbook will inspire new sociological work.

OVERVIEW OF THE VOLUME

The volume begins by exploring the theoretical contributions sociologists make to conceptualizations of the digital self, digital economy, and digital society. Judy Wajcman, for example, challenges current theoretical accounts of time, arguing that the experience of time is best understood through a sociological lens (Chapter 1). She posits that the experience of time is structured by social institutions and varies across social cleavages. Power dynamics, in short, affect how an individual or group experiences time. Jenny L. Davis makes a similar point, noting that social processes, such as that of curation, can be used to understand power, or how information flows (Chapter 3). Stefania Milan and Emiliano Treré extend this observation and outline how power as expressed through datafication negatively affects those at the margins of society such as refugees, racialized individuals, gig workers, and citizens of authoritative regimes (Chapter 5). The authors present an analytical matrix for identifying non-mainstream data vulnerabilities, which they call "data at the margins," and three lenses through which power, poverty, and inequality might be better understood.

The second section of the volume unpacks how digital media affect key social institutions, including education, mass media, family, religion, and work. The contributions in this section highlight how digital media reinforce—and create new forms of—inequality. For instance, Cassidy Puckett and Matthew Rafalow argue that sociologists should focus less on the relative impact of technology use in schools and more on how technology use can shape and be shaped by existing inequalities (Chapter 6). This, they posit, shifts the emphasis away from research that assesses the ability of educational technologies to increase school efficiency and focuses more squarely on how educational technologies reinforce processes of social stratification. Similarly, Raelene Wilding argues that sociologists cannot understand the effects of digital media on family without contextualizing familial practices in global social forces, such as changing gender roles and migration, that simultaneously reinforce existing inequalities and create new asymmetries in power (Chapter 8). Jamie Woodcock rounds out the section, suggesting that sociologists look to history to better understand how technology, labor, and the gig economy interact to produce different outcomes for workers (Chapter 10). One way to do so, he argues, is to focus on how the structure of and organizational practices associated with a platform, as well as the social and political contexts informing its creation, influence gig work.

The section on digital media in everyday life explores how these technologies have become integral to our most basic routines. Deborah Lupton uses multiple theoretical lenses to draw out the sociocultural and political dimensions of the mobile apps woven into our daily practices (Chapter 11). Similarly, Elizabeth Wissinger shows the way social inequalities and power dynamics are embedded in wearable technologies (Chapter 16). Other contributions show that digital media are now part of even our most intimate social interactions. In her chapter, for instance, Shantel Buggs outlines how online spaces and dating apps are critical to members of marginalized groups seeking to minimize discriminatory interactions as they pursue romance and sexual fulfillment (Chapter 13).

The fourth section of the volume addresses how digital media change our understandings of community and identity. Some of the chapters problematize hegemonic understandings of community, which largely reflect White, Anglo, and heterosexual perspectives. Brady Robards, Paul Byron, and Sab D'Souza, for example, argue that LGBTQ+ individuals' digital media use varies cross-nationally, reflecting the local customs, legal frameworks, and cultural norms of those using the technologies (Chapter 17). Xiaoli Tian and Qian Li extend this insight, exploring how "face" is given and maintained on- and offline in China (Chapter 18). They argue that while "face" is universally relevant, it is particularly salient in Chinese society because of its hierarchical social structure and its emphasis on mutual dependence and collaboration. As such, they show that developing rules around giving and maintaining face in different virtual settings is a cultural priority. Other contributions highlight how digital identities and communities can provide a framework for political participation. Thomas Maher's exploration of fan communities shows how participants use digital technologies to mobilize pressure on producers and shape the representations that emerge (Chapter 20). Not all political engagement, however, benefits a society writ large. Jessica Beyer explains how digital platforms such as 4chan were used to create identities that valued disruption, using racism, sexism, and anti-immigrnt rhetoric, among others, to mobilize their communities to engage in everything from voting to attending alt-right rallies (Chapter 21).

The next section is dedicated to the role of digital media in the (re)production of social inequality. David Pellow examines electronic waste, and e-waste trading and processing, from an environmental justice perspective (Chapter 24). He uses recycling as a powerful illustration of "slow violence," showing how the economics of e-waste have shifted, making them, to some degree, less exploitative of poorer nations over time. Matias Dodel also employs a global perspective to explore how digital skills (or lack thereof) reinforce inequality within and across national contexts (Chapter 27). Other contributors address the way digital media reinforce inequality at the intersections of gender, race, ethnicity, sexuality, and class. Sophie Bishop and Brooke Erin Duffy show the way gender inequality shapes the labor in the context of social media (Chapter 23). Many tasks performed online, for instance, are denigrated as "women's work," and subsequently devalued. Stephanie Ortiz centers whiteness and masculinity in gaming, arguing that sociologists can only understand inequality in virtual settings using intersectional and interactional approaches (Chapter 26).

The final section of the volume probes the relationships between power, politics, and digital media. The contributions in this section underscore the ways complex interactions among authorities, citizens, and technology shape individual political empowerment, efforts for social change, and the functioning of democratic processes. Jennifer Earl, Sam Scovill, and Elliot Ramo, for example, demonstrate that digital technologies can make political engagement more inclusive and equitable (Chapter 32). Surveying the research across five forms of political engagement, they find more evidence of youth engagement than disengagement. For her part, Alice Mattoni argues that more interdisciplinary pollination is needed to understand—and adequately conceptualize—global, grassroots efforts—in this case, anti-corruption campaigns (Chapter 31). Not all of the chapters, however, inspire optimism. Gabrielle Lim and Joan Donovan provide a critical synthesis of disinformation and media manipulation research and call for researchers to employ a sociotechnical perspective to better understand the effects of bad content on liberal democracies (Chapter 29). Likewise, Sarah Sobieraj shows that training a sociological lens on identity-based harassment online reveals a set of negative democratic outcomes that demand as much attention as individual impacts. (Chapter 30).

THE ROAD AHEAD

The authors in this volume invite readers to bring a sociological lens to the social contexts that create and are created by digital media. On the one hand, this presents an opportunity for sociologists to apply their disciplinary perspectives to better understand how digital technologies influence core power dynamics. Many of the contributions in this volume do just that, highlighting the different ways that power manifests and its differential effects at the intersection of race, ethnicity, social class, gender identity, sexual identity, and citizenship. More importantly, in mapping sociological inquiry into digital media, these chapters identify areas where sociological research could make particularly significant contributions. Olga Boichak's chapter on digital war (Chapter 25), for example, outlines how sociologists can contribute to an emerging field of inquiry, including challenging the construction of virtual battles as clean and bloodless.

Having said that, sociologists' late arrival requires us to proceed with care. Now more than ever, digital sociology is an interdisciplinary endeavor. Sociologists must engage with colleagues from other disciplines, and do so with the recognition that they are entering a set of debates that have been going on for quite some time. This is particularly important if they hope to inform inquiry regarding the implications of digital media for society, culture, politics, and individuals' daily lives. As Stef Aupers and Lars de Wildt point out in their chapter on digital religion (Chapter 9), sociologists too often treat digital media as a constant and, in doing so, remove themselves from important conversations involving the consequences of technologies in a rapidly changing world.

Unpacking the effects of digital technologies on global society will also require more research on countries beyond North America, Europe, and Australia. For example, countries in Latin America and Africa that are leveraging digital technologies to grow their economies will provide important insight into the effects of technological investment on the workforce, education, and society more broadly. Likewise, more cross-national engagement among scholars is critical for exploring global power dynamics and their effects on inequalities in localities as well as countries around the world. As the contributors in this volume remind us, relational dynamics shape everything from our conceptualizations of self and community to global economic and political practices.

REFERENCES

Brienza, Casey, and Matthias Revers. 2016. "The Field of American Media Sociology: Origins, Resurrection, and Consolidation." *Sociology Compass* 10, no. 7: 539–552.

Katz, Elihu. 2009. "Why Sociology Abandoned Communication." *The American Sociologist* 40, no. 3: 167–174.

PART I
THEORETICAL EXPLORATIONS OF DIGITAL LIFE

CHAPTER 1

TECHNOLOGY AND TIME

JUDY WAJCMAN

Across the social science and humanities disciplines there is a strong resurgence of interest in temporality. Much of this literature focuses on the impact of networked technologies and digital media on the contemporary experience of time. The extent to which personal computers, smartphones, and tablets are now the means or "medium" by which we accomplish more and more tasks of daily life has no historical precedent. Neither do the constant multichannel communications with multiple audiences that have become habitual, a quotidian fact of life.

As a result, there is a widespread preoccupation with the speeding up of everyday life in modern societies. The belief that ubiquitous technologies are colonizing our time, causing a time-pressure epidemic, is a constant theme in both mainstream sociological accounts of postmodern society and popular commentary (Agger 2004; Bauman 2000; Crary 2013; Rosa 2013; Tomlinson 2007; Wajcman 2015). Concepts such as "timeless time" (Castells 2010), "network time" (Hassan 2009), and "instantaneous time" (Urry 2000) abound to describe a purportedly new digital temporality of incessant acceleration. Yet, the idea that more and more aspects of our lives—technological and economic, cultural and political, public and private—are speeding up is rarely questioned.

This chapter will bring a much needed sociological perspective to bear on the interrelationship between technology and time. It will begin by situating claims about our acceleration society in a historical perspective, tracing how speed first became identified with modernity in classical social theory. Particularly prescient is Simmel's analysis of modern time consciousness as one involving immediacy, simultaneity, and presentism. His early writing resonates with contemporary speed theory that is outlined in the following section. The chapter will then argue that extant sociological analyses of acceleration commonly exhibit a tendency toward technological determinism. The shared idea is that speed is driven by digitalization, resulting in a one-dimensional view of time, as if everything is speeding up. In other words, the cultural condition of contemporary capitalism is characterized simply as one of acceleration.

By contrast, scholars writing under the rubric of science and technology studies (STS) conceive of the relationship between time and technology as one of mutual shaping or co-constitution. Fundamentally, this involves understanding temporality as not only social but also sociotechnical or sociomaterial. Focusing on the materiality of time, including investigating the technical and institutional infrastructure that underpins speed, is key given the extent to which temporality today is experienced via multiple media modalities. Adopting this approach enables us to consider whether the growing centrality of electronic mediations produces acceleration across all sectors of society and all aspects of life or whether the distribution and experience of time vary profoundly across social cleavages. A central claim of acceleration theorists is that 24/7 mobile connectivity has dissolved the traditional boundary between public and private spheres. Empirical evidence will be presented that tells a more complicated, multifaceted story about the causes of harriedness and temporal fragmentation. Contra to speed theory, we will see that digital temporal regimes are perceived and practiced in specific and variable concrete contexts.

The chapter concludes by examining the contemporary cultural valorization of speed. To this point the chapter has emphasized the extent to which our lived time is inextricably entangled with digital materiality. However, our modern orientation or philosophy of time, in which time is treated as a scarce resource that must be optimally utilized, is also a moral imperative. Busyness has become a badge of honor. And, in the twenty-first century, this mindset has become integral to Silicon Valley ideology, in which digital devices are designed and marketed primarily as time-saving tools. Our obsession with timekeeping and time management, our quest for efficiency, is constantly fed by cybergurus. In order to counter and resist the dominant time regime, we must begin by interrogating the moral, economic, and cultural logics of a fast-paced modernity.

THE TEMPO OF MODERNITY

We tend to think of high-speed society as a recent phenomenon, associated with the growth of digital technologies. However, claims about technology annihilating time and space are not new. Indeed, the role of technologies in radically speeding up the social world's tempo around the turn of the twentieth century has been the subject of a vast literature. Social theorists and historians, ranging from Adam (2004) and Nowotny (1996) to Thompson (1967) and Schivelbusch (1987) have described how the clock, the railway, the telegraph, and the telephone were the metronomes of a major historical shift in modern time consciousness. Time, once distinguished by seasons and tasks, became clock time and engendered the pursuit of a frugal use of time. In the quest for efficiency, people were constituted as temporal subjects, "as both having an orientation *to* time, and being disciplined *by* time" (Lash and Urry 1994, 226). No wonder Mumford ([1934] 2010, 14) saw the clock, not the steam engine, as the key invention of the industrial age.

Most sociological explanations of acceleration begin with the character of the capitalist economy, entailing the commodification of (clock) time. Following Marx, they argue that the regulation and exploitation of labor time means that saving time is equivalent to making profit: "when time is money then faster is better" (Adam 2004, 39). And it is through the historical lens of Thompson's (1967) essay, "Time, Work-Discipline, and Industrial Capitalism," that social scientists primarily view modern time in economic terms, as market time. According to Thompson, prior to industrialization, people depended on "natural rhythms" oriented to a variety of tasks related to an agricultural economy, task-oriented time. These older notations were gradually replaced by a new manufacturers' time, a commodity measured in monetary terms and regarded as precious. He saw this as the result both of advances in timekeeping and of a Puritan ethic which helped people internalize the idea that time was not to be wasted. By the nineteenth century, this idea of time thrift had become culturally embedded and came to seem natural. Our modern obsession with timekeeping in the quest for efficiency can be traced to this historical shift to the clock culture that developed in modernity.

One of the pioneers of the sociology of time, Zerubavel (1986) defines this orientation to time, which has come to characterize Western civilization, as the *quantitative philosophy of time*. This philosophy conceives of time as an entity that is "segmentable into various quantities of duration and, therefore, is countable and measurable." And in this process, he argues, the invention of the schedule was key. It enabled time to be calibrated at the microscopic level of the hour and minute. Schedules epitomize this quantitative view of time as they require rigid durations or *time slots* into which we fit fixed activities and events. This temporal exactitude is a unique feature of modern life: The schedule made the modern art of time management possible. This art in turn relies on us having internalized a socially sanctioned norm of time discipline in which, to paraphrase Weber, wasting time is the deadliest of sins. Schedules thus materialize the highly rationalized temporal order in which time is viewed as a scarce resource that must be optimally utilized. And once this linear system of time was set, "acceleration became the experience of modernisation overshadowing and shaping everything else" (Nowotny 1996, 84).

These accounts rightly focus on the dynamics of the capitalist economy and processes of rationalization as key to the formation of modern time consciousness. However, a vital addition to these explanations is provided by the German sociologist Simmel (1997), who, as early as 1900, identified the modern metropolis as the site where modernity is fully experienced. As we move into an era where more than half the world's population live in cities and the urban experience is becoming ever more pervasive, Simmel's writings have once again become resonant. His insights about the increasing pace of life in fin-de-siècle Europe, his take on the zeitgeist, have such affinity with postmodern theories about the significance and allure of speed that it is worth recalling them here.

In *The Philosophy of Money*, Simmel (2004, 450) analyzes the ephemerality and briefness that have become signifiers of the temporality of modernity. For him, there is an intrinsic connection between the increased pace of life in the city and the circulation of money, which speeds up every activity connected with it. Production, transportation, sales, and consumption all have to be constantly on the move; and this revolutionizes the time–space coordinates of social relations. The totally dynamic impetus of the money economy creates a transitory constellation of relations in which everything is in flux, with no secure resting points.

What is particularly fascinating is Simmel's description of the modern personality types that this social turbulence generates. The classic metropolitan type, the blasé individual, suffers from the *"intensification of nervous stimulation* which results from the swift and uninterrupted change of outer and inner stimuli" (Simmel 1997, 175). The cornucopia of possibilities and distractions available within the capitalist metropolitan milieu makes it the locale in which "stimulations, interests, fillings in of time and consciousness" are offered in profusion. In stark contrast to the slow rhythm of rural life, each crossing of the city street creates "the rapid crowding of changing images, the sharp discontinuity in the grasp of a single glance, and the unexpectedness of onrushing impressions."

Simmel was acutely aware of the inherent ambiguity of modern city life: that it promotes individualization and standardization at the same time. For example, in his exploration of fashion and style, we find the dialectical interplay of individual imitation and differentiation, the desire to be like others and the desire for difference. Fashion requires continuous reproduction to accelerate the turnover time of new commodities, making its newness its simultaneous death. As such, it exemplifies the modern cultural fixation with the "eternal present," with immediacy, with transitory, perpetual motion. Simmel was thus highly attuned to the emergent time consciousness of the modern individual: "the dominion of presentism—erasure of the past, effacement of inherited connections, domination by the immediately invisible sublime—is an integral part of modernity" (Scaff 2005, 18). The point I will return to is that this condition of immediacy is taken today as being wholly a consequence of digital technologies.

Strikingly absent from Simmel's prescient analysis, however, is how the experience of the metropolis is highly stratified by social class, status, gender, and ethnicity—in other words, power relations. The realization of simultaneity as a phenomenon of the perception of time, the awareness of everything happening in the moment, was reserved for the privileged few. The acceleration of the pace of life was not then, and is not now, a uniform condition of existence. As I will elaborate, time as a resource remains differentially distributed, accessed and interpreted by different groups, depending on their circumstances.

CONTEMPORARY SPEED THEORY

At the beginning of the twenty-first century, there is once again intense interest across the disciplines in how technologies, principally digital media and networked technologies, are transforming the human perception of time. The idea that digitalization has wrought a new temporal regime of acceleration, immediacy, and instantaneity is widespread. Among social theorists, concepts such as "timeless time" (Castells 2010), "instantaneous time" (Urry 2000), "network time" (Hassan 2009), and "chronoscopic time" (Virilio 1986) abound to describe the pace of high-speed society in which we are all constantly pressed for time. The third wave of the mediatization of time—how the digitalization and datafication of communication shape temporalities—is also attracting increasing attention in media studies (Couldry and Hepp 2017; Fornäs 2016; Hartmann et al. 2019; Pentzold 2018). While theoretical analyses of a high-speed society differ in their emphasis, there is a shared thematic that new technologies and faster-moving capital are increasing the tempo of daily life.

Probably the best-known theorist of the "acceleration society" is Rosa (2013), who draws on elements from both classical and late modernist literature. In his discussion of the social processes of acceleration, Rosa refers to three mutually reinforcing processes of change characterizing late modernity: technological acceleration (the speeding up of transport, communication, and production), acceleration in the rate of societal change (in the family and occupations, for example), and acceleration of the pace of life. The "pace" of (social) life refers to the speed and compression of actions and experiences in everyday life.

Now the most intriguing question is how these three types of acceleration relate to each other. As Rosa points out, there is clearly a paradox between the first and third processes. If technological acceleration means that less time is needed, this should entail an increase in free time, which in turn would slow down the pace of life. Rather than time becoming abundant, however, time seems to be increasingly scarce. Accordingly, it only makes sense to apply the term "acceleration society" to a society if "technological acceleration and the growing scarcity of time (that is, an acceleration of the 'pace of life') occur simultaneously" (Rosa 2003, 10). This has become known as the "time pressure paradox" and is the subject of much debate (Wajcman 2015).

Most general analyses of contemporary society can be read as versions of the acceleration society thesis. In other words, they make a direct, causal link between technological acceleration, especially the speed of electronic communication systems, and the harriedness of everyday life. In contrast to an earlier literature about "industrial society" that predicted a "leisure revolution" driven by automation in industry and the home (Bell 1973), contemporary debates are concerned with time poverty and the paucity of leisure. The fact that our social interactions in both work and leisure time are increasingly mediated by networked technologies and social media platforms, that we live in a state of constant connectivity, is a recurring theme. For example, the geographer David Harvey (1990, 240) conceived of "time–space compression" as being at the heart of modernity, or, in some formulations, postmodernity: "I use the term 'compression' because ... the history of capitalism has been characterized by speed-up in the pace of life, while ... space appears to shrink to a 'global village.'" This echoes McLuhan's ([1964] 1994) famous prophecy in the 1970s that the speed of electronic communication would culminate in the harmonization and connection of all humanity into a global village

However, it was Castells' (2010) vision of how the accelerating speed of ICTs (information and communication technologies) annihilate time in *The Rise of the Network Society*, which became mainstream in social science. For him, the revolution in ICTs has given rise to a new network society in which labor and capital are replaced by informational networks and knowledge. Information is the key ingredient of organizations, and flows of electronic messages and images between networks now constitute the basic thread of social structure. He defines the space of flows as the technological and organizational possibility of practicing simultaneity without contiguity. These circuits come to dominate the organization of activity in individual places such that the site of networks and their relationship to other networks become more important than the characteristics of place itself.

At the core of this argument is the disappearance of time: that we are increasingly moving away from the clock time of the industrial age in which time was a method of demarcating and ordering sequences of events. Instead, he argues, the world is increasingly organized in the space of flows: flows of merchandise, people, money, and information around dispersed and distributed networks. The sheer velocity and intensity of these global flows, interactions, and networks dissolve time, resulting in simultaneity and instant communications—what he terms "timeless time." While this new "timeless time" emerged in financial markets, it is spreading to every realm. No wonder then, Castells opines, that life is a frantic race as people multitask and multi-live by means of technology to reach "timeless time: the social practice that aims at negating sequence to install ourselves in perennial simultaneity and simultaneous ubiquity" (Castells 2010, xii). In true postmodern rhetoric, society becomes eternally ephemeral as space and time are radically compressed to the point where, at least with regard to the latter, it ceases to exist.

While such conceptions of time do capture something important about the extent to which the extraordinary speed of technologies is transforming the economy, financial markets, politics, and patterns of production and consumption, it is far less clear what this speeding up means for the experience of lived time and how it concretely relates to the actual use of ICTs in everyday life. In part, this is because sociological theories of acceleration too often take the form of grand, totalizing narratives, "techno-epics heralding techno-epochs," with little substantive interest in the specific, located settings in which temporality is made together with devices and instruments (Thrift 1996, 1467). A similar critique has been leveled at the burgeoning literature in media studies on the temporality of social media platforms. As Pentzold (2018) notes, the customary practices through which time is produced in the interplay of communicative texts, media technologies, and social relations, the "temporal scaffoldings" of daily life, are mostly ignored. It is to these issues that I will turn in the remainder of this chapter.

But I want to foreshadow here that "speed theory," as Sharma's (2014, 15) astute critique shows, has become a genre in itself, a circulating discourse that masks the "chronographies of power" (see also Rosa and Scheuerman 2009; Vostal 2014; Wajcman and Dodd 2017). That is, it both obscures the socially differentiated lived experience of time and legitimates the cultural fixation on the control of time. In other words, this regime of speed can be understood both as a cultural imperative and as emergent sociotechnical affordances that facilitate and promote our sped-up lives. While digital technologies do drive speed, these sociological theories of acceleration are inadequate to capture the complexity of lived time. We need to know how digital temporalities are experienced and constructed, negotiated and transformed, in modern timescapes (Adam 1990).

TIME AS A SOCIOTECHNICAL PRACTICE

What role, then, does digital technology play in shaping people's experience of time? Does technological acceleration necessarily hasten the pace of our everyday lives? To answer these questions, let us look more generally at how the relationship between technology and society has been conceived.

The most influential common-sense assumption about the relationship between technology and society is "technological determinism." Key here is the idea that technology impinges on society from the outside, that technical change is autonomous and itself causes social change, that technology is not part of society but a separate, external sphere, so to speak, advancing according to its own logic. Although some speed theorists distance themselves from a technologically determinist stance, they tend to discuss how ICTs have major "irreversible" effects, ushering in disruptive social revolutions. For example, the idea that technical innovation is the most important cause of social change permeates Castells' analysis of the network society. The common assumption is that the social acceleration dynamic is all-encompassing: that technologies are used in a uniform way across all sectors of society and all dimensions of life.

By contrast, a more nuanced conversation about technology and temporality has been going on under the rubric of STS.[1] While sociologists have always emphasized that time is a social entity, formed through collective rhythms of human engagement with the world, technology is rarely accorded the same treatment. Technology is too often seen as outside of social relations. Yet, modern patterns of time can scarcely be conceived of without the use of technology. From simple tools to large technological systems, our lives are intertwined with technology. Our actions and society itself are built on and with technical artifacts. We make the world together with technology, and so it is with time.

In challenging technological determinism, STS scholars do not deny the profound influence that technical systems have had on reconfiguring time. Rather, the aim has been to reconceptualize the complex interrelationship between the two. Adopting an STS perspective points the way to understanding time as not only fundamentally social but also a fundamentally sociotechnical or sociomaterial practice (Bijker, Hughes, and Pinch 1987; Latour 2005; MacKenzie and Wajcman 1999). It makes sense, then, to think about the relationship between time practices and technology as one of ongoing mutual shaping: that the contours and rhythms of our lives are calibrated by and with machines. It is simply impossible to disentangle our notions of time from our embodied habitual involvement with the sociomaterial world. In other words, we cannot comprehend the social organization of time separately from technology.

In a similar vein, media scholars increasingly emphasize that material objects and technical assemblages are "active participants and intermediaries" in the production of time (Leong et al. 2009, 1281). Focusing on materiality, including investigating the technical and institutional infrastructure that underpins speed, is especially critical today given the extent to which temporality is experienced via multiple media modalities. It also enables us, as I will elaborate, to go beyond the notion that technology itself is driving our cultural obsession with speed and optimization.

I begin by examining the ways in which mobile networked technologies are reconfiguring the conventional distinctions between family time and work time as this is a major subject of sociological studies on the impact of technology on temporality.

Technology and Temporal Boundaries

Over the last decade, a major current in the sociological literature on technology and time has focused on individual well-being and family functioning (Ollier-Malaterre, Jacobs, and Rothbard 2019). Many scholars argue that digital technologies have transformed the temporal boundaries that once allowed us to separate our lives by creating distinct times and places in which we engage in various activities (Beckman and Mazmanian 2020; Chesley 2005; Kossek 2016; Turkle 2011). Before the diffusion of cell phones, the boundary between work and nonwork life was reflected in the separation of business and home phone lines. This was one of the principal ways that many people organized their time. The most widely noted feature of the mobile/cell phone, arguably the most rapidly diffused technological artifact in history, is that it affords perpetual contact, thereby disturbing the divisions between private and public realms. The capacity for 24/7 communication "anytime, anywhere" is widely seen as fostering harriedness and temporal fragmentation.

Consistent with theories of the acceleration society, then, constant connectivity is viewed as potentially an oppressive feature of smart devices. A large body of research in the work–family domain has highlighted the potential for negative spillover from one role to another, exacerbating work–life conflict and creating negative family dynamics (Chesley and Siibak 2003; Kelly and Moen 2020). The contention is that blurring work–family boundaries is bad for individuals and families because it promotes overwork, individual isolation, accelerated family life, and continual interruption. More recently, others have begun to examine the potential for positive spillover or enrichment that can occur between these domains (Erickson and Mazmanian 2017). Connection technologies enable us to more flexibly navigate the boundaries between our work and nonwork lives, which may enhance family and work performance for individuals who are comfortable integrating work and life roles.

The argument about the work-extending effects of ICTs coincided with a public debate about major changes that were occurring in working time regimes, sparked by the publication of books such as Schor's (1991) *The Overworked American* and Hochschild's

(1997) *The Time Bind*. The overall trend identified was an increasing polarization of working time, between those who work very long hours or overwork and others who work few or no hours (Clawson and Gerstel 2014). Contra to Schor, however, the substantial increases in overall workloads since the 1970s have mainly been a feature of specific socioeconomic groups, those who are more highly educated and in higher-status jobs (Gershuny and Sullivan 2019; Jacobs and Gerson 2005). As these are the groups who spend the most time using a digital device at work (Mullan 2019), many scholars and pundits concluded that such intensified working conditions are perpetuated by the capacities of ever more ubiquitous, wearable, networked, and multifunctional ICTs (Perlow 2012; Ticona 2015).

This perspective reflects at least a soft technological determinism by its direct linkage of the emergence of wireless computing to specific temporal impacts on individuals and organizations. While there is little doubt that technology is helping to shape modern forms of work, we are only beginning to understand how those sociotechnical forms of work are reconfiguring temporality. A common finding is that frequently working under stress, working at speed to tight deadlines, and time pressure are significantly correlated. However, an STS perspective should make us wary of making facile assumptions about the casual direction of the association. Even the time we spend on email may be as much a cultural symbol of overload as it is the source of it (Barley, Meyerson, and Grodal 2011). Rather than seeing ICTs as the culprit, workers are likely to experience the intensification of work, long working hours, time pressure, and heavy technology use as a single package.

Moreover, when theorists of the acceleration society refer to the hastening pace of life, they have in mind a universal abstract subject. They are not attuned to the detailed manner and circumstances in which time is organized into daily routines by gendered individuals and negotiated within households. Consequently, they fail to see that what happens to an individual's average hours of work is not the same as what happens to work collectively within households. The vicissitudes of scheduling and the intricacy with which our lives are tied to others can only be fully understood by treating the household, rather than the individual, as the unit of analysis.

One of the most striking findings of time-use surveys is that gender, rather than technology use per se, is the major predictor of time pressure. A much higher proportion of women than men report "always" feeling rushed, and "women's time is both more fragmented and involves more multi-tasking than that of men's" (Sullivan and Gershuny 2019, 295). As feminist literature has long documented, women perform a disproportionate amount of unpaid domestic work; and as more women enter the labor market, they experience greater work–family conflict than men (Bianchi, Robinson, and Milkie 2006). As a result, the working woman is much busier than either her male colleagues or her household counterpart.

In addition, a much overlooked source of time pressure, which again illustrates the socially patterned character of time, is the difficulty of synchronizing diverse temporal schedules or "temporal dis-organization" (Southerton 2020; Young and Lim 2014). When it comes to the individual experience of time, the ability to coordinate one's time with others may matter as much as having a particular amount of free time. This is particularly apposite given the extent to which collective social practices, derived from institutionally stable temporal rhythms, have been eroded. With the rise of flexible working patterns and the predominance of dual-earner families, the need for people to coordinate and mesh the temporal regimes of paid work, family life, and leisure has never been more important. Indeed, these major structural changes in the labor market and the household proved to be the ideal environment for the diffusion of the mobile phone. Unsurprisingly, studies of mobile telephony reveal that its major use is for the microcoordination of everyday life, allowing for tighter and more efficient "real-time" planning of activities, thus "softening" precise schedules (Green and Haddon 2009; Ling 2004). As household coordination is an important contributor to the time squeeze, cell phones provide unique tools for temporal management that could alleviate feelings of time pressure.

Although a schedule may appear to be an individual affair, a schedule is collective—based on shared and negotiated relations within the family and within workplaces and organizations as well as across them. These relations together make up a "web of time" in which changes in one person's schedule cascade to create changes in the schedule of another person (Clawson and Gerstel 2014, 6). Our time is entangled with the time of others, and the power to control time varies by class, gender, and other dimensions of inequality. For example, while knowledge workers may welcome digital technologies for the temporal and spatial flexibility they offer, service workers may experience these same technologies as increasing employers' control over their time. An individual's power to control their temporal boundaries is heavily constrained by the nature of their work. As Woodcock's chapter in this volume elaborates, automated systems have been critical to the rise of the "gig" economy and the spread of precarious scheduling, making the timing of work a critical form of control within the workplace.

Suffice it to say that while ubiquitous technologies of acceleration are now the "natural" ecology of our sociomaterial world, they do not result in a uniform experience of the shortage of time. Nor do we have the same ability and resources to exert control over our lived time. Time pressure may be experienced by employed lone mothers, by two-job, two-parent families who work shifts, and by dual-career managerial/professional couples; but the sense of time squeeze and the mechanisms causing it may differ. The extent to which money can be deployed to alleviate time pressure also differs greatly between these diverse groups. In order to unpack the time-pressure paradox, we need to recognize that digital temporal regimes are perceived and practiced in specific and variable concrete contexts.

Finally, a somewhat related debate takes the form of an anxiety about whether the fact that we now spend almost half of our waking hours on digital devices leaves us less time to talk face to face. As this topic is covered in Wilding's chapter in this volume, I will briefly allude to the issue of technology's impact on communication. Largely sparked by Turkle's (2011, 2015) books *Alone Together* and *Reclaiming Conversation*, the claim is that the constant connection afforded by mobile modalities leads to a reduction in the amount and quality of our intimate and family-based communication time.

Hardly a month goes by in which there isn't a new article or book on the subject of whether digital devices bring us together or push us apart. Just as in some early debates about the impact of television, many express the view that smartphones/tablets/laptops are hollowing out our personal relationships and family time. In these scenarios, media use is portrayed as a replacement for, rather than a complement to, co-present family contact. For example, Turkle argues that ICTs dilute the quality of time families spend together because individual family members are glued to a screen instead of socializing with each other. Far from allowing us to communicate better, she views technology as isolating us in a cyber-reality that is a poor imitation of the human world. Addicted to multitasking on their smartphones, parents do not give children their full attention, and teenagers have become scared of the immediacy of talking on the telephone.

What is important to note is that such debates adopt a quantitative view of the time, see technology as having a unilinear deterministic impact, and treat communication as taking only one form. As a result, time spent in face-to-face communication is set up as separate from and superior to mediated communication. A more productive way of thinking about these issues from an STS perspective would be to reframe such debates around the relationship between mediated communication and forms of close personal ties. This involves questioning the primacy typically accorded to direct, in-person interaction, which tends to obscure the role of material objects in the dynamics of affiliation. A sociotechnical approach treats communication as embedded in various technologies that cannot be separated in terms of pure and mediated, with the former assumed to be more "real" than the latter. Digital devices and social media can then be understood as fostering new patterns of social contact, providing new tools for intimacy (Baym 2014; Livingstone and Blum-Ross 2020).

Up to this point, I have examined the lived experience of acceleration in relation to the temporal affordances that are emphasized, favored, and encouraged by digital technologies. However, as indicated at the outset, the dominant temporal regime of speed is also a discursive construct and cultural imperative. For the remainder of this chapter, therefore, we take the important step of bringing changing cultural norms about busyness to bear on the paradox of time pressure.

The Culture of Optimization

"The permanent struggle for optimisation is surely one of the most significant cultural principles operative in contemporary Western societies" (King, Gerisch, and Rosa 2019, 1). Indeed, the allure of metropolitan speed, doing the most with the time one has and realizing as many options as possible from the vast possibilities that the world has to offer, is indissolubly linked to the dominant ideals of modernity. This orientation to, and valorization of, the fast-paced, full life as the good life is constantly fueled by the headlong developments in digitalization. Although the hyperconnectivity of electronic devices is typically blamed for time pressure, paradoxically, the most common solution to time scarcity involves using more and more technologies to make our lives more efficient.

This chapter began by tracing our obsession with timekeeping and time management to the clock culture that developed in industrial capitalism. Much has been written about how this *quantitative* philosophy of time was perfected in the early twentieth century by the time-and-motion studies of Taylorism or scientific management (Gregg 2018). From punch clocks and timetables to the assembly line, work became marked and measured by clock time. Crucially, however, as Weber well understood, Protestant ascetics were attracted to clocks and schedules, not only as tools to coerce labor but because of their role in developing and internalizing time discipline as a moral enterprise. While Taylor "is deservedly (in)famous for having pushed the agenda of Chronos the taskmaster to the extreme, Taylor also clearly had in mind an ambition to instil the moralizing face of Chronos into the industrial workplace" (Snyder 2016, 40). Over the course of several hundred years, the modern orthodoxy that "all things should act efficiently" became entrenched in Western culture (Alexander 2008). Accordingly, Tomlinson (2007, 47) argues, the idea of progress itself became identified with speed and, combined with technological innovation, constructs a "hugely powerful cultural narrative of social acceleration."

That notions of speed and progress are still so intertwined in contemporary political discourse is integral to the insistent sense of time pressure. Cultural discourses that value action-packed lives lead people to pursue busy lives that are at once both stressful and affirming. The increasing salience of consumption for modern identity formation also fuels the demand for faster, hyper-consumption. In the new spirit of capitalism, "to be doing something, to move, to change—that is what enjoys prestige" (Boltanski and Chiapello 2007, 155). The "promise of a good life" puts a premium on *activity* as a necessary condition of a fulfilling lifestyle.

So, has the notion of busyness acquired a new positive meaning in our culture? In an intriguing argument, Gershuny (2005) claims that whereas at the turn of the twentieth century those in the upper income bracket were defined by their leisure, in a reversal of Veblen's (1899) classic *Theory of the Leisure Class*, nowadays prestige accords to those who work long hours and are busiest at work. In other words, busyness has become a badge of honor, a status symbol, and a form of self-validation. As Gregg (2018) shows, time mastery permeates the very subjectivity of today's knowledge professionals, for whom productivity has become a self-affirming logic of action. Time-management techniques in the form of self-help manuals and more recently mobile apps were crucial in encouraging a personalized relationship to efficiency, providing the necessary cultural weight and authority to normalize such practices as management common sense.

In the twenty-first century, the quest for efficiency, with employing every minute wisely, has become an integral element of Silicon Valley ideology and is manifest in its products. Digital commodities are routinely designed and marketed for a busy life on the move: as tools for self-optimization. The accelerating pace of technological innovation promises to solve all social problems, including navigating the problem of time scarcity in this apparently sped-up world. The proliferation of time-management apps are endless. Each presents the possibility of allowing us to do many more things at once, faster and better. We are constantly expected to work on our relationship to time, especially with the aid of technology.

The widespread use of self-tracking devices, for example, encourages self-discipline by providing data on all aspects of one's daily life (Lupton 2016; Neff and Nafus 2016). These apps treat time as a quantitative resource to be maximized and place the responsibility for well-being onto the individual. Indeed, the ethic of busyness, doing more in less time, is so ingrained that these productivity tools perform an affective role, helping people constitute themselves as valuable and accomplished individuals. The belief that machines can be profitably deployed to control and manage time has a long history, but today, in the acceleration society, it is fueled by the cybergurus of Silicon Valley who envisage that they will ultimately deliver it.

Conclusion

There is now an entire stream of literature that analyzes the interrelationship between technology and temporalities in a wide variety of contexts. For instance, the journal *Time & Society*, set up in 1992, publishes papers across a range of disciplines and increasingly includes the impact of digital technology as a central theme. The same can be said of media and communications journals. Across these different fields there is a shared interest in examining the ways in which the social experience of time is mediated and shaped by digital materialities. As a result, some of the most lively and productive work on the topic is taking place at the intersections between sociology, STS, and media studies.

Despite the promising research reviewed in this chapter, greater scrutiny is still required regarding how technology-related changes in temporal, spatial, and relationship arrangements are structured by the dynamics of power. While the rhetoric of speed and busyness is pervasive, time pressure is in reality experienced very differently by diverse social groups, depending on their resources and capacities. Not everyone can equally avail themselves of the temporal offerings of digital technologies.

The point is particularly salient with respect to how temporal sovereignty or control over one's time varies across jobs and occupations, on the one hand, and across families, on the other. Firstly, in relation to paid work, we need to better understand the differences in connectivity and the subsequent blurring of boundaries across blue-collar and white-collar jobs and different types of work arrangements and contracts. The rise of the gig or platform economy during the 2010s has markedly shifted how labor time is deployed. Jobs with relatively stable schedules are also increasingly characterized by unpredictability. Algorithmic systems have made the timing of work ever more critical, and we need more research on how such systems of control are established, maintained, and resisted. More generally, the ways in which digital technologies are being incorporated into work processes themselves merit continuous inquiry, especially as the very meaning of work changes over time as people innovate and modify their usage of technology.

Secondly, future research should examine the allocation and distribution of time in relation to different family configurations as they vary between social classes and cultural backgrounds. The undervaluing of time spent performing housework and caring activities remains a source of gender inequality, and more research should be aimed at investigating how this might influence the nature of private, leisure time. Variations by age, including teenagers and older adults, will also give us insights into the evolution of intrafamily mediated communication practices. In sum, we need more intersectional research on how differently situated individuals and social groups within households experience and access time.

Finally, the contemporary allure of speed and the imperative of optimization are ripe for scrutiny. In particular, the notion that ever more high-tech innovations will solve the problem of time scarcity needs questioning. Digital devices for time management are premised on the assumption that time is an individual, quantitative resource open to the engineering solutions of planning and maximization. However, even intelligent machines can only operationalize time according to an instrumental philosophy in which an efficient life is morally equated to a good life. Countering this dominant time regime does not require disconnecting from technology and social media, but rather challenging the cultural logics of a fast-paced modernity. We are still in the early days of the digital revolution, and many of the salient issues reviewed here will no doubt take on unforeseen forms as technologies continue to evolve and are integrated into our everyday sociomaterial time practices.

Postscript

At the time of writing, we are in the midst of the coronavirus pandemic, and there is much speculation about how the experience of lockdown is affecting our sense of time. Some have dubbed this a period of "deceleration." The media are full of recipes for baking bread, apps for identifying bird song, and other diversions for the months in confinement. There is also much discussion about the phenomenal growth of Zoom and other virtual meetings and more generally how fundamental digital communication has become to sociability at a distance. There are wide variations in how the slowdown resulting from lockdown is being experienced. Some groups report having additional discretionary time at their disposal and that this is provoking reflection on their priorities and activities. Some report the feeling that time is slowing down, while others explore the reasons as to why Zoom meetings are so tiring. There is also much speculation about the end of the office and increased home-based working.

It is hard to predict how long-lasting any of these changes will be. But perhaps it is wise to end on a word of caution. As I have commented, we need more research on the broad variations in access to time, how it differs both within families and across social classes and other dimensions of inequality. In general, however, it is clear that the pressure on parents' time during lockdown is immense. On average, parents are doing child care during nine hours of the day and housework during three (Andrew et al. 2020). While fathers have nearly doubled the time they spend on child care, mothers are more likely to have quit or lost their job during the crisis and are disproportionately bearing the time involved in home schooling and other domestic work. The sharp time divide between households with children and those without has also grown.

Furthermore, the interrelated class and racial composition of the labor force has resulted in a widening polarization between white-collar workers who are able to work remotely and so-called service workers who cannot. The service sector encompasses a wide variety of jobs, from health service workers such as doctors and nurses to the vast army who are delivering goods at ever greater volume and speed. At both ends of the spectrum, for very different reasons, time is more pressured than ever. And then there are the millions who are furloughed from work or have lost their jobs, for whom time hangs heavy. The distribution of time is political in every sense.

Over the last decade or so, there has been increasing attention in political philosophy to the idea that the ability to choose how you allocate your time lies at the core of a positive notion of freedom. In *Free Time*, for example, Rose (2017) argues that a just society must guarantee all citizens their fair share of free time. She defines discretionary free time as a resource: an all-purpose means to pursue one's conception of the good, whatever it may be. Having more time at home as a result of a public health crisis is not the same as having more control over how we spend our time. The time of a pandemic is a time of anxiety and thus has a very different quality from the concept of discretionary time or temporal sovereignty. Instead of focusing on the experience of speed-up or slow-down, we should be looking at the changing dynamics in the distribution of time.

Note

1. STS is a broad field with distinct theoretical positions. A sample of the research can be found in journals such as *Social Studies of Science*; *Science, Technology, & Human Values*; the book series *Inside Technology* (MIT Press); and Felt et al. (2017).

References

Adam, Barbara. 1990. *Time and Social Theory*. Cambridge: Polity.
Adam, Barbara. 2004. *Time*. Cambridge: Polity.
Agger, Ben. 2004. *Speeding Up Fast Capitalism*. Boulder, CO: Paradigm.
Alexander, Jennifer K. 2008. *The Mantra of Efficiency: From Waterwheel to Social Control*. Baltimore, MD: John Hopkins University Press.
Andrew, Alison, Sarah Cattan, Monica Costa Dias, Christine Farquharson, Lucy Kraftman, Sonya Krutikova, Angus Phimister, and Almudena Sevilla. 2020. "How Are Mothers and Fathers Balancing Work and Family under Lockdown?" Institute for Fiscal Studies. https://www.ifs.org.uk/publications/14860.

Barley, Stephen R., Debra E. Meyerson, and Stine Grodal. 2011. "E-mail as a Source and Symbol of Stress." *Organization Science* 22, no. 4: 887–906.

Bauman, Zygmunt. 2000. *Liquid Modernity*. London: Blackwell.

Baym, Nancy K. 2014. *Personal Connections in the Digital Age*. Cambridge: Polity.

Beckman, Christine, and Melissa Mazmanian. 2020. *Dreams of the Overworked*. Stanford, CA: Stanford University Press.

Bell, Daniel. 1973. *The Coming of Post-Industrial Society*. New York: Basic Books.

Bianchi, Suzanne M., John P. Robinson, and Melissa A. Milkie. 2006. *The Changing Rhythm of American Family Life*. New York: Russell Sage Foundation.

Bijker, Wiebe, Thomas Hughes, and Trevor Pinch, eds. 1987. *The Social Construction of Technological Systems*. Cambridge, MA: MIT Press.

Boltanski, Luc, and Eve Chiapello. 2007. *The New Spirit of Capitalism*. London: Verso.

Castells, Manuel. 2010. *The Rise of the Network Society*. 2nd ed. Malden, MA: Blackwell.

Chesley, Noelle. 2005. "Blurring Boundaries? Linking Technology Use, Spillover, Individual Distress, and Family Satisfaction." *Journal of Marriage and Family* 67, no. 5: 1237–1248.

Chesley, Noelle, and Andra Siibak. 2003. "Information and Communication Technology Use and Work–Life Integration." In *Handbook of Work–Life Integration of Professionals: Challenges and Opportunities*, edited by Debra A. Major and Ronald J. Burke, 245–266. Cheltenham, UK: Elgar.

Clawson, Dan, and Naomi Gerstel. 2014. *Unequal Time*. New York: Russell Sage Foundation.

Couldry, Nick, and Andreas Hepp. 2017. *The Mediated Construction of Reality*. Cambridge: Polity.

Crary, Jonathan. 2013. *24/7: Late Capitalism and the End of Sleep*. London: Verso.

Erickson, Ingrid, and Melissa Mazmanian. 2017. "Bending Time to a New End: Investigating the Idea of Temporal Entrepreneurship." In *The Sociology of Speed: Digital, Organizational, and Social Temporalities*, edited by Judy Wajcman and Nigel Dodd, 152–168. Oxford: Oxford University Press.

Felt, Ulrike, Rayvon Fouché, Clark A. Miller, and Laurel Smith-Doerr, eds. 2017. *The Handbook of Science and Technology Studies*. Cambridge: MIT Press.

Fornäs, Johan. 2016. "The Mediatization of Third-Time Tools." *International Journal of Communication* 10: 5213–5232.

Gershuny, Jonathan. 2005. "Busyness as the Badge of Honor for the New Superordinate Working Class." *Social Research* 72, no. 2: 287–314.

Gershuny, Jonathan, and Oriel Sullivan. 2019. *What We Really Do All Day: Insights from the Centre for Time Use Research*. London: Pelican.

Green, Nicola, and Leslie Haddon. 2009. *Mobile Communications: An Introduction to New Media*. New York: Berg.

Gregg, Melissa. 2018. *Counterproductive: Time Management in the Knowledge Economy*. Durham, NC: Duke University Press.

Hartmann, Maren, Elizabeth Prommer, Karin Deckner, and Stephan O. Görland, eds. 2019. *Mediated Time: Perspectives on Time in a Digital Age*. London: Palgrave.

Harvey, David. 1990. *The Condition of Postmodernity*. Oxford: Blackwell.

Hassan, Robert. 2009. *Empires of Speed: Time and the Acceleration of Politics and Society*. Leiden, The Netherlands: Brill.

Hochschild, Arlie. 1997. *The Time Bind: When Work Becomes Home and Home Becomes Work*. New York: Henry Holt.

Jacobs, Jerry A., and Kathleen Gerson. 2005. *The Time Divide: Work, Family and Gender Inequality*. Cambridge, MA: Harvard University Press.

Kelly, Erin L., and Phyllis Moen. 2020. *Overload: How Good Jobs Went Bad and What We Can Do about It*. Princeton, NJ: Princeton University Press.

King, Vera, Benigna Gerisch, and Hartmut Rosa, eds. 2019. *Lost in Perfection*. London: Routledge.

Kossek, Ellen. 2016. "Managing Work–Life Boundaries in the Digital Age." *Organizational Dynamics* 45, no. 3: 258–270.

Lash, Scott, and John Urry. 1994. *Economies of Signs and Space*. London: Sage Publications.

Latour, Bruno. 2005. *Reassembling the Social: An Introduction to Actor-Network Theory*. Oxford: Oxford University Press.

Leong, Susan, Teodor Mitew, Marta Celetti, and Erika Pearson. 2009. "The Question Concerning (Internet) Time." *New Media & Society* 11, no. 8: 1267–1285.

Ling, Rich. 2004. *The Mobile Connection: The Cell Phone's Impact on Society*. San Francisco: Morgan Kaufmann.

Livingstone, Sonia, and Alicia Blum-Ross. 2020. *Parenting for a Digital Future: How Hopes and Fears about Technology Shape Children's Lives*. London: Oxford University Press.

Lupton, Deborah. 2016. *The Quantified Self*. Cambridge: Polity.

MacKenzie, Donald, and Judy Wajcman, eds. 1999. *The Social Shaping of Technology*. Milton Keynes, UK: Open University Press.

McLuhan, Marshall. (1964) 1994. *Understanding Media*. New York: McGraw-Hill.

Mullan, Kilian. 2019. "Technology in the Daily Lives of Adults." In *What We Really Do All Day: Insights from the Centre for Time Use Research*, edited by Jonathan Gershuny and Oriel Sullivan, 237–264. London: Pelican.

Mumford, Lewis. (1934) 2010. *Technics and Civilization*. Chicago: University of Chicago Press.

Neff, Gina, and Dawn Nafus. 2016. *Self-Tracking*. Cambridge, MA: MIT Press.

Nowotny, Helga. 1996. *Time: The Modern and Postmodern Experience*. Cambridge: Polity.

Ollier-Malaterre, Ariane, Jerry A. Jacobs, and Nancy P. Rothbard. 2019. "Technology, Work, and Family: Digital Cultural Capital and Boundary Management." *Annual Review of Sociology* 45: 425–447.

Pentzold, Christian. 2018. "Between Moments and Millennia: Temporalising Mediatisation." *Media, Culture and Society* 40, no. 6: 927–937.

Perlow, Leslie A. 2012. *Sleeping with Your Smartphone: How to Break the 24/7 Habit and Change the Way You Work*. Boston: Harvard Business Review.

Rosa, Hartmut. 2003. "Social Acceleration: Ethical and Political Consequences of a Desynchronized High-Speed Society." *Constellations* 10, no. 1: 3–33.

Rosa, Hartmut. 2013. *Social Acceleration: A New Theory of Modernity*. New York: Columbia University Press.

Rosa, Hartmut, and William Scheuerman, eds. 2009. *High-Speed Society: Social Acceleration, Power, and Modernity*. University Park: Pennsylvania State University Press.

Rose, Julie. 2017. *Free Time*. Princeton, NJ: Princeton University Press.

Scaff, Lawrence. 2005. "The Mind of the Modernist: Simmel on Time." *Time & Society* 14, no. 1: 5–23.

Schivelbusch, Wolfgang. 1987. *The Railway Journey: The Industrialization of Time and Space in the Nineteenth Century*. Oakland: University of California Press.

Schor, Juliet B. 1991. *The Overworked American: The Unexpected Decline of Leisure*. New York: Basic Books.

Sharma, Sarah. 2014. *In the Meantime: Temporality and Cultural Politics*. Durham, NC: Duke University Press.

Simmel, Georg. 1997. "The Metropolis and Mental Life." In *Simmel on Culture: Selected Writings*, edited by David Frisby and Mike Featherstone, 174–186. London: Sage.

Simmel, Georg. 2004. *The Philosophy of Money*. London: Routledge.

Snyder, Benjamin. 2016. *The Disrupted Workplace: Time and the Moral Order of Flexible Capitalism*. Oxford: Oxford University Press.

Southerton, David. 2020. *Time, Consumption and the Coordination of Everyday Life*. London: Palgrave.

Sullivan, O. and Gershuny, J. 2019 in "Feeling Rushed" in Gershuny, Jonathan, and Oriel Sullivan. 2019. *What We Really Do All Day: Insights from the Centre for Time Use Research*. London: Pelican, 299-305.

Thompson, E. P. 1967. "Time, Work-Discipline, and Industrial Capitalism." *Past and Present* 38: 56–97.

Thrift, Nigel. 1996. "New Urban Eras and Old Technological Fears: Reconfiguring the Goodwill of Electronic Things." *Urban Studies* 33, no. 8: 1436–1493.

Ticona, Julia. 2015. "Strategies of Control: Workers' Use of ICTs to Shape Knowledge and Service Work." *Information, Communication & Society* 18: 509–523.

Tomlinson, John. 2007. *The Culture of Speed: The Coming of Immediacy*. London: Sage.

Turkle, Sherry. 2011. *Alone Together*. New York: Basic Books.

Turkle, Sherry. 2015. *Reclaiming Conversation*. New York: Penguin.

Urry, John. 2000. *Sociology Beyond Societies: Mobilities for the Twenty-First Century*. London: Routledge.

Veblen, Thorstein. 1899. *The Theory of the Leisure Class: An Economic Study of Institutions*. New York: Macmillan.

Virilio, Paul. 1986. *Speed and Politics*. New York: Semiotext(e).

Vostal, Filip. 2014. "Thematizing Speed: Between Critical Theory and Cultural Analysis." *European Journal of Social Theory* 17, no. 1: 95–114.

Wajcman, Judy. 2015. *Pressed for Time: The Acceleration of Life in Digital Capitalism*. Chicago: University of Chicago Press.

Wajcman, Judy, and Nigel Dodd, eds. 2017. *The Sociology of Speed: Digital, Organizational and Social Temporalities*. Oxford: Oxford University Press.

Young, Cristobal, and Chaeyoon Lim. 2014. "Time as a Network Good: Evidence from Unemployment and the Standard Workweek." *Sociological Science* 1: 10–27.

Zerubavel, Eviatar. 1986. *Hidden Rhythms: Schedules and Calendars in Social Life*. Berkeley: University of California Press.

CHAPTER 2

MEDIA AND THE SOCIAL CONSTRUCTION OF REALITY

NICK COULDRY AND ANDREAS HEPP

SOCIOLOGICAL bestsellers were more common in the 1960s than they are today: one example was Peter Berger and Thomas Luckmann's *The Social Construction of Reality* (Berger and Luckmann 1966). This introduced a wider audience to the tradition of phenomenological sociology and to the then-shocking idea that what counts as social reality is itself the result of an ongoing process of social construction. A key premise of their book was that social construction works through human interaction, and more specifically through "a conversational apparatus that ongoingly maintains, modifies and reconstructs . . . . social reality" (1966, 172). For Berger and Luckmann, quite literally, human beings make their social reality through how they talk face to face about the world. They went further and insisted that the core sources of our social knowledge are human beings' interpretations of the world: "everyday life presents itself as a reality interpreted by men and subjectively meaningful to them as a coherent world . . . it is a world that originates in their thoughts and acts, and is maintained as real by these" (1966, 33). A core question for sociology today is whether these two premises—about how social reality is maintained and social knowledge produced—still hold in a world characterized by intense reliance on digital media. If they do not, the viability of a phenomenological sociology is in doubt.

In this chapter, we argue that those premises still hold to a degree—so that the relevance of a phenomenological approach to sociology is preserved—*but only* if we develop a version of phenomenological sociology that takes seriously the existence of media and the entanglement of digital media technologies and interfaces in every aspect of daily life. That means, in turn, taking seriously the roles that data extraction and data processing play in both the operations of digital media and the production of what counts as knowledge of the social world. If so, then some adjustments to other key assumptions must be made, for example, about the social world's transparency. But those adjustments are worth making in order to preserve the project of phenomenological sociology, which still has much to contribute to our sense of the tensions at work in the social world and its forms of knowledge. A key step toward making those adjustments will be to introduce the concept of "deep mediatization," a term explained in the section "Deep Mediatization as a Sensitizing Concept".

The Consequences of a Mediated Life for Social Theory

Let's consider a typical day in a rich country where possession of a smartphone and an internet connection at home can be taken for granted by most people. For now, let's take the case of an adult living alone without children. How is social reality constructed and maintained during that typical day?

Without us trying to give an exhaustive account, just a few details bring out a basic dependence on media devices and interfaces. Many wake up to the sound of the alarm function on their smartphone: An uncharged phone battery can be the difference between re-entering the conscious world on time and not! Many people, depending on age, immediately check their phone for messages on social media platforms and emails received overnight; alternatively, or at the same time, they may listen to media, whether in the form of broadcast news or entertainment, often relayed via their phone or other digital device. Work (including work for school or college) may well involve attending a distant institution: If not, it will almost certainly involve reliance on a computer and an internet connection so that emails can be received and sent, remote information accessed, and documents produced and exchanged. Work away from home is also very likely to involve a computer of some sort: maybe in an office or classroom setting or using computer devices to track manual work (for example, goods trackers in warehouses) or to enter task completion into handheld devices. Relaxation from work during the day could involve a walk or eating without media, but very often it will involve catching up once more with nonwork messages from friends and family and scanning online news, scrolling social media, or using gaming apps. When we find interesting items, we are likely to pass them on to others (Boczkowski 2010), using our phone, laptop, or tablet. Travel to and from work is likely to involve media too: whether listening to podcasts or audio books, reading a book on an e-reader, consuming preloaded music or film on a portable device, exchanging SMS texts or other instant messages, or once more checking up on social media newsfeeds. Evening relaxation, as it was before the age of digital media, is likely to involve watching television content of some sort; but this may not now be watched on a television set but rather via a laptop or phone or, if it is watched on a TV, it may well be a smart TV with internet connection. There is a strong possibility that what is watched is taken from a live broadcasting schedule but via some sort of catchup system (such as in the United Kingdom the BBC i-Player) or a large-scale video on-demand service such as Netflix.

That is enough detail to illustrate the entanglement of media with everyday practices during a typical adult day, without even considering the role that media play in the lives of children or parents. None of these media uses were reflected in Berger and Luckmann's model of how social reality is maintained, which is curious because television, radio, and newspaper consumption were already very widespread when they wrote. Their almost complete silence about media, however, reflected a long disinterest in mainstream sociology, which—apart from a few early classics from the likes of Ernest Manheim (1933)—only began to be challenged by social theorists such as Anthony Giddens in the early 1990s (Giddens 1990, 1991) and political sociologists such as William Gamson (Gamson et al. 1992). Already by then, the study of media and communications technologies was expanding rapidly, and fundamental insights were emerging, for example, about the role of electronic media in reshaping space and time in everyday life (Meyrowitz 1985; Scannell 1988).

We cannot in this chapter survey how sociology as a discipline gradually adapted to the existence of modern media, especially in terms of the relationship between sociology and the emerging field of media and communication studies (Wahl-Jorgensen 2013). But it is worth noting that one of the very first sociologists to think seriously about media's importance for social order was a predecessor of Berger and Luckmann, Alfred Schütz (1967, 88, 177), to whom they strongly refer in their social theory of the everyday world. Schütz had already discussed the question of how social relations can extend to the telephone and other media and shape the everyday.[1] It is even more striking therefore that media played such a minor role in Berger and Luckmann's work. Nor is there space here to survey the history of how media's role in everyday life expanded from broadcast media to internet-based media in the 1990s and onward.[2] What is more urgent is to think conceptually about the dimensions along which everyday life—or, as Berger and Luckmann put it, the social construction of reality—has been reshaped in the twenty-first century through the massive proliferation of media use in daily life across all generations. So, while we need, for brevity, to offer a more general discussion, we are aware of the considerable differences in usage between "media generations" (Bolin 2017).

Media use is important today for almost every aspect of daily life, from its most intimate to its most public aspects. There are many ways of categorizing media use, for example, from the perspective of basic individual actions (McQuail and Deuze 2020) or in terms of how media enable people to fulfill basic needs and capabilities (Couldry 2012, 156–179, discussing Sen). Since in this chapter our concern is with how social reality is constructed and social knowledge produced, we will offer a typology focused on dimensions of media use that play a core role in sustaining individuals in a relational social order. How do media help individuals sustain their place not just in the world but in what feels like, and works as, a social reality?

Social Relations, Digital Media, and the Mediated Construction Reality

For an understanding of current processes of social construction, it seems fundamental to us that today's social relations are to a large extent established and maintained by digital media and their infrastructures. In this sense, such social relations are *mediated* and we are therefore dealing with a mediated construction of reality. The implications of this seemingly far-reaching sentence become more apparent if we look more closely, drawing on recent research.

One of the most basic ways in which we sustain our place in the social world is through the interactions we undertake to survive. We can start our reflection with financial transactions: Offline cash transactions, at least until the COVID-19 crisis, remained common, but an increasing number of transactions have been taking place online, relying on interconnections between computers. As Craig Calhoun (1992) noted in a useful survey essay, such "tertiary" relations became increasingly important in late modernity (building on top of the primary and secondary relations that US sociologist Cooley saw in face-to-face relations). In some parts of the world (for example, China), financial and commercial transactions are now occurring online on a colossal scale through digital platforms like Alibaba which combine social media interfaces, retail shopping sites, and financial services But commercial transactions are only one type of basic interaction that sustain our sense of belonging to a social world. Another type encompasses the social relations that we increasingly sustain through digital platforms designed for mediated connection such as Facebook, Twitter, WeChat, and so on. We have become used not merely to sustaining particular connections through media such as the telephone and email but to communicating on multiple scales with extended networks of people that may be larger than the set of people we know face to face. "Personal connections" sustained precisely through media become a fundamental feature of how social reality is maintained in the twenty-first century (Baym 2015). From a basic web of social connections sustained in large part online, we are able to coordinate and build the events and achievements which make up social life, from birthday parties to group gatherings to fundraising. Lynn Schofield Clark (2013) has provided a vivid account of the essential role that digital media now play in the basic *organization* of family life by parents and equally the organization by children of *their* social life within and beyond the confines of the family.

Social relations are based on identity, but *how* we establish or sustain our identity is, very often, shaped through the process of sustaining connections with diverse others under the pressures of daily life. As we connect with each other in particular ways, for example, by sharing information or telling others what we are up to, we communicate aspects of our identity. The proliferation of digital media and digital platforms for presenting aspects of the self has radically expanded the means available to individuals to show aspects of their lives to close and distant others. Increasingly, we are used to sharing photos just taken, news articles just read, music tracks just heard, shoe recommendations just found online or perhaps encountered *right now* in a shop. What we send to others may be just a link, or it may be something more organized, accounting in some way for our life. How we do this will itself depend on the medium as Facebook, Instagram, and TikTok, for example, each have different styles, requirements, and typical modes of reception. The result is a new digital space for "the accounting of everyday life," which, as Lee Humphreys (2018) argues, is not entirely new but certainly rivals in importance the extensive written diaries and letter exchanges that characterized middle-class life in the eighteenth and nineteenth centuries. In formative years, these types of self-accounting may be of huge importance to self-identity and self-worth, with various commercial forces competing to shape those accounts in distinctive and sometimes questionable ways (Banet-Weiser 2012).

The performance of identity through media is equally important at a group level. The increasing ease with which we share images, ideas, and media via media has arguably facilitated the formation of new types of groups among people who would otherwise have remained physically distant from each other. While there has been a long-standing discussion in media and communications research on how all "imagined communities" (Anderson 1983), such as the community of a particular region, a nation, or Europe, are constructed through mass media, the processes of construction became more diverse with digital media and their infrastructures. For example, "platform collectivities" (Hepp 2020, 138) emerged, that is, alignments of humans that form around a platform such as Airbnb and Facebook who share a certain orientation in practice but are essentially "collectivities without communitization" (Couldry and Hepp 2016, 183). Digital media and their infrastructures also come to play an important role in sustaining the intimate routines and rhythms of family communication, from SMS texts to WhatsApp messages and image exchanges (Pertierra 2018, 100–118). When digital media enable someone to send a photo of a beautiful sunset across the world to close family in other time zones and feel their immediate reactions, a new type of family situation has emerged which has the capacity to enrich the order of family life in surprising ways, sustaining a sense of continuous group connection that would otherwise have been absent during long-distance travel. Just as easily, however, digital media can be used to harm and hurt others who are close to us (Gershon 2010).

In addition to these intimate dimensions of reality maintenance through media, there are more public-facing uses of media. For a century or more in rich nations people have used media to sustain some sense of "public connection," that is, a connection to a world beyond them of shared importance (Couldry, Livingstone, and Markham 2010). Increasingly, however, in a world of proliferating media, this sense of "connection" needs to be sustained not through attending to a broadcast schedule but through improvised personal choices of information source, creating something less like a Habermasian public sphere (Habermas 1989) and more like a "private sphere" (Papacharissi 2010), whose sustainability may be fragile. There are many forms that this private sphere can take: keeping up with Twitter, sharing news links among friends on Facebook, consuming one's own "playlist" of blogs and podcasts, or, if one has the time and resources to compile it, drawing on one's personally curated set of non-mainstream news sources. Without extensive further research, there is no ground for assuming that my form of mediated connection maps much, or at all, onto yours: This constitutes a major difference in how media now contribute to our sense of public connection compared with the mass media era.

Another use of media beyond the immediate contours of individual or group life that helps maintain social reality involves memory practices. People have always held onto mementos and special items which help them sustain a sense of continuity within life's flux. But digital media have massively increased our capacity to store images, texts, video and sound recordings, and so on (Hajek, Lohmeier, and Pentzold 2016). The result, as Jose Van Dijck (2007) argues, is not just to increase our archiving of the past but to reshape our memories around the forms of media storage and exchanges that the digital era has made available. The remarkable new growth of computer memory and the ease with which what is stored on one computer can be sent to another has created radical new challenges for sustaining identity in the face of memories that those individuals perhaps do *not* want to encounter again. What Kate Eichhorn (2019) calls "the end of forgetting" is a particular challenge for children who, as they grow up, undergo profound transformations and reflexive growth whose success may depend on those around them *forgetting* how they once were, something that computer archives may refuse to do. Just as a generation ago Meyrowitz showed that the spatial contours of family life were changed by television, so today the *temporal* contours of family development are being reconfigured by computers.

Finally, media provide reasons to enable all of us to reflect on our experiences of social relations and the world that media are transforming. We are increasingly able to layer our own commentary onto the mediated world, and we often do so by circulating yet more media, with or without our own commentary. All media, as Henry Jenkins and colleagues argue, are now "spreadable" (Jenkins, Ford, and Green 2013), and this spreadability adds an important aspect to the dynamics of our collective understanding and indeed imagination of the social world (Frosh 2019). We grasp this when we recall that, until the age of digital media, sharing media was difficult: It involved perhaps cutting out an article from a newspaper and posting it in an envelope to a friend or calling someone to alert them to watch a TV program at a certain time (once broadcast, programs were generally subsumed into history and so beyond sharing). Now, media sharing across past, present, and future is just a matter of sending a digital link via email or social media message.

In all these aspects of how social relations are being transformed by digital media and their infrastructures, we must be aware that the latter are no longer merely a means of communication. Due to their software-based character, digital media are always simultaneously means of generating data, and much of today's reality construction has to do with collecting and processing this data, which is by and large data that relates to social relationships (Beer 2019). As an example, one can think of the discussion about "big data" (boyd and Crawford 2012), which is based on the hope that by evaluating large amounts of data, "direct access" (for companies, government agencies, and other organizations) can be gained to some form of social reality. From a social constructivist point of view, however, things are different: The significance of this data in today's societies stands for the extent to which its (automated) collection and processing has become part of the construction of reality. In this sense, it can be argued that while Berger and Luckmann focused solely on "knowledge," it is crucial to consider the importance of data for social domains such as education, health, the economy in particular, and social relations in general (Couldry and Hepp 2016, 122–142), when dealing with today's mediated construction of reality.

It is the role of sociology to unpack these many dimensions along which social relations are configured and enacted through media. Very often they just happen without us being consciously aware, as we get on with life, because of how digital devices, such as the smartphone, are "reified" in social description. Richard Ling makes exactly this point by referring to the concept of "reification" that Berger and Luckmann borrowed from Marxist sociology (Ling 2012, 178, citing Berger and Luckmann 1966, 79). The irony is that Berger and Luckmann themselves did not integrate the impact of this media reification into their own thinking, although it was already under way when they wrote in the 1960s.

At this point, to help us further appreciate the implications of media for the order of social life, we need a broader concept: that of "mediatization," and specifically "deep" mediatization. That is the topic of the next section.

Deep Mediatization as a Sensitizing Concept

"Mediatization" as a concept refers to the everyday experience we have discussed up to this point: The making and maintenance of social relations are increasingly entangled with and transformed by digital media and their infrastructures. More specifically, "mediatization" refers to the relationship between the transformation of media and communication, on the one hand, and culture and society, on the other (Krotz 2007; Hjarvard 2013; Lundby 2014). Digitalization and its related datafication have seen emerge a new stage of mediatization, which we can identify as "deep" mediatization: an advanced stage of the process in which all elements of our social world are intricately related to media and their underlying infrastructures (Couldry and Hepp 2016, 7, 34). As a concept, the term "deep mediatization" captures how the mediated construction of reality has changed with the establishment of digital media.

Mediatization can therefore be understood as a "sensitizing concept." A sensitizing concept "gives the user a general sense of reference and guidance in approaching empirical instances" (Blumer 1954, 7) and draws their attention to (present) phenomena in culture and society. On these terms, mediatization "sensitizes" us to fundamental transformations we experience in the context of today's media environment, and this occurs in three ways: the historical depth of the process of media-related transformations, the diversity of media-related transformations in different domains of society, and the connection of media-related transformations with further processes of modernization (Lunt and Livingstone 2016, 465). In addition, deep mediatization sensitizes us to the extent to which digital media and their infrastructures are entangled with the construction of today's social reality. In this light, the term "deep mediatization" also resonates with various other uses of "deep" in the everyday world, such as "deep learning" (which is understood as a new level of automated learning based on algorithmic processes) or "deep analytics" (which is applied to data mining).

As previous research has shown, mediatization is not a linear process (Krotz 2007; Hjarvard 2013; Lundby 2014; Couldry and Hepp 2016, 34–56; Hepp 2020): It occurs via various "waves" of fundamental change to the media environment. The most current wave of mediatization is digitalization, which stimulated the trend toward increasing datafication. Media are increasingly computerized, and objects not previously considered as media, such as a car, are made "media" by virtue of their digital connectivity. Since—as we have argued—digital media are now software-based, they are no longer simply communicative tools; they also act as generators of data, demonstrating clearly how the advanced stage of deep mediatization is firmly grounded in media's digital character.

It is clear that media's pervasiveness in our lives is made possible largely as a consequence of them being refashioned into the digital realm. These software-based media are shaped in a wide variety of digital devices. "Radio" as a medium, for example, is no longer tied to the radio receiver. With a variety of software solutions, we can use a whole range of digital devices to listen to the radio. Some still look like radios (the digital radio as a discrete device), and some are representations on our screens through specific software (a radio app on a smartphone); and we can apply the same principle to television, telephony, and the entire breadth of media services and devices we make use of. Together they make up today's media environment, which is characterized by a "media manifold" (Couldry 2012, 16): a multitude of different media which are intricately connected by internet infrastructure, continuously "innovating" in a recursive process, and, in addition to affording communication, serve the ongoing processing of data.

THE RE-FIGURATION OF SOCIETY

A figurational approach helps us understand how the social construction of reality changes with deep mediatization. A figurational approach understands the individual and society not as discrete entities but as fundamentally entangled with each other (Elias 1978, 129). The various institutions that make up society only exist in and through the social practices of individuals, and the individual only exists in light of the social relations in which they engage. Society does not consist of entities external to and independent from the individual from which they are isolated. All social institutions are made up of individuals who are oriented toward and linked with each other in diverse ways. This is what we can understand as "webs of interdependencies" or, as Elias (1978, 15) puts it, "figurations." If we follow Elias' train of thought, the traditional institutions of family, school, and workplace are no longer positioned "around" individuals but are constituted as figurations of individuals. Each individual lives at the intersection of the different figurations of which they are a part and develops an identity through the subjective narration of the self on the basis of their involvements.

Today, many figurations are constructed around media use. The figurations of collectivities (families, peer groups, communities, etc.) and organizations (media companies, churches, schools, etc.) are entangled with specific media ensembles that potentially transform the figurations of which they are a part. Deep mediatization also makes new figurations possible, such as online gatherings in chat threads, on various platforms, or through apps. Some figurations are even entirely constructed around media technologies. For example, "collectivities of taste" (Passoth, Sutter, and Wehner 2014, 282) represent the calculation of groups of individuals brought together because they share product interests on online stores such as Amazon.

Communication practices are highly relevant when it comes to the social construction of each figuration. Figurations are typically articulated through practices of communication that take place across a variety of media. Family members, for example, can be separated in space but connected through multimodal communication such as (mobile) phone calls, email, and sharing on digital platforms, which all work to maintain the everyday dynamism of family relationships. Organizations, considered as figurations, are preserved through the use of databases, communication across an intranet, as well as printed flyers and other media for internal and external communication. Individuals are involved in these figurations according to the role and position they occupy in their respective actor constellations.

"Transformation" at this point refers to a more fundamental, structural shift of human relationships and practices, something more than mere "change" in the sense that tomorrow is somehow different from today. From a figurational point of view, what we are talking about here is the idea of "re-figuration" (Knoblauch and Löw 2017; Hepp 2020). Broadly speaking, "re-figuration" refers to the transformation of figurations and their interrelatedness to society. Re-figuration is more than a functional adjustment; rather, it is a process related to questions of power, tension, and conflict. Any re-figuration also refers to the significance of powerful individual and supraindividual actors as well as the power of discursive constructions over what form figurations should take. It is not just a question of how, for example, organizations change when digital media are introduced. It is also the question of how they *should* change—and how they orient themselves to normative discourses when implementing digital media (Fredriksson and Pallas 2017).

As our discussion up to this point shows, in these times of deep mediatization we are confronted with a particular form of transformation which we can call "recursive transformation." "Recursivity" indicates that rules are reapplied to the entity that generated them (Couldry and Hepp 2016, 217; Davies 2017). In many respects, the social world has always been recursive, at least insofar as it is based on rules and norms: We sustain it, and repair it when problems arise, by replaying once again the rules and norms on which it was previously based. However, with deep mediatization, recursivity intensifies in tune with its fundamental relation to technology. Many practices are now entangled with digital media, and the algorithms they are based on involve a new kind of recursivity. Human practice, when incorporating digital media and their infrastructures, leads to a continuous processing of data, which, in turn, is the basis for adapting these media. A continuous technology-based monitoring of social practices takes place, changes in which depend on the further development of these technologies, which can work to stabilize particular practices and question others. We can see this happening in the way platforms like Facebook function: User behavior on these platforms is continuously tracked, which not only leads to friend suggestions but is also the basis for generating new functions. The fact that we are dealing with digital media as a process drives this recursivity. Developers' visions of sociality play an important role here: implicit ideas of how society should be inscribed into algorithms which are then reapplied to social practices. Through these development loops, the transformation of society becomes in many ways a transformation that occurs through digital media and their infrastructures.

Conclusion: A Materialist Phenomenology

Such an approach to deep mediatization and the associated re-figuration of society demonstrates the extent to which the original understanding of the *social* construction of reality and the related "phenomenology," as developed by Berger and Luckmann, needs expanding. To put it bluntly, we need a "materialist phenomenology" (Couldry and Hepp 2016, 5–8) to better understand the *mediated* construction of reality. Just as with Raymond Williams' (1990) idea of "cultural materialism," it is fundamental for any analysis of the mediated construction of reality to consider both the material and the symbolic: The "materiality" of today's media concerns not only the various devices, cable networks, and satellites that bring us content. As we have emphasized, since today's media are largely software-based, it is important to note that complex tasks can and most likely will be "shifted" to algorithms. It is necessary, therefore, to think much more rigorously about the materiality of media and to pose questions on which kind of agency is involved and at what times. A materialist phenomenology scrutinizes media technologies and infrastructures through and on the basis of contemporary communications.

Despite the important role played by data and algorithms, questions of human meaning and sense-making remain a central issue for any analysis of social construction. Financial products that make up much of today's globalized stock exchanges, for example, are often completely based on processed data and are wholly intangible without a visual, computer-based representation of the processed data (Knorr Cetina and Reichmann 2015). But that data is only given significance as a financial product through the attribution of meaning, meaning given to it by people. For this reason, it is important to not lose sight of the symbolic: that is, the construction of *meaning* in times of deep mediatization. A materialist phenomenology means understanding that, whatever its appearance of complexity and opacity, the social world remains accessible to interpretation and understanding by human actors. Indeed, it is a structure built up, in part, through those interpretations and understandings. Insofar as that world is not open to interpretation and understanding, this opacity (a growing feature of the world of big data) is a source of tension and contradiction.

One of material phenomenology's key concerns should be the respective actors involved, whether they be individuals or supraindividual actors such as corporations and collectives. Deep mediatization is not a process that just "happens." While this process involves a variety of technologies and some of the most complex infrastructures in history, it remains one made by humans who give it meaning: individual actors as single humans, corporative actors as organizations, companies and state agencies, as well as collective actors such as pioneer communities or social movements. Adopting an actor's viewpoint onto deep mediatization means trying to gain an understanding of how mediatization takes place when the actions of a variety of actors intersect. The result is to change the starting points for both social theory and interpretive sociology.

NOTES

1. For discussion, see Couldry and Hepp (2016, 83–84).
2. For a survey, see Couldry and Hepp (2016, 34–56).

REFERENCES

Anderson, B. 1983. *Imagined Communities: Reflections on the Origins and Spread of Nationalism.* New York: Verso.

Banet-Weiser, S. 2012. *Authentic˜: The Politics of Ambivalence in a Brand Culture.* New York: New York University Press.

Baym, N. 2015. *Personal Connections in the Digital Age.* 2nd ed. Cambridge: Polity.

Beer, D. 2019. *The Data Gaze. Capitalism, Power, Perception.* London: Sage.

Berger, P., and T. Luckmann. 1966. *The Social Construction of Reality.* Harmondsworth, UK: Penguin.

Blumer, H. 1954. "What Is Wrong with Social Theory?" *American Sociological Review* 19: 3–10.

Boczkowski, P. 2010. *News at Work.* Chicago: Chicago University Press.

Bolin, G. 2017. *Media Generations.* London: Routledge.

boyd, d., and K. Crawford. 2012. "Critical Questions for Big Data: Provocations for a Cultural, Technological, and Scholarly Phenomenon." *Information, Communication & Society* 15, no. 5: 662–679.

Calhoun, C. 1992. "The Infrastructure of Modernity." In *Social Change and Modernity*, edited by H. Haferkamp and N. Smelser, 205–236. Berkeley: University of California Press.
Clark, L. Schofield. 2013. *The Parent App: Understanding Families in the Digital Age*. Oxford: Oxford University Press.
Couldry, N. 2012. *Media, Society, World: Social Theory and Digital Media Practice*. Cambridge: Polity.
Couldry, N., and A. Hepp. 2016. *The Mediated Construction of Reality*. Cambridge: Polity.
Couldry, N., S. Livingstone, and T. Markham. 2010. *Media Consumption and Public Engagement*. 2nd ed. Basingstoke, UK: Macmillan.
Davies, S. R. 2017. *Hackerspaces. Making the Maker Movement*. Cambridge: Polity.
Eichhorn, K. 2019. *The End of Forgetting: Growing Up with Social Media*. Cambridge, MA: Harvard University Press.
Elias, N. 1978. *What Is Sociology?* London: Hutchinson.
Fredriksson, M., and J. Pallas. 2017. The localities of mediatization: How organizations translate mediatization into everyday practices. In *Dynamics of Mediatization*, edited by O. Driessens, G. Bolin, A. Hepp, and S. Hjarvard, 119–136. London: Palgrave Macmillan.
Frosh, P. 2019. *The Poetics of Digital Media*. Cambridge: Polity.
Gamson, W., D. Croteau, W. Hoynes, and T. Sasson. 1992. "Media Images and the Social Construction of Reality." *American Sociological Review* 18: 373–393.
Gershon, I. 2010. *The Breakup 2.0*. Ithaca, NY: Cornell University Press.
Giddens, A. 1990. *The Consequences of Modernity*. Cambridge: Polity.
Giddens, A. 1991. *Modernity and Self-Identity*. Cambridge: Polity.
Habermas, J. 1989. *The Structural Transformation of the Public Sphere: An Inquiry into a Category of Bourgeois Society*. Cambridge, MA: MIT Press.
Hajek, A., C. Lohmeier, and C. Pentzold, eds. 2016. *Memory in a Mediated World: Remembering and Reconstruction*. Basingstoke, UK: Palgrave Macmillan.
Hepp, A. 2020. *Deep Mediatization*. London: Routledge.
Hjarvard, S. 2013. *The Mediatization of Culture and Society*. London: Routledge.
Humphreys, L. 2018. *The Qualified Self: Social Media and the Accounting of Everyday Life*. Cambridge, MA: MIT Press.
Jenkins, H., S. Ford, and J. Green. 2013. *Spreadable Media: Creating Value and Meaning in a Networked Culture*. New York: New York University Press.
Knoblauch, H., and M. Löw. 2017. "On the Spatial Re-figuration of the Social World." *Sociologica* 11, no. 2: 1–27.
Knorr Cetina, K., and W. Reichmann. 2015. "Living Data in Financial Markets: Concepts and Consequences." In *Die Gesellschaft der Daten: Über die digitale Transformation der sozialen Ordnung*, edited by F. Süssenguth, 147–172. Bielefeld, Germany: Transcript.
Krotz, F. 2007. "The Meta-Process of Mediatization as a Conceptual Frame." *Global Media and Communication* 3, no. 3: 256–260.
Ling, R. 2012. *Taken for Grantedness: The Embedding of Mobile Communication into Society*. Cambridge, MA: MIT Press.
Lundby, K., ed. 2014. *Mediatization of Communication*. Berlin: de Gruyter.
Lunt, P., and S. Livingstone. 2016. "Is 'Mediatization' the New Paradigm for Our Field?" *Media, Culture & Society* 38, no. 3: 462–470.
Manheim, E. 1933. *Die Träger der öffentlichen Meinung. Studien zur Soziologie der Öffentlichkeit*. Vienna: Verlag Rudolf M. Rohrer.

McQuail, D., and M. Deuze. 2020. *McQuail's Media and Mass Communication Theory*. London: Sage.

Meyrowitz, J. 1985. *No Sense of Place*. New York: Oxford University Press.

Papacharissi, Z. 2010. *A Private Sphere*. Cambridge: Polity.

Passoth, J.-H., T. Sutter, and J. Wehner. 2014. "The Quantified Listener: Reshaping Providers and Audiences with Calculated Measurement." In *Mediatized Worlds*, edited by A. Hepp and F. Krotz, 271–287. London: Palgrave.

Pertierra, A. 2018. *Media Anthropology for the Digital Age*. Cambridge: Polity.

Powers, D. 2017. "First! Cultural Circulation in the Age of Recursivity." *New Media & Society* 19, no. 2: 165–180.

Scannell, P. 1988. "Radio Times: The Temporal Arrangements of Broadcasting in the Modern World." In *Television and Its Audiences: International Research Perspectives*, edited by Philip Drummond and Richard Paterson, 15–31. London: British Film Institute.

Schütz, A. 1967. *The Phenomenology of the Social World*. New York: Northwestern University Press.

Van Dijck, J. 2007. *Mediated Memories in the Digital Age*. Stanford, CA: Stanford University Press.

Wahl-Jorgensen, K. 2013. "The Chicago School of Sociology and Mass Communication Research." In *The International Encyclopedia of Media Studies*, edited by Fabienne Darling-Wolf, 554–577. Hoboken, NJ: John Wiley & Sons.

Williams, R. 1990. *Television: Technology and Cultural Form*. London and New York: Routledge.

CHAPTER 3

THEORIZING CURATION

JENNY L. DAVIS

DIGITAL technologies—which both run on and generate data—have become integrated into personal, public, and institutional life. Data production is seamless and persistent as the data corpus exponentially expands. Gone is the problem of information scarcity, displaced by the challenge of information glut (Andrejevic 2013). Under these data-saturated conditions, curation emerges as a central process.

Broadly defined, "curation" is the discriminate selection and organization of materials. Humans are ontologically curatorial and always have been. The world is full of sensory stimuli that subjects filter, evaluate, highlight, background, and ignore. These are curatorial practices that rely on and reinforce shared meaning systems (Berger and Luckmann 1991; Blumer 1969; Zerubavel 1996). Indeed, curation is intrinsic to the human condition, far predating the "digital turn." However, in a networked and data-driven social context, curation is amplified, explicit, and acute.

Through a targeted review of theoretical and empirical research, I show how curation undergirds and weaves together diverse elements of personal and public life as they manifest with and through the hardware and software of digital technologies. I situate this review within a single theoretical framework, the "curatorial matrix." This general theoretical scaffolding, introduced in Davis (2017a), positions curation as a basic social process that spans and is integral to the foundational dynamics of everyday life in a digitized world.

Situating curation within a single theoretical framework is valuable in two regards. First, it facilitates a coherent conversation between scholarly subfields, creating a common vocabulary that connects diverse but interrelated empirical sites of study. Second, it provides dexterity for curation research moving forward. Technological change occurs regularly and at a rapid pace. New hardware and software habitually roll out, while existing systems are tweaked, revamped, and subject to shifts in legal and political imperatives. Theories of technology need dynamic and transferrable conceptual tools. The curatorial matrix is designed to move with technology theorists as objects of study develop in yet unknowable ways.

I use the curatorial matrix as a common foundation for substantive inquiry into distinct but overlapping bodies of work that address key social phenomena for which curation plays a central role. Specifically, I address curation in identity performance, content moderation, distributions of news and information, and recommender systems. Rather than a comprehensive treatment of each substantive area, I select and highlight writings that exemplify the respective scholarly literatures.

Curatorial Matrix

The curatorial matrix is an existing framework that breaks curation into two kinds of curatorial practice (production and consumption), bound by two extrinsic forces (networks and code) (Davis 2017a): "productive curation" refers to the selection of materials for sharing and display (p. 772); "consumptive curation" refers to the allocation of attention (p. 773); "networked curation" is how social networks shape the data landscape (p. 775); and "curatorial code" is how data organize through inbuilt policies, architectures, and algorithms (p. 776). Although separated for analytic clarity, the boundaries of the matrix are porous, and all elements are entwined with and inform the others (see also Bayer and Hofstra 2020; Jansson 2019; Weiner et al. 2020).

People produce a lot of data. Sometimes data production is intentional (e.g., composing a tweet), and sometimes it is incidental (e.g., geolocational data automated to the cloud). "Productive curation" refers to the way people allocate their content. It is how, when, where, and with whom people share and how, when, where, and from whom people withhold.

Of all the data produced, each individual can consume a mere fraction. The course of daily life presents a constant stream of information, far beyond what anyone could reasonably digest. "Consumptive curation" refers to the choices people make about how to allocate their attention within a crowded information economy—following, muting, skimming, and/or deep-diving through websites, newsfeeds, platforms, and individual content-creators' accounts.

Although individuals actively traverse digital environments and make explicit and tacit choices about production and consumption, these choices are constrained. Choices about production and consumption are constrained because social life is networked (entangled with other people) and shaped by the affordances of hardware and software that mediate social interaction. Within the curatorial matrix, these constraints are represented by networked curation and curatorial code.

"Networked curation" refers to the way productive and consumptive practices are bound by other people within a social network. For example, one is unlikely to encounter content that is set to private but highly likely to encounter content that others send through direct messages. In this way, a person cannot productively contribute to discussions if that individual has been blocked or is actively ignored. However, one may be hypervisible if others follow, "upvote," and/or otherwise boost that person's content through acts such as sharing and tagging.

"Curatorial code" refers to the ways that policies, hardware, and software shape content creation and distribution. Curatorial code ties directly to affordances, or how the design of technical systems enable and constrain the use of those systems with ripple effects onto broader social dynamics (Gibson 1979; Norman 1988; Nagy and Neff 2015; Evans et al. 2017). More specifically, affordances are how artifacts *request*, *demand*, *encourage*, *discourage*, *refuse*, and *allow* particular lines of action for socially situated subjects (Davis and Chouinard 2016; Davis 2020). Technical design features are inextricably social. They are the material outcomes of choices made by developers and engineers, who are often embedded within institutions, which are embedded within societies. Technological objects are thus infused with human values and reflect complex webs of relations between those who make technologies, organizational and institutional bodies, and real and imagined users (see Benjamin 2019; Costanza-Chock 2020; Nagy and Neff 2015; Orr and Davis 2020; Schraube 2009). Together, these relational dynamics have material effects on curation.

Design features of hardware and software set the terms for content production and consumption (Costanza-Chock 2020; Friedman and Hendry 2019; Shilton 2013; Wajcman 2000). For example, social media platforms may nudge users to produce certain kinds of content (e.g., Twitter's "What's happening?" prompt) or, alternatively, prevent a type of content by not supporting it on the platform (e.g., a text-based site will *refuse* the production of images). In turn, the design of hardware and software can *encourage* content consumption by making it seamless to encounter (e.g., Facebook recommending Friends and Groups to follow) but *discourage* or *refuse* consumption by making that content less accessible (e.g., digital paywalls).

Of note, these extrinsic factors (network and code) are not determinative, nor do they apply uniformly across all persons and contexts. Rather, their effects vary between individuals and across social circumstances (Abras, Maloney-Krichmar, and Preece 2004; Hassenzahl 2013). What is celebrated in one networked community may be disparaged in another; what a platform *demands* of me it may *request* of you. Far from neutral, variations are entwined with broader sociostructural arrangements, which are imbued with cultural norms, community practices, and relations of politics and power (Benjamin 2019; Brock 2020; Costanza-Chock 2020; Davis 2020; Irani et al. 2010). Data, information, and attention are all valuable resources and potential vulnerabilities. The distribution of these resources and vulnerabilities reveals and affects broader opportunity structures and patterns of inequality in the larger social order.

In what follows, I overlay the curatorial matrix onto representative works from a range of scholarly subfields. Throughout, I weave a discussion of the power and politics that manifest socially, materially, and symbolically through intersections of race, class, gender, sexuality, (dis)ability, and geography. Overall, this review situates curation as an integral process which reflects and affects sociostructural arrangements. The review also provides a simple vocabulary—production, consumption, networks, and code—to address and identify the agentic and structural elements at play in curatorial processes across time, subjects, and circumstances.

IDENTITY CURATION

For sociologists, curation has always been part of self and identity processes. Rather than intrinsic or essential, sociologists understand the self as a collaborative accomplishment, situated within and developed through complex social relations that make up a social structure. Accomplishing a self means managing multiple identities, across multiple audiences, through performances that are believable, authentic, and verifiable (Mead 1934; Goffman 1959; Stryker and Burke 2000; Burke and Stets 2009). This includes selecting which elements of the self to reveal and conceal, when, how, and to whom.

Canonical theories of self and identity were constructed pre-internet, predicated on face-to-face, physically co-present interaction. Although these theories retain explanatory value, they need reconsideration in light of new forms of communication. Social media scholars have readily taken up this task. In doing so, theorists of identity curation online situate microprocesses of the self within a macro-level information economy, connected by meso-level networks that are shaped and constituted through digitally mediated sites of sociality.

One of the early and influential works on the topic of identity curation online is Bernie Hogan's "Presentation of Self in the Age of Social Media" (2010). Building on Goffman's (1959) dramaturgical perspective, Hogan defines social media platforms as "exhibition" spaces in which users leave data traces and interact with the data traces left by one another.[1] For Hogan, exhibitions are distinct from the spatially and temporally bound "performances" that characterize physically co-present interaction.

Curation is central to Hogan's theorizing. He conceptualizes curation as a collaboration between actors, audiences, and algorithms—or, recast in the language of the curatorial matrix—production, consumption, networks, and code. Algorithmic systems facilitate the curatorial functions of filtering, ordering, and searching (Hogan 2010, 381). These systems, using complex and black-boxed calculations, deliver content of presumed interest and appropriateness to those within a social network, who can manipulate their feeds to make content more or less central.

By default, the algorithms leave content producers with little control over whom their posts reach. This is complicated by the context collapse endemic to social media at the time of Hogan's writing. "Context collapse" refers to the convergence of diverse networks within a shared social space (boyd 2010; Davis and Jurgenson 2014). Hogan thus identifies the lowest common denominator approach as the predominant interactive norm for content production. The "lowest common denominator approach" refers to the practice of producing content that will be acceptable to *all* members of a broad network, calibrated by the network's most sensitive members (e.g., employer, grandparent, religious leader). The lowest common denominator approach significantly curtails both productive and consumptive curatorial practices.

Curating performances to the lowest common denominator means filtering out much of the depth, nuance, and dynamism that enrich social relationships. Actors are constrained in their presentations, and audiences may select from a limited and shallow view. However, there is evidence that the lowest common denominator approach is but one strategy among many and that, in contrast to Hogan's early contentions, identity curation on social media has retained a vibrant character. In particular, Hogan's theorizing has been complicated by the expansion and diversification of social media ecologies, increased digital literacies, and critical intellectual turns which together paint a complex and intricate picture of productive and consumptive identity curation on social media.

The social media landscape is populated by multiple platforms, each with its own norms, affordances, and dynamics. These platforms are not mutually exclusive, nor have they displaced one another (Perrin and Anderson 2019). Rather, legacy social network sites (e.g., Facebook) coexist with emergent and niche platforms which together make up an ecology that is greater than the sum of its parts. Thus, the norms of identity performance are different on Snapchat from Tumblr, both of which diverge from Facebook and all of which maintain a different sensibility from Reddit. These platforms coexist and (at least partially) define each other in their interrelation. For example, Facebook is now the banal family-friendly platform *because* one can goof off on TikTok, spread snark on Twitter, and "fangirl" on Twitch. The point is that each platform serves a different facet of self and identity, situates users amid distinct audiences, and thus fosters various practices of identity curation.

The capacity to regain control over a multifaceted self is a product of diversified social media platforms and users' capacity to manage their platform-mediated identities (Vitak 2012; Marwick and boyd 2014; Treptе, Scharkow, and Dienlin 2020). Productive and consumptive identity curation and their manifestation in light of both networks and code vary with access to, and skill with, sociotechnical systems (Hargittai and Marwick 2016). Identity management is not evenly available, as indicated by critical scholarship in digital inequality (Davis 2017b; Marwick, Fontaine, and boyd 2017, Stevens et al. 2017).

Digital inequalities affect technological access in a variety of ways and toward a variety of ends (Robinson et al. 2015). Laura Robinson's work is unique in its focus on how digital inequalities affect identity curation processes and the entanglement between identity curation and emotion (Robinson 2018). While Hogan (2010) ties identity curation to platform affordances, Robinson approaches curation from a socioeconomic perspective, situating curatorial practice within a broader resource structure.

Through a study of differentially resourced youth, Robinson (2018) identifies identity curation as a central "game" among adolescents. The game contains a set of implicit rules, which are set by those with the highest levels of capital: constantly update, engage in reciprocal identity-affirming interactions, and repair failed identity performances (p. 661). These productive and consumptive identity moves are readily available to those with personal home computers and multiple "smart" devices with reliable internet connectivity. Such agility with identity is more challenging (or impossible) when access is sporadic, unpredictable, and/or nonexistent. When identity curation is unsuccessful, youth pay social and emotional costs, suppressing their own negative feelings and managing the social expectations of their peers. Thus, identity curation varies in ways that reflect and exacerbate structural inequalities through subtle dynamics of everyday interaction.

For people with marginalized identities, social media presents both opportunities and liabilities. Sites like Facebook, with "default publicness" and collapsed network walls (Cho 2018), threaten to expose people in ways that may cause harm. That is, the curatorial code can be damaging. At the same time, social media offers resources to marginalized groups including community building, subcultural knowledge, and the space to express the self within a supportive environment (Dobson, Robards, and Carah 2018). For example, Hanckel et al. (2019) show how "LGBTIQ+ young people curate their identities [across multiple platforms], thereby enhancing the value of their social media experiences ... that are supportive, comfortable and, at times, political" (p. 1263). In this vein, Brock (2020) highlights Black technocultures that are joyful, intimate, and empowering.

In sum, people make choices about what to share, with whom, and on which platforms (productive curation) while consuming content from that which is on offer (consumptive curation). Identity production and consumption are shaped by what others do (and do not) share about each other and about themselves (networked curation), along with algorithms and architectural design features that affect content availability (curatorial code). In some ways, the conditions of identity curation on social media present vulnerabilities that exacerbate existing social and economic disparities. However, these same conditions also provide opportunities for individual identity development, community building, and collective identity formation (Brock 2020; Davis, Love, and Fares 2019; Dobson, Robards, and Carah 2018; Rohlinger and Bunnage 2018). The curatorial matrix situates these elements together such that identity online is at once entwined with material digital architectures, complex social networks, sociostructural circumstances, and interpersonal interaction.

Content Moderation

The early promise of an open web characterized by unfettered and direct expression quickly revealed itself to be untenable. Left unchecked, web technologies do not facilitate rich discussion and debate but a cacophony of noise peppered with explicit, offensive, harmful, hurtful, and dangerous content (Caplan, Hanson, and Donovan 2018; Donovan 2020; Lewis 2018; Nagle 2017). Social media platforms have emerged as systematic filters, and their content moderation practices regulate how this filtering takes shape.

Content moderation organizes content based on policies (terms of service), norms (user feedback), and the values—ideological and economic—of a platform's designers, developers, and executives. User content is preemptively structured by platform architectures and continually (re)shaped by moderation decisions enacted by both humans (networked curation) and machines (curatorial code). Moderation decisions affect what people can produce and share and what is available for consumption. These infrastructural decisions are not neutral but intrinsically political (Gillespie 2010; Plantin and Punathambekar 2019; Duguay, Burgess, and Suzor 2020). They reflect implicit and explicit agendas and taken-for-granted logics within which users operate (Van Dijck and Poell 2013).

Gillespie (2018) asserts that platforms are defined by their content moderation practices and policies. Decisions about what to moderate, with how much force, under what conditions, and for whom are how platforms differentiate themselves from one another. Moderation can take myriad forms, intersecting social and technical elements with varying emphasis on each. Content moderation can be internally driven by network norms and/or enforced by professional moderators who are formally compensated for their labor.

Informal network-based moderation relies on community volunteers and rating mechanisms that signal evaluation while affecting algorithms that sort and distribute user-generated content (Matias 2019; Squirrell 2019). Volunteer moderators can have special technical privileges which enable them to remove content. They may post warnings, ban users, and arbitrate on internal community disagreements. Informal community-based moderation can also be facilitated through rating features—"hearts," "likes," up- and downvotes—with which community participants indicate agreement or dissent while amplifying or diminishing content centrality (Leavitt and Clark 2014; Leavitt and Robinson 2017). This labor is distributed throughout community networks rather than concentrated in the hands of high-status moderators. In practice, community moderation is often a hybrid of volunteer moderators and rating systems, as is the case with Reddit subcommunities in which votes affect content centrality and subreddit community moderators set the rules and enforce them at will.

Informal, community-based moderation presents a version of the democratic ideal: Content is not extrinsically regulated from above but curated from within based on community feedback and a set of implicitly and/or explicitly agreed-upon values (Poor 2005; Goode 2009). In seeming paradox, community-based moderation has also proven highly normalizing in ways that stifle and exclude marginalized voices. Rather than inviting a diversity of perspectives, (sub)communities converge toward the mean and reinforce the status quo. For example, Julien (2017) showed how participants in a community on the image-sharing site Imgur upvoted content that adhered to color-blind race ideologies while ignoring and/or downvoting content with White supremacist leanings and critical race messaging. This largely hetero, upper-middle-class, White user group thus resisted the worst racist impulses but at the same time stifled content (and content producers) that approached race and racism with a critical lens.

With vast economic growth and expanding user populations, many platforms supplement community-based moderation with paid workers. This emergent labor force represents a new field of commercial content moderation. Commercial content moderators are "professional people paid to screen content uploaded to the internet's social media sites on behalf of the firms that solicit user participation" (Roberts 2019, 1). Workers moderate content delivered to them through automated detection systems and by users who flag content as problematic (Crawford and Gillespie 2016).

Commercial content moderation intersects mundane practices of curation with a changing global economy that trades in data and information. Commercial content moderators are largely invisible and engage in what Mary L. Gray and Siddharth Suri (2019) refer to as "ghost work." "Ghost work" is the human labor that closes the gap between services provided by a technical system and that system's actual technical capacities. Indeed, there are many tasks for which humans remain far better suited than machines. Content moderation, with its requirement for nuanced cultural readings, is one such task. Although many large platforms include automated detection systems that screen for prohibited content, these automated systems are decidedly blunt and imprecise and thus operate as tools for human moderators rather than stand-alone (or even primary) moderation devices.

Commercial content moderation can take many forms, from in-house embedded employees to contract workers to piece-workers located around the globe moderating content through discrete tasks assigned via micro-labor platforms such as Upwork or Amazon's Mechanical Turk. Increasingly, piece-work is becoming the norm. The working conditions for piece-work moderators are characterized by a tension between flexibility and autonomy, on the one hand, and exploitative relations in which moderators receive low wages, little training, and even less institutional or collegial support, on the other. Although both autonomy and exploitation are at play, research shows that, on balance, the latter generally outweighs the former (Chen 2014; Gray and Suri 2019; Roberts 2019). Disproportionately, these jobs distribute to those already disadvantaged within the existing global economy (e.g., people living in the Global South, people with care responsibilities, people with disabilities that curtail traditional forms of employment, people whose full-time jobs do not cover the necessities of basic living, etc.) (Anwar and Graham 2020; Gray and Suri 2019; Roberts 2016; Zyskowski et al. 2015).

Although the status quo for commercial content moderation relies on low-paid workers implementing corporate guidelines, other models are conceivable. Joan Donovan (2020), for example, has called for a professionalization of the field, pointing to librarians as expert curators with skill sets ideally suited to platform filtering. Rather than simply *removing* undesirable material, professional librarians have the capacity to intentionally curate content based on relevance, helpfulness, and veracity. This idea, and other re-imaginings, are crucial in a social–historical moment plagued by mediated hate, violence, and mis/disinformation.

In sum, content moderation is an infrastructural form of content curation with micro, macro, material, and social-relational elements that emerge through the constituent parts of the curatorial matrix. Moderation relies on interplays between the technical features of curatorial code (algorithms, rating features, automated detection), micro-networks of community participants (volunteer moderators, voting, flagging), and macro-networks of a global workforce (piece-workers, embedded employees, contract workers). Content moderation, as it affects both production and consumption, is political. Moderation reflects the values of large social media companies, the judgments of dispersed individuals, and the status quo logics of community users. These sociostructural dynamics affect who can produce content, what is on offer for consumption, and, more generally, the shape of public discourse (Gillespie 2018; Massanari 2017; Matamoros-Fernández 2017). Although most platforms draw on a narrow range of moderation practices, alternative models are possible, plausible, and worth consideration (Donovan 2020).

News and Information

News and information have always been curated. Library sciences have long studied the ways information is classified, categorized, and granted relevance (Black and Muddiman 2016; Burke 2007; Mattern 2014; Rubin 2017), while traditional media studies have trained attention on how newspapers and television broadcasters curate stories, construct narratives, and thus shape the public conversation (Matthes 2009; McCombs and Shaw 1972; Park and Pooley 2008). These foundational forms of curation remain relevant. However, the contemporary information landscape is qualitatively distinct from previous epochs in both scale and kind. News and information now flow through commercial search engines and social media platforms, where they are curated by complex algorithms, vast and often unidentifiable networks, and individual users whose practices reflect varied engagements between social networks and multifaceted sociotechnical systems (Barnard 2018; Bruns 2018; Christin 2018, 2020). A critical point when analyzing the flows of news and information across digital platforms and infrastructures is that these curatorial systems are, first and foremost, powerful commercial enterprises. Thus, "truth" necessarily takes form through a prism of capitalist logic (Fuchs 2017; Vaidhyanathan 2018).

Social media has emerged as a central source of news and information. In 2017, Facebook founder Mark Zuckerberg issued a "manifesto" in which he touted the platform as a premier site of global civic engagement by which "community governance might work at scale." "Just as TV became the primary medium for civic communication in the 1960s," Zuckerberg (2017) wrote, "social media is becoming this in the 21st century." Indeed, almost 70% of Americans report getting news on social media, especially Facebook, Twitter, and Reddit (Shearer and Matsa 2018), while users of these platforms productively curate news landscapes by sharing, commenting on, and contextualizing news stories. However, the function of social media as a form of "community governance ... at scale" remains unsubstantiated.

Although social media present opportunities for users to express themselves and discuss, debate, and gather information, there are also real concerns about how platform design features curate materials, in whose interests, and toward what ends (Vaidhyanathan 2018). Facebook—the most powerful and prominent social media platform—shapes the political landscape through interrelated processes of productive and consumptive curation, operating within complex networks and black-boxed code (Vaidhyanathan 2018). Facebook trades in data and attention. Its financial prerogative is to generate as much data as possible from user participation and to harness user attention for the benefit of advertisers. The platform's curatorial algorithms reflect these interests.

Relying on its EdgeRank algorithms, Facebook highlights content that will generate attention and clicks (Bucher 2012, 2018). It does so by amplifying emotionally charged and sensationalist posts (Jones, Libert, and Tynski 2016) and by microtargeting users based on a complex amalgamation of individual and collective usage histories (Ribeiro et al. 2019). Facebook users are thus delivered a semi-personalized feed, derived from their own prior behaviors and the behaviors of others like them. Technically, each individual can share freely with their networks, thus enacting an ideal of open expression through productive curatorial practice. Yet, this ostensible productive agency has not resulted in a robust public sphere. Instead, the curatorial systems of Facebook and other mainstream social media platforms foster widespread mis/disinformation and distrust (Marwick and Lewis 2017), undue political influence (Martin and Hutchinson 2020), and filter-bubbles (Pariser 2011) in which information is disproportionately self-affirmatory (Vaidhyanathan 2018). This is not to say that users cannot "bump" into diverse perspectives—they do (Lu and Lee 2019)—but by default, the Facebook platform and other mainstream social media sites curate feeds toward confirmation bias and thus deepen ideological positions and related social divides (Vaidhyanathan 2018).

Although people regularly access news and information on social media, these sites are primarily designed for *social* engagement. In contrast, commercial search engines are designed as information systems. Commercial search engines act as conduits to the internet and the means by which users navigate a saturated information economy (Halavais 2017; Hillis, Petit, and Jarrett 2012; Mager 2012). Google is by far the most prominent commercial search engine and thus carries outsized control over information flows (Vaidhyanathan 2012).

Search engines are not impartial delivery systems but economically driven and politically charged corporate products (Halavais 2017). The political dynamics of search engines—and Google in particular—are outlined in Noble's (2018) *Algorithms of Oppression*. Noble shows the tension between a general population who understand Google search results as objectively relevant and/or true and an algorithmic system that is deeply biased in ways that reinforce and amplify inequalities at the intersection of race and gender (see also Brock 2020, chap. 2). To be sure, Google Inc. is not invested in promoting racist or sexist content. Rather, Google is in the data and advertising business, and this business capitalizes on clicks and links. Using the PageRank system, Google curates content based on incoming and outgoing links, tinged with input from individual usage histories. Because information is entrenched within the cultural systems from which it derives, the inequalities of a society infuse the Google search system. That is, in a racist–sexist (classist, heteronormative, ableist) society, Google's information landscape will reproduce inequality by default.

Two points are critical to qualify this discussion. First, social media and Google have not displaced mainstream broadcast outlets but joined with them in a multifaced information ecosystem. Second, even within a complex and highly corporatized information infrastructure, users maintain curatorial agency (albeit differentially distributed).

Digital information systems and traditional news are not mutually exclusive but intertwined. Traditional news outlets use algorithms to curate stories, with a bidirectional flow between social media and broadcast media. Stories that gain traction on social media are picked up by mainstream outlets, and mainstream news outlets produce stories for social media virality (Barnard 2018; Christin 2018, 2020); Google search results disproportionately direct users to mainstream news outlets (Hindman 2008); and mainstream journalists often maintain active social media profiles, weaving between traditional broadcasters and direct-to-consumer communications (Barnard 2016).

Although powerful conglomerates enact substantial control over the information landscape, users do maintain the capacity for agency and subversion. For instance, social media users may engage with platform settings to control how their own content distributes (O'Meara 2019; Petre, Duffy, and Hund 2019), they may strategically amplify and/or diminish particular users and content, and they may play with the algorithm by actively scrolling, clicking, and commenting in ways that affect their subsequent newsfeeds (Vaidhyanathan 2018; Bruns 2019). In turn, individuals and organizations may engage in search engine optimization to amplify that which they produce within a search query and/or undermine the system by flooding, spamming, or otherwise confusing the clear connection between search terms and search results (Vaidhyanathan 2012; Noble 2018). Such practices, of course, are resource-dependent and vary across subjects and circumstances.

Overall, social media platforms and commercial search engines are formidable knowledge systems with significant shaping effects. They affect how people come to know the world and the likelihood that ideas, news, and information will be available. Read through the curatorial matrix, the delivery of news and information is predicated on individual practices, identity indicators, and collective patterns of search terms and clicks (i.e., various forms of networked curation), all of which are algorithmically guided by documented use histories, platform architectures, and complex data infrastructures (curatorial code). Users remain active as both productive and consumptive curators but always in relation to, embedded within, and in the context of powerful, commercially driven, political–economic infrastructures.

Recommender Systems

Recommendations help people make decisions when the available choices are unclear, when information is incomplete, and/or when the options are too vast. People have long sought advice about where to eat, which doctors to visit, which schools to attend, and many other choices that occupy daily life. With the rise of digital technologies, recommendations have been automated at scale as a way to manage immense information streams.

Recommender systems algorithmically select and deliver content to users based on individual data histories and broader patterns derived from large data sets. These are the video, book, song, research article, and network recommendations that populate apps, platforms, and services. Recommender algorithms curate for users from an unwieldy content corpus in ways that optimize "stickiness" (Gladwell 2006) or sustained user attention and engagement. These systems curate based on user behaviors, thus involving users productively within the consumptive curatorial process. That is, user behaviors and feedback and the behaviors and feedback of connected social networks (i.e., productive curation) fuel recommender systems' curatorial code. In turn, user-generated content is filtered through algorithmic and networked processes, making user outputs differentially available for consumption.

The history of recommender systems follows an evolution from content-filtering devices, through user rating metrics, to the current infrastructural system of "captology," in which algorithms operate as a form of material–psychological trap (Seaver 2018). At the end of the twentieth century, developers created recommender systems as filtering tools for immense information catalogs on the web (Resnick et al. 1994). Commercially, recommender systems became a means of delivering to users what they ostensibly want, channeling desires into automated code. In the first decade of the new millennium, recommender algorithms were based on user evaluations, with developers measuring effectiveness by the coincidence between actual and predicted user ratings, as indicated by the "root mean square error" (RMSE). However, user ratings proved troublesome as a curatorial device. Users can be fickle in their evaluations (Amatriain, Pujol, and Oliver 2009) while remaining susceptible to limitations of self-knowledge and divergences between attitudes and behaviors (Herlocker et al. 2004).[2] For these reasons, RMSE has been displaced by implicit measures of user behavior—clicks, time spent, content not consumed—while the goal of recommender systems has become that of "captivation."

For Seaver (2018), captivation is a form of entrapment that blurs the lines between coercion and persuasion, gratification and control. Commercial enterprises use data traces to curate content in ways that keep users hooked. These curatorial algorithms encode users' implicit desires and propensities based on individual and collective behavioral patterns, ensnaring users in pathways of pleasure, affective excitation, discovery, and intrigue (Drott 2018; Milano, Taddeo, and Floridi 2020).

As curatorial devices, recommender systems are deeply socio-material and blur the lines between consumption and production, networks, and code. Recommendations are fueled by user-produced data, "nudging" users toward particular consumptive actions and away from others. These behaviors produce new data, which inform recommender algorithms, and so on.

Recommender systems can paradoxically expand and reinforce consumption habits and in turn expand and reinforce subjects' lens on the world. Based on historical behavioral data, recommender systems deliver content that appeals to existing proclivities and preferences. At the same time, recommendations can be surprising and serendipitous, especially when they are predicated on appeal and entrapment rather than, necessarily, eliciting positive content evaluations (Kotkov, Wang, and Veijalainen 2016). The extent to which recommender systems are reinforcing versus expansive can be a product of the algorithmic system itself (e.g., algorithms based on discovery versus history), the consumptive practices of agentic user-subjects (e.g., users who seek out versus skip over unfamiliar content), and, most often, a complex combination of users and algorithms, differing in relative emphasis.

Research shows that people do not uncritically accept algorithmic recommendations but instead mistrust automated systems that are likely to err (Dietvorst, Simmons, and Massey 2015) and which defy clear explanation (Yeomans et al. 2017). Indeed, recommender systems have integrated with personal, political, and professional life; yet algorithms do not necessarily give the best (or even good/right) recommendations, and they often operate through impenetrable code. Thus, there is reason for people to be wary of recommended content and clear motivation for people to navigate recommender systems with vigilance and care (Harambam, Helberger, and van Hoboken 2018).

One's understanding of recommender systems and how these systems operate can, and often does, affect the process of content production. Indeed, a powerful industry is emerging to help content producers optimize their likelihood of "recommendation," while best practices across many sites of content production include considerations of encoded content delivery systems. For example, it behooves journalists, bloggers, and even academics to choose titles, keywords, and references/links that strategically connect one piece of work to popular topics and networks, thus bolstering the chances that an article, book, or post is delivered to potential consumers through automated recommender algorithms (Beel, Gipp, and Wilde 2010; Blanchett Neheli 2018; Christin 2018, 2020).

Ultimately, recommender systems are deployed by commercial enterprises for the purposes of data collection, attention containment, and the economic capital that data and attention engender. At the same time, however, recommender systems feed on and respond to organic user behaviors and the pleasures entailed therein. Thus, recommender algorithms are at once capitalist curatorial tools and distinctly human artifacts that, for many individuals, markedly improve consumption on the web and increase content centrality in a crowded attention economy.

Recommender systems are characterized by tensions of persuasion and coercion, gratification and control. Within the curatorial matrix, this is reflected as a fluid relation between content production and consumption, delivered through networks, via curatorial code. For those who make content (productive curation), recommender systems may alternatively hide that which is produced or deliver content to those who may not have otherwise encountered it. Dexterity with the sociotechnical system and the economic resources to optimize the system work in a content producer's favor. Consumptively, those who can opt out, restructure, toggle between, and push back on content recommendations maintain greater agency and a closer proximity to persuasion than do those with fewer digital skills and resources, whose experiences veer closer to coercion with little recourse for escape. The capacity to navigate sociotechnical recommender systems thus makes these systems more pliable, while resource deficits render them rigid.

Conclusion

In a data- and information-saturated social environment, the practice and process of curation is normative, necessary, and integral. Grounded theoretically in the curatorial matrix, we can understand curatorial processes as interrelated dynamics of production and consumption within complex social networks and encoded digital infrastructures. In this review, I have discussed how curation figures into identity, content moderation, distributions of news and information, and recommender systems that draw on user data and deliver it back to them in repackaged form. Throughout, I have highlighted the ways in which curation is imbricated with sociostructural variables and political-economic realities.

As a conceptual tool, the curatorial matrix assumes a critical orientation. This is essential for any conceptual device in the social study of technology. Technologies develop with and through existing social systems. By default, the power dynamics of those social systems are thus embedded in, reproduced through, and amplified by sociotechnical apparatuses (e.g., Winner 1980; Eubanks 2018; Benjamin 2019; Costanza-Chock 2020). These dynamics are clear in the scholarly contributions reviewed in this chapter. Curatorial relations—productive and consumptive, networked and encoded—privilege user-subjects with more resources and higher standing within the existing social order. At the same time, curatorial processes can serve as mechanisms of empowerment and subversion by marginalized groups, breaching boundaries of inequality and oppression.

Going forward, the curatorial matrix can be put to use (and potentially amended) through application in multiple and divergent fields of sociotechnical study. Curation is central to the practices of everyday social life in contemporary societies. Understanding human social dynamics necessarily entails attention to how information flows, to whom, and under what circumstances.

I conclude with a note about the limitations of this chapter, wrapped in the curatorial theme around which the argument is based. Although I considered and reported on a variety of literatures and highlighted influential works, these represent a partial, indeed *curated*, depiction of the academic landscape. In selecting each topical focus and the relevant, representative texts, I necessarily relied on curatorial decisions from scholars before me and in turn foreclosed alternate intellectual configurations, with reverberating effects on the field of curation studies and digital media studies more broadly. Not only will readers be affected by my referencing choices—even in disagreement and critique—but the selected fields and works will be bolstered through increased citation numbers and a related boost in attention, whereas those omitted enter into an opposite, invisiblizing cycle. Of course, this is just one chapter, in one handbook, by one author, making the direct effects relatively minor. However, at scale, scholarly practices matter. In a data-driven context, scholarly practice is inextricable from the curatorial systems that shape knowledge, bestow status, and threaten obscurity for that which slips through the nets and webs of curatorial hold.

Notes

1. See also Humphreys' (2018) *The Qualified Self: Social Media and the Accounting of Everyday Life*, in which Humphreys demonstrates how users translate data into personal narratives.
2. For a broader discussion of the social–psychological processes that underlie limitations of self-knowledge and divergence between attitudes and behaviors, see Kutner, Wilkins, and Yarrow (1952) and Wilson and Dunn (2004).

References

Abras, Chadia, Diane Maloney-Krichmar, and Jenny Preece. 2004. "User-Centered Design." In *Encyclopedia of Human–Computer Interaction*, edited by William Sims Bainbridge, 445–456. Thousand Oaks, CA: Sage Publications.

Amatriain, Xavier, Josep M. Pujol, and Nuria Oliver. 2009. "I Like It . . . I Like It Not: Evaluating User Ratings Noise in Recommender Systems." Paper presented at the International Conference on User Modeling, Adaptation, and Personalization, Trento, Italy, June 22–26.

Andrejevic, Mark. 2013. *Infoglut: How Too Much Information Is Changing the Way We Think and Know*. New York and London: Routledge.

Anwar, Mohammad Amir, and Mark Graham. 2020. "Between a Rock and a Hard Place: Freedom, Flexibility, Precarity and Vulnerability in the Gig Economy in Africa." *Competition & Change*. Published ahead of print April 1, 2020. https://doi.org/10.1177/1024529420914473.

Barnard, Stephen. 2018. *Citizens at the Gates*. New York: Palgrave Macmillan.

Barnard, Stephen R. 2016. "'Tweet or Be Sacked': Twitter and the New Elements of Journalistic Practice." *Journalism* 17, no. 2: 190–207.

Bayer, Joseph B., and Bas Hofstra. 2020. "Toward Curation and Personality-Driven Social Networks." *Nature Human Behaviour* 4, no. 2: 123–125.

Beel, Jöran, Bela Gipp, and Erik Wilde. 2010. "Academic Search Engine Optimization (ASEO): Optimizing Scholarly Literature for Google Scholar & Co." *Journal of Scholarly Publishing* 41, no. 2: 176–190.

Benjamin, Ruha. 2019. *Race after Technology: Abolitionist Tools for the New Jim Code*. Cambridge: Polity.

Berger, Peter L., and Thomas Luckmann. 1991. *The Social Construction of Reality: A Treatise in the Sociology of Knowledge*. London: Penguin.

Black, Alistair, and Dave Muddiman. 2016. *The Early Information Society: Information Management in Britain before the Computer*. London and New York: Routledge.

Blanchett Neheli, Nicole. 2018. "News by Numbers: The Evolution of Analytics in Journalism." *Digital Journalism* 6, no. 8: 1041–1051.

Blumer, Herbert. 1969. *Symbolic Interactionism: Perspective and Method*. Englewood Cliffs, NJ: Prentice-Hall.

boyd, danah. 2010. "Social Network Sites as Networked Publics: Affordances, Dynamics, and Implications." In *A Networked Self: Identity, Community, and Culture on Social Network Sites*, edited by Zizi Papacharissi, 39–58. New York and London: Routledge.

Brock, André, Jr. 2020. *Distributed Blackness: African American Cybercultures*. New York: New York University Press.

Bruns, Axel. 2018. *Gatewatching and News Curation: Journalism, Social Media, and the Public Sphere*. New York: Peter Lang Publishing.

Bruns, Axel. 2019. *Are Filter Bubbles Real?* Cambridge: Polity.

Bucher, Taina. 2012. "What to Be on Top? Algorithmic Power and the Threat of Invisibility on Facebook." *New Media & Society* 14, no. 7: 1164–1180.

Bucher, Taina. 2018. *If . . . Then: Algorithmic Power and Politics*. New York: Oxford University Press.

Burke, Colin. 2007. "History of Information Science." *Annual Review of Information Science and Technology* 41, no. 1: 3–53.

Burke, Peter J., and Jan E. Stets. 2009. *Identity Theory*. Oxford: Oxford University Press.

Caplan, Robyn, Lauren Hanson, and Joan Donovan. 2018. *Dead Reckoning: Navigating Content Moderation after Fake News*. New York: Data & Society Research Institute. https://datasociety.net/pubs/oh/DataAndSociety_Dead_Reckoning_2018.pdf.

Chen, Adrian. 2014. "The Laborers Who Keep Dick Pics and Beheadings out of Your Facebook Feed." *Wired*. https://www.wired.com/2014/10/content-moderation/.

Cho, Alexander. 2018. "Default Publicness: Queer Youth of Color, Social Media, and Being Outed by the Machine." *New Media & Society* 20, no. 9: 3183–3200.

Christin, Angèle. 2018. "Counting Clicks: Quantification and Variation in Web Journalism in the United States and France." *American Journal of Sociology* 123, no. 5: 1382–1415.

Christin, Angèle. 2020. *Metrics at Work: Journalism and the Contested Meaning of Algorithms*. Princeton, NJ: Princeton University Press.

Costanza-Chock, Sasha. 2020. *Design Justice: Community-Led Practices to Build the Worlds We Need*. Cambridge, MA: MIT Press.

Crawford, Kate, and Tarleton Gillespie. 2016. "What Is a Flag For? Social Media Reporting Tools and the Vocabulary of Complaint." *New Media & Society* 18, no. 3: 410–428.

Davis, Jenny L. 2017a. "Curation: A Theoretical Treatment." *Information, Communication & Society* 20, no. 5: 770–783.

Davis, Jenny L. 2017b. "The End of What People Do Online." *New Criticals*. http://www.newcriticals.com/the-end-of-what-people-do-online.

Davis, Jenny L. 2020. *How Artifacts Afford: The Power and Politics of Everyday Things*. Cambridge, MA: MIT Press.

Davis, Jenny L., and James B. Chouinard. 2016. "Theorizing Affordances: From Request to Refuse." *Bulletin of Science, Technology & Society* 36, no. 4: 241–248.

Davis, Jenny L., and Nathan Jurgenson. 2014. "Context Collapse: Theorizing Context Collusions and Collisions." *Information, Communication & Society* 17, no. 4: 476–485.

Davis, Jenny L., Tony P. Love, and Phoenicia Fares. 2019. "Collective Social Identity: Synthesizing Identity Theory and Social Identity Theory Using Digital Data." *Social Psychology Quarterly* 82, no. 3: 254–273.

Dietvorst, Berkeley J., Joseph P. Simmons, and Cade Massey. 2015. "Algorithm Aversion: People Erroneously Avoid Algorithms after Seeing Them Err." *Journal of Experimental Psychology: General* 144, no. 1: 114.

Dobson, Amy Shields, Brady Robards, and Nicholas Carah. 2018. *Digital Intimate Publics and Social Media*. New York: Springer.

Donovan, Joan. 2020. "You Purged Racists from your Website? Great, Now Get to Work." *Wired*. https://www.wired.com/story/you-purged-racists-from-your-website-great-now-get-to-work/.

Drott, Eric. 2018. "Why the Next Song Matters: Streaming, Recommendation, Scarcity." *Twentieth-Century Music* 15, no. 3: 325–357.

Duguay, Stefanie, Jean Burgess, and Nicolas Suzor. 2020. "Queer Women's Experiences of Patchwork Platform Governance on Tinder, Instagram, and Vine." *Convergence* 26, no. 2: 237–252.

Evans, Sandra K., Katy E. Pearce, Jessica Vitak, and Jeffrey W. Treem. 2017. "Explicating Affordances: A Conceptual Framework for Understanding Affordances in Communication Research." *Journal of Computer Mediated Communication* 22, no. 1: 35–52.

Eubanks, V. 2018. *Automating Inequality: How High-Tech Tools Profile, Police, and Punish the Poor*. New York: St. Martin's Press.

Friedman, Batya, and David G. Hendry. 2019. *Value Sensitive Design: Shaping Technology with Moral Imagination*. Cambridge, MA: MIT Press.

Fuchs, Christian. 2017. *Social Media: A Critical Introduction*. London: Sage.

Gibson, J. J. 1979. "The Theory of Affordances." In *The Ecological Approach to Visual Perception*, 127–143. Boston: Houghton Mifflin.

Gillespie, Tarleton. 2010. "The Politics of 'Platforms.'" *New Media & Society* 12, no. 3: 347–364.

Gillespie, Tarleton. 2018. *Custodians of the Internet: Platforms, Content Moderation, and the Hidden Decisions That Shape Social Media*. New Haven, CT: Yale University Press.

Gladwell, Malcolm. 2006. *The Tipping Point: How Little Things Can Make a Big Difference*. New York: Little, Brown.

Goffman, Erving. 1959. *The Presentation of Self in Everyday Life*. New York: Doubleday.

Goode, Luke. 2009. "Social News, Citizen Journalism and Democracy." *New Media & Society* 11, no. 8: 1287–1305.

Gray, Mary L., and Siddharth Suri. 2019. *Ghost Work: How to Stop Silicon Valley from Building a New Global Underclass*. New York: Houghton Mifflin Harcourt.

Halavais, Alexander. 2017. *Search Engine Society*. Cambridge: Polity.

Hanckel, Benjamin, Son Vivienne, Paul Byron, Brady Robards, and Brendan Churchill. 2019. "'That's Not Necessarily for Them': LGBTIQ+ Young People, Social Media Platform Affordances and Identity Curation." *Media, Culture & Society* 41, no. 8: 1261–1278.

Harambam, Jaron, Natali Helberger, and Joris van Hoboken. 2018. "Democratizing Algorithmic News Recommenders: How to Materialize Voice in a Technologically Saturated Media Ecosystem." *Philosophical Transactions of the Royal Society A: Mathematical, Physical and Engineering Sciences* 376, no. 2133: 20180088.

Hargittai, Eszter, and Alice Marwick. 2016. "'What Can I Really Do?' Explaining the Privacy Paradox with Online Apathy." *International Journal of Communication* 10, no. 21: 3737–3757.

Hassenzahl, Marc. 2013. "User Experience and Experience Design." *The Encyclopedia of Human-Computer Interaction*. 2nd ed. Interaction Design Foundation. https://www.researchgate.net/profile/Marc_Hassenzahl/publication/259823352_User_Experience_and_Experience_Design/links/56a7352d08ae997e22bbc807/User-Experience-and-Experience-Design.pdf.

Herlocker, Jonathan L., Joseph A. Konstan, Loren G. Terveen, and John T. Riedl. 2004. "Evaluating Collaborative Filtering Recommender Systems." *ACM Transactions on Information Systems* 22, no. 1: 5–53.

Hillis, Ken, Michael Petit, and Kylie Jarrett. 2012. *Google and the Culture of Search*. New York and London: Routledge.

Hindman, Matthew. 2008. *The Myth of Digital Democracy*. Princeton, NJ: Princeton University Press.

Hogan, Bernie. 2010. "The Presentation of Self in the Age of Social Media: Distinguishing Performances and Exhibitions Online." *Bulletin of Science, Technology & Society* 30, no. 6: 377–386.

Humphreys, Lee. 2018. *The Qualified Self: Social Media and the Accounting of Everyday Life*. Cambridge MA: MIT Press.

Irani, Lilly, Janet Vertesi, Paul Dourish, Kavita Philip, and Rebecca E. Grinter. 2010. "Postcolonial Computing: A Lens on Design and Development." In *Proceedings of the SIGCHI Conference on Human Factors in Computing Systems*, 1311–1320. New York: ACM.

Jansson, Johan. 2019. "The Online Forum as a Digital Space of Curation." *Geoforum* 106, no. 1: 115–124.

Jones, Kerry, K. Libert, and K. Tynski. 2016. "The Emotional Combinations That Make Stories Go Viral." *Harvard Business Review*. Accessed June 9, 2016. https://hbr.org/2016/05/research-the-link-between-feeling-in-controland-viral-content.

Julien, Christopher M. 2017. "The Iconic Ghetto, Color-Blind Racism and White Masculinities: A Content and Discourse Analysis of Black Twitter on www.imgur.com." Master's thesis, University of North Carolina, Greensboro.

Kotkov, Denis, Shuaiqiang Wang, and Jari Veijalainen. 2016. "A Survey of Serendipity in Recommender Systems." *Knowledge-Based Systems* 111, no. 1: 180–192.

Kutner, Bernard, Carol Wilkins, and Penny Rechtman Yarrow. 1952. "Verbal Attitudes and Overt Behavior Involving Racial Prejudice." *Journal of Abnormal and Social Psychology* 47, no. 3: 649–652.

Leavitt, Alex, and Joshua A. Clark. 2014. "Upvoting Hurricane Sandy: Event-Based News Production Processes on a Social News Site." *Proceedings of the SIGCHI Conference on Human Factors in Computing Systems*, 1495–1504. New York: ACM.

Leavitt, Alex, and John J. Robinson. 2017. "Upvote My News: The Practices of Peer Information Aggregation for Breaking News on Reddit.com." *Proceedings of the ACM on Human–Computer Interaction*. Article 65.

Lewis, Rebecca. 2018. "Alternative Influence: Broadcasting the Reactionary Right on YouTube." *Data & Society*. https://datasociety.net/library/alternative-influence.

Lu, Yanqin, and Jae Kook Lee. 2019. "Stumbling Upon the Other Side: Incidental Learning of Counter-Attitudinal Political Information on Facebook." *New Media & Society* 21, no. 1: 248–265.

Mager, Astrid. 2012. "Algorithmic Ideology: How Capitalist Society Shapes Search Engines." *Information, Communication & Society* 15, no. 5: 769–787.

Martin, Fiona, and Jonathon Hutchinson. 2020. "Deep Data: Analyzing Power and Influence in Social Media Networks." In *Second International Handbook of Internet Research*, edited by Jeremy Hunsinger, Matthew M. Allen, and Lisbeth Klastrup, 857–877. Dordrecht, The Netherlands: Springer.

Marwick, Alice E., and danah boyd. 2014. "Networked Privacy: How Teenagers Negotiate Context in Social Media." *New Media & Society* 16, no. 7: 1051–1067.

Marwick, Alice, Claire Fontaine, and danah boyd. 2017. "'Nobody Sees It, Nobody Gets Mad': Social Media, Privacy, and Personal Responsibility among Low-SES Youth." *Social Media + Society* 3, no. 2. doi: 10.1177/2056305117710455.

Marwick, Alice, and Rebecca Lewis. 2017. *Media Manipulation and Disinformation Online.* New York: Data & Society Research Institute. https://datasociety.net/library/media-manipulation-and-disinfo-online/.

Massanari, Adrienne. 2017. "#Gamergate and the Fappening: How Reddit's Algorithm, Governance, and Culture Support Toxic Technocultures." *New Media & Society* 19, no. 3: 329–346.

Matamoros-Fernández, Ariadna. 2017. "Platformed Racism: The Mediation and Circulation of an Australian Race-Based Controversy on Twitter, Facebook and Youtube." *Information, Communication & Society* 20, no. 6: 930–946.

Matias, J. Nathan. 2019. "The Civic Labor of Volunteer Moderators Online." *Social Media + Society* 5, no. 2. https://doi.org/10.1177/2056305119836778.

Mattern, Shannon. 2014. "Library as Infrastructure." *Places Journal.* https://placesjournal.org/article/library-as-infrastructure/.

Matthes, Jörg. 2009. "What's in a Frame? A Content Analysis of Media Framing Studies in the World's Leading Communication Journals, 1990–2005." *Journalism & Mass Communication Quarterly* 86, no. 2: 349–367.

McCombs, Maxwell E., and Donald L. Shaw. 1972. "The Agenda-Setting Function of Mass Media." *Public Opinion Quarterly* 36, no. 2: 176–187.

Mead, George Herbert. 1934. *Mind, Self and Society.* Chicago: University of Chicago Press.

Milano, Silvia, Mariarosaria Taddeo, and Luciano Floridi. 2020. "Recommender Systems and Their Ethical Challenges." *AI & Society.* https://doi.org/10.1007/s00146-020-00950-y.

Nagle, Angela. 2017. *Kill All Normies: Online Culture Wars from 4chan and Tumblr to Trump and the Alt-Right.* Winchester, UK: Zero Books.

Nagy, Peter, and Gina Neff. 2015. "Imagined Affordance: Reconstructing a Keyword for Communication Theory." *Social Media + Society* 1, no. 2. https://doi.org/10.1177/2056305115603385.

Noble, Safiya Umoja. 2018. *Algorithms of Oppression: How Search Engines Reinforce Racism.* New York: New York University Press.

Norman, D. A. 1988. *The Psychology of Everyday Things.* New York: Basic Books.

O'Meara, Victoria. 2019. "Weapons of the Chic: Instagram Influencer Engagement Pods as Practices of Resistance to Instagram Platform Labor." *Social Media + Society* 5, no. 4. https://doi.org/10.1177/2056305119879671.

Orr, Will, and Jenny L. Davis. 2020. "Attributions of Ethical Responsibility by Artificial Intelligence Practitioners." *Information, Communication & Society* 23, no. 5: 719–735.

Pariser, Eli. 2011. *The Filter Bubble: What the Internet Is Hiding from You.* London: Penguin.

Park, David W., and Jefferson Pooley. 2008. *The History of Media and Communication Research: Contested Memories.* New York: Peter Lang.

Perrin, A., and M. Anderson. 2019. "Share of US Adults Using Social Media, Including Facebook, Is Mostly Unchanged Since 2018." Pew Research Center. https://www.pewresearch.org/fact-tank/2019/04/10/share-of-u-s-adults-using-social-media-including-facebook-is-mostly-unchanged-since-2018/.

Petre, Caitlin, Brooke Erin Duffy, and Emily Hund. 2019. "'Gaming the System': Platform Paternalism and the Politics of Algorithmic Visibility." *Social Media + Society* 5, no. 4. https://doi.org/10.1177/2056305119879995.

Plantin, Jean-Christophe, and Aswin Punathambekar. 2019. "Digital Media Infrastructures: Pipes, Platforms, and Politics." *Media, Culture & Society* 41, no. 2: 163–174.

Poor, Nathaniel. 2005. "Mechanisms of an Online Public Sphere: The Website Slashdot." *Journal of Computer-Mediated Communication* 10, no. 2. https://academic.oup.com/jcmc/article/10/2/JCMC1028/4614448

Resnick, Paul, Neophytos Iacovou, Mitesh Suchak, Peter Bergstrom, and John Riedl. 1994. "GroupLens: An Open Architecture for Collaborative Filtering of Netnews." In *Proceedings of the 1994 ACM Conference on Computer Supported Cooperative Work*, 175–186. New York: ACM.

Ribeiro, Filipe N., Koustuv Saha, Mahmoudreza Babaei, Lucas Henrique, Johnnatan Messias, Fabricio Benevenuto, Oana Goga, Krishna P. Gummadi, and Elissa M. Redmiles. 2019. "On Microtargeting Socially Divisive Ads: A Case Study of Russia-Linked Ad Campaigns on Facebook." In *Proceedings of the Conference on Fairness, Accountability, and Transparency*, 140–149. New York: ACM.

Roberts, Sarah T. 2016. "Digital Refuse: Canadian Garbage, Commercial Content Moderation and the Global Circulation of Social Media's Waste." *Wi: Journal of Mobile Media* 10, no. 1: 1–11.

Roberts, Sarah T. 2019. *Behind the Screen: Content Moderation in the Shadows of Social Media.* New Haven, CT: Yale University Press.

Robinson, Laura. 2018. "The Identity Curation Game: Digital Inequality, Identity Work, and Emotion Management." *Information, Communication & Society* 21, no. 5: 661–680.

Robinson, Laura, Shelia R. Cotten, Hiroshi Ono, Anabel Quan-Haase, Gustavo Mesch, Wenhong Chen, Jeremy Schulz, Timothy M. Hale, and Michael J. Stern. 2015. "Digital Inequalities and Why They Matter." *Information, Communication & Society* 18, no. 5: 569–582.

Rohlinger, Deana A., and Leslie A. Bunnage. 2018. "Collective Identity in the Digital Age: Thin and Thick Identities in Moveon.org and the Tea Party Movement." *Mobilization* 23, no. 2: 135–157.

Rubin, Richard E. 2017. *Foundations of Library and Information Science.* Chicago: American Library Association.

Schraube, Ernst. 2009. "Technology as Materialized Action and Its Ambivalences." *Theory & Psychology* 19, no. 2: 296–312.

Seaver, Nick. 2018. "Captivating Algorithms: Recommender Systems as Traps." *Journal of Material Culture* 24, no. 4: 421–436.

Shearer, Elisa, and Katerina Eva Matsa. 2018. "News Use across Social Media Platforms 2018." Pew Research Center, Journalism and Media. https://www.journalism.org/2018/09/10/news-use-across-social-media-platforms-2018/.

Shilton, Katie. 2013. "Values Levers: Building Ethics into Design." *Science, Technology, & Human Values* 38, no. 3: 374–397.

Squirrell, Tim. 2019. "Platform Dialectics: The Relationships between Volunteer Moderators and End Users on Reddit." *New Media & Society* 21, no. 9: 1910–1927.

Stevens, Robin, Stacia Gilliard-Matthews, Jamie Dunaev, Marcus K. Woods, and Bridgette M. Brawner. 2017. "The Digital Hood: Social Media Use among Youth in Disadvantaged Neighborhoods." *New Media & Society* 19, no. 6: 950–967.

Stryker, Sheldon, and Peter J. Burke. 2000. "The Past, Present, and Future of an Identity Theory." *Social Psychology Quarterly* 63, no. 4: 284–297.

Trepte, Sabine, Michael Scharkow, and Tobias Dienlin. 2020. "The Privacy Calculus Contextualized: The Influence of Affordances." *Computers in Human Behavior* 104, no. 1: 106–115.

Vaidhyanathan, Siva. 2012. *The Googlization of Everything (And Why We Should Worry)*. Los Angeles: University of California Press.

Vaidhyanathan, Siva. 2018. *Antisocial Media: How Facebook Disconnects Us and Undermines Democracy*. Oxford: Oxford University Press.

Van Dijck, José, and Thomas Poell. 2013. "Understanding Social Media Logic." *Media and Communication* 1, no. 1: 2–14.

Vitak, Jessica. 2012. "The Impact of Context Collapse and Privacy on Social Network Site Disclosures." *Journal of Broadcasting & Electronic Media* 56, no. 4: 451–470.

Wajcman, Judy. 2000. "Reflections on Gender and Technology Studies: In What State Is the Art?" *Social Studies of Science* 30, no. 3: 447–464.

Weiner, Kate, Catherine Will, Flis Henwood, and Rosalind Williams. 2020. "Everyday Curation? Attending to Data, Records and Record Keeping in the Practices of Self-Monitoring." *Big Data & Society* 7, no. 1. https://doi.org/10.1177/2053951720918275.

Wilson, Timothy D., and Elizabeth W. Dunn. 2004. "Self-Knowledge: Its Limits, Value, and Potential for Improvement." *Annual Review of Psychology* 55: 493–518.

Winner, Langdon. 1980. "Do Artifacts Have Politics?" *Daedalus* 109, no. 1: 121–136.

Yeomans, Michael, Anuj Shah, Sendhil Mullainathan, and Jon Kleinberg. 2017. "Making Sense of Recommendations." *Journal of Behavioral Decision Making* 32, no. 4: 403–414.

Zerubavel, Eviatar. 1996. "Lumping and Splitting: Notes on Social Classification." *Sociological Forum* 11, no. 3: 421–433.

Zuckerberg, Mark. 2017. "Building Global Community." Facebook. https://www.facebook.com/notes/mark-zuckerberg/building-global-community/10154544292806634/.

Zyskowski, Kathryn, Meredith Ringel Morris, Jeffrey P. Bigham, Mary L. Gray, and Shaun K. Kane. 2015. "Accessible Crowdwork? Understanding the Value in and Challenge of Microtask Employment for People with Disabilities." In *Proceedings of the 18th ACM Conference on Computer Supported Cooperative Work & Social Computing*, 1682–1693. New York: ACM.

CHAPTER 4

AFFECTIVE PUBLICS

Solidarity and Distance

ZIZI PAPACHARISSI

THE problem is democracy. The answer to that problem is often technology. Unfortunately, this path of understanding and seeking to solve the problems of democracy leads us down erroneous assumptions about what technology can and cannot achieve as well as what the condition of democracy is really about. It is common to evoke the theory of the public sphere when examining the civic potential of technology. Yet this logic is flawed, for it assigns technology a deterministic part in this equation that existing research does not support. The public sphere is a metaphor, useful for comprehending the form conversation can take in democratic societies (Habermas [1962] 1991). Critics of the public sphere (e.g., Calhoun 1992; Fraser 1992) contest the viability of the public sphere model, arguing that a true public sphere, in the manner that Habermas described it, never truly existed. They point to subaltern counterpublics or smaller, marginal, or semi-marginal spheres of interaction, parallel to dominant discourse, from which democratizing initiatives emerge as more meaningful (Fraser 1992; Warner 2002). Others argue that conversation does not present the soul of democracy (Schudson 1998) and that deliberation can only advance democracy so long as it supports agonistic and not antagonizing perspectives (Mouffe 2000). This chapter is not an overview of public sphere theory as an entryway to analyzing the meaning of technology for democracy. What is important is not whether the public sphere ever existed but, rather, that at the present moment the conditions for it to ever come into being have become extinct. Habermas has abandoned the concept in favor of the contemporary idea of "lifeworlds," that is, socioculturally structured environments where individual experiences materialize (Habermas [1962] 1991). Technology, including the internet and the many platforms that it supports, does not render a public sphere; but it does afford public space in societies, democratic and non. This chapter therefore explores the relevance of technology as public space, as a civic architecture that supports democratically sourced expression, connection, and engagement.

Social science is vested in the potential technology carries for expression and connection. Indeed, the overwhelming majority of research on media, social media, and communication technologies indicates that, above all, human beings utilize these technologies for expression and connection (Baym 2015; Papacharissi 2010a, 2018a, 2018b, 2018c, 2018d). That is indeed the expectation, although it often is not the outcome. We approach technology in earnest, and we often abandon it with indignation. We focus on the political yet forget that civic activity merges all spheres of interaction to advance by shifting the cultural ground. For some time now, I have been studying the social and political consequences of communication technologies. Lately, I have taken an interest in the *soft* structures of feeling that these technologies filter, conduct, and enable. It is through these soft structures of feeling that I would like to tell a different story about civic engagement afforded through technology, one that has led me to the development of the construct of "affective publics" and its companion term, "affective news." These concepts have been adopted in a multitude of studies that examine the relationship between technology and politics.[1] In this chapter, I explicate these two concepts and present them as alternatives to understanding the place of technology in societies, democratic and non.

SOLIDARITY AND DISTANCE

It is best that one begins by establishing an understanding of what the communicative interfaces that the internet enables do and what they do not. The connective thread in the argument I am formulating is one that begins at solidarity and arrives at distance, only so that it may find itself back to solidarity, in an ongoing loop that fuels human connection and expression. So, let's begin with the underpinnings of this argument, long documented by the social sciences.

First, the internet is not a magical space. It cannot create something out of nothing, nor can it create something that does not exist. Technology cannot create democracy. It is also incapable of destroying democracy. It does open up pathways, digital and non, to democratization, to authoritarianism, to populism, and to a variety of other potential outcomes (e.g., Bimber 2003; Howard and Hussain 2013). Humans may choose to construct these pathways, wonder on them, or block them. Technology may offer them up, but the choice is ours, even though our ability to exercise that agency may be negated.

Second, and further lending clarity to our understanding of how technology, democracy, and equality may coexist, the internet pluralizes, but it does not democratize (e.g., Chadwick 2013; Chadwick and Howard 2008). Platforms that the internet supports and others that may follow it are as likely to populate our information sphere with items with value as they are to fill it with garbage. Gatekeepers, curators, and filters certainly channel information flows, yet those reflect bias, interest, and subjectivities, much like everything in our everyday lives (e.g., Rohlinger 2019a, 2019b). The internet opens up pathways to connection and expression. These may bring together democratically oriented people, and they can also assemble fascists (e.g., Boatright et al. 2019). Plurality is a necessary, yet not sufficient, condition for democracy.

Third, much like the internet cannot create something out of nothing, it is also not capable of extinguishing social problems. The net does not create hate speech, toxicity, cyberbullying. Those are the work of human beings. It does, however, make these problems more spreadable, more visible, and, in so doing, possibly more harmful to a greater number of human beings. The internet does amplify everything. It augments voice for all, and it often does so in unequal terms (e.g., Nakamura 2007; Brock 2020; Sobiearaj 2011). We all have voice online, but the voice of some is louder than the voice of others (Earl and Kimport 2011; Earl and Papacharissi 2019).

I have often said that the internet provides a public space but not a public sphere (e.g., Papacharissi 2010b). A healthy and functional public sphere has never existed (e.g., Fraser 1992). Still, in the sense that Habermas described it, which was as a metaphor and not as a tangible condition, it serves as a premise for democracy. The internet is not a space where rational discourse leads to consensus, if that is how we define a public sphere. Let's keep in mind that Habermas used the German word *Öffentilichkeit*, which roughly translates as "openness." The term "public sphere" translates rather poorly in Greek, even though ancient Greece is viewed by many as the root of the concept. Greek philosophers spoke of concepts like δήμος and Αγορά, both of which evoke ideas of openness and include an intersection of publicity and commerce. The internet certainly provides openness, one that is not free of commercial and other interests. Whether we ever enjoyed public deliberation in open spaces that were completely devoid of commercial bias is certainly up for debate (Schudson 1998). There is also no historical precedent of spaces that inherently support reason and successfully thwart all attempts at toxicity. Quite the opposite—history is rife with examples of public spaces being overrun with emotion. Human beings inhabit spaces, and we enter them with all of our preexisting problems on hand. Still, there is no point to studying technology if we cannot come up with ways of using it to help improve the human condition. So, what does technology offer toward solidarity and distance, privacy and publicity, reason and emotion, democracy and authority, and finally personal autonomy? Something, but the conventional political vocabulary does not permit me to capture the nuance of this very elusive something.

Affect

I stumbled on the idea of affect by accident. With my colleagues and students at the University of Illinois at Chicago, I became involved in a number of studies designed to understand social media and social movements. We were particularly interested in how movements were controlling gatekeeping online, how they were managing content injections and hashtag hijacking by counterpublics, and how they were using social media to frame a narrative about how they were. We began by examining various aspects of the Egyptian uprisings that led to the resignation of Hosni Mubarak (Papacharissi and de Fatima Oliveira 2012; Meraz and Papacharissi 2013). We then turned our attention to the Occupy movement, focusing on prominent actors and frames (Meraz and Papacharissi 2016). We were particularly interested in the stories various actors told about the movements and how those produced overlapping, parallel, or contradicting frames.

We quickly realized that framing was of the essence and that curators were integral to producing narratives that were coherent, consistent, and cohesive. Fundamental to our line of thinking was the idea that there are events, and there are the stories we tell about events. This assumption is picked up in several studies that utilized the affective publics concept (e.g., Bucher 2017; Flew 2018; Massanari 2017; Siapera 2017). These stories may differ and can be multilayered, multifaceted, or even completely distinct, depending on the medium and the actors involved in telling them (e.g., Meyer 2007; Polletta 2006). Following John Hartley's (2012) definition of news values as the things that turn events into stories, we analyzed news values that emerged and dominated modalities of storytelling online. Using big data analysis to identify core trends and deep, qualitative analysis to study those trends closely, we traced frames and followed how those frames were reinforced, reproduced, or negotiated online over time. We quickly evolved Entman's (1993) paradigmatic definition of framing into what we understood as a process of networked framing: a process through which a particular problem definition, causal interpretation, moral evaluation, and/or treatment recommendation attains prominence through crowdsourcing practices (Meraz and Papacharissi 2016).

Resting on a long tradition of agenda setting, framing, and gatekeeping research, we were drawn to a nexus of constant information negotiation, curation, and contestation that we interpreted as networked gatekeeping: a process through which actors are crowdsourced to prominence via the use of conversational, social practices that symbiotically connect elite and crowd in the determination of information-relevant practices (Meraz and Papacharissi 2016). Networked framing and networked gatekeeping are fundamental to our understanding of how publics negotiated power, discourses, and agency online, through frontstage and backstage interactions. They allowed us to trace information flows, track power distributions, and map information hierarchies or heterarchies that were in formation. We understood these processes as both cognitively and affectively enabled. Our theoretical framework guided us as we shifted through large amounts of data and led us to conclude that while social media do not tell us what to think, do not make or break revolutions, and do not win or lose elections, they certainly modulate information flows that are formative in what we think about, what we direct our attention to, and how we think about it. The application of agenda setting and framing theories provided us with important theoretical vocabulary that informed our interpretations (e.g., Gamson 1992; Gitlin 1980; Reese, Gandy, and Grant 2001; Snow and Benford 1992).

Still, as I immersed myself in qualitative analysis of the data, I noticed patterns that led to the intensification of communication rhythms and rituals that developed.

There were co-occurring turns of connection and disconnection that were rhythmical and repetitive. Stories were told but often in terms, tonalities, or textures that intensified feelings that brought together some publics and divided others. Narratives were intensified, often attaining populistic tone and tenor. Performative tendencies and tensions developed, and these usually helped identify micro-publics on the rise. The term "collective action" seemed simply inadequate to describe what was taking place. I was looking for words to describe what I was observing and did not want to invent a new term if what I was describing had already been talked about. It seemed that publics were entranced by a developing process of anticipation and enamorment with what might happen, what might follow. The potentiality of what tomorrow would bring seemed intoxicating for these publics and drove the rhythms of communication. That is how I stumbled into affect and engaged in explanations that often confused my colleagues, until I learned enough and I understood this well enough so as to explain it succinctly.

I combine approaches from psychology, philosophy, and political science to understand affect as sentiment, mood, atmosphere—all indicative of things that we are about to experience but can't quite finding the feelings or words to describe (Seigworth and Gregg 2010). I define this potentiality as a pre-emotive intensity subjectively experienced and connected to processes of anticipation of events prior to their occurrence (Karatzogianni and Kuntsman 2012). Affect is not the same as emotion. It is the intensity with which we feel. It is the difference between a poke, a shove, and a push to the ground. I like to say that it is the difference between a caress of the check and a slap to the face—same gesture yet applied with a different intensity, revealing distinct intentions and yielding divergent outcomes.

It seemed that political theory was prompting me to label many of the conversational modalities that I was studying online as rational or emotional, when in fact so many of them were affective in nature. I understood that many of these conversational natures were phatic and spontaneous in nature. They were similar to a tap of the foot to a tune that we like. They reminded me of a nod of the head intended not as agreement but as a mere indication that one is following along. Similarly, retweets were often gestures meant to amplify intensity, ways of turning the sound up. Often, they were ways of being seen and of revealing to others, affectively, presence. Likes or hearts were ways of nodding in or tuning into the rhythm of a stream. They did not indicate agreement as much as they indicated an effort to chime in. The result of all these affective reactions, of these cumulative phatic gestures, was always intensity. The stream changed in tonality, in texture, in the overall effect it possessed, evoked, and generated. The mood became different. The atmosphere changed. I was often asked, early on, whether a news stream or a conversational stream can have affect. Of course it can. Does a record not have its own affect when one plays it? Does a conversation does not have its own tonality? How can an exchange of ideas not possess its own air, aesthetic, atmosphere, and potential, sensed and shared among those participating in it?

It struck me that the recurring word that came to mind in describing the mood of the news streams I was studying was "intensity." Feelings are subjective, and human creatures read this intensity into different emotions, through processes that combine reason with emotion. But the intensity, the affect, with all the potential it contains prior to its inevitable categorization, is there and sets the beat to which these publics converse. I had understood and studied *what* these publics were saying, through the logics of networked framing and gatekeeping. I gradually became more interested in *how* they were saying it, the tonality and texture of expression. At this stage, I came across the theory of connective action and had the pleasure of co-keynoting an event with Lance Bennett so that I could receive a more nuanced explanation for it. If I was trying to understand what sort of tendency this intensity was creating, then it became apparent to me that foundational energy was connective. Connective, and not collective, was that word to describe the primal rhythmicality of what I was encountering. These were people who were chatting for the mere sake of connection, identification, and disconnection. They were online to be seen, heard, counted, and felt. The overwhelming sentiment was the need to affectively presence oneself and connect with others. Connective action explained to me where this intensity was headed, but I still was looking for a theoretical vernacular to describe the stories the liminally connected publics were telling. They were "networked publics" of course, but that term struck me as too descriptive.

"Premediation" was an illuminating term. It was as enlightening its predecessor, "remediation," had been in helping me interpret how social media weave into the fabric of our everyday lives. Grusin (2010) developed the term post-9/11, to describe the form that events take on before they turn into stories. This sent me back to my original interest in storytelling and my fascination with what an event looks like before it turns into a story. Grusin explained that premediation is rich in affect as it emerges in anticipation of events that are happening or are about to happen. News media are always immersed in processes of premediation so as to foretell and scoop the news. With the litany of news scrollers that it introduced into structures of news storytelling, 9/11 thrived on the uncertainty and potentiality of tomorrow. Insecurity prevailed as news outlets tried to anticipate what might happen, through providing always-on, ambient, linear, and endless updates that introduced a texture of storytelling that had previously only been reserved for emergencies and resembled the logic of reporting on the stock market. The constant updates that repeated, instead of refreshing, information drummed up the intensity levels of news storytelling. In the absence of new news, the scrollers were for us what clickbait and news feeds are now: linear, flat updates on infinite repeat, introducing the rhythms of intensity that make us feel like something is always about to happen and do little to alleviate our anxiety. The news feeds I studied on Twitter mimicked that structure, through blending broadcasting conventions with the traditions of interpersonal conversation and reconciling a primary and a secondary orality into something that can only be described as a digital orality: news, fact, drama, opinion, and mood blend into one, to the point where distinguishing one from the other is impossible and doing so is irrelevant (Papacharissi 2017a). I termed this form of news "affective" (Papacharissi 2014a).

Affective News

Our studies of social media and social movements were driven by the need to understand how online platforms facilitated news storytelling. In our research, we were drawn to the news values that prevailed online as events turned into stories and how those stories were shared, reframed, and broadcast to the world. The trends we observed led us to define the form of online news as affective. The tendencies and tensions of affective news are by no means new or specific to the internet, but they are amplified by the mediality online platforms possess.

Affective news is defined as the blend of news, fact, sentiment, and opinion that is produced, reproduced, and reinforced through shareable and collaborative news streams. It is rendered as subjective experience, opinion, and sentiment coalesce. It sustains and is sustained by ambient, hybrid, and polymedia news environments. Characterized by premediation, affective news streams contain anticipatory gestures that are not predictive of the future but communicate a predisposition to frame it and, in doing so, lay claim to latent forms of agency that are also affective and networked (Papacharissi 2014b).

Affective news is typically flat, repetitive, and intense. Information curation online and across media often takes the form of affective news, recognizable as clickbait, listicles, news scrollers, or news feeds mounting in intensity. Affective news is designed to grab attention and is driven by the need to anticipate the future. It is characterized by repetition, absence of context, lack of substance, brevity, and instantaneity. In fact, affective news is rewarded by and further contributes to a culture of instantaneity in news reporting. It is characterized by rhythms that are instantaneous, emotive, and phatic. Repetition and intensity, enabled through retweeting, endorsing, mimicking, scrolling, and a variety of similar affective gestures set the pace of news storytelling. Phrases, terms, and the vernacular of broadcast news serve to dress up the rituals of interpersonal conversation so as to produce a stream of news that carries a more immediate and intimate tone (Papacharissi 2015).

On the one hand, these collaboratively generated streams present pluralistic arguments on what should be news and how news stories should be told. We could interpret affective news gestures as indicative of political statements of dissent with a mainstream news culture. More importantly, the infusion of affect into news marks the return of affect to the paradigm of news neutrality, which often leaves citizens cynical about news and wanting more. But it also provides a way of turning affective statements of disagreement into atomized political gestures that can be networked, to piece together a contemporary understanding of the political. In this manner, affective news streams discursively render spaces where the long-disconnected publics of citizens and journalists may reconnect (Papacharissi 2017b).

On the other hand, these streams can be curated to inform and to misinform. Ambient and always-on streams of misinformation can be algorithmically enhanced to flood the news infoscape with garbage. Herein lies a problem for both audiences and journalists who are not accustomed to navigating news markets populated by waste. Neither audiences nor journalists possess the tools or time to figuratively sweep the garbage away. Journalists are trained to fact-find, confirm, and investigate. Audiences, on the other hand, possess the critical skills to read and evaluate the news; but no one has the time to find the news when there is a heap of rubbish obstructing it. I am using a metaphor to illustrate that affective news may empower both citizens and journalists to work together, but it can also be susceptible to manipulation that deepens the cynical void separating citizens from journalists (e.g., Cappella and Jamieson 1997; Carey 1995; Patterson 1993).

At this stage it becomes essential to draw a distinction between affective reactions and the news. Affect represents a mood. This mood may be the result of news or somehow associated with news of a certain nature, but it is not the news. Affective reactions or gestures that may read as affective news are not news or de facto newsworthy. Affective reactions, even when woven into affective news streams, are precisely that: reactions, gestures, and ways for citizens to feel their way into the story. Things become problematic when we confuse affective gestures for news and report them as the news. Some affective gestures are newsworthy—not all. Several are ways of sense-making and feeling our way through the news infoscape. When we confuse affective gestures as news, we tend to repeat the same headlines over and over again. We report presidential or politicians' tweets that are not newsworthy in staccato and frenetic rhythms. We flood the infoscape with lines that were manufactured to manipulate publics and should not turn into headlines. Affect, with all the intensity and potentiality that it envelops, can sustain feelings of community, which can then further reflexively drive publics forward or entrap them in a state of engaged passivity. Curational acumen, context, and literacy will determine that outcome.

Affective Publics

Affective publics are networked publics that come together, are identified, and disband through shared sentiment. Even though affective publics may endorse affective news, what unites, identifies, and potentially divides these publics is the sentiment that drives them and the stories that they come together to tell.

A first point to make is that affective publics materialize uniquely and leave distinct digital footprints. This may appear obvious to the reader, yet it is a point worth repeating. All too often, we are impressed with the social media presence certain publics attain online. We then presume that all public formations will evolve into movements and achieve similar online status. This is not the case. Every movement is unique. Every movement will call upon its own affective publics and draw energy, ambience, and a sense of always-on presence from them. And every movement will therefore generate its own distinct digital imprint.

A second element that is essential to how affective publics are rendered into being revolves around their ability to support connective, yet not collective, action. There is no overarching authority that determines how the news streams generated by these publics turn into stories. The process is collaborative and connective, which is why the narratives that are associated with affective publics are frequently fragmented. For example, the Occupy movement, one that energized numerous affective formations, produced a narrative that lacked cohesion and frequently confused media striving to report on it. Yet the point of Occupy was not to produce a unified narrative. The point of that movement was to present a call for people to come together, be counted, and feel like their voice was heard. The heterarchical structure of the movement was reflected in the open signifier of #occupy, designed to generate diverse presence and amplified dissent. This tends to be the case for most affective public formations, unless curators are crowdsourced to prominence so as to help collate a cohesive narrative. For instance, the Egyptian uprisings that led to the resignation of Hosni Mubarak benefited, in their early days, from people tweeting on the street and others curating from abroad, who worked together to fact-check, correct, and broadcast a stream that framed the movement as a revolution well before it had brought in regime reversal—and despite the fact that it ultimately never did (Papacharissi and Blasiola 2016). Likewise, journalists and celebrities working together managed to inoculate the #metoo narrative against attempts to hashtag hijack and divert the narrative of that movement. By contrast, windows of opportunity for change that were opened up by the #BlackLivesMatter movement were frequently interrupted by counterpublics flooding that stream with content injections aimed at disrupting the continuity of that movement's narrative (Freelon, McIlwain, and Clark 2016; Papacharissi and Trevey 2018).

Third, the digital texture of mobilized support varies, depending on sociocultural context and political economy systemic factors. Nonetheless, these public formations will be powered by affective statements of opinion or fact or a blend of the two, which in turn produce ambient, always-on feeds that further connect and pluralize expression in regimes, democratic and non.

Fourth, these publics will typically produce disruptions/interruptions of dominant political narratives by *presencing* underrepresented viewpoints. In other words, the meaning of affective publics derives from their ability to allow humans to come together and be seen. Their modus operandi is gestural and anticipatory. They are powered by people who feel they are unseen and want to become more visible. Some of these people are the *indignados* in Spain and the Occupy crowds that first started gathering in Zuccotti Park. Others also include the folks that Arlie Hochschild (2016) termed "strangers in their own land" and that Kathlyn Cramer (2016) described in "the politics of resentment." They include people who sided with #maga and #brexit, who seized those opportunities to present their own affective gestures of dissent and presence.

Finally, affective publics will convene around streams sustained by affective commonalities. Their impact will be of a symbolic nature, the agency they afford will be semantic, and the power they access will be liminal. These publics will not bring about change that is instantaneous; political, sociocultural, economic; or long term. They are an impactful yet evanescent formation. This point is worth emphasizing because all too often we are swayed by the pathos that these publics use to move information, by the virality of it all. We then expect change to follow in an equally speedy manner, and when it does not, we are disappointed in our media, our politicians, and our systems of governance. Still, it is not just those institutions that have let us down but our own exuberant expectations as well. Change is slow. And revolutions, in the words of Raymond Williams (1961), are long. They have to be long, in order to acquire meaning. In repressive regimes, an affective gesture of dissent may result in a death sentence for those brave enough to claim it. In democratic regimes, an affective gesture of repression reminds us that there are crucial problems of inequality, racism, and sexism that persist. So to say that something carries symbolic meaning or enables semantic agency is no small thing. In order to change our institutions, we must reimagine them first. And once we reimagine them, we need to renegotiate our terms for individual autonomy. Technologies network us, yes; but it is our stories that connect us, identify us, and ultimately divide us. There is solidarity that is affectively enabled, but there is also distance that we are daily and affectively reminded of. Information and technology alone cannot mend that distance, and our primary forms of storytelling have a tendency to amplify it.

AFFECTIVE PUBLICS AND POPULISM

Affective sustain feelings of community that can effectively propel a movement forward or entrap it in a state of still motion, constantly revving up but not heading anywhere. Recent elections, referenda, and uprisings have revealed how affective publics can sustain forms of engagement that advance, stall, or derail democracies. Populist rhetoric works by appealing to sentiment and, in so doing, thrives by motivating affective publics to act, even if it is for a mere fleeting moment. For democracies to move forward, publics, the media, and politicians must learn to read appeals to sentiment and use technology to redeploy them in a civically meaningful manner.

Affective gestures offer ways for publics to be seen, heard, and recognized. It is these very gestures that can be potentially empowering for citizens and that render affective publics vulnerable to populist rhetoric. Populism promises easy solutions premised on a false sense of closeness or intimacy. In contemporary societies, characterized by growing cynicism, citizens are often counted but do not feel like they count, in the words of Stephen Coleman (2013). Populism thrives because it speaks to the insecurities of everyday citizens. It makes empty promises that soothe affective drives of insecurity.

The connection between affectivity and populism becomes clear if we examine the meaning of populism. Laclau understood populism as a dialectic, a political logic that could be co-opted by a variety of right-wing, centrist, or left-wing ideologies. Similarly, affective publics are susceptible to potentialities that emerge across the entire political spectrum, extreme right to extreme left. It is telling that Laclau titled his most influential work on populism *On Populist Reason* (2005). Some people presume that populism lacks reason, but Laclau argued that it has a logic, that it is a progression of its own. Populists rely on discourse and utilize refrains to attract attention and distract from the complexity of issues. Refrains are central to how affective drives are called into being. Repetitive headlines or hashtags that appear at the closing of every tweet are such refrains that drum up the rhythms of affective news streams and the publics that convene around them.

Refrains often take the form of an empty signifier, that is, words that semantically open enough to be appealing to diverse crowds. Empty signifiers do not possess an ideology, nor are they the property of left- or right-wing inclinations. They are effective precisely because they are open enough to be filled with meaning by the individuals who adopt them. Laclau (1996) explained that populists often use *empty signifiers* to allow the masses to connect around abstract ideas. Claude Lévi-Strauss (1987, 63–64) uses the "open" or "floating signifier" to describe a term that lacks any real meaning and thus is open to multiple interpretations.

Empty signifiers reproduce and reinforce popular ideas by turning them into affective refrains. An empty signifier is a vessel of populist sentiment because it is barren of ideology. It beckons people to align behind an abstract idea that is interpretable in a way that suits their personal issue politics. "Brexit" presented one such signifier embraced by populist sentiment and supported by affectively driven publics. It is an abstraction that allowed people to unite, despite their own complex feelings and reasons for wanting to leave the European Union. The term itself offers no solutions, nor does it invite complex discussion. "Occupy" is yet another open signifier. It works because it hails people and invites them to stand up and be counted, no matter what their individual reasons for wanting to line up behind this refrain may be. As Laclau explained (2005), populist reason is promiscuous when it comes to ideological affiliation and so are affective drives. Affective publics have reflexively pushed forward left-wing, centrist, and right-wing movements. I developed the concept as I was studying how a revolution in the making overthrew a dictator in Egypt, only to replace him with a regime that remained authoritative. I further finetuned the construct through studying the Occupy movement. Finally, I recognized it again as I was observing the affective rhythms of #maga, the Make America Great Again movement that climaxed with the election of US president Donald Trump.

Populist rhetoric makes constant use of empty signifiers as slogans. Populist strategies become alive as they attain affective refrains of their own. These refrains are usually introduced by a leading figure, someone who, per Laclau (2005), is frequently anointed a populist messiah: an individual who rhetorically and emotionally connects with a crowd and emerges as someone who can magically put an end to all problems. Every era, country, and context has its own populist messiahs. They are elevated to prominence through mechanisms that combine interpersonal conversational conventions with traditional practices of broadcasting opinion. These mechanisms sound familiar because they are the very mechanisms that support affective news.

The collaborative logic of affective news combines legacy and new media in ways that facilitate populist reason. Populists are most successful when they work around traditional channels of communication, in ways that simultaneously provoke and circumvent them. Populist messiahs prefer to engage publics directly to call attention to and evoke the messianic rhetoric of promise (Laclau 1996). They introduce and affectively repeat an empty signifier of symbolic significance, typically disseminated via an independent channel designed to engage in direct communication with constituents (Laclau 2005). Populists will explain that they only do so to avoid intermediaries who are polluting the purity of their message and create binaries, divisions that thrive on an *us versus them* mentality.

Conclusion

In developing *affective publics* as a theoretical construct I have traversed through a variety of affective states. I first used the term to capture the potentialities formed around new democracies possibly emerging, with some help from technology. I then applied it to social movements motivated by the need to reinvent democracies that were exhausting the citizens sustaining them. I have lately been tracing it in populist oeuvres that are deeply threatening to democratic infrastructures. The term is theoretically related to theories of agenda setting, framing, and connective action. It is deeply informed by affect theory and the concept of premediation in particular. Finally, it further explicates how mechanisms of populism attain momentum.

Affect is about movement—movement before it has taken on direction and movement that perhaps never will assume a particular direction. It is about the intensity of movement and all that intensity energizes. Technologies that are always new, as Gitelman (2006) suggests, inherently lay an affective claim to the future. We use technology for a variety of things, mundane and exceptional. We further use technology to affectively lay claim to what we want our future to look like, and this is the unique civic potential of technology that I have described here.

Note

1. For a full list, please see the Google Scholar listing for "Papacharissi/affective publics."

References

Baym, Nancy. 2015. *Personal Connections in the Digital Age*. 2nd ed. Cambridge: Polity Press.
Bimber, Bruce. 2003. *Information and American Democracy: Technology in the Evolution of Political Power*. Cambridge: Cambridge University Press.
Boatright, Robert, Tim Shaffer, Sarah Sobieraj, and Dannagal Goldwaite Young, eds. 2019. *A Crisis of Civility: Political Discourse and its Discontents*. London and New York: Routledge.

Brock, André, Jr. 2020. *Distributed Blackness: African American Cybercultures*. New York: New York University Press.

Bucher, Taina. 2017. "The Algorithmic Imaginary: Exploring the Ordinary Affects of Facebook Algorithms." *Information, Communication and Society* 20, no. 1: 30–44. doi: 10.1080/1369118X.2016.1154086

Calhoun, Craig. 1992. "Introduction: Habermas and the Public Sphere." In *Habermas and the Public sphere*, edited by Craig Calhoun, 1–48. Cambridge, MA: MIT Press.

Cappella, Joe, and Kathleen Jamieson. 1997. *Spiral of Cynicism: The Press and the Public Good*. New York: Oxford University Press.

Carey, James. 1995. "The Press, Public Opinion, and Public Discourse." In *Public Opinion and the Communication of Consent*, edited by Theodore L. Glasser and Charles T. Salmon, 373–402. New York: Guilford.

Chadwick, Andrew. 2013. *The Hybrid Media System: Politics and Power*. London: Oxford University Press.

Chadwick, Andrew, and Philip N. Howard, eds. 2008. *Routledge Handbook of Internet Politics*. London and New York: Routledge.

Cramer, Katherine J. 2016. *The Politics of Resentment: Rural Consciousness in Wisconsin and the Rise of Scott Walker*. Chicago: University of Chicago Press.

Coleman, Stephen. 2013. *How Voters Feel*. Cambridge: Cambridge University Press.

Earl, Jennifer, and Katrina Kimport. 2011. *Digitally Enabled Social Change: Activism in the Internet Age*. Cambridge, MA: MIT Press.

Earl, Jennifer, and Zizi Papacharissi. 2019, April 26. "Participatory Politics in an Age of Crisis: What's in a Name?" In *Confessions of an ACA-Fan* (blog, edited by H. Jenkins). http://henryjenkins.org/blog/2019/4/21/participatory-politics-in-an-age-of-crisis-jennifer-earl-amp-zizi-papacharissi.

Entman, Robert M. 1993. "Framing: Toward Clarification of a Fractured Paradigm." *Journal of Communication* 43, no. 4: 51–58.

Flew, Terry. 2018. *Understanding Global Media*. London: Palgrave.

Fraser, Nancy. 1992. "Rethinking the Public Sphere: A Contribution to the Critique of Actually Existing Democracy." In *Habermas and the Public Sphere*, edited by Craig Calhoun, 109–142. Cambridge, MA: MIT Press.

Freelon, Deen, Charlton D. McIlwain, and Meredith Clark. 2016. *Beyond the Hashtags: #Ferguson, #Blacklivesmatter, and the Online Struggle for Offline Justice*. Washington, DC: Center for Media and Social Impact, American University. http://archive.cmsimpact.org/sites/default/files/beyond_the_hashtags_2016.pdf

Gamson, William A. 1992. *Talking Politics*. New York: Cambridge University Press.

Gitelman, Lisa. 2006. *Always Already New: Media, History, and the Data of Culture*. Cambridge, MA: MIT Press.

Gitlin, Todd. 1980. *The Whole World Is Watching: Mass Media in the Making and Unmaking of the New Left*. Berkeley: University of California Press.

Grusin, Richard. 2010. *Premediation: Affect and Mediality after 9/11*. New York: Palgrave Macmillan.

Habermas, Jürgen. (1962) 1991. *The Structural Transformation of the Public Sphere: An Inquiry into a Category of Bourgeois Society*. Translated by Thomas Burger with the assistance of Frederick Lawrence. Cambridge, MA: MIT Press. http://egalitarianism.no/wp-content/uploads/2014/10/The-Structural-Transformation-of-the-Public-Sphere.pdf

Hartley, John. 2012. *Communication, Cultural and Media Studies: The Key Concepts*. London and New York: Routledge.
Hochschild, Arlie Russell. 2016. *Strangers in Their Own Land: Anger and Mourning on the American Right*. New York: New Press.
Howard, Philip N., and Muzammil M. Hussain. 2013. *Democracy's Fourth Wave? Digital Media and the Arab Spring*. New York: Oxford University Press.
Karatzogianni, Athina, and Adi Kuntsman. 2012. *Digital Cultures and the Politics of Emotion: Feelings, Affect and Technological Change*. London: Palgrave Macmillan.
Laclau, Ernesto. 1996. *Emancipation(s)*. London: Verso.
Laclau, Ernesto. 2005. *On Populist Reason*. London: Verso.
Lévi-Strauss, Claude. 1987. *Introduction to Marcel Mauss*. London: Routledge.
Massanari, Adrienne. 2017. "#Gamergate and the Fappening: How Reddit's Algorithm, Governance, and Culture Support Toxic Technocultures." *New Media and Society* 19, no. 3: 329–346. https://doi.org/10.1177/1461444815608807.
Meraz, Sharon, and Zizi Papacharissi. 2013. "Networked Gatekeeping and Networked Framing on #Egypt." *International Journal of Press and Politics* 18, no. 2: 138–166.
Meraz, Sharon, and Zizi Papacharissi. 2016. "Networked Framing and Gatekeeping." In *The Sage Handbook of Digital Journalism*, edited by Tamara Witschge, C. W. Anderson, David Domingo, and Alfred Hermida, 95–112. London: Sage.
Meyer, David. 2007. *The Politics of Protest: Social Movements in America*. New York: Oxford University Press.
Mouffe, Chantal. 2000. *The Democratic Paradox*. London: Verso.
Nakamura, Lisa. 2007. *Digitizing Race: Visual Cultures of the Internet*. Minneapolis: University of Minnesota Press.
Papacharissi, Zizi, ed. 2010a. *A Networked Self: Identity, Community, and Culture on Social Network Sites*. New York and London: Routledge.
Papacharissi, Zizi. 2010b. *A Private Sphere: Democracy in a Digital Age*. Cambridge: Polity Press.
Papacharissi, Zizi. 2014a. *Affective Publics: Sentiment, Technology, and Politics*. New York: Oxford University Press.
Papacharissi, Zizi. 2014b. "Toward New Journalism(s): Affective News, Hybridity, and Liminal Spaces." *Journalism Studies*, 16, no. 1: 27–40.
Papacharissi, Zizi. 2015. "Affective Publics and Structures of Storytelling: Sentiment, Events and Mediality." *Information, Communication and Society* 19, no. 3: 307–324.
Papacharissi, Zizi. 2017a. "A Forum on Digital Storytelling: Interview with Zizi Papacharissi." By Mark C. Lashley and Brian Creech. *International Journal of Communication* 11: 1069–1073.
Papacharissi, Zizi. 2017b. "Commentary: Remaking Events, Storytelling, and News." In *Remaking the News: Essays on the Future of Journalism Scholarship in the Digital Age*, edited by Pablo J. Boczkowski and C. W, Anderson, 147–154. Cambridge, MA: MIT Press.
Papacharissi, Zizi, ed. 2018a. *A Networked Self: Platforms, Stories, Connections*. London and New York: Routledge.
Papacharissi, Zizi, ed. 2018b. *A Networked Self: Love*. London and New York: Routledge.
Papacharissi, Zizi, ed. 2018c. *A Networked Self: Birth, Life, Death*. London and New York: Routledge.
Papacharissi, Zizi, ed. 2018d. *A Networked Self: Human Augmentics, Artificial Intelligence, Sentience*. London and New York: Routledge.
Papacharissi, Zizi, and Stacy Blasiola. 2016. "Structures of Feeling, Storytelling, and Social Media: The Case of #Egypt." In *The Routledge Companion to Social Media and Politics*, edited

by Axel Bruns, Gunn Enli, Eli Skogerbø, Anders Olof Larsson, and Christian Christiansen, 211–222. London and New York: Routledge.

Papacharissi, Zizi, and Maria de Fatima Oliveira. 2012. "Affective News and Networked Publics: The Rhythms of News Storytelling on #Egypt." *Journal of Communication* 62, no. 2: 266–282.

Papacharissi, Zizi, and Meggan Trevey. 2018. "Affective Publics and Windows of Opportunity: Social Movements and the Potential for Social Change." In *The Routledge Companion to Media and Activism*, edited by Graham Meikle, 87–96. London and New York: Routledge.

Patterson, Thomas E. 1993. *Out of Order: An Incisive and Boldly Original Critique of the News Media's Domination of America's Political Process*. New York: Knopf.

Polletta, Francesca. 2006. *It Was Like a Fever: Storytelling in Protest and Politics*. Chicago: University of Chicago Press.

Reese, Stephen D., Oscar H. Gandy, and August E. Grant. 2001. *Framing Public Life: Perspectives on Media and Our Understanding of the Social World*. Mahwah, NJ: Lawrence Erlbaum Associates.

Rohlinger, Deana A. 2019a. "Symposium on Political Communication and Social Movements: Ships Passing in the Night." *Information, Communication and Society* 22, no. 5: 724–738. doi: 10.1080/1369118X.2019.1568514.

Rohlinger, Deana A. 2019b. *New Media and Society*. New York: New York University Press.

Schudson, Michael. 1998. *The Good Citizen: A History of American Civic Life*. New York: Free Press.

Siapera, Eugenia. 2017. *Understanding New Media*. London: Sage.

Seigworth, Gregory J., and Melissa Gregg. 2010. "An Inventory of Shimmers." In *The Affect Theory Reader*, edited by Melissa Gregg and Gregory J. Seigworth, 1–28. Durham, NC: Duke University Press.

Snow, David A., and Robert D. Benford. 1992. "Master Frames and Cycles of Protest." In *Frontiers in Social Movement Theory*, edited by Aldon D. Morris and Carol McClurg Mueller, 133–155. New Haven, CT: Yale University Press.

Sobieraj, Sarah. 2011. *Soundbitten: The Perils of Media-Centered Political Activism*. New York: New York University Press.

Warner, Michael. 2002. "Publics and Counterpublics." *Public Culture* 14, no. 1: 49–90. doi: 10.1215/08992363-14-1-49

Williams, Raymond. 1961. *The Long Revolution*. London: Chatto and Windus.

CHAPTER 5

BIG DATA FROM THE SOUTH(S)

An Analytical Matrix to Investigate Data at the Margins

STEFANIA MILAN AND EMILIANO TRERÉ

THE computational turn witnessed since the 1960s has spectacularly accelerated since the 2010s, thanks to the increase in computing power and the advances in automation and artificial intelligence (AI). Through this omnipresent digital infrastructure, more and more aspects of human existence and social life are transmuted into data points, in a process known as "datafication." Cities become "smart" (Gupta, Panagiotopoulos, and Bowen 2020), service work moves to the "platform" (van Doorn 2017), and citizens are increasingly "datafied" (Hintz, Dencik, and Wahl-Jorgensen 2018). These developments are typically associated with positive outcomes and accompanied by flamboyant narratives of empowerment. They yield the promise of flexible income generation, media content targeted to personal preferences, and increased efficiency in the use of public resources. However, there exists an "asymmetric relationship between those who collect, store, and mine large quantities of data, and those whom data collection targets" (Andrejevic 2014, 1673). This data trade, often invasive of people's privacy, is at the core of "surveillance capitalism," an exploitative economic system that benefits a handful of tech corporations at the expense of the majority of users (Zuboff 2019).

While these exploitative dynamics affect societies across the globe regardless of geography, census, or education, communities in the fringes of the neoliberal system appear to suffer the worst consequences—in the so-called Global South as much as in the north of the hemisphere. Migrants and refugees, racialized groups, indigenous peoples, subjects with disabilities, children and minors, women and non-gender-conforming individuals, and impoverished households are increasingly at risk of discrimination. Take the example of data-driven policymaking, whereby public policies are based on data automatically generated by dashboards and devices. Ethnic prejudices are reproduced in racially biased decision-making software adopted by judiciary systems worldwide, targeting especially minority communities (Gangadharan and Jędrzej 2018). Also, citizens of countries with weak rule of law, under authoritarian governments, or simply with poor sovereignty over digital infrastructure are exposed to data exploitation, which might result in human rights violations and the (re-)production of inequality. Think of the pervasive data infrastructure run by the state for the management of digital identity like Aadhaar in India, the world's largest biometric identity system (Masiero 2020). "Citizen scoring" schemes such as the Social Credit System in China (Dencik et al. 2018) are another case in point: Algorithms amenable to false positives are used to segment population groups according to their "risk profile." Both systems might eventually generate social exclusion. Yet, individuals and communities at the margins are not merely paying the social costs of datafication. On the contrary, they increasingly explore the potential of "counter data action" (Currie et al. 2016) and "data resistance" (Vera et al. 2018) to defy and subvert the pervasive datafication of social life.

How can we understand the multiple ways in which the disempowered are impacted by and seek to confront data exploitation? To date, research tends to rely on a limited set of *Western* conceptual tools to make sense of the specificities of these novel types of social vulnerability and resistance. Frameworks, epistemologies, and ontologies used to decode what large-scale data collection does to people at the margins or to determine what data infrastructure–impoverished communities might need to "develop" (Taylor and Broeders 2015) emerge almost entirely from "a world economy of knowledge structured by the history of colonialism and current north–south global inequalities" (Connell 2014, 210). They reproduce the "digital sublime" of Silicon Valley narratives, meaning the allure exerted by digital technologies that often obfuscates their drawbacks (Mosco 2004). This fascination is often uncritically extended to include also the dispossessed, ignoring the relevance of situated knowledge and contextual differences. In other words, we tend to extend theories and categorizations developed in a handful of centers of epistemic power in liberal democracies and wealthy countries to make sense of the datafied society in the fringes of the neoliberal system. We thus risk "universalizing" both the interpretation of the problem and the proposed solutions (Milan and Treré 2019), instead of trying to "decolonize" our approach (Ali 2016). In addition, most scholarship on these subject matters circulates merely in English, which acts as lingua franca for critical thinking on these matters (Suzina 2020). Significant interventions from academia and nonprofits within Latin America (e.g., Castro-Gómez and Grosfoguel 2007; Herrera Huérfano, Sierra Caballero, and Del Valle Rojas 2016), Africa (e.g., Cheruiyot and Ferrer-Conill 2018; Rodrigues et al. 2018), or Asia (e.g., Thorat 2021) circulate poorly or pay the price of linguistic diversity.

This chapter argues that we need to critically interrogate and redefine our conceptual toolbox if we are to understand non-mainstream data vulnerabilities and practices. To explore this claim, the essay promotes an interdisciplinary dialogue between critical data studies, sociology, science and technology studies, and decolonial thinking. The result is an analytical matrix which allows us to approach non-mainstream engagement with data from a sociological standpoint. More specifically, the matrix takes into consideration three key aspects of the datafied society: firstly, data infrastructure, meaning the *structural* dimension of datafication (e.g., the technical and governance arrangements imposed on data subjects, their governmentality consequences, and any potential self-organized alternatives); secondly, data practices, which allow us to understand how *agency* unfolds when people relate to datafication (e.g., how people and communities incorporate data in their action repertoires); and thirdly, data imaginaries, which stand in for the *cultural and symbolic* dimension of data at the margins (e.g., meaning-making processes as they are mediated by data and data infrastructure). Furthermore, the matrix mobilizes three lenses of interpretation which may help in overcoming the blind spots in current "Western" analyses of the datafied society, namely decoloniality, or the decolonial "thinking and doing" (Mignolo 2011, xxiv); race, intersectionality, and feminism; and the "pluriverse," which stands in for the myriad of "alternative" epistemologies that emerge outside the mainstream (Escobar 2018).

The chapter is organized as follows. Firstly, we review useful literature to approach and further define the margins, also evoking the concept of a "plural" south. Secondly, we present our three-pronged approach which accounts for three fundamental aspects of the datafied society, namely infrastructure, practices, and imaginaries. Finally, we sketch three valuable lenses of interpretations to read data at the margins, questioning power dynamics and making room for distinct epistemologies.

Thinking from the Margins: A Critical Literature Review

Only 53% of the world population is connected to the internet today (International Telecommunication Union 2019). But in our increasingly datafied society, reducing the problem to the dichotomy between the "big data rich" and the "have nots" (boyd and Crawford 2012) would be a mistake. It is also more than simply lacking access to digital infrastructure, as the classical literature on digital divide seems to suggest (Van Dijk 2020)—for three reasons. Firstly, policymakers increasingly rely on "calculated publics," that is to say publics evoked by automatized quantification exercises (Crawford 2015), to make decisions and allocate public resources. As a result, people's existence is more and more tied to data, as the COVID-19 global health crisis has made evident (Milan, Treré, and Masiero 2021). Being "datafied" during a pandemic (e.g., visible to the state, gaining access to social welfare and vaccines) has turned into a necessary condition for survival and care (Milan and Treré 2020). For example, undocumented migrants in many EU countries are invisible to government data sets, which prevents them from accessing healthcare or unemployment benefits (Pelizza, Milan, and Lausberg forthcoming). While this new type of "data poverty" (Milan and Treré 2020) has to do with fundamental forms of inequality that predate the datafied society, it is aggravated by the limited citizen agency in the complex ecosystem of data extractivism and commodification (Sadowski 2019). Secondly, many individuals and communities lack the data literacy and sociocultural capital to situate their voices in the public sphere. Thus, they struggle to engage with the challenges of an increasingly datafied policymaking process where it is often impossible to seek redress. Finally, technology innovation itself may paradoxically contribute to worsen the problem. To name just one example, the emergence of digital technology breaking the boundaries between the networking infrastructure and the application data, such as the celebrated fifth generation of cellular networks (5G), risks limiting the possibilities of end users to run and/or use the infrastructure as they want, deepening the gulf between the "haves" and the "have nots."

Scholars of disciplines as diverse as media studies, law, sociology, and informatics are increasingly devoting their attention to the implications of datafication from a critical perspective. They have denounced the novel forms of exploitation of those "at the bottom of the data pyramid" (Arora 2016) and exposed how these mechanisms contribute to reproduce colonial power relations (Thatcher, O'Sullivan, and Mahmoudi 2016). They have brought under the spotlight a variety of bottom-up data justice projects which emerged in the Global South as well as in the plurality of "Souths"—in other words, pockets of marginality—that survive in the fringes of Western democracies. These grassroots projects expand the space of possibilities of citizen action (Sun and Yan 2020), promote social justice through data (Heeks and Renken 2018), reclaim citizenship through transparency activism (Torres 2019), and seek ways of decolonizing data and technology (Awori et al. 2016). Instead of replicating the mainstream, they generate novel data epistemologies and alternative ways of participating in the datafied society (Milan and van der Velden 2016). Regrettably, in the literature these disparate case studies seldom result in wide-ranging theory development. They remain siloed in distinct disciplines which rarely converse with each other, with sociologists often overlooking the social affordances of technology and media scholars disregarding fundamental questions of power.

This chapter offers an analytical grid that combines insights from four disciplines—sociology, science and technology studies, critical data studies, and postcolonial and decolonial studies. An interdisciplinary approach is required because investigating the impact of datafication on people at the margins means taking a deep dive into complex processes at the intersection of several dimensions, including the infrastructural, cultural, political, and legal. Sociology, especially political sociology and social movement studies, allows us to center human agency with respect to data, infrastructure, and software (Couldry 2014). Science and technology studies reminds us that data infrastructure is not merely the outcome of decisions of technical nature but embodies the values and preferences of its designers, producers, and shareholders (Winner 1999). Critical data studies, at the crossroads of the humanities, social sciences, and informatics, brings under the spotlight the potential exclusion, discrimination, and unfairness embedded in the datafied society (Dalton, Taylor, and Thatcher 2016). Finally, scholarship on colonialism and decoloniality, especially its Latin American strand, invites us to question the narratives of technology as "imported magic" (Medina, Marques, and Holmes 2014) pushed onto the Global South. It forces us to consider the colonial rationalities (Quijano 2007) embedded also in the datafied society and to give voice to diversity and multiplicity (Mignolo 2000).

To situate these "non-mainstream" forms of engagement with data, in our earlier work we proposed taking the plurality of the South as a frame of reference. South is "not merely a geographical or geopolitical marker (as in 'Global South'). Rather, it is a plural entity subsuming *also* the different, the underprivileged, the alternative, the resistant, the invisible, and the subversive" (Milan and Treré 2019, 321). This flexible and expansive definition of the South(s) identifies "*a place of (and a proxy for) alterity, resistance, subversion, and creativity*" (2019, 325, original italics). It empowers us to take into consideration inequality as "it transcends boundaries and known geographies" (2019, 321). However, to avoid the potential reductionism harbored by a spatial metaphor, here we summon a second, broader frame of reference: the margins. "[T]he margin," claims Colombian citizen media scholar Clemencia Rodríguez, is "a shortcut to speak of complex dynamics of power inequality. Processes of asymmetrical access to material and symbolic resources shape differentiated and unequal access to the public sphere" (Rodriguez 2017, 49). The margins are understood as complex sites of struggle, where the challenges of datafication unfold in distinctive ways but also where particular data ecologies divergent from the mainstream emerge and thrive.

Using the media analogy introduced by Rodríguez, we can identify a first distinction between "data at the center" and "data at the margins," whereby the latter questions technological and data universalism, or the tendency to gloss over diversity and impose Western epistemologies (Milan and Treré 2019). Nonetheless, current interpretation of forms of resistance and inequality associated with data tend to flatten the intrinsic multiplicity of data at the margins. They overgeneralize the features of people's engagement with data and overlook key differences between distinct types of data practices, imaginaries, and infrastructure. Data at the margins are grounded in local time, social geography, values, and agendas that might be diametrically opposed to "global" trends and market imperatives. At the margins, data generally exist out of sight, rendered invisible by the glitter, hype, and excitement that characterize "data at the center." Data at the margins hardly ever looks like one might expect. Instead, it is frequently used in unpredictable ways that differ from its originally intended purpose. It might even be absent because people lack the infrastructure or skills needed to produce, share, or make sense of it. Journeying into data at the margins is "stepping into the land of otherwise" (Rodriguez 2017, 49). Thus, how can we understand datafication as it unfolds at the margins of our increasingly interconnected world?

Three Building Blocks to Investigate the Land of Otherwise

To explore peripheral ways of engaging with data, we propose a three-pronged approach that allows for locating three fundamental aspects of the datafied society. These can be seen as the building blocks for a comprehensive analysis of the interplay between

Table 1. Building Blocks to Analyze Data at the Margins and Illustrative Examples

Data infrastructure	• Data infrastructures in the Global South (e.g., citizen scoring systems) • Creation of autonomous data infrastructure (e.g., cell networks, data sets) • Experiments with local data sovereignty
Data imaginaries	• Fear and resignation associated with surveillance • Facial recognition technology as dehumanizing • #AbolishBigData2009, connecting datafication to abolitionism
Data practices	• Data activism • Citizen sensing of environmental degradation • Rituals associated with everyday encounters with data (e.g., self-tracking)

datafication and inequality—one that is able to knit together the research loci of the four disciplines inspiring our work. These building blocks can be studied both as a whole and in isolation. In this section we introduce each building block, reviewing useful concepts for its analysis and identifying potential areas of investigation. Table 1 provides an overview of the building blocks, offering illustrative examples as they relate specifically to data at the margins.

Data Infrastructure: Investigating Structure in the Datafied Society

The first building block concerns the *material* dimension of data at the margins. We can think of physical infrastructure from large (e.g., corporate data centers) to small (e.g., personal devices like smartphones) but also of the mechanisms generating, collecting, and processing data and the related governance arrangements. The material dimension of the datafied society is also made visible in a myriad of software-based "sociotechnical assemblages" (Akrich 1992) like social media platforms and their "infrastructures of tracking" (Helles, Lomborg, and Lai 2020) or COVID-19 data sets and dashboards (Milan 2020). These data assemblages are "composed of many apparatuses and elements that are thoroughly entwined, and develop and mutate over time and space," shaping "what is possible, desirable and expected of data" (Kitchin 2014, 24–25). Data infrastructure, rising out of and existing in a complex web of relationships, can be sociologically understood as the recurrent yet mutable *structure* of the datafied society determining the environment, choices, and opportunities available to social actors.

How can we understand infrastructure at the margins? Useful concepts include the popular notions of "surveillant assemblage," indicating how individuals are profiled from information collected in a variety of digital places such as social media (Haggerty and Ericson 2000); "dataveillance," or surveillance through data infrastructure (van Dijck 2014); and "governmentality" as applied to big data (Aradau and Blanke 2017). Alternative perspectives include the Latin American critical ecology approach

(Barranquero and Baeza 2017), which connects resistance to the Western-led, one-way vision of development with sustainability and "environmental rationality" concerns (Leff 1994). The latter directions are particularly promising given the growing environmental footprint of the datafied society, and AI in particular (Dauvergne 2020).

In the field, we may focus our attention on the features of data infrastructure in the Global South, investigating, for instance, citizen scoring systems to regulate access to welfare like Sisbén in Colombia (López 2020) and the emergence of digital identity systems in the African continent (Schoemaker et al. 2020). One could analyze the discriminatory effects of the governance by data infrastructure by means of "immunity passports" (Voo, Clapham, and Tam 2020), the governmentality consequences of the securitization of migration (Bigo 2002), or local experiments in data ownership and technological sovereignty seeking to empower individuals to control their data as experimented in Barcelona, Spain (Lynch 2020). But we can also investigate the emergence of alternative data infrastructure, ranging from the self-organized cellular networks operated by indigenous communities in Oaxaca, Mexico (Baca-Feldman et al. 2019) to the citizen-led curation of a feminist index of domestic violence in Argentina (Chenou and Cepeda-Másmela 2019) or a data set of human rights violations in the Syrian conflict (Deutch and Habal 2018).

Data Imaginaries: Meaning-Making in the Datafied Society

Social actors, both individually and collectively, seek to make sense of their datafied environment. To mobilize people, sense-making (i.e., the process of interpretation of the complex reality of datafication) must be paired with meaning attribution (i.e., the generation of shared insights and beliefs). In this process, the perception of some form of injustice plays a key role (Gamson 1992). Movement frames might also help in attributing mobilizing value to otherwise technical or expert issues (Milan 2013). Examples of narratives associated with datafication include empowerment (Baack 2015), unfairness (O'Neil 2017), and fear or resignation (Dencik 2018). Popular mobilizing frames include state resistance and data appropriation and transparency (Torres 2019) and seek to counteract the mainstream narratives of securitization and self-empowerment. Recent examples include characterizing period-tracking mobile applications as "unpaid work" that "must be considered in light of the historic lack of recognition for women's sexual, reproductive and relational labor" (Felizi and Varon, n.d.) and biometric surveillance in public space as objectifying, commodifying, and dehumanizing people rather than increasing their safety (ReclaimYourFace 2020).

Suitable notions to capture how social actors engaging in resistant data practices make sense of datafication include "alternative epistemologies" as applied to datafication (Milan and van der Velden 2016), "social imaginaries" (Lehtiniemi and Ruckenstein 2018), and "counter imaginaries" (Kazansky and Milan 2021). Despite illuminating distinct ways of "feeling out" datafication, these notions similarly capture collective visions that connect "intentions and projects as well as utopias and ideologies" (Flichy 2007, 4). Knitting together the "technological" and the "social," they embody a normative dimension which often has mobilizing potential (Milan and ten Oever 2017). Venues to study emerging data imaginaries include initiatives to come to terms with surveillance (e.g., Duffy and Chan 2018), tools and platforms designed by activists to support other activists (e.g., Aouragh et al. 2015), and events like digital rights festivals and security training workshops (Daskal 2018).

Examples of alternative imaginaries of datafication at the margins include interventions like #AbolishBigData2009, promoted by grassroots organizations representing or working with racialized and minoritized communities in the United States. The initiative aims at changing the way big data and AI are conceived in society by connecting the mainstream discourse to abolitionism (Crooks 2019; see also Mohamed, Png, and Isaac 2020). Groups like Data 4 Black Lives, mobilizing data as "protest" and as "accountability," contribute to change the perception of data itself by positing data tools as statistical modeling as "powerful instruments for fighting bias, building progressive movements, and promoting civic engagement" (Data for Black Lives n.d.). Indigenous perspectives, too, provide alternative points of entry able to promote the decolonization of mainstream approaches to data, arguing for indigenous data sovereignty (Walker et al. 2021). Among others, the indigenous social philosophy of Andean origin known as *el buen vivir* ("good living")—"a way of doing things that is community-centric, ecologically-balanced and culturally-sensitive" (Balch 2013)—can be fruitfully adapted to reconcile humanism, sustainability, and the ecological imperative (Gudynas 2011; Arcila Calderón, Barranquero, and González Tanco 2018) in the datafied society.

Data Practices: Reclaiming Agency in the Datafied Society

But far from passively losing out to the sweeping structure of datafication, social actors may engage in resistant, subversive, and creative practices that reclaim their political agency. Political agency has to do with the ability of social actors in "making sense of the world so as to act within it" (Couldry 2014, 891). It is "transformative of the structures within which it is embedded" as it makes "use of knowledge and resources in creative and often radical ways" (Kaun, Kyriakidou, and Uldam 2016, 2). The dynamics of datafication forces us to rethink the very same conditions of political agency. In particular, it encourages us to focus on the interstitial spaces between institutionalized politics and the datafied public sphere (including social media platforms). Looking at practices of engagement with data offers a point of entry to track the manifestations of agency in the datafied society as social actors renegotiate their possibilities of intervention. Data practices point to routinized and creative sociotechnical practices of engagement with data, understood both in their guise of objects (e.g., data sets, data visualizations) and in their processes (e.g., surveillance, self-quantification) (see also Mattoni and Treré 2014 on media practices). Practices emerge within hybrid informational ecologies (Treré 2019) and can be individual or collective or both.

In the search for ways of exercising agency in the datafied society, we can explore how variably skilled users engage with data. Examples include data activism, data journalism, citizen sensing, and rituals associated with everyday encounters with data. Data activism appropriates or generates data to exert social change (Gutierrez 2018) or seeks to resist surveillance often by means of technical solutions such as communication encryption (Milan 2017). Data journalism points to the use of data for journalistic storytelling, often with an investigative goal (Baack 2015). Citizen sensing concerns the engagement of citizens in the collection of evidence to support, for example, environmental preservation campaigns (Berti Suman and van Geenhuizen 2020). Finally, everyday encounters with data include the rituals of the quantified self, whereby individuals engage in self-tracking by means of wearable devices (Lupton 2016), but also the efforts of making sense of the many data visualizations that populate pop culture today (Kennedy et al. 2016).

"Contentious data politics," pointing to the sociocultural mobilizations that critically interrogate datafication from the bottom up (Beraldo and Milan 2019), offers a useful framework to understand data practices. Furthermore, a range of notions allows us to zoom in on what people do with information and technology. These include the idea of "acting on" data and data infrastructures as a politics of intervention (Kubitschko 2017; Milan 2019), as well as "emancipatory communication practices" (Milan 2013) and "critical technical practice" (Dunbar-Hester 2012) foregrounding hands-on, do-it-yourself modes of engagement with data and data infrastructures. Martin-Barbero's (1993) analysis of "mediations" as opposed to "media," pointing to autonomous ways of appropriating media products, can help us in thinking about the grammar of grassroots appropriation and subversion when applied to datafication. Finally, Latin American movement praxis that foregrounds community understood as "common-unit (*común-unidad*)" (Barranquero and Baeza 2017) can help us to rethink collective agency in the datafied society.

Interpretative Lenses to Understand Data at the Margins

The horizontal axis of our matrix identifies three fruitful lenses of interpretation to explore emerging peripheral ways of making sense of data, namely decoloniality and race, intersectionality and feminism, and the pluriverse. Mobilizing these lenses of interpretation pursues two main goals. Firstly, it helps to overcome the blind spots in current "Western" analyses of the datafied society, zeroing in on specific genealogies of dispossession by means of a sociohistorical approach. Secondly, and most importantly, asking why and how certain social groups are oppressed through data and data infrastructure nurtures ongoing efforts to uncover viable pathways toward justice and equality in the datafied society. In other words, by evoking these perspectives to interrogate datafication, we want to make room for thinking along the lines of the "activist work that is required to turn that belief [of equality and justice] into reality" (D'Ignazio and Klein 2020, 3). It is worth noting, however, that there are other possible interpretative lenses that one might adopt to investigate data at the margins: Our other selection is situated and by no means conclusive.

The first lens of interpretation we acknowledge is the broad domain of decoloniality and race. Decoloniality and race identify two interconnected perspectives that give voice to those "options confronting and delinking from ... the colonial matrix of power" (Mignolo 2011, xxvii). They represent a concrete call to think from and at the margins and peripheries of the world system (Bhambra 2007). They also point to a process of "epistemic reconstruction" (Quijano 2007, 176) that outlines reparative measures and invites redress. Inspired by decolonial and critical race theorists, we can question the persistence of (European and Western) colonial structures in the contemporary datafied society. These colonial structures are visible, for example, in the reproduction of racial bias in search engine algorithms (Noble 2018) or in the use of high-tech tools in predictive policing that profile and punish the poor (Eubanks 2018). Concretely, adopting a decoloniality and race perspective entails interrogating how human characteristics like ethnicity and class are encoded in web applications designed to mediate the relation between the state and its citizens that mirror the colonial lineages of a country like The Netherlands (van Schie, Smit, and López Coombs 2020). It means critically approaching the data infrastructure designed to curb the COVID-19 pandemic by asking in what ways it renders migrants and minorities invisible (Pelizza 2020).

The second lens of interpretation is offered by intersectional and feminist scholarship and movement praxis. Intersectionality and feminism point to traditions that forefront the situated and contextual nature of datafication, grounding it on an analysis of social change (D'Ignazio and Klein 2020). Feminism, often referred to with the plural "feminisms" to emphasize the vast diversity of critical feminist thinking, upholds the idea of equality between the sexes, while challenging sexism and other forces of oppression. Intersectionality broadens the scope of the critique, considering also other aspects of privilege and dispossession that characterize any individual identity. Taken together, these approaches encourage us to "center embodiment and situatedness in relation to disempowerment" (Milan and Treré 2019, 327). Grounded on the feminist imperative of equality, data feminism is "a way of thinking about data, both their uses and their limits, that is informed by direct experience, by a commitment to action, and by intersectional feminist thought" (D'Ignazio and Klein 2020, 8). The art project *Feminist Data Set* by Caroline Sinders (2017) offers a practical example of an intersectional approach to datafication: It purports to collect cultural material about feminism to train AI systems to locate feminist and other intersectional ways of thinking across online media content. Adopting a data feminist perspective might also entail interrogating the gender data gap, exposing how women's contributions to society have been historically silenced and investigating how said gender data gap concretely impacts their lives today (Criado Perez 2019).

Finally, the third lens of interpretation we put forward addresses the need to make room for distinct ways of seeing and interpreting the world we inhabit, interrogating emerging "southern" (as in the plurality of Souths) epistemologies in our analysis of datafication from the bottom up. Rather than "a fixed set of propositions," giving voice to southern epistemologies represents "a challenge to develop new knowledge projects and new ways of learning with globally expanded resources" (Connell 2014, 210). The notion of the pluriverse, which foregrounds ontological difference, comes in handy. Advanced by anthropologist Arturo Escobar, the pluriverse is a "world where many worlds fit" and "a tool for reimagining and reconstructing local worlds" (Escobar 2018, xvi). Engaging with the pluriverse paves the way for "an ethical and political practice of alterity that involves a deep concern for social justice, the radical equality of all beings, and nonhierarchy" (p. xvi). And because "culture sits in places" (Escobar 2001, 139), localizing data knowledge and data uses is a first step toward recognizing place as a sociocultural object of struggle also in the datafied society. Concretely, adopting a pluriverse lens to interpret datafication asks, for instance, what *buen vivir* with data might mean in practice, in an effort to reconcile distinct cosmogonies and local specificities with datafication as a Global North project with a high environmental footprint (Milan and Treré 2021). But a pluriversal approach represents also an invitation to question the epistemology of research itself, paying close attention to relation-building with communities and methods that empower research subjects (Kazansky et al. 2019). It may mean, for example, bridging the agenda of astronomy researchers in rural Brazil with the needs of the local indigenous groups during a global pandemic (Cortesi et al. 2021).

Table 2 presents our analytical matrix populated with the illustrative example discussed in the chapter. The vertical axis details the three components of data at the margins, whereas the horizontal axis identifies the three lenses of interpretation we detected.

Table 2. Analytical Matrix

	Lenses of Interpretation		
Components of Data at the Margins	Decoloniality and Race	Intersectionality and Feminism	The Pluriverse
Data infrastructure	Algorithmic racism in facial recognition technology	Feminist index of domestic violence in Argentina	Servers for local data sovereignty (e.g., Barcelona)
Data imaginaries	Data as accountability for Black lives	Period tracking apps as data exploitation	*Buen vivir* with data
Data practices	Creation of "southern" autonomous data infrastructure	*Feminist Data Set* by Caroline Sinders (2017)	Indigenous data sovereignty initiatives

CONCLUSION

Far from being merely an economic resource of global interest, big data and associated technological innovations, including AI applications, might alter citizen agency, jeopardize human rights, and reproduce or create new forms of discrimination. They might also flatten the richness, plurality, and diversity of data cultures, visions, and infrastructure emerging in the fringes of society. This chapter introduced the notion of data at the margins as a starting point to redefine our conceptual toolbox to address non-mainstream data vulnerabilities. It offered an analytical matrix to study the complex entanglements of infrastructures, imaginaries, and practices. It argued that for a sociological understanding of data at the margins we ought to dialogue with distinct scholarly fields, including critical data, algorithms, and AI studies but also decolonial, feminist, critical race, and critical design studies. In so doing, it sketched a research agenda able to future-proof our understanding of the complex relation between people and technology.

Much work remains to be done. Sociology is particularly well placed to bring valuable insights in this timely debate, in virtue of its long-standing engagement with power, poverty, inequality, and social justice and its tradition of investigating social movements, forms of collective solidarity, and resistance. Particularly promising are recent developments in global sociology, where scholars increasingly complement their postcolonial approach with an anti-authoritarian ethos, articulating also the urgency of a dialogue between different national sociologies (Hanafi 2019).

REFERENCES

Akrich, Madeleine. 1992. "The De-Scription of Technical Objects." In *Shaping Technology/Building Society. Studies in Sociotechnical Change*, edited by W. E. Bijker and J. Law, 205–224. Cambridge, MA: MIT Press.

Ali, Syed Mustafa. 2016. "Algorithmic Racism: A Decolonial Critique." *Proceedings of the 10th International Society for the Study of Religion*. http://www.academia.edu/14124452/Algorithmic_Racism_-_A_Decolonial_Critique.

Andrejevic, Mark. 2014. "Big Data, Big Questions: The Big Data Divide." *International Journal of Communication* 8: 1673–1689.

Aouragh, Miriyam, Seda Gürses, Jara Rocha, and Femke Snelting. 2015. "Let's First Get Things Done! On Division of Labour and Techno-Political Practices of Delegation in Times of Crisis." *Fiberculture* 26: 208–235. https://doi.org/10.15307/fcj.26.196.2015.

Aradau, Claudia, and Tobias Blanke. 2017. "Politics of Prediction: Security and the Time/Space of Governmentality in the Age of Big Data." *European Journal of Social Theory* 20, no. 3: 373–391.

Arcila Calderón, Carlos, Alejandro Barranquero, and Eva González Tanco. 2018. "From Media to Buen Vivir: Latin American Approaches to Indigenous Communication." *Communication Theory* 28, no. 2: 180–201.

Arora, Payal. 2016. "The Bottom of the Data Pyramid: Big Data and the Global South." *International Journal of Communication* 10: 1681–1699. https://ijoc.org/index.php/ijoc/article/viewFile/4297/1616

Awori, Kagonya, Nicola J. Bidwell, Tigist Sherwaga Hussan, Satinder Gill, and Silvia Lindtner. 2016. "Decolonising Technology Design." In *Proceedings of the First African Conference on Human Computer Interaction (AfriCHI'16)*, 226–228. New York: ACM. https://doi.org/10.1145/2998581.2998622.

Baack, Stefan. 2015. "Datafication and Empowerment: How the Open Data Movement Rearticulates Notions of Democracy, Participation, and Journalism." *Big Data & Society* 2, no. 2. https://doi.org/10.1177/2053951715594634.

Baca-Feldman, Carlos F., Erick Huerta Velázquez, María Álvarez Malvido, Daniela Parra Hinojosa, and Karla Velasco Ramos. 2019. "Weaving Technological Autonomy in Indigenous Peoples: Community Cellular Telephony in Oaxaca, Mexico." In *Internet Governance and Regulations in Latin America*, edited by L. Belli and O. Cavalli, 275–288. Rio de Janeiro: FGV Direito Rio.

Balch, Oliver. 2013. "Buen Vivir: The Social Philosophy Inspiring Movements in South America." *The Guardian*, February 4. https://www.theguardian.com/sustainable-business/blog/buen-vivir-philosophy-south-america-eduardo-gudynas.

Barranquero, Alejandro Carretero, and Chiara Saez Baeza. 2017. "Latin American Critical Epistemologies toward a Biocentric Turn in Communication for Social Change: Communication from a Good Living Perspective." *Latin American Research Review* 52, no. 3: 431–445. https://doi.org/10.25222/larr.59.

Beraldo, Davide, and Stefania Milan. 2019. "From Data Politics to the Contentious Politics of Data." *Big Data & Society* 6, no. 2. https://doi.org/10.1177/2053951719885967.

Berti Suman, Anna, and Marina van Geenhuizen. 2020. "Not Just Noise Monitoring: Rethinking Citizen Sensing for Risk-Related Problem-Solving." *Journal of Environmental Planning and Management* 63, no. 3: 546–567. https://doi.org/10.1080/09640568.2019.1598852.

Bhambra, Gurminder K. 2007. *Rethinking Modernity: Postcolonialism and the Sociological Imagination*. Basingstoke, UK, and New York: Palgrave MacMillan.

Bigo, Didier. 2002. "Security and Immigration: Toward a Critique of the Governmentality of Unease." *Alternatives* 27, no. 1: 63–92. https://doi.org/10.1177/03043754020270S105.

boyd, danah, and Kate Crawford. 2012. "Critical Questions for Big Data. Provocations for a Cultural, Technological, and Scholarly Phenomenon." *Information, Communication & Society* 15, no. 5: 662–679.

Castro-Gómez, Santiago, and Ramón Grosfoguel, eds. 2007. *El giro decolonial. Reflexiones para una diversidad epistémica más allá del capitalismo global*. Bogota, Colombia: Siglo del Hombre Editores.

Chenou, Jean-Marie, and Carolina Cepeda-Másmela. 2019. "#NiUnaMenos: Data Activism from the Global South." *Television & New Media* 20, no. 4: 396–411. https://doi.org/10.1177/1527476419828995.

Cheruiyot, David, and Raul Ferrer-Conill. 2018. "Fact-Checking Africa. Epistemologies, Data and the Expansion of Journalistic Discourse." *Digital Journalism* 6, no. 8: 964–975.

Connell, R. 2014. "Using Southern Theory: Decolonizing Social Thought in Theory, Research and Application." *Planning Theory* 13, no. 2: 210–223.

Cortesi, Arianna, Claudia Magnani, Roberto Romero, Paula C.P. Silva, Sueli Maxakali, Isael Maxakali, and Ana Maria R. Gomes. 2021. "Under other Skies: Astronomy as a Tool to Face COVID-19-Induced Isolation in the Indigenous Village of Aldeia Verde, Brazil." In

COVID-19 from the Margins: Pandemic Invisibilities, Policies and Resistance in the Datafied Society, edited by S. Milan, E. Treré, & S. Masiero, 259–262. Amsterdam: Institute of Network Cultures.

Couldry, Nick. 2014. "A Necessary Disenchantment: Myth, Agency and Injustice in a Digital World." *Sociological Review* 62, no. 4: 880–897.

Crawford, Kate. 2015. "Can an Algorithm be Agonistic? Ten Scenes from Life in Calculated Publics." *Science, Technology & Human Values* 41, no. 1: 77–92. https://doi.org/10.1177/0162243915589635.

Criado Perez, Caroline. 2019. *Invisible Women. Exposing Data Bias in a World Designed for Men*. London: Vintage.

Crooks, Roderic. 2019. "What We Mean When We Say #AbolishBigData2019." *Medium*, March 22. https://medium.com/@rncrooks/what-we-mean-when-we-say-abolishbigdata2019-d030799ab22e.

Currie, Morgan, Brittany Paris, I. Pasquetto, and J. Pierre. 2016. "The Conundrum of Police Officer-Involved Homicides: Counter-data in Los Angeles County." *Big Data & Society* 3, no. 2. https://doi.org/10.1177/2053951716663566.

Dalton, Craig M., Linnet Taylor, and Jim Thatcher. 2016. "Critical Data Studies: A Dialog on Data and Space." *Big Data & Society* 3, no. 1. https://doi.org/10.1177/2053951716648346.

Daskal, Efrat. 2018. "Let's Be Careful out There . . . : How Digital Rights Advocates Educate Citizens in the Digital Age." *Information, Communication & Society* 21, no. 2: 241–256. https://doi.org/10.1080/1369118X.2016.1271903.

Data for Black Lives. n.d. "About Us." http://d4bl.org/about.html.

Dauvergne, Peter. 2020. "Is Artificial Intelligence Greening Global Supply Chains? Exposing the Political Economy of Environmental Costs." *Review of International Political Economy*. Published ahead of print September 3, 2020. https://doi.org/10.1080/09692290.2020.1814381.

Dencik, Lina. 2018. "Surveillance Realism and the Politics of Imagination: Is There no Alternative?" *Krisis: Journal for Contemporary Philosophy* 1: 31–43.

Dencik, Lina, Arne Hintz, Joanna Redden, and Harry Warne. 2018. *Data Scores as Governance: Investigating Uses of Citizen Scoring in Public Services*. Cardiff, UK: Data Justice Lab. http://orca.cf.ac.uk/117517/1/data-scores-as-governance-project-report2.pdf.

Deutch, Jeff, and Hadi Habal. 2018. "The Syrian Archive: A Methodological Case Study of Open-Source Investigation of State Crime Using Video Evidence from Social Media Platforms." *State Crime* 7, no. 1: 46–76.

D'Ignazio, Catherine, and Lauren Klein. 2020. *Data Feminism*. Cambridge, MA: MIT Press.

Duffy, Brooke Erin, and Ngai Keung Chan. 2018. " 'You Never Really Know Who's Looking': Imagined Surveillance across Social Media Platforms." *New Media & Society* 21, no. 1: 119–138. https://doi.org/10.1177/1461444818791318.

Dunbar-Hester, Christina. 2012. "Soldering toward Media Democracy. Technical Practice as Symbolic Value in Radio Activism." *Journal of Communication Inquiry* 36, no. 2: 149–169.

Escobar, Arturo. 2001. "Culture Sits in Places: Reflections on Globalism and Subaltern Strategies of Localization." *Political Geography* 20, no. 2: 139–174. https://doi.org/10.1016/S0962-6298(00)00064-0.

Escobar, Arturo. 2018. *Designs for the Pluriverse. Radical Interdependence, Autonomy, and the Making of Worlds*. Durham, NC: Duke University Press.

Eubanks, Virginia. 2018. *Automating Inequality: How High-Tech Tools Profile, Police, and Punish the Poor*. New York: St. Martin's Press.

Felizi, Natasha, and Joana Varon. n.d. "MENSTRUAPPS—How to Turn Your Period into Money (for Others)." Coding Rights. https://chupadados.codingrights.org/en/menstruapps-como-transformar-sua-menstruacao-em-dinheiro-para-os-outros/.

Flichy, Patrice. 2007. *The Internet Imaginaire*. Cambridge, MA: MIT Press.

Gamson, William A. 1992. *Talking Politics*. Cambridge: Cambridge University Press.

Gangadharan, Seeta P., and Niklas Jędrzej. 2018. *Between Antidiscrimination and Data: Understanding Human Rights Discourse on Automated Discrimination in Europe*. London: London School of Economics. http://eprints.lse.ac.uk/88053/13/Gangadharan_Between-antidiscrimination_Published.pdf.

Gudynas, Eduardo. 2011. "Buen Vivir: Today's Tomorrow." *Development* 54, no. 4: 441–447. https://link.springer.com/article/10.1057/dev.2011.86.

Gupta, Anushri, Panos Panagiotopoulos, and Frances Bowen. 2020. "An Orchestration Approach to Smart City Data Ecosystems." *Technological Forecasting and Social Change* 153: 119929. https://doi.org/10.1016/j.techfore.2020.119929.

Gutierrez, Miren. 2018. *Data Activism and Social Change*. London: Palgrave MacMillan.

Haggerty, Kevin D., and Richard V. Ericson. 2000. "The Surveillant Assemblage." *British Journal of Sociology* 51, no. 4: 605–622.

Hanafi, Sari. 2019. "Global Sociology Revisited: Toward New Directions." *Current Sociology* 68, no. 1: 3–21. https://doi.org/10.1177/0011392119869051.

Heeks, Richard, and Jaco Renken. 2018. "Data Justice for Development: What Would It Mean?" *Information Development* 34, no. 1: 90–102. https://doi.org/10.1177/0266666916678282.

Helles, Rasmus, Stine Lomborg, and Signe Sophus Lai. 2020. "Infrastructures of Tracking: Mapping the Ecology of Third-Party Services across Top Sites in the EU." *New Media & Society* 22, no. 11: 1957–1975. https://doi.org/10.1177/1461444820932868.

Herrera Huérfano, Eliana, Francisco Sierra Caballero, and Carlos Del Valle Rojas. 2016. "Hacia una epistemología del sur. Decolonialidad del saberpoder informativo y nueva comunicología Latinoamericana. Una lectura crítica de la mediación desde las culturas indígenas." *Chasqui. Revista Latinoamericana de Comunicación* 131: 77–105.

Hintz, Arne, Lina Dencik, and Karin Wahl-Jorgensen. 2018. *Digital Citizenship in a Datafied Society*. Cambridge: Polity.

International Telecommunication Union. 2019. "Statistics." https://www.itu.int/en/ITU-D/Statistics/Pages/stat/default.aspx.

Kaun, Anne, Maria Kyriakidou, and Julie Uldam. 2016. "Political Agency at the Digital Crossroads?" *Media and Communication* 4, no. 4: 1–7.

Kazansky, Becky, and Stefania Milan. 2021. " 'Bodies not Templates': Contesting Mainstream Algorithmic Imaginaries." *New Media & Society* 23, no. 2: 363–381. https://doi.org/10.1177/1461444820929316.

Kazansky, Becky, Guillén Torres, Lonneke van der Velden, Kersti R. Wissenbach, and Stefania Milan. 2019. "Data for the Social Good: Toward a Data-Activist Research Agenda." In *Good Data*, edited by A. Daly and M. Mann, 244–259. Amsterdam: Institute of Network Cultures.

Kennedy, Helen, Rosemary Lucy Hill, William Allen, and Andy Kirk. 2016. "Engaging with (Big) Data Visualizations: Factors That Affect Engagement and Resulting New Definitions of Effectiveness." *First Monday* 21, no. 11. https://firstmonday.org/article/view/6389/5652

Kitchin, Rob. 2014. *The Data Revolution: Big Data, Open Data, Data Infrastructures and Their Consequences*. London: Sage.

Kubitschko, Sebastian. 2017. "Acting on Media Technologies and Infrastructures: Expanding the Media as Practice Approach." *Media, Culture & Society* 40, no. 4: 629–635. https://doi.org/10.1177/0163443717706068.

Leff, Enrique. 1994. *Ecología y capital: Racionalidad ambiental, democracia participativa y desarrollo sustentable*. Mexico City: Siglo XXI.

Lehtiniemi, Tuukka, and Minna Ruckenstein. 2018. "The Social Imaginaries of Data Activism." *Big Data & Society* 6, no. 1. https://journals.sagepub.com/doi/full/10.1177/2053951718821146.

López, Joan. 2020. *Experimentando con la pobreza: El sisbén y los proyectos de analítica de datos*. Bogota, Colombia: Fundación Karisma. https://web.karisma.org.co/wp-content/uploads/download-manager-files/Experimentando%20con%20la%20pobreza.pdf.

Lupton, Deborah. 2016. *The Quantified Self*. Cambridge: Polity.

Lynch, Casey R. 2020. "Contesting Digital Futures: Urban Politics, Alternative Economies, and the Movement for Technological Sovereignty in Barcelona." *Antipode* 52, no. 3: 660–680. https://doi.org/10.1111/anti.12522.

Martin-Barbero, Jesus. 1993. *Communication, Culture and Hegemony: From the Media to Mediations*. London: Sage:

Masiero, Silvia. 2020. "Biometric Infrastructures and the Indian Public Distribution System." *South Asia Multidisciplinary Academic Journal* 23. https://doi.org/10.4000/samaj.6459.

Mattoni, Alice, and Emiliano Treré. 2014. "Media Practices, Mediation Processes, and Mediatization in the Study of Social Movements." *Communication Theory* 24, no. 3: 252–271.

Medina, Eden, Ivan da Costa Marques, and Christina Holmes, eds. 2014. *Beyond Imported Magic. Essays on Science, Technology, and Society in Latin America*. Cambridge, MA: MIT Press.

Mignolo, Walter D. 2000. *Local Histories/Global Designs: Essays on the Coloniality of Power, Subaltern Knowledges and Border Thinking*. Princeton, NJ: Princeton University Press.

Mignolo, Walter D. 2011. *The Darker Side of Western Modernity: Global Futures, Decolonial Options*. Durham, NC: Duke University Press.

Milan, Stefania. 2013. *Social Movements and Their Technologies: Wiring Social Change*. London: Palgrave Macmillan.

Milan, Stefania. 2017. "Data Activism as the New Frontier of Media Activism." In *Media Activism in the Digital Age*, edited by G. Yang and V. Pickard, 151–163. London and New York: Routledge.

Milan, Stefania. 2019. "Acting on Data(fication)." In *Citizen Media and Practice: Currents, Connections, Challenges*, edited by H. Stephansen and E. Treré, 212–226. London and New York: Routledge.

Milan, Stefania. 2020. "Techno-solutionism and the Standard Human in the Making of the COVID-19 Pandemic." *Big Data & Society* 7, no. 2. https://doi.org/10.1177/2053951720966781.

Milan, Stefania, and Niels ten Oever. 2017. "Coding and Encoding Rights in Internet Infrastructure." *Internet Policy Review* 6, no. 1. https://doi.org/10.14763/2017.1.442.

Milan, Stefania, and Emiliano Treré. 2019. "Big Data from the South(s): Beyond Data Universalism." *Television & New Media* 20, no. 4: 319–335. https://doi.org/10.1177/1527476419837739.

Milan, Stefania, and Emiliano Treré. 2020. "The Rise of the Data Poor: The COVID-19 Pandemic Seen from the Margins." *Social Media + Society* 6, no. 3. https://doi.org/10.1177/2056305120948233.

Milan, Stefania, and Emiliano Treré. 2021. "Latin American Visions for a Digital New Deal: Learning from Critical Ecology, Liberation Pedagogy and Autonomous Design." In *A

Digital New Deal. Visions of Justice in a Post-Covid World, edited by S. Sarkar and A. Korjan, 101–111. Bangalore, India: IT for Change.

Milan, Stefania, Emiliano Treré, and Silvia Masiero. 2021. *COVID-19 from the Margins: Pandemic Invisibilities, Policies and Resistance in the Datafied Society*. Amsterdam: Institute of Network Cultures.

Milan, Stefania, and Lonneke van der Velden. 2016. "The Alternative Epistemologies of Data Activism." *Digital Culture & Society* 2, 57–74. https://doi.org/10.14361/dcs-2016-0205.

Mohamed, Shakir, Marie-Therese Png, and William Isaac. 2020. "Decolonial AI: Decolonial Theory as Sociotechnical Foresight in Artificial Intelligence." *Philosophy & Technology* 33, no. 4: 659–684. https://doi.org/10.1007/s13347-020-00405-8.

Mosco, Vincent. 2004. *The Digital Sublime: Myth, Power, and Cyberspace*. Cambridge, MA: MIT Press.

Noble, Safiya Umoja. 2018. *Algorithms of Oppression: How Search Engines Reinforce Racism*. New York: New York University Press.

O'Neil, Cathy. 2017. *Weapons of Math Destruction: How Big Data Increases Inequality and Threatens Democracy*. New York: Broadway Books.

Pelizza, Annalisa. 2020. " 'No Disease for the Others": How COVID-19 Data Can Enact New and Old Alterities." *Big Data & Society* 7, no. 2: 2053951720942542. https://doi.org/10.1177/2053951720942542.

Pelizza, Annalisa, Stefania Milan, and Yoren Lausberg. Forthcoming. "Undocumented Migrants in COVID-19 Counting: Rethinking the Data-(In)Visibility Nexus." *Data & Policy*.

Quijano, Anibal. 2007. "Coloniality and Modernity/Rationality." *Cultural Studies* 21, no. 2–3: 168–178.

ReclaimYourFace. 2020. "Secretive. Unlawful. Inhumane." https://reclaimyourface.eu/the-problem/.

Rodrigues, Gemma F., Christopher Csikszentmihalyi, Daniel Mwesigwa, Jude Mukundane, and Michelle Kasprzak. 2018. *Social Tech Ecosystems in Sub-Saharan Africa*. Funchal, Madeira: Madeira Interactive Technologies Institute. https://doi.org/10.5281/zenodo.1244086.

Rodriguez, Clemencia. 2017. "Studying Media at the Margins: Learning from the Field." In *Media Activism in the Digital Age*, edited by V. Pickard and G. Yang, 49–60. London and New York: Routledge.

Sadowski, Jathan. 2019. "When Data Is Capital: Datafication, Accumulation, and Extraction." *Big Data & Society* 6, no. 1. https://doi.org/10.1177/2053951718820549.

Schoemaker, Emrys, Dina Baslan, Bryan Pon, and Nicola Dell. 2020. "Identity at the Margins: Data Justice and Refugee Experiences with Digital Identity Systems in Lebanon, Jordan, and Uganda." *Information Technology for Development* 27, no. 1: 13–36. https://doi.org/10.1080/02681102.2020.1785826.

Sinders, Caroline. 2017. *Feminist Data Set*. https://carolinesinders.com/feminist-data-set/.

Sun, Y., and W. Yan. 2020. "The Power of Data from the Global South: Environmental Civic Tech and Data Activism in China." *International Journal of Communication* 14: 2144–2162.

Suzina, Ana Cristina. 2020. "English as *Lingua Franca*. Or the Sterilisation of Scientific Work." *Media, Culture & Society* 43, no. 1: 171–179. https://doi.org/10.1177/0163443720957906.

Taylor, Linnet, and Dennis Broeders. 2015. "In the Name of Development: Power, Profit and the Datafication of the Global South." *Geoforum* 64: 229–237. https://doi.org/10.1016/j.geoforum.2015.07.002.

Thatcher, Jim, David O'Sullivan, and Dillon Mahmoudi. 2016. "Data Colonialism through Accumulation by Dispossession: New Metaphors for Daily Data." *Environment and Planning D: Society and Space* 34, no. 6: 990–1006. https://doi.org/10.1177/0263775816633195.

Thorat, Dhanashree. 2021. "Modalities of Data Colonialism and South Asian Hashtag Publics." *Feminist Media Studies* 21, no. 1: 151–153. https://doi.org/10.1080/14680777.2021.1864874.

Torres, Guillén. 2019. "Institutional Resistance to Transparency: The Quest for Public Sector Information in Mexico." *Journal of Resistance Studies* 5, no. 2: 68–96.

Treré, Emiliano. 2019. *Hybrid Media Activism*. London and New York: Routledge.

van Dijck, José. 2014. "Datafication, Dataism and Dataveillance: Big Data between Scientific Paradigm and Ideology." *Surveillance and Society* 12, no. 3: 197–208.

Van Dijk, Jan. 2020. *The Digital Divide*. Cambridge: Polity Press.

van Doorn, Niels. 2017. "Platform Labor: On the Gendered and Racialized Exploitation of Low-Income Service Work in the 'On-Demand' Economy." *Information, Communication & Society* 20, no. 6: 898–914. https://doi.org/10.1080/1369118X.2017.1294194.

van Schie, Gerwin, Alex Smit, and Nicolás López Coombs. 2020. "Racing through the Dutch Governmental Data Assemblage: A Postcolonial Data Studies Approach." *Global Perspectives* 1, no. 1: 12779. https://doi.org/10.1525/gp.2020.12779.

Vera, Lourdes A., Lindsey Dillon, Sara Wylie, Jennifer Liss Ohayon, Aaron Lemelin, Phil Brown, et al. 2018. "Data Resistance: A Social Movement Organizational Autoethnography of the Environmental Data and Governance Initiative." *Mobilization: An International Quarterly* 23, no. 4: 511–529. https://doi.org/10.17813/1086-671X-24-4-511.

Voo, Teck Chuan, Hannah Clapham, and Clarence C Tam. 2020. "Ethical Implementation of Immunity Passports during the COVID-19 Pandemic." *Journal of Infectious Diseases* 222, no. 5: 715–718. https://doi.org/10.1093/infdis/jiaa352.

Walker, Maggie, Tahu Kukutai, Stephanie Russo Carroll, and Desi Rodriguez-Lonebear, eds. 2021. *Indigenous Data Sovereignty and Policy*. London and New York: Routledge.

Winner, Langdon. 1999. "Do Artefacts Have Politics?" In *The Social Shaping of Technology*, edited by D. MacKenzie and J. Wajcman, 28–40. Buckingham, UK, and Philadelphia: Open University Press.

Zuboff, Shoshana. 2019. *The Age of Surveillance Capitalism*. London: Profile Books.

PART II
DIGITAL MEDIA AND SOCIAL INSTITUTIONS

PART II

DIGITAL MEDIA AND SOCIAL INSTITUTIONS

CHAPTER 6

FROM "IMPACT" TO "NEGOTIATION"

Educational Technologies and Inequality

CASSIDY PUCKETT AND MATTHEW H. RAFALOW

In this chapter, we use frame theory to argue for a shift in the way research and policy understands technology use in schools. The dominant frame currently used by researchers and policymakers focuses on "impact," suggesting that the adoption of technological innovations can improve the efficiency and effectiveness of core content area teaching, typically measured through standardized test scores. We instead argue for a nuanced understanding of technology use in schools as a sociopolitical negotiation, linking technology use to broader processes of social stratification deeply embedded in the fabric of educational systems, rather than an add-on to increase schools' efficiency. While most research narrowly asks, "What is the impact of technology use in schools on achievement?" the approach we propose asks, instead, "How does the negotiation of existing inequalities shape unequal use and unequal outcomes?" Overall, we show precisely why this new reframing is necessary and how it can be applied.

Further, rather than focusing on the introduction of personal computers into schools in the 1980s, as is often the case in the discussion of technology use in schools, the negotiation frame we propose takes a longer view of how educational policies, schools, educators, and students construct meaning around technologies. This, we argue, occurs in historically patterned ways that are both shaped by and influence race- and class-based inequalities. Indeed, these negotiations started with the founding of public education, when educational philosophers and policymakers debated about the meaning of technological activity, its match to particular social classes and racial groups, and what this meant for the structuring of schools (Labaree 2010). This negotiation extends into the present day with continued debates over issues as broad as funding particular forms of technology in schools to policies about at-school cell phone usage or, more recently in the context of the global pandemic, what it means to be a school online (Moyer 2020; Strauss 2018; Baig 2020; Dinsmore 2019).

In what follows, we first explain frame theory, then describe the impact frame in greater detail, explaining how this became the dominant view in educational research and policy and clarifying what it misses. We next compare it to our formulation of the negotiation frame and how this alternate frame reveals a very different way of understanding technology use in schools, drawing on empirical cases from high-tech and low-tech schools across the country. Viewed as negotiation in the context of preexisting inequalities, research using the negotiation frame reveals that school technology use involves three dynamics: the ongoing categorization of technology use as vocational, risky, or innovative/academic; the matching of privileged groups to privileged technology uses; and the linking of micro- and meso-level processes and macro-level social stratification. Finally, we apply the negotiation frame to the recent coronavirus pandemic to show how a narrow focus on impact will cut off fruitful lines of research and apply the negotiation frame to identify opportunities for future research. Overall, we highlight the need for research on educational technologies that takes a critical perspective on the intimate connection between schools, technology use, and social stratification, in contrast to narrower conceptualizations of the impact of technologies in schools.

Frame Theory

We draw upon scholarship on frame theory, applied to the context of organizations and institutions, to analyze how researchers and policymakers make sense of technology use in schools. Frame theory in organizations often looks at three separate levels of action: micro-level organizational decision-making (Nutt 1998; Hodgkinson et al. 1999), meso-level strategic framing across groups and social movements (Benford and Snow 2000; Kaplan 2008), and macro-level processes where cultural templates of understanding (field-level frames) are changed and/or institutionalized (Fligstein and McAdam 2012). Here, we draw upon literature that emphasizes the interconnection between macro-, meso-, and micro-level processes to understand how field-level framing has shaped research on technology use in schools. This work suggests that institutional schema—broader logics that are embedded in complex relations of power—shape how individuals think about how institutions and organizations should and do work (Polletta and Ho 2006; Polletta 2008). These "cognitive frames" are used by individuals and organizations to guide action (Friedland and Alford 1991; Polletta 2008; Scott 2014). One such cognitive frame is how technologies are used in schools, by whom, and for what purpose.

Applying the idea of framing to research on technologies in schools, we argue that the main way researchers in education—including sociologists of education—have understood these technologies is through an "impact" frame where technologies are used to shape student learning, particularly (quantified) academic achievement. This idea of the "impact" of technologies and student learning has shaped scholars' research design, data collection, analysis, and findings. While important given large public investments in the acquisition of technologies to support student learning and the fact that this frame has motivated concerns over the "digital divide," this framing leaves out a consideration of broader sociopolitical forces in education where technology use can both shape and be shaped by existing inequalities.

The impact frame also assumes a technological determinism where media efficiently and uniformly influence children. Known as "media effects" literature and motivated by concerns over the negative effects of television and video gaming, scholars have long argued that this framing of technologies and their influence fundamentally undertheorizes their social nature (Selwyn 2012). As Selwyn notes,

> Looking back over the past three decades of academic work on young people, education and technology, it could be argued that the social nature of technology itself has been decidedly under-theorised. ... Throughout the 1980s and 1990s the majority of academic writing was content to imbue educational technologies such as the television and computer with a range of inherent qualities. These qualities were then seen to 'impact' (for better or worse) on young users in ways which were consistent regardless of circumstance or context. The crude but compelling 'technologically determinist' perspective that 'social progress is driven by technological innovation, which in turn follows an "inevitable" course' (Smith, 1994, p. 38) has a long lineage in academic research—not least in terms of widely held assumptions about 'media effects'. For example, a determinist way of thinking underpins the wealth of claims that video games cause violent behaviour, or that online tuition enhances learning. (2012, 83)

Yet, despite the calls for a shift in how school technology use is understood, since the 1980s research has largely focused on whether or not devices impact student learning in core academic subject areas (mathematics, science, English, social studies) (Schacter 1999; Wenglinsky 2006; Hedges, Konstantopoulis, and Thoreson 2003; Niemiec and Walberg 1987). We first describe the impact frame in greater detail, including its strengths and weaknesses, offering an alternate way of understanding school technology use that focuses on the historical and contemporary connections between school technology use and inequality.

THE IMPACT FRAME

We define the "impact frame" as the view that adopting technological innovations in the classroom might improve the efficiency and effectiveness of teaching content areas—typically measured as impact on certain forms of measured educational achievement (Niemiec and Walberg 1992; Skryabin et al. 2015). Such a view is in line with historical debates over the use of classroom technologies—from radio to television to computers—for the purpose of classroom efficiency. As educational historian Larry Cuban explains in his 1986 book *Teachers and Machines: The Classroom Use of Technology since 1920*, such a position "offers a view of teaching as a mechanical process of applying knowledge, skills, and tools to students" (p. 56) and follows "the engineer's dream of individual instruction through a machine" that efficiently and cheaply "drill[s] and tutor[s] each student ... while simultaneously record[ing] and report[ing] achievement" (p. 75). This perspective follows the historical pattern of school reformers applying the principles of scientific management to schooling as a "philosophy and set of tools with which to transform American schools into productive businesses" (Cuban 1986, p. 86). In other words, this framework for educational technologies is predicated on the idea that schools are bureaucracies that can be "managed like corporations" (p. 86).

Substantial research has used and continues to use the impact frame, and it is particularly influential to policy analysis and decision-making. While most work using the impact frame has been conducted by economists of education (Bulman and Fairlie 2016; Goolsbee and Guryan 2006; Fairlie and Robinson 2013), the idea that technology can impact achievement has also greatly influenced how sociologists understand and examine technology use in education (Camerini, Schulz, and Jeannet 2018; Gonzales, Calarco, and Lynch 2020). This way of framing educational technology in research began with the introduction of the personal computer into schools in the 1980s, when researchers and policymakers focused on what digital technologies could add to the efficiency of content delivery and student achievement, as well as in standardized testing (Niemiec and Walberg 1987). For example, early studies of the Apple Classrooms of Tomorrow program in the 1980s and 1990s suggested that with the use of computers students performed better on standardized tests, as well as "competencies not usually measured" (Baker, Gearhart, and Herman 1990; Sandholtz, Ringstaff, and Dwyer 1997).

This same impact framing continues in work today. For example, studies look at how technologies like 1:1 laptop programs influence motivation and learning (Warschauer 2006; Silvernail and Gritter 2007). Such work has, in a positive sense, helped motivate research and policy discourse on the "digital divides," at school and home, and how students without access, skill, or specific styles of technology use might suffer in terms of their achievement (Fairlie, Beltran, and Das 2010; Vigdor, Ladd, and Martinez 2014). Yet, in their comprehensive study of the impact of educational technology on student learning since 1984, economists George Bulman and Robert Fairlie (2016) conclude that "results suggest that increasing access to home computers among students who do not already have access is unlikely to greatly improve educational outcomes but is also unlikely to negatively affect outcomes" (p. 275). While informative, such an approach misses critical questions about how technologies are understood and engaged with in schools—which likely shapes these mixed results and misses how inequalities shape and are shaped by technology use.

However, some studies do note that whether or not technology impacts learning largely depends on how (and if) educators use technology. For example, in a nationally representative study of students using the 1996 National Assessment of Educational Progress—a gold standard in assessment—research scientist at Educational Testing Services Harold Wenglinsky (1998) found overall that "technology could matter [for mathematics achievement], but . . . this depended on how it was used" (p. 3). Wenglinsky noted that overall "findings indicate that computers are neither a cure-all for problems facing the schools nor mere fads without impact on student learning" (1998, p. 4). Indeed, he found that inequities in the benefit of technology use depend not on frequency of use but on how technologies were used in classrooms—already disadvantaged students are less likely to be exposed to "higher-order" uses of computers than more affluent students.

Further, since 1980 there has been very limited technology use in schools. As early as 1983, a National Education Association study reported little classroom use despite high teacher interest in teaching with and about technology (Euchner 1983). Another national survey of schools conducted in 2009 by the National Center for Educational Statistics reported that 29% of teachers never or rarely use computers during instructional time (Gray et al. 2010). Much of the blame for these trends in low technology use is placed on teachers. As Cuban (1986) argues,

> The temptation to blame teachers for the uneven penetration of computers into classrooms is, indeed, seductive. How infuriating it must be for true believers in the machine's liberating qualities and sheer productivity to find teachers blocking classroom doors, preventing the entry of this magical innovation, this panacea for the school's problems. If uncritical admirers of this electronic technology succumb to the temptation, they, like their forbears, will overlook the importance of settings in shaping instructional behavior. Limited teacher use of new technology may be due to organizational constraints built into classrooms and schools as workplaces. (p. 81)

In other words, a focus primarily on "impact" ignores more concrete realities in the negotiation of technology use in classrooms. Concerns about technology maintenance and the stability of critical infrastructure—such as if the internet will function during a key lesson—can preclude teachers from relying too heavily on these tools. Further, such a framing treats teachers as unskilled laborers, merely delivering content into the heads of students, rather than as actors making sense of the role of technology and technology learning within complex organizational and institutional contexts.

Like the technological determinism of media effects literature, the impact frame also treats students as passive recipients of subject area content. This ignores the negotiation of technology learning altogether, as though learning to use the technology itself—and the differences among students in their ability to do so—is simply not a concern. Teachers, negotiating organizational commitments and challenges in students' ability to use technologies, often selectively use computers for their own administrative tasks or for simple tasks (Gray et al. 2010). But for teachers to use technologies to their fullest extent—to learn about technology and use it in creative ways to support subject-area learning—requires in-depth investments of instructional time and funding, precisely the opposite of an "efficiency" paradigm within which technologies are framed. Cuban suggests that although teachers may be enthusiastic about technology use, to "instruct students in programming, to use the computer as a problem-solving tool, to learn procedural reasoning, and to encourage students to work alone with the machine in order to learn new content and skills" ultimately stretch too far beyond what teachers must do in the classroom and the "persistent imperatives tucked away in the DNA of classroom life" (p. 81).

Yet, even when an organization makes such a holistic approach possible by fully integrating technologies into all classrooms, a lingering concern remains about the use of technologies in learning. Is their use purely intended for students to learn mathematics, English, science, and social studies more efficiently? Or should students learn technologies for their own sake? What do these choices say about what counts as legitimate and illegitimate technology use? What is considered vocational or risky (lower status) or academic and innovative (higher status) technology use? These questions continue to pervade technology use in schools—and in the process of resolving this ambiguity, as we show in the next section, schools often respond in ways that exacerbate existing inequalities.

The Negotiation Frame

Given the predominant focus on the impact frame, much less research on technology use in schools considers how processes within schools might unequally allocate or legitimate its use. Thus, in contrast to focusing on educational technologies' impact on achievement, a critical way of understanding technology use in schools is as a sociopolitical negotiation, with deep historical roots in the structuring and function of schooling described in the introduction. This negotiation can involve teachers, students, and parents—who draw upon broader organizational, institutional, and societal categorizations of technologies, their uses, and the groups best suited to use them in unequal ways (Dinsmore 2019).

This "negotiation" perspective bridges different literatures. It draws upon communication and science and technology studies scholarship that argues technologies "have politics" (Winner 1980) and connects this to stratification theory in education that views schools as sites of social and political negotiation (Bourdieu and Passeron [1977] 1990; Lareau [2003] 2011; Meyer 1977). As communication scholar Katie Day Good (2020) describes,

> This approach acknowledges that media technologies operate neither in isolation from each other nor according to preordained use values, but rather in dynamic relation with other devices and objects, in daily practices of use and disuse, and embedded with complex social, political, and material contexts. (Good 2020, p. 7)

Thus, the negotiation frame links sociotechnical theories and educational stratification theories to argue that the ways technologies are understood and structured in schools can fundamentally shape and be shaped by the broader organization of society.

What does this negotiation about technology use in schools look like, and what are the benefits of this frame? To answer this question, we delve into the historical roots of these negotiations and then provide contemporary examples of negotiations over technology that are shaped by and contribute to inequalities. These examples show how negotiations occur among different kinds of actors/stakeholders (e.g., policymakers, teachers, students) and play a role in the reproduction or exacerbation of inequities at the intersection of race and class. With both historical and contemporary examples, we demonstrate the benefits of using a negotiation frame to understand technologies in schools to clarify how existing social inequalities shape technology use and vice versa.

Historical Negotiations and Technology in Schools

Looking at historical debates about the broader range of technology use in schools reveals that these negotiations are deeply embedded in the structure and functioning of schools. Negotiation over the meaning of technological activities and their purpose in schooling was at the heart of debates over the purpose and organization of education as: an engine of democratic equality (to educate citizens), a means for social efficiency (to train workers), or a lever for social mobility (to help individuals get ahead) (Labaree 1997). Deliberations following the Civil War centered on how to understand and organize technological activities and if these activities—most of which became categorized as "career and technical education" (CTE)—should be included in publicly funded schools at all or if employers should educate future workers in "job-related" technical skills (Goldin 1999; Hayward and Benson 1993; Gordon 2014). These debates centered on the categorization of technological activities, to whom such activities should be matched, and, especially, what this meant for the social mobility function of schools. For example, in the late nineteenth century W. E. B. Du Bois and Booker T. Washington debated the role of technology education for African Americans' upward mobility. Washington took the position that "practical education" could meet the more immediate needs of African Americans in the south. while Du Bois advocated non-technical "classical education" and racial uplift through the training of a smaller group of elite students who could become leaders of Black society (Anderson 1988; Frantz 1997).

Similar debates arose into the late nineteenth and early twentieth centuries with the expansion and rapid influx of lower-class and immigrant students into public schools during the Progressive Era. The most famous and explicit debate during this time was between educational philosopher and University of Chicago professor John Dewey and educational sociologist and education commissioner of Massachusetts David Snedden. They argued about how schooling and technical activities should be understood and organized—if technological activities should be considered "hands-on" experiences everyone should have (Dewey's position) or if these experiences were purely vocational and therefore should occur in separate vocational schools for students most suited to vocational roles (Snedden's position) (Labaree 2010).

Early opponents of CTE worried that its expansion would lead to a dual educational system stratified by social class. To prevent this, reformers created a policy compromise in the form of comprehensive schools serving CTE and academic tracks that physically integrated all students into the same building but at the same time separated them via educational tracking (Oakes 2005; Labaree 2010)—as well as the creation of separate vocational schools with a funding structure and decision-making bodies separate from local school districts. Unfortunately, a dual system did emerge within (and between) schools, confirming fears that CTE would reproduce the inequalities it sought to address:

> [W]ith very few exceptions, [these schools] were comprehensive in name only. Most schools gradually evolved into the United States version of a "dual system," consisting of one branch for pupils who planned to enter postsecondary educational institutions and one for students who were preparing for the world of work. The early fears about separation and stratification were slowly realized. (Hayward and Benson 1993, p. 6)

This institutional tracking of lower-achieving students in comprehensive high schools into CTE made defensible by standardized testing also expanded into "vocationalization" at the community college level (Brint and Karabel 1989; Karabel 1986). Scholars have characterized this as "submerged class conflict," with testing justifying the stratification of students by the categorization of technological activity at all educational levels, from elementary through college (Karabel 1972, p. 526; Rosenbaum 2001; Oakes 2005). Thus, the negotiation of the meaning of technological activities and their place in schools has been central to public schooling since its very beginning—and links directly to processes of social stratification deeply embedded in educational systems.

These same debates and negotiations continue to the present day, complicated by the introduction of the science, technology, engineering, and mathematics, or "STEM," category of higher-status academic activity in the 1990s (Sanders 2009). US policymakers have used the STEM term as a framework for international competitiveness in the globalized economy and to call for increased federal funding in these higher-status areas (Gonzalez and Kuenzi 2012; Xie, Fang, and Shauman 2015). Yet, under the umbrella of both lower-status CTE and higher-status STEM, the meaning and valuation of technologies in schools depend heavily on negotiation processes within institutional and organizational settings, as well as how racial and socioeconomic groups of students are understood in terms of their match and valuation in engaging in technological activities. Thus, through these negotiations over the meaning and valuation of technologies and their match to different groups, educational actors define the terms upon which the structuring and practice of education are formulated—and how inequities are addressed, reified, or exacerbated in schools.

Contemporary Negotiations and Technology in Schools

These same debates about the role of technology in schools and their match to students continue into research on contemporary schooling. Here, we highlight three cases to show how these negotiations occur in both tech-rich and tech-poor schools. First, in a 3-year study of a technology-focused school in New York, communication scholar Christo Sims (2014) studied the negotiation of the meaning and valuation of technology use in an organizational context. Sims found that while students had roughly equal access to technologies at school "only certain uses of digital media were considered educationally legitimate," where more privileged students and their media uses were more valued than disadvantaged students (p. 678). He explains that processes of negotiation where supporting and legitimating some students' technology interests and practices while overlooking or stigmatizing other students' technology use shows how even the most potentially impactful use of integrated technology in schools can help remake the educational divisions (i.e., addressing inequities among students) that they hope to address.

On the one hand were the more affluent cliques of students, groups separated by gender. The girls were the "goody two shoes" group and the boys were the "gamer" or "geeky" group. Their technology practices relied on extensive access outside of school and were legitimated by peers and teachers' approval of their technology use—reinforcing preexisting differences between students. For example, of the geeky boys group, Sims said that the group "routinely differentiated themselves as distinctively enthusiastic for, and expert at, gaming, and increasingly digital technology more broadly" by referencing technological activities they did at home "that were not available to all" (p. 677). Through these negotiations in group formation at the school, technological practices served to differentiate groups on the basis of gender as well as by social class, where only those who were more affluent could participate in the geeky boys' clique.

On the other hand were the "cool kids" from less affluent families, separated into the "cool girls" and "cool boys." In contrast to the more affluent cliques, the cool kids' technological activities were instead devalued by adults at the school. While "most of the participants in the 'cool kids' cliques made extensive use of digital media in their out-of-school lives, [this was] just not in the ways that were valued by educators at school" (p. 678). The clique included students who were high achieving and highly technologically skilled, but educators did not consider their technology practices "educational." For example, the cool girls clique used social and communications media (e.g., Facebook, a video-chat program called ooVoo, mobile phones, instant messenger apps, etc.) in sophisticated ways, but educators "stigmatized these uses in lessons about online safety and civility" (p. 678). Thus, their practices were not legitimized at school, and their technological prowess did not become a defining feature of their individual or group identity like the geek boys' group and further pushed the less affluent students away from technology learning opportunities like the after-school program.

These negotiation processes, where some forms of technology use were viewed as higher-status "educational" and others viewed as lower-status "unsafe" and "uncivil" communicated which activities and, therefore, which students were valued in the school. This process eventually encouraged many of the "cool kids" to leave the school, while those in the more affluent cliques remained in the middle school through their eighth-grade year. This story could be missed entirely if focusing on impact alone, with a narrow focus on test scores. Instead, negotiation captures how different uses of technology are understood and valued within the context of the school—and how this shapes broader outcomes, like persistence and continuity in students' educational experiences. Overall, Sims argues that "without a better understanding of how different digital media uses contribute to the production of privilege in different situations, misdiagnoses are likely to prevail," and causes of the reification or even exacerbation of educational inequities are likely to be overlooked and to go unchallenged (p. 679).

A second empirical case similarly takes a negotiation frame to understand how different organizational contexts can produce very different meanings for technology use, where processes of categorization and differentiation reify existing privilege, even in heavily funded "innovative" schools oriented toward addressing equity. In a yearlong study of three different technology-rich middle schools in California, sociologist Matt Rafalow (2018, 2020) found that each school viewed similar technologies and technology uses in very different ways. These perceptions varied by the racial-ethnic and socioeconomic background of the student population, as well as how the organizations framed their technology use, despite students having similar technological access and skill. These differences ultimately shaped the extent to which students' technology skill and use translated into academic and social rewards (Rafalow 2018).

For example, Rafalow found that most interviewed students at each school had a similar profile of technology access and learned "digital basics," like online communication and digital production, from play online with peers. Such an equitable picture might suggest that students' skills and use in their technology-rich schools might lead to direct impacts on achievement—whether by helping students in their learning or, as research shows, by inflating teachers' perception of student ability and inflating their grades.

However, this was not the case. Instead, teachers at Heathcliff viewed their predominately White, wealthy students as tech geniuses and encouraged their technology use; teachers at Sheldon thought of mostly Asian American, middle-class students as risky hackers and technology use as a distraction from academic learning; and Chávez teachers constructed their primarily Latinx, working-class students' use of technology as "21st-century laborers" who might rely on digital skills for working-class jobs, rather than be tech geniuses like Heathcliff students. Perceptions of student race-ethnicity and social class, inflected through constructions of students as different types of technology users, led to educational inequalities. Thus, through organization-specific negotiation, Rafalow found that while students in all three schools were skillful and used technology in similar ways, based on the organization-specific understanding of students and their technology use, benefits translated in very different ways.

If instead of focusing on negotiation, Rafalow or Sims had studied the same schools with an impact frame, they might assume that equally technologically endowed schools should result in equal benefit to students. Yet, that is clearly not the case. Such findings are entirely dependent upon taking a negotiation perspective on research—and may be equally beneficial in terms of how policymakers and educators craft technological interventions. Here, where technologies are widely available at home and at school, their benefit to students is entirely contingent upon social processes of meaning-making—shaped by perceptions of student groups, valuation of technological activities (as twenty-first-century labor, as risk, or as cutting-edge innovation), and how groups are matched to these activities. Thus, digital access and digital skills are not enough—organizational negotiation of the value of technology use shapes whether such access and skills net students educational gains.

Finally, in a third empirical case using a negotiation frame to understand how organizational context shapes the meaning and value of technology use, sociologist Cassidy Puckett (2015, 2019) looked at a contrastingly technology-poor, low-income school in the Midwest. In a multiyear study, Puckett found that tech use was contingent upon students' primary categorization as "good students" coupled with preexisting interests in technology based on experiences outside of school. Because technology use was limited to teachers' selective use—common across the large majority of schools, as described by Cuban and others—opportunities for more in-depth technology learning experiences were understood as an "extra" reward and given to students the teachers thought had earned the prize and signaled some form of interest in technology (Puckett and Nelson 2019; Puckett 2015).

Such students were very few in number. One was a girl named Sumalee, who was higher achieving and engaged in extensive technology use at home. Unlike many other students at her school, Sumalee was given many opportunities to engage in in-depth problem-solving with computers—including helping to troubleshoot the teachers' laptop when it had problems. In fact, she did this so often that she knew the password to her teacher's computer. She was also given additional opportunities to learn programming languages and engage in conversation about various technologies with the computer teacher, whose regular computer curriculum was compromised by months of standardized test prep and testing. In fact, in a month of observations, Puckett saw just one technology course in which students learned how to use computers, but this was via step-by-step instruction rather than the more creative uses that Sumalee experienced both at home and at school.

In contrast, there were many students the teachers felt did not "earn" this extra experience with computers or who were unaware of their technology interests—both largely shaped by whether or not students were considered sufficiently "good" (in terms of academic performance and classroom behavior). For example, a student named Rafael, who was considered a "distracted" student but who was very interested in technology, was not given the same level of access to technology learning as Sumalee. Instead, he, like his classmates, used computers at school primarily for test prep during what was otherwise supposed to be a technology class. For the few limited times when technology was used as an aid for instruction in science by creating PowerPoint presentations about extinction, students were given little guidance. In this way technology had little impact on many students' learning but played a larger role for select students who earned the privilege—exacerbating preexisting divisions by academic achievement within the predominantly low-income school.

In this third study—while occurring in an entirely different school context where technology use was quite low—Puckett found precisely the same negotiation processes as in the Rafalow and Sims studies. Indeed, institutional and organizational contexts shaped how teachers understood specific forms of technology use and their match to specific students—as less central to the function of schools and therefore only an added reward for deserving students. This, like the other two studies, points out a process that again advantages more privileged students—although in this case it was according to already-established academic performance combined with their technology experiences outside of school. Indeed, without this framework it might be unclear how technology use might amplify learning so unevenly, despite student background being homogeneously low-income.

Benefits of the Negotiation Frame

Overall, a negotiation frame shows the intricacies of technology use in schools beyond its mere impact on student learning—and why it is necessary to reframe research on the impact of educational technology use in schools as a sociopolitical negotiation. Understanding technologies in this way has several benefits. First, it avoids the assumption of technological determinism suggested by "media effects" literature—and of teachers and students as passive, neutral recipients of these technologies (Selwyn 2012). Such a view has long been criticized in media scholarship and in children's use of media and technology outside of schools, but it continues to hold sway inside school, particularly among policymakers trying to justify financial investments (National Telecommunications and Information Administration 1995). Although such concerns have motivated important investigations into digital divides, the impact frame ultimately does a disservice to research and policy by undertheorizing the social and political nature of these technologies—and why and how they might address inequality or not (Light 2001).

Second, it creates possible lines of research on how negotiations over the place of technology in schools are intricately embedded in structural racism, classism, sexism, ableism, and other dynamics of inequality. By applying a negotiation frame, researchers and policymakers can understand how processes of social stratification embedded in educational systems—and implicated in how we understand technological activities and their match with students—continue to shape schooling to the present day. If research asks more narrowly, "What is the impact of technology use in schools?" it misses the central function of technology in schools. Thus, we argue that scholars should instead ask, "How does the negotiation of existing inequalities shape unequal use and unequal outcomes?" Viewed as the negotiation of preexisting inequality, this dynamic includes the ongoing categorization of technology use as vocational or technical (and risky or beneficial) and the consistent matching of privileged groups to privileged technology uses and therefore links micro- and meso-level processes to macro-level social stratification in ways that a simple impact framework does not.

The Negotiation Frame and Online Learning in the Global Pandemic

Thus far we have argued for the importance of a negotiation framework by describing what a focus on impact misses and what a focus on negotiation can reveal, based on past research studies. Looking forward, we turn our attention to current and future work, by describing how a negotiation frame might be better suited to understanding the dynamics at play during the global pandemic and the rapid shift to online learning. While many might ask about the impact of schools moving online on their achievement—and while surely this is an important consideration—it fails to identify the negotiation dynamics at play. It again misses the same considerations that Sims, Rafalow, Puckett, Cuban, and many others argue are key—namely, how organizations and the educators and students within them negotiate the meaning of forms of legitimate and illegitimate technology use, as well as allocate rewards for use. Instead, we describe how applying a negotiation frame can reveal dynamics in the move to online schooling that can shape outcomes from early childhood through college and beyond, by considering the issues of access, skills, and reward.

The first and most obvious issue is negotiations over access to technologies. While access gaps have been shrinking over time, recent findings from the Pew Research Center's Internet & American Life Project show that at least 15% of US households with children in school lack high-speed internet at home and one in three low-income families lack any kind of internet access (Anderson and Perrin 2018). Further, there are ongoing access issues of stability and maintenance (Gonzales 2015). Taking a negotiation perspective, gaps in access arose from historical debates about whether technologies should be considered a consumer good or a public utility, resulting in uneven and unreliable access for many. Given that private industry and policymaking bodies are intimately intertwined, even if technology is reframed as a public good during the pandemic, the goal of access will likely be for purposes of private benefit. As technology historian Joy Lisi Rankin explains in *A People's History of Computing in the United States*, this is precisely what happened in schools when early computing shifted from collaborative school- and university-based networks to personal machines in the 1980s. Some corporations took advantage of tax breaks via educational donations to expand the consumer base for not-yet-popular personal computers through schools. Ultimately, this negotiation resulted in the greatest benefit to companies—under the guise of educational equity and potential public economic benefit (Rankin 2018).

Looking at negotiations over access to technologies during the pandemic suggests that how people understand technological infrastructure may shift in dramatic ways, but it will be important to track precisely how these negotiations play out. Will there be an argument for tying such utilities to local taxes, in much the same way children benefit from being in more affluent neighborhoods where tax bases buoy local schools? What about the effect of these negotiations in more rural areas? How will private industry and political lobbyists shape how access is understood and put into practice? How might local politicians, including school board members, also shape the conversation around computer and internet access now and into the future? If past negotiation is any indication, future research should pay close attention to how tech businesses and policymakers negotiate for their interests in the shift to online learning during the pandemic, shaping equity in access for years to come.

Beyond negotiations around the meaning and formulation of access, there are likely other negotiations around differences in technological readiness, skills, and literacies that shape how well individuals can utilize technological resources. In this moment where all schools are online, technological competence on the part of educators and students shapes how effectively teachers can teach and how easily students can learn online. Research has long documented that schools are woefully underprepared in terms of technology education, particularly in lower-performing schools where attention is focused on standardized test preparation, even if these schools offer computer classes. This is coupled with a broader dismissive assumption that kids born into the digital age are naturally skillful with technology—suggesting kids do not need to be explicitly taught digital skills in school. Yet, research shows many are underprepared for technology-based learning, even in districts implementing new policies requiring that students demonstrate technological skill to graduate high school (Puckett 2019). This research also notes the importance of home practices in shaping students' technology learning, and this is likely to be key in the shift online as well. Future research could shed light on how families, students, and teachers negotiated the rapid shift to online learning—and if some were more prepared than others for this change.

Other negotiations around technology use pertain to unequal reward for students' technology use. Some research suggests that social class position can shape styles of technology use that reify existing inequities where more affluent students might use it in ways that are more beneficial. Other research, like the Sims, Rafalow, and Puckett studies, focuses on how social contexts allocate reward in unequal ways. Applied to the context of the pandemic and the shift to online learning, social class position can reify existing inequities and may even be amplified. For example, some students may not know how to ask for help—in their classes, in job and college applications, etc. Likewise, teachers might reward technology use among affluent students (or allow them to opt out of online learning) and police technology use among less affluent students, even as their families face more challenges during the pandemic (Rafalow 2018; Sims 2014). These "digital distinctions" operate in much the same way that long-documented educational distinctions are made among students by social class and race, where lower-income and minoritized students are more heavily policed in schools (Shedd 2015; Gonzalez 2018). We understand the seriousness of these problems offline—future research may address these issues in ways that a focus on impact would miss entirely.

Finally, beyond teaching and learning, there are many other issues that arise in the shift to online learning during the pandemic when viewing it as a negotiation (e.g., how privatization leads to commercial interests gaining consumer information and shaping consumer preferences). Following sociotechnical research that understands technological systems as artifacts with multiple interests shaping their development and use raises all sorts of ethical and legal questions (Winner 1980; Benjamin 2019; Umoja Noble 2018). For example, what kinds of information are being collected in online spaces? How do technological systems uphold the Family Education Rights and Privacy Act? How are students protected from such practices as so-called Zoombombing? Who holds the intellectual property created by educators in these online spaces? Who benefits and who is disadvantaged by private technological systems as we move an entire national K–12 educational system and colleges and universities online without fully understanding the implications of doing so? Again, these are serious questions that are entirely missed in the simple conceptualization of educational technologies as (potentially) more efficient content delivery systems—but can be better investigated and understood through a negotiation frame.

Conclusion

In this chapter, we reframe the impact of educational technology use more broadly as a matter of sociopolitical negotiation where technology use can both shape and be shaped by existing inequalities. Such a shift may provide a way to link how people understand and use technologies to processes of social stratification long embedded in the structures and practices of educational systems, rather than an add-on to increase schools' efficiency. This viewpoint takes very seriously the argument of science and technology scholar Langdon Winner (1980) in his oft-cited article, "Do Artifacts Have Politics?"

> The things we call "technologies" are *ways of building order in our world*. ... Consciously or not, deliberately or inadvertently, societies choose structures for technologies that influence how people are going to work, communicate, travel, consume, and so forth over a very long time. In the process by which structuring decisions are made, different people are differently situated and possess unequal degrees of power as well as unequal levels of awareness.
> [C]hoices ... become strongly fixed in material equipment, economic investment, and social habit ... once the initial commitments are made. In that sense, *technological innovations are similar to legislative acts ... that establish a framework for public order that will endure over many generations.* ... The issues that divide or unite people in society are settled not only in the institutions and practice of politics proper but also, and less obviously, in tangle arrangements of ... wires and transistors, nuts and bolts (127–128, Emphasis added).

Comparing past scholarship to more recent research that uses a negotiation approach, we highlighted the benefits of this reframing. Viewed through the lens of negotiation, research shows that educational technology use involves not simply delivering educational content in more (or less) efficient ways. Instead, what is involved is the ongoing categorization of technologies and the unequal matching of students to technologies and technological activities that often advantages already privileged groups, thereby linking decisions at the individual and organizational levels to broader processes of social stratification.

Using a negotiation frame, future research can better understand the conditions that support more equitable access, skill development, and valuation and reward for students' technological skill—academically and in other dimensions of social life. Such an approach also adds further nuance to understanding how institutional and organizational context can shape how the educators and students within them negotiate the meaning of technologies, such that certain forms of technology use may be viewed as riskier or less valued than uses deemed more acceptable and valued. It also offers policymakers insight into what matters for technology use beyond whether or not a school has a particular ratio of student to computer access—particularly since in the past computers have often been "oversold and underused" in schools (Cuban 2003). Instead, research and policy might turn attention to how educators are trained, particularly with regard to equity in technology use and its reward across groups of students, in different types of classrooms, and within and between schools.

Given these opportunities in using a negotiation frame, future research could investigate not just the impact of technology use on standardized measures of academic learning in K–12 education and higher education during the coronavirus epidemic but also why and how more advantaged students may in fact unequally benefit from online schooling during this crisis. For example, how, if at all, are families providing support to students as they transition online? Are they coaching their children on particular means to interact with teachers and to ask for help and in ways that may map to inequities? And how might teachers' approaches to online instruction cement into particular hidden standards for appropriate participation that may reward some students over others?

Further, negotiations are additive—educational research shows that how students are rewarded in K–12 shapes their life trajectories (Deil-Amen and López Turley 2007). The same is likely true for online participation. In the critical transitions from K–12 to higher education and beyond, what are the ways that students and their families translate their "worth" to college admissions officers through the internet? Are some students curating online presences that reflect their candidacy for college admission? Further, how do students today learn about colleges—including whether they would like to attend but also crucially how they can best apply—given how much information is available online? How do they vet which information is helpful or not? And who, if anyone, is coaching students through these processes? In higher education, how do students negotiate the important aspects of college beyond the impact of courses delivered online? And how are students negotiating technology use in their transition into graduate education or the working world?

Of course, there are other important considerations beyond negotiations, such as more concrete outcomes. For example, how might the "natural educational experiment" of moving all students online and the very different organizational policies implemented as a result—like some medical schools accepting pass/fail grades from college students who shifted to online learning in the spring of 2020, while other medical schools did not (Burke 2020)—affect admissions? Such considerations are similar to concerns about impact, but we highlight how they may be better understood by following negotiation patterns at key stages of students' academic, social, and economic careers. Thus, a negotiation framing moves beyond the concerns of well-meaning bodies of work on the impact of technologies in schools and focuses on the more critical question of how negotiations shape the very meaning of education itself—a critical concern historically but all the more poignant in the new paradigm of immediate and future technology-based schooling.

REFERENCES

Anderson, James D. 1988. *The Education of Blacks in the South, 1860–1935*. Chapel Hill: University of North Carolina Press.

Anderson, Monica, and Andrew Perrin. 2018. "Nearly One-in-Five Teens Can't Always Finish Their Homework Because of the Digital Divide." Pew Research Center. https://www.pewresearch.org/fact-tank/2018/10/26/nearly-one-in-five-teens-cant-always-finish-their-homework-because-of-the-digital-divide/.

Baig, Edward C. 2020. "Phones at School: Should You Let Your Kids Have a Cellphone in School?" *USA Today*, February 5. https://www.usatoday.com/story/tech/2020/02/05/should-kids-have-cellphones-at-school/4669488002/

Baker, Eva L., Maryl Gearhart, and Joan L. Herman. 1990. *Assessment: Apple Classrooms of Tomorrow (ACOT) Evaluation Study, First and Second Year Findings*. Cupertino, CA: UCLA Center for Technology Assessment and Apple Computer. http://www.appleclassrooms.com/wp-content/uploads/2020/02/rpt7.pdf

Benford, Robert D., and David A. Snow. 2000. "Framing Processes and Social Movements: An Overview and Assessment." *Annual Review of Sociology* 26: 611–639.

Benjamin, Ruha. 2019. *Captivating Technology: Race, Carceral Technoscience, and Liberatory Imagination in Everyday Life*. Durham, NC: Duke University Press.

Bourdieu, Pierre, and Jean-Claude Passeron. (1977) 1990. *Reproduction in Education, Society, and Culture*. London: Sage Publications.

Brint, Steven, and Jerome D. Karabel. 1989. *The Diverted Dream: Community Colleges and the Promise of Educational Opportunity in America, 1900–1985*. New York: Oxford University Press.

Bulman, George, and Robert W. Fairlie. 2016. "Technology and Education: Computers, Software, and the Internet." In *Handbook of the Economics of Education*, edited by Eric A. Hanushek, Stephen Machin, and Ludger Woessmann, 5:239–280. Oxford: Elsevier. https://doi.org/https://doi.org/10.1016/B978-0-444-63459-7.00005-1.

Burke, Lilah. 2020. "The Asterisk Semester." *Inside Higher Education*, April 13. https://www.insidehighered.com/news/2020/04/13/how-will-passfail-affect-students-future.

Camerini, Anne-Linda, Peter J. Schulz, and Anne-Marie Jeannet. 2018. "The Social Inequalities of Internet Access, Its Use, and the Impact on Children's Academic Performance: Evidence from a Longitudinal Study in Switzerland." *New Media & Society* 20, no. 7: 2489–2508.

Cuban, Larry. 1986. *Teachers and Machines: The Classroom Use of Technology since 1920.* New York: Teachers College Press.

Cuban, Larry. 2003. *Oversold and Underused: Computers in the Classroom.* Cambridge, MA: Harvard University Press.

Day Good, Katie. 2020. *Bring the World to the Child: Technologies of Global Citizenship in American Education.* Cambridge, MA: MIT Press.

Deil-Amen, Regina, and Ruth N. López Turley. 2007. "A Review of the Transition to College Literature in Sociology." *Teachers College Record* 109: 2324–2366.

Dinsmore, Brooke. 2019. "Contested Affordances: Teachers and Students Negotiating the Classroom Integration of Mobile Technology." *Information, Communication & Society* 22, no. 5: 664–677.

Euchner, Charles. 1983. "Teachers' Interest in Computers Is High, but Usage Is Low." *Education Week* 2, no. 16. https://www.edweek.org/ew/articles/1983/01/12/03030021.h02.html

Fairlie, Robert W., Daniel O. Beltran, and Kuntal K. Das. 2010. "Home Computers and Educational Outcomes: Evidence from the NLSY97 and CPS." *Economic Inquiry* 48, no. 3: 771–779.

Fairlie, Robert W., and Jonathan Robinson. 2013. "Experimental Evidence on the Effects of Home Computers on Academic Achievement among Schoolchildren." *American Economic Journal: Applied Economics* 5, no. 3: 211–240.

Fligstein, Neil, and Doug McAdam. 2012. *A Theory of Fields.* New York: Oxford University Press.

Frantz, Nevin R., Jr. 1997. "The Contributions of Booker T. Washington and W. E. B. Du Bois in the Development of Vocational Education." *Journal of Industrial Teacher Education* 34, no. 4: 87–91.

Friedland, Roger, and Robert R. Alford. 1991. "Bringing Society Back in: Symbols, Practices, and Institutional Contradictions." In *The New Institutionalism in Organizational Analysis*, edited by Walter Powell and Paul J. DiMaggio, 232–266. Chicago: University of Chicago Press.

Goldin, Claudia. 1999. *A Brief History of Education in the United States.* Cambridge, MA: National Bureau of Economic Research.

Gonzales, Amy. 2015. "The Contemporary US Digital Divide: From Initial Access to Technology Maintenance." *Information, Communication & Society* 19, no. 2: 234–248.

Gonzales, Amy, Jessica McCrory Calarco, and Teresa Lynch. 2020. "Technology Problems and Student Achievement Gaps: A Validation and Extension of the Technology Maintenance Construct." *Communication Research* 45, no. 5: 750–770. https://doi.org/https://doi.org/10.1177/0093650218796366.

Gonzalez, Catherine Lizette. 2018. "The Urgent Need to Dismantle School Policing in Communities of Color." *Colorlines*, September 13. https://www.colorlines.com/articles/report-urgent-need-dismantle-school-policing-communities-color.

Gonzalez, Heather B., and Jeffrey J. Kuenzi. 2012. *Science, Technology, Engineering, and Mathematics (STEM) Education: A Primer.* Washington, DC: Congressional Research Service.

Goolsbee, Austan, and Jonathan Guryan. 2006. "The Impact of Internet Subsidies in Public Schools." *Review of Economics and Statistics* 88, no. 2: 336–347.

Gordon, Howard R. D. 2014. *The History and Growth of Career and Technical Education in America.* 4th ed. Longrove, IL: Waveland Press.

Gray, Lucinda, Nina Thomas, Laurie Lewis, and Peter Tice. 2010. *Teachers' Use of Educational Technology in U.S. Public Schools: 2009.* Washington, DC: National Center for Educational Statistics, Institute for Educational Sciences, US Department of Education.

Hayward, Gerald C., and Charles S. Benson. 1993. *Vocational-Technical Education: Major Reforms and Debates 1917–Present*. Washington, DC: Office of Vocational and Adult Education.

Hedges, Larry V., Spyros Konstantopoulis, and Amy Thoreson. 2003. *Computer Use and Its Relation to Academic Achievement in Mathematics, Reading and Writing*. Washington, DC: National Center for Education Statistics.

Hodgkinson, Gerard P., Nicola J. Bown, A. John Maule, Keith W. Glaister, and Alan D. Pearman. 1999. "Breaking the Frame: An Analysis of Strategic Cognition and Decision Making Under Uncertainty." *Strategic Management Journal* 20: 977–985.

Kaplan, Sarah. 2008. "Framing Contests: Strategy Making under Uncertainty." *Organization Science* 19, no. 5: 729–752. https://doi.org/10.1287/orsc.1070.0340.

Karabel, Jerome D. 1972. "Community Colleges and Social Stratification." *Harvard Educational Review* 42, no. 4: 521–562.

Karabel, Jerome D. 1986. "Community Colleges and Social Stratification in the 1980s." In *The Community College and Its Critics*, edited by Stephen Zwerling, 13–30. San Francisco: Jossey-Bass.

Labaree, David F. 1997. "Public Goods, Private Goods: The American Struggle over Educational Goals." *American Educational Research Journal* 34, no. 1: 39–81.

Labaree, David F. 2010. "How Dewey Lost: The Victory of David Snedden and Social Efficiency in the Reform of American Education." In *Pragmatism and Modernities*, edited by Daniel Trohler, Thomas Schlag, and Fritz Osterwalder, 163–188. Rotterdam, The Netherlands: Sense Publishers.

Lareau, Annette. (2003) 2011. *Unequal Childhoods: Class, Race, and Family Life*. 2nd ed. Los Angeles: University of California Press.

Light, Jennifer. 2001. "Rethinking the Digital Divide." *Harvard Educational Review* 71, no. 4: 710–734.

Meyer, John W. 1977. "The Effects of Education as an Institution." *American Journal of Sociology* 83, no. 1: 55–77.

Moyer, Melissa. 2020. "Not Everyone Can Write Off a School Year. Who Should Be Worried about Their Kids Falling Behind?" *Slate*, April 9. https://slate.com/human-interest/2020/04/online-school-remote-learning-inequality-falling-behind.html

National Telecommunications and Information Administration. 1995. *Falling through the Net: A Survey of the "Have Nots" in Rural and Urban America*. Washington, DC: US Department of Commerce.

Niemiec, Richard P., and Herbert J. Walberg. 1987. "Comparative Effects of Computer-Assisted Instruction: A Synthesis of Reviews." *Journal of Educational Computing Research* 3, no. 1: 19–37.

Niemiec, Richard P., and Herbert J. Walberg. 1992. "The Effect of Computers on Learning." *International Journal of Education* 17, no. 1: 99–108.

Nutt, Paul C. 1998. "Framing Strategic Decisions." *Organization Science* 9: 195–216.

Oakes, Jeannie. 2005. *Keeping Track: How Schools Structure Inequality*. 2nd ed. New Haven, CT: Yale University Press.

Polletta, Francesca. 2008. "Culture and Movements." *Annals of the American Academy of Political and Social Science* 619: 78–96.

Polletta, Francesca, and M. Kai Ho. 2006. "Frames and Their Consequences." In *The Oxford Handbook of Contextual Political Analysis*, edited by Robert E. Goodin and Charles Tilly, 187–209. Oxford: Oxford University Press.

Puckett, Cassidy. 2015. "Technological Change, Digital Adaptability, and Social Inequality." Phd diss., Northwestern University.

Puckett, Cassidy. 2019. "CS4Some? Differences in Technology Learning Readiness." *Harvard Educational Review* 89, no. 4: 554–587.

Puckett, Cassidy, and Jennifer L. Nelson. 2019. "The Geek Instinct: Theorizing Cultural Alignment in Disadvantaged Contexts." *Qualitative Sociology* 42, no. 1: 25–48.

Rafalow, Matthew H. 2018. "Disciplining Play: Digital Youth Culture as Capital at School." *American Journal of Sociology* 123, no. 5: 1416–1452.

Rafalow, Matthew H. 2020. *Digital Divisions: How Schools Create Inequality in the Tech Era*. Chicago, IL: University of Chicago Press. https://press.uchicago.edu/ucp/books/book/chicago/D/bo57273552.html

Rankin, Joy Lisi. 2018. *A People's History of Computing in the United States*. Cambridge, MA: Harvard University Press.

Rosenbaum, James. 2001. *Beyond College for All*. New York: Russell Sage Foundation.

Sanders, Mark. 2009. "STEM, STEM Education, STEMmania." *The Technology Teacher* 68, no. 4: 20–26.

Sandholtz, Judith Haymore, Cathy Ringstaff, and David C. Dwyer. 1997. *Teaching with Technology: Creating Student-Centered Classrooms*. New York: Teachers College Press.

Schacter, John. 1999. *The Impact of Education Technology on Student Achievement: What the Most Current Research Has to Say*. Santa Monica, CA: Milken Exchange on Educational Technology.

Scott, W. Richard. 2014. *Institutions and Organizations: Ideas, Interests, and Identities*. 4th ed. Thousand Oaks, CA: Sage Publications.

Selwyn, Neil. 2012. "Making Sense of Young People, Education and Digital Technology: The Role of Sociological Theory." *Oxford Review of Education* 38, no. 1: 81–96. https://doi.org/10.1080/03054985.2011.577949.

Shedd, Carla. 2015. *Unequal City: Race, Schools, and Perceptions of Injustice*. New York: Russell Sage Foundation.

Silvernail, David L., and Aaron K. Gritter. 2007. *Maine's Middle School Laptop Program: Creating Better Writers*. Gorham, ME: Maine Education Policy Research Institute, University of Southern Maine.

Sims, Christo. 2014. "From Differentiated Use to Differentiating Practices: Negotiating Legitimate Participation and the Production of Privileged Identities." *Information, Communication & Society* 17, no. 6: 670–682. https://doi.org/10.1080/1369118X.2013.808363.

Skryabin, M., Zhang, J., Liu, L., & Zhang, D. 2015. "How the ICT Development Level and Usage Influence Student Achievement in Reading, Mathematics, and Science." *Computers & Education* 85: 49–58.

Strauss, Valerie. 2018. "Students Protest Zuckerberg-Backed Digital Learning Program and Ask Him: 'What Gives You This Right?'" *Washington Post*, 2018. https://www.washingtonpost.com/education/2018/11/17/students-protest-zuckerberg-backed-digital-learning-program-ask-him-what-gives-you-this-right.

Umoja Noble, Safiya. 2018. *Algorithms of Oppression: How Search Engines Reinforce Racism*. New York: New York University Press.

Vigdor, Jacob L., Helen F. Ladd, and Erika Martinez. 2014. "Scaling the Digital Divide: Home Computer Use and Student Achievement." *Economic Inquiry* 52, no. 3: 1103–1119.

Warschauer, Mark. 2006. *Laptops and Literacy: Learning in the Wireless Classroom*. New York: Teachers College Press.

Wenglinsky, Harold. 1998. *Does It Compute? The Relationship between Educational Technology and Student Achievement in Mathematics*. Princeton, NJ: Educational Testing Service.

Wenglinsky, Harold. 2006. "Technology and Achievement: The Bottom Line." *Educational Leadership* 63, no. 4: 29–32.

Winner, Langdon. 1980. "Do Artifacts Have Politics?" *Daedalus* 109, no. 1: 121–136.

Xie, Yu, Michael Fang, and Kimberlee Shauman. 2015. "STEM Education." *Annual Review of Sociology* 41: 331–357.

CHAPTER 7

JOURNALISM IN THE AGE OF TWITTER

STEPHEN R. BARNARD

On any given day, people across the world—average citizens, trained journalists, and influential politicians alike—use Twitter to follow the latest news, share information, and stay in touch with others in their network. Twitter, for its part, knows how important its platform is to the news business. In response to public criticism for its failures in slowing the spread of misinformation, it revamped its "trending topics" feature in September 2020 to include more context and to ensure that those topics highlighted were professionally curated (Conger and Perlroth 2020). Weeks later, it launched an "election hub," which features journalists' posts, including Twitter-native updates as well as links to longer-form articles, on a variety of election-related issues (McNamara 2020).

Although most journalists undoubtedly give priority to their primary channels, Twitter plays a profoundly important role in many reporters' day-to-day work. According to scholarship on Twitter and journalism, more than half of American journalists used the platform regularly (Willnat, Weaver, and Wilhoit, 2017), and over 70% of America's largest newspapers had formal policies governing reporters' Twitter usage (Santana and Hopp 2016). While professional and civic cultures vary greatly, other studies have found similar trends in Twitter usage by journalists in other national contexts (Hedman and Djerf-Pierre 2013; Gulyas 2013; Bloom, Cleary, and North 2016).

As might be expected for any disruptive technology, Twitter became the focus of much conversation within the profession. Amid Twitter's meteoric rise in journalism, many working in and around the news business spent years debating the pros and cons of the social networking service. Yet, those discussions did little to slow its foray in the field. Ironically, these debates may have actually increased pressure for reporters to jump on the Twitter bandwagon since they often took place on the platform.[1] Accordingly, Twitter quickly became the de facto digital "water cooler" for many media professionals. It was a place journalists could gather—asynchronously and from across the globe—to discuss matters of relevance to their occupation.

Despite Twitter's popularity among media professionals and other political actors, it is hardly representative of the public writ large (Wojcik and Hughes 2019). Still, the medium carries particular sociological significance. In addition to its capacity to provide researchers with rich social data, Twitter's prominence within the field of journalism has piqued the interest of many media sociologists.[2] Whether situated squarely within the field of sociology or at its margins, scholars have been drawn to questions regarding journalism and Twitter because of the window it provides into everyday practices, institutional processes, and power relations, as well as the role it plays in reshaping them.

This chapter critically examines Twitter's journalistic significance, taking stock of the myriad ways the platform has shaped media work and grappling with the implications this has had for scholarship in the field. After reviewing some of the most salient sociological contributions to the study of journalism before social media, the chapter offers an evaluation of Twitter's popularity among journalists and an assessment of its implications for the profession as well as scholarship on it. Then, it looks beyond Twitter and journalism to examine how the emerging hybrid media system is changing journalism's relationship with the public. The chapter concludes by offering some reflections on the state of the field before as well as some suggestions to help guide future research.

Sociology of Journalism before Twitter

Journalism is currently undergoing remarkable change due to a combination of political, economic, technological, and professional forces. Although it may appear that journalism's heightened sociological significance sets the current historical moment apart—news and information have never been more ubiquitous in public life, after all—it has long been of particular significance to sociologists. Journalism's notable role in our vocation can be traced back to some of the discipline's early pioneers. Indeed, Max Weber, Robert Park, and Ferdinand Tönnies were studying journalism well before the birth of modern media (Marocco 2005; Hardt 2001). While Weber's and Park's interest in the subject emerged in part from the time they spent working as reporters, they were also drawn to studying journalism because of its organizational makeup and the privileged position it holds in most political systems (Dickinson 2013; Jacobs 2009).

Building on this line of inquiry, sociologists have since brought the discipline's unique toolkit to bear on the practice and profession of journalism. Beyond offering insights that could translate to other professional fields, analyses of journalism have generated profound knowledge about the particular ways information and power flow through media. Whatever their theoretical and methodological approach, sociological analyses of journalism typically focus on at least one stage (Lindner and Barnard 2020) of the mediation process: production (e.g., Christin 2020; Klinenberg 2007), reception (e.g.,

Butsch 2008; Peters 2011), and the content itself (e.g., Jacobs 2000; Kendall 2011). Many such studies have furthered our collective understanding of media work and industries, media content, and audiences, proving how useful the sociological toolkit can be, especially for those situated outside the discipline (i.e., in the media professions) (Anderson 2015; Zelizer 2004).

One of the most distinctive characteristics of a sociological approach is the tendency to interrogate the forces shaping everyday reality, which are often maintained through normative pressures and implicit assumptions. For example, in "Social Control in the Newsroom," Warren Breed (1955) sought to explain why reporters typically followed newspaper policies despite frequently disagreeing with them. Based on his observations and interviews, Breed concluded that the most effective social control mechanisms for newsworkers are the ones followed in their immediate working environment (rather than imposed by broader societal or professional standards) because of the value placed on status and group solidarity. Such insights were hard to come by in less sociological analyses yet deeply valuable in contextualizing journalistic phenomena within the broader framework of social relations.

During the 1970s and early 1980s, sociological studies of news organizations were common, and they frequently discovered that the organizational structures shaping newsrooms were more often driven by the institutions' profit and efficiency goals rather than by democratic goals of informing the public (Tuchman 1978; Fishman 1980). Outside the United States, a number of scholars studied professional news cultures, focusing on British print (Tunstall 1971) and television newsrooms (Elliott 1972; Schlesinger 1978), as well as on comparing media organizations across national contexts (Golding and Elliott 1979). In addition to providing a thick description of the structure and culture of newswork, such as the role rituals play in professional journalistic life (Elliott 1972; Tuchman 1972), one of the most noteworthy findings to emerge was the realization that the press had subtly shifted its conception of its primary product from news to audience attention. Indeed, given that most news companies generated the bulk of their revenue through advertising, newswork was increasingly structured to ensure that workers produced stories that would be recognizable by and of interest to their target audience (Stonbely 2015; Fishman 1980; Tuchman 1978).

If one thread of sociological inquiry pertains to journalism's professional cultures and organizational makeup, another has to do with its position in the political system. Scholars of social movements have taken a keen interest in media and journalism due to their symbolic and agenda-setting power. Whereas some sociological studies have used quantitative measures to establish how much news attention social movements receive (Amenta et al. 2009; Andrews and Caren 2010; Oliver and Meyer 1999), others examine how media shape social movements' framing and tactics (Gamson and Wolfsfeld 1993; Ryan 2004; Rohlinger 2006). Still others have combined ethnographic studies of movements with media to paint an even more detailed picture of the tenuous and ever-evolving relationship between movements and the media that cover them (Gitlin 1980; Sobieraj 2011)—a dynamic that has grown even more complex in an era of hybrid media.

Despite the rise in complaints about media's "liberal bias" (Sands 2020), many sociological analyses have shown that journalism is more likely to reinforce existing power structures than to challenge them (Stonbely 2015). Whether intentionally or not, one of the most consequential ways journalism can help maintain the status quo is by relying on official sources to shape a narrative (Fishman 1980; Herman and Chomsky 2002). Furthermore, rather than serving as a mere reflection of reality, journalists actively construct it in a variety of ways, such as by adhering to professional norms about what constitutes news, where it originates, and which perspectives should be treated as (il)legitimate (Tuchman 1978; Stonbely 2015; cf. Berger and Luckmann 1967). Other culture-oriented analyses have shed much needed light on the ethos of journalism as a practice and profession.

In his landmark book *Discovering the News*, Michael Schudson (1978) provided a rich description of American journalism's "critical culture"—most notably, its commitment to the professional norms of objectivity—as well as of how that work was organized. Although others had already called attention to journalistic objectivity's more latent functions (Tuchman 1972), Schudson and others (Gans 2004) provided a detailed account of how the norm of objectivity became institutionalized and how it relates to other news values. Still, other culturally attuned accounts of journalism helped explain how members of the profession operated as interpretive communities (Zelizer 1993) and how their reporting shaped the collective meaning of events across a variety of cultures (Dayan and Katz 1992). Emerging out of the tradition of British cultural studies, which brought much needed attention to the ways meaning was not inherent to cultural objects but rather encoded and decoded against the often-invisible backdrop of ideology (Hall 1980), a new wave of media scholarship began with a sharper critical edge. For example, Ronald Jacobs' (2000) examination of culturally salient news events—the Watts uprising in 1965, the police beating of Rodney King in 1991, and the subsequent unrest following the police officers' acquittal in 1992—helped establish a greater understanding of how news representations can vary depending on who is doing the reporting and what implications that can have for the (African American) public sphere.

While there is much to learn by studying journalism's distinct cultures and their influence on social life, scholars adopting a "new institutionalist" perspective have also added much to the conversation. For example, Paul Starr's (2005) analysis of early American and European media showed how a combination of political and economic conditions laid the foundation for the creation of unique informational environments. This point was also laid bare in Hallin and Mancini's (2004) ambitious modeling of how political and economic contexts combine to shape media in various societies across the globe. Others, like Sparrow (2006) and Cook (2006), have articulated comparable visions for how to understand journalism's relationship with other spheres of social life, such as politics, culture, technology, and the economy.

Similarly, in Rodney Benson's (1999) pathbreaking application of Pierre Bourdieu's (1993) "field theory" to the media industries, he demonstrated how sociological analyses aimed at the "mezzo-level" can simultaneously account for dynamics often addressed dichotomously, such as production and reception, macro-level structural forces, and micro-level organizational cultures, as well as constancy and change (p. 463). The basic premise of field theory—that spheres of social action can be simultaneously separate and interrelated (Benson and Neveu 2005; cf. Fligstein and McAdam 2015)—along with its unique interest in the interrelatedness of structures and practices provided a useful framework for scholars to explain the changes the journalistic field would undergo in the decade that followed (Couldry 2003; Saguy, Gruys, and Gong 2010). These changes included greater political–economic constraints following the rise of new information communication technologies (ICTs) as well as the loss of advertising revenue and jobs, the shifting boundaries and practices of professional journalism as bloggers and other internet users began entering the field, and the growing importance of technology use and real-time public engagement in journalistic routines (Barnard 2018a).

Altogether, media sociology helped establish a canon of knowledge about journalism's professional cultures and the organization of media work, the structure of the news industry and its relationship to other fields, trends in media representations, and the bearing these have on the public sphere.[3] Nevertheless, much of this knowledge—from the routines and values of reporters to the pressures that bear upon newsworkers and even to the role citizens play in processes of mediation—would soon be called into question thanks to the emergence of a new, disruptive innovation.

Twitter and Journalism: Professional Journalists

Twitter's intervention in the field of journalism may be described as complex and contradictory, helping to bring about relatively equal parts of collaboration, competition, and contestation (Barnard 2018a). By the early 2010s, social media sites had established themselves as spaces where users could gather to collect and share information, complicating the established structure and practices of the media industries. Twitter had a number of features that made it particularly appealing to news junkies, including its immediacy, reverse-chronological structure, and customizability—users could follow hashtags along with individual or "lists" of accounts related to their interests—as well as its capacity to highlight "trending topics." These features, alongside the cultures of sharing and public engagement they encouraged, helped make Twitter a uniquely important platform for the news industry. Yet, as with all aspects of social change, little was known about what effects the platform's rise was having on the production and distribution of news. Given this, early scholarship regarding the phenomenon aimed to both document its role in the field as well as theorize its implications.

Much of this early work examined questions regarding if, how, and to what extent Twitter adoption was changing journalistic norms and practices. Beyond providing journalists opportunities to build and maintain social ties with other media professionals (Barnard 2016; Deprez and Van Leuven 2018; Hanusch and Nölleke 2019) and members of the public (Lasorsa, Lewis, and Holton 2012; cf. Hanusch and Tandoc 2017), Twitter has also afforded many more practical uses. They include the ability to monitor and verify breaking news in real time (Hermida 2010, 2012; Coddington, Molyneux, and Lawrence 2014), to connect with potential sources (Broersma and Graham 2013; Deprez and Van Leuven 2018; Hermida et al. 2014), to provide additional context and transparency (Hedman 2016; Lasorsa 2012), to strengthen ties with audiences (Lysak, Cremedas, and Wolf 2012; López-Rabadán and Mellado 2019), to build and manage their personal or organizational brands (Molyneux 2015; Hanusch 2017; Hanusch and Bruns 2017; Jukes 2019; Olausson 2018) and even to share news published by competing outlets (Barthel, Moon, and Mari 2015).

Considering the breadth of Twitter usage by journalists, it is not surprising that its foray into the field would be accompanied by alterations to journalistic norms. Although the maturation of the internet had already made a tremendous amount of digital information available to consumers at no (direct) cost, Twitter's place as a de facto news wire accessible to anyone with an internet connection inevitably added to the pressure placed on news organizations seeking to find new business models for the digital age. But, on a practical level, journalists' Twitter use led to revisions of how they express themselves as well as their relationship with the public. While research has found that journalists' Twitter usage has contributed to moderate improvements in transparency, providing the public with glimpses into the reporting process, most reporters are limited in their use of Twitter to increase transparency with regard to their personal lives or to encourage public participation in the newsmaking process (Hedman 2016; Lawrence et al. 2014; cf. Lasorsa 2012). One study of political journalists' use of Twitter during the 2012 Republican and Democratic national conventions found that reporters tended to express personal opinions on Twitter in somewhat new and surprising ways, even if the increased importance of social media did not upend other professional norms (Lawrence et al. 2014). Nevertheless, other studies found that many reporters mixed personal opinion and commentary with news updates, especially following acts of police aggression against members of the press, such as during their coverage of the 2014 protests in Ferguson, Missouri (Araiza et al. 2016; Barnard 2018b). Furthermore, some noted how many reporters used Twitter to openly reflect on the state of journalism as a profession (Barnard 2016), as well as a tendency among reporters to treat social media content as a proxy for public opinion (Dubois, Gruzd, and Jacobson 2018; McGregor 2019; Wojcik and Hughes 2019).

By combining content, network, and hyperlink analyses, Barnard (2018a) found that journalists' use of Twitter helped them build personal platforms that were relatively independent from their news organizations' typical distribution channels. Although this allowed them greater autonomy over the kinds of information they shared and the language they used to describe it, their frequent decisions to amplify already-prominent political narratives—namely, controversial tweets by Donald Trump—led them to test the boundaries of objectivity while reinforcing Trump's status as an elite agenda-setter. Other studies also found Twitter to be a significant force for sourcing and agenda-setting. In their examination of Belgian health journalists, Deprez and Van Leuven (2018) found that reporters primarily used Twitter as a means to monitor fellow reporters' accounts but also that Twitter helped connect them to widely recognized health experts, thus reinforcing the influence of elites as agenda-setters.

Journalists also used Twitter to boost their own influence. Multiple studies have documented Twitter's role in journalists' self-branding efforts (Molyneux 2015), their generation of social and economic capital (Hanusch and Bruns 2017), as well as their "celebrification" (Olausson 2018). Considering Twitter's salience in the journalistic and political fields, enterprising uses of Twitter allowed reporters a unique opportunity to build status, which might then be used to generate other opportunities (Barnard 2018a). While such developments may carve out pockets of autonomy for journalists in a time of increased professional pressure, there are downsides as well. For example, some studies have found that journalists' use of Twitter reinforces preexisting boundaries such as segregation by gender and organizational affiliation—barriers that can systematically limit individuals' ability to grow their networks (Hanusch and Nölleke 2019; Usher, Holcomb, and Littman 2018). Still, others lament journalists' self-promotion, viewing it as a sign that the metaphorical wall separating the production and sale of journalistic products is eroding (Jukes 2019).

Although many journalists joined Twitter voluntarily, use of Twitter and other social media for professional purposes was also mandated in many newsrooms. In one extreme case, BBC editor Peter Horrocks enthusiastically directed members of his newsroom to "tweet or be sacked" (Miller 2011). While it is unlikely that this directive was solidified in formal policy, many news organizations developed social media policies that more clearly governed its use in professional newswork. In a 2013 survey of 480 US newspaper reporters, over 70% stated that their newsroom had a policy governing their use of Twitter, while just under 20% said their organization restricts their use of the platform for reporting (Santana and Hopp 2016). Similarly, a 2010 survey of local TV newsrooms found that a majority had a policy requiring (17%) or encouraging (51%) its staff to have a social media presence (Lysak, Cremedas, and Wolf 2012). Some news organizations offered detailed training and guidelines, at times mandating what kinds of content journalists can post, when (i.e., no breaking news on Twitter), and to which accounts (i.e., personal or organizational), while others relied on dated policy or had none at all. Others simply instructed reporters to apply the same judgment they do when deciding what to share on the air (Bloom, Cleary, and North 2016).

Given the diversity of the journalistic field in an international context, previous research has found substantial variation in journalists' Twitter usage. Some studies have found disparities in how different types of news organizations use Twitter—print versus broadcast, regional versus local or national (Armstrong and Gao 2010)—or how, and how much, they interacted with members of the audience (Russell 2019). Others have found variation across national contexts (Bloom, Cleary, and North 2016; Bodrunova, Litvinenko, and Blekanov 2018; Broersma and Graham 2013). In addition to finding differences in Twitter use across newspapers as well as across types of news stories (i.e., soft vs. hard news), Broersma and Graham (2013) found that newspapers in the United Kingdom and The Netherlands frequently, albeit to varying degrees, included tweets in their stories to represent public opinion or statements by public figures. In Bodrunova, Litvinenko, and Blekanov's (2018) analysis of the role Twitter plays in elite and regional responses to conflicts in the public sphere, they used a combination of content analysis and network analysis to show disparities across countries as well as within individual organizations. Furthermore, a study by Bloom, Cleary, and North (2016) of news agencies in many parts of the world found that a majority of their interviewees' employers expected them to use Twitter more for promotion and public relations than newsgathering.

In addition to the breadth of organization-level approaches to journalism via Twitter, there exists another set of differences regarding individual perspectives on the platform's relevance to the profession, its products, and its members' daily practices. Despite Twitter's normalization within the profession (Lasorsa, Lewis, and Holton 2012), newsworkers are often disincentivized from treating tweets as a primary journalistic product. Beyond the possible risks associated with shifting notable portions of their work to a space that is common or amateurish—recall the debate over citizen journalism and its perceived devaluing of professional newswork—many journalists face mounting pressures to drive traffic to a news organization's website, therefore generating revenue for their employers via digital advertising. In their ethnography of an American metropolitan newspaper, Liu and Berkowitz (2018) found differences in Twitter usage based on a reporter's age (it is more popular with younger journalists) and the type of news they produce (feature writers are less reliant on it than are breaking news reporters). Liu and Berkowitz also discovered that despite Twitter's extraordinary significance to everyday newswork, there was notable disagreement about whether or not tweets themselves were to be considered a legitimate form of journalism. Furthermore, they saw journalists' interpretation of Twitter's significance to their profession as telling of the kinds of boundary work common in a variety of fields.

Given the ever-evolving convergence of digital media and the pace at which many social networks rise and fall, scholarly inquiries often take a dual focus, highlighting the unique implications of specific media while speaking more broadly to the social, political, economic, and technological contexts they are embedded within. This pattern is fitting of most scholarship on journalism in the age of Twitter, which has sought to grapple with the platform's distinctive footprint in the field while remaining attuned to the ways its potential effects intersect with other social forces. While much of this research has focused on Twitter's influence on professional journalistic pressures, practices, norms, and values, the increasing role played by citizens and other technologies has led to new areas of inquiry. The introduction of the concept of "hybridity"—a term meant to signal the convergence of technologies, social roles, practices, and institutional contexts, among other things—was one intervention meant to redirect attention away from individual media and toward their shared logics, practices, and institutional junctures (see Chadwick 2011, 2017; Russell 2013; Barnard 2016). The significance of such an intervention becomes clear when we consider what functions Twitter serves at the borders of the journalistic field.

Open Gates? Information, Politics, Activists, and the "Audience"

As should be apparent by now, Twitter and other digital media platforms have proven relevant to sociological analyses of media because of the influence they (or, rather, uses of them) have on social processes. Thanks to the rise of Twitter and other social media, it has become increasingly common for users to document and share their experiences, as well as to offer commentary on the news as both a product and a process. This practice, broadly characterized as "citizen journalism" (Goode 2009), spelled consequences for the profession of journalism as well as its relationship to the broader public sphere.

The popularizing of digital media as a tool for the public sharing of information gave rise to what Alfred Hermida termed "ambient journalism," which he described as "an awareness system that offers diverse means to collect, communicate, share and display news and information" (2010, 301). For Hermida, Twitter was an early example of the way the widespread adoption of ICTs could broaden the kinds of information and sources available to reporters, which posed potential challenges to how public opinion was understood and what effects this had on journalistic products and processes. Furthermore, the ability for journalists and "the people formerly known as the audience" (Rosen 2006) to remain plugged into their newsfeeds contributed to an emergent "awareness system" where users could monitor updates specific to their particular interests, potentially leading to increased public knowledge, more shared experiences, and a heightened sense of community (Hermida 2010).

Although many questions remain about exactly what effects Twitter or other social media have had on the public sphere, there is little doubt that they have fundamentally altered our understanding of the audience. Whereas twentieth-century journalists had limited opportunities to interact with the public, audiences in the age of Twitter were more visible, accessible, and participatory. In addition to grappling with the benefits and costs of user-generated content, much of the early scholarship on Twitter's intervention in the space between journalists and the public was interested in the potential it had to facilitate audience engagement (Lewis, Holton, and Coddington 2014) as well as collaborations between professional and amateur reporters (Bruns and Highfield 2012; Hermida 2012; Barnard 2018a). Furthermore, members of the networked public also have the capacity to influence what stories reporters tell as well as how they tell them, whether through audience measurement metrics (Christin 2020; Petre 2018) or through acts of "gatewatching," where they observe, amplify, and critique the work of media professionals (Barnard 2018a; Bruns 2015). While serious apprehensions about nefarious actors (think disinformation and fake news) were still far on the horizon, there were many questions about what consequences might follow from lowering barriers to entry in journalism, which included concerns about accuracy and the devaluing of professional reporting.

Building on the notion of increasingly active audiences, another notable aspect of social media's significance is how deeply these media are embedded in relations and contestations of power—in the field of journalism and beyond. While traditional one-way media have garnered attention for their potential to shape public opinion, social media have been viewed simultaneously as channels of domination and resistance. Whereas establishment organizations, elected officials, and celebrities typically hold greater sway over public discourse, enterprising activists and unorthodox politicians have found ways to use social media to generate attention and advocate for social change. For example, studies have demonstrated how social movement activists use Twitter and other online media to generate press coverage in order to reach politicians with particular messages or otherwise filter out into public discourse (Freelon, McIlwain, and Clark 2018). Although these are often good-faith efforts to raise awareness about issues of social and political importance, digital media also afford bad actors with an abundance of opportunities to wage media manipulation campaigns (Donovan and Friedberg 2019). Indeed, in addition to serving as tools for assisting with processes of public accountability and justice-oriented coalition-building, digital media like YouTube, Facebook, Twitter, and Google have aided efforts to circulate extremist rhetoric, propaganda, and disinformation (Donovan and Friedberg 2019; Marwick and Lewis 2017; Nadler, Crain, and Donovan 2018). These examples provide a vivid illustration of the contradictory roles that Twitter and other digital media play in the contemporary public sphere.

Another related site of contestation has to do with the control of information. Whereas the press has traditionally monopolized the "gatekeeping" role, deciding what information should (and should not) be shared with the public (Shoemaker and Vos 2009), the rise of ICTs has led to a redistribution of some of that power. In addition to the journalism profession ceding a considerable portion of its gatekeeping power to digital media platforms, whose algorithms and editorial teams filter information based on their own unique criteria, internet users who create and share content play a growing role in determining what information reaches their personal audiences. For example, Twitter affords users with the potential to "gatecrash," circumventing professional media's gatekeeping power in order to reach audiences directly using their own channels (Barnard 2018a; Bruns 2015). Of course, this power is far from equally distributed (Rogstad 2016). Through an analysis of tweets by activists, political journalists, and public officials, Barnard (2018a) showed that networked activists have the potential to generate outsized influence relative to their social capital, often through collaboration. More importantly, public figures can use Twitter to reach even larger audiences by speaking directly to their followers while also generating additional attention through amplification.

These capabilities speak to the potential of Twitter and other digital media to assist in the process of "agenda-setting"—that is, using the power of media to tell the public what to think about (McCombs and Shaw 1972). Furthermore, they also demonstrate the opportunities digital media afford users to cultivate inverse effects, or "agenda-building," where those on the peripheries of journalism shape media coverage (Parmelee 2014; Russell et al. 2015). Although elite media undoubtedly hold the upper hand, journalists' overrepresentation on Twitter opens up potential for networked activists to affect decisions about framing and newsworthiness. More broadly, the frequency with which many such exchanges occur on Twitter—a platform whose data remains remarkably accessible in comparison to other social media sites—also provides researchers with extraordinary opportunities to address a wide array of questions about the complex and ever-evolving relationship between journalism and democracy.

Conclusion: Sociology of Journalism Going Forward

As this chapter has shown, journalism has long been an important topic of sociological inquiry, and multiple indicators suggest this trend will continue. Whether through analyses of individual practices, professional norms and values, or the field's structural composition and boundary relations, sociological studies of journalism have borne substantial fruit. We have already learned much about the political and economic pressures placed on journalistic work, about the mundane significance of newsworkers' daily routines, and about how the press interfaces with the public sphere. Like many critical interventions that have come before it, Twitter has added a new chapter to this enduring saga—one that is still being written. This concluding section offers some reflections and suggestions to guide sociological analyses of journalism and digital media going forward.

In order to continue making valuable contributions to our collective understanding of contemporary social life, sociologically oriented scholarship on media and journalism should continue to re-examine its assumptions and reorient its focus. Just as others have encouraged media scholars to shirk our implicit assumptions about journalism as the center of social life (Tandoc 2019) or about political discourse representing good-faith communication and rational deliberation (Lewis and Molyneux 2018), the future health of our subfield requires that we broaden our frames beyond a single profession (journalism), platform (Twitter), or variable (technology) so that we may more clearly see other influences. Furthermore, although Twitter provides a window into social relations that have previously been difficult for researchers to investigate, there is good reason to widen our focus beyond Twitter (and other social media) *content*. As Lewis and Molyneux put it, "time spent analyzing tweets could be coming at the expense of analyzing the logic of algorithms, the political economy of technology giants, and other organizational and institutional arrangements that are reshaping the contexts for news subsidy," among other things (p. 18). Despite Twitter's significance to journalism and the relative ease with which researchers can access its data, many conversations regarding shifting power relations in media and politics are already being framed in ways that look beyond Twitter to focus instead on digital media in general (Broersma and Eldridge 2019). Others have found creative ways to broaden the scope of their research by incorporating other sources of data alongside their analysis of tweets (Revers 2014;

Chacon, Giasson, and Brin 2018; cf. Snelson 2016). While such approaches bode well for the future of scholarship on digital media and journalism, they are a necessary but insufficient condition for strengthening our shared analytical toolkit.

Despite the influx of new actors discussed in the previous section, scholarship on Twitter and journalism has often skewed toward a focus on professional and elite actors, has often lacked adequate attention to matters of power, and has at times unnecessarily reified the boundaries defining the traditional journalistic field. The latter tendency is at times driven by researchers' hesitance to critically assess and contextualize the attempted distinctions of journalistic actors. Certainly, journalists' claims that a tweet is (or is not) a "legitimate artifact of journalism" (Liu and Berkowitz 2018, 653) can contribute to the collective understanding of journalism's normative framework—even as much of it remains contradictory and in flux. Although these claims may indeed represent meaningful attempts at boundary work (Liu and Berkowitz 2018), their value is limited if viewed as expressions of (social) fact. Indeed, while there is little value in "arguing with the members" (Gubrium and Holstein 2012, 87), it is imperative of sociological analyses to critically examine the ways structure and culture shape meaning and social action (Griswold 2013) and to maintain a reflexive awareness of "vocabularies of motive" (Mills 1940) when studying meta-journalistic discourse (Carlson 2016; Barnard 2016).

Thus, the field would also benefit from additional research that further problematizes the ways unequal power relations shape users' dispositions toward the networked world (Rafalow 2018; Sobieraj 2020; Broersma and Eldridge 2019; Cohen 2019; Compton and Benedetti 2010). Although media professions are often privileged spaces, they are not insulated from the social world; and the social relations that occur within them are inevitably shaped by the institution's enduring pressures, such as those of patriarchy, profit, and professionalism. Given that many of these phenomena are admittedly difficult to decipher using existing repertoires of digital data collection and analysis, we must build the theoretical and methodological tools to better triangulate these divergent points to generate a more common body of knowledge about the flow of power and information in an age of hybrid media.

To be clear, much of what has been proposed here is already underway, and its impact on the field has not gone unnoticed. The success of this work is further evidence of its ability to help us raise new questions, adopt new perspectives, and fashion new frameworks to address hybrid media's growing role in social life. For example, although sociological research has already uncovered how emergent logics are shaping the culture of newsrooms (Christin 2020; Petre 2018), there is a need for research to more carefully examine how the growth of "surveillance capitalism" (Zuboff 2019; cf. Couldry and Mejias 2019) affects the structure, culture, and practices of journalism, politics, and other social institutions. Furthermore, in light of the recent rise of propaganda and disinformation, which infamously invaded public discourse related to the 2016 US presidential election, the United Kingdom's Brexit referendum, and many other political contests around the world, assumptions about social media platforms serving as a boon to democracy are much less common. Although we now know how disinformation can move from the fringes of the internet to mainstream public discourse via established journalism outlets (Lukito et al. 2019; Benkler, Faris, and Roberts 2018) and what methods media manipulators use to attract reporters' attention (Donovan and Friedberg 2019), there is room to develop a much greater understanding of *why* and *to what effect(s)*.

In sum, sociological analyses of journalism in the age of Twitter have contributed much to our collective understanding of how the combination of political, economic, technological, cultural, and other factors reshape what occurs in and around one of society's most important social institutions. Sociology stands to contribute far more than novel empirical, theoretical, and methodological insights to the study of journalism and hybrid media; it offers a critical view of how the dynamics of continuity and change work in institutions that are always-already in the making. There is little doubt these social processes will endure, though there is reason to question which factors will prove most consequential for media, journalism, and beyond. Although we must continue to fashion forward-looking lenses and to shine a critical light on what occurs in the current moment, we must resist the temptation to place too great an emphasis on the extraordinary at the cost of overlooking the ordinary (Brekhus 2000). Sometimes, what is new is newsworthy; other times, it is not.

Notes

1. Despite professional journalists' criticism of the platform and its affordances, journalists were also credited with helping boost Twitter's profile among the public in its early years (Arceneaux and Schmitz Weiss 2010).
2. In fact, a Google Scholar search for "Twitter journalism" yields roughly 133,000 citations, and although sociological approaches play a predominant role in much of this literature, the vast majority originate from neighboring fields like communication, media studies, and journalism.
3. For a more detailed review of the literature on the sociology of journalism, see Zelizer (2004).

References

Amenta, Edwin, Neal Caren, Sheera Joy Olasky, and James E. Stobaugh. 2009. "All the Movements Fit to Print: Who, What, When, Where, and Why SMO Families Appeared in the New York Times in the Twentieth Century." *American Sociological Review* 74, no. 4: 636–656. https://doi.org/10.1177/000312240907400407.

Anderson, C. W. 2015. "Drawing Boundary Lines between Journalism and Sociology, 1895–2000." In *Boundaries of Journalism*, edited by Matt Carlson and Seth C. Lewis, 201–217. New York and London: Routledge.

Andrews, Kenneth T., and Neal Caren. 2010. "Making the News: Movement Organizations, Media Attention, and the Public Agenda." *American Sociological Review* 75, no. 6: 841–866. https://doi.org/10.1177/0003122410386689.

Araiza, José Andrés, Heloisa Aruth Sturm, Pinar Istek, and Mary Angela Bock. 2016. "Hands Up, Don't Shoot, Whose Side Are You On? Journalists Tweeting the Ferguson Protests." *Cultural Studies ↔ Critical Methodologies* 16, no. 3: 305–312. https://doi.org/10.1177/1532708616634834.

Arceneaux, Noah, and Amy Schmitz Weiss. 2010. "Seems Stupid until You Try It: Press Coverage of Twitter, 2006–9." *New Media & Society* 12, no. 8: 1262–1279. https://doi.org/10.1177/1461444809360773.

Armstrong, Cory L., and Fangfang Gao. 2010. "Now Tweet This: How News Organizations Use Twitter." *Electronic News* 4, no. 4: 218–235. https://doi.org/10.1177/1931243110389457.

Barnard, Stephen R. 2016. " 'Tweet or Be Sacked': Twitter and the New Elements of Journalistic Practice." *Journalism* 17, 2: 190–207. https://doi.org/10.1177/1464884914553079.

Barnard, Stephen R. 2018a. *Citizens at the Gates: Twitter, Networked Publics, and the Transformation of American Journalism*. Cham, Switzerland: Springer.

Barnard, Stephen R. 2018b. "Tweeting #Ferguson: Mediatized Fields and the New Activist Journalist." *New Media & Society* 20, no. 7: 2252–2271. https://doi.org/10.1177/1461444817712723.

Barthel, Michael L., Ruth Moon, and William Mari. 2015. "Who Retweets Whom: How Digital and Legacy Journalists Interact on Twitter." Accessed March 6, 2015. https://issuu.com/saladeprensa/docs/who_retweets_whom__how_digital_and_legacy_journali.

Benkler, Yochai, Robert Faris, and Hal Roberts. 2018. *Network Propaganda: Manipulation, Disinformation, and Radicalization in American Politics*. New York: Oxford University Press.

Benson, Rodney. 1999. "Field Theory in Comparative Context: A New Paradigm for Media Studies." *Theory and Society* 28, no. 3: 463–498.

Benson, Rodney, and Erik Neveu. 2005. *Bourdieu and the Journalistic Field*. Cambridge and Malden, MA: Polity.

Berger, Peter L., and Thomas Luckmann. 1967. *The Social Construction of Reality: A Treatise in the Sociology of Knowledge*. New York: Anchor.

Bloom, Terry, Johanna Cleary, and Michael North. 2016. "Traversing the 'Twittersphere.' " *Journalism Practice* 10, no. 3: 343–357. https://doi.org/10.1080/17512786.2015.1017408.

Bodrunova, Svetlana S., Anna A. Litvinenko, and Ivan S. Blekanov. 2018. "Please Follow Us." *Journalism Practice* 12, no. 2: 177–203. https://doi.org/10.1080/17512786.2017.1394208.

Bourdieu, Pierre. 1993. *The Field of Cultural Production: Essays on Art and Literature*. New York: Columbia University Press.

Breed, Warren. 1955. "Social Control in the Newsroom: A Functional Analysis." *Social Forces* 33, no. 4: 326–335.

Brekhus, Wayne. 2000. "A Mundane Manifesto." *Journal of Mundane Behavior* 1, no. 1: 89–106.

Broersma, Marcel, and Scott A. Eldridge II. 2019. "Journalism and Social Media: Redistribution of Power?" *Media and Communication* 7, no. 1: 5.

Broersma, Marcel, and Todd Graham. 2013. "Twitter as a News Source." *Journalism Practice* 7, no. 4: 446–464. https://doi.org/10.1080/17512786.2013.802481.

Bruns, Axel. 2015. "Gatekeeping, Gatewatching, Real-Time Feedback: New Challenges for Journalism." *Brazilian Journalism Research* 10, no. 2 EN: 224–237.

Bruns, Axel, and Tim Highfield. 2012. "Blogs, Twitter, and Breaking News: The Produsage of Citizen Journalism." In *Producing Theory in a Digital World: The Intersection of Audiences and Production in Contemporary Theory*, edited by Rebecca Ann Lind, 15–32. New York: Peter Lang.

Butsch, Richard. 2008. *The Citizen Audience: Crowds, Publics, and Individuals*. New York and London: Routledge.

Carlson, Matt. 2016. "Metajournalistic Discourse and the Meanings of Journalism: Definitional Control, Boundary Work, and Legitimation." *Communication Theory* 26, no. 4: 349–368. https://doi.org/10.1111/comt.12088.

Chacon, Geneviève, Thierry Giasson, and Colette Brin. 2018. " 'That's What I'm Talking about': Twitter as a Promotional Tool for Political Journalists." *Popular Communication* 16, no. 4: 276–292. https://doi.org/10.1080/15405702.2018.1535657.

Chadwick, Andrew. 2011. "The Political Information Cycle in a Hybrid News System: The British Prime Minister and the 'Bullygate' Affair." *International Journal of Press/Politics* 16, no. 1: 3–29. https://doi.org/10.1177/1940161210384730.

Chadwick, Andrew. 2017. *The Hybrid Media System: Politics and Power*. 2nd ed. New York: Oxford University Press.

Christin, Angèle. 2020. *Metrics at Work: Journalism and the Contested Meaning of Algorithms*. Princeton, NJ: Princeton University Press.

Coddington, Mark, Logan Molyneux, and Regina G. Lawrence. 2014. "Fact Checking the Campaign: How Political Reporters Use Twitter to Set the Record Straight (or Not)." *International Journal of Press/Politics* 19, no. 4: 391–409. https://doi.org/10.1177/1940161214540942.

Cohen, Nicole S. 2019. "At Work in the Digital Newsroom." *Digital Journalism* 7, no. 5: 571–591. https://doi.org/10.1080/21670811.2017.1419821.

Compton, James R., and Paul Benedetti. 2010. "Labour, New Media and the Institutional Restructuring of Journalism." *Journalism Studies* 11, no. 4: 487–499. https://doi.org/10.1080/14616701003638350.

Conger, Kate, and Nicole Perlroth. 2020. "Twitter to Add Context to Trending Topics." *New York Times*, September 1. https://www.nytimes.com/2020/09/01/technology/twitter-trending-topics.html.

Cook, Timothy E. 2006. "The News Media as a Political Institution: Looking Backward and Looking Forward." *Political Communication* 23, no. 2: 159–171. https://doi.org/10.1080/10584600600629711.

Couldry, Nick. 2003. "Media Meta-Capital: Extending the Range of Bourdieu's Field Theory." *Theory and Society* 32, no. 5/6: 653–677.

Couldry, Nick, and Ulises A. Mejias. 2019. *The Costs of Connection: How Data Is Colonizing Human Life and Appropriating It for Capitalism*. 1st edition. Stanford, CA: Stanford University Press.

Dayan, Daniel, and Elihu Katz. 1992. *Media Events: The Live Broadcasting of History*. Cambridge, MA: Harvard University Press.

Deprez, Annelore, and Sarah Van Leuven. 2018. "About Pseudo Quarrels and Trustworthiness." *Journalism Studies* 19, no. 9: 1257–1274. https://doi.org/10.1080/1461670X.2016.1266910.

Dickinson, Roger. 2013. "Weber's Sociology of the Press and Journalism: Continuities in Contemporary Sociologies of Journalists and the Media." *Max Weber Studies* 13, no. 2: 197–215.

Donovan, Joan, and Brian Friedberg. 2019. "Source Hacking: Media Manipulation in Practice." Data & Society. https://datasociety.net/output/source-hacking-media-manipulation-in-practice/.

Dubois, Elizabeth, Anatoliy Gruzd, and Jenna Jacobson. 2018. "Journalists' Use of Social Media to Infer Public Opinion: The Citizens' Perspective." *Social Science Computer Review* 38, no. 1: 57–74. https://doi.org/10.1177/0894439318791527.

Elliott, Philip. 1972. *The Sociology of the Professions*. London: Macmillan International Higher Education.

Fishman, Mark. 1980. *Manufacturing the News*. Austin: University of Texas Press.

Fligstein, Neil, and Doug McAdam. 2015. *A Theory of Fields*. New York: Oxford University Press.

Freelon, Deen, Charlton McIlwain, and Meredith Clark. 2018. "Quantifying the Power and Consequences of Social Media Protest." *New Media & Society* 20, no. 3: 990–1011. https://doi.org/10.1177/1461444816676646.

Gamson, William A., and Gadi Wolfsfeld. 1993. "Movements and Media as Interacting Systems." *The ANNALS of the American Academy of Political and Social Science* 528, no. 1: 114–25. https://doi.org/10.1177/0002716293528001009.

Gans, Herbert J. 2004. *Deciding What's News: A Study of CBS Evening News, NBC Nightly News, Newsweek, and Time*. Evanston, IL: Northwestern University Press (initially published in 1979).

Gitlin, Todd. 1980. *The Whole World Is Watching: Mass Media in the Making & Unmaking of the New Left*. Berkeley: University of California Press.

Golding, Peter, and Philip Elliott. 1979. *Making the News*. New York: Longman.

Goode, Luke. 2009. "Social News, Citizen Journalism and Democracy." *New Media & Society* 11, no. 8: 1287–1305. https://doi.org/10.1177/1461444809341393.

Griswold, Wendy. 2013. *Cultures and Societies in a Changing World*. 4th ed. Sociology for a New Century Series. Thousand Oaks, CA: SAGE Publications.

Gubrium, Jaber F., and James A. Holstein. 2012. "Don't Argue with the Members." *American Sociologist* 43, no. 1: 85–98.

Gulyas, Agnes. 2013. "The Influence of Professional Variables on Journalists' Uses and Views of Social Media." *Digital Journalism* 1, no. 2: 270–285. https://doi.org/10.1080/21670811.2012.744559.

Hall, Stuart. 1980. "Encoding/Decoding." In *Culture, Media, Language: Working Papers in Cultural Studies*, edited by Stuart Hall, Dorothy Hobson, Andrew Lowe, and Paul Willis, 117–127. London and New York: Routledge.

Hallin, Daniel C., and Paolo Mancini. 2004. *Comparing Media Systems: Three Models of Media and Politics*. Cambridge: Cambridge University Press.

Hanusch, Folker. 2017. "Political Journalists' Corporate and Personal Identities on Twitter Profile Pages: A Comparative Analysis in Four Westminster Democracies." *New Media & Society* 20, no. 4: 1488–1505. https://doi.org/10.1177/1461444817698479.

Hanusch, Folker, and Axel Bruns. 2017. "Journalistic Branding on Twitter." *Digital Journalism* 5, no. 1: 26–43. https://doi.org/10.1080/21670811.2016.1152161.

Hanusch, Folker, and Daniel Nölleke. 2019. "Journalistic Homophily on Social Media." *Digital Journalism* 7, no. 1: 22–44. https://doi.org/10.1080/21670811.2018.1436977.

Hanusch, Folker, and Edson C. Tandoc, Jr. 2017. "Comments, Analytics, and Social Media: The Impact of Audience Feedback on Journalists' Market Orientation." *Journalism* 20, no. 6: 695–713. https://doi.org/10.1177/1464884917720305.

Hardt, Hanno. 2001. *Social Theories of the Press: Constituents of Communication Research, 1840s to 1920s*. Lanham, MD: Rowman & Littlefield.

Hedman, Ulrika. 2016. "When Journalists Tweet: Disclosure, Participatory, and Personal Transparency." *Social Media + Society* 2, no. 1: 2056305115624528. https://doi.org/10.1177/2056305115624528.

Hedman, Ulrika, and Monika Djerf-Pierre. 2013. "The Social Journalist: Embracing the Social Media Life or Creating a New Digital Divide?" *Digital Journalism* 1, no. 3: 368–385. https://doi.org/10.1080/21670811.2013.776804.

Herman, Edward S., and Noam Chomsky. 2002. *Manufacturing Consent: The Political Economy of the Mass Media*. New York: Pantheon.

Hermida, Alfred. 2010. "Twittering the News: The Emergence of Ambient Journalism." *Journalism Practice* 4, no. 3: 297–308. https://doi.org/10.1080/17512781003640703.

Hermida, Alfred. 2012. "Tweets and Truth: Journalism as a Discipline of Collaborative Verification." *Journalism Practice* 6, nos. 5–6: 659–668. https://doi.org/10.1080/17512786.2012.667269.

Hermida, Alfred, Seth C. Lewis, and Rodrigo Zamith. 2014. "Sourcing the Arab Spring: A Case Study of Andy Carvin's Sources on Twitter during the Tunisian and Egyptian Revolutions." *Journal of Computer-Mediated Communication* 19, no. 3: 479–499. https://doi.org/10.1111/jcc4.12074.

Jacobs, Ronald N. 2000. *Race, Media, and the Crisis of Civil Society: From Watts to Rodney King*. Cambridge: Cambridge University Press.

Jacobs, Ronald N. 2009. "Culture, the Public Sphere, and Media Sociology: A Search for a Classical Founder in the Work of Robert Park." *American Sociologist* 40, no. 3: 149–166. https://doi.org/10.1007/s12108-009-9070-5.

Jukes, Stephen. 2019. "Crossing the Line between News and the Business of News: Exploring Journalists' Use of Twitter." *Media and Communication* 7, 1: 248–258. https://doi.org/10.17645/mac.v7i1.1772.

Kendall, Diana. 2011. *Framing Class: Media Representations of Wealth and Poverty in America*. Lanham, MD: Rowman & Littlefield.

Klinenberg, Eric. 2007. *Fighting for Air: The Battle to Control America's Media*. New York: Henry Holt and Company.

Lasorsa, Dominic. 2012. "Transparency and Other Journalistic Norms on Twitter." *Journalism Studies* 13, no. 3: 402–417. https://doi.org/10.1080/1461670X.2012.657909.

Lasorsa, Dominic L., Seth C. Lewis, and Avery E. Holton. 2012. "Normalizing Twitter: Journalism Practice in an Emerging Communication Space." *Journalism Studies* 13, no. 1: 19–36. https://doi.org/10.1080/1461670X.2011.571825.

Lawrence, Regina G., Logan Molyneux, Mark Coddington, and Avery Holton. 2014. "Tweeting Conventions: Political Journalists' Use of Twitter to Cover the 2012 Presidential Campaign." *Journalism Studies* 15, no. 6: 789–806. https://doi.org/10.1080/1461670X.2013.836378.

Lewis, Seth C., Avery E. Holton, and Mark Coddington. 2014. "Reciprocal Journalism: A Concept of Mutual Exchange between Journalists and Audiences." *Journalism Practice* 8, no. 2: 229–241. https://doi.org/10.1080/17512786.2013.859840.

Lewis, Seth C., and Logan Molyneux. 2018. "A Decade of Research on Social Media and Journalism: Assumptions, Blind Spots, and a Way Forward." *Media and Communication* 6, no. 4: 11–23. https://doi.org/10.17645/mac.v6i4.1562.

Lindner, Andrew M., and Stephen R. Barnard. 2020. *All Media Are Social: Sociological Perspectives on Mass Media*. New York and London: Routledge.

Liu, Zhaoxi (Josie), and Dan Berkowitz. 2018. "Blurring Boundaries: Exploring Tweets as a Legitimate Journalism Artifact." *Journalism* 21, no. 5: 652–669. https://doi.org/10.1177/1464884918775073.

López-Rabadán, Pablo, and Claudia Mellado. 2019. "Twitter as a Space for Interaction in Political Journalism. Dynamics, Consequences and Proposal of Interactivity Scale for Social Media." *Communication & Society* 32, no. 1: 1–16. https://doi.org/10.15581/003.32.1.1-18.

Lukito, Josephine, Jiyoun Suk, Yini Zhang, Larissa Doroshenko, Sang Jung Kim, Min-Hsin Su, Yiping Xia, Deen Freelon, and Chris Wells. 2019. "The Wolves in Sheep's Clothing: How

Russia's Internet Research Agency Tweets Appeared in U.S. News as Vox Populi." *International Journal of Press/Politics* 25, no. 2: 196–216. https://doi.org/10.1177/1940161219895215.

Lysak, Suzanne, Michael Cremedas, and John Wolf. 2012. "Facebook and Twitter in the Newsroom: How and Why Local Television News Is Getting Social With Viewers?" *Electronic News* 6, no. 4: 187–207. https://doi.org/10.1177/1931243112466095.

Marocco, Beatriz. 2005. "The Social Theories of the Press: Journalism and Society." *Brazilian Journalism Research* 1, no. 1: 195–216. http://dx.doi.org/10.25200/BJR.v1n1.2005.38.

Marwick, Alice, and Rebecca Lewis. 2017. "Media Manipulation and Disinformation Online." Data & Society. https://datasociety.net/output/media-manipulation-and-disinfo-online/.

McCombs, Maxwell E., and Donald L. Shaw. 1972. "The Agenda-Setting Function of Mass Media." *Public Opinion Quarterly* 36, no. 2: 176–187.

McGregor, Shannon C. 2019. "Social Media as Public Opinion: How Journalists Use Social Media to Represent Public Opinion." *Journalism* 20, no. 8: 1070–1086. https://doi.org/10.1177/1464884919845458.

McNamara, Audrey. 2020, September 15. "Twitter Launches 'Election Hub' to Battle Disinformation." *CBS News* (blog). https://www.cbsnews.com/news/twitter-launches-election-hub-battle-disinformation/.

Miller, Charles. 2011, May 11. "#bbcsms: Changing Journalists' Social Media Mindset." *BBC* (blog). https://www.bbc.co.uk/blogs/collegeofjournalism/entries/c25df279-74ed-3174-8db0-6d7a38613499.

Mills, C. Wright. 1940. "Situated Actions and Vocabularies of Motive." *American Sociological Review* 5, no. 6: 904–913. https://doi.org/10.2307/2084524.

Molyneux, Logan. 2015. "What Journalists Retweet: Opinion, Humor, and Brand Development on Twitter." *Journalism* 16, no. 7: 920–935. https://doi.org/10.1177/1464884914550135.

Nadler, Anthony, Matthew Crain, and Joan Donovan. 2018. "Weaponizing the Digital Influence Machine: The Political Perils of Online Ad Tech." Data & Society. https://datasociety.net/output/weaponizing-the-digital-influence-machine/.

Olausson, Ulrika. 2018. "The Celebrified Journalist: Journalistic Self-Promotion and Branding in Celebrity Constructions on Twitter." *Journalism Studies* 19, no. 16: 2379–2399. https://doi.org/10.1080/1461670X.2017.1349548.

Oliver, Pamela E., and Daniel J. Meyer. 1999. "How Events Enter the Public Sphere: Conflict, Location, and Sponsorship in Local Newspaper Coverage of Public Events." *American Journal of Sociology* 105, no. 1: 38–87. https://doi.org/10.1086/210267.

Parmelee, John H. 2014. "The Agenda-Building Function of Political Tweets." *New Media & Society* 16, no. 3: 434–450. https://doi.org/10.1177/1461444813487955.

Peters, Chris. 2011. "Emotion aside or Emotional Side? Crafting an 'Experience of Involvement' in the News." *Journalism* 12, no. 3: 297–316. https://doi.org/10.1177/1464884910388224.

Petre, Caitlin. 2018. "Engineering Consent: How the Design and Marketing of Newsroom Analytics Tools Rationalize Journalists' Labor." *Digital Journalism* 6, no. 4: 509–527. https://doi.org/10.1080/21670811.2018.1444998.

Rafalow, Matthew H. 2018. "Disciplining Play: Digital Youth Culture as Capital at School." *American Journal of Sociology* 123, no. 5: 1416–1452. https://doi.org/10.1086/695766.

Revers, Matthias. 2014. "The Twitterization of News Making: Transparency and Journalistic Professionalism." *Journal of Communication* 64, no. 5: 806–826. https://doi.org/10.1111/jcom.12111.

Rogstad, Ingrid. 2016. "Is Twitter Just Rehashing? Intermedia Agenda Setting between Twitter and Mainstream Media." *Journal of Information Technology & Politics* 13, no. 2: 142–158. https://doi.org/10.1080/19331681.2016.1160263.

Rohlinger, Deana A. 2006. "Friends and Foes: Media, Politics, and Tactics in the Abortion War." *Social Problems* 53, no. 4: 537–561. https://doi.org/10.1525/sp.2006.53.4.537.

Rosen, Jay. 2006, June 27. "The People Formerly Known as the Audience." *PressThink* (blog). http://archive.pressthink.org/2006/06/27/ppl_frmr.html.

Russell, Adrienne. 2013. "Innovation in Hybrid Spaces: 2011 UN Climate Summit and the Expanding Journalism Landscape." *Journalism* 14, no. 7: 904–920. https://doi.org/10.1177/1464884913477311.

Russell, Frank Michael. 2019. "Twitter and News Gatekeeping." *Digital Journalism* 7, no. 1: 80–99. https://doi.org/10.1080/21670811.2017.1399805.

Russell, Frank Michael, Marina A. Hendricks, Heesook Choi, and Elizabeth Conner Stephens. 2015. "Who Sets the News Agenda on Twitter? Journalists' Posts during the 2013 US Government Shutdown." *Digital Journalism* 3, no. 6: 925–943. https://doi.org/10.1080/21670811.2014.995918.

Ryan, Charlotte. 2004. "It Takes a Movement to Raise an Issue: Media Lessons from the 1997 U.P.S. Strike." *Critical Sociology* 30, no. 2: 483–511. https://doi.org/10.1163/156916304323072189.

Saguy, Abigail C., Kjerstin Gruys, and Shanna Gong. 2010. "Social Problem Construction and National Context: News Reporting on 'Overweight' and 'Obesity' in the United States and France." *Social Problems* 57, no. 4: 586–610. https://doi.org/10.1525/sp.2010.57.4.586.

Sands, John. 2020, August 6. "Americans Are Losing Faith in an Objective Media. A New Gallup/Knight Study Explores Why." *Medium* (blog). https://medium.com/trust-media-and-democracy/americans-are-losing-faith-in-an-objective-media-a-new-gallup-knight-study-explores-why-8bc87139648e.

Santana, Arthur D., and Toby Hopp. 2016. "Tapping into a New Stream of (Personal) Data: Assessing Journalists' Different Use of Social Media." *Journalism & Mass Communication Quarterly* 93, no. 2: 383–408. https://doi.org/10.1177/1077699016637105.

Schlesinger, Philip. 1978. *Putting "Reality" Together: BBC News*. Constable & Co., Ltd. London.

Schudson, Michael. 1978. *Discovering The News*. Basic Books.

Shoemaker, Pamela J., and Timothy Vos. 2009. *Gatekeeping Theory*. New York and London: Routledge.

Snelson, Chareen L. 2016. "Qualitative and Mixed Methods Social Media Research: A Review of the Literature." *International Journal of Qualitative Methods* 15, no. 1: 1609406915624574. https://doi.org/10.1177/1609406915624574.

Sobieraj, Sarah. 2011. *Soundbitten: The Perils of Media-Centered Political Activism*. New York: New York University Press.

Sobieraj, Sarah. 2020. *Credible Threat: Attacks against Women Online and the Future of Democracy*. New York: Oxford University Press.

Sparrow, Bartholomew H. 2006. "A Research Agenda for an Institutional Media." *Political Communication* 23, no. 2: 145–157. https://doi.org/10.1080/10584600600629695.

Starr, Paul. 2005. *The Creation of the Media: Political Origins of Modern Communications*. New York: Basic Books.

Stonbely, Sarah. 2015. "The Social and Intellectual Contexts of the U.S. 'Newsroom Studies,' and the Media Sociology of Today." *Journalism Studies* 16, no. 2: 259–274.

Tandoc, Edson C., Jr. 2019. "Journalism at the Periphery." *Media and Communication* 7 (4): 138–143. https://doi.org/10.17645/mac.v7i4.2626.

Tuchman, Gaye. 1972. "Objectivity as Strategic Ritual: An Examination of Newsmen's Notions of Objectivity." *American Journal of Sociology* 77, no. 4: 660–679. https://doi.org/10.1086/225193.

Tuchman, Gaye. 1978. *Making News: A Study in the Construction of Reality*. New York: Free Press.

Tunstall, Jeremy. 1971. *Journalists at Work: Specialist Correspondents: Their News Organizations, News Sources, and Competitor-Colleagues*. London: Constable.

Usher, Nikki, Jesse Holcomb, and Justin Littman. 2018. "Twitter Makes It Worse: Political Journalists, Gendered Echo Chambers, and the Amplification of Gender Bias." *International Journal of Press/Politics* 23, no. 3: 324–344. https://doi.org/10.1177/1940161218781254.

Willnat, Lars, David H. Weaver, and G. Cleveland Wilhoit. 2017. *The American Journalist in the Digital Age: A Half-Century Perspective*. New York: Peter Lang.

Wojcik, Stefan, and Adam Hughes. 2019. "How Twitter Users Compare to the General Public." Pew Research Center, April 24. https://www.pewresearch.org/internet/2019/04/24/sizing-up-twitter-users/.

Zelizer, Barbie. 1993. "Journalists as Interpretive Communities." *Critical Studies in Mass Communication* 10, no. 3: 219–237. https://doi.org/10.1080/15295039309366865.

Zelizer, Barbie. 2004. *Taking Journalism Seriously: News and the Academy*. Thousand Oaks, CA: SAGE Publications.

Zuboff, Shoshana. 2019. *The Age of Surveillance Capitalism: The Fight for a Human Future at the New Frontier of Power*. New York: PublicAffairs.

CHAPTER 8

FAMILIES, RELATIONSHIPS, AND TECHNOLOGY

RAELENE WILDING

On July 9, 2020, the residents of Melbourne, Australia, went into a strict lockdown for what turned out to be 12 weeks. In the interest of public health, people were instructed to remain in their homes and practice "social distancing." New rules prevented them from visiting each other, sharing meals in restaurants, or going shopping together. Most people complied with these instructions. However, they were not necessarily practicing *social* distancing. While they were certainly remaining physically distant, they were also using a wide range of digital media tools and platforms to connect with each other socially on a regular basis. They were virtually visiting each other's homes in order to eat together and play board games or video games and keeping in touch throughout the day using voice calls, video calls, text messages, emojis, memes, and photographs and watching movies and television together on streaming services. Celebrations such as birthdays, weddings, and funerals were relocated to platforms such as Zoom or Skype, grandparents played peekaboo or supervised online school from a distance, and couples joined each other for online dates.

This experience in Melbourne was not unique. Around the world, governments and health authorities were adopting strict lockdown measures aimed at containing the spread of COVID-19, a disease caused by a virus that was highly infectious as well as deadly. In response, growing numbers of people across the world were turning to their digital devices for social contact. This turn to digital media was also far from unique. Indeed, this reliance on digital media for social interactions was just a further intensification of patterns that had been established over several decades, in which digital devices have become an increasingly common feature in family life. In this chapter, we explore what this shift to the digital means for the family and for family relationships. Why are families using digital media? How are families using digital media? And what does this tell us about the role of digital media in transforming family life?

To answer these questions, this chapter begins by outlining an approach to understanding the family that takes into account the social and cultural diversity of contemporary family forms. Then, a particular perspective on digital media is outlined, one that uses a techno-social approach to avoid assumptions that technology determines family life or that family life is somehow separate from technological transformations. Finally, the approaches outlined in the opening sections form the basis of an exploration of digital media practices in families across the life span, from partnering to pregnancy and adoption to parenting, family support, and aged care.

From "the Family" to Family Practices

In the 1950s, there was a strong consensus regarding "the family," captured in Murdock's ([1949] 1965, 1) definition of the family:

> A social group characterized by common residence, economic cooperation and reproduction. It includes adults of both sexes, at least two of whom maintain a socially approved sexual relationship, and one or more children, own or adopted, of the sexually cohabiting adults

Murdock was attempting to provide a definition of the family that encompassed the full variety of family forms from around the world. However, he included a fundamental assumption that the family was a heterosexual couple responsible for the shared raising of children. This is perhaps not surprising. In Murdock's time and place—1950s America—the dominant family form (both ideologically and demographically) was the nuclear family, made up of the breadwinner father, his stay-home wife, and their dependent children (Lasch 1977; Coontz 2016).

Fast-forward to the twenty-first century. Across the world, what is considered to be "normal" family life has been transformed. Families now include same-sex couples and parents, single-parent families, step and blended families, stay-home fathers and working mothers, couples who "live apart together," and transnational families who live in different homes in different countries (e.g., Weeks, Heaphy, and Donovan 2001; Beck-Gernsheim 2002; Baldassar, Baldock, and Wilding 2007; Beck and Beck-Gernsheim 2013; Holmes 2014; Wilding 2018). Reproductive technologies have transformed what it means to be a mother or a father, by enabling the work of conception, pregnancy, and childrearing to be separated across individuals and dispersed across nations. Shifts in gendered norms increasingly expect women to sustain careers while raising children and men to contribute to child care while building careers. Norms of parenting, aged care, and family support are also transforming, contributing to concerns about the emergence of intensive mothering, sandwich generations, and care crises.

These complex changes to the family are of interest here for at least two reasons. First, these transformations in family forms are closely linked to the emergence of digital media. For example, it is difficult to imagine a global movement supporting LGBTQI+ rights of marriage and parenting without the capacity to use digital media to raise awareness, share information, and offer support across distance. Similarly, it is difficult to imagine how family members might connect with each other across distance without telephones, the internet, and communication apps. Family is no longer lived only in the family home. It is also increasingly and simultaneously lived online. Second, this complex picture of family life doesn't allow for an easy definition of "the family." It is no longer possible to say that the family is made up of a household containing a man, a woman, and their children. There are too many configurations of family to allow for a single, simple definition. So how do sociologists respond to this complex and messy picture of family life? How do we continue to research "the family," when the nature of the family is so diverse across the world, and its shared features are far from clear?

With social and cultural change happening around the world, rapidly and unevenly, sociologists have been grappling with new concepts and theoretical frameworks to help make sense of these new relational contexts. Some sociologists have sought to avoid the term "family" by using other terms, such as "intimacy" or "personal life" (Giddens 1991, 1992; Smart 2007; Jamieson 2011; May and Nordqvist 2019). However, this use of new terms is not ideal, not least because it fails to fully account for the fact that people still refer to their families as "family" (Gilding 2010). An alternative approach, captured most clearly in the work of David Morgan (1996, 2013), is to stop focusing on "family" and instead pay attention to "family practices." This approach leaves aside the question of how to define "the family" and instead draws attention to "those relationships and activities that are constructed as having to do with family matters" (Morgan 1996, 192). Instead of thinking about what family "is," this approach asks us to pay attention to what family "does," or what people do in the name of family.

The advantage of this approach is that it provides a means of thinking about family that allows for current and continuing social and cultural change. Family becomes defined by and evident in the everyday things that people do as part of maintaining and being part of a family, whatever form that family takes, including sharing family meals and celebrations, calling each other by particular familial terms, taking and displaying family photographs, contributing to family decisions, or creating and participating in a WhatsApp group of family members (Weeks, Heaphy, and Donovan 2001; Finch 2007). A focus on family practices does not need to include any assumptions about those family practices. Instead, it investigates what people consider to be "family" and how they enact that vision of family. For social researchers, this allows an analysis of the role of gender, sexuality, ethnicity, class, culture, and other differences in those meanings and practices of family life. Family practices, then, might be perceived as fluid and changeable at the level of individual families. However, they can also be observed and analyzed for the ways in which they contribute to or are shaped by larger social structures and cultural norms. This means that the concept of family practices is particularly useful for thinking about social change and cultural diversity in families, relationships, and intimacy. It is also useful for thinking about the ways in which digital media are shaping and being shaped by family life. Before further exploring this last point, it is necessary to outline a useful approach to thinking about digital media.

Digital Media: A Techno-Social Approach

It is relatively common for new technologies, including digital media, to be understood as innovations that are reshaping the world, transforming not only how we do things but also what we do, how we see ourselves, and what we consider to be important (Wajcman 1991). Thus, we hear claims that digital media are doing everything from giving children short attention spans to providing them with unprecedented opportunities for creativity, from undermining democracy to empowering marginalized voices. Such arguments tend to rely on a form of technological determinism, which assumes that the technologies with which we live are shaping the worlds in which we live.

In contrast, this chapter draws on alternative sociological arguments to think about the role and impact of digital media. This approach assumes that, while technologies do impact upon and reshape the worlds in which they are used, we also need to acknowledge that technologies are simultaneously impacted upon and shaped by the social worlds in which they are designed and adopted. This occurs in at least two ways. First, technologies are formed within particular sets of social arrangements that shape not only who is designing and manufacturing them but also which new technologies are considered valuable and worth designing, who is expected to have access to and make use of those technologies, and what purposes are intended and legitimate uses of those technologies. Second, it is important to note that, once released into society, new technologies are almost always adopted and appropriated by users who were not initially imagined or anticipated and for purposes that were not built into the original design (e.g., Kramarae 1988). The example of the humble telephone helps to illustrate this point.

The landline telephone was invented by men, to replace the telegraph and support masculine endeavors in commerce and industry (Fischer 1988). When it was first introduced into the domestic home, it was not perceived as a familial technology. Indeed, until at least the 1920s, there was a strong resistance to the idea that the telephone might be used for such "frivolous" (feminine) purposes as the domain of social interactions (Wajcman 1995; de Sola Pool 1977). However, women did use this new tool in their homes. Furthermore, they used it to perform the unpaid and distinctly feminine labor that di Leonardo (1987) has aptly termed "kinwork," such as keeping in touch, providing support, and maintaining social relations of care across families and communities. Women also used the telephone to reduce the loneliness of lives that were spent largely within the home, alone, performing domestic labor and child care tasks (de Sola Pool 1977; Rakow 1988). Yet, the telephone was not designed for these uses. As Rakow (1988, 183) suggests, "If there had been a genuine interest in easing farm women's isolation, telephone sets would have been designed differently so that women could talk together while they worked."

This history of the telephone helps us to understand that all technologies are produced within social relations, are used within social and cultural contexts, and contribute to the shaping of social lives and interactions. Thus, while technology might contribute to change, it is always only one factor among many in those changes. Technologies are always social, because they are always embedded in and contribute to existing sets of social, cultural, and political relations (MacKenzie and Wajcman 1999). We can see this in analyses of the development and uses of digital media. For example, there is clear evidence that broader social and economic inequalities are typically reproduced in the digital sphere, tending to favor the wealthy over the poor, men over women, and younger adults over those aged 60+ (e.g., Ragnedda and Mutsvairo 2018; Thomas et al. 2019). However, it is also the case that some affordances of digital media are disrupting some sites of inequality. For example, mobile phones and internet access have become essential resources for refugees, providing them with valuable access to both economic resources and a sense of connection to families and communities dispersed around the world (e.g., Harney 2013; Marlowe 2019; Udwan, Leurs, and Alencar 2020). At the same time, other forms of digital media are simultaneously creating new opportunities for states to monitor and constrain refugee and migrant mobility, further reinforcing entrenched power and inequalities (e.g., Ajana 2013; Wilding and Gifford 2013; Latonero and Kift 2018).

An analysis of the role of digital media within the space of families and intimacy, then, requires attention to multiple dimensions at once. On the one hand, it is important to be alert to the ways in which preexisting inequalities are embedded in the digital media that people are using and the ways in which they shape the affordances available to users. On the other hand, we must also pay attention to the ways in which users navigate, resist, and transform digital media to suit their own needs and maximize their own opportunities. Finally, we must also pay attention to this dynamic of affordances and resistances within larger social, cultural, political, and economic contexts. It is this balancing act of reflecting on the ways in which digital media both shape and are shaped by family practices that are explored in the following examples of family life, from partnering to childbirth and adoption to parenting, family support, and aged care.

Family Practices, Intimacy, and Digital Media across the Life Course

It is not possible to do justice here to the large and growing body of literature examining the intersections of family, intimacy, and digital media (but see, for example, Neves and Casimiro 2018; Van Hook, McHale, and King 2018). Rather than attempting a comprehensive account, this section instead reviews examples from across three moments in the life course: partnering, childbirth and parenting, and family support and aged care. The examples are selected to support an exploration of the larger questions that will be the focus of the concluding section: How and why are families using digital media? And what does this tell us about the role of digital media in transforming family life?

Partnering

By the 1990s, online dating was rapidly emerging as a multibillion-dollar industry (Arvidsson 2006). Online dating services made it possible for subscribers to access large numbers of potential partners, while sophisticated algorithms made it possible to streamline the search for a preferred partner by applying ever more refined criteria (Illouz 2007), including sex and gender diversity, ethnic and religious identities, specific age groups, and international cross-cultural online relationships (Rochadiat, Tong, and Novak 2017; Chen and Liu 2019; Pananakhonsab 2016). Online dating was not a completely new phenomenon. Rather, it continued a pattern that had been well established during the twentieth century, of using media such as newspapers to advertise for a marital or dating partner. By the 1980s, advertisements to attract a romantic or marriage partner had become a relatively commonplace practice, providing an efficient way of finding a partner in a work-focused late modern world (Jagger 2001).

By the 2010s, the online dating scene was further transformed by mobile dating apps. While some were simply an extension of existing online dating sites, others were a completely new product (Albury et al. 2017). In the past, advertising for a partner had been typically framed as part of a romantic quest for a life partner. However, mobile dating apps instead emphasized the pleasures of a gamified experience of dating and normalized a "hook-up" culture in which sexual intimacy was freely available and intimate partners were easily discarded (Albury 2017). In response, various commentators raised concerns about increased promiscuity and about the inherent risks in meeting strangers for casual sex, while young people were reporting a sense of pressure to conform to new norms of short-term sexual intimacy (Farvid and Braun 2017).

For some scholars, online dating and dating apps are evidence of a commoditization of the self that has moved beyond the world of work, where we routinely sell our skills and expertise to potential employers. Now, it seems we are required to package and sell ourselves to potential intimate partners (Coupland 1996; Illouz 2007). This might suggest a certain democratization of the search for a partner, with everyone having equal capacity to present themselves and to select from the available partners on offer. However, not all players in the relationship marketplace are positioned equally. This becomes particularly clear in the case of international online dating sites. Feminists have raised concerns that online dating websites objectify and commodify women from poorer nations, presenting them as products to be consumed by men in wealthier nations (Halualani 2015).

This straightforward picture of exploitation is somewhat challenged by ethnographic researchers who pay attention to women's motivations for participating in online cross-cultural dating. They suggest that online dating, while clearly hierarchical and unequal, also does provide opportunities for some women to assert agency in their intimate lives and avoid constraints they face in their local contexts (Constable 2003). For example, a Thai woman who has been divorced is highly unlikely to find a male partner in Thailand but remains attractive to men in Australia or the United States, where divorce is not associated with the same level of stigma (Pananakhonsab 2016). She is able to meet these potential partners using digital media. However, at the same time, women in poorer nations have less power than men in wealthier nations to determine the course of the relationship. They must try and distinguish between (desirable) men seeking marriage or a long-term relationship and (undesirable) men who are seeking a holiday girlfriend or who might be an abusive partner. While online dating helps to expand opportunities, women remain embedded in global inequalities of class, race, and gender that impact their opportunities and outcomes (Constable 2003; Pananakhonsab 2016).

Online dating tools are changing what it means to have an intimate relationship so that some scholars now argue that digital media have placed more emphasis on "looks" (David and Cambre 2016). This emphasis on what is "seen" encourages people to focus on preconfigured fantasies about their partners, rather than adjusting to the actual person who sits behind the image. This creates a danger that online daters might be responding to internalized sets of expectations about others, rather than the realities of social interaction. In the process, online dating apps might be reproducing stereotypes of gender, sexuality, ethnicity, race, and so forth that reinforce social inequalities (David and Cambre 2016).

This notion of relationships being about the self rather than about the couple is not a new one. Indeed, theorists such as Anthony Giddens (1991, 1992) were suggesting something similar long before online dating apps were even possible. Giddens argued that broader processes of individualization and detraditionalization were breaking down social categories such as gender and class that had previously shaped key moments in the life course, including partnering. Instead, he suggested that marriage and romantic relationships were being replaced by the "pure relationship," a relationship "entered into for its own sake, for what can be derived by each person from a sustained association with another; and which is continued only in so far as it is thought by both parties to deliver enough satisfactions for each individual to stay within it" (Giddens 1992, 58). Unlike the 1950s heterosexual marriage relationship, which required men and women to divide into breadwinner and caregiver, the pure relationship does not assume that partners will fulfill a particular role. Instead, intimacy in the pure relationship is built through mutual disclosure and the sharing of innermost thoughts about the self. Also unlike 1950s expectations about marriage, the pure relationship does not rely on an expectation of a long-term relationship. Rather, each partner is expected to leave once that relationship is no longer satisfying.

Digital media and online dating appear to be uniquely suitable for the pure relationship. Online tools allow people to meet on equal terms, enter into only those relationships that deliver satisfaction, and only remain for as long as a relationship delivers satisfaction. It also seems that each partner has equal power to exit that relationship, having the capacity to block contact with the other person at the click of a button.

Mutual disclosure is also the primary mode of interacting, with people relying primarily on the sharing of innermost thoughts to sustain online intimacies.

However, the online pure relationship is not necessarily as pleasurable or even as equal as it might at first appear. Fears abound that mutual disclosure in online environments might be inauthentic, with evidence of online intimacies being used to steal money as well as hearts (e.g., Duguay 2017). The capacity to leave a relationship easily and without consequence means that relationships are now equivalent to other consumer products that can be easily thrown away (Bauman 2003). Meanwhile, it is not clear that the pure relationship is actually as equal as Giddens suggested. Inequalities of gender, class, race, sexuality, and so forth continue to shape people's opportunities (Jamieson 1998; Cherlin 2020). Not everyone has equal power to enter or exit relationships or to participate in them on their own terms. For example, women are still expected to allow men to initiate contact and lead the progression of a heterosexual relationship in order to avoid being perceived as too "pushy," older people are perceived as less desirable than younger people, and lighter skins are consistently given preference over darker skins (e.g., Jha and Adelman 2009; Chen and Liu 2019). In practice, online interactions and representations are often highly normative, even in non-heteronormative communities, with dating apps such as Tinder supporting detrimental gendered and sexual identities (Thompson 2018; Ferris and Duguay 2019). Moreover, the underlying logics of the algorithms that shape people's experiences and apparent agency in who and how they meet others online remain invisible (David and Cambre 2016; Macleod and McArthur 2019). This leaves some digital media users feeling ambivalent about the digital media that are increasingly ubiquitous in their search for intimate partners (Miles 2017).

At the same time, there is evidence that digital media are an important tool for maintaining long-term long-distance relationships. Labor market constraints require growing numbers of intimate partners to live at a distance in order to access employment and build careers. In this case, digital media provide an essential tool for maintaining the relationship. In particular, digital media allow couples to sustain "incidental intimacy" at a distance, by sending each other short messages on a regular basis, checking in with each other throughout the day, sending links to amusing videos or social media posts, and photographs of their meals, setting, or other events throughout the day (Holmes 2014). For cross-cultural international couples who meet through online dating sites, digital media allow them to interact with each and build their relationship, including by using digital translation tools to help communicate across language barriers or using video calls to "meet" each other in an online date (Pananakhonsab 2016). On the other hand, phones can also facilitate intimate partner surveillance. This was clear in a project exploring the long-distance marriages of women in Senegal and their husbands working in other countries (Hannaford 2015). Jealous husbands would use communication tools to monitor their intimate partners, requiring women to constantly be available to be seen and respond immediately to messages and calls, in order to provide reassurance of their fidelity. This included one young woman whose outfit required daily approval by her husband via a Skype call.

In sum, digital media are providing new means of meeting new partners and appear to be influencing new modes of relating and intimacy. In some cases, this appears to enhance agency, as in the case of women escaping local gendered norms that would otherwise limit their partnering options (Pananakhonsab 2016; Amundsen 2020; Chen and Liu 2019; Hobbs, Owen, and Gerber 2017). However, there is another side to this story, one in which existing inequalities are further exacerbated, including the reinforcing of heteronormative, gendered, classed, racial, and ethnic hierarchies.

Parenting

Digital media are just one of the technologies involved in transforming family life. Advances in reproductive technologies have also created new opportunities for a broader range of people to become parents. This has facilitated social, cultural, and legal changes in the meanings of parenthood, such as the separation of different biological and social modes of motherhood and fatherhood. While reproductive technologies are not the focus in this chapter, they do intersect in important ways with digital media. This is because, alongside attention to the separation of parental roles, there is a renewed interest in identifying the mechanisms and processes through which parenting roles are established, affirmed, and enacted. It is in this respect that digital media have come to play an increasingly important role, by making more explicit the family practices (Morgan 2013) and processes of kinning (Howell 2006) that construct both parents and parent–child relationships.

Becoming a new parent for the first time is an inherently anxious time, requiring adjustment to a new role and an accompanying revision of existing identities and practices. This sense of anxiety has arguably intensified over the past century, evident in the emergence of "intensive motherhood" (Hays 1996) and "involved fatherhood" (Jackson 2012), which are united by an expectation that parents will invest in optimum outcomes for their children. Even prior to conception, new parents are encouraged to pay attention to their own health choices in order to maximize the prospects of their children. Arguably, this anxiety is a key factor in prompting new parents to engage with websites, online forums, and mobile apps in order to access information and reassurance to support and shape their parenting practices, not just during pregnancy and childbirth but throughout the life course (Doty and Dworkin 2014).

Mobile apps and internet sites for pregnancy and parenting are highly diverse and serve multiple purposes for their users (Lupton, Pedersen, and Thomas 2016). For example, they enable parents to monitor and record the changes in their bodies during pregnancy and the changes in their babies after birth. These include nutritional information, weight changes, ultrasound scans, sleep patterns, and milestones. They also provide an opportunity to record photographs of changing bodies of both mother and child. In addition, some apps enable parents to connect with others who are going through similar experiences, providing opportunities to generate social networks that are relevant to their new social roles as parents. These networks are particularly important for parents of children with health conditions or parents from migrant and ethnic communities, by providing an opportunity for exchanging and exploring experiences that are outside of the local social and cultural norm (Swallow et al. 2012; Williams Veazey 2020).

The impact of parenting and pregnancy apps also goes beyond simple access to information or social networks. They are also used to establish a relationship between parent and child as members of a family. This begins even before the baby is born, with digital media providing parents with opportunities to imagine their child as an interactive contributor to the family. This is arguably another instance of the "preconfigured fantasies" of others that are associated with online dating apps, this time applied to the parent–child relationship instead of the couple relationship. For example, parents can receive app-generated messages that are purported to come from the baby, such as "Hi Mommy! When will I see you for the first time?" or animated versions of ultrasound scans that translate medical images into aesthetic and emotionally charged tools for the imagination (Lupton and Thomas 2015). As in the case of online dating imagery, the object here is not so much to generate a "real" relationship with the fetus as to support the fantasy work of the parents in imagining and preparing for the arrival of the new infant. These practices are particularly evident for parents using a transnational surrogate, who rely on regular images and updates via digital media to help them track, monitor, and engage with the development of their prospective child from a distance (Carone, Baiocco, and Lingiardi 2017). As one Italian parent said of their overseas surrogacy experience,

> We didn't say "we are pregnant" right away, we needed time, a multitude of Skype calls with our surrogate, a collection of ultrasounds of our baby . . . [surrogate's name] played her role very well, she helped us to turn "that" child into "our" child week by week.
>
> (Carone, Baiocco, and Lingiardi 2017, 185)

Other parents, too, rely on digital media to help them sustain their identities as parents across distance. The phenomenon of long-distance parenting has grown with the expansion of temporary labor migration (Parreñas 2005). In the 1970s and 1980s, labor migration markets encouraged men to leave behind their families in order to work overseas in industries such as construction, mining, and seafaring. Nations such as the Philippines benefited economically from the remittances being sent back. Meanwhile, the impact on families was rarely discussed, possibly because the absent father was a relatively culturally acceptable extension of the male breadwinner household that was prevalent at the time. Instead of leaving for work each morning and coming home each evening, fathers would leave for months or years at a time in order to fulfill their paternal role as providers. While there was some acknowledgment of his reduced opportunity to establish intimate relationships with his children, this was not presented as a public crisis (Parreñas 2008). However, by the early 2000s the majority of temporary migrant labor opportunities were in feminized industries, such as nursing, child care, aged care, and domestic service (Asis, Huang, and Yeoh 2004). Economies such as the Philippines were already heavily reliant on the remittances of overseas foreign workers. To continue this source of income, large numbers of women began to travel overseas to work. The combination of high costs of living in the countries where they worked and the restrictions on family reunion migration means that often these women were required to leave their children behind to be cared for by others (Yeates 2012). Widespread concerns were raised about the public crisis of abandoned children left without mothers and emasculated men who relied on the earnings of their wives (Parreñas 2005). Children reported feeling that they had missed out on an essential part of their childhood as a result of lacking their mother as the "light of the home" (Asis, Huang, and Yeoh 2004). Rather than fathers, it was grandmothers, aunts, and paid domestic servants who filled the gap left behind by the overseas foreign worker. The gendered norms of the family household remained firmly intact, even as women became empowered as income earners to make broader contributions to their extended families.

With the expansion of digital media in recent years, the situation of overseas foreign workers has been further transformed (Parreñas 2014). It is now possible for migrant parents to engage in and monitor the lives of their children on a daily basis through social media, to share meals with them via video call, and to exchange frequent text messages in order to provide emotional support during key moments in a child's life (Madianou and Miller 2012). Overseas workers can now be virtually "present" at family events, such as Christmas, birthdays, and funerals through Skype or Zoom (McKay 2017). The flow of information is also more diffused throughout the extended family network, with all members of the family posting updates through apps such as WhatsApp, rather than overseas foreign workers relying on the letters sent and received from one key family member (Wilding 2006). The result of this new "polymedia" environment is that mothers now report feeling that they are able to both earn an income and be full and complete mothers who can perform the expectations of "intensive mothering" that usually prompted their migration in the first place, to earn more income to invest in their children's future success (Madianou and Miller 2012). Children also report feeling that they have an intimate relationship with their mother, that they can rely on her in times of difficulty, and that it feels almost as if she were physically present (Madianou and Miller 2012). In fact, in some cases, children feel that there is almost too much contact, with intensive mothering from afar sometimes experienced as a claustrophobic overinvolvement. New obligations to be seen and to keep in touch sometimes impinge on their sense of freedom to live their life locally, instead requiring constant attention to key family members who are living in a different time zone.

Parenting in non-migrant families has also been transformed by access to digital media. For example, the practices of intensive parenting have been expanded, to include monitoring the location of children with geolocational apps, maintaining a record of their physical activity or mental health using apps and websites, and providing social media accounts for displaying the achievements of children to the public (Haddon 2013; Mascheroni 2013, 2020; Lupton, Pedersen, and Thomas 2016; Lupton and Williamson 2017). There is some debate about the implications of these affordances for parenting and for the lives of children. Some suggest that the increased digital surveillance of children leaves them vulnerable to a loss of privacy and the exploitation of their data by digital media companies (Mascheroni 2020). Access to digital media has also become a site of conflict and contestation between parents and children, with the management of screen time and access to mobile phones and the internet presenting a new domain for intergenerational conflict between children, parents, and grandparents (Haddon 2013; Elias, Nimrod, and Lemish 2019; Mukherjee 2020). The ubiquitous presence of digital media in the lives of parents also adds another challenge, by blurring the division between work and family. Parents are increasingly working at home, during time that was previously allocated to family, leading to new opportunities for work–family conflicts and pressures, reflecting an ongoing broader process of change that is squeezing the family out of work–life balance and changing the temporal routines of the family home (Sakamoto 2018; Chambers 2019).

The processes of individualization evident in relation to online dating are also evident in relation to children's uses of digital media. In past generations, media consumption was typically located within a family household environment. For example, parents controlled the television remote and socialized their children into viewing the same types of content they were consuming themselves (Morley 1986). In this respect, media access was shaped by the gender and age hierarchies that dominated other aspects of family life. The introduction of digital media and digital devices has disrupted the hierarchies that previously shaped media consumption. Because digital devices are aimed at individual users, they provide more opportunities for children and parents to separate into independent practices of media consumption. This raises important questions about the potential loss of the family practices that constitute the family. Does individualized media consumption provide fewer opportunities for parents and children to interact and, thus, undermine their relationships? While this is always a possibility, research continues to suggest that one of the main uses of digital media and digital devices is in fact to stay connected with family and to coordinate family activities (Kennedy and Wellman 2007).

A more positive interpretation of the impact of individualization of media consumption alerts us to the potential democratizing of the family, including a reduction in hierarchies based on age and generation. For example, individualized access to digital media means that children are no longer completely reliant on their parents for knowledge about their world. They have a greater capacity to independently access the education and information that they deem relevant to them (Nathanson 2018). Furthermore, children increasingly play a role in introducing their parents to new devices and content, drawing on their own skills in media consumption to share alternative mediated worlds and practices with family members (Worrell 2021). This helps to disrupt generational hierarchies, by replacing dependent relationships with interdependent relationships, in which each member of the family is able to both contribute and receive different types of digital and non-digital support, regardless of age. Each family member is also able to participate in (and is subject to) the practices of "intimate surveillance" that constitute digital family practices (Sinanan and Hjorth 2018).

Intergenerational Support and Aging

Relationships between dependent children and their caregiver parents are not the only family domain transformed by digital media. Broader patterns of intergenerational contact and support are also undergoing change, including between adult children and their aging parents (Knodel 2014; Baldassar and Wilding 2020). One of the challenges of the twentieth century, acknowledged by classic sociological theorists such as Talcott Parsons (1949), was the impact of labor markets on intergenerational support within the family. Increasingly, access to employment required moving some distance away from the parental home, leading to questions about who would provide care and support to aging parents. The expansion of women's employment participation further exacerbated this trend, leading some to question whether family solidarity might undergo a steep decline.

However, a series of recent studies of intergenerational support suggests that, in fact, family contact and support between adult children and their parents are either remaining steady or increasing—especially across distance (Treas and Gubernskaya 2018; see also Baldassar, Baldock, and Wilding 2007; Albertini, Kohli, and Vogel 2007; Swartz 2009; Gubernskaya and Treas 2016; Peng et al. 2018). Moreover, digital devices such as the mobile phone appear to be central to this pattern (Treas and Gubernskaya 2018). It is becoming increasingly clear that a majority of people continue to value their family relationships and engage in regular phone calls, text messages, and video calls in order to sustain those relationships across time and space. For example, men and women from India leave their aging parents behind in order to earn incomes that can pay for medicines, accommodation, and ongoing support for daily needs (Ahlin 2018a). For them, digital media are an essential part of the family's routines and practices, allowing migrants and aging parents to benefit from both close contact and distant employment opportunities.

Nevertheless, it is important to recognize that not all family members have equal access to digital media (Cabalquinto 2018; Lim 2016). For example, according to the Australian Digital Inclusion Index, adults aged 55 and over are among the least digitally included populations. While their engagement with mobile phones and the internet is increasing, the gap in usage rates between older adults and younger adults continues to grow. This gap is even more problematic when older adults are on a low income or are living in rural areas, where accommodation is more affordable (Malta and Wilding 2018). As a result, some family members might be less able to participate in intergenerational relations of support than others. However, research demonstrates that families work hard at mitigating these inequalities (Cabalquinto 2018), including by giving help to older adults to access digital devices and platforms (Worrell 2021) and "tinkering" with available technologies and platforms to identify the ones that best suit the needs of all family members (Ahlin 2018a). In the process, the devices that family members use in order to keep in touch become objects of care themselves, with "good care" across distance requiring attention to caring both for people and for the objects of communication (Ahlin 2018b; Wilding et al. 2020).

The global asymmetries of power that shape and are shaped by digital media practices are particularly evident in the families of forced migrants and refugees. Increasingly, forced migrants consider access to mobile phones and the internet to be just as fundamentally essential as food, water, and shelter (UNHCR 2016). In cases of forced migration, digital media become a lifeline for maintaining the family and providing reassurance that family members are safe and well. One woman, living in Australia with her older mother, explained that regular phone calls to their family members in Myanmar was essential: "They get sick very often and my mother wants to hear their voice, so I call them once a day. ... If we use the internet, we can see each other when we talk ... it's like medicine when they get to talk and see each other. It can cure diseases" (Wilding et al. 2020, 649; see also Robertson, Wilding, and Gifford 2016). At the same time, not all kin within transnational families of forced migrants have equal access to the tools of communication. For some, using digital media is risky, creating a new means of state surveillance of vulnerable people. Thus, family members acknowledge that they simultaneously inhabit online and offline worlds, each with its own power asymmetries, risks, and opportunities that require careful navigation and negotiation (Lim, Bork-Huffer, and Yeoh 2016).

Transformations of Family, Intimacy, and Digital Media

These examples make it abundantly clear that digital media have transformed family practices. Kin who are separated by distance can now engage in everyday practices of incidental intimacy, providing them with a sense of familyhood and connection. However, it is less clear that these practices are contributing to more equal lives and worlds. There is little evidence, for example, that heteronormative gender roles in the family are shifting. Online dating practices tend to amplify existing gendered and sexual norms and inequalities. Women who migrate for work remain responsible for intensive mothering of their children and do so with digital media. While digital media are often associated with young people, this has not contributed to young people feeling empowered, with many subject to greater levels of surveillance. Neither have digital media reshaped global political or economic inequalities. For example, while refugee families are now more able to keep in touch with kin dispersed across the world, there is no evidence that this new capacity is contributing to a fairer world in which they and their family members can more easily escape persecution or access reunion on a temporary or permanent basis.

Recent decades have been characterized by increasing diversity of family forms and family practices. However, as digital media become a more common part of everyday family life for both migrants and non-migrants, it is worth asking whether the individualizing tendencies embedded in them are bringing a halt to that diversity and perhaps contributing to new forms of homogenization of intimacy and family practices. More research needs to be done to explore this possibility. There is almost no consideration of indigenous or other uses of digital media to sustain non-individualistic relational modes of family and community (but see Carlson and Dreher 2018; Carlson and Frazer 2020). To what extent are colonial forces of marginalization, racialization, and individualization reinforced through digital media devices and platforms and with what impacts on kinship and family networks? Similarly, there is a gap in understandings of non-heterosexual practices of digital media to enact family practices, including across distance (but see Andreassen 2017). Are these distinct from those of heterosexual families? Or is there a narrowing of diversity in the doing of family, even as the forms that family take are growing in variety?

Questions also need to be asked about the role that highly influential digital media companies and creators might be playing in the shaping of the future of the family. Will recent gains in the democratizing of family and intimate relationships be reversed as a result of a narrowing of digital media discourses about gender, generation, and family? Will the relatively recent patterns of involved fatherhood continue with digital media engagement, or will they revert to more distant surveillance practices that reassert gendered and generational hierarchies? How is emotion work being transformed by the growing reliance on digital media to demonstrate affection and care? Will care—including the care of older adults—increasingly be relegated to autonomous robots that allow family members to monitor patterns of everyday behavior from a distance? If so, will this result in less caring families?

Questions such as these allude to science fiction dystopias of loss of familial and intimate connections and reinforcement of strict hierarchies of surveillance and authority. We have not reached that point yet. However, such a future remains within reach, particularly if digital media designers are allowed to continue to work invisibly to implement their visions of the world through new devices and communication technologies. What is needed now is social science research that examines the ways in which not just users but also designers and distributors of digital media are shaping social and cultural norms of intimate and family life. In the domain of users, there is also a need for more attention to effective strategies for resisting the norms and assumptions of intimacy and family that are built into digital media devices and platforms. Such research requires attention to what people "do" in creating their families and intimate lives. But it also requires attention to what is not said, to the constellations of fantasies, assumptions, and predispositions that underlie and shape those practices of doing family and intimacy. This might require more attention to creative methods of documenting the imaginings and fantasies of new possibilities in relationships and intimate lives.

In conclusion, digital media have become central features in families across the life course. They support family practices of reciprocity, care, and support and facilitate commitment to others across time and space. At the same time, they enable surveillance and control and contribute to the extension of hierarchies and inequalities across distance. This helps to explain the rapid and widespread adoption of digital media practices. They serve the diverse interests of relationships across the world. In the process, they appear to be reinforcing entrenched inequalities, with only a few moments of escape into alternative, potentially more liberating and more culturally diverse futures. We now need new explanations of these patterns of normativity and constraint, to enable family members and intimate partners to pursue more satisfying and diverse futures for all, that do not simply reproduce uncritical assumptions about families and intimacy that might otherwise be designed into the ubiquitous digital media tools of everyday life.

REFERENCES

Ahlin, Tanja. 2018a. "Only Near Is Dear? Doing Elderly Care with Everyday ICTs in Indian Transnational Families." *Medical Anthropology Quarterly* 32, no. 1: 85–102.

Ahlin, Tanja. 2018b. "Frequent Callers: 'Good Care' with ICTs in Indian Transnational Families." *Medical Anthropology* 39, no. 1: 69–82.

Ajana, Btihaj. 2013. "Asylum, Identity Management and Biometric Control." *Journal of Refugee Studies* 26, no. 4: 576–595.

Albertini, Marco, Martin Kohli, and Claudia Vogel. 2007. "Intergenerational Transfers of Time and Money in European Families: Common Patterns–Different Regimes?" *Journal of European Social Policy* 17, no. 4: 319–334.

Albury, Kath. 2017. "Heterosexual Casual Sex: From Free Love to Tinder." In *The Routledge Companion to Media, Sex and Sexuality*, edited by Clarissa Smith, Feona Attwood, and Brian McNair, 81–90. London and New York: Routledge.

Albury, Kath, Jean Burgess, Ben Light, Kane Race, and Rowan Wilken. 2017. "Data Cultures of Mobile Dating and Hook-Up Apps: Emerging Issues for Critical Social Science Research." *Big Data & Society* 4, no. 2. https://doi.org/10.1177/2053951717720950.

Amundsen, Rikke. 2020. "Hetero-Sexting as Mediated Intimacy Work: 'Putting Something on the Line.'" *New Media & Society*. Published ahead of print September 30, 2020. https://doi.org/10.1177/1461444820962452.

Andreassen, Rikke. 2017. "New Kinships, New Family Formations and Negotiations of Intimacy via Social Media Sites." *Journal of Gender Studies* 26, no. 3: 361–371.

Arvidsson, Adam. 2006. "'Quality Singles': Internet Dating and the Work of Fantasy." *New Media & Society* 8, no. 4: 671–690.

Asis, Maruja, Shirlena Huang, and Brenda S. A. Yeoh. 2004. "When the Light of the Home Is Abroad: Unskilled Female Migration and the Filipino Family." *Singapore Journal of Tropical Geography* 25, no. 2: 198–215.

Baldassar, Loretta, Cora Vellekoop Baldock, and Raelene Wilding. 2007. *Families Caring across Borders: Migration, Ageing and Transnational Caregiving*. Basingstoke, UK, and New York: Palgrave.

Baldassar, Loretta, and Raelene Wilding. 2020. "Migration, Ageing and Digital Kinning." *The Gerontologist* 60, no. 2: 313–321.

Bauman, Zygmunt. 2003. *Liquid Love: On the Frailty of Human Bonds*. Cambridge: Polity Press.

Beck-Gernsheim, Elisabeth. 2002. *Reinventing the Family: In Search of New Lifestyles*. Cambridge: Polity Press.

Beck, Ulrich, and Elisabeth Beck-Gernsheim. 2013. *Distant Love*. Cambridge: Polity Press.

Cabalquinto, Earvin Charles B. 2018. " 'We're not Only Here but We're There in Spirit': Asymmetrical Mobile Intimacy and the Transnational Filipino Family." *Mobile Media & Communication* 6, no. 1: 37–52.

Carlson, Bronwyn, and Tanja Dreher. 2018. "Introduction: Indigenous Innovation in Social Media." *Media International Australia* 169, no. 1: 16–20.

Carlson, Bronwyn, and Ryan Frazer. 2020. " 'They Got Filters': Indigenous Social Media, the Settler Gaze and a Politics of Hope." *Social Media + Society* 6, no. 2. https://doi.org/10.1177/2056305120925261.

Carone, Nicola, Roberto Baiocco, and Vittorio Lingiardi. 2017. "Italian Gay Fathers' Experiences of Transnational Surrogacy and Their Relationship with the Surrogate Pre- and Post-birth." *Reproductive Biomedicine Online* 34, no. 2: 181–190.

Chambers, Deborah. 2019. "Emerging Temporalities in the Multiscreen Home." *Media, Culture & Society*. Published ahead of print August 18, 2019. https://doi.org/10.1177/0163443719867851.

Chen, Xu, and Tingting Liu. 2019. "On 'Never Right-Swipe Whites' and 'Only Date Whites': Gendered and Racialized Digital Dating Experiences of the Australian Chinese Diaspora." *Information, Communication & Society* 24, no. 9: 1247–1264. https://doi.org/10.1080/1369118X.2019.1697341.

Cherlin, Andrew J. 2020. "Degrees of Change: An Assessment of the Deinstitutionalization of Marriage Thesis." *Journal of Marriage and Family* 82: 62–80.

Constable, Nicole. 2003. *Romance on a Global Stage: Pen Pals, Virtual Ethnography and "Mail Order" Marriages*. Berkeley: University of California Press.

Coontz, Stephanie. 2016. *The Way We Never Were*. New York: Basic Books.

Coupland, Justine. 1996. "Dating Advertisements: Discourses of the Commodified Self." *Discourse & Society* 7, no. 2: 187–207.

David, Gaby, and Carolina Cambre. 2016. "Screened Intimacies: Tinder and the Swipe Logic." *Social Media + Society* 2, no. 2: https://doi.org/10.1177/2056305116641976.

de Sola Pool, Ithiel. 1977. *The Social Impact of the Telephone*. Cambridge, MA: MIT Press.

di Leonardo, Micaela. 1987. "The Female World of Cards and Holidays: Women, Families, and the Work of Kinship." *Signs* 12, no. 3: 440–453.

Doty, Jennifer L., and Jodi Dworkin. 2014. "Online Social Support for Parents: A Critical Review." *Marriage & Family Review* 50, no. 2: 174–198.

Duguay, Stefanie. 2017. "Dressing up Tinderella: Interrogating Authenticity Claims on the Mobile Dating App Tinder." *Information, Communication & Society* 20, no. 3: 351–367.

Elias, Nelly, Galit Nimrod, and Dafna Lemish. 2019. "The Ultimate Treat? Young Israeli Children's Media Use under Their Grandparents' Care." *Journal of Children and Media* 13, no. 4: 472–483.

Farvid, Pantea, and Virginia Braun. 2017. "Unpacking the 'Pleasures' and 'Pains' of Heterosexual Casual Sex: Beyond Singular Understandings." *Journal of Sex Research* 54, no. 1: 73–90.

Ferris, Lindsay, and Stefanie Duguay. 2019. "Tinder's Lesbian Digital Imaginary: Investigating (Im)Permeable Boundaries of Sexual Identity on a Popular Dating App." *New Media & Society* 22, no. 3: 489–506.

Finch, Janet. 2007. "Displaying Families." *Sociology* 41, no. 1: 65–81.

Fischer, Claude S. 1988. " 'Touch Someone': The Telephone Industry Discovers Sociability." *Technology and Culture* 29, no. 1: 32–61.

Giddens, Anthony. 1991. *Modernity and Self-Identity: Self and Society in the Late Modern Age*. Stanford, CA: Stanford University Press.

Giddens, Anthony. 1992. *The Transformation of Intimacy: Sexuality, Love and Eroticism in Modern Societies.* Cambridge: Polity Press.

Gilding, Michael. 2010. "Reflexivity over and above Convention: The New Orthodoxy in the Sociology of Personal Life, Formerly Sociology of the Family." *British Journal of Sociology* 61, no. 4: 757–777.

Gubernskaya, Zoya, and Judith Treas. 2016. "Call Home? Mobile Phones and Contacts with Mother in 24 Countries." *Journal of Marriage and Family* 78, no. 5: 1237–1249.

Haddon, Leslie. 2013. "Mobile Media and Children." *Mobile Media & Communication* 1, no. 1: 89–95.

Halualani, Rona Tamiko. 2015. "The Intersecting Hegemonic Discourses of an Asian Mail-Order Bride Catalog: Pilipina 'Oriental Butterfly' Dolls for Sale." *Women's Studies in Communication* 18, no. 1: 45–64.

Hannaford, Dinah. 2015. "Technologies of the Spouse: Intimate Surveillance in Senegalese Transnational Marriages." *Global Networks* 15, no. 1: 43–59.

Harney, Nicholas. 2013. "Precarity, Affect and Problem Solving with Mobile Phones by Asylum Seekers, Refugees and Migrants in Naples, Italy." *Journal of Refugee Studies* 26, no. 4: 541–557.

Hays, Sharon. 1996. *The Cultural Contradictions of Motherhood.* New Haven, CT: Yale University Press.

Hobbs, Mitchell, Stephen Owen, and Livia Gerber. 2017. "Liquid Love? Dating Apps, Sex, Relationships and the Digital Transformation of Intimacy." *Journal of Sociology* 53, no. 2: 271–284.

Holmes, Mary. 2014. *Distance Relationships: Intimacy and Emotions amongst Academics and Their Partners in Dual Locations.* Basingstoke, UK, and New York: Palgrave.

Howell, Signe. 2006. *The Kinning of Foreigners.* New York and Oxford: Berghahn Books.

Illouz, Eva. 2007. *Cold Intimacies: The Making of Emotional Capitalism.* Cambridge: Polity Press.

Jackson, Brian. 2012. *Fatherhood.* New York and London: Routledge.

Jagger, Elizabeth. 2001. "Marketing Molly and Melville: Dating in a Postmodern, Consumer Society." *Sociology* 35, no. 1: 39–57.

Jamieson, Lynn. 1998. *Intimacy: Personal Relationships in Modern Societies.* Cambridge: Polity Press.

Jamieson, Lynn. 2011. "Intimacy as a Concept." *Sociological Research Online* 16, no. 4: 151–163.

Jha, Sonora, and Mara Adelman. 2009. "Looking for Love in All the White Places: A Study of Skin Color Preferences on Indian Matrimonial and Mate-Seeking Websites." *Studies in South Asian Film & Media* 1, no. 1: 65–83.

Kennedy, Tracy L. M., and Barry Wellman. 2007. "The Networked Household." *Information, Communication & Society* 10: 645–670.

Knodel, John. 2014. "Is Intergenerational Solidarity Really on the Decline? Cautionary Evidence from Thailand." *Asian Population Studies* 10, no. 2: 176–194. https://doi.org/10.1080/17441730.2014.902160.

Kramarae, Cheris. 1988. "Gotta Go Myrtle, Technology's at the Door." In *Technology and Women's Voices—Keeping in Touch*, edited by Cheris Kramarae, 1–11. London and New York: Routledge.

Lasch, Christopher. 1977. *Haven in a Heartless World.* New York: Basic Books.

Latonero, Mark, and Paula Kift. 2018. "On Digital Passages and Borders: Refugees and the New Infrastructure for Movement and Control." *Social Media & Society* 4, no. 1. https://doi.org/10.1177/2056305118764432.

Lim, Sun Sun. 2016. "Asymmetries in Asian Families' Domestication of Mobile Communication." In *Mobile Communication and the Family: Asian Experiences in Technology Domestication*, edited by S. S. Lim, 1–12. London: Springer.

Lim, Sun Sun, Tabea Bork-Huffer, and Brenda. S. A. Yeoh. 2016. "Mobility, Migration and New Media: Manoeuvring through Physical, Digital and Liminal Spaces." *New Media & Society* 18, no. 10: 2147–2154.

Lupton, Deborah, Sarah Pedersen, and Gareth M. Thomas. 2016. "Parenting and Digital Media: From the Early Web to Contemporary Digital Society." *Sociology Compass* 10, no. 8: 730–743.

Lupton, Deborah, and Gareth. M. Thomas. 2015. "Playing Pregnancy: The Ludification and Gamification of Expectant Motherhood in Smartphone Apps." *M/C Journal* 18, no. 5. https://doi.org/10.5204/mcj.1012

Lupton, Deborah, and Ben Williamson. 2017. "The Datafied Child." *New Media & Society* 19, no. 5: 780–794.

MacKenzie, Donald, and Judy Wajcman. 1999. *The Social Shaping of Technology*. 2nd ed. Buckingham, UK, and Philadelphia: Open University Press.

Macleod, Caitlin, and Victoria McArthur. 2019. "The Construction of Gender in Dating Apps: An Interface Analysis of Tinder and Bumble." *Feminist Media Studies* 19, no. 6: 822–840.

Madianou, Mirca, and Daniel. Miller. 2012. *Migration and New Media: Transnational Families and Polymedia*. London and New York: Routledge.

Malta, Sue, and Raelene. Wilding. 2018. "Not so Ubiquitous: Digital Inclusion and Older Adults in Australia." In *Digital Inclusion: An International Comparative Analysis*, edited by Massimo Ragnedda and Bruce Mutsvairo, 19–38. Lanham, MD: Lexington Books.

Marlowe, Jay. 2019. "Social Media and Forced Migration: The Subversion and Subjugation of Political Life." *Media and Communication* 7, no. 2: 173–183.

Mascheroni, Giovanna. 2013. "Parenting the Mobile Internet in Italian Households." *Journal of Children and Media* 8, no. 4: 440–456.

Mascheroni, Giovanna. 2020. "Datafied Childhoods." *Current Sociology* 68, no. 6: 798–813.

May, Vanessa, and Petra Nordqvist. 2019. *Sociology of Personal Life*. London: Macmillan.

McKay, Deirdre. 2017. *An Archipelago of Care: Filipino Migrants and Global Networks*. Bloomington: Indiana University Press.

Miles, Sam. 2017. "Sex in the Digital City: Location-Based Dating Apps and Queer Urban Life." *Gender, Place & Culture* 24, no. 11: 1595–1610.

Morgan, David H. J. 1996. *Family Connections*. Cambridge: Polity Press.

Morgan, David H. J. 2013. *Rethinking Family Practices*. Basingstoke, UK: Palgrave Macmillan.

Morley, David. 1986. *Family Television: Cultural Power and Domestic Leisure*. London and New York: Routledge.

Mukherjee, Utsa. 2020. "Navigating Children's Screen-Time at Home: Narratives of Childing and Parenting within the Familial Generational Structure." *Children's Geographies*. Published ahead of print December 21, 2020. https://doi.org/10.1080/14733285.2020.1862758.

Murdock, George Peter. (1949) 1965. *Social Structure*. New York: Free Press.

Nathanson, Amy I. 2018. "How Parents Manage Young Children's Mobile Media Use." In *Families and Technology*, edited by J. Van Hook, S. M. McHale, and V. King, 3–22. Cham, Switzerland: Springer Nature.

Neves, Barbara Barbosa, and Claudia Casimiro, eds. 2018. *Connecting Families? Information and Communication Technologies, Generations and the Life Course*. Bristol, UK: Policy Press.

Pananakhonsab, Wilasinee. 2016. *Love and Intimacy in Online Cross-Cultural Relationships: The Power of Imagination.* Basingstoke, UK: Palgrave.

Parreñas, Rhacel Salazar. 2005. *Children of Global Migration: Transnational Families and Gendered Woes.* Stanford, CA: Stanford University Press.

Parreñas, Rhacel Salazar. 2008. "Transnational Fathering: Gendered Conflicts, Distant Disciplining and Emotional Gaps." *Journal of Ethnic and Migration Studies* 34, no. 7: 1057–1072.

Parreñas, Rhacel Salazar. 2014. "The Intimate Labour of Transnational Communication." *Families, Relationships and Societies* 3, no. 3: 425–442.

Parsons, Talcott. 1949. "The Social Structure of the Family." In *The Family: Its Function and Destiny*, edited by Ruth Nanda Anshen, 173–201. New York: Harper.

Peng, Siyun, Merril Silverstein, J. Jill Suitor, Megan Gilligan, Woosang Hwang, Sangbo Nam, and Brianna Routh. 2018. "Use of Communication Technology to Maintain Intergenerational Contact: Toward an Understanding of 'Digital Solidarity.'" In *Connecting Families? Information and Communication Technologies, Generations and the Life Course*, edited by Barbara Barbosa Neves and Claudia. Casimiro, 1–19. Bristol, UK: Policy Press. DOI:10.1332/policypress/9781447339946.003.0009

Ragnedda, Massimo, and Bruce Mutsvairo, eds. 2018. *Digital Inclusion: An International Comparative Analysis.* Lanham, MD: Lexington Books.

Rakow, L. F. 1988. "Women and the Telephone: The Gendering of a Communications Technology." In *Technology and Women's Voices—Keeping in Touch*, edited by Cheris Kramarae, 179–199. London and New York: Routledge.

Robertson, Zoe, Raelene Wilding, and Sandra Gifford. 2016. "Mediating the Family Imaginary: Young People Negotiating Absence in Transnational Refugee Families." *Global Networks* 16, no. 2: 219–236.

Rochadiat, Aannisa M.P., Stephanie Tom Tong, and Julie M. Novak. 2017. "Online Dating and Courtship among Muslim American Women: Negotiating Technology, Religious Identity and Culture." *New Media & Society* 20, no. 4: 1618–1639.

Sakamoto, Yuka. 2018. "Permeability of Work–Family Borders: Effects of Information and Communication Technologies on Work–Family Conflict at the Childcare Stage in Japan." In *Connecting Families?*, edited by Barbara Barbosa Neves and Claudia Casimiro, 1–15. Bristol, UK: Policy Press. DOI:10.1332/policypress/9781447339946.003.0014

Sinanan, Jolynna, and Larissa Hjorth. 2018. "Careful Families and Care as 'Kinwork': An Intergenerational Study of Families and Digital Media Use in Melbourne, Australia." In *Connecting Families?*, edited by Barbara Barbosa Neves and Claudia Casimiro, 1–15. Bristol, UK: Policy Press. DOI:10.1332/policypress/9781447339946.003.0010

Smart, Carol. 2007. *Personal Life: New Directions in Sociological Thinking.* Cambridge: Polity Press.

Swallow, Veronica, Kathleen Knafl, Sheila Sanatacroce, Andrew Hall, Trish Smith, Malcolm Campbell and Nicholas J. A. Webb. 2012. "The Online Parent Information and Support Project, Meeting Parents Information and Support Needs for Home-Based Management of Childhood Chronic Kidney Disease." *Journal of Advanced Nursing* 68, no. 9: 2095–2102.

Swartz, Teresa Toguchi 2009. "Intergenerational Family Relations in Adulthood: Patterns, Variations, and Implications in the Contemporary United States." *Annual Review of Sociology* 35: 191–212.

Thomas, J., J. Barraket, C. K. Wilson, E. Rennie, S. Ewing, and T. MacDonald. 2019. *Measuring Australia's Digital Divide: The Australian Digital Inclusion Index 2019.* Melbourne: RMIT University and Swinburne University of Technology.

Thompson, Laura. 2018. " 'I Can Be Your Tinder Nightmare': Harassment and Misogyny in the Online Marketplace." *Feminism & Psychology* 28, no. 1: 69–89.

Treas, Judith, and Zoya Gubernskaya. 2018. "Did Mobile Phones Increase Adult Children's Maternal Contact?" In *Families and Technology*, edited by J. Van Hook, S. M. McHale, and V. King, 139–153. Cham, Switzerland: Springer.

Udwan, Ghadeer, Koen. Leurs, and Amanda Alencar. 2020. "Digital Resilience Tactics of Syrian Refugees in The Netherlands: Social Media for Social Support, Health and Identity." *Social Media & Society* 6, no. 2. https://doi.org/10.1177/2056305120915587.

UNHCR. 2016. *Connecting Refugees*. Geneva: UNHCR.

Van Hook, Jennifer, Susan M. McHale, and Valarie King, eds. 2018. *Families and Technology*. Cham, Switzerland: Springer.

Wajcman, Judy. 1991. *Feminism Confronts Technology*. Cambridge: Polity.

Wajcman, Judy. 1995. "Feminist Theories of Technology." In *Handbook of Science and Technology Studies*, edited by Sheila Jasanoff, Gerald E. Markle, James C. Peterson, and Trevor Pinch, 189–204. Thousand Oaks, CA: Sage.

Weeks, Jeffrey, Brian Heaphy, and Catherine Donovan. 2001. *Same Sex Intimacies: Families of Choice and Other Experiments*. New York and London: Routledge.

Wilding, Raelene 2006. " 'Virtual' Intimacies? Families Communicating across Transnational Contexts." *Global Networks* 6, no. 2: 125–142.

Wilding, Raelene. 2018. *Families, Intimacy and Globalization: Floating Ties*. Basingstoke, UK: Palgrave.

Wilding, Raelene, Loretta Baldassar, Shashini Gamage, Shane Worrell, and Samiro Mohamud. 2020. "Digital Media and the Affective Economies of Transnational Families." *International Journal of Cultural Studies* 23, no. 5: 639–655. https://doi.org/10.1177/1367877920920278.

Wilding, Raelene, and Sandra. M. Gifford, eds. 2013. "Special Issue: Forced Displacement, Refugees and ICTs: Transformations of Place, Power and Social Ties." *Journal of Refugee Studies* 26, no. 4: 495–595.

Williams Veazey, Leah. 2020. "Migrant Mothers and the Ambivalence of Co-ethnicity in Online Communities." *Journal of Ethnic and Migration Studies*. Published ahead of print June 22, 2020. https://doi.org/10.1080/1369183X.2020.1782180.

Worrell, Shane. 2021. "From Language Brokering to Digital Brokering." *Social Media & Society* 7, no. 2. https://doi.org/10.1177/20563051211012365.

Yeates, Nicola. 2012. "Global Care Chains: A State-of-the-Art Review and Future Directions in Care Transnationalization Research." *Global Networks* 12, no. 2: 135–154.

CHAPTER 9

DIGITAL RELIGION

STEF AUPERS AND LARS DE WILDT

> The new religions are unlikely to emerge from the caves of Afghanistan or from the madrasas of the Middle East. Rather, they will emerge from research laboratories.
>
> —Harari (2016, 351)

IN his worldwide bestseller *Homo Deus*, the historian Yuval Noah Harari claims that religions of the future will be digital. He argues that humans will self-consciously fuse with digital technology to enhance their potential and consequently turn into post-human deities. Indeed, over the last decades the increased power of computer technology and developments in the fields of biotech, artificial intelligence, and virtual reality have motivated religious dreams about technology-enhanced salvation from human suffering, illness, and even death (Aupers and Houtman 2010).

Developments such as these conflict with theoretical insights in classical and modern sociology where it is still a mainstay that secular technologies and the otherworldly orientation of religion are incompatible. More than that, it is generally held that the widespread application of technological principles, tools, and devices in everyday life is a powerful force in the progressive secularization, rationalization, and disenchantment of Western societies. In his analysis of the long-standing cultural trajectory of goal or instrumental rationality in the West, Max Weber already pointed out that, particularly, modern science and technology are a "motive force" ([1919] 1948, 139) in the "disenchantment of the world" (*Entzauberung der Welt*). He famously argued in this respect

> that principally there are no mysterious incalculable forces that come into play, but rather that one can, in principle, master all things by calculation. This means that the world is disenchanted. One need no longer have recourse to magical means in

order to master or implore the spirits, as did the savage, for whom such mysterious powers existed. Technical means and calculations perform the service.

(Weber [1919] 1948, 139)

Weber understood rationalization as a Faustian bargain: On the one hand, we know more about the world through science, while technology greatly enhances effectiveness, efficiency, and our control over nature; on the other hand, their spread and prominence in modern society inevitably disenchant the world and rob it of its ultimate meaning. Unlike religion, modern science and technology cannot provide answers to "the only question important for us: 'What shall we do and how shall we live?' " (Weber [1919] 1948, 143). Quite the contrary: From the nineteenth century's application of steam-driven technology in modern factories onward, Weber argued, technology increasingly became an autonomous force beyond human control. Intrinsically connected to the industrial mode of production, modern technology allegedly "determine(s) the lives of all the individuals who are born into this mechanism" ([1930] 2005, 123). This connection between modern technology and disenchantment has become almost a truism in the social sciences. Jacques Ellul, for instance, argued that "The mysterious is merely that which has not yet been technicized" (1967, 142), while Bryan Wilson, just like other defenders of the thesis of secularization, typically commented that "Secularization is in large part intimately involved with the development of technology, since technology is itself the encapsulation of human rationality.... The instrumentalism of rational thinking is powerfully embodied in machines" (1976, 88).

In this article, we will reconsider the modern dichotomy between technology and religion and the long-standing sociological assumption that technological progress undermines religious worldviews, beliefs, and "ultimate" meaning. More particularly, we will demonstrate the elective affinity between digital technology and religion and, based on our review of contemporary literature, argue that the rise and omnipresence of digital media in everyday life co-constitutes a shift toward a "post-secular" society (Habermas 2008). Ideal-typically we distinguish three forms of the digitalization of religion that contribute to this development: firstly, traditional religions globally spread and transform *through* digital media; secondly, religious contents play a prominent role *in* digital media texts; and, thirdly, there is an emergence of religions *of* digital media—placing digital technology itself at the center of religious speculation and spiritual imagination.

POST-SECULAR SOCIETY?

Already since the 1960s, the classical thesis of secularization came to be widely debated and severely scrutinized on several grounds. Sociologists of religion have increasingly problematized linear processes of religious decline at the hands of modern science, industrialism, and technology. Late in his career, Peter Berger looks back on the secularization debate as a whole:

> Since its inception, presumably to be dated in the classical period of Durkheim and Weber, the sociology of religion has been fascinated by the phenomenon of *secularization*. This term, of course, has been endlessly debated, modified and occasionally repudiated. But for most purposes it can be defined quite simply as a process in which religion diminishes in importance both in society and in the consciousness of individuals. And most sociologists looking at this phenomenon have shared the view that secularization is the direct result of modernization. Put simply, the idea has been that the relation between modernity and religion is inverse—the more of the former, the less of the latter.
>
> (Berger 2005, 336, italics original)

Different critical objections have been raised against the secularization thesis. A first major argument is that secularization is an ideological construct rather than an empirically grounded fact. Secularization, from this perspective, is typically debunked as a modernist, Western, or even colonialist wish-dream informed by the desire that modern Enlightenment, science, and technology have to conquer religion. Gerhard Lenski, for instance, argues that sociology "from its inception was committed to the positivist view that religion in the modern world is merely a survival from man's primitive past, and doomed to disappear in an era of science and general enlightenment" (1961, 3). Jeffrey Hadden calls classical secularization theory for this reason "sacralised" (1987, 594), judging it "an ideological preference rather than a systematic theory" (p. 587). Empirically, sociologists showed that secularization is primarily a local, perhaps temporary but certainly exceptional northwestern European phenomenon. They point out that "organized religion thrives in the United States in an open market system" (Warner 1993, 1044; e.g., Stark and Bainbridge 1985), whereas Christian and non- Christian forms of religion (i.e., Protestant evangelicals, Islam, Buddhism) flourish worldwide (Berger 2005; Martin 1990).

A second cluster of objections is that secularization may undermine the Christian institutions, dogmas, and rituals but that this is a symptom of religious change rather than the decline of religion in general. Secularization, from this stance, is a "self-limiting" process (Stark and Bainbridge 1985). Indeed, in Europe it is verified that increasingly fewer (young) individuals are baptized and attend the services of churches, mosques, synagogues, and so on (Archbishops' Council 2012; Brenner 2016; Hooghe, Quintelier, and Reeskens 2006), nor do they identify with any organized or "institutionalized" religion such as Christianity or Islam (Pew Research Center 2018). Rather than a decline in religious beliefs, however, this indicates a shift toward less institutional, more privatized, and alternative forms of religion (Altinordu and Gorski 2008; Dobbelaere 1981; Parsons 1977; Shiner 1967; Tschannen 1991). Already over half a century ago Thomas Luckmann argued that the decline of the monopoly of the Christian church in Western countries was accompanied by the rise of non-institutional and, hence, "invisible religion" (1967, 103). Religion takes a new social form on an open "market of ultimate significance" where religious movements, groups, and producers offer their religious worldviews and "consumers" are involved in constructing their own privatized religious packages based on personal taste and preference (p. 103). This "bricolage" or "picking and choosing" of religious elements has been referred to as "do-it-yourself-religion" (Baerveldt 1996), "pick-and mix religion" (Hamilton 2000), "religious consumption à la carte" (Possamai 2003), and a "spiritual supermarket" (Lyon 2000; cf. Aupers and Houtman 2006). It is argued that this type of privatized bricolage is particularly characteristic of the growing group of people who refer to themselves as "not religious, but spiritual" (Ammerman 2013). These "spiritual seekers" delve into Buddhism, paganism, esotericism, New Age, and holistic health; and their beliefs can be considered a form of "post-traditional spirituality" (Heelas 1996), "alternative spirituality" (Sutcliffe and Bowman 2000), or "progressive spirituality" (Lynch 2007). In Europe, this type of spirituality is prominent in countries where Christian churches are in decline, such as France, Sweden, and The Netherlands (Houtman and Aupers 2007)—a development that motivated the assumption in academia that we are witnessing a veritable "spiritual revolution" (Heelas and Woodhead 2005) or "Easternization of the West" (Campbell 2007).

The transformation and revitalization of religion in late-modern society have brought academics such as Jürgen Habermas (2006, 2008) to the claim that we are now living in a "post-secular" world. In addition to privatized forms of religion, he argues, religion in all its forms and varieties features increasingly in the public sphere of politics, media, and journalism (e.g., Casanova 1994). In this article, we suggest that the process of digitalization contributes to this "post-secular" society in, at least, three different ways.

The Spreading of Religion *through* Digital Media

First of all, religion spreads *through* digital media—a development that leads to a transformation of religion from local churches to potentially global communities. The internet is not only a tool to efficiently communicate religious messages and to connect believers from different countries and cultures through prayer apps like Azan Basic or rabbinic consultations on chabad.org. The internet also radically transforms religions' conventions, practices and rituals. Religion and media scholar Heidi Campbell argues that rather than rejecting new media, Christian, Muslim, and Jewish communities use media to globally spread and reshape religious traditions (2010). Through the lens of what she calls the "religious-social shaping of technology" she studies the negotiation of media in light of (Semitic) religious institutions' history, beliefs, practices, and communal discourses, resulting in media uses such as digitalizing religious texts (an incorporation of old practices in new technologies) to televangelism (which actively makes use of media to appropriate and spread faith).

Campbell demonstrates in her work that this religious-social shaping is not a homogenous process for all religions and denominations. Embedded in different traditions, religious organizations and groups appropriate digital technology in various ways. Thus, Islamic prayer guidelines led to the creation of specific prayer alert programs for the Muslim community, calculating prayer times and the direction to Mecca (Campbell 2010, 184–186), while strict kosher laws among Jewish Orthodox communities led to the creation of a "kosher phone," which disables internet access, text messaging, and other "services that many rabbinical authorities felt would expose members of this conservative religious community to dubious, unmonitored secular content" (p. 213). Outside of religious institutions, Stig Hjarvard comments on this spread and transformation of religion online by adding that even the predominantly secular Nordic countries have seen an increased visibility of religion "due to the presence of religion in the media" (2016, 8). He calls this the "mediatization of religion," referring to the processes "through which religious beliefs, agency, and symbols are becoming influenced by the workings of various media," rather than the other way around (p. 8).

This transformation from local religious practice to globally mediatized audiences is, of course, not entirely new. It already starts with televangelism, Christian music, and other predigital religious media. Stewart Hoover showed that for Christian television in the 1980s there was "the more general sense among the leaders of this new movement that in order to have its desired outcomes it needed to be something that took the public sphere—and particularly the media—seriously" (2006, 58). Campbell and Vitullo (2016) indeed show that religious institutions have always been among the first to adopt internet technologies, from online forums to video conferencing; and this has changed the way in which churches operate offline as well, such as through the use of multisite churches to stream services to wider, disparate, and diasporic communities (Bruce 2019; Vitullo 2019). Daniel Stout demonstrates that while the internet provides greater access to studying religion individually, in many cases classical religious leadership's authority remains intact. To use Stout's own example, Mormon websites "are highly controlled in terms of social networking features in order to protect the hierarchical leadership structure within the denomination" by restricting network interactions between regular users (2012, 76). Other institutions similarly reassert themselves on digital media through cyberchurches, e-commerce, and online rituals such as prayer and "online confession, although discouraged by some," while organizing religious fellowships and reading groups on social media such as Facebook and Twitter (Stout 2012, 77).

In sum, established religious institutions and organizations appropriate the internet and shape it in their own image: the doctrines of the Roman Catholic church, Protestant churches, sects, and new religious movements all provide different dilemmas on how to spread the message online and impose authority over individual believers (Noomen, Houtman, and Aupers 2011). Such worries and dilemmas of religious leaders are understandable. Outside of formal religious institutions and organizations, digital media transform religion by allowing individuals more agency, freedom, and control over how they practice religion. Indeed, given the non-hierarchical nature of the internet, it is impossible to control the idiosyncratic ways in which individual believers express their religious identity in blogs, vlogs, and audiovisual clips on social media (Evolvi 2018) or how religious tweets or memes travel the internet (Aguilar et al. 2017). Birgit Meyer and Annelies Moors argue in this respect that the media-specific forms and affordances of digital media shape the modes in which consumers and believers are able to interact with religion: "modes that are difficult to control by religious establishment [so that] new media may both have a destabilizing and an enabling potential for established practices for religious mediation" (2006, 11). In the same year, Hoover found that the way in which individual consumers perform this "negotia[tion of] media material into their spiritual and religious lives" is with "*playfulness* rather than *deliberation*":

> Consistent with ideas about media practice such as Henry Jenkins's well-known notion of "textual poaching," these interviewees can be seen to approach media with a sense of experiment, testing, and appropriation ... the media are a playful context in that they seem to provide a relatively "low-stakes" place to explore.
>
> (Hoover 2006, 145–150, italics original)

Across interviews with various religious families, Hoover's interviewees reveal that they constantly negotiate their religious beliefs with their consumption of music and TV shows such as *South Park*, internet blogs, and "trash TV": Their attitudes range from reluctantly giving up such media (because *South Park* insults the Christian God even though it is "a really funny cartoon. I mean, a funny, funny cartoon" [p. 124]) to being a safe space to explore Buddhism through monastic blogs as a (former) Catholic (p. 138) or simply to revel in stories of aliens and the supernatural as a Catholic (p. 142). The internet serves to motivate such forms of individual experimentation and bricolage. Lövheim concludes in a study on young Swedes' religious identity that the internet provides them with "experiences that enrich young people in their efforts to create their own religious identity" (2004, 70; cf. Droogers 2014). Johan Roeland and co-authors (2010) even show that such digital religious identity-formation can lead young people, such as Salafists and New Agers, to seek a privatized, more "purified" version of their religion outside of institutions. Additional research shows that other media, such as video games, encourage believers to not only explore their own religious identities but also to role-play as differently religious—in some cases to the point of conversion (de Wildt and Aupers 2019).

Religion is changed by this spread and appropriation of religion through digital media. Whether digital media are used to reproduce institutional religious authority or to engage in individual bricolage, religion's relocation from a local to a global affair transforms the way it is practiced. An overview of the literature provides ample empirical examples including online church services, prayer, confession, and other rituals in which old religious practices and digital media are combined. The Roman Catholic

Confession app, for instance, invites users not just to confess their sins but to keep track of them too (Cheong and Ess 2012)—much like a to-do list app. The Church of England has launched its Daily Prayer app for iOS and Android, which is more accessible and portable and makes textual comparison of different translations easier; it is also argued, by Joshua Mann (2012), that it takes away the traditional "sacredness" of ornately designed praying books. In Kerstin Radde-Antweiler's study of worship in *Second Life*, the presence of digital avatars in virtual synagogues, churches, mosques, and temples leads to practical transformations (too many churchgoers leads to internet connectivity problems, leading in turn to the organization of smaller, more intimate services) as well as pluralistic ones: the virtually coexistent places of worship of Judaism, Christianity, Islam, and Hinduism lead to a "patchwork" of religious practices that becomes more than "an accumulation of separate religious structures or in other words as an analysis of individual religiousness" (2008, 207).

Religion *in* Digital Media Text

While religious traditions increasingly go digital, digital media also increasingly go religious. More concretely, religious narratives, symbols, and rituals play a significant role *in* (secular) contemporary media texts (Partridge 2005) and in digital media specifically (e.g., Bosman 2015; Geraci 2014).

Christopher Partridge observed a "re-enchantment of the West" through film, television, and popular music, designating such pop-cultural influences as George Harrison and *Buffy the Vampire Slayer* as popularizing spirituality, the occult, and other alternatives to institutionalized religion, a "return to a form of magical culture" through popular media (2005, 40). Indeed, just as popular music of the 1970s introduced tropes from oriental spirituality, so did television in the late 1990s introduce a preoccupation with the occult and alternative religions such as Wicca, continuing well into the twenty-first century. Examples by Partridge are hit series such as *Charmed*, *True Blood*, and *Vampire Diaries*. We may see the same kind of use of what Partridge calls "occulture" in the popular books and films of Dan Brown and the *Assassin's Creed* videogames—the latter of which came out at the height of Dan Brown's popularity. Both engage in speculative fictions that suggest that more is going on beneath the surface of our own societies' history, by using the mystery of the Catholic Church to unearth all types of plots and conspiracies in Jerusalem, the Vatican, and old French churches that reveal the magical, mysterious secrets of Opus Dei or the Templars. Lynn Schofield Clark (2005) documented ethnographically how teens deal with such interweaving of the supernatural and religion in fiction and found that teens' engagement with series like *Angel*, *Buffy*, and *The X-Files* leads them often to reconsider their religious stance against (or sometimes back in line with) organized religion, while speculating about the place of magic and the supernatural in their own belief systems.

Material religion scholar David Morgan goes as far as to argue that digital media consumption and religious experience are, in many ways, structurally similar, if not fundamentally intertwined. According to Morgan:

> Religion has come to be widely understood as embodied practices that cultivate relations among people, places, and non-human forces—nature, spirits, ancestors, saints, gods—resulting in communities and sensibilities that shape those who participate. . . . By the same token, media have come to be understood as technologies of sensation, as embodied forms of participation in extended communities joined in imagination, feeling, taste, affinity, and affect.
>
> (Morgan 2013, 347)

By media communities, Morgan refers to the kind of shared community of meanings that Jenkins describes as "participatory culture" (2012) and that Stolov describes as "a body of readers (and embodied readers)" (2005).

Digital media and their communities are especially vibrant modern religious media landscapes. Beside the *appearance* of religion in media, as Partridge shows, digital media show consumers' increasingly active ways of engaging with religious identities and discourses. Video games especially, Rachel Wagner argues, are functionally similar to religious rituals more than predigital media such as cinema because they offer an escape from the "vicissitudes of contemporary life" in which "practitioners give themselves over to a predetermined set of rules that shape a world view and offer a system of order and structure that is comforting for its very predictability" (2012, 193), providing clear objectives and a unified purpose. Much of the research on religion in digital media, then, is unsurprisingly about video games as ideal-typical spaces for exploring religious identities and worlds, not in the least because it is the largest cultural industry of the world (Entertainment Retailers Association 2018; Entertainment Software Association 2018). Moreover, they can present consumers with an encyclopedic range of cultural heritage to populate their worlds (de Wildt and Aupers 2021), resulting in an eclectic combination of Christian, Muslim, Hindu, and other religious worldviews alongside each other. A notable example is the genre of Japanese role-playing games such as the *Final Fantasy* and *Persona* series, which, as de Wildt and Aupers show, represent "multiple religious traditions presented together" in what they call "eclectic religion"; it is unavoidable for players of *Final Fantasy XV* to encounter Leviathan, Shiva, Arabic djinn, and Christian choir music all in the same play session (p. 14). Empirically, interviews with players show that they use this temporary worldview and structure to experiment with religious identities outside of their own culture and upbringing, inside media (de Wildt and Aupers 2019; Schaap and Aupers 2017). Confronted with new religious identities to experiment with, digital media provide players with a "liminal zone" in which "serious" issues of everyday life, culture, and politics are transgressed, reversed, and renegotiated (e.g., Geertz 2005; Turner 2010; van Bohemen, van Zoonen, and Aupers 2014). Online identity play is in this sense often compared to a "laboratory" where adolescents try out new personal identities (Turkle 1995). By playing at being atheists, Christians, Hindus, or Muslims in games, media consumers may become aware that the absolute truths they were raised with are culturally contingent and replaceable by alternatives—both historical and fantastical. In addition, such experimentation with religion in media texts may "provide(s) inspiration at a metaphorical level and/or is a source of beliefs for everyday life" (Possamai 2012, 20).

This experimentation with religion in and through media, however, is not only a personal quest; it has social and public significance. Firstly, the prominence of religion in popular media culture—film, series, and video games—may be understood as a form of institutionalization. Religion becomes a commodity, packaged and sold to global audiences, to be eagerly swept up by consumers in search of meaning (Aupers and Houtman 2006; Davidsen 2018; Hoover 2006; Schultze 2003; Wagner 2012). Secondly, the experimentation with religion in games and online media texts is done not alone but as a deeply social endeavor (e.g., Geraci 2014). Young people actively discuss the meanings of religion in popular games such as *World of Warcraft*, *Assassins Creed*, *Dark Souls*, *Dante's Inferno*, and *Final Fantasy* collectively on the internet in online fora and social media platforms (de Wildt and Aupers 2017). Although they do not necessarily share the collective meanings, moralities, and communal functions of religion, players with different (non-)religious backgrounds respectively reject, debunk, debate, and connect with religion online—performing a "pop theology" in which they actively relate to and debate god(s) and religious meanings (de Wildt and Aupers 2020). Such online religious talk contradicts theories of "invisible religion" (e.g., Luckmann 1967): After all, in such cases religion is returned from privatized systems of belief to a vivid public debate. In a similar vein, Kelly Besecke (2005) noted that we can visibly "see religion" in the public conversation about it in self-help books, magazines, and other mass media featuring religion and spirituality. Digital media platforms facilitate such public debates even better: The non-hierarchical structure and "participatory culture" of the internet (Jenkins 2012) invite laypeople and amateurs to openly voice their opinions on religion and worldviews.

Notwithstanding different positions, players are in dialogue about the "real" meanings of religion in media, showing that media inspire conversations on religion. It is important to note, however, that the arguments players are making in this conversation are neither noncommittal nor arbitrary. Quite the contrary. What they express online about in-game content is strongly motivated by their (non)religious identity in offline life. Hence, religion in media becomes a way to relate to religion without having to believe in it—exactly because (young) people in the West do not "believe" anymore (Dentsu Communication Institute 2006; Zuckerman 2006). Considering those statistics, it is as counterintuitive as it is true to say that young people in the West are now more likely to encounter religion and experience enchantment in video games than in a place of worship (cf. Newzoo 2017; Pew Research Center 2018). Moving beyond the classical dichotomies of "believing or not believing," secular or sacred, atheism or religion, we may argue that religious narratives *in* media texts do motivate a generation of "digital natives" to relate to religion in different ways: They reflect, experiment, and individually play with religious worldviews without believing and collectively debate religious meaning in online domains. As such, we may observe a process of religious change rather than of a progressive secularization and disenchantment.

Religion *of* Digital Technology

In addition to the spread and transformation of traditional religion through media and its manifestation in digital media texts, there is a third, by and large unacknowledged, development indicating the elective affinity between digital technology and religion: a religion *of* digital technology. In his book *The Religion of Technology* (1999), the historian David Noble demonstrates that the relation between technological progress and a "disenchantment of the world" is problematic. He actually reverses the Weberian thesis by stating that "modern technology and religion have evolved together and that, as a result, the technological enterprise has been and remains suffused with religious belief" (p. 5). In his work he primarily describes in empirical detail how Christian millennialist movements provided the cultural blueprint for technological salvation; how technological inventions, such as nuclear weapons, aerospace technology, and artificial intelligence (AI), were engineered by devoted Christians and inspired by otherworldly longings for a "return to Eden," the (original) "divinity of man," or—in futurist terms—the destiny of man as *imago dei* (p. 15).

Technology, from this historical perspective, is neither opposed to spiritual worldviews nor an "irreligious power," as Max Weber would have it. Indeed, there are many other historical studies demonstrating such affinities and convergence, for example, on the "spiritual telegraph" in the nineteenth century (Davis 1999; Stolov 2008), chemistry and modern alchemy (Morrisson 2007), and other hybrids between science-based technology and religion at the beginning of the twentieth century that indicate "the problem of disenchantment" (Asprem 2014). The opposition between technology and religion may be particularly difficult to uphold when applied to digital technology—(personal) computers, the internet, and AI. The short history of these digital technologies indicates a cultural shift from perceiving them as source of alienation to a tool for spiritual salvation and re-enchantment (e.g., Aupers and Houtman 2010; Davis 1999; Harari 2016; Roszak 2000).

In the 1950s, the first large IBM computers were still owned and deployed by the companies, governments, or the so-called military–industrial complex and, as such, exemplified the status of technology as a supraindividual and alienating system for many people. This discourse changed during the 1960s and 1970s with the attempts of hackers at MIT to bring "computer power to the people" (Levy 2010, 144); the fusion of hippies, hackers, and psychedelics in the Californian counterculture (Dery 1996; Roszak 2000; Rushkoff 1994); and, ultimately, the privatization and personalization of computer technology (Aupers and Houtman 2006). Recent studies addressing the roots of spirituality in the counterculture of the 1960s and 1970s, for instance, argue that human-made products, science, and technology were *not* unambiguously considered as alienating in the countercultural spiritual milieu. In *From Satori to Silicon Valley* (2000) Theodore Roszak even revised his own interpretation: Beside nature-celebrating "luddites," he argues, the counterculture featured many "technophiles"— hippies, hackers, and information and communication technology (ICT) gurus who projected the spiritual imagination on digital technology as a tool of salvation (e.g., Aupers, Houtman, and Pels 2008; Rushkoff 1994). Key figures of the early Californian spiritual milieu, like Ken Kesey, Terrence McKenna, and, most notably, Timothy Leary, fall within this category. Leary argued that "hard technology" may in fact promise a more effective avenue toward the goal of personal salvation than "soft techniques" like yoga, tai chi, or chakra healing. He compared the personal computer to LSD (e.g., Dery 1996) and suggested in the 1990s that one can escape an "alienating" and "repressive" society by immersing oneself in the new otherworldly realm of cyberspace that was opened up by computer networks:

> Recite to yourself some of the traditional attributes of the word "spiritual": mythic, magical, ethereal, incorporeal, intangible, non-material, disembodied, ideal, platonic. Is that not a definition of the electronic-digital? ... These "spiritual" realms, over centuries imagined, may, perhaps, now be realized!
>
> (Leary 1994, 5)

And Leary was no exception. He was but the *eminence grise* of a much broader "technophile" wing of the counterculture that, especially in the early 1990s, gathered around hackers, internet gurus, and cyberpunk writers like William Gibson and Rudy Rucker— a group of people who constituted "counter culture 2.0" (Dery 1996) or "cyberian counter culture" (Rushkoff 1994, 6–7). With the rise of the internet in the 1990s, renowned technicians and academics also heralded the newly emerging realm of cyberspace as a spiritual space with an immaterial and ephemeral ontology. It was described as a 'paradise' where we "(W)ill all be angels, and for eternity!" (Stenger 1992, 52), a "new Jerusalem" (Benedikt 1992, 14), and a "technological substitute of the Christian space of heaven" (Wertheim 2000, 16).

Such otherworldly dreams about spiritual liberation are a permanent feature of the culture in Silicon Valley and co-evolve with and are "updated" by new developments in the domain of digital technology. Most notable, contemporary spiritual groups like Scientology and the Raelian movement and ICT gurus like Ray Kurzweil (1999) and Hans Moravec (1988) are promising the end of human suffering and eternal life through the uploading of consciousness (Aupers and Houtman 2010; Geraci 2012). Much of this type of techno-spirituality falls under the heading of trans- or post-humanism: Based on radical materialist interpretations of the brain/human consciousness as being "just" information that can be copied, saved, and transferred to a computer, robot, or internet, it is held in this milieu that we can become like gods online. Given the large investments of tech companies like Google in these forms of digital religion, *Time* magazine formulated the question in 2013: "Can Google solve death?"

And yet these spiritual worldviews based on a belief in technical salvation are complemented by the picture of AI, viruses, and algorithms as ultimately opaque, invisible, evasive, and permanently out of control. To paraphrase Max Weber, technology may (or may not) "master all things by calculation," but it itself becomes a manifestation of "mysterious incalculable forces" (Weber [1919] 1948, 139). Early twenty-first-century Silicon Valley discourse, in particular, faced the increasingly "smaller, less tangible or even invisible" displacement of technology to the level of software, in which "the program itself is an abstraction, it doesn't exist in any form anywhere" (Aupers 2010a, 160). Enchanted discourse extends to such early techno-cultural tropes as calling installation software "wizards" and IT experts "magicians," and in Kevin Kelly's terms, enchantment extends into a discourse of "nerd theology" (1999). In addition, ICT pioneers, programmers, and developers of digital technology in Silicon Valley often frame AI, virtual reality, viruses, algorithms, and our surrounding digital ecology in magical and animistic terms (Aupers 2002, 2010a, 2010b). Like nature, they are considered a mysterious, overpowering force that can be experienced as deeply spiritual. Exemplary are programmers referring to themselves as "techno-pagans" (Aupers 2002, 2010a, 2010b; e.g., Davis 1999; Dery 1996), arguing that "The force is great, and especially the programmers, laser jocks, scientists, and silicon architects can feel it. The technology has a spirit of its own, as valid as the spirit of any creature of the goddess" (Aupers 2010a). And whereas the opaque "spiritual power" of technology is often imagined to be a good, creative force, it can also, like nature, be considered a "dark" and "destructive" power. We can think in this respect about theories featuring the overpowering force of AI and robotics in the new age of "spiritual machines" (Kurzweil 1999) and techno-apocalyptic and millennialist scenarios advocated by ICT gurus (Geraci 2012).

From the personal computer in the 1970s to the internet and the immaterial realm of cyberspace in the 1990s to complex AI, invisible algorithms, and robotics in the new millennium, it is demonstrated that digital technology has been a staple of the religious imagination and a source of veritable enchantment over the decades. This religion *of* digital technology, we argue, is a third development that contributes to a post-secular society.

Conclusion: The Digitalization of Religion

Long-standing sociological theories about a progressive secularization and disenchantment of Western society have been scrutinized over the last decades on different grounds. One of the main arguments in this debate is that the religious quest for transcendence and the construction of "ultimate meaning" in the face of illness, human suffering, and death is a "universal constant" or an "anthropological condition" (Yinger 1970; Luckmann 1967). From this perspective, "the process of secularization is self-limiting" since the decline of particular social forms of religion goes hand in hand with "religious revival" and "religious innovation" (Stark and Bainbridge 1985, 2–3). Indeed, religion is not necessarily related to membership in a church, mosque, or other institution: Since the 1960s and 1970s we have witnessed the rise of new religious movements, sects, cults, and a "cultic milieu" of heterodox religious beliefs (Campbell [1972] 2002), whereas religion has become more personal and privatized on a "market of ultimate significance" (Luckmann 1967).

Building on this sociological assumption that we are witnessing religious change instead of secularization, we reviewed the academic literature, focusing on the way digital media impede on traditional "churched" religion and spiritual beliefs, rituals, and practices. Notwithstanding modernist perspectives framing technology and religion as incompatible forces, we argued that the process of digitalization both revives and transforms religion/spirituality in three ways. Firstly, traditional religions, organizations, and groups increasingly complement or even replace their offline services in local churches with online communities. Notwithstanding their virtual and nonphysical nature—including the use of apps, digital icons, and symbols—such online religious meetings are globally accessible and may enhance Durkheimian "collective effervescence" between church members. In addition, online religion further motivated individual bricolage as envisioned by Luckmann: individual Muslims, Christians, pagans, and spiritual seekers rejecting churched dogmas and constructing their own privatized and "purified" religion (Roeland et al. 2010).

Secondly, we demonstrated that not only are traditional religious organizations, churches, and texts moving online but vice versa (digital) media texts are also incorporating religious narratives and worldviews. Such encounters with religion *in* digital media, we argued, are not trivial or even alienating simulations of religion: Being part of an online "participatory culture" (Jenkins 2012), it engages young consumers to actively reflect on the value of religion (Schaap and Aupers 2017), try out different worldviews through role-playing (de Wildt and Aupers 2019), or discuss the issues on fora, social media, and offline in an unacknowledged manifestation of "pop theology" (de Wildt and Aupers 2020).

Finally, we demonstrated that religious engagement and enchantment and the search for ultimate meaning have been relocated from traditional religious texts and holy scriptures not only to online media texts but also to digital technology itself. Instead of being framed as alienating forces, the personal computer, internet, virtual reality, and AI are often appropriated as tools of religious salvation—ultimately promising the end of human illness, suffering, and death of a technologically enhanced "Homo Deus" (Harari 2016).

Overall, then, our threefold argumentation on the digitalization of religion leads us to the claim that it becomes increasingly problematic to sustain the long-standing sociological dichotomies between religion and modernity, spirituality and technology (e.g., Aupers and Houtman 2010). It may and will, of course, be argued that what we call "digital religion" here is not "real," "true," or "authentic" religion and only a weak derivate or bleak substitution of religion. Indeed, particularly the second and third arguments discussed in this article—religion *in* digital media texts and religion *of* digital technology—are all too easily deconstructed as "hyper-real testaments" of religion (Possamai 2005) or a verification of secularization rather than a confirmation of the persistence of religion in contemporary society.

From a cultural sociological perspective this common perception is problematic. Implicitly or explicitly such critical notions on "digital religion" are always grounded in a comparison with traditional (and often Christian) forms of "churched" religion that have a long-standing historical tradition, are institutionalized, and are grounded in real-life social interactions and rituals. Such critiques, then, are hardly open to social-cultural diversity and historical change or, in other words, the possibility that the social manifestation of religion differs per time and place. Why should such comparative perspectives and (overly moral) interpretations of digital religion be revised? Given the "social construction of reality" (Berger and Luckmann 1966), we argue, the religious quest for ultimate meaning has countless different faces; but its manifestations are not arbitrary. Quite the contrary. Both the content and form of religion are always grounded in and shaped by a particular social-cultural context. In the 1960s, Thomas Luckmann (1967) wrote in this respect about the emergence of a privatized social form of religion in an increasingly fragmented, pluriform, and individualistic society. Now, more than half a century later, we live with what Couldry and Hepp call the "mediated construction of reality" (2016)—a Western society in which many of our institutions, organizations, cultures, social networks, and activities are embedded in and informed by digital media. Religion, from this perspective, is not only thoroughly "mediatized" (Hjarvard 2016) but can only be understood in relation to our expanding digital media environment that embraces it, to paraphrase Peter Berger (1967), like an overarching "secular canopy." With this article, we contribute to this argument—that the mediatization of religion or, rather, its "digitalization" spreads, shapes, and transforms religion in contemporary society. Building on this state-of-the-art scholarship, we have set an agenda for further research, calling for robust, empirical, sociological research on what religious institutions, organizations, and individual people actually do with digital media; how religious texts, narratives, and rituals in games and the virtual world are appropriated by "secular" youngsters; and what the motivations are of technicians, AI specialist, ICT gurus, and post-humanists in Silicon Valley who are actually building those "brave new religions" of the future (Harari 2016, 351). Issues such as these, we conclude, should be high on the research agenda of sociologists of religion.

References

Aguilar, Gabriëlle K., Heidi A. Campbell, Maria Stanley, and Ellen Taylor. 2017. "Communicating Mixed Messages about Religion through Internet Memes." *Information, Communication & Society* 20, no. 10: 1498–1520.

Altinordu, Ates, and Philip S. Gorski. 2008. "After Secularization." *Annual Review of Sociology* 34: 55–85.

Ammerman, Nancy T. 2013. "Spiritual but not Religious? Beyond Binary Choices in the Study of Religion." *Journal for the Scientific Study of Religion* 52, no. 2: 258–278.

Archbishops' Council. 2012. *Statistics for Mission 2011*. London: Archbishops' Council, Research and Statistics Central Secretariat.

Asprem, Egil. 2014. *The Problem of Disenchantment: Scientific Naturalism and Esoteric Discourse 1900–1939*. Leiden, The Netherlands, and Boston: Brill.

Aupers, Stef. 2002. "The Revenge of the Machines: On Modernity, Digital Technology and Animism." *Asian Journal of Social Science* 30, no. 2: 199–220.

Aupers, S. 2010a. " 'The Force Is Great': Enchantment and Magic in Silicon Valley." *Masaryk University Journal of Law and Technology* 3, no. 1: 153–173.

Aupers, S. 2010b. " 'Where the Zeroes Meet the Ones': Exploring the Affinity between Magic and Computer Technology." In *Religions of Modernity: Relocating the Sacred to the Self and the Digital*, edited by Stef Aupers and Dick Houtman, 219–238. Leiden, The Netherlands: Brill.

Aupers, Stef, and Dick Houtman. 2006. "Beyond the Spiritual Supermarket: The Social and Public Significance of New Age Spirituality." *Journal of Contemporary Religion* 21, no. 2: 201–222.

Aupers, Stef, and Dick Houtman, eds. 2010. *Religions of Modernity: Relocating the Sacred to the Self and the Digital*. Leiden, The Netherlands: Brill.

Aupers, Stef, Dick Houtman, and Peter Pels. 2008. "Cybergnosis: Technology, Religion and the Secular." In *Religion: Beyond a Concept*, edited by Hent de Vries, 687–703. New York: Fordham University Press.

Baerveldt, Cor. 1996. "New Age-religiositeit als individueel constructieproces." In *De kool en de geit in de nieuwe tijd: Wetenschappelijke reflecties op New Age*, edited by Miranda Moerland, 19–31. Utrecht, Netherlands: Van Arkel.

Benedikt, Michael. 1992. "Introduction." In *Cyberspace: First Steps*, edited by Michael Benedikt, 1–26. Cambridge, MA: MIT Press.

Berger, Peter L. 1967. *The Sacred Canopy: Elements of a Sociological Theory of Religion*. New York: Doubleday.

Berger, Peter L. 2005. "Secularization and De-Secularization." In *Religions in the Modern World: Traditions and Transformations*, edited by Linda Woodhead, Paul Fletcher, Hiroko Kawanami, and David Smith, 336–344. London and New York: Routledge.

Berger, Peter L., and Thomas Luckmann. 1966. *The Social Construction of Reality: A Treatise in the Sociology of Knowledge*. London and New York: Penguin Books.

Besecke, Kelly. 2005. "Seeing Invisible Religion: Religion as a Societal Conversation about Transcendent Meaning." *Sociological Theory* 23, no. 2: 179–196.

Bosman, Frank G. 2015. " 'Playing God.' On God & Game." *Online-Heidelberg Journal of Religions on the Internet* 7: 185–189.

Brenner, Philip S. 2016. "Cross-National Trends in Religious Service Attendance." *Public Opinion Quarterly* 80, no. 2: 563–583.

Bruce, Steve. 2019. *Pray TV: Televangelism in America*. Vol. 7, *Routledge Library Editions: Sociology of Religion*. London and New York: Routledge.

Campbell, Collin. (1972) 2002. "The Cult, the Cultic Milieu and Secularization." In *The Cultic Milieu: Oppositional Subcultures in an Age of Globalization*, edited by J. Kaplan and H. Lööw, 12–25. Oxford: Rowman Altamira.

Campbell, Collin. 2007. *The Easternization of the West: A Thematic Account of Cultural Change in the Modern Era*. Boulder, CO: Paradigm Publishers.

Campbell, Heidi A. 2010. *When Religion Meets New Media*. London and New York: Routledge.

Campbell, Heidi A., and Alessandra Vitullo. 2016. "Assessing Changes in the Study of Religious Communities in Digital Religion Studies." *Church, Communication and Culture* 1, no. 1: 73–89.

Casanova, José. 1994. *Public Religions in the Modern World*. Chicago: University of Chicago Press.

Cheong, Pauline Hope, and Charles Ess. 2012. "Introduction: Religion 2.0?: Relational and Hybridizing Pathways in Religion, Social Media, and Culture." In *Digital Religion, Social Media and Culture: Perspectives, Practices and Futures*, edited by Pauline Hope Cheong, Peter Fischer-Nielsen, Stefan Gelfgren, and Charles Ess, 1–21. New York: Peter Lang.

Clark, Lynn Schofield. 2005. *From Angels to Aliens: Teenagers, the Media, and the Supernatural*. New York: Oxford University Press.

Couldry, Nick, and Andreas Hepp. 2016. *The Mediated Construction of Reality*. Cambridge: Polity Press.

Davidsen, Markus Altena, ed. 2018. *Narrative and Belief: The Religious Affordance of Supernatural Fiction*. London and New York: Routledge.

Davis, Erik. 1999. *TechGnosis: Myth, Magic and Mysticism in the Age of Information*. London: Serpent's Tail.

Dentsu Communication Institute. 2006. 世界60カ国価値観データブック [World 60 values databook]. Tokyo: Dentsu Research Institute.

Dery, Mark. 1996. *Escape Velocity: Cyberculture at the End of the Century*. New York: Grove Press.

de Wildt, Lars, and Stef Aupers. 2017. "Bibles and BioShock: Affording Religious Discussion on Video Game Forums." In *CHI PLAY '17: Proceedings of the Annual Symposium on Computer-Human Interaction in Play*, edited by Ben Schouten, Panos Markopoulos and Zachary Toups, 463–475. New York: ACM Press. doi: 10.1145/3116595.3116625.

de Wildt, Lars, and Stef Aupers. 2019. "Playing the Other: Role-Playing Religion in Videogames." *European Journal of Cultural Studies* 22, no. 5-6: 867–884. doi: 10.1177/1367549418790454.

de Wildt, Lars, and Stef Aupers. 2020. "Pop Theology: Forum Discussions on Religion in Videogames." *Information, Communication & Society* 23, no. 10: 1444–1462. doi: 10.1080/1369118X.2019.1577476.

de Wildt, Lars, and S. D. Aupers. 2021. "Eclectic Religion: The Flattening of Religious Cultural Heritage in Videogames." *International Journal of Heritage Studies* 27, no. 3: 312–330. doi: 10.1080/13527258.2020.1746920.

Dobbelaere, Karel. 1981. "Trend report: Secularization: A Multi-Dimensional Concept." *Current Sociology* 29, no. 2: 3–153.

Droogers, André. 2014. *Religion at Play: A Manifesto*. Eugene, OR: Wipf and Stock Publishers.

Ellul, Jacques. 1967. *The Technological Society*. New York: Vintage Books.

Entertainment Retailers Association. 2018. *2018 Yearbook*. London: Entertainment Retailers Association.

Entertainment Software Association. 2018. *2018 Essential Facts About the Computer and Video Game Industry*. Washington, DC: Entertainment Software Association.

Evolvi, Giulia. 2018. *Blogging My Religion: Secular, Muslim, and Catholic Media Spaces in Europe*. New York: Routledge.

Geertz, Clifford. 2005. "Deep Play: Notes on the Balinese Cockfight." *Daedalus* 134, no. 4: 56–86.

Geraci, Robert M. 2012. *Apocalyptic AI: Visions of Heaven in Robotics, Artificial Intelligence, and Virtual Reality*. New York: Oxford University Press.

Geraci, Robert M. 2014. *Virtually Sacred: Myth and Meaning in World of Warcraft and Second Life*. New York: Oxford University Press.

Habermas, Jürgen. 2006. "Religion in the Public Sphere." *European Journal of Philosophy* 14, no. 1: 1–25.

Habermas, Jürgen. 2008. "Notes on Post-Secular Society." *New Perspectives Quarterly* 25, no. 4: 17–29.

Hamilton, Malcolm B. 2000. "An Analysis of the Festival for Mind-Body-Spirit, London." In: *Beyond New Age: Exploring Alternative Spirituality*, edited by Steven Sutcliffe and Marion Bowman, 188–200. Edinburgh, UK: Edinburgh University Press.

Harari, Yuval Noah. 2016. *Homo Deus. A Brief History of Tomorrow*. London: Harvill Secker.

Heelas, Paul. 1996. *The New Age Movement*. Oxford: Blackwell.

Heelas, Paul, and Linda Woodhead. 2005. *The Spiritual Revolution: Why Religion Is Giving Way to Spirituality*. With Benjamin Seel, Bronislaw Szerszynski, and Karin Tusting. Oxford: Blackwell.

Hjarvard, Stig. 2016. "Mediatization and the Changing Authority of Religion." *Media, Culture & Society* 38, no. 1: 8–17.

Hooghe, Marc, Ellen Quintelier, and Tim Reeskens. 2006. "Kerkpraktijk in Vlaanderen." *Ethische Perspectieven* 16, no. 2: 113–123.

Hoover, Stewart M. 2006. *Religion in the Media Age*. London and New York: Routledge.

Houtman, Dick, and Stef Aupers. 2007. "The Spiritual Turn and the Decline of Tradition: The Spread of Post-Christian Spirituality in Fourteen Western Countries (1981–2000)." *Journal for the Scientific Study of Religion* 46, no. 3: 305–320.

Jenkins, Henry. 2012. *Textual Poachers: Television Fans and Participatory Culture*. London and New York: Routledge.

Kelly, Kevin. 1999. "Nerd Theology." *Technology in Society: An International Journal* 21, no. 4: 349–354.

Kurzweil, Ray. 1999. *The Age of Spiritual Machines: When Computers Exceed Human Intelligence*. New York: Penguin Books.

Leary, Timothy. 1994. *Chaos and Cyberculture*. Berkeley, CA: Ronin Publishing.

Lenski, G. E. 1961. *The Religious Factor*. New York: Doubleday.

Levy, Steven. 2010. *Hackers: Heroes of the Computer Revolution*. Sebastopol, CA: O'Reilly Media.

Lövheim, Mia. 2004. "Young People, Religious Identity, and the Internet." In *Religion Online: Finding Faith on the Internet*, edited by Lorne L. Dawson and Douglas E. Cowan, 59–74. London and New York: Routledge.

Luckmann, Thomas. 1967. *The Invisible Religion: The Problem of Religion in Modern Society*. New York and London: Macmillan.

Lynch, Gordon. 2007. *The New Spirituality: An Introduction to Progressive Belief in the Twenty-First Century*. London and New York: I. B. Tauris.

Lyon, D. 2000. *Jesus in Disneyland: Religion in Postmodern Times*. Cambridge: Polity Press.

Mann, Joshua L. 2012. "Mobile Liturgy—Reflections on the Church of England's Daily Prayer App." *Online-Heidelberg Journal of Religions on the Internet* 12: 42–59.

Martin, David. 1990. *Tongues of Fire: The Explosion of Pentecostalism in Latin America*. Oxford and Cambridge, MA: Blackwell.

Meyer, Birgit, and Annelies Moors. 2006. *Religion, Media, and the Public Sphere*. Bloomington: Indiana University Press.

Moravec, Hans. 1988. *Mind Children. The Future of Robot and human Intelligence*. Cambridge, MA: Harvard University Press.

Morgan, David. 2013. "Religion and Media: A Critical Review of Recent Developments." *Critical Research on Religion* 1, no. 3: 347–356.

Morrisson, Mark S. 2007. *Modern Alchemy: Occultism and the Emergence of Atomic Theory.* New York: Oxford University Press.

Newzoo. 2017. *Global Games Market Report.* Utrecht, The Netherlands: Newzoo.

Noble, David. 1999. *The Religion of Technology: The Divinity of Man and the Spirit of Invention*, New York and London: Penguin Books.

Noomen, Ineke, Dick Houtman, and Stef Aupers. 2011. " 'In Their Own Image': Catholic, Protestant and Holistic Spiritual Appropriations of the Internet." *Information, Communication and Society* 14, no. 8: 1097–1117.

Parsons, Talcott. 1977. *The Evolution of Societies.* Edited by Jackson Toby. Upper Saddle River, NJ: Prentice-Hall.

Partridge, Christopher. 2005. *The Re-enchantment of the West.* Vol. 1, *Understanding Popular Occulture.* London. Continuum.

Pew Research Center. 2018. *The Age Gap in Religion around the World.* Washington, DC: Pew Research Center.

Possamai, Adam. 2003. "Alternative spiritualities and the cultural logic of late capitalism." *Culture and Religion* 4, no. 1: 31–45.

Possamai, Adam. 2005. *Religion and Popular Culture: A Hyper-Real Testament.* New York: Peter Lang.

Possamai, Adam. 2012. *Handbook of Hyper-Real Religions.* Leiden, The Netherlands, and Boston: Brill.

Radde-Antweiler, Kerstin. 2008. "Virtual Religion: An Approach to a Religious and Ritual Topography of Second Life." *Online-Heidelberg Journal of Religions on the Internet* 3, no. 1: 174–211.

Roeland, Johan, Stef Aupers, Dick Houtman, Martijn De Koning, and Ineke Noomen. 2010. "The Quest for Religious Purity in New Age, Evangelicalism and Islam Religious Renditions of Dutch Youth and the Luckmann Legacy." In *Annual Review of the Sociology of Religion*, 289–306. Leiden, The Netherlands: Brill.

Roszak, Theodor. 2000. *From Satori to Silicon Valley: San Francisco and the American Counterculture.* Redwood City, CA: Stanford University Press.

Rushkoff, Douglas. 1994. *Cyberia: Life in the Trenches of Cyberspace.* San Francisco: Harper Collins.

Schaap, Julian, and Stef Aupers. 2017. " 'Gods in World of Warcraft Exist': Religious Reflexivity and the Quest for Meaning in Online Computer Games." *New Media & Society* 19, no. 11: 1744–1760.

Schultze, Quentin J. 2003. *Televangelism and American Culture: The Business of Popular Religion.* Eugene, OR: Wipf and Stock Publishers.

Shiner, Larry. 1967. "The Concept of Secularization in Empirical Research." *Journal for the Scientific Study of Religion* 6, no. 2: 207–220.

Stark, Rodney, and William Sims Bainbridge. 1985. *The Future of Religion: Secularization, Revival and Cult Formation.* Berkeley: University of California Press.

Stenger, Nicole. 1992. "Mind Is a Leaking Rainbow." In: *Cyberspace: First Steps*, edited by Michael Benedikt, 49–58. Cambridge, MA: MIT Press.

Stolov, Jeremy. 2005. "Religion and/as Media." *Theory, Culture & Society* 22, no. 4: 119–145.

Stolov, Jeremy. 2008. "Salvation by Electricity." In *Religion: Beyond a Concept*, edited by Hent de Vries, 668–687. New York: Fordham University Press.

Stout, Daniel A. 2012. *Media and Religion: Foundations of an Emerging Field*. London and New York: Routledge.

Sutcliffe, Steven, and Marion Bowman, eds. 2000. *Beyond New Age: Exploring Alternative Spirituality*. Edinburgh: Edinburgh University Press.

Tschannen, Olivier. 1991. "The Secularization Paradigm: A Systematization." *Journal for the Scientific Study of Religion* 30, no. 4: 395–415.

Turkle, S. 1995. *Life on the Screen: Identity in the Age of the Internet*. New York: Simon & Schuster.

Turner, Fred. 2010. *From Counterculture to Cyberculture: Stewart Brand, the Whole Earth Network, and the Rise of Digital Utopianism*. Chicago: University of Chicago Press.

van Bohemen, Samira, Liesbet van Zoonen, and Stef Aupers. 2014. "Negotiating Gender through Fun and Play: Radical Femininity and Fantasy in the Red Hat Society." *Journal of Contemporary Ethnography* 43, no. 5: 582–600.

Vitullo, Alessandra. 2019. "Multisite Churches." *Online-Heidelberg Journal of Religions on the Internet* 14: 41–60.

Wagner, Rachel. 2012. *Godwired: Religion, Ritual and Virtual Reality*. London and New York: Routledge.

Warner, R. Stephen. 1993. "Work in Progress toward a New Paradigm for the Sociological Study of Religion in the United States." *American Journal of Sociology* 98 no. 5: 1044–1093.

Weber, Max. (1919) 1948. "Science as a Vocation." In *From Weber: Essays in Sociology*, edited by H. H. Gerth and C. Wright Mills, 29–156. London: Routledge.

Weber, Max. (1930) 2005. *The Protestant Ethic and the Spirit of Capitalism*. London: Routledge.

Wertheim, Margaret. 2000. *The Pearly Gates of Cyberspace: A History of Space from Dante to the Internet*. London: Virago Press.

Wilson, Bryan. 1976. *Contemporary Transformations of Religion*. Oxford: Oxford University Press.

Yinger, J. M. 1970. *The Scientific Study of Religion*. London: Macmillan.

Zuckerman, P. 2006. "Atheism: Contemporary Numbers and Patterns." In *The Cambridge Companion to Atheism*, edited by Michael Martin, 47–66. New York: Cambridge University Press.

CHAPTER 10

TECHNOLOGY, LABOR, AND THE GIG ECONOMY

JAMIE WOODCOCK

The "gig economy" has become a popular term, often involving a debate about how technology is changing labor and what work is like today. This chapter takes a broader view of the way that work has changed since 1980. This history provides an important backdrop to contemporary discussions about digital technology (which is often what is being referred to in these debates) and work, as well as defining the terms involved in the debates on the future of work.

Once these basic terms and backdrop have been established, the chapter examines the key digital trends that are reshaping work. The most important of these are digital platforms—a new form of hosting and distributing media, and increasingly organizing work. While the gig economy is broader than platform work, companies such as Uber have come to symbolize the changes introduced by the gig economy. Drawing on existing research with platform-based workers, the different experiences of work are explored, providing an outline of the gig economy. The last part of the chapter explores the sociological significance of the changing relationship between technology, labor, and the gig economy. This provides a series of different analytical angles on the problem, as well as drawing out important sociological concerns. It concludes with some predictions about how work may change in the future, as well as putting forward possible research questions.

Understanding the Changes in Work and Labor

The emergence of the gig economy is rooted in longer-term changes to work. In the context of the Global North, the work relation is often normalized in terms of the "standard employment relationship." Broadly speaking, this refers to the arrangements following World War II, in which workers could expect a "stable, socially protected, dependent, full-time job . . . the basic conditions of which (working time, pay, social transfers) are regulated to a minimum level by collective agreement or by labour and/or social security law" (Bosch, 2004, 618–619). This experience is limited mainly to workers in the Global North—and more often than not to white male citizens. In much of the Global South, there has not been this experience of work (Webster, Lambert, and Bezuidenhout 2008). Furthermore, within the Global North, it is worth noting that many people were not able to access or were excluded from these forms of stable work, including many women, migrants, and otherwise marginalized workers. Therefore, "for most people, most of the time, work has been a precarious relationship" (Woodcock and Graham 2019, 16). Despite this, the existence of some form of stable employment relationship had implications for many. For example, this work entailed a "link" between the work relationship and the "wider risk-sharing role of the welfare or social state," which developed in the same postwar period (Fudge 2017, 379).

The collapse—or at least undermining—of this relationship is often attributed to the success of neoliberalism from the 1970s onward. However, as Jamie Peck (2013, 133) notes, neoliberalism is a kind of "rascal concept" that is often deployed with "pejorative intent" to critique changes. However, as Peck (2013, 153) continues, using neoliberalism as a term "must not be a substitute for explanation; it should be an occasion for explanation." David Harvey (2007, 2) argues that neoliberalism is "in the first instance a theory of political economic practices that propose that human well-being can best be advanced by liberating individual entrepreneurial freedoms and skills within an institutional framework characterized by strong private property rights, free markets, and free trade." This has had concrete effects on the experience of work, often implemented through "shock doctrine" reforms quickly introduced after crises (Klein 2008). There are three important dynamics that this has introduced: first, undermining and attacking the terms and conditions of work, often resulting in shifts away from the standard employment contract; second, cutting back on the welfare state, seeking to break the link between work and welfare discussed before; and third, privatization programs and introduction of market forces and competition (Harvey 2007, 12).

The outcome has been a series of detrimental changes to the work relationship for workers. For example, in the United Kingdom there has been a significant increase in temporary work across the public sector, including health, public administration, and education (McDowell, Batnitzky, and Dyer 2009, 9). This has involved "a general move away from the full employment goal towards activation policies" (MacGregor 2005, 144). There has been a polarization of job types (Kaplanis 2007), with a growth of what have been called "lousy jobs" (Goos and Manning 2007) that are stigmatized and considered low quality—as well as being low paid. Many of these shifts accelerated after the 2008 financial crisis—which provided another opportunity for neoliberal "shock" changes. For example, across the European Union recommendations argued that "EU member states should develop measures within a policy framework informed by the principles of 'flexicurity' " (Heyes 2011, 643). However, as Heyes (2011, 643) argues, the "dominant trend has been towards less security." This is differentiated: less security for workers, alongside less obligation for employers.

Although keeping in mind Peck's warning about neoliberalism, much of this has been captured by the idea of precarious work. Mitropoulos (2005, 13) notes this, arguing that using the term "precarious" for work can be "both unwieldy and indeterminate. If it is possible to say anything for certain about precariousness, it is that it teeters." As the International Labour Organization (2011, 5) definition states:

> In the most general sense, precarious work is a means for employers to shift risks and responsibilities on to workers. It is work performed in the formal and informal economy and is characterized by variable levels and degrees of objective (legal status) and subjective (feeling) characteristics of uncertainty and insecurity. Although a precarious job can have many faces, it is usually defined by uncertainty as to the duration of employment, multiple possible employers or a disguised or ambiguous employment relationship, a lack of access to social protection and benefits usually associated with employment, low pay, and substantial legal and practical obstacles to joining a trade union and bargaining collectively.

This is an attempt to capture the shift from "lifelong full-time work"—whether experienced, expected, or demanded—toward a "risk-fraught system of flexible, pluralized, decentralized underemployment, which, however, will possibly no longer raise the problem of unemployment in the sense of being completely without a paid job" (Beck 1992, 144). These changes are the result of "social, economic, and political forces" that "have aligned to make work more precarious" (Kalleberg 2009, 2). For Bourdieu (1998, 95) this precariousness is a "new mode of domination in public life ... based on the creation of a generalized and permanent state of insecurity aimed at forcing workers into submission, into the acceptance of exploitation."

The precariousness of work is also experienced differently across sectors of the economy and kinds of work. For example, the same kinds of marginalized workers who were excluded from the standard employment relationship also experience precarity in sharper ways. For example, lack of legal migration status places many workers at risk (Ryan 2005), meaning many are "often forced to accept the most precarious contracts, in jobs incommensurate with their skill levels" (McDowell, Batnitzky, and Dyer 2009, 4). Migrant cleaners in London, for example, are often not covered by existing regulator regimes (Woodcock 2014). This kind of reproductive work, like cleaning or domestic work, is often "invisible," lacking either employment protection or collective bargaining (Pollert and Charlwood 2009). This stands in contrast to some forms of creative work considered highly skilled that can also be precarious.

There are disagreements about the scope and implications of precarious work. For example, Kevin Doogan (2009, 91) has argued that there is a "broad public perception of the end of jobs for life and the decline of stable employment" which operates alongside "the rise in long-term employment." While Doogan uses this to argue that not much has really changed—a point that will be returned in the two sections on platform work (see "Key Sociological Dimensions of the Gig Economy and Platform Work")—this misses the importance of the experience of work. Likewise, Kalleberg (2009, 8) notes that the "growth in perceived job insecurity" is an important component. As Seymour (2012, quoted in Woodcock 2017, 136) notes, the feeling that work is more precarious can change how people act within the work relationship. For example, even if a worker has not actually lost their job, the fear of losing it may make someone less likely to engage in collective action to change their conditions. Increasingly precarious work is a specter—both real and experienced—that hangs behind the debates on the gig economy.

Key Sociological Dimensions of the Gig Economy and Platform Work

The growth of the platforms and the gig economy is deeply entwined in a longer history of changes to the nature of work. Platforms, as Nick Srnicek (2017, 48) has argued, are

> a new type of firm; they are characterized by providing the infrastructure to intermediate between different user groups, by displaying monopoly tendencies driven by network effects, by employing cross-subsidization to draw in different user groups, and by having designed a core architecture that governs the interaction possibilities.

This organizational innovation builds upon technology, but as Woodcock and Graham (2019, 19) have argued, "there is "a complex and interconnected set of preconditions that shape how the gig economy emerges in practice." Although there is a temptation to place much of the emphasis on the role of technology, the growth of the gig economy is driven by "underlying factors of technology, society, political economy, or a combination"—each indicated in parentheses after the preconditions in the following quotation. The nine preconditions identified by Woodcock and Graham (2019, 20) are as follows:

> platform infrastructure (technology), digital legibility of work (technology), mass connectivity and cheap technology (technology and social), consumer attitudes and preferences (social), gendered and racialized relationships of work (social), desire for flexibility for/from workers (social and political economy), state regulation (political economy), worker power (political economy), and globalization and outsourcing (political economy and technology).

It is worth noting here that although platforms are at the sharp edge of the gig economy, there remain many areas of the gig economy that are not platformized. A key requirement for introducing the platform as an intermediary is digital legibility. There are therefore some kinds of work that are particularly suitable for "routinization, reorganization, and rebundling" (Peck 2017, 207), while others are more resistant to this. However, understanding platforms is necessary for tracing the latest developments of this model of organizing work—both platformized and not—as well as the potential implications for other kinds of work.

While there are many kinds of platforms reshaping society at present, in the context of the gig economy the focus needs to be on work platforms. These involve platforms which provide "tools to bring together the supply of, and demand for, labour" (Graham and Woodcock 2018, 242), most commonly involving an application (whether on a smartphone or browser), the digital infrastructure underpinning the interactions, and algorithms for managing the work. Algorithmic management has become a key area of research (Lee et al. 2015; Rosenblat and Stark 2016; Rosenblat 2018), as well as considering how ranking and reputation systems increasingly regulate interactions at work (Gandini 2016) and aspects of gamification at work (Woodcock and Johnson 2018).

The application of platform technology to the gig economy has scaled up the organization of this kind of work. However, one of the empirical challenges is effectively gauging how many people are now involved in this kind of work. At the high end, it has been predicted that by 2025 one-third of all labor transactions will take place on digital platforms (Standing 2016) or that "540 million people could benefit from online talent platforms by 2025" (Manyika et al. 2016). In the Global North exact figures can be difficult to come by, with significant differences between estimates (Organisation for Economic Co-operation and Development 2019). In one study, 1.5% of respondents in France, Germany, Spain, Sweden, the United Kingdom, and the United States reported earning income from working on a platform (Manyika et al. 2016), while another study estimated that 11% of UK workers had (Huws and Joyce 2016) and that 8% of Americans worked on an online platform—an estimate that rises to 16% for those under the age of 29 (Smith 2016). In the broader gig economy, it has been estimated there are 1.1 million UK workers, a similar number to those working in the National Health Service (Balaram, Warden, and Wallace-Stephens 2017). Beyond this, Heeks (2017) estimated that 70 million had found work via platforms across the world. A study of seven African countries—Ghana, Kenya, Nigeria, Rwanda, South Africa, Tanzania, Uganda—found that 1.3% of people had worked on platforms.

Despite the lack of clarity on the absolute numbers involved, there has been a range of recent empirical studies that have shown much needed insights into the operation of platforms and the gig economy. In a review of empirical research, Vallas and Schor (2020, 273) identified four types of employment and labor market conditions involved in the gig economy. The first involves those who design platforms. This kind of digital labor is often hidden from view in discussions of platforms, although there have been studies that have sought to unpack this (Irani 2015; Cockayne 2016; Kelkar 2018). The second involves gig workers who provide services in-person (see "Geographically Tethered Work" below). The third is freelance cloud workers who "offer professional services via platforms," while the fourth are microworkers, completing short tasks online (Vallas and Schor 2020, 273) (these latter two are discussed in the section "Cloudwork" below). By distinguishing between the work completed in these two main ways, we can unpack the relationships between technology and labor in the gig economy.

Geographically Tethered Work

It is worth pointing out here that there are two different forms of platform work. The first is "geographically tethered work" that "takes existing forms of work that happen in particular places and reorganizes them through a digital platform" (Woodcock and Graham 2019, 51). This involves tasks like driving and delivery, as well as in-person activities like cleaning and care. Most work has historically been connected to a place because "labour-power has to go home every night" (Harvey 1989, 19). Place has therefore played a key role in the organization of work (Massey 1984, 8).

The most visible example of this kind of work can be found with Uber. The platform positions itself as a technology company, using a strategy of "regulatory entrepreneurship," that involves "changing the law" as "a significant part of the business plan" (Pollman and Barry 2016). The former chief executive officer of Uber, Travis Kalanick, compared the company to a political campaign in which they competed with an "incumbent . . . an asshole called 'taxi' " (Kalanick and Swisher 2014). Often, these companies emphasize the newness of what they are doing—found in the regular use of the term "disruption." The lack of platform regulation, again as Kalanick (2013) explained, has resulted in "massive regulatory ambiguity leading to one-sided competition which Uber has not engaged in to its own disadvantage." This ambiguity has been identified by Scholz (2017a, 44), who argues that "Uber is a labor company, not simply a tech startup, which means that it is reliant on the availability of an abundance of cheap labor and a permissive regulatory environment." This remains, as the chapter will return to, a point of disagreement in the courts and in practice. There has also been a significant growth of platforms providing services like food delivery. Similar to Uber, these platforms have become a site of research on algorithmic management and new conditions of work (Waters and Woodcock 2017; Woodcock 2020), as well as the dangers of working in this way while navigating city streets (Christie and Ward 2018). In Callum Cant's (2019) ethnography of working for Deliveroo, he argues that these platforms have also become a laboratory in which new management techniques are being tested.

While there has been significant focus on these kinds of platform work, it is important to remember that there are other kinds of work that can be much less visible. As Ticona and Mateescu (2018) have argued, the focus on "Uberization" misses what is happening with domestic work platforms. They suggest a gendered bias in the literature. This develops from a longer-standing marginalization of domestic work, as Dalla Costa and James (1971, 10) argue, "where women are concerned, their labor appears to be a personal service outside of capital." This can either be as a "second shift" of work for women (Hochschild 1989) or involve systematically undervalued emotional labor (Hochschild 1983). In the context of platform work, Hunt and Samman (2019) have argued, "on the whole it represents the continuation (and in some cases deepening) of long-standing structural, and gendered, inequalities." While Uber is often mentioned in debates about platforms, Care.com rarely is, despite having 12.7 million "caregivers" registered on the website (Care.com 2018). The development of domestic work platforms is creating new positives and negatives for workers who sign up. For example, they may have more flexibility and options for work, but the evidence so far points to low incomes and lack of employment protections (Hunt and Machingura 2016, 5). Additionally, this kind of work is "among the fastest growing and perhaps the most resistant to automation" (Ticona and Mateescu 2018) as "the machine doesn't exist that makes and minds children" (Dalla Costa and James 1971, 11).

Cloudwork

The second kind of platform work is "cloudwork." This differs from geographically tethered work because as "markets for digital work are created, ties between service work and particular places can be severed" (Woodcock and Graham 2019, 54). Cloudwork can involve microwork, comprising tasks like "image identification, transcription and annotation; content moderation; data collection and processing; audio and video transcription; and translation" (Berg et al. 2018, xv). Platforms like Amazon Mechanical Turk allow clients to "post bulk tasks" that are split into smaller parts of a crowd of workers to complete (Berg et al. 2018, xv). This builds on longer relationships of outsourcing—shifting work to other locations that might be cheaper—and crowdsourcing (Kaganer et al. 2013, 23), involving "taking a function once performed by employees and outsourcing it to an undefined (and generally large) network of people in the form of an open call" (Howe 2006). What is interesting about Mechanical Turk is that it is presented as though it already uses automation. As Scholz (2015) argues, Amazon's "crowd sorcerers work with coolness and the spectacle of innovation to conceal the worker." It is therefore a kind of "artificial artificial intelligence," in which humans are treated as software. For many applications, it can be cheaper and quicker to utilize human labor in this way, rather than developing an artificial intelligence alternative (Solon 2018). As Lanier (2014, 178) notes, this involves "a sense of magic, as if you can just pluck results out of the cloud at an incredibly low cost." Unsurprisingly, this means the work receives very low pay (Hara et al. 2018), with much work going unpaid (Irani and Silberman 2013). There is also an important relationship between this kind of work and the promise (or threat, depending on the perspective) of automation that is present with transport platform work. The tasks completed on microwork platforms are crucial for the development of machine learning and algorithms that will automate these tasks (Gray and Suri 2019).

Cloudwork can also involve longer freelance tasks like writing, website creation, or software development. This is often project-based work (Christin 2018; Osnowitz 2011). One debate is whether these kinds of platforms are replacing temporary employment agencies (Corporaal and Lehdonvirta 2017) or encouraging outsourcing from the traditional economy (Drahokoupil and Piasna 2019). Either way, the technology allows for this kind of work to be coordinated across "planetary labour markets" (Graham and Anwar 2019). The platforms that organize this kind of freelance work have also grown rapidly in scale. For example, Upwork claims to have 12 million registered workers and

Freelancer 25 million (Graham and Anwar 2019). As noted, it can be difficult to estimate how many of those are actually able to work. The numbers signing up are often not the same as the levels of work available. However, in this kind of work, like microwork, it is important to remember that place still matters. Even if these workers can be engaged over the internet, the work is still requested and still happens in particular places. As Graham and Anwar (2018) argue, it does not take place in some digital space, instead building upon previous economic, social, and political relationships. Similarly, Ettlinger (2017) has found geographic clustering of work relationships on platforms. For example, much of the work is requested by companies in the Global North, with increasing numbers of workers located in the Global South, mirroring prior relationships of colonial exploitation.

Implications of Platform Work

When platforms were being introduced to organize work, many commentators saw this as a positive development. For example, the term "sharing economy" (Sundararajan 2017) was often used, implying a collaborative and optimistic sense of what these developments would involve. Similarly, as Kessler (2018, x) explained, a startup founder at the time claimed the gig economy meant "we could work for our neighbours, connect with as many projects as we needed to get by, and fit those gigs between band rehearsals, gardening, and other passion" projects. However, as these platforms have grown in scope and public awareness, there have been increasing criticisms of the model for work (Slee 2015; Schor 2020). Hill (2017, 4) summarizes the outcome as a "raw deal" for workers in the United States. Instead of seeing sharing at the core of the relationship, van Doorn (2017, 901) notes that these are "platform labour intermediaries that, despite their self-presentation as tech companies, operate as new players in a dynamic temporary staffing industry." Similarly, Ravenelle (2019, 6) argues that "despite its focus on emerging technology," the resulting gig economy "is truly a movement forward to the past" for employment protections.

There has been considerable debate on the employment status of workers in the gig economy (Cherry 2016; Rogers 2016; Dubal 2017a; Aloisi 2018; De Stefano 2018). This has included academic debates as well as legal challenges, with only some recently proving successful (Collier, Dubal, and Carter 2017; Dubal 2017b). For gig workers, as Woodcock and Graham (2019, 32) argue,

> Constructing the relationship in this way has involved the widespread use of a different kind of relationship, far removed from the 'standard employment relationship'. Instead of an employment relationship, many kinds of gig work instead use versions of self-employment and independent contractor status. This goes further than the removal of stable employment that we have traced since the 1970s, representing a breaking of the employment relationship and the freeing of platforms from many of the responsibilities and requirements that used to be involved.

In many cases, this means not being covered by regulations for minimum wages, holiday pay, sick pay, parental leave, trade union rights, protections against dismissal, and so on. The use of self-employment status can be seen as an extension of the wider shifts in the context of employment discussed at the beginning of the chapter. There have been some cases of reclassification of gig economy workers, mainly in transportation, although in general there has been "relative quiet at a national policy level" (Countouris and De Stefano 2019, 57).

In most of the world this involves a debate between employment and self-employment, posing two different ways of organizing the work. However, in the United Kingdom, as Jason Moyer-Lee (2018), the general secretary of the Independent Workers' Union of Great Britain, has argued, platforms have argued that,

> the problem is confusion in the law, or the inability of the law to keep up with the times, which can result in workers being inadvertently deprived of rights to which they're entitled. On the other side of the debate, you have those of us who have been submitting and repeatedly winning tribunal cases establishing the 'gig economy's' labourers as limb (b) workers, in particular the Independent Workers' Union of Great Britain ... and of course the judges who are writing these decisions. We say the law is pretty clear and the companies are clearly on the wrong side of it.

This status of "worker"—or to use the legal term "limb (b) worker"[1]—is an intermediate status, between employment and self-employment, involving some aspects of employment law protection, while retaining the flexibility that many workers are looking for in the gig economy. Vallas and Schor (2020, 285) warn that "if platforms are forced to convert workers to employees, it will result in major changes and may be a threat to profitability." Even without legal victories, there have been some instances of stricter regulation, including the introduction of a minimum wage for drivers in New York City (Schor 2020).

These courtroom battles over employment status have not been the only indication of resistance to platforms in the gig economy. There have been challenges to the operation of the platform model. For example, Trebor Scholz (2017b, 47) has argued for "platform cooperatives" as democratic and cooperatively owned alternatives to the current organization of platforms. He ask us to "just for one moment imagine that the algorithmic heart of any of these citadels of anti-unionism could be cloned and brought back to life under a different ownership model, with fair working conditions, as a humane alternative to the free market model."

From another angle, there has also been a marked increase in worker resistance on platforms. As has been well documented, there have been waves of strikes on food delivery platforms, starting in London in 2016 (Waters and Woodcock 2017) and spreading across Europe (Cant 2018). There have now been globally coordinated strikes of food and transport platform workers (Woodcock 2020). Workers have successfully found new and innovative ways to organize on these platforms, starting from the tensions already present in the work (Woodcock 2018). Often, this has involved mobilizing and organizing through WhatsApp and other "mass self-communication networks" (Wood 2015). As Kurt Vandaele (2018, 16) has argued, these "networks are serving as a 'breeding ground' for self-organized courier associations boosting their associational power." While these networks can be most obviously found with geographically tethered work and the meeting points around the city, there is increasing evidence of widespread networks in cloudwork too. Online communication and forums are an important part of this work (Gupta et al. 2014; Gray et al. 2016; Yin et al. 2016; Wood et al. 2018).

One of the remaining debates about the implications of platform work hinges on what they represent. For some theorists, platforms are understood as marking a break from previous forms of employment and organization—a future of work that is rapidly becoming a present. This can be seen in the use of the term "Uberization" to capture how these changes have swept beyond the taxi industry (see Davis 2016a, 2016b; Kornberger, Pflueger, and Mouritsen 2017). For example, Vallas and Schor (2020, 282) argue that "platforms represent a distinctively new form of economic activity. In advancing this argument, we caution that platforms represent a nascent and highly dynamic economic form characterized by high levels of instability whose future is difficult to foresee." However, there are many aspects of platforms and the gig economy that hark back to previous ways of organizing work. For example, precarious and on-call work has a long history in the dock industry (Woodcock and Graham 2019). Similarly, Vallas and Schor (2020, 282) argue that the "extraction of value rests on a new structural form in which platforms remain powerful even as they cede control over aspects of the labor process." However, piecework is not a new phenomenon, nor is drawing upon alternative methods of supervision and surveillance at work. In order to address these questions, further empirical research is necessary.

The Next Steps for Sociological Research on Technology, Labor, and the Gig Economy

Platforms and the gig economy are often presented as a clear break from the past. This chapter has outlined the longer history and preconditions of how technology, labor, and the gig economy combine to produce different outcomes for workers in these kinds of work. However, the effects of the gig economy extend far beyond just delivery drivers and online cloudworkers. New models of organizing work are rarely isolated to one sector. As Kim Moody (2017, 69) has noted, there is a risk of only focusing on this kind of work because it is new. This can "trivialize the deeper reality of capitalism, its dynamics, and the altered state of working-class life." One way to protect against this is to try and understand the broader implications of platforms. More empirical research is, of course, to be welcomed here. After all, the methods and techniques that become successful in the platform-driven gig economy will increasingly be applied more widely—both to other kinds of work and to social life more generally.

As Vallas and Schor (2020, 285) point out, "although research on platform work has grown rapidly, much remains unknown. To some extent, such uncertainty reflects the inchoate nature of the phenomenon itself." Work is undergoing changes in which different actors are fighting for their own interests and the changes are far from complete. However, through this survey of existing research, it is possible to point toward some key areas that further research can unpack. First, little is known about the relationships of work involved in the creation and maintenance of platforms. When we talk of "platform work" we focus on those workers providing the services for the platform, rather than the workers who are analyzing the data, writing code, or designing systems. In a sense, this labor has become hidden, despite the clear importance it has for making sense of the labor process of workers on the platform. In a similar vein, there has been little research connecting the traditional parts of the economy with platforms other than cyclical changes between the two (Farrell and Greig 2016; Farrell, Greig, and Hamoudi 2018; Huang et al. 2019), and this is something likely to further transform, particularly following the COVID-19 pandemic.

A second important area for future research involves unpacking the roles of algorithms and data at work. There is a growing body of literature emerging (Pasquale 2015; O'Neil 2017; Eubanks 2019; Noble 2018; Benjamin 2019) that has drawn attention to the ways in which algorithms are reproducing existing biases, including gender, race, and class. The use of ratings in platform work has already been widely critiqued (Gandini 2016; Hannák et al. 2017; Cansoy 2018; Ajunwa and Greene 2019), but these metrics are increasingly being applied beyond platforms to other forms of work (Moore 2018).

Following on from this, the final area that demands urgent sociological attention is the ability for the current state of the gig economy to be reshaped. While there is emerging evidence of resistance and collective organizing across a range of sectors in the gig economy, there is still little agreement about the implications for this. The early commentators who argued that collective organizing had been defeated by algorithmic management are increasingly being disproven in practice. For example, Vallas and Schor (2020, 287) suggest that "early views about the potential for collective action have been too negative." Sociological inquiry would benefit from connecting the wider literatures on resistance and organizing at work to the current research on the gig economy, understanding how the dynamics differ and converge.

Note

1. For more information on the differences between employment statuses and the definition of "limb (b) worker", see Section 230(3) of the Employment Rights Act 1996. Available here: https://www.legislation.gov.uk/ukpga/1996/18.

References

Ajunwa, Ifeoma, and Daniel Greene. 2019. "Platforms at Work: Automated Hiring Platforms and Other New Intermediaries in the Organization of Work." In *Research in the Sociology of Work*. Vol. 33, *Work and Labor in the Digital Age*, edited by Steve P. Vallas and Anne Kovalainen, 61–91. Bingley, UK: Emerald.

Aloisi, Antonio. 2018. "Dispatch No. 13—Italy—'With great power comes virtual freedom': A Review of the First Italian Case Holding That (Food-Delivery) Platform Workers Are Not Employees." *Comparative Labor Law and Policy Journal*, December 3. https://cllpj.law.illinois.edu/dispatches.

Balaram, Brhmie, Josie Warden, and Fabian Wallace-Stephens. 2017. *Good Gigs: A Fairer Future for the UK's Gig Economy*. London: Royal Society of Arts.

Beck, Ulrich. 1992. *Risk Society: Towards a New Modernity*. London: Sage.

Benjamin, Ruha. 2019. *Race after Technology: Abolitionist Tools for the New Jim Code*. Cambridge: Polity.

Berg, Janine, Marianne Furrer, Ellie Harman, Uma Rani, and M. Six Silberman. 2018. *Digital Labour Platforms and the Future of Work: Towards Decent Work in the Online World*. Geneva: International Labour Organization.

Bosch, Gerhard. 2004. "Towards a New Standard Employment Relationship in Western Europe." *British Journal of Industrial Relations* 42, no. 4: 617–636.

Bourdieu, Pierre. 1998. *Contre Feux*. Paris: Raisons d'agir.

Cansoy, M. 2018. " 'Sharing' in Unequal Spaces: Short-Term Rentals and the Reproduction of Urban Inequalities." PhD diss., Boston College.

Cant, Callum. 2018. "The Wave of Worker Resistance in European Food Platforms 2016–17. *Notes from Below* 1. https://notesfrombelow.org/article/european-food-platform-strike-wave.

Cant, Callum. 2019. *Riding for Deliveroo: Resistance in the New Economy*. Cambridge: Polity.

Care.com. 2018. "Company Overview." https://www.care.com/company-overview.

Cherry, Miriam A. 2016. "Beyond Misclassification: The Digital Transformation of Work." *Comparative Labor Law Policy Journal* 37, no. 3: 577–602.

Christie, Nicola, and Heather Ward. 2018. *The Emerging Issues for Management of Occupational Road Risk in a Changing Economy: A Survey of Gig Economy Drivers, Riders and Their Managers*. London: UCL Centre for Transport Studies.

Christin, Angèle. 2018. "Counting Clicks: Quantification and Variation in Web Journalism in the United States and France." *American Journal of Sociology* 123, no. 5: 1382–1415.

Cockayne, Daniel G. 2016. "Sharing and Neoliberal Discourse: The Economic Function of Sharing in the Digital On-Demand Economy." *Geoforum* 77: 73–82.

Collier, Ruth Berins, V. B. Dubal, and Christopher Carter. 2017. "Labor Platforms and Gig Work: The Failure to Regulate." Working Paper 106–17, Institute for Research on Labor and Employment, University of California, Berkeley. https://www.irle.berkeley.edu/files/2017/Labor-Platforms-and-Gig-Work.pdf.

Corporaal, Greetje F., and Vili Lehdonvirta. 2017. *Platform Sourcing: How Fortune 500 Firms Are Adopting Online Freelancing Platforms*. Oxford: Oxford Internet Institute. https://www.oii.ox.ac.uk/publications/platformsourcing.pdf.

Countouris, Nicola, and Valerio De Stefano. 2019. *New Trade Union Strategies for New Forms of Employment*. Brussels: European Trade Union Confederation.

Dalla Costa, Mariarosa, and Selma James. 1971. *The Power of Women and the Subversion of the Community*. Brooklyn, NY: Pétroleuse Press.

Davis, Gerald F. 2016a. *The Vanishing American Corporation: Navigating the Hazards of a New Economy*. San Francisco: Berrett-Kohler.

Davis, Gerald F. 2016b. "What Might Replace the Modern Corporation? Uberization and the Web Page Enterprise." *Seattle University Law Review* 39: 501–515.

De Stefano, Valerio. 2018. "A More Comprehensive Approach to Platform-Work Litigation." *Regulating for Globalisation* (blog), November 28. http://regulatingforglobalization.com/2018/11/28/a-more-comprensive-approach-to-platform-work-litigation/.

Doogan, Kevin. 2009. *New Capitalism? The Transformation of Work*. London: Polity.

Drahokoupil, Jan, and Agnieszka Piasna. 2019. "Work in the Platform Economy: Deliveroo Riders in Belgium and the SMart Arrangement." Working Paper 2019.01, European Trade Union Institute, Brussels, Belgium.

Dubal, Veena B. 2017a. "Wage-Slave or Entrepreneur? Contesting the Dualism of Legal Worker Categories." *California Law Review* 105: 65–126.

Dubal, Veena B. 2017b. "Winning the Battle, Losing the War: Assessing the Impact of Misclassification Litigation on Workers in the Gig Economy." *Wisconsin Law Review* 239: 739–802.

Ettlinger, Nancy. 2017. "Paradoxes, Problems and Potentialities of Online Work Platforms." *Work Organisation, Labour & Globalisation* 11, no. 2: 21–34.

Eubanks, Virginia. 2019. *Automating Inequality: How High-Tech Tools Profile, Police, and Punish the Poor*. New York: St. Martin's Press.

Farrell, Diana, and Fiona Greig. 2016. "The Online Platform Economy: Has Growth Peaked?" Working Paper, JPMorgan Chase Institute, New York.

Farrell, Diana, Fiona Greig, and Amar Hamoudi. 2018. "The Online Platform Economy in 2018: Drivers, Workers, Sellers, and Lessors." Working Paper, JPMorgan Chase Institute, New York.

Fudge, Judy. 2017. "The Future of the Standard Employment Relationship: Labour Law, New Institutional Economics and Old Power Resource Theory." *Journal of Industrial Relations* 59, no. 3: 374–392.

Gandini, Alessandro. 2016. *The Reputation Economy: Understanding Knowledge Work in Digital Society*. London: Palgrave Macmillan.

Goos, Maarten, and Alan Manning. 2007. "Lousy and Lovely Jobs: The Rising Polarization of Work in Britain." *Review of Economics and Statistics* 89, no. 1: 118–133.

Graham, Mark, and Mohammad Amir Anwar. 2018. "Digital Labour." In *Digital Geographies*, edited by James Ash, Rob Kitchin, and Agnieszka Leszczynski, 177–187. London: Sage.

Graham, Mark, and Mohammad Amir Anwar. 2019. "The Global Gig Economy: Towards a Planetary Labour Market?" *First Monday* 24, no. 4. doi.org/10.5210/fm.v24i4.9913.Graham, M., and J. Woodcock. 2018. "Towards a Fairer Platform Economy: Introducing the Fairwork Foundation." *Alternate Routes* 29: 242–253.

Gray, Mary L., and Siddharth Suri. 2019. *Ghost Work: How to Stop Silicon Valley from Building a New Global Underclass*. New York: Houghton Mifflin Harcourt.

Gray, Mary L., Siddharth Suri, Syed Shoaib Ali, and Deepti Kulkarni. 2016. "The Crowd Is a Collaborative Network." In *CSCW'16: Proceedings of the 19th ACM Conference on Computer-Supported Cooperative Work & Social Computing, San Francisco, CA, 27 February–2 March*, 134–147. New York: ACM Press.

Gupta, Neha, David Martin, Benjamin V. Hanrahan, and Jacki O'Neill. 2014. "Turk-Life in India." In *Proceedings of the ACM International Conference on Supporting Group Work (GROUP'14), Sanibel Island, 9–12 November*, 1–11. New York: ACM Press.

Hannák, Anikó, Claudia Wagner, David Garcia, Alan Mislove, Markus Strohmaier, and Christo Wilson. 2017. "Bias in Online Freelance Marketplaces: Evidence from TaskRabbit and Fiverr." In *Proceedings of the 2017 ACM Conference on Computer Supported Cooperative Work and Social Computing*, 1914–1933. Portland, OR: ACM.

Hara, Kotaro, Abigail Adams, Kristy Milland, Saiph Savage, Chris Callison-Burch, and Jeffrey P. Bigham. 2018. "A Data-Driven Analysis of Workers' Earnings on Amazon Mechanical Turk." In *CHI'18: Proceedings of the 2018 CHI Conference on Human Factors in Computing Systems*, 114. New York: ACM Press.

Harvey, David. 1989. *The Urban Experience*. Oxford: Blackwell.

Harvey, David. 2007. *A Brief History of Neoliberalism*. Oxford: Oxford University Press.

Heeks, Richard. 2017. "Decent Work and the Digital Gig Economy: A Developing Country Perspective on Employment Impacts and Standards in Online Outsourcing, Crowdwork, etc." Development Informatics Working Paper 71. Centre for Development Informatics, Global Development Institute, SEED, Manchester, UK.

Heyes, Jason. 2011. "Flexicurity, Employment Protection and the Jobs Crisis." *Work, Employment and Society* 25, no. 4: 642–657.

Hill, Steven. 2017. *Raw Deal: How the "Uber Economy" and Runaway Capitalism Are Screwing American Workers*. New York: St Martin's Press.

Hochschild, Arlie Russell. 1983. *The Managed Heart: The Commercialisation of Human Feeling*. Berkeley: University of California Press.

Hochschild, Arlie. 1989. *The Second Shift: Working Families and the Revolution at Home*. With Anne Machung. New York: Penguin.

Howe, Jeff. 2006. "The Rise of Crowdsourcing." *Wired*, June 1. http://www.wired.com/2006/06/crowds/.

Huang, Ni, Gordon Burtch, Yili Hong, and Paul A. Pavlou. 2019. "Unemployment and Worker Participation in the Gig Economy: Evidence from an Online Labor Platform." *Information Systems Research* 31, no. 2. https://pubsonline.informs.org/doi/10.1287/isre.2019.0896.

Hunt, Abigail, and Fortunate Machingura. 2016. "A Good Gig? The Rise of On-Demand Domestic Work." ODI Development Progress Working Paper 7. Overseas Development Institute, London.

Hunt, Abigail, and Emma Samman. 2019. "Gender and the Gig Economy." ODI Working Paper 546. Overseas Development Institute, London.

Huws, Ursula, and Simon Joyce. 2016. *Crowd Working Survey: Size of the UK's "Gig Economy" Revealed for the First Time*. Hatfield, UK: University of Hertfordshire.

International Labour Organization. 2011. *Policies and Regulations to Combat Precarious Employment*. Geneva: International Labour Organization.

Irani, Lilly. 2015. "Difference and Dependence among Digital Workers: The Case of Amazon Mechanical Turk." *South Atlantic Quarterly* 114, no. 1: 225–234.

Irani, Lilly C., and M. Six Silberman. 2013. "Turkopticon: Interrupting Worker Invisibility in Amazon Mechanical Turk." *Proceedings of CHI 2013*, 28 April–2 May, 611–620. New York: ACM Press.

Kaganer, Evgeny, Erran Carmel, Rudy Hirscheim, and Timothy Olsen. 2013. "Managing the Human Cloud." *MIT Sloan Management Review* 54, no. 2: 23–32.

Kalanick, T. 2013. "Uber Policy White Paper 1.0." April 12. http://www.benedelman.org/uber/uber-policy-whitepaper.pdf.

Kalanick, Travis, and Kara Swisher. 2014. "Uber CEO: We're in a Political Battle with an 'Assh*le.'" *Mashable*, May 28. http://mashable.com/2014/05/28/travis-kalanick-co-founder-and-ceo-of-uber/.

Kalleberg, Arne L. 2009. "Precarious Work, Insecure Workers: Employment Relations in Transition." *American Sociological Review* 74, no. 1: 1–22.

Kaplanis, Ioannis. 2007. *The Geography of Employment Polarisation in Britain*. London: Institute for Public Policy Research.

Kelkar, S. 2018. "Engineering a Platform: The Construction of Interfaces, Users, Organizational Roles, and the Division of Labor." *New Media & Society* 20, no. 7: 2629–2646.

Kessler, Sarah. 2018. *Gigged: The Gig Economy, the End of the Job and the Future of Work*. New York: St. Martin's Press.

Klein, Naomi. 2008. *The Shock Doctrine: The Rise of Disaster Capitalism*. London: Penguin Books.

Kornberger, Martin, Dane Pflueger, and Jan Mouritsen. 2017. "Evaluative Infrastructures: Accounting for Platform Organization." *Accounting Organisations and Society* 60: 79–95.

Lanier, Jaron. 2014. *Who Owns the Future?* New York: Simon & Schuster.

Lee, Min Kyung, Daniel Kusbit, Evan Metsky, and Laura Dabbish. 2015. "Working with Machines: The Impact of Algorithmic, Data-Driven Management on Human Workers." In *Proceedings of the 33rd Annual ACM SIGCHI Conference*, edited by B. Begole, J. Kim, K. Inkpen and W. Wood, 1603–1612. New York: ACM Press.

MacGregor, Susanne. 2005. "The Welfare State and Neoliberalism." In *Neoliberalism: A Critical Reader*, edited by Alfredo Saad-Filho and Deborah Johnston, 142–148. London: Pluto Press.Manyika, James, Susan Lund, Jacques Bughin, Kelsey Robinson, Jan Mischke, and Deppa Mahajan. 2016. *Independent Work: Choice, Necessity, and the Gig Economy*. Washington, DC: McKinsey Global Institute. https://www.mckinsey.com/featured-insights/employment-and-growth/independent-work-choice-necessity-and-the-gig-economy.

Manyika, James, Susan Lund, Kelsey Robinson, John Valentino and Richard Dobbs. 2015. Connecting talent with opportunity in the digital age. Washington, DC: McKinsey & Company. https://www.mckinsey.com/featured-insights/employment-and-growth/connecting-talent-with-opportunity-in-the-digital-age.

Massey, Doreen. 1984. *Spatial Divisions of Labor: Social Structures and the Geography of Production*. New York: Routledge.

McDowell, Linda, Adina Batnitzky, and Sarah Dyer. 2009. "Precarious Work and Economic Migration: Emerging Immigrant Divisions of Labour in Greater London's Service Sector." *International Journal of Urban and Regional Research* 33, no. 1: 3–25.

Mitropoulos, Angela. 2005. "Precari-Us." *Mute: Precarious Reader* 2: 12–19.

Moody, Kim. 2017. *On New Terrain: How Capital Is Reshaping the Battleground of Class War*. Chicago: Haymarket.

Moore, Phoebe V. 2018. *The Quantified Self in Precarity: Work, Technology and What Counts*. Routledge Advances in Sociology. London and New York: Routledge.

Moyer-Lee, Jason. 2018. "When Will 'Gig Economy' Companies Admit That Their Workers Have Rights?" *The Guardian*, June 14. https://www.theguardian.com/commentisfree/2018/jun/14/gig-economy-workers-pimlico-plumbers-employment-rights.

Noble, Safiya Umoja. 2018. *Algorithms of Oppression: How Search Engines Reinforce Racism*. New York: New York University Press.

O'Neil, Cathy. 2017. *Weapons of Math Destruction: How Big Data Increases Inequality and Threatens Democracy*. London: Penguin.

Organisation for Economic Co-operation and Development. 2019. "Measuring Platform Mediated Workers." OECD Digital Economy Papers 282. OECD Publishing, Paris.

Osnowitz, Debra. 2011. *Freelancing Expertise: Contract Professionals in the New Economy*. Ithaca, NY: Cornell/ILR.

Pasquale, Frank. 2015. *The Black Box Society: The Secret Algorithms That Control Money and Information*. Cambridge, MA: Harvard University Press.

Peck, Jamie. 2013. "Explaining (with) Neoliberalism." *Territory, Politics, Governance* 1, no. 2: 132–157.

Peck, Jamie. 2017. *Offshore: Exploring the Worlds of Global Outsourcing*. Oxford: Oxford University Press.

Pollert, Anna, and Andy Charlwood. 2009. "The Vulnerable Worker in Britain and Problems at Work." *Work, Employment and Society* 23, no. 2: 343–362.

Pollman, Elizabeth, and Jordan M. Barry. 2016. "Regulatory Entrepreneurship." *Southern California Law Review* 90: 383–442.

Ravenelle, Alexandrea. 2019. *Hustle and Gig: Struggling and Surviving in the Sharing Economy*. Oakland, CA: University of California Press.

Rogers, Brishen. 2016. "Employment Rights in the Platform Economy: Getting Back to Basics." *Harvard Law Policy Review* 10: 479–520.

Rosenblat, Alex. 2018. *Uberland: How Algorithms are Rewriting the Rules of Work*. Oakland, CA: University of California Press.

Rosenblat, Alex, and Luke Stark. 2016. "Algorithmic Labor and Information Asymmetries: A Case Study of Uber's Drivers." *International Journal of Communication* 10: 3758–3784.

Ryan, Bernard. 2005. *Labour Migration and Employment Rights*. Liverpool, UK: Institute of Employment Rights.

Scholz, Trebor. 2015. "Think Outside the Boss: Cooperative Alternatives to the Sharing Economy." Public Seminar, April 5. https://www.publicseminar.org/2015/04/think-outside-the-boss.

Scholz, Trebor. 2017a. *Uberworked and Underpaid: How Workers are Disrupting the Digital Economy*. Cambridge: Polity.

Scholz, Trebor. 2017b. "Platform Cooperativism vs. the Sharing Economy." In *Big Data & Civic Engagement*, edited by Nicolas Douay and Annie Wan, 47–54. Rome: Planum.

Schor, Juliet B. 2020. *After the Gig: How the Sharing Economy Got Hijacked and How to Win It Back*. Oakland, CA: University of California Press.

Slee, Tom. 2015. *What's Yours Is Mine: Against the Sharing Economy*. London: OR Books.

Smith, Aaron. 2016. "Gig Work, Online Selling and Home Sharing." Pew Research Centre, November 17. http://www.pewinternet.org/2016/11/17/gig-work-online-selling-and-home-sharing/.

Solon, Olivia. 2018. "The Rise of 'Pseudo-AI': How Tech Firms Quietly Use Humans to Do Bots' Work." *The Guardian*, July 6. https://www.theguardian.com/technology/2018/jul/06/artificial-intelligence-ai-humans-bots-tech-companies.

Srnicek, Nick. 2017. *Platform Capitalism*. Cambridge: Polity.

Standing, Guy. 2016. *The Corruption of Capitalism: Why Rentiers Thrive and Work Does Not Pay*. London: Biteback Publishing.

Sundararajan, Arun. 2017. *The Sharing Economy: The End of Employment and the Rise of Crowd-Based Capitalism*. Cambridge, MA: MIT Press.

Ticona, Julia, and Alexandra Mateescu. 2018. "Trusted Strangers: Carework Platforms' Cultural Entrepreneurship in the On-Demand Economy." *New Media & Society* 20, no. 11: 4384–4404.

Vallas, Steven, and Juliet B. Schor. 2020. "What Do Platforms Do? Understanding the Gig Economy." *Annual Review of Sociology* 46: 273–294.

Vandaele, Kurt. 2018. "Will Trade Unions Survive in the Platform Economy? Emerging Patterns of Platform Workers' Collective Voice and Representation in Europe." Working Paper. European Trade Union Institute, Brussels, Belgium.

van Doorn, Niels. 2017. "Platform Labor: On the Gendered and Racialized Exploitation of Low-Income Service Work in the 'On-Demand' Economy." *Information, Communication & Society* 20, no. 6: 898–914.Waters, Facility, and Jamie Woodcock. 2017. "Far from Seamless: A Workers' Inquiry at Deliveroo." *Viewpoint Magazine*, September 20. https://viewpointmag.com/2017/09/20/far-seamless-workers-inquiry-deliveroo/.

Webster, Edward, Rob Lambert, and Andries Bezuidenhout. 2008. *Grounding Globalization: Labour in the Age of Insecurity*. Oxford: Blackwell.

Wood, Alex J. 2015. "Networks of Injustice and Worker Mobilisation at Walmart." *Industrial Relations Journal* 46, no. 4: 259–274.

Wood, Alex J., Vili Lehdonvirta, and Mark Graham. 2018. "Workers of the Internet Unite? Online Freelancer Organisation Among Remote Gig Economy Workers in Six Asian and African Countries." New Technology, Work and Employment 33, no 2. 95–112.

Woodcock, Jamie. 2014. "Precarious Work in London: New Forms of Organisation and the City." *City: Analysis of Urban Trends, Culture, Theory, Policy, Action* 18, no. 6: 776–788.

Woodcock, Jamie. 2017. *Working the Phones: Control and Resistance in Call Centres*. London: Pluto.

Woodcock, Jamie. 2018. "Digital Labour and Workers' Organisation." In *Global Perspectives on Workers' and Labour Organizations*, edited by Maurizio Atzeni and Immanuel Ness, 157–173. Singapore: Springer.

Woodcock, Jamie. 2020. "The Algorithmic Panopticon at Deliveroo: Measurement, Precarity, and the Illusion of Control." *Ephemera* 20, no. 3: 67–95.

Woodcock, Jamie, and Mark Graham. 2019. *The Gig Economy: A Critical Introduction*. Cambridge: Polity.

Woodcock, Jamie, and Mark R. Johnson. 2018. "Gamification: What It Is, and How to Fight It." *Sociological Review* 66, no. 3: 542–558.

Yin, Ming, Mary L. Gray, Siddharth Suri, and Jennifer Wortman Vaughan. 2016. "The Communication Network within the Crowd." Proceedings of the 25th International World Wide Web Conference (WWW), Montreal, Canada, April 11.

PART III

DIGITAL MEDIA IN EVERYDAY LIFE

CHAPTER 11

THE SOCIOLOGY OF MOBILE APPS

DEBORAH LUPTON

MOBILE applications (better known as "apps") are digital media commodities. They are small bits of software, microprograms designed to work quickly and easily on mobile devices such as smartphones, tablet computers, and wearable devices, with little effort required from users to upload them and put them into action. Since their introduction in 2008 (first by Apple, quickly followed by Google), apps have become popular forms of software. The two major app stores—Google Play and the Apple App Store—now offer millions of apps with a huge range of purposes and functions, receiving billions of downloads worldwide. Apps differ from other software in having limited functions but offering people easy access to software through the mobile devices that they often carry with them throughout their days and nights. Unlike other software, they are often free to use or else require only a small up-front fee or in-app purchases: Some app developers offer free "lite" versions as well as paid versions with more features. Just as mobile devices have become ubiquitous and permanently connected to the internet, so too are the apps that are downloaded onto this hardware. Apps are designed to be media artifacts that are quick to acquire on impulse and just as easily discarded or relinquished (Morris and Elkins 2015). They have been characterized as both mundane and stylish (Morris and Murray 2018) and as "charming junkware" (Bardini 2014).

This chapter presents a sociological analysis of apps. I draw on social and cultural theory and empirical research to discuss the ways in which apps can be understood as sociocultural and political phenomena. This sociological approach to apps departs from other approaches in that rather than focusing on design, instrumental, or utilitarian user-experience issues (such as how well-designed, popular, or effective apps are or how accurate their content), it views apps as sociocultural and political artifacts that are created and experienced in complex relationships and networks involving app users, app designers and developers, app stores, app blogs and news reports, as well as the broader sociopolitical environment involving government agencies, regulators, digital infrastructures, social institutions, and many other entities. This chapter will demonstrate that, like other media, apps are material objects invested with meaning and affective forces. They are designed and marketed with certain types of uses and users in mind and offer various promises to entice downloads and use but are not always taken up in these ways by users. This approach to apps incorporates sociological theory and research as well as new interdisciplinary fields of research such as science and technology studies, software studies, internet studies, and surveillance studies.

Three major perspectives presented in the social research literature on apps are outlined: (1) political economy, (2) Foucauldian perspectives, and (3) sociomaterial approaches. Each perspective adopts a different focus, but all elucidate important aspects of the sociocultural and political dimensions of apps. The outlined approaches range from a macro- to a micropolitical focus. Scholars engaging with the political economy approach are principally interested in the macropolitical dimensions of apps. These are the broad social, economic, and political structures (age, gender, social class, sexual identity, race/ethnicity, geographical location) and institutions (the workplace, educational sites, the family, the economy, the mass media, healthcare systems, and so on) in which apps are developed, promoted, and used. Foucauldian researchers often seek to bring the macro- together with the micropolitical elements of apps in understanding their biopolitical dimensions. The micropolitical focus dominates for scholars taking up sociomaterial perspectives to examine people's lived experiences as they come together with apps. The chapter ends with an overview of key insights and suggestions concerning where sociological app research might head in the future.

Background: The App Economy and Patterns of App Use

The rapid expansion of smartphone ownership globally—with over 3 billion users in 2019 (O'Dea 2020)—has been accompanied by a growing interest in apps. The app economy is thriving and expanding, in terms of both the number of apps published and downloaded and their commercial value (Dieter et al. 2019; Morris and Murray 2018). Consumers' interest in apps has continued to increase over time. Hundreds of billions of app downloads each year occur across the world (Clement 2020), with over 2 billion downloads in 2019 alone, representing the highest number of any year (Sydow 2020b). A report published by the app analytics company App Annie revealed that in 2019 US $120 billion had been spent by consumers on app purchases globally: twice that spent on commodities offered by the global music industry (Sydow 2020b). The app economy is global, with successful app publishers distributed across the world, including not only Silicon Valley in the United States but also Europe, Israel, and Asia. Indeed, two Chinese companies topped the list of the most lucrative app publishers in 2019 (App Annie 2020).

Most apps fulfill a solutionist approach to software development: They are designed to deal with a specific microproblem that has been identified by the app developer (Morris and Murray 2018). Above all, apps offer entertainment and convenience: helping people to engage in work activities, use social media, find their destinations, do their online shopping, seek romantic or sexual partners, check the weather forecast, find a ride, order food delivery, send and receive messages, play games, make and share photographs and videos, listen to music, manage their finances, monitor their health and physical activity, and many more services. As the Apple App Store famously put it in early app promotional efforts, "There's an app for that." An analysis of apps categorized in the Apple App Store revealed that game apps were far and above the most commonly offered, followed by business, education, and lifestyle apps (a large and diverse category including digital home assistant, shopping, service and job seeking, job makeover, astrology, and dating apps but not health or fitness, which have their own category) (Clement 2019). In terms of popularity (how many apps are downloaded), video streaming, content sharing, messaging, social media, and work-related apps rank at the top. Apple's top 10 free downloaded apps for 2019 (excluding game apps) were listed as YouTube, Instagram, Snapchat, TikTok, Messenger, Gmail, Netflix, Facebook, Google Maps, and Amazon (Stolyar 2020). A list of the all-time most popular apps on rival app store Google Play similarly identified the top 10 as dominated by apps for messaging, social media and work: WhatsApp, Facebook, Messenger, Instagram, the Subway Surfers game, Facebook Lite, SHAREit (a file-sharing app), Microsoft Excel, Microsoft PowerPoint, and Microsoft Word (Price 2020).

For many people, apps have become incorporated into their everyday lives. It is estimated that app users spend an average of 3.7 hours a day on their apps (Sydow 2020b). However, despite very large download metrics, only a small number of apps are used regularly (Morris and Murray 2018). Given this crowded and competitive marketplace and the burgeoning numbers of apps coming onto the market each day, app developers must work hard to make their products attractive to consumers (Whitson 2019). They attempt to lure users to download and use them with promissory narratives referring to almost magical properties offered by the app and colorful graphical designs that invite interest and engagement (Bardini 2014; Lupton 2014, 2019b; Rose 2014). The visual appearance of the app and its description in app stories are key elements that must appeal to people browsing the stores. These promissory narratives suggest that almost any human need or desire can be "appified" (Morris and Murray 2018), or fulfilled by a well-designed app.

The strategies of "gamification" and "ludification" are central to the design of many apps, in their attempts to attract and maintain people's interest by offering elements of fun and play. Gamification involves incorporating game-like elements into apps that are designed for purposes other than games so as to encourage interest and involvement (Murray 2018). A multitude of apps have included gamification elements, including productivity apps (Murray 2018) and health and fitness apps (Maturo and Setiffi 2016). Popular dating apps such as Tinder also mobilize some gamification strategies, presenting the quest for romantic and sexual relationships or short-term hookups as a competition based on physical attractiveness (Hobbs, Owen, and Gerber 2017; Tziallas 2015). Ludification, on the other hand, is a broader strategy that goes beyond the specific endeavor of including game-like elements in apps. "Ludification" is a term used in cultural and media studies literature to describe the adoption of a child-like, playful approach to aspects of life that may otherwise have been considered adult and serious. Ludification is not (solely) about motivating people to use media such as apps or change their behavior but rather has a wider cultural resonance beyond the digital that involves an attitude to life itself. It has been argued that ludic approaches have begun to permeate Western cultures across most domains, including education, the workplace, politics, and even warfare (Dippel and Fizek 2017; Frissen et al. 2015). Examples of apps employing ludification include apps designed for little girls that involve making a game of pregnancy and childbirth. In these games, players are invited to glamorize pregnant women to prepare them for birth by performing "makeovers" on the game avatars, and then to assist in performing a cesarean section on the avatar to deliver her baby: the successful birth is a "win" (Lupton and Thomas 2015).

The need to market apps that are new and excite consumers' interest can sometimes result in ludicrous novelty apps such as the "Is it Tuesday" app that offers the sole function of informing the user whether it is Tuesday or another day of the week. The app is offered to users simply as a joke but simultaneously highlights the often trivial functions of apps made available in the app stores and the "problems" they claim to "solve" (Morris 2018). At the other extreme, however, are apps developed by reputable medical publishers, such as WebMD, which provide vast reams of medical information for people worried about symptoms they are experiencing; apps used by women with young children to measure their growth, food consumption, and development; and those offered to people with chronic health conditions such as diabetes, continuing pain, mental health conditions, or high blood pressure to manage their health and engage in self-care (Lupton 2017a). Far from trivial, these types of apps are important complements to or sometimes even replacements of traditional face-to-face healthcare. Many of these apps allow for a far more participatory approach to health and medical information generation and sharing, in contrast to the traditional top-down dissemination of advice from trained healthcare professionals to patients and laypeople. In my research with Australian users of health and fitness apps, I found that they highly valued the support, convenience, and information the apps offered (Lupton 2018b, 2019b; Lupton and Maslen 2019; Lupton and Smith 2018).

Dating apps have also risen in prominence to become one of the major ways in which people meet sexual and romantic partners. The Pew Research Center (Vogels 2020) conducted a survey of American adults in late 2019 about their use of dating apps and sites. Findings revealed the high popularity of using these media for intimate relationships. Three in 10 respondents had ever used a dating app or site, with almost half of those aged between 18 and 20 years reporting use, as well as 38% of people aged 30 to 49 years. People who identified as lesbian, gay, or bisexual were approximately twice as likely than heterosexuals to have used a dating app or site. Dating apps can be racist (Carlson 2020; Mason 2016) and misogynist (Hess and Flores 2018; Shaw 2016). However, people of diverse gender and sexual identities have reported enjoying the feelings of empowerment and freedom to meet like-minded people, explore their sexuality, and facilitate intimacy and sexual encounters that dating apps can offer them (Hobbs, Owen, and Gerber 2017; Ferris and Duguay 2019; Jaspal 2016; Tziallas 2015).

The app marketplace is dynamic. App developers are often responsive to social changes as part of attempting to gain a foothold in consumer attention. A key example is the changes that occurred in the app marketplace and consumption of apps during the first stages of the COVID-19 pandemic in early to mid-2020. In these unusual circumstances, apps offered solutions to many problems faced by countries seeking to control the spread of the coronavirus and help people manage quarantine and physical distancing requirements. For example, following hygiene, isolation, and other restrictions brought in to contain the spread of the coronavirus, download and time spent using health and fitness apps increased to record levels. At-home fitness apps were particularly popular. App publishers moved to change the names and content of their apps to appeal to the new market of people confined to their homes and wanting workout routines and tips (Sydow 2020a). Finance and banking, shopping, video streaming, video conferencing, and game apps also received higher levels of engagement across the globe during the COVID lockdown period (Venkatraman 2020). In China (the first country to be affected by the pandemic), time spent on apps increased by 30% to 5 hours a day during its lockdown period, while other people in other countries experiencing similarly long social isolation periods (such as Italy, France, Germany, and the United States) soon followed in devoting more time to app use (Venkatraman 2020).

THE POLITICAL ECONOMY APPROACH

The political economy approach adopts a macropolitical perspective on apps, focusing on the social structural, geographical, and economic dimensions of their development, promotion, and use. This perspective builds on the foundational work of German philosopher Karl Marx. Writing in the nineteenth century, Marx ([1867] 1977) drew attention to the political and economic dimensions of the relations of work in the emergent capitalist economy spawned by the Industrial Revolution. He emphasized the exploitation of what he called "the proletariat," or the wage laborers, by their employers, the wealthy owners of the means of production (capitalists, or the bourgeoisie): In those days, principally industrialists who owned and operated factories. With his collaborator Friedrich Engels, Marx argued that the industrialists profited handsomely from using the labor power of the proletariat by failing to compensate them adequately for their work and keeping them in conditions of destitution. He called for the proletariat to rise up against their oppressors as the only option to improve their poor working and living conditions (Marx [1867] 1977; Marx and Engels [1848] 1968).

Contemporary scholars who adopt a political economy approach build on Marx's critique by focusing not only on labor relations but also on other socioeconomic determinants of people's lives: their gender, age, race/ethnicity, place of residence, and health or disability status. When applied to digital media, political economists have drawn attention to what they perceive as the exploitation of workers and consumers by the internet empires (Apple, Facebook, Google, Amazon, and Microsoft). They have examined the sociopolitical and economic dimensions of the app marketplace, demonstrating that workers are often poorly paid, while the major corporations profit handsomely from their labor. For example, as the title suggests, in his book *Digital Labour and Karl Marx* (2014), Fuchs directly applies a Marxian lens to analyzing how workers and citizens engage in "digital labor" across a variety of practices, including people in the Democratic Republic of Congo extracting minerals for hardware such as laptops, tablets, and mobile devices and Chinese employees working on production lines assembling them. Fuchs also examines the relations of production in the Indian and Silicon Valley software industries, where apps are among the artifacts generated in conditions of long working hours. While some of these workers are paid better and have more favorable working conditions than others, Fuchs argues that they are all exploited for the benefit of the owners and shareholders of the major corporations for whom they work.

Political economy researchers have also highlighted the processes of datafication and dataveillance that occur when people use apps and the opportunities for exploitation or privacy breaches that can result. "Datafication" refers to rendering people's activities, preferences, and habits into digital data, while "dataveillance" is a term used to describe the many ways in which people can be placed under surveillance using their digitized information (van Dijck 2014). Many types of app use generate flows of personal data: about people's movements in space and place and their name, age, gender, contacts, relationships, everyday routines, and a plethora of other features of their lives. Zuboff's (2019) *The Age of Surveillance Capitalism* is often cited in critical analyses of datafication and dataveillance. Zuboff defines "surveillance capitalism" as a new form of capitalism, developed by the major internet corporations in Silicon Valley. These corporations, she argues, exploit internet and app users by extracting their personal information from them and selling it to third parties for data profiling and targeted advertising purposes. According to Zuboff, people who use the internet or apps are manipulated by profiling and targeted advertising conducted by these corporations and have little power to challenge this use of their personal data.

Other researchers have drawn attention to the third-party use of the personal information that is generated when people use apps, identifying the potential for personal privacy to be breached by insufficient protection of users' data. The highly sensitive information collected by health tracking and dating apps is particularly vulnerable to privacy breaches or misuse (Brandtzaeg, Pultier, and Moen 2019; Kuntsman, Miyake, and Martin 2019; Lutz and Ranzini 2017). People who are already experiencing socioeconomic disadvantage are often the worst affected by such privacy breaches or by the use of their personal data by government or commercial agencies to exclude them from opportunities such as special offers, social security support, insurance, quality housing, and employment (Arora 2019; Gangadharan 2017; Petty et al. 2018). Human rights advocates have drawn attention to the risks of supplying devices with monitoring apps to displaced peoples as part of digitized humanitarian initiatives. The rights of such marginalized groups to opt out of datafication and dataveillance of their movements and biometrics are often not considered by these initiatives. People in these situations rarely have control over who collects their personal data and how it is used (Sandvik 2020).

The app industry has also been criticized for its exploitation of what are often referred to as "gig workers": people who depend on apps such as the ride-sharing app Uber, the freelance work app TaskRabbit, or one of the multitude of food delivery apps now available for finding ill-paid, short-term and casual work and have little job security or protections in place (Sharma 2018). This mode of employment often offers little choice to people who have signed up to be gig workers. Their working conditions are controlled by the app and platform through which they seek jobs. Gig workers are often at the mercy of dataveillance and profiling algorithms used in the apps and platforms for finding and maintaining regular work in a context of labor oversupply and competition (Gandini 2018; Wood et al. 2018). Further, people working as software engineers developing and publishing apps also frequently face job insecurity if they are attempting to engage in kickstarter initiatives rather than working for large software companies (Whitson 2019). App developers who live in the Global South and focus on local content can have great difficulties challenging the corporate power of major multinational companies in the Global North when they are attempting to attract the attention of local markets to their products (Wagner and Fernández-Ardèvol 2015).

During the COVID-19 crisis, as the coronavirus spread around the world, generating health, social, and economic disruptions, the tension between top-down health imperatives and the need to preserve the capitalist economic system in how the crisis was managed using apps drew much attention from the political economy perspective (French and Monahan 2020). In response to social changes resulting from the COVID crisis, including many more people using digital technologies to work from home, Fuchs (2020) applied his political economy critique to what has been called "coronavirus capitalism." He raised the concern that the turn to videoconferencing apps such as Skype and Zoom to conduct social life is a poor substitute for in-person communication and a way of commodifying the need to communicate with others using commercial enterprises. Fuchs suggested that these kinds of apps operate to colonize the domestic space, blurring the boundaries between the home and the workplace. He argued that from a political economy perspective, such blurring of boundaries can work to "extend the logic of capital into spheres outside the traditional workplace" (Fuchs, 2020). The rapid expansion or tweaking of apps to meet the needs of people in self-isolation or quarantine conditions may also be viewed as an element of coronavirus capitalism, with app publishers seeking to profit from people's changed consumption needs.

A range of apps were used for health-related purposes by governments and health authorities seeking to manage the spread of COVID-19. These included apps designed to assist with providing information to publics, contact tracing of people infected with the virus, and the surveillance and monitoring of populations, including enforcing quarantine restrictions. In China, for example, apps were used that calculated a personal risk rating that could be used to prevent people deemed potentially to be contagious from entering public spaces, while South Korea introduced an app that publicized the movements of people with COVID-19, and the Israeli government monitored the movements of citizens using geolocational smartphone data to enforce self-isolation (Calvo, Deterding, and Ryan 2020). In India, some government agencies and workplaces insisted that citizens register with a contact tracing app using a unique digital identification number linked to their personal details and to carry a smartphone or wear a wristband with the app installed if they wanted to enter certain regions or engage in some work activities (Das 2020).

Adopting a political economy perspective, privacy and surveillance scholars raised the alarm about the breaches of privacy and human rights these apps could engender and the potential for ever-greater restrictions of rights and freedoms (Calvo, Deterding, and Ryan 2020; French and Monahan 2020). Critics pointed out that people living in disadvantaged conditions (in overcrowded housing, needing to go out of the home to earn money) could not readily engage in the social isolation measures that were monitored by these apps and were therefore rendered more vulnerable to social discrimination and poverty (Fuchs 2020). Others drew attention to the dataveillance overreach of companies using apps and other digital monitoring systems to check on their employees' activities and monitor their productivity, geolocation, sanitation, social distancing practices, and health status during the pandemic (Chyi 2020).

Foucauldian Perspectives

The scholarship of the late French philosopher Michel Foucault has been employed in numerous critical analyses of the sociocultural and political implications of app design and use. Foucauldian approaches are interested in both the macropolitical and micropolitical dimensions of apps, often seeking to bring them together in analyzing the implications of apps for discourses and practices of identity and embodiment. While Foucault was writing well before the advent of mobile devices and apps, his focus on biopolitics and biopower has been taken up by other scholars to examine how apps operate to encourage users to engage in practices of self-responsibility. The concept of "biopolitics" refers to the ways in which people's bodies are managed and monitored by themselves but in alignment with the objectives and imperatives of state agencies and commercial enterprises. "Biopower" is a term Foucault uses to describe the power relations that are exercised with and through biopolitical strategies and practices. Both concepts focus on how human bodies are measured, disciplined, controlled, regulated, and brought into fields of visibility (Foucault 2008).

An important difference between the political economy approach and that of Foucauldian theory is that Foucault positions power as essentially part of all relationships and as productive as well as repressive. Political economists tend to represent publics as lacking power, autonomy, and agency in their relationships with internet corporations or app publishers. Foucault (1991) argues that through discourses and practices of biopolitics, certain kinds of identities and bodily practices are brought into existence—often in ways that encourage people to take responsibility for managing their own lives and bodies in their own interests rather than being forced to do so by powerful institutions. In this way, personal objectives—to be healthy, productive citizens—are often aligned with institutional interests as part of governing populations through everyday practices that are directed at "the care of the self" (Foucault 1986). It is here that the micropolitical and the macropolitical converge.

Foucauldian analyses examine how apps are marketed and used as ways to help people engage in practices related to the care of the self in their efforts to be responsible, productive, and careful citizens. In my work on the sociological dimensions of self-tracking practices and "the quantified self" movement, I have discussed how practices of digitized self-monitoring using apps for health and fitness tracking can be viewed from a Foucauldian perspective as supporting and encouraging people to conform to these ideals of citizenship. Self-tracking apps devoted to body functions and attributes such as activity levels, food and alcohol consumption, sleep patterns, mood, pregnancy, and indicators of fertility such as ovulation and menstruation are often predicated on the biopolitical imperative to establish a norm of behavior against which users are encouraged to measure themselves (Lupton 2016a, 2016b, 2017a). These apps suggest that achieving the goals or targets established by the app (often involving arbitrary metrics such as "10,000 steps a day") is a way of achieving the ideals of self-control, optimization, and responsibility (Esmonde and Jette 2020; Fotopoulou and O'Riordan 2017; Lupton 2016b; Millington 2014; Toner 2018).

The affordances offered in health and fitness apps assume that users have access to resources such as up-to-date smartphones, time and space in which to exercise or engage in other forms of health-related self-care such as mediation and mindfulness, and the physical capacity to operate apps and perform the activities suggested by the app. People who are already advantaged and able to make use of these resources often appreciate being able to use health and fitness apps to feel more in control of their health, physical fitness, and well-being (Fotopoulou and O'Riordan 2017; Lupton 2018b, 2019b; Lupton and Smith 2018; Pink et al. 2017). For example, in one of my projects involving interviews with Australian self-trackers, the notion that one can become a "much better" and "more responsible person" by engaging in practices of self-monitoring was frequently espoused by participants (Lupton and Smith 2018). These assumptions suggest that app users are well-off people living in safe neighborhoods with plenty of green space available for walking and other forms of exercise, with enough disposable income to support gym memberships or exercise equipment and clothing, and not living with a chronic health problem, injuries, or disabilities. Foucauldian critiques point out that the state's responsibility for protecting the health of its citizens is glossed over in this emphasis on personal responsibility and autonomy (Esmonde and Jette 2020; Lupton 2018b; Millington 2014; Thornham 2019). The social determinants of ill health, such as socioeconomic disadvantage and living in crowded and polluted urban environments, are ignored in this overweening focus on individual consumerist and lifestyle behaviors. Further, this is a concept of personhood that ascribes to the Western models of the individual, health, and embodiment. It excludes worldviews from non-Western cultures, in which people are viewed as inextricably part of their communities, kinship networks, and environment and health is a collective and relational state (Christie and Verran 2014; Kuoljok 2019; Nahar et al. 2017).

Feminist critiques point to the ways that many health and fitness apps are gendered. There are apps for self-monitoring sexual and reproductive activity, for example, which encourage people to view their sexual behavior and fertility as bodily functions that can and should be quantified and compared against norms of behavior, even in a competitive way in terms of monitoring and measuring sexual performance. Sex-tracking apps often position women as reproductive subjects, while men are portrayed as sexually competitive, interested in comparing their performance with other men (Lupton 2015). Beauty apps, designed to help users improve their physical attractiveness and to rank, analyze, monitor, or measure people's appearance, are largely targeted at women. These apps adhere closely to ideals of self-improvement by recommending practices of self-surveillance and dataveillance from others (Elias and Gill 2018). Pregnancy apps are mostly designed with the overt assumption that women are willing and able to engage in the pursuit of intensive self-monitoring of their bodies and that of their fetus as part of a responsibilized focus on protecting their fetus's health (Barassi 2017; Thomas and Lupton 2016; Thornham 2019). Here again, however, these apps can be helpful: Women can also appreciate using these kinds of apps as a way to avoid risk, perform the ideal of the caring and responsible mother, cope with the challenges and chaos of new motherhood, and feel in control of their fertility and reproductive cycles (Karlsson 2019; Lupton 2017b; Thornham 2019).

The biopolitical dimensions of apps are particularly overt in health crises, in which publics are often encouraged to engage in practices of self-care as a way of alleviating the burden they may pose to societal resources if they become ill. During the "obesity crisis," for example, citizens across the Global North were the subject of campaigns by health agencies and commercial enterprises to engage in activities to monitor their body weight and reduce it if they were deemed to be "too fat." Calorie counting and physical activity apps were promoted as one avenue for achieving these weight loss expectations by supporting people to engage in self-surveillance and disciplinary practices (Didžiokaitė, Saukko, and Greiffenhagen 2018; Lupton 2018a). As several commentators have noted, social and government responses to the COVID-19 pandemic can be viewed from a Foucauldian perspective as an example of biopolitics and biopower (Coeckelbergh 2020; Raffaetà 2020; Sarasin 2020). A combination of "raw" power (exercised from the top down by governments) and the more subtle "soft" power (involving voluntary actions from citizens encouraged by governments) was characteristic of many countries' experiences of the pandemic (Coeckelbergh 2020). As part of efforts to protect populations from infection and minimize the burden on healthcare services, governments initiated measures that required their citizens to engage in self-management and self-discipline to conform to strategies such as hygiene, distancing, and self-isolation practices as well as using contact tracing and other COVID-related apps.

The discourse around these portrayals of health crises and suggested measures to improve public health and reduce the burden on the healthcare system often focuses on messages that "we are all in this together" and that individual behavioral change is needed for the protection of the larger polity. For example, while engaging in COVID-related app use and other measures was productive and beneficial in helping people feel as if they were contributing to reducing the spread of the virus and simultaneously protecting themselves and their families, there was also a moralistic undertone to these discourses that implied that people who could not or would not engage in these practices were lacking in self-discipline or civility (Ali 2020; Manderson and Levine 2020). Similarly, fat people targeted by digital media measures designed to counter the "obesity epidemic" were frequently represented as moral failures, toxic and undisciplined bodies, and burdens on the economy, requiring greater reserves of self-discipline than the general population (Lupton 2018a).

SOCIOMATERIAL PERSPECTIVES

Sociomaterial perspectives have only recently been taken up to understand the micropolitical and sociocultural dimensions of apps. Sociomaterialism perspectives devote close attention to the ways in which humans live with and through apps. This approach builds on Marxian concepts of the importance of the materiality of power relations and Foucauldian insights into the relationships between the discursive and material elements of biopolitics but extend this work by devoting greater attention to nonhuman agents as they come together with people in the context of the broader sociotechnical worlds in which apps are imagined, developed, tested, published, marketed, and incorporated into everyday lives and routines. These worlds include the economic and regulatory contexts, the digital ecosystem, the people working on making and promoting apps, the app stores, other agents and agencies that advocate for app use (such as government departments, schools, gyms, medical professionals), the people who connect with each other on apps (such as those engaging on social media, content sharing or gaming apps), and, in the case of apps designed for monitoring pets, livestock, or wildlife, animals other than humans.

Scholars drawing on science and technology studies, and particularly actor-network theory based on Bruno Latour's work, have investigated the infrastructural dimensions of app ecologies. Actor-network theory positions both people and things as active agents in shifting networks (Latour 2005). These human and nonhuman entities together make up the social world. Actor-network theory is often less interested than are other sociological theories in social structures such as social class or social institutions and more interested in noticing and documenting the specific details of how entities relate to each other (Michael 2016). While they do not adopt an overtly critical Marxian analysis, studies of app infrastructures have frequently focused on questions of relational power in the context of digital economies—that is, how apps are positioned within and interact with the broader sociotechnical operational networks, computational cultures, and systems in which they are sited (Gerlitz et al. 2019a). This focus on how the social and the technological are entangled includes exploring the ways mundane experiences are ordered by technologies such as digital devices and apps and how apps operate as "digital objects" (Dieter et al. 2019; Gerlitz et al. 2019b; Morris and Elkins 2015).

As researchers engaged in science and technology studies demonstrate, while apps might be presented as self-contained entities on app stores and mobile devices, they are products of a complex network of diverse agents that are constantly relating to each other. These include flows of digitized information and the broader digital platforms, interfaces, hardware, regulatory environments, network protocols, algorithms, and other infrastructures within which apps operate (Dieter et al. 2019; Gerlitz et al. 2019a; Gillespie, Boczkowski, and Foot 2014; Morris and Elkins 2015). A sociotechnical approach to apps can show, for example, how app stores create specific situations in which apps are developed and published. Each app store—whether it is the two major stores Apple App Store and Google Play or the plethora of smaller app stores in Western countries and larger app stories in countries like China and Russia—has its own regulatory environment, logics, access points, recommendation systems, topic categories, and rules with which app publishers must engage, including how they describe the app on the store (Dieter et al. 2019; Morris and Murray 2018). At a different level—that of the platform—social media companies and platforms such as Facebook, Snapchat, Twitter, and Instagram have intersecting platforms and apps that work with and across each other on multiple devices: mobile devices, desktop and laptop computers, and smartwatches. Studies of "app–platform relations" that observe how apps interact with app stories and web-based platforms have drawn attention to these entanglements, which can often be messy and contingent. They have shown that app developers need to structure their working practices and the content and design of their apps in response to the demands of the app stores and other platforms (Gerlitz et al. 2019b).

The role played by humans, other living things, and non-digital objects is often neglected in these analyses of the sociomaterial networks in which apps are developed and marketed. Feminist materialism scholars (Barad 2007; Bennett 2009; Braidotti 2019; Haraway 2016) and perspectives building on age-old indigenous and non-Western cosmologies (Bawaka Country et al. 2015; Kuoljok 2019; Todd 2016) offer a somewhat different perspective, sometimes referred to as "vital materialism" (Bennett 2010; Coole 2013; Lupton 2019b). Vital materialism emphasizes the interrelationships between humans and nonhuman things, including objects, place and space, and other living things. Drawing on the philosophy of Giles Deleuze, affective forces are understood in this body of work as shared intensities of sensation and emotion that propel human action. These forces flow between humans and nonhuman things (Ott 2017). "Relational connections" are the relationships that are continually formed and reformed as people come together with other people but also with nonhuman agents. Barad (2003) uses the term "intra-action" to describe "how matter comes to matter," that is, how assemblages (groupings) of human and nonhuman agents work together to generate forces and action. Bennett's concept of "thing-power" also acknowledges the flows of vibrancies and intensities that human–nonhuman assemblages can configure: "the curious ability of inanimate things to animate, to act, to produce effects dramatic and subtle" (2004: 351). Bennett (2001) describes the force of this thing-power as the capacity to create enchantment in everyday things.

Sociomaterial theoretical perspectives drawing on vital materialism theory focus on the micropolitics of the lived experiences of people when engaging with apps (Lupton 2018b, 2019b; Salmela, Valtonen, and Lupton 2018). The affective dimensions and relational connections of human–app encounters are identified in some analyses, as well as their agential capacities, or what they allow people to do. The potential to enchant users is an essential element of the successful app, in attracting interest and affective intensities that lead to continued use from app consumers (Lupton 2019b). From a vital materialism perspective, when humans come together with apps, they are creating new worlds of movement and place. Human–app assemblages are lively, opening up thing-power that configures capacities (Esmonde and Jette 2020; Fullagar et al. 2017; Lupton 2018b, 2019b; Salmela, Valtonen, and Lupton 2018). It depends on the affordances of the app (the features it is designed to offer users), the affordances of human bodies (the capacity for movement, learning, memory, and sensory perception), and the situated contexts in which the app is used (where, when, for what reason, at what time) how these vitalities and capacities may be opened or closed (Lupton 2019b).

Another insight from vital materialism is the concept of distributed agencies. Agency is viewed not as a force that belongs only to humans or only to some humans and not others. Instead, agential capacities are continually and dynamically generated with and between people and nonhuman agents. Various forms of agencies, therefore, are configured as human–app assemblages come together. They are brought into being as these agents assemble and can just as quickly dissolve and re-form as people move through space and time. Human–app assemblages, therefore, are lively, dynamic, and responsive to the situated contexts in which they are configured. They generate relational connections between the agents in the assemblages, between the humans moving around in the spaces and places in relation to each other. This is intra-action and thing-power in action. Apps, from this perspective, have affordances that offer humans certain capacities; but humans may resist, reinvent, ignore, or improvise with these affordances, drawing on their bodily capacities.

Thus, for example, building on Bennett's theory, in my analysis of the thing-power of what I called "the human–app health assemblage" (Lupton 2019b), I drew on several of my empirical research studies with people who use health, parenting, and fitness tracking apps. I found that my participants' personal biographies and life trajectories were important in their use: for example, the key moments of becoming a parent for the first time, receiving a diagnosis, having a major birthday such as turning 40, or deciding to attempt a major fitness or athletic goal or achievement. When deciding to use health apps, the affective forces and relational connections generated by coming together with people's life experiences, personal relationships, and the affordances offered by the apps opened capacities for these participants such as feeling as they had taken control over their bodies, performed as a responsible citizen or parent, and invested in their own futures. It is in these findings that a vital materialism focus on the vitalities generated by human–app assemblages and how these forces can motivate human action accords with the Foucauldian emphasis on biopolitics and the government of bodies.

Apps can generate strong affective responses and relational connections. Game apps, together with apps involving gamification or ludification elements, frequently attempt to incite intense affects to incite download and regular use of the apps. Excitement and the spirit of competition are often a key affective force driving game app use, which offer incentives such as badges, rewards, and favorable comparisons with other users as evidence of "winning." For example, the location-based augmented reality game app Pokémon GO was initially highly popular because it worked to draw in users by combining the affective force of "finding all" the characters and earning rewards with moving around in space and place, allowing users to explore new domains, find new friends within their locale, and turning neighborhoods into gaming fields (Hjorth and Richardson 2017). The Strava athletic tracking app is designed to create supportive and competitive communities of runners or cyclists who can measure and publicly display their feats, record their personal bests, win segments of their route by proving they have achieved the fastest time (thereby becoming "King of the Mountain"), and give and receive congratulatory messages in response to other users (Lupton 2018c).

In contrast, the developers of the darkly humorous productivity "CARROT" suite of apps seek to inspire the affects of guilt, humiliation, and shame. These apps work to gamify productivity by stimulating these feelings as well as offering rewards for tasks and goals that are achieved by the user. Users (referred to as "meatbags") are greeted with insulting messages from the apps if they fail to achieve set tasks, with the less-than-subtle rationale for such messages on the part of the developers being that evoking these affects can be motivating for people, inspiring them to adhere to the ideals of self-responsibility and high productivity (Murray 2018). The developer's website describes the app as embodied in a forceful female personality, describing it as "she" and noting "be careful! Slackers make CARROT upset" (Meet Carrot 2020). According to the information on the Apple App Store posted by the app developer, these messages include "It's been 18 hours since you did anything useful" (CARROT To-Do app) and "Obey your mistress. Do not try to sleep in. Otherwise ... I will be upset" (CARROT Alarm). As these messages suggest, the voice of "Carrot" is that of a dominatrix. This portrayal is further emphasized in the text used in the app store description for a third CARROT app—CARROT Fit—in which the app is anthropomorphized in the following description:

> CARROT is a sadistic AI construct with one simple goal: to transform your flabby carcass into a Grade A specimen of the human race. She will do whatever it takes—including threatening, inspiring, ridiculing, and bribing you—to make this happen. You will get fit—or else.

Even when they are using apps that provide rewards such as flashing lights or badges for achieving goals rather than belittling criticism, ambivalent feelings can also feature in people's lived experiences of using apps. In my study on women's use of food-tracking apps, the participants expressed their feelings of pleasure, control, and achievement in losing weight or monitoring their food intake, which motivated them to continue using the apps. However, the forces of disappointment and frustration, as well as a fear of becoming too obsessive about counting calories, were also expressed by some women, sometimes leading to giving up or avoiding app use (Lupton 2018b). Further, apps can sometimes feel invasive or somehow "wrong," creating feelings of discomfort. A study involving autoethnographic accounts of using a sleep-tracking "smart ring" and app (Salmela, Valtonen, and Lupton 2018) drew attention to intense feelings in response to considering incorporating this type of self-monitoring technology into the private space of the bed and bedroom.

A vital materialism approach highlights the ways in which apps are responsive and change as they intra-act with the people who design and use them, just as people's bodies, activities, and feelings can be changed by apps (Esmonde and Jette 2020; Fox 2017; Fullagar et al. 2017; Lupton 2019a). Self-tracking apps, for example, operate synergistically with the people who use them. The sensors and algorithms designed into the apps provide opportunities for people to monitor and measure their bodies and activities in certain defined ways. The digitized information generated by these gatherings of people and apps is itself lively and ever-changing, responding to people's movements in time and place (Lupton 2018c, 2019a). People who use these apps can review the data they generate, which can contribute to their sense of embodiment, place, and space. In turn, the app responds to further changes in the human users' quotidian activities (Lupton 2012). Some apps generate thing-power that changes the ways people move in time and space. For example, geolocation apps such as Apple Map or Google Map and physical activity self-tracking apps such as Strava and Fitbit can help people find their way in the world and document their movements and in turn rely on the information relayed to them by humans and their devices to locate the human body. When people are using these kinds of apps, they are working with the app and the physical environment in which they are located and through which they move in intra-active ways to generate capacities for movement, spatial location, and wayfinding (Lupton 2019c). This is a synergistic relational connection of change and response that repeats itself so that people make data and data make people (Lupton 2019a).

FUTURE DIRECTIONS FOR SOCIOLOGICAL APP RESEARCH

As I have demonstrated in this chapter, while apps may be considered to be mundane software, for many people across the globe, they are integral to social worlds, social relationships, concepts of selfhood and embodiment, and the performance of everyday life. Taken together, the three theoretical perspectives discussed in this chapter offer rich and diverse insights into the sociocultural and political dimensions of apps. While an important body of empirical research by sociologists and other social researchers has been published, important gaps in the literature remain. Given the sheer volume and diversity of apps in the marketplace, with a bewildering array of new apps being published every day, it is a difficult task to maintain a close engagement with changes in the app industry. Apps for social media, health and fitness, games, pregnancy and parenting, and dating have attracted the highest level of attention by social researchers. There are still many categories of apps that have yet to be examined in detail. These include apps that are extremely popular and used regularly: weather, education, messaging, and banking apps, for example. More nuanced research on how people across the different life stages are using apps and on users from marginalized and disadvantaged backgrounds and from non-white and non–Global North regions would make an important contribution. Finally, close attention to the types of apps that are published in the future—and particularly those that attract popularity or are responses to crises and other major social problems such as the COVID pandemic—remains an important area of research for the sociology of digital media.

References

Ali, I. 2020. "The COVID-19 Pandemic: Making Sense of Rumor and Fear." *Medical Anthropology* 39, no. 5: 376–379.
App Annie. 2020. "App Annie Announces Its Top Publisher Award Winners of 2020." Accessed May 15, 2020. https://www.appannie.com/en/insights/app-annie-news/top-52-app-publishers-2020/.
Arora, P. 2019. "Decolonizing Privacy Studies." *Television and New Media* 20: 366–378.
Barad, K. 2003. "Posthumanist Performativity: Toward an Understanding of How Matter Comes to Matter." *Signs* 28: 801–831.
Barad, K. 2007. *Meeting the Universe Halfway: Quantum Physics and the Entanglement of Matter and Meaning*. Durham, NC: Duke University Press.
Barassi, V. 2017. "BabyVeillance? Expecting Parents, Online Surveillance and the Cultural Specificity of Pregnancy Apps." *Social Media + Society* 3, no. 2. Accessed August 28, 2017. http://dx.doi.org/10.1177/2056305117707188.
Bardini, T. 2014. "Apps as 'charming junkware'?" In *The Imaginary App*, edited by P. D. Miller and S. Matviyenko, 205–216. Cambridge, MA: MIT Press.
Bawaka Country, S. Wright, S. Suchet-Pearson, K. Lloyd, L. Burarrwanga, R. Ganambarr, M. Ganambarr-Stubbs, B. Ganambarr, and D. Maymuru. 2015. "Working with and Learning from Country: Decentring Human Authority." *Cultural Geographies* 22: 269–283.
Bennett, J. 2001. *The Enchantment of Modern Life: Attachments, Crossings, and Ethics*. Princeton, NJ: Princeton University Press.
Bennett, J. 2004. "The Force of Things: Steps toward an Ecology of Matter." *Political Theory,* 32: 347–372.
Bennett, J. 2009. *Vibrant Matter: A Political Ecology of Things*. Durham, NC: Duke University Press.

Bennett, J. 2010. "A Vitalist Stopover on the Way to a New Materialism." In *New Materialisms: Ontology, Agency and Politics*, edited by D. Coole and S. Frost, 47–69. Durham, NC: Duke University Press.

Braidotti, R. 2019. "A Theoretical Framework for the Critical Posthumanities." *Theory, Culture and Society* 36: 31–61.

Brandtzaeg, P. B., A. Pultier, and G. M. Moen. 2019. "Losing Control to Data-Hungry Apps: A Mixed-Methods Approach to Mobile App Privacy." *Social Science Computer Review* 37: 466–488.

Calvo, R. A., S. Deterding, and R. M. Ryan. 2020. "Health Surveillance during Covid-19 Pandemic." *British Medical Journal* 369: m1373. https://www.bmj.com/content/369/bmj.m1373.

Carlson, B. 2020. "Love and Hate at the Cultural Interface: Indigenous Australians and Dating Apps." *Journal of Sociology* 56, no. 2: 133–150.

Christie, M., and H. Verran. 2014. "The Touch Pad Body: A Generative Transcultural Digital Device Interrupting Received Ideas and Practices in Aboriginal Health." *Societies* 4. Accessed July 11, 2014. http://www.mdpi.com/2075-4698/4/2/256.

Chyi, N. 2020. "The Workplace-Surveillance Technology Boom." *Slate*. Accessed May 21, 2020. https://slate.com/technology/2020/05/workplace-surveillance-apps-coronavirus.html.

Clement, J. 2019. "Most Popular Apple App Store Categories 2019." Statista. Accessed May 8, 2020. https://www.statista.com/statistics/270291/popular-categories-in-the-app-store/.

Clement, J. 2020. "Annual Number of Global Mobile App Downloads 2016–2019." Statista. Accessed May 8, 2020. https://www.statista.com/statistics/271644/worldwide-free-and-paid-mobile-app-store-downloads/.

Coeckelbergh, M. 2020. "The Postdigital in Pandemic Times: A Comment on the Covid-19 Crisis and Its Political Epistemologies." *Postdigital Science and Education*. https://link.springer.com/content/pdf/10.1007/s42438-020-00119-2.pdf

Coole, D. 2013. "Agentic Capacities and Capacious Historical Materialism: Thinking with New Materialisms in the Political Sciences." *Millennium* 41, 451–469.

Das, S. 2020. "Surveillance in the Time of Coronavirus: The Case of the Indian Contact Tracking App Aarogya Setu." Datactive. Accessed May 15, 2020. https://data-activism.net/2020/04/bigdatasur-covid-surveillance-in-the-time-of-coronavirus-the-case-of-the-indian-contact-tracing-app-aarogya-setu/.

Didžiokaitė, G., P. Saukko, and C. Greiffenhagen. 2018. "The Mundane Experience of Everyday Calorie Trackers: Beyond the Metaphor of Quantified Self." *New Media and Society* 20: 1470–1487.

Dieter, M., C. Gerlitz, A. Helmond, N. Tkacz, F. N. Van Der Vlist, and E. Weltevrede. 2019. "Multi-situated App Studies: Methods and Propositions." *Social Media + Society* 5. Accessed January 4, 2019. https://doi.org/10.1177/2056305119846486.

Dippel, A., and S. Fizek. 2017. "Ludification of Culture: The Significance of Play and Games in Everyday Practices of the Digital Era." In *Digitisation: Theories and Concepts for the Empirical Cultural Analysis*, edited by G. Koch, 276–292. London: Routledge.

Elias, A. S., and R. Gill. 2018. "Beauty Surveillance: The Digital Self-Monitoring Cultures of Neoliberalism." *European Journal of Cultural Studies* 21: 59–77.

Esmonde, K., and S. Jette. 2020. "Assembling the "Fitbit Subject": A Foucauldian-Sociomaterialist Examination of Social Class, Gender and Self-Surveillance on Fitbit Community Message Boards." *Health* 24: 299–314.

Ferris, L., and S. Duguay. 2019. "Tinder's Lesbian Digital Imaginary: Investigating (Im) Permeable Boundaries of Sexual Identity on a Popular Dating App." *New Media and Society* 22: 489–506.

Fotopoulou, A., and K. O'Riordan. 2017. "Training to Self-Care: Fitness Tracking, Biopedagogy and the Healthy Consumer." *Health Sociology Review* 26: 54–68.

Foucault, M. 1986. *The Care of the Self: The History of Sexuality*. Vol. 3. New York: Pantheon.

Foucault, M. 1991. "Governmentality." In *The Foucault Effect: Studies in Governmentality*, edited by G. Burchell, C. Gordon, and P. Miller, 87–104. Hemel Hempstead, UK: Harvester Wheatsheaf.

Foucault, M. 2008. *The Birth of Biopolitics: Lectures at the Collège de France, 1978–79*. Houndmills, UK: Palgrave Macmillan.

Fox, N. 2017. "Personal Health Technologies, Micropolitics and Resistance: A New Materialist Analysis." *Health* 21: 136–153.

French, M., and T. Monahan. 2020. "Dis-ease Surveillance: How Might Surveillance Studies Address COVID-19?" *Surveillance and Society* 18. https://ojs.library.queensu.ca/index.php/surveillance-and-society/article/view/13985.

Frissen, V., S. Lammes, M. De Lange, J. De Mul, and J. Raessens. 2015. "Homo ludens 2.0: Play, Media and Identity." In *Playful Identities: The Ludification of Digital Media Cultures*, edited by V. Frissen, S. Lammes, M. De Lange, J. De Mul, and J. Raessens, 9–50. Amsterdam: University of Amsterdam Press.

Fuchs, C. 2014. *Digital Labour and Karl Marx*. London: Routledge.

Fuchs, C. 2020. "Everyday Life and Everyday Communication in Coronavirus Capitalism." *tripleC* 18: 375–399.

Fullagar, S., E. Rich, J. Francombe-Webb, and A. Maturo. 2017. "Digital Ecologies of Youth Mental Health: Apps, Therapeutic Publics and Pedagogy as Affective Arrangements." *Social Sciences* 6: 135. Accessed November 14, 2017. http://www.mdpi.com/2076-0760/6/4/135.

Gandini, A. 2018. "Labour Process Theory and the Gig Economy." *Human Relations* 72: 1039–1056.

Gangadharan, S. P. 2017. "The Downside of Digital Inclusion: Expectations and Experiences of Privacy and Surveillance among Marginal Internet Users." *New Media and Society* 19: 597–615.

Gerlitz, C., A. Helmond, D. B. Nieborg, and F. N. Van Der Vlist. 2019a. "Apps and Infrastructures: A Research Agenda." *Computational Culture* 7. Accessed June 14, 2020. http://computationalculture.net/apps-and-infrastructures-a-research-agenda/.

Gerlitz, C., A. Helmond, F. N. Van Der Vlist, and E. Weltevrede. 2019b. "Regramming the Platform: Infrastructural Relations between Apps and Social Media." *Computational Culture* 7. Accessed June 14, 2020. http://computationalculture.net/regramming-the-platform/.

Gillespie, T., P. J. Boczkowski, and K. A. Foot. 2014. "Introduction." In *Media Technologies: Essays on Communication, Materiality, and Society*, edited by T. Gillespie, P. J. Boczkowski, and K. A. Foot, 1–17. Cambridge, MA: MIT Press.

Haraway, D. 2016. *Staying with the Trouble: Making Kin in the Chthulucene*. Durham, NC: Duke University Press.

Hess, A., and C. Flores. 2018. "Simply More Than Swiping Left: A Critical Analysis of Toxic Masculine Performances on Tinder Nightmares." *New Media and Society* 20: 1085–1102.

Hjorth, L., and I. Richardson. 2017. "Pokémon GO: Mobile Media Play, Place-Making, and the Digital Wayfarer." *Mobile Media and Communication* 1: 3–14.

Hobbs, M., S. Owen, and L. Gerber. 2017. "Liquid Love? Dating Apps, Sex, Relationships and the Digital Transformation of Intimacy." *Journal of Sociology* 53: 271–284.

Jaspal, R. 2016. "Gay Men's Construction and Management of Identity on Grindr." *Sexuality and Culture* 21: 187–204.

Karlsson, A. 2019. "A Room of One's Own? Using Period Trackers to Escape Menstrual Stigma." *Nordicom Review* 40: 111–123.

Kuntsman, A., E. Miyake, and S. Martin. 2019. "Re-thinking Digital Health: Data, Appisation and the (Im)Possibility of 'Opting Out.'" *Digital Health* 5. Accessed January 1, 2019. https://doi.org/10.1177/2055207619880671.

Kuoljok, K. 2019. "Without Land We Are Lost: Traditional Knowledge, Digital Technology and Power Relations." *AlterNative: An International Journal of Indigenous Peoples* 15: 349–358.

Latour, B. 2005. *Reassembling the Social: An Introduction to Actor-Network-Theory.* Oxford: Clarendon.

Lupton, D. 2012. "M-Health and Health Promotion: The Digital Cyborg and Surveillance Society." *Social Theory and Health* 10: 229–244.

Lupton, D. 2014. "Apps as Artefacts: Towards a Critical Perspective on Mobile Health and Medical Apps." *Societies* 4: 606–622.

Lupton, D. 2015. "Quantified Sex: A Critical Analysis of Sexual and Reproductive Self-Tracking Using Apps." *Culture, Health and Sexuality* 17: 440–453.

Lupton, D. 2016a. "The Diverse Domains of Quantified Selves: Self-Tracking Modes and Dataveillance.: *Economy and Society* 45: 101–122.

Lupton, D. 2016b. *The Quantified Self: A Sociology of Self-Tracking.* Cambridge: Polity Press.

Lupton, D. 2017a. *Digital Health: Critical and Cross-Disciplinary Perspectives.* London: Routledge.

Lupton, D. 2017b. "'It Just Gives Me a Bit of Peace of Mind': Australian Women's Use of Digital Media for Pregnancy and Early Motherhood." *Societies* 7: 25. Accessed December 10, 2017. http://www.mdpi.com/2075-4698/7/3/25.

Lupton, D. 2018a. *Fat.* London: Routledge.

Lupton, D. 2018b. "'I Just Want It to Be Done, Done, Done!' Food Tracking Apps, Affects, and Agential Capacities." *Multimodal Technologies and Interaction* 2: 29. Accessed May 23, 2018. http://www.mdpi.com/2414-4088/2/2/29/htm.

Lupton, D. 2018c. "Lively Data, Social Fitness and Biovalue: The Intersections of Health Self-Tracking and Social Media." In *The Sage Handbook of Social Media*, edited by J. Burgess, A. Marwick, and T. Poell, 562–578. London: Sage.

Lupton, D. 2019a. *Data Selves: More-than-Human Perspectives.* Cambridge: Polity Press.

Lupton, D. 2019b. "The Thing-Power of the Human-App Health Assemblage: Thinking with Vital Materialism." *Social Theory and Health* 17: 125–139.

Lupton, D. 2019c. "Toward a More-than-Human Analysis of Digital Health: Inspirations from Feminist New Materialism." *Qualitative Health Research* 29: 1998–2009.

Lupton, D., and S. Maslen. 2019. "How Women Use Digital Technologies for Health: Qualitative Interview and Focus Group Study." *Journal of Medical Internet Research* 21: e11481. Accessed April 7, 2019. http://www.jmir.org/2019/1/e11481/.

Lupton, D., and G. J. D. Smith. 2018. "'A Much Better Person': The Agential Capacities of Self-Tracking Practices." In *Metric Culture: Ontologies of Self-Tracking Practices*, edited by B. Ajana, 57–76. London: Emerald Publishing.

Lupton, D., and G. M. Thomas. 2015. "Playing Pregnancy: The Ludification and Gamification of Expectant Motherhood in Smartphone Apps." *M/C Journal* 18. Accessed October 22, 2015. http://journal.media-culture.org.au/index.php/mcjournal/article/viewArticle/1012.

Lutz, C., and G. Ranzini. 2017. "Where Dating Meets Data: Investigating Social and Institutional Privacy Concerns on Tinder." *Social Media + Society* 3. https://doi.org/10.1177/2056305117697735

Manderson, L., and S. Levine. 2020. "COVID-19, Risk, Fear, and Fall-out." *Medical Anthropology* 39: 367–370.

Marx, K. (1867) 1977. *Capital: A Critique of Political Economy*. New York, Vintage.

Marx, K., and F. Engels. (1848) 1968. *Selected Works in One Volume*. London: Lawrence and Wishart.

Mason, C. L. 2016. "Tinder and Humanitarian Hook-ups: The Erotics of Social Media Racism." *Feminist Media Studies* 16: 822–837.

Maturo, A., and F. Setiffi. 2016. "The Gamification of Risk: How Health Apps Foster Self-Confidence and Why This Is not Enough." *Health, Risk and Society* 17: 477–494.

Meet Carrot. 2020. https://www.meetcarrot.com/todo/.

Michael, M. 2016. *Actor-Network Theory: Trials, Trails and Translations*. London: Sage.

Millington, B. 2014. "Smartphone Apps and the Mobile Privatization of Health and Fitness." *Critical Studies in Media Communication* 31: 479–493.

Morris, J. W. 2018. "Is It Tuesday? Novelty Apps and Digital Solutionism." In *Appified: Culture in the Age of Apps*, edited by J. W. Morris and S. Murray, 91–102. Ann Arbor: University of Michigan Press.

Morris, J. W., and E. Elkins. 2015. "There's a History for That: Apps and Mundane Software as Commodity." *The Fibreculture Journal*. Accessed April 15, 2017. http://twentyfive.fibreculturejournal.org/fcj-181-theres-a-history-for-that-apps-and-mundane-software-as-commodity/.

Morris, J. W., and S. Murray. 2018. "Introduction." In *Appified: Culture in the Age of Apps*, edited by J. W. Morris and S. Murray, 1–22. Ann Arbor: University of Michigan Press.

Murray, S. 2018. "Carrot: Productivity Apps and the Gamification of Shame." In *Appified: Culture in the Age of Apps*, edited by J. W. Morris and S. Murray, 72–81. Ann Arbor: University of Michigan Press.

Nahar, P., N. K. Kannuri, S. Mikkilineni, G. V. S. Murthy, and P. Phillimore. 2017. "mHealth and the Management of Chronic Conditions in Rural Areas: A Note of Caution from Southern India." *Anthropology and Medicine* 24: 1–6.

O'Dea, S. 2020. "Smartphone Users Worldwide 2016–2021." Statista. Accessed May 14, 2020. https://www.statista.com/statistics/330695/number-of-smartphone-users-worldwide/.

Ott, B. L. 2017. "Affect in Critical Studies." *Oxford Research Encyclopedia of Communication*. https://oxfordre.com/communication/view/10.1093/acrefore/9780190228613.001.0001/acrefore-9780190228613-e-56.

Petty, T., M. Saba, T. Lewis, S. P. Gangadharan, and V. Eubanks. 2018. "Reclaiming Our Data." Accessed March 21, 2019. https://www.odbproject.org/wp-content/uploads/2016/12/ODB.InterimReport.FINAL_.7.16.2018.pdf.

Pink, S., S. Sumartojo, D. Lupton, and C. Heyes Labond. 2017. "Mundane Data: The Routines, Contingencies and Accomplishments of Digital Living." *Big Data and Society* 4. Accessed March 28, 2017. http://dx.doi.org/10.1177/2053951717700924.

Price, D. 2020. "The 20 Most Popular Android Apps in the Google Play Store." MUO.com. Accessed May 11, 2020. https://www.makeuseof.com/tag/most-popular-android-apps/.

Raffaetà, R. 2020. "Another Day in Dystopia. Italy in the Time of COVID-19." *Medical Anthropology* 39: 371–373.

Rose, D. 2014. *Enchanted Objects: Design, Human Desire, and the Internet of Things*. New York: Scribner.

Salmela, T., A. Valtonen, and D. Lupton. 2018. "The Affective Circle of Harassment and Enchantment: Reflections on the ŌURA Ring as an Intimate Research Device." *Qualitative Inquiry* 25: 260–270.

Sandvik, K. B. 2020. "Humanitarian Wearables: Digital Bodies, Experimentation and Ethics." In *Ethics of Medical Innovation, Experimentation, and Enhancement in Military and Humanitarian Contexts*, edited by D. Messelken and D. Winkler, 87–104. Cham, Switzerland: Springer International Publishing.

Sarasin, P. 2020. "Understanding the Coronavirus Pandemic with Foucault?" Accessed April 2, 2020. https://www.fsw.uzh.ch/foucaultblog/essays/254/understanding-corona-with-foucault?fbclid=IwAR27MNjW4yggm1WNl2NZf9umJL-NpUczdmcMUcJUyStQPPILFwnl-KGCcUA.

Sharma, S. 2018. "TaskRabbit: The Gig Economy and Finding Time to Care Less." In *Appified: Culture in the Age of Apps*, edited by J. W. Morris and S. Murray, 63–71. Ann Arbor: University of Michigan Press.

Shaw, F. 2016. " 'Bitch I Said Hi': The Bye Felipe Campaign and Discursive Activism in Mobile Dating Apps." *Social Media + Society* 2. Accessed April 15, 2017. http://journals.sagepub.com/doi/abs/10.1177/2056305116672889.

Stolyar, B. 2020. "Apple Unveils the Most Popular iPhone Apps of 2019." Mashable. Accessed March 11, 2020.

Sydow, L. 2020a. "At-Home Fitness Apps in Demand admidst Coronavirus Lockdowns." App Annie. Accessed March 11, 2020. https://www.appannie.com/en/insights/market-data/at-home-fitness-apps-in-demand-coronavirus/.

Sydow, L. 2020b. "The State of Mobile in 2020: The Key Stats You Need to Know." App Annie. Accessed May 13, 2020. https://www.appannie.com/en/insights/market-data/state-of-mobile-2020-infographic/.

Thomas, G. M., and D. Lupton. 2016. "Threats and Thrills: Pregnancy Apps, Risk and Consumption." *Health, Risk and Society* 17: 495–509.

Thornham, H. 2019. "Algorithmic Vulnerabilities and the Datalogical: Early Motherhood and Tracking-as-Care Regimes. *Convergence* 25: 171–185.

Todd, Z. 2016. "An Indigenous Feminist's Take on the Ontological Turn: "Ontology" Is Just Another Word for Colonialism." *Journal of Historical Sociology* 29: 4–22.

Toner, J. 2018. "Exploring the Dark-Side of Fitness Trackers: Normalization, Objectification and the Anaesthetisation of Human Experience." *Performance Enhancement and Health* 6: 75–81.

Tziallas, E. 2015. "Gamified Eroticism: Gay Male "Social Networking" Applications and Self-Pornography." *Sexuality and Culture* 19: 759–775.

Van Dijck, J. 2014. "Datafication, Dataism and Dataveillance: Big Data between Scientific Paradigm and Ideology." *Surveillance and Society* 12: 197–208.

Venkatraman, A. 2020. "Weekly Time Spent in Apps Grows 20 Percent Year over Year as People Hunker Down at Home." App Annie. Accessed May 15, 2020. https://www.appannie.com/en/insights/market-data/weekly-time-spent-in-apps-grows-20-year-over-year-as-people-hunker-down-at-home/.

Vogels, E. A. 2020. "10 Facts about Americans and Online Dating." Pew Research Center. Accessed May 20, 2020. https://www.pewresearch.org/fact-tank/2020/02/06/10-facts-about-americans-and-online-dating/.

Wagner, S., and M. Fernández-Ardèvol. 2015. "Local Content Production and the Political Economy of the Mobile App Industries in Argentina and Bolivia." *New Media and Society* 18: 1768–1786.

Whitson, J. R. 2019. "The New Spirit of Capitalism in the Game Industry." *Television and New Media* 20: 789–801.

Wood, A. J., M. Graham, V. Lehdonvirta, and I. Hjorth. 2018. "Good Gig, Bad Gig: Autonomy and Algorithmic Control in the Global Gig Economy." *Work, Employment and Society* 33: 56–75.

Zuboff, S. 2019. *The Age of Surveillance Capitalism: The Fight for the Future at the New Frontier of Power*. London: Profile Books.

CHAPTER 12

FOLDING AND FRICTION

The Internet of Things and Everyday Life

MURRAY GOULDEN

> *The clock on the microwave reads 6:40 a.m. For me—never a morning person—this is uncomfortably early. I navigate around the kitchen in a sleep-deprived fugue, assembling the kids' breakfast. Announcing its presence with a beep, the Amazon Echo on the worktop lights up and transmits my daughter's overamplified voice from the sitting room: "Daaaad! Where's our toast?"*

THE *internet of things* (IoT)—succinctly, the embedding of networked computing into the material world around us—reimagines the quotidian infrastructure of everyday life. Even the most mundane of objects, like shower heads (Shove 2003) or washing machines (Cowan 1985), shape and are shaped by the social worlds in which they circulate, changing society in ways both big and small. In the IoT the "social life" of objects becomes more complicated still—no longer inert, they become two-way nodes in globe-spanning networks through which flows data but also much, much more besides. This chapter is primarily concerned with unpacking that "more" and understanding the implications of this connectivity for everyday life. In the process it seeks to show what sociology brings to our understanding of what the IoT is and what it does.

Amazon's Echo "smart" speaker—better known for the Alexa conversational bot it hosts—is perhaps the pre-eminent IoT device today. Amazon claimed 100 million had been sold by 2019, and this had doubled again by early 2020 (Rubin 2020). These devices are fast becoming a standard fixture of homes in the Global North, and there are countless other IoT devices besides—commonly appended with a "smart" label—which target the home or some other domain of everyday life.

The interaction with an Echo described in the opening vignette above took place in summer 2019 as my family lived alongside a set of IoT technologies as part of a study I was running. In that moment two Echos collapsed the distinction between our sitting room and kitchen, creating a conversation that otherwise would not have happened. What struck me momentarily was the irony that—far from being the user portrayed in IoT-enabled "smart home" visions as a heroic master of technology, empowered by informationalism and automation (Strengers 2014; Strengers and Nicholls 2018)—I was in this instant just another *thing*, an automaton in a 6-year-old's personal IoT.

The first thing I did was to finish buttering the toast; the second was to explain to my daughter that from now on if she wanted to ask something of me, she would have to do so face to face, without the help of Echo. In this anecdote there are a number of themes we shall return to over the course of this chapter: the dissolution of boundaries social and spatial, the (re)distribution of agency and power between entities both obvious and more unexpected, the resistance or pushback that follows such shifts.

Before proceeding, we have our own task of demarcation to conduct. Why the IoT? Why take it as our unit of enquiry? The question confronts us immediately because so much of what is captured by the label "IoT" has already its own established treatment. Algorithms, artificial intelligence (AI), platforms—all are intrinsic aspects of the IoT, and all have, to date, attracted more attention. In this chapter I take the position that to address the IoT is to address the material interface between the global digital networks which these phenomena in part constitute and everyday life—by which I mean the mundane doings, affects, experiences which occupy the great majority of our existence. With this in mind, and the need to render our task tractable, we shall take domestic IoT, the so-called smart home, as our focus. Doing so necessarily requires that we neglect other sites at which the IoT has materialized—such as the smart city, wearables, the gig economy. While this focus inevitably colors the account which follows, I argue that the key properties of the IoT are, as hinted at in our opening, all readily identifiable in this most familiar of settings.

Our claim for the suitability of the smart home as our exemplar in part hinges on a rejection of the temptation to read the IoT as simply an intensification of existing trends, the ongoing extension of computing connectivity which has already jumped from mainframe to desktop to laptop to smartphone. In breaking out of the constraints of any single *personal* device, no matter how mobile, the IoT not only further dissolves the spatial and temporal distance between different social domains but also profoundly implicates social life within those domains, between the members of the setting. The IoT is constitutionally *social* in a way in which no type of social media is. The home, with its (idealized) history as a simultaneously intimate and private space (Mallett 2004), in which so much of life is spent, is well suited to demonstrate this.

In our treatment, the home is taken to be a shared setting. It is, of course, a feature of modern societies that many live alone; but even in such cases, the home is a social setting. Such homes still house pets and host guests and visitors who leave their own (data) traces (Tolmie et al. 2016). They also house the technologies which concern us here. The period of rolling COVID-19 lockdowns during which this chapter was written is testament to how these technologies allow the outside world to share the home with us.

The chapter is divided into three sections. First, I offer a consideration of the role of technologies in everyday life, drawing on social practice theory (SPT) (Reckwitz 2002).

This section also highlights some key features of the IoT most broadly. I then review the literature on the smart home, briefly contextualizing matters via a consideration of the political economy at play, before addressing everyday life in terms of information management, control, domestic labor, and resistance. In the final section I present two aspects of the IoT that have emerged from our analysis, as particularly worthy of future research—the world folding undertaken by the IoT and its misconceived efforts to erase the social frictions of everyday life.

Technology, Everyday Life, and the IoT

To appreciate the role of the IoT in everyday life it is first worth considering the sociality of objects more broadly. Sociology and related disciplines—most notably science and technology studies—have in recent decades undertaken a "material turn," in which objects are recognized as playing an important role. Influential conceptualizations like actor-network theory (Latour 1987) and SPT (Reckwitz 2002) emphasize—in different ways—the interactional, experiential, and agentic properties of objects and their role in the constitution of social worlds.

The latter is particularly useful for understanding the everyday, which we focus on here. In seeking to escape sociology's enduring analytical tension between explanations favoring individual agency, on the one hand, or social structure, on the other, SPT instead takes practices to be its subject. *Practices* are the activities we undertake in the conduct of day-to-day life—cooking a meal, commuting to work, internet dating. Through these practices we not only complete tasks and fulfill goals but also make and remake the social norms that give coherence to our shared realities (Shove and Pantzar 2007, 155). Each practice consists of three components—objects, meanings, and skills (Shove, Pantzar, and Watson 2012). The practice of showering then includes the material dimension of pipes, hot water systems, shower cubicles; meanings such as the social importance of bodily hygiene; and skills like the knowledge of how to turn on the shower without being blasted by cold water. These components are interdependent—changes to one commonly entail changes to another—and this interlinking gives practices a durability and a routineness which characterize the everyday. While only a subset of the sources cited in this chapter are themselves written explicitly as SPT texts, we read all of them through an SPT-informed lens. Recognizing the interlinkages between technologies and other practice components is vital to understanding the role of technology in everyday life—that technologies cannot be understood in isolation or as determining how the social takes shape around them but, rather, that they are adopted, routinized, discarded as part of a bundle of ways of knowing, ways of doing, and ways of feeling (Pink 2004). Technology simultaneously constitutes and is constituted by the sociality of everyday life.

The IoT serves to multiply the number of practices in which any such device is enmeshed. Lindley et al. (2019, 10) speak of things in the IoT living "double lives," simultaneously readily tangible objects in the everyday and digital entities invisibly reporting on this particular day to some server farm half a planet away. As such, seemingly simple queries as to their status become complex, such as who their *user* is (the individual interacting with the device or the company harvesting its data) and what it is they *do* (a smart toothbrush might simultaneously clean teeth, inform the skills involved in teeth cleaning practices, order replacement heads, drive advertising, and shape future toothbrush design). Considered in its entirety, we might conceive of the IoT's materiality constituting a "hyperobject," something "massively distributed in time and space relative to humans" (Morton 2013, 1), like climate change or nuclear power. Our interactions with such things have consequences that will stretch far beyond our own horizons, and indeed beyond our own lifetimes. As such, it is simply too vast to govern, or even simply conceptualize, in any traditional manner.

Dodge and Kitchin (2009) offer a means of anchoring this ethereality back to the home and the everyday. Their work recognizes homes as already existing as "metamachines of literally thousands of different technological components" (p. 1352) but draws attention to the IoT's coding of these components and the spatial reconfiguration which follows "the deepening and widening of dwellings as nodes in a variety of networks of utilities, entertainment, health and communication" (p. 1359). While the permeability of the home is not novel (Mallett 2004), the nature of these information flows as two-way, where everyday domestic practices become subject to corporate surveillance, is.

Mapping the IoT

Before focusing on applications of the IoT within the home, a broader view is needed. Greenfield's (2017, chap. 2) treatment addresses the IoT at three different scales—the individual (wearables), the room (the smart home), and the city (the smart city). Scale is a key feature of the IoT but not in the sense of globe-spanning, which one could argue has been a feature of information and communication technologies (ICTs) at least as far back as the telegram. Instead, it is the promise of the IoT's seemingly infinite scaling between different domains and resolutions. Mosco (2017) sketches the implications of this technology in realms as diverse as warfare, the environment, privacy, and working conditions—from drones over battlefields to the heartbeats of joggers. It is this populating of everywhere between skin and sky above with sensors, processors, and actuators that leads Greenfield to define the IoT as "the colonisation of everyday life by information technologies" (2017, 32). Furszyfer Del Rio et al.'s (2020) typology of business models for smart home technologies alone extends to 15 different types, including everything from energy service provision, healthcare, security, and electric vehicles to platform subscriptions, advertising, and insurance.

In early coverage, Cameron (2016, 87) declared the IoT to carry "an almost unbelievable opaqueness in a transparency-driven digital world," whilst Bunz (2016) noted the disparity between declarations of IoT as the next big thing and the paucity of real-world cases. Certainly, where such cases have become established, analysis has quickly followed—wearables, in the form of devices like Fitbits, were already established in the literature at this point (e.g., Gilmore 2016), part of a larger conversation around the "quantified self" (Swan 2013). As IoT technologies, wearables are distinct, however, in being singular (networked) devices, in contrast to the all-encompassing visions of smart homes and cities which call for the assembly of entire ecosystems. The reality of "in the wild" smart homes today is of piecemeal assemblages of both networked and "dumb" devices and appliances, with limited interoperability. The ultimate impacts of the IoT in these spaces will only emerge if and when the ambition of ubiquitous connectivity is fulfilled.

Lupton's (2020) review of the social dimensions of IoT does demonstrate a growing interest in this domain, though reflecting the IoT's still inchoate nature, Lupton chooses to structure her work largely around the imaginaries attached to it, from techno-utopian promises of seamless connectivity and process optimization to dystopian fears of its capacity for enabling surveillance, dataveillance, and even physical harm. The exception to this framing, and a sign that the IoT *is* finding material forms, is the section on lived experience. Lupton raises the important point that existing treatments of the IoT—as this chapter's literature review attests—are overwhelmingly limited to homes and cities in the Global North, failing to reflect the global reach of these technologies.

Finally, it would be remiss to not also acknowledge the IoT's environmental impact. Its connective infrastructure is rarely visible to the end user—its material form most visible in vast data centers located in often nondescript hinterland sheds—and the direct energy cost of any individual device limited. However, the embodied carbon in the construction and transportation of devices is found to be several times greater than their direct energy demand (Bates et al. 2014, 2015). Furthermore, the appeal to convenience and "pleasance" (Strengers and Nicholls 2018) made by many smart home technologies has the effect of increasing homeowner expectations of comfort and ease, with the result that demand for energy-using services is liable to increase (Goulden et al. 2014; Nyborg and Ropke 2011). The consequence is that far from being a source of energy reduction, as is often claimed of IoT technologies—particularly smart heating systems—there is a risk of energy intensification (Hargreaves, Wilson, and Hauxwell-Baldwin 2017).

The Smart Home

The smart home imaginary is premised on a "smart ontology," which does not leverage technology simply as a material feature of its visions but as a cornerstone of the reality it constructs (Strengers 2013). Social action here occurs not through human activities situated in materially constituted social practices—our "everyday"—but via a rationalistic model of technology-driven informationalism. The bulk of this review will be devoted to exploring the tensions inherent in these competing notions of domestic life, but first I briefly address the political economy in which this smart ontology circulates, to contextualize what follows.

Political Economy

The IoT cannot be understood without the recognition that, even in a world scaffolded by the internet, most of our interactions happen outside a valorization process of profit generation (Srnicek 2017). Srnicek identifies digital platforms as a means of changing this state, but it is the ubiquity of the IoT which provides the infrastructural means of actually capturing these exchanges. Couldry and Mejias (2018) push this argument further, declaring these technologies the preconditions for a new stage of capitalism "that as yet we can barely imagine, but for which the appropriation of human life through data will be central" (p. 337). Their description of this "data colonialism" does not simply invoke a world of pervasive corporate surveillance but—echoing Strengers—identifies the production of the social for capital, "that is, a form of 'social' that is ready for appropriation and exploitation for value as data" (p. 3).

We have then a web between the mundane interactions of everyday sociality and a political economy which valorizes these exchanges, through, for example, the creation of "behavioural futures markets" (Zuboff 2019) that trade in predicted behaviors. This web consists in large part of the IoT as an infrastructure that traces the digital footprints of the everyday and feeds them into the platforms' economies, which, having processed and exchanged them, work back through the web into everyday life various forms of intervention which seek to effect change. The processing of these traces is in itself performative—epistemologies have ontological consequences; they reshape the world they seek to describe (Law 2009). In the political economy of the IoT these epistemologies take the form of systems of metrics, through which we are said to be made and remade: "Metrics facilitate the making and remaking of judgements about us, the judgements we make of ourselves and the consequences of those judgements as they are felt and experienced in our lives" (Beer 2016, 3). Bringing our discussion back to domestic settings, Sadowski (2020) riffs on the IoT label with his description of an "Internet of landlords," in which the IoT enables the massive expansion of rentier capitalism into all areas of life. Sadowski identifies three mechanism through which this occurs: data extraction, capital convergence (the novel assemblage of different sources of capital), and digital enclosure (the capture of social domains). Using smart home examples of each in turn, West (2019) describes Amazon's pursuit of "surveillance-as-service" through the IoT—Echo and its Alexa conversational assistant specifically. Rather than pursue data collection surreptitiously, Amazon effectively promotes it as a means of personalizing services. It harnesses this personalization, in combination with Alexa's affective human-like presentation, to generate and leverage intimacy between household and brand (p. 31). Demonstrating capital convergence, Maalsen and Sadowski (2019) show how Amazon and Google's domestic IoT creates a bridgehead for the finance, insurance, and real estate sector. In bringing together different types of capital, such as the venture capital of platforms and real estate capital, new institutional forms are generated. An example is given of Rentberry, a rental platform which serves to discipline tenants through the generation of detailed data profiling and the fostering of competitive bidding for properties (p. 122).

Turning to digital enclosure finally, Goulden (2019) describes how Amazon and Google's smart home platforms attempt to capture a standardized domestic life in order to render it amenable to the market, most strikingly through their family user accounts, which formalize a set of roles and responsibilities between members of the household and coordinate an "engineered simulacra of domesticity ... serving simultaneously as a vehicle for domestic consumption, and a vehicle for consuming domestic life" (p. 1). Very real tensions are highlighted between this formalized enclosure of domestic forms and the vernacular diversity of households that characterizes modern society, which Chambers (2012) notes have proliferated despite government attempts to homogenize them through housing policies, tax breaks for married couples, divorce laws, etc.

These tensions, and the forms they take, will become a recurring theme in this chapter. In contrast to the vision of ease and empowerment projected by smart home imaginaries, these technologies are found to be disruptive of home life and demanding of users (Hargreaves, Wilson, and Hauxwell-Baldwin 2017). Their adoption into any specific setting is only achieved despite standardization, through the multifaceted improvisation work of householders (Cameron and Goulden n.d.). Ultimately, smartness does not reside in the technology itself but is emergent from users' everyday lives and the ways in which technology is woven into them (Wilson, Hargreaves, and Hauxwell-Baldwin 2015). In the remainder of this review, we turn to these everyday settings.

Information Management

> *Carol and James are study participants. As part of our research, we gave them several pieces of smart home kit to live with. When I visited 2 weeks after bringing them an Echo Show—Amazon's melding of smart speaker and display—they had a question: how was it that the day after installing it in the kitchen it had begun to show them pictures from a family holiday several years earlier? They hadn't even seen these photos in years.*

Privacy and surveillance have been well-worn lenses through which to gaze upon the smart home project. The temptation when turning to the everyday is to carry this language forward, but the titling of this section is deliberate. Privacy so often plays the role of shibboleth in discussions of the impact of digital data on users. My discomfort lies in the assumption—usually implicit—that it is the withholding of information from others which should form the underlying principle in the management of our digital traces. When the "other" is a corporate or state actor, there is merit in this belief; but among members of a setting scaffolded by the IoT, it is my view that the underlying principle is far less absolutist. In the home, it is the *negotiated* management of data between parties and *how* those negotiations are conducted in a dynamic, sociomaterially complex environment, in which social agency and technical skills are unevenly distributed among the members implicated by the data captured by the IoT around them. In domestic information management, what is at stake is not simply the privacy of individuals but the moral ordering of the group (Kilic et al. Forthcoming).

These negotiations take place in the context of contemporary Western societies where families have undergone a "democratization" in which traditional hierarchies have been weakened in favor of individual agency and "mutual disclosure" between parties has become the ideal of intimacy (Giddens 1992). The reality is more complex however. While, for example, parents can no longer rely on authority alone to structure their relationship with their children, and respect must be earned—in part through practices of mutual disclosure which reveal inner thoughts and feelings—domestic relations remain unequal in myriad ways (Jamieson 1999). For example, Brannen et al. (1994) show how middle-class British parents walk a tightrope between cultivating an emotional transparency with their child, so as to really *know* them, and maintaining control and influence over them.

We argue then that the very process of negotiated disclosure between household members is a fundamental aspect of the moral ordering of domestic life, where accountability is demonstrated and the at times mercurial, at times obdurate dynamism of intimate relations is recognized as, for example, children become teenagers become young adults. Enter stage right the IoT, in which "smart" features rely on the *automated* collection, processing, and dissemination of data. Floridi's (2005) metaphor of a house transformed into perfectly transparent glass (p. 188) by digital ICTs holds a certain appeal here, given the smart home's capacity for events like that described below (see "Control"). Floridi argues that pervasively digitalized environments are able to erase *ontological friction*—the forces which limit the flow of information within a setting (p. 186)—hence the glass house. Floridi goes on to argue, however, that contemporary technologies, through gatekeepers like biometrics and passwords, and underpinned by supportive data protection laws (DPLs) like the European Union's General Data Protection Regulation, actually increase ontological friction, which is to say increase the agency of *individual* users to manage *their* data.

While this particular work predates the language of the IoT and current realizations of smart home technology, we use it as an example of the problematic application of individualistic notions of privacy to the home. Both Goulden et al. (2018) and Barassi (2020) identify a characteristic of domestic IoT being the blurring of data subject demarcations, which they term, respectively, "interpersonal data" and "home life data." Both concepts serve to show how the notion of *personal* data, born of an era of personal computers and smartphones in which device and user (singular) are entwined, translates poorly to a setting in which devices (plural) are entwined within a *space* of potentially many users. This is messy data, generated by, and generative of, members of the setting. Barassi's concern is primarily with how the mixing of children's data with their parents' within the smart home allows platform operators to ignore DPL prohibitions on harvesting minors' data. Goulden et al., motivated by the recognition that it is often not what remote corporations know about us but what those closest to us know which is of most concern (boyd 2014, 56), focus instead on the implications for information management within the group. This is driven in part by DPL regimes themselves, which operationalize the same individualistic framing. These laws seek to empower individual users by increasing their access to the data that is collected on them, but when that data is interpersonal, the result is to effectively transgress the delicate information management practices which characterize domestic life (Goulden et al. 2018, 1582–1583). These practices are, between intimates, deeply nuanced, balancing on one side the pragmatic need and/or desire to share devices and practices as part of the conduct of coordinating and experiencing everyday shared lives and, on the other, the need to keep some information strictly private (Jacobs, Cramer, and Barkhuus 2016).

The experience of Carol and James, in the vignette above speaks to these concerns. From what the family and the researcher could piece together, at some point those holiday snaps ended up on an Amazon tablet the family owned previously and from there Amazon's cloud service. Neither Carol nor James had any idea they had been uploaded and were living a second life on a distant server drive. When they logged the Show into the Amazon account they shared, it redownloaded the images and—in its role as a digital photo frame—presented them to anyone in the vicinity. As Barassi's (2020) work highlights, their children—also captured in these pictures—gave no permission for this processing as no discussion between members could take place during what was an automated, "smart" process. For Goulden et al. (2018), the questions raised concern the accountability between members that is implicated when such automated observation is created. While these photos were considered innocuous, had they been, for example, intimate photos of a family member or a member's collection of pornography, the transgression of local moral order would have been consequential for all involved. Finally, for both interpersonal and home life data, and contrasting the rational "new economic actor" (Crabtree et al. 2016) suggested by Floridi (2005) as master of their informational domain, this case speaks to the messy, often confused collision of intimate lives and pervasive data collection *and dissemination* that the smart home enacts, a situation more akin to *data incontinence*, in which the work of making "uncomfortable truths" unremarkable, so as not to continually have to account for them, becomes increasingly demanding (Tolmie and Crabtree 2018, 304). As domestic environments become saturated by these technologies, understanding what information is captured, where it is stored, and how it is used becomes increasingly overwhelming, as Huang, Obada-Obieh, and Beznosov (2020) find for smart speaker users.

From the perspective of the corporate or state actor looking in, the construction of the glass house can be considered intentional design. From the perspective of members within the setting, these new translucencies are better read as accidental corollaries of misplaced individualism, automation, and system complexity. One means by which ontological friction *is* reinserted is via members' own mutual practices of demonstrating trust and respect for autonomy. In a study of domestic CCTV, Mäkinen (2016) introduces, alongside functional and playful uses of these technologies between members, "sincere surveillance," to describe the manner in which the use of these technologies is mediated by members' recognition of "democratized" (Giddens 1992) relations. In a similar manner Goulden et al. (2018) highlight the deployment of "discretion" in these situations, which acknowledges that the watcher is subject to local moral ordering just as the watched is (Tolmie et al. 2016).

The important exception to this picture is where trust and respect are not recognized locally, in situations of domestic coercion or violence. Here there is little to prevent abuse by fellow house members, who can use the remote control of smart devices to gaslight their victims by surreptitiously changing connected devices like thermostats, locks, and lights or do so openly as a demonstration of power (Bowles 2018). One of the challenges of responding to this form of abuse is, for support services, overcoming the designs of these systems, which complacently assume all homes are havens of mutual trust (Lopez-Neira et al., 2019).

Control

> *A Saturday afternoon. I'm in the sitting room on the couch, watching a Youtuber's game stream on my phone. In a Battlegrounds match 100 players face off on an island strewn with guns—last one standing wins. I shift in my seat and accidentally hit the Cast button on screen. I quickly cancel the message that pops up and continue. A minute later a text arrives from my neighbor—she asks if it was me whose warfare interrupted the cartoon their daughter was watching on their smart TV.*

This really happened. Jessie was watching *PAW Patrol* when I commandeered her TV with a video game about competitive murder. All it took was my accidental screen press and the presence of her parents' WiFi password on my phone—a product of babysitting Jessie previously. For the smart home, social norms and brick walls are equally invisible, and there are *no* secrets between password holders.

This anecdote speaks most obviously to the glass house metaphor, but it also raises questions of what control looks like in IoT-mediated environments, what the limits of individual agency are in spaces girded by technologies rendered sociopathic by their inability to recognize moral constraint, and designed to frictionlessly empower their undifferentiated user. As in the case of information management, in the absence of technology able to parse social context, it falls on users themselves to reconcile the IoT with the moral economy of the home. This process is performed with reference to participants' own relative positioning within this economy—whether a couple, a parent and child, roommates, etc. (Geeng and Roesner 2019)—as well as their positioning in regard to the practices implicated by the technology and, associated with that, respective access to relevant resources like time and skills (Cameron and Goulden n.d.; Hargreaves, Wilson, and Hauxwell-Baldwin 2017). An important way in which these disparities are manifested is in initial purchase and installation—the member carrying out device setup commonly takes on a dominant role in regard to the ongoing control of the device (Geeng and Roesner 2019). Zeng, Mare, and Roesner (2017) note that these figures, particularly "early adopters," "often treat the technology as a personal hobby, [but] smart homes are fundamentally not personal technologies" (p. 73). The consequences of these dynamics can be enduring disparities—for example, Google's Families group account allows up to two Parent roles and four Family Members, but only one of the former, the Family Manager, has the executive agency to remove any other member or dissolve the group entirely. This status is conferred upon whoever sets up the account originally, which, given the existing masculinized gendering of ICT, effectively imposes patriarchal relations on the digital family (Goulden 2019).

Hine (2020, 23) provides a powerful autoethnographic account of how these affordances of IoT technologies can trample over the social topography of what are often delicate domestic ecosystems. Her mother, a dementia sufferer, lives alone, supported locally by two of her children, with a third across the country. The distant sibling visits one weekend to install, without consultation, a smart heating system. The acrimony is immediate—the agency of their mother and the local siblings has been transgressed. Life goes on, and things settle into a new rhythm:

> But we're not the same. The temperature of the house has become a new feature in the family relationships, thanks to the heating system . . . . [H]igh on the wall in the hallway, a smart thermostatic controller is mounted, controlled by an app on the smartphone of the sibling 200 miles away. Before, when I visited and the house temperature felt wrong I could do something about it—open a window, turn on a gas fire, but now I can't. The controller sits there mute, a blank shiny black plaque . . . . Next visit, there's no doubt the house strikes chill as soon as you step inside. I phone my sibling. The house is cold. They check their phone—it's set at 26°, that's right. No, really, I insist, it is freezing cold. No heating at all. After they give me a speech about how I must expect that the heating will go on and off throughout the day because that's how thermostats work, I insist again, it is cold. They recheck—actually the controller is offline.

I reproduce this account in detail because it goes to the heart of how the IoT's material forms are—contra the rationalist ordering of the smart ontology—deeply, irrevocably enmeshed in the sensory production of "home" and its affective regimes. They are also, like Hine's thermostat, constitutive of those human actors they are associated with. Material things are "an integral and inseparable aspect of all relationships. People exist for us in and through their material presence" (Miller 2008, 286).

Finally, in this section, it would be remiss to neglect the unique challenge that connected things pose for notions of control over their material selves. They depend on software for core functionality, which is commonly governed under different regulatory regimes than hardware (Tusikov 2019). Manufacturers use copyright law and licensing agreements to maintain enduring agency over the functioning of the device, which can be exercised through changes to the product, even to the extent of temporarily or permanently "bricking it," as smart speaker manufacturer Sonos did with its "Recycle Mode," which permanently deactivated otherwise working devices, as part of an upselling scheme (BBC News 2019).

Domestic Labor

The *work* of maintaining a household—ensuring the sufficient flow of goods into the home, preparing meals, meeting expectations of cleanliness and orderliness, coordinating members' schedules, etc.—has long been recognized as a subject of academic study (Oakley 1974). The gender divisions Oakley described, in which women were found to work a 77-hour week, were stark. In the subsequent decades women have entered the paid workforce in large numbers and yet are still found to hold the main responsibility for domestic work, even if the division is not as stark as it once was (Chambers 2012, 30). The consequence of this shift is that households in which two parents work *and* seek to meet high expectations of parenting and household management are now common (Hansen 2005).

It is not coincidental that some of the major appeals of smart home manufacturers target this space. iRobot's popular Roomba smart vacuum is advertised with images of the device set against a backdrop of a mother escorting her child out the front door (iRobot 2020)—liberated from domestic labor by smart automation to meet her other demands of parental and waged labor. Amazon's advertising of its Household family account similarly shows parents' juggling of multiple demands eased by its affordances (see Goulden 2019, fig. 2).

One question raised by these efforts is their likely efficacy in freeing householders from unwanted work, but this requires unpacking. In her seminal account of the "industrialisation of the home," Cowan (1985) highlights how the first wave of home automation—in the form of appliances like washing machines—failed to reduce the time women spent on housework. Instead, these technologies largely served to reduce the work that had previously fallen on husbands, children, and servants, while wives faced rising expectations of domestic cleanliness. Given the inchoate nature of the IoT currently, it remains to be seen how this wave of technologies will impact domestic labor. There are some suggestions that it might play out differently however. Successfully incorporating, and maintaining, digital technologies in the home generates its own work—"digital housekeeping" (Tolmie et al. 2007). Feminist scholars have long noted the "genderscripting" (Oudshoorn and Pinch 2005, 10) of devices, in which male-dominated design teams create technologies for which they are the imagined user (Oudshoorn, Rommes, and Stienstra 2004). The increasing diffusion of masculinized digital technologies throughout the home may ultimately generate "more work for father" (Strengers and Nicholls 2018, 78), though this in turn might result in other household members taking a greater share of traditional housework (Kennedy et al. 2015), as part of the trading of work with the domestic economy (Rode, Toye, and Blackwell 2004).

The potential impact of IoT on domestic labor is not simply a question of time commitments, of course. There is also the matter of the qualities of this labor and the broader relations of production in which domestic labor exists. In Srnicek's (2017) typology of digital platforms, it is "industrial" which most appropriately describes the smart home: "the embedding of sensors and computer chips into the production process and of trackers ... into the logistics process" (p. 64), in the name of optimization. Recognition of parallels between the factory and domestic work go back to Oakley's (1974) original study, which notes that due to the monotony, fragmentation, and speed of the work described, domestic labor most closely paralleled the alienation of assembly-line work (p. 82).

Perhaps the most iconic form of the assembly line in contemporary capitalism is the Amazon logistics center, the point at which the usually ethereal platform takes on titanic material form. Here, the IoT has a crucial role in tracking and cajoling each individual worker through every moment of their shift. The impact of these technologies is not simply to intensify work; it also changes the lived experience of work, fostering the "quantified self at work"—"an attempt to quantify the affective field so as to render it more predictably exploitable" (Moore and Robinson 2016, 2775).

We must exercise caution in attempting to transpose factory on to home—industrialization played out in very distinct ways in the home (Cowan 1985)—but the two-way flows enabled by the IoT which Dodge and Kitchin highlight in their notion of codespace (2009) further dissolve the already permeable boundaries between these domains. This is demonstrated clearly in Johnson's (2020) telling account of a "smart grid" demand-side response[1] (DSR) trial. Inverting the visions of feminized AI assistants automating domestic chores projected by entities like Amazon's Alexa, Johnson describes how grid response in the low-income households studied hinged instead on the situated knowledge and labor of women. In other words, the "smart" in this system resided not in technology but in "Flexibility Woman":

> She had knowledge about her family's consumption habits, the loads in home and the schedules of life that shaped her household's electricity demand profile. She may not have talked in these terms or made such connections explicitly, but she had this knowledge because she knew when the laundry had to be done and when it could wait, she knew when meals were to be eaten and therefore when food needed to be cooked .... She differentiated between necessary and indulgent consumption, she arbitraged between gas and electricity, and she developed strategies to recruit other household members into her response. (p. 6)

Johnson's study highlights the need to factor an appreciation of everyday domestic life into the design of IoT technologies. It also—using the example of a mother who is applauded by her family for securing £13 credit through her skillful management of domestic practices during the DSR trial—highlights the affectivities of chore work and its capacity to performatively express identity (Pink 2004) and care for others (Miller 2008). Oakley's work hints at this in the finding that the *autonomy* of housework—"you're your own boss"—was the most highly valued aspect of it (1974, 38). In light of this, and the contrast of the quantified self at work, new means of IoT-enabled oversight of domestic labor raise questions about how it might be commodified or (further) routinized to the detriment of those performing it. Whether the new boss is a remote algorithm (Woodcock 2020) or a 6-year-old demanding toast, there is a danger that, far from liberating us from domestic labor, the smart home simply renders it more alienating. In delegating practices to automated devices, the temporal rhythms, relations, and identities involved in them also become subject to the smart ontology which birthed them (Davidoff et al. 2006).

Resistance

These darker visions bring us naturally to the question of resistance to such interventions. Explicitly performative challenges to the politics of the smart home are emerging (see, for example, Malliaraki's [2019] creation of a "feminist Alexa," which subverts the submissive femininity encoded in Amazon's creation). Our interests here though are more specific: What does everyday resistance to the IoT look like? Our opening anecdote showed us a most mundane demonstration of resistance—a father's objection to the sense that his parental duties were rendered transgressively transactional by the addition of remote demands to work faster. Or perhaps it was simply the bald inversion of the remaining vestiges of domestic hierarchy which motivated his rejection—a refusal to be the *thing* on the end of this chain of command. Regardless, after this discomfort was relayed to his human would-be overseer, it never repeated. The life of this IoT-mediated practice was a short one.

In approaching this question of resistance, we need to recognize that praxis here is unlikely to be directed in explicit opposition to the smart ontology (Strengers 2013) or the political economy of the IoT but rather to ameliorating the unwelcome consequences which their juxtapositions create. In several of the studies we have discussed, constraints on the utilization of connected devices stemmed from householders' *selective* incorporation of them into existing moral and practical orderings (Goulden et al. 2018; Hargreaves and Wilson 2017; Mäkinen 2016; Tolmie and Crabtree 2018). The result of these quotidian tapestries of use can nevertheless be just as systemically consequential as overt resistance, whether for platforms' intentions to "re-engineer" domestic life (Goulden 2019) or simply to extract data from it (West 2019), with the result that their perspective on domestic life is less Bentham-esque glass house and instead consists of a "myopic" view limited to a subset of users and a subset of practices (Pridmore and Mols 2020).

The curating of smart home engagement has echoes of Nafus and Sherman's (2014) account of "soft resistance" among the quantified self movement. Rather than accept the role of passive subject to dominant big data modalities, quantified self participants develop their own practices for generating personal insights from these technologies, in which they are simultaneously project designers, data collectors, and sense-makers. Just as with the examples we have discussed, this has the effect of disrupting the platforms' intentions by, for example, fragmenting data sets. Nevertheless, the "softness" of this resistance reflects that it is "always necessarily partial, firmly rooted in many of the same social logics that shape the categories [it] seek[s] to escape" (p. 1785). Adopting these technologies necessarily involves adopting aspects of their ontological framing, including here a radical individualism and a project of optimizing well-being through quantification. A similarly dialectical relationship between designer and user can be found in Hansen and Hauge's (2017) study of a Danish DSR trial, in which system control was contested between designers and users through processes of in-scripting and de-scripting (Akrich 1992).

In considering resistance then, we must recognize that it is often not enacted as an overt challenge to an identified external force but rather simply emerges out of the everyday durability of practices which refuse to remake themselves according to someone else's intentions. In Scott's (2014) wonderful (caveated) celebration of anarchism, he highlights the role of "infrapolitics"—so called because it takes place outside recognized forms of political activity—in shaping history:

> By infrapolitics I have in mind such acts as foot-dragging, poaching, pilfering, dissimulation, sabotage, desertion, absenteeism, squatting, and flight . . . . Why openly petition for rights to wood, fish, and game when poaching will accomplish the same purpose quietly? . . . [T]he accumulation of thousands or even millions of such petty acts can have massive effects on warfare, land rights, taxes, and property relations. (p. xx)

In the smart home, such mundane subversions can also take many forms. Sonos' plan to brick working devices was ultimately abandoned in the face of unorganized, if very open, rebellion by its users (BBC News 2020); but more covert actions take place continuously in the everyday workings of the smart home. Just as past resistance might be registered through reports of missing trees or game, in the smart home it is missing data. When users chose not to share with Alexa their credit card details (Huang, Obada-Obieh, and Beznosov 2020, 7) or shop for goods through it, instead utilizing it as nothing more than a glorified cooking timer, Amazon's intentions—underwritten by its regular steep discounting of Echo products—are thwarted.

This affordance is, of course, a double-edged sword however. These acts of non-use, or subversive use, register *because* connected devices serving the needs of remote corporate and state masters are becoming ubiquitous. The possibility of escaping these tethers, whether in the home or outside it, is ever diminishing (Kuntsman and Miyake 2019). The darkest questions posed by the IoT are what the possibilities of infrapolitics are, in a world of listening lampposts (Tkacik 2020) and "unauthorised bread" (Doctorow 2020).

Future Research: Friction and Folding

In this closing section we seek to tie threads together, in order to present two features of the IoT which call for ongoing investigation. Seeking out examples of these phenomena, and charting their impacts, is a primary task for a sociology of the IoT.

World Folding

Urquhart and Chen (forthcoming) pose a seemingly absurd question: How might transnational data protection laws be applied to everyday domestic interactions? They invoke teenagers lodging "right to be forgotten" demands with their parents in response to embarrassing social media posts and flatmates exchanging "data portability" requests when they move out. The European Union's DPL regulation has long included a "household exemption" clause, in recognition that laws formulated to ensure that organizations do not transgress individuals' rights are unsuitable for domestic settings lacking formal structures and deep technical resources; but the authors note that, as the IoT has increasingly eroded distinctions between home and world outside, court decisions have chipped away at the exemption clause, such that its survival is now in doubt.

This argument is a striking demonstration of an affordance of the IoT we have seen repeatedly in this chapter, whereby very different ontologies are brought into uneasy co-presence. This recognition owes a debt to boyd's much cited notion of "context collapse" (Marwick and boyd 2011), in which social media platforms compress together a user's multiple different networks, creating a Frankenstein audience of peers, parents, and bosses without predigital equivalent. This remaking of audience seems out of proportion with what I describe here. More fitting is Lee et al.'s (2019) metaphor of algorithmic work as "folding." When the IoT draws international laws into the minutia of domestic relations through DPL or into domestic practices through the enforcement of digital rights management and copyright law (Goulden 2019; Tusikov 2019), reconfigures domestic chores around national energy grids (Johnson 2020), or more fundamentally still, captures and plays back domestic life through a rationalized smart ontology (Strengers 2013), the juxtapositions we see are a consequence of *world folding*. These foldings take place at far more intimate scales as well, when collapsing together my daughter in the sitting room and me in the kitchen, or my phone and my neighbor's TV. In both cases the sociality of the spaces' integrity was transgressed—my daughter's space of leisure with mine of labor, my device with *their* TV.

The notion of IoT as ubiquitous connectivity which we began with is misleading as it implies an easy separation between realms. "Folding" does not imply a loss of domain distinction but rather a layering of one domain atop or through another. Indeed, it is the efforts of inhabitants of these worlds to maintain vernacular idiosyncrasies in these circumstances that prompt so much of what is described in this chapter.

The Friction of Frictionless Homogeneity

Our concern to recognize the enduring integrity of domains stands in contrast to the purposes of the IoT, which operates under a logic of minimizing transaction costs—"the keyword is *frictionless* interfaces" (Sadowski 2020, 565, original emphasis). This work requires standardization across domain boundaries. Friction is the peculiar and the specific, which refuses homogenization. This logic runs throughout the IoT's political economy, but it is equally present in its recipe for optimizing the everyday of domestic life, through the automation of practices. The reduction of friction is in-scripted (Akrich 1992) in YouTube's Cast button, which—with a single press—takes control of devices in others' houses, just as it is in a robotic vacuum cleaner which lessens the load of keeping your single-floor apartment free of dust.

Social friction, though, is *valuable*. Friction is where the politics of the everyday happens, in the loaded, sometimes painful interactions between members that draw and redraw relations, obligations, freedoms. In refusing my daughter's leveraging of Echo, a lesson was given about the mutuality of accountability that in some immeasurable way will contribute to her socialization as a fully formed human. Friction also purposefully accumulates at significant social boundaries, such as between one house and the next. Friction is often unwelcome, even boring, in the effort of monotonous housework, for example; but it is simultaneously where pleasure *can* be found and where meaning and identity forged (Pink 2004). When rational ontologies like the smart home seek process optimization, they make the "fatal assumption that in any such activity there is *only one thing going on*" (Scott 2014, 42–43, original emphasis), neglecting the multivalent nature of all practices.

Scott's work gives us a broader perspective, within which the smart home can be read as but the latest incarnation of the troubled attempt to apply modern rationalist control in settings which cannot be controlled. Scott contrasts the success of Ford's minutely standardized Model-T factory, where the environment could be re-engineered to suit the process, with the abject failure of Ford's application of the same approach to Fordlandia—his rubber plantations in the Amazon (pp. 35–40). Under a sociological lens, the home's enduring heterogeneity looks far more like the forest than the factory.

Note

1. DSR entails the attempted remote management of domestic energy consumption in order to balance the energy grid at a system level through the use of IoT technologies.

References

Akrich, Madeleine. 1992. "The De-scription of Technical Objects." In *Shaping Technology/Building Society: Studies in Sociotechnical Change*, edited by Wiebe E. Bijker and John Law, 205–224. Cambridge, MA: MIT Press.
Barassi, Veronica. 2020. *Child Data Citizen: How Tech Companies Are Profiling Us from Before Birth*. Cambridge, MA: MIT Press.
Bates, Oliver, Mike Hazas, Adrian Friday, Janine Morley, and Adrian K. Clear. 2014. "Towards an Holistic View of the Energy and Environmental Impacts of Domestic Media and IT." In *Proceedings of the SIGCHI Conference on Human Factors in Computing Systems, CHI '14*, 1173–1182. New York: ACM Press. https://doi.org/10.1145/2556288.2556968.

Bates, Oliver, Caroline Lord, Bran Knowles, Adrian Friday, Adrian Clear, and Mike Hazas. 2015. "Exploring (Un)Sustainable Growth of Digital Technologies in the Home." In *Proceedings of EnviroInfo and ICT for Sustainability 2015*, 300–309. Amsterdam: Atlantis Press. https://doi.org/10.2991/ict4s-env-15.2015.34.

BBC News. 2019. "Sonos in Bricked Speaker 'Recycling' Row." December 31. Accessed July 30, 2020. https://www.bbc.com/news/technology-50948868.

BBC News. 2020. "Sonos U-Turn over 'Bricking' Its Smart Speakers." March 6. Accessed July 30, 2020. https://www.bbc.com/news/technology-51768574.

Beer, David. 2016. *Metric Power*. London: Palgrave Macmillan.

Bowles, Nellie. 2018. "Thermostats, Locks and Lights: Digital Tools of Domestic Abuse." *New York Times*, June 23.

boyd, danah. 2014. *It's Complicated: The Social Lives of Networked Teens*. New Haven, CT: Yale University Press.

Brannen, Julia, Kathryn Dodd, Ann Oakley, and Pamela Storey. 1994. *Young People, Health and Family Life*. Buckingham, UK, and Philadelphia, PA: Open University Press.

Bunz, Mercedes. 2016. "Book Review: The Internet of Things: Tracing a New Field of Enquiry." *Media Culture & Society* 38, no. 8: 1278–1282. https://doi.org/10.1177/0163443716667066.

Cameron, L., and M. Goulden. n.d. "Improvising the Smart Home: Overcoming Standardisation through Improvisations-in-Practice." Unpublished manuscript.

Cameron, Nigel. 2016. "A Tangled Web." *Issues in Science and Technology* 32, no. 3: 87–89.

Chambers, Deborah. 2012. *A Sociology of Family Life*. Cambridge and Malden, MA: Polity Press.

Couldry, Nick, and Ulises A. Mejias. 2018. "Data Colonialism: Rethinking Big Data's Relation to the Contemporary Subject." *Television & New Media* 20, no 4: 336–349. https://doi.org/10.1177/1527476418796632.

Cowan, Ruth Schwartz. 1985. *More Work for Mother: The Ironies of Household Technology from the Open Hearth to the Microwave*. 2nd ed. New York: Basic Books.

Crabtree, Andy, Tom Lodge, James Colley, Chris Greenhalgh, Richard Mortier, and Hamed Haddadi. 2016. "Enabling the New Economic Actor: Data Protection, the Digital Economy, and the Databox." *Personal and Ubiquitous Computing* 20: 947–957. https://doi.org/10.1007/s00779-016-0939-3.

Davidoff, Scott, Min Kyung Lee, Charles Yiu, John Zimmerman, and Anind K. Dey. 2006. "Principles of Smart Home Control." In *UbiComp 2006: Ubiquitous Computing*. Lecture Notes in Computer Science, edited by Paul Dourish and Adrian Friday, 19–34. Berlin: Springer. https://doi.org/10.1007/11853565_2.

Doctorow, Cory. 2020. "Unauthorized Bread: Real Rebellions Involve Jailbreaking IoT Toasters." Ars Technica, January 22, 2020. Accessed August 1, 2020. https://arstechnica.com/gaming/2020/01/unauthorized-bread-a-near-future-tale-of-refugees-and-sinister-iot-appliances/.

Dodge, Martin, and Rob Kitchin. 2009. "Software, Objects, and Home Space." *Environment and Planning A: Economy and Space* 41, no. 6: 1344–1365. https://doi.org/10.1068/a4138.

Floridi, Luciano. 2005. "The Ontological Interpretation of Informational Privacy." *Ethics and Information Technology* 7: 185–200. https://doi.org/10.1007/s10676-006-0001-7.

Furszyfer Del Rio, Dylan D., Benjamin K. Sovacool, Noam Bergman, and Karen E. Makuch. 2020. "Critically Reviewing Smart Home Technology Applications and Business Models in Europe." *Energy Policy* 144: 111631. https://doi.org/10.1016/j.enpol.2020.111631.

Geeng, Christine, and Franziska Roesner. 2019. "Who's in Control? Interactions in Multi-User Smart Homes." In *Proceedings of the 2019 CHI Conference on Human Factors in Computing*

Systems, CHI '19, 1–13. Glasgow, UK: Association for Computing Machinery. https://doi.org/10.1145/3290605.3300498.

Giddens, Anthony. 1992. *The Transformation of Intimacy: Sexuality, Love, and Eroticism in Modern Societies.* Cambridge: Polity Press.

Gilmore, James N. 2016. "Everywear: The Quantified Self and Wearable Fitness Technologies." *New Media & Society* 18: 2524–2539. https://doi.org/10.1177/1461444815588768.

Goulden, Murray. 2019. " 'Delete the Family': Platform Families and the Colonisation of the Smart Home." *Information, Communication & Society.* Published ahead of print September 26, 2019. https://doi.org/10.1080/1369118X.2019.1668454.

Goulden, Murray, Ben Bedwell, Stefan Rennick-Egglestone, Tom Rodden, and Alexa Spence. 2014. "Smart Grids, Smart Users? The Role of the User in Demand Side Management." *Energy Research & Social Science* 2: 21–29. https://doi.org/10.1016/j.erss.2014.04.008.

Goulden, Murray, Peter Tolmie, Richard Mortier, Tom Lodge, Anna-Kaisa Pietilainen, and Renata Teixeira. 2018. "Living with Interpersonal Data: Observability and Accountability in the Age of Pervasive ICT." *New Media & Society* 20: 1580–1599. https://doi.org/10.1177/1461444817700154.

Greenfield, Adam. 2017. *Radical Technologies: The Design of Everyday Life.* London and New York: Verso.

Hansen, Karen V. 2005. *Not-so-Nuclear Families: Class, Gender, and Networks of Care.* New Brunswick, NJ: Rutgers University Press.

Hansen, Meiken, and Bettina Hauge. 2017. "Scripting, Control, and Privacy in Domestic Smart Grid Technologies: Insights from a Danish Pilot Study." *Energy Research & Social Science* 25: 112–123. https://doi.org/10.1016/j.erss.2017.01.005.

Hargreaves, Tom, and Charlie Wilson. 2017. *Smart Homes and Their Users.* New York: Springer.

Hargreaves, Tom, Charlie Wilson, and Richard Hauxwell-Baldwin. 2017. "Learning to Live in a Smart Home." *Building Research & Information* 46, no. 1: 127–139. https://doi.org/10.1080/09613218.2017.1286882.

Hine, Christine. 2020. "Strategies for Reflexive Ethnography in the Smart Home: Autoethnography of Silence and Emotion." *Sociology* 54, no. 1: 22–36. https://doi.org/10.1177/0038038519855325.

Huang, Yue, Borke Obada-Obieh, and Konstantin Beznosov. 2020. "Amazon vs. My Brother: How Users of Shared Smart Speakers Perceive and Cope with Privacy Risks." In *CHI '20: Proceedings of the 2020 CHI Conference on Human Factors in Computing Systems*, 1–13. New York: ACM Press.

iRobot. 2020. "Roomba i Series." Accessed July 31, 2020. https://www.irobot.co.uk/en-GB/roomba/i-series.

Jacobs, Maia, Henriette Cramer, and Louise Barkhuus. 2016. "Caring about Sharing: Couples' Practices in Single User Device Access." In *Proceedings of the 19th International Conference on Supporting Group Work, GROUP '16*, 235–243. New York: ACM Press. https://doi.org/10.1145/2957276.2957296.

Jamieson, Lynn. 1999. "Intimacy Transformed? A Critical Look at the 'Pure Relationship.'" *Sociology* 33: 477–494. https://doi.org/10.1177/S0038038599000310.

Johnson, Charlotte. 2020. "Is Demand Side Response a Woman's Work? Domestic Labour and Electricity Shifting in Low Income Homes in the United Kingdom." *Energy Research & Social Science* 68: 101558. https://doi.org/10.1016/j.erss.2020.101558.

Kennedy, Jenny, Bjorn Nansen, Michael Arnold, Rowan Wilken, and Martin Gibbs. 2015. "Digital Housekeepers and Domestic Expertise in the Networked Home." *Convergence* 21: 408–422. https://doi.org/10.1177/1354856515579848.

Kilic, Damla, Lewis Cameron, Glenn McGarry, Murray Goulden, and Andy Crabtree. Forthcoming. "The Socially Negotiated Management of Personal Data in Everyday Life". In *Privacy by Design for the Internet of Things: Building Accountability and Security*, edited by A. Crabtree, R. Mortier, and H. Haddadi. London: IET Press.

Kuntsman, Adi, and Esperanza Miyake. 2019. "The Paradox and Continuum of Digital Disengagement: Denaturalising Digital Sociality and Technological Connectivity." *Media Culture & Society* 41: 901–913. https://doi.org/10.1177/0163443719853732.

Latour, Bruno. 1987. *Science in Action*. Cambridge, MA: Harvard University Press.

Law, John. 2009. "Seeing Like a Survey." *Cultural Sociology* 3: 239–256. https://doi.org/10.1177/1749975509105533.

Lee, Francis, Jess Bier, Jeffrey Christensen, Lukas Engelmann, Claes-Fredrik Helgesson, and Robin Williams. 2019. "Algorithms as Folding: Reframing the Analytical Focus." *Big Data & Society* 6: 2053951719863819. https://doi.org/10.1177/2053951719863819.

Lindley, Joseph Galen, Paul Coulton, Haider Akmal, Duncan Hay, Max Van Kleek, Sara Cannizzaro, and Reuben Binns. 2019. *The Little Book of Philosophy for the Internet of Things*. Lancaster, UK: Lancaster University.

Lopez-Neira, Isabel, Trupti Patel, Simon Parkin, George Danezis, and Leonie Tanczer. 2019. " 'Internet of Things': How Abuse Is Getting Smarter." *Safe—The Domestic Abuse Quarterly* 63: 22–26.

Lupton, Deborah. 2020. "The Internet of Things: Social Dimensions." *Sociology Compass* 14: e12770. https://doi.org/10.1111/soc4.12770.

Maalsen, Sophia, and Jathan Sadowski. 2019. "The Smart Home on FIRE: Amplifying and Accelerating Domestic Surveillance." *Surveillance & Society* 17: 118–124. https://doi.org/10.24908/ss.v17i1/2.12925.

Mäkinen, Lisa A. 2016. "Surveillance On/Off: Examining Home Surveillance Systems from the User's Perspective." *Surveillance & Society* 14: 59–77.

Mallett, Shelley. 2004. "Understanding Home: A Critical Review of the Literature," *Sociological Review* 52: 62–89. https://doi.org/10.1111/j.1467-954X.2004.00442.x.

Malliaraki, Eirini. 2019. "Making a Feminist Alexa." SAGE Ocean, January 31. Accessed February 11, 2019. https://ocean.sagepub.com/blog/2019/1/14/making-a-feminist-alexa.

Marwick, Alice E., and danah boyd. 2011. "I Tweet Honestly, I Tweet Passionately: Twitter Users, Context Collapse, and the Imagined Audience." *New Media & Society* 13: 114–133. https://doi.org/10.1177/1461444810365313.

Miller, Daniel. 2008. *The Comfort of Things*. Cambridge, UK, and Malden, MA: Polity Press.

Moore, Phoebe, and Andrew Robinson. 2016. "The Quantified Self: What Counts in the Neoliberal Workplace." *New Media & Society* 18: 2774–2792. https://doi.org/10.1177/1461444815604328.

Morton, Timothy. 2013. *Hyperobjects: Philosophy and Ecology after the End of the World*. Minneapolis: University of Minnesota Press.

Mosco, Vincent. 2017. "After the Internet: New Technologies, Social Issues, and Public Policies." *Fudan Journal of the Humanities and Social Sciences* 10: 297–313. https://doi.org/10.1007/s40647-016-0156-5.

Nafus, Dawn, and Jamie Sherman. 2014. "This One Does Not Go up to 11: The Quantified Self Movement as an Alternative Big Data Practice." *International Journal of Communication* 8: 1784–1794.

Nyborg, Sophie, and Inge Ropke. 2011. "Energy Impacts of the Smart Home—Conflicting Visions." In *Energy Efficiency First: The Foundation of a Low-Carbon Society*, 1849–1860. Stockholm: European Council for an Energy-Efficient Economy.

Oakley, Ann. 1974. *The Sociology of Housework*. Oxford: Wiley-Blackwell.

Oudshoorn, Nelly, and Trevor Pinch, eds. 2005. *How Users Matter: The Co-Construction of Users and Technology*. Cambridge, MA: MIT Press.

Oudshoorn, Nelly, Els Rommes, and Marcelle Stienstra. 2004. "Configuring the User as Everybody: Gender and Design Cultures in Information and Communication Technologies." *Science, Technology, & Human Values* 29: 30–63. https://doi.org/10.1177/0162243903259190.

Pink, Sarah. 2004. *Home Truths: Gender, Domestic Objects and Everyday Life*. Oxford: Berg.

Pridmore, Jason, and Anouk Mols. 2020. "Personal Choices and Situated Data: Privacy Negotiations and the Acceptance of Household Intelligent Personal Assistants." *Big Data & Society* 7: 2053951719891748. https://doi.org/10.1177/2053951719891748.

Reckwitz, Andreas. 2002. "Toward a Theory of Social Practices: A Development in Culturalist Theorizing." *European Journal of Social Theory* 5: 243–263. https://doi.org/10.1177/13684310222225432.

Rode, Jennifer A., Eleanor F. Toye, and Alan F. Blackwell. 2004. "The Fuzzy Felt Ethnography—Understanding the Programming Patterns of Domestic Appliances." *Personal and Ubiquitous Computing* 8: 161–176. https://doi.org/10.1007/s00779-004-0272-0.

Rubin, Ben Fox. 2020. "Amazon sees Alexa devices more than double in just one year." CNET. Accessed September 14, 2020. https://www.cnet.com/news/amazon-sees-alexa-devices-more-than-double-in-just-one-year/.

Sadowski, Jathan. 2020. "The Internet of Landlords: Digital Platforms and New Mechanisms of Rentier Capitalism." *Antipode* 52: 562–580. https://doi.org/10.1111/anti.12595.

Scott, James C. 2014. *Two Cheers for Anarchism: Six Easy Pieces on Autonomy, Dignity, and Meaningful Work and Play*. Princeton, NJ: Princeton University Press.

Shove, Elizabeth. 2003. *Comfort, Cleanliness and Convenience: The Social Organization of Normality*. Milton Keynes: Berg.

Shove, Elizabeth, and Mika Pantzar. 2007. "Recruitment and Reproduction: The Careers and Carriers of Digital Photography and Floorball." *Human Affairs* 17: 154–167. https://doi.org/10.2478/v10023-007-0014-9.

Shove, Elizabeth, Mika Pantzar, and Matt Watson. 2012. *The Dynamics of Social Practice: Everyday Life and How It Changes*. London: SAGE Publications.

Srnicek, Nick. 2017. *Platform Capitalism*. Cambridge: Polity Press.

Strengers, Yolande. 2013. *Smart Energy Technologies in Everyday Life*. New York: Palgrave Macmillan.

Strengers, Yolande. 2014. "Smart Energy in Everyday Life: Are You Designing for Resource Man?" *ACM Interactions* (July–August): 24.

Strengers, Yolande, and Larissa Nicholls. 2018. "Aesthetic Pleasures and Gendered Tech-Work in the 21st-Century Smart Home." *Media International Australia* 166: 70–80. https://doi.org/10.1177/1329878X17737661.

Swan, Melanie. 2013. "The Quantified Self: Fundamental Disruption in Big Data Science and Biological Discovery." *Big Data* 1: 85–99. https://doi.org/10.1089/big.2012.0002.

Tkacik, Daniel. 2020. "How Much Control Are People Willing to Grant to a Personal Privacy Assistant?" Cylab, June 18. Accessed August 1, 2020. https://www.cylab.cmu.edu/news/2020/06/18-control-privacy-assistance.html.

Tolmie, Peter, and Andy Crabtree. 2018. "The Practical Politics of Sharing Personal Data." *Personal and Ubiquitous Computing* 22: 293–315. https://doi.org/10.1007/s00779-017-1071-8.

Tolmie, Peter, Andy Crabtree, Tom Rodden, James Colley, and Ewa Luger. 2016. " 'This Has to Be the Cats': Personal Data Legibility in Networked Sensing Systems." In *Proceedings of* the 19th ACM Conference on Computer-Supported Cooperative Work & Social Computing, CSCW '16, 491–502. New York: ACM Press. https://doi.org/10.1145/2818048.2819992.

Tolmie, Peter, Andy Crabtree, Tom Rodden, Chris Greenhalgh, and Steve Benford. 2007. "Making the Home Network at Home: Digital Housekeeping." In *ECSCW 2007*, edited by L. J. Bannon, I. Wagner, C. Gutwin, R H. R. Harper, and K. Schmidt, 331–350. London: Springer. https://doi.org/10.1007/978-1-84800-031-5_18.

Tusikov, Natasha. 2019. "Precarious Ownership of the Internet of Things in the Age of Data." In *Information, Technology and Control in a Changing World: Understanding Power Structures in the 21st Century*, edited by B. Haggart, K. Henne, and N. Tusikov, 121–148. International Political Economy Series. Cham, Switzerland: Springer International. https://doi.org/10.1007/978-3-030-14540-8_6.

Urquhart, Lachlan, and Jiahong Chen. Forthcoming. "On the Principle of Accountability: Challenges for Smart Homes & Cybersecurity." In *Privacy by Design for the Internet of Things: Building Accountability and Security*, edited by A. Crabtree, R. Mortier, and H. Haddadi. London: IET Press.

West, Emily. 2019. "Amazon: Surveillance as a Service." *Surveillance & Society* 17: 27–33. https://doi.org/10.24908/ss.v17i1/2.13008.

Wilson, Charlie, Tom Hargreaves, and Richard Hauxwell-Baldwin. 2015. "Smart Homes and Their Users: A Systematic Analysis and Key Challenges." *Personal and Ubiquitous Computing* 19: 463–476. https://doi.org/10.1007/s00779-014-0813-0.

Woodcock, Jamie. 2020. "The Algorithmic Panopticon at Deliveroo: Measurement, Precarity, and the Illusion of Control." *Ephemera* 20, no. 3: 67–95.

Zeng, Eric, Shrirang Mare, and Franziska Roesner. 2017. "End User Security and Privacy Concerns with Smart Homes." In *SOUPS '17: Proceedings of the Thirteenth USENIX Conference on Usable Privacy and Security*, 65–80. New York: ACM Press.

Zuboff, Shoshana. 2019. "Surveillance Capitalism and the Challenge of Collective Action." *New Labor Forum* 28: 10–29. https://doi.org/10.1177/1095796018819461.

CHAPTER 13

NEGOTIATING INTIMACY VIA DATING WEBSITES AND APPS

Digital Media in Everyday Life

SHANTEL GABRIEAL BUGGS

WITH the ever-increasing number of online dating websites and phone applications (from here on referred to as "apps") launching regularly, the popularity of online dating can be traced to a decrease in the stigma associated with it, as well as an entire global generation of people who have "grown up online" driving increased usage (Vogels 2019). A 2016 Singles in America study conducted by the oldest online dating website, Match.com, found that 53% of single people have a dating profile and that Millennials are 57% more likely to have an online dating profile than any other generation (Fisher and Garcia 2017). Another study found that 44% of Millennial college students use the app Tinder for "confidence boosting procrastination" (Fellizar 2017), suggesting that the use of online dating platforms is a highly normalized and widespread practice, resembling an "evil but satisfying" game that psychologically conditions users to seek the "reward" of a match (Purvis 2017).

According to a 2016 report from *Consumer Reports*, over 40% of people who have engaged in online dating say it led to a serious long-term relationship or marriage, and most people surveyed stated that they prefer free sites/apps like OkCupid and Tinder over costly subscription sites like Match and eHarmony (Dickler 2017). One nationally representative psychology study claims that one-third of all marriages in the United States begin online (Cacioppo et al. 2013) and that, compared to marriages that began offline, those who met online were less likely to break up (separation or divorce). These marriages also were associated with somewhat higher marital satisfaction. The television and film industry has certainly picked up on the generational and cultural shifts that have come with increased popularity of online dating, with dozens of movies and television shows from the 1990s, early aughts, and through the 2010s exploring the successes, failures, and traumas of meeting people online (examples include 2020's *Love Guaranteed* and *I May Destroy You*, 2018's *Swiped*, 2009's *He's Just Not That Into You*, 2005's *Must Love Dogs*, and 1998's *You've Got Mail*). It remains evident from these trends that online dating will continue to be a fixture of contemporary everyday life, even as some degree of stigma persists (see Albury and Byron 2016; Cali, Coleman, and Campbell 2013; Hasinoff 2015; Gibbs, Ellison, and Lai 2011; Hess and Flores 2018) and users contend with social anxiety (Pitcho-Prelorentzos, Heckel, and Ring 2020). Various parties—including researchers and business investors—continue to seek answers about what people get out of dating via technological intervention, how the experience can be improved, and to what degree, if at all, online daters differ from those who do not date online (Sautter, Tippett, and Morgan 2010). Focused on the central question of what intimacy looks like when mediated by technology, this chapter provides an assessment of existing research on online dating. In an effort to illuminate the ways that dating websites and apps are shaping contemporary relationship formation, this article contends with the ways that race, gender, class, and sexuality, among other factors, shape the pursuit of these relationships and how research can continue to move beyond mostly an exploration of the interactions, encounters, and power dynamics among heterosexuals and gay men. Expanding the focus of research on online dating is even more pressing when considering the dating behaviors of younger generations who are more likely to identify as LGBTQ+ (Jones 2021) or, at minimum, engage in sexual behavior that is not considered "heterosexual," particularly Millennial and Gen Z women (Bridges and Moore 2019).

Dating Markets and the In(ter)vention of Online Dating

Sociologists typically evaluate dating "markets" as part of assessing marriage markets and their associated pools of marriageable singles. Developed to model the economics of marriage (Becker 1974), marriage/dating markets focus on people who are seeking relationships and assess their mate-selection behaviors—particularly whether they marry and/or divorce or marry interracially (Qian and Lichter 2001, 2007, 2011). Increasingly, analysis of dating has required a particular focus on the impact of online dating websites (Hitsch, Hortaçsu, and Ariely 2006) and, with the increase in smartphone usage, typically geolocation-driven dating apps. Researchers Rosenfeld, Thomas, and Hausen (2019) argue that so-called traditional ways of meeting heterosexual romantic partners have consistently declined since World War II. Instead of meeting a partner through one's family, church, neighborhood, or even friends, daters are meeting online. This is a significant change from even a decade earlier, when friends were still the primary means for facilitating heterosexual couplings (Rosenfeld and Thomas 2012).

Though there is much debate about whether the displacing of friends and family as romantic intermediates is a good thing (Bauman 2003; Turkle 2016) and whether the "matching algorithms" of many sites are even scientific (Finkle et al. 2012), it is clear that online dating offers a significantly more expansive pool of choices—a "paradox of choice" comedian Aziz Ansari compares to the endless selection of restaurants one can research on the internet in his 2015 book (with sociologist Eric Klinenberg) *Modern Romance* (pp. 123–127). Ansari's analogy is an uncomfortable extension of psychologist Barry Schwartz's 2004 assessment of the relationship between happiness and goal achievement; in arguing that consumers suffer anxiety as a result of too many available options as shoppers, Schwartz suggests that people would be happier with fewer options (because they can make decisions more easily). This framing perhaps ignores how race, gender, sexuality, and disability inform who even gets these endless options. Rosenfeld (2017) argues that everyone finds value in having more options available; this is particularly the case for those who experience greater difficulty locating partners, such as gays and lesbians (Rosenfeld and Thomas 2012). Of course, not all users are on dating apps to find romantic partners but, rather, casual sexual partners. What some scholars refer to as "hook-up" culture (Christensen 2020; Hamilton and Armstrong 2009; Lundquist and Curington 2019; Spell 2017; Wade 2017; Wade et al. 2021) or "party and play" (Race 2015) others refer to as "digital cruising" (Ahlm 2017; Gudelunas 2012; Mowlabocus 2010), effectively a technology-enhanced version of gay subcultural sexual practice that typically occurs in bars, clubs, or other public spaces wherein men signal sexual interest (Tewksbury 2002; Orne 2017). Apps like Grindr facilitate cruising in seemingly heterosexual spaces (Crooks 2013; Mowlabocus 2010) but still deal with tensions between "public" and "private" behaviors as users navigate the politics of respectability (Ahlm 2017). The app developers themselves are aware of this, either capitalizing on reputations as hook-up apps (like Tinder) or providing a variety of options for what types of relationships people are looking for (like Bumble, OkCupid).

Certainly, the observed increase in the use of online dating websites/apps can also be attributed to factors like ease, control, and safety. The advent of geolocation apps enables users to easily track down potential dates or hookups within as little as a mile of where they live or the bar they are grabbing a drink in. Today, all dating websites have a smartphone app (reducing the need to use web browsers to access the websites), and nearly all dating platforms have some aspect that is free to use. However, some, like Zoosk, Match, and eHarmony, require pricey subscriptions to get full use of the website. Widely used geolocation apps like Plenty of Fish, OkCupid, Tinder, Bumble, Hinge, and Coffee Meets Bagel began as completely free services; however, as usage has increased, companies began to commodify certain aspects of the apps, employing subscription-based additions that charge fluctuating monthly fees (see Table I) to gain access to features like the ability to see "intro" messages before you match with someone, search by "attractiveness" or body type, remove ads, or get "boosts" that increase the traffic to your profile to drive up "likes."

Based on my own research with multiracial female and white male online daters, these costs do seem to act as "push factors," making users leave expensive services like Match for "free" services like OkCupid. However, users who have experienced harassment note the appeal of services that grant them control over messages or being able to

Table 1. Examples of Online Dating Platform Subscription Services (as of 2020)

Service	Cost	Features Include
A-List (OkCupid)	US$14.99 per month for A-list, US$2.99 per "boost"	View "intro" messages before you match with someone, search by "attractiveness" or body type, remove ads, "boosts" that increase the traffic to profile to drive up "likes"
Bumble Boost (Bumble)	US$24.99 per month	Extend a match's expiration, rematch with expired matches, access unlimited "advanced" filters, see users who have already "liked" you
eHarmony—Basic	US$59.99 per month	Send and receive messages (free accounts can only view profiles and receive compatible matches), see if matches are logged in
eHarmony—Total Connect	US$44.95 per month for 3 months	Includes all Basic features in addition to the ability to make secure voice calls from the app and verification of membership information ("RelyID")
Grindr Premium (Grindr)	US$49.99 per month	All XTRA features plus seeing everyone who has viewed a profile, "incognito" mode, "unsend" messages
Grindr XTRA (Grindr)	US$29.99	No pop-up ads, view up to 600 people on the "grid," unlimited blocks and favorites, read receipts for messages, PIN lock option for added security
Match—Standard	US$31.99 per month for 3 months	Send and receive messages (only liking a profile is free), track users you send "winks" to, remove users from search results
Match—Premium	US$34.99 per month for 3 months	All Standard plan features in addition to a yearly review of profile from Match staff, monthly profile "boosts" to increase views, notifications when an email is read, voice calling through the app
Tinder Gold (Tinder)	US$29.99 per month	All Plus features in addition to being able to see who likes you before you "like" (swipe right) or "nope" (swipe left)
Tinder Platinum (Tinder)	Approximately US$39.99 per month; varies by location	All Plus and Gold features in addition to "Priority Likes" where your "like" is prioritized over others
Tinder Plus (Tinder)	US$9.99 per month	Unlimited "likes," taking back a "like" or a "nope" if you accidentally pass on a profile ("Rewind"), no ads, the ability to swipe users all over the world ("Passport")
Zoosk	US$29.95 per month	Seeing who has viewed a profile, advanced safety features such as photo and Facebook verification

browse discreetly (Buggs 2017a). Whether a user ignores these costs or has the income to afford them, these platforms provide the potential to disclose a user's "true" self in ways they may not be able to in face-to-face settings (McKenna, Green, and Gleason 2002) and to have up-to-date information about the availability of (in theory) millions of people rather than just the dozen or so people their friends and family know (Rosenfeld, Thomas, and Hausen 2019).

Being able to vet partners based on the contents of their online profile or via features like "match questions" provides a means of control but also protection for structurally marginalized daters (e.g., LGBTQ people, people of color, people with disabilities) who want to avoid daters with certain stances on social issues such as the Black Lives Matter movement (Buggs 2017b). Certainly, structurally empowered users—white, heterosexual, cisgender, politically conservative—also utilize these filter features to avoid undesirable partners. These empowered users' reasons are less about "safety" as they are about purging undesirables from their purview, what researchers have referred to as cyber "cleansing" in the interest of racialized and classed "personal preference" (Robinson 2015). Survey research indicates that women are much more likely than men to say dating websites/apps are not a safe way to meet people, with Black and Hispanic daters and those with a high school diploma or less also viewing them as less safe (Anderson, Vogels, and Turner 2020). Kuperberg and Padgett (2015) note that even though partners who met over the internet were more likely to result in dates compared to those who met in bars and at parties (which were associated with hooking up), finding partners online was associated with lower levels of trust. As was illustrated by the controversy over a sexual encounter between Aziz Ansari and a woman only known as "Grace," navigating sex as part of dating can tread ambiguous lines between sexual assault and seemingly acceptable or even expected behavior as part of heterosexual dating (Patil and Puri 2021). Accordingly, users—especially heterosexual women—will utilize their friend groups and social media to check up on the authenticity of their matches as well as employ other protective behaviors such as sharing the location of dates with friends (Hanson 2021). Various scholars (see extensive reviews from Choi, Wong, and Fong 2017; Gillett 2018; Phan, Siegfried-Spellar and Choo 2021) note the potential for abuse, sexual violence, stalking, and negative psychological effects due to online dating.

Further, those who do not wish for family members or friends to be made aware of what they desire in a partner may perceive online dating as a discreet option (Rosenfeld, Thomas, and Hausen 2019) despite the fact that websites/apps claim rights to user data. Users often have the ability to block and/or report users who say or send something inappropriate via the online messaging built into these apps; apps like Tinder have developed a reputation where heterosexual men tend to bombard women matches with unrequested "dick pics"—typically close up, staged photos of penises—or expectations for sex or "sexting"—the sending and sharing of sexual photos online or via other digital technology (Ybarra and Mitchell 2014)—leading to a general distaste for the platform among many online daters despite its widespread popularity. In fact, in response to the sexual harassment she experienced in the workplace, Tinder co-founder Whitney Wolfe went on to found the "feminist Tinder" platform Bumble, where only women users can initiate the conversation in the hopes of preventing the violent or misogynist outbursts that have characterized Tinder, OkCupid, and other apps' heterosexual exchanges (Haywood 2018; Thompson 2018; Yashari 2015). Apps like OkCupid also have algorithms that detect potentially offensive language and prompt users to report what makes them uncomfortable, which OkCupid's privacy policy states are part of the platform's efforts to "prevent, detect and fight" misbehavior on- and off-platform or what some scholars might call "trolling" (March et al. 2017). These efforts seem less successful at preventing "revenge porn"—nonconsensual dissemination of sexually explicit videos or images—that has been found to more frequently victimize gay and bisexual men on online dating apps (Waldman 2019). Therefore, as much as online dating apps can provide a semblance of safety or control, there is still work to be done to make the platforms safer, as well as assess whether these dangers are "truly caused by dating app usage" (Phan, Siegfried-Spellar, and Choo 2021).

It is among these less appealing aspects that many heterosexual women choose platforms that provide the most information up front. Research suggests that women are more likely to value information on the type of relationship someone is looking for and a person's religious beliefs, racial background, occupation, and political affiliation (Anderson, Vogels, and Turner 2020). Few empirical studies have investigated the motivations behind signing up for Tinder, but communications scholars Sumter, Vandenbosch, and Ligtenberg (2017) state that love is a stronger motivator than casual sex, especially for women users (pp. 73–74). To better create matches, researchers are even developing the capability for websites/apps to establish two-sided matching based on "learning" user preferences from the content of their message exchanges and profile content (Tu et al. 2014) or in the case of one new app, Iris, use artificial intelligence (AI) to determine a user's "AttractionDNA" to connect people who will likely be compatible based on past swiping preferences and face scanning analysis (Iris 2021). Despite the potential for negative experiences, a Pew Research Center study reports that a majority of users in the United States have had overall positive experiences with online dating; those most likely to report a positive experience are those with at least a bachelor's degree (Anderson, Vogels, and Turner 2020). Further, those who have ever used dating websites/apps to find partners are much more likely to be younger (under 30) and lesbian, gay, or bisexual.

Taking into account all of these factors, the contours of the online dating market are deeply complex. The constant reminder that one is participating in a market from the websites/apps themselves aids in perpetuating the notion that people are "shopping" for potential romantic partners and "selling" themselves in an online supermarket or catalog (Heino, Ellison, and Gibbs 2010). The development of "filtering instincts" as part of the shopping culture of online dating "saps energy" from daters trying to determine whether profiles are inaccurate before they've invested too much time in someone (Best and Delmege 2012). Others argue that the websites frame people like commodities—as "experience goods" instead of by their experiential attributes like sense of humor—when they make searchable attributes like income or religion the primary ways to filter through users (Frost et al. 2008). These market logics work against those who are not desirably positioned in a society rooted in patriarchal, heteronormative, racist, classist, and ableist ideologies; and as research has shown, certain groups experience far more discrimination and sidelining than others.

Dominant and Developing Trends in Online Dating Research

Online dating is more common among all sexual orientations today, but the vast majority of research has explored the experiences and behaviors of heterosexuals and gay men. Issues related to assortative mating—the tendency to marry people of similar backgrounds and beliefs—and recent trends in heterosexual women online daters "marrying down" in education (Hitsch, Hortaçsu, and Ariely 2010) indicate that there continues to be a wealth of research to be done on the role of online dating in how people match across a variety of social boundaries, particularly how inequality manifests within and between generations, long-term population changes, and relationship quality and dissolution (Schwartz 2013). *Modern Romance*, a text that pulls together original data collected by Ansari and Klinenberg, data from existing surveys, and data from OkCupid—arguably one of the more ambitious publications on online dating in terms of data—focuses pretty exclusively on heterosexuals. Ansari excuses this by claiming they "wouldn't be able to do the topic justice" (p. x) if they covered all sexual orientations. Directing more attention to marginalized groups' dating practices will continue to clarify not only how power operates within these online spaces but how the structures of these websites facilitate social inequality offline. Further, as with most spaces on the internet, online dating apps are constantly evolving—new apps are released, new features are added to existing apps, and, more recently, apps have had to be more proactive about how they respond to social concerns (e.g., anti-racism and gun control). Arguably, though, there are three areas that have become of greater concern to contemporary understandings of online dating and that will push the direction of the research on technology-mediated dating going forward: (1) issues of discrimination and exclusion, (2) the influence of politics and political context, and (3) the experiences of populations underserved by the apps and underrepresented in the literature. Some of these issues have only begun to be discussed by scholars in communication, journalists, or other forms of online media; in my view, it will be the task of future scholarship to provide sociological analysis of these topics, particularly in light of the impact of a global coronavirus pandemic on mediated forms of dating and developing intimacy.

Discrimination and Exclusion within Online Dating Websites/Apps

The primary focus of research on discrimination in online dating has been on sexual racism, particularly discrimination against Black and Asian daters (see Buggs 2019; Lundquist and Lin 2015; Feliciano, Robnett, and Komaie 2009). Research into the racial aspects of marriage/dating markets tends to focus on the prevalence of interracial relationships (intermarriage in particular) rather than how gender, sexuality, and (perceived) race come together to influence dating and marriage outcomes. While some scholars have determined that the likelihood of interracial relationships for white daters is influenced by family approval (Miller et al. 2021), many researchers assess the selection of romantic partners across racial and ethnic lines as indicative of social and political progressiveness, even when limited by structural inequalities. In their study of same-sex daters, Rafalow, Feliciano, and Robnett (2017) state that racialized gender hierarchies are especially salient for white gay and lesbian daters, with lesbians of color being the most open in their dating preferences. Scholarship on gay men has been particularly attentive to issues of discrimination where users—rather than being free from the constraints of social structures of difference (Chow-White 2006)—must contend with power dynamics (Callander, Holt, and Newman 2012; Nakamura 2001, 2008; Phua and Kaufman 2003; Robinson 2015) and body objectification (Anderson et al. 2018; Breslow et al. 2020). Legal scholar Sonu Bedi (2015) attests that sexual racism—the prioritizing of possible romantic partners in a way that reinforces racial hierarchies or racial stereotypes (p. 998)—is a matter of injustice, a reflection of the problematic conditions that structure society, and an insidious issue that renders online dating websites as sites of public concern. Amid this debate about whether racial preferences in romantic and sexual partners is equitable to so-called generic racism (Callander, Newman, and Holt 2015), it has even been suggested by some researchers (Wu, Chen, and Greenberger 2015) that those who date interracially are more attractive than those who date intraracially.

The sexual stereotypes that inform how sexual racism plays out among heterosexual and gay daters, particularly in qualitative studies (Buggs 2017b; Robnett and Feliciano 2011; Han 2007; Robinson 2015; Smith and Morales 2018), invoke the white "ethnosexual adventurers" (Nagel 2003) who have little intention of seriously dating or marrying people of color. As much as these stereotypes have the potential to increase a given dater's appeal, there is the risk that the appeal is in pursuit of the fulfillment of some fantasy rather than a desire for genuine connection (Alexander 2005; Battle and Barnes 2009; Courtney 2005; Kempadoo 1999). As Lin and Lindquist (2013) demonstrate, heterosexual white men and women are least likely to respond to messages from Black men and women, while heterosexual white men are more receptive of messages from Asian and Latina women. Thus, a number of factors come into play to determine how any non-white online dater will be treated when trying to find dating partners, and this is heavily dependent upon phenotype, degree of racial fetishization, and, likely to an extent, investment in culturally specific knowledge (Rockquemore, Laszloffy, and Noveske 2006). The "exoticness" of a potential partner increases if they have cultural knowledge—such as speaking a language other than English—that can be deployed to shore up a particular racial identity or stereotype. Dating apps facilitate this with the information made available on profiles and whether users can filter out others based on race or ethnicity, body type, or attractiveness ratings—the "cleansing" Robinson (2015) notes on gay dating apps. These findings provide evidence of the ways power dynamics determine how intimate certain relationships can be, not only along the lines of race and ethnicity but also skin tone and other aspects of physical appearance. New developments in dating apps, such as the late 2020 offering Iris, tout the implementation of AI to scan faces to confirm identity (no more pesky catfishing!) and to confirm one's "AttractionDNA"—where the algorithm determines who users find attractive based on their individual swiping preferences and uses this information to filter inbox messages. Iris also utilizes what it calls "Trust Ratings," where profiles that are "honest" and "respectful" display a badge and can garner full access to app features for free (PR Newswire 2020). Given what we already know about how AI technology's tendency to replicate racist and sexist logics due to the lack of women, queer people, and people of color behind their programming (Nobel 2018; Benjamin 2019), if greater use of algorithms and AI in dating apps is the future, there will likely be considerable issues with discrimination.

Lighter-skinned people of color have been found to experience preferential treatment in dating and marriage markets (Hunter 2005). People from Western nations who pursue sexual relationships with racial Others reify the superiority of whiteness and Western-ness through their sex tourism (Davidson and Taylor 1999) and today increasingly facilitate this through international dating websites like Elite Singles and popular apps like Badoo. Tinder's "passport" feature makes it easier for sex workers around the globe to locate clients and avoid the dangers of brothel raids in certain countries like the Philippines, while clients can make arrangements for trysts before even arriving at their destinations (Muthia 2019). Preliminary work on queer men users of Badoo in Brazil suggests that a rejection of "gay identity" due to the negative media representation of gay men in the Global South as "sissies" (Nascimento and de Carvalho Figueiredo 2013) contrasts with the fact that apps like Grindr offer within-app chat translation as part of the premium subscription packages in order to facilitate communication in the event of a language barrier. These global racialized gender notions illustrate the far-reaching implications of dating apps and influence romantic and sexual pairing trends in the West, such as the likelihood of heterosexual exogamy for racial minorities in places like the United States. Black men are still overwhelmingly more likely to marry whites than Black women are to marry whites, and Asian men are significantly less likely than Asian women to marry whites (Qian and Lichter 2001; Livingston and Brown 2017). Interracial relationships have also been found to be more common among gay-, lesbian-, and bisexual-identified individuals (Horowitz and Gomez 2018). The factors shaping interracial intimacy in the West and elsewhere are further illustrated by findings regarding the appeal of certain groups in online dating, where Black women and Asian men are found to be rated the least attractive (Feliciano, Robnett, and Komaie 2009; Rafalow, Feliciano, and Robnett 2017; Robnett and Feliciano 2011; Rosenfeld and Kim 2005; Rudder 2014; Tsunokai, McGrath, and Kavanagh 2014) and the least likely to garner responses to their messages (Lin and Lundquist 2013; Rudder 2014). This manifestation of sexual racism and colorism is particularly important to consider in the face of recent research that suggests that multiracial people experience an increase in favorability in comparison to monoracial daters (Curington, Lin, and Lundquist 2015; Lewis 2010; McGrath et al. 2016; Rudder 2014). To this end, sociologist Cynthia Feliciano (2016) states that despite the growth of the multiracial population in the United States, observers tend to place people—specifically online daters—in single-race categories associating "medium" skin tones with Latinx identities and dark skin tones with Blackness (pp. 409–411).

Influence of Politics and Political Context on Online Dating

As online dating platforms have gained popularity, researchers have maintained their interest in understanding whether people form relationships based on political similarity. Dating websites/apps provide an opportunity to observe partnerships in formation; the current political context—which has seen the development of "pro-Trump" dating websites (Evans 2019) and profile "banners" supporting the American Civil Liberties Union, Planned Parenthood, and the Black Lives Matter movement (Moore 2020; OkCupid 2017, 2018)—only further emphasizes the need to evaluate how people navigate selecting potential dating partners in an increasingly politically polarized environment. In response to OkCupid's partnership with Planned Parenthood, conservative media outlet *The Federalist* posted a viral article titled "Your Refusal to Date Conservatives Is One Reason We Have Donald Trump," which argued that a badge on a dating website is "political protest" when a private admission of one's support for abortion rights is more appropriate (Roberts 2017).

Research has explored the impact of political affiliation on attraction and mate selection (Anderson et al. 2014; Huber and Malhotra 2017; Iyengar, Konitzer, and Tedin 2018; Klofstad, McDermott, and Hatemi 2012, 2013), with some scholars suggesting that political attitudes are tied to genetics (Eaves and Hatemi 2008). Overwhelmingly, scholars note the extreme polarization of US politics and how these ideological differences are becoming further entrenched as daters aim to date people like themselves. So, in some ways, the appearance of platforms like Bernie Singles, Where white People Meet, Righter, Donald Daters, and Trump Singles does not necessarily signal a new shift in political preferences. However, given the fact that hate crimes have spiked since Trump's 2016 election (Cohen 2017; Edwards and Rushin 2018) and that social movements have had enough of a mainstream impact that online dating platforms are responding with changes—whether that be OkCupid's banners or Grindr's decision to eliminate the ability to filter for race and ethnicity at all (Woodyatt 2020)—it is imperative for social scientists to contextualize the impact of political ideology and whether this polarization can be bridged or is further exacerbated by online dating, where a dater can ascertain a potential partner's politics before even going on a date. Some research finds that political participation and knowledge are now sexual capital on dating apps, with self-censorship of social media use emerging in some contexts as a means of influencing the partner-vetting behaviors of other online daters seeking politically like-minded partners (Chan 2021). Further, it is clear that online dating platforms care; Match's "Singles in America" study released prior to the 2016 election reported that those who talked about politics on a first date had a 91% chance of getting a second date, and survey results released by Tinder suggest that 71% of online daters find differing politics to be a deal-breaker compared to 66% of offline daters (Spira 2017). So, there are strong implications that online daters might be even more politically polarized than those who meet in more traditional venues, likely a result of the younger, more educated demographics comprising online dating populations. This is evident in emerging research on Reddit's communities of "incels"—involuntary celibates—that situates misogynistic and heteropatriarchal relationship logics and seduction strategies within a political and social context that continues to grapple with the shifting politics of desirability and, in particular, accessibility to romantic and sexual partners (see Krendel 2020; Menzie 2020; Van Valkenburgh 2021).

Of course, political context also shapes what role dating apps fulfill. The app Hornet, for example, was created to serve queer men in countries where homosexuality is a criminal offense (Levesley 2020); in these places, better-known and less discreet gay apps like Grindr are banned, so a platform like Hornet, which also hosts curated LGBTQ+ news and content, facilitates more than hookups for users (Braidwood 2018). Other research post-election of Donald Trump argues that political leadership and their policies create "structural stigma," particularly for sexual and gender minorities (Fredrick et al. 2021)—this stigma at the societal and/or policy level can have negative health outcomes, suggesting that there is an assortment of consequences that inform the ways political context shapes sexual and romantic encounters and, of course, family formation processes. It will be even more pressing for future research to go beyond analyzing indicated political party affiliations (e.g., is someone a Democrat, Republican, or Independent) and instead explore shifting political contexts and commitments, especially as aspects of users' social media lives (e.g., hashtags) make their way into dating profile content and the apps themselves respond to social movement concerns and shifts in political leadership.

Underrepresented Populations in Online Dating Literature

As I have noted in previous sections, there is a clear skew to sociological online dating literature that foregrounds heterosexual and gay men's experiences, particularly those who are cisgender, disproportionately well-educated, and white. Though quantitative work often cannot account for the physical appearances or relative attractiveness of daters (see Curington, Lin, and Lundquist 2015; Lin and Lundquist 2013; Lundquist and Lin 2015), qualitative work does have this capacity and seems to include many respondents who can access conventional attractiveness (thin or fit, not showing any visible disabilities) even as their race often modifies their ability to translate this into dating success (see Buggs 2017a; Robinson 2015; Smith and Morales 2018). The reasons for this focus are certainly rooted in accessibility; the largest and oldest dating apps began by catering exclusively to heterosexuals, and many eventually expanded to include gay, lesbian, and bisexual daters. Dating apps targeting gay (and presumably bisexual) men have much greater visibility in popular consciousness, with outlets like *Men's Health* (Ellis 2020) and *GQ* (Levesley 2020) providing lists of the most popular apps. There are equivalent lists for queer women at outlets like *Women's Health* (Kassel 2020) and *Good Housekeeping* (Schumer 2021), but most of the suggested apps are platforms that cater to heterosexuals as well, such as Bumble, Hinge, Tinder, and OkCupid. This suggests that developing platforms specifically for queer women is not as prioritized by developers (Murray and Ankerson 2016), and this marginalization in the market extends to research focused on users of lesbian apps.

Though sociological dating research seems to be consistent in the attention to differences between Black, Hispanic, and white daters—and, to an extent, Asian daters—many other racialized groups are rarely included in comparative studies due to small samples or just generally being ignored as singular populations of study. Arabs/North Africans/Middle Easterners, South and West Asians, and Native Americans, Hawai'ians, or Pacific Islanders find some mention in the online dating research outside of sociology but not anywhere near the rate of Black, Hispanic, East Asian, and white populations. The lack of attention to these unique racialized experiences is a detriment to the sociological literature and the exploration of online dating overall. In the case of Muslim daters, they experience racialization and stigmatization as a result of their religion in most Western contexts (Rochadiat, Tong, and Novak 2018) and are relegated to Islam-specific matrimonial websites (Abdel-Fadil 2015; Al-Saggaf 2013). These facts suggest that removing the race and ethnicity filters may not be sufficient to eliminate sexual racism masquerading as "personal preference" online (Robinson 2015); other factors such as language and religion can communicate racialized identity, and overwhelmingly accounts of sexual racism are focused on mainstream websites and apps rather than, for instance, religion-specific ones (e.g., Christian Mingle, J-Date, Hipster Shaadi/Ishqr). Additionally, utilizing large data sets of interactions online is limited in the capacity to evaluate the influence of phenotype as photos are often not made available to researchers (Curington, Lin, and Lundquist 2015), and different groups' racialization in offline contexts shifts depending on political, social, and institutional context, as well as the personal racial and ethnic identity of users themselves (Buggs 2019).

The limited research on queer women who utilize online dating platforms to seek women partners primarily notes the lack of lesbian-identified apps (Murray and Ankerson 2016) and the perceived scarcity of potential partners (Duguay 2019), though lesbian, gay, and bisexual daters are said to be more likely to flirt online and to use online dating websites/apps than heterosexuals (Johnson, Vilceaunu, and Pontes 2017). Cultural norms around dating also influence whether lesbian and bisexual women are able to locate romantic partners (Tang 2017), and many women daters lament the use of more "mainstream" websites/apps (Tinder, OkCupid, Match, etc.) due to concerns around having men, couples, and heterosexual women appear in their search results (Duguay 2019; Ferris and Duguay 2020; Pond and Farvid 2017), requiring almost exaggerated online performances of non-heterosexuality. The little comparative research between gay, lesbian, and heterosexual online daters (Rafalow, Feliciano, and Robnett 2017; Lundquist and Lin 2015) both suggests that lesbians are less likely to be explicit about racial preferences and shows that they have a similar pattern of same-race pairing as other groups. Older adults who utilize online dating also vary in their motivations and self-presentations, with those seeking same-sex relationships emphasizing romance and shared experience more in their profiles compared to heterosexuals (Griffin and Fingerman 2018). Some research (Stephure et al. 2009) suggests that participating in online dating increases with age due to "diminishing satisfaction" with conventional relationship formation via friends, bars or clubs, or church. Even with the stigma younger users report with online dating, Stephure and colleagues (2009) note this may have to do with greater access and larger pools of potential partners; for those older users who do decide to use the internet to pursue romantic partners, they are more serious in their intent than their younger counterparts. Scholars like Rafalow and Kizer (2018) have explored how race shapes the preferences of lesbians who have children, finding that more highly educated queer Black and Latinx women are more likely than white women to indicate an openness for women with children. This openness is suggested to result from the differing life trajectories of white lesbians and non-white lesbians—Black women are more likely to have had heterosexual relationships that resulted in children (Moore 2011), making them more accepting of women with children than women who came out first and then seek a partner with whom to have children. However, because there are so few studies investigating lesbians, Rafalow and Kizer (2018, 307) argue that more work needs to be done, particularly for Asian and Latina women, in order to explain these apparent preferences.

Similar silences around the experiences of transgender, nonbinary, and other gender expansive online daters are endemic to the literature. In recent years, several dating apps (and other social media platforms) have expanded their options for gender identity and sexual orientation, with apps like OkCupid offering 22 gender identities and 12 sexual orientation options with glossaries that define each term and provide explanations from users who use the labels (OkCupid n.d.). However, research suggests that dating apps construct gender as a rigid category for the function of matching profiles rather than reflecting identity (MacLeod and McArthur 2019). Therefore, it should not be surprising that apps like Tinder have repeatedly come under fire for informally excluding transgender and nonbinary users, even after announcing an effort to be more inclusive in 2016 by offering 50 gender identity options (Riotta 2019). Prominent trans women have noted that these informal "bans" result from being mass reported by transphobic men and Tinder failing to support trans users (Spellings 2018). Writing on transgender people's intimate lives tends to be one part of larger projects on gender identity (Abelson 2019) or focus on their experiences as sexual deviants (Melendez and Pinto 2007; Operario et al. 2008; Serano 2007) and the existing relationships they navigate while transitioning (Bischof et al. 2016; Pfeffer 2008, 2017). Some research has focused specifically on dating (Buggs 2020; Zamantakis 2019, 2020), but the sample sizes remain small, limiting the ability to generalize more broadly. Scholars argue that for some transgender people who seek relationships with cisgender partners, those embodying binary masculinity or femininity will further affirm the gender identities of trans partners (Abelson 2019; Glynn et al. 2016; Sevelius 2013). Others argue that these stakes are even higher for trans women of color due to racialized and classed notions of femininity that marginalize even cisgender women (Buggs 2020; Collins 2000, 2005).

Sexual orientation and gender identity are not the only axes along which online daters experience differential romantic and sexual opportunities, however. There is a significant dearth of research on the dating experiences of fat-identified people and even less on the influence of a fat body in terms of online dating experiences. Schoemaker Holmes (2016, 374) discusses the notion of "fat authenticity," wherein heterosexual women engage in online performance that constructs them as "authentically" fat or thin in order to be seen as realistic and desirable romantic partners. Women are obligated to "spoil" their bodies within their profiles to avoid rejection and being perceived as deceptive; men, alternatively, are not expected to engage in this type of performance to be deemed datable. An example would be describing oneself as "cute and curvy" in order to direct attention to body size as depicted in full-body profile photos (Dupere 2019). Ellison, Hancock, and Toma (2011) describe this moderation of self-presentation in online dating profiles as "profile as promise"—potential dates are more forgiving of discrepancies in characteristics that are likely to change by the time people meet in person (e.g., hairstyle), but significant discrepancies are not forgivable (p. 51–52). However, being upfront about one's body can have negative consequences. Many women have described in blogs, opinion pieces, or other media interviews how online dating websites and apps subject them to specific harassment from fat fetishizers (Silvester 2014). In my own research, larger-bodied multiracial women describe immense pressure to be "honest" about their bodies to ward off undesirable partners even as they worry about being fetishized (Buggs 2017a). Gay men experience extensive body shaming on apps like Grindr and Tinder, developing body image issues as a result of the weight stigma and objectification that occurs (Filice et al. 2019).

Body-positive activists emphasize the need for fat sexuality—not fat fetishism—to be recognized, noting that there are "fat people out there somewhere joyously getting their freak on. Not only that, but fat people are falling in love, having hook-ups, being crushed-out, putting on sexy lingerie, being objects of other people's lust, flirting, primping before hot dates . . . seducing and being seduced, and having shuddering, toe-curling orgasms that are as big as they are" (quoted in Khandpur 2015). Fat women in one study noted that they did not begin to have satisfactory sex lives until they began to embody fat pride (Gailey 2012). The fascination with fat people—particularly women—having sex or being in loving relationships has gained enough attention in the mainstream that the problematic term "mixed-weight relationships" has gained traction (Almendrala 2013; Wong 2018) to the point that a reality show, *Hot and Heavy*, premiered on TLC in January 2020. Curiously, every couple used to evidence this "phenomenon" both in the show and in any other news coverage of mixed-weight couples involves a larger-bodied woman with a man who is smaller-bodied than her, not necessarily that these men are particularly fit. This perpetuates the notion that fat-bodied people—especially ones read as feminine—are a spectacle or a fetish.

Lastly, the experiences of people with chronic illnesses, mental health issues, and other disabilities are typically relegated to specific subfields within the social sciences and rarely are discussed as part of broader analyses of sexual and romantic intimacy. Recently, one analysis of Twitter hashtags found that content related to dating and disability was severely limited compared to content around dating with no reference to disability (Kearney, Darling, and Dukes 2020). Further, sociologists have been called to task for not including disability within intersectional analysis (see Frederick and Shifrer 2019), and disability activists have been calling for marriage equality for people with disabilities for several decades (Evans n.d.). Historically, people with a variety of disabilities were forcibly sterilized and prohibited from marrying; in many US states today, people with disabilities are effectively denied the right to marriage because of regulations around Supplemental Security Income (SSI) and Medicaid. When someone is married to a partner not on those programs, both incomes and assets are used to determine eligibility (Star 2019). This creates issues because, in most cases, these combined incomes will render people ineligible for their SSI and Medicaid benefits. These embedded inequalities are one of many reasons to explore the romantic and sexual lives of people with disabilities as they fall at the intersection of varied social institutions. In fact, AddHealth data indicates that type of disability influences people's chances of getting married, with those with multiple disabilities reporting the lowest likelihood of entry into a first marriage in adulthood (MacInnes 2011). Other research (see Vaughn et al. 2015) argues for deeper understanding of the ways disability overlaps with marginalized sexual identities and how this impacts quality of life.

Research that has explored the online dating experiences of people with disabilities notes that these individuals are often pushed to dating websites specifically for people with disabilities, such as the websites Dating4Disabled or Disabled Passions. Advice about pursuing relationships outside of "disability-centric" dating sites notes that users of mainstream platforms "may face a bit more questioning or even receive higher rejection rates" despite mainstream sites having larger pools (Vantage Mobility 2017). This reinforces assumptions that these individuals should not match with people without disabilities (Goyal 2016). Individuals with disabilities describe feeling pressured to disclose their status to people they meet via online dating with greater expectation to discuss "visible" disabilities upfront as opposed to "invisible" disabilities (Porter et al. 2017; Saltes 2013). However, for some populations, online dating may have advantages over face-to-face dating, such as easing the social anxiety of those with autism spectrum disorder (Gavin, Rees-Evans, and Brosnan 2019; Roth and Gillis 2015) or facilitating the constructing of the dater's idealized self by highlighting their most attractive characteristics (Milbrodt 2019). Advantages aside, people with disabilities often are expected to perform additional labor to manage the feelings and perceptions of potential dates (Porter et al. 2017) and must navigate conflicting spaces and perceptions as they move between insular websites geared toward daters with disabilities and mainstream websites (Milbrodt 2019) that replicate ableist cultural logics (Ellis and Kent 2013). Of course, users with disabilities not only have to contend with the stigma of disability while dating; their experiences are also complicated by sexual orientation, race, gender, and class. Research suggests that people without disabilities do not fear stigma by association so much as they perceive the relationship not satisfying their physical and emotional needs or not being equitable between partners (Collisson et al. 2019). Though people with disabilities often try to preemptively disclose their disability to weed out undesirable partners on mainstream dating websites/apps (Porter et al. 2017; Milbrodt 2019), it is evident that there is an unfair burden that could be alleviated by restructuring how online dating websites/apps operate.

Conclusion

This article demonstrates how deeply embedded technology, specifically websites and smartphone apps designed to facilitate social interaction, has become in modern-day life. For some groups, meeting romantic and/or sexual partners would be practically impossible without the aid of dating websites and apps. However, it is telling that there remain so many groups who are understudied within sociological and communication/media studies research. The continued marginalization of the lives and experiences of transgender and nonbinary people, people racialized as nonwhite, people with disabilities, and, of course, people at the intersection of all of these positions makes it evident that researchers need to reconsider centering heterosexual, cisgender, white online daters without disabilities as the standard users of online dating websites/apps. Not only do developers of the more widely used, accessible, and better-resourced platforms fail to consider how they cater to these marginalized populations in order to make sure marginalized daters feel included and equally capable of finding the relationships they desire but developers continue to reproduce and facilitate some of the most vicious aspects of offline interactions through the use of incentivized filtering of characteristics like race, body type, and arbitrary measures of "attractiveness" based on how many other users pay a particular user attention (Rudder 2014). Some platforms have attempted to be responsive in the midst of continued pressure to address sexual racism, an increasingly politically polarized context in the United States and elsewhere with the rise of right-wing movements and violent mass shootings. Grindr first announced its intention to combat sexual racism in 2017 with its "Kindr Grindr" campaign that banned the use of phrases like "No Blacks" or "No Asians" in users' profiles. In light of the resurgence of Black Lives Matter protests in the United States in 2020, the app announced it would finally remove its "ethnicity" filter in order to show support for the protests and continue to address sexual racism (Lim, Robards, and Carlson 2020). In response to several mass shootings and calls for gun control—particularly the devastating attack at Marjory Stoneman Douglas High School in Parkland, Florida, in 2018—Bumble opted to ban photos of firearms and knives unless users were members of the military or law enforcement and the photo of their weapons included them in uniform (Hsu 2018). Bumble's founder claimed this choice was made to "create a community where people feel at ease, where they do not feel threatened" rather than it being a "politically driven decision," a stance that seems at odds with the company's actual policy of allowing military and law enforcement to pose with weapons in uniform and the lived experiences of users who have been harassed by members of these professions on- and offline (see Buggs 2017a).

That some platforms have responded to pressure from disgruntled users, social science findings, and/or sociopolitical upheaval illustrates that one reason to continue to expand the research of *who* uses dating apps, *how* people use them, and *what* people experience is that this work can influence direct change from dating service providers. In the midst of a global coronavirus pandemic where populations that had an easier time translating online matches into offline interactions have had to resort to more exclusively online courting practices (Vinopal 2020), there is a wealth of sociological knowledge to gain about how dating is shaped by both factors outside of and within users' and the dating platform's control. More directly addressing political context and providing needed attention to understudied groups' experiences not only fleshes out the realities of online dating; moving away from a heteronormative focus in particular allows for nuanced exploration of what it means for desires and norms to be both oppressive and potentially empowering for structurally marginalized people and what shifts in family formation are occurring outside of the nuclear family structure sold by many dating apps. Comparative, trans- and nonbinary-inclusive, and transnational work will especially be needed as this area of research moves forward.

REFERENCES

Abdel-Fadil, Mona. 2015. "Counselling Muslim Selves on Islamic Websites: Walking a Tightrope between Secular and Religious Counselling Ideals?" *Journal of Religion, Media and Digital Culture* 4, no. 1: 1–38.

Abelson, Miriam. 2019. *Men in Place: Trans Masculinity, Race, and Sexuality in America.* Minneapolis: University of Minnesota Press.

Ahlm, Jody. 2017. "Respectable Promiscuity: Digital Cruising in an Era of Queer Liberalism." *Sexualities* 20, no. 3: 364–379.

Albury, Kath, and Paul Byron. 2016. "Safe on My Phone? Same-Sex Attracted Young People's Negotiations of Intimacy, Visibility, and Risk on Digital Hook-up Apps." *Social Media and Society* 2, no. 4. doi: 10.1177/2056305116672887.

Alexander, M. Jacqui. 2005. *Pedagogies of Crossing: Meditations on Feminism, Sexual Politics, Memory and the Sacred.* Durham, NC: Duke University Press.

Almendrala, Anna. 2013. "Mixed-Weight Relationships: No One Prepared Us for the Biggest Conflict in Our Marriage." *Huffington Post*, January 29. https://www.huffpost.com/entry/mixed-weight-relationship_b_2567988.

Al-Saggaf, Yeslam. 2013. "Males' Trust and Mistrust of Females in Muslim Matrimonial Sites." *Journal of Information, Communication and Ethics in Society* 11, no. 3: 174–192.

Anderson, Ashton, Sharad Goel, Gregory Huber, Neil Malhotra, and Duncan J. Watts. 2014. "Political Ideology and Racial Preferences in Online Dating." *Sociological Science* 1: 28–40.

Anderson, Joel R., Elise Holland, Yasin Koc, and Nick Haslam. 2018. "iObjectify: Self- and Other-Objectification on Grindr, a Geosocial Networking Application Designed for Men who Have Sex with Men." *European Journal of Social Psychology* 48, no. 5: 600–613.

Anderson, Monica, Emily A. Vogels, and Erica Turner. 2020. "The Virtues and Downsides of Online Dating." Pew Research Center, February 6. https://www.pewresearch.org/internet/2020/02/06/the-virtues-and-downsides-of-online-dating/.

Ansari, Aziz. 2015. *Modern Romance*. With Eric Klinenberg. New York: Penguin Books.

Battle, Juan, and Sandra L. Barnes, eds. 2009. *Black Sexualities: Probing Powers, Passions, Practices and Policies*. New Brunswick, NJ: Rutgers University Press.

Bauman, Zygmunt. 2003. *Liquid Love: On the Frailty of Human Bonds*. Cambridge: Polity Press.

Becker, Gary S. 1974. "A Theory of Marriage." In *Economics of the Family: Marriage, Children, and Human Capital*, edited by Theodore W. Schultz, 299–351. Chicago: University of Chicago Press.

Bedi, Sonu. 2015. "Sexual Racism: Intimacy as a Matter of Justice." *Journal of Politics* 77, no. 4: 998–1011.

Benjamin, Ruha. 2019. *Race after Technology. Abolitionist Tools for the New Jim Code*. Boston: Polity Press.

Best, Kirsty, and Sharon Delmege. 2012. "The Filtered Encounter: Online Dating and the Problem of Filtering through Excessive Information." *Social Semiotics* 22, no. 3: 237–258.

Bischof, Gary H., Codie Stone, Mariam M. Mustafa, and Theodore J. Wampuszyc. 2016. "Couple Relationships of Transgender Individuals and Their Partners: A 2017 Update." *Michigan Family Review* 20, no. 1: 37–47.

Braidwood, Ella. 2018. "What Is Hornet? The Gay Dating App that Lets You 'Sting' Men." Pink News, April 6. https://www.pinknews.co.uk/2018/04/06/what-is-hornet-the-gay-dating-app-that-lets-you-sting-men/.

Breslow, Aaron S., Riddhi Sandil, Melanie E. Brewster, Mike C. Parent, Anthea Chan, Aysegul Yucel, et al. 2020. "Adonis on the Apps: Online Objectification, Self-Esteem, and Sexual Minority Men." *Psychology of Men and Masculinities* 21, no. 1: 25–35.

Bridges, Tristan, and Mignon Moore. 2019. "23% of Young Black Women Now Identify as Bisexual." *The Conversation*, June 11. https://theconversation.com/23-of-young-black-women-now-identify-as-bisexual-116116.

Buggs, Shantel Gabrieal. 2017a. "Utopic Subjects, Post-Racial Desires: Mixed-Race, Intimacy, and the On-line Dating Experience." PhD diss., University of Texas at Austin. https://repositories.lib.utexas.edu/handle/2152/60461.

Buggs, Shantel Gabrieal. 2017b. "Dating in the Time of #BlackLivesMatter: Exploring Mixed-Race Women's Discourses of Race and Racism." *Sociology of Race and Ethnicity* 3, no. 4: 538–551.

Buggs, Shantel Gabrieal. 2019. "Color, Culture, or Cousin: Multiracial Americans and Framing Boundaries in Interracial Relationships." *Journal of Marriage and Family* 81, no. 5: 1221–1236.

Buggs, Shantel Gabrieal. 2020. "(Dis)Owning Exotic: Navigating Race, Intimacy, and Trans Identity." *Sociological Inquiry* 90, no. 2: 249–270.

Cacioppo, John T., Stephanie Cacioppo, Gian C. Gonzaga, Elizabeth L. Ogburn, and Tyler J. VanderWeele. 2013. "Marital Satisfaction and Break-ups Differ across On-line and Off-line Meeting Venues." *Proceedings of the National Academy of Sciences of the United States of America* 110, no. 25: 10135–10140.

Cali, Billie E., Jill M. Coleman, and Catherine Campbell. 2013. "Stranger Danger? Women's Self-Protection Intent and the Continuing Stigma of Online Dating." *Cyberpsychology, Behavior, and Social Networking* 16, no. 12: 853–857.

Callander, Denton, Martin Holt, and Christy E. Newman. 2012. "Just a Preference: Racialized Language in the Sex-Seeking Profiles of Gay and Bisexual Men." *Culture, Health & Sexuality* 14, no. 9: 1049–1063.

Callander, Denton, Christy E. Newman, and Martin Holt. 2015. "Is Sexual Racism *Really* Racism? Distinguishing Attitudes toward Sexual Racism and Generic Racism among Gay and Bisexual Men." *Archives of Sexual Behavior* 44: 1991–2000.

Chan, Lik Sam. 2021. "Looking for Politically Like-Minded Partners: Self-Presentation and Partner-Vetting Strategies on Dating Apps." *Personal Relationships*. Published ahead of print March 30, 2021. https://doi.org/10.1111/pere.12375.

Choi, E. P. H., J. Y. H. Wong, and D. Y. T. Fong. 2017. "The Use of Social Networking Applications of Smartphone and Associated Sexual Risks in Lesbian, Gay, Bisexual, and Transgender Populations: A Systematic Review." *AIDS Care: Psychological and Socio-medical Aspects of AIDS/HIV* 29, no. 2: 145–155.

Chow-White, Peter A. 2006. "Race, Gender and Sex on the Net: Semantic Networks of Selling and Storytelling Sex Tourism." *Media Culture Society* 28, no. 6: 883–905.

Christensen, MacKenzie A. 2020. " 'Tindersluts' and 'Tinderellas': Examining the Digital Affordances Shaping the (Hetero)Sexual Scripts of Young Womxn on Tinder." *Sociological Perspectives* 64, no. 3: 432–449.

Cohen, Richard. 2017. "Hate Crimes Rise for Second Straight Year; Anti-Muslim Violence Soars Amid President Trump's Xenophobic Rhetoric." Southern Poverty Law Center, November 13. https://www.splcenter.org/news/2017/11/13/hate-crimes-rise-second-straight-year-anti-muslim-violence-soars-amid-president-trumps.

Collins, Patricia Hill. 2000. *Black Feminist Thought: Knowledge, Consciousness and the Politics of Empowerment*. New York: Routledge.

Collins, Patricia Hill. 2005. *Black Sexual Politics: African Americans, Gender and the New Racism*. New York: Routledge.

Collisson, Brian, Julianne M. Edwards, Lara Chakrian, Jennifer Mendoza, Alexandra Anduiza and Ashley Corona. 2019. "Perceived Satisfaction and Inequity: A Survey of Potential Romantic Partners of People with a Disability." *Sexuality and Disability* 38: 405–420. https://doi.org/10.1007/s11195-019-09601-7.

Courtney, Susan. 2005. *Hollywood Fantasies of Miscegenation: Spectacular Narratives of Gender and Race, 1903–1967*. Princeton, NJ: Princeton University Press.

Crooks, Roderic N. 2013. "The Rainbow Flag and the Green Carnation: Grindr in the Gay Village." *First Monday*, 18, no. 11. https://firstmonday.org/ojs/index.php/fm/article/view/4958/3790.

Curington, Celeste Vaughan, Ken-Hou Lin, and Jennifer Hickes Lundquist. 2015. "Positioning Multiraciality in Cyberspace: Treatment of Multiracial Daters in an Online Dating Website." *American Sociological Review* 80, no. 4: 764–788.

Davidson, Julia O'Connell and Jacqueline Sanchez Taylor. 1999. "Fantasy Islands: Exploring the Demand for Sex Tourism" in *Sun, Sex and Gold: Tourism and Sex Work in the Caribbean*, edited by Kamala Kempadoo, 37–54. Lanham, MD: Rowman and Littlefield.

Dickler, Jessica. 2017. "How to Land a Date for Valentine's Day." CNBC News, February 14. https://www.cnbc.com/2017/02/08/the-best-and-worst-online-dating-sites.html.

Duguay, Stefanie. 2019. " 'There's No One New Around You': Queer Women's Experiences of Scarcity in Geospatial Partner-Seeking on Tinder." In *The Geographies of Digital Sexuality*, edited by Catherine J. Nash and Andrew Gorman-Murray, 93–114. Singapore: Palgrave Macmillan.

Dupere, Katie. 2019. "Yes, I Want You to Notice I'm Fat before Liking Me on Tinder." Swipe Life (Tinder), November 16. https://swipelife.tinder.com/post/fat-woman-dating.

Eaves, Lindon, and Peter K. Hatemi. 2008. "Transmission of Attitudes toward Abortion and Gay Rights: Effects of Genes, Social Learning and Mate Selection." *Behavior Genetics* 38: 247–256.

Edwards, Griffin Sims, and Stephen Rushin. 2018. "The Effect of President Trump's Election on Hate Crimes." SSRN, January 18. https://papers.ssrn.com/sol3/papers.cfm?abstract_id=3102652.

Ellis, Katie, and Mike Kent. 2013. *Disability and New Media*. London: Routledge.

Ellis, Philip. 2020. "The 8 Best LGBTQ-Friendly Dating and Hookup Apps for Queer Men." *Men's Health Magazine*, August 28. https://www.menshealth.com/sex-women/g33759654/best-lgbtq-dating-apps-sites/.

Ellison, Nicole B., Jeffrey T. Hancock, and Catalina L. Toma. 2011. "Profile as Promise: A Framework for Conceptualizing Veracity in Online Dating Self-Presentations." *New Media & Society* 14, no. 1: 45–62.

Evans, Dominick. n.d. "Marriage Equality." Center for Disability Rights. http://cdrnys.org/blog/disability-dialogue/the-disability-dialogue-marriage-equality/.

Evans, Erica. 2019. "We Checked Out These Dating Apps for Trump Supporters. Here's What We Found." *Deseret News*, October 9. https://www.deseret.com/indepth/2019/10/9/20903269/trump-supporters-dating-apps-online.

Feliciano, Cynthia. 2016. "Shades of Race: How Phenotype and Observer Characteristics Shape Racial Classification." *American Behavioral Scientist* 60, no. 4: 390–419.

Feliciano, Cynthia, Belinda Robnett, and Golnaz Komaie. 2009. "Gendered Racial Exclusion among White Internet Daters." *Social Science Research* 38, no. 1: 39–54.

Fellizar, Kristine. 2017. "So *This* Is Why Millennials Really Use Tinder." Bustle, April 4. https://www.bustle.com/p/the-real-reason-millennials-use-tinder-for-a-confidence-boost-survey-says-46715.

Ferris, Lindsay, and Stefanie Duguay. 2020. "Tinder's Lesbian Digital Imaginary: Investigating (Im)Permeable Boundaries of Sexual Identity on a Popular Dating App." *New Media & Society* 22, no. 3: 489–506.

Filice, Eric, Amanda Raffoul, Samantha B. Meyer, and Elena Neiterman. 2019. "The Influence of Grindr, a Geosocial Networking Application, on Body Image in Gay, Bisexual and Other Men who Have Sex with Men: An Exploratory Study." *Body Image* 31: 59–70.

Finkle, Eli J., Paul W. Eastwick, Benjamin R. Karney, Harry T. Reis, and Susan Sprecher. 2012. "Online Dating: A Critical Analysis from the Perspective of Psychological Science." *Psychological Science in the Public Interest* 13, no. 1: 3–66.

Fisher, Helen, and Justin R. Garcia. 2017. "Singles in America." Match.com. https://www.match.com/dnws/cpx/en-us/singlesinamerica/2017/

Frederick, Angela, and Dara Shifrer. 2019. "Race and Disability: From Analogy to Intersectionality." *Sociology of Race and Ethnicity* 5, no. 2: 200–214.

Fredrick, Emma G., Abbey K. Mann, Byron D. Brooks, and Jameson K. Hirsch. 2021. "Anticipated to Enacted: Structural Stigma against Sexual and Gender Minorities Following the 2016 Presidential Election." *Sexuality Research and Social Policy*. Published ahead of print February 16, 2021. https://doi.org/10.1007/s13178-021-00547-0.

Frost, Jeana H., Zoë Chance, Michael I. Norton, and Dan Ariely. 2008. "People Are Experience Goods: Improving Online Dating with Virtual Dates." *Journal of Interactive Marketing* 22, no. 1: 51–61.

Gailey, Jeannine A. 2012. "Fat Shame to Fat Pride: Fat Women's Sexual and Dating Experiences." *Fat Studies: An Interdisciplinary Journal of Body Weight and Society* 1, no. 1: 114–127.

Gavin, Jeff, Daisie Rees-Evans, and Mark Brosnan. 2019. "Shy Geek, Likes Music, Technology, and Gaming: An Examination of Autistic Males' Online Dating Profiles." *Cyberpsychology, Behavior and Social Networking* 22, no. 4: 344–348.

Gibbs, Jennifer L., Nicole B. Ellison, and Chih-Hui Lai. 2011. "First Comes Love, Then Comes Google: An Investigation of Uncertainty Reduction Strategies and Self-Disclosure in Online Dating." *Communication Research* 38, no. 1: 70–100.

Gillett, Rosalie. 2018. "Intimate Intrusions Online: Studying the Normalization of Abuse in Dating Apps." *Women's Studies International Forum* 69: 212–219.

Glynn, Tiffany R., Kirsti E. Gamarel, Christopher W. Kahler, Mariko Iwamoto, Don Operario, and Tooru Nemoto. 2016. "The Role of Gender Affirmation in Psychological Well-Being among Transgender Women." *Psychology of Sexual Orientation and Gender Diversity* 3, no. 3: 336–344.

Goyal, Nidhi. 2016. "Is Access Real? Disability, Sexuality, and the Digital Space." *Arrow for Change* 22, no. 1: 31–33.

Griffin, Eden M., and Karen L. Fingerman. 2018. "Online Dating Profile Content of Older Adults Seeking Same- and Cross-Sex Relationships." *Journal of GLBT Family Studies* 14, no. 5: 446–466.

Gudelunas, David. 2012. "There's an App for That: The Uses and Gratifications of Online Social Networks for Gay Men." *Sexuality & Culture* 16: 347–365.

Hamilton, Laura, and Elizabeth A. Armstrong. 2009. "Gendered Sexuality in Young Adulthood: Double Binds and Flawed Options." *Gender and Society* 32, no. 5: 589–616.

Han, Chong-suk. 2007. "They Don't Want to Cruise Your Type: Gay Men of Color and the Racial Politics of Exclusion." *Social Identities: Journal for the Study of Race, Nation and Culture* 13, no. 1: 51–67.

Hanson, Kenneth R. 2021. "Collective Exclusion: How White Heterosexual Dating App Norms Reproduce Status Quo Hookup Culture." *Sociological Inquiry*. Published ahead of print April 12, 2021. https://doi.org/10.1111/soin.12426.

Hasinoff, Amy Adele. 2015. *Sexting Panic: Rethinking Criminalization, Privacy, and Consent*. Champaign: University of Illinois Press.

Haywood, Chris. 2018. "Mobile Romance: Tinder and the Navigation of Masculinity." In *Men, Masculinity and Contemporary Dating*, 131–166. London: Palgrave Macmillan.

Heino, Rebecca D., Nicole B. Ellison, and Jennifer L. Gibbs. 2010. "Relationshopping: Investigating the Market Metaphor in Online Dating." *Journal of Social and Personal Relationships* 27, no. 4: 427–447.

Hess, Aaron, and Carlos Flores. 2018. "Simply More than Swiping Left: A Critical Analysis of Toxic Masculine Performances on *Tinder Nightmares*." *New Media and Society* 20, no. 3: 1085–1102.

Hitsch, Gunter J., Ali Hortaçsu, and Dan Ariely. 2006. "What Makes You Click? Mate Preferences and Matching Outcomes in Online Dating." MIT Sloan Research Paper 4603-06. SSRN, April 11. https://papers.ssrn.com/sol3/papers.cfm?abstract_id=895442.

Hitsch, Gunter J., Ali Hortaçsu, and Dan Ariely. 2010. "Matching and Sorting in Online Dating." *American Economic Review* 100, no. 1: 130–163.

Horowitz, Adam L., and Charles J. Gomez. 2018. "Identity Override: How Sexual Orientation Reduces the Rigidity of Racial Boundaries." *Sociological Science* 28, no. 5: 669–693.

Hsu, Tiffany. 2018. "Bumble Dating App Bans Gun Images after Mass Shootings." *New York Times*, March 5. https://www.nytimes.com/2018/03/05/business/bumble-dating-app-gun-images.html.

Huber, Gregory A., and Neil Malhotra. 2017. "Political Homophily in Social Relationships: Evidence from Online Dating Behavior." *Journal of Politics* 79, no. 1: 269–283.

Hunter, Margaret L. 2005. *Race, Gender, and the Politics of Skin Tone*. New York: Routledge.

Iris. 2021. "Our Story." https://www.irisdating.com.

Iyengar, Shanto, Tobias Konitzer, and Kent Tedin. 2018. "The Home as a Political Fortress: Family Agreement in an Era of Polarization." *Journal of Politics* 80, no. 4: 1326–1338.

Johnson, Kristine, M. Olguta Vilceanu, and Manuel C. Pontes. 2017. "Use of Online Dating Websites and Dating Apps: Findings and Implications for LGB Populations." *Journal of Marketing Development and Competitiveness* 11, no. 3: 60–66.

Jones, Jeffrey M. 2021. "LGBT Identification Rises to 5.6% in Latest U.S. Estimate." Gallup, February 24. https://news.gallup.com/poll/329708/lgbt-identification-rises-latest-estimate.aspx.

Kassel, Gabrielle. 2020. "The Best Lesbian Dating Apps for the 21st Century." *Women's Health Magazine*, May 12. https://www.womenshealthmag.com/relationships/g32435296/lesbian-dating-apps/.

Kearney, Kelly B., Sharon M. Darling, and Charles Dukes. 2020. "Disability and Dating: Exploring the Twittersphere." *Inclusion* 8, no. 4: 293–302.

Kempadoo, Kamala, ed. 1999. *Sun, Sex and Gold: Tourism and Sex Work in the Caribbean*. Lanham, MD: Rowman and Littlefield.

Khandpur, Gurleen. 2015. "Fat and Thin Sex: Fetishized Normal and Normalised Fetish." *M/C Journal: A Journal of Media and Culture* 18, no. 3. http://www.journal.media-culture.org.au/index.php/mcjournal/article/view/976.

Klofstad, Casey, Rose McDermott, and Peter K. Hatemi. 2012. "Do Bedroom Eyes Wear Political Glasses? The Role of Politics in Human Mate Attraction." *Evolution and Human Behavior* 33, no. 2: 100–108.

Klofstad, Casey, Rose McDermott, and Peter K. Hatemi. 2013. "The Dating Preferences of Liberals and Conservatives." *Political Behavior* 35: 519–538.

Krendel, Alexandra. 2020. "The Men and Women, Guys and Girls of the 'Manosphere': A Corpus-Assisted Discourse Approach." *Discourse and Society* 31, no. 6: 607–630.

Kuperberg, Arielle, and Joseph E. Padgett. 2015. "Dating and Hooking Up in College: Meeting Contexts, Sex, and Variation by Gender, Partner's Gender, and Class Standing." *Journal of Sex Research* 52, no. 5: 517–531.

Levesley, David. 2020. "The Best Apps for Gay Dating, Gay Sex and Gay Romance." *GQ Magazine*, August 22. https://www.gq-magazine.co.uk/article/best-gay-dating-apps.

Lewis, Michael B. 2010. "Why Are Mixed-Race People Perceived as More Attractive?" *Perception* 39, no. 1: 136–138.

Lim, Gene, Brady Robards, and Bronwyn Carlson. 2020. "Grindr Is Deleting Its 'Ethnicity Filter'. But Racism Is Still Rife in Online Dating." *The Conversation*, June 7. https://theconve

rsation.com/grindr-is-deleting-its-ethnicity-filter-but-racism-is-still-rife-in-online-dating-140077.

Lin, Ken-Hou, and Jennifer Lundquist. 2013. "Mate Selection in Cyberspace: The Intersection of Race, Gender, and Education." *American Journal of Sociology* 119, no. 1: 183–215.

Livingston, Gretchen, and Anna Brown. 2017. Intermarriage in the U.S. 50 Years after *Loving v. Virginia*. Pew Research Center, May 18. https://www.pewresearch.org/social-trends/2017/05/18/intermarriage-in-the-u-s-50-years-after-loving-v-virginia/

Lundquist, Jennifer H., and Ken-Hou Lin. 2015. "Is Love (Color) Blind? The Economy of Race among Gay and Straight Daters." *Social Forces* 93, no. 4: 1423–1449.

Lundquist, Jennifer Hickes, and Celeste Vaughan Curington. 2019. "Love Me Tinder, Love Me Sweet." *Contexts* 18, no. 4: 22–27.

MacInnes, Maryhelen D. 2011. "Altar-Bound? The Effect of Disability on the Hazard of Entry into a First Marriage." *International Journal of Sociology* 41, no. 1: 87–103.

MacLeod, Caitlin, and Victoria McArthur. 2019. "The Construction of Gender in Dating Apps: An Interface Analysis of Tinder and Bumble." *Feminist Media Studies* 19, no. 6: 822–840.

March, Evita, Rachel Grieve, Jessica Marrington, and Peter K. Jonason. 2017. "Trolling on Tinder (and Other Dating Apps): Examining the Role of the Dark Tetrad and Impulsivity." *Personality and Individual Differences* 110: 139–143.

McGrath, Allison R., Glenn T. Tsunokai, Melinda Schultz, Jillian Kavanaugh, and Jake A. Tarrence. 2016. "Differing Shades of Colour: Online Dating Preferences of Biracial Individuals." *Ethnic and Racial Studies* 39, no. 11: 1920–1942.

McKenna, Katelyn Y. A., Amie S. Green, and Marci E. J. Gleason. 2002. "Relationship Formation on the Internet: What's the Big Attraction?" *Journal of Social Issues* 58, no. 1: 9–31.

Melendez, Rita M., and Rogério Pinto. 2007. " 'It's Really a Hard Life': Love, Gender, and HIV Risk among Male-to-Female Transgender Persons." *Culture, Health & Sexuality: An International Journal for Research, Intervention and Care* 9, no. 3: 233–245.

Menzie, Lauren. 2020. "Stacys, Beckys, and Chads: The Construction of Femininity and Hegemonic Masculinity within Incel Rhetoric." *Psychology and Sexuality*. Published ahead of print August 18, 2020. https://doi.org/10.1080/19419899.2020.1806915.

Milbrodt, Teresa. 2019. "Dating Websites and Disability Identity: Presentations of the Disabled Self in Online Dating Profiles." *Western Folklore* 78, no. 1: 66–100.

Miller, Byron, Savanah Catalina, Sara Rocks, and Kathryn Tillman. 2021. "It Is Your Decision to Date Interracially: The Influence of Family Approval on the Likelihood of Interracial/Interethnic Dating." *Journal of Family Issues*. Published ahead of print March 6, 2021. https://doi.org/10.1177/0192513X21994130.

Moore, Cortney. 2020. "OkCupid Adds Black Lives Matter Profile Badge for Users." FOX Business, June 12. https://www.foxbusiness.com/technology/okcupid-black-lives-matter-badge.

Moore, Mignon. 2011. *Invisible Families: Gay Identities, Relationships, and Motherhood among Black Women*. Berkeley: University of California Press.

Mowlabocus, Sharif. 2010. *Gaydar Culture: Gay Men, Technology, and Embodiment in the Digital Age*. Burlington, VT: Ashgate.

Murray, Sarah, and Megan Sapnar Ankerson. 2016. "Lez Takes Time: Designing Lesbian Geosocial Networking Apps." *Critical Studies in Media Communication* 33, no. 1: 53–69.

Muthia, Risyiana. 2019. " 'Tinder Tourists': Indonesian Sex Workers Turn to Online Dating Apps for Safety and to Set Their Own Rules." *South China Morning Post*, October 2. https://

www.scmp.com/lifestyle/travel-leisure/article/3031096/tinder-tourists-indonesian-sex-workers-turn-online-dating.

Nagel, Joane. 2003. *Race, Ethnicity, and Sexuality: Intimate Intersections, Forbidden Frontiers*. New York: Oxford University Press.

Nakamura, Lisa. 2001. "Head Hunting in Cyberspace." *Women's Review of Books* 18, no. 5: 10–11.

Nakamura, Lisa. 2008. "Cyberrace." *Publications of the Modern Language Association of America* 123, no. 5: 1673–1682.

Nascimento, Fábio Santiago, and Débora de Carvalho Figueiredo. 2013. "Queer Masculinities on the Dating Website Badoo.com: A Preliminary Study." Unpublished manuscript. http://www.fg2013.wwc2017.eventos.dype.com.br/resources/anais/old_20/1373338783_ARQUIVO_NASCIMENTO-FIGUEIREDO.FazendoGenero2013.pdf.

Nobel, Safiya. 2018. *Algorithms of Oppression: How Search Engines Reinforce Racism*. New York: New York University Press.

OkCupid. n.d. "Identity." https://www.okcupid.com/identity.

OkCupid. 2017. "Our New Profile Badge Helps You Filter for Planned Parenthood Supporters." *The OkCupid Blog* (blog), September 13. https://theblog.okcupid.com/our-new-profile-badge-helps-you-filter-for-planned-parenthood-supporters-e40f5c4d6e8f.

OkCupid. 2018. "What It Means When Your OkCupid Match Has the ACLU #RightToLove Badge." *The OkCupid Blog* (blog), June 28. https://theblog.okcupid.com/what-it-means-when-your-okcupid-match-has-the-aclu-righttolove-badge-184a209b6190.

Operario, Don, Jennifer Burton, Kristen Underhill, and Jae Sevelius. 2008. "Men Who Have Sex with Transgender Women: Challenges to Category-Based HIV Prevention." *AIDS and Behavior* 12: 18–26.

Orne, Jay. 2017. *Boystown: Sex and Community in Chicago*. Chicago: University of Chicago Press.

Patil, Vrushali, and Jyoti Puri. 2021. "Colorblind Feminisms: Ansari-Grace and the Limits of #MeToo Counterpublics." *Signs: Journal of Women in Culture and Society* 46, no. 3: 689–713.

Pfeffer, Carla A. 2008. "Bodies in Relation—Bodies in Transition: Lesbian Partners of Trans Men and Body Image." *Journal of Lesbian Studies* 12, no. 4: 325–345.

Pfeffer, Carla A. 2017. *Queering Families: The Postmodern Partnerships of Cisgender Women and Transgender Men*. New York: Oxford University Press.

Phan, Anh, Kathryn Siegfried-Spellar, and Kim-Kwang Raymond Choo. 2021. "Threaten Me Softly: A Review of Potential Dating App Risks." *Computers in Human Behavior Reports* 3: 100055: 1–12.

Phua, Voon Chin, and Gayle Kaufman. 2003. "The Crossroads of Race and Sexuality: Date Selection among Men in Internet 'Personal' Ads." *Journal of Family Issues* 24, no. 8: 981–994.

Pitcho-Prelorentzos, Shani, Christian Heckel, and Lia Ring. 2020. "Predictors of Social Anxiety among Online Dating Users." *Computers in Human Behavior* 110: 106381.

Pond, Tara, and Panteá Farvid. 2017. " 'I Do Like Girls, I Promise': Young Bisexual Women's Experiences of Using Tinder." *Psychology of Sexualities Review* 8, no. 2: 6–24.

Porter, John R., Kiley Sobel, Sarah E. Fox, Cynthia L. Bennett, and Julie A. Kientz. 2017. "Filtered Out: Disability Disclosure Practices in Online Dating Communities." *Proceedings of the ACM on Human–Computer Interaction* 1: 87.

PR Newswire. 2020. "Dating App Iris Launches New 'Trust Rating' Feature Ahead of Dating Sunday." https://www.prnewswire.com/news-releases/dating-app-iris-launches-new-trust-rating-feature-ahead-of-dating-sunday-301199770.html

Purvis, Jeanette. 2017. "Why Tinder Is so 'Evilly Satisfying.'" *The Conversation*, February 10. https://theconversation.com/why-tinder-is-so-evilly-satisfying-72177.

Qian, Zenchao, and Daniel T. Lichter. 2001. "Measuring Marital Assimilation: Intermarriage among Natives and Immigrants." *Social Science Research* 30: 289–312.

Qian, Zenchao, and Daniel T. Lichter. 2007. "Social Boundaries and Marital Assimilation: Interpreting Trends in Racial and Ethnic Intermarriage." *American Sociological Review* 72: 68–94.

Qian, Zenchao, and Daniel T. Lichter. 2011. "Changing Patterns of Interracial Marriage in a Mixed-Race Society." *Journal of Marriage and Family* 73: 1065–1084.

Race, Kane. 2015. " 'Part and Play': Online Hook-up Devices and the Emergence of PNP Practices among Gay Men." *Sexualities* 18, no. 3: 253–275.

Rafalow, Matthew H., Cynthia Feliciano, and Belinda Robnett. 2017. "Racialized Femininity and Masculinity in the Preferences of Online Same-Sex Daters." *Social Currents* 4, no. 4: 306–321.

Rafalow, Matthew H., and Jessica M. Kizer. 2018. "Mommy Markets: Racial Differences in Lesbians' Dating Preferences for Women with Children." *Journal of Lesbian Studies* 22, no. 3: 297–312.

Riotta, Chris. 2019. "Tinder Still Banning Transgender People Despite Pledge of Inclusivity." *The Independent*, December 12. https://www.independent.co.uk/news/world/americas/tinder-ban-trans-account-block-report-lawsuit-pride-gender-identity-a9007721.html.

Roberts, Molly. 2017. "No, Liberal Women who Refuse to Date Conservatives Are not to Blame for Trump." *Washington Post*, September 19. https://www.washingtonpost.com/blogs/post-partisan/wp/2017/09/19/no-liberal-women-shouldnt-date-antiabortion-men-to-avoid-more-trumps/.

Robinson, Brandon Andrew. 2015. " 'Personal Preference' as the New Racism: Gay Desire and Racial Cleansing in Cyberspace." *Sociology of Race and Ethnicity* 1, no. 2: 317–330.

Robnett, Belinda, and Cynthia Feliciano. 2011. "Patterns of Racial–Ethnic Exclusion by Internet Daters." *Social Forces* 89, no. 3: 807–828.

Rochadiat, Annisa M. P., Stephanie Tom Tong, and Julie M. Novak. 2018. "Online Dating and Courtship among Muslim American Women: Negotiating Technology, Religious Identity, and Culture." *New Media and Society* 20, no. 4: 1618–1639.

Rockquemore, Kerry Ann, Tracey Laszloffy, and Julia Noveske. 2006. "It All Starts at Home: Racial Socialization in Multiracial Families." In *Mixed Messages: Multiracial Identities in the "Color-Blind" Era*, edited by David Brunsma, 203–216. Boulder, CO: Lynne Rienner.

Rosenfeld, Michael J. 2017. "Marriage, Choice, and Couplehood in the Age of the Internet." *Sociological Science* 4: 490–510.

Rosenfeld, Michael J., and Byung-Soo Kim. 2005. "The Independence of Young Adults and the Rise of Interracial and Same-Sex Unions." *American Sociological Review* 70, no. 4: 541–562.

Rosenfeld, Michael J., and Reuben J. Thomas. 2012. "Searching for a Mate: The Rise of the Internet as a Social Intermediary." *American Sociological Review* 77: 523–547.

Rosenfeld, Michael J., Reuben J. Thomas, and Sonia Hausen. 2019. "Disintermediating Your Friends: How Online Dating in the United States Displaces Other Ways of Meeting." *Proceedings of the National Academy of Sciences of the United States of America* 116, no. 36: 17753–17758.

Roth, Matthew E., and Jennifer M. Gillis. 2015. " 'Convenience with the Click of a Mouse': A Survey of Adults with Autism Spectrum Disorder on Online Dating." *Sexuality and Disability* 33: 133–150.

Rudder, Christian. 2014. *Dataclysm: Who We Are (When We Think No One's Looking)*. New York: Crown Publishers.

Saltes, Natasha. 2013. "Disability, Identity and Disclosure in the Online Dating Environment." *Disability & Society* 28, no. 1: 96–109.

Sautter, Jessica M., Rebecca M. Tippett, and S. Philip Morgan. 2010. "The Social Demography of Internet Dating in the United States." *Social Science Quarterly* 91, no. 2: 554–575.

Schoemaker Holmes, Jacqueline. 2016. "Fat Authenticity and the Pursuit of Hetero-romantic Love in Vancouver: The Case of Online Dating." In *Obesity in Canada: Critical Perspectives*, edited by Jenny Ellison, Deborah McPhail, and Wendy Mitchinson, 373–398. Toronto: University of Toronto Press.

Schumer, Lizz. 2021. "12 Popular Lesbian Dating Apps to Help You Find Love." *Good Housekeeping Magazine*, May 19. https://www.goodhousekeeping.com/life/relationships/g32070139/best-lesbian-dating-apps/.

Schwartz, Barry. 2004. *The Paradox of Choice: Why More Is Less*. New York: Harper Collins.

Schwartz, Christine R. 2013. "Trends and Variation in Assortative Mating: Causes and Consequences." *Annual Review of Sociology* 39: 451–470.

Serano. Julia. 2007. *Whipping Girl: A Transsexual Woman on Sexism and the Scapegoating of Femininity*. Emeryville, CA: Seal Press.

Sevelius, Jae M. 2013. "Gender Affirmation: A Framework for Conceptualizing Risk Behavior among Transgender Women of Color." *Sex Roles* 68: 675–689.

Silvester, Jessica. 2014. "I'd Been Fat All My Life, but Tinder Taught Me I Had a 'Fetish Body.'" *The Cut, New York Magazine*, September 5. https://www.thecut.com/2014/09/tinder-taught-me-that-plus-size-is-a-fetish.html.

Smith, Jesus Gregorio, and Maria Cristina Morales. 2018. "Racial Constructions among Men Who Have Sex with Men: The Utility of the Latin Americanization Thesis and Colorblind Racism on Sexual Partner Selection." *Issues in Race and Society* 6: 25–44.

Spell, Sarah A. 2017. "Not Just Black and White: How Race/Ethnicity and Gender Intersect in Hookup Culture." *Sociology of Race and Ethnicity* 3, no. 2: 172–187.

Spellings, Sarah. 2018. "Transgender Woman Sues Tinder after Her Account Is Deleted." *The Cut, New York Magazine*, March 14. https://www.thecut.com/2018/03/transgender-woman-sues-tinder-after-her-account-was-deleted.html.

Spira, Julie. 2017. "SURVEY: Singles Care about Politics and Education When Dating Online." *Huffington Post*, August 25. https://www.huffpost.com/entry/singles-care-about-politics-and-education-when-dating_b_59a079f4e4b0a62d0987aed7.

Star, Eryn. 2019. "Marriage Equality Is Still Not a Reality: Disabled People and the Right to Marry." *The Advocacy Monitor*, November 14. https://advocacymonitor.com/marriage-equality-is-still-not-a-reality-disabled-people-and-the-right-to-marry/.

Stephure, Robert J., Susan D. Boon, Stacey L. MacKinnon, and Vicki L. Deveau. 2009. "Internet Initiated Relationships: Associations between Age and Involvement in Online Dating." *Journal of Computer-Mediated Communication* 14, no. 3: 658–681.

Sumter, Sindy, Laura Vandenbosch, and Loes Ligtenberg. 2017. "Love Me Tinder: Untangling Emerging Adults' Motivations for Using the Dating Application Tinder." *Telematics and Informatics* 34: 67–78.

Tang, Denise Tse-Shang. 2017. "All I Get Is an Emoji: Dating on Lesbian Mobile Phone App Butterfly." *Media, Culture & Society* 39, no. 6: 816–832.

Tewksbury, Richard. 2002. "Bathhouse intercourse: Structural and behavioral aspects of an erotic oasis." *Deviant Behavior* 23, no. 1: 75–112.

Thompson, Laura. 2018. " 'I Can Be Your Tinder Nightmare': Harassment and Misogyny in the Online Sexual Marketplace." *Feminism and Psychology* 28, no. 1: 69–89.

Tsunokai, Glenn T., Allison R. McGrath, and Jillian K. Kavanagh. 2014. "Online Dating Preferences of Asian Americans." *Journal of Social and Personal Relationships* 31, no. 6: 796–814.

Tu, Kun, Bruno Ribeiro, David Jensen, Don Towsley, Benyuan Liu, H. Jiang, et al. 2014. "Online Dating Recommendations: Matching Markets and Learning Preferences." In *Proceedings of the 23rd International Conference on World Wide Web*, 787–792. New York: ACM Press.

Turkle, Sherry. 2016. *Reclaiming Conversation: The Power of Talk in a Digital Age*. New York: Penguin Books.

Vantage Mobility. 2017. "Expert Dating Tips for the Best Disabled Dating Websites." Vantage Mobility News and Press, January 4. https://www.vantagemobility.com/blog/dating-tips-and-sites-for-people-with-disabilities.

Van Valkenburgh, Shawn P. 2021. "Digesting the Red Pill: Masculinity and Neoliberalism in the Manosphere." *Men and Masculinities* 24, no. 1: 84–103.

Vaughn, Mya, Barbara McEntee, Barbara Schoen, and Michele McGrady. 2015. "Addressing Disability Stigma within the Lesbian Community." *Journal of Rehabilitation* 81, no. 4: 49–56.

Vinopal, Courtney. 2020. "Coronavirus Has Changed Online Dating. Here's Why Some Say That's a Good Thing." *PBS News Hour*, May 15. https://www.pbs.org/newshour/nation/coronavirus-has-changed-online-dating-heres-why-some-say-thats-a-good-thing.

Vogels, Emily A. 2019. "Millennials Stand Out for Their Technology Use, but Older Generations Also Embrace Digital Life." Pew Research Center, September 9. https://www.pewresearch.org/fact-tank/2019/09/09/us-generations-technology-use/.

Wade, Lisa. 2017. *American Hookup: The New Culture of Sex on Campus*. New York: W. W. Norton.

Wade, T. Joel, Maryanne L. Fisher, Catherine Salmon, and Carly Downs. 2021. "Want to Hookup? Sex Differences in Short-term Mate Attraction Tactics." *Evolutionary Psychological Science*. Published ahead of print April 20, 2021. https://doi.org/10.1007/s40806-021-00282-0.

Waldman, Ari Ezra. 2019. "Law, Privacy, and Online Dating: 'Revenge Porn' in Gay Online Communities." *Law and Social Inquiry* 44, no. 4: 987–1018.

Wong, Brittany. 2018. "9 Things You Should Never Say to Mixed-Weight Couples." *Huffington Post*, May 2. https://www.huffpost.com/entry/things-you-should-never-say-to-mixed-weight-couples_n_5a983ab6e4b0479c0250543e.

Woodyatt, Amy. 2020. "Grindr Pulls Feature That Lets Users Sort by Race. It Says It's Supporting Black Lives Matter." CNN Business, June 3. https://www.cnn.com/2020/06/03/tech/grindr-ethnicity-filter-intl-scli/index.html.

Wu, Karen, Chuansheng Chen, and Ellen Greenberger. 2015. "The Sweetness of Forbidden Fruit: Interracial Daters Are More Attractive than Intraracial Daters." *Journal of Social and Personal Relationships* 32, no. 5: 650–666.

Yashari, Leora. 2015. "Meet the Tinder Co-Founder Trying to Change Online Dating Forever." *Vanity Fair*, August 7. https://www.vanityfair.com/culture/2015/08/bumble-app-whitney-wolfe.

Ybarra, Michele L., and Kimberly J. Mitchell. 2014. "'Sexting' and Its Relation to Sexual Activity and Sexual Risk Behavior in a National Survey of Adolescents." *Journal of Adolescent Health* 55, no. 6: 757–764.

Zamantakis, Alithia. 2019. "'I Try Not to Push It Too Far': Trans and Nonbinary Individuals Negotiating Race and Gender within Intimate Relationships." In *Expanding the Rainbow: Exploring the Relationships of Bi+, Trans, Ace, Poly, Kink, and Intersex People*, edited by B. L. Simula, J. E. Sumerau, and A. Miller, 293–308. Boston: Sense Publishers.

Zamantakis, Alithia. 2020. "Queering Intimate Emotions: Trans/Nonbinary People Negotiating Emotional Expectations in Intimate Relationships." *Sexualities*. Published ahead of print December 15, 2020. https://doi.org/10.1177/1363460720979307.

CHAPTER 14

DIGITAL PORNOGRAPHY AND EVERYDAY LIFE

JENNIFER A. JOHNSON

Driven almost exclusively by the rise of the internet and the corresponding birth of the modern digital pornography industry, pornography has transformed from magazines and videos hidden behind counters to digital media that are both hyperaccessible and hypersexualized. Almost any type of sexual behavior involving any type of body is available to anyone, regardless of age, at any given time and in any given social context with few, if any, regulatory barriers. As a consequence, digital pornography is a ubiquitous experience beginning in early adolescence, in which it now serves as the primary, if not sole, source of sexual education (Chen et al. 2013; Hunter, Figueredo, and Malamuth 2010; Kubicek et al. 2010; Morgan 2011; Sabina, Wolak, and Finkelhor 2008; Weber, Quiring, and Daschmann 2012). Yet sociological scholarship on this powerful form of media is relatively scarce compared to the literature in medicine, psychology, and cultural studies. Research on digital pornography largely focuses on health and safety implications for individuals and relationships (Gouvernet et al. 2020) as well as theoretical explorations on the scope and breadth of polysemic meanings and audience interpretations embedded in the content (Attwood 2005, 2007). Critical research on the structural and material conditions that produce digital pornography as a technological and commercial artifact and how this artifact then impacts the macro and micro levels is critically necessary given the large role it plays in sexual politics, relationships, and identities (Dines 2010; McRobbie 2008).

To speak of material conditions is to recognize that the means of production, including such things as labor power, technology, and economic conditions, directly shape and impact, not only the artifact that is produced, but also the larger institutional structures and social relationships implicated in the production and consumption of that artifact. To engage in this form of critique is to examine the political economy of the sociocultural and material processes of production and consumption. To speak of the political economy of pornography is to recognize that it is, at its core, a commercial artifact produced at a unique intersection of technological, economic, and sociopolitical forces. Pornography has always been a major driver for the development of new technologies and business models (Barss 2011; Coopersmith 2006). With expanding personal access to broadband internet circa the year 2000, digital pornography is at the center of the new digital economy (Johnson 2011; Ogas and Gaddam 2011; Tarrant 2016). Digital pornography occupies an estimated 4–20% of digital media (Buchholz 2019; Kamvar and Baluja 2006; Ogas and Gaddam 2011) and generates an estimated $15 billion per year (Naughton 2018). Pornhub.com, the largest and most popular digital pornography site, reports 42 billion visits to the site, an average of 115 million per day, and an additional 6.83 million new videos uploaded in 2019, thus bringing the total amount of data transferred through its content to 6,597 petabytes (Pornhub Insights 2019). The industry is developing sophisticated bots and algorithms to manage and curate this massive amount of content in ways that maximize the visibility of content that is most profitable (Hassan 2018). And, like all algorithms and bots, the result is the production and promotion of content that represents and reproduces inequalities, particularly those related to gender and race (Bridges 2019; Brown and L'Engle 2009).

These modern technologies and resulting online economies raise new questions related to the role of pornography in everyday life. Conventional debates related to freedom of expression, personal choice, and innate sexual desire are less relevant to understanding digital pornography. As a commercial enterprise, digital pornography is more about technology, profit, and new online economies than sex, sexuality, or relationships. Therefore, as an economic means of production, distribution, and consumption, the digital pornography industry should be subject to the same critical sociological analysis as other capitalist structures and products. Exploring the hyperreality of digital pornography as a commercial and technological artifact that shapes our everyday life in both manifest and hidden ways will require a revisiting of questions related to individual sexual behaviors and interpersonal relationships across intersecting identities, as well as taking advantage of new forms of digital data to ask larger questions related to systems of power and inequality.

I have two distinct goals for this chapter. The first is to contribute to the growing intellectual work of digital sociology, a new subfield in the discipline focused on understanding how digital media inform our concepts of self and personal relationships as well as how digital media may produce and/or reproduce social patterns, inequalities, and systems of power (Lupton 2014; Wynn 2009). The digital traces left as consumers interact with online content, as well as the network connections established by the industry itself, concatenate into what digital sociologists call "native digital data" (Lupton 2014, 55). Native digital data is data generated and oftentimes captured through naturally occurring activities, interactions, and other online "doings" across various devices and/or platforms. These new forms of digital data allow for deeper insights into the sexual attitudes, choices, and experiences of pornography users as well as the political economy of an industry that typically operates in the shadows of algorithms and bots. By situating personal and relational questions inside the techno-economic environment created by the modern digital pornography industry, I aim to illustrate how the digital has transformed the experience of pornography in everyday life.

My second goal is to situate current research on digital pornography in the everyday life of individuals. How does the political economy of digital pornography shape the everyday sexual experiences of individuals? This review of current research is not intended to be exhaustive. Instead, the scope is narrowed by time and topic. In terms of time, I concentrate on empirical research conducted since around 2010, corresponding with patterns of consumer access; that is, pornography exposure is now almost entirely via the internet and digital devices (Sun et al. 2016). In terms of topic, I focus on empirical research related to personal and relational health and behavior. Given that we no longer face a pornographic landscape that is restrictive, hidden, and controllable by conventional moral and regulatory frameworks, theoretical questions related to representation, access, and speech are less pressing. We must now turn attention to improving our understanding of the impact of digital pornography on the lived realities of individuals across intersecting identities.

Terminology: What Is Digital Pornography?

While there are varied terms used in the literature to study pornographic material, including "sexually explicit internet material," "sexually explicit material," and "internet pornography," I am deliberate in my use of the term "digital pornography" for several reasons. First, I am following the common nomenclature of the industry, consumers, and other scholars who use the term "pornography" to describe a type of commercial media product with distinct form and style that is concerned with the explicit representation of human sexuality (Hardy 2008). Second, my use of the term "digital" refers to how this commercial product is accessed primarily via digital devices and platforms. Third, I use the term as a means of emphasizing the potential for digital sociology, as a new disciplinary subfield, to reveal the new online economies and technological intermediaries that shape digital pornography, in terms of both access and content.

Digital Sociology: New Theory and Data for the Study of Digital Pornography

Research and theory on pornography as a form of media has largely been captured by serious political and ideological chasms within the feminist community. The heated debate, oftentimes characterized as the "porn wars," largely centers on the impact of pornography on women. Is pornography a pathway toward sexual and economic empowerment for women, as well as a means of resistance to repressive, heteronormative sexual practices (Attwood 2005; McKee 2009; Williams 2004)? Or is pornography the (re)entrenchment of the sexual and economic domination and oppression of women and the (mis)education of boys into hegemonic ideals of masculinity (Dines 2010; Dworkin 1981; Jensen 2009; MacKinnon 1996)? These debates have largely revolved around questions of representation—who is represented, and how are they being portrayed?—questions of speech—whose voices are allowed, and what are they saying?—and questions of power—who has a choice, what are their options, and what do they choose? The intensity of this debate has created a hostile research environment among scholars (Paasonen 2011) and a fragmented literature base (Gouvernet et al. 2020) undercut by citation bias (Ferguson, Nielsen, and Markey 2017).

The early rise of digital pornography seemingly resolved many of these questions related to representation, freedom, and power. In the late 1990s and early 2000s, new content was being digitized so fast it appeared as if sexuality had finally been unleashed from conventional moral, legal, and religious social controls. Guided by initial excitement about the potential of the internet to "democratize" access to information and reduce inequality (Shirky 2008), early descriptions characterized the rise of digital pornography as "a thousand cybersex flowers [blooming], exploring and tinkering to create new services, products, technologies, and organizational forms" (Coopersmith 2006, 5). Content analysis of select websites described how "new porn professionals" were creating "new sex taste cultures" by deploying pornography as tools of self-expression, community-building, and recreation (Attwood 2005, 2007). This analysis of digital pornography as innovative and empowering was predicated on the belief that this new revolution in pornography was being driven by DIY (do-it-yourself) pornography created and uploaded by everyday people who were now free to express and explore highly diverse sexual desires (Jacobs 2007; Wilkinson 2017). These new possibilities were described as a "democratization of desire"; the digital collapsed the boundaries between those who controlled the definition and presentation of "normal" forms of desire and those who embody and express diverse forms of desire, thus allowing for greater, more democratic, representation of sexuality (McNair 2013).

However, as the initial optimism about the potential for the internet to promote democracy and challenge conventional systems of inequality waned (Van Dijk and Hacker 2018), a need for more sophisticated critical structural analysis of digital media crystallized across a variety of disciplines including media studies (McChesney 2013, 2016), political science (Hindman 2018), and sociology and economics (Castells et al. 2017). Among sociologists, the growing interest in a critical approach to studying the digital environment as a specific site of analysis has coalesced into the use of the term "digital sociology" to describe a new subfield in the discipline (Lupton 2014). Digital sociology includes the study of how individuals use digital technologies to construct and express their sense of self and their relationships as well as a critical analysis of how digital media (re)produce social institutions, social structures, and systems of inequality (Daniels, Gregory, and Cottom 2016). What makes digital sociology so transformative for social science research are the new forms and scope of data that are produced through digital interactions as well as the new computational and technological means of collecting and analyzing digital data, including big data (Felt 2016; Selwyn 2019). Digital sociology has been described as a fundamental "reinvention of social research" (Marres 2017) and a "revolution" in the social sciences (Davidson 2017).

To take a digital sociology approach to digital pornography is to emphasize the digital in asking questions about pornography and/or utilizing digital data to answer questions. It is to move beyond noting that the digital has created an explosion of easily accessible pornography to critically thinking about how the digital has transformed user experiences with content that is produced by the digital for the digital. It is also to move beyond the individual experience with digital pornography to include larger, more structural questions related to new economies, networks, politics, and intersectional inequalities. These larger questions are made possible by more expansive forms of digital data that allow for new questions to be asked as well as a new means of revisiting vexing questions related to representation, speech, and (dis)empowerment. Most importantly, a digital sociology approach applies critical sociological theory, both old and new, to these questions to better understand the role of digital pornography as a ubiquitous agent of socialization and dominant force in structuring our everyday experiences with digital media.

Digital Pornography as a Technological and Commercial Artifact

A digital sociology approach begins with an understanding of digital pornography as a sociopolitical artifact of technological and economic processes. Digital pornography has come to define and dominate the sexual landscape through technological innovation, competitive marketing strategies, and the deliberative commodification of gender politics. Beginning in 1953, with the first publication of *Playboy* magazine featuring Marilyn Monroe, the modern commercialized pornography industry pioneered the use of women's bodies as a tool for selling men a commercialized lifestyle complete with advice, products, and images of modern masculinity. All subsequent iterations of the pornography industry have worked to refine this capitalist practice of men selling other men a type of masculinity for profit. *Penthouse* and *Hustler* launched in 1969 and 1974, respectively, as market competitors of *Playboy*. Each relied on increasing levels of explicit sexual content, nudity, vulgarity, and aggression toward women to distinguish itself and carve out a share of the market (Dines 2010; Dines and Levy 2015). This escalation in the level of vulgarity and aggression culminated in the use of gonzo pornography, which was pioneered in the 1990s and came to dominate the industry in the early 2000s. "Gonzo" pornography is an industry term that is synonymous with the concept of hardcore, which is defined by how much damage is done to a woman's body (Purcell 2012).

The level of violence toward women is a product of underlying economic and technological developments as opposed to changes in authentic sexual desire, individual agency, and the politics of free speech. The rise of MindGeek is a perfect exemplar of how these techno-economic forces come to shape consumers' encounters with particularized content. MindGeek (formerly known as Manwin) is currently the largest distributor of pornography on the web. It is a multinational, privately held technology company that bills itself as a leader in web design, information technology, web development, and search engine optimization. With headquarters in Luxembourg, MindGeek controls 8 of the top 10 pornographic websites including PornHub.com, YouPorn.com, and RedTube.com as well as large production companies including Playboy Plus Entertainment, Vivid, and Brazzers (Pinsker 2016). On its website, MindGeek.com, the company reports approximately 115 million daily visitors to its various sites, exposing them to 3 billion advertising impressions as they browse 15 terabytes of pornographic material. MindGeek did not arrive at such prominence in the industry through the production of pornographic material. Rather, it came to dominate the industry through software development and a mastery of algorithms and online analytics (Auerbach 2014; Hassan 2018).

MindGeek's origins, circa the late 1990s, can be traced to the development of software which allowed for the tracking and directing of consumers across multiple websites in order to collect and monetize user data on preferences (Auerbach 2014; Forrester 2016; Tarrant 2016). The software developers used pornography as a means to test and refine the software; pornography was a means to an economic end rather than a political end itself. One piece of software, titled Next-Generation Affiliate Tracking Software (NATS), organized the backend of membership-based websites in order to aggregate them into affiliate programs, offering paying members access to a set of curated sites organized by types or "niches" of pornographic content. Through the NATS software, webmasters were likewise able to tailor and refine the curation of content across those sites based on user data, motivated to attract paying members in an increasingly competitive online marketplace. Niche hypersexualized markets were—and still are—effective at drawing traffic in crowded, noisy environments (Dery 2007), and the type of material most likely to attract paying consumers was the gonzo/hardcore niche (Dines 2006; Johnson 2011).

Circa 2008, once again in an effort to stand out among the increasingly crowded market, affiliate programs began to move bits of content out from behind the paywall to offer free teasers in order to entice curious clickers (Johnson 2011). There were multiple consequences to this economic decision. First, sexual content, most often hardcore, became freely available without cost or age verification. "Free porn" became easily available to anyone, at any age. However, "free porn" is not actually free; rather, it became the feeder not only to enclose users within affiliate program websites but also the mass input needed to fuel MindGeek's new advertising software, TrafficJunky.com, that was designed to facilitate "ad impressions" through newly developing search engine optimization analytics, push marketing, and pay-to-click monetization schemes (Johnson

2010). Essentially, "free porn" allows the digital pornography industry to track, manage, and profit from anyone who clicks on an image, even, and especially, curious adolescents.

Second, while providing easy access to copious amounts of content had short-term payoffs for webmasters of affiliate programs in terms of driving traffic and increasing membership, the long-term consequence was the rise of now dominant aggregate sites such as PornHub.com or YouPorn.com, created, yet again, through software development by MindGeek. Tube or aggregator sites use algorithms to scoop up free content from across the web, which is then organized into thumbnails for easy browsing, tracking, and advertising. Essentially, MindGeek pirated all the free content made available by affiliate programs and then used search engine optimization to redirect traffic to newly formed aggregator tube sites, thus effectively putting webmasters out of business (Auerbach 2014). Affiliate programs are now relatively obsolete, having been consumed by MindGeek's aggregation bots, pirating algorithms, and mastery of search engine optimization. Through what is essentially a hostile takeover, a technology company now dominates the digital pornography industry (Forrester 2016; Tarrant 2016).

There are several important consequences of a digital pornography landscape that is more corporate and technological than personal and sexual. First, MindGeek bills itself as an expert in the use of search optimization analytics, which ensures that the content that is most likely to draw traffic and produce a profit will be the most visible and easily accessible. Thus, the presentation of content is skewed toward the sexual choices of the most frequent, experienced, and invested users. Research shows that acts of aggression such as choking, gagging, slapping, biting, pinching, bondage, and spanking are quite common in digital pornography (Bridges 2019; Bridges et al. 2010), with the overwhelming majority of acts (93%) targeting women (Klaassen and Peter 2015), including in non-heterosexual digital pornography (Carrotte, Davis, and Lim 2020). This raises serious concerns about the impact of digital pornography on the sexual development of adolescents, whose first encounter with sex will be curated by the tastes of a select group of high-frequency, advanced pornography users (Johnson et al. 2019).

Digital data collection represents a second set of concerns pertaining to the issues of privacy and safety. MindGeek operates one of the most sophisticated digital data collection and analysis operations on the web. The privately held company collects large amounts of highly personal and intimate information, which is fed to sophisticated algorithms in order to monetize both casual and serious users. MindGeek now collects, aggregates, and mines more user data than Netflix and Hulu combined (Hassan 2018). The industry leader remains on the cutting edge of technology including new artificial intelligence facial recognition of performers to provide more nuanced curation of content for users (Vincent 2017) and push marketing on social media such as Snapchat and Instagram, thus targeting adolescents (Berr 2018). There have been some attempts to install legal barriers such as user age verification or opt-in policies for cable and internet companies; however, technical and political difficulties have stymied these efforts (Golden 2016; Waterson 2019). MindGeek has acknowledged that 80% of the content collected and curated by bots and algorithms comes from unverifiable sources (Cole

2021) and has admitted that content featuring underage teenagers and child pornography is present on its websites (Caruso-Moro 2021). Given that algorithms and bots have been shown to deepen systems of inequality (Noble 2018; O'Neil 2016), the technological underpinnings of digital pornography directly challenge claims that it is a democratic representation of authentic sexual desire or a healthy environment for sexual exploration. This is particularly concerning for adolescents, who most likely first encounter pornography around middle school (Allen and Lavender-Stott 2015), before their first romantic relationship (Cheng, Ma, and Missari 2014), and whose only counternarrative is abstinence-only heteronormative sex education (Hunter, Figueredo, and Malamuth 2010; Kubicek et al. 2010; Morgan 2011).

Data Considerations and New Theoretical Possibilities

While the digital has clearly transformed the way in which pornography is encountered and consumed, there is very little in the way of critical analysis of how these new economic and technological forces have (re)shaped the individual's relationship with pornography. Research on digital pornography is quite copious, yet it centers largely on an exhaustive list of quantitative measures of individualized patterns, predictors, and outcomes of consumption (Wright 2020b). While early research on digital pornography did acknowledge the digital transformation, it did so most commonly to explain how exposure to digital pornography has become an almost ubiquitous experience for adolescents (Chen et al. 2013; Sabina, Wolak, and Finkelhor 2008; Weber, Quiring, and Daschmann 2012). In addition, it commonly sought to confirm that pornography consumption, even in the digital space, is still an overwhelmingly male phenomenon (Grubbs et al. 2019; Ševčíková and Daneback 2014).

Most other research on digital pornography renders invisible these new digital forces in terms of both measures and analysis, instead focusing on adding greater nuance to questions of impact (Wright 2021). Does digital pornography consumption relate to sexual behaviors, attitudes, and relationships? If so, in what way and through what pathways? Research on the associations between digital pornography consumption and sexual behavior is robust. Studies regularly find higher rates of digital pornography consumption to be associated with higher rates of risky sexual behaviors including earlier sexual debut, higher number of overall sexual partners, lower rates of condom use, use of drugs and/or alcohol during sex, increased likelihood of an extramarital affair, increased likelihood to have engaged in group sex or paid sex, and higher rates of sexually transmitted infections (Braithwaite et al. 2015; Hald, Malamuth, and Lange 2013; Harkness, Mullan, and Blaszczynski 2015; Peter and Valkenburg 2011; Wright 2013; Wright, Sun, and Steffen 2018). Exposure at younger ages increases the likelihood of risk (Sinković, Štulhofer, and Božić 2013). At minimum, the strength and consistency of the associations indicate that digital pornography consumption is a reliable indicator of sexual risk-taking and thus should be considered an important public health concern (Nelson and Rothman 2020).

Much care is taken in asking these questions, to hedge against causal arguments. In fact, so much care is taken that it becomes difficult to declare much of anything specific about individual experiences with pornography (Marshall and Miller 2019). Instead, focus is directed at slicing variables into smaller and smaller pieces in order to navigate the difficult political terrain that underlies the academic study of pornography (Ferguson, Nielsen, and Markey 2017; Wright 2020b). This political tension has produced a contested evidence base that makes it difficult to develop a clear understanding of how to respond politically, academically, or medically (Fisher and Kohut 2020; Nelson and Rothman 2020). A perfect example of this empirical quandary is research on the relationship between pornography and attitudes toward sexuality, gender roles, and violence. Those who consume digital pornography generally have more progressive attitudes toward sexuality, including more openness to diverse sexualities, support for gay marriage, and an overall less conservative approach to relationships (Kohut, Baer, and Watts 2016; Tokunaga, Wright, and Roskos 2018; Wright, Tokunaga, and Bae 2014). However, attitudes toward women are seemingly more hostile and regressive, with consumption rates having been shown to be associated with greater acceptance of violence toward women, greater endorsement of rape myths, and more regressive gender roles (Borgogna et al. 2019; Mikorski and Szymanski 2017; Wright, Tokunaga, and Kraus 2016). Additionally, several recent meta-analyses which included cross-sectional, longitudinal, and/or experimental studies found that digital pornography consumption was associated with an increased likelihood of verbal and physical aggression in relationships (Bridges 2019; Hald, Malamuth, and Yuen 2010; Wright, Tokunaga, and Kraus 2016). In other words, individual perceptions do not match empirical outcomes, and each outcome aligns with one side of the "porn war" debate; thus, engaging in any discussion about pornography is politically fraught.

Part of the reason for the "consistently inconsistent" findings in the literature may also have to do with the limitations of data, particularly related to generalizability and causality (Marshall and Miller 2019). For example, research that relies on user self-perceptions reports positive outcomes from consumption (Dwulit and Rzymski 2019; Miller, Hald, and Kidd 2018; Weinberg et al. 2010), while data that draws associations reveals diminished feelings of intimacy during sex (Johnson et al. 2019; Sun et al. 2016) and increased feelings of bodily insecurity during sexual relations (Johnson et al. 2019). Several recent systematic analyses have revealed that associational data on digital pornography consumption is overwhelmingly cross-sectional and thus can only speak to associations rather than causality. Data is also mostly drawn from convenience samples or clinical populations (Owens et al. 2012; Peter and Valkenburg 2016). The General Social Survey, the leading nationally representative longitudinal survey, contains a question about pornography use; but it is dated in its language in that it asks about viewing X-rated movies (Smith et al. 2020). However, it is one of the only publicly available measures of pornography use that does not rely on cross-sectional or clinical samples.

The definition of the concept of digital pornography is also inconsistent in its use and measurement, with virtually all studies using a researcher-generated definition and use measurements (Marshall and Miller 2019; Short et al. 2011).

Furthermore, questions related to digital pornography are almost always asked as empirical questions rather than theoretical ones, with very little in the way of new theory development (Wright 2013). The dominant theoretical framework in the study of sexual media is "sexual scripts theory," which holds that sexualized media images and narratives codify what counts as sexual behavior and desire and concatenate to form a heuristic processing model that is activated in the mind during sexual encounters to interpret and navigate situational behaviors and responses (Berger, Simon, and Gagnon 1973; Simon and Gagnon 1986; Wright 2020a). Heuristic processing of media describes how information is processed quickly, easily, and without much effort or deliberation, as opposed to systemic processing, which is about deliberation, weighing of fact, and conscious analysis (Hetsroni 2010). In other words, through the viewing of sexual media, individuals come to learn a script that shapes their understanding of their sexuality as well as their sexual worldview. These sexual scripts then function as an easily accessible mental model for sexual decision-making used to understand their own choices and preferences as well as to navigate situations with others. While the sexual scripts model is a reliable and robust theoretical framework for understanding sexual behavior across multiple disciplines (Simon and Gagnon 2003), it is grounded in theory that predates digital media and is a generalized theory applicable to all forms of media.

Recent theoretical work by Wright (2011, 2020a) has sought to integrate the sexual scripts framework with new theory and research from media and communications to study pornography specifically. In his 3AM theory of sexual media socialization, Wright (2020a) outlines pathways for the acquisition, activation, and application of the sexual script, with moderators and mediators operating at each stage of the process. Work using Wright's 3AM theory, for example, has demonstrated that gender is not a straightforward moderator of digital pornography as once thought. Men's relationship with pornography is more direct and operates more heuristically (Sun et al. 2016), whereas women's relationship requires some deliberation and intentionality with regard to activating the pornographic script into their sexual lives (Johnson et al. 2019). Once activated, however, the pornographic sexual script is similarly applied to the sexual experiences of heterosexual men and women; both are equally as likely to express interest in trying sexual behaviors learned via the pornographic sexual script and equally likely to have tried them (Bridges et al. 2016). Yet, when it comes to enjoyment of the more extreme forms of sexual behaviors commonly found in the modern pornographic script, heterosexual men and women differ significantly in their levels of enjoyment, with men showing greater enjoyment of extreme sexual acts (Ezzell et al. 2020).

While Wright's 3AM adaptation of the sexual scripts model represents new theory in the study of pornography, it does not apply directly to digital pornography or consider how the digital environment may (re)shape the social learning process of sexual scripts. For example, the structure of MindGeek's algorithm has significant implications for understanding the relationship between personality traits and digital pornography. Research demonstrates that adolescents, particularly boys, who are "sensation-seeking" (defined as eager to experience new, intense, or novel experiences or take heightened risks in search of new sensations) are more likely to use pornography and use it more often than non-sensation-seeking peers (Beyens, Vandenbosch, and Eggermont 2015; Ševčíková and Daneback 2014). Low self-control (Holt, Bossler, and May 2012), low self-esteem (Bőthe et al. 2020), a lower sense of personal autonomy (Weber, Quiring, and Daschmann 2012), and less satisfaction with life (Bőthe et al. 2020; Peter and Valkenburg 2006) are all negatively correlated with rates of pornography use, particularly for men. Additionally, adolescents whose peer group contains more delinquent behaviors are more likely to consume pornography (Hasking, Scheier, and Abdallah 2011; Holt, Bossler, and May 2012). In other words, males who are most likely to be reckless, impulsive, and cause trouble have higher rates of pornography consumption. As has been discussed, MindGeek's algorithm is recursively responsive to high-frequency users; those who consume the most have the most influence on what type of content is most prominent on the sites. Understanding these different pathways for the acquisition, activation, and application of particular sexual scripts in a digital environment is important given that pornography consumption is consistently associated with high-risk patterns of sexual behaviors (for reviews, see Grubbs et al. 2019; Wright et al. 2017), including violence and aggression (Bridges 2019; Hald, Malamuth, and Yuen 2010; Wright, Tokunaga, and Kraus 2016).

These empirical and theoretical challenges are both a reflection and a result of the fractious political environment surrounding the study of pornography. Anchored down by two opposing positions related to the impact of pornography on women's lives, research is now sorted into disciplinary enclaves with little empirical overlap. Gouvernet et al. (2020) evaluated 2,457 articles from 850 different journals using social network analysis to map patterns in the lexicon of pornography scholarship from 2006 to 2017, dates which deliberately corresponded to technological developments in the digital pornography industry. Based on keyword and cluster analysis, the authors concluded that there was a decline in the coherence of the literature base and a greater number of articles emphasizing the health risks for individuals and relationships. The disciplines that presented a coherent literature base included medicine and behavioral sciences, media studies, and criminal justice. The social sciences did not present as such a discipline; there are very few sociologists directly engaged in the study of digital pornography. These ideological tensions and empirical gaps indicate a need for (re)engagement by critical sociology to expand discussions beyond content and associations to empirically explore the complex ways in which the digital has transformed pornography, as a form of power, commerce, technology, and hypersexualized media. In other words, the study of digital pornography needs the attention of digital sociologists.

Digital Sociology: New Theory and Data for the Study of Digital Pornography

There are few examples of the application of a comprehensive digital sociological approach to the study of digital pornography. Early pioneers include Rimm (1994) and Mehta (2001), who randomly downloaded thousands of pornographic images from Usenet newsgroups to illustrate both the diversity and commercialization of pornography at the start of the internet age. Brubaker and Johnson (2008) as well as Paasonen (2006) decoded unsolicited email messages advertising male enhancement and/or pornography websites to discuss hegemonic gender ideology and power. More recent work utilizes digital data on pornography to evaluate the effectiveness of new "big data" measurements (Morichetta, Trevisan, and Vassio 2019) or to test new computer science tools for collecting social media data (Barfian et al. 2017) including digital forensics (Karamizadeh and Arabsorkhi 2018). There are a few studies that foreground the digital in their analysis of pornography, including understanding how algorithms can racialize the policing of child pornography (Thakor 2018), the impacts of computer-generated pornography on the video game experience (Saunders 2019), and, more commonly, to theorize how the digital has transformed the feminist pornographic debates (Paasonen et al. 2017). However, studies that marry a theoretical approach to the study of digital pornography with the immense power of digital data are needed to fully illustrate the potential of a digital sociological approach to the study of digital pornography.

My work is an early example of the application of critical sociological theory to the study of digital pornography through a social network analysis of digital data (Johnson 2010, 2011). Consulting with a computer scientist, I scraped the daily business reports published between 2007 and 2008 from X-Biz and AVN News, two major digital pornography industry trade publications. These daily reports document new and established connections between and among organizations, companies, and other business entities involved in the production, distribution, marketing, and monetization of digital pornography. We extracted 808 nodes with 1,076 relationships among them and coded the ties based on functionality (i.e., production, distribution, financial, marketing, etc.). We then used common social network analysis measures and sociograms to describe and visualize the network.

The analysis revealed a "core–periphery network" anchored by two strong "hubs" which operate as centers of power in these types of networks (see Johnson 2011 for a visual socio-gram of this network structure). This type of network structure is characterized by a set of highly interconnected powerful nodes called the "core" surrounded by a set of loosely or singularly connected nodes which constitute the "periphery" (Barabási 2002). The two dominant nodes—*Playboy* and *Hustler*—had not only the most connections (high-degree centrality) but also the most nodes in the core that were connected through them (high-betweenness centrality). The core of the network consisted entirely of business entities focused on production, technology, finance, and marketing. The periphery of the network serviced the consumers and consisted entirely of distribution sites where users found niche content. The nodes that coordinated between the core and the periphery were the affiliate program websites that eventually became subsumed by MindGeek, beginning around 2008. In other words, techno-economic concerns are the core organizing principles of the digital pornography industry; sexuality is literally a peripheral issue.

This core–periphery structure also provides insight into why research on pornography is "consistently inconsistent" (Marshall and Miller 2019) and why both sides of the "porn wars" debate may find validation. When a consumer seeks out digital pornography, they visit the nodes on the periphery where the niche websites are deliberately scattered to attract the curious clicker. To the consumer, these websites appear random, diverse, never-ending, and based on their personal choices. The political economy of user experience is materially designed to be empowering, individualized, and never-ending. Thus, when scholars ask users about their experiences, users report positive feelings of exploration and empowerment. And when scholars approach digital pornography from the vantage point of a consumer, the content and experience appear diverse and reflective of user preference. These consumer perspectives are not accidental; rather, they are by design.

However, when approached from the perspective of the industry, the network reveals a tightly organized techno-economic core composed of software developers, search engine optimization analytics, bots, algorithms, and financial and marketing companies. Using various monetization strategies including push marketing, advertising, memberships, and free click-bait content, the core of the network directs users across a labyrinth of niche content in order to optimize user data for maximum profit. The goal of the industry is not sexual empowerment or sexual health. Rather, just like any other capitalist enterprise, the goal is profit and expanding market share. Thus, when research is focused on the impact of digital pornography on sexual health, research captures the negative consequences of commodified sexuality.

More recent analysis of the political economy of the digital pornography industry reveals a maturing industry that has more effectively concentrated power (Dines and Levy 2015, 2019; Johnson et al. 2019). Through a series of mergers and acquisitions, MindGeek has now replaced *Playboy* and *Hustler* as the core organizing node of the digital pornography industry and is now considered to have single monopolistic power over the industry (Auerbach 2014; Constine 2019). MindGeek's monopoly has come through pirating content, exploitative labor practices, and manipulative cross-platform tracking, all of which have essentially put most other independent and/or DIY pornography agencies out of business. MindGeek has almost complete market dominance over the production and distribution of digital pornography. Even among those scholars who were most optimistic about the democratization potential of digital pornography, there is a growing awareness of the ways in which hidden techno-economic structures are creating more abusive and exploitive labor and user practices (Paasonen et al. 2017). Most recently, there have been several legal actions taken to mitigate user risks created by MindGeek including challenging the company's ability to ensure that all content on its sites abides by the age and consent statutes (Batty 2018; Cole 2021; Dines and Levy 2018).

To fully realize the promise of digital sociology requires the application of critical sociological theory to big data. To my knowledge, the only big data exploration of digital pornography is by Ogas and Gaddam (2011) in their book *A Billion Wicked Thoughts*, in which two neuroscientists analyze a year's worth of search terms found through a search engine aggregator. What is essentially a sorting and counting of 55 million sexual terms (out of a total of 400 million), the conclusions drawn were unremarkable and reified traditional hegemonic notions of gender—that is, humans like sex; men like pornography, particularly involving young girls; and women like romance novels. Such conventional understandings of sex and gender are the path of least resistance without engagement from critical social scientists, particularly sociologists who are most adept at empirical macro-analysis related to how social structures and social interactions produce and reproduce power and inequality.

Summary and Conclusion

In sum, research shows that digital pornography functions as a powerful sexual script in the lives of both adolescents and adults. While research demonstrates consistency in associations with risky sexual behavior and declining sexual satisfaction and relational intimacy, it also reveals positive self-reports about the effects of consumption and feelings of empowerment. Recent empirical work on mediators and moderators indicates that the pathways for sexual script socialization are complex, especially for women. These mixed signals stem from methodological limitations in the data as well as from the fractious ideological debates that have long dominated the field of study, all of which has led to a lack of innovation in theory and data. Furthermore, the political economy of digital pornography presents significant challenges to the development of a cohesive narrative about the role of digital pornography in everyday life. First, the core–periphery structure of the network allows for opposing interpretations of empowerment and choice, thus providing little resolution to the "porn wars" debate. Second, the hidden technological underpinnings that create the massive scope and chaotic presentation of content make it difficult to comprehensively evaluate either the diversity of content or the impact on users through conventional social science sampling methodologies.

Thus, the study of digital pornography is open for a paradigm readjustment, which I argue should be led by digital sociology. My work on the political economy of the digital pornography industry reveals the power of digital data and new methodologies to reveal hidden structures in the online economy of digital pornography. Research has become bifurcated into either a broad cultural studies approach focused on how diverse content can be read by diverse audiences or an individual/social-psychological approach focused on behaviors and relationships. What is missing is a critical analysis of the structural and material realities of a commercialized media form that has become ubiquitous in the sexual lives of adolescents. Given that digital pornography now serves as the normative framework for understanding sexuality and sexual interactions as well as the primary, if not sole, source of sexual education in a time of heteronormative abstinence-only curricula, a digital sociologist approach is essential to effectively challenge intersecting systems of inequality and power in order to ensure access to non-commodified comprehensive sexual education and positive sexual health for everyone.

REFERENCES

Allen, Katherine R., and Erin S. Lavender-Stott. 2015. "Family Contexts of Informal Sex Education: Young Men's Perceptions of First Sexual Images." *Family Relations* 64, no. 3: 393–406.

Attwood, Feona. 2005. "What Do People Do with Porn? Qualitative Research into the Consumption, Use, and Experience of Pornography and Other Sexually Explicit Media." *Sexuality and Culture* 9, no. 2: 65–86.

Attwood, Feona. 2007. "No Money Shot? Commerce, Pornography and New Sex Taste Cultures." *Sexualities* 10, no. 4: 441–456.

Auerbach, David. 2014. "Vampire Porn: MindGeek is a cautionary tale of consolidating production and distribution in a single, monopolistic owner." *Slate*, October 23. https://slate.com/technology/2014/10/mindgeek-porn-monopoly-its-dominance-is-a-cautionary-tale-for-other-industries.html.

Barabási, Albert-László. 2002. *Linked: The New Science of Networks*. Cambridge: Perseus.

Barfian, Edo, Bambang Heru Iswanto, and Sani Muhamad Isa. 2017. "Twitter Pornography Multilingual Content Identification Based on Machine Learning." *Procedia Computer Science* 116:129–36.

Barss, Patchen. 2011. *The Erotic Engine How Pornography Has Powered Mass Communication, from Gutenberg to Google*. Toronto: Anchor Canada.

Batty, David. 2018. "Child Abuse Images Increasingly Hidden on Adult Pornography Sites." *The Guardian*, April 17. http://www.theguardian.com/society/2018/apr/18/child-abuse-images-increasingly-hidden-on-adult-pornography-sites.

Berger, Alan S., William Simon, and John H. Gagnon. 1973. "Youth and Pornography in Social Context." *Archives of Sexual Behavior* 2, no. 4: 279–308.

Berr, Jonathan. 2018. "Despite 'No Nudity Rule,' Instagram Is Chock Full of Pornography." *Forbes*, September 28. https://www.forbes.com/sites/jonathanberr/2018/09/28/despite-no-nudity-rule-instagram-is-chock-full-of-pornography/.

Beyens, Ine, Laura Vandenbosch, and Steven Eggermont. 2015. "Early Adolescent Boys' Exposure to Internet Pornography: Relationships to Pubertal Timing, Sensation Seeking, and Academic Performance." *Journal of Early Adolescence* 35, no. 8: 1045–1068.

Borgogna, Nicholas C., Ryon C. McDermott, Brandon R. Browning, Jameson D. Beach, and Stephen L. Aita. 2019. "How Does Traditional Masculinity Relate to Men and Women's Problematic Pornography Viewing?" *Sex Roles* 80, no. 11: 693–706. https://doi.org/10.1007/s11199-018-0967-8.

Bőthe, Beáta, István Tóth-Király, Marc N. Potenza, Gábor Orosz, and Zsolt Demetrovics. 2020. "High-Frequency Pornography Use May Not Always Be Problematic." *Journal of Sexual Medicine* 17, no. 4: 793–811. https://doi.org/10.1016/j.jsxm.2020.01.007.

Braithwaite, Scott R., Gwen Coulson, Krista Keddington, and Frank D. Fincham. 2015. "The Influence of Pornography on Sexual Scripts and Hooking Up among Emerging Adults in College." *Archives of Sexual Behavior* 44, no. 1: 111–123.

Bridges, Ana J. 2019. "Pornography and Sexual Assault." In *Handbook of Sexual Assault and Sexual Assault Prevention*, edited by W. T. O'Donohue and P. A. Schewe, 129–149. Cham, Switzerland: Springer International. https://doi.org/10.1007/978-3-030-23645-8_8.

Bridges, Ana J., Chyng F. Sun, Matthew B. Ezzell, and Jennifer Johnson. 2016. "Sexual Scripts and the Sexual Behavior of Men and Women Who Use Pornography." *Sexualization, Media, & Society* 2, no. 4. https://doi.org/10.1177%2F2374623816668275.

Bridges, Ana J., Robert Wosnitzer, Erica Scharrer, Chyng Sun, and Rachael Liberman. 2010. "Aggression and Sexual Behavior in Best-Selling Pornography Videos: A Content Analysis Update." *Violence Against Women* 16, no. 10: 1065–1085.

Brown, Jane D. and Kelly L. L'Engle. 2009. "X-Rated: Sexual Attitudes and Behaviors Associated with US Early Adolescents' Exposure to Sexually Explicit Media." *Communication Research* 36, no. 1: 129–151.

Brubaker, Sarah J. and Jennifer A. Johnson. 2008. " 'Pack a More Powerful Punch' and 'Lay the Pipe': Erectile Enhancement Discourse as a Body Project for Masculinity." *Journal of Gender Studies* 17, no. 2: 131–146. https://doi.org/10.1080/09589230802008899.

Buchholz, Katharina. 2019. "Infographic: How Much of the Internet Consists of Porn?" Statista, February 11. https://www.statista.com/chart/16959/share-of-the-internet-that-is-porn/.

Carrotte, Elise R., Angela C. Davis, and Megan S. C. Lim. 2020. "Sexual Behaviors and Violence in Pornography: Systematic Review and Narrative Synthesis of Video Content Analyses." *Journal of Medical Internet Research* 22, no. 5. https://doi.org/10.2196/16702.

Caruso-Moro, Luca. 2021. "MindGeek Executives Testify before Ethics Committee over Allegations of Illegal Content on Pornhub." CTV News, February 5. https://montreal.ctvnews.ca/mindgeek-executives-testify-before-ethics-committee-over-allegations-of-illegal-content-on-pornhub-1.5296887.

Castells, Manuel, Sarah Banet-Weiser, Sviatlana Hlebik, Giorgos Kallis, Sarah Pink, Kristen Seale, Lisa J. Servon, Lana Swartz, and Angelos Vavarousiset al. 2017. *Another Economy Is Possible: Culture and Economy in a Time of Crisis*. Cambridge: Polity.

Chen, An-Sing, Mark Leung, Chih-Hao Chen, and Shu Ching Yang. 2013. "Exposure to Internet Pornography among Taiwanese Adolescents." *Social Behavior and Personality: An International Journal* 41, no. 1: 157–164.

Cheng, Simon, Josef (Kuo-Hsun) Ma, and Stacy Missari. 2014. "The Effects of Internet Use on Adolescents' First Romantic and Sexual Relationships in Taiwan." *International Sociology* 29, no. 4: 324–347.

Cole, Samantha. 2021. "Watch Pornhub Execs Being Grilled for Abuse on Their Platform." Vice, February 8. https://www.vice.com/en/article/93wmjy/pornhub-executives-parliament-hearing.

Constine, Josh. 2019. "Why You Don't Want Tumblr Sold to Exploitative Pornhub." TechCrunch, May 2. https://social.techcrunch.com/2019/05/02/porns-secret-monopoly/.

Coopersmith, Jonathan. 2006. "Does Your Mother Know What You Really Do? The Changing Nature and Image of Computer-Based Pornography." *History and Technology* 22, no. 1: 1–25.

Daniels, Jessie, Karen Gregory, and Tressie McMillan Cottom, eds. 2016. *Digital Sociologies*. Bristol, UK: Policy Press.

Davidson, Cathy N. 2017. "Revolutionizing the University for the World We Live in Now." HigherEdJobs, September 27. https://www.higheredjobs.com/blog/postDisplay.cfm?post=1415&blog=20.

Dery, Mark. 2007. "Naked Lunch: Talking Realcore with Sergio Messina." In *C'lickme: A Netporn Studies Reader*, edited by K. Jacobs, M. Janssen, and M. Pasquinelli, 17–30. Institute of Network Cultures.

Dines, Gail. 2006. "The White Man's Burden: Gonzo Pornography and the Construction of Black Masculinity." *Yale Journal of Law and Feminism* 18, no. 1: 283–297.

Dines, Gail. 2010. *Pornland: How Pornography Has Hijacked Our Sexual Culture*. Boston: Beacon Press.

Dines, Gail and David L. Levy. 2015. "Why Your Father's Playboy Can't Compete in Today's World of Hardcore Porn.: Scroll. In, October 23. http://scroll.in/article/764164/why-your-fathers-playboy-cant-compete-in-todays-world-of-hardcore-porn.

Dines, Gail and David L. Levy. 2018. "Child Pornography May Make a Comeback after Court Ruling Guts Regulations Protecting Minors." The Conversation, August 23. http://theconversation.com/child-pornography-may-make-a-comeback-after-court-ruling-guts-regulations-protecting-minors-101763.

Dines, Gail and David L. Levy. 2019. "Porn 'Disruption' Makes Stormy Daniels a Rare Success in Increasingly Abusive Industry." The Conversation, April 9. http://theconversation.com/porn-disruption-makes-stormy-daniels-a-rare-success-in-increasingly-abusive-industry-94534.

Dworkin, Ronald. 1981. "Is There a Right to Pornography?" *Oxford Journal of Legal Studies* 1, no. 2: 177–212.

Dwulit, Aleksandra D. and Piotr Rzymski. 2019. "Prevalence, Patterns and Self-Perceived Effects of Pornography Consumption in Polish University Students: A Cross-Sectional Study." *International Journal of Environmental Research and Public Health* 16, no. 10:1861. https://doi.org/10.3390/ijerph16101861.

Ezzell, Matthew B., Jennifer A. Johnson, Ana J. Bridges, and Chyng F. Sun. 2020. "I (Dis)Like It Like That: Gender, Pornography, and Liking Sex." *Journal of Sex & Marital Therapy* 46, no. 5: 460–473.

Felt, Mylynn. 2016. "Social Media and the Social Sciences: How Researchers Employ Big Data Analytics." *Big Data & Society* 3, no. 1. https://doi.org/10.1177/2053951716645828.

Ferguson, Christopher J., Rune K. L. Nielsen, and Patrick M. Markey. 2017. "Does Sexy Media Promote Teen Sex? A Meta-Analytic and Methodological Review." *Psychiatric Quarterly* 88, no. 2: 349–358. https://doi.org/10.1007/s11126-016-9442-2.

Fisher, William A., and Taylor Kohut. 2020. "Reading Pornography: Methodological Considerations in Evaluating Pornography Research." *Journal of Sexual Medicine* 17, no. 2: 195–209. https://doi.org/10.1016/j.jsxm.2019.11.257.

Forrester, Katrina. 2016. "Making Sense of Modern Pornography." The New Yorker, September 19. https://www.newyorker.com/magazine/2016/09/26/making-sense-of-modern-pornography.

Golden, Hallie. 2016. "Utah Lawmaker Wants Opt-In Requirement for Porn." AP News, May 20. https://apnews.com/a0cbec8aab324f31b9dce2ff6b657e0c.

Gouvernet, Brice, Yassamine Hentati, Maria Teresa Rebelo, Amine Rezrazi, Fabrice Sebbe, and Serge Combaluzier. 2020. "Porn Studies or Pornology? Network Analysis of the Keywords of Scientific Articles Published between 2006 and 2017." *Porn Studies* 7, no. 2: 228–246.

Grubbs, Joshua B., Samuel L. Perry, Joshua A. Wilt, and Rory C. Reid. 2019. "Pornography Problems due to Moral Incongruence: An Integrative Model with a Systematic Review and Meta-Analysis." *Archives of Sexual Behavior* 48, no. 2: 397–415.

Hald, Gert M., Neil M. Malamuth, and Theis Lange. 2013. "Pornography and Sexist Attitudes among Heterosexuals." *Journal of Communication* 63, no. 4: 638–660.

Hald, Gert M., Neil M. Malamuth, and Carlin Yuen. 2010. "Pornography and Attitudes Supporting Violence against Women: Revisiting the Relationship in Nonexperimental Studies." *Aggressive Behavior* 36, no. 1: 14–20. https://doi.org/10.1002/ab.20328.

Hardy, Simon. 2008. "The Pornography of Reality." *Sexualities* 11, no. 1–2: 60–64.

Harkness, Emily L., Barbara Mullan, and Alex Blaszczynski. 2015. "Association between Pornography Use and Sexual Risk Behaviors in Adult Consumers: A Systematic Review." *Cyberpsychology, Behavior, and Social Networking* 18, no. 2: 59–71.

Hasking, Penelope A., Lawrence M. Scheier, and Arbi B. Abdallah. 2011. "The Three Latent Classes of Adolescent Delinquency and the Risk Factors for Membership in Each Class." *Aggressive Behavior* 37, no. 1: 19–35.

Hassan, Aisha. 2018. "Porn Sites Collect More User Data than Netflix or Hulu. This is What They Do with It." Quartz, December 13. https://qz.com/1407235/porn-sites-collect-more-user-data-than-netflix-or-hulu-this-is-what-they-do-with-it/?utm_source=reddit.com.

Hetsroni, Amir. 2010. "Violence in Mainstream TV Advertising: A Comparison of the Representation of Physical Aggression in American and Israeli Commercials." *Communications* 35, no. 1: 29–44.

Hindman, Matthew. 2018. *The Internet Trap: How the Digital Economy Builds Monopolies and Undermines Democracy*. Princeton, NJ: Princeton University Press.

Holt, Thomas J., Adam M. Bossler, and David C. May. 2012. "Low Self-Control, Deviant Peer Associations, and Juvenile Cyberdeviance." *American Journal of Criminal Justice* 37, no. 3: 378–395.

Hunter, John A., Aurelio J. Figueredo, and Neil M. Malamuth. 2010. "Developmental Pathways into Social and Sexual Deviance." *Journal of Family Violence* 25, no. 2: 141–148.

Jacobs, Katrien. 2007. *Netporn: DIY Web Culture and Sexual Politics*. Lanham, MD: Rowman & Littlefield.

Jensen, Robert. 2009. *Getting Off: Pornography and the End of Masculinity*. Boston: South End Press.

Johnson, Jennifer A. 2010. "To Catch a Curious Clicker: A Social Network Analysis of the Online Pornography Industry." In *Everyday Pornography*, edited by K. Boyle, 159–175. London and New York: Routledge.

Johnson, Jennifer A. 2011. "Mapping the Feminist Political Economy of the Online Commercial Pornography Industry: A Network Approach." *International Journal of Media & Cultural Politics* 7, no. 2: 189–208.

Johnson, Jennifer A., Matthew B. Ezzell, Ana J. Bridges, and Chyng F. Sun. 2019. "Pornography and Heterosexual Women's Intimate Experiences with a Partner." *Journal of Women's Health* 28, no. 9: 1254–1265. https://doi.org/10.1089/jwh.2018.7006.

Kamvar, Maryam and Shumeet Baluja. 2006. "A Large Scale Study of Wireless Search Behavior: Google Mobile Search." In *CHI '06: Proceedings of the SIGCHI Conference on Human Factors in Computing Systems*, 701–709. New York: ACM Press. https://doi.org/10.1145/1124772.1124877.

Karamizadeh, Sasan and Abouzar Arabsorkhi. 2018. "Methods of Pornography Detection: Review." In *ICCMS 2018: Proceedings of the 10th International Conference on*

Computer Modeling and Simulation, 33–38. New York: ACM Press. https://doi.org/10.1145/3177457.3177484.

Klaassen, Marleen J. E., and Jochen Peter. 2015. "Gender (In)Equality in Internet Pornography: A Content Analysis of Popular Pornographic Internet Videos." *Journal of Sex Research* 52, no. 7: 721–735.

Kohut, Taylor, Jodie L. Baer, and Brendan Watts. 2016. "Is Pornography Really about 'Making Hate to Women?' Pornography Users Hold More Gender Egalitarian Attitudes than Nonusers in a Representative American Sample." *Journal of Sex Research* 53, no. 1: 1–11. https://doi.org/10.1080/00224499.2015.1023427.

Kubicek, Katrina, William J. Beyer, George Weiss, Ellen Iverson, and Michele D. Kipke. 2010. "In the Dark: Young Men's Stories of Sexual Initiation in the Absence of Relevant Sexual Health Information." *Health Education & Behavior* 37, no. 2: 243–263.

Lupton, Deborah. 2014. *Digital Sociology*. London and New York: Routledge.

MacKinnon, Catharine A. 1996. *Only Words*. Cambridge, MA: Harvard University Press.

Marres, Noortje. 2017. *Digital Sociology: The Reinvention of Social Research*. Cambridge: Polity Press.

Marshall, Ethan A., and Holly A. Miller. 2019. "Consistently Inconsistent: A Systematic Review of the Measurement of Pornography Use." *Aggression and Violent Behavior* 48: 169–179. https://doi.org/10.1016/j.avb.2019.08.019.

McChesney, Robert W. 2013. *Digital Disconnect: How Capitalism Is Turning the Internet against Democracy*. New York: New Press.

McChesney, Robert W. 2016. *Rich Media, Poor Democracy: Communication Politics in Dubious Times*. New York: New Press.

McKee, Alan. 2009. "Social Scientists Don't Say 'Titwank.'" *Sexualities* 12, no. 5: 629–646.

McNair, Brian. 2013. *Porno? Chic!: How Pornography Changed the World and Made It a Better Place*. New York and London: Routledge.

McRobbie, Angela. 2008. "Young Women and Consumer Culture." *Cultural Studies* 22, no. 5: 531–550. https://doi.org/10.1080/09502380802245803.

Mehta, M. D. 2001. "Pornography in Usenet: A Study of 9,800 Randomly Selected Images." *CyberPsychology & Behavior* 4, no. 6: 695–703.

Mikorski, Renee and Dawn M. Szymanski. 2017. "Masculine Norms, Peer Group, Pornography, Facebook, and Men's Sexual Objectification of Women." *Psychology of Men & Masculinity* 18, no. 4: 257–267. https://doi.org/10.1037/men0000058.

Miller, Dan J., Gert M. Hald, and Garry Kidd. 2018. "Self-Perceived Effects of Pornography Consumption among Heterosexual Men." *Psychology of Men & Masculinity* 19, no. 3: 469–476. https://doi.org/10.1037/men0000112.

Morgan, Elizabeth M. 2011. "Associations between Young Adults' Use of Sexually Explicit Materials and Their Sexual Preferences, Behaviors, and Satisfaction." *Journal of Sex Research* 48, no. 6: 520–530. https://doi.org/10.1080/00224499.2010.543960.

Morichetta, Andrea, Martino Trevisan, and Luca Vassio. 2019. "Characterizing Web Pornography Consumption from Passive Measurements." In *PAM 2019: Passive and Active Measurement*, edited by D. Choffnes and M. Barcellos, 304–316. Cham, Switzerland: Springer. https://doi.org/10.1007/978-3-030-15986-3_20.

Naughton, John. 2018. "Growth of Internet Porn Tells Us More about Ourselves than Technology." *The Guardian*, December 30. http://www.theguardian.com/commentisfree/2018/dec/30/internet-porn-says-more-about-ourselves-than-technology.

Nelson, Kimberly M., and Emily F. Rothman. 2020. "Should Public Health Professionals Consider Pornography a Public Health Crisis?" *American Journal of Public Health* 110, no. 2: 151–153. https://doi.org/10.2105/AJPH.2019.305498.

Noble, Safiya U. 2018. *Algorithms of Oppression: How Search Engines Reinforce Racism*. New York: New York University Press.

Ogas, Ogi and Sai Gaddam. 2011. *A Billion Wicked Thoughts: What the World's Largest Experiment Reveals about Human Desire*. New York: Dutton.

O'Neil, Cathy. 2016. *Weapons of Math Destruction: How Big Data Increases Inequality and Threatens Democracy*. New York: Broadway Books.

Owens, Eric W., Richard J. Behun, Jill C. Manning, and Rory C. Reid. 2012. "The Impact of Internet Pornography on Adolescents: A Review of the Research." *Sexual Addiction & Compulsivity* 19, no. 1–2: 99–122.

Paasonen, Susanna. 2006. "Email from Nancy Nutsucker: Representation and Gendered Address in Online Pornography." *European Journal of Cultural Studies* 9, no. 4: 403–420.

Paasonen, Susanna. 2011. "Online Pornography: Ubiquitous and Effaced." In *The Handbook of Internet Studies*, edited by M. Consalvo and C. Ess, 424–439. Chichester, UK: Wiley-Blackwell.

Paasonen, Susanna, Kath Albury, Zahra Stardust, John Mercer, Sharif Mowlabocus, Brady Robards, and Clarissa Smith. 2017. "Digital Networks, Digital Pub(l)ics (1): Labour, Pleasure, Porn." Paper presented at Networked Publics: 18th Annual Conference of the Association of Internet Researchers, Tartu, Estonia, October 19–21.

Peter, Jochen and Patti M. Valkenburg. 2006. "Adolescents' Exposure to Sexually Explicit Material on the Internet." *Communication Research* 33, no. 2: 178–204. https://doi.org/10.1177/0093650205285369.

Peter, Jochen and Patti M. Valkenburg. 2011. "The Use of Sexually Explicit Internet Material and Its Antecedents: A Longitudinal Comparison of Adolescents and Adults." *Archives of Sexual Behavior* 40, no. 5: 1015–1025.

Peter, Jochen and Patti M. Valkenburg. 2016. "Adolescents and Pornography: A Review of 20 Years of Research." *Journal of Sex Research* 53, no. 4–5: 509–531.

Pinsker, Joe. 2016. "The Hidden Economics of Porn." The Atlantic, April 4. https://www.theatlantic.com/business/archive/2016/04/pornography-industry-economics-tarrant/476580/.

Pornhub Insights. 2019. "The 2019 Year in Review." December 11. https://www.pornhub.com/insights/2019-year-in-review.

Purcell, Natalie J. 2012. *Violence and the Pornographic Imaginary: The Politics of Sex, Gender, and Aggression in Hardcore Pornography*. London and New York: Routledge.

Rimm, Marty. 1994. "Marketing Pornography on the Information Superhighway: A Survey of 917,410 Images, Descriptions, Short Stories, and Animations Downloaded 8.5 Million Times by Consumers in over 2000 Cities in Forty Countries, Provinces, and Territories." *Georgetown Law Journal* 83, no. 5: 1849.

Sabina, Chiara, Janis Wolak, and David Finkelhor. 2008. "The Nature and Dynamics of Internet Pornography Exposure for Youth." *CyberPsychology & Behavior* 11, no. 6: 691–693.

Saunders, Rebecca. 2019. "Computer-Generated Pornography and Convergence: Animation and Algorithms as New Digital Desire." *Convergence* 25, no. 2: 241–259. https://doi.org/10.1177/1354856519833591.

Selwyn, Neil. 2019. *What Is Digital Sociology?* Cambridge: Polity Press.

Ševčíková, Anna and Kristian Daneback. 2014. "Online Pornography Use in Adolescence: Age and Gender Differences." *European Journal of Developmental Psychology* 11, no. 6: 674–686.

Shirky, Clay. 2008. *Here Comes Everybody: The Power of Organizing without Organizations*. New York: Penguin Press.

Short, Mary B., Lora Black, Angela H. Smith, Chad T. Wetterneck, and Daryl E. Wells. 2011. "A Review of Internet Pornography Use Research: Methodology and Content from the Past 10 Years." *Cyberpsychology, Behavior, and Social Networking* 15, no. 1: 13–23. https://doi.org/10.1089/cyber.2010.0477.

Simon, William and John H. Gagnon. 1986. "Sexual Scripts: Permanence and Change." *Archives of Sexual Behavior* 15, no. 2: 97–120.

Simon, William and John H. Gagnon. 2003. "Sexual Scripts: Origins, Influences and Changes." *Qualitative Sociology* 26, no. 4: 491–497. https://doi.org/10.1023/B:QUAS.0000005053.99846.e5.

Sinković, Matija, Aleksandar Štulhofer, and Jasmina Božić. 2013. "Revisiting the Association between Pornography Use and Risky Sexual Behaviors: The Role of Early Exposure to Pornography and Sexual Sensation Seeking." *Journal of Sex Research* 50, no. 7: 633–641.

Smith, Tom W., Michael Davern, Jeremy Freese, and Stephen L. Morgan. 2020. General social surveys, 1972–2018. National Science Foundation, GSS Data Explorer. Chicago: NORC, 2018: NORC at the University of Chicago [producer and distributor]. Data accessed from the GSS Data Explorer website at gssdataexplorer.norc.org.

Sun, Chyng, Ana Bridges, Jennifer A. Johnson, and Matthew B. Ezzell. 2016. "Pornography and the Male Sexual Script: An Analysis of Consumption and Sexual Relations." *Archives of Sexual Behavior* 45, no. 4: 983–994. https://doi.org/10.1007/s10508-014-0391-2.

Tarrant, Shira. 2016. *The Pornography Industry: What Everyone Needs to Know*. New York: Oxford University Press.

Thakor, Mitali. 2018. "Digital Apprehensions: Policing, Child Pornography, and the Algorithmic Management of Innocence." *Catalyst: Feminism, Theory, Technoscience* 4, no. 1: 1–16.

Tokunaga, Robert S., Paul J. Wright, and Joseph E. Roskos. 2018. "Pornography and Impersonal Sex." *Human Communication Research* 45, no. 1: 78–118. https://doi.org/10.1093/hcr/hqy014.

Van Dijk, Jan A.G.M., and Kenneth L. Hacker. 2018. *Internet and Democracy in the Network Society*. London and New York: Routledge.

Vincent, James. 2017. "Pornhub Is Using Machine Learning to Automatically Tag Its 5 Million Videos." The Verge, October 11. https://www.theverge.com/2017/10/11/16459646/pornhub-machine-learning-ai-video-tagging.

Waterson, Jim. 2019. "UK Drops Plans for Online Pornography Age Verification System." *The Guardian*, October 16. https://www.theguardian.com/culture/2019/oct/16/uk-drops-plans-for-online-pornography-age-verification-system.

Weber, Mathias, Oliver Quiring, and Gregor Daschmann. 2012. "Peers, Parents and Pornography: Exploring Adolescents' Exposure to Sexually Explicit Material and Its Developmental Correlates." *Sexuality & Culture* 16, no. 4: 408–427.

Weinberg, Martin S., Colin J. Williams, Sibyl Kleiner, and Yasmiyn Irizarry. 2010. "Pornography, Normalization, and Empowerment." *Archives of Sexual Behavior* 39, no. 6: 1389–1401. https://doi.org/10.1007/s10508-009-9592-5.

Wilkinson, Eleanor. 2017. "The Diverse Economies of Online Pornography: From Paranoid Readings to Post-Capitalist Futures." *Sexualities* 20, no. 8: 981–998. https://doi.org/10.1177/1363460716675141.

Williams, Linda, ed. 2004. *Porn Studies*. Durham, NC: Duke University Press. https://muse.jhu.edu/book/69560.

Wright, Paul J. 2011. "Mass Media Effects on Youth Sexual Behavior Assessing the Claim for Causality." *Annals of the International Communication Association* 35, no. 1: 343–385. https://doi.org/10.1080/23808985.2011.11679121.

Wright, Paul J. 2013. "US Males and Pornography, 1973–2010: Consumption, Predictors, Correlates." *Journal of Sex Research* 50, no. 1: 60–71.

Wright, Paul J. 2020a. "Media and sexuality." In *Media Effects: Advances in Theory and Research*, 4th ed., edited by M. B. Oliver, A. A. Raney, and J. Bryant, 227–242. London and New York: Routledge.

Wright, Paul J. 2020b. "Pornography and Sexual Behavior: Do Sexual Attitudes Mediate or Confound?" *Communication Research* 47, no. 3: 451–475. https://doi.org/10.1177/0093650218796363.

Wright, Paul J. 2021. "Overcontrol in Pornography Research: Let It Go, Let It Go . . . " *Archives of Sexual Behavior* 50, no. 2: 387–392. https://doi.org/10.1007/s10508-020-01902-9.

Wright, Paul J., Chyng Sun, and Nicola Steffen. 2018. "Pornography Consumption, Perceptions of Pornography as Sexual Information, and Condom Use." *Journal of Sex & Marital Therapy* 44, no. 8: 800–805.

Wright, Paul J., Robert S. Tokunaga, and Soyoung Bae. 2014. "More than a Dalliance? Pornography Consumption and Extramarital Sex Attitudes among Married U.S. Adults." *Psychology of Popular Media Culture* 3, no. 2: 97–109. https://doi.org/10.1037/ppm0000024.

Wright, Paul J., Robert S. Tokunaga, and Ashley Kraus. 2016. "A Meta-Analysis of Pornography Consumption and Actual Acts of Sexual Aggression in General Population Studies." *Journal of Communication* 66, no. 1: 183–205. https://doi.org/10.1111/jcom.12201.

Wright, Paul J., Robert S. Tokunaga, Ashley Kraus, and Elyssa Klann. 2017. "Pornography Consumption and Satisfaction: A Meta-Analysis." *Human Communication Research* 43, no. 3: 315–343. https://doi.org/10.1111/hcre.12108.

Wynn, Jonathan R. 2009. "Digital Sociology: Emergent Technologies in the Field and the Classroom." *Sociological Forum* 24, no. 2: 448–456.

CHAPTER 15

USE OF INFORMATION AND COMMUNICATION TECHNOLOGIES AMONG OLDER ADULTS

Usage Differences, Health-Related Impacts, and Future Needs

ALEXANDER SEIFERT AND SHELIA R. COTTEN

We live in a society where we are surrounded by technological innovations and digital content. On a daily basis, individuals may read the latest news on a tablet, text with social ties, track daily activities through wearable activity trackers (e.g., smartwatches, Fitbit, Garmin, and other wearable technologies), or pay digitally with smartphone apps. The digitalization of society yields opportunities to maintain daily life activities and stay engaged with social ties. However, for individuals who are not adept at using technology or find it difficult to adapt to technological innovations, living in a digitalized society may be problematic (Lupton 2015). In addition, specific portions of the US population (and worldwide) do not have direct or immediate access to such new technologies and, thus, have fewer opportunities to use these devices to garner additional benefits for their daily lives (Francis et al. 2019a). This "digital divide" can be understood as a globally applicable term for the perceived gap between those who have access to the latest information and communication technologies (ICTs) and those who do not (Compaine 2001). Alongside sociodemographic characteristics (e.g., age, gender, education, income) and personal factors (e.g., health, attitudes toward technologies, anxiety related to using ICTs), there are also environmental factors, such as the ICT infrastructure and the wealth status of the region, that shape the digital divide (Warschauer 2004; Korupp and Szydlik 2005; Wang, Rau, and Salvendy 2011; Mitzner et al. 2019).

This chapter focuses on one group that often falls on the wrong side of the digital divide—older adults. Though there are myriad ways to classify older adults, we focus on individuals aged 65 and older as this is a common age classification by federal agencies and other organizations that work with older adults. Compared to younger adults, who are often very familiar with the newest technologies (e.g., smartphones, apps, social media), older adults in general are less familiar and skilled in using ICTs in general (e.g., internet, smartphone) and newer to market ICTs (e.g., smartwatches, virtual reality tools) in particular. Approximately 75% of older adults who reside in the community report using the internet, while 64% report having access to broadband (Pew Research Center 2021a). Mobile phones, and smartphones in particular, have been increasingly used by individuals. In the United States, 92% of community-dwelling individuals aged 65 and above have a mobile phone of some type; however, only 61% report owning a smartphone (Pew Research Center 2021c). While access to a mobile phone can be beneficial for communicating with social ties who are in varying locations, smartphones include substantial other features which expand the capabilities for individuals to complete a range of activities (e.g., collect and manage fitness data, engage in videocalls with social ties, buy and sell items). For older adults without access to and/or skills to use smartphones, this may result in them being left behind in our increasingly digitalized society.

Currently, the COVID-19 pandemic has reminded us of the significance and persistence of the "digital divide" and fostered discussion about the positive and negative outcomes of using or not using technologies during a time of physical distancing. When physical distancing mandates were put in place during COVID-19, older adults, one of the most at-risk groups for COVID-19, were not able to interact with their social ties in person and were told to refrain from going out to stores, restaurants, and so forth. Older adults who had access to and could use ICTs could still maintain contact with social ties, purchase food and groceries, and stay engaged in organizations with a digital presence (e.g., many churches began broadcasting their services online). Older adults who had health and mobility limitations were already at risk of social exclusion due to these limitations. Older adults who do not use ICTs in addition to having these health and/or mobility limitations were likely to struggle with a double burden of social exclusion (Seifert, Cotten, and Xie 2021). This struggle with online participation influences whether older adults can access online services and content, such as health information, social events, social networking, social tie interaction, and online shopping, during a time when digital solutions could compensate for missing physical and social interactions (Marston, Musselwhite, and Hadley 2020). Though using ICTs can help older adults to maintain social interaction and engagement during a pandemic, for older adults who do not have access to and/or the skills to use ICTs a feeling of social exclusion from society is likely (Robinson et al. 2020).

As the COVID-19 pandemic has reinforced, having access to and being able to use ICTs are critical for participation in society on many levels. Understanding usage differences and how ICT usage relates to a range of health outcomes is critical for identifying which older adults may be disadvantaged and those who could potentially benefit from using ICTs. In this chapter, we provide a broad overview of existing research and present findings about usage differences, health-related impacts, and future forward-thinking research needs. We first define what we mean by the concepts of ICTs and the digital divide. Next, we delineate patterns of ICT use among older adults. We also note ecological differences in ICT use among those who are living in private households and those who are living in long-term care facilities (LTCFs). Furthermore, we provide an overview of the impacts of ICT use on different health-related and well-being outcomes. We bring attention to how digital exclusion may also lead to social exclusion for older adults. After detailing this broad overview of the literature, we discuss some challenges of the nascent research on ICT use and older adults by presenting current gaps in knowledge and data sources. Finally, we offer suggestions for advancing research on ICT use and outcomes among older adults.

Defining ICTs and the Digital Divide

At the most basic level, technology is simply a product, tool, or application that helps people accomplish things they need to accomplish (Derry and Williams 1993). While this is a broad conceptualization of technology, we primarily, though not exclusively, focus in this chapter on ICTs. By ICTs, we refer to devices and applications that can be used to communicate with others, gather and exchange information, and entertain individuals. Examples of ICTs include things such as landline telephones, mobile phones, smartphones, computers, internet, tablets, television,[1] and information and communication apps (e.g., news apps on a tablet). The types of, access to, and usage of ICTs, such as smartphones, have increased at a rapid pace over the past decade.

Existing research has focused on understanding the use and impacts of ICTs as well as the causes and consequences of digital inequalities (Robinson et al. 2015). The concept of digital inequality highlights the multiple dimensions of the digital divide—moving from the most basic level involving access to ICTs to a more evolved understanding of the differences in how people use ICTs and which resources (e.g., skills) people have to use ICTs (i.e., the second-level digital divide) to the third level of the digital divide, which focuses on the outcomes of ICT use for the user's life (Helsper and van Deursen 2015; Scheerder, van Deursen, and van Dijk 2017). DiMaggio et al. (2004) coined the term "digital inequalities" to describe the multidimensional digital divide, subdividing it into usage, skills, social support, and self-perception. "Usage" refers to the variety of online content that can be used for a variety of different purposes, while "skill" refers to individuals' internet-specific knowledge. "Social support" relates to the resources, whether emotional, instrumental, or tangible, obtained from family members, friends, and professionals. "Self-perception" encompasses the individual's attitudes toward internet use. "Digital inequality" thus refers not only to having or not having access to digital technologies but also to participating either actively or passively in the digital society and the rewards that are reaped as a function of using technologies.

As more and more older adults embrace ICTs, it is important to explore how the different ways they use ICTs may relate to their well-being and the maintenance of their everyday activities. Schulz et al. (2015) stated that modern technologies "can be helpful for maintaining functioning, independence, and motivating engagement with important life goals" (p. 732). This use is important because an increasing number of services, such as banking, shopping, and buying tickets for public transport, are available (sometimes solely) on the internet. Furthermore, modern ICTs, specifically the internet, have been proposed as a potential major gateway for social participation and social inclusion among older adults in society. Thus, understanding ICT use patterns is a necessary prerequisite to determining the ways that ICT use can enhance older adults' lives.

ICT Use among Older Adults

Based on Elder's (1995) life course paradigm, we examine how different formative experiences at various points in life shape older adults' lives. Understanding when ICTs were developed and proliferated across society, as well as the historical context, helps us understand why a significant segment of older adults do not use ICTs. Many older adults are part of a *cohort*, a group of people within a population who have experienced similar life events within certain time periods. Every cohort has its own experience with technology, which leads to different technical skills and adaptation between generations. Based on the life course paradigm, Sackmann and Winkler (2013) presented the following technical generations[2]: (1) the mechanical generation (born before 1939), (2) the generation of the household revolution (born 1939–1948), (3) the generation of technology spread (born 1949–1963), (4) the computer generation (born 1964–1978), and the internet generation (born after 1978). This concept of different cohort-specific relationships with technology illustrates the importance of ICT exposure as a function of historical timing and technology proliferation. This historical timing and the stage of the life course influence what types of ICTs are used within different age cohorts. Furthermore, many individuals in these cohorts did not encounter ICTs in the workforce. For example, they may have historically relied extensively upon landline telephones rather than cellphones, smartphones, and computers.

The foundation of the internet and the beginning of its public use in the 1990s opened up new dimensions of ICT uses worldwide. With the internet, social interactions over a long distance were made possible; for instance, video chatting via the internet can be useful for visual interactions when geographic distance or health limitations prevent in-person interactions. For older adults, using the internet allows them to find information to make important life decisions, locate health information, and connect with others via online communities and social media (Hogeboom et al. 2010; Berkowsky and Czaja 2018).

Though there is an increasing trend in internet usage among older adults, a digital gap remains between age groups (Anderson and Perrin 2017). For example, a recent US study found that 25% of community-dwelling individuals aged 65 years and above still did not use the internet, compared to less than 4% of 50- to 64-year-olds, 2% of 30- to 39-year-olds, and 1% of individuals aged 18–29 (Pew Research Center 2021a).

While the gap in internet usage between emerging and advanced economies has narrowed in recent years, there are still regions in the world, especially within developed countries, where a significant number of older adults do not use the internet (Poushter, Bishop, and Chwe 2018). For example, a representative survey conducted across EU countries showed that only 49% of people aged 50 years and above used the internet; nevertheless, there is a divide between northwest European countries (e.g., 83% in Denmark use the internet) and southeast European countries (e.g., 27% in Croatia use the internet) (König, Seifert, and Doh 2018). In this study, internet use among older adults was influenced by personal factors, such as age, gender, education, and income. Participants older than 80 years reported spending less time online than individuals aged 65–79 years. Additionally, men and older adults with higher educational and economic status were more likely to use the internet. Individuals' health, prior experience with technology, social salience (internet use among the members of one's social network), and the communication technology infrastructure of the country the participants lived in were also predictors of internet usage by older adults (König, Seifert, and Doh 2018). An additional study with newer European data (among 13 countries) shows that 53% of people aged 50 years and above use the internet; however, health limitations (e.g., subjective health, grip strength) are important factors that affect whether older adults are able to remain online (König and Seifert 2020).

Though these studies provide basic illustrations as to *which older adults* use ICTs, the question remains: What do older adults actually *do* on the internet?[3] It might be expected that they do the same things on the internet that younger adults do, but research has shown that younger and older adults differ. For example, in their cross-country study, Büchi, Just, and Latzer (2016) found that age was by far the most important predictor of usage *frequency of different internet services*; overall, their findings indicated that younger people (<60 years old) use the internet for social, informational, entertainment, and transactional purposes more frequently than older people (60 years and older). However, in a representative Swiss study, adults aged 65 years and above reported using the internet for general functions, such as writing emails, searching for information, and searching for train schedules, while specific applications, such as multimedia content (music, video, games), social networking sites, or platforms for buying or selling goods, were used less frequently (Seifert, Ackermann, and Schelling 2020).

Previous findings also showed that use of the internet for social networking is becoming increasingly more common across people aged 50 years and above (Yu et al. 2016). Recent Pew Research Center (2021b) results report that 45% of community-dwelling individuals in the United States aged 65 and above use at least one form of social media compared to 73% of 50- to 64-year-olds, 81% of 30- to 49-year-olds, and 84% of 18- to 29-year-olds. However, the use of social media, such as Facebook, differs between cohorts; most Millennials (born 1981–1996) use Facebook, whereas only 37% of the Silent Generation (born 1928–1945) uses these social media sites (Vogels 2019). Study results from the United States show that those 80+ years old were more motivated to use the internet for social connectivity than for information-seeking (Sims, Reed, and Carr 2017). Participation in online communities to seek social support could be considered an intervention that may help older adults avoid social isolation (Leist 2013).

In addition to being a means of social exchange, the internet is a platform for active social and political participation, and internet users can be creators of online content. Despite this, studies have found that a digital divide exists between generations, in which older adults are less likely to be creators of online content (Brake 2014; Brewer, Morris, and Piper 2016). However, studies have also shown the positive effects (e.g., social inclusion in an online community) of creating online content, such as Wikipedia, web blogs, and forums, for older adults (Brewer and Piper 2016; Nielek et al. 2017).

Similar differences in use of the internet are seen with other ICTs, including smartphones, tablets, and smartwatches. In all advanced economies, a large majority of the population under the age of 35 owns a smartphone (Taylor and Silver 2019). In contrast, smartphone ownership among older populations varies widely but overall lags behind the ownership rates of younger adults. Though smartphone ownership among older cohorts is increasing in the United States, they still lag behind younger age cohorts (i.e., 61% of community-dwelling individuals aged 65 years and above own a smartphone versus 96% of individuals between 18 and 29 years old in 2021) (Pew Research Center 2021c); furthermore, 83% of individuals aged 50–64 and 95% of the those aged 30–49 own a smartphone. Slightly over half of Baby Boomers (born 1946–1964) (52%) and 33% of the Silent Generation own a tablet in the United States (Vogels 2019). However, though tablet ownership and usage are less than for other ICTs, the interface design may be easier for older adults to learn to use compared to laptops and computers (Tsai et al. 2015). Though smartphone and tablet use have increased, at least in Switzerland smartwatch use remains low among older adults. A secondary analysis of two Swiss surveys shows that only 6% of people aged 50 years and above and 4% of people aged 60 years and above use a smartwatch (Seifert 2020). The study shows that education, interest in technology, and the use of smartphones or tablets predicted smartwatch usage.

ICT Use among Older Adults Living in Long-Term Care Facilities

The majority of existing studies that examine older adults' use of ICTs focus on healthy, community-dwelling individuals who are in the younger-old age group (60–79 years old) (Hunsaker and Hargittai 2018). Fewer studies examine individuals with comorbidities and functional impairments and those in advanced old age (e.g., aged 80 and above), who are the primary residents of long-term care facilities (LTCFs) (Cotten et al. 2017; Seifert and Cotten 2020; Seifert, Doh, and Wahl 2017; Francis et al. 2019b). One of the limited studies examining LTCFs and ICT use, Seifert and Cotten (2020) have shown that only 21% of retirement home residents in Zurich (Switzerland) use the internet. The authors also found that, compared to non-users, internet users were more likely to be younger, healthier, and more functionally unimpaired. Of the LTCF participants in the study, only 12.8% reported owning a smartphone, and even fewer reported owning a tablet (4.5%) (Seifert and Cotten 2020). Schlomann et al. (2020b) also recently conducted a study using data from Germany that involved 1,863 people aged 80 years and above living in private households and LTCFs. Fewer than 3% of individuals in LTCFs in this study reported using internet-connected ICT devices. ICT device adoption was associated with the living environment (people aged 80 years and above living in LTCFs were using ICTs less often than those living in private households) and individual characteristics, including better functional health, higher education, and more technology interest (Schlomann et al. 2020a). These results indicate that individual characteristics and the living environment are both related to technology usage among the oldest age groups. Moreover, studies from the United States have found that older age, increased frailty (measured through limitations in daily-living activities), and participation in non-ICT activities were related to discontinued ICT use within LTCFs (Rikard, Berkowsky, and Cotten 2018; Berkowsky et al. 2013; Berkowsky, Rikard, and Cotten 2015).

Individual LTCF residents' ability and willingness to use ICTs are important. However, attention should also be focused on the ICT infrastructure of LTCFs as this is an important factor concerning whether residents may be able to access and use ICTs. The availability of ICTs is limited in many LTCFs, thus highlighting a significant deficiency in ICT infrastructure (Moyle et al. 2018; Powell et al. 2019). Another factor related to gaps in ICT infrastructure is a lack of ICT skills among some LTCF staff (Konttila et al. 2019). Furthermore, the ongoing COVID-19 pandemic has created awareness of the existing limitations of these facilities' current ICT infrastructures and how these limitations may negatively impact social interaction with social ties and social engagement among older adults who reside in LTCFs (Chen 2020; Eghtesadi 2020; Siette, Wuthrich, and Low 2020; Seifert, Cotten, and Xie 2021).

Factors Predicting ICT Use among Older Adults

A range of factors have been related to whether individuals use ICTs. Although age is a key factor in the digital divide, previous research has highlighted that other factors, such as education and income, also affect access to and use of ICTs; individuals with lower levels of education and income typically have less access to ICTs as well as lower levels of proficiency in ICT usage (Korupp and Szydlik 2005; Robinson et al. 2015). Social inequalities and differing access to new technologies are related to socioeconomic resources (Mingo and Bracciale 2018; Perrin and Atske 2021).

Additionally, personal resources, such as cognitive reserves, disabilities, and motivations and attitudes toward technology, are factors that may influence the adoption of ICTs (Kamin and Lang 2018; Seifert, Kamin, and Lang 2020; Hargittai and Dobransky 2017; Mitzner et al. 2019). Technology attitudes (e.g., an openness to adapting to new technologies) and environmental factors (e.g., getting support to learn new technology) are related to technology usage (Davis 1989; Venkatesh et al. 2003). Skill differences have been found among older adults as well, with younger older adults having more digital skills than older adults (Hargittai, Piper, and Morris 2019). This is partially due to the fact that cohorts younger than 65 are more likely to have encountered ICTs in the workforce and may continue to use them after retirement (Cotten 2021). Health declines and limitations in instrumental activities of daily living (e.g., managing finances and medications, cooking, maintaining a home) may also lead some older adults to discontinue ICT usage over time (Francis et al. 2019a; Rikard, Berkowsky, and Cotten 2018; Berkowsky et al. 2013).

In addition to individual factors, meso-level factors, such as social and technical support, and macro-level influences, like ICT infrastructure, are relevant for the successful adoption of ICTs. Older adults who have social network members (like relatives and acquaintances) who use the internet and receive informal support (and advice) in its proper use are more likely to use the internet independently (König, Seifert, and Doh 2018; Kamin, Beyer, and Lang 2020). Support from family and friends is also important for older adults to learn to use tablets (Tsai, Shillair, and Cotten 2017). Regarding macro-level influences, rural areas often have a less robust ICT infrastructure and thus have restricted access to the internet (Berner et al. 2015; Robinson et al. 2015), as well as lower rates of broadband internet access—which has been related to the types and amounts of online activities (Davison and Cotten 2010). Moreover, economically weaker or developing countries are often characterized by an underdeveloped ICT infrastructure (Poushter, Bishop, and Chwe 2018).

As the research detailed in this section illustrates, a range of factors are related to whether older adults use ICTs. Given this, there is no easy solution to ensure that all older adults are able to access and effectively use ICTs. Organizations and groups that seek to encourage older adults to use ICTs must take into account access as well as socioeconomic, personal, and meso- and macro-level factors that impact whether someone can access and effectively use ICTs.

IMPACT OF ICT USE ON OLDER ADULTS' HEALTH AND QUALITY OF LIFE

Though ICT use is increasing among older adults, less is known about the impacts of ICT use on older adults' lives and how these effects may change over time. Seifert and Schelling (2018), however, examined the attitudes of older adults (65 years and older) who used the internet and whether they viewed it as a resource for coping with everyday life situations. The study's findings confirmed that (a) many of the respondents viewed the internet as useful, both in general and for coping with everyday situations, and (b) 53% of the respondents agreed with the statement "The Internet allows me to stay independent longer into old age." These findings along with other studies (Cotten, Anderson, and McCullough 2013; Erickson and Johnson 2011; Forsman and Nordmyr 2017; Sims, Reed, and Carr 2017; Schlomann et al. 2020b; Cotten 2021) suggest that ICT use could be a resource to promote successful aging and to compensate for functional declines as individuals progress through older age. This potential role for ICTs seems to exist regardless of the living situation, such as living in the community versus a retirement home (Cotten et al. 2017; Seifert, Doh, and Wahl 2017).

Psychosocial Impacts

One of the areas that we believe ICT use has the potential to have the most impact for older adults concerns maintaining social connections with social ties. Older adults are at an increased risk of loneliness and social isolation when they are not able to maintain social interactions, such as visiting with friends and family members. As families have become more geographically dispersed and the rates of chronic health conditions have increased among older adults, mobility and staying connected may be more challenging for many older adults (Cotten 2021). Using ICTs, particularly to maintain contact with social ties, can help older adults enhance their social connections and well-being (Marston, Musselwhite, and Hadley 2020; Hogeboom et al. 2010) and their sense of mattering to others (Francis et al. 2019b). Increasing evidence suggests that perceived social isolation and loneliness are major risk factors for physical and mental illness in later life (Ong, Uchino, and Wethington 2016). Therefore, finding ways to decrease loneliness and isolation is critical for enhancing well-being among older adults. ICTs may be one way to enhance connections and well-being; however, older adults must have access to and be able to effectively use ICTs in order to reap the rewards from ICT use (Schulz et al. 2015).

Moreover, each ICT has distinct features that are perceived as either beneficial or detrimental for enhancing social connectedness and well-being (Cotten 2017). ICT devices are designed for social interaction over distances, and social networking applications, sending text messages, and engaging in video chats provide opportunities for social contact. In this way, ICT use can enable new forms of social interaction, especially for older adults (Antonucci, Ajrouch, and Manalel 2017). However, the empirical evidence on the relationship between loneliness and ICT use among older adults is mixed. Some studies have found that internet use is associated with reduced loneliness (e.g., Cotten, Anderson, and McCullough 2013; Szabo et al. 2019). Other researchers have found that social networking site use enhances well-being—usually by reducing loneliness (Sims, Reed, and Carr 2017; Chopik 2016). In contrast, a systematic review demonstrated that the use of computers and the internet in randomized controlled trial designs was not significantly related to lower levels of loneliness (Chen and Schulz 2016).

These mixed results might be related to the question of whether real-life social interactions are replaced by interactions via ICTs, which might lead to higher experiences of loneliness. However, a review of social relations and technology studies concludes that technology use is more likely to expand traditional forms of social interactions than to replace them (Antonucci, Ajrouch, and Manalel 2017). In addition, recent studies have found that accessing services, finding information, and learning about new opportunities through the use of ICTs are related to participating in social gatherings and enhanced social engagement, such as visiting family or friends and volunteering in the community, that are offline for older adults (Ihm and Hsieh 2015; Schehl 2020). Given mobility and health limitations that are more typically experienced by older adults, using ICTs may also help them to overcome spatial and social barriers, which could lead to enhancements in their contact with social ties and well-being, in addition to being able to access needed information and resources (Cotten et al. 2017; Winstead et al. 2013).

ICT use has been related to a sense of mattering—perceiving that you are important and relied upon by others—in older adults who reside in LTCFs; for these older adults, ICT use helps keep them connected with their social ties and support networks, which is related to increased mattering (Francis et al. 2019b). Given that mattering refers to how individuals recognize their value and importance to their social ties, a sense of mattering may also help to stave off depressive symptoms. Research using the US Health and Retirement Survey has shown that even when controlling for prior depression levels, older retired adults who use the internet and/or email were less likely to be classified as depressed (Cotten et al. 2012, 2014).

Even though ICT use has been positively associated with older adult psychosocial well-being, the mechanisms through which ICT use impacts well-being have not been clearly articulated in prior studies. As more extensive longitudinal data is available to assess changes over time, we anticipate that the specific mechanisms will be better identified and tested. We suggest that additional longitudinal studies that are theoretically designed, test a diverse range of potential mechanisms through which ICT use may impact psychosocial well-being, and include a range of global and differentiated measures of psychosocial well-being outcomes as well as potential mediators and moderators of these relationships are needed. Focusing on specific aspects of mental health, social support, mattering, social connection, life satisfaction, and self-efficacy, in addition to global measures of well-being, social ties, and social connections, can help researchers to better distinguish the pathways through which varying types of ICT use impact well-being for older adults.

Physical Health Outcomes

Although research is increasingly focused on psychosocial well-being and ICT use, fewer studies examine how ICT use is related to physical health outcomes. There are various ways that using ICTs could, theoretically, potentially impact physical health outcomes. A primary way that ICT use may impact health is through the use of online health information. Whether found through an online support group, a healthcare website, or government websites, these resources could enable individuals to find information to maintain or manage their health conditions, find healthy behaviors to help them stay more active and engaged, use telemedicine, and find information related to disease risk and medications (Berkowsky and Czaja 2018; Batsis et al. 2019). A recent study found that subjective health and functional limitations, two aspects of physical health, were related to using more ICT devices and applications—through the mechanism of using ICTs to gain new skills and information (Sims, Reed, and Carr, 2017). Social uses of ICTs, however, were not related to physical health.

In addition to positive impacts on physical health, there may be negative impacts. Though the negative impacts are not frequently examined, it is likely that if ICT use continues to increase among older adults, we may see more negative impacts on a range of physical health aspects. For example, we anticipate increases in repetitive motion issues, sleep deficits, and reduced mobility.

Furthermore, for both positive and negative outcomes, we suggest that the manner in which older adults engage in the digital world matters (Szabo et al. 2019). Engaging with ICTs to find information to make important decisions (health-related and otherwise), stay connected to social ties, and stay integrated into society are likely to be the most health-promoting types of activities. We encourage other researchers to examine both positive and negative effects of ICT use on psychosocial and physical health among older adults, given the shortage of research on these topics.

Social Exclusion through Digital Exclusion

In addition to its positive influence on maintaining everyday life activities for older adults, technology use has the potential to perpetuate ageism (e.g., older non-users of technology are viewed as outsiders) (Cutler 2005). If inclusion in today's society means active participation in the digital world, then older adults who do not have access to a smartphone or are not active on the internet are at risk of social exclusion. However, little is known about whether a lower level of internet use among older adults is accompanied by lower degrees of social inclusion or by subjective perceptions of social exclusion. For example, a study among 1,037 adults aged 65 years and above living in Switzerland found that 33% of the participants who used the internet reported that they would feel socially excluded if they stopped using it; in comparison, 14% of the participants who did not use the internet felt socially excluded because of their lack of internet usage (Seifert, Hofer, and Rössel 2018). Furthermore, the authors identified that the attitudes of non-users toward internet usage and their feelings of loneliness in general were associated with the sense of social exclusion resulting from not using the internet (Seifert, Hofer, and Rössel 2018).

A sense of exclusion can also be experienced with smartphone use. For youth, smartphones are an extension of their selves, and they use them at extremely high levels, relative to other age groups, to stay connected with social ties, coordinate activities, engage with social media, and so forth. However, older adults are less likely to use smartphones (Pew Research Center 2021c; Taylor and Silver 2019), and they use them, on average, in more basic ways than do younger age groups (Seifert and Schelling 2015). A consequence of these generational differences in the ways that smartphones are used is that older adults may experience phubbing (e.g., phone snubbing) when in the presence of their social ties who are using smartphones (Ball et al. 2019; Kadylak et al. 2018). This may result in disrupted co-presence and a physical–digital divide—even though they are in the same physical space with younger social ties, a digital divide still exists, with the younger social ties focused on smartphone use rather than engaging in social interaction with the older adult social tie (Ball et al. 2019).

These results indicate that a form of social pressure exists among the older adult population concerning internet and smartphone usage, in particular, and perhaps other types of ICT usage. As an increasing number of service providers begin to offer specific information and services on an online-only basis (or charge an extra fee for offline services), older adults who are offline could become increasingly disadvantaged as the internet's societal pervasiveness progresses (Peacock and Künemund 2007; Seifert, Cotten, and Xie 2021). And as younger age groups continue embracing smartphones and social media at high levels, older adults may continue to experience a physical–digital divide, which may result in fewer strong social ties across these generational groups. Sociologists, gerontologists, and policymakers must therefore work together to minimize the risk of social exclusion in relation to new technology use and new digital content on the internet, especially among the older adult population. Furthermore, research is needed to evaluate not only the positive outcomes of ICT use among older adults but also the negative consequences of not using ICTs within our digitally based society.

Advancing Research on ICT Use and Outcomes among Older Adults

In this section, we briefly suggest areas that we have identified as critical for expanding research on older adults and technologies and offer recommendations for future studies.

Missing Target Groups

Most of the studies that have targeted the use of ICTs among older adults have focused mainly on community-dwelling adults and not on those living in LTCFs (for an exception, see Cotten et al. 2017; Cotten 2021). We suggest that researchers must make efforts to include harder-to-reach older adult populations living in LTCFs in their studies. Recruitment protocols should include individuals living in supportive care settings as context-based disparities might occur for these older adults; for example, some LTCFs may not have WiFi available for residents or individuals to help older adults when technical difficulties arise. The oldest-old individuals, aged 80 and above, are also often excluded from studies, regardless of whether they reside in community settings or in LTCFs (Hunsaker and Hargittai 2018; Seifert and Cotten 2020). Often, studies have an age cap of 95 years and do not include a representative sample of the oldest-old (Schlomann et al. 2020a). Furthermore, population groups among the older adult population who are often neglected in ICT studies should also be included (e.g., homeless individuals, migrants, people with disabilities, surrogate users, and people living in prisons). If we are to fully understand ICT use and the impacts of ICT use among older adults, ensuring that we have representative samples that include all segments of older adults is necessary, not merely the ones who are easiest to access or those who are online. However, given that these populations are harder to access, including them may result in more costly studies due to increased recruitment costs and time to collect data. Nevertheless, participatory research with older adults is necessary to develop technology to meet the needs of older adults (Merkel and Kucharski 2019).

Measures and Data

Most existing data sets that include older adults include very few measures of technology usage (Cotten 2021; Hunsaker and Hargittai 2018). At best, measures of internet and email use are typically included. Less often, smartphone and social media use are included. Assessing the functions, motivations for use, and timing of use across devices and time is typically absent from data sets (Cotten 2021). Additionally, measurements of ICT usage remain largely unstandardized; even when examining access, differing temporal approaches and definitions of use complicate and even hinder cross-study comparisons (Hunsaker and Hargittai 2018).

At a minimum, further longitudinal research is needed to examine how technology use changes over time and how these changes may relate to a range of health and well-being outcomes. However, focusing on one or two technologies is not sufficient. We need studies that include a range of ICTs that are prevalently used for specific groups in society, as well as the myriad ways in which older adults use technology on a regular basis. For instance, given the pervasiveness and multimodal nature of technology use, it is possible for individuals to check their email and social media (among other things) via their laptops, smartphones, tablets, and smartwatches across the course of a single day. From a self-report and recall perspective, this makes it incredibly hard to accurately measure the amount, timing, and range of ICT uses even on a daily basis for individuals who use multiple devices to do certain activities. This also makes it harder for researchers to determine if it is the types of ICT being used, the amounts of certain activities, or other factors that may be related to various health outcomes (Hofer 2017). This is a critical area that needs better measurement moving forward. Cotten (2021) has suggested that access to device use data could be helpful in alleviating the recall bias that is likely inherent in self-report measurement tools. In addition, understanding the functions being served by the use of these ICTs may be pivotal to understanding how and why specific health outcomes are or are not affected. As noted, we also need studies that include a range of behavioral and health (psychosocial and physical health) outcomes.

One way to collect information on daily ICT usage and its possible outcomes is the approach of using smartphones or other wearables as data collection devices. Mobile data collection—part of the methodological family of ambulatory assessment—is an approach to assessing and tracking people's ongoing thoughts, feelings, behaviors, or environments, including in the context of older adults' daily life (Seifert and Harari 2019). The primary goal of this method is to collect in-the-moment actively logged (i.e., self-reported survey responses) and/or passively sensed data (e.g., data collected from mobile sensors or phone logs) directly from people's smartphones or wearables in their natural environments (Harari et al. 2016). Mobile data collection is possible because smartphones are now widely available and come with the computational power and embedded sensors needed to obtain real-world information (Cartwright 2016; Miller 2012). A main advantage of this approach is that it permits ecologically valid research designs because data are collected during people's day-to-day lives (Wrzus and Mehl 2015). By using a smartphone to collect the data, the researchers can capture self-reports by setting random, continuous, or event-based notifications that prompt participants to respond to questions as they go about their day (Seifert, Hofer, and Allemand 2018). These ecological momentary assessments (i.e., in-the-moment reports) are less prone to memory bias than retrospective assessments and provide important information, such as the dynamic patterns of real-life ICT use. Moreover, intensive repeated measurements of one participant capture information at the within-person level (i.e., the extent to which a person varies from themselves over time). Mobile data is also rich in contextual information because it allows for the combination of subjective self-reports and more objective assessments, such as daily activities or social interactions via apps on the smartphone, using the sensors that are built into smartphones. The combination of subjective and objective data is likely to yield better information for determining how ICT use is changing over time and how it is related to various health outcomes and real-world contexts (Wolf et al. 2021).

New Areas of ICT Use

Digital assistants and wearables are increasing in market penetration to older adults. Limited large-scale studies have examined which older adults are willing to use these ICTs (for an exception, see Kadylak and Cotten 2020). In addition, privacy and security concerns with digital assistants and wearables need to be examined in greater detail, as well as what happens to the substantial data that these devices generate (National Academies of Sciences, Engineering, and Medicine 2020). Further research is clearly warranted to enable researchers to determine how or if older adults' behaviors can be changed by using these devices as well as potential impacts on health and quality of life. Ideally, device manufacturers would work with researchers in developing health-related interventions and data collection with wearables, including the individual needs of older adult users (Cotten 2021; Seifert, Reinwand, and Schlomann 2019). Further, having social and behavioral scientists work with computer scientists to mine data from devices and evaluate the potential to use the data to predict behavioral and health outcomes will be needed. The data collected from wearables, like fitness trackers or smartwatches, can then be used for designing and tailoring interventions for older adult populations with specific health conditions (Seifert, Christen, and Martin 2018).

While research has shown that smartwatches today are not widely used by older adults (Seifert 2020), opportunities for their assistance in health-related behavioral change interventions have been discussed (Antos et al. 2019; Fernández-Ardèvol and Rosales 2017). For example, the importance of augmented reality (AR) and virtual reality (VR) for older adults' health and well-being has steadily increased in recent years (Seifert and Schlomann 2021). Drivers for this development have included the technological evolution of smartphones and tablets and the success of AR-based games, such as Pokémon GO. AR game concepts can also be used for health-related purposes among older adults (Schlomann et al. 2019). For instance, serious games with an AR approach can include physical activity–related interventions so that older adults who play the games are motivated to do physical activities. Therefore, there are potential benefits to developing physical activity–related games for older adults. However, developers of AR games for older adults have to keep in mind that older adults are a specific population with distinctive characteristics, interests, technology backgrounds, and specific preferences regarding usefulness and usability (Schlomann et al. 2019).

Moreover, some of the existing ICTs and future emerging technologies for older adults (e.g., robots, VR, digital voice assistants, AR, smart home technologies, telehealth applications) may help them with disabilities as well as their caregivers (Cotten et al. 2017). Cotten (2021) noted that ICTs could be useful for remote home access, monitoring of mobility patterns, and check-ins through video conferencing platforms. Given current and projected direct-care caregiver shortages, it is likely that there will be increased pressure for development and dissemination of new ICTs to help in monitoring and care of individuals as well as to help compensate for caregiver shortages and the increasing older adult population with chronic health conditions in society. Hopefully, these ICTs can help older adults and individuals with disabilities to age in place even as chronic health conditions increase and physical health declines. However, research will be needed to determine whether these types of ICTs can substitute for direct-care caregiving shortages for monitoring and care and how older adult health changes over time by using these ICTs.

Challenges Associated with Maintaining ICT Use

Though the development of new technologies has potential to help older adults to maintain independence and age in place, older adults must be able to use these technologies. Getting older adults to use ICTs is one challenge; however, once they are online, helping them to continue to use ICTs is another challenge. Maintaining devices and maintaining use over time are understudied but critical areas. When ICTs stop working properly, need repairs, require software and password updates, and change layout and appearance through software interface updates, this can result in some older adults not being able to maintain use over time (Houston, Richardson, and Cotten 2019). During these times, older adults may need assistance from IT professionals or from social ties who can help them resolve the issues and successfully begin using the technology again (Cotten 2021). If these sources of instrumental support are not available, older adults may end up using the technology less frequently or not at all (König and Seifert 2020). These cognitive and emotional challenges related to ICT maintenance need to be accounted for by groups seeking to eliminate the digital divide, informal sources of support who may be called upon to assist older adults with these issues, and researchers who provide ICTs as part of intervention studies (Gonzales, Ems, and Suri 2016; Gonzales 2016; Kamin and Lang 2018).

As people aged 60–70 years grow older, it will be interesting to see how their use evolves as new ICTs continue to be developed and disseminated and whether they will be able to maintain the types and functions of various types of ICT usage. Here, it is important to keep in mind that ICT usage may not be stable over time and that after the acceptance and usage of a device or the internet, health-related, social support, or technical limitations can lead to a pause or termination of use (König and Seifert 2020).

Technology is constantly evolving; the fast-paced nature of technology development leaves researchers challenged with staying abreast of the latest developments in technology and how use is evolving over time. This also contributes to the primitive understanding of the impacts of technology use on older adults and how to maintain this use over time. Interdisciplinary research as well as cooperative studies between technology developers and researchers will be needed in the future if we are to more fully comprehend the myriad ways that older adults use ICTs, how use waxes and wanes over time, and the complex pathways through which ICT use may impact older adults' lives.

Conclusion

New technologies are being created around the world every day. Many of these technologies will help older adults live at home, stay connected to their social ties and caregivers, overcome functional limitations, and continue to be mobile as they age and to actively engage in society through driving, buying products, socializing, being entertained, and finding information. Future research can help to map this diversity in everyday ICT use, creating models and solutions that enable older adults to live independently into old age. We encourage other researchers to continue to push the boundaries of examining our technologically mediated lives and to understand how individuals and groups can harness technology to enhance older adults' health and well-being.

Notes

1. Though landline telephones and television are considered ICTs, for the purposes of this article, we do not include these technologies in our discussion.
2. Though these are referred to as "generations" by Sackmann and Winkler, they are technically age cohorts.
3. While research is increasingly examining this issue, there are differences in sampling designs, measurement approaches, and time frames examined which limit the ability to make generalizations across older adults.

References

Anderson, Monica, and Andrew Perrin. 2017. "Tech Adoption Climbs among Older Adults." Pew Research Center, May 17. http://www.pewinternet.org/wp-content/uploads/sites/9/2017/05/PI_2017.05.17_Older-Americans-Tech_FINAL.pdf.

Antonucci, Toni C., Kristine J. Ajrouch, and Jasmine A. Manalel. 2017. "Social Relations and Technology: Continuity, Context, and Change." *Innovation in Aging* 1, no. 3. https://doi.org/10.1093/geroni/igx029.

Antos, Stephen A., Margaret K. Danilovich, Amy R. Eisenstein, Keith E. Gordon, and Konrad P. Kording. 2019. "Smartwatches Can Detect Walker and Cane Use in Older Adults." *Innovation in Aging* 3, no. 1. https://doi.org/10.1093/geroni/igz008.

Ball, Christopher, Jessica Francis, Kuo-Ting Huang, Travis Kadylak, Shelia R. Cotten, and R. V. Rikard. 2019. "The Physical–Digital Divide: Exploring the Social Gap between Digital Natives and Physical Natives." *Journal of Applied Gerontology* 38, no. 8: 1167–1184. https://doi.org/10.1177/0733464817732518.

Batsis, John A., Peter R. DiMilia, Lillian M. Seo, Karen L. Fortuna, Meaghan A. Kennedy, Heather B. Blunt, et al. 2019. "Effectiveness of Ambulatory Telemedicine Care in Older Adults: A Systematic Review." *Journal of the American Geriatrics Society* 67, no. 8: 1737–1749. https://doi.org/10.1111/jgs.15959.

Berkowsky, Ronald W., Shelia R. Cotten, Elizabeth A. Yost, and Vicki P. Winstead. 2013. "Attitudes towards and Limitations to ICT Use in Assisted and Independent Living Communities: Findings from a Specially-Designed Technological Intervention." *Educational Gerontology* 39, no. 11: 797–811. https://doi.org/10.1080/03601277.2012.734162.

Berkowsky, Ronald W., and Sara J. Czaja. 2018. "Challenges Associated with Online Health Information Seeking among Older Adults." In *Aging, Technology and Health*, edited by R. Pak and A. C. McLaughlin, 31–48. Cambridge, MA: Academic Press. https://doi.org/10.1016/B978-0-12-811272-4.00002-6.

Berkowsky, Ronald W., R. V. Rikard, and Shelia R. Cotten. 2015. "Signing Off: Predicting Discontinued ICT Usage among Older Adults in Assisted and Independent Living." In *Human Aspects of IT for the Aged Population. Design for Everyday Life*, edited by Jia Zhou and Gavriel Salvendy, 389–398. Cham, Switzerland: Springer International. https://doi.org/10.1007/978-3-319-20913-5_36.

Berner, Jessica, Mikael Rennemark, Claes Jogréus, Peter Anderberg, Anders Sköldunger, Maria Wahlberg, et al. 2015. "Factors Influencing Internet Usage in Older Adults (65 Years and above) Living in Rural and Urban Sweden." *Health Informatics Journal* 21, no. 3: 237–249. https://doi.org/10.1177/1460458214521226.

Brake, David R. 2014. "Are We All Online Content Creators Now? Web 2.0 and Digital Divides." *Journal of Computer-Mediated Communication* 19, no. 3: 591–609. https://doi.org/10.1111/jcc4.12042.

Brewer, Robin, Meredith Ringel Morris, and Anne Marie Piper. 2016. " 'Why Would Anybody Do This?': Understanding Older Adults' Motivations and Challenges in Crowd Work." In *CHI '16: Proceedings of the 2016 CHI Conference on Human Factors in Computing Systems*, 2246–2257. Santa Clara, CA: ACM Press. https://doi.org/10.1145/2858036.2858198.

Brewer, Robin, and Anne Marie Piper. 2016. " 'Tell It Like It Really Is': A Case of Online Content Creation and Sharing among Older Adult Bloggers." In *CHI '16: Proceedings of the 2016 CHI Conference on Human Factors in Computing Systems*, 5529–5542. Santa Clara, CA: ACM Press. https://doi.org/10.1145/2858036.2858379.

Büchi, Moritz, Natascha Just, and Michael Latzer. 2016. "Modeling the Second-Level Digital Divide: A Five-Country Study of Social Differences in Internet Use." *New Media & Society* 18, no. 11: 2703–2722. https://doi.org/10.1177/1461444815604154.

Cartwright, Jon. 2016. "Technology: Smartphone Science." *Nature* 531, no. 7596: 669–671. https://doi.org/10.1038/nj7596-669a.

Chen, Ke. 2020. "Use of Gerontechnology to Assist Older Adults to Cope with the COVID-19 Pandemic." *Journal of the American Medical Directors Association* 21, no. 7: 983–984. https://doi.org/10.1016/j.jamda.2020.05.021.

Chen, Yi-Ru Regina, and Peter J. Schulz. 2016. "The Effect of Information Communication Technology Interventions on Reducing Social Isolation in the Elderly: A Systematic Review." *Journal of Medical Internet Research* 18, no. 1: e18. https://doi.org/10.2196/jmir.4596.

Chopik, William J. 2016. "The Benefits of Social Technology Use among Older Adults Are Mediated by Reduced Loneliness." *Cyberpsychology, Behavior, and Social Networking* 19, no. 9: 551–556. https://doi.org/10.1089/cyber.2016.0151.

Compaine, Benjamin M., ed. 2001. *The Digital Divide: Facing a Crisis or Creating a Myth?* MIT Press Sourcebooks. Cambridge, MA: MIT Press.

Cotten, Shelia R. 2017. "Examining the Roles of Technology in Aging and Quality of Life." *Journals of Gerontology: Series B* 72, no. 5: 823–826. https://doi.org/10.1093/geronb/gbx109.

Cotten, Shelia R. 2021. "Technologies and Aging: Understanding Use, Impacts, and Future Needs." In *Handbook of Aging and the Social Sciences*, edited by D. Carr and Kenneth F. Ferraro, 373–392. New York: Academic Press.

Cotten, Shelia R., William A. Anderson, and Brandi M. McCullough. 2013. "Impact of Internet Use on Loneliness and Contact with Others among Older Adults: Cross-Sectional Analysis." *Journal of Medical Internet Research* 15, no. 2: e39. https://doi.org/10.2196/jmir.2306.

Cotten, Shelia R., George Ford, Sherry Ford, and Timothy M. Hale. 2012. "Internet Use and Depression among Older Adults." *Computers in Human Behavior* 28, no. 2: 496–499. https://doi.org/10.1016/j.chb.2011.10.021.

Cotten, S. R., G. Ford, S. Ford, and T. M. Hale. 2014. "Internet Use and Depression among Retired Older Adults in the United States: A Longitudinal Analysis." *Journals of Gerontology Series B: Psychological Sciences and Social Sciences* 69, no. 5: 763–771. https://doi.org/10.1093/geronb/gbu018.

Cotten, Shelia R., Elizabeth A. Yost, Ronald W. Berkowsky, Vicki Winstead, and William A. Anderson. 2017. *Designing Technology Training for Older Adults in Continuing Care Retirement Communities*. Boca Raton, FL: CRC Press.

Cutler, Stephen J. 2005. "Ageism and Technology." *Generations* 29, no. 3: 67–72.

Davis, Fred D. 1989. "Perceived Usefulness, Perceived Ease of Use, and User Acceptance of Information Technology." *MIS Quarterly* 13, no. 3: 319–340. https://doi.org/10.2307/249008.

Davison, Elizabeth L., and Shelia R. Cotten. 2010. "Connection Disparities: The Importance of Broadband Connections in Understanding Today's Digital Divide." In *Handbook of Research on Overcoming Digital Divides: Constructing an Equitable and Competitive Information Society*, edited by Enrico Ferro, Yogesh K. Dwivedi, J. Ramon Gil-Garcia, and Michael D. Williams, 346–358. Hershey, PA: IGI Global. https://doi.org/10.4018/978-1-60566-699-0.

Derry, T. K., and Trevor Illtyd Williams. 1993. *A Short History of Technology: From the Earliest Times to A.D. 1900*. New York: Dover Publications.

DiMaggio, P., E. Hargittai, C. Celeste, and S. Shafer. 2004. "Digital Inequality: From Unequal Access to Differentiated Use." In *Social Inequality*, edited by K. M. Neckermann, 335–400. New York: Russel Sage Foundation.

Eghtesadi, Marzieh. 2020. "Breaking Social Isolation amidst COVID-19: A Viewpoint on Improving Access to Technology in Long-Term Care Facilities." *Journal of the American Geriatrics Society* 68, no. 5: 949–950. https://doi.org/10.1111/jgs.16478.

Elder, Glen H. 1995. "The Life Course Paradigm: Social Change and Individual Development." In *Examining Lives in Context: Perspectives on the Ecology of Human Development*, edited by Phyllis Moen, Glen H. Elder, and Kurt Lüscher, 101–139. Washington, DC: American Psychological Association. https://doi.org/10.1037/10176-003.

Erickson, Julie, and Genevieve M. Johnson. 2011. "Internet Use and Psychological Wellness during Late Adulthood." *Canadian Journal on Aging* 30, no. 2: 197–209. https://doi.org/10.1017/S0714980811000109.

Fernández-Ardèvol, Mireia, and Andrea Rosales. 2017. "My Interests, My Activities: Learning from an Intergenerational Comparison of Smartwatch Use." In *Human Aspects of IT for the Aged Population. Applications, Services and Contexts*, edited by Jia Zhou and Gavriel Salvendy, 114–129. Cham, Switzerland: Springer International. https://doi.org/10.1007/978-3-319-58536-9_10.

Forsman, Anna K., and Johanna Nordmyr. 2017. "Psychosocial Links between Internet Use and Mental Health in Later Life: A Systematic Review of Quantitative and Qualitative Evidence." *Journal of Applied Gerontology* 36, no. 12: 1471–1518. https://doi.org/10.1177/0733464815595509.

Francis, Jessica, Christopher Ball, Travis Kadylak, and Shelia R. Cotten. 2019a. "Aging in the Digital Age: Conceptualizing Technology Adoption and Digital Inequalities." In *Ageing and Digital Technology*, edited by Barbara Barbosa Neves and Frank Vetere, 35–49. Singapore: Springer. https://doi.org/10.1007/978-981-13-3693-5_3.

Francis, Jessica, R. V. Rikard, Shelia R. Cotten, and Travis Kadylak. 2019b. "Does ICT Use Matter? How Information and Communication Technology Use Affects Perceived Mattering among a Predominantly Female Sample of Older Adults Residing in Retirement

Communities." *Information, Communication & Society* 22, no. 9: 1281–1294. https://doi.org/10.1080/1369118X.2017.1417459.

Gonzales, Amy. 2016. "The Contemporary US Digital Divide: From Initial Access to Technology Maintenance." *Information, Communication & Society* 19, no. 2: 234–248. https://doi.org/10.1080/1369118X.2015.1050438.

Gonzales, Amy L., Lindsay Ems, and Venkata Ratnadeep Suri. 2016. "Cell Phone Disconnection Disrupts Access to Healthcare and Health Resources: A Technology Maintenance Perspective." *New Media & Society* 18, no. 8: 1422–1438. https://doi.org/10.1177/1461444814558670.

Harari, Gabriella M., Nicholas D. Lane, Rui Wang, Benjamin S. Crosier, Andrew T. Campbell, and Samuel D. Gosling. 2016. "Using Smartphones to Collect Behavioral Data in Psychological Science: Opportunities, Practical Considerations, and Challenges." *Perspectives on Psychological Science* 11, no. 6: 838–854. https://doi.org/10.1177/1745691616650285.

Hargittai, Eszter, and Kerry Dobransky. 2017. "Old Dogs, New Clicks: Digital Inequality in Skills and Uses among Older Adults." *Canadian Journal of Communication* 42, no. 2. https://doi.org/10.22230/cjc.2017v42n2a3176.

Hargittai, Eszter, Anne Marie Piper, and Meredith Ringel Morris. 2019. "From Internet Access to Internet Skills: Digital Inequality among Older Adults." *Universal Access in the Information Society* 18, no. 4: 881–890. https://doi.org/10.1007/s10209-018-0617-5.

Helsper, Ellen J., and Alexander J. A. M. van Deursen. 2015. "The Third-Level Digital Divide: Who Benefits Most from Being Online?" In *Communication and Information Technologies Annual*, edited by Laura Robinson, Shelia R. Cotten, Jeremy Schulz, Timothy M. Hale, and Apryl Williams, 29–52. Studies in Media and Communications 10. Bingley, UK: Emerald Group. https://doi.org/10.1108/S2050-206020150000010002.

Hofer, Matthias. 2017. "Older Adults' Media Use and Well-Being: Media as a Resource in the Process of Successful Aging." In *The Routledge Handbook of Media Use and Well-Being*, edited by Leonard Reinecke and Mary Beth Oliver, 384–395. New York and London: Routledge.

Hogeboom, David L., Robert J. McDermott, Karen M. Perrin, Hana Osman, and Bethany A. Bell-Ellison. 2010. "Internet Use and Social Networking among Middle Aged and Older Adults." *Educational Gerontology* 36, no. 2: 93–111. https://doi.org/10.1080/03601270903058507.

Houston, Thomas K., Lorilei M. Richardson, and Shelia R. Cotten. 2019. "Patient-Directed Digital Health Technologies: Is Implementation Outpacing Evidence?" *Medical Care* 57, no. 2: 95–97. https://doi.org/10.1097/MLR.0000000000001068.

Hunsaker, Amanda, and Eszter Hargittai. 2018. "A Review of Internet Use among Older Adults." *New Media & Society* 20, no. 10: 3937–3954. https://doi.org/10.1177/1461444818787348.

Ihm, Jennifer, and Yuli Patrick Hsieh. 2015. "The Implications of Information and Communication Technology Use for the Social Well-Being of Older Adults." *Information, Communication & Society* 18, no. 10: 1123–1138. https://doi.org/10.1080/1369118X.2015.1019912.

Kadylak, Travis, and Shelia R. Cotten. 2020. "United States Older Adults' Willingness to Use Emerging Technologies." *Information, Communication & Society* 23, no. 5: 736–750. https://doi.org/10.1080/1369118X.2020.1713848.

Kadylak, Travis, Taj W. Makki, Jessica Francis, Shelia R. Cotten, R. V. Rikard, and Young June Sah. 2018. "Disrupted Copresence: Older Adults' Views on Mobile Phone Use during

Face-to-Face Interactions." *Mobile Media & Communication* 6, no. 3: 331–349. https://doi.org/10.1177/2050157918758129.

Kamin, Stefan T., Anja Beyer, and Frieder R. Lang. 2020. "Social Support Is Associated with Technology Use in Old Age." *Zeitschrift Für Gerontologie Und Geriatrie* 53: 256–262. https://doi.org/10.1007/s00391-019-01529-z.

Kamin, Stefan T., and Frieder R. Lang. 2018. "Internet Use and Cognitive Functioning in Late Adulthood: Longitudinal Findings from the Survey of Health, Ageing and Retirement in Europe (SHARE)." *Journals of Gerontology: Series B* 75, no. 3: 534–539. https://doi.org/10.1093/geronb/gby123.

König, Ronny, and Alexander Seifert. 2020. "From Online to Offline and Vice Versa: Change in Internet Use in Later Life across Europe." *Frontiers in Sociology* 5, no. 4: 1–12. https://doi.org/10.3389/fsoc.2020.00004.

König, Ronny, Alexander Seifert, and Michael Doh. 2018. "Internet Use among Older Europeans: An Analysis Based on SHARE Data." *Universal Access in the Information Society* 17, no. 3: 621–633. https://doi.org/10.1007/s10209-018-0609-5.

Konttila, Jenni, Heidi Siira, Helvi Kyngäs, Minna Lahtinen, Satu Elo, Maria Kääriäinen, et al. 2019. "Healthcare Professionals' Competence in Digitalisation: A Systematic Review." *Journal of Clinical Nursing* 28, no. 5–6: 745–761. https://doi.org/10.1111/jocn.14710.

Korupp, S. E., and M. Szydlik. 2005. "Causes and Trends of the Digital Divide." *European Sociological Review* 21, no. 4: 409–422. https://doi.org/10.1093/esr/jci030.

Leist, Anja K. 2013. "Social Media Use of Older Adults: A Mini-Review." *Gerontology* 59, no. 4: 378–384. https://doi.org/10.1159/000346818.

Lupton, Deborah. 2015. *Digital Sociology*. London and New York: Routledge.

Marston, H. R., Charles Musselwhite, and Robin Hadley. 2020. "COVID-19 vs Social Isolation: The Impact Technology Can Have on Communities, Social Connections and Citizens." British Society of Gerontology, *Ageing Issues* (blog), March 18. https://ageingissues.wordpress.com/2020/03/18/covid-19-vs-social-isolation-the-impact-technology-can-have-on-communities-social-connections-and-citizens/.

Merkel, Sebastian, and Alexander Kucharski. 2019. "Participatory Design in Gerontechnology: A Systematic Literature Review." *The Gerontologist* 59, no. 1: e16–e25. https://doi.org/10.1093/geront/gny034.

Miller, Geoffrey. 2012. "The Smartphone Psychology Manifesto." *Perspectives on Psychological Science* 7, no. 3: 221–237. https://doi.org/10.1177/1745691612441215.

Mingo, Isabella, and Roberta Bracciale. 2018. "The Matthew Effect in the Italian Digital Context: The Progressive Marginalisation of the 'Poor.'" *Social Indicators Research* 135, no. 2: 629–659. https://doi.org/10.1007/s11205-016-1511-2.

Mitzner, Tracy L., Jyoti Savla, Walter R. Boot, Joseph Sharit, Neil Charness, Sara J. Czaja, et al. 2019. "Technology Adoption by Older Adults: Findings from the PRISM Trial." *The Gerontologist* 59, no. 1: 34–44. https://doi.org/10.1093/geront/gny113.

Moyle, Wendy, Cindy Jones, Jenny Murfield, Toni Dwan, and Tamara Ownsworth. 2018. "'We Don't Even Have Wi-Fi': A Descriptive Study Exploring Current Use and Availability of Communication Technologies in Residential Aged Care." *Contemporary Nurse* 54, no. 1: 35–43. https://doi.org/10.1080/10376178.2017.1411203.

National Academies of Sciences, Engineering, and Medicine. 2020. *Mobile Technology for Adaptive Aging: Proceedings of a Workshop*. Washington, DC: National Academies Press. https://doi.org/10.17226/25878.

Nielek, Radoslaw, Marta Lutostańska, Wiesław Kopeć, and Adam Wierzbicki. 2017. "Turned 70?: It Is Time to Start Editing Wikipedia." In *WI '17: Proceedings of the International Conference on Web Intelligence*, 899–906. München, Germany: ACM Press. https://doi.org/10.1145/3106426.3106539.

Ong, Anthony D., Bert N. Uchino, and Elaine Wethington. 2016. "Loneliness and Health in Older Adults: A Mini-Review and Synthesis." *Gerontology* 62, no. 4: 443–449. https://doi.org/10.1159/000441651.

Peacock, Sylvia E., and Harald Künemund. 2007. "Senior Citizens and Internet Technology: Reasons and Correlates of Access versus Non-Access in a European Comparative Perspective." *European Journal of Ageing* 4, no. 4: 191–200. https://doi.org/10.1007/s10433-007-0067-z.

Perrin, Andrew, and Sara Atske. 2021. "7% of Americans don't use the internet. Who are they?." Pew Research Center, April 2. https://www.pewresearch.org/fact-tank/2021/04/02/7-of-americans-dont-use-the-internet-who-are-they/

Pew Research Center. 2021a. "Internet/Broadband Fact Sheet." https://www.pewresearch.org/internet/fact-sheet/internet-broadband/.

Pew Research Center. 2021b. "Social Media Fact Sheet." https://www.pewresearch.org/internet/fact-sheet/social-media/.

Pew Research Center. 2021c. "Mobile Fact Sheet." https://www.pewresearch.org/internet/fact-sheet/mobile/.

Poushter, Jacob, Caldwell Bishop, and Hanuy Chwe. 2018. "Social Media Use Continues to Rise in Developing Countries but Plateaus across Developed Ones." Pew Research Center, June 19. http://www.pewglobal.org/2018/06/19/2-smartphone-ownership-on-the-rise-in-emerging-economies/.

Powell, Kimberly Ryan, Gregory Lynn Alexander, Richard Madsen, and Chelsea Deroche. 2019. "A National Assessment of Access to Technology among Nursing Home Residents: A Secondary Analysis." *JMIR Aging* 2, no. 1: e11449. https://doi.org/10.2196/11449.

Rikard, R. V., Ronald W. Berkowsky, and Shelia R. Cotten. 2018. "Discontinued Information and Communication Technology Usage among Older Adults in Continuing Care Retirement Communities in the United States." *Gerontology* 64, no. 2: 188–200. https://doi.org/10.1159/000482017.

Robinson, Laura, Shelia R. Cotten, Hiroshi Ono, Anabel Quan-Haase, Gustavo Mesch, Wenhong Chen, et al. 2015. "Digital Inequalities and Why They Matter." *Information, Communication & Society* 18, no. 5: 569–582. https://doi.org/10.1080/1369118X.2015.1012532.

Robinson, Laura, Jeremy Schulz, Aneka Khilnani, Hiroshi Ono, Shelia R. Cotten, Noah McClain, et al. 2020. "Digital Inequalities in Time of Pandemic: COVID-19 Exposure Risk Profiles and New Forms of Vulnerability." *First Monday* 25, no. 7. https://doi.org/10.5210/fm.v25i7.10845.

Sackmann, R., and O. Winkler. 2013. "Technology Generations Revisited: The Internet Generation." *Gerontechnology* 11, no. 4: 493–503. https://doi.org/10.4017/gt.2013.11.4.002.00.

Scheerder, Anique, Alexander van Deursen, and Jan van Dijk. 2017. "Determinants of Internet Skills, Uses and Outcomes. A Systematic Review of the Second- and Third-Level Digital Divide." *Telematics and Informatics* 34, no. 8: 1607–1624. https://doi.org/10.1016/j.tele.2017.07.007.

Schehl, Barbara. 2020. "Outdoor Activity among Older Adults: Exploring the Role of Informational Internet Use." *Educational Gerontology* 46, no. 1: 36–45. https://doi.org/10.1080/03601277.2019.1698200.

Schlomann, Anna, Peter Rasche, Alexander Seifert, Katharina Schäfer, Matthias Wille, Christina Bröhl, et al. 2019. "Augmented Reality Games for Health Promotion in Old Age." In *Augmented Reality Games II*, edited by Vladimir Geroimenko, 159–177. Cham, Switzerland: Springer International. https://doi.org/10.1007/978-3-030-15620-6_7.

Schlomann, Anna, Alexander Seifert, Susanne Zank, and Christian Rietz. 2020a. "Assistive Technology and Mobile ICT Usage among Oldest-Old Cohorts: Comparison of the Oldest-Old in Private Homes and in Long-Term Care Facilities." *Research on Aging* 42, no. 5–6: 163–173. https://doi.org/10.1177/0164027520911286.

Schlomann, Anna, Alexander Seifert, Susanne Zank, Christiane Woopen, and Christian Rietz. 2020b. "Use of Information and Communication Technology (ICT) Devices among the Oldest-Old: Loneliness, Anomie, and Autonomy." *Innovation in Aging* 4, no. 2: igz050. https://doi.org/10.1093/geroni/igz050.

Schulz, Richard, Hans-Werner Wahl, Judith T. Matthews, Annette De Vito Dabbs, Scott R. Beach, and Sara J. Czaja. 2015. "Advancing the Aging and Technology Agenda in Gerontology." *The Gerontologist* 55, no. 5: 724–734. https://doi.org/10.1093/geront/gnu071.

Seifert, Alexander. 2020. "Smartwatch Use among Older Adults: Findings from Two Large Surveys." In *Human Aspects of IT for the Aged Population. Technologies, Design and User Experience*, edited by Qin Gao and Jia Zhou, 372–385. Lecture Notes in Computer Science 12207. Cham, Switzerland: Springer International. https://doi.org/10.1007/978-3-030-50252-2_28.

Seifert, Alexander, Tobias Ackermann, and Hans R. Schelling. 2020. *Digitale Senioren III—2020/Nutzung von Informations- Und Kommunikationstechnologien (IKT) Durch Menschen Ab 65 Jahren in Der Schweiz*. Zürich: Zentrum für Gerontologie.

Seifert, Alexander, Markus Christen, and Mike Martin. 2018. "Willingness of Older Adults to Share Mobile Health Data with Researchers." *GeroPsych* 31, no. 1: 41–49. https://doi.org/10.1024/1662-9647/a000181.

Seifert, Alexander, and Shelia R. Cotten. 2020. "In Care and Digitally Savvy? Modern ICT Use in Long-Term Care Institutions." *Educational Gerontology* 46, no. 8: 473–485. https://doi.org/10.1080/03601277.2020.1776911.

Seifert, Alexander, Shelia R. Cotten, and Bo Xie. 2021. "A Double Burden of Exclusion? Digital and Social Exclusion of Older Adults in Times of COVID-19." *Journals of Gerontology: Series B* 76, no. 3: e99–e103. https://doi.org/10.1093/geronb/gbaa098.

Seifert, Alexander, Michael Doh, and Hans-Werner Wahl. 2017. "They Also Do It: Internet Use by Older Adults Living in Residential Care Facilities." *Educational Gerontology* 43, no. 9: 451–461. https://doi.org/10.1080/03601277.2017.1326224.

Seifert, Alexander, and Gabriella M. Harari. 2019. "Mobile Data Collection with Smartphones." In *Encyclopedia of Gerontology and Population Aging*, edited by Danan Gu and Matthew E. Dupre, 1–3. Cham, Switzerland: Springer International. https://doi.org/10.1007/978-3-319-69892-2_562-1.

Seifert, Alexander, Matthias Hofer, and Mathias Allemand. 2018. "Mobile Data Collection: Smart, but Not (Yet) Smart Enough." *Frontiers in Neuroscience* 12: 971. https://doi.org/10.3389/fnins.2018.00971.

Seifert, Alexander, Matthias Hofer, and Jörg Rössel. 2018. "Older Adults' Perceived Sense of Social Exclusion from the Digital World." *Educational Gerontology* 44, no. 12: 775–785. https://doi.org/10.1080/03601277.2019.1574415.

Seifert, Alexander, Stefan T. Kamin, and Frieder R. Lang. 2020. "Technology Adaptivity Mediates the Effect of Technology Biography on Internet Use Variability." *Innovation in Aging* 4, no. 2: igz054. https://doi.org/10.1093/geroni/igz054.

Seifert, Alexander, Dominique Alexandra Reinwand, and Anna Schlomann. 2019. "Designing and Using Digital Mental Health Interventions for Older Adults: Being Aware of Digital Inequality." *Frontiers in Psychiatry* 10: 568. https://doi.org/10.3389/fpsyt.2019.00568.

Seifert, Alexander, and Hans R. Schelling. 2015. "Mobile Use of the Internet Using Smartphones or Tablets by Swiss People over 65 Years." *Gerontechnology* 14, no. 1: 57–62. https://doi.org/10.4017/gt.2015.14.1.006.00.

Seifert, Alexander, and Hans Rudolf Schelling. 2018. "Seniors Online: Attitudes toward the Internet and Coping with Everyday Life." *Journal of Applied Gerontology* 37, no. 1: 99–109. https://doi.org/10.1177/0733464816669805.

Seifert, Alexander, and Anna Schlomann. 2021. "The Use of Virtual and Augmented Reality by Older Adults: Potentials and Challenges." *Frontiers in Virtual Reality* 2: 639718. https://doi.org/10.3389/frvir.2021.639718.

Siette, Joyce, Viviana Wuthrich, and Lee-Fay Low. 2020. "Social Preparedness in Response to Spatial Distancing Measures for Aged Care during COVID-19." *Journal of the American Medical Directors Association* 21, no. 7: 985–986. https://doi.org/10.1016/j.jamda.2020.04.015.

Sims, Tamara, Andrew E. Reed, and Dawn C. Carr. 2017. "Information and Communication Technology Use Is Related to Higher Well-Being among the Oldest-Old." *Journals of Gerontology Series B: Psychological Sciences and Social Sciences* 72, no. 5: 761–770. https://doi.org/10.1093/geronb/gbw130.

Szabo, Agnes, Joanne Allen, Christine Stephens, and Fiona Alpass. 2019. "Longitudinal Analysis of the Relationship between Purposes of Internet Use and Well-Being among Older Adults." *The Gerontologist* 59, no. 1: 58–68. https://doi.org/10.1093/geront/gny036.

Taylor, Kyle, and Laura Silver. 2019. "Smartphone Ownership Is Growing Rapidly around the World, but Not Always Equally." Pew Research Center, February 5. https://www.pewresearch.org/global/wp-content/uploads/sites/2/2019/02/Pew-Research-Center_Global-Technology-Use-2018_2019-02-05.pdf

Tsai, Hsin-yi Sandy, Ruth Shillair, and Shelia R. Cotten. 2017. "Social Support and 'Playing Around': An Examination of How Older Adults Acquire Digital Literacy with Tablet Computers." *Journal of Applied Gerontology* 36, no. 1: 29–55. https://doi.org/10.1177/0733464815609440.

Tsai, Hsin-yi Sandy, Ruth Shillair, Shelia R. Cotten, Vicki Winstead, and Elizabeth Yost. 2015. "Getting Grandma Online: Are Tablets the Answer for Increasing Digital Inclusion for Older Adults in the U.S.?" *Educational Gerontology* 41, no. 10: 695–709. https://doi.org/10.1080/03601277.2015.1048165.

Venkatesh, V., M. G. Morris, G. B. Davis, and F. D. Davis. 2003. "User Acceptance of Information Technology: Toward a Unified View." *MIS Quarterly* 27, no. 3: 425–478. https://doi.org/10.2307/30036540.

Vogels, Emily A. 2019. "Millennials Stand out for Their Technology Use, but Older Generations Also Embrace Digital Life." Pew Research Center, September 9. https://www.pewresearch.org/fact-tank/2019/09/09/us-generations-technology-use/.

Wang, Lin, Pei-Luen Patrick Rau, and Gavriel Salvendy. 2011. "Older Adults' Acceptance of Information Technology." *Educational Gerontology* 37, no. 12: 1081–1099.

Warschauer, Mark. 2004. *Technology and Social Inclusion: Rethinking the Digital Divide*. Cambridge, MA: MIT Press.

Winstead, Vicki, William A. Anderson, Elizabeth A. Yost, Shelia R. Cotten, Amanda Warr, and Ronald W. Berkowsky. 2013. "You Can Teach an Old Dog New Tricks: A Qualitative Analysis of How Residents of Senior Living Communities May Use the Web to Overcome Spatial and

Social Barriers." *Journal of Applied Gerontology* 32, no. 5: 540–560. https://doi.org/10.1177/0733464811431824.

Wolf, Friedrich, Alexander Seifert, Mike Martin, and Frank Oswald. 2021. "Considering Situational Variety in Contextualized Aging Research—Opinion about Methodological Perspectives." *Frontiers in Psychology* 12: 570900. https://doi.org/10.3389/fpsyg.2021.570900.

Wrzus, Cornelia, and Matthias R. Mehl. 2015. "Lab and/or Field? Measuring Personality Processes and Their Social Consequences." *European Journal of Personality* 29, no. 2: 250–271. https://doi.org/10.1002/per.1986.

Yu, Rebecca P., Nicole B. Ellison, Ryan J. McCammon, and Kenneth M. Langa. 2016. "Mapping the Two Levels of Digital Divide: Internet Access and Social Network Site Adoption among Older Adults in the USA." *Information, Communication & Society* 19, no. 10: 1445–1464. https://doi.org/10.1080/1369118X.2015.1109695.

CHAPTER 16

THE SOCIOLOGY OF SELF-TRACKING AND EMBODIED TECHNOLOGIES

How Does Technology Engage Gendered, Raced, and Datafied Bodies?

ELIZABETH WISSINGER

In the age of COVID-19, one of the top 10 wearables of 2020 was an air purifier you can strap on your face. Called the "Atmos" (Aō Air 2020), the mask claims to offer air filtration that is 50 times better than the leading masks. It has all the typical earmarks of wearable tech. It's clunky. It's funny looking. It's expensive. It has a "high-tech" aesthetic, with sleek metallic lines, glowing lights, and a vaguely spaceshippy vibe. It is Bluetooth-connected, so it can casually spew data to be parsed for corporate ends. Of course, it has received a ton of hype. Fawning articles from *Fast Company* (Schwab 2019), *Forbes* (Walmsley 2019), and the BBC (Kelion 2020) touted it as lifestyle protection against disease, pollution, and anything else the twenty-first century can throw at us. As with many other wearable technologies, the Atmos exemplifies many of the issues identified by scholars analyzing wearable tech: it pushes responsibility for socially caused risk onto individuals; its functioning benefits the company that manufactured it as much as, if not more than, the wearer; it assumes the wearer needs protection from the world; and it is designed more for show than for the actual comfort of the person using it.

This essay provides an overview of the issues raised by wearable technology as a social phenomenon through a survey of current sociological analyses of the subject. Since it is a complex site of study, whose hybrid nature can defy categorization, we must first delineate what, exactly, we mean by the term. Are we talking about garments? Gadgets? Medical devices? Computers? Should a study of technology worn on the body exclude technologies inserted into the body? Is "embodied technology" a better term? To make sense of the research on wearable tech, I will first give an overview of the kinds of technologies scholars have studied and then highlight three groups of studies that best represent the literature that has emerged to analyze wearable technology in social context.

This chapter offers an overview of the areas of sociological analysis focusing on self-tracking technologies, to give the reader a better sense of this burgeoning part of the field. Many scholars have examined products that enable self-tracking, by studying devices such as the smart watches and fitness trackers populating the wrists of folks who want to better themselves through data monitoring for self-optimization. Of devices that facilitate body/self interaction, the Apple watch and the Fitbit are the best-known examples—though the field has seen many different versions of self-tracking technology come and go. All areas of the body have been fair game, from smart rings and bracelets (Oura 2021; GripBeats 2020; Fossil 2021) to devices one tucks in one's bra (Matsakis 2017), wears on one's head (InteraXon 2021; Philips 2021; LIFTiD 2021), or wears on one's feet in the form of a *Get Smart*–like shoe.[1] Generally, the most common wearables aim to optimize body and self to achieve top-notch personal health, fitness, productivity, communicative capacity, wellness, and stress reduction (Chibuk 2020; FitTo Health 2020; Tap Systems 2021; G2T 2017; Bellabeat 2020; Taison Digital 2021; Apple Inc. 2020; Xenoma 2021; Wearable X 2021; Allison 2020; Digitsole Smartshoe 2020). At a recent meeting of the January Consumer Electronics Show, for example, developers wowed attendees with wearable technologies for wireless payment (Keyble 2021), personal safety (SEAM 2021), vision enhancement (smart eyewear), and health (smart clothing) and even devices one can strap on one's dog (Nuzzle 2019).

As discussed in the examples cited in this chapter, these self-tracking studies sometimes focus on user experience, in terms of the effects of data collection on how bodies are lived and interact with the surrounding world. Some of these studies also offer analysis from the critical data studies perspective. Since wearables are by definition technology worn on the body, they can render bodies legible to technological networks, making the wearable-enabled body a node in the internet of things. This aspect of wearable tech lends itself to the study of the datafication of bodies by technology. As I will discuss, the overarching theme of these studies elucidates how the power of wearables to reveal the inner workings of a body, tracking biometrics such as heartbeat, step count, and calories burned, can be a two-edged sword. While offering the user new forms of personal control over self and body, they also afford new avenues of corporate control in a Faustian deal to which many unwittingly agree the moment they strap on a device. As these studies point out, bringing technology into constant and direct contact with the body makes the personal political: Even as it offers the wearer intimate details about body and self, it exposes these same details to unchecked corporate data mining and behavioral control. The studies discussed in this essay reveal how the data exploitation model informing most wearable tech design is rife with issues surrounding big data, privacy, and surveillance. Viewed in this way, the seemingly innocuous self-tracking smart watch, pinging a text message alert, is in fact riddled with controversial issues, of which the sociologists under consideration here have taken note.

In addition to issues of data ownership, some of the studies consider how bodies in society are forcibly raced and gendered, which brings the question of who gets to choose personal technology that is designed with them in mind into sharp relief. The sociologists cited here who study wearables as cultural artifacts have uncovered values baked into designs that make broad assumptions about users, which are not always accurate or equitable. Investigating the origins of wearables' design and function has proven a fruitful avenue of sociological analysis of technology, data, and gender. As I shall discuss, however, empirical studies focused specifically on wearables and race are less common and represent an area of study in which sociologists are poised to make a valuable contribution.

Looking at these aspects of wearables—as facilitators of body/self interactions, data gathering devices that open the body to concerns about big data, and designed devices that sometimes offer highly gendered and raced functions and content as "neutral"— reveals how wearables trouble boundaries that sociologists frequently seek to map and analyze: work/leisure, public/private, nature/culture, body/self. Wearables are also a focus in ongoing debates about medicalization (Sandvik 2020a), the conversion of soldiers into a form of robocop in the military (Hambling 2020), and ethical issues raised by the use of ankle bracelets to limit movement in the case of house arrest (Jethani 2020) and immigration control. The focus of this section in the volume, however, is on everyday life, in which wearing a device is a personal choice. Of course, just how voluntary, informed, and equitable that choice can possibly be is itself a subject of debate, as the discussion here will assess.

Most of the work covered here is relatively recent, in part because the technology is so new but also because sociologists have come to see the value in studying digital technologies somewhat later than their colleagues in other fields. As digital sociologists Jessie Daniels, Karen Gregory, and Tressie McMillan Cottom (2017, xix) have pointed out, "As a discipline, sociology has been less concerned with redefining itself through its understanding of the digital, and has instead been content to cede its terrain" to a wide array of other disciplines, such as fashion studies, critical data studies, information studies, and communication and media studies, all of which have engaged quite readily with wearable tech. Until quite recently, getting a sense of the social issues surrounding wearable tech demanded taking a multidisciplinary point of view. Sociologists have had a more difficult time of it, in part because the discipline's traditions are so deeply mired in the fanciful assumption that there exist in the world distinct "ontological zones: that of human beings on the one hand; that of nonhumans on the other" (Latour 1993). Wearable tech troubles these divides in a manner that questions some of the underlying assumptions of sociological analysis, namely that human beings exist as a unit of study, which proper sociological methods can isolate from the writing, imaging, and knowledge technologies that make those humans legible in the first place. Sociologists have a unique contribution to make to the conversation, however. Sociological analyses of wearable technologies put the social sorting mechanisms of race, class, and gender front and center, thereby adding a needed dimension to a rich and growing field of analysis that can help us understand the complexities of everyday life and perhaps help guide where it is headed.

In sum, the studies considered in this chapter highlight important issues at stake in the realm of wearable tech, including the emergence and cultural meaning of the quantified self (QS) movement (e.g., groups of people united in their belief that self-mastery and empowerment can be achieved through self-tracking); the rise of wearables at work in the form of enforced data gathering and the subsequent labor issues it entails; the threat of corporate profiteering from personal data gathered through surveillance hidden as personal empowerment and connection; and finally, the issue of wearables and women, where researchers uncovered sexism about female-identified people baked into the design of the devices themselves. The essay concludes by discussing the dearth of studies on wearables and race and offers suggestions for avenues of inquiry in this much needed area of analysis. The following sections will take up each of these areas in turn, to offer a brief overview and enhanced understanding of the issues highlighted by sociological analysis of wearable technologies.

Wearable Tech, the Body, and the Quantified Self

The emergence of vibrating, chirping, tapping, and other forms of human machine interface, dramatically increase the speed and computational power of devices, making "personalized health" into a new watchword. As the studies in this section point out, health is being reconfigured from a public good into a luxury commodity as entrepreneurs vying for new markets in "wellness" have explored strategies for human biological optimization and enhancement, hoping to commercialize many aspects of this process. These studies of the QS in particular have outlined how data-mining personalization protocols have intensified internet and social media entanglements in the name of convenience and control. These studies identify how wearable tech pushes the envelopes of tracking and management, amplifying how technologically enmeshed bodies are nudged and cajoled, metered and managed, protected and surveilled, or coerced and connected.

In one of the first sociological monographs to tackle these issues, *The Quantified Self* (2016), sociologist Deborah Lupton examined self-tracking cultures and practices by means of analyzing portrayals of self-tracking in popular media and exploring "app and software descriptions, product reviews, news reports, white papers, social media and blog discussions" (p. 6). She tracked hashtags, such as #quantifiedself, #lifelogging, and #selftracking; attended exhibitions and websites of artists and designers engaged in self-tracking; and synthesized a broad range of empirical studies of Fitbits, activity trackers, and devices that monitor human physical states.

In contrast to the hype surrounding wearables that was common at the time,[2] the book's take on wearable tech was not a rosy one. Lupton sought to cut through some of the boosterism surrounding wearables by examining the processes of forced data collection, disputes over data ownership, and the politics of bodily control in public and private life enabled by commercially available self-tracking devices. The book touches on themes that thread throughout the sociological literature on wearable tech and are noted here as a grounding for categorizing the work that will be discussed in the following sections. Calling on some of the major theoretical formulations that have deeply affected sociological analysis, Lupton theorized data gathering as a form of "free labor" (Terranova 2000); a means of control invoked by the figure of the panopticon, achieving an intensified form of surveillance (Foucault 2012); and a form of "biopower," which incites personal bodily management to fall into lockstep with population-wide demands for regulation and control (Foucault 2008). Lupton found data ownership to be a central issue, focusing on what she termed the "data politics" involved in adjudicating who can rightfully claim ownership of personal information generated by means of commercially available devices. The book argues that freely generated data taken up for corporate profit is the price users pay for enjoying "free" content, experiences, or self-monitoring provided by interacting with a device. This issue of voluntary generation of data that is subsequently exploited resonates with many later studies which explore coercive data generation of the kind that explicitly benefits employers; it also touches on the murkier issue of "opting in" to get perks in exchange for sharing data with corporate third parties, as I will discuss. The book ends by invoking Donna Haraway's figure of the cyborg (Haraway 1991) to call for "self-tracking to be transformed into a political act" (Lupton 2016, 147). Lupton argued that we all must engage in "citizen hacktivism, in the service of agitating for social change and acknowledging the social determinants of health, productivity, and well-being" (2016, 147).

Since her first forays into analyzing wearable tech, Lupton's take on it has become increasingly complex. Her recent work has moved toward a feminist materialist stance to explore the exchange of power and agency between humans and non-humans that wearables facilitate (Lupton 2020). Covering a range of topics, Lupton is currently the most prolific sociologist working in this area. Readers interested in reading more may refer to Lupton's chapter in this volume.

Lupton is not the only scholar to analyze wearable technology from a social scientific stance. Lupton's monograph came out within a 2-year span that produced a bumper crop of books on wearables. These works are defined by their focus on the spread of self-tracking from an underground culture to a widespread society practice. It should be noted that only one of these books can claim authorship by a sociologist—the rest are works by anthropologists. Gina Neff (sociologist and communication scholar) and Dawn Nafus' (anthropologist) *Self-Tracking* (2016) took a clear-eyed look at the fraught relationship between the QS movement and the corporate interests seeking to profit from their community's innovations. The QS community grew out of a small number of meet-ups in the San Francisco area in the early 2000s, gatherings of individuals interested in "taking advantage of the enhanced availability of technology for self-tracking"

(Neff and Nafus 2016, 33). Within a larger cultural move toward the uncritical acceptance of self-quantification as a means to self-optimization, QSers asked questions, posed problems, and hacked themselves in creative ways. Taking this community and the quasi-medical aspects of self-tracking as their primary point of analysis, Neff and Nafus' findings made a substantial contribution to debates about data and social justice, by describing how their respondents carved out a space of empowerment via self-quantification and coordinated data collection for the benefit of the community and fought for opportunities for more equitable participation in data gathering and interpretation.

Similarly, anthropologist Josh Berson's *Computable Bodies: Instrumented Life and the Human Somatic Niche* (2015) argued that although the QS movement's focus on "self-instrumentation" seemed to privilege individual behavioral change, its practice of wielding data as a means to optimization might be turned toward fostering the social dimensions of well-being as well. Within the year, anthropologist Dawn Nafus' edited collection *Quantified: Biosensing Technologies in Everyday Life* (2016) broadened the focus on tracking technologies to encompass the body in its environment, to present analyses of "data, personhood, and the urge to self-quantify" that ranged from the cellular level of microbiomes to the macro level of water treatment plants. Anthropologist Natasha Dow Schüll's investigation of self-tracking also made the QS the primary unit of analysis. Her focus on designers and users in tandem offered a fresh perspective that attempted to dispel the doom and gloom about data ownership and control by big corporations, which animates so much of the work on this topic. Rather, Schüll saw these technologies in terms of a "micro-nudge" that helps the user to carve out personal space within Big Brother's overarching influence (Schüll 2016, 2019). In one of her takes on the subject, Schüll's user-centered stance argued for a nuanced approach:

> Rather than dismiss self-quantifiers—as life-avoiding and robotically inclined, as victims of data capitalism and its surveillance apparatus, or as symptomatic figures of neoliberal subjectivity and its self-mastering, entrepreneurial ethos—we might regard them as pioneers in the art of living with and through data. (2019, 925)

Overall, the initial wave of sociological analysis focused mainly on the emergence of self-tracking as a cultural practice. Studies of the QS movement documented its nerdy, whacky, individualistically inflected origins, whose respondents tracked biometrics through cobbled-together systems of do-it-yourself body sensors connected, for instance, to Christmas lights that flickered with the wearer's changing mood (see Dougherty 2012). They then went on to trace the contours of the power struggles over data as wearable trackers proliferated in a burgeoning market. Researchers found neoliberal pressures driving the coercive nature of wearable technology, by looking at how these pressures shaped data relations and data gatherers' rights. While these issues continue to surface in more recent studies, they have been less focused on the QSers as a movement. These studies have instead documented and analyzed the normalization of self-quantification in an increasingly digitized world. Since 2015, sociological research on wearables and self-tracking has branched into several ongoing debates, to which I will now turn.

The first studies take up issues of data ownership, property, and personhood within debates about meaning-making and management of body and self by looking specifically at the coerced use of self-tracking at work, while also considering the generation of data as work; the second group considers wearables as a form of surveillance within the context of big data debates; and finally, in the third area of research, scholars of gender and race have taken issue with designs that originate in the all too familiar "bro-culture" of venture capital–funded startups to reveal "a certain blindness" when it comes to women (Lupton 2015) and uncovered a failure to confront problems emanating from the #DesignSoWhite world that so often ignores the needs of Blacks, the indigenous, and people of color (or Blacks, Asians, and other minority ethnic groups) when bringing wearables, or most technology for that matter, to market (Benjamin 2019; McIlwain 2019; Broussard 2018; Noble 2018; Browne 2015; Nakamura 2014).

Wearable Tech and Work, Where Living Becomes Living™

On his deathbed, Steve Jobs had a vision of the dawn of a new era: "The biggest innovations of the twenty-first century will be the intersection of biology and technology. A new era is beginning, just like the digital one when I was [my son's] age" (Isaacson 2011). Some have called this the "fourth Industrial Revolution," coming after the first three, in which we moved from mechanical to electrical to digital forms of production.[3] As the fourth Industrial Revolution of biological production unfolds, it brings new intimacy with, and exposure to, technology that is altering social relations on a scale not seen since the dawn of the internet.

Within the sociology of work and labor, the disruptive effects of digitization have been well documented. Starting in the mid-1990s when internet technology was relatively new, analyses of the internet and subsequently social media have tracked the changing nature of work in a digitizing world. Scholars in the area uncovered conceptions of "new" forms of labor, such as immaterial labor (Lazzarato 1996), affective labor (Clough and Halley 2007), free labor (Terranova 2000), playbour (Scholz 2013), and cultural labor (Zukin 1995; Hesmondhalgh 2013; Fuchs 2014). These analyses revealed how divisions between labor and leisure were blurred by the boundaryless nature of digital interactions, allowing increasing levels of "off" time to be co-opted into the labor process, creating new inequities and levels of exploitation.

Scholars of work in communication, media studies, and sociology subsequently examined the proliferation of the co-optation of life itself, revealing how the hungry maw of social media sucked as much of life as possible into monetization processes online. Combining insights from the broad literature on cultural labor and gendered work, scholars such as Duffy (2015, 2017), Banet-Weiser (2012), Abidin (2016), Marwick (2015), and Senft (2008, 2012) explored the new modes of opportunity and exploitation, innovation, and evolving forms of inequality these technologies provoked. These analyses of the brief age of blogging and its usurpation by social media prompted further excavations of the exploitative aspects of digital work, such as aspirational labor (Duffy 2017), glamour labor (Wissinger 2015), status labor (Marwick 2015), self-branding labor (Senft 2012), and visibility labor (Abidin 2016). Against this backdrop, sociological analysis of wearable tech has taken up the notion of data production as a form of work, to explore new modes of productivity that are not easily identified as work.

How can converting a body into data be considered a form of labor? Sociological analyses of work and labor have traditionally focused on the management of bodily labor power within coercive circumstances. The notion that merely moving around, breathing, eating, or sleeping can become a form of work was somewhat controversial. Several sociologists tackled this idea to produce research indicating that wearables proved definitively that this was indeed the case.

The initial sociological studies found that the QS movement set in motion a complicated dance between empowerment through self-knowledge, on the one hand, and co-optation by its dependence on tools that threaten the privacy and ownership of that knowledge, on the other. Within these intricate relations of pleasure and power, studies of commercial fitness trackers made it clear that data was a form of free labor, with the lion's share of benefits from data mining going to corporations, not users. The consequent proliferation of wearables, as they migrated beyond the wrist to colonize every inch of the body, developed in an environment where taking up bodily data as a resource for profit became normalized (Wissinger 2017a,b, 2018).

Sociologists' subsequent studies of commercially available personal tech wearables shed light on how these technologies converted areas of life in which the body was not considered to be at work, the sleeping, eating, exercising, and emoting body, into yet another resource to be tossed into the whirring hoppers of corporate profit-seeking. Examining the inter-imbrication of the goals for self-management through self-care with corporate goals for managing workers, digital sociologist Karen Gregory and co-authors argued that this new set of relations "turn[ed] the body into an investment property":

> From the perspective of the new spirit of capitalism, using fitness trackers is a logical, cost-saving practice: If every body is to be a business and each individual an entrepreneur of the self, then each body-factory needs a managerial process to gather and analyze data in hopes of running the business better, maximizing efficiency, and minimizing risk. But by engaging with tracking devices and their associated services, the user interacts with a black-box ecosystem of data circulation that co-opts the act of self-care for corporate ends.
>
> (Gregory et al. 2017)

The authors go on to point out the following:

> Under this logic—one that sees bodies as "owned" by selves—care becomes entangled with a sense of duty to make the body endlessly productive, an investment capable of yielding returns. Each individual must be a manager of the self and an investor in the body as a capital stock.
>
> (Gregory et al. 2017)

Gregory and her co-authors' essay identified a theme that has appeared frequently and added further nuance by the ongoing sociological analysis of self-tracking and the lived body. Researchers in this area have repeatedly found that tracking technologies amplified the murky intermingling of self-entrepreneurial impulses that benefit the wearer, with forces converting users and workers into body-factories whose efforts at self-care were quickly co-opted not only for the benefit of the corporations where they worked but also for the benefit of the corporations which produced the devices that converted the body's self-care into work.

Sociologist Btihaj Ajana noted this structure/agency tension in the turn to metrics and measurement as an unquestioned social good useful for the management of both individuals and populations in her book *Metric Culture: Ontologies of Self-Tracking Practices* (2018).

> What is striking about this metric culture is that not only are governments and private companies the only actors interested in using metrics and data to control and manage individuals and populations, but individuals themselves are now choosing to voluntarily quantify themselves and their lives more than ever before, happily sharing the resulting data with others and actively turning themselves into projects of (self-) governance and surveillance.
>
> (Ajana 2018)

To put these findings in context, we must think about how voluntary self-quantification rose with the tides of self-optimization, which sociologist Nikolas Rose (2006) identified as endemic to neoliberal forces that contributed to the popularization of self-branding as a way of life. Within this social trend, the line between "turning" oneself "into a project" and the personal demands of seeking project-based (or gig) work became increasingly blurred. Wearable devices' monitoring and metric conversion of bodily processes at all times, not just while at work, served to strengthen these forces within what surveillance studies scholar Jose van Dijck famously termed the "datafication of everyday life" (van Dijck 2014). Amidst this widespread datafication, researchers seeking to examine these issues have found them particularly pronounced in the workplace.

Social scientist Thomas Calvard examined several social scientific perspectives on the "quantified employee self" and found practices of "embodied sensemaking" where employees self-consciously used big data to try to make sense of themselves within "wider digital and organizational environments" (Calvard 2019, 1). He looked at "employers' big data strategies for governing and managing the performance of quantified digital employee selves" (p. 1) and argued that the self-conscious use of technologies that feed seamlessly into intensified employee surveillance and control created a tension that must be addressed, to protect employee agency within and against these corporate interests.

Interestingly, several researchers followed this tension straight to the individualization of risk and the management of the fallibility of bodies in the insurance industry. Cultural studies scholar Constantine Gidaris examined the relationship between "interactive life insurance companies and their policyholders" and found that "wearable fitness devices are deployed by these companies as data-generating surveillance technologies instead of personal health and fitness devices" (Gidaris 2019, 132). Looking specifically at "the labour of the interactive life insurance policyholder" (p. 135), Gidaris identified the data generation by means of tracking physical activity and biometrics through wearing a fitness device as a form of unremunerated "free labor." The interactive life insurance policyholders Gidaris studied were incentivized through a system of rewards and punishments to give away their bodily data tracked by wearable devices through playing games that accumulated "vitality points" (p. 136), which could lower their insurance premiums. In this process, he argued, "wearable fitness devices do not operate in social or financial isolation, free from the clutches of surveillance capitalism"; rather, they turn "bodies into data flows that can be exchanged, purchased, and sold in the digital economy," essentially converting the body to "a digital site, one whose value is predicated entirely on its capacity to yield profitable information" (p. 137). In other words, producing data in exchange for gaining reasonable access to life insurance protection is a coerced form of data mining that should be considered work, no matter how much it looks like playful, voluntary engagement.

Similarly, sociologist Liz McFall and media studies scholar Liz Moor looked at "efforts by health insurers to incentivize health behaviours (for example through the use of fitness trackers), and insurance companies' own marketing materials" to "assess the current state of play in the field of 'personalized' insurance pricing" and found that these "new methods of pricing and premium setting that are claimed to follow from the availability of self-tracking technologies and new volumes of customer data" troubled distinctions between "property" and "personhood" (McFall and Moor 2018, 193) in a manner that found surveillance to be a key factor in the process.

These trade-offs are some of the many "costs of connection" which sociologists Nick Couldry and Ulises Mejias (2019) enumerated in their book analyzing these society-wide issues. In the process of what they call "data colonialism," hapless citizen/workers must engage in "data relations" in which they have but little choice to submit:

> There are indeed plenty of hard incentives to submit to data relations: lower insurance premiums, the availability of workplace health insurance only if an employee accepts tracking of their health, or perhaps the unavailability of household goods that can function without connection.
>
> (Couldry and Mejias 2019, 133)

Citing how wearables collapse the distance between technologies of quantification and a social actor's body by means of sensors on the body, Couldry and Mejias position wearables within forms of data colonialism that rely on the intimacy enabled by wearables. They argue that wearables are "only the start" of a broader phenomenon in which

> data relations increasingly strive to erase the distance between the social actor's body and the precisely targeted sensor system that serves it (or more accurately, which that body serves) . . . . The gathering and processing of personal data and its conversion into a targeted marketing offer (here's a coupon for smart water, since you're sweating) has all happened before we can reflect on any of this.
>
> (Couldry and Mejias 2019, 129)

The result, they argue, is a disturbing loss of agency to fight against the growing "power of the social quantification sector" (2019, 17) that wearables and body tracking devices have made possible.

In sum, wearables are among the several technologies that privacy specialist Bruce Schneier has termed an "intimate form of surveillance" (2015, 1). They are part and parcel of the constant trade-off between exposing data about one's physical state, location, and proclivities in exchange for, say, free access to an internet search to locate the nearest donut shop, the seamless convenience of paying for a baker's dozen using contactless payment on your smart watch, and increased motivation to work off the aftermath of such sweet consumption by strapping on a fitness tracker. Among the advertisements for donuts, digital payment apps, fitness trackers, and weight loss apps that will soon spring up in the margins of your every digital interaction, the intimacy of digital surveillance becomes quite clear.

While sociologists of work highlighted wearables' role in surveillance at work, the next section considers these forms of data intimacy in other life sectors. Taking the work of wearables beyond the workplace, some scholars have examined wearables' role in privacy violation by means of both societal and personal surveillance made possible by the turn to "metric culture," in a "datafied" world in which wearables have become a common facet of everyday life. In these studies, sociologists highlight how wearables trouble understandings of the social construction of privacy and raise important questions about where the line between private and public is now drawn.

PRIVACY AND SURVEILLANCE STUDIES

As wearables augment data's value, it has become urgently important to expose the exploitative origins of that value, via concerted scholarship and public-facing inquiry. In the trend toward digitization, surveillance studies has become a field in its own right, attracting scholars from a range of disciplines, including sociologists and those who take sociological concerns of public/private divides surrounding privacy and personhood to heart in their research. Within the overarching message that, when it comes to data privacy and personhood, "it's complicated" (boyd 2014), sociologists have sought to identify the tensions and travails embodied by the use of wearable tech and the personal data that is its modus operandi.

Among the most influential concepts informing these studies has been sociologists Haggerty and Ericson's (2000) formulation of the "surveillant assemblage," in which they argue that surveillance systems have converged to create discrete and virtual "data doubles" that transform the contours of surveillance, making it far more flexible and pervasive than previous modes. This formulation has informed several sociological studies including recent studies of wearables and sport (Esmonde 2020), fashion (Wissinger 2018), health (Rich and Miah 2017), children (Sandvik 2020b), and the way agency is complicated when using wearables, making it a moving target that is hard to pin down (Young 2018).

Many analyses of privacy and wearables have been informed by scholars in information science, such as Helen Nissenbaum's oft-cited 2004 formulation of "contextual integrity." This was a "new construct" proposed as an

> alternative benchmark for privacy, to capture the nature of challenges posed by information technologies. Contextual integrity ties adequate protection for privacy to norms of specific contexts, demanding that information gathering and dissemination be appropriate to that context and obey the governing norms of distribution within it.
>
> (Nissenbaum 2004, 119)

This rather fluid definition of information privacy reflects the norms of technological embodiment within which scholars have faced the complex task of arguing for the public's right to have access to the criteria for adjudicating whose data or what forms of data should be protected. As sociologists have noted, alongside scholars from other disciplines with similar concerns, users frequently have little idea of the risks involved when strapping on a device.

Wearables marketed to the public as something they not only want but need profit from the fact that users' knowledge about their data vulnerability is dim at best. Some users, for instance, reported not realizing that the data collected by their Fitbit went any further than their own phones (Zimmer et al. 2020). A Pew Research Center study found that half of Americans do not know what a privacy policy is (Smith 2014). Others have pointed out the low level of knowledge and high levels of resignation evidenced in actual versus stated privacy behaviors. Some scholars found high levels of cynicism, documenting users who faced a paradox—they knew their privacy was compromised by their use of devices, yet they neglected to try to protect themselves (Hoffmann, Lutz, and Ranzini 2016)—while others found forms of apathy (Hargittai and Marwick 2016) or privacy fatigue (Choi, Park, and Jung 2018) and varying and fluid conditions of data protection (Lupton and Michael 2017).

Along with scholars who have been sounding the alarm about the risk of possible data loss, leakage, or compromise inherent to wearable health technologies, others have highlighted how wearables play easily into forms of biopolitics, which connect micropractices of individual control and empowerment with broader structures of management that tend to disempower the individual. Recent analyses have highlighted the trade-off between increased self-knowledge and the loss of autonomy involved in gaining that knowledge through commercial fitness trackers (Lanzing 2016); biopolitical aspects of fitness trackers as a form of digital health (Ajana 2017); and the way "digital self-tracking devices ... expand individuals' capacity for self-knowledge and self-care at the same time that they facilitate unprecedented levels of biometric surveillance, extend the regulatory mechanisms of both public health and fashion/beauty authorities, and enable increasingly rigorous body projects devoted to the attainment of normative femininity" (Sanders 2017). Overall, looking at wearables in terms of biopolitics illustrates how they take "a new socio-technical grip on the human body" that targets "habits of moving, eating and drinking, sleeping, working and relaxing" as "the common ground for governance and optimization," which represents a "remarkable shift" in focus from " 'life itself' to 'life as it is lived' " (Lindner 2020).

The overall takeaway of the sociology of surveillance by means of wearable-enabled data tracking is that data design and privacy are urgent social issues in need of careful examination and scholarly discussion. As feminists Catherine D'Ignazio and Lauren F. Klein have passionately argued in their advance publicity for their book *Data Feminism* (2020),

> Today, data science is a form of power. It has been used to expose injustice, improve health outcomes, and topple governments. But it has also been used to discriminate, police, and surveil. This potential for good, on the one hand, and harm, on the other, makes it essential to ask: Data science by whom? Data science for whom? Data science with whose interests in mind? The narratives around big data and data science are overwhelmingly white, male, and techno-heroic.

The authors make a strong case for finding a "new way of thinking about data science and data ethics—one that is informed by intersectional feminist thought." As such scholarship makes very clear, "the data never, ever 'speak for themselves' " (D'Ignazio and Klein 2020), and new modes of analysis are needed to open pathways for more specifically sociological studies of data, privacy, and the wearables that blur the boundaries between the two.

Wearable Tech and Women

We have seen the internet's dreams of improved society promised by the free exchange of information devolve into a free-for-all in which online misogyny is commonplace and your personal data is up for sale to the highest bidder. That tech is a boy's game continues to be a depressing constant in findings studying technology, and wearables are no exception. As Caroline Criado-Perez points out in her entertainingly upsetting book *Invisible Women: Data Bias in a World Designed for Men*, "In the tech world, the implicit assumption that men are the default human remains king" (2019, 176). Sociologist Gina Neff and co-author Becca Schwartz have termed these "gendered affordances," which they define as "social affordances that enable different users to take different actions based on the gendered social and cultural repertoires available to users and technology designers" (Schwartz and Neff 2019).

In my research on wearables, I spoke to early adopters, hackers, technophiles, fashionistas, and design freaks in interviews and at fashion and technology gatherings, meet-ups, and summits. I asked attendees and participants about why and how gender shapes what we put onto—and into—the body. I too found the "default" male body that shaped the "gendered affordances" of wearable tech; wearables aimed at women were inflected by deep-seated cultural ambivalence about women in public space, women in relationships, and women in tech (Wissinger 2017a, 2017b)[4]. Body alarms, and smart jewelry that dials 911 at the first sign of distress were typical of early iterations of wearables for women. As one user experience expert explained to me, technologies that assume women in public are all potential victims of violence come from "sort of an understandable first wave of things, but it is colored by 'Damsel in Distress' gender associations." My research found little evidence that these technologies could move beyond gendered assumptions limiting this technology's potential, precluding exploration of avenues for moving the field toward more equitable and socially just ends.

Recent sociological studies of wearable tech have uncovered similar issues. Feminist scholars Rena Bivens and Amy Hasinoff's study of over 200 mobile phone apps designed to prevent sexual violence found that the "anti-rape app design generally reinforces and reflects pervasive rape myths, by both targeting potential victims and reinforcing stranger-danger" (Bivens and Hasinoff 2018). Similarly, cultural sociologist Renee Marie Shelby's clever study of international patent and historical records of anti-rape technologies from 1850 to 2016 found that inventors subscribe to what she termed "techno-physical feminism—or strategies that utilize technoscience to seemingly transform the wearer's psychology, corporeal resilience, and agency" (Shelby 2019). With a clear nod toward Judy Wajcman's (2004) articulation of technofeminism, Shelby argued that recent iterations of wearable anti-rape technology "reinforced traditional gender ideologies and re-inscribed feminine bodies as passive." The "damsel in distress" still needs protection by means of her wearable alarms, speed dial to 911, and automatic SOS calls silently broadcasting her distress to friends near and far.

Wearable Tech and Race

Sociologist Ruha Benjamin's study summed up her research findings regarding racially biased algorithms, programming assumptions, and projected user behavior as the "new Jim Code" (Benjamin 2019). Her book joins several critical race studies of technology that are building a much needed canon (McIlwain 2019; Broussard 2018; Noble 2018; Browne 2015). Excepting Benjamin's book, these works emanate from outside of the field of sociology. In particular, Jim Code seems to have affected the availability of sociological research on wearable technology. Given some of its obvious problems, sociological analysis of wearable tech with regard to race should be much easier to find and cite than it is as of this writing.

Consider a recent article in *Forbes*, which argues that Black-centered design is the future of business, if somebody would just pay attention (Winchester 2020). The problems are not just a few. Citing recent studies (Hailu 2019), Winchester enumerates as follows:

> Many wearable heart rate trackers rely on technology that could be less reliable for users with darker skin, which negatively impacts people of color whose employers incentivize employees' use of fitness trackers with extra vacation days, gear, or even lower health insurance premiums. Recent studies on facial recognition technologies find that many of these systems perform poorly on Black faces.... Even within the sectors of the tech community that advocate for human-centered design, such as human–computer interaction, little has been done to grapple with racism.
>
> (Winchester 2020)

Little has been done to address these problems in sociology either, it would seem. Despite her comprehensive catalogue of articles about wearables in general, a search of the Deborah Lupton literature turned up nothing that focused specifically on race as a variable. Many scholars refer to race as one variable among many, but empirical sociological studies focused on race as the main variable to examine users of wearable tech are hard to come by. Winchester is not a sociologist, but he has published a case study of an "Afrofuturistic reimagining" of "connected fitness technologies for Black/African-American women that addresses the often socially and culturally exclusionary form of current designs," arguing that "engaging Afrofuturism 2.0 would support the development of future technologies that are more relevant and responsive to the Black mind, body, and spirit" (Winchester 2019, 55). Similarly, information scientists Sofiya Noble and Sarah T. Roberts have identified that "nuanced, intersectional analyses of power along race, class, and gender must be at the forefront of future research on wearable technologies" (Noble and Roberts 2016), pointing out that race and class taken together are urgently important in the "face of unending rollouts of new wearable products designed to integrate seamlessly with everyday life—for those, of course, who can afford them."

Sociologists are incredibly well positioned to address inequities baked into the design of wearable technology, and more research is needed, especially on the effects of race on design and use. Rather than leaving the work for Black sociologists, making race the focal point of technological usage and effects should be of primary concern for all researchers interested in investigating the social impacts of technologies such as wearables, which are so intimately connected to how the body is perceived, managed, and lived. While sociology is now paying more attention to the ramifications of our digitized world, wearable tech presents a field that is still ripe for analysis. Bringing the unique ability of sociological research to identify problems on the ground, as they are lived, with rigorously gathered empirical evidence for backup, sociologists have much to offer to conversations about wearable technology and fights over data ownership, problems with privacy and surveillance, sexism in design, and racial inequities in the design and use of these devices that have promised empowerment to so many.

Notes

1. *Get Smart* was a 1960s television show in which the spy was equipped with a phone in his shoe—a ridiculously hilarious idea at the time that is now embodied by the Bluetooth-enabled smart shoe. It isn't a phone, but it can definitely "talk" to one (Under Armour 2021); Marsan (2008) is another discussion of the *Get Smart* transition into reality.
2. The years 2014 (Spence 2013), 2015 (Gibbs 2014), and 2016 (Ingham 2015) were each in turn deemed "the year for wearable technology."
3. The phrase "fourth Industrial Revolution" was first coined by Schwab in *The Fourth Industrial Revolution* (2016) and introduced the same year at the World Economic Forum.
4. I use the term "women" here as it is used in marketing to woman-identified persons, while acknowledging that marketing terms import problematic assumptions about gender normativity that affect a variety of bodies, queer and heterosexual, trans and cis, which thus far have not fit into the established markets.

References

Abidin, Crystal. 2016. "Visibility Labour: Engaging with Influencers' Fashion Brands and #OOTD Advertorial Campaigns on Instagram." *Media International Australia* 161, no. 1: 86–100. https://doi.org/10.1177/1329878X16665177.

Ajana, Btihaj. 2017. "Digital Health and the Biopolitics of the Quantified Self." *Digital Health* 3 (January): 205520761668950. https://doi.org/10.1177/2055207616689509.

Ajana, Btihaj, ed. 2018. *Metric Culture: Ontologies of Self-Tracking Practices*. Bingley, UK: Emerald Publishing.

Allison, Conor. 2020. "Asics Smart Running Shoe Offers Real-Time Running Data." Wareable, January 8. Accessed December 2020 at https://www.wareable.com/wearable-tech/asics-smart-running-shoe-prototype-ces-7853.

Aō Air. 2020. "The Atmos." Accessed July 2021 at https://www.ao-air.com.

Apple Inc. 2020. "Apple Watch." Accessed December 2020 at https://www.apple.com/watch/.

Banet-Weiser, Sarah. 2012. *Authentic™: Politics and Ambivalence in a Brand Culture*. Critical Cultural Communication. New York: New York University Press.

Bellabeat. 2020. "Bellabeat: Sync Your Body & Mind." Accessed July 2021 at https://shop.bellabeat.com/.

Benjamin, Ruha. 2019. *Race after Technology: Abolitionist Tools for the New Jim Code*. Medford, MA: Polity.

Berson, Josh. 2015. *Computable Bodies: Instrumented Life and the Human Somatic Niche*. London: Bloomsbury Academic.

Bivens, Rena, and Amy Adele Hasinoff. 2018. "Rape: Is There an App for That? An Empirical Analysis of the Features of Anti-Rape Apps." *Information, Communication & Society* 21, no. 8: 1050–1067.

boyd, danah. 2014. *It's Complicated: The Social Lives of Networked Teens*. New Haven, CT: Yale University Press.

Broussard, Meredith. 2018. *Artificial Unintelligence: How Computers Misunderstand the World*. Cambridge, MA: MIT Press.

Browne, Simone. 2015. *Dark Matters: On the Surveillance of Blackness*. Durham, NC: Duke University Press.

Calvard, Thomas. 2019. "Integrating Social Scientific Perspectives on the Quantified Employee Self." *Social Sciences* 8, no. 9: 262. https://doi.org/10.3390/socsci8090262.

Chibuk, John David. 2020. "Blueberry: Smart Glasses That Help You Relax and Perform." Kickstarter, November 3. https://www.kickstarter.com/projects/jdchibuk/smart-glasses-that-help-you-relax-and-perform.

Choi, Hanbyul, Jonghwa Park, and Yoonhyuk Jung. 2018. "The Role of Privacy Fatigue in Online Privacy Behavior." *Computers in Human Behavior* 81: 42–51. https://doi.org/10.1016/j.chb.2017.12.001.

Clough, Patricia Ticineto, and Jean O'Malley Halley. 2007. *The Affective Turn: Theorizing the Social*. Durham, NC: Duke University Press.

Couldry, Nick, and Ulises Ali Mejias. 2019. *The Costs of Connection: How Data Is Colonizing Human Life and Appropriating It for Capitalism*. Culture and Economic Life. Stanford, CA: Stanford University Press.

Criado-Perez, Caroline. 2019. *Invisible Women: Data Bias in a World Designed for Men*. New York: Abrams Press.

Daniels, Jessie, Karen Gregory, and Tressie McMillan Cottom, eds. 2017. *Digital Sociologies*. London: Policy Press.

Digitsole Smartshoe. 2020. "Digitsole Smartshoe." Kickstarter, October 2. https://www.kickstarter.com/projects/141658446/digitsole-smartshoe-the-worlds-first-intelligent-s.

D'Ignazio, Catherine, and Lauren F. Klein. 2020. *Data Feminism*. Strong Ideas Series. Cambridge, MA: MIT Press. For language quoted here, see https://data-feminism.mitpress.mit.edu/.

Dougherty, Nancy. 2012. "Technology for Mindfulness." Quantified Self: Self-Knowledge through Numbers. Video, 16:36. https://quantifiedself.com/show-and-tell/?project=43.

Duffy, Brooke. 2015. "Amateur, Autonomous, and Collaborative: Myths of Aspiring Female Cultural Producers in Web 2.0." *Critical Studies in Media Communication* 32, no. 1: 48–64. https://doi.org/10.1080/15295036.2014.997832.

Duffy, Brooke Erin. 2017. *(Not) Getting Paid to Do What You Love: Gender, Social Media, and Aspirational Work*. New Haven, CT: Yale University Press.

Esmonde, Katelyn. 2020. " 'There's Only so Much Data You Can Handle in Your Life': Accommodating and Resisting Self-Surveillance in Women's Running and Fitness Tracking Practices." *Qualitative Research in Sport, Exercise and Health* 12, no. 1: 76–90. https://doi.org/10.1080/2159676X.2019.1617188.

FitTo Health. 2020. "FitTo Vibrating Weight Loss Device." Indiegogo, January 13. https://www.indiegogo.com/projects/2551665.

Foucault, Michel. 2008. *The Birth of Biopolitics: Lectures at the Collège de France, 1978–1979*. Translated by Graham Burchell. London: Palgrave.

Foucault, Michel. 2012. *Discipline and Punish: The Birth of the Prison*. New York: Vintage.

Fuchs, Christian. 2014. *Digital Labour and Karl Marx*. New York and London: Routledge.

G2T. 2017. "N2—Portable Air Conditioning with a Personal Sound Space." Kickstarter, February 8. Accessed December 2020 at https://www.kickstarter.com/projects/1079165658/n2-a-stylish-electric-scarf-from-the-future.

Gibbs, Samuel. 2014. "2015 Gears up to Be the Year of Wearable Tech." *Guardian*, December 25. http://www.theguardian.com/technology/2014/dec/25/apple-watch-spring-launch-wearable-technology.

Fossil GEN5E Smart Wartch with Jeweled band. Accessed July 2021 at https://www.fossil.com/en-us/products/gen-5e-smartwatch-blush-silicone/FTW6066.html

Gidaris, Constantine. 2019. "Surveillance Capitalism, Datafication, and Unwaged Labour: The Rise of Wearable Fitness Devices and Interactive Life Insurance." *Surveillance & Society* 17, no. 1/2: 132–138. https://doi.org/10.24908/ss.v17i1/2.12913.

Gregory, Karen, Kirsty Hendry, Jake Watts, and Dave Young. 2017. "Selfwork." *Real Life Magazine*, February 2. https://reallifemag.com/selfwork/.

GripBeats. 2020. "GripBeats: Turn Your Hands into a Musical Instrument!" Kickstarter, October 8. https://www.kickstarter.com/projects/gripbeats/gripbeats-the-multi-functional-wearable-musical-instrument.

Haggerty, Kevin D., and Richard V. Ericson. 2000. "The Surveillant Assemblage." *British Journal of Sociology* 51, no. 4: 605–622. https://doi.org/10.1080/00071310020015280.

Hailu, Ruth. 2019. "Fitbits and Other Wearables May Not Accurately Track Heart Rates in People of Color." *STAT* (blog), July 24. https://www.statnews.com/2019/07/24/fitbit-accuracy-dark-skin/.

Hambling, David. 2020. "Battlefield Augmented Reality Getting Real for U.S. Army." *Forbes*, May 22. https://www.forbes.com/sites/davidhambling/2020/05/22/battlefield-augmented-reality-gets-real/.

Haraway, Donna. 1991. *Simians, Cyborgs, and Women: The Reinvention of Nature*. New York: Routledge.

Hargittai, Eszter, and Alice Marwick. 2016. " 'What Can I Really Do?' Explaining the Privacy Paradox with Online Apathy." *International Journal of Communication* 10: 3737–3757.

Hesmondhalgh, David. 2013. *The Cultural Industries*. 3rd ed. London: Sage.

Hoffmann, Christian Pieter, Christoph Lutz, and Giulia Ranzini. 2016. "Privacy Cynicism: A New Approach to the Privacy Paradox." *Cyberpsychology: Journal of Psychosocial Research on Cyberspace* 10, no. 4: 7. https://doi.org/10.5817/CP2016-4-7.

Ingham, Lucy. 2015. "2016 Will Be the Year of Wearable Technology." *Factor* (blog), November 12. https://www.factor-tech.com/wearable-technology/20578-2016-will-be-the-year-of-wearable-technology/.

InteraXon. 2021. "Meditation Made Easy." Muse. Accessed July 2021 at https://choosemuse.com/.

Isaacson, Walter. 2011. *Steve Jobs*. New York: Simon & Schuster.

Jethani, S. 2020. "Doing Time in the Home-Space: Ankle Monitors, Script Analysis, and Anticipatory Methodology." In *Embodied Computing: Wearables, Implantables, Embeddables, Ingestibles*, edited by Isabel Pedersen and Andrew Iliadis, 161–186. Cambridge, MA: MIT Press.

Kelion, Leo. 2020. "CES 2020: Preview of Tomorrow's Tech on Show in Las Vegas." BBC News, January 4. https://www.bbc.com/news/technology-50952021.

Keyble. 2021. "Flywallet Contactless Payment." Accessed July 2021 at https://www.flywalletpay.com/en/.

Lanzing, Marjolein. 2016. "The Transparent Self." *Ethics and Information Technology* 18, no. 1: 9–16. https://doi.org/10.1007/s10676-016-9396-y.

Latour, Bruno. 1993. *We Have Never Been Modern*. Cambridge, MA: Harvard University Press.

Lazzarato, Maurizio. 1996. "Immaterial Labor." In *Radical Thought in Italy: A Potential Politics*. Vol. 7, *Theory out of Bounds*, edited by Paolo Virno, Michael Hardt, Sandra Buckley, and Brian Massumi, 133–147. Minneapolis: University of Minnesota Press.

LIFTiD. 2021. "LIFTiD Neurostimulation." Accessed July 2021 at https://www.getliftid.com/.

Lindner, Peter. 2020. "Molecular Politics, Wearables, and the *Aretaic* Shift in Biopolitical Governance." *Theory, Culture & Society* 37, no. 3: 71–96. https://doi.org/10.1177/0263276419894053.

Lupton, Deborah. 2015. "The Cultural Specificity of Digital Health Technologies." *This Sociological Life* (blog), January 25. https://simplysociology.wordpress.com/2015/01/25/the-cultural-specificity-of-digital-health-technologies/.

Lupton, Deborah. 2016. *The Quantified Self: A Sociology of Self-Tracking*. Cambridge: Polity.

Lupton, Deborah. 2020. "Wearable Devices: Sociotechnical Imaginaries and Agential Capacities." In *Embodied Computing: Wearables, Implantables, Embeddables, Ingestibles*, edited by Isabel Pedersen and Andrew Iliadis, 49–69. Cambridge, MA: MIT Press.

Lupton, Deborah, and Mike Michael. 2017. " 'Depends on Who's Got the Data': Public Understandings of Personal Digital Dataveillance." *Surveillance & Society* 15, no. 2: 254–268. https://doi.org/10.24908/ss.v15i2.6332.

Marsan, Carolyn Duffy. 2008. "10 'Get Smart' Phones You Can Actually Get." *PC World*, June 17. https://www.pcworld.idg.com.au/slideshow/225264/10-get-smart-phones-can-actually-get/.

Marwick, Alice E. 2015. *Status Update: Celebrity, Publicity, and Branding in the Social Media Age*. New Haven, CT: Yale University Press.

Matsakis, Louise. 2017. "This Smart Bra Can Tell When You're Getting Stressed." *Mashable*, April 11. https://mashable.com/2017/04/11/vitali-smart-bra-kickstarter/.

McFall, Liz, and Liz Moor. 2018. "Who, or What, Is Insurtech Personalizing?: Persons, Prices and the Historical Classifications of Risk." *Distinktion: Journal of Social Theory* 19, no. 2: 193–213. https://doi.org/10.1080/1600910X.2018.1503609.

McIlwain, Charlton D. 2019. *Black Software: The Internet and Racial Justice, from the AfroNet to Black Lives Matter*. New York: Oxford University Press.

Nafus, Dawn, ed. 2016. *Quantified: Biosensing Technologies in Everyday Life*. Cambridge, MA: MIT Press.

Nakamura, Lisa. 2014. "Gender and Race Online." In *Society and the Internet: How Networks of Information and Communication Are Changing Our Lives*, edited by Mark Graham and William H. Dutton, 81–96. Oxford: Oxford University Press.

Neff, Gina, and Dawn Nafus. 2016. *Self-Tracking*. MIT Press Essential Knowledge Series. Cambridge, MA: MIT Press.

Nissenbaum, Helen. 2004. "Privacy as Contextual Integrity." *Washington Law Review* 79, no. 1: 119–157.

Noble, Safiya Umoja. 2018. *Algorithms of Oppression: How Search Engines Reinforce Racism*. New York: New York University Press.

Noble, Safiya Umoja, and Sarah T. Roberts. 2016. "Through Google-Colored Glass(es): Design, Emotion, Class, and Wearables as Commodity and Control." In *Emotions, Technology, and Design*, edited by Sharon Y. Tettegah, 187–212. Emotions and Technology. London: Elsevier.

Nuzzle. 2019. "Nuzzle: The Smartest Pet Collar with No Fees." Indiegogo. Accessed May 2019 https://www.indiegogo.com/projects/1451922.

Oura. 2021. "Oura Ring: Wellness, wrapped around your finger." Accessed July 2021 at https://ouraring.com.

Philips. 2021. "SmartSleep Deep Sleep Headband." Accessed July 2021 at https://www.usa.philips.com/c-e/smartsleep/deep-sleep-headband.html.

Rich, Emma, and Andy Miah. 2017. "Mobile, Wearable and Ingestible Health Technologies: Towards a Critical Research Agenda." *Health Sociology Review* 26, no. 1: 84–97. https://doi.org/10.1080/14461242.2016.1211486.

Rose, Nikolas S. 2006. *Politics of Life Itself: Biomedicine, Power, and Subjectivity in the Twenty-First Century*. Information Series. Princeton, NJ: Princeton University Press.

Sanders, Rachel. 2017. "Self-Tracking in the Digital Era: Biopower, Patriarchy, and the New Biometric Body Projects." *Body & Society* 23, no. 1: 36–63. https://doi.org/10.1177/1357034X16660366.

Sandvik, Kristin Bergtora. 2020a. "Humanitarian Wearables: Digital Bodies, Experimentation and Ethics." In *Ethics of Medical Innovation, Experimentation, and Enhancement in Military and Humanitarian Contexts*, edited by Daniel Messelken and David Winkler, 87–104. Military and Humanitarian Health Ethics. Cham, Switzerland: Springer International Publishing. https://doi.org/10.1007/978-3-030-36319-2_6.

Sandvik, Kristin Bergtora. 2020b. "Wearables for Something Good: Aid, Dataveillance and the Production of Children's Digital Bodies." *Information, Communication & Society* 23, no. 14: 2014–2029. https://doi.org/10.1080/1369118X.2020.1753797.

Schneier, Bruce. 2015. *Data and Goliath: The Hidden Battles to Collect Your Data and Control Your World*. New York: W.W. Norton.

Scholz, Trebor, ed. 2013. *Digital Labor: The Internet as Playground and Factory*. New York: Routledge.

Schüll, Natasha D. 2019. "The Data-Based Self: Self-Quantification and the Data-Driven (Good) Life." *Social Research: An International Quarterly* 86, no. 4: 909–930.

Schüll, Natasha Dow. 2016. "Data for Life: Wearable Technology and the Design of Self-Care." *BioSocieties* 11, no. 3: 317–333. https://doi.org/10.1057/biosoc.2015.47.

Schwab, Katharine. 2019. "A Pollution Mask So Sleek It Debuted on the Fashion Week Runways of New York and Seoul." *Fast Company*, September 9. https://www.fastcompany.com/90396769/a-pollution-mask-so-sleek-it-debuted-on-the-fashion-week-runways-of-new-york-and-seoul.

Schwab, Klaus. 2016. *The Fourth Industrial Revolution*. New York: Crown Business and World Economic Forum.

Schwartz, Becca, and Gina Neff. 2019. "The Gendered Affordances of Craigslist 'New-in-Town Girls Wanted' Ads." *New Media & Society* 21, no. 11–12: 2404–2421. https://doi.org/10.1177/1461444819849897.

SEAM. 2021. "Lotus—Panic Button Meets Smart Speaker." Accessed July 2021 at https://www.seamtechnic.com/lotus-by-seam/.

Senft, Theresa M. 2008. *Camgirls: Celebrity and Community in the Age of Social Networks*. Vol. 4, *Digital Formations*. New York: Lang.

Senft, Theresa M. 2012. "Microcelebrity and the Branded Self." In *A Companion to New Media Dynamics*, edited by John Hartley, Jean Burgess, and Axel Bruns, 346–354. Chichester, UK: John Wiley & Sons.

Shelby, Renee Marie. 2019. "Techno-Physical Feminism: Anti-Rape Technology, Gender, and Corporeal Surveillance." *Feminist Media Studies* 20, no. 8: 1088–1109.

Smith, Aaron. 2014. "Half of Online Americans Don't Know What a Privacy Policy Is." Pew Research Center, December 4. https://www.pewresearch.org/fact-tank/2014/12/04/half-of-americans-dont-know-what-a-privacy-policy-is/.

Spence, Ewan. 2013. "2014 Will Be the Year of Wearable Technology." *Forbes*, November 2. http://www.forbes.com/sites/ewanspence/2013/11/02/2014-will-be-the-year-of-wearable-technology/#31e0ba823e53.

Taison Digital. 2021. "Upmood: The First Live Emotion Detection Wearable and App." Accessed July 2021 at https://upmood.com/.

Tap Systems. 2021. "Meet Tap." Accessed July 2021 at https://www.tapwithus.com/.

Terranova, Tiziana. 2000. "Free Labor: Producing Culture for the Digital Economy." *Social Text* 18, no. 2: 33–58.

Under Armour. 2021. "Run Connected." Accessed July 2021 at https://www.underarmour.com/en-us/t/connected-shoes-page.html.

van Dijck, J. 2014. "Datafication, Dataism and Dataveillance: Big Data between Scientific Paradigm and Ideology." *Surveillance and Society* 12, no. 2: 197–208.

Wajcman, Judy. 2004. *TechnoFeminism*. Cambridge: Polity.

Walmsley, Julie. 2019. "Facewear to Clean Your Breathing Space and More Futuristic Ideas for Urban Commuters." *Forbes*, February 2. https://www.forbes.com/sites/juliewalmsley/2019/02/24/these-3-startups-are-making-nerdy-urban-commute-necessities-stylish/?sh=730cbac677a1.

Wearable X. 2021. "Nadi X." Accessed July 2021 at https://www.wearablex.com/.

Winchester, Woodrow III. 2020. "Black-Centered Design Is the Future of Business." *Fast Company*, June 8. https://www.fastcompany.com/90513962/black-centered-design-is-the-future-of-business.

Winchester, Woodrow W III. 2019. "Engaging the Black Ethos: Afrofuturism as a Design Lens for Inclusive Technological Innovation." *Journal of Futures Studies* 24, no. 2: 55–62.

Wissinger, Elizabeth. 2015. *This Year's Model: Fashion, Media, and the Making of Glamour*. New York: New York University Press.

Wissinger, Elizabeth. 2017a. "From 'Geek' to 'Chic': Wearable Technology and the Woman Question." In *Digital Sociologies*, edited by Jessie Daniels, Karen Gregory, and Tressie McMillan Cottom, 369–386. London: Policy Press.

Wissinger, Elizabeth. 2017b. "Wearable Tech, Bodies, and Gender." *Sociology Compass* 11, no. 11: e12514. https://doi.org/10.1111/soc4.12514.

Wissinger, Elizabeth. 2018. "Blood, Sweat, and Tears: Navigating Creepy versus Cool in Wearable Biotech." *Information, Communication & Society* 21, no. 5: 779–785. https://doi.org/10.1080/1369118X.2018.1428657.

Xenoma. 2021. "e-skin Smart Apparel." Accessed July 2021 at https://xenoma.com/.

Young, Sarah. 2018. "Agency and the Digital Alter Ego: Surveillance Data and Wearable Technologies." *International Journal of Sociotechnology and Knowledge Development* 10, no. 3: 41–53. https://doi.org/10.4018/IJSKD.2018070103.

Zimmer, Michael, Priya Kumar, Jessica Vitak, Yuting Liao, and Katie Chamberlain Kritikos. 2020. "'There's Nothing Really They Can Do with This Information': Unpacking How Users Manage Privacy Boundaries for Personal Fitness Information." *Information, Communication & Society* 23, no. 7: 1020–1037. https://doi.org/10.1080/1369118X.2018.1543442.

Zukin, Sharon. 1995. *The Cultures of Cities*. Cambridge, MA: Blackwell.

PART IV

DIGITAL MEDIA, COMMUNITY, AND IDENTITY

CHAPTER 17

LGBTQ+ COMMUNITIES AND DIGITAL MEDIA

BRADY ROBARDS, PAUL BYRON, AND SAB D'SOUZA

For many lesbian, gay, bisexual, transgender, and queer (LGBTQ+[1]) people, the internet enables connection, support, and friendship and hosts vital resources for learning and practicing diverse genders and sexualities. For people who feel marginalized, isolated, and invisible, the connections afforded by digital media can offer support that is lacking or absent in other parts of their lives. The internet can be a space for identity work, friendship, and connecting to different communities, cultures, and ways of being. Through social media, LGBTQ+ people can see their experiences reflected in the shared lives of others, learn language and skills to connect to their own experiences of the world with others, and find spaces of refuge, comfort, and solidarity. Such spaces can foster greater self-acceptance and help when dealing with a range of aggressions, prejudices, and structural barriers to social participation.

For Berger (1998), the sociological approach to community has been about contrasting a sense of community with society: "community is tradition; society is change. Community is feeling; society is rationality. Community is female; society is male. Community is warm and wet and intimate; society is cold and dry and formal. Community is love; society is business" (Berger 1998, 324). While these binaries sit uncomfortably with us (precisely because they inscribe a gendered binary that, as we explain and explore in this chapter, is not at all stable), it does point to the attention in sociological approaches to community on affect and feeling. Bruhn (2011) suggests that a sociological interest in community has persisted because of the way experiences of community are bound up in "emotional attachment to place" at the same time as conceptualizations of community offer "ideal guidelines for human relationships" (p. 29). While our attention in this chapter seeks to look beyond physical places, certainly many of the examples we explore here are centered on emotional attachments to digitally mediated places, platforms, sites, and apps. So too do some of these digital spaces provide what might be understood as "guidelines for human relationships," although this feels to us to be potentially constraining. Instead, in the case of LGBTQ+ people's experiences of these spaces and places, there exists a set of opportunities around connection, safety, and self-expression that might otherwise be impossible or at least riskier in physical spaces.

This chapter maps some of the ways digital media are used by LGBTQ+ people in three key intersecting domains. The first section examines how LGBTQ+ people use digital media to forge connections and find and build communities. While "community" is a contested term in digital media studies (for a summary, see Baym 2015, 82), we recognize that many LGBTQ+ people use it to describe their experiences of digital networks (Byron et al. 2019; Pym, Byron, and Albury 2020). Second, we explore how LGBTQ+ people use digital media in their romantic and sexual lives, from dating/hook-up apps to popular social media. We consider the challenges, pleasures, and opportunities found here and how these intersect with aspects of LGBTQ+ communities and identities. Third, we reflect on how digital media use relates to ongoing and shifting approaches to LGBTQ+ identities and how LGBTQ+ people develop shared languages and understandings of identities through digital media that foster expansive modes of self-representation. In particular, we examine this identity work through shifting understandings of "coming out." Throughout this chapter we also consider how the affective aspects of digital media use among LGBTQ+ people contribute to contemporary understandings and negotiations of gender and sexuality and how social media play a significant role in expanding queerness as a site of feeling (beyond simply being) queer.

In this chapter, we are conscious of important differences in cultural contexts and in the practices, affordances, and structures of different digital media platforms. Thus, we acknowledge that the experiences of LGBTQ+ people vary enormously, modulated by race, gender, class, age, culture, laws, and other social and cultural experiences and structures in people's lives. A wide diversity of experiences and media settings ensures different uses of media platforms and diverse digital media literacies. It is also important to recognize that digital media landscapes constantly change, including media infrastructures and governance, platform regulation, transglobal economies, data privacy legislations, many forms of surveillance, the logic of algorithms, moderation practices and their guiding "community standards," and the ongoing revision of platform content policies. Different platform affordances for privacy and visibility also inform how LGBTQ+ people use these media.

"LGBTQ+ identities" and "digital media" are not static monoliths, and we wish to emphasize the diversity of practices, platforms, identities, and networks involved in digital media use among LGBTQ+ people. Due to this, our chapter does not attempt to synthesize decades of digital media scholarship with far-reaching global discussions of gender, sexuality, and queer studies. Instead, we present some key accounts of LGBTQ+ digital connections and practices. By pointing to many more research examples than we are able to discuss in depth, we flag for readers a range of adjacent challenges and opportunities. Before we move on to these substantive sections and to round out our introduction, we briefly outline some of the rich background and history of digital media use among LGBTQ+ people.

Background and History

Wakeford (2000, 408) pointed out that "cyberqueer spaces" operate as sites of "resistance against the dominant assumption of the normality of heterosexuality," and decades later the same still holds true. While there have been a number of achievements in the fight for queer and gender-diverse people to be visible, accepted, and represented in society, LGBTQ+ people continue to experience poor mental health (Russell and Fish 2016; Wilson and Cariola 2020), personal harassment (Mallory, Hasenbush, and Sears 2015), structural barriers to social participation, and active vilification in many parts of the world (Steinmetz 2019). These experiences are also powerfully modulated by race, ethnicity, class, culture, age, and gender, among other factors. As such, the importance of an intersectional approach to researching LGBTQ+ people's digital media practices is increasingly recognized (Haimson et al. 2020; Jackson, Bailey, and Foucault Welles 2017).

Digital media practices have changed considerably in recent decades, yet digitally mediated spaces continue to be vital to mitigate experiences of isolation and marginalization and to foster and support intimate connections. Online spaces continue to be theorized as a "safety net" (Hillier, Mitchell, and Ybarra 2012), especially for LGBTQ+ young people; however, the "default publicness" of major social media platforms, like Facebook, presents new and ongoing challenges to safety (Cho 2018). As Cho (2018, citing Browne) highlights, the default publicness built into platforms (and pivotal to their profits) poses significant risks to queer people of color (POC),[2] given that public spaces are inherently "shaped for and by whiteness" (p. 3186).

Considering digital spaces for LGBTQ+ safety, Fraser (2010) refers to these as "closet" spaces that are not simply oppressive but also offer safety that can generate important queer learning and knowledge. More recently, Rubin and McClelland (2015) discuss Facebook use among queer women of color as a contemporary negotiation of "the closet," where many of their participants choose the safety of nondisclosure. These are two of many examples of how existing concepts of closets, outness, authenticity, and safe space have expanded or shifted to accommodate increasingly digital aspects of everyday life. Despite (often neoliberal) discourses of being "out and proud" and "living our authentic lives," the persistent need for safe spaces is an ongoing queer negotiation, digitally and otherwise. This chapter gestures to many key discussions of these practices and tensions.

Despite many forms and practices of safety that digital media offer to LGBTQ+ people, new challenges and threats to safety have also emerged. This includes the mobilization of conservative, alt-right groups through digital media, where homophobia, transphobia, and misogyny are dominant (Jones, Trott, and Wright 2020; Nicholas and

Agius 2018), and the "sterilization" of many digital spaces—like Tumblr (Bronstein 2020; Southerton et al. 2021; Haimson et al. 2020)—to ostensibly appeal to (heteronormative) family-friendly advertising (Paasonen, Jarrett, and Light 2019, 170). This kind of "sterilization," such as Tumblr's movement away from "not safe for work" content like pornography, kink material, and "female presenting nipples" (Duguay 2018), is ostensibly about making these platforms more "family" (read: children) friendly but also risks erasing significant queer and gender-diverse content, and thus communities of connection.

These technical and discursive disturbances to LGBTQ+ experiences online muddy previous utopic conceptualizations of LGBTQ+ digital space as safer. As Dasgupta notes of early discussions of online community safeties, "[t]he idea of a utopian world being created through the Internet envisages cyberspace as a safe and accommodating sphere, where communities can interact and grow" (2018, 189). However, the perceived safety of any space (digital or otherwise) also holds the potential for harm (Anzaldúa 2002). As new intimacies and connections open users up to one another in any counterpublic, new tensions and challenges emerge, including lateral violence and policing that disrupts the imagined "LGBTQ+ community" that we explore in this chapter. This relates to discussions of "calling out" (Zamanian 2014) and public pushbacks among conservatives who feel challenged by having their privileges (such as being White and cisgender) brought into question. Such public discussions are not new but can extend their reach through networked discussions on sites like Tumblr (Ringrose and Lawrence 2018).

The following sections outline some key research discussions, while also addressing gaps in existing literature of LGBTQ+ people's uses of digital media. Much of the literature available centers on gay and, to a slightly lesser extent, lesbian digital communities, especially in the United States (Szulc 2014). Recent research highlights a lack of attention to trans communities in early internet practices, despite trans people being early adopters and key players in digital media histories (Cavalcante 2016; Dame-Griff 2019; Haimson et al. 2020). This also holds true for LGBTQ+ communities that prioritize the identity work and connection of their Black, First Nations, and POC users.

Community and Connection

Identity often emerges from and operates in concert with experiences of belonging and connection. The concept of community mediated by the digital has been hotly contested. Turkle (2011, 238) argues that communities must be "constituted by physical proximity, shared concerns, real consequences, and common responsibilities" and that scholars—herself included—have been too quick to label digitally mediated connections "communities." Sites like MySpace and Facebook or online worlds like Second Life, she contends, are the realm of "weak ties" (Turkle 2011, 239), and thus cannot offer a true sense of community. Banks (2012) has critiqued Turkle's (2011) oscillation toward a more pessimistic view of the internet and technology in our lives by drawing attention to how she inscribes binaries between "real" and "virtual." Instead, Banks (2012) and previously Jurgenson (2011) suggest that the digital and the physical are so enmeshed that Turkle's "digital dualism" is untenable. Much of the research we discuss throughout this chapter highlights a constant interplay between the digital and the physical.

The notion of a singular community—"*the* LGBTQ+ community"—is often mobilized in political and research discussions. Critics argue that there is no singular community, and this understanding can foreclose our attention to considerable lateral exclusion, marginalization, harassment, and violence between people ostensibly within this "rainbow community." Ahmed and Fortier (2003, 251) complicate singular notions of community, explaining that community can be about "the promise of a universal togetherness" or commonality or living together in difference. However, community can also represent "a failed promise insofar as the appeal to community assumes a way of relating to others that violates rather than supports the ethical principle of alterity" (2003, 251). They go on to explain that it is important to distinguish between multiple sets of complex social relationships that cannot simply be "folded into 'community'":

> When are relationships and encounters and exchanges and dialogues, forms of co-presence and coexistence, about "'community'" and when are they about family, the reenactment of "'tradition'", remembrances, dreams, sites of momentary connections or disconnections, political mobilization, imitations of past lives and imagined futures? For us, to be unsettled by the very word "'community'" is to remind ourselves that the word "'community'" might not name all it is that we can do and be when we "'get together.'"
>
> (Ahmed & and Fortier 2003:, 257)

For many LGBTQ+ people, coming to terms with identity can be a uniquely isolating experience, and thus the search for connection and some semblance of belonging or community is often digitally mediated. Whereas many other marginalized groups—marginalized, for instance, by social structures around race, class, religion—are usually born into families who share that experience of marginalization, queer and gender-diverse young people are mostly born into heterosexual and cisgender families. Seeking out external representations of queer life is a key part of forming connections, identities, and imagined futures. Historically these representations have often not readily been found in traditional media like film, television, and music (although there have been a range of important changes in this space, see, for instance, Monaghan [2016]), so instead, young LGBTQ+ people find these connections and representations through social media and, in doing so, learn shared languages to articulate their own experiences (Robards et al. 2020).

Robards et al. (2018), in their study of young LGBTIQ+ social media users in Australia ($n = 1,304$), found that "cyberqueer" spaces—as Wakeford (2000, 408) described them—continue to be critical for young queer and gender-diverse people, two decades on. Their participants variously described how different social media platforms afforded different connections, introduced them to important concepts and ideas, and made them feel like they were not alone. One respondent, for instance, explained that "Before Tumblr, I had no idea that lgbt+ people existed (my parents are quite homophobic and very strict ...) and by using Tumblr I was able to fully immerse myself within its very lgbt+ culture" (17, lesbian female). Another powerfully described how "social media helped me embrace my sexuality and feel like I am not alone" (18, bisexual female) (Robards et al. 2018, 162).

Earlier research on the mediation of gay and lesbian "community" online was interested in whether the digital was *displacing* physical experiences of connection. Gudelunas (2005) studied 200 personal advertisements on PlanetOut, a website that sought to become a "national electronic town square that people can access from the privacy of their closet—from any small town, any suburb, any reservation in America" (Rielly, cited in Gudelunas 2005, 8). The language here is dated now, with its narrow focus on American gay men and lesbians, as the visibility of other experiences—of trans and nonbinary people, of bisexual and pansexual people—has increased. Similarly, in the modern context of the mobility of the internet through smartphones, the "newness" of being able to access the internet from anywhere has been superseded. And yet, it's important to note—as Gudelunas did at the time—that sites like PlanetOut, made possible because of the internet, were revolutionary at the time because of their capacity to link "gays and lesbians" in a way that was previously impossible to comprehend.

Ultimately, Gudelunas (2005) concluded that the users on PlanetOut did not consider themselves to be part of this "virtual community" and that the website was not a "threat" to the "brick and mortar gay and lesbian community" (p. 30) constituted by bars, bookstores, and clubs. Instead, Gudelunas points to "the interplay between online and offline space" (2005, 25), where his own respondents talk about connecting with people online and meeting them in physical spaces. This resonates with later arguments that we have highlighted here already, about the "enmeshed" nature of the digital and physical developed by Jurgenson (2011) and Banks (2012) in response to Turkle's (2011) criticisms of digitally mediated experiences of community. However, this implication of a conflict between digital and physical spaces (the "threat" of the digital) also works to inscribe that dualism.

How else might we conceptualize digitally mediated connection beyond the concept of "community"? As "participatory" media (Jenkins, Ito, and boyd 2015), social media are more explicitly connective than previous forms of mass media centered on broadcast (such as radio, television, and film). However, a focus on participation is also limited when we consider how people inhabit or use a range of digital and social media without actively participating through direct communication in these spaces—a form of use often described as "lurking" but that we think is more productively framed as "listening" (Crawford 2009). This is particularly the case for many LGBTQ+ people who may use, learn from, and exist anonymously on sites like Tumblr and Reddit, as described by our (Robards et al.'s 2018) research participants. For many such users, the issue of feeling connected is a key aspect of their uses of these technologies, and so we argue that "connection" can often be a more useful term than "community" since it can involve connection to a sense of community, as well as to information, resources, and insight into one's own identity (Byron et al. 2019); and this connection need not involve actively communicating with others.

According to Byron et al. (2019), for many young LGBTQ+ people, communities are understood as more bounded in their membership and spatial parameters, and therefore some Tumblr users they interviewed felt ambivalent about using the term "community" to describe their use of such platforms. However, others continued to use the term, suggesting a more porous and less bounded sense of community. These divergent uses point to the differently affective aspects of communities and how they're imagined.

Since Warner's work on "counterpublics" (2002), many have used this term to more broadly conceptualize queer digital spaces (Cavalcante 2016; Jackson, Bailey, and Foucault Welles 2017; Jenzen 2017; Renninger 2015). Counterpublics are various kinds of publics (such as audiences) "constituted through a conflictual relation to the dominant public . . . structured by different dispositions or protocols from those that obtain elsewhere in the culture, making different assumptions about what can be said or what goes without saying" (Warner 2002, 86). Renninger (2015), for instance, takes up the concept of the counterpublic to understand the mobilization of asexuals and their allies on Tumblr. According to Renninger, Tumblr provides a forum for discussing asexuality that is important because there are few offline forums for these discussions. For asexuals, people who do not experience sexual attraction in a society and culture where sexual attraction is normalized and essentialized, digitally mediated counterpublics—like Tumblr—can allow users to "be myself" (Renninger 2015, 1520). Further, though, these counterpublics can provide opportunities to map "ideologies, thoughts, and subjectivities among people, mostly strangers, that share an awareness of similar countercultural referents" (Renninger 2015, 1526) that can go on to have wider purchase in other spaces and discourses.

More recent research has begun to further account for early internet trans communities on usenet (Dame-Griff 2019), queer African migrants in autonomous Facebook groups (Asante 2018), and queer, asexual, and trans young people's use of Tumblr hashtags for identity work (Schudson and van Anders 2019). These studies demonstrate how differing platform affordances still share community-building practices like breakaway groups and internal factions. They also make evident that digital spaces cannot escape the normative systems of power that interpolate their LGBTQ+ users offline. Most importantly, they reveal that digital communities, in their rhizomatic formation, speak to an ease of movement from which intimacies emerge and tether users to one another. LGBTQ+ life online is inherently fraught and always shifting. Further to this, attention to digital media connections must consider different kinds of connections—for example, social or sexual connections and where these may differ or overlap. The following section looks closely at sexual and romantic connections, how digital media (especially dating/hook-up apps) have facilitated a range of intimacies beyond "communities," and how their use encompasses a sense of community through users participating in shared cultural practices of sex, dating, and media use.

Sex, Romance, and Dating

As important sites of connection, online personal ads, dating websites, and dating apps have been central to understandings of LGBTQ+ identities and digital media; and research on their uses is vast. In the 2010s, a significant portion of this research focused on Grindr as the first geo-locative hook-up app launched in 2009. Grindr was initially marketed as a hook-up app for gay men but expanded its user identity options to include nonbinary and female users in 2017, as well as a range of cis/transgender options (Hall 2017). Tinder arrived in 2012, and while commonly framed as a dating app for heterosexuals, it also has many LGBTQ+ users (Duguay 2019; MacKee 2016).

The use of dating apps, now considered common among LGBTQ+ populations, overlaps with everyday practices of identity and engagements with community, as well as broader social media use (Byron, Albury, and Pym 2021). App use also entangles with queer politics of visibility and safety, with many users comfortably representing their queerness (including details of their sexual interests, desires, and preferences) among peers. With limited places to safely express these details in everyday life, these apps offer space for queer ontologies and representations. Yet, we should not simply see dating/hook-up apps as spaces to be "out and proud" as they can also intensify other forms of discrimination and disconnection, including racism, misogyny, and transphobia, which we explore in this section. Ferris and Duguay's (2020) research on Tinder considers how queer women must filter out and avoid intrusive and unwelcome interactions, particularly with cisgender-presenting men. Male infiltration of queer women's digital spaces is similarly noted elsewhere (Albury and Byron 2016; Pond and Farvid 2017), as well as bisexual women's app-based experiences of biphobia (Pond and Farvid 2017). Queer women evidently face different challenges from queer men in negotiating safeties and identities in dating/hook-up apps (Pym, Byron, and Albury 2020).

Research attention to LGBTQ+ people's uses of dating apps predominantly centers on gay/queer men from the Global North. Much of this literature focuses on Grindr as the most popular gay hook-up app for men in North America, Australia, the United Kingdom, and much of Europe. Researchers often consider Grindr's value in generating a sense of "queer space" that is less obvious or available to non-app users. Grindr, Scruff, and similar apps have been discussed in terms of generating a "queer cartography" (Batiste 2013) or a new social setting for gay men to convene and connect (Crooks 2013). Many note the hybridity of these spaces in relation to the layering of physical and virtual spaces that generates experiences of "co-situation" (Blackwell, Birnholtz, and Abbott 2015). Correlations have been drawn between apps and offline spaces through discussing these as "the new gay bar" (Miller 2015), with gay press commonly blaming hook-up apps for the death of gay scenes (Renninger 2019). For many, Grindr and other sites that have been key to gay men's digital connections (e.g., gay.com, Gaydar, Manhunt, GayRomeo) constitute a form of private cruising, as opposed to traditional cruising that relies on reinscribing (or queering) public space. Mowlabocus'

(2010) research on Gaydar explores "digital cruising," as does that of Miles (2018, 2), who notes that these platforms have "deeply impacted" gay communities and cruising culture. Elsewhere, Møller and Nebeling Petersen (2018) consider how hook-up app uses among non-monogamous gay couples further disrupt normative boundaries between public and private sexual practices.

Notably, a focus on cruising and "gay bar" comparisons highlights a set of dominant research principles and frameworks that do not translate to many parts of the world or to nonurban environments. Beyond the Global North, queer dating/hook-up apps have been just as important for generating a range of connections and identity negotiations, with less concern for what these platforms may take away from historicized and celebrated queer cultures (as was Gudelunas' [2005] line of inquiry around the "threat" digital spaces pose to physical ones). Broader global and transnational research accounts have similarly highlighted the hybridity of these spaces, along with their role within, and influence of, transnational negotiations of space and identity. Much of this research also considers strategic and creative uses of hook-up apps for community-building and social interactions that may counterpose nondigital opportunities to connect, convene, and forge intimacies. For many LGBTQ+ people, social, political, and/or family pressures ensure nondisclosure of one's gender/sexual identities; and this can limit sexual, community, and political engagements.[3]

In his research on men's use of Hornet in Turkey, Phua (2020) found that "making friends" was a priority of app use for a large majority (91%) of locals and tourists. This percentage matched that of participants who used Hornet for "seeking sexual contacts." Some tourists in the study strategically used Hornet to connect with locals prior to visiting Turkey, highlighting the affordances of some apps for building transglobal intimacies from afar. Elsewhere, through interviews and ethnographic research with foreign aid workers and locals in post-typhoon Philippines, Ong (2017) considers the queer cosmopolitanism that Grindr offers. Through participants' experiences, Ong draws our attention to new situational opportunities for queer intimacies that cut across cultural, racial, and class-based divisions within queer cosmopolitanism. Yet Ong also proposes the need to further explore the uneven experiences of middle-class and low-income LGBTQ+ people within such intimacies.

Dating apps and their integration or overlap with broader social media in China and Hong Kong have facilitated greater connection to queer communities, sex, and relationships. This is discussed in relation to Momo, which rebranded as a "friendship app" in an attempt to escape its reputation for being a sex app (Chan 2020; Liu 2016; Xue et al. 2016). As noted by Chan (2020), this rebranding offered users the potential to use Momo for sex, with the opportunity to explain their use of the app as friendship-oriented, if necessary. This offers strategic benefit to fostering sexual and queer connections that are also found through WeChat and other popular social media platforms that have a "people nearby" feature suitable for facilitating hook-ups (Xue et al. 2016). These examples speak to different strategies of platform use to ensure privacy, while also offering a source of denial since these are "social media" rather than "hook-up" media—yet can invariably be used for both. There has been less attention to uses of popular social media for dating and hooking up in the Global North, though recent research from Australia highlights this overlap, particularly among LGBTQ+ young people (Albury et al. 2019; Byron, Albury, and Pym 2021).

This overlap of social media and apps commonly understood to be sexual is also apparent in Castañeda's (2015) research on young gay men's use of Grindr in the Philippines. Castañeda found that many participants used Grindr not only for sex and dating but also to socialize, chat about sexuality, and "learn how to be gay." Elsewhere, Tang's (2017) research on lesbian and bisexual women's use of the Hong Kong app Butterfly (an app specifically for lesbian and bisexual women in Hong Kong) also highlighted a range of nonsexual interactions such as self-disclosure, finding friends, and offering intergenerational intimacies. Choy's (2018) research further explores Butterfly's use as a construction of lesbian space in Hong Kong, while exploring user tensions in negotiating co-situational spaces as public and private, along with conflicting user agendas for visibility and privacy. Meanwhile, another dating app called Butterfly was launched in late 2019 in the United Kingdom (but for an international user base), specifically designed for trans users. This app focuses on safety and "serious relationships" and promises trans users a site less conditioned by trans-fetishization, as is common to apps where trans users are a minority (Paper 2020). This follows other dating apps targeting or including trans people as a key user base, including Lex (formerly Personals), which is marketed as "a lo-fi, text-based dating and social app for womxn, trans, genderqueer, two spirit, and non-binary people for meeting lovers and friends" (thisislex.app). At the time of writing, little research has been published on these apps, and most published research on trans users' experiences of apps relates to Grindr use and HIV risk among trans women (usually grouped with gay men). One notable recent exception is the work of Albury et al. (2020), based on interviews with 14 Australian trans dating app users, examining negotiations of personal safety and sexual health on these platforms. A key reason that gay men and Grindr continue to dominate LGBTQ+ dating/hook-up app research is a strong public health concern about these media, particularly regarding HIV prevention (Albury and Byron 2016). This focus is distinct from sociological or cultural studies' attention to these media as "safer" spaces for socializing and connecting. Somewhat related to this "health risk approach" to hook-up apps are recent concerns about the mental health risks of app use among gay men (Goldenberg 2019). Interestingly, such concerns are rarely expressed in relation to other user groups, including queer women.

Many studies discuss forms of user exclusion and harassment on dating apps, including racism. This research typically references gay cultures in which Whiteness is privileged in an economy of desire (Raj 2011). Key studies have focused on app cultures of racial exclusion (Han and Choi 2018), sexual racism (Callander, Holt, and Newman 2016; Carlson 2020), homonationalism (Barrett 2020), threats of colonial violence among Indigenous users (Carlson 2020), intersections of racism and femmephobia (Han et al. 2014), and racial fetishization (Han and Choi 2018; Raj 2011). While experiences of racism, marginalization and harassment vary among users and locations, and associated cultural biases, it has been argued that dating/hook-up app interactions exaggerate cultural marginalizations that precede these apps (Conner 2019).

All of the men of color in Callander, Holt, and Newman's (2016) Australian study reported accounts of sexual racism, though sexual racism had a wide range of interpretations among these participants, from subtle to blatant forms of racism. While some participants withstood experiences of sexual racism, others discontinued their use of hook-up apps on account of this. Discussing sexual racism experienced among her Indigenous gay male participants on Grindr, Carlson (2020) highlights how these played out not only in app-based interactions but also in sex and dating that followed. As some participants indicated, racism only occurred once they revealed that they were Indigenous (2020). This speaks to the ongoing impacts of colonialism, including the endurance of settler violence and racist stereotypes that pervade Indigenous-settler relations and can be further intensified through a digital "proliferation of colonial, racist discourse" (2020, 134).

As Conner (2019) argues, despite the possibilities for change that new media platforms offer, apps such as Grindr typically reproduce existing prejudices, including racism, HIV stigma, and ageism. Gay male cultures of femmephobia also intersect with racism on hook-up apps (Barrett 2020; Han, Proctor, and Choi 2014). As Han, Proctor, and Choi (2014) outline, there is a pervasive gay male stereotype in North America (and potentially all White-majority countries) that Asian men are submissive, feminine, and only desiring of White men. This stereotype is indicative of White gay men seeking to distance themselves from femininity. Elsewhere, Han and Choi (2018) argue that when men of color participate in these spaces, their desirability often comes to be associated with their race. Many of their participants of color noted having to play to such stereotypes when seeking sexual partners. Raj (2011) also discusses this, arguing that Whiteness on Grindr is a privileged form of desiring capital. Through his autoethnographic approach, Raj considers some of the affective experiences and potentials of being non-White within a space that operates through a normalized erotics of White bodies. Many researchers have interrogated the argument for "sexual racism" versus "just a preference" in dating/hook-up app dynamics (Callander, Holt, and Newman 2016; Robinson 2015), and Wang's (2020) analysis of online discussion of sexual racism highlights how more dialogic social media (outside these apps) hosts much exploration of these tensions, as do sites such as "douchebags of Grindr" (McGlotten 2013).

Geo-locative dating/hook-up apps can also offer maps or knowledge of the cities they're used in, as per Batiste's (2013) concept of a queer cartography. These aspects can be traced through location-specific research on such apps, including studies from Los Angeles (Crooks 2013), Montreal (Arroyo 2016), London (Miles 2017), Tacloban (Ong 2017), and Sydney (Race 2010). Migrant experiences of new home cities have also been researched in relation to apps, such as Asian diasporic experiences of queer life in Canada (Kojima 2014) and gay male immigrant experiences of Grindr in Belgium (Dhoest and Szulc 2016; Dhoest 2018) and Copenhagen (Shield 2017). In these accounts, apps provide more than an indication of how queer a location is; they also offer representations of queer life and identities in these locations.

Unlike research on users' experiences of Grindr, studies of queer women's use of Tinder report a scarcity of queer women in such spaces (Duguay 2019). Duguay's (2017) research on Tinder focuses on how queer women move between and across a range of digital spaces, including Instagram. For Duguay (2017), this suggests practices that are more amenable to networking, where social media and dating are connected practices. This can also be seen in earlier research on young lesbians' uses of MySpace (Crowley 2010) and Livejournal (Driver 2006). For Pond and Farvid (2017), participants in their study of bisexual young women's use of Tinder suggested this site was a "heteronormative and biphobic domain," like broader social spaces in which bisexual women's identities are erased or challenged. In an Australian study, queer female participants reported discomfort in assessing other women's queerness on dating apps and often assumed some bisexual women were straight or "experimenting" (Pym, Byron, and Albury 2020).

Literature on dating apps often builds on and intersects with literature on earlier dating websites and enfolds much research on LGBTQ+ people's broader uses of social media. Examples provided here point to many key research discussions, both historical and recent, and intersecting discussions of community, friendship, politics, representation, and identity—as themes explored elsewhere in this chapter. This literature also speaks to many intersecting sociological issues including race, gender, geopolitics, cultural affiliations and differences, health and well-being, transnational migrations, cross-cultural negotiations, and a range of social inequities. In our final section, we bring these open threads together to discuss the role of the digital in mediating "coming out."

Closets and Outings and Queer Becomings

From the emergence of digital media and the proliferation of social media platforms (such as Instagram, Facebook, Tumblr, and Reddit) has come an array of spaces with unique affordances that LGBTQ+ people negotiate to construct a range of self-representations. This follows on from hopeful queer and feminist theorizations of digital media in the 1990s, where cyberspace was envisioned as a place where those marginalized by race, gender, sexuality, access, and class might manage and ultimately hide gender or sexual identities in order to more freely belong and participate in new media environments (Haraway 1990). As mentioned earlier in the section "Background and History," identity is inextricably tethered to an individual's sense of belonging and community (be that familial, friends, workplace, etc.). LGBTQ+ identities are interpolated through these attachments to communities or belonging, with keen interest given to the differing performances of identity between those within and outside queer counterpublics.

For decades, researchers have focused on the potential for digital media to support or host acts of "coming out" which inevitably transform these attachments. While the closet remains a prevalent metaphor for LGBTQ+ people's experiences of disclosure (or their expectations to disclose) and is entangled with cultural discourses of authenticity (as in being "true to oneself"), digital media have complicated these understandings of disclosure and authenticity. As Fortier notes, "queer and diasporic narratives of belonging often deploy 'homing desires' ... the widespread narrative of migration as homecoming within queer culture, establishes an equation between leaving and becoming" (2001, 410). Here, Fortier ties the journey toward queer becoming (as in being your authentic self) to the act of leaving what you once were (or were perceived to be). This tension between leaving and becoming is further exemplified by Gray: "what we call 'the closet' springs from the idea that identities are waiting to be discovered and unfold from the inside out. Authenticity hinges on erasing the traces of others from our work to become who we 'really' are" (2009, 1182). Gray complicates the configurations of "the closet" space as unrealized authenticity and suggests that there is a generative nature to queer becoming located within the constant reworking of identity with no fixed endpoint. Clare (2017) further highlights the neoliberal aspects of "coming out" discourse, while others elaborate on the digital media spaces and practices now involved (Lovelock 2019).

Many digital media scholars draw upon Orne's concept of "strategic outness" (2011), discussing how using a range of apps and platforms enables being "out" in some digital spaces and interactions but not in others (see Carlson 2020, for example). These movements between spaces, through which we can strategically represent our queer selves through multiple "publics," challenge binary and simplistic notions of "outness." Through the mirrors and feedback loops that digital media offer, authenticity is also understood as a genre of self-representation—one that can be strategically used to maintain certain privacies and intimacies. Self-disclosures can produce intimacies but can also be meted out carefully and opportunistically for social capital and audience development. Many examples of digital media disclosures, such as trans vlogging on YouTube, offer and produce intimacy while also building large audience bases that challenge traditional understandings of intimacy (as private) (Horak 2014). Whether or not LGBTQ+ people build and manage large audiences, digital media—enabling connection to multiple publics through multiple platforms—simultaneously offer the safety of "closet spaces" and opportunities for public self-disclosure, and these need not compromise each other.

With greater mobile access to digital connection, many young LGBTQ+ people's lives are not easily compartmentalized into neat offline/online encounters. Instead, "life online" is porous. As a result, much research into LGBTQ+ identity construction is concerned with how users negotiate, encourage, and refuse this enmeshment across multiple platforms, contexts, and audiences. For example, McConnell et al. (2018) extrapolate on Orne's (2011) "strategic outness" as a spectrum constantly negotiated by young LGBTQ+ people on Facebook. Impression management practices (privacy settings, multiple accounts, monitoring self-presentation) employed by young LGBTQ+ people seek to emulate the many contexts they inhabit in their face-to-face interactions. McConnell et al. (2018) found that common practices among LGBTQ+ users have been useful in revealing how specific platforms stipulate certain types of queer identity (and their construction) over others through design, moderation, and user guidelines/policy.

In relation to YouTube, Alexander and Losh (2010) suggest that the proliferation of "coming out" videos invites a form of queer participation that could present new ways of constructing identity through a pooling of queer experiences. These generative interactions collated together challenge the overarching narrative of "outness" wherein queer authenticity is tied to a static identity. Elsewhere, research on trans young people's use of YouTube points to how the corporate control of the platform strategically filters out certain forms of expression, while privileging Whiteness and linear accounts of transitioning (Horak 2014; Raun 2016). More recently, Lovelock (2019) argues that the visibility of normative "LGB scripts" within the genre reveals greater platform vernaculars of YouTube vlogging that preferences the sharing of "authentic" queer feelings. He notes that the affective intimate nature of the genre demonstrates the continued structuring of queer life through its situatedness within public heteronormativity ("feeling queer" in a straight world). While Lovelock shows how these videos help situate coming out as "less a process of self-revelation than a journey to self-validation" (2019, 14), he also warns that vlogging's currency of authenticity (present across all digital media platforms) interpolates LGBTQ+ users as recognizably queer through their public negotiation of identities.

Still, digital media hold great potential in their capacity to network and connect those kept separate by location, opportunity, and visibility. As Duguay (2014) contends, both the social conditions and architectural affordances of platforms inform LGBTQ+ performances of identity to digital audiences. Discussions of coming out also relate to disclosures of trans status or a focus on the personal and political practices of trans visibility, supported through social media networks (Raun 2016). This work highlights a more contemporary approach to "coming out" as an ongoing digital process rather than an event one might rehearse online—in safely anonymous settings—prior to offline disclosure. As such, the concept of "queer becomings"—as ongoing, iterative, and performative practices of identity—might better capture the complexities of "coming out," if that term still holds relevance. Like closets, these spatial metaphors are still rich in meaning and can be used to make sense of our lives. However, we suspect that all such metaphors have varied degrees of resonance for LGBTQ+ people today, especially younger people and those whose situations don't sit comfortably with White, middle-class cultures of "pride" and self-acceptance or the expectations of family and community acceptance of LGBTQ+ identities. This can be seen in Rubin and McClelland's (2015) research with queer women of color on Facebook and Cho's (2018) discussion of the "default publicness" of many social media platforms that offer particular challenges for queer young POC.

Research into "real-name" social media platforms such as Facebook reveals how these rely upon the offline identities of users in order to authenticate and facilitate preexisting connections (Clark-Parsons 2018). In other words, these platforms prioritize encounters between previously networked users by connecting those perceived to be in close social proximity (like Facebook's "people you may know" feature). In contrast, research into semiprivate platforms, like Tumblr (Cho 2018) and Reddit (Triggs, Møller, and Neumayer 2019) tend to highlight the productive affordance of anonymity granted within these platforms for counterpublic address. Indeed, much work on trans and queer communities of Tumblr highlights how these spaces are not just a testing ground for gender and sexuality but are "community spaces" in which LGBTQ+ people live, engage, form relationships, produce knowledge, and learn about self and future possibilities (Byron et al. 2019; Cavalcante 2018). As such, these can be sites of ongoing gender/sexuality practices, beyond simply offering a safe space to get through difficult times, though some young people in the research by Byron et al. (2019) did discuss the value of "lurking" in these spaces to learn, without engaging in explicit community-building practices or making friends on sites like Tumblr.

Renninger's (2015) study of asexual communities on Tumblr extends upon boyd's (2011 theorization of networked publics to explore how the platform has supported more legibility, recognition, and inclusion of asexuals in LGBTQ+ spaces and communities. Tumblr blogs are not automatically tied to singular "real-name" profiles (like Facebook) as usernames take the form of URL-pseudonyms. Tumblr also grants further agency to the user's self-representation through its customizable interfaces. These technical affordances differentiate the platform from other social networking sites and encourage Tumblr's positioning as a site for learning and queer world–building (Fox and Ralston 2016). Schudson and van Anders' (2019) study of asexual, queer, and/or trans young people's use of Tumblr found that participants employed language pertaining to gender and sexual identity in order to represent parts of themselves that were previously un-named or ignored in hegemonic identity discourse. LGBTQ+ identities readily "try on" new labels via Tumblr's tagging function, which simultaneously generates and restricts the identification process. Triggs, Møller, and Neumayer (2019) found that hashtags allowed emergent identity cultures to occur simultaneously on a singular platform through a "bracketing" of counterpublics. Tagging practices reflect a rhizomatic under-standing of identity as one label emerges from another and goes on to be shaped by the people who use them. As Dame (2016) argues, trans hashtags on Tumblr offer strategic visibility, ensure that trans content is searchable, and contribute to trans ontologies. The browsing strategies employed by young LGBTQ+ people to navigate these terms engenders more specified language when naming one's conditions of sexual, romantic, and gender identities.

This practice of "trying on" new labels on Tumblr in the work of Bates, Hobman and Bell (2019, 72) is reminiscent of Turkle's (1995) earlier, more optimistic work on the possibilities of the internet—and the text-only "multi-user dungeons" she studied—to be an "identity laboratory" where people could explore and experiment with their own identities. Despite Turkle's later turn to a more pessimistic line on the role of social and digital media in our lives (as discussed in the section "Community and Connection"), these spaces continue to offer opportunities for the reflexivity, introspection, and self-learning that is key to identity work. While the digital media landscape has evolved con-siderably and various inequalities and structural considerations have been brought into stark contrast, capacities for identity work and an array of queer becomings remain.

Conclusion and Future Directions

By way of conclusion, we want to highlight some new and emerging directions in the research on LGBTQ+ identity and digital media and flag some important areas for future work. First, it is clear that new bodies of research in this area are rapidly growing in a range of different national, social, and cultural contexts. The work we have pointed to here from Turkey, the Philippines, China, and other non-English-speaking countries reveals patterns and practices of use that intersect with local customs, legal frameworks, and cultures. These variations in use must be accounted for in research from the "Global North" too, in order to better understand and learn across cultural and national boundaries. It is important that this research is not siloed off but is instead attended to, built on, and incorporated into our understandings of LGBTQ+ digital media use beyond predominantly White Anglo research hubs.

Second, research on LGBTQ+ people's uses of digital media must continue to question and push boundaries and categorizations according to people's experiences, especially around gender identity. For instance, Bivens (2017) explained how while in 2014 Facebook updated its gender identification options from 2 to 58, at the deep level of the database users were still configured into a binary system of male or female. These processes of technical categorization and conflation erase or reclassify nonbinary people, and it is important that researchers avoid this in the future. This includes attending to the experiences of trans, gender-fluid, agender, and nonbinary people in research in this space and being open to new and emerging configurations of gender and sexuality for which languages will no doubt develop (and are developing) in the kinds of digital spaces we have discussed here.

Finally, as we hope to have demonstrated, it is important to seek out the complexity in experiences of LGBTQ+ people's uses of digital media and avoid collapsing these under a single "rainbow family" banner. We have pointed to Ahmed and Fortier's (2003, 251) useful complication of the concept of community and have suggested—following others—that Warner's (2002) conceptualization of counterpublics may be a productive way forward in understanding queer mobilizations in digital spaces.

It is clear that digital media continue to offer LGBTQ+ people opportunities to connect to, learn from, and find each other—for friendship, dating, sex, and more. These sites and channels are vital for personal reflection and identity work in an otherwise largely hetero- and cis-normative social world. Everyday sites such as workplaces or schools can sometimes be hostile to LGBTQ+ people, and even in perceivably queer/trans-friendly settings, this friendliness may rely on limited forms of disclosure. As such, digital spaces are often experienced as safer spaces to engage with queer selves and people with shared experiences, connecting with diverse communities and an unlimited range of information. However, as we have discussed here, they are also spaces of violence and exclusion, both from dominant actors (be they high school bullies or presidents) and laterally, from other LGBTQ+ people. Further complicating the relational dynamics here is an ever-evolving and quickly moving social and digital media landscape from a platforms perspective, driven by opaque algorithmic decision-making and the logic of constant expansion and motivated by advertising and other forms of revenue generation under capitalism. Taken together, these forces have led to a sterilization of many queer digital spaces—from Facebook to Tumblr—to ostensibly appeal to (heteronormative) family-friendly advertising (Paasonen, Jarrett, and Light 2019, 170). The future of research on LGBTQ+ digital media use must seek to hold all of these complexities together, while being open to new complexities on the horizon.

Notes

1. We use "LGBTQ+" as a recognized acronym, but we also acknowledge (and have documented) the growing diversity and complexity captured in the "+," including intersex people and people who identify as gender nonbinary, fluid, nonconforming, and agender, as well as people who identify as asexual, pansexual, demisexual, and more. For a longer discussion, see Robards et al. (2018).
2. We use the term "POC" as a recognized acronym for people of color, while acknowledging the term's complexity in critical race studies today. We use this term with reference to its origins, as a means to give a name to the collective identity and solidarity between racialized people subjugated by White supremacy to various degrees.
3. However, "non-disclosure" is a problematic term that fails to register the cultural aspects of "coming out" discourse and practice that do not resonate for many people.

References

Ahmed, S., and A. M. Fortier. 2003. "Re-imagining Communities." *International Journal of Cultural Studies* 6, no. 3: 251–259.

Albury, K., and P. Byron. 2016. "Safe on My Phone? Same-Sex-Attracted Young People's Negotiations of Intimacy, Visibility and Risk on Digital Hook-up Apps." *Social Media + Society* 2, no. 4. https://journals.sagepub.com/doi/full/10.1177/2056305116672887

Albury, K., P. Byron, A. McCosker, T. Pym, J. Walshe, K. Race, et al. 2019. *Safety, Risk and Wellbeing on Dating Apps: Final Report.* Melbourne: Swinburne University of Technology. https://apo.org.au/node/268156.

Albury, K., C. Dietzel, T. Pym, S. Vivienne, and T. Cook. 2020. "Not Your Unicorn: Trans Dating App Users' Negotiations of Personal Safety and Sexual Health." *Health Sociology Review* 30, no. 1: 72–86.

Alexander, J., and E. Losh. 2010. "A YouTube of One's Own? Coming Out Videos as Rhetorical Action." In *LGBT Identity and Online New Media*, edited by C. Pullen and M. Cooper, 37–50. New York and London: Routledge.

Anzaldúa, G. 2002. "(Un)natural Bridges, (Un)safe Spaces." In *This Bridge We Call Home: Radical Visions for Transformation*, edited by G. E. Anzaldúa and A. Keating, 1–5. New York and London: Routledge.

Arroyo, B. 2016. "Sexual Affects and Active Pornographic Space in the Networked Gay Village." *Porn Studies* 3, no. 1: 77–88.

Asante, G. 2018. "'Where is home?' Negotiating Comm(unity) and Un/Belonging Among Queer African Migrants on Facebook." *Borderlands*, 17, no. 1, 1–22.

Banks, D. 2012. "Sherry Turkle's Chronic Digital Dualism Problem." Cyborgology, April 23. Accessed February 12, 2020. https://thesocietypages.org/cyborgology/2012/04/23/sherry-turkles-chronic-digital-dualism-problem/.

Barrett, E. L. R. 2020. "Sexing the Margins: Homonationalism in Gay Dating Apps." In *Gender, Sexuality and Race in the Digital Age*, edited by D. N. Farris, D. L. R. Compton, and A. P. Herrera, 115–136. Cham, Switzerland: Springer International.

Bates, A., T. Hobman and B. T., Bell 2019. "Let Me Do What I Please With It ... Don't Decide My Identity For Me": LGBTQ+ Youth Experiences of Social Media in Narrative Identity Development. *Journal of Adolescent Research* 31, no. 1: 51–83.

Batiste, D. P. 2013. " '0 Feet Away': The Queer Cartography of French Gay Men's Geo-social Media Use." *Anthropological Journal of European Cultures* 22, no. 2: 111–132.

Baym, N. K. 2015. *Personal Connections in the Digital Age*. 2nd ed. Cambridge: Polity Press.

Berger, B. M. 1998. "Disenchanting the Concept of Community." *Society* 35, no. 2: 324–327.

Bivens, R. 2017. "The Gender Binary Will Not Be Deprogrammed: Ten Years of Coding Gender on Facebook." *New Media & Society* 19, no. 6: 880–898.

Blackwell, C., J. Birnholtz, and C. Abbott. 2015. "Seeing and Being Seen: Co-situation and Impression Formation Using Grindr, a Location-Aware Gay Dating App." *New Media & Society* 17, no. 7: 1117–1136.

boyd, d. 2011. "Social network sites as networked publics: Affordances, dynamics, and implications." In *Networked self: Identity, community, and culture on social network sites*, edited by Zizi Papacharissi, 39–58. New York and London: Routledge.

Bronstein, C. 2020. "Pornography, Trans Visibility, and the Demise of Tumblr." *TSQ: Transgender Studies Quarterly*, 7, no. 2, 240–254.

Bruhn, J. G. 2011. *The Sociology of Community Connections*. Dordrecht, Netherlands: Springer.

Byron, P., K. Albury, and T. Pym. 2021. "Hooking Up with Friends: LGBTQ+ Young People, Dating Apps, Friendship and Safety." *Media, Culture and Society*, 43, no. 3, 497–514.

Byron, P., B. Robards, B. Hanckel, S. Vivienne, and B. Churchill. 2019. " 'Hey, I'm Having These Experiences': Tumblr Use and Young People's Queer (Dis)connections." *International Journal of Communication* 13, 2239–2259.

Callander, D., M. Holt, and C. E. Newman. 2016. " 'Not Everyone's Gonna Like Me': Accounting for Race and Racism in Sex and Dating Web Services for Gay and Bisexual Men." *Ethnicities* 16, no. 1: 3–21.

Carlson, B. 2020. "Love and Hate at the Cultural Interface: Indigenous Australians and Dating Apps." *Journal of Sociology* 56, no. 2: 133–150.

Castañeda, J. G. M. 2015. "Grindring the Self: Young Filipino Gay Men's Exploration of Sexual Identity through a Geo-social Networking Application." *Philippine Journal of Psychology* 48, no. 1: 29–58.

Cavalcante, A. 2016. " 'I Did it All Online': Transgender Identity and the Management of Everyday Life." *Critical Studies in Media Communication* 33, no. 1: 109–122.

Cavalcante, A. 2018. "Tumbling into Queer Utopias and Vortexes: Experiences of LGBTQ Social Media Users on Tumblr." *Journal of Homosexuality* 66, no. 12: 1715–1735.

Chan, L. S. 2020. "Multiple Uses and Anti-purposefulness on Momo, a Chinese Dating/Social App." *Information, Communication & Society* 23, no. 10: 1515–1530.

Cho, A. 2018. "Default Publicness: Queer Youth of Color, Social Media, and Being Outed by the Machine." *New Media & Society* 20, no. 9: 3183–3200.

Choy, C. H. Y. 2018. "Smartphone Apps as Cosituated Closets: A Lesbian App, Public/Private Spaces, Mobile Intimacy, and Collapsing Contexts." *Mobile Media & Communication* 6, no. 1: 88–107.

Clare, S. D. 2017. " 'Finally, She's Accepted Herself!' Coming Out in Neoliberal Times." *Social Text* 35, no. 2: 17–38.

Clark-Parsons, R. 2018. "Building a Digital Girl Army: The Cultivation of Feminist Safe Spaces Online." *New Media & Society* 20, no. 6: 2125–2144.

Conner, C. T. 2019. "The Gay Gayze: Expressions of Inequality on Grindr." *Sociological Quarterly* 60, no. 3: 397–419.

Crawford, K. 2009. "Following You: Disciplines of Listening in Social Media." *Continuum* 23, no. 4: 525–535.

Crooks, R. N. 2013. "The Rainbow Flag and the Green Carnation: Grindr in the Gay Village." *First Monday*, 18, no. 11. doi: 10.5210/fm.v18i11.

Crowley, M. S. 2010. "How r u??? Lesbian and Bi-identified Youth on MySpace." *Journal of Lesbian Studies* 14, no. 1: 52–60.

Dame, A. 2016. "Making a Name for Yourself: Tagging as Transgender Ontological Practice on Tumblr." *Critical Studies in Media Communication* 33, no. 1: 23–37.

Dame-Griff, A. 2019. "Herding the 'Performing Elephants': Using Computational Methods to Study Usenet." *Internet Histories* 3, no. 3–4: 223–244.

Dasgupta, R. K. 2018. "Online Romeos and Gay-dia: Exploring Queer Spaces in Digital India." In *Mapping Queer Space(s) of Praxis and Pedagogy*, edited by Elizabeth McNeil, James E. Wermers, and Joshua O. Lunn, 183–200. London: Palgrave Macmillan.

Dhoest, A. 2018. "Complicating Cosmopolitanism: Ethno-cultural and Sexual Connections among Gay Migrants." *Popular Communication* 16, no. 1: 32–44.

Dhoest, A., and L. Szulc. 2016. "Navigating Online Selves: Social, Cultural, and Material Contexts of Social Media Use by Diasporic Gay Men." *Social Media + Society*, 2, no. 4. https://doi.org/10.1177/2056305116672485.

Driver, S. 2006. "Virtually Queer Youth Communities of Girls and Birls: Dialogical Spaces of Identity Work and Desiring Exchanges." In *Digital Generations: Children, Young People, and New Media*, edited by D. Buckingham and R. Willett, 229–245. Mahwah, NJ: Lawrence Erlbaum Associates.

Duguay, S. 2014. " 'He Has a Way Gayer Facebook than I Do': Investigating Sexual Identity Disclosure and Context Collapse on a Social Networking Site." *New Media & Society* 18, no. 6: 891–907.

Duguay, S. 2017. "Identity Modulation in Networked Publics: Queer Women's Participation and Representation on Tinder, Instagram, and Vine." PhD thesis, Queensland University of Technology.

Duguay, S. 2018. "Why Tumblr's Ban on Adult Content Is Bad for LGBTQ Youth." The Conversation, December 6. Accessed January 12, 2020. https://theconversation.com/why-tumblrs-ban-on-adult-content-is-bad-for-lgbtq-youth-108215.

Duguay, S. 2019. " 'There's No One New Around You': Queer Women's Experiences of Scarcity in Geospatial Partner-Seeking on Tinder." In *The Geographies of Digital Sexuality*, edited by C. J. Nash and A. Gorman-Murray, 93–114. Singapore: Springer.

Ferris, L., and S. Duguay. 2020. "Tinder's Lesbian Digital Imaginary: Investigating (Im)Permeable Boundaries of Sexual Identity on a Popular Dating App." *New Media & Society* 22, no. 3: 489–506. https://doi.org/10.1177/1461444819864903.

Fortier, Anne-Marie. 2001. " 'Coming Home': Queer Migration and Multiple Evocations of Home." *European Journal of Cultural Studies* 4, no. 4: 405–424.

Fox, J., and R. Ralston. 2016. "Queer Identity Online: Informal Learning and Teaching Experiences of LGBTQ Individuals on Social Media." *Computers in Human Behavior* 65: 635–642.

Fraser, V. 2010. "Queer Closets and Rainbow Hyperlinks: The Construction and Constraint of Queer Subjectivities Online." *Sexuality Research and Social Policy* 7, no. 1: 30–36.

Goldenberg, D. 2019. "Disconnected Connectedness: The Paradox of Digital Dating for Gay and Bisexual Men." *Journal of Gay and Lesbian Mental Health* 23, no. 3: 360–366.

Gray, M. L. 2009. "Negotiating Identities/Queering Desires: Coming Out Online and the Remediation of the Coming-Out Story." *Journal of Computer-Mediated Communication* 14, no. 4: 1162–1189.

Gudelunas, D. 2005. "Online Personal Ads: Community and Sex, Virtually." *Journal of Homosexuality* 49, no. 1: 1–33.

Haimson, O. L., A. Dame-Griff, E. Capello, and Z. Richter. 2020. "Tumblr Was a Trans Technology: The Meaning, Importance, History, and Future of Trans Technologies." *Feminist Media Studies*. https://doi.org/10.1080/14680777.2019.1678505.

Hall, J. 2017. "So, Grindr Has Opened Its Doors to All—What Does That Mean?" *i-D Vice*, December 8. Accessed June 16, 2020. https://i-d.vice.com/en_au/article/d3xp5k/so-grindr-has-opened-its-doors-to-all-what-does-that-mean.

Han, C.-S., and K.-H. Choi. 2018. "Very Few People Say 'No Whites': Gay Men of Color and the Racial Politics of Desire." *Sociological Spectrum* 38, no. 3: 145–161.

Han, C.-S., K. Proctor, and K.-H. Choi. 2014. "I Know a Lot of Gay Asian Men Who Are Actually Tops: Managing and Negotiating Gay Racial Stigma." *Sexuality and Culture* 18, no. 2: 219–234.

Han, C. S., S. E. Rutledge, L. Bond, J. Lauby, and A. B. LaPollo. 2014. "You're Better Respected When You Carry Yourself as a Man: Black Men's Personal Accounts of the Down Low 'Lifestyle.' " *Sexuality and Culture* 18, no. 1: 89–102.

Haraway, D. 1990. "A Manifesto for Cyborgs: Science, Technology, and Socialist Feminism in the 1980s." In *Feminism/Postmodernism*, edited by Linda J. Nicholson (190–233). New York: Routledge.

Hillier, L., K. J. Mitchell, and M. L. Ybarra. 2012. "The Internet as a Safety Net: Findings from a Series of Online Focus Groups with LGB and non-LGB Young People in the United States." *Journal of LGBT Youth* 9, no. 3: 225–246.

Horak, L. 2014. "Trans on YouTube: Intimacy, Visibility, Temporality." *Transgender Studies Quarterly* 1, no. 4: 572–585.

Jackson, S. J., M. Bailey, and B. Foucault Welles. 2017. "#GirlsLikeUs: Trans Advocacy and Community Building Online." *New Media and Society* 20, no. 5: 1868–1888.

Jenkins, H., M. Ito, and d. boyd. 2015. *Participatory Culture in a Networked Era: A Conversation on Youth, Learning, Commerce, and Politics*. Cambridge: Polity Press.

Jenzen, O. 2017. "Trans youth and social media: moving between counterpublics and the wider web." *Gender, Place & Culture*, 24, no. 11, 1626–1641.

Jones, C., V. Trott, and S. Wright. 2020. "Sluts and Soyboys: MGTOW and the Production of Misogynistic Online Harassment." *New Media & Society* 22, no. 10: 1903–1921.

Jurgenson, N. 2011. "Digital Dualism versus Augmented Reality." *Cyborgology: The Society Pages* https://thesocietypages.org/cyborgology/2011/02/24/digital-dualism-versus-augmented-reality/.

Kojima, D. 2014. "Migrant Intimacies: Mobilities-in-Difference and Basue Tactics in Queer Asian Diasporas." *Anthropologica* 56, no. 1: 33–44.

Liu, T. 2016. "Neoliberal Ethos, State Censorship and Sexual Culture: A Chinese Dating/Hook-Up App." *Continuum* 30, no. 5: 557–566.

Lovelock, M. 2019. " 'My Coming Out Story': Lesbian, Gay and Bisexual Youth Identities on YouTube." *International Journal of Cultural Studies* 22, no. 1: 70–85.

MacKee, F. 2016. "Social Media in Gay London: Tinder as an Alternative to Hook-Up Apps." *Social Media + Society* 2, no. 3. https://journals.sagepub.com/doi/full/10.1177/2056305116662186

Mallory, C., A. Hasenbush, and B. Sears. 2015. *Discrimination and Harassment by Law Enforcement Officers in the LGBT Community*. Los Angeles: Williams Institute, University of California. Accessed October 14, 2019. https://escholarship.org/uc/item/5663q0w1#main.

McConnell, E., B. Néray, B. Hogan, A. Korpak, A. Clifford, and M. Birkett. 2018. " 'Everybody Puts Their Whole Life on Facebook': Identity Management and the Online Social Networks of LGBTQ Youth." *International Journal of Environmental Research and Public Health* 15, no. 6: 1078.

McGlotten, S. 2013. *Virtual Intimacies: Media, Affect, and Queer Sociality*. Albany: State University of New York Press.

Miles, S. 2017. "Sex in the Digital City: Location-Based Dating Apps and Queer Urban Life." *Gender, Place & Culture* 24, no. 11: 1595–1610.

Miles, S. 2018. Still Getting It on Online: Thirty Years of Queer Male Spaces Brokered through Digital Technologies." *Geography Compass* 11, no. 12: e12407.

Miller, B. 2015. " 'They're the Modern-Day Gay Bar': Exploring the Uses and Gratifications of Social Networks for Men who Have Sex with Men." *Computers in Human Behavior* 51, Part A, 476–482.

Møller, K., and M. Nebeling Petersen. 2018. "Bleeding Boundaries: Domesticating Gay Hook-Up Apps." In *Mediated Intimacies: Connectivities, Relationalities and Proximities*, edited by R. Andreassen, M. Nebeling Petersen, K. Harrison, and T. Raun, 208–223. London and New York: Routledge.

Monaghan, W. 2016. *Queer Girls, Temporality and Screen Media: Not "Just a Phase."* London: Springer.

Mowlabocus, S. 2010. *Gaydar Culture: Gay Men, Technology and Embodiment in the Digital Age*. Farnham, UK: Ashgate.

Nicholas, L., and C. Agius. 2018. "#Notallmen, #Menenism, Manospheres and Unsafe Spaces: Overt and Subtle Masculinism in Anti-'PC' Discourse." In *The Persistence of Global Masculinism*, 31–59. Cham, Switzerland: Springer.

Ong, J. C. 2017. "Queer Cosmopolitanism in the Disaster Zone: 'My Grindr Became the United Nations.'" *International Communication Gazette* 79, no. 6–7: 656–673.

Orne, J. 2011. " 'You Will Always Have to 'Out' Yourself': Reconsidering Coming Out through strategic Outness." *Sexualities* 14, no. 6: 681–703.

Paasonen, S., K. Jarrett, and B. Light. 2019. *NSFW: Sex, Humor, and Risk in Social Media*. Cambridge, MA: MIT Press.

Paper. 2019. "This Trans Dating App Focuses on Safety and Serious Relationships." November 12. Accessed June 3, 2020. https://www.papermag.com/butterfly-dating-app-2641315990.

Phua, V. C. 2020. "The Use of Hornet and 'Multi-Apping' in Turkey." *Sexuality & Culture* 24: 1376–1386.

Pond, T., and P. Farvid. 2017. " 'I Do Like Girls, I Promise': Young Bisexual Women's Experiences of Using Tinder." *Psychology of Sexualities Review* 8, no. 2: 6–24.

Pym, T., P. Byron, and K. Albury. 2020. " ' I Still Want to Know They're Not Terrible People': Negotiating 'Queer Community' on Dating Apps." *International Journal of Cultural Studies*. Published ahead of print October 3, 2020. https://doi.org/10.1177/1367877920959332.

Race, K. 2010. "Click Here for HIV Status: Shifting Templates of Sexual Negotiation." *Emotion, Space and Society* 3, no. 1: 7–14.

Raj, S. 2011. "Grindring Bodies: Racial and Affective Economies of Online Queer Desire." *Critical Race and Whiteness Studies* 7: 55–67.

Raun, T. 2016. *Out online: Trans Self-Representation and Community Building on YouTube*. London and New York: Routledge.

Renninger, B. J. 2015. " 'Where I Can Be Myself … Where I Can Speak My Mind': Networked Counterpublics in a Polymedia Environment." *New Media & Society* 17, no. 9: 1513–1529.

Renninger, B. J. 2019. "Grindr Killed the Gay Bar, and Other Attempts to Blame Social Technologies for Urban Development: A Democratic Approach to Popular Technologies and Queer Sociality." *Journal of Homosexuality* 66, no. 12: 1736–1755.

Ringrose, J., and E. Lawrence. 2018. "Remixing Misandry, Manspreading, and Dick Pics: Networked Feminist Humour on Tumblr." *Feminist Media Studies* 18, no. 4: 686–704.

Robards, B., P. Byron, B. Churchill, B. Hanckel, and S. Vivienne. 2020. "Tumblr as a Space of Learning, Connecting, and Identity Formation for LGBTIQ+ Young People." In *A Tumblr Book: Platform and Cultures*, edited by A. McCracken, A. Cho, L. Stein, and N. Indira, 281–292. Ann Arbor: University of Michigan Press.

Robards, B., B. Churchill, S. Vivienne, B. Hanckel, and P. Byron. 2018. "Twenty Years of 'Cyberqueer': The Enduring Significance of the Internet for Young LGBTIQ+ People." In *Youth, Sexuality and Sexual Citizenship*, edited by P. Aggleton, R. Cover, D. Leahy, D. Marshall, and M. L. Rasmussen, 151–167. London and New York: Routledge.

Robinson, B. A. 2015. " 'Personal Preference' as the New Racism: Gay Desire and Racial Cleansing in Cyberspace." *Sociology of Race and Ethnicity* 1, no. 2: 317–330.

Rubin, J. D., and S. I. McClelland. 2015. " 'Even though It's a Small Checkbox, It's a Big Deal': Stresses and Strains of Managing Sexual Identity(s) on Facebook." *Culture, Health and Sexuality* 17, no. 4: 512–526.

Russell, S. T., and J. N. Fish. 2016. "Mental Health in Lesbian, Gay, Bisexual, and Transgender (LGBT) Youth." *Annual Review of Clinical Psychology* 12: 465–487.

Schudson, Z., and S. van Anders. 2019. " 'You Have to Coin New Things': Sexual and Gender Identity Discourses in Asexual, Queer, and/or Trans Young People's Networked Counterpublics." *Psychology & Sexuality* 10, no. 4: 354–368.

Shield, A. D. 2017. "New in Town: Gay Immigrants and Geosocial Dating Apps." In *LGBTQs, Media and Culture in Europe*, edited by A. Dhoest, L. Szulc, and B. Eeckhout, 244–261. London and New York: Routledge.

Southerton, C., D. Marshall, P. Aggleton, M. L. Rasmussen, and R. Cover. 2021. "Restricted Modes: Social Media, Content Classification and LGBTQ Sexual Citizenship." *New Media & Society*, 23, no. 5, 920–938.

Steinmetz, K. 2019. "A Victim of the Anti-Gay Purge in Chechnya Speaks Out: 'The Truth Exists.' " *Time*, July 26. Accessed October 14, 2019. https://time.com/5633588/anti-gay-purge-chechnya-victim/.

Szulc, L. 2014. "The Geography of LGBTQ Internet Studies." *International Journal of Communication* 8, no. 5: 2927–2931.

Tang, D. T. S. 2017. "All I Get Is an Emoji: Dating on Lesbian Mobile Phone App Butterfly." *Media, Culture & Society* 39, no. 6: 816–832.

Triggs, A. H., K. Møller, and C. Neumayer. 2019. "Context Collapse and Anonymity among Queer Reddit Users." *New Media & Society* 23, no. 1: 5–21.

Turkle, S. 1995. *Life on the Screen: Identity in the Age of the Internet.* New York: Touchstone.

Turkle, S. 2011. *Alone Together: Why We Expect More from Technology and Less from Each Other.* New York: Basic Books.

Wakeford, N. 2000. "Cyberqueer." In *The Cybercultures Reader*, edited by D. Bell and B. M. Kennedy, 401–415. London and New York: Routledge.

Wang, P.-H. 2020. "Negotiating Racialized Sexuality through Online Stancetaking in Text-Based Communication." In *Gender, Sexuality and Race in the Digital Age*, edited by D. N. Farris, D. L. R. Compton, and A. P. Herrera, 187–203. Cham, Switzerland: Springer.

Warner, M. 2002. "Publics and Counterpublics." *Public Culture* 14, no. 1: 49–90.

Wilson, C., and L. A. Cariola. 2020. "LGBTQI+ Youth and Mental Health: A Systematic Review of Qualitative Research." *Adolescent Research Review* 5, 187–211.

Xue, M., L. Yang, K. W. Ross, and H. Qian. 2016b. "Characterizing User Behaviors in Location-Based Find-and-Flirt Services: Anonymity and Demographics." *Peer-to-Peer Networking and Applications* 10, 357–367.

Zamanian, P. 2014. "Queer Lives: The Construction of Queer Self and Community on Tumblr." Master's thesis, Sarah Lawrence College.

CHAPTER 18

FACEWORK ON SOCIAL MEDIA IN CHINA

XIAOLI TIAN AND QIAN LI

GOFFMAN (1955, 213; 1956) defined "face" as "an image of self, delineated in terms of approved social attributes." Face is a universal phenomenon across cultural contexts. However, sociologists and anthropologists suggest that face plays an even more central role in Chinese interactions (Hsu 1996). Chinese people are particularly motivated to do facework during social interactions; that is, protect their own face and avoid discrediting the face of others. Unlike Western cultures where individuals tend to form a "core self" and can therefore more easily remove themselves from their roles, the "self" and its dignity in China are validated based on not only one's role but also the evaluation of others (Fei 1992).

This brings about a fascinating question in modern times: What does facework look like in online social spaces? In recent decades, many social interactions have moved online, especially in China. By the end of January 2020, there were 1.04 billion active social media users in China, which makes 72% of its population (We Are Social and Hootsuite 2020). As of December 2019, the most popular social media site in China, WeChat, reported 1.16 billion active users every month[1] (Tencent 2020); and another popular social media site, Weibo, saw 516 million active monthly users (Sina 2020).

Given these statistics, social media are compelling sites for studying facework, other interpersonal interactions, and the presentation of the self in online settings. Furthermore, social media usually involve interacting with physically invisible others. Without a corporeal co-presence, interactants are ignorant of exactly who reads what and when they read it, especially where they are engaging in asynchronous interactions with disembodied others (Zhao 2005). So the question deepens: How does the existence of "undetectable others" influence self-presentation and interaction on social media? Without a physical co-presence, will Chinese users consider facework less important?

In this chapter, we review the literature on the importance of face and facework in Chinese interpersonal interactions online. Specifically, we discuss the extent to which and the reasons why face is more salient in the Chinese context; explain the characteristics of major Chinese social media sites, such as Weibo and WeChat; and elaborate upon how their attributes influence the way people interact and present themselves online. We use empirical cases to discuss how Chinese users protect their own face and give face to others, as well as how they avoid discrediting the face of others on social media. This is followed by a discussion of the conditions under which there is less emphasis on face, when compared to offline social contexts, as well as a review of the different methods used to study facework online, offline, and cross-nationally. We conclude with a brief discussion of how sociological research has contributed to the study of social media in China and directions for future research.

FACE: A UNIVERSAL SOCIAL PHENOMENON

Generally speaking, "face" refers to the positive social images that are formed in the gaze of others. Goffman (1955, 213) defined "face" as "the positive social value a person effectively claims for himself by the line others assumes he has taken during a particular contact." His definition points to three essential factors that revolve around the sociological concept of face. First, face is presenting a favorable self-image to others. Second, face is acted and performed during interactions based on mutual acknowledgment and acceptance of an assumed situated identity. Finally, face is situational and dynamic and, thus, can be saved or lost depending on the exhibited behavior in certain situations.

Ultimately, face is not self-determined because it is influenced by interactions with others (Qi 2011). Rather than a private self-presentation, face is a public self-image (Brown and Levinson 1987) and a "social self" (Ting-Toomey and Kurogi 1998). To claim face during an interaction, one must present a preferred self-image that is consistent with societal expectations in a situation. And, to ensure amicable encounters, one must modify their actions so that they are consistent with face. As long as the performance is accepted, face is maintained and saved. Otherwise, face is lost, which is embarrassing. The awareness of others plays an essential role in this process. In this sense, appropriate self-presentation is critical for preventing loss of face (Goffman 1967).

Facework involves not only self-presentation but also the performance of others. For example, when demonstrating self-respect, facework is used to save one's own dignity (a defensive orientation). In contrast, when one speaks and acts considerately, facework is being used to save the face of others (a protective orientation). As such, Goffman (1967) suggested that "maintenance of face is a condition of interaction" (p. 12) and performance of facework shows "the hallmark of his socialization as an interactant" (p. 31).

Although numerous studies have shown that face is a universal concept, the interpretation of face and facework strategies varies across different cultural settings. To understand cultural variations, Ting-Toomey (1988) proposed face negotiation theory (FNT), which distinguished self-oriented and other-oriented/mutual-oriented facework. Specifically, FNT suggests that in collectivist countries the subordinates are more compliant to those with more power in the social hierarchy, like China, usually prefer to use other- or mutually oriented facework strategies, while individualist countries with a small power distance, like the United States, tend to adopt self-oriented strategies. For example, some cross-cultural comparisons have found that Americans place more importance on maintaining self-face and behave more aggressively and arbitrarily in conflicts. In contrast, the Chinese prioritize relational bonds and group-face and may even sacrifice their own face to meet in-group goals (Cocroft and Ting-Toomey 1994; Oetzel and Ting-Toomey 2016; Oetzel et al. 2001; Ting-Toomey 1988; Ting-Toomey and Kurogi 1998). Similarly, Sun Park and Guan (2006) found that the Chinese are more inclined to apologize, which is a self-effacing practice when the face of the other party is threatened.

Face and Facework in China

Social scientists consistently find that the Chinese are preoccupied with face, so much so that it permeates every aspect of social life and interpersonal relationships (Hu 1944; Ho 1976; Hsu 1996). Face is so important that a significant loss of face can lead to suicide (Hu 1944; Ho 1976). On the one hand, the preoccupation with face makes sense. The Confucian cultural background, hierarchical social structure, and close individual–group relationship not only define the values attached to a positive social image but also create an environment where people are motivated to maintain and gain face without hurting that of others (Kinnison 2017; Hsu 1996; Cheng 1986). On the other hand, face has social consequences. Scholars argue that face is a form of symbolic capital that is circulated in relationship networks based on *renqing* (obligations among *guanxi* members) (Hwang 1987; Hsu 1996). As a result, facework in China is not merely about self-presentation in an isolated situation. It is embedded in relational networks with lasting influence. Therefore, Chinese social interactions emphasize consideration of others, individual–group relationships, and power dynamics.

The extant research shows that traditional Chinese society is dominated by relationship networks, such as *guanxi* (Fei 1992; Hwang 1987). Families, kinship, neighbors, acquaintances, and strangers are given different weight according to their relational distance. Consequently, different social groups are clearly demarcated through interaction norms and face concerns (*cha xu ge ju*). More importantly, network members monitor and evaluate the behaviors of others; and because they anticipate future interactions, they are obligated to maintain harmonious relationships. To do so, reciprocity-driven rules of *renqing* are applied: When a favor is asked, one may grant the request to give face and facilitate future exchanges of face or other resources (Hwang 1987).

In Chinese society, the significance of face is further reinforced by the hierarchical structure of social networks. Those in a higher position have more *guanxi*, which also means that the social consequences for hurting their face are higher. As a result, they exert more control and can oblige others to distribute resources through facework. In this sense, they participate in the power game with expectations that the relationship will have an enduring impact. Subordinates also participate, lest they be perceived as refusing to give face and, thus, are sanctioned. Still, face is reciprocal with *renqing*. Motivated by possible reciprocity, subordinates are driven to perform in their prescribed roles, such as showing deference (Hsu 1996; Ho 1976; Hwang 1987). Consequently, face and *renqing* are prioritized in everyday life. Those who stray from the principles of face and *renqing* upset the harmony of relationships and the parameters of *renqing*. Worse, they might be considered immoral and become ostracized (Hwang 1987; Hsu 1996; Kinnison 2017).

While face still dominates and shapes behaviors in contemporary Chinese social interactions (Hsu 1996; Zhai 2004), the rapid development of information and communication technologies (ICTs) has altered social interactions because the presence of others is not always known and because the public and private boundaries have blurred.

Facework on the Internet

Since face is interactional and relational (Arundale 2006), the facework strategies people adopt are situational and depend on the audience. In the virtual world, facework is more challenging. The internet has significantly altered face concerns, facework practices, and the consequences of facework.

Online Self-Presentation and Facework

Symbolic interactionists suggest that in social interactions certain situated identities are adopted and that behavior is continuously modified based on the response of others (Mead 1934; Cooley 1902; Goffman 1959). This is exactly how face manifests and operates in social encounters. To ensure that one's behaviors are consistent with expectations, facework is done. In other words, to claim face, facework inevitably involves self-presentation and impression management.

Social media offer individuals more control over their online self-presentations. For instance, individuals can edit their profiles and conceal flaws in order to present a more desirable image (Davis 2010; Walther 1996, 2007, 2011). Individuals, in other words, can effectively craft or curate a more ideal self in digital spaces (Turkle 1984; Zhao, Grasmuck, and Martin 2008). Self-presentation facework, however, requires a performance to be accepted by others. This means that the high visibility and public nature of social media can enhance an individual's face. Approval from the audience is obtained through likes, comments, follower counts, and other mechanisms facilitated by the technical affordances of social media. The accumulation of face through these means is kindred with prestige and reputation and can, if metrics such as number of followers are high, signal an increase in power and status. Moreover, neoliberalism and social media are creating a Web 2.0 culture which ties public acknowledgment to economic benefits by rewarding visibility and attention (Marwick 2013; Davenport and Beck 2001). To reap the rewards, individuals are motivated to engage in strategic self-presentation, self-promotion, and self-branding, which commodify and commercialize the self as a brand and then frame and edit that brand to cater to a lucrative audience or employees (Whitmer 2019). Interestingly, empirical research has suggested that individualist North Americans tend to adopt a positive self-presentation in comparison to collectivist South Koreans, which supports the assumptions of FNT in self-oriented facework (Lee-Won et al. 2014).

Increasing Risks of Inconsistency and New Challenges

Social media also increase the risk of losing face since facework requires the acknowledgment of others. The loss of face is sometimes related to assessments regarding an individual's authenticity. Users often scrutinize the performances of others in digital spaces and look for (in)consistencies (Ellison, Heino, and Gibbs 2006; Ellison, Hancock, and Toma 2012; Tian and Menchik 2016). Of course, the chance of being regarded as inconsistent is relatively high in a digital environment. Individuals typically have a number of social groups to which they belong, and they tailor their performances to group members. Inconsistent performance is not the only threat to an individual's face. Individuals sometimes make inappropriate comments online, and these comments can be searched and viewed. If other users confirm that a performance disappoints them, they will invalidate the performance, which leads to loss of face.

Other challenges to maintaining face include the recordability, asynchronism, and searchability of social media interactions. Online self-presentation increasingly is an "artifact in an exhibition" rather than an "interactive performance" (Goffman 1959). Images, videos, and comments, once posted online, cannot be monitored and modified as easily as performance in face-to-face (FTF) interactions since the audience for posted content remains elusive (Hogan 2010). This means that facework strategies used in FTF interactions, such as avoidance, are less effective on social media. Absent an immediate and known audience, individuals cannot alter their performances and, instead, must try to determine how potential viewers in the future will interpret what they do and say (Davis and Jurgenson 2014; boyd 2010; Tian and Menchik 2016). As a result, the imagined audience plays a vital role in online facework (Davis 2014; boyd 2010). For instance, the ratio of actual to total friends is an important predictor that affects the behavior of South Korean Facebook users because there is a tendency to use different facework strategies based on familiarity and intimacy. As the ratio of actual friends increases, self-enhancing presentations are reduced (Lee-Won et al. 2014).

Giving Face on Social Media

The rule of considerateness (the protective orientation) in facework is also important online. Although considerateness appears more frequently in collectivist cultures such as that of China (Ting-Toomey and Kurogi 1998), other-/mutually oriented facework is not a culturally unique phenomenon. Across cultures, hurting the face of others not only causes embarrassment but can also end further interaction.

This protective orientation is prevalent in online facework. For instance, Ditchfield (2020) found that Facebook users intentionally engage in both defensive and protective facework in the "rehearsal stage" of the online interaction. Respondents repeatedly scrutinized messages sent to friends, occasionally deleted unkind words, and rewrote messages to avoid hurting the face of others during pre-post editing. That is, the technical affordances of social media have allowed face-threatening acts to be reduced, which maintains relationships. Likewise, clicking "like" on a post is also a means to give face and for "doing friendship" online (Davies 2012). Thus, individuals often feel obliged to give face to others in order to maintain relationships and show group solidarity (Lim et al. 2012).

In sum, digital media present new opportunities and challenges for doing facework online. Next, we discuss what online facework looks like in China and how the unique layouts and settings of social media platforms affect how facework is done.

FACEWORK ON SOCIAL MEDIA IN CHINA

With the development of the internet and ICTs, online interactions have become an increasingly important entity in everyday life. According to the China Internet Network Information Center (2020), the three most popular social media platforms in China are WeChat Moments (a feature of WeChat), QQ Zone, and Sina Weibo, with usage rates of 85.1%, 47.6%, and 42.5%, respectively. While these are all social media platforms, they have different technical affordances and audience designs.

Specifically, WeChat is used for social gratification, while Sina Weibo is used for content gratification (Gan and Wang 2015). QQ Zone users, in contrast, flock to the platform because it promises high levels of social interaction (Wang et al. 2015). The user composition also varies from platform to platform. WeChat is more private due to its distinct "networked privacy" design, which means that there is no "social searching" or "social browsing" function. Both WeChat and QQ, however, allow users to easily connect with individuals they know in the real world. In fact, users report that 95% of their contacts on WeChat and QQ are real-life acquaintances. Weibo, in contrast, is more anonymous and public insofar as it is a microblogging platform (like Twitter) that allows strangers to follow, or just observe, others (Lin and Tian 2019; DeLuca, Brunner and Sun 2016; Tian and Guo 2021).

Video sharing and live streaming increasingly have become popular in China. Most notably, Douyin, or TikTok, is tremendously popular (China Internet Network Information Center 2020). As new forms of social interaction develop, it is important to determine their impact on facework, online communication, and personal relationships.

Performing the Idealized Self: Self-Presentation and Impression Management

Previous research suggests that the Chinese tend to present themselves modestly because arrogance might negatively affect their own face as well as the face of others (Hu 1944). However, this is not true on Chinese social media. Chinese youths, in particular, are becoming more at ease with presenting their idealized selves, although less frequently and extensively than their American counterparts (Mazur and Li 2016; Chen 2010). For instance, they edit their profile pictures (Zhao and Jiang 2011) and use strategies such as self-promotion, enhancement, and competitive self-presentation to attract and build relationships on social media sites (Chen 2010; Chu and Choi 2010; Wong 2012).

Similarly, Tian and Guo (2021) found that many WeChat Moments posts are oriented toward face enhancement. In these posts users lavishly display their wealth, status, and other desirable attributes. Positive comments and "likes" by other users on the platform not only allow individuals to "feel like somebody" but also serve as a validation of face. Individual users can also manipulate the privacy settings of WeChat in ways that are face-enhancing. For example, WeChat allows users to hide post replies and then comment on their own posts. Users can pretend that they are replying to someone, allowing them to appear more popular and influential (Tian and Guo 2021).

That said, social scientists find that Chinese social media users increasingly note that, as their online network grows in number and diversity, a modest online self-image is better than a face-enhancing one. Users also employ more strategies that maintain the face of other users. Similar to FTF communication, the comments and posts of others are mostly positive and friendly. Users explain that they choose their words with great care so that they can maintain harmonious relationships on- and offline (Fossati 2014). For example, Chen (2010) found that Taiwanese use more ingratiation strategies in their self-presentations on blogs than Americans and that they do so to preserve the face of others (Jones and Pittman 1982). Similarly, a study by Wong (2012) on the self-presentation of Hong Kong students found that social media users preferred to use ingratiation strategies to maintain relationships with Facebook friends they knew in the real world and enhancement and supplication strategies when they were trying to make new friends.

To Give or Not to Give Face

Differences in self-presentation strategies are not only a result of changing cultural expectations around positive social images. As with protective facework, the effect of an imagined audience also plays an essential role in considerateness. Although the audience cannot be directly detected on social media, individuals gauge their relationships with their online contacts and do facework accordingly. In Chinese culture, engaging in facework is more important with acquaintances than it is with strangers.

Tian (2017), for example, found that the imagined audience influenced Chinese self-presentation and facework on social media. Her study, which is among the few studies that address facework on social media directly, compares the self-presentation of Chinese students on Renren and Facebook. Renren is a Chinese social networking site where most of the users are close friends and family members. Since users know their audience, they tend to present themselves more modestly. Specifically, Tian found that users calculated their status relative to others and, if they had a higher status than a friend or family member, avoided face-threatening behaviors, such as showing off. Instead, they opted to engage lower-status users in safe topics, such as entertainment. This, Tian found, allowed the higher-status user to present an amicable and "equal" image in front of *ziji ren* (in-group persons). This facework not only allowed users to maintain their relationships but also allowed users of different status to seek—and receive—assistance from one another. This, Tian notes, is very different from Facebook, where users tend to present themselves positively in order to prevent the loss of face.

Facework varies across social media platforms. For example, since most Weibo users participate anonymously, they assume that the imagined audience consists mostly of strangers and, consequently, express their opinions with ease (DeLuca, Brunner, and Sun 2016). In this context, users are less concerned about maintaining relationships with others on the forum, and users debate issues freely (Lin and Tian 2019). As discussed above (see "Performing the Idealized Self: Self-Presentation and Impression Management"), this is not true of forums such as WeChat Moments. Since users can control who views their posts, facework and concerns over maintaining offline friendships influence how users interact (Zhu et al. 2014). The lack of anonymity as well as the overlap of online and offline networks motivate users to avoid conflict and discrediting the face of others. Additionally, users on WeChat are more likely to engage in face-giving strategies, such as "liking" a friend's post (Gan 2017; Tian and Guo 2021).

Flattery is not enough to maintain good relationships. On WeChat, users must determine how often to interact with their friends, what to disclose to friends, and how they might respond to their posts. For example, liking one friend's post and not indicating a similar level of support for another friend could cause damage to the relationship. As such, individuals must constantly consider the intricacies of the social relationships when doing facework on social media.

Face and Favors: *Renqing*, Reciprocity, and Power Structure

The hierarchical power structures and face culture of Chinese society have transferred online. As mentioned, *renqing* is a reciprocal social exchange, and its maintenance requires facework. An individual gives face to others, in part because it creates good will and could ultimately enhance their own status. Refusal to grant a favor damages not only the face of the other person but also one's own because others will condemn such disharmonious behavior as *bu hui zuo ren* (lacking the basic ability to act like a human being) and marginalize that person in the social network.

In their research on WeChat Moments, Tian and Guo (2021) found that the rules of *renqing* continue to define online facework. Users "like" and comment on the posts as well as repost the comments of others in their network with whom they wish to maintain good relationships. In China, the assumption is that these behaviors enhance the status and prestige of others, so they are considered online favors that need to be returned in the future. For example, Au (2020) found that the exchange of "likes" on Facebook among Hong Kong youths is considered a digital form of *renqing*, through which ties are formed or maintained. That said, from time to time, *renqing* requests may not align with one's ideal self-image and could harm one's own face. Consequently, individuals must develop strategies to balance face with favor, such as selectively sharing *renqing* posts with friends in a network (Tian and Guo 2021).

Giving *renqing* can become a dilemma with which individuals must contend. Sociologists find that, when facing this dilemma, individuals consider the degree of familiarity with another user and the relative status of another user when determining what facework strategies to employ. For example, stronger social ties mean more obligation to engage in facework, as well as more frequent participation in reciprocal exchanges (Au 2020). Similarly, facework is more salient in exchanges between superiors and subordinates, regardless of whether the interactions are online or offline. Tian (2020) found that WeChat is increasingly used in the workplace, reinforcing hierarchies during work and after hours. Subordinates report that they deliberately flatter, "like," or show deference to their superiors and that they do so on nights and weekends. In fact, many employees reported that they felt compelled to constantly check, and respond to, their WeChat messages for "WeChat Virtual Red Packets" from their workplace superiors during Chinese New Year. Tian (2020) found that the pressure to engage in facework with superiors is increasing and that Chinese middle-class workers are willing to use flattery in the hope of garnering a favor in the future.

Interestingly, Tian (2020) also found that there are benefits associated with online facework. Some WeChat users indicated that less emotional energy is involved in other-oriented facework online; namely, it is less interactional and emotionally taxing than offline interactions. Smiling at the boss is affective labor, but sending a smiley-faced emoji is more physical than affective labor. In the digital age awkward real-life interactions can be replaced with texts, pictures, and emojis. Additionally, many employees reported that they actively take advantage of WeChat as a communication channel to establish relationships with superiors and that they find face-giving strategies such as flattery less demeaning because they can be disguised as playfulness. One of Tian's respondents, for instance, reported that when the supervisor posted on Moments that he was stuck in a traffic jam and his car got scratched by the car behind, his colleagues all declared they were "defending their supervisor to the bitter end." In FTF contexts, such an exchange might lead to negative sanctions from other employees (Coser 1961). Online, however, such facework can be disguised as playfulness.

While other-oriented facework displaying deference and subordination on WeChat might require less emotional effort, it does require a great deal of attention (Lanham 2006). However, attention is a scarce resource. Among middle-class Chinese workers attention is increasingly understood as relational currency. Liking, commenting on, and interacting with superiors online can lead to promotions and other benefits in the real world. Of course, this facework is one-sided. While employees must spend a great deal of time acknowledging the positions of their superiors, superiors are under no obligation to return the favor.

Methodology Revisited

Face is interactional and relational (Arundale 2006). New digital technologies have not only changed the strategies and forms of facework but also provided unprecedented opportunities to observe social interactions (Golder and Macy 2014). In this section we briefly note how facework has been studied in the past and address the challenges associated with studying this "fundamental communication phenomenon" in the digital age (Ting-Toomey 1994, 325).

Early research on facework adopted a linguistic approach (e.g., Hu 1944; Brown and Levinson 1987; Matsumoto 1988). Scholars studied the language used in interactions and outlined how facework strategies varied across different cultural settings. Other social scientists used psychological approaches, such as experimentation, to understand the micro-processes of facework, such as the emotional and cognitive reactions associated with giving and receiving face (e.g., Modigliani 1971). Finally, some scholars used ethnomethodology to explore the structural and cultural factors that influence facework. This line of research linked micro-phenomena to a broader context, illustrating how facework is socially and interactionally constructed. The latter research animates much of the current conceptual understanding of facework because it underscores that how facework is managed depends on the power dynamics and embedded relational networks (e.g., Goffman 1967; Ho 1976; Hsu 1996).

Current research on facework largely uses qualitative methods. Posts on personal profiles and homepages, user names, "likes," comments, and other online behaviors are primary data sources; and social scientists use textual and content analyses to analyze facework. For example, Helfrich (2014) studied comments about a video clip to discuss how "flaming," a seemingly face-damaging behavior, can sometimes enhance users' face. In this instance, commenters were united against the individual who posted the video, and flaming become a way for users to complement one another as they insulted a common enemy. Ditchfield (2020) used screen-captured recordings to explore when and how individuals edited posts on Facebook. She found that individuals spent a fair amount of time editing content in order to enhance the face of their friends. Sociologists find that in-depth interviews are also a useful method for understanding facework online because researchers can gain valuable insight into the role of facework in identity construction and relationship maintenance (e.g., Tian and Guo 2021; Au 2020; Lim et al. 2012).

While observations of online interaction provide direct and real-time data rather than retrospective self-reports, it is not always clear how facework online affects offline relationships. Consequently, social science research increasingly uses a mixed-method approach, which combines data regarding individual behavior online and offline. For example, Beneito-Montagut (2011) suggests that scholars adopt a user-centered approach to study relationships online and, specifically, focus on the various ways and places individuals engage with one another. Similarly, Tian (2017) advocates for a combination of online observation (both real-time observation and textual analyses) and in-depth interviews so that researchers can understand how facework done in an online setting links to the broader social and cultural structures in which users are situated.

Conclusion

As social creatures, we constantly seek to interact with others and build relationships. As long as we seek the recognition of others, we want others to see us in a positive light. While face is universally relevant, it is particularly salient in Chinese society because the social structure is hierarchical and higher-ranking individuals control resources. China is also traditionally an acquaintance society where long-term relationships are the norm. In the Chinese context, facework is expected since the survival of the community rests on mutual dependence and collaboration.

In recent decades, China has rapidly modernized and urbanized. Sociologists argue that Chinese society has transformed from an "acquaintance society" to a "quasi-acquaintance society" or even a "stranger society" (Simmel 1950; Zhai 2004; Chen 2019). Despite these changes, face culture and the rules around giving face remain; only now social interactions occur online. In the digital age, although co-presence is not necessary, offline acquaintance communities reassemble and move to online domains.

Future research on facework should explore the following questions: What are the perceived and real consequences of not giving face to others or if someone loses face to a public audience? In a society that is undergoing rapid social change, how do sociocultural changes influence face concerns and facework strategies? Will the consequences of losing face diminish in severity with China's continued urbanization? And finally, how are facework strategies in China different from or similar to those in other cultural contexts? Given that the COVID-19 pandemic has forced even more social interaction online, it is imperative that we understand how social media influence our relationships and our understandings of ourselves.

Note

1. This is the combined total number of domestic (Weixin) and international (WeChat) active accounts. Additionally, a user may have more than one account simultaneously on WeChat.

References

Arundale, Robert. 2006. "Face as Relational and Interactional: A Communication Framework for Research on Face, Facework, and Politeness." *Journal of Politeness Research* 2: 193–216.

Au, Anson. 2020. "Guanxi 2.0: The Exchange of Likes in Social Networking Sites." *Information, Communication & Society*. Published ahead of print April 8, 2020. https://doi.org/10.1080/1369118X.2020.1748091.

Beneito-Montagut, Roser. 2011. "Ethnography Goes Online: Towards a User-Centred Methodology to Research Interpersonal Communication on the Internet." *Qualitative Research* 11, no. 6: 716–735.

boyd, danah. 2010. "Social Network Sites as Networked Publics: Affordances, Dynamics, and Implications." In *A Networked Self: Identity, Community, and Culture on Social Network Sites*, edited by Zizi Papacharissi, 39–58. New York: Routledge.

Brown, Penelope, and Stephen Levinson. 1987. *Politeness: Some Universals in Language Usage*. Cambridge: Cambridge University Press.

Chen, Baifeng. 2019. *Ban shuren shehui: Zhuanxing qi xiangcun shehui xingzhi shenmiao* [The quasi-acquaintance society: A thick description of the rural society in transition]. Beijing: Social Sciences Academic Press.

Chen, Yi-Ning Katherine. 2010. "Examining the Presentation of Self in Popular Blogs: A Cultural Perspective." *Chinese Journal of Communication* 3, no. 1: 28–41.

Cheng, Chung-ying. 1986. "The Concept of Face and Its Confucian Roots." *Journal of Chinese Philosophy* 13, no. 3: 329–348.

Chu, Shu-Chuan, and Sejung Marina Choi. 2010. "Social Capital and Self-Presentation on Social Networking Sites: A Comparative Study of Chinese and American Young Generations." *Chinese Journal of Communication* 3, no. 4: 402–420.

China Internet Network Information Center. 2020. *The 45th China Statistical Report on Internet Development*. Accessed June 17, 2020. http://www.cnnic.net.cn/hlwfzyj/hlwxzbg/hlwtjbg/202004/P020200428596599037028.pdf.

Cocroft, Beth-Ann, and Stella Ting-Toomey. 1994. "Facework in Japan and the United States." *International Journal of Intercultural Relations* 18, no. 4: 469–506.

Cooley, Charles Horton. 1902. *Human Nature and the Social Order*. New York: C. Scribner's Sons.

Coser, Rose. 1961. "Insulation from Observability and Types of Social Conformity." *American Sociological Review* 26, no. 1: 28–39.

Davenport, Thomas, and John Beck. 2001. *The Attention Economy: Understanding the New Currency of Business*. Cambridge, MA: Harvard Business School Press.

Davies, Julia. 2012. "Facework on Facebook as a New Literacy Practice." *Computers & Education* 59, no. 1: 19–29.

Davis, Jenny. 2010. "Architecture of the Personal Interactive Homepage: Constructing the Self through Myspace." *New Media & Society* 12, no. 7: 1103–1119.

Davis, Jenny. 2014. "Triangulating the Self: Identity Processes in a Connected Era." *Symbolic Interaction* 37, no. 4: 500–523.

Davis, Jenny, and Nathan Jurgenson. 2014. "Context Collapse: Theorizing Context Collusions and Collisions." *Information, Communication & Society* 17, no. 4: 476–485.

DeLuca, Kevin Michael, Elizabeth Brunner, and Ye Sun. 2016. "Weibo, Wechat, and the Transformative Events of Environmental Activism on Chinese Wild Public Screens." *International Journal of Communication* 10: 321–339.

Ditchfield, Hannah. 2020. "Behind the Screen of Facebook: Identity Construction in the Rehearsal Stage of Online Interaction." *New Media & Society* 22, no. 6: 927–943.

Ellison, Nicole, Jeffrey T. Hancock, and Catalina L. Toma. 2012. "Profile as Promise: A Framework for Conceptualizing Veracity in Online Dating Self-Presentations." *New Media & Society* 14, no. 1: 45–62.

Ellison, Nicole, Rebecca Heino, and Jennifer Gibbs. 2006. "Managing Impressions Online: Self-Presentation Processes in the Online Dating Environment." *Journal of Computer-Mediated Communication* 11, no. 2: 415–441.

Fei, Hsiao-t'ung. 1992. *From the Soil: The Foundations of Chinese Society. A Translation of Fei Xiaotong's Xiangtu Zhongguo*. Translated by Gary G. Hamilton and Wang Zheng. Berkeley: University of California Press.

Fossati, Serena. 2014. "Identity Construction Online: A Study of the Chinese Social Networking Site Renren." *Comunicazioni Sociali* 2: 336–346.

Gan, Chunmei. 2017. "Understanding Wechat Users' Liking Behavior: An Empirical Study in China." *Computers in Human Behavior* 68: 30–39.

Gan, Chunmei, and Weijun Wang. 2015. "Uses and Gratifications of Social Media: A Comparison of Microblog and Wechat." *Journal of Systems and Information Technology* 17, no. 4: 351–363.

Goffman, Erving. 1955. "On Face-Work: An Analysis of Ritual Elements in Social Interaction." *Psychiatry* 18, no. 3: 213–231.

Goffman, Erving. 1956. "Embarrassment and Social Organization." *American Journal of Sociology* 62, no. 3: 264–271.

Goffman, Erving. 1959. *The Presentation of Self in Everyday Life*. Harmondsworth, UK: Penguin.

Goffman, Erving. 1967. *Interaction Ritual: Essays on Face-to-Face Interaction*. Garden City, NY: Doubleday.

Golder, Scott, and Michael Macy. 2014. "Digital Footprints: Opportunities and Challenges for Online Social Research." *Annual Review of Sociology* 40, no. 1: 129–152.

Helfrich, Uta. 2014. "Face Work and Flaming in Social Media." In *Face Work and Social Media*, edited by Gudrun Held, Kristina Bedijs, and Christiane Maaß, 297–322. Münster, Germany: LIT Verlag.

Ho, David Yau-fai. 1976. "On the Concept of Face." *American Journal of Sociology* 81, no. 4: 867–884.

Hogan, Bernie. 2010. "The Presentation of Self in the Age of Social Media: Distinguishing Performances and Exhibitions Online." *Bulletin of Science, Technology & Society* 30, no. 6: 377–386.

Hsu, Chuanhsi Stephen. 1996. " 'Face': An Ethnographic Study of Chinese Social Behavior." PhD diss., Yale University.

Hu, Hsien Chin. 1944. "The Chinese Concepts of 'Face.' " *American Anthropologist* 46, no. 1: 45–64.

Hwang, Kwang-kuo. 1987. "Face and Favor: The Chinese Power Game." *American Journal of Sociology* 92, no. 4: 944–974.

Jones, Edward, and Thane Pittman. 1982. "Toward a General Theory of Strategic Self-Presentation." *Psychological Perspectives on the Self* 1, no. 1: 231–262.

Kinnison, Li Qing. 2017. "Power, Integrity, and Mask—An Attempt to Disentangle the Chinese Face Concept." *Journal of Pragmatics* 114: 32–48.

Lanham, Richard. 2006. *The Economics of Attention: Style and Substance in the Age of Information*. Chicago and London: University of Chicago Press.

Lee-Won, Roselyn, Minsun Shim, Yeon Kyoung Joo, and Sung Gwan Park. 2014. "Who Puts the Best 'Face' Forward on Facebook? Positive Self-Presentation in Online Social Networking and the Role of Self-Consciousness, Actual-to-Total Friends Ratio, and Culture." *Computers in Human Behavior* 39: 413–423.

Lim, Sun Sun, Shobha Vadrevu, Yoke Hian Chan, and Iccha Basnyat. 2012. "Facework on Facebook: The Online Publicness of Juvenile Delinquents and Youths-at-Risk." *Journal of Broadcasting & Electronic Media* 56, no. 3: 346–361.

Lin, Tony Zhiyang, and Xiaoli Tian. 2019. "Audience Design and Context Discrepancy: How Online Debates Lead to Opinion Polarization." *Symbolic Interaction* 42, no. 1: 70–97.

Marwick, Alice E. 2013. *Status Update: Celebrity, Publicity, and Branding in the Social Media Age*. New Haven, CT: Yale University Press.

Matsumoto, Yoshiko. 1988. "Reexamination of The Universality of Face: Politeness Phenomena in Japanese." *Journal of Pragmatics* 12, no. 4: 403–426.

Mazur, Elizabeth, and Yidi Li. 2016. "Identity and Self-Presentation on Social Networking Web Sites: A Comparison of Online Profiles of Chinese and American Emerging Adults." *Psychology of Popular Media Culture* 5, no. 2: 101–118.

Mead, George Herbert. 1934. *Mind, Self and Society*. Edited by Charles W. Morris. Chicago: University of Chicago Press.

Modigliani, Andre. 1971. "Embarrassment, Facework, and Eye Contact: Testing a Theory of Embarrassment." *Journal of Personality and Social Psychology* 17, no. 1: 15–24.

Oetzel, John, and Stella Ting-Toomey. 2016. "Face Concerns in Interpersonal Conflict." *Communication Research* 30, no. 6: 599–624.

Oetzel, John, Stella Ting-Toomey, Tomoko Masumoto, Yumiko Yokochi, Xiaohui Pan, Jiro Takai, and Richard Wilcox. 2001. "Face and Facework in Conflict: A Cross-Cultural Comparison of China, Germany, Japan, and the United States." *Communication Monographs* 68, no. 3: 235–258.

Qi, Xiaoying. 2011. "Face: A Chinese Concept in a Global Sociology." *Journal of Sociology* 47, no. 3: 279–295.

Simmel, Georg. 1950. *The Sociology of Georg Simmel*. New York: Free Press.

Sina. 2020. *Annual Report 2019*. Accessed June 17, 2020. http://ir.sina.com/static-files/f97b9f1f-f122-4a7d-a47e-f57f9b19d21f.

Sun Park, Hee, and Xiaowen Guan. 2006. "The Effects of National Culture and Face Concerns on Intention to Apologize: A Comparison of the USA and China." *Journal of Intercultural Communication Research* 35, no. 3: 183–204.

Tencent. 2020. *2019 Annual Report*. Accessed June 17, 2020. https://cdc-tencent-com-1258344 706.image.myqcloud.com/uploads/2020/04/02/ed18b0a8465d8bb733e338a1abe76b73.pdf.

Tian, Xiaoli. 2017. "Face-Work on Social Media in China: The Presentation of Self on Renren and Facebook." In *Chinese Social Media*, edited by Mike Kent, Katie Ellis, and Jian Xu, 92–105. New York and London: Routledge.

Tian, Xiaoli. 2020. "An Interactional Space of Permanent Observability: Wechat and Reinforcing the Power Hierarchy in Chinese Workplaces." *Sociological Forum*. Published ahead of print November 2, 2020. https://doi.org/10.1111/socf.12662.

Tian, Xiaoli, and Yanan Guo. 2021. "An Online Acquaintance Community: The Emergence of Chinese Virtual Civility." *Symbolic Interaction*. Published ahead of print January 3, 2021. https://doi.org/10.31235/osf.io/rhwm3.

Tian, Xiaoli, and Daniel Menchik. 2016. "On Violating One's Own Privacy: *N*-Adic Utterances and Inadvertent Disclosures in Online Venues." In *Communication and Information Technologies Annual: [New] Media Cultures*, edited by Laura Robinson, Jeremy Schulz, Shelia R. Cotten, Timothy M. Hale, Apryl A. Williams, and Joy L. Hightower, 3–30. Studies in Media and Communications 11. Bingley, UK: Emerald Group.

Ting-Toomey, Stella. 1988. "Intercultural Conflict Styles: A Face Negotiation Theory." In *Theory in Intercultural Communication*, edited by Y. Kim and W. Gudykunst, 213–235. Newbury Park, CA: Sage.

Ting-Toomey, Stella, ed. 1994. *The Challenge of Facework: Cross-Cultural and Interpersonal Issues*. Albany: State University of New York Press.

Ting-Toomey, Stella, and Atsuko Kurogi. 1998. "Facework Competence in Intercultural Conflict: An Updated Face-Negotiation Theory." *International Journal of Intercultural Relations* 22, no. 2: 187–225.

Turkle, Sherry. 1984. *The Second Self: Computers and the Human Spirit*. New York: Simon & Schuster.

Walther, Joseph B. 1996. "Computer-Mediated Communication: Impersonal, Interpersonal, and Hyperpersonal Interaction." *Communication Research* 23, no. 1: 3–43.

Walther, Joseph. 2007. "Selective Self-Presentation in Computer-Mediated Communication: Hyperpersonal Dimensions of Technology, Language, and Cognition." *Computers in Human Behavior* 23, no. 5: 2538–2557.

Walther, Joseph. 2011. "Theories of Computer-Mediated Communication and Interpersonal Relations." In *The Sage Handbook of Interpersonal Communication*, 4th ed., edited by Mark L. Knapp and John A. Daly, 443–479. Thousand Oaks, CA: SAGE Publications.

Wang, Jin-Liang, Linda Jackson, Hai-Zhen Wang, and James Gaskin. 2015. "Predicting Social Networking Site (SNS) Use: Personality, Attitudes, Motivation and Internet Self-Efficacy." *Personality and Individual Differences* 80: 119–124.

We Are Social and Hootsuite. 2020. *Digital 2020 China*. Accessed June 17, 2020. https://wearesocial-cn.s3.cn-north-1.amazonaws.com.cn/digital2020-china.pdf.

Whitmer, Jennifer. 2019. "You Are Your Brand: Self-Branding and the Marketization of Self." *Sociology Compass* 13, no. 3: e12662.

Wong, Winter Ka Wai. 2012. "Faces on Facebook: A Study of Self-Presentation and Social Support on Facebook." Outstanding Academic Papers by Students, City University of Hong Kong. http://dspace.cityu.edu.hk/handle/2031/6847.

Zhai, Xuewei. 2004. "Renqing, mianzi, yu quanli de zai shengchan: Qingli shehui zhong de shehui jiaohuan fangshi" [Favor, face and reproduction of power: A way of social exchange in a reasonableness society]." *Sociological Research* 5, no. 4: 48–57.

Zhao, Chen, and Gonglue Jiang. 2011. "Cultural Differences on Visual Self-Presentation through Social Networking Site Profile Images." In *Proceedings of the SIGCHI Conference on Human Factors in Computing Systems*. 1129–1132. New York: ACM Press.

Zhao, Shanyang. 2005. "The Digital Self: Through the Looking Glass of Telecopresent Others." *Symbolic Interaction* 28, no. 3: 387–405.

Zhao, Shanyang, Sherri Grasmuck, and Jason Martin. 2008. "Identity Construction on Facebook: Digital Empowerment in Anchored Relationships." *Computers in Human Behavior* 24, no. 5: 1816–1836.

Zhu, W., D. Zheng, W. Wang, and H. Zhou. 2014. "The Differences between Weibo and Wechat: The Evidence from the Social Capital Theory." *Journal of Intelligence* 33, no. 6: 138–143.

CHAPTER 19

VIDEO GAMES AND IDENTITY FORMATION IN CONTEMPORARY SOCIETY

DANIEL MURIEL

IDENTITY can be understood as how we think about ourselves, a collective construction of meaning, and the process by which individuals *identify with* and *differentiate from* others. Although we might live in times where more flexible and elusive forms of identity prevail, other identity configurations have not completely disappeared; and there are still questions that interpellate subjects in powerful ways.

In this chapter, I explore the gamer construct in order to understand the processes of identity formation in video game culture and, more generally, contemporary society. Video games provide a vantage point to observe the always elusive processes of meaning construction. The chapter begins with a brief review of some of the contemporary theoretical discussions on identity and its crisis. I then review some of the most relevant empirical works on gaming and identity, connecting them with the main sociological discussions on the matter. Finally, the chapter will help devise new ways to approach the question of meaning construction in contemporary society and shed light on the new (and subaltern) kinds of identity formations around gaming.

IDENTITY AND ITS CRISIS

With all its nuances, "identity" is a concept that allows us to think of certain aspects of social reality in sociological terms. Thus, I would like to start this section with a formal definition of identity[1]:

> Identity is our understanding of who we are and who other people are, and, reciprocally, other people's understanding of themselves and of others (which

includes us). It is a very practical matter, synthesising relationships of similarity and difference.

(Jenkins 2014, 19)

Jenkins defines identity in its fundamental form: identity as a way to represent ourselves and others, an understanding formed around the tension between what makes us similar and different. Once this elementary conceptual infrastructure is set, the question of identity is on the table and subject to debate. In relation to its form, identity can be represented as either strong, solid, and permanent or flexible, fragmented, and temporary. When it comes to discussing its nature, identity can be seen as essentialist—what someone is (Parsons 1968; Durkheim [1953] 2010)—or as a disposition—a process of identification (Hall 1996; Butler 1999; Bauman 2004; Haraway 1991; Sen 2007). Thus, identity can be understood as both a position from where we act and speak—a starting point—and a process that (re)produces and articulates a sense of identity—an outcome.

In this section, I will focus on identity as a notion in crisis. There is a widely spread diagnosis among contemporary social theorists that suggests that some of the fundamental institutions of modernity are in crisis or decline (Giddens 2002; Lyotard 1984; Bauman 2000; Beck 1992; Dubet 2006)—a reality that is portrayed by the failure of society as the project of "living together" (Thévenot 2004). According to these theoretical developments, social reality becomes liquid, unstable, risky, aimless, and meaningless. In particular, the models of identity construction dramatically change, and contemporary societies face a crisis in the processes of meaning construction. New kinds of identities emerge.

The crisis of meaning is connected, to a greater or lesser extent, with the development of the Enlightenment's project taken to the extreme, the same project that undermined the (in)securities of the traditional world: from a—probably idealized—sociological version of reality in which the meaning of social life was *taken for granted* to a sociological form where social meaning is problematized and planned and has to be constructed (Berger and Luckmann 1995, 80).

Society emerges, therefore, as a planned reality. The social is explicitly designed (Bauman 1989, 54), deploying a myriad of methods, techniques, and processes in order to govern and act on it (Rose 1999, 51–55). However, as a result of this constant control and planning, not only does the ambivalence decrease, but it grows exponentially (Bauman 1993, 214).

It is in this context, in the dawn of the modern state, when, as Bauman suggests (2004, 20), identity as a problem and, moreover, as a task is born. In premodern societies, it was not possible to think in terms of identity because asking "who you are" only makes sense if "you believe that you can be someone other than you are" (Bauman 2004, 19). Identity was determined by birth, something taken for granted. Therefore, identity as a notion acquired full meaning in modernity and became a task "which individuals had to perform" through their "biographies" (Bauman 2004, 49). It is the "quest of self-identity" (Giddens 1990, 121) or the "construction of the self as a reflexive project," where individuals must find their "identity amid the strategies and options provided by abstract systems" (Giddens, 1990, 124).

Presenting identity as a task, a project, or a quest was, in comparison to the premodern identity ascription at birth, an act of relative liberation. Although these were identities that individuals needed to choose and pursue, implying they should be constantly maintained and reproduced, their trajectories were "unambiguously laid out" (Bauman 2004, 49), which means, I would suggest, that identities were relatively unambiguous.

However, Bauman argues (2004, 53), as the idea of a "cohesive, firmly riveted and solidly constructed identity" progressively became a limitation on "the freedom to choose," identities began to liquefy. Similarly to what happened with the obsession to control and administer every aspect of the social, the constant problematization of identity is the cause of its fragmentation, multiplication, and loss of stability.

In this regard, within a context of advanced modernity or postmodernity, identities are reinvented in strange, fragmented, and multiple ways. According to Bauman (2000, 82), the "search for identity" turns into a "struggle to arrest or slow down the flow, to solidify the fluid, to give form to the formless." In Latour (1993), this process can be read as the multiplication of hybrids, associations, and enrollments between different kinds of actors, while in Haraway (1991), it can be understood as the proliferation of cyborgs and the articulation between heterogeneous elements that challenge the notion of identity through the emergence of "inappropriate/d others" (Haraway 2004, 47–61; Trinh 1986–1987). Therefore, identities understood as an essence—those fragments of the self that are always identical to themselves—are not possible anymore. The pleasant, secure, and harmonic image of identity falls apart:

> Whenever we speak of identity, there is at the back of our minds a faint image of harmony, logic, consistency: all those things which the flow of our experience seems—to our perpetual despair—so grossly and abominably to lack.
>
> (Bauman 2000, 82)

Identity is, therefore, a notion in crisis and under scrutiny in contemporary society, a crisis that the culture around gaming helps to analyze in depth.

Gaming and Identity

Identity-formation processes within gaming practices are powerful because they take, to a greater or lesser degree, the forms of political, cultural, and social articulations but also because they refer to other formulations that take into account the ideas of consumption, the ludic, and the trivial. For some, video games have become a significant part of their lives, defining, at least partially, how they see themselves and who they are.

Gaming provides identity structures that are both solid and volatile and fosters, paradoxically, both unswerving loyalties and identity promiscuity. At times, identities can be so restrictive that they become exclusionary categories, while, on other occasions, they present themselves as soft labels that become broadly inclusive and all-encompassing. This means that studying gaming practices and communities helps challenge traditional notions of identity and facilitates the understanding of how meaning construction works in today's digital mediated society.

In recent years, there has been considerable empirical research on gaming and identity, examining, among other topics, important questions of gender, race, sexuality, and class. In this section, I summarize some of the most relevant findings on gaming and identity in relation to those questions and link them to the main sociological debate on identity and its crisis.

The Solid Identities of Gaming: Hardcore Gamer and Its Exclusions

In video gaming communities, there are groups of people who are heavily involved in the culture and consider video games as central to their identity. Klimmt, Hefner, and Vorderer (2009, 363), in their research on the way players deal with characters and social roles in video games, find that "models of interactive video game experiences can claim the utility of 'identification' with an especially strong legitimization," while Gee (2003, 58) characterizes the identification of video game players with game characters as "quite powerful," transcending the identification processes that take place "in novels or movies." Similarly, King and Krzywinska (2006, 168–169), summarizing previous theoretical and empirical research experience in a book that aims to contribute to the academic analysis of games, consider that, due to the "active nature of play," players seem to be more "directly implicated than traditional media consumers." These authors explain that games are "potent sources of interpellation" and players are "more literally interpellated" (King and Krzywinska 2006, 197), turning mere *players* into *gamers*. This promotes a generalized and strong awareness of the gamer as a subject-position that can be occupied for those who play video games.

Within the solid forms of identities that are created around the practice of video gaming, there is a particularly relevant category that stands out: the hardcore gamer. This could be also referred to as the classic or canonical version of the gamer, the one that was born in the "historical anomaly of the 1980s and 1990s when video games were played by only a small part of the population" (Juul 2010, 20). This is a notion of gamer that operates inside the coordinates of a traditional and essentialist definition of identity, in contrast to more diffused, diluted, and contemporary definitions. The hardcore gamer is probably the most problematic definition of gamer, the quintessential stereotyped gamer identity, rousing irate debates around the category but essential to understanding it. It is problematic for various reasons: first of all, the hardcore gamer as the prototypical gamer obscures a more diverse reality of gamers who relate to video games in a different way; it also becomes a conceptual barricade from where certain exclusionary and hostile practices are developed; finally, it becomes problematic for some individuals who would identify as gamers but prefer to distance themselves from the label because they do not feel comfortable with some of the attributes associated with it.

The hardcore gamer is principally defined—by both the individuals who identify with the category and an important part of society—according to their dedication and passion for video games. King and Krzywinska (2006, 220) suggest that those "who invest a great deal of time, money and energy in playing games are more inclined to identify themselves as part of a distinct category of 'gamers.' " In his research on casual video gaming practices and their relationship with gaming identities, Juul (2010, 29) finds that this identification process follows a *hardcore* ethic: "spend as much time as possible, play as difficult games as possible, play games at the expense of everything else." This is an approach that certain behavioral studies, such as the one conducted by Kapalo et al. (2015), who studied how hardcore gamers differ from casual gamers, have used to distinguish between dedicated and casual gaming practices. In their research, hardcore gamers were mainly defined by the time and money they invest in gaming. This particular set of ideals, along with the practices they encompass, emerged inside specific and relatively closed gaming communities (as Juul's in-depth interviews with developers, designers, and ex–hardcore gamers show), but it was rapidly disseminated and consolidated throughout society's stereotyped vision of gamers and the specialized media (Kirkpatrick 2015).

In this sense, the hardcore gamer is inseparable from the formation of the gaming culture that was produced in the 1980s. Kirkpatrick (2015) has shown how specialized gaming magazines fundamentally contributed to the creation, in the 1980s, of a gaming culture as a separated reality, magazines that teach "how to be a gamer" (Consalvo 2007, 22).

Thus, the popularization of the "gameplay" notion among journalists, developers, and expert gamers in the second half of the 1980s was particularly important in this process, which marked a tendency "to assess games in terms of their feel" (Kirkpatrick 2015, 64), understood as experiences (Crawford, Muriel, and Conway 2019). Gameplay, Kirkpatrick (2015, 66–67) argues, becomes central to "gaming's bid for autonomy as a cultural practice" and "signifies the tastes and preferences of the authentic gamer." Therefore, gameplay serves to "affirm and to regulate gamer identity" (Kirkpatrick 2015, 69), which outlines the shape of the "real gamer" as the experienced and knowledgeable individual whose performance with games places them on a superior plane in relation to the novice gamer or nongamer. This, along with the paratextual aspects of gaming, creates—building on Bourdieu's work—a "gaming capital" (Consalvo 2007), excluding those who cannot accumulate it.

Equally relevant is the role of gaming magazines when it comes to producing the average or ideal representation of the gamer as "young, male, and heterosexual" (Consalvo 2007, 22). In her analysis of *Nintendo Power* magazine in the second half of the 1990s, Amanda Cote (2018, 480) suggests that its discourse frames women "as outsiders to gaming, and men and boys as central components." If gamers are mainly imagined in male terms, women are not going to consider gaming as a key aspect of their identities, "undermining efforts to broaden the gaming community" (Cote 2018, 484) and making the gaming identity a "firmly masculinized" one (Cote 2018, 496).

This is how the traditional image of the gamer (equated to the hardcore gamer type) as a young, White, heterosexual male was forged in the light of an emerging gaming culture during the 1980s and 1990s, which still resonates in the 2020s (even though it is more questioned than ever, as I will show), an image that has been historically reinforced by the way the gaming industry advertises and presents video games. Chess, Evans, and Baines (2017) studied almost 200 commercials in 2013 (the year in which there was a generational shift, with the commercialization of the PS4, the Xbox One, and the Wii-U) and found that when someone was presented as a gamer or an advocate for video games, "that person was overwhelmingly white and male" (p. 50). Even though there might be a more diverse group of actors in video game commercials, the central role or the prototypical representation of the gamer is still mostly unchanged.

This kind of marketing and the problematic portrayal of gender, race, and sexuality in video games make the solid form of the gamer identity particularly exclusionary. The hardcore gamer has been traditionally seen as immature. Although a majority of individuals consider that video gaming is a widely extended and accepted activity in our societies, the ideal gamer is often represented as a solitary young male with scarce social skills; in sum, the gamer is what Bergstrom, Fisher, and Jenson (2016, 234) call "That Guy." This is a stereotypical perception, fixed in popular culture, of the archetypal video game player as a White, "male teen, likely overweight and socially awkward or isolated." Kowert, Griffiths, and Oldmeadow (2012, 473) sustain a similar portrayal of gamers as "socially anxious and incompetent, mentally stunted and withdrawn, and physically unhealthy."

The gamer figure is often associated, literally and metaphorically, with White, male adolescence and immaturity. The gamer is then linked to immature and impulsive behaviors. Not only is this a category imagined as mainly formed by a group of White male teenagers, but it is also shaping a mental state, a mode of conduct, and a way to represent the world. In a previous study of video game culture, we found that gamers were portrayed as an extremely territorial group of individuals who antagonize anyone who might be threatening the status quo because they might feel that "they are losing their cultural and social space" (Muriel and Crawford 2018, 153).

In this context, people who do not identify with that specific demographic perceive and experience exclusion and discrimination. The interviewees in Cote's (2017, 138) research considered that gaming was still part of men's spaces, "with women thought to be interlopers into that space." Equally, Lisa Nakamura (2019, 131) argues that "the world of video games self-identifies, and is seen by many of its players of both genders, as fundamentally masculine." Furthermore, when sexuality and ethnic background come into play, these discriminations are even more evident. This is the case of the Black lesbians who Kishonna Gray (2018, 193) studied, who were made particularly "hypervisible and hypervulnerable to the impacts of racialized, heteronormative, heterosexist, patriarchy" within gaming contexts.

When women (and other individuals who do not fit with the hardcore stereotype) are deemed to be a strange body inside the gaming community, it marks "them as potentially threatening outsiders" (Cote 2017, 139), making them be seen as an instance of gender, race, or sexuality deviation that would require a *correction*. This is why "women, ethnic minorities, or lesbian, gay, bisexual, and transgender (LGBT) players, for instance, are frequently targeted for harassment" (Cote 2017, 137).

This was particularly visible during the Gamergate phenomenon (Braithwaite 2016; Mortensen 2018; Perreault and Vos 2018; Shepherd et al. 2015), which took place in the second half of 2014. Despite presenting themselves as advocates for ethics in games journalism, a great number of Gamergate supporters engaged "in concentrated harassment of game developers, feminist critics, and their male allies on Twitter and other platforms" (Massanari 2017, 334). Due to the intensity and violence of Gamergate's supporters toward those groups, the increasing fragmentation of the prototypical gamer identity was made spectacularly visible.

While video games, their culture, and the people who play them became more and more diverse, the category of gamer remained mostly invariable (Golding 2014). Because of this, when the hegemony of White, male hardcore gamers was challenged in gaming culture, they reacted furiously against the non-White, female, and LGBT players and all of those who sustain feminist, LGBT, and postcolonial points of view. In any case, previous movements and changes inside the gaming culture, along with outbursts like Gamergate, have made clear that identities around gaming are more complex and nuanced than the social imaginary of the hardcore gamers, and some of their actions, indicate.

The Fragmented Identities of Gaming: Casual Gamers and the Subalterns

Gamers, as a solid identity, are normally understood as knowledgeable about the gaming culture and dedicate a significant part of their time to playing video games and exploring the medium. Video gaming is, in these cases, a planned activity that is complemented with other video game-related pursuits (such as reading specialized websites, watching video game content on YouTube and Twitch channels, and collecting video game memorabilia). From the point of view of those who embrace the hardcore gaming identity, casual gaming practices are negatively considered because they connote the idea of video games as a pastime. Some hardcore gamers consider this offensive, as if people were picking up "stones from the ground and throw[ing] them into a river" (Muriel and Crawford 2018, 159).[2]

This derogatory description matches what Juul (2010, 8) describes as the stereotype of a *casual gamer*, who has "a preference for positive and pleasant fictions, has played few games, is willing to commit little time and few resources toward playing video games, and dislikes difficult games." This established then a correlation between the habit of playing certain video games that are described as casual and the figure of the casual gamer, who follows specific behavioral patterns that entail gaming practices that require "shorter commitments" (Juul 2010, 9). As the research conducted by Chess and Paul (2019, 109–110) shows, casual gamers are defined from the core gaming communities within a "dismissive set of descriptors," where the "casual" label is used as "a slur to police what kinds of games should be judged as proper and which are not worth the time." In this sense, Paul (2018) extensively explores the toxic nature of the hardcore approach to video games, which usually rewards "skill and effort," diminishing other alternatives. However, this is just a symptom of an identity that has begun to fragment and points to other ways of being a gamer, including gaming practices that develop more fluid and unstable identities.

At the beginning of the 2000s, the industry stopped focusing exclusively on the young male niche target, which "was perceived as the key to dominance in the whole business" (Kline, Dyer-Whiteford, and De Peuter 2003, 250) in the 1980s and 1990s. This, along with the launch of video game consoles like Nintendo Wii (2006) and the popularization of smartphones, promoted a first implosion of the gamer category, giving way to more flexible definitions and self-identifications—different gamer mentalities.

Kallio, Mäyrä, and Kaipainen (2011) show that there are various gamer mentalities (dependent on context) rather than just one monolithic mindset. They found that the majority of video gaming practices take place "between 'casual relaxing' and 'committed entertaining'" (Kallio, Mäyrä, and Kaipainen 2011, 347), which challenges the stereotype of the gamer only as someone who is completely immersed in the game and committed to its culture. This draws a reality defined by fluid mentalities and situated practices that are realized inside the everyday life of gamers. Video games are inexorably becoming normalized parts "of the invisible everyday social realities for large groups of peoples" (Kallio, Mäyrä, and Kaipainen 2011, 348).

These open definitions do not use any gaming practice as an excuse to expel someone from the now more diverse (and fragmented) population of gamers (as happens with the more restrictive definitions). When part of the gaming community and society in general let new types enter the semantic field of gamers, even after facing the resistance and harassment of individuals who are actively using their privileges that stem from their dominant social position, the category is widened to the point of causing important fissures in the former gamer's solid identity shell.

This means that any category that strides from the hardcore gamer identity is, in fact, constituted in relation to it: to reaffirm the hardcore gamer identity, to oppose or question it, to distance from it, to propose alternative gaming practices, or to explore new kinds of relations with video games and their culture. As I have shown, the "casual" label has been used by those who see themselves as hardcore gamers to delimit and reaffirm their identities, excluding all those who do not fit their hegemonic representation (such as non-dedicated, female, racialized, and LGBT gamers). At the same time, others use the casual notion to distance themselves from some of the implications that are usually associated with the (hardcore) gamer identity (geekiness, social isolation, immaturity), even though they are heavily involved in gaming practices and consider video games to be an important part of their identities. Furthermore, there are those who have been actively excluded from the category and create their own identity space and set of gaming practices in contrast with the hardcore gamer category, including players who seek to explore new types of practices and create communities that do not reproduce the exclusions associated with hardcore gaming.

Therefore, even though the *casual revolution* reimagined the act of gaming as *for everyone*, there are still difficulties for those "who are not the stereotypical straight, white, male gamer" (Cote 2017, 136), and it is not unusual that "men who play less often than women may identify with gaming and as gamers more strongly than women" (Nakamura 2019, 131). For all these reasons, other kinds of gamers develop their own strategies to cope with this situation and approach the gamer identity differently.

A few scholars have studied how women (including racialized, LGBT, and working-class women) try to fit in the cracks of the solid instances of the gamer identity. Cote (2017, 137), for example, lists a set of coping strategies that women put into motion in order to make online gaming more pleasant: "leaving online gaming, avoiding playing with strangers, camouflaging their gender, deploying their skill and experience, or adopting an aggressive persona." Similarly, Tiercelin and Remy (2019, 32) described the ideal types that self-identifying female gamers adopted when it comes to coping with harassment in online gaming: tomboy (defines herself as having qualities generally attributed to men), camouflaged girl (to avoid stigmatization, hides her gaming practices in society and plays *like a man* during gaming sessions), and authentic girl (defines herself as a woman who plays and does not hide her feminine character in both the world of gaming and society).

All of these are mainly elusive strategies, which usually reflect the devaluation of their gender and gamer identities (Tiercelin and Remy 2019, 34). This means that if women want to fit into the normative gamer identity, they have to hide, camouflage, or avoid their gender identity; on the other hand, if they want to keep their gender identity intact, they are probably going to lose part of the recognition of their gamer identity. Other identity formations around class, race, and sexuality face similar devaluations.

Nevertheless, the fragmentation of the canonical gamer identity also gives way to more proactive and confrontational strategies, applying more pressure to the already battered solid forms of the gamer identity (even if this means new backlashes against subaltern identity positions). In this sense, Gray (2018, 291) points to the transgressive forms of play that Black women who identified as lesbian carry out in order to "resist the patriarchy." As Aarseth (2014, 182) states, it is a way to "regain their sense of identity and uniqueness through the mechanisms of the game itself." Some of the strategies to reclaim their space within gaming communities and be part of the gamer identity without diminishing other aspects of their identity spectrum are those online websites that denounce abusive players, "exposing them to semi-public ridicule and shame" (Nakamura 2019, 139).

From the gaps and cracks of the fragmented identities, new identification possibilities emerge, such as "gaymers" (Pulos 2013), "grrrl gamers" (Bryce and Rutter 2005), and

"Todas Gamers" (Muriel 2018, 159–167), that is, different ways to reappropriate the gamer category from the margins of the gaming community (Shaw 2014). Fighting between the interstices of once solid identities, these individuals are able to strengthen their subaltern identities by fragmenting the hegemonic ones.

Thus, the universe of potential gamers grows, and the definition of a gamer is immensely widened by the fragmentation of the hardcore gamer identity and the emergence and multiplication of more diverse meaning construction types linked to gaming. In his research, Juul (2010, 152) describes the "cultural moment when video games became normal; when it is no longer exceptional to play games." If this was already happening at the beginning of the 2010s, it is possible to acknowledge that, in the 2020s, this tendency has done nothing but grow. We are witnessing the "loss of the isolated gamer" (Woodcock 2019, 155). One of the most obvious consequences of this normalization is the weakening of the gamer category, which loses its defining ability and becomes so generic and fragmented that it becomes more difficult to create a proper sense of belonging in traditional terms.

Ian Bogost (2011, 154) argues that, as video games become more entangled in the general fabric of society and a more diverse pool of individuals play them, the idea of gamers as an identity will lose strength and will not be deemed "as a primary part of one's identity." Normalization of video games brings the fragmentation of its communities and identities. It is then the perfect moment to "redefine who gamers are and change expectations for who plays games" because it will help visualize marginalized groups as "essential members of the audience, rather than as outsiders or anomalies" (Cote 2017, 152).

The gamer identity is, at the same time, strong and weak, solid and liquid, bounded and limitless. "Gamer" is part of the struggles between dominant and subaltern positions, a field for marginalization and resistance and yet a category that defines individuals and communities as much as it does not say anything (relevant) about them. Hence, it is not surprising to find that "gamer" is, above all, a category that individuals increasingly do not know whether they (want to) occupy or not. It becomes a floating identity.

The Floating Identities of Gaming: The Volatile Gamer and Beyond Identity

The fragmentation of the gamer identity creates doubts and insecurities about who can occupy it. Although many see the gamer as a strongly bounded identity, the increasing indefiniteness and fragmentation of the category foster a sense of indeterminacy when it comes to understanding what a gamer is or who can be considered one. Gamers seem not to know if they, or others, are, in fact, gamers. The variety and changing possibilities of *gamer positions*, which do not usually fit the stereotype of gamer (as in the hardcore gamer type), make it "impossible for most gamers to identify themselves as 'gamers' "

(Kallio, Mäyrä, and Kaipainen 2011, 64) in terms of the images that the current public discussion produces about them. Gamer becomes, in this way, a floating identity.

The self-perception of an individual as a gamer depends on different factors that do not always align, particularly between the opposing forces that imply the processes of self-identification and external interpellation (Hall 1996; Butler 1999). The tension between the multiple definitions of gamer, including the elitist and solid approaches of the hardcore type and those that rely on the openness and fragility of the category, only contributes to this generalized uncertainty. The boundaries of the gamer identity are drawn with blurred lines.

One way or another, the gamer identity figuratively dances around the various versions of identity imagined by social scientists without settling on any particular type; it's obstinate, solid, and perennial but also open, free, and ethereal. It reproduces the hegemonic but also gives way to the subaltern. In any case, the disjunction of the act of playing and the identification as gamer evince some of the contemporary debates around identity, where, for instance, work (traditionally, what you do) and nationality or citizenship (traditionally, what you are) do not necessarily define people's identity. Identity becomes part of the insecurities that populate contemporary society, and the gamer identity reflects and promotes those processes.

This turns the gamer identity into a paradox; an identity categorization that does not define the identity of those who are defined by it. Like any paradox, the gamer identity is a tricky one and full of contradictions: A nondefining definition? An identity without a sense of belonging? As surprising and counterintuitive as it might seem, this is the corollary of the gamer identity and the principal lesson we can learn from it in order to understand the identity nowadays. In their research, Muriel and Crawford (2018, 167) found individuals who put the constitutive contradiction of the gamer identity (and identity in general) into words: "Gamer is a fair way to summarize that I love video games and am able to say: 'I'm a lifelong gamer'. But not as a way to define myself."

According to this person, gamer is, at the same time, a category that perfectly summarizes an important part of their life (to the point of presenting themselves as a "lifelong gamer") and something that does not define themselves. They identify with an identity that does not necessarily define them—the nondefining identity of the volatile gamer. This is not a solid identity, but it is neither a fragmented nor a fluid one. The gamer identity floats; it is a fringe identity. We are faced with a volatile and floating identity that produces a quantic gamer: individuals who are at the same time gamers and non-gamers.

In the end, the paradox of the volatile gamer embodies the paradox of identity. Identity is still a necessary concept to make some aspects of social reality thinkable, but, simultaneously, identity does not allow us to properly approach those very aspects. It seems that we need to talk about identity in order to talk about things that identity cannot explain. Video games prefigure, then, the post-identity scenario that is emerging in contemporary society.

As mentioned, the notion of identity can be approached using two axes of analysis. The first axis analyzes identity in relation to its shape: from its more solid, stable, and consolidated forms to its more fragmented, unstable, and liquid ones. The second axis refers to how identity is assembled: identity as a position, a starting point from where individuals are able to enunciate and act, or identity as a point of arrival, the non-preexisting outcome of different associations, mediations, and processes.

The gamer identity, I would argue, can be understood as the prototypical example of an emerging social reality dominated by a post-identity scenario, where the two axes crumble as soon as they attempt to capture a sense of identity.

For example, the gamer identity cannot find accommodation in the spectrum of solidity/liquidity of the first axis. It jumps from solid and rounded definitions of gamer (hardcore gamer) to radically liquid and fragmented ones (casual gamer, gaymers, grrrl gamers, transgressive players), to the point of finding individuals who abandon the categorization almost the very moment they occupy it (the volatile gamer). The gamer identity restlessly circulates between these two poles and, eventually, escapes their coordinates to stay in an undetermined state. The quantic theory reaches identity formation, questioning some of the fundamental aspects of its traditional articulation.

In relation to the second axis, the video gamer identity is incapable of providing a definite and (at least moderately) stable outcome to become a position from which to enunciate or act for the individuals that identify (or are identified) with it. It seems that it is not possible to reach the gamer identity, and instead, it turns into a perennial struggle to become a gamer or fight the gamer category. The gamer identity is, thus, an assemblage of an essence, the articulation of different discourses, practices, and experiences that allows individuals to (partially) occupy the category without any previous condition of belonging.

However, individuals will approach it from a variety of subject positions: promiscuous, mixed, hybrid, precarious. As Dyer-Whiteford and de Peuter (2011, 94) suggest, gamer nomadism that "produces unpredictable effects, unforeseen permutations of desire and capacity that give cyborgs degrees of autonomy, latitudes of action."

Therefore, video games and their culture question the very notion of identity and foresee a coming post-identity scenario. We are defined by what does not (essentially) define us, and that is the fundamental paradox video gaming practices are making spectacularly visible. The gamer is what Agamben (1993, 65) calls "a singularity without identity," which overcomes the idea of the search for an "individual property" with "a proper identity"—gamer as a notion that unites a group of people so different that they cannot be united under any notion.

A post-identity approach challenges both the essentialism of the modernist subject and the re-essentialization that some of the postmodern theorists reintroduce in their radical deconstruction of the former (Hekman 2000; Martínez de Albeniz 2017). However, this approach does not look for a middle-ground identity (another re-essentialization of sorts), such as Hekman's (2000, 298–302) thesis on identity and her idea of an "ungrounded ground." In this case, I argue, individuals and collectives are confronted and realized through a sequence of related experiences that never fully materializes in an identity. This is similar to what Martínez de Albeniz (2017, 3) calls "identity 3.0," an "identity that expresses by means of its unfolding," an identity as a "circulating reference" (Latour 1999, 24–79), without a beginning or an end. This would allow us to "keep interrogating the role of the 'gamer' as a cultural archetype" (Chess, Evans, and Baines 2017, 53) in order to facilitate new kinds of identifications beyond the limited scope of the gamer stereotype.

Conclusion

Bogost (2011, 154) thinks that "gamer" will be soon an anomaly, even a category that will probably disappear. Despite this being a plausible hypothesis, "gamer" will neither necessarily disappear nor become an anomaly. The gamer category might even become more relevant than ever but emptied of its identity meaning. Identity, as a concept, will become the anomaly, not the questions of gender, politics, race, class, sexuality, body, work, leisure, or consumption, as certain post-identity politics rhetoric suggests (Oh and Kutufam 2014). These issues will not necessarily pass through the "identity filter" but will be equally, if not more, relevant. In the post-identity scenario, our research should look beyond identity but without avoiding the central questions that affect how individuals construct meaning and produce determined power relations.

Identity is following a path that it can no longer see. Social reality has fragmented, made flexible, multiplied, and liquefied identity; but we have not dared to discard it completely when it was necessary. This has happened at both the scientific and the sociopolitical levels. Definitely, if identity is not (completely) useful for articulating scientific representations or political actions, it might be time to part with it. We need to problematize social reality and understand the processes that forge and break bonds, links, and meanings without thinking in terms of identity (in all its forms) as what remains identical throughout time or what equals or differentiates us from others.

In this sense, video game culture shows us how to think outside the coordinates of identity, which is not a headlong rush to theorize about the ethereal nature of contemporary life but a theoretical, political, and social stance that allows us to think of social reality under a new light, letting marginalized subject positions reach new horizons. Research on gaming and identity should distance itself from the prototypical (exceptional and in decline) gamer figure and explore its extended margins (whether understood in terms of the gamer category or not), including the multiple and diverse possibilities that dwell in the video game culture.

The next steps for sociological research on this matter, then, should include both qualitative and quantitative studies that focus on gaming practices and meaning-construction processes that are not carried out on the basis of the core gamer identity. The priority is to understand the labile, ever-changing, and diluted gamer positions and, consequently, approach them not as predefined or substantive positions but as in-progress articulations. This means looking for individuals and groups that create, play, read about, and speak of video games (including those games that are not considered hardcore such as mobile phone games, free to play games, experimental games, and so on) who do not necessarily identify as gamers and have been, historically, obscured by gaming communities and scholarship: women, LGBT and racialized individuals, older people, and those who might match the gamer stereotype but distance themselves from their given attributes, behaviors, and representations.

NOTES

1. Since the literature on identity in the social sciences is so abundant and varied that it is almost impossible to cover it all, I recommend the works of Jenkins (2014), Lawler (2014), Hall and Du Gay (1996), Burke and Stets (2009), Giddens (1991), and Bauman (2004) as relevant points of entry to the main debates on the issue.
2. This comparison made by hardcore gamers seeks to ridicule casual gamers, but this author believes there is no better way to spend one's time than doing something as satisfactory as throwing stones into a river.

REFERENCES

Aarseth, Espen. 2014. "I Fought the Law: Transgressive Play and the Implied Player." In *From Literature to Cultural Literacy*, edited by Naomi Segal and Daniela Koleva, 180–188. London: Palgrave Macmillan.

Agamben, Giorgio. 1993. *The Coming Community*. Minneapolis: University of Minnesota Press.

Bauman, Zygmunt. 1989. *Legislators and Interpreters*. Cambridge: Polity Press.

Bauman, Zygmunt. 1993. *Modernity and Ambivalence*. Cambridge: Polity Press.

Bauman, Zygmunt. 2000. *Liquid Modernity*. Cambridge: Polity Press.

Bauman, Zygmunt. 2004. *Identity*. Cambridge: Polity Press.

Beck, Ulrich. 1992. *Risk Society: Towards a New Modernity*. London: SAGE.

Berger, Peter L., and Thomas Luckmann. 1995. *Modernity, Pluralism and the Crisis of Meaning*. Gütersloh, Germany: Bertelsman Foundation Publishers.

Bergstrom, Kelly, Stephanie Fisher, and Jennifer Jenson. 2016. "Disavowing 'That Guy': Identity Construction and Massively Multiplayer Online Game Players." *Convergence*, 22, no. 3: 233–249.

Bogost, Ian. 2011. *How to Do Things with Videogames*. Minneapolis: University of Minnesota Press.

Braithwaite, Andrea. 2016. "It's about Ethics in Games Journalism? Gamergaters and Geek Masculinity." *Social Media + Society* 2, no. 4: 1–10.

Bryce, Jo, and Jason Rutter. 2005. "Gendered Gaming in Gendered Space." In *Handbook of Computer Game Studies*, edited by Joost Raessens and Jeffrey Goldstein, 301–310. Cambridge, MA: MIT Press.

Burke, Peter J., and Jan E. Stets. 2009. *Identity Theory*. Oxford: Oxford University Press.

Butler, Judith. 1999. *Gender Trouble. Feminism and the Subversion of Identity*. 2nd ed. New York and London: Routledge.

Chess, Shira, Nathaniel J. Evans, and Joyya JaDawn Baines. 2017. "What Does a Gamer Look Like? Video Games, Advertising, and Diversity." *Television & New Media* 18, no. 1: 37–57.

Chess, Shira, and Christopher A. Paul. 2019. "The End of Casual: Long Live Casual." *Games and Culture* 14, no. 2: 107–118.

Consalvo, Mia. 2007. *Cheating. Gaining Advantage in Videogames*. Cambridge, MA: MIT Press.

Cote, Amanda. 2017. "'I Can Defend Myself': Women's Strategies for Coping With Harassment While Gaming Online." *Games and Culture* 12, no. 2: 136–155.

Cote, Amanda. 2018. "Writing 'Gamers': The Gendered Construction of Gamer Identity in Nintendo Power (1994–1999)." *Games and Culture* 13, no. 5: 479–503.

Crawford, Garry, Daniel Muriel, and Steve Conway. 2019. "A Feel for the Game. Exploring Gaming 'Experience' through the Case of Sports-Themed Video Games." *Convergence* 25, no. 5–6: 937–952.

Dubet, François. 2006. *El declive de la institución*. Barcelona, Spain: Gedisa.

Durkheim, Émile. (1953) 2010. *Sociology and Philosophy*. London and New York: Routledge.

Dyer-Whiteford, Nick, and Greig de Peuter. 2011. *Games of Empire: Global Capitalism and Video Games*. Minneapolis: University of Minnesota Press.

Gee, James Paul. 2003. *What Video Games Have to Teach Us about Learning and Literacy*. New York: Palgrave MacMillan.

Giddens, Anthony. 1990. *The Consequences of Modernity*. Cambridge: Polity Press.

Giddens, Anthony. 1991. *Modernity and Self-Identity*. Cambridge: Polity Press.

Giddens, Anthony. 2002. *Runaway World: How Globalisation Is Reshaping Our Lives*. 2nd ed. London: Profile Books.

Golding, Dan. 2014. "The End of Gamers." Tumblr, August 28. Accessed January 26, 2021. https://dangolding.tumblr.com/post/95985875943/the-end-of-gamers.

Gray, Kishonna L. 2018. "Gaming Out Online: Black Lesbian Identity Development and Community Building in Xbox Live." *Journal of Lesbian Studies* 22, no. 3: 282–296.

Hall, Stuart. 1996. "Who Needs Identity?" In *Questions of Cultural Identity*, edited by Stuart Hall and Paul Du Gay, 1–17. London: SAGE.

Hall, Stuart, and Paul Du Gay, eds. 1996. *Questions of Cultural Identity*. London: SAGE.

Haraway, Donna. 1991. *Simians, Cyborgs, and Women: The Reinvention of Nature*. London and New York: Routledge.

Haraway, Donna. 2004. *The Haraway Reader*. London and New York: Routledge.

Hekman, Susan. 2000. "Beyond Identity: Feminism, Identity and Identity Politics." *Feminist Theory* 1, no. 3: 289–308.

Jenkins, Richard. 2014. *Social Identity*. 4th ed. London and New York: Routledge.

Juul, Jesper. 2010. *A Casual Revolution: Reinventing Video Games and Their Players*. Cambridge, MA: MIT Press.

Kallio, Kirsi P., Frans Mäyrä, and Kirsikka Kaipainen. 2011. "At Least Nine Ways to Play: Approaching Gamer Mentalities." *Games and Culture* 6, no. 4: 327–353.

Kapalo, Katelynn A., Alexis Dewar, Michael A. Rupp, and James L. Szalma. 2015. "Individual Differences in Video Gaming: Defining Hardcore Video Gamers." *Proceedings of the Human Factors and Ergonomics Society 59th Annual Meeting* 59, no. 1: 878–881.

King, Geoff, and Tanya Krzywinska. 2006. *Tomb Raiders and Space Invaders. Videogame Forms and Contexts*. New York: I. B. Tauris.

Kirkpatrick, Graeme. 2015. *The Formation of the Gaming Culture: UK Gaming Magazines, 1981–1995*. London: Palgrave.

Klimmt, Christoph, Dorothée Hefner, and Peter Vorderer. 2009. "The Video Game Experience as 'True' Identification: A Theory of Enjoyable Alterations of Players' Self-Perception." *Communication Theory* 19: 351–373.

Kline, Stephen, Nick Dyer-Whiteford, and Greig De Peuter. 2003. *Digital Play. The Interaction of Technology, Culture, and Marketing*. Montreal: McGill-Queen's University Press.

Kowert, Rachel, Mark D. Griffiths, and Julian A. Oldmeadow. 2012. "Geek or Chic? Emerging Stereotypes of Online Gamers." *Bulletin of Science, Technology and Society* 32, no. 6: 471–479.

Latour, Bruno. 1993. *We Have Never Been Modern*. Cambridge, MA: Harvard University Press.

Latour, Bruno. 1999. *Pandora's Hope. Essays on the Reality of Science Studies*. Cambridge, MA: Harvard University Press.

Lawler, Steph. 2014. *Identity. Sociological Perspectives*. 2nd ed. Cambridge: Polity Press.

Lyotard, Jean-François. 1984. *The Postmodern Condition*. Minneapolis: University of Minnesota Press.

Martínez de Albeniz, Iñaki. 2017. "¡Funtziona! La identidad como ensamblaje." Unpublished manuscript.

Massanari, Adrienne. 2017. "#Gamergate and the Fappening: How Reddit's Algorithm, Governance, and Culture Support Toxic Technocultures." *New Media and Society* 19, no. 3: 329–346.

Mortensen, Torill Elvira. 2018. "Anger, Fear, and Games: The Long Event of #GamerGate." *Games and Culture* 13, no. 8: 787–806.

Muriel, Daniel. 2018. *Identidad gamer. Videojuegos y construcción de sentido en la sociedad contemporánea*. Barcelona, Spain: AnaitGames.

Muriel, Daniel, and Garry Crawford. 2018. *Video Games as Culture*. London and New York: Routledge.

Nakamura, Lisa. 2019. "Gender and Race in the Gaming World." In *Society and the Internet: How Networks of Information and Communication Are Changing Our Lives*, 2nd ed., edited by Mark Graham and William Dutton, 127–145. Oxford: Oxford University Press.

Oh, David C., and Doreen V. Kutufam. 2014. "The Orientalized 'Other' and Corrosive Femininity: Threats to White Masculinity in 300." *Journal of Communication Inquiry* 38, no. 2: 149–165.

Parsons, Talcott. 1968. "The Position of Identity in the General Theory of Action." In *The Self in Social Interaction*, edited by Chad Gordon and Kenneth Gergen, 1:11–24. New York: Wiley.

Paul, Christopher A. 2018. *The Toxic Meritocracy of Video Games: Why Gaming Culture Is the Worst*. Minneapolis: University of Minnesota Press.

Perreault, Gregory P., and Tim P. Vos. 2018. "The GamerGate Controversy and Journalistic Paradigm Maintenance." *Journalism* 19, no. 4: 553–569.

Pulos, Alexis. 2013. "Confronting Heteronormativity in Online Games: A Critical Discourse Analysis of LGBTQ Sexuality in World of Warcraft." *Games and Culture* 8, no. 2: 77–97.

Rose, Nikolas. 1999. *Politics of Freedom. Reframing Political Thought*. Cambridge: Cambridge University Press.

Sen, Amartya. 2007. *Identity and Violence: The Illusion of Destiny*. London: Penguin Books.

Shaw, Adrienne. 2014. *Gaming at the Edge. Sexuality and Gender at the Margins of Gamer Culture*. Minneapolis: University of Minnesota Press.

Shepherd, Tamara, Alison Harvey, Tim Jordan, Sam Srauy, and Kate Miltner. 2015. "Histories of Hating." *Social Media + Society* 1, no. 2: 1–10.

Thévenot, Laurent. 2004. "Une science de la vie ensemble dans le monde." *Revue du MAUSS* 24: 115–126.

Tiercelin, Alexandre, and Eric Remy. 2019. "The Market between Symbolic Violence and Emancipation: The Case of Female Hardcore Gamers." *Recherche et Applications en Marketing* 34, no. 2: 24–41.

Trinh, T. Minh-Ha. 1986–1987. "Introduction." *Discourse* 8: 3–10.

Woodcook, Jamie. 2019. *Marx at the Arcade*. Chicago: Haymarket Books.

CHAPTER 20

FANS AND FAN ACTIVISM

THOMAS V. MAHER

In 2020, as the COVID-19 pandemic shut down the economy and society, many people turned to the television, music, film, and sports cultures they love—and the fan communities built around them—to bolster spirits, feel a sense of community, and inspire pro-social behavior. To offer just a few examples, people shared uplifting quotes from the *Lord of the Rings* books (Cooper 2020), fans of the *Doctor Who* television series held watch parties (BBC News 2020), Orlando City soccer club fans organized video game tournaments (Poe 2020), and the Harry Potter Alliance—a group of fans inspired by the world of Harry Potter—held teach-ins that explained how to make cloth masks (Harry Potter Alliance 2020). From film, sports, and music's roles as cultural touchstones to their place on the T-shirts and bumper stickers that signal our affections and in the fan conventions and message boards that have emerged to bring fans and enthusiasts together, fandom has become a nearly ubiquitous part of social life (Harrington and Bielby 1995; Jenkins 2006; Kustritz 2015). At its most basic level, media fandom "is the recognition of a positive, personal, relatively deep emotional connection with a mediated element of popular culture" (Duffett 2013, 2). But what it means to be a fan and how being a fan influences participation in parts of social life like consumption and political participation are ongoing debates.

Research on fans and fan communities has expanded considerably as fandom has become a more prominent part of our culture. Fandom research and fan studies is a growing field that covers several disciplines including sociology, cultural studies, psychology, and communication (Barton and Lampley 2013; Duffett 2013; Gray, Sandvoss, and Harrington 2017). Yet as the field has grown, scholars have disagreed over what it means to be a fan and whether a general definition of "fandom" is even possible (Abercrombie and Longhurst 1998; Hellekson and Busse 2006; Jenkins 2014; Sandvoss 2005a). This chapter will synthesize these approaches by arguing that we should consider fandom as an ideal type where—aside from the consumption of fan objects[1] — there are no necessary or sufficient elements of fandom. Rather, fandom is based on a set of common characteristics including knowledge of the fan object and its media world, engagement with the object beyond appreciation, participation in the objects' fan community, self-identification as a fan, and an emotional connection with the object. Not only will fans embody most of these elements, but it is also through them that we can understand how fan communities are sustained and how they connect with other aspects of social life.

Building on the conceptualization of fandom as an ideal type, this chapter will review two parts of the fandom literature. First, it will review research on axes of racial, class, and gender inequities in fandom. As subcultures of broader society, fan communities, and practices are reflective of many of the inequities of broader society (Fine and Kleinman 1979) but not perfectly so (Chin 2018; Sandvoss 2005a; Thornton 1996). Indeed, fandom researchers have outlined how gender, class, and race shape the sometimes reciprocal relationship between fans and the books, television, movies, and teams they love (Brown 2001; Harrington and Bielby 1995; Martin 2019; Thomas and O'Shea 2010), as well as how fan communities themselves can be sites of conflict, collaboration, and exploration (A. Cox 2017; McInroy 2019; Scott 2019).

This chapter will then turn its attention to how fandom itself has emerged as a site of (and source for) political participation and activism. Inspired by their fan objects or drawing on the skills they developed as a part of fan communities, fans have participated in institutional and non-institutional politics for several decades (Bird and Maher 2017; Harrington and Bielby 1995; Hinck 2019; Jenkins et al. 2018). This has increasingly taken the form of fan activism, and this chapter will conclude by discussing how—through technological affordances, cultural acupuncture, and bloc recruitment—fans and fan activists have been able to make fan communities fertile sites for political engagement.

What Is a Fan?

The term "fan" first appeared in seventeenth-century England as an abbreviated description for religious zealots ("fanatics"). It took hold in the United States as a description for baseball spectators who many saw as particularly devoted and deranged (Abercrombie and Longhurst 1998; A. Cox 2017; Jenson 1992). In many ways, fandom research has emerged as a rejection of the normal/fanatic conceptualization and has grown into an active area that incorporates several disciplines and two well-cited journals: the *Journal of Fandom Studies* and the open-source *Transformative Works and Cultures*.

Scholars have identified three waves of fandom research (Duffett 2013; Gray, Sandvoss, and Harrington 2007, 2017).[2] The first wave—referred to as the "fandom is beautiful" era—rejected the notion that fandom is deviant and argued for the validity and coherence of fandom as a research topic (Bacon-Smith 1992; Fiske 1992; Jenkins 2012b; Penley 1997). The first wave's central thesis is that fandom is creative, thoughtful, and productive and that fans actively participant in their fan worlds by attending conventions, writing fan fiction, joining letter-writing campaigns, and dressing up as their favorite characters (Harrington and Bielby 1995; Jenkins 2012b). The second wave of fandom research contends that, while beautiful, fandom is not inherently a space of resistance and cultural autonomy (Harris 1998; Jancovich 2002). Building from this premise, second-wave scholars argued that fandom research needed to consider inequalities between and within fan cultures more seriously. This is because fan communities, like other subcultures, are shaped by the same class, race, gender, sexuality, and sexual identity distinctions that influence broader society (Abercrombie and Longhurst 1998; Pande 2020; Thomas and O'Shea 2010; Thornton 1996).

The third wave of fandom research incorporates "multiple projects with multiple trajectories that *combined* still have the force of a new wave" (Sandvoss, Gray, and Harrington 2017, 6; emphasis in original). Drawing from cultural studies, several scholars have focused on how fans read and construct meaning from texts (Sandvoss 2005b, 2017), how fandom changes with different types of fan objects (Brooker 2005; Hills 2003), and intertextuality (i.e., the ties, conversations, references, and connections between textual objects) (Gray 2005; Sandvoss 2017). Other scholars have focused on how the expansion of fandom helps explain broader social, cultural, and economic transformations including learning outcomes (Ito et al. 2018), strengthening global/local connections (Sandvoss 2004; Shresthova 2011), and reshaping political participation (Hinck 2019; Jenkins et al. 2018). These three waves are more conceptual than they are temporal, and several texts tap into the spirit of multiple waves.

Defining what it means to be a fan has been surprisingly challenging. More succinct definitions focus on the subject and emphasize the fan's passion. For example, for Cavicchi, fandom is the "special feeling of 'connection'" one has with the fan object (1998, 40; see also Hinck 2019, 9). Others expand their definitions to require action—such as play and "cultural creativity" (Hills 2003, 90) or "the regular, emotionally involved consumption of a given popular narrative or text" (Sandvoss 2005a, 8). Abercrombie and Longhurst emphasize attachment by conceptualizing fandom as "people who become particularly attached to certain programs or stars within the context of relatively heavy mass media use" (1998, 138).[3] Embodying this challenge, Duffett offers two definitions in his text on fandom. The first, emphasizes emotion and action (2013, 18), but the latter instead emphasizes identity by stating a fan is a "self-identified enthusiast, devotee or follower of a particular media genre, text, person, or activity" (p. 293).

Although many of these definitions touch on shared themes and points of emphasis, scholars continue to disagree over a general definition of fandom. Busse and Hellekson (2006, 6) contend that "it is impossible, and perhaps even dangerous, to speak of a single fandom" because fandom itself is not cohesive and its fan objects—and thus how fans interact with them—vary considerably. Indeed, Bruce Springsteen and Beyoncé fans, college football fans, and Harry Potter fans engage with their fan objects in vastly different ways (Cavicchi 1998; Duffett 2013; Jenkins 2012b). Further, definitions of fandom need to account for how changing technological affordances reshape what it means to be a fan (Click, Lee, and Holladay 2013; Jenkins 2006). While several prior studies have offered multipart explanations of what it means to be a fan (Duffett 2013; Harrington and Bielby 1995; Hills 2003; Hinck 2019), these "yardstick" approaches can suggest that fandom is hierarchical, with some seen as being more "true" fans than others. Any definition of fandom must encompass these various evolving fandoms. This is a tall order for any singular definition.

Fandom as an Ideal Type

Fandom is best thought of as an ideal type rather than an identity or set of behaviors that can be defined in a way that is sufficiently broad and yet succinct. By synthesizing the array of definitions of fandom, we can see that what it means to be a fan is organized around six core components: consumption, knowledge, engagement, community, identity, and an emotional connection. While consumption is necessary, none of these components are sufficient for fandom. Thinking of fandom as an ideal type is useful because an ideal type acknowledges that the phenomenon is an abstract—even fictional—construct and helps scholars pursuing terminological specificity, establishing heuristics, and classification processes (Swedberg 2018). Fandom is constantly evolving, and few, if any, fans will be the perfect embodiment, especially now that fandom is a part of mass culture. Treating fandom as multifaceted supports exploration into *types* of fandoms and helps us identify spaces for conceptual and theoretical expansion.

Consumption

Fandom is about fans meaningfully engaging with the comics, film, literature, music, and sports teams they love. This makes economic and cultural consumption of these or other fan objects necessary but not sufficient for fandom. Fan engagement is often economic. Fans buy books, records, and tickets; attend conventions and games; and collect art, toys, and memorabilia, among many other activities. General attendance at concerts, sporting events, and theaters helps make these industries—and individual artists—sustainable; but dedicated fans are often responsible for a large part of book, ticket, and media sales. Indeed, studios target fans for new releases because of their willingness to attend repeated screenings, buy collectibles and memorabilia, and, in the process, generate attention from others (Duffett 2013).

Yet consumption is non-monetary too (Booth 2010). Fandom is about more than just passive consumption or collection; it is when fans make these fan objects a part of their identities. "Commodities are easily and frequently commuted into personal possessions which excite commitment, investment, and meaning" (Warde 2015, 121). As Duffett (2013) notes, fans integrate these fan objects into their identities by reading, listening, watching, and participating with these objects in ways that deepen their understanding of them as well as their connections to them. This means that everyone, regardless of economic status, has the potential to be a fan. Anyone with a library card or an internet connection has access to books, television, and a world of music and movies; and our connections often start from these everyday beginnings (Hills 2003). Further, like the modern rock group Radiohead, the American punk musician Jeff Rosenstock and rap duo Run the Jewels have also released their albums for free online to encourage this sort of cultural consumption. Digital media have also produced their own, cheaply accessible objects of fandom. We have seen an explosion of online celebrities from Youtubers and Twitch streamers like the gaming streamers Pokimane, Pewdiepie, and Arcus to food/cooking streamers like Binging with Babish to those who give makeup tutorials like Zoella and Michelle Phan. Economic consumption may be a part of these fandoms, but cultural consumption is a crucial element in the process.

Knowledge

The second element of fandom is a deep knowledge of the fan object and its universe. Fandom is often about exceptional readings more so than exceptional texts (Jenkins 2012b), and exceptional readings require repeatedly returning to the text (Sandvoss 2005a).[4] Deep engagement with the fan objects produces the technical, analytic, and interpretative understanding of them that distinguishes fans from enthusiasts and consumers (Abercrombie and Longhurst 1998). Fans devote themselves to learning the rules of magic systems, the syntax of languages like Elvish or Valyrian, Youtubers' inside jokes, and historical and biographical references in song lyrics. It is this core knowledge that establishes fan communities as subcultures rather than subsocieties. Its members share an understanding of the clearly defined cultural world and the values, beliefs, and practices that are tied to it (Fine and Kleinman 1979). Indeed, many fans' antagonism toward franchise reboots stems from what they feel is an inconsistent appreciation for the rules and values of the objects' universe (Johnson 2017).[5] For fans, such knowledge is not trivia. These rules and belief systems are the building blocks they use to produce, poach, remix, and reimagine stories, art, songs, and breakdowns. As Jenkins explains, "watching television as a fan involves different levels of attentiveness and evokes different viewing competencies than more casual viewing of the same material" (2012b, 56). As a fan, you watch to discuss with your friends, to formulate your own fan theories, to be inspired to write your own version of the story. While it is hard to imagine a fan with limited knowledge, our conceptualization of fandom should account for fans at all stages in the fandom life course (Duffett 2013; Harrington and Bielby 2010). This means capturing the new fans who are emotionally engaged, self-identified fans who participate with the fan community as well as the veterans of those communities.

Engagement

Participation is a crucial part of being a fan. Individuals may watch or read a lot from a series and know a lot about its universe, but fandom is about what you do as well. Indeed, fandom is a type of "skilled audience," and fans distinguish themselves from enthusiasts or collectors by repurposing, remixing, and dissecting the fan objects that excite them (Abercrombie and Longhurst 1998; Baym 2018; Fiske 1992; Jenkins 2006). Duffett (2013) outlines three aggregate types of fan engagement. The first type is the pleasure of connection. These are actions that bring fans closer to their fan objects (often celebrities for this type) like autograph hunting and star encounters. The second type—acts of appropriation—is when fans subvert texts and media. These include activities like writing fan fiction or slash fiction[6] and spoiling plot points in stories for others (Bacon-Smith 1992; Jenkins 2006, 2012b). Fans write and remix these stories for the joy of storytelling, to connect them to their own experiences, and as form of escapism. The final type is performance. Performance incorporates the largest range of activities, from collecting and writing zines or blogs to writing story-inspired songs (*filking*) and dressing up as characters from movies, books, or shows (i.e., cosplay), among other acts. Regardless of the form, as Coppa emphasizes, fandom is a pro-active consumption that is "just boatloads of fun: this century's equivalent of the sing-a-long, the backyard show, the community dance" (2014, 78, emphasis in the original). As with knowledge, it may be hard to imagine an inactive fan, but there are certainly enthusiastic and knowledgeable, but otherwise inactive, self-identified fans that we should try to capture in our conceptualizations (for examples, see Ang 1989; Jenkins 2012b).

Perhaps more than other aspects of fandom, the proliferation of digital media has expanded opportunities for engagement. Fans excited by the pleasures of connection can use Twitter, Instagram, and YouTube for new types of celebrity connections like replying to celebrity posts, pursuing celebrity retweets, selfies with celebrities, and obsessive or overzealous celebrity fandom (i.e. stanning) (Baym 2018; Click, Lee, and Holladay 2013; A. Cox 2017). Digital media have also made acts of appropriation easier. It is undoubtedly easier to find and share fan fiction or spoil stories through social media. Plus, fans have used the new medium for updated types of creative subversion. For example, parody Twitter accounts have turned Kylo Ren, the villain of the most recent *Star Wars* trilogy, into an emo teenager (@KyloR3n); Lord Voldemort, the antagonist in the *Harry Potter* series, into a sassy and sarcastic figure (@Lord_Voldemort7); and President Snow, the autocratic ruler in the *Hunger Games* series, into a parody of Donald Trump (@realprezsnow). These embody the same creative energy as fan fiction in a new form. Finally, digital media have enhanced old forms of participation, while also offering opportunities to create new ways to participate like coding, archiving, making gifs, video-log reviews of books and episodes, editing wikis, and filling roles for the community like moderating, organizing, and promoting.

Community

Fandom is also communal, participatory, and highly networked (Jenkins 2014; Morimoto and Chin 2017; Schreyer 2015). Fan communities may be informal networks connected by message boards, listservs, and social media or more organized groups like the Harry Potter Alliance and Starfleet (a fan group dedicated to the television series *Star Trek*).⁷ Fans participate in communities to share their collective enthusiasm for the bands, books, teams, and other fan objects they love (Grossberg 1992). Much of fan participation is inherently interactive with other people in addition to the fan objects. Fans share stories, debate on message boards and social media, watch and listen to each other's songs and videos, and generally share their collective love for artists, stories, and teams. Indeed, community ties are one of the things that distinguish fans from followers (Tulloch and Jenkins 1995, 23). The result for many fan communities is a sort of imagined community with shared enthusiasm and sets of practices, norms, and beliefs tied to the fan object (Duffett 2013; Jindra 1994; Schreyer 2015).⁸ Of course, some individuals are not yet in contact with these communities or are only connected through mass-produced literature (teenage magazines, for example). Like prior studies (Ang 1989; Jenkins 2012b), our conceptualization of fandom should incorporate them, especially if they display other aspects of being a fan.

Digital media have made fandom even more participatory (Jenkins 2006). In addition to the expanded forms of participation, fans simply have more contact with other parts of their cultural "field" (Bourdieu 1984). With the internet and social media, fans can interact with other fans, react in real time as producers release content and information, and have more direct contact with their fan objects. Fans of Korean pop (K-Pop) acts like BTS and Blackpink interact through hashtags on Twitter and TikTok to celebrate group members' birthdays, hype release dates, and support one another. European football supporters have more direct contact with clubs and individual players through Twitter (Price, Farrington, and Hall 2013). As Click, Lee, and Holladay (2013) highlight, artists like the American musician Lady Gaga have built a dedicated fanbase on this level of availability (see also Baym 2018). Further, we see digital media produce new spaces for community-building. Sites like YouTube, Reddit, and fan-run wikis help fan communities, for example, fans of the *Game of Thrones* books and television series organize and facilitate the documentation of the books' lore, discussions of fan theories, and access to videos remixing the show to suggest alternate endings and storylines (Hein 2019).

Identity

One's identity as a fan is simultaneously one of the most straightforward elements of fandom and one of the most complicated. Several scholars argue that self-identifying as a fan is a necessary condition for being a fan [in contrast to "followers" or enthusiasts (Coppa 2014; Tulloch and Jenkins 1995)] and suggest that "we need to see *identifying* as *one* of the central personal and cultural processes of fandom" (Duffett 2013, 25, emphasis in original). Fandom may be best conceptualized as a role-based identity (Stryker and Burke 2000; Stryker and Serpe 1994). That is, being a fan is something you do and not something you are. A considerable amount of work focuses on how fans enact these identities through cosplay (Lamerichs 2011) and totems like fannish tattoos (Jones 2015) and how identities create sustained in-groups and out-groups around teams, ethnicity, and class (Brown 1998; Porat 2010; Sandvoss 2004).

But identity is an inconsistent indicator of fandom because not all fans are willing to publicly identify as fans, and some may not see themselves as fans at all. Fans may be slow to publicly self-identify for fear of their fandom being associated with the stereotypes of celebrity stalkers and sports violence that continue to hold sway in the public imagination (Harrington and Bielby 1995; Jung 2012; Schimmel, Harrington, and Bielby 2007). Fans may also hesitate to self-identify due to concerns over how others perceive their fan objects. Being a fan of sports, award-winning television like *Breaking Bad*, or a Grammy-winning rapper like Kendrick Lamar is celebrated; but some fandoms—like soap operas, comic books, and musicians like Celine Dion—continue to be looked down upon because of what they signal about cultural taste (Harrington and Bielby 1995; Hills 2003; Wilson 2007). Finally, some who behave like fans may not identify as fans at all. As Harrington and Bielby explain, "one can do fan activity without being a fan, and vice versa. Fanship is not merely about activity. It involves parallel processes of activity and identity" (1995, 86–87). In sum, identity is an important aspect of fandom, but we should be cautious about treating it as a necessary or sufficient condition as action and self-identification are not enough on their own.

Emotional Connection

The final element of fandom as an ideal type is an emotional connection to the fan object. At its heart, fandom is *fun*. It is impossible to read the literature on fandom and not recognize that people are fans because they *love* the books, movies, music, or teams. For fans, this is more than just an academic appreciation; it is about connecting with their fan objects in ways that they do not connect with other media (Abercrombie and Longhurst 1998). This is obviously an important part of fandom (Harrington and Bielby 1995), but it is one that often gets overlooked or explained away (Hills 2003). Fans typically connect with a single object like a specific set of texts—such as *Star Trek*, *Star Wars*, or soap operas—or a musical artist like Lady Gaga or Phish (Bacon-Smith 1992; Cavicchi 1998; Jenkins 2012b). Until recently, music fandom was less common because music fans were more likely to focus on a style than a single artist (Abercrombie and Longhurst 1998; Cavicchi 1998). This has changed as social media have expanded access to celebrities and facilitated more music fan communities in the process (Click, Lee, and Holladay 2013). The emotional connection is the lifeblood of fandom. While fans may vary in knowledge, participation, and self-identification, we would be hard-pressed not to see them as a fan if they *love* the story, artist, or team. Indeed, it is often the emotional connection that drives knowledge accumulation, fan engagement, and their sense of identity.

Researchers have identified contexts where fandom can operate without this emotional connection. Fandom for some extends beyond a focus on a primary text to other texts and media. These "cultural nomads" are committed not to particular texts but rather to a set of practices that define how they interact with texts (Coppa 2014; Jenkins 2012b). While they may have a favorite, these fans circulate from one object to another in cyclical patterns picking up ideas, experiences, and points of reference that they use to make sense of their social and fan worlds (Hills 2003). This sort of analytic fandom is less likely to hold the same emotional connections. Instead, the joy may come from being versed in enough fandoms to recognize the intra-textual and inter-textual connections. A range of media—including television shows like *Community* and *Stranger Things*, books like Ernest Cline's *Ready Player One*, and films like the Marvel-verse films and the Star Wars reboots—are built around these types of intra-franchise and inter-franchise references (with varying levels of quality and success). Music communities thrive on these kinds of intra- and inter-genre references too (Lena 2012).

In sum, no one element of fandom is sufficient to make someone a fan, and, aside from economic and cultural consumption, we can envision individuals missing specific elements who we would be comfortable referring to as a fan. Indeed, all of these elements of fandom build on one another, and it is likely that, as Henry Jenkins (2007, 361) points out, the future of fan research is in how these elements are organized into a collective experience. But this opens a range of questions about how that collective experience operates. How do fan communities balance stability and change within the community as well as with the life course of the books, artists, and series they follow? How do the aspects of fandom that are championed vary across communities? Established fan communities like those for *Star Wars* and *Doctor Who* may value encyclopedic knowledge of the fan world, whereas passion and dedication may be more central to the fan communities of K-Pop artists or the British singer Harry Styles. Further, how are fandoms changing with the ever-expanding possibilities of the internet and social media? While digital media may expand who has access, they may also produce class and generational divides in what fandom looks like.

Fandom and Axes of Inequality

Fandoms are subcultures that embody many of the same inequalities that are a part of the broader society. These inequalities have not been overlooked by fandom researchers. A subset of fandom research has focused on the sociological aspects of how gender, class, and race are depicted in media as well as how they shape perceptions of fan communities and fans' experiences within them.

Fandom researchers have focused extensively on gender and sexual identity in fan communities and how fan objects are often gendered. Harrington and Bielby (1995) demonstrate how media—like soap operas—orient themselves toward women through the style of storytelling (often relationship- and dialogue-focused) and close-up camera work (see also Thomas and O'Shea 2010). Others have highlighted how gory, excessively violent, or "difficult" films and television shows are often coded as male, creating gendered fan communities in the process (Cherry 1999; Duffett 2013). These substantive and demographic differences can make fan communities sites of gender conflict (Duffett 2013; Pugh 2005). Scott (2019) argues that these conflicts are often most severe as fans police the proverbial borders of who counts as a true fan (see also Busse 2013). In order to participate in fan communities, and sometimes in response to this style of authenticity policing, women often have to carve out their own spaces in male-gendered roles and activities (Bacon-Smith 1992), downplay their gender identities (Jones 2008), or gravitate toward more gendered forms of engagement like writing fan fiction, cosplay, and participating in celebrity infatuation (Jenkins 2006; Thomas and O'Shea 2010). Indeed, Kashtan (2018) argues that debates over issues like gendered comic book covers by "traditional" and progressive" comic book fans are, like Gamergate, a microcosm of larger divisions in American society. Of course, fan communities can be spaces of gender affirmation and exploration too. For example, McInroy (2019) finds that fandom communities can increase connection and a sense of support for LGBTQ youth. Similarly, Palmer (2019) finds that fan communities like the one dedicated to the *My Little Pony* toy and media franchise can act as spaces where men can challenge masculinity but cautions that these spaces can reinforce gender inequalities in other ways.[9]

The role of class in fandom research is more complex. In a strict sense, discussion of fans' socioeconomic status is surprisingly limited. Jenkins (2012b, 212–213) discusses the role of class in the stories but not the fan community, and several studies acknowledge that fans tend to be solidly middle class or relatively affluent, potentially shaping their responses (Brooker 2005; Harrington and Bielby 1995, 189; Jancovich 2002). Instead, fandom studies focus on class through the lens of Bourdieuian taste and cultural capital (Bourdieu 1984). Indeed, several studies use cultural taste to understand football, film, and pop music fans (Brown 1998; Jancovich 2002; Wilson 2007). Several fandom researchers argue that, despite their increasing prevalence, fans and fandom are associated with the marginalized and subordinated in society because fan objects and forms of fan participation often skew closer to "popular" culture (Fiske 1992; Hills 2003; Jenkins 2012b). Many of these studies argue that subcultural knowledge and taste are more important than an individual's socioeconomic class for understanding hierarchies within fan communities (Longhurst 2007; Pearson 2007; Thornton 1996). While this may be true, it leaves open space for considering how fandom fits with more recent work on class and taste (Lamont and Molnár 2002; Lena 2012; Warde 2015). Specifically, consumption scholars find that upper-class individuals are more likely to engage in "omnivorous consumption" or consuming high culture and pop culture (Peterson and Kern 1996). This indicates that fandom may be associated with the marginalized and incorporated into elite tastes, opening potentially interesting questions about how fans determine what is worthy of geekery—especially in an era of mass fandom.

While scholars have thoroughly considered gender- and class-related tastes in fan communities, race has been a historically understudied aspect of fan culture (Brown 2001; Lopez 2012; Pande 2020; Wanzo 2015). "Fan studies in the West has largely been organized around white bodies" as well as White fan objects, and there has only recently been an explosion of work on race and fandom (Stanfill 2011; Wanzo 2015). As Wanzo (2015) argues, reconsidering fan identity with Black people as the focal fan reveals new perspectives on fandom, such as the subversive potential of consumption (through boycotts and opting out of consumption), Black cultural criticism like Black Twitter as a type of anti-fandom, and how Black fans have to negotiate often demeaning or problematic depictions to participate. Indeed, Black fandom's relationship with fan objects like movies, comics, and music differs from that of White fans because Black fans are compelled to see the Blackness of these objects and to evaluate their ability to teach others about the Black experience (Martin 2019).

This is particularly evident as digital media have offered new spaces for fan engagement. On the one hand, this has been positive. Sites like Tumblr have expanded opportunities for fandom formation around non-White characters like Ms. Marvel (a Pakistani American comic character), Miles Morales (a Black boy who becomes Spider Man), and the Black Panther and facilitate the forms of civic resistance they inspire (C. M. Cox 2017; Martin 2019). On the other hand, digital spaces can also be toxic for fans—and actors—of color. Similar to the gendered boundary policing already discussed, fans have used online platforms like Twitter to subject non-White actors like Kelly Marie Tran and Leslie Jones to racist harassment for their roles in the *Star Wars* and *Ghostbusters* films, highlighting the potential toxicity of fandom (Pande 2020). Further, while not as extreme, social media force the K-Pop, *Magic the Gathering* card game, European football, and the metal fan communities to more publicly reckon with their histories of cultural misappropriation (Anderson 2016), blind spots for racist subgroups (Bassam 2020; Moynihan 2019), and racist art and characters (Pietsch 2020). This ongoing reckoning of race and fandom highlights potential areas for future research such as how people of color negotiate often White fan spaces, how predominantly White fan communities reflect on (or fail to reflect on) the historic and contemporary racism in their community, and how integrating people of color into new and old fan universes helps and complicates these processes.

PARTICIPATORY POLITICS AND FAN ACTIVISM

Fandom is a community-based, networked experience that is active and engaging and encourages fans to join in; and its participatory nature is increasingly evident in spaces like politics as well (Jenkins 2006). Scholars like Henry Jenkins and his co-authors contend that participatory politics—or "that point where political change is promoted through social and cultural mechanisms rather than through established political institutions, and where citizens see themselves as capable of expressing their political concerns—often through the production and circulation of media" (Jenkins et al. 2018, 2)—is increasingly common. Participatory politics operates through nontraditional political channels—like fan communities—and utilizes the cultural repertoires, knowledge, skills, and habits that participants are familiar with (rather than traditional political behavior) to participate in the political process (Chatman 2017; Hinck 2019; Lopez 2012; Scardaville 2005). Just as there are multiple ways to be a fan, participatory politics emphasizes that there are multiple ways to participate in politics. Participants might share news and information; post, tweet, or talk about political issues; make memes, videos, or other civically oriented content; participate in online petitions; or change their online avatars (Cohen and Kahne 2012; Kahne, Lee, and Feezell 2013; Kahne, Middaugh, and Allen 2015). This approach contrasts sharply with traditional "apprentice"-style models of political socialization (Kirshner 2008) in that it is participant-driven rather than hierarchical.

Fandom intersects with participatory politics in several different ways. First, fandom helps people develop a political imagination. Fiction writers like Ursula LeGuin, Kurt Vonnegut, and Octavia Butler have used the medium to explore alternative political, social, and technological systems; and fans—as active consumers—are well practiced at considering the costs and benefits of these imaginary worlds (Brooker 2005; Hills 2010). These same practices can be applied to imagining a more just society. Fandom scholars repeatedly point to the power of the story as an impetus for more deliberate civic and political action (Bird and Maher 2017; Kligler-Vilenchik et al. 2012; Slack 2010), and the values and beliefs embedded in these fan worlds can shape individuals' political beliefs (Dessewffy and Mezei 2020; Moore and Roberts 2009). Fandom has also become an increasingly important discursive source for citizens as they draw on pop culture like *Star Wars* and *Game of Thrones* to express disgust, joy, and outrage with the current political climate (Hunting 2020; Jenkins 2012a).

Second, fandom and fan communities offer non-political gateways into civic and political participation. Many fan communities have incorporated civically engaged elements into their fan cultures. As of May 2021, the semiannual video game speedrunning marathon *Games Done Quick* has raised more than $31 million in donations for Doctors Without Borders, CARE, and the Prevent Cancer Foundation.[10] The Harry Potter Alliance has tapped into the story to organize get-out-the-vote campaigns (Wizard Rock the Vote), library book drives (Accio Books), and support for trans kids through fan posts, media, and fan art. The punk community routinely holds benefit shows and encourages activist organizations to distribute literature at concerts (Haenfler 2006; Moore and Roberts 2009).

Fan communities have been particularly adept at using expanding technology for political expression. Video game players have applied the focus developed through long hours of "grinding" a game (performing repetitive tasks to improve your characters' levels or status) to repeatedly post political messages on Reddit, Twitter, Facebook, and other sites online. Libertarians have used YouTube to share fan songs about Hayek and Ayn Rand and informational videos about the 2008 economic crash (Jenkins et al. 2018). Other fans have remixed media content—for example, mashing up Hillary Clinton footage and songs by the feminist punk band Bikini Kill (Davisson 2016)—to counter prominent political narratives. Recognizing and analyzing these actions are especially important for fandom and political researchers alike because young people are increasingly turning toward these less traditional, more networked forms of political engagement (Earl, Maher, and Elliott 2017; Jenkins et al. 2018; Kahne, Lee, and Feezell 2013). Further, these forms of participatory politics are having an impact on politics and public discourse (Hunting 2020).

Fan Activism

Alongside participatory politics, fan activism also emerged as a vital topic for researchers interested in fandom and social movements more broadly. The earliest work in this area emphasized biographical and cultural—rather than political—outcomes. These studies focused on how fans adopt nontraditional political tactics to influence studios and executives tied to their fan objects (Earl and Kimport 2009; Harrington and Bielby 1995). For example, Scardaville's (2005) pathbreaking work focused on how fans of the soap opera *Another World*—who were not activists before the campaign— used social movement tactics like petitions, call-in campaigns, and boycotts to pressure executives to keep the show on the air. Her work also highlighted how participating in the campaign tightened participants' friendship bonds and heightened their sense of agency. Yet fan activism operates in a broader context of fan participation. "Soap activism is not an evolutionary step on the fan activity ladder but instead, one of many tools employed by fans who want to take action" (Scardaville 2005, 899). Indeed, the use of protest tactics for these types of entertainment-oriented goals has grown considerably (Earl and Kimport 2009). Earl and Kimport (2009) attribute much of this growth to the spread of the internet and social media, making these campaigns easier to organize, and the growth of the "social movement society," where social movements and protest campaigns are increasingly a part of social and political life.

More recent work on fan activism has emphasized its potential impact on the political realm. Brough and Shrestova (2012) push the concept of fan activism forward. They argue that fan activism is political because even "nonpolitical" cultural issues (like who gets represented in film and media) have political aspects and that fan activism is defined by its form— "engagement with and strategic deployment of popular culture content"—not its target (see also Jenkins and Shresthova 2012). Subsequent research has demonstrated how cultural targets are often politically potent. Lopez (2012) demonstrates that who gets cast for films—especially films based on non-White characters, like *The Last Airbender*—has important racial and political implications. Gross (2020) shows that ostensibly apolitical fandoms, like Harry Styles fans, can be a venue for engaging in political discourse.

Scholars interested in fan activism have focused on how fan communities are mobilized, particularly how fans take advantage of technology, engage in what they call "cultural acupuncture," and bloc recruit from fan communities. Many fans are well versed with the internet and social media and can work within digital spaces to achieve political aims. Fans revel in learning the intricacies of how games operate, optimize search results, and convince large groups to participate in events and campaigns. In many ways, fan activism is simply applying these same tactics for political ends. For example, Collister (2017) documents the "running of the gnomes," an event in the multiplayer online role-playing game *World of Warcraft* which coincides with the Race for the Cure (a breast cancer awareness event) where players race pink-haired gnome characters through the online world while posting in the chatlog about breast cancer awareness. The event disrupts other players, often crashes the servers, and draws attention to the cause in the process. In June of 2020, K-Pop fans drew national attention for organizing on Twitter and TikTok to sign up for free tickets to Donald Trump's re-election rally in Tulsa, Oklahoma, artificially inflating attendance projections considerably (Lorenz, Browning, and Frenkel 2020). Around this same time, K-Pop fans also rendered the #whitelivesmatter and #alllivesmatter Twitter hashtags useless for racist organizing by spamming them with Fancam videos, posts about their favorite groups, and memes mocking racists (Hou 2020). While some have dismissed the effectiveness of these actions (Andrews 2020), there is no doubt that the fans' efforts influenced the political narrative, disrupted racist organizing, and further reinforced youth and fan activist perceptions that they could influence the political process.

Media, fandom, and culture are also a site where activists influence people's beliefs and perspectives. Scholars and practitioners have referred to attempts to tap into mass pop culture events to mobilize fan activists, attract media and public interest, and connect to fans' emotional investments in their fan objects as "cultural acupuncture." Andrew Slack, the co-founder of the Harry Potter Alliance, defines cultural acupuncture as "finding where the psychological energy is in the culture, and moving that energy towards creating a healthier world" (2010). The Harry Potter Alliance has been especially adept at this practice, tapping into Harry Potter book and movie release dates and special events to spark activism and attention for causes like fair trade sourcing for Harry Potter–licensed chocolate treats and advocating for net neutrality, and other fandoms—like the Hunger Games community—have adopted similar tactics (Bird and Maher 2017; Hinck 2019). Jenkins (2012a) adds that cultural acupuncture is not just about the media events; it is the ability to map the fictional events—the stories that inspire fans—onto real-world issues. This highlights the importance of fandom for the success of cultural acupuncture and makes the tactic a lasting resource even after the story is finished being told.

The final element of recent work on fan activism focuses on fan communities as a source of potential activists. A wide range of social movements, from the civil rights movement to the animal rights movement have tapped into non-political constituencies like the Black church and the punk community for mobilization (Moore and Roberts 2009; Morris 1986). This type of recruitment—where social movement organizers often recruit participants among groups already organized for some other purpose—is known as *bloc recruitment* (Oberschall 1993, 24). For bloc recruitment to be effective, activists and mobilizers need to have authentic connections with the communities being recruited (Bird and Maher 2017). Indeed, part of what makes the Harry Potter Alliance effective at bloc recruiting from the Harry Potter fan community is its ability to identify resonant obscure characters and events, quote particularly meaningful dialogue, and connect with existing forms of fan participation (like Wizard Rock and fan viding) to mobilize otherwise politically inactive individuals (Bird and Maher 2017; Jenkins 2012a). Further, bloc recruitment of fan communities often facilitates more participation by incorporating lower-cost forms of activism that are connected to everyday fan activities. For example, the aforementioned K-Pop fans were already talking about their bands, posting fan videos, and trying to manipulate search engine results; adding a hashtag is an easy change to make, especially if lots of other people are doing it too. Of course, not all participants will be participating because they care about the issue. Some may participate because they agree, others may participate to draw attention to their fandom, and more may participate just because it is fun. Regardless of motivation, the impact on the hashtag is the same.

Fan activism and participatory politics are an exciting but nascent area of fandom research as well as social movement research, and there is still an incredible amount of research to be done in the area. First, I support Brough and Shresthova's (2012) call for more analysis of transnational non-Western analysis of fan activism. Transnational activism and global framing (i.e., messages that can resonate across cultural and linguistic barriers) are difficult but important mechanisms to organize (Tarrow 2005), but human rights activists have drawn on pop culture like the *Hunger Games*, *Harry Potter*, and Indian Bollywood films to try to build these connections with varying degrees of success (Datta 2019; Mydans 2014). How does fandom act as a shared touchstone across countries, and what are its strengths and limitations in "signal boosting" protest messages globally? Further, are these attempts building from efforts to mobilize local fan communities, strategic attempts to tap into transnational cultural scripts, or something in between?

Second, recent trends and analyses suggest that politics is taking on elements of fandom. While not a new phenomenon, recent political figures like Ron Paul, Barack Obama, Bernie Sanders, and Donald Trump have garnered fanbases that are closer to the media-driven fan communities described in this chapter. Indeed, these communities are organized around fandom for the individual rather than any larger ideology (Miller 2020), and, more broadly, political participation is adopting broader elements of fandom like rooting for one's "team," stanning, and participatory practices (Burwell and Boler 2008; Miller 2020). Recent work by Eitan Hersh (2020) contends that politically engaged individuals—particularly those on the left—are increasingly passive consumers of political knowledge who read the news, support their "teams," and discuss with friends but rarely act on these interests. These trends toward centering individual "objects" of political fandom suggest that the analytic tools of fandom research are useful for understanding contemporary political conditions.

Finally, while scholars have identified how fan activism works, we still know little about the long-term prospects of participating in fan activism for individuals and fan activist organizations. Social change is hard, and movement campaigns often last for years, if not decades. How does the fandom life course (Harrington and Bielby 1995) intersect with activist and movement timelines? In an internal survey, 57% of Harry Potter Alliance members had never participated in activism before joining, and they reported feeling more comfortable identifying as a "wizard activist" than with the more general term (Bird and Maher 2017). While fan activism expands opportunities for young people to get involved and think of themselves as activists (Earl, Maher, and Elliott

2017), what does that increased comfort mean for subsequent behavior and their sense of political efficacy? Further, movement success takes time. How does that expanded time frame influence how fan activist organizations adopt causes and their ability to maintain engagement after the series has completed? Fan activist organizations like the Harry Potter Alliance are still active, making it even more important to understand how the life course of fandom intersects with movement and political timelines.

Conclusion

Research on fan communities and fan activism has grown considerably since the beginning of the 21st century, and it has yielded a range of insights into how fandom is a central aspect of contemporary culture. While scholars have not agreed on a general definition of a what fan is, their definitions revolve around being a fan as an "ideal type" where individuals demonstrate some combination of economic or cultural consumption; literacy of their fan objects' stories, histories, and nuances; active engagement with the books, films, and artists they care about; fan community participation; self-identification as a fan; and an emotional attachment to the fan object. While only consumption is necessary for being a fan, none of these aspects is sufficient. Fan communities are subcultures that embody many of the broader gender, sexual identity, race, disability, and class inequities that define the broader society; and they can be sites of conflict around these issues (Abercrombie and Longhurst 1998; Fine and Kleinman 1979). However, they do not perfectly mirror these broader inequities, and they have the potential to support and encourage marginalized groups as well (Brown 2001; McInroy 2019; Tulloch and Jenkins 1995). Finally, this chapter reviewed more recent work on the intersection between politics, activism, and fan communities. Fans are using activist tactics and participating in the political process more often (Earl and Kimport 2009; Jenkins et al. 2018), and recent work in the area has emphasized how fandom has taken advantage of technological affordances, tapped into public enthusiasm for pop culture events, and mobilized fellow fans to increase participation and draw attention to social problems. This chapter will hopefully spark new and exciting research in these areas.

Notes

1. A *fan object* is the specific person, text, or team attracting fan attention (Duffett 2013). I will use this term throughout this chapter to represent all the different forms of fandom.
2. Fandom scholars draw a distinction between fandom research (a broad topic drawing on sociology, psychology, and communication that focuses on fandom as a topic) and fan studies [an approach that draws from cultural studies to focus on the relationship between the fan and the text (Duffett 2013)]. While I will focus primarily on the sociologically oriented work, I will discuss these as one holistic field of research.

3. Abercrombie and Longhurst (1998) thoroughly unpack the differences between enthusiasts, fans, and "cultists." Although there are differences, their conceptualization of cultists—a group of heavily engaged individuals with a specific focus—is similar to our contemporary understanding of fans. This suggests that there has been a meaningful drift in the conceptualization and expectations around being a fan.
4. Fan studies has consistently argued that fandom is interactive with the texts and focused on the readers' relationship with the text rather than the authors' intent (Hellekson and Busse 2006; Sandvoss 2017). The decision of Harry Potter fan sites like the Leaky Cauldron to stop posting about J. K. Rowling after a series of anti-transgender statements is a contemporary example of how fandom distinguishes between the text and its author (Anelli 2020).
5. Fans' antagonism toward franchise updates may also be connected to the updates including women and people of color in prominent roles. Indeed, the authenticity policing that I describe in the section on inequality and fan communities applies to who gets to play prominent roles as much as it applies to who counts as a true fan.
6. *Slash fiction* is fan fiction that depicts fictional characters in (often homosexual) intimate and/or sexual scenarios.
7. Abercrombie and Longhurst (1998) refer to these more organized fan communities as "cultists," but—despite the stigmatizing terminology—their description seems to suit a more committed subset of fans.
8. More recent work has questioned treating fan communities—especially transcultural fan communities—as imagined communities because they often omit marginalized voices and people while emphasizing commonalities among fans (Morimoto and Chin 2017).
9. While I do not discuss it here, there is also a growing subset of this literature that focuses on disability and fandom. Much of this work focuses on how disability is depicted in specific media like television (Cook 2019), comedy (Nevárez Araújo 2019), and comics (Bryan 2019). But some, like Nevárez Araújo (2019), do focus on how disability influences individuals' fandoms and disabled people's membership in fan communities.
10. https://gamesdonequick.com/tracker/

References

Abercrombie, Nicholas, and Brian J. Longhurst. 1998. *Audiences: A Sociological Theory of Performance and Imagination*. London: SAGE.

Anderson, Crystal S. 2016. "Hybrid Hallyu: The African American Music Tradition in K-Pop." In *Global Asian American Popular Cultures*, edited by Shilpa Davé, Leilani Nishime, and Tasha Oren, 290–303. New York: New York University Press.

Andrews, Travis. 2020. "Did TikTokers and K-Pop Fans Foil Trump's Tulsa Rally? It's Complicated." *Washington Post*, June 21.

Anelli, Melissa. 2020. "Addressing J. K. Rowling's Recent Statements." The Leaky Cauldron.org, July 1. Accessed August 11, 2020. http://www.the-leaky-cauldron.org/2020/07/01/addressing-j-k-rowlings-recent-statements/.

Ang, Ien. 1989. *Watching Dallas: Soap Opera and the Melodramatic Imagination*. London and New York: Routledge.

Bacon-Smith, Camille. 1992. *Enterprising Women: Television Fandom and the Creation of Popular Myth*. Philadelphia: University of Pennsylvania Press.

Barton, Kristin M., and Jonathan Malcolm Lampley. 2013. *Fan Culture: Essays on Participatory Fandom in the 21st Century*. Jefferson, NC: McFarland.

Bassam, Tom. 2020. "Sharp Rise in Football Racism as Incidents Go up by More than 50% in One Year." *The Guardian*, January 30.

Baym, Nancy K. 2018. *Playing to the Crowd: Musicians, Audiences, and the Intimate Work of Connection*. New York: New York University Press.

BBC News. 2020. "Doctor Who's Online Viewing Convention." Accessed June 23. https://www.bbc.com/news/av/entertainment-arts-52050569/doctor-who-fans-unite-with-an-online-viewing.

Bird, Jackson, and Thomas V. Maher. 2017. "Turning Fans into Heroes: How the Harry Potter Alliance Uses the Power of Story to Facilitate Fan Activism and Bloc Recruitment." In *Studies in Media and Communications*. Vol. 14, *Social Movements and Media*, edited by Jennifer Earl and Deana A. Rohlinger, 23–54. Bingley, UK: Emerald Publishing.

Booth, Paul. 2010. *Digital Fandom: New Media Studies*. New York: Peter Lang.

Bourdieu, Pierre. 1984. *Distinction: A Social Critique of the Judgement of Taste*. Cambridge, MA: Harvard University Press.

Brooker, Will. 2005. " 'It Is Love': The Lewis Carroll Society as a Fan Community." *American Behavioral Scientist* 48, no. 7: 859–880.

Brough, Melissa M., and Sangita Shresthova. 2012. "Fandom Meets Activism: Rethinking Civic and Political Participation." *Transformative Works and Cultures* 10: 1–27.

Brown, Adam, ed. 1998. *Fanatics! Power, Identity, & Fandom in Football*. London and New York: Routledge.

Brown, Jeffrey A. 2001. *Black Superheroes, Milestone Comics, and Their Fans*. Jackson: University Press of Mississippi.

Bryan, Peter Cullen. 2019. "Purple Healing Rays and Paralysis: Intersections of Disability and Gender Theory in Comics." *Journal of Fandom Studies* 7, no. 1: 21–34.

Burwell, Catherine, and Megan Boler. 2008. "Calling on the Colbert Nation: Fandom, Politics and Parody in an Age of Media Convergence" *Electronic Journal of Communication* 18, no. 2: 3–25.

Busse, Karen, and Karen Hellekson. 2006. "Introduction: Work in Progress." In *Fan Fiction and Fan Communities in the Age of the Internet*, edited by K. Hellekson and Kristina Busse, 5–32. Jefferson, NC: McFarland.

Busse, Kristina. 2013. "Geek Hierarchies, Boundary Policing, and the Gendering of the Good Fan." *Participations* 10, no. 1: 73–91.

Cavicchi, Daniel. 1998. *Tramps Like Us: Music and Meaning among Springsteen Fans*. New York: Oxford University Press.

Chatman, Dayna. 2017. "Black Twitter and the Politics of Viewing Scandal." In *Fandom: Identities and Communities in a Mediated World*, edited by J. Gray, C. Sandvoss, and C. L. Harrington, 299–314. New York: New York University Press.

Cherry, Brigid. 1999. "Refusing to Refuse to Look: Female Viewers of the Horror Film." In *Identifying Hollywood Audiences: Cultural Identity and the Movies*, edited by M. Stokes and R. Maltby, 187–203. London: British Film Institute.

Chin, Bertha. 2018. "It's about Who You Know; Social Capital, Hierarchies, and Fandom." In *A Companion to Media Fandom and Fan Studies*, edited by P. Booth, 243–255. New York: John Wiley & Sons.

Click, Melissa A., Hyunji Lee, and Holly Willson Holladay. 2013. "Making Monsters: Lady Gaga, Fan Identification, and Social Media." *Popular Music and Society* 36, no. 3: 360–379.

Cohen, Cathy J., and Joseph Kahne. 2012. *Participatory Politics: New Media and Youth Political Action*. Chicago: MacArthur Foundation.

Collister, Lauren B. 2017. "Transformative (h)Activism: Breast Cancer Awareness and the 'World of Warcraft' Running of the Gnomes." *Transformative Works and Cultures* 25. http://dx.doi.org/10.3983/twc.2017.990.

Cook, Tanya N. 2019. " 'All Dwarfs Are Bastards': *Game of Thrones* as Disability Studies Pedagogy." *Journal of Fandom Studies* 7, no. 1: 35–46.

Cooper, Gael Fashingbauer. 2020. "Lord of the Rings Is Lifting Spirits during These Dark Coronavirus Times." CNET. Accessed June 23. https://www.cnet.com/news/lord-of-the-rings-is-lifting-spirits-during-these-dark-coronavirus-times/.

Coppa, Francesca. 2014. "Fuck Yeah, Fandom Is Beautiful." *Journal of Fandom Studies* 2, no. 1: 73–82.

Cox, Annabel. 2017. "Stereotyped Fans and Social Critique: Miguel de Cervantes's Don Quixote and Eminem's 'Stan.'" *Journal of Fandom Studies* 5, no. 1: 113–128.

Cox, Christopher M. 2017. " 'Ms. Marvel,' Tumblr, and the Industrial Logics of Identity in Digital Spaces." *Transformative Works and Cultures* 27. https://dx.doi.org/10.3983/twc.2018.1195.

Datta, Tiyashi. 2019. "Pune Protests against CAA: Harry Potter to GoT, Millennials Find Creative Ways to Carry On." *Indian Express*, December 26.

Davisson, Amber. 2016. "Mashing up, Remixing, and Contesting the Popular Memory of Hillary Clinton." *Transformative Works and Cultures* 22. http://dx.doi.org/10.3983/twc.2016.0965.

Dessewffy, Tibor, and Mikes Mezei. 2020. "Fans and Politics in an Illiberal State." *Transformative Works and Cultures* 32. https://dx.doi.org/10.3983/twc.2019.1757.

Duffett, Mark. 2013. *Understanding Fandom: An Introduction to the Study of Media Fan Culture*. New York: Bloomsbury Publishing.

Earl, Jennifer, and Katrina Kimport. 2009. "Movement Societies and Digital Protest: Fan Activism and Other Nonpolitical Protest Online." *Sociological Theory* 27, no. 3: 220–243.

Earl, Jennifer, Thomas V. Maher, and Thomas Elliott. 2017. "Youth, Activism, and Social Movements." *Sociology Compass* 11, no. 4: e12465.

Fine, Gary Alan, and Sherryl Kleinman. 1979. "Rethinking Subculture: An Interactionist Analysis." *American Journal of Sociology* 85, no. 1: 1–20.

Fiske, John. 1992. "The Cultural Economy of Fandom." In *The Adoring Audience: Fan Culture and Popular Media*, edited by Lisa A. Lewis, 30–49. London and New York: Routledge.

Gray, Jonathan. 2005. "Antifandom and the Moral Text: Television without Pity and Textual Dislike." *American Behavioral Scientist* 48, no. 7: 840–858.

Gray, Jonathan Alan, Cornel Sandvoss, and C. Lee Harrington. 2007. *Fandom: Identities and Communities in a Mediated World*. New York: New York University Press.

Gray, Jonathan, Cornel Sandvoss, and C. Lee Harrington. 2017. *Fandom, Identities and Communities in a Mediated World*. 2nd ed. New York: New York University Press.

Gross, Allyson. 2020. "To Wave a Flag: Identification, #BlackLivesMatter, and Populism in Harry Styles Fandom." *Transformative Works and Cultures* 32. https://doi.org/10.3983/twc.2020.1765.

Grossberg, Lawrence. 1992. "Is There a Fan in the House? The Affective Sensibility of Fandom." In *The adoring audience: Fan culture and popular media*, edited by Lisa A. Lewis, 50–65. London and New York: Routledge.

Haenfler, Ross. 2006. *Straight Edge: Clean-Living Youth, Hardcore Punk, and Social Change*. New Brunswick, NJ: Rutgers University Press.

Harrington, C. Lee, and Denise D. Bielby. 1995. *Soap Fans: Pursuing Pleasure and Making Meaning in Everyday Life*. Philadelphia: Temple University Press.

Harrington, C. Lee, and Denise D. Bielby. 2010. "A Life Course Perspective on Fandom." *International Journal of Cultural Studies* 13, no. 5: 429–450.

Harris, Cheryl. 1998. "A Sociology of Television Fandom." *Theorizing Fandom: Fans, Subculture and Identity* 41: 42.

Harry Potter Alliance. 2020. "*Shield Charms and Sewing Spells: Creating Your Own Face Mask.*" April 6. YouTube. Accessed May 18, 2021. (https://www.youtube.com/watch?v=gKWOp4dsChk).

Hein, Michael. 2019. " 'Game of Thrones' Fan Rewrites Show's Ending, and Fans Are Here for It." PopCulture, August 12. Accessed July 12, 2020. https://popculture.com/tv-shows/news/game-of-thrones-fan-rewrites-series-finale-ending/.

Hellekson, Karen, and Kristina Busse. 2006. *Fan Fiction and Fan Communities in the Age of the Internet: New Essays*. Jefferson, NC: McFarland.

Hersh, Eitan. 2020. *Politics Is for Power: How to Move Beyond Political Hobbyism, Take Action, and Make Real Change*. New York: Scribner.

Hills, Matt. 2010. *Triumph of a Time Lord: Regenerating Doctor Who in the Twenty-First Century*. London: I. B. Tauris.

Hills, Matthew. 2003. *Fan Cultures*. London and New York: Routledge.

Hinck, Ashley. 2019. *Politics for the Love of Fandom: Fan-Based Citizenship in a Digital World*. Baton Rouge, LA: LSU Press.

Hou, Kathleen. 2020. "The K-Pop Stans Are Radicalizing." The Cut, June 4. Accessed June 23, 2020. https://www.thecut.com/2020/06/k-pop-stans-spam-police-take-over-whitelivesmatter-hashtag.html.

Hunting, Kyra Osten. 2020. "The Role of Popular Media in 2016 US Presidential Election Memes." *Transformative Works and Cultures* 32. https://doi.org/10.3983/twc.2020.1785.

Ito, Mizuko, Crystle Martin, Rachel Cody Pfister, Matthew H. Rafalow, Katie Salen, and Amanda Wortman. 2018. *Affinity Online: How Connection and Shared Interest Fuel Learning*. New York: New York University Press.

Jancovich, Mark. 2002. "Cult Fictions: Cult Movies, Subcultural Capital and the Production of Cultural Distinctions." *Cultural Studies* 16, no. 2: 306–322.

Jenkins, Henry. 2006. *Convergence Culture: Where Old and New Media Collide*. New York: New York University Press.

Jenkins, Henry. 2007. "The Future of Fandom." In *Fandom: Identities and Communities in a Mediated World*, edited by J. Gray, C. Sandvoss, and C. L. Harrington, 357–364. New York: New York University Press.

Jenkins, Henry. 2012a. " 'Cultural Acupuncture': Fan Activism and the Harry Potter Alliance." *Transformative Works and Cultures* 10. https://doi.org/10.3983/twc.2012.0305.

Jenkins, Henry. 2012b. *Textual Poachers: Television Fans and Participatory Culture*. London and New York: Routledge.

Jenkins, Henry. 2014. "Fandom Studies as I See It." *Journal of Fandom Studies* 2, no. 2: 89–109.

Jenkins, Henry, and Sangita Shresthova. 2012. "Up, up, and Away! The Power and Potential of Fan Activism." *Transformative Works and Cultures* 10. https://doi.org/10.3983/twc.2012.0435.

Jenkins, Henry, Sangita Shresthova, Liana Gamber-Thompson, Neta Kligler-Vilenchik, and Arely Zimmerman. 2018. *By Any Media Necessary: The New Youth Activism*. Vol. 3. New York: New York University Press.

Jenson, Joli. 1992. "Fandom as Pathology: The Consequences of Characterization." In *The Adoring Audience: Fan Culture and Popular Media*, edited by Lisa A. Lewis, 9–29. London and New York: Routledge.

Jindra, Michael. 1994. "Star Trek Fandom as a Religious Phenomenon." *Sociology of Religion* 55, no. 1: 27–51.

Johnson, Derek. 2017. "Fantagonism: Factions, Institutions, and Constitutive Hegemonies of Fandom." In *Fandom: Identities and Communities in a mediated world*, vol. 2, edited by J. Gray, C. Sandvoss, and C. L. Harrington, 369–386. New York: New York University Press.

Jones, Bethan. 2015. "Fannish Tattooing and Sacred Identity." *Transformative Works and Cultures* 18. https://doi.org/10.3983/twc.2015.0626.

Jones, Katharine W. 2008. "Female Fandom: Identity, Sexism, and Men's Professional Football in England." *Sociology of Sport Journal* 25, no. 4: 516–537.

Jung, Sun. 2012. "Fan Activism, Cybervigilantism, and Othering Mechanisms in K-Pop Fandom." *Transformative Works and Fan Activism* 10. https://doi.org/10.3983/twc.2012.0300.

Kahne, Joseph, Nam-Jin Lee, and Jessica T. Feezell. 2013. "The Civic and Political Significance of Online Participatory Cultures among Youth Transitioning to Adulthood." *Journal of Information Technology & Politics* 10, no. 1: 1–20.

Kahne, Joseph, Ellen Middaugh, and Danielle Allen. 2015. "Youth, New Media, and the Rise of Participatory Politics." In *From Voice to Influence: Understanding Citizenship in a Digital Age*, vol. 35, edited by Danielle Allen and Jennifer S. Light, 35–58. Chicago: University of Chicago Press.

Kashtan, Aaron. 2018. "Change the Cover: Superhero Fan Identity in an Age of Diversification." *Journal of Fandom Studies* 6, no. 3: 243–261.

Kirshner, Ben. 2008. "Guided Participation in Three Youth Activism Organizations: Facilitation, Apprenticeship, and Joint Work." *Journal of the Learning Sciences* 17, no. 1: 60–101.

Kligler-Vilenchik, Neta, Joshua McVeigh-Schultz, Christine Weitbrecht, and Chris Tokuhama. 2012. "Experiencing Fan Activism: Understanding the Power of Fan Activist Organizations through Members' Narratives." *Transformative Works and Cultures* 10. https://doi.org/10.3983/twc.2012.0322.

Kustritz, Anne. 2015. "Transnationalism, Localization, and Translation in European Fandom: Fan Studies as Global Media and Audience Studies." *Transformative Works and Cultures* 19. https://doi.org/10.3983/twc.2015.0682.

Lamerichs, Nicolle. 2011. "Stranger than Fiction: Fan Identity in Cosplay." *Transformative Works and Cultures* 7. https://doi.org/10.3983/twc.2011.0246.

Lamont, Michèle, and Virág Molnár. 2002. "The Study of Boundaries in the Social Sciences." *Annual Review of Sociology* 28, no. 1: 167–195.

Lena, Jennifer C. 2012. *Banding Together: How Communities Create Genres in Popular Music*. Princeton, NJ: Princeton University Press.

Longhurst, Brian. 2007. *Popular Music and Society*. Cambridge: Polity.

Lopez, Lori Kido. 2012. "Fan Activists and the Politics of Race in The Last Airbender." *International Journal of Cultural Studies* 15, no. 5: 431–445.

Lorenz, Taylor, Kellen Browning, and Sheera Frenkel. 2020. "TikTok Teens and K-Pop Stans Say They Sank Trump Rally." *New York Times*, June 21.

Martin, Alfred L. 2019. "Fandom while Black: Misty Copeland, Black Panther, Tyler Perry and the Contours of US Black Fandoms." *International Journal of Cultural Studies* 22, no. 6: 737–753.

McInroy, Lauren B. 2019. "Building Connections and Slaying Basilisks: Fostering Support, Resilience, and Positive Adjustment for Sexual and Gender Minority Youth in Online Fandom Communities." *Information, Communication & Society* 23, no. 13: 1874–1891.

Miller, Lucy. 2020. " 'Wolfenstein II' and MAGA as fandom." *Transformative Works and Cultures* 32. https://doi.org/10.3983/twc.2020.1717.

Moore, Ryan, and Michael Roberts. 2009. "Do-It-Yourself Mobilization: Punk and Social Movements." *Mobilization: An International Quarterly* 14, no. 3: 273–291.

Morimoto, Lori Hitchcock, and Bertha Chin. 2017. "Reimagining the Imagined Community." In *Fandom: Identities and Communities in a Mediated World*, edited by J. Gray, C. Sandvoss, and C. L. Harrington, 174–190. New York: New York University Press.

Morris, Aldon D. 1986. *Origins of the Civil Rights Movements*. New York: Free Press.

Moynihan, Colin. 2019. "Heavy Metal Confronts Its Nazi Problem." *The New Yorker*, February 19. Accessed August 1, 2020. https://www.newyorker.com/culture/culture-desk/heavy-metal-confronts-its-nazi-problem.

Mydans, Seth. 2014. "Thai Protesters Are Detained after Using 'Hunger Games' Salute." *New York Times*, November 20.

Nevárez Araújo, Daniel. 2019. "Nervous Laughter: Comedy, Disabilities and the Reconstitution of Space." *Journal of Fandom Studies* 7, no. 1: 7–19.

Oberschall, Anthony. 1993. *Social Movements: Ideologies, Interests, and Identities*. New Brunswick, NJ: Transaction Publishers.

Palmer, Zachary D. 2019. "Gender in Equestria: An Examination of Reconstituted Forms of Masculinity and Their Consequences for Gender Relations in the Brony Community." PhD diss., Purdue University.

Pande, Rukmini. 2020. "How (Not) to Talk about Race: A Critique of Methodological Practices in Fan Studies." *Transformative Works and Cultures* 33. https://doi.org/10.3983/twc.2020.1737.

Pearson, Roberta. 2007. "Bachies, Bardies, Trekkies, and Sherlockians." *Fandom: Identities and Communities in a Mediated World* 102: 98–109.

Penley, Constance. 1997. *NASA/Trek: Popular Science and Sex in America*. New York: Verso.

Peterson, Richard A., and Roger M. Kern. 1996. "Changing Highbrow Taste: From Snob to Omnivore." *American Sociological Review* 61, no. 5: 900–907.

Pietsch, Bryan. 2020. " 'Magic: The Gathering' Pulls Racist Playing Cards from Popular Game." *New York Times*, June 22.

Poe, Julia. 2020. "Fans Organize FIFA 20 Tournament to Fill Void during Coronavirus Break." *Orlando Sentinel*, March 31.

Porat, Amir Ben. 2010. "Football Fandom: A Bounded Identification." *Soccer & Society* 11, no. 3: 277–290.

Price, John, Neil Farrington, and Lee Hall. 2013. "Changing the Game? The Impact of Twitter on Relationships between Football Clubs, Supporters and the Sports Media." *Soccer & Society* 14, no. 4: 446–461.

Pugh, Sheenagh. 2005. *The Democratic Genre: Fan Fiction in a Literary Context*. Bridgend, UK: Seren.

Sandvoss, Cornel. 2004. *A Game of Two Halves: Football Fandom, Television and Globalisation*. London and New York: Routledge.

Sandvoss, Cornel. 2005a. *Fans: The Mirror of Consumption*. Cambridge: Polity.

Sandvoss, Cornel. 2005b. "One-Dimensional Fan: Toward an Aesthetic of Fan Texts." *American Behavioral Scientist* 48, no. 7: 822–839.

Sandvoss, Cornel. 2017. "The Death of the Reader? Literary Theory and the Study of Texts in Popular Culture." In *Fandom: Identities and Communities in a Mediate World*, edited by J. Gray, C. Sandvoss, and C. L. Harrington, 29–44. New York: New York University Press.

Sandvoss, Cornel, Jonathan Gray, and C. Lee Harrington. 2017. "Introduction: Why Still Study Fans?" In *Fandom: Identities and Communities in a Mediated World*, edited by J. Gray, C. Sandvoss, and C. L. Harrington, 1–26. New York: New York University Press.

Scardaville, Melissa C. 2005. "Accidental Activists: Fan Activism in the Soap Opera Community." *American Behavioral Scientist* 48, no. 7: 881–901.

Schimmel, Kimberly S., C. Lee Harrington, and Denise D. Bielby. 2007. "Keep Your Fans to Yourself: The Disjuncture between Sport Studies' and Pop Culture Studies' Perspectives on Fandom." *Sport in Society* 10, no. 4: 580–600.

Schreyer, Christine. 2015. "The Digital Fandom of Na'vi Speakers." *Transformative Works and Cultures* 18. https://doi.org/10.3983/twc.2015.0610.

Scott, Suzanne. 2019. *Fake Geek Girls: Fandom, Gender, and the Convergence Culture Industry*. New York: New York University Press.

Shresthova, Sangita. 2011. *Is It All about Hips? Around the World with Bollywood Dance*. New Delhi, India: SAGE Publishing.

Slack, Andrew. 2010. "Cultural Acupuncture and a Future for Social Change." *Huffington Post*, July 2.

Stanfill, Mel. 2011. "Doing Fandom, (Mis)Doing Whiteness: Heteronormativity, Racialization, and the Discursive Construction of Fandom." *Transformative Works and Cultures* 8. https://doi.org/10.3983/twc.2011.0256.

Stryker, Sheldon, and Peter J. Burke. 2000. "The Past, Present, and Future of an Identity Theory." *Social Psychology Quarterly* 63, no. 4: 284–297.

Stryker, Sheldon, and Richard T. Serpe. 1994. "Identity Salience and Psychological Centrality: Equivalent, Overlapping, or Complementary Concepts?" *Social Psychology Quarterly* 57, no. 1: 16–35.

Swedberg, Richard. 2018. "How to Use Max Weber's Ideal Type in Sociological Analysis." *Journal of Classical Sociology* 18, no. 3: 181–196.

Tarrow, Sidney. 2005. *The New Transnational Activism*. Cambridge: Cambridge University Press.

Thomas, Lynne M., and Tara O'Shea, eds. 2010. *Chicks Dig Time Lords: A Celebration of Doctor Who by the Women Who Love It*. Des Moines, IA: Mad Norwegian Press.

Thornton, Sarah. 1996. *Club Cultures: Music, Media, and Subcultural Capital*. Middletown, CT: Wesleyan University Press.

Tulloch, John, and Henry Jenkins. 1995. *Science Fiction Audiences: Watching Doctor Who and Star Trek*. London and New York: Routledge.

Wanzo, Rebecca. 2015. "African American Acafandom and Other Strangers: New Genealogies of Fan Studies." *Transformative Works and Cultures* 20. https://doi.org/10.3983/twc.2015.0699.

Warde, Alan. 2015. "The Sociology of Consumption: Its Recent Development." *Annual Review of Sociology* 41: 117–134.

Wilson, Carl. 2007. *Celine Dion's Let's Talk about Love: A Journey to the End of Taste*. New York: Continuum.

CHAPTER 21

TROLLS AND HACKTIVISTS

Political Mobilization from Online Communities

JESSICA L. BEYER

IN 2008, when Anonymous emerged as an activist movement, the collective operated within the lineage of hacktivist movements, aesthetics, and tactics (Coleman 2012a, 2014; Beyer 2014a; Sauter 2014). Anonymous' birthplace was 4chan and other chans—posting boards with highly offensive content that had come to represent trolling culture online (Phillips 2015 Norton 2011). Anonymous appeared from chan culture at a time when scholars were grappling with the changes the internet and digital media were causing in social movement organization, focus, and form (Bennett and Segerberg 2012; Earl and Kimport 2011) and so immediately drew interest as a new kind of movement, born wholly from the internet (Beyer 2014a; Coleman 2014).

Anonymous' star has long since been eclipsed, its numbers diminished, and its direct impact relatively spent. However, Anonymous' tactics and mode of political action, born from the chans and refined through Gamergate and the politics of the 2016 election, have continued to provide a template for organized online movements. As the anti-censorship and freedom of information movements that came out of these websites in the late aughts have faded, spaces such as 4chan have instead fostered extremists, have become fruitful sites for White supremacist recruiting, and have been deeply intertwined with the rise of the alt-right. The continued impact of these spaces means it is important to understand the role that highly populated online communities have and continue to play in politics.

As the linked cases in this chapter illustrate, mobilizations build on each other, group identity is durable, and changing political and social contexts shape events. In the sections that follow I discuss the theory that informs the study of online groups and mobilization. Then, I examine 4chan, its so-called trolling culture, and the development of collective action repertoires there that later online mobilizations have refined and used as core tactics. I follow this with a discussion of the emergence and separation of Anonymous from 4chan and trace the cultural elements from 4chan that continued to shape Anonymous' public presentation. Finally, I discuss the refinement of a set of violent forms of action from the original 4chan mobilization template combined with new allies and networks more closely tied to partisan politics in sections on Gamergate and the 2016 US presidential election.

UNDERSTANDING POLITICAL MOBILIZATION IN ONLINE COMMUNITIES

Scholars attempting to understand political mobilization arising from online communities initially focused on Anonymous. Anonymous has served as a focus not only because it was the first major primarily online movement but also because it emerged from chan culture at a time when scholars were working to understand the role the internet played in traditional politics writ large (Bennett, Freelon, and Wells 2010; Beyer 2014a; Bimber and Davis 2003; Chadwick and Howard 2010; Diani 2000; Earl and Kimport 2011; Milan 2013). Prior to 2012, many scholars thought of hybrid online–offline movements as positive, although some were beginning to warn that internet affordances granted capacity not only to activists but also to repressive governments (Howard 2011; Morozov 2011a). Utopic ideals about internet technology, hacktivist histories, and the role of the internet in the Arab Spring shaped a sense of optimism regarding the role the internet could have in democracy and democratic movements among those studying the internet.

Much of the work looking at the internet vis-à-vis social movements has focused on the ways in which internet affordances have changed the organizational form that is necessary for a successful social movement (Bennett and Segerberg 2012; Nicholls, Uitermark, and van Haperen 2016; Tufekci 2017), the tools that activists and others have gained for collective action because of the internet (Daniels 2009; Earl and Kimport 2011; Ray et al. 2017), the ways in which overall societal change and political shocks have worked in concert with the rise of the internet's role in movements (Castells 2000, 2015; Rohlinger and Brown 2009), and whether organizing via social media translates into political power (Freelon, McIlwain, and Clark 2018; Schradie 2019). Research that has focused on how online tools, communities, and networks facilitate offline political action has found clear impacts (Tufekci and Wilson 2012). For instance, the Black Lives Matter movement, which draws on social media to circulate movement narratives, succeeded in educating casual observers in places such as Twitter (Freelon, McIlwain, and Clark 2016). Freelon, McIlwain, and Clark (2018) using Bennett and Segerberg's (2013 typology argued that Black Lives Matter is an "organizationally enabled network" because it operates both online and in the streets. In another example, Howard and Hussain (2013) argued that digital media were integral to the Arab Spring because they built solidarity networks, shamed political elites, organized large numbers of protesters, and in the aftermath, offered competing visions for the future from various sectors of society.

In relation to the impact of the internet on movements, scholars have also focused on how broader cultural changes have meant a rise of "self-directed versus organizationally directed political consumption" (Earl, Copeland, and Bimber 2017; Boy and Uitermark 2019) and how the surges of engagement without organization-building—or the problem of "weak ties" (Diani 2000)—within movements can hurt movement sustainability (Beyer 2014a; Tufekci 2017). Research has also addressed the issues with separating online and offline movements into different categories (Jurgenson 2012; Maher and Earl 2019) as well as how participants' sometimes contradictory feelings about the role of social media influence participant longevity (Rohlinger and Bunnage 2017).

All four of the cases examined in this chapter engage with the literature outlined so far in this section, but all four cases are also distinct in that the mobilization related to each occurred nearly entirely online. When considering collective action that was purely online, such as that emerging from online fandom, Earl and Kimport (2011) and Earl and Schussman (2002) argued that this type of behavior should be considered a social movement. In their examination of the strategic voting movement in 2000, a campaign that was run almost entirely online, Earl and Schussman (2002, 2004; Schussman and Earl 2004) found that online resources included educational sites, sites that linked voters to each other, and sites where voters could "pledge" their votes from a "safe" state. They also found that the people starting and running these sites were not longtime activists but people who had only some political experience.

Earl and Kimport (2011) built upon these findings to show how the internet facilitates a range of activism with a continuum of action. First, Earl and Kimport (2011, 12) argued that e-mobilizations are instances in which the internet is used to "facilitate the sharing of information in the service of an offline protest action." Second, they argued that "e-tactics" include on- and offline elements such as petitions, boycotts, email campaigns, and letter writing campaigns. These actions are mostly low-cost and do not necessitate that people be co-located. Finally, they asserted that there are *e-movements*, or movements that occur entirely online. Each of these points on Earl and Kimport's continuum captures the leverage internet affordances provide in different ways, but all illustrate the transformative impact the internet has had on organizing. All four of the cases discussed in this chapter could be considered "e-movements," and in one of the four cases, Anonymous, participants engaged in e-tactics as well as offline protest.

Also working to understand the role of the internet in social movements, Bennett and Segerberg (2012) argued that there has been a rise of personalized collective action that digital tools facilitate—something they contrast with collective action from traditional social movements. To understand contemporary political action, they argued that we must consider personal action frames and social media networks—instances where the reasons for action are personalized rather than based on higher-level identities such as social group. Bennett and Segerberg (2012, 748) named this the "logic of connective action," arguing that formal organizational power has diminished as social media have gained power, allowing for action without "the symbolic construction of a united 'we.'" Under the rubric that Bennett and Segerberg developed (2012, 756), mobilizations such as Anonymous and others arising from 4chan would be considered "self-organizing networks," which they defined as entities with

> Little or no organizational coordination of action; large scale personal access to multi-layered social technologies; communication content centers on emergent inclusive personal action frames; personal expression shared over social networks; collectivities often shun involvement of existing formal organizations.

While the action that arose from the chans—both the earlier, less focused collective action and the later, more politically motivated action—fulfills Bennett and Segerberg's definition of a self-organizing network, in contrast with their overall framework, the action also operates under a clear understanding of a united "we." That "we" is structured not within organizational boundaries or as connected to an existing social category but rather as a collective identity related to the online community. To understand this collective identity, or "we-ness," I use Polletta and Jasper's (2001, 285) definition:

> An individual's cognitive, moral, and emotional connection with a broader community, category, practice, or institution. It is a perception of a shared status or relation, which may be imagined rather than experienced directly, and it is distinct from personal identities, although it may form part of a personal identity ... collective identities are expressed in cultural materials—names, narratives, symbols, verbal styles, rituals, clothing, and so on.

As will be discussed, the collective action from the chans was possible due to a strong sense of community culture that developed in anonymous and ephemeral spaces. Shared discourse, affirmation of group values, and a history of collective action on the chans created an identity that became a base for mobilization, with many of the cultural trademarks visible in the chans remaining a part of other movements, such as Anonymous (Beyer 2014a).

The affordances of some online spaces help build a sense of "we" that allows for resolution of what Bennett and Segerberg (2012) called "frame conflicts." In every case in this chapter, centrally articulated community values, underpinned by a strong sense of collective identity, serve as a type of "boundary object." A boundary object is an object that has local meaning but also meaning across many communities (Star and Griesemer 1989). In each case, a particular community value may not mean the same thing to all participants, but its role as a boundary object serves to bridge potential conflict (Beyer 2014a). As will be discussed, in the case of 4chan, this boundary object is the "lulz." For Anonymous, it is a conception of freedom of information and, possibly, helping those who cannot help themselves. For Gamergate, the boundary object is an articulation of a set of grievances with the idea that feminism and "PC culture" are ruining gaming. In the case focusing on support for Donald Trump's campaign in the 2016 election, the articulation of a set of mobilizing ideas such as anti-feminism, anti-immigration, racism, and misogyny serves as the boundary object.

In all of these cases, as Bennett and Segerberg (2012) argued, digital media sit as a central organizing agent. But in the cases of online communities, this centrality is not only the ways in which, as Earl and Kimport (2011) argued, internet affordances are leveraged to disseminate a movement's message or organize a particular action. The affordances of each website—such as 4chan—first shape the participants on that site itself, creating distinct community cultures that react to and use the opportunities the internet presents in community-based ways. For the cases in this chapter, these include, most importantly, anonymity and lack of extensive content moderation in core community and organizing spaces, which help to generate communities more likely to engage in collective action vis-à-vis the outside world and traditional politics (Beyer 2014a).

As Tilly (1986) argued, organizers and activists operate using a "repertoire of contention" that is intimately wrapped up in a given historical moment. In later work, Tilly (1995, 26) argued that repertoires are "learned cultural creations." In social movements, these repertoires have included tactics such as sit-ins, petitions, media statements, and boycotts. Tilly also points out that activists are products of their environments, and the historical moments in which they find themselves shape how they choose to perform protest. It is true that within the cultural framework of the chans, users mobilized against an opponent using methods that were "traditional" for that community. However, the users on 4chan and other chans were not activists in 2008 when the subsection of the community that became Anonymous began mobilizing against the Church of Scientology. Instead, each group of actors drew upon sets of collective behaviors that had been refined in the community through years of non-political collective action, including group "raids" on other websites, cooperative creation of memes and cultural content, and targeted harassment of individuals. As political mobilizations emerged from the chans—Anonymous, Gamergate, and the 2016 "trolling" armies—each drew on 4chan's collective action model to build repertoires of contention, but each refined them in relation to their political goals.

What has made the Anonymous and post-Anonymous 4chan mobilizations effective politically is their ability to draw on the affordances of the internet to facilitate participatory online culture (Burgess 2008), the use of the overall social media ecology to move messages to new audiences, and the connection of online communities to existing political action networks (Marwick and Lewis 2017). For instance, the effectiveness of 4chan, 8chan, and other online communities in mobilizing on behalf of Donald Trump's presidential campaign was due to their linking to an existing fringe right-wing informational ecosystem and that ecosystem's activists—a process that began during Gamergate. However, Gamergate and the 2016 US presidential election brought new and chilling tactics to modern partisan politics. These tactics used original 4chan templates for collective action but refined these templates through Gamergate and the support of Donald Trump's presidential campaign, creating highly effective forms of digital abuse (Sobieraj 2018, 2020) and networked harassment (Lewis, Marwick, and Partin 2021).

4CHAN AND TROLLING CULTURE

Studies of 4chan and chan culture often have argued that 4chan as a community was perfectly representational of trolling culture online—so much so that 4chan has become synonymous with the term "trolling" (Phillips 2015). It is this trolling culture that provided the basis for collective mobilization from 4chan.

However, discussions of trolling as an online phenomenon predate 4chan's existence—and trolling has always been understood as a characteristic of all online communities (Bartle 1996; Dibbell 1993, 2008; Donath 1999; Herring et al. 2002). Early trolling scholars would probably not have even called themselves "trolling" scholars because bad behavior online was differentiated into categories such as "flaming" (Bartle 1996; Kayany 1998), which happened in many kinds of online spaces; "griefing" (Bakioğlu 2009; Bartle 1996; Dahlberg 2001; Yee 2005), which tended to be confined to online games; and a more performance-based, playful type of trolling that could be benign and performative in nature (Bergstrom 2011; Hardaker 2010), as well as generally abusive behavior that appeared across online communities.

As the conversation about trolling developed, another conception of trolling emerged as well—the idea that trolls were playing a game for their own enjoyment, a game often at the expense of others (Dibbell 2008; Donath 1999; Hardaker 2010, 237). In line with this, scholars have examined the transgressive nature of trolling culture (Beyer 2014a; Coleman 2014, 2016, 2017; Phillips 2015) and the role of humor in trolling as a focus of community mobilization in relation to 4chan (Coleman 2012a, 2012b; Sauter 2014). Researchers also focused on trolling as a subculture and as a characteristic of a broader set of political activities that emerged from some online communities, including 4chan, during the early 2000s (Bakioğlu 2012; Beyer 2014a; Coleman 2014; Phillips 2015).

As academic work refined the concept of trolling as related to collective mobilization from online communities, the term moved into popular discourse and has come to mean any bad behavior both online and off (Phillips 2020; Phillips, Beyer, and Coleman 2017). The popularization of the term "trolling" also led to the abandonment of terms that referred to subtypes of trolling that earlier work focused on—for example, discussions of "flaming" more or less disappeared and conversations about "griefing" became confined to discussions about gaming (Bakioğlu 2019; Bergstrom 2020). Scholars, notably Phillips (2016), have sounded the alarm at the flattening of trolling as a concept because it collapses all bad behavior into a single category. This single category can then include everything from pranks to the use of language that does harm to individuals or groups to *swatting* (the practice of attempting to compel a SWAT team to show up at someone's house). Flattening all bad behavior into one category compounds the more serious harmful behavior with the trivial (Phillips 2016; Phillips, Beyer, and Coleman 2017). As Phillips and Milner (2017, 7) argued, "it would appear that trolls are everywhere, doing everything."

4chan and a United "We"

The cohesive "trolling" culture that developed on 4chan was used as a basis for mobilization. 4chan was born in 2003 when Christopher Poole, then a high school student, created it as an English-language version of the Japanese anime-focused website Futaba Channel or 2chan (Beyer 2014a; Coleman 2014). Quickly 4chan's no-topic or /b/ board became its heart, with the bulk of the traffic to the board ending up there. 4chan was built on an open-source image-board framework, and over time others built other "chans" such as 7chan, 420chan, and 711chan. Some of these sites had large audiences and were stable and long-lived, such as 7chan. Some were gated, with people allowed only by invitation (Beyer 2014a). Many were unstable, appearing and disappearing as those hosting the sites stopped maintaining them (Beyer 2014a). These sites were related in the sense that they shared cultural characteristics, including a commitment to anonymity and low levels of content moderation. Content moderation, although universally low, could vary from board to board. For instance, on some of the chans administrators allowed people to talk about and organize attacks on other online communities, share resources about how to hack people, and post content that could be of interest to law enforcement. But other chan systems did not allow this type of content (Beyer 2014a).

4chan and the other chans tended to be anonymous, without user names or other features that were present in many other online forums (Auerbach 2012; Bernstein et al. 2011; Beyer 2014a; Coleman 2012c, 2014). On 4chan, each poster posted as the user name "Anonymous." The combination of anonymity and little content moderation meant that the content on these sites was often offensive and disturbing. Posters regularly used racial slurs, posted misogynist content, constantly used homophobic language, and then co-opted the ubiquitous offensive material as part of community inside jokes (Beyer 2014a; Manivannan 2013; Milner 2013). Following is a quote that captures the boards' particular posting style from a different board than 4chan but a board that became central to Anonymous' 2008 anti-Scientology mobilization (please be warned: This quotation contains offensive and upsetting language) (Beyer 2014a, 30):

> WE ARE AN INTERNETZ HAET MACHINE, NOT SOME FUCKING MERCENARY GROUP THAT JUST ATTACKS SHIT YOU DISAGREE WITH AND THAT WILL HAVE NO LULZ-POTENTIAL. PEOPLE YOU WANT TO EXALT YOUR REVENGE ON AND THAT MAD YOU BAWWWWWWWWW. WE DON'T CARE. GO CRY SOME MORE, EMOKID. PEOPLE YOU WANT TO EXALT ANYSHIT ON, THAT PROVIDE NO FUCKING LUZ FOR ANYONE EXCEPT FOR YOU, YOU FAG: SUCH AS YOUR RETARDED TEACHER, YOUR MAMA, YOUR 5-YEAR OLD BROTHER BECAUSE HE DIDN'T WANT TO SUCK YOUR COCK ETC. LULZ AND RAIDWORTHY TARGETS: -CHATROOMS, WEBSITES, WEBCAM CHATS, FAGGY FAGS WHO ARE EVIDENTLY FAGGING MY INTERWUBZ UP WITH THEIR BULLSHIT AND RETARDEDNESS SO THAT IT IS VISIBLE FOR ANYONE, SOCIAL NETWORKING SITES, GAMES, GAMESITES, BDSM-FAGS, ISLAMISTS, CHRISTUNS, BUDDISTS, VEGANS,

BEEFEATERS, RETARDED PEOPLE, ANYTHING AS LONG AS IT IS TRULY FUCKING FUNNY AND NOT JUST BASED NO YOUR VERY OWN DISLIKE. Reposted. And yes, this scientology raids fucking suck. This needs sticky. Everyone who participated in them should be ashamed of themselves.

Site affordances also shaped chan culture (Beyer 2014a). Posts on 4chan and other chans are ephemeral. They are not saved and disappear quickly, so they are not searchable (Bernstein et al. 2011; Beyer 2014a). This means that there is no way for new members to access community history without reading old members' current accounts of that history or without consulting off-site repositories that were and are not reliable—such as Encyclopedia Dramatica. People posting on 4chan and the other chans have no ability to signal their own distinct identity through user names, post counts, or other identifiers (Beyer 2014a). Spaces with identification elements such as user names cause users to protect their online identities, even when they are posting under a pseudonym because the pseudonym itself gains a reputation (Beyer 2014a). However, in the anonymous chans, users instead signal their status as community members through proper use of a dense lexicon, citation of community jokes and stories, and ability to articulate community values (Beyer 2014a). All of this is done under conditions of anonymity and without any in-board features that allow one-on-one conversation, thus replacing one's individual or group indicators with a collective identity (Beyer 2014a). Unlike other online communities, such as World of Warcraft realms, the 4chan community is cohesive in presentation but with fewer personal bonds (Beyer 2014a). Even so, the shared discourse, behaviors, repetition of group values, and history of collective action create a high level of group cohesion and tools that can be drawn on for collective action (Beyer 2014a).

4chan and Repertoires of Contention

Scholars identified the core cultural value on 4chan as entertainment for entertainment's sake, or what the community called "lulz" (Auerbach 2012; Beyer 2014a; Coleman 2014; Knuttila 2011, 2015; Simcoe 2012). In pursuit of the lulz, 4chan and the other chans engaged in collective action—usually in the form of "raids" against other online communities. Raids included a range of attack tactics but were meant to disrupt the service of other websites. The raids were sometimes on behalf of a community member, but most of the chans included a note/rule posted on their boards along the lines of, "We are not your personal army, we will not raid your ex or some rando person without lulzy motivation" (Beyer 2014a, 30). Some scholars (Phillips, Beyer, and Coleman 2017; Simcoe 2012) have argued that these raids sometimes had a proto-political flavor. However, although they included attacks on White supremacists such as Hal Turner or were sometimes related to animal protection, as the community frequently targeted people who posted videos of animal cruelty, there were no clear cohesive political agendas in these raids. For every raid on a White supremacist there were more raids characterized by banal cruelty, such as gaining access to naked photos of young women online and then distributing them to people they knew (Beyer 2014a).

On the chans, a set of "raid" tactics—or repertoires of contention—developed. The central tactics include doxing, brigading, distributed denial of service (DDOS) attacks, astroturfing, and organized griefing and harassment (Beyer 2014a).[1] A set of these tactics focuses on obtaining information about someone and using it to harm them—such as trying to make someone lose their job—through the practice of doxing. *Doxing* involves uncovering information about an individual such as their legal name, address, family information, place of employment, and other personal details and then making these details public. Making the information public allows anyone to pick up the information and harass the person who has been doxed. Doxing is tied to other types of harassment, such as *brigading*, which is an organized harassment tactic where a group of people work together to target someone in a sustained way. Common brigading practices include mailing a large number of pizzas to a target's house or faxing reams of black paper to a target. Doxing also is tied to the practice of uncovering private, and often embarrassing, information and making it public (Beyer 2014a; Sobieraj 2020). In the case of the chans, people would look for embarrassing materials associated with someone who was a doxing target already or, in other instances, look for embarrassing materials such as naked photographs and then attempt to dox the person in the photos in order to harass them (Beyer 2014a).

Other central raid tactics are less individually focused but are also harmful, such as DDOS attacks, astroturfing, and griefing (Beyer 2014a). *DDOS attacks* involve flooding a computational system with so many requests that it ceases to function. DDOS attacks are both a cybercriminal and a hacktivist tactic that predates 4chan but that became a 4chan raid tactic. 4chan used DDOS attacks to target the websites of rival online communities and other perceived enemies (Sauter 2014). In the past it was possible for an organized group of people to successfully DDOS a system and bring it offline, but in 2021 this is usually impossible without the help of a botnet.[2] *Astroturfing* is making a coordinated campaign meant to express political sentiment appear to be a spontaneous and earnest swelling of sentiment rather than one that is coordinated. Organized *griefing* occurs when large numbers of people flood online video games and disrupt gameplay, as was done during the Habbo Hotel raid in 2006 (Beyer 2014a).

4chan and the other chans are not the only examples of online communities where collective action was present. On other posting boards, people organized complex gift-giving activities around holidays (Beyer 2014a). In online video games, people organized gay pride parades that spanned warring factions and were protected by the broader community (Beyer 2014a). However, it was 4chan's tactics that became the template for online community political mobilization.

Anonymous and the Move to Hacktivism

As the previous section illustrates, 4chan and the other chans were unlikely places to give birth to Anonymous, an online movement that became grounded in ideas such as speaking for those who could not speak for themselves, anti-censorship, and freedom of expression. Although Anonymous was born out of 4chan, Anonymous left 4chan behind. But Anonymous used and expanded the tactics and tools that were developed as part of 4chan raids.

Anonymous emerged in 2008 after the Church of Scientology successfully petitioned most news organizations and websites to take down an unflattering video of Tom Cruise talking about the benefits of Scientology (Beyer 2014a; Coleman 2014; Olson 2012). In response to what was seen as censorship, 4chan and other chan users calling themselves "Anonymous" began to mobilize against the Church of Scientology. Anonymous' foray into political action began with "traditional" 4chan raid tactics such DDOS attacks and moved to street protests and letter-writing campaigns to request that the Church of Scientology's tax-free status be revoked.

Anonymous' United "We"

Key to Anonymous' mobilization was the strong identity that emerged from 4chan and its shared history of collective action. Anonymous operated within the same cultural context, particularly initially. However, although Anonymous and the chans had a shared iconography, Anonymous was not necessarily a single unified group, nor was it tied to the chans after 2008. Before 2008, posters on 4chan—as well as other chans—often referred to themselves collectively as "Anonymous" (Phillips 2015; Beyer 2014a; Coleman 2012c, 2013, 2014). After 2008, the people who rejected the anti-Scientology mobilization no longer used the name Anonymous. Instead, it came to refer only to the political collective that now contained both people who had come out of the chan systems as well as those who had come across Anonymous as a political actor, liked what they saw, and joined (Beyer 2014a; Coleman 2014).

As Anonymous incorporated new participants—many of whom had never visited a chan—there were debates about how to engage with these new people (Beyer 2014a). Some proposed cleaning up the shared language developed on 4chan so as not to "scare" away new people. Others argued that Anonymous had to remain true to its roots (Beyer 2014a). In the end, the influx of new participants changed Anonymous, although many of its shared cultural characteristics with 4chan remained (Beyer 2014a; Coleman 2014). For instance, Anonymous continued to use iconography such as the Guy Fawkes mask, retained a commitment to anonymity, and remained committed to participatory culture. Furthermore, like 4chan's raids, Anonymous' structure was non-hierarchical with no clear internal structure or boundaries between the many groups that made up Anonymous. Although there were experts who designed tools, hosted websites, led educational efforts, created press releases, and helped the community, there were no real leaders (Beyer 2014b; Coleman 2014; Norton 2012). Decisions to mobilize were informal and involved someone proposing an activity, and then if enough people agreed to do it, it was done. Different factions within Anonymous rose and fell, and it was possible for different factions to disagree (Coleman 2014).

Anonymous' Repertoire of Contention

The action that marked the birth of Anonymous began as a "raid" against the Church of Scientology in January 2008. The action drew upon the repertoire of tactics that had been developed over Anonymous members' time on the chans. These tactics included doxing the Church of Scientology for potentially incriminating and secret church materials, doxing church officials, DDOS attacks on Church of Scientology websites, faxing reams of black paper to church offices, and sending hundreds of pizzas to church offices (Beyer 2014a).

Initial language around the action was in line with community values, framing it as an entertaining raid. However, Anonymous quickly began to shift orientation—adopting new tactics that were more in line with traditional movement practices. Organically, the language used in the community to discuss the action began to change to articulate a set of higher principles for the action, such as speaking for people who could not speak for themselves—such as the church's victims (Beyer 2014a). At the same time, among complaints from 4chan users who were not participating in the anti-Scientology action that the Scientology raid was neither entertaining nor something that belonged on 4chan, 4chan's administrator banned discussion of the operation entirely. Public organization and recruiting then moved to other board systems in the chan ecosystem (Beyer 2014a) and to Internet Relay Chat (IRC) channels (Coleman 2014). Simultaneously, new people began to join the anti-Scientology actions, including longtime anti-Scientology activists. In response, divisions began to appear among Anonymous about the types of tactics that should be used. A combination of new participants and existing Anonymous members began to argue that use of the "traditional" 4chan raid tactics was weakening the overall movement. Others maintained that Anonymous needed to remain true to its origins and pursue tactics that were both in line with their political goals as well as entertaining (Beyer 2014a).

Along with the new influx of people, participants began proposing and enacting more traditional movement tactics such as petitions, letter-writing campaigns, and in-person protests (Beyer 2014a). On February 10, 2008, street protests were held in front of Church of Scientology offices around the world at 11:00 a.m. local time in 108 cities across 17 countries (Beyer 2014a). These protests involved 5,000–8,000 people who arrived with signs showing the same messaging, handed out flyers that were the same but were customized to locality, and, when interviewed, framed the issue and the protest in the same ways. Monthly protests followed the February protest. Underpinning the protests were active online educational campaigns about how to protest safely, how to obey local laws, and how to talk about the action if asked (Beyer 2014a).

As time went on, Anonymous attempted to recruit new people to its varied "ops" and disseminated its message broadly (Beyer 2014a; Coleman 2014). To do this, Anonymous used social media platforms such as Twitter and YouTube. On Twitter, Anonymous accounts shared information about objectives, coordinated action, and disseminated political messages. On YouTube, Anonymous members created news stations and produced information both for those involved in Anonymous action and people interested in joining. In places such as the IRC, people engaged in collective decision-making, coordinated actions such as DDOS attacks, and collectively produced memes and other materials to disseminate on other platforms (Beyer 2014a, 2014b; Coleman 2014).

Many viewed Anonymous' actions in relation to the broader societal context and an optimistic view of the internet's role in democracy—seeing it as an example of how political power could be formed and exercised online in ways that were positive for democracy—in spite of 4chan, its birthplace. Overall societal context was key to this assessment. Anonymous emerged at the tail end of the Bush administration when the dramatic expansion of the surveillance state had the backdrop of the increasingly ubiquitous nature of internet technology in the United States and abroad. At the same time, the internet appeared to be fostering major democratizations in places such as Egypt (Howard and Hussain 2013) and our current pessimistic understanding of online interaction had not yet taken hold (Persily 2017). Nor had concerns about the ways in which the internet would facilitate deeper surveillance become a major element of public conversation, although some such as Morozov (2011b) as well as activist groups were pointing it out. The Swedish Pirate Party's 2009 election into the European Parliament seemed to indicate that the digital rights movement was gaining wider leverage (Beyer 2014a). It was a time of optimism about the power of the internet to transform politics in positive ways.

After the Scientology protests and its break with 4chan, Anonymous engaged in actions on behalf of the file-sharing site The Pirate Bay, supported protests during the Arab Spring, mobilized on behalf of WikiLeaks, worked on behalf of Occupy Wall Street, breached and then leaked documents from organizations such as the Ku Klux Klan, and engaged in innumerable other actions on behalf of freedom of information, anti-censorship, transparency, and democracy (Coleman 2014). While the behavior in the chans had been largely without political focus, Anonymous focused on freedom of information and anti-censorship. In this, its ethos was formed and operated in the lineage of the overall historical arc of hacktivist movements (Beyer 2014b; Beyer and McKelvey 2015; Coleman 2014; Sauter 2014; Söderberg 2008). *Hacktivists* are activists that use hacking to further activist goals (Manion and Goodrum 2000). Well-known hacktivist groups include the Electronic Disturbance Theater and the Cult of the Dead Cow (Menn 2019; Sauter 2014). Other activities are also often considered in the lineage of hacktivism, such as phreaking (Coleman 2014; Donovan 2016; Lapsley 2013).[3]

Anonymous also fits into a broader history of hackers in general. While there is a debate about whether there is a single "hacker" politics (Coleman 2014), there is a vein of hacker politics that emphasizes open information flow, freedom of speech, and transparency. These are some of the elements that Coleman (2012b) named as the "productive freedom" that hackers are committed to. Coleman (2012b, 3) argued that this productive freedom is the "institutions, legal devices, and moral codes that hackers have built in order to autonomously improve on their peers' work, refine their technical skills, and extend craftlike engineering traditions." Coleman (2012b) asserted that hackers challenge a core element of liberal jurisprudence, intellectual property; therefore, hacking is inherently a political project even if that is not explicitly articulated.

In addition, Anonymous' actions had a relationship to freedom of information sentiment (Jordan and Taylor 2004; Levy 1984) and the protection of the information commons (Earl and Beyer 2014). Elements of this relationship include an open-source culture and a focus on radical transparency (Coleman 2012b; Kelty 2008; Raymond 2001; Sauter 2014). Anonymous also was tied to the digital rights movement (Gillespie 2007; Postigo 2012) as well as to the pirate movements that were a part of the overall digital rights landscape (Beyer and McKelvey 2015; Burkart 2014; McKelvey 2015).

Gamergate and the Diffusion of Tactics

The optimism about 4chan and Anonymous was quickly proven wrong. Anonymous became a separate political force and moved out of the chans, and what remained in the chans were the same site affordances and offensive content but without members interested in political action focused on freedom of information (Phillips, Beyer, Coleman 2017; Beyer 2014a; Coleman 2014). In addition, the societal context was changing. As Anonymous was diminishing in size and impact around 2012, the same affordances of 4chan and other sites like it were fostering other political mobilizations, this time more in line with offensive site content. By 2012, mobilizations from 4chan and the other chans, such as Gamergate, had less to do with concerns about surveillance and freedom of information and more to do with a perceived loss of White, straight, cismale, hegemonic control of cultural production, likely tied to racism and Barack Obama's election (Daniels 2018), masculinity threat (Carian and Sobotka 2018), and misogyny (Dignam and Rohlinger 2019; Sobieraj 2020). These movements built on larger political ecosystems and networks, drawing together political affinity groups online (Marwick and Lewis 2017)—such as topic-specific sub-reddits where people aired grievances about "PC" culture, advocated for men's rights, argued about women's right to criticize online video games, and, ultimately, embraced extreme right news sources. These affinities laid the groundwork for what Marwick (2021) and Lewis, Marwick, and Partin (2021) refer to as "networked harassment," harassment with a foundation in moral outrage at perceived violations of an imagined social order.

Although scholars and journalists had focused on 4chan's culture and site affordances as elements in the emergence of Anonymous, the offensive content often was a side note to the story of chaotic online communities and the generation of political power online. Scholars studying 4chan and Anonymous mentioned it, most with concern (Beyer 2014a, 28, n3; Coleman 2014, 21, 26, 31–32, 41–42; Phillips 2015, 3); but they did not necessarily focus on the offensive content as a political position. In addition, as Anonymous emerged from 4chan, there was a debate about whether the language in online spaces such as 4chan was an example of boundary policing, meant to keep non-members out, or a genuine expression of belief (Auerbach 2012; Norton 2011). At the time, some mistakenly took the general 4chan ethos that nothing was serious combined with Anonymous' political orientation toward more leftist action as an indication that most people on 4chan might not actually mean the offensive language and imagery that they posted.

Gamergate's United "We"

Gamergate emerged from 4chan and other online spaces like it and drew on the same sense of online community-fostered identity. In 2011, 4chan's owner created the "politically incorrect" board or /pol/. It had been in existence in 2010, but he had deleted and re-created it because, as he said, it had become overrun with White supremacist posts (Scolyer-Gray 2018). However, after its re-creation in 2012, White supremacists began to notice the volume of offensive content and wondered if that meant there might actually be a sympathetic audience on 4chan. They then started successfully recruiting on the /pol/ board, in particular (Phillips, Beyer, and Coleman 2017). With the creation of the /pol/ board and boards with a deeply misogynistic "involuntary celibates" or "incels" focus such as /r9k/, the center of 4chan mobilization moved from the miscellaneous board (/b/) to places such as /pol/. The politically incorrect board, like the broader set of online forums such as racist sub-reddits, provided a place for extremist recruiters to potentially find inchoate White heterosexual cismale anger and channel it. One of the best examples of this was Gamergate, which was born not just from 4chan but from 4chan along with other sympathetic online forums such as Reddit forums (Gray, Buyukozturk, and Hill 2016; Massanari 2017).

Most scholars argue that Gamergate began in August 2014 following a lengthy post by Eron Kjoni in which he discussed a failed relationship with a female game developer (Gray, Buyukozturk, and Hill 2016; Massanari 2017). The post by Kjoni became a catalyst for many who felt that feminists and other progressives were trying to change (i.e., ruin) gaming. The argument loosely ran that "social justice warriors," particularly feminists, were infecting the gaming space with their agenda. These complaints could be seen in sub-reddits, in the comments on video game reviews, and on other posting boards prior to Gamergate itself. While the Gamergate party line was that its movement was about collusion between gaming developers and the journalists who review games, the major impact and focus of Gamergate was on women—developers, writers, critics, and academics—some of whom had to go into hiding because the organized harassment and threats against them were so terrifying and explicit that they feared for their safety (Murphy 2015). On Twitter, people were afraid to even use the term "Gamergate" for fear that it would draw organized harassment (McDonald 2014). Although initial conversations about Gamergate were seen on 4chan, 4chan's owner quickly banned the topic. Those sympathetic to the Gamergate movement then moved to 8chan—a site whose owner argued that he was defending radical freedom of speech and anonymity.

Gamergate organization also occurred on sub-reddits such as r/KotakuInAction and on Twitter (Gray, Buyukozturk, and Hill 2016; Massanari 2017).

As happened with Anonymous in 2008, existing networks of individuals with compatible agendas found each other and, buoyed by the opportunities offered by anonymous online spaces with little content moderation, organized (Massanari 2020). In this case, the baked-in hostility to people of color, women, and other minoritized groups that scholars such as Gray (2012a, 2012b, 2013, 2014), Beyer (2012), and Cote (2015) had documented in online spaces related to gaming became organized and virulent, spreading across sympathetic online spaces. Like Anonymous, although there were some prominent proponents of the movement, it was non-hierarchical and without a clear structure (Mortensen 2018, 792). However, in a major difference from Anonymous' mobilization, extreme right-wing activists, many already involved in long-standing men's rights mobilizations (O'Donnell 2020), helped to articulate Gamergate's political platform (Chess and Shaw 2015; Massanari 2017; Mortensen 2018; Salter 2018).

People who played games and who spent time in gaming spaces before 2012 were quite familiar with the set of ideas Gamergate encapsulated (Beyer 2012; Consalvo 2012; Gray 2014; Gray, Buyukozturk, and Hill 2016), which meant that the earlier understanding of 4chan's content as ambient but not mobilizing was wrong. Right-wing and White supremacist activists had been correct—people really did mean the terrible things they were posting and could be mobilized into collective action.

Gamergate's Repertoire of Contention

As had happened in Anonymous' initial mobilization, participants organized on public boards. The campaign also drew on similar tactics to those Anonymous used to spread messages outside the internet subcultures where Gamergate had been born. Users drew on Twitter hashtags and publicity campaigns, YouTube videos, and other more popular platforms to spread Gamergate's message and recruit allies (Social Justice Bread 2014; Johnson 2014).

Much of the mobilization consisted of organized harassment campaigns that used many of the same methods that had been developed on 4chan and other chans prior to 2008 as "raid" tactics. For instance, Gamergate doxed, or uncovered and publicized information about, perceived opponents, opening them up to violent threats and harassment. Gamergate engaged in swatting as a central tactic and worked to collectively identify targets and then engage in organized harassment. Anyone who criticized Gamergate was targeted (Hern 2015), prominent women who worked in the video game industry were targeted (Stuart 2014), and academics using feminist or critical lenses to understand video game culture were targeted (Straumsheim 2014).

Most of these tactics, and others used, harkened back to 4chan. However, by 2012 these tactics had been refined. While 4chan users had moved between targets and had varied intent, Gamergate turned them into a singular focus tied to a single political agenda. Much as Anonymous had been made up of many subparts, often working together and sometimes apart toward a single overarching set of ideals grounded in freedom of information and anti-censorship, a single unifying articulation of a culture war mobilized Gamergate. In embracing that single articulation, harassment tactics were refined and focused. And these refined harassment tactics continue to be used against individuals from minoritized groups online (Sobieraj 2020).

Internet Subcultures and the 2016 US Presidential Election

If Gamergate was the moment in which the traditional repertoires of contention, built and refined over time, began to connect to broader right-wing movements that were able to articulate grievance as a political stance, then the 2016 election was the culmination of this movement. Users across similar online spaces—4chan's /pol/ board, 8chan, right-wing sub-reddits—with common political interests, articulated and honed through Gamergate, connected firmly to a faction of the right in the United States.

The 2016 US Presidential Election and a United "We"

During the 2016 election, users across online communities used the same techniques that had long characterized 4chan and other online spaces' creation of collaborative memes and cultural materials to support Trump's campaign—the same process that produced internet cultural phenomena such as lolcats (originally, Caturday). Using participatory culture practices, people working together build cultural content, and this material gained a life of its own as it was shared and iterated by others (Marwick and Lewis 2017).

Gamergate had marked a turn for 4chan and other major online communities because extreme right activists realized that there was sentiment in these communities that could be channeled into more organized action (Reid, Valasik, and Bagavathi 2020).[4] These activists were first the White supremacists who recruited on the /pol/ board, then men's rights activists (O'Donnell 2020) from the "manosphere" (Marwick and Lewis 2017; Dignam and Rohlinger 2019), and finally the so-called alt-right (Dignam and Rohlinger 2019; Reid, Valasik, and Bagavathi 2020). Alt-right figures such as Steve Bannon identified large, anonymous, and pseudo-anonymous online forums like the chans and reddit as places to recruit. As Bannon said, "You can activate that army. They come in through Gamergate or whatever and then get turned onto politics and Trump" (Snider 2017). People in these forums then helped to create and spread pro-Trump memes, harass Trump critics, and otherwise work collectively (Marwick and Lewis 2017).

Colley and Moore (2020) studied the content on the /pol/ board to understand the relationship between the /pol/ board and the alt-right. Their research, which involved qualitative discourse analysis of a single large thread on the board that was created in response to a research presentation they were giving about /pol/, found that while the posters produced content that was in line with alt-right and far right ideology, there appeared to be more variation in belief. In their study, they found that there were four political ideologies and identities that recurred: "commitment to extreme freedom of speech; belief that the community possesses a superior understanding of the world to outsiders; critique of the hypocrisies of liberalism, and belief in the community's ability to 'redpill' site visitors" (p. 9). *Redpilling* is a reference to the scene in *The Matrix* when Neo is given the choice between taking the red pill and seeing harsh reality or taking the blue pill and living in ignorance (Dignam and Rohlinger 2019, 595).

In his research of 4chan users, with a particular focus on four boards (/b/, /int/, /pol/, /r9k/) that included observational research, a survey, and interviews, Scolyer-Gray (2018) noted that very few of the people he interacted with articulated their political beliefs as "alt-right." However, he also found that a significant block of users expressed beliefs that mapped onto a general alt-right platform—particularly ideas of anti-progressivism and a collection of ideas he called "xenophobia" that included anti-multiculturalism, anti-immigration, racism, and anti-globalism as well as clear misogyny and anti-feminist beliefs. In the surveys and interviews, Scolyer-Gray connected the content on the boards to these individually articulated beliefs.

Dignam and Rohlinger's (2019) work ties the political ideals outlined in Colley and Moore's (2020) and Scolyer-Gray's (2018) work to political action. They found that prior to the 2016 election users on Reddit's TheRedPill had rejected political action as too closely tied to men's rights movements. However, in the months leading up to the 2016 US presidential election, Dignam and Rohlinger (2019, 602) found that elite users such as moderators recast the beliefs of the community and the community's identity in terms of political action, specifically the action of voting for Donald Trump. The reframing of existing belief and behavior as political as a precursor to mobilization has also been found in other online communities, such as The Pirate Bay and file-sharing communities (Beyer 2014a).

Repertoires of Contention in the US 2016 Election

The existing well of belief that Scolyer-Gray (2018) identified, combined with long developed collective action tactics, the political articulation and awakening that happened through Gamergate, and the ties to existing right-wing movements and networks set the stage for the process of message amplification that occurred during the 2016 presidential election. Both Marwick and Lewis (2017) and Benkler, Faris, and Roberts (2018) articulated a process by which information moved from "internet subcultures" (Marwick and Lewis 2017) or the "internet's periphery" (Benkler, Faris, and Roberts 2018) into the mainstream.

In their description of this process, Marwick and Lewis (2017) show the various factions and networks that workshopped and experimented with developing conspiracies, memes, and political framings. Much of the collaborative work occurred on public-facing board systems but also on Discord, which served a similar purpose for coordination and collective work as the IRC had for Anonymous. Content that was developed, such as memes and conspiracy theories, was then broadcast across social media, drawing on Twitter hashtags and YouTube channels. As Benkler, Faris, and Roberts (2018) found, successful materials moved out of places such as 8chan into major fringe amplification sites like Infowars where large audiences accessed the content. The most successful memes were shared broadly across social media platforms, usually by people who would have never heard of the chans and who would have been shocked by their content.

In the wake of the 2016 election, there were claims that "4chan" won the election for President Trump (Beran 2017). While there is little evidence that 4chan and other online communities won the election "for" Trump (Phillips, Beyer, and Coleman 2017; Benkler, Faris, and Roberts 2018), the election certainly illustrated the power of online communities to shape public discourse, impact political events, and work in concert with traditional political actors. In addition, it illustrated the susceptibility of democracies to organized online efforts to create and spread conspiracy theories.

Future Research

Online political mobilization may arise from any online community, even the most unlikely. As I write this chapter in January 2021, users on a sub-reddit named WallStreetBets, dedicated to day trading and with no real history of collective action, have brought at least one major hedge fund to the brink of bankruptcy in a coordinated effort to frustrate short selling of GameStop stock and to drive up GameStop's stock prices (Barrett 2021; Schneider 2021). In the description of the sub-reddit, WallStreetBets describes itself as "like 4chan found a bloomberg terminal illness."

As WallStreetBets turned its attention to GameStop, the sub-reddit filled with memes framing the activity as political action against corrupt Wall Street firms. People began making posts with comments along lines such as "I don't think of my purchase as an investment, but as putting my own skin in the game as a fuck you against a rigged system." People reported buying one or two or three shares just to "do their part." Users repeatedly posted a reference to the film *300*: "WE HOLD." As the events were being covered across most major news sources, numerous political figures tweeted or stated their support for the WallStreetBets users (Newmyer and Denham 2021), and congressional hearings were planned on the events (Shepardson 2021).

Similar to the moment when Anonymous mobilized on behalf of WikiLeaks, as the WallStreetBets events began to hit major news sources, journalists and academics speculated about the reasons for the sudden rise of collective action from the sub-reddit. Some read the "4chan" label, noticed mentions of lulz, and speculated that these actions were just for entertainment. Others pointed out that the majority of posts in the subreddit were framing the events as political. Still others noted that WallStreetBets was formed to make money and clearly included community members who worked in the financial sector, concluding that, in the end, the users were primarily after profit. As the events unfolded, WallStreetsBets membership swelled from 1.7 million to over 7 million in a matter of days.

Reddit and other major online platforms face more state and public scrutiny over issues such as their privacy standards, their relationship to Section 230 of the US Communications Decency Act of 1996, and their content moderation methods; but we can expect to see existing online systems remain highly populated and new online community spaces to appear. Understanding these online spaces—their culture, their political power, and their impact on societies—requires research, often ethnographic. Key questions remain: Why do some of these communities mobilize and others do not? Why are some of these mobilizations sustained, while others are not? What is the interplay between online affordances and offline context in producing these movements?

As An Xiao Mina (2019) argues, the internet makes movements visible to themselves and to each other. The chans' modes of cultural production and collective action, including organized harassment, have long since become memeified. They have been adopted by political actors of all kinds. The internet's affordances combined with the unique cultural elements and historical moments that created Anonymous, Gamergate, and WallStreetBets will create other movements. It seems no one had been studying WallStreetBets as a place of a potential mobilization with the capacity to shape markets and politics before its January 2021 public action. And why would they? It is like so many communities on the internet—made up of people brought together around a common interest who have spent enough time together online to develop some shared stories, community identity, and values but who have not engaged in any overtly political action. Until they did.

Notes

1. Note, while the activities were present on 4chan prior to 2008, terms such as "brigading" were not necessarily in wide use. "Swatting" was also in use prior to 2008 but not widely enough to be part of the core set of raid tactics commonly used.
2. A *botnet* is a collection of internet-connected devices that have been infected with malware, allowing someone to control them.
3. *Phreaking*, in practice from the 1950s through the 1980s, involves reverse-engineering the tones used to make long-distance calls—allowing those involved to make free calls (Lapsley 2013).
4. There is a collection of computational studies examining content on 4chan's /pol/ board, most of which are largely methodological in nature and have little to say about the issue of political power (Chandrasekharan et al. 2017; Papasavva et al. 2020).

References

Auerbach, David. 2012. "Anonymity as Culture: Treatise." Triple Canopy. Accessed August 1, 2020. https://www.canopycanopycanopy.com/contents/anonymity_as_culture__treatise.

Bakioğlu, Burcu. 2009. "Spectacular Interventions of Second Life: Goon Culture, Griefing, and Disruption in Virtual Spaces." *Journal for Virtual Worlds Research* 1, no. 3: 4–21.

Bakioğlu, Burcu. 2012. "Negotiating Governance in Virtual Worlds: Grief Play, Hacktivism, and LeakOps in Second Life." *New Review of Hypermedia and Multimedia* 18, no. 4: 237–259.

Bakioğlu, Burcu. 2019. "Lore of Mayhem: Griefers and the Radical Deployment of Spatial Storytelling." *Journal of Gaming & Virtual Worlds* 11, no. 3: 231–250.

Barrett, Brian. 2021. "Robinhood Restricts GameStop Trading—In a Bid to Save Itself." Wired, January 28. https://www.wired.com/story/robinhood-gamestop-stock/.

Bartle, Richard. 1996. "Hearts, Clubs, Diamonds, Spades: Players Who Suit MUDs." *Journal of MUD Research* 1, no. 1: 19.

Benkler, Yochai, Robert Faris, and Hal Roberts. 2018. *Network Propaganda: Manipulation, Disinformation, and Radicalization in American Politics*. New York: Oxford University Press.

Bennett, W. Lance, Deen Freelon, and Chris Wells. 2010. "Changing Citizen Identity and the Rise of a Participatory Media Culture." In *Handbook of Research on Civic Engagement in Youth*, edited by Lonnie R. Sherrod, Judith Torney-Purta, and Constance A. Flanagan, 393–423. Hoboken, NJ: John Wiley & Sons.

Bennett, W. Lance, and Alexandra Segerberg. 2012. "The Logic of Connective Action: Digital Media and the Personalization of Contentious Politics." *Information, Communication & Society* 15, no. 5: 739–768.

Bennett, W. Lance, and Alexandra Segerberg. 2013. *The Logic of Connective Action: Digital Media and the Personalization of Contentious Politics*. New York: Cambridge University Press.

Beran, Dale. 2017. "4chan: The Skeleton Key to the Rise of Trump." Medium.com, February 14. https://medium.com/@DaleBeran/4chan-the-skeleton-key-to-the-rise-of-trump-624e7cb798cb.

Bergstrom, Kelly. 2011. " 'Don't Feed the Troll': Shutting Down Debate about Community Expectations on Reddit.com." *First Monday* 16, no. 8. https://firstmonday.org/article/view/3498/3029

Bergstrom, Kelly. 2020. "Destruction as Deviant Leisure in EVE Online." *Journal for Virtual Worlds Research* 13, no. 1. https://journals.tdl.org/jvwr/index.php/jvwr/article/view/7403

Bernstein, Michael, Andrés Monroy-Hernández, Drew Harry, Paul André, Katrina Panovich, and Gregory Vargas. 2011. "4chan and /b/: An Analysis of Anonymity and Ephemerality in a Large Online Community." In *Proceedings of the International AAAI Conference on Web and Social Media* Vol. 5, no. 1: 50–57. Burnaby, Canada: PKP Publishing Services.

Beyer, Jessica L. 2012. "Women's (Dis)embodied Engagement with Male-Dominated Online Communities." In *Cyberfeminism 2.0*, edited by R. Gajjala and Y. Ju Oh, 153–170. New York: Peter Lang.

Beyer, Jessica L. 2014a. *Expect Us: Online Communities and Political Mobilization*. New York: Oxford University Press.

Beyer, Jessica L. 2014b. "The Emergence of a Freedom of Information Movement: Anonymous, WikiLeaks, the Pirate Party, and Iceland." *Journal of Computer-Mediated Communication* 19, no. 2: 141–154.

Beyer, Jessica L., and Fenwick McKelvey. 2015. "You Are Not Welcome among Us: Pirates and the State." *International Journal of Communication* 9: 890–908.

Bimber, Bruce, and Richard Davis. 2003. *Campaigning Online: The Internet in US Elections*. New York: Oxford University Press.

Boy, John D., and Justus Uitermark. 2019. "Theorizing Social Media with Elias: Status Displays, Mutual Monitoring, and the Genesis of New Sensibilities." SocArXiv Papers. https://doi.org/10.31235/osf.io/phm5x.

Burgess, Jean. 2008. " 'All Your Chocolate Rain Are Belong to Us'?: Viral Video, YouTube and the Dynamics of Participatory Culture." In *Video Vortex Reader: Responses to YouTube*, edited by G. Lovink and S. Niederer, 101–109. Amsterdam: Institute of Network Cultures.

Burkart, Patrick. 2014. *Pirate Politics: The New Information Policy Contests*. Cambridge, MA: MIT Press.

Carian, Emily K., and Tagart Cain Sobotka. 2018. "Playing the Trump Card: Masculinity Threat and the US 2016 Presidential Election." *Socius* 4. https://doi.org/10.1177/2378023117740699

Castells, Manuel. 2000. "Toward a Sociology of the Network Society." *Contemporary Sociology* 29, no. 5: 693–699.

Castells, Manuel. 2015. *Networks of Outrage and Hope: Social movements in the Internet Age*. Hoboken, NJ: John Wiley & Sons.

Chadwick, Andrew, and Philip. N. Howard, eds. 2010. *Routledge Handbook of Internet Politics*. London and New York: Routledge.

Chandrasekharan, Eshwar, Mattia Samory, Anirudh Srinivasan, and Eric Gilbert. 2017. "The Bag of Communities: Identifying Abusive Behavior Online with Preexisting Internet Data." In *Proceedings of the 2017 CHI Conference on Human Factors in Computing Systems*, 3175–3187. New York: ACM Press.

Chess, Shira, and Adrienne Shaw. 2015. "A Conspiracy of Fishes, or, How We Learned to Stop Worrying about #GamerGate and Embrace Hegemonic Masculinity." *Journal of Broadcasting & Electronic Media* 59, no. 1: 208–220.

Coleman, Gabriella. 2012a. "Phreaks, Hackers, and Trolls and the Politics of Transgression and Spectacle." In *The Social Media Reader*, edited by Michael Mandiberg, 99–119. New York: New York University Press.

Coleman, Gabriella. 2012b. *Coding Freedom: The Ethics and Aesthetics of Hacking*. Princeton, NJ: Princeton University Press.

Coleman, Gabriella. 2012c. "Our Weirdness Is Free." Triple Canopy. https://www.canopycanopycanopy.com/contents/our_weirdness_is_free.

Coleman, Gabriella. 2013. "Anonymous in Context: The Politics and Power behind the Mask." Internet Governance Papers, 3. September. Centre for International Governance Innovation, Waterloo, Canada. https://www.cigionline.org/sites/default/files/no3_8.pdf.

Coleman, Gabriella. 2014. *Hacker, Hoaxer, Whistleblower, Spy: The Many Faces of Anonymous*. New York: Verso Books.

Coleman, Gabriella. 2016. "Hacker." In *Digital Keywords: A Vocabulary of Information Society and Culture*, edited by B. Peters, 158–172. Princeton, NJ: Princeton University Press.

Coleman, Gabriella. 2017. "From Internet Farming to Weapons of the Geek." *Cultural Anthropology* 58, no. 15: 91–102.

Colley, Thomas, and Martin Moore. 2020. "The Challenges of Studying 4chan and the Alt-Right: 'Come on in the Water's Fine.' " *New Media & Society*. https://doi.org/10.1177/1461444820948803.

Consalvo, Mia. 2012. "Confronting Toxic Gamer Culture: A Challenge for Feminist Game Studies Scholars." *Ada: A Journal of Gender, New Media, and Technology* 1, no. 1: 1–6.

Cote, Amanda. 2015. " 'I Can Defend Myself' Women's Strategies for Coping with Harassment while Gaming Online." *Games and Culture* 12, no. 2: 136–155.

Dahlberg, Lincoln. 2001. "Computer-Mediated Communication and the Public Sphere: A Critical Analysis." *Journal of Computer-Mediated Communication* 7, no. 1: JCMC714.

Daniels, Jessie. 2009. *Cyber Racism: White Supremacy Online and the New Attack on Civil Rights*. Lanham, MD: Rowman & Littlefield.

Daniels, Jessie. 2018. "The Algorithmic Rise of the 'Alt-Right.' " *Contexts* 17, no. 1: 60–65.

Diani, Mario. 2000. "Social Movement Networks Virtual and Real." *Information, Communication & Society* 3, no. 3: 386–401.

Dibbell, Julian. 1993. "A Rape in Cyberspace or How an Evil Clown, a Haitian Trickster Spirit, Two Wizards and a Cast of Dozens Turned a Database." *Village Voice* 21: 36–42.

Dibbell, Julian. 2008. "Mutilated Furries, Flying Phalluses: Put the Blame on Griefers, the Sociopaths of the Virtual World." *Wired* 16, no. 2: 1–7.

Dignam, Pierce Alexander, and Deana A. Rohlinger. 2019. "Misogynistic Men Online: How the Red Pill Helped Elect Trump." *Signs: Journal of Women in Culture and Society* 44, no. 3: 589–612.

Donath, Judith S. 1999. "Identity and Deception in the Virtual Community." In *Communities in Cyberspace*, edited by Marc A. Smith and Peter Kollock, 29–59. New York and London: Routledge.

Donovan, Joan. 2016. " 'Can You Hear Me Now?' Phreaking the Party Line from Operators to Occupy." *Information, Communication & Society* 19, no. 5: 601–617.

Earl, Jennifer, and Jessica L. Beyer. 2014. "The Dynamics of Backlash Online: Anonymous and the Battle for WikiLeaks." In *Intersectionality and Social Change*, edited by Lynne M. Woehrle, 207–234. Bingley, UK: Emerald Group.

Earl, Jennifer, Lauren Copeland, and Bruce Bimber. 2017. "Routing around Organizations: Self-Directed Political Consumption." *Mobilization: An International Quarterly* 22, no. 2: 131–153.

Earl, Jennifer, and Katrina Kimport. 2011. *Digitally Enabled Social Change: Activism in the Internet Age*. Cambridge, MA: MIT Press.

Earl, Jennifer, and Alan Schussman. 2002. "The New Site of Activism: On-line Organizations, Movement Entrepreneurs, and the Changing Location of Social Movement Decision Making." *Research in Social Movements, Conflicts and Change* 24: 155–187.

Earl, Jennifer, and Alan Schussman. 2004. "Cease and Desist: Repression, Strategic Voting and the 2000 US Presidential Election." *Mobilization: An International Quarterly* 9, no. 2: 181–202.

Freelon, Deen, Charlton D. McIlwain, and Meredith Clark. 2016. *Beyond the Hashtags: #Ferguson, #Blacklivesmatter, and the Online Struggle for Offline Justice*. Washington, DC: Center for Media & Social Impact, American University.

Freelon, Deen, Charlton D. McIlwain, and Meredith Clark. 2018. "Quantifying the Power and Consequences of Social Media Protest." *New Media & Society* 20, no. 3: 990–1011.

Gillespie, Tarleton. 2007. *Wired Shut: Copyright and the Shape of Digital Culture*. Cambridge, MA: MIT Press.

Gray, Kishonna L. 2012a. "Deviant Bodies, Stigmatized Identities, and Racist Acts: Examining the Experiences of African-American Gamers in Xbox Live." *New Review of Hypermedia and Multimedia* 18, no. 4: 261–276.

Gray, Kishonna L. 2012b. "Intersecting Oppressions and Online Communities: Examining the Experiences of Women of Color in Xbox Live." *Information, Communication & Society* 15, no. 3: 411–428.

Gray, Kishonna L. 2013. "Collective Organizing, Individual Resistance, or Asshole Griefers? An Ethnographic Analysis of Women of Color in Xbox Live." *Ada: A Journal of Gender, New Media, and Technology* no. 2. https://adanewmedia.org/2013/06/issue2-gray/.

Gray, Kishonna L. 2014. *Race, Gender, and Deviance in Xbox Live: Theoretical Perspectives from the Virtual Margins*. London and New York: Routledge.

Gray, Kishonna L., Bertan Buyukozturk, and Zachary G. Hill. 2016. "Blurring the Boundaries: Using Gamergate to Examine 'Real' and Symbolic Violence against Women in Contemporary Gaming Culture." *Sociology Compass* 11, no. 3: e12458.

Hardaker, Claire. 2010. "Trolling in Asynchronous Computer-Mediated Communication: From User Discussions to Academic Definitions." *Journal of Politeness Research* 6, no. 2: 215–242.

Hern, Alex. 2015. "Gamergate Hits New Low with Attempts to Send SWAT Teams to Critics." *The Guardian*, January 13. https://www.theguardian.com/technology/2015/jan/13/gamergate-hits-new-low-with-attempts-to-send-swat-teams-to-critics.

Herring, Susan, Kirk Job-Sluder, Rebecca Scheckler, and Sasha Barab. 2002. "Searching for Safety Online: Managing 'Trolling' in a Feminist Forum." *The Information Society* 18, no. 5: 371–384.

Howard, Philip N. 2011. "Review: The Net Delusion: The Dark Side of Internet Freedom by Evgeny Morozov." *Perspectives on Politics* 9, no. 4: 895–897.

Howard, Philip N., and Muzammil M. Hussain. 2013. *Democracy's Fourth Wave? Digital Media and the Arab Spring*. New York: Oxford University Press.

Johnson, Casey. 2014. "Chat Logs Show How 4chan Users Created #GamerGate Controversy." Ars Technica, September 9. https://arstechnica.com/gaming/2014/09/new-chat-logs-show-how-4chan-users-pushed-gamergate-into-the-national-spotlight/.

Jordan, Tim, and Paul Taylor. 2004. *Hacktivism and Cyberwars: Rebels with a Cause?* London: Routledge.

Jurgenson, Nathan. 2012. "When Atoms Meet Bits: Social Media, the Mobile Web and Augmented Revolution." *Future Internet* 4, no. 1: 83–91.

Kayany, Joseph M. 1998. "Contexts of Uninhibited Online Behavior: Flaming in Social Newsgroups on Usenet." *Journal of the American Society for Information Science* 49, no. 12: 1135–1141.

Kelty, Christopher M. 2008. *Two Bits: The Cultural Significance of Free Software*. Durham, NC: Duke University Press.

Knuttila, Lee. 2011. "User Unknown: 4chan, Anonymity and Contingency." *First Monday* 16, no. 10. https://firstmonday.org/article/view/3665/3055

Knuttila, Lee. 2015. "Trolling Aesthetics: The Lulz as Creative Practice." PhD diss., York University. https://yorkspace.library.yorku.ca/xmlui/handle/10315/30682.

Lapsley, Phil. 2013. *Exploding the Phone: The Untold Story of the Teenagers and Outlaws Who Hacked Ma Bell*. New York: Grove Press.

Levy, Steven. 1984. *Hackers: Heroes of the Computer Revolution*. New York: Anchor Press/Doubleday.

Lewis, Rebecca, Alice E. Marwick, and William Clyde Partin. 2021. "We Dissect Stupidity and Respond to It": Response Videos and Networked Harassment on YouTube. *American Behavioral Scientist* 65, no. 5: 735–756.

Maher, Thomas V., and Jennifer Earl. 2019. "Barrier or Booster? Digital Media, Social Networks, and Youth Micromobilization." *Sociological Perspectives* 62, no. 6: 865–883.

Manion, Mark, and Abby Goodrum. 2000. "Terrorism or Civil Disobedience: Toward a Hacktivist Ethic." *Computers and Society* 30, no. 2: 14–19.

Manivannan, Vyshali. 2013. "FCJ-158 Tits or GTFO: The Logics of Misogyny on 4chan's Random-/b." *The Fibreculture Journal* 22. https://twentytwo.fibreculturejournal.org/fcj-158-tits-or-gtfo-the-logics-of-misogyny-on-4chans-random-b/

Marwick, Alice E. 2021. "Morally Motivated Networked Harassment as Normative Reinforcement." *Social Media + Society*.

Marwick, Alice E., and Rebecca Lewis. 2017. *Media Manipulation and Disinformation Online*. New York: Data & Society Research Institute. https://datasociety.net/library/media-manipulation-and-disinfo-online/

Massanari, Adrienne. 2017. "#Gamergate and The Fappening: How Reddit's Algorithm, Governance, and Culture Support Toxic Technocultures." *New Media & Society* 19, no. 3: 329–346.

Massanari, Adrienne. 2020. "Gamergate." In *The International Encyclopedia of Gender, Media, and Communication*, edited by K. Ross, I. Bachmann, V. Cardo, S. Moorti, and C. Scarcelli, 1–5. Hoboken, NJ: John Wiley & Sons.

McDonald, Soraya Nadia. 2014. "Gamergate Targets Felicia Day after She Expresses Fear of Being Targeted." *Washington Post*, October 24. https://www.washingtonpost.com/news/morning-mix/wp/2014/10/24/gamergate-targets-felicia-day-after-she-expresses-fear-of-being-targeted/.

McKelvey, Fenwick. 2015. "We Like Copies, Just Don't Let the Others Fool You: The Paradox of the Pirate Bay." *Television & New Media* 16, no. 8: 734–750.

Menn, Joseph. 2019. *Cult of the Dead Cow: How the Original Hacking Supergroup Might Just Save the World*. New York: Public Affairs.

Milan, Stefania. 2013. *Social Movements and Their Technologies: Wiring Social Change*. Basingstoke, U.K.: Palgrave Macmillan.

Milner, Ryan M. 2013. "FCJ-156 Hacking the Social: Internet Memes, Identity Antagonism, and the Logic of Lulz." *The Fibreculture Journal* no. 22. http://twentytwo.fibreculturejournal.org/fcj-156-hacking-the-social-internet-memes-identity-antagonism-and-the-logic-of-lulz/.

Mina, An Xiao. 2019. *Memes to Movements: How the World's Most Viral Media Is Changing Social Protest and Power*. Boston: Beacon Press.

Morozov, Evgeny. 2011a. "Response to Philip N. Howard's Review of *The Net Delusion: The Dark Side of Internet Freedom*." *Perspectives on Politics* 9, no. 4: 897–897.

Morozov, Evgeny. 2011b. *The Net Delusion: The Dark Side of Internet Freedom*. New York: Public Affairs.

Mortensen, Torill Elvira. 2018. "Anger, Fear, and Games: The Long Event of #GamerGate." *Games and Culture* 13, no. 8: 787–806.

Murphy, Shaunna. 2015. "One Year Later, the Women of Gamergate Open UP: There's a Lot of Work to Do, Still." MTV News, August 24. http://www.mtv.com/news/2245633/gamer-gate-one-year-later/.

Newmyer, Tory, and Hannah Denham. 2021. "GameStop and Other Stocks Targeted by Reddit Users Plummet." *Washington Post*, January 28. https://www.washingtonpost.com/business/2021/01/28/gamestop-stocks-reddit/.

Nicholls, Walter J., Justus Uitermark, and Sander van Haperen. 2016. "The Networked Grassroots. How Radicals Outflanked Reformists in the United States' Immigrant Rights Movement." *Journal of Ethnic and Migration Studies* 42, no. 6: 1036–1054.

Norton, Quinn. 2011. "Anonymous 101: Introduction to the Lulz." *Wired*, November 8. https://www.wired.com/2011/11/anonymous-101/.

Norton, Quinn. 2012. "How Anonymous Picks Targets, Launches Attacks, and Takes Powerful Organizations Down." *Wired*, June 3. https://www.wired.com/2012/07/ff-anonymous/.

O'Donnell, Jessica. 2020. "Militant Meninism: The Militaristic Discourse of Gamergate and Men's Rights Activism." *Media, Culture, & Society* 42, no. 5: 654–674.

Olson, Parmy. 2012. *We Are Anonymous: Inside the Hacker World of LulzSec, Anonymous, and the Global Cyber Insurgency*. New York: Little, Brown.

Papasavva, Antonis, Savvas Zannettou, Emiliano De Cristofaro, Gianluca Stringhini, and Jeremy Blackburn. 2020. "Raiders of the Lost Kek: 3.5 Years of Augmented 4chan Posts from the Politically Incorrect Board." In *Proceedings of the International AAAI Conference on Web and Social Media*, 14:885–894. Palo Alto, CA: AAAI Press.

Persily, Nathaniel. 2017. "The 2016 US Election: Can Democracy Survive the Internet?" *Journal of Democracy* 28, no. 2: 63–76.

Phillips, Whitney. 2015. *This Is Why We Can't Have Nice Things: Mapping the Relationship between Online Trolling and Mainstream Culture*. Cambridge, MA: MIT Press.

Phillips, Whitney. 2016. "Donald Trump Is Not a Troll." *Slate*, June 23. https://slate.com/technology/2016/06/the-problems-with-calling-donald-trump-a-troll.html.

Phillips, Whitney. 2020. "A Brief History of Trolls." Daily Dot, March 2. https://www.dailydot.com/unclick/phillips-brief-history-of-trolls/.

Phillips, Whitney, Jessica L. Beyer, and Gabriella Coleman. 2017. "Trolling Scholars Debunk the Idea that Alt-Right Shitposters Have Magic Powers." Motherboard, March 27. https://www.vice.com/en/article/z4k549/trolling-scholars-debunk-the-idea-that-the-alt-rights-trolls-have-magic-powers.

Phillips, Whitney, and Ryan M. Milner. 2017. *The Ambivalent Internet: Mischief, Oddity, and Antagonism Online*. Boston: Polity Press.

Polletta, Francesca, and James M. Jasper. 2001. "Collective Identity and Social Movements." *Annual Review of Sociology* 27, no. 1: 283–305.

Postigo, Hector. 2012. *The Digital Rights Movement: The Role of Technology in Subverting Digital Copyright*. Cambridge, MA: MIT Press.

Ray, Rashawn, Melissa Brown, Neil Fraistat, and Edward Summers. 2017. "Ferguson and the Death of Michael Brown on Twitter: #BlackLivesMatter, #TCOT, and the Evolution of Collective Identities." *Ethnic and Racial Studies* 40, no. 11: 1797–1813.

Raymond, Eric S. 2001. *The Cathedral and the Bazaar: Musings on Linux and Open Source by an Accidental Revolutionary*, rev. ed. Sebastopol, CA: O'Reilly.

Reid, Shannon. E., Matthew Valasik, and Arunkumar Bagavathi. 2020. "Examining the Physical Manifestation of Alt-Right Gangs: From Online Trolling to Street Fighting." In *Gangs in the Era of Internet and Social Media*, edited by Chris Melde and Frank Weerman, 105–134. Cham, Switzerland: Springer.

Rohlinger, Deana A., and Jordan Brown. 2009. "Democracy, Action, and the Internet after 9/11." *American Behavioral Scientist* 53, no. 1: 133–150.

Rohlinger, Deana A., and Leslie Bunnage. 2017. "Did the Tea Party Movement Fuel the Trump-Train? The Role of Social Media in Activist Persistence and Political Change in the 21st Century." *Social Media + Society* 3, no. 2. https://doi.org/10.1177/2056305117706786

Salter, Michael 2018. "From Geek Masculinity to Gamergate: The Technological Rationality of Online Abuse." *Crime Media Culture* 14, no. 2: 247–264.

Sauter, M. R. 2014. *The Coming Swarm: DDOS Actions, Hacktivism, and Civil Disobedience on the Internet*. New York: Bloomsbury Publishing.

Schneider, Avie. 2021. "GameStop Stock Mania: Why Everyone Is Talking about It and Many Are Worried." NPR, January 28. https://www.npr.org/2021/01/28/961349400/gamestop-how-reddit-traders-occupied-wall-streets-turf.

Schradie, Jen. 2019. *The Revolution that Wasn't: How Digital Activism Favors Conservatives.* Cambridge, MA: Harvard University Press.

Schussman, Alan, and Jennifer Earl. 2004. "From Barricades to Firewalls? Strategic Voting and Social Movement Leadership in the Internet Age." *Sociological Inquiry* 74, no. 4: 439–463.

Scolyer-Gray, Patrick. 2018. "Interpreting 'Artistic Works of Fiction and Falsehood': A Sociological Analysis of the Production and Consumption of Knowledge on 4chan." PhD diss., La Trobe University.

Shepardson, David. 2021. "U.S. Congress to Hold Hearings on GameStop Trading, State of Stock Markets." Reuters, January 28. https://www.reuters.com/article/us-retail-trading-usa-congress/u-s-congress-to-hold-hearings-on-gamestop-trading-state-of-stock-markets-idUSKBN29X33T.

Simcoe, Luke. 2012. "The Internet Is Serious Business: 4chan's /b/ Board and the Lulz as Alternative Political Discourse on the Internet." PhD diss., Ryerson University.

Snider, Mike. 2017. "Steve Bannon Learned to Harness Troll Army from 'World of Warcraft.'" *USA Today*, July 18. https://www.usatoday.com/story/tech/talkingtech/2017/07/18/steve-bannon-learned-harness-troll-army-world-warcraft/489713001/.

Sobieraj, Sarah. 2018. "Bitch, Slut, Skank, Cunt: Patterned Resistance to Women's Visibility in Digital Publics." *Information, Communication & Society* 21, no. 11: 1700–1714.

Sobieraj, Sarah. 2020. *Credible Threat: Attacks against Women Online and the Future of Democracy.* New York: Oxford University Press.

Social Justice Bread. 2014. "Zoe Quinn Blows #GamerGate Wide Open." Storify. Accessed December 2014.

Söderberg, Johan. 2008. *Hacking Capitalism: The Free and Open Source Software Movement.* London and New York: Routledge.

Star, Susan Leigh, and James R. Griesemer. 1989. "Institutional Ecology, 'Translations' and Boundary Objects: Amateurs and Professionals in Berkeley's Museum of Vertebrate Zoology, 1907–39." *Social Studies of Science* 19, no. 3: 387–420.

Straumsheim, Carl. 2014. "#Gamergate and Games Research." Inside Higher Ed, November 11. https://www.insidehighered.com/news/2014/11/11/gamergate-supporters-attack-digital-games-research-association.

Stuart, Keith. 2014. "Brianna Wu and the Human Cost of Gamergate: 'Every Woman I Know in the Industry Is Scared.'" *The Guardian*, October 17. https://www.theguardian.com/technology/2014/oct/17/brianna-wu-gamergate-human-cost.

Tilly, Charles. 1986. *The Contentious French.* Cambridge, MA: Harvard University Press.

Tilly, Charles. 1995. "Contentious Repertoires in Great Britain. 1758–1834." In *Repertoires and Cycles of Collective Action*, edited by Mark Traugott, 15–42. Durham, NC: Duke University Press.

Tufekci, Zeynep. 2017. *Twitter and Tear Gas: The Power and Fragility of Networked Protest.* New Haven, CT: Yale University Press.

Tufekci, Zeynep., and Christopher Wilson. 2012. "Social Media and the Decision to Participate in Political Protest: Observations from Tahrir Square." *Journal of Communication* 62, no. 2: 363–379.

Yee, Nick. 2005. "Motivations of Play in MMORPGs." In *DiGRA '05—Proceedings of the 2005 DiGRA International Conference: Changing Views: Worlds in Play*, Vol. 3. http://www.digra.org/digital-library/publications/motivations-of-play-in-mmorpgs/.

CHAPTER 22

NETWORKED STREET LIFE

JEFFREY LANE AND WILL MARLER

The "triple revolution" of online social networking, mobile communication, and always-on connectivity has reshaped life in the twenty-first century (Rainie and Wellman 2012), including in the context of urban poverty. How social life in urban poor communities becomes "networked" and how the phenomenon might be studied practically and ethically is the subject of this chapter. We identify networked street life as an emergent area of research that links the inequality concerns of urban sociologists and digital scholars. "Street life" refers to the role of urban public space in shaping how people relate to one another and forge collective identities in the face of inequalities that in many ways define contemporary urban life (Ross 2018). As street life becomes digitized, the "neighborhood effects" of urban poverty (Sampson 2012) and digital inequities (DiMaggio et al. 2004) increasingly come to bear on one another (Stuart 2020a). In this handbook chapter, we propose a way to investigate this reciprocal relationship by focusing on the unique circumstances of networked street life for the urban poor.

We begin this chapter by setting up the street as a key social setting of urban life and reviewing research which theorizes the extension of street life into the digital arena. Building on these lines of research, we propose an integration of urban and digital research to examine inequalities of access, uses, and outcomes of technology use. We make two theoretical moves to set this unified agenda for the study of networked street life. The first reimagines the typical concepts of digital inequality to regard individual-level measures of access, use, and outcomes as embedded in neighborhood street life and local communication ecologies. Second, we move away from normative categories of what technology can or should do in the hands of the urban poor. Instead, this agenda focuses on the role of digital technologies in the opportunities and challenges of neighborhood street life, where the stakes are highest for members of poor, urban communities, especially communities of color. To support our points, we draw on topic areas and findings related to mobile internet access, social support and resource mobilization, neighborhood violence and outreach work, and surveillance and punishment. In the remainder of the chapter, we discuss some ethical considerations around studying networked street life. We raise concerns over the proximity of digital ethnography to digital surveillance and show how robust informed consent and reviewing digital data with participants can distinguish researchers and bring participants into the process of meaning-making around their online expressions. Finally, we look ahead by suggesting three lines of future research to strengthen and develop the study of networked street life going forward.

Background on Street Life of the Urban Poor

Urban ethnographers study the role of street life in the social order of urban neighborhoods and whole cities (Duneier, Kasinitz, and Murphy 2014). Everyday street life, such as residents out on their stoops or gathered together to socialize in the park, connects residents and reduces social isolation (Jacobs 1961; Jerolmack 2013). Interactions as simple as nodding or saying hello to a passing neighbor can generate durable relations and a shared sense of community belonging (Felder 2020). Street life, however, can also be tense and troubling (Duneier and Molotch 1999), from men harassing women on the street to racialized stop-and-frisk policing practices (Rios, Prieto, and Ibarra 2020). These street-level experiences are key to how everyday people and institutional actors relate to each other and the urban environment.

Streets both connect and divide cities into distinct neighborhoods and "parts of town." Ethnographers describe the social stratification of neighborhoods by examining differences in street life, emphasizing its more robust role in poor neighborhoods where the street affords opportunities to socialize beyond cramped housing units (Bell 1983). By contrast, more affluent communities tend to cut off these social possibilities outside the home, using the streets as "pathways rather than places" (Bell 1983, 57–58). The street enables market opportunities where formal market access may be limited (Venkatesh 2006) and a staging area for the negotiation of respect and reputations (Anderson 1999).

Socioeconomic differences engender fundamentally different ways of accessing and using the streets. Unhoused persons, for instance, identify upward of "one hundred categories of [public] sleeping places" (Spradley 1970, 99) that housing-secure residents would never need to think about. Ross and colleagues (2019, 2) write that the study of street life is fundamentally focused on "individuals and groups in specific, mostly disadvantaged, spatial relationships," which we can see, for instance, in Manhattan's Greenwich Village, where the more affluent residents discard quality books and magazines that poor, Black men resell (Duneier 1999).

Inequality takes shape in street life and both disadvantages and sustains the urban poor. With the street as our key setting for understanding inequality, we discuss now various perspectives on digital street life.

Online Extension and Digitization of Street Life

Urban life and the life of city streets are increasingly shaped by the relationships that people and institutions have vis-à-vis networked technologies. Researchers have studied a number of digital technologies for their role in shaping urban life. These have included social media (Boy and Uitermark 2020), mobile phone applications (Sutko and de Souza e Silva 2011), online neighborhood forums (Hampton 2010; Morelli 2019), and big data and algorithms (Coletta and Kitchin 2017).

There are ways that networked technologies shape the experience of the street for any urban resident with a smartphone, social media account, and data plan or Wi-Fi access. The use of technologies that link geospatial location and internet, especially smartphones, augments the experience of the street by introducing "annotations and connections, information and orientations from a network of people and devices" (Gordon and de Souza e Silva 2011, 1). Such "net locality" is a new form of locational awareness in which "[t]he street is no longer limited to the perceptual horizon of the person walking down it" (Gordon and de Souza e Silva 2011, 3). Street spaces are "hybrid spaces" of digital information and physical spatiality with entrance to the internet based on street location (de Souza e Silva and Sheller 2014, 6). People source information and impressions from online platforms and apply them in real time to shape the routes they take through the city (Bertel et al. 2017), the businesses they patronize (Zukin, Lindeman, and Hurson 2017), and their meetups with existing and new ties (Humphreys 2010; Saker and Frith 2018). Neighborhood online forums have been shown to make neighborhood streets more social by facilitating additional interactions between neighbors (Morelli 2019) and local problem-solving (Hampton 2010).

The digitally networked nature of urban life reflects both the divisions and integrations of urban society (Georgiou 2013). Hepp, Breiter, and Hasebrink (2018) describe how digital social media supports local city life in its segregated, unequal, and differentiated forms as "figurations" of friend groups and media ensembles highly attuned to each other in the same online and urban places. Boy and Uitermark (2017) have taken an aerial view of the streets of Amsterdam as depicted on the visual social media platform Instagram, noting the role of Instagram as both a *membrane*, filtering and making more visible already popular street scenes, and a *stage* for urban residents to present themselves and their relationships in unequal urban spaces. When assessed against urban geography, social media activities reflect and may even play an active role in the stratification of urban life, for example, the digital labeling of "ghetto" areas and residents (Boy and Uitermark 2020; Shelton, Poorthuis, and Zook 2015; Zukin, Lindeman, and Hurson 2017).

Other recent studies have specifically examined how digital social media are changing social life within poor, Black neighborhoods. Based on his ethnography of Harlem, Lane (2019) shows how neighborhood street life extends online through the activity of young

Black teenagers on social media sites as well as concerned Black adults and the police, who use to different ends the online visibility and access to the same teens on the street. Lane conceptualizes two layers of street life that unfold on the physical and digital streets of the neighborhood, with each layer playing out in relation to the other. He argues that "the digital street" on social media allows teenagers to preview, shape, and even displace neighborhood interactions in person. For instance, by "meeting" first on social media, girls and boys signal whether they are interested in talking when they pass each other in person. Stevens and her collaborators (2017) theorize a "digital hood" on social media characterized by primarily negative interactions associated with peer aggression and sexual bullying, findings that suggest that social media amplifies neighborhood risks. By contrast, in *Ballad of the Bullet*, Stuart (2020a) argues that gang-associated, Black youth in Chicago perform violence online in the hopes of monetizing these racial stereotypes of urban gang violence in the attention economy of rap "drill music."

These approaches to studying the particular processes of networked street life for the urban poor draw closely on a tradition of urban inequality research, such as research on the outcomes associated with neighborhood effects and concentrated disadvantage (Sampson, Morenoff, and Gannon-Rowley 2002; Sharkey and Faber 2014). As we consider how the neighborhood life of stratified cities extends online, we find it useful to source our study of networked street life in an additional, younger research tradition on *digital* inequality. Digital inequality research over the last several decades shows how the diffusion of digital technologies influences existing patterns of socioeconomic inequality and introduces new patterns (DiMaggio et al. 2004; Robinson et al. 2015). While the "digital divide" between internet haves and have-nots first drew researchers' attention (National Telecommunications and Information Administration 1995), in the 2000s, researchers of digital inequality have pointed to differences in digital skills and predominant uses of the internet across socioeconomic groups (Hargittai 2002; DiMaggio et al. 2004), as well as the differential consequences of different uses and of digital harms and surveillance (Gangadharan 2017). Access, uses, and outcomes of technology use become the framework for assessing how networked technologies enter into the equation of socioeconomic inequality (van Deursen and Helsper 2015). As the social life of urban neighborhoods has digitized, we see a fruitful opportunity to integrate urban and digital inequality research by examining how the urban poor adapt to networked street life.

Street-Level Integration: Redefining Digital Inequality Measures as Urban-Digital Inequality Measures

Research on the digital side of neighborhood street life and neighborhood effects underscores the value of a more ecological approach to digital inequality. Since the early 2000s, digital inequality has primarily been studied at the individual level based on a set of variables measured in survey research (Hargittai and Hsieh 2013; Scheerder, van Deursen, and van Dijk 2017). However, urban communication scholars—building on the inequality concerns of urban sociologists—have pointed to the importance of studying digital inequality at multiple levels of community (Katz and Gonzalez 2016; Katz and Hampton 2016).

Urban communication ecology scholars emphasize that urban communities are organized through a "storytelling network" of neighborhood residents, organizations, and local/ethnic media within a structural context that facilitates or hinders the actions of the network (Kim et al. 2018). The agenda we propose integrates urban communication with the "symbolic interactionism" (Fine 1995) that shapes neighborhood order—the traditional focus of street ethnography. Given the role of social media, this agenda also incorporates research on "networked publics" (Ito 2008; boyd 2011; Lane 2019) and "attention economy" (Marwick 2013; Tufekci 2013; Stuart 2020a) to account for the changing scale of neighborhood interaction.

We set this agenda for the study of networked street life by making two theoretical moves. The first reconsiders the definitions of access, uses, and outcomes to regard these individual-level measures as embedded in local street life and neighborhood communication ecologies. Second, we transition away from normative categories of how the urban poor should use technology. For instance, surveys are unlikely to ask respondents if they use technology to "campain for respect" (Anderson 1999; Lane 2019) on the street, nor would this street-level use be marked as human capital; but ethnographic research suggests this form of internet use bears on public safety and serves as an economic strategy in the attention economy (Stuart 2020a).

We acknowledge also that these street-level categories overlap with urban-digital poverty broadly and, to a lesser degree, universal aspects of networked life (Rainie and Wellman 2012). The categories we propose also capture forms of inequality that operate as compounding and sequential (van Deursen et al. 2017) and mutually constitutive. For instance, threatening online behavior may incite violence or circumvent street violence in person, which further bears upon social media use going forward. With these acknowledgments, we propose an agenda around networked street life that reframes conventional digital inequality categories along these lines:

Access. "Access" means not only access to technology and the internet but connectivity in the broader social sense of neighborhood relationships and access to people and information that emanates from the street. Technology is part of the ecology of street life, including as operated "by individuals and organizations that spend a disproportionate amount of time on the streets of large urban centers" (Ross, 2018, 8). *Uses.* Street-level "use" refers to how these street-level actors use technology relative to neighborhood threat and opportunity structures. Examples of street-level uses include getting respect, seeking social and material support, staying abreast of local gossip, and managing risks. These uses track closely with the cognitive frameworks and specialized skills and knowledge learned firsthand to get by in contentious urban spaces—what scholars have termed, for instance, being "streetwise" (Anderson 1990) and "copwise" (Stuart 2016), street "efficacy" (Sharkey 2006), and street "capital" (Ross 2018, see also for further examples and discussion).

Outcomes. Street-level "outcome" refers to the consequences of street-level access and uses of technology and the mediating role of technology in exposure to multiple forms of violence and surveillance. Examples of street-level outcomes include victimization and physical harm, discrimination and discrediting, criminal justice contact, and getting scammed. The outcomes are often negative, but they can also take positive or protective forms, such as anti-violence intervention.

Emerging Research Topics and Key Findings

The three-part conceptual framework introduced above offers a way to integrate currently disparate threads of research on digital and urban inequality. This section reviews emerging concerns and findings at the intersection of these research traditions. It explains and illustrates how digital issues of technology access, uses, and outcomes and urban issues of neighborhood connectivity, conflict and support, and intervention and surveillance interlock on the street.

Street-Level Technology Access

Where typically, digital-inequality research frames access in terms of technological connectivity, we propose access in terms of both the technological and social aspects of neighborhood street life because of their interconnections. In this section, we pose street-level access as a matter of technological connectivity nested within community connectivity more broadly, focusing on those relationships and flows of information that matter to street survival and support. First, we address the conventional concept of access inequality and propose its relation to networked street life. We then turn to our concept and elaboration of community connectivity as a framework better suited to addressing urban-digital inequality.

People in poverty tend to lack privileged access to the internet, and this stands to shape their digital engagements in several ways. Privileged access to technology means having a range of devices and locations from which to go online and the confidence that one will have consistent access to the internet over time (Hassani 2006; DiMaggio et al. 2004; Gonzales 2016). People with lower incomes tend to lack such options, consistency, and autonomy in their internet access (Hassani 2006; Gonzales 2016; Marler 2018). For example, people in poverty in the United States are more likely to be "smartphone-dependent," relying entirely on smartphones to go online (Pew Research Center 2019; Tsetsi and Rains 2017). From this, researchers have theorized a "mobile underclass" of poor who are restricted to mobile internet applications (Napoli and Obar 2014). In lieu of private avenues for computer access, people in poverty more often rely on public and shared means of internet access, including public libraries and commercial Wi-Fi hotspots (Dailey et al. 2010; Humphry 2019). Similarly, in the 1990s, low-income urban residents reported relying on public payphones when lacking service in their own home; in turn, residents often found the closest payphones to be out of service, already occupied, or charging unaffordable rates (Mueller and Schement 1996). In the internet era, the poor have precarious relationships to cafes and other Wi-Fi hotspots as their presence is more often policed at these public sites of internet access (Humphry 2019; Stuart 2014).

Inferior and unstable access to the internet conditions the networked street lives of the urban poor in several ways. One is to shape daily routines and movements throughout the city. Infrastructure studies direct our attention to the often-unseen relationship between the built systems of society and the social level (Star et al. 1999). Similarly, the search for free Wi-Fi draws people on the economic margins as well as their more privileged neighbors to cafes, shopping centers, trains, public squares, and other sites where Wi-Fi is freely available, in addition to libraries and nonprofits (Humphry 2019; Hampton, Livio, and Sessions Goulet 2010). For the more privileged, these stays in public spaces are stopgaps between access to the internet at work and home access (Hampton, Livio, and Sessions Goulet 2010). For the urban poor and for the homeless, the search for Wi-Fi becomes a burdensome portion of the daily routine, bringing them into contact with public and commercial places where their presence is more highly policed (Humphry 2019).

At the same time, the work to maintain an internet connection becomes part of the solidarity expressed in street life. In his fieldwork with adults experiencing homelessness in north-side Chicago, Marler (2019) observes how the street is both a site of disconnection from digital technology and a site (along with the community rooms of nonprofits where people seek refuge from the street) to reconnect. As payphones have disappeared from the public way in major cities, people living on and off the street in Chicago cooperate to make sure that mobile phones are available, whether by sharing one's own device or keeping an extra phone on hand for the purpose of lending to those in need (Marler 2019). In a similar vein, Lane (2020) describes how JayVon, an 18-year-old Black teenager with food and housing insecurity issues, relies on the help of multiple social ties from the same street corner to acquire a second-hand BlackBerry phone and compatible SIM card and pay the reactivation and service costs.

Networked street life is thus shaped by gaps in people's reliable and consistent access to a suitable range of networked technologies. From the starting point of technology access and inequality, we wish to expand the access lens to incorporate the social and community aspect. To explicate our concept of community connectivity, we draw on the communication infrastructure perspective and its lens on neighborhoods as contexts for communication action (Ball-Rokeach, Kim, and Matei 2001). Ball-Rokeach, Kim, and Matei (2001) learned from Los Angeles neighborhood residents of the features of their neighborhoods that constrained or enabled communication among residents. Physical factors included the layout of streets and the presence of "communication-incipient" places such as parks, grocery stores, and libraries that tended to bring people together for conversation. Whether or not people felt comfortable or fearful engaging with one another comprised a psychological dimension, which was closely related to the sociocultural makeup and economic resources of a neighborhood. Finally, the authors were interested in the technological factors, such as internet connections and transport options. Different combinations of people, places, resources, and technologies produced neighborhoods that were more and less open to communication and thus self-definition through stories told about the neighborhood (Ball-Rokeach, Kim, and Matei 2001).

The communication infrastructure perspective aligns with urban street ethnographies and their long-standing focus on communication channels (Suttles 1968) and community connectivity through the activities of public characters and neighborhood brokers (Jacobs 1961). Lane (2019) updates a classic, street-level communication system involving youth and adult authority figures that was once rooted in local stores where outreach workers collected and disseminated neighborhood gossip pertaining to risky youth behavior. With the availability of mobile and social media communication, outreach figures can gather information on their neighborhood rounds, as well as through various communication technologies to, in a sense, be in more than one place at a time. The street pastor Lane (2019) shadowed in his study engaged multiple neighborhood stakeholders in different physical and digital locations to gather gossip about violence and mobilize interventions. To conceptualize access as a street-level category requires thinking holistically about the technological and social aspects of connectivity in light of poverty constraints and the particular problems and actors involved in street life.

Street-Level Uses of Technology

In describing street-level access, we have shown how technology access is one component of a broader orientation people have to the communication channels that shape and sustain neighborhood life. We turn now to particular uses of technology, extending and reframing the study of technology uses in digital inequality research. Researchers of digital inequality began to ask in the 2000s whether differences were emerging beyond mere technology access to the ways that people of different socioeconomic backgrounds used the internet. Studies showed that privileged socioeconomic groups used the internet more for information resources and less privileged groups more for socializing and entertainment (van Dijk and Hacker 2003; Zillien and Hargittai 2009; van Deursen and van Dijk 2014). These researchers raised concerns over the potential for different uses to magnify inequalities stemming from internet use, with informational uses thought to contribute to socioeconomic mobility and social and entertainment uses to socioeconomic stagnancy.

In this section, we describe street-level uses of technology that both resonate with and depart from typical uses of technology by more privileged internet users. Doing so, we hope to improve on both digital inequality research and street ethnography by illustrating the limits to a normative account of "legitimate" uses (Livingstone and Helsper 2007, 692) of technology use for the urban poor or any other marginalized community. We describe in this section how amid street life, the urban poor use networked technologies to maintain and develop their social networks in the interest of social and material support, to manage street reputations and conflicts, to keep up with what is happening in the neighborhood, and to intervene against violence as it breaks out. Street-level uses of technology shift our attention from the orientation of people, places, and technologies in neighborhood communication channels to the opportunities and risks that entail particular ways of adapting networked technologies to the concerns of street life.

The first area of interest is online networking and social support and social capital that extends outside the neighborhood. A long-standing concern of urban sociologists is how members of low-income urban communities derive the support they need to manage the hardships of poverty (Desmond 2012; Edin and Lein 1997; Stack 1975). Drawing on theories of social networks and social capital (Granovetter 1973; Lin 2001), researchers have studied the interpersonal networks of people in poverty as the potential source for both "coping" resources, such as the sharing of food, clothing, child care, and places to sleep, as well as "leverage" resources, such as job contacts or educational sponsorship (Briggs 1998). The findings have been that low-income residents of urban poor communities regularly and creatively help one another survive poverty, yet neighbors and other social ties of the same social status are rarely sources of resources for upward mobility (Briggs 1998; Snow and Anderson 1993).

There are two ways that online communication and networking might shift the situation for people to cope with or overcome poverty through their social networks. The first is that social network sites (SNSs) like Facebook might make resources that a person has within their existing social network more visible and easier to access. People who more often use Facebook and instant messaging report receiving more social support from their close social ties (Lu and Hampton 2017) and better access to weak ties (Ellison et al. 2011). Scholars point to "pervasive awareness" within personal networks as well as the reduced labor required to maintain a larger number of offline contacts over time and across life changes as explanations for this relationship between technology use and gains in social support and capital (Hampton 2016; Donath 2007). The second potential for networked technologies in this regard is for SNS use to actually expand and diversify the number of social ties to include people of higher social status outside the neighborhood, rather than merely maintain existing ties. This potential is less supported in the existing studies, which focus on the middle class and primarily find that SNSs support existing offline relationships (Ellison et al. 2011; Burke, Marlow, and Lento 2010). Yet more recent sociological literature points to previously overlooked sources of social support and capital for members of low-income communities, including from relative strangers (Desmond 2012) and community organizations (Small 2009). The networked publics (boyd 2011) of SNSs may be a frontier for unanticipated sources of diverse social connections and thus survival and upward mobility resources for members of urban poor communities.

Emerging research on street-level uses of social media to tap into social resources suggests that Facebook may improve within-neighborhood support, while doing little for network diversity of the kind to provide resources for upward mobility. While focused on rural rather urban marginality, Rickman and Sandvig (2014) illustrate how adolescent women of lower socioeconomic status run into dead ends when attempting to bridge networks with college students over social media as their requests for aid in college advice from their Facebook networks found no suitable audience there in terms of ties with college backgrounds. Marler's (2020) research shows how middle-aged and older adults living on and off the street in north-side Chicago similarly perceive and pursue, yet have difficulty securing, the potential for their Facebook account to act as a network diversifier. The "connective ambition" that organizers within the homeless community express operates as largely a false promise, drawing people experiencing homelessness into large webs of online strangers through their Facebook friends lists, contacts who are likely to be scammers or others eager for far-flung connections to translate into money or romance.

Another primary line of networked street life research concerns the uses of social media relative to neighborhood gang violence and new opportunities for outreach and intervention. Gang social media researchers have described the phenomenon of "internet banging" (Patton, Eschmann, and Butler 2013) and online mechanisms of gang violence in neighborhoods characterized by racialized poverty and higher rates of violence (Lauger and Densley 2018; Pyrooz, Decker, and Moule 2015; Storrod and Densley 2017; Urbanik and Haggerty 2018). Some research identifies real-time links between threats online and gun violence offline (Patton et al. 2017) and incidents in which neighborhood youth attribute physical violence to online conflict (Patton et al. 2020). Studies also show how neighborhood youth use social media to manage neighborhood violence by calibrating the threat levels of provocative content (Lane 2019). Stuart (2020b) theorizes a "code of the tweet" based on the deployment of different online strategies that are more or less likely to provoke physical violence. Neighborhood youth devote significant time and effort to their respect campaigns on social media (Anderson 1999; Lane 2019), monitoring feedback, watching their rivals' feeds (Stuart 2020a), and interpreting online threats (Patton et al. 2019).

Neighborhood youth appear then to use social media to both escalate and de-escalate conflict, including by signaling to outreach workers for help. Such intergenerational communication between neighborhood youth and trusted adults is key to informal social control (Lane 2019). Patton et al. (2018) find a critical 2-day window for outreach work after a gang homicide during which loss expressions on Twitter give way to more aggressive tweets suggestive of retaliation. Digital street outreach may be most productive when linked to media arts programming (Lane 2019; Stuart 2020a) and equally responsive to prosocial expressions (Lane 2019). By addressing technology use as a street-level category we can capture the time and effort that goes into this type of neighborhood communication. We note also that this form of "street capital" (Ross 2018) rarely converts into human capital in formal labor markets and generally serves to sustain inequality.

Street-Level Outcomes of Technology

Access to problem situations and the visibility of street violence online raise questions about what we as a society choose to do with this information and whether we use this visibility to further surveil, stigmatize, and punish the poor or channel resources and support equitably and effectively (Eubanks 2018; Stuart, Riley, and Pourreza 2020). To study the outcomes of technology at the street level is to examine the social and institutional responses to intended and unintended online disclosures or context collusions and collisions (Davis and Jurgenson 2014) of neighborhood street life. This focus on digital-urban inequality entails also thinking about how street-level uses of technology are based upon and shaped by the audiences and potential outcomes that users anticipate or fear. Urban ethnographies have documented the labeling of neighborhood youth, especially Black and Latinx youth, as street- or gang-involved by many of the adults and institutional actors in their lives and the alienation that may follow (cf. Anderson 1999; Garot 2007; Jones 2009). These studies also examine the code-switching strategies youth use to deflect and manage such labeling. The networked publics literature describes how imagined communities of people and places are reconfigured with the design of the internet and SNSs, opening up new and unanticipated audiences for presentations of self (Ito 2008; boyd 2011). boyd (2011) points to persistence, replicability, scalability, and searchability to distinguish the SNS environment from what previous media afforded a communication environment.

The digitization of neighborhood street life raises especially the issue of context collapse relative to these visibility affordances (Flyverbom et al. 2016). The teenagers in Lane's (2019) study were not only using social media to manage peer threats but also switching between "street" and "decent" codes to manage conflicting forms of accountability. The teens partitioned the drama of street life by platform and censored what they said online to protect their reputations at home, school, and work. Or they took another approach by disclosing the violence they were in to enlist help from neighborhood adults they trusted (e.g., outreach workers), at the risk of being discredited by adults who were less sympathetic. How the adult world interprets locally nuanced threats and facework poses potential problems for youth from poor, urban neighborhoods seeking employment, college admissions, and other opportunities for upward mobility (boyd 2014).

Street culture is often a liability for urban Black and Latinx youth crossing over into the mainstream (Bourgois 2003) even as White, middle-class consumers have readily adopted street styles and culture (Lane 2018; Ross 2018). Social media afford a new stage on which urban culture and experience become objects of mainstream consumption. Stuart (2020a) discusses how and why poor, Black youth in Chicago play up violent stereotypes in the do-it-yourself "drill music" scene. Stuart points to the wider market for hyper-violent, hyper-local representations of urban, Black poverty, evident also in the appeal of racialized and sexualized fight videos on WorldStarHipHop.com (Hitchens 2019). Some of the young men Stuart studied were able to monetize online notoriety and find social validation, but they all faced ongoing economic marginalization and threats of physical violence and criminal liability.

Research in US, Canadian, and European cities documents the surveillance and use of social media by law enforcement to define, monitor, and prosecute street gangs (Densley and Pyrooz 2020; Lane 2019; Stuart 2020a; Urbanik and Roks 2020). Tactics include police use of social media to identify and "friend" presumptive gang members and the use of defendants' social media activity by prosecutors as criminal evidence. Lane, Ramirez, and Pearce (2018) found that the visibility of associations on social media can help gang prosecutors meet the legal requirements for the crime of conspiracy, which raises a number of concerns about the increased criminalization of young people of color who socialize on the same platforms with gang-involved peers. It also raises questions about the ability of law enforcement to reliably interpret Black youth on social media. The actual or potential criminal outcomes of social media have also shaped the communication practices of youth under police surveillance. For instance, youth may encode messages posted to social media in popular rap lyrics or delete potentially incriminating content (Lane 2019; Lane, Ramirez, and Pearce 2018).

Peers, family, fans, and police populate the social media worlds of street-involved youth and adults, offering challenges, penalties, and supportive interventions. Yet there are still other online actors shaping the outcomes of digital participation for the urban poor. Scammers and predatory lenders rely on digital tools to target low-income internet users, who tend to lack the digital preparedness to protect themselves from these practices (Gangadharan 2017). For example, one survey found that low-income US households are twice as likely as the highest-earning US households to say they lost money due to an online scam, including those that are perpetrated over social media (Madden 2017). Similarly, it is those who are already poor that are targeted with subprime and predatory loans, a form of targeting that relies on predictive modeling based on a person's past online activity (Gangadharan 2014).

The social and economic life of the street shapes people's interactions with these online bad actors in a number of ways. On the one hand, the lack of economic opportunities for the poor in inner cities drives a curiosity around money to be made and clout to be gained through online ties and audiences (Lane 2019; Stuart 2020a; Marler 2020). In Marler's (2020) fieldwork with unstably housed adults in Chicago, men living on the street or in shelters who had few romantic options in the neighborhood were highly susceptible to the online advances of Facebook accounts posing as attractive women. These online accounts posing as women asked men for money in order to come and visit them where they live, a common pattern of online "romance scams" (Sorell and Whitty 2019).

At the same time, street knowledge and lived experiences of urban poverty may help guard against scams and other online violations. Marler (2020) found that, while men experiencing homelessness were susceptible to romance scams on Facebook, they also adapted street wisdom to the networked environment. Men in search of online romance used mutual friends and profile elements in an attempt to root out "legit" from "fake" Facebook users seeking romantic involvement. Similarly, social media users may use street life not only as a reference to gauge online scams but also to estimate their online privacy risks and guard against privacy predations (Marwick, Fontaine, and boyd 2017; Spiller 2020). It is troubling to find, thus, that low-income urban youth appear to underestimate the harms of online surveillance precisely in comparison to their experiences of persistent and more visceral forms of surveillance by police and other authorities in their offline lives (Marwick, Fontaine, and boyd 2017).

Research and Ethics in the Study of Networked Street Life

The local nuances of technology and the vulnerability of the urban poor underscore the importance of grounded knowledge and attention to context in the study of networked street life. Field relationships, we argue, are an essential entry point not only into understanding local context but also, as we discuss in this section, into conducting ethical research into the networked lives of the urban poor. Urban ethnographers make it a priority to discuss with readers how they think their positionality (marked by age, race, class, gender, etc.) has shaped their fieldwork and the perspectives they are privy to and ultimately how they understand the communities they write about, comparing unique ethnographic relationships against histories of marginalization (Duneier, Kasinitz, and Murphy 2014).

Less writing has emerged to explore the role of an ethnographer's positionality in regard to fieldwork that extends online in urban poor communities. We propose as a key ethical issue in the ethnographic study of networked street life the proximity to means of digital surveillance active in the community. People who are poor and people of color are already subject to disproportionate surveillance by state and market institutions, from law enforcement to the welfare state to predatory businesses. These means of surveillance are adapted to networked technologies through predictive policing (Brayne 2020), welfare case management systems (Eubanks 2018), and commercial data profiling (Gangadharan 2014). Studying street life through digital observation risks positioning researchers similarly to law enforcement and other surveilling institutions, which, unlike researchers, often bend their data collection toward punishment and sanctioning of members of poor and minoritized communities.

The concern over surveillance may be multiplied for white researchers entering into poor communities of color asking for permission to observe and record aspects of offline and digital life. Members of Black and Latinx communities may look with suspicion on White researchers given histories of unequal urban race relations and local references to White people as police and in other authority roles. Many influential urban ethnographies by White researchers discuss efforts to form meaningful relationships in the community even in the face of irreconcilable racial differences and inequalities (see especially Bourgois 2003 on "violating apartheid"). At the same time, White ethnographers, like all ethnographers, can never know exactly what they mean to the people in their studies; and ultimately the ethnographer moves forward as they themselves feel more comfortable and confident (Liebow 1967).

Addressing issues of data access and use head-on with participants can help all ethnographers build trust by reinforcing distinctions between ethnography and state surveillance. Important to the distinction is that law enforcement and other surveilling state institutions do not (a) discuss openly the extent, nature, and the ends of data collection or (b) seek input into the meaning of that data. Ethnographers can do the opposite of state practices by continually showing participants what data they have collected, saying why, and interpreting participants' data with them.

These iterative discussions help also to maintain informed consent on an ongoing basis (Thorne 1980) by continuously addressing the scope of the fieldwork and adjusting the boundaries if necessary. This is particularly important in digital fieldwork as an ethnographer's presence may be less apparent in social media feeds than on the street. By printing off social media posts and using them as interview prompts with the participants who had posted them, Lane (2019) and Marler (2020) felt they were able to normalize their presence online as well as check their assumptions about online expressions. "Member checks" in this context perform a double duty by differentiating ethnography from surrounding surveillance and improving the quality of the fieldwork.

Checking data with participants can also enrich the accounts of networked street life in a way that aids in dispelling myths and biases circulated in media and in the courts about social life in poor urban neighborhoods. Lane (2019) and Stuart (2020a) discuss the stakes of observing the social media activity of youth in urban neighborhoods where gang activity is more common. Many youth in these neighborhoods who are active on social media tend to exaggerate their involvement in drug dealing, gun violence, and gang activity on sites like Twitter and YouTube in a bid to win respect and fame among their peers and a digital audience. Law enforcement and news media may accept these exaggerations on face, leading to prosecutions and an inflated sense of violence among youth in places like Harlem and Chicago's south side. Lane (2019) found that his member checks with gang-involved youth around their social media posts provided him an additional stream of evidence that often challenged the simplified accounts of Black youth in the neighborhood published in news reports and legal documents. Non-ethnographic studies of networked street life can benefit as well from efforts to link digital interaction to the neighborhood context, such as through the use of "domain experts" (e.g., formerly gang-involved youth) to analyze social media data (Frey et al. 2020).

Finally, initial choices about how to engage with participants online can shape trust and reciprocity. Ethnographers of networked street life face novel choices around personal boundaries in the digital sphere of fieldwork. To conduct their social media observations, ethnographers may choose to use a research-only account devoid of personal information rather than a personal account. This approach, likened to a one-way mirror by Urbanik and Roks (2020), reflects a reasonable concern over maintaining personal boundaries as well as over protecting the anonymity of participants and even researcher safety. On the other hand, researchers may consider using their personal social media account to connect to and interact with participants over social media.

Connecting to participants with personal accounts has the risk of de-anonymizing participants to the researcher's network based on visible interactions on platforms like Facebook and Twitter. Where this concern is relevant, a researcher connecting over a personal account with participants should be diligent in communicating with participants about actions such as hiding comments and reactions from participants (Urbanik and Roks 2020; Marler 2020).

Despite these risks, we suggest that connecting over personal accounts has the benefits of mutual visibility in the ethnographic relationship. For example, seeing updates from the researcher's own social media activity in their feeds, participants might be more likely to recall a researcher's presence as a digital observer in the participants' own feeds. As another benefit, participants have the chance, if they choose, to represent the researcher to networked publics through their own posts, providing the researcher additional evidence of how they are seen from the perspective of participants. The use of personal accounts also distinguishes the ethnographer's account from "fake pages" created by police detectives (Lane 2019) or digital scammers (Marler 2020) and suspicious accounts with sparse content presumed to be forms of surveillance (Urbanik and Roks 2020).

Our understanding of networked street life improves with fieldwork conducted in social media feeds as well as on the streets. Researchers should pursue digital streams of ethnographic data while remaining sensitive to the ethical issues that stem from unequal power relations and state surveillance practices targeting poor communities and communities of color. To distinguish the ethnographer from law enforcement requires approaches built around ongoing informed consent and member checks of digital (and all) ethnographic data. By developing offline relationships, being candid about the scope of online ethnography, and working through interpretations of this data together, ethnographers of networked street life can provide opportunities for participants to shape the use and meaning of their own digital data. These efforts can help sustain ethnographic relationships across positional differences.

FUTURE RESEARCH DIRECTIONS

Our goal with this handbook chapter was to set an agenda for the study of networked street life that bridges urban and digital inequality research. We reframed three standard measures of digital inequality usually grounded in schools and workplaces by moving the focus onto the street where major differences and disparities in access, uses, and outcomes of technology also disadvantage the urban poor. This street-level perspective helps contextualize and explain "usage gaps" (Hargittai and Hinnant 2008; van Deursen and van Dijk 2014) by pointing to the social and legal costs of street capital and acknowledging the daily efforts to manage neighborhood risks and precarious support networks. We have by no means outlined all aspects and examples of each revamped category, but we hope to have provided the theoretical and methodological starting points.

We conclude by laying out three directions for future street-level research that we think can add nuance and richness to the study of urban and digital inequality going forward.

Street Intersectionality

To strengthen this line of inequality research, we need to further theorize how race, gender, and other power relations are encoded (Benjamin 2019) in the technologies of street life. Future research can further clarify and disentangle the dimensions of difference (Dill and Zambrana 2009) that stratify street-level access, uses, and outcomes of technology. Research has shown how gender organizes networked street life for Black teenagers in Harlem (Lane 2019) and Chicago (Patton et al. 2020), with young women rather than men being the more central figures in neighborhood networks. These findings are based on traditional, heteronormative gender roles, which prompts questions about LGBTQ+ youth and networked street life across racial/ethnic groups. Although the increased racialization of poverty has drawn more attention to poor, urban, Black neighborhoods, the study of networked street life would benefit from more comparative study sites, including in poor, White, urban areas. Comparative research can help disentangle race and guard against our scholarly use of "the street" as a pejorative label for Black people, as we have seen in school (Dance 2002) and corporate (Negus 1999) settings. As the authors of this agenda, we have also drawn largely on the US context and call on more international perspectives to balance our knowledge of the literature.

Networked Inequality

The tension between networked individuals liberated from place-based social life and support (Rainie and Wellman 2012), on the one hand, and the boundedness of urban poverty and street life, on the other hand, is ripe for further theorization and empirical study. We observe the qualities of "networked individuals" (Rainie and Wellman 2012) in our studies of street life, such as when gang-involved youth and unhoused adults tap into global music audiences and far-flung networks of financial support (Stuart 2020a; Marler 2020). At the same time, we report on the heavy bearing of street encounters with local actors and law enforcement and the importance of highly localized support systems and interventions. The challenge for future research is not to settle on physical place or digital networks as the primary force shaping the lives of young people and adults living in low-income urban neighborhoods. Rather, it is to understand the linkages between expression and action as they emanate across geographic scales and through diffuse communicative pathways while remaining attuned to the local constraints and resources. A focus on networked street life, we propose, helps parse these linkages. Here, we emphasize that uses of technology may address local concerns to audiences outside the neighborhood, taking both intended and unintended paths through networked publics. For example, boosting the perception of one's neighborhood as a hyper-violent place to global audiences on social media can garner monetary and social rewards for gang-involved youth close to home; the same expressions can garner evidence against young people in court (Stuart 2020a; Lane 2019). Future research should further explicate the savvy with which members of urban poor communities understand and balance neighborhood concerns and global audiences as networked individuals.

Police Violence

Although we have primarily discussed gang violence, police violence and all forms of institutional violence must be understood side by side and as a root cause of interpersonal violence (Bourgois and Schonberg 2009). In the wake of the 2020 police killings of George Floyd and Breonna Taylor and calls to defund police, street-level questions about the use and impact of mobile video recordings of violent street encounters between police and Black residents and between police and protesters appear newly relevant. This brand of street-level videography and citizen journalism (Tufekci and Wilson 2012) can be compared against the institutional transparency of police body cameras and public access to this footage (Ramirez 2018). As we continue to theorize context collapse in urban neighborhoods, we suggest studying the wider responses of White populations and governments to online videos showing police violence and the actions or inactions that follow. We want to watch for and protect against the role of technology in amplifying existing institutional power (Toyama 2011) as technology factors more prominently in urban policing.

We hope these suggested lines of research and the broader agenda of the handbook chapter stimulate further theoretical discussion of urban-digital inequality and empirical study of street-level access, uses, and outcomes of technology. To this end, we advocate for the synchronous, ethnographic study of street life online and offline and an ongoing evaluation of our methods in order to keep up methodologically with changes in the networked lives of our participants. Networked street life holds great promise for a grass-roots approach to studying digital inequality embedded in urban communities and the interconnectedness of digital and neighborhood disadvantages.

REFERENCES

Anderson, Elijah. 1990. *Streetwise: Race, Class, and Change in an Urban Community*. Chicago: University of Chicago Press.

Anderson, Elijah. 1999. *Code of the Street: Decency, Violence, and the Moral Life of the Inner City*. New York: W. W. Norton.

Ball-Rokeach, Sandra J., Yong-Chan Kim, and Sorin Matei. 2001. "Storytelling Neighborhood: Paths to Belonging in Diverse Urban Environments." *Communication Research* 28, no. 4: 392–428.

Bell, Michael Joseph. 1983. *The World from Brown's Lounge: An Ethnography of Black Middle-Class Play*. Urbana: University of Illinois Press.

Benjamin, Ruha. 2019. *Race after Technology: Abolitionist Tools for the New Jim Code*. Cambridge: Polity Press.

Bertel, Sven, Thomas Dressel, Tom Kohlberg, and von Vanessa Jan. 2017. "Spatial Knowledge Acquired from Pedestrian Urban Navigation Systems." In *Proceedings of the 19th International Conference on Human–Computer Interaction with Mobile Devices and Services*, 1–6. New York: ACM.

Bourgois, Philippe. 2003. *In Search of Respect: Selling Crack in El Barrio*. Cambridge: Cambridge University Press.

Bourgois, Philippe I., and Jeffrey Schonberg. 2009. *Righteous Dopefiend*. Berkeley: University of California Press.

Boy, John D., and Justus Uitermark. 2017. "Reassembling the City through Instagram." *Transactions of the Institute of British Geographers* 42, no. 4: 612–624.

Boy, John D., and Justus Uitermark. 2020. "Lifestyle Enclaves in the Instagram City?" *Social Media + Society* 6, no. 3. doi: 10.1177/2056305120940698.

boyd, danah. 2011. "Social Network Sites as Networked Publics." In *A Networked Self: Identity, Community, and Culture on Social Network Sites*, edited by Zizi. Papacharissi, 39–58. New York and London: Routledge.

boyd, danah. 2014. *It's Complicated: The Social Lives of Networked Teens*. New Haven, CT: Yale University Press.

Brayne, Sarah. 2020. *Predict and Surveil: Data, Discretion, and the Future of Policing*. New York: Oxford University Press.

Briggs, Xavier de Souza. 1998. "Brown Kids in White Suburbs: Housing Mobility and the Many Faces of Social Capital." *Housing Policy Debate* 9, no. 1: 177–221.

Burke, Moira, Cameron Marlow, and Thomas Lento. 2010. "Social Network Activity and Social Well-Being." In *Proceedings of the SIGCHI Conference on Human Factors in Computing Systems*, 1909–1912. New York: ACM.

Coletta, Claudio, and Rob Kitchin. 2017. "Algorhythmic Governance: Regulating the 'Heartbeat' of a City Using the Internet of Things." *Big Data & Society* 4, no. 2: 2053951717742418.

Dailey, Dharma, Amelia Bryne, Alison Powell, Joe Karaganis, and Jaewon Chung. 2010. *Broadband Adoption in Low-Income Communities*. New York: Social Science Research Council.

Dance, Lory Janelle. 2002. *Tough Fronts: The Impact of Street Culture on Schooling*. New York and London: RoutledgeFalmer.

Davis, Jenny L., and Nathan Jurgenson. 2014. "Context Collapse: Theorizing Context Collusions and Collisions." *Information Communication and Society* 17, no. 4: 476–485. https://doi.org/10.1080/1369118X.2014.888458.

Densley, James A., and David C. Pyrooz. 2020. "The Matrix in Context: Taking Stock of Police Gang Databases in London and Beyond." *Youth Justice* 20, no. 1–2: 11–30.

Desmond, Matthew. 2012. "Disposable Ties and the Urban Poor." *American Journal of Sociology* 117, no. 5: 1295–1335.

de Souza e Silva, Adriana, and Mimi Sheller. 2014. *Mobility and Locative Media: Mobile Communication in Hybrid Spaces*. London and New York: Routledge.

Dill, Bonnie Thornton, and Ruth Enid Zambrana. 2009. "Critical Thinking about Inequality: An Emerging Lens." In *Emerging Intersections: Race, Class, and Gender in Theory,*

Policy, and Practice, edited by Bonnie Thornton Dill and Ruth Enid Zambrana, 1–21. New Brunswick, NJ: Rutgers University Press.

DiMaggio, Paul, Eszter Hargittai, Coral Celeste, and Steven Shafer. 2004. "Digital Inequality: From Unequal Access to Differentiated Use." In *Social Inequality*, edited by Kathryn M. Neckerman, 355–400. New York: Russell Sage Foundation.

Donath, Judith. 2007. "Signals in Social Supernets." *Journal of Computer-Mediated Communication* 13, no. 1: 231–251. https://doi.org/10.1111/j.1083-6101.2007.00394.x.

Duneier, Mitchell. 1999. *Sidewalk*. New York: Farrar, Straus and Giroux.

Duneier, Mitchell, Philip Kasinitz, and Alexandra Murphy, eds. 2014. *The Urban Ethnography Reader*. New York: Oxford University Press.

Duneier, Mitchell, and Harvey Molotch. 1999. "Talking City Trouble: Interactional Vandalism, Social Inequality, and the 'Urban Interaction Problem.'" *American Journal of Sociology* 104, no. 5: 1263–1295.

Edin, Kathryn, and Laura Lein. 1997. *Making Ends Meet: How Single Mothers Survive Welfare and Low-Wage Work*. New York: Russell Sage Foundation.

Ellison, Nicole B., Cliff Lampe, Charles Steinfield, and Jessica Vitak. 2011. "With a Little Help from My Friends: How Social Network Sites Affect Social Capital Processes." In *A Networked Self: Identity, Community and Culture on Social Network Sites*, edited by Zizi Papacharissi, 124–146. New York and London: Routledge.

Eubanks, Virginia. 2018. *Automating Inequality: How High-Tech Tools Profile, Police, and Punish the Poor*. New York: St. Martin's Press.

Felder, Maxime. 2020. "Strong, Weak and Invisible Ties: A Relational Perspective on Urban Coexistence." *Sociology* 54, no. 4: 675–692. https://doi.org/10.1177/0038038519895938.

Fine, Gary Alan. 1995. *A Second Chicago School? The Development of a Postwar American Sociology*. Chicago: University of Chicago Press.

Flyverbom, Mikkel, Paul M. Leonardi, Cynthia Stohl, and Michael Stohl. 2016. "The Management of Visibilities in the Digital Age." *International Journal of Communication* 10, no. 1: 98–109.

Frey, William R., Desmond U. Patton, Michael B. Gaskell, and Kyle A. McGregor. 2020. "Artificial Intelligence and Inclusion: Formerly Gang-Involved Youth as Domain Experts for Analyzing Unstructured Twitter Data." *Social Science Computer Review* 38, no. 1: 42–56. https://doi.org/10.1177/0894439318788314.

Gangadharan, Seeta Pena, ed. 2014. *Data and Discrimination: Collected Essays*. With Virginia Eubanks and Solon Barocas. Washington, DC: Open Technology Institute.

Gangadharan, Seeta Peña. 2017. "The Downside of Digital Inclusion: Expectations and Experiences of Privacy and Surveillance among Marginal Internet Users." *New Media and Society* 19, no. 4: 597–615. https://doi.org/10.1177/1461444815614053.

Garot, Robert. 2007. "Non-Violence in the Inner City: 'Decent' and 'Street' as Strategic Resources." *Journal of African American Studies* 10, no. 4: 94–111.

Georgiou, Myria. 2013. *Media and the City: Cosmopolitanism and Difference*. Cambridge: Polity.

Gonzales, Amy. 2016. "The Contemporary US Digital Divide: From Initial Access to Technology Maintenance." *Information, Communication & Society* 19, no. 2: 234–248.

Gordon, Eric, and Adriana de Souza e Silva. 2011. *Net Locality: Why Location Matters in a Networked World*. Chichester, UK: John Wiley & Sons.

Granovetter, Mark S. 1973. "The Strength of Weak Ties." *American Journal of Sociology* 78, no. 6: 1360–1380. https://doi.org/10.1086/225469.

Hampton, Keith N. 2010. "Internet Use and the Concentration of Disadvantage: Glocalization and the Urban Underclass." *American Behavioral Scientist* 53, no. 8: 1111–1132. https://doi.org/10.1177/0002764209356244.

Hampton, Keith N. 2016. "Persistent and Pervasive Community: New Communication Technologies and the Future of Community." *American Behavioral Scientist* 60, no. 1: 101–124.

Hampton, Keith N., Oren Livio, and Lauren Sessions Goulet. 2010. "The Social Life of Wireless Urban Spaces: Internet Use, Social Networks, and the Public Realm." *Journal of Communication* 60, no. 4: 701–722. https://doi.org/10.1111/j.1460-2466.2010.01510.x.

Hargittai, Eszter. 2002. "Second-Level Digital Divide: Differences in People's Online Skills." *First Monday* 7, no. 4. https://firstmonday.org/article/view/942/864.

Hargittai, Eszter, and Amanda Hinnant. 2008. "Digital Inequality: Differences in Young Adults' Use of the Internet." *Communication Research* 35, no. 5: 602–621.

Hargittai, Eszter, and Yuli Patrick Hsieh. 2013. "Digital Inequality." In *The Oxford Handbook of Internet Studies*, edited by William H Dutton, 129–150. Oxford: Oxford University Press.

Hassani, Sara Nephew. 2006. "Locating Digital Divides at Home, Work, and Everywhere Else." *Poetics* 34, no. 4–5: 250–272. https://doi.org/10.1016/j.poetic.2006.05.007.

Hepp, Andreas, Andreas Breiter, and Uwe Hasebrink. 2018. "Rethinking Transforming Communications: An Introduction." In *Communicative Figurations: Transforming Communications in Times of Deep Mediatization*, edited by Andreas Hepp, Andreas Breiter, and Uwe Hasebrink, 3–14. Cham, Switzerland: Springer Nature.

Hitchens, Brooklynn K. 2019. "Girl Fights and the Online Media Construction of Black Female Violence and Sexuality." *Feminist Criminology* 14, no. 2: 173–197. https://doi.org/10.1177/1557085117723705.

Humphreys, Lee. 2010. "Mobile Social Networks and Urban Public Space." *New Media & Society* 12, no. 5: 763–778.

Humphry, Justine. 2019. "Looking for Wi-Fi: Youth Homelessness and Mobile Connectivity in the City." *Information Communication and Society*. https://doi.org/10.1080/1369118X.2019.1670227.

Ito, Mizuko. 2008. "Introduction." In *Networked Publics*, edited by Kazys Varnelis, 1–14. Cambridge, MA: MIT Press.

Jacobs, Jane. 1961. *The Death and Life of Great American Cities*. New York: Random House.

Jerolmack, Colin. 2013. *The Global Pigeon*. Chicago: University of Chicago Press.

Jones, Nikki. 2009. *Between Good and Ghetto: African American Girls and Inner-City Violence*. New Brunswick, NJ: Rutgers University Press.

Katz, Vikki S., and Carmen Gonzalez. 2016. "Toward Meaningful Connectivity: Using Multilevel Communication Research to Reframe Digital Inequality." *Journal of Communication* 66, no. 2: 236–249. https://doi.org/10.1111/jcom.12214.

Katz, Vikki S., and Keith N. Hampton. 2016. "Communication in City and Community: From the Chicago School to Digital Technology." *American Behavioral Scientist* 60, no. 1: 3–7. https://doi.org/10.1177/0002764215601708.

Kim, Yong-Chan, Matthew D. Matsaganis, Holley A. Wilkin, and Joo-Young Jung, eds. 2018. *The Communication Ecology of 21st Century Urban Communities*. New York: Peter Lang.

Lane, Jeffrey. 2018. "Rethinking the Brand–Community Relationship: Wearing a Biggie in Harlem." *Journal of Consumer Culture*. https://doi.org/10.1177/1469540518773823.

Lane, Jeffrey. 2019. *The Digital Street*. New York: Oxford University Press.

Lane, Jeffrey. 2020. "A Smartphone Case Method: Reimagining Social Relationships with Smartphone Data in the U.S. Context of Harlem." *Journal of Children and Media*. https://doi.org/10.1080/17482798.2019.1710718.

Lane, Jeffrey, Fanny A. Ramirez, and Katy E. Pearce. 2018. "Guilty by Visible Association: Socially Mediated Visibility in Gang Prosecutions." *Journal of Computer-Mediated Communication* 23, no. 6: 354–369. https://doi.org/10.1093/jcmc/zmy019.

Lauger, Timothy R., and James A. Densley. 2018. "Broadcasting Badness: Violence, Identity, and Performance in the Online Gang Rap Scene." *Justice Quarterly* 35, no. 5: 816–841. https://doi.org/10.1080/07418825.2017.1341542.

Liebow, Elliot. 1967. *Tally's Corner: A Study of Negro Streetcorner Men*. Lanham, MD: Rowman & Littlefield.

Lin, Nan. 2001. *Social Capital: A Theory of Social Structure and Action*. Cambridge: Cambridge University Press.

Livingstone, Sonia, and Ellen Helsper. 2007. "Gradations in Digital Inclusion: Children, Young People and the Digital Divide." *New Media and Society* 9, no. 4: 671–696. https://doi.org/10.1177/1461444807080335.

Lu, Weixu, and Keith N. Hampton. 2017. "Beyond the Power of Networks: Differentiating Network Structure from Social Media Affordances for Perceived Social Support." *New Media & Society* 19, no. 6: 861–879. https://doi.org/10.1177/1461444815621514.

Madden, Mary. 2017. *Privacy, Security, and Digital Inequality*. New York: Data & Society Research Institute. https://datasociety.net/pubs/prv/DataAndSociety_PrivacySecurityandDigitalInequality.pdf.

Marler, Will. 2018. "Mobile Phones and Inequality: Findings, Trends, and Future Directions." *New Media & Society* 20, no. 9: 3498–3520. https://doi.org/10.1177/1461444818765154.

Marler, Will. 2019. "Accumulating Phones: Aid and Adaptation in Phone Access for the Urban Poor." *Mobile Media & Communication* 7, no. 2: 155–174. https://doi.org/10.1177/2050157918800350.

Marler, Will. 2020. "Urban Digital Inequality: Adversity and Adaptation in the Network Society." Northwestern University.

Marwick, Alice, Claire Fontaine, and danah boyd. 2017. " 'Nobody Sees It, Nobody Gets Mad': Social Media, Privacy, and Personal Responsibility among Low-SES Youth." *Social Media and Society* 3, no. 2. https://doi.org/10.1177/2056305117710455.

Marwick, Alice E. 2013. *Status Update: Celebrity, Publicity, and Branding in the Social Media Age*. New Haven, CT: Yale University Press.

Morelli, Niccolò. 2019. "Creating Urban Sociality in Middle-Class Neighborhoods in Milan and Bologna: A Study on the Social Streets Phenomenon." *City & Community* 18, no. 3: 834–852.

Mueller, M. L., and J. R. Schement. 1996. "Universal Service from the Bottom Up: A Study of Telephone Penetration in Camden, New Jersey." *Information Society* 12, no. 3: 273–292. https://doi.org/10.1080/019722496129468.

Napoli, Philip M., and Jonathan A. Obar. 2014. "The Emerging Mobile Internet Underclass: A Critique of Mobile Internet Access." *Information Society* 30, no. 5: 323–334. https://doi.org/10.1080/01972243.2014.944726.

National Telecommunications and Information Administration. 1995. "Falling through the Net: A Survey of the 'Have Nots' in Rural and Urban America." Washington, DC: US Department of Commerce.

Negus, Keith. 1999. "The Music Business and Rap: Between the Street and the Executive Suite." *Cultural Studies* 13, no. 3: 488–508.

Patton, Desmond Upton, Robert D. Eschmann, and Dirk A. Butler. 2013. "Internet Banging: New Trends in Social Media, Gang Violence, Masculinity and Hip Hop." *Computers in Human Behavior* 29, no. 5: A54–A59. https://doi.org/10.1016/j.chb.2012.12.035.

Patton, Desmond Upton, Patrick Leonard, Caitlin Elaesser, Robert D. Eschmann, Sadiq Patel, and Shantel Crosby. 2019. "What's a Threat on Social Media? How Black and Latino Chicago Young Men Define and Navigate Threats Online." *Youth and Society* 51, no. 6: 756–772. https://doi.org/10.1177/0044118X17720325.

Patton, Desmond Upton, Owen Rambow, Jonathan Auerbach, Kevin Li, and William Frey. 2018. "Expressions of Loss Predict Aggressive Comments on Twitter among Gang-Involved Youth in Chicago." *NPJ Digital Medicine* 1, no. 1: 1–2.

Patton, Desmond Upton, Robin Stevens, Jocelyn R. Smith Lee, Grace Cecile Eya, and William Frey. 2020. "You Set Me Up: Gendered Perceptions of Twitter Communication among Black Chicago Youth." *Social Media and Society* 6, no. 2. https://doi.org/10.1177/2056305120913877.

Patton, Desmond Upton, Douglas-Wade Brunton, Andrea Dixon, Reuben Jonathan Miller, Patrick Leonard, and Rose Hackman. 2017. "Stop and Frisk Online: Theorizing Everyday Racism in Digital Policing in the Use of Social Media for Identification of Criminal Conduct and Associations." *Social Media + Society* 3, no. 3: 205630511773334. https://doi.org/10.1177/2056305117733344.

Pew Research Center. 2019. "Mobile Fact Sheet." Internet and Technology. https://www.pewresearch.org/internet/fact-sheet/mobile/.

Pyrooz, David C., Scott H. Decker, and Richard K. Moule. 2015. "Criminal and Routine Activities in Online Settings: Gangs, Offenders, and the Internet." *Justice Quarterly* 32, no. 3: 471–499. https://doi.org/10.1080/07418825.2013.778326.

Rainie, Harrison, and Barry Wellman. 2012. *Networked: The New Social Operating System*. Cambridge, MA: MIT Press.

Ramirez, Fanny A. 2018. "Social Media Affordances in the Context of Police Transparency: An Analysis of the First Public Archive of Police Body Camera Videos." *Journal of Applied Communication Research* 46, no. 5: 621–640.

Rickman, Aimee, and Christian Sandvig. 2014. "Broke and Buying Rides: Adolescent Girls and Social Media Brokering." In *Proceedings of the Eighth International AAAI Conference on Weblogs and Social Media*, 1–10. Palo Alto, CA: AAAI Press.

Rios, Victor M., Greg Prieto, and Jonathan M. Ibarra. 2020. "Mano Suave–Mano Dura: Legitimacy Policing and Latino Stop-and-Frisk." *American Sociological Review* 85, no. 1: 58–75.

Robinson, Laura, Shelia R. Cotten, Hiroshi Ono, Anabel Quan-Haase, Gustavo Mesch, Wenhong Chen, et al. 2015. "Digital Inequalities and Why They Matter." *Information, Communication & Society* 18, no. 5: 569–582. https://doi.org/10.1080/1369118X.2015.1012532.

Ross, Jeffrey Ian. 2018. "Reframing Urban Street Culture: Towards a Dynamic and Heuristic Process Model." *City, Culture and Society* 15: 7–13.

Ross, Jeffrey Ian, G. James Daichendt, Sebastian Kurtenbach, Paul Gilchrist, Monique Charles, and James Wicks. 2019. "Clarifying Street Culture: Integrating a Diversity of Opinions and Voices." *Urban Research and Practice*. https://doi.org/10.1080/17535069.2019.1630673.

Saker, Michael, and Jordan Frith. 2018. "Locative Media and Sociability: Using Location-Based Social Networks to Coordinate Everyday Life." *Architecture_MPS* 14, no. 1. https://doi.org/10.14324/111.444.amps.2018v14i1.001.

Sampson, Robert J. 2012. *Great American City: Chicago and the Enduring Neighborhood Effect*. Chicago University of Chicago Press.

Sampson, Robert J., Jeffrey D. Morenoff, and Thomas Gannon-Rowley. 2002. "Assessing 'Neighborhood Effects': Social Processes and New Directions in Research." *Annual Review of Sociology* 28, no. 1: 443–478.

Scheerder, Anique, Alexander van Deursen, and Jan van Dijk. 2017. "Determinants of Internet Skills, Uses and Outcomes. A Systematic Review of the Second- and Third-Level Digital Divide." *Telematics and Informatics* 34, no. 8: 1607–1624. https://doi.org/10.1016/j.tele.2017.07.007.

Sharkey, Patrick, and Jacob W. Faber. 2014. "Where, When, Why, and for Whom Do Residential Contexts Matter? Moving away from the Dichotomous Understanding of Neighborhood Effects." *Annual Review of Sociology* 40: 559–579.

Sharkey, Patrick T. 2006. "Navigating Dangerous Streets: The Sources and Consequences of Street Efficacy." *American Sociological Review* 71, no. 5: 826–846.

Shelton, Taylor, Ate Poorthuis, and Matthew Zook. 2015. "Social Media and the City: Rethinking Urban Socio-Spatial Inequality Using User-Generated Geographic Information." *Landscape and Urban Planning* 142: 198–211. https://doi.org/10.1016/j.landurbplan.2015.02.020.

Small, Mario Luis. 2009. *Unanticipated Gains: Origins of Network Inequality in Everyday Life*. New York: Oxford University Press.

Snow, David A., and Leon Anderson. 1993. *Down on Their Luck: A Study of Homeless Street People*. Berkeley: University of California Press.

Sorell, Tom, and Monica Whitty. 2019. "Online Romance Scams and Victimhood." *Security Journal* 32: 342–361. https://doi.org/10.1057/s41284-019-00166-w.

Spiller, Keith. 2020. " 'Putting Everything up There': Framing How We Navigate the Intricacies of Privacy and Security on Social Media." *Humanity & Society*. https://doi.org/10.1177/0160597620904502.

Spradley, James P. 1970. *You Owe Yourself a Drunk: An Ethnography of Urban Nomads*. Boston: Little, Brown.

Stack, Carol B. 1975. *All Our Kin: Strategies for Survival in a Black Community*. New York: Basic Books.

Star, Susan, Lucy Suchman, Jeanette Blomberg, Julian Orr, Randall Trigg, Nicola Green, et al. 1999. "The Ethnography of Infrastructure." *American Behavioral Scientist* 43, no. 3: 377–392.

Stevens, Robin, Stacia Gilliard-Matthews, Jamie Dunaev, Marcus K. Woods, and Bridgette M. Brawner. 2017. "The Digital Hood: Social Media Use among Youth in Disadvantaged Neighborhoods." *New Media & Society* 19, no. 6: 950–967.

Storrod, Michelle L., and James A. Densley. 2017. " 'Going Viral' and 'Going Country': The Expressive and Instrumental Activities of Street Gangs on Social Media." *Journal of Youth Studies* 20, no. 6: 677–696.

Stuart, Forrest. 2014. "From 'Rabble Management' to 'Recovery Management': Policing Homelessness in Marginal Urban Space." *Urban Studies* 51, no. 9: 1909–1925.

Stuart, Forrest. 2016. "Becoming 'Copwise': Policing, Culture, and the Collateral Consequences of Street-Level Criminalization." *Law & Society Review* 50, no. 2: 279–313.

Stuart, Forrest. 2020a. *Ballad of the Bullet: Gangs, Drill Music, and the Power of Online Infamy*. Princeton, NJ: Princeton University Press.

Stuart, Forrest. 2020b. "Code of the Tweet: Urban Gang Violence in the Social Media Age." *Social Problems* 67, no. 2: 191–207.

Stuart, Forrest, Alicia Riley, and Hossein Pourreza. 2020. "A Human–Machine Partnered Approach for Identifying Social Media Signals of Elevated Traumatic Grief in Chicago Gang Territories." *PLoS One* 15, no. 7: e0236625.

Sutko, Daniel M., and Adriana de Souza e Silva. 2011. "Location-Aware Mobile Media and Urban Sociability." *New Media and Society* 13, no. 5: 807–823. https://doi.org/10.1177/1461444810385202.

Suttles, Gerald D. 1968. *The Social Order of the Slum: Ethnicity and Territory in the Inner City.* Chicago: University of Chicago Press.

Thorne, Barrie. 1980. " 'You Still Takin' Notes?' Fieldwork and Problems of Informed Consent." *Social Problems* 27, no. 3: 284–297.

Toyama, Kentaro. 2011. "Technology as Amplifier in International Development." *iConference '11: Proceedings of the 2011 iConference*, 75–82. New York: ACM. https://doi.org/10.1145/1940761.1940772.

Tsetsi, Eric, and Stephen A. Rains. 2017. "Smartphone Internet Access and Use: Extending the Digital Divide and Usage Gap." *Mobile Media and Communication* 5, no. 3: 239–255. https://doi.org/10.1177/2050157917708329.

Tufekci, Zeynep. 2013. " 'Not This One' Social Movements, the Attention Economy, and Microcelebrity Networked Activism." *American Behavioral Scientist* 57, no. 7: 848–870.

Tufekci, Zeynep, and Christopher Wilson. 2012. "Social Media and the Decision to Participate in Political Protest: Observations from Tahrir Square." *Journal of Communication* 62, no. 2: 363–379. https://doi.org/10.1111/j.1460-2466.2012.01629.x.

Urbanik, Marta Marika, and Kevin D. Haggerty. 2018. " '#It's Dangerous': The Online World of Drug Dealers, Rappers and the Street Code." *British Journal of Criminology* 58, no. 6: 1343–1360. https://doi.org/10.1093/bjc/azx083.

Urbanik, Marta Marika, and Robert A. Roks. 2020. "GangstaLife: Fusing Urban Ethnography with Netnography in Gang Studies." *Qualitative Sociology* 43: 213–233. https://doi.org/10.1007/s11133-020-09445-0.

van Deursen, Alexander J. A. M., and Ellen J. Helsper. 2015. "The Third-Level Digital Divide: Who Benefits Most from Being Online?" In *Communication and Information Technologies Annual: Digital Distinctions and Inequalities*, edited by Laura Robinson, Sheila R. Cotten, Jeremy Schulz, Timothy M. Hale, and Apryl Williams, 29–53. Studies in Media and Communications 10. Bingley, UK: Emerald Group. https://doi.org/10.1108/S2050-206020150000010002.

van Deursen, Alexander J. A. M., Ellen J. Helsper, Rebecca Eynon, and Jan A. G. M. Van Dijk. 2017. "The Compoundness and Sequentiality of Digital Inequality." *International Journal of Communication* 11: 452–473. http://eprints.lse.ac.uk/id/eprint/68921

van Deursen, Alexander J. A. M., and Jan A. G. M. van Dijk. 2014. "The Digital Divide Shifts to Differences in Usage." *New Media & Society* 16, no. 3: 507–526. https://doi.org/10.1177/1461444813487959.

van Dijk, Jan, and Kenneth Hacker. 2003. "The Digital Divide as a Complex and Dynamic Phenomenon." *The Information Society* 19, no. 4: 315–326. https://doi.org/10.1080/01972240309487.

Venkatesh, Sudhir Alladi. 2006. *Off the Books: The Underground Economy of the Urban Poor.* Cambridge, MA: Harvard University Press.

Zillien, Nicole, and Eszter Hargittai. 2009. "Digital Distinction: Status-Specific Types of Internet Usage." *Social Science Quarterly* 90, no. 2: 274–291. https://doi.org/10.1111/j.1540-6237.2009.00617.x.

Zukin, Sharon, Scarlett Lindeman, and Laurie Hurson. 2017. "The Omnivore's Neighborhood? Online Restaurant Reviews, Race, and Gentrification." *Journal of Consumer Culture* 17, no. 3: 459–479.

PART V

SOCIAL INEQUALITIES IN THE DIGITAL LANDSCAPE

CHAPTER 23

THE FEMINIZATION OF SOCIAL MEDIA LABOR

SOPHIE BISHOP AND BROOKE ERIN DUFFY

DURING a 2010 TED talk that garnered more than 1.5 million views and generated a steady stream of media coverage, entertainment researcher Johanna Blakley offered a provocative prediction about the advent of social media: It marked the waning significance of gender. To Blakley, media models long powered by crude demographic categories were being supplanted by tools of customization promising to "free us from absurd assumptions about gender" (Blakley 2010). Less than a decade later, an essay published in *The Business of Fashion* offered a strikingly similar appraisal of a media ecology wrought by digitization. Headlined "Is This the End of Gendered Media?" and penned by former *New York Times* style writer Chantal Fernandez, the article contended that niche economic models, coupled with more fluid gender roles, were rendering identity-based constructions of the audience less and less relevant (Fernandez 2019). Signaling the implications of these new media logics for progressive identity politics, Fernandez contended that we "feel less defined by gender norms than they did in the past" (para. 5).

Though accounts of a media environment unencumbered by traditional gender norms and stereotypes are beguiling, they are by no means unprecedented; rather, they index an early perspective about the trappings of identity play and performativity enabled by new media technologies (e.g., Turkle 1999; Hine 2000). Summarizing early optimism about the internet's provisions for users to *be anyone*, Baym (2015) writes

> On a societal level, anonymity opens the possibility of liberation from the divisions that come about from seeing one another's race, age, gender, abilities and so on.... Early rhetoric about the internet often speculated that the reduction of social cues would lead to people valuing one another's contributions for their intrinsic worth rather than the speaker's status. (pp. 38–39).

In more recent years, the techno-optimism of the 1990s and the early 2000s has been supplanted by critical attention to the profoundly undemocratic nature of digital communication and information. Not only are online environments mired by identity-based bias and discrimination (e.g., Banet-Weiser 2018; Massanari 2017; Nakamura 2015; Sobieraj 2018, 2020) but examples of unabashedly feminine and masculine subcultures are rife across Instagram, YouTube, TikTok, and more (e.g., Bishop 2019; Duffy and Hund 2015; Stuart 2020). Accordingly, we take the perspective that gender remains as relevant as ever to digital sociologists as well as to those users who rely on social media platforms for creativity, community, and career prospects. By examining key features and contradictions of social media labor, we show how traditional gender codes persist—and, in some cases, are amplified—on mainstream social media platforms.

This chapter begins by summarizing sociologies of "women's work" (e.g., Daniels 1987; Acker 1990; Cohen and Huffman 2003) that illuminate the patterned social and economic devaluation of feminized labor; social histories of both the media and technology industries, we contend, are especially relevant precursors to social media. Then, to systematize our discussion of the mechanisms and implications of such devaluation, we explore four interrelated features of feminized labor: (1) the demand for emotional and affective expressions, (2) the discipline of aesthetics through the fraught ideal of "visibility," (3) mandates for flexibility and an always-on stance, and (4) a deep imbrication with consumer capitalism. In exploring each of these features, we show how the devaluation of gender-coded labor is exacerbated along other axes of social inequality, including age, race, class, ethnicity, ability, and sexuality.

In exploring social media's requirements for emotional and affective expressions, we invoke Hochschild's ([1983] 2012) original formulation of emotional labor, wherein (overwhelmingly women) laborers are called upon to manage their own emotional state—often within strict organizational boundaries—in an effort to elicit the desired response of another. In many commercial online spaces, carefully managed projections of the self have much in common with the perpetually upbeat, neatly groomed, empathetic flight attendants who took center stage in Hochschild's study. However, we should also consider how feminized online labor encompasses a diversity of social norms or "feeling rules." As such, we show how other enactments of social media labor are thus reminiscent of Hochschild's comparatively under-cited account of bill collectors, who avoided the strategic perception of closeness, instead maintaining a perception of aloofness and distance in order to manage unruly and potentially dangerous clientele. Accounts of online community moderators and social media managers serve as illustrative case studies.

While emotional and affective labor are often conceptualized as instantiations of *invisible* labor, the second section draws attention to the fraught politics of *visibility*. On the one hand, we show how social media personalities are compelled to "put themselves out there" in ways that reaffirm heteronormative codes of femininity (Bishop 2019; Duffy and Hund 2019). At the same time, such visibility makes them more vulnerable to a host of negative consequences: from economic exploitation (Duffy 2017) to increased mechanisms of surveillance and moderation (Nakamura 2015; Gill 2019) to expressions of misogyny and targeted harassment (Sobieraj 2018; Banet-Weiser 2018; Lawson 2020).

Greater still is the level of vulnerability experienced by women of color, the LGBTQ community, and members of other marginalized groups.

The third section offers a critical reflection on the worker ideal of flexibility, wherein social media users and laborers are expected to exhibit nimbleness in the face of platforms' constant push to "innovate." We tie these flexibility directives to discourses that construct women as uniquely adaptable and primed for multitasking (Mayer 2013; Bridges 2018; Morgan and Nelligan 2015). In addition to highlighting the demand for always-on worker-personae willing to collapse personal and professional boundaries, we note how platforms' unanticipated tweaks and updates have amped up the requirements for flexibility. Finally, we examine how various modes of social media activity—from product sharing to brand advocacy—deploy thinly veiled promises of creativity and participation while ultimately directing users toward consumptive ends. As we contend in this section, the historical conflation of women and shopping—as well as twentieth-century debates about the media's provisions of "the audience commodity"—gets revived in the context of social media's prescriptions for the "shoppable life" (Hund and McGuigan 2019).

In closing, we outline future directions for researching the intersection of gender, social media, and labor—including the politics of "visibility," unevenly applied content moderation, and the invisible labor required to navigate perpetual harassment and abuse. The need for such research seems all the more urgent at the present historical juncture; indeed, social media work is highly compatible with neoliberal mandates for entrepreneurial individualized work, which redouble during economic recessions. Traditionally "feminized" occupations can now be organized and marketed through social media platforms (e.g., Duffy and Pruchniewska 2017); yet, the platformization of women's work places women at risk of erasure through uneven systems of moderation (Gerrard and Thornham 2020). As such, critical interventions into inequities in both society and the labor economy have been made all the more pressing.

Contextualizing "Women's Work"

Though the term "women's work" is laden with normative value judgments, it is also a profoundly relative concept; that is, what counts as "women's work" varies considerably across historical, geographic, and sociocultural contexts. Activities ranging from unwaged domestic and care labor (e.g., Federici 2002; Weeks 2011) to waged service work (Hochschild [1983] 2012; Duffy 2007) to jobs that foreground "soft skills" (e.g., Andrews 2016; Hill 2016; Mayer 2013) have been critically examined through the lens of "women's work." Despite such conceptual ambiguity, we invoke the term to refer to activities in the labor market that are (1) overwhelmingly (though, not exclusively) performed by women and, thus, have been (2) socially and economically devalued within capitalist economies (Daniels 1987; Webster 2014; Weeks 2011). As feminist scholars have made clear, there is nothing natural or inevitable about the particular tasks and professions that get designated—or, more aptly, denigrated—as "women's work." Rather, as Webster (2014) usefully reminds, the devaluation of women-coded career sectors occurs "no matter how much individual jobs may involve competence, skill, and technological knowledge" (p. 143; see also Mayer 2013). Accordingly, examples abound from the realm of waged work wherein professional sectors have undergone progressive feminizations or masculinizations alongside fluctuations in their workforce compositions, salaries, and statuses (e.g., Hicks 2017; Arndt and Bigelow 2005).

Especially relevant to the present analysis are accounts of feminized labor within the media and technology industries. Both historical and contemporary research into the cultural industries, for instance, reveal a division of labor that falls sharply along gender lines: While women have traditionally been relegated to administrative, clerical, and communications- oriented positions, men are overrepresented in creative, executive, and technological roles (Banks 2018; Mayer 2013; Hesmondhalgh and Baker 2015). As Hill (2016) chronicles of the early film industry, early twentieth-century Hollywood was marked by a

> *de facto* occupational segregation that links women to certain types of media production work [while] effectively dissociat[ing] them from others, thereby perpetuating male domination in fields with the greatest prestige and power, the most creative status, and the highest incomes. (p. 6)

Such forms of gendered clustering—or what labor sociologists term "occupational segregation" (e.g., Bielby and Baron 1986)—are not unique to the early studio system. Rather, gendered divisions of labor are pervasive in TV and movies (Mayer 2013; Banks 2018; Ouellette and Wilson 2011), journalism/publishing (Steiner 2012; Hesmondhalgh and Baker 2015), and broadcasting (Coventry 2004), among others. What weaves these industry-based studies together is a shared recognition that the positions wherein women cluster have been systematically devalued—be it through reduced wages, a lack of respect, or assumptions that this work is less central to the fundamentals of the business.

Gender is not the only system of exclusion that sullies the cultural industries' spirit of "cool, creative, [and] egalitarian" (Gill, 2002) work. Hill (2016) notes how the film industry operated like so many other American businesses during that era: with a "tacit policy of workplace segregation, under which it was understood black men would not be hired in most positions and would be the only type of employees hired for others" (p. 72). The legacy of US Jim Crow—and structures of occupational segregation—persists in contemporary Hollywood. As Erigha (2019) details of the contemporary film industry, opportunities for African Americans are largely confined to "movies that regularly devalue, label unbankable, marginalize, and ghettoize" (p. 71). Black women, moreover, experience double exclusion, so much so that they are often relegated to a "permanent underclass" (p. 109). Even when they *do* break into creative industries, Black women confront cultural intermediaries who seek to "brand" them in accordance with discriminatory cultural stereotypes. As Balaji (2009) notes of American pop singer

Keke Palmer, her career was shaped by her refusal of Atlantic Records' desire to market her as sexualized and "urban"—despite her White contemporaries' proven successes as highly commercial "good girls." Together, these accounts demonstrate the spectrum of social and economic forces which shape cultural production by reaffirming dominant systems of inclusion and exclusion.

Social histories of computing reveal similar patterns of gender- and race-based marginalization (e.g., Light 1999; Hicks 2017; Edwards and Harris 2017). In her aptly titled, "When Computers Were Women," Light (1999) elucidates how the usage of "computer" in reference to a technological artifact is a relatively recent development. During the mid-twentieth century, the term "computers" described the women technicians deployed by US and British governments. These early-generation tech workers were called upon for their (perceived) detail and patience; hence, the occupational clusters of the early computing industry were staggeringly different from the masculinist cultures of Silicon Valley (Marwick 2013). In calling attention to this particular phase of computing as "women's work," Hicks (2017) offers the important reminder that "gender and class, much more than skill, determined workers' roles in the computing hierarchy" (p. 230).

In more recent decades and in the context of a sprawling digital economy, there has been a growing consensus that the framework of "women's work" is apt to describe the various activities that propel the social media economy (e.g., Jarrett 2017; Cirucci 2018; Shepherd 2014). As Lisa Nakamura (2015, 106) put it, "cheap female labor is the engine that powers the internet." To be clear, we are not suggesting that women are the only devalued participants in the social media economy. Rather, digital media enliven all of us to participate in economically exploitative, undercompensated labor—forms wrought by the complexities of the pleasures and connection that forms of engagement can afford. In other words, social media can be understood through the framework of cultural feminization (Adkins 2001; see also Baym 2015).

Four Features of Feminized Social Media Labor

In what follows, we discuss four particular features of social media labor—both waged and unwaged—that testify to its feminine-coded nature.

Emotional and Affective Performances

As evinced by the "social" descriptor, social media platforms impel participation in public registers of emotion and affect: from mundane practices of "liking" Facebook posts to the raw emotional expressions furnished by YouTubers and TikTok creators.

Here, it seems important to acknowledge the slippage between the terms "emotional labor" and "affective labor"; while these terms have been used inconsistently (see Mears 2014, for a review of various subcategories of emotional labor), Joanne Entwistle and Elizabeth Wissinger (2006) supply an especially productive distinction between affective labor's emphasis on *the self* and emotional labor's desired impact on *the other*. It is in this vein that researchers have noted that social media's requirements for visible affective expressions—likes, comments, shares—alongside social forms of "identity work" (Humphreys 2018) are akin to the emotional maintenance disproportionately shouldered by women in the domestic sphere (Campbell 2011; Hillis, Paasonen, and Petit 2015). Kylie Jarrett (2017) offers the rhetorical device of "The Digital Housewife" to show how digital capitalism hinges on the uncompensated labor—likes, clicks, and ultimately data—of its users. Through the lens of Marxist feminism, Jarrett contends that these activities are both economically devalued (i.e., unpaid) yet essential to the capitalist economy—much like the role of women in the system of social reproduction.

Other research focuses on narrower domains of feminized social media labor, including community organization, activism, and social media management. Studies of early internet communities, for instance, noted how community moderators—overwhelmingly women and scarcely compensated—played a vital role in the emotional management of communities (Terranova 2000; Postigo 2009). More recently—and in line with the communicative affordances of social media—scholars have noted the enduring reliance on women for emotionally intensive digital community support. For instance, Kerr and Kelleher's (2015) analysis shows that the community managers of gaming sites is a role not only where women are overrepresented but also wherein "'soft' skills of verbal and written communication, management of emotions, diplomacy, and empathy are valued and exploited" (p. 180). deWinter, Kocurek, and Vie (2017), similarly, describe how the emotional labor requirements of community management tend to confine workers to a "liminal space between fan and company shill" (p. 41). Collective efforts at social change—including online activism and participation in call-out culture—demand similar provisions of emotional labor, often from socially vulnerable populations (Nakamura 2015; Lawson 2020). Of the "call-out culture" that provides a system of accountability in online environments, Nakamura (2015) contends that it often hinges upon "the hidden and often-stigmatized and dangerous labor performed by women of color, queer and trans people, and racial minorities who call out, educate, protest, and design around toxic social environments in digital media" (para. 1).

Meanwhile, the fast-growing field of social media management enlists "hidden workers" to wildly different ends, namely brand promotion. Often young and overwhelmingly women, social media editors/managers are tasked with carrying the mantle of their respective company's brand across the social media ecology as they ratchet up Instagram followers, Twitter favorites, and other quantified indices of affect. In the popular imagination at least, social media editing is disparaged as a "girly job," with frivolous worker activities located within a proverbial "pink ghetto" (Levinson 2015). Drawing on an analysis of social media job advertisements, Duffy and Schwartz (2018) conclude that the ideal social media worker subjectivity is constructed as a feminized one, in part through requirements for emotional labor. Explicit calls for "enthusiasm" and "positivity" invoke Hochschild's ([1983] 2012) assessment that in service work, "seeming to 'love the job' becomes part of the job." What is more, calls for employees to remain "cool under pressure" with a "calm and steady disposition" may also signal the need to endure the emotional difficulties of labor behind-the-screen (p. 2984).

Accordingly, and as we discuss further in the section on "visibility politics," women's participation in the (digital) public sphere has opened them up to networked hate and harassment—adding a new layer of emotional burden for workers to shoulder (Massanari 2018; Nakamura 2015; Sobieraj 2018). As Marta Martinez (2020) wrote in an essay titled, "The Social Media Managers Are Not Ok," the invisible workers who manage branded accounts are the frequent target of audiences' misdirected ire. In a profile of Alexya, a Black woman hired to manage social media for a news company, Martinez describes the profound emotional toll of being the voice behind the brand during Black Lives Matter protests in the United States. In addition to receiving dozens of photos, messages, and quotes from reporters on the ground, Alexya also had to monitor protest hashtags and online conversations, which were full of abusive and racist comments. As Alexya shared, "I feel threatened by the fact that people feel like they can say [racist comments] online very boldly, and I'm the target audience for that person inciting some sort of negative emotions."

But while social media managers remain concealed behind the screens, other social media professionals are compelled to provide highly visible expressions of emotional labor, including the strategic management of their digitally networked audiences. In her multiyear study of musicians, Nancy Baym (2018) notes the increased demands for cultural producers to engage in "relational labor"—or the ongoing efforts to build and sustain connections—on social media. These relationships, Baym usefully reminds, can be—and often are—simultaneously meaningful and instrumental.

Another example demonstrating the interlinked nature of affective and strategic labor can be found in Instagram's "Support Small Businesses" initiative, launched in May 2020 as the COVID-19 crisis began to unfold. Promoted as an answer to the "immense challenges" that businesses were facing during COVID-19, Instagram invited users to adorn posts with the Support Small Businesses "sticker" (Instagram 2020). The scheme refused more tangible forms of financial support, instead steering creators and their audiences to engage with Instagram's affordances in labor-intensive and affective ways: through integrating the sticker into personal posts and stories to promote the small businesses that they love (the stickers, notably, are pink-hued and heart-adorned). Despite the prosocial draped pitches, such initiatives encourage profit-generating content production for commercial platforms. More pressingly, they also ignore the real structural hardships of entrepreneurship, predominantly affecting Black business owners as they operate in the sectors worst hit by the pandemic (such as retail and healthcare), with reduced access to state support and private capital—further fraying their financial safety nets (Umoh 2020). Despite such hardships, small business owners must continue to solicit support and post regularly and positively on social media—redoubling the deep and consistent emotional labor already mandated by entrepreneurial economies.

Visibility Politics

By inviting users to "share," "post," and "update" their lives in a patterned fashion, social media platforms prod all of us to *put ourselves out there*. But as the emancipatory potential of web 2.0 for identity politics has been dimmed, the highly uneven attention economies sustained by social media platforms—in which only a small number of users can achieve a meaningful level of visibility—have been brought to bear (Glatt, forthcoming) (Goldhaber 1997). As we have argued elsewhere (Duffy 2017; Bishop 2018), the most successful women cultural producers tend to reaffirm normative standards of beauty and aesthetics and, in many cases, draw upon existing reserves of economic and social capital. We thus consider "visibility"—and its relationship to "vulnerability"—to be a second key feature of feminized social media labor.

Social media influencers—content creators who blend coverage of their personal lives with advertorial content—help to illustrate the fraught politics of digitally mediated *visibility*. Not only do mainstream influencers feel compelled to project a self-image that is simultaneously aspirational and accessible, but they are also called upon to *make public* elements of their domestic life, aesthetic labor, and daily activities to ensure a continuous stream of content (Abidin 2016; Duffy and Hund 2015). The public manifestation of this highly personal image dovetails with a need to be recognizable and desirable to potential brand sponsors (Carah and Angus 2018; Craig and Cunningham 2019). In this vein, social media platforms such as Instagram work to enforce social media's "digital double bind" which (in part) mandates "female entrepreneurs" (and arguably women more broadly) to work within "traditional prescriptions for femininity, including modesty, sociality, and an aura of decorum" (Duffy and Pruchniewska 2017, 845).

Of course, the visibility affordances of social media can also be a form of productive resistance, particularly for members of communities long underrepresented within "mainstream" media. However, examining platform work through the critical lens of *labor* demonstrates how social media's commercial context presents particular pressures on Black influencers and content creators (Sobande, Fearfull, and Brownlie 2019). Taking into account the strains of emotional and affective labor outlined in the preceding section, we can see that influencers working on YouTube are interpellated to show authentic love and enthusiasm for products that they promote. Yet these demands are complicated by the fact that beauty and fashion brands underserve women of color in numerous ways, often offering limited shades and products suitable for certain skin tones, hair types, and body shapes. Within this context, influencers who respond with critically honest product tryouts and reviews assume the risk of being designated as commercially unfriendly or "brand unsafe" (Bishop 2021; Lawson 2020). The line between commercially viable and authentic is thus more laborious and affectively charged for women of color; such uncertainty, moreover, impels consistent, often emotive, labor from content creators to strategize toward visibility.

As such, we contend that any reflection on platform-contingent labor and visibility must also acknowledge the increased risks and potential vulnerabilities. More pointedly, those who experience structural forms of marginalization must work more to negotiate embodied risks—such as the increased risk of "policing, abuse and harassment" in digital spaces (Duffy and Hund 2019, 4987; see also, Massanari 2018; Nakamura 2015; Sobieraj 2018). This work is redoubled for women of color—platform comment sections have been identified as spaces of "networked racialized hostility" (Murthy and Sharma 2019); Amnesty International found that Black women were 84% more likely to be mentioned in abusive tweets than White women (Amnesty International 2018). Furthermore, social media platforms and their uneven attention economies reify long-standing material social and cultural inequalities, particularly along the lines of class and race (Noble 2018). YouTube and Instagram, in particular, have been critiqued for the Whiteness of their "top" creators; several of YouTube's flagship creators publicly apologized in mid-2020 for historic racist content, for example, producing videos in blackface and using slurs (Kiefer 2020). Across commercial creator economies, female Black influencers have reported sizable pay gaps, consistently reporting being told that there is "no budget" by brands when White peers earn sizable fees for collaborations and sponsored posts (Deighton 2020).

Another instance of the uneven politics of social media visibility relates to platform-based assessments of *problematic content*; decisions about "appropriateness" often fall along gendered lines of respectability (Cook, 2019). Take, for example, Tumblr's 2018 ban on images of "female presenting nipples, which rendered the platform uninhabitable for female and queer artists who sought to post 'educational and political' sexual content" (Tiidenberg 2019). Platforms often determine and restrict so-called "problematic" content based on concerns about their public image, alongside worries about offending commercial stakeholders, particularly advertisers and app stores. Platforms' governance of content may also be underpinned by national policy decisions. For example, the US 2018 Fighting Online Sex Traffic Act has promoted a catch-all approach to the moderation of adult content across social media platforms; as such, *voluntary* forms of sex work and performance are subject to bans, in addition to the exploitative sex trafficking that this law ostensibly supports (Tiidenberg 2019). In this vein, moderation affects the livelihoods and labor of sex workers and performers (often women and queer people), who use platforms such as Instagram to vet clients, sell merchandise, and substitute *digital* sex work for *more risky* forms of in-person sex work. It is thus important to recognize that decisions often unevenly redistribute labor onto those already marginalized, as the latter must work to maintain access to platformed visibility and legibility.

Social media, for their part, deploy complex automated and human decision-making processes to moderate content, and as a result, the decisions made can often be confusing and unclear to those affected (Gillespie 2018; Myers West 2018; Roberts 2019). But for content producers, *contesting* such moderation is subject to laborious and timely administrative processes—amplifying the vulnerability of an already precarious career sector.

Flexibility

As the example of content moderation makes clear, social media creators and influencers are called upon to continuously negotiate the affordances—that is, features, design, and broader environment (Bucher and Helmond 2017)—of various platforms. Indeed, platform-dependent careers hinge on being contingent or anticipating and molding one's labor to changes wrought by platform evolution (Nieborg and Poell 2018). In a reappraisal of the cultural expectation that social media–dependent workers effortlessly navigate the public and private spheres, social media–dependent workers must stay abreast of structures, changes, and updates—with neither input nor recourse on how these manifest (O'Meara 2019). At the same time, that they are beholden to the constant tweaks that platform operators make to their algorithmic systems—often without warning. As such, social media laborers must be adaptable, exhibiting an orientation that Morgan and Nelligan (2015) called "labile laborers": "mobile, spontaneous, malleable, and capable of being aroused by new vocational possibilities" (p. 66). To take one example, in 2019, Instagram tested the removal of visible "likes" for users across Canada, the United States, and Brazil. These significant (and unevenly applied) changes presented considerable difficulties for influencers who have orientated their activities toward collecting a specific kind of engagement—impelling their followers toward symbiotic "visibility labor," which often includes activities orientated toward inviting likes, comments, and shares (Abidin 2016). This action particularly complicates working practices in feminized ecologies, which are underpinned by expectations to maintain accessibility and intimacy with their followers. The removal of likes thus reordered conceptions of value and its measurement in commercial contexts for key stakeholders in digital marketing industries.

Although all users maintain uneven relationships with social media platforms, inequalities (and the labor required to mitigate them) are exacerbated across existing lines of marginalization. Theorists have outlined the diverse ways that women, in particular, have strategized to reclaim power and agency in the face of instability. Bucher (2018), for instance, outlines a case study of the YouTube Reply Girls, who systematically posted "cleavage-bearing bodies as thumbnails to drive traffic" in their responses to popular YouTube videos. These young women deployed tried and tested attention-grabbing strategies (breasts) to cultivate engagement (clicks), propelling their videos further in the YouTube algorithm and earning them money through the platform's revenue-sharing program. The technique of cleavage-bearing was effective, but also controversial, prompting other YouTube users to express frustration with the Reply Girls' allegedly "spammy" strategies. The Reply Girls were young women responding to platform conditions, "[building] their businesses and practices around the existing culture of clicks and reply videos"; yet, crucially, they caused strategic algorithmic overhaul on YouTube (Bucher 2018). In this vein, the Reply Girls raise broader questions about *what* practices, undertaken by *whom*, are designated as spam by platform gatekeepers.

The demand to be flexible in the face of platforms' changing priorities disproportionately impacts already marginalized users. For example, many LGBTQI+ creators title, promote, and otherwise label their content with "queer" keywords in order to navigate platforms' algorithmic structures of visibility (Craig and Cunningham 2019). Although this practice strategically impels interested audiences, tagged queer content is also routinely censored or demonetized by platforms. At different times, these videos have been identified as not "family-friendly" by YouTube (Hunt 2017) or cautiously removed amid concerns that such videos put creators at risk of bullying on TikTok (Hern 2019). In producing these videos, YouTube creators performed the feminized affective labor described in a preceding section of this chapter: supplying advice, offering support, and signposting to resources (Fish et al. 2020; Homant and Sender 2019). In addition to this community work and the visibility labor addressed in the previous sections, queer creators are required to stay vigilant for LGBTQI+ censorship. For example, when YouTube's "family-friendly" mode was found to block queer content, creators pieced together screengrabs and shared information on Twitter to amass proof of suppression that was later presented to a dubious YouTube (Hunt, 2017).

Algorithmic changes are often implemented by platforms to encourage creators to be complicit with monetized systems—and, ultimately—to encourage them to pay for promotion (Bishop, 2020). Creators' efforts to sidestep calls for paid content distribution are often heavily critiqued by platforms, couched in moralized critiques of cheating or manipulation (Petre, Duffy, and Hund 2019). Yet, instead, these activities can be viewed as a site of platform *resistance*. Turning to examples of explicitly *collective* responses to algorithmic precarity, O'Meara (2019) views the work undertaken by Instagram influencers to "mutually like, comment on or share" as a form of "alternative labor organizing." Like the example of the Reply Girls, O'Meara recognizes that influencer work has arisen out of a drive toward precarious, entrepreneurial, individualized work that erases company-supported worker protections. She identifies a form of labor collective action in these economies—influencer "pods" or collectives that engender mutual support to improve appearances for advertisers, increase algorithmic visibility, and share strategies (Cotter 2018). This example also reveals how gender contributes to the framing of technological engagement (Bishop 2019; Hicks 2017). Technical processes of information-sharing about software and even activities that could be described as engineering or hacking are arguably taken less seriously as they intersect with feminized affective labor. Algorithmically boosting mutual support intersects with caring and emotive work in complex and far-reaching ways.

Gendered Consumer Economies

More than four decades ago, political economist Dallas Smythe (1977) contended that commercial media industries construct the so-called "commodity audience." Capturing the then model of broadcast television advertising, Smythe argued that media provide a proverbial "free lunch" of television shows to attract audience attention, which is then packaged and sold to advertisers. As audiences create surplus value through their consumption of media, viewing time can thus be reframed as labor. Refining Smythe's thesis, Eileen Meehan (2012) drew attention to the industries' gendered hierarchies of value, with a male prime time audience being more highly sought by advertisers and thus more aptly catered to by broadcasters. But while broadcast media companies deployed measurement technologies to present audience data according to advertiser preferences, social media's demographic data consists of algorithmically approximated profiles (Baym 2015; Sender 2018).

On the surface at least, these profiles seem less fixed than traditional gender categories as they are based on individual clicks, preferences, and browsing history. Yet, such datafied approximations "inevitably [harden] into something that works for advertisers" (Bivens and Oliver 2016). Indeed, upon opening Facebook's advertising tool, the first targeting category offered is binary gender. Facebook's guide to using "audience insights" extolls client success stories such as SkinLabo, which targets "women aged 35 and older with an interest in cosmetics and skincare," and Leeway Motor Company, which shows ads to "car-based interest audiences (segmented by gender and age)" (Facebook 2021).

In this vein, it seems important to recognize that social media platforms such as Facebook, Instagram, and YouTube do not simply *reflect* audience interests and identities; rather, they reify these categories by encouraging participation in the consumer marketplace. These categories are drawn from data, but they arguably remain based on "prevailing stereotypes" about audience likes, dislikes, and preferences (Shepherd 2014, 159). As women conduct their activities on social media platforms, this labor is hardened into demographics data, which then shapes the gendered commercial content that they consume. Such categorizations contribute to the gendered social media economy, wherein women's contributions skew toward feminized ecologies of cosmetics, fashion, luxury travel, domestic activities, and "mommy blogs" (García-Rapp 2017; Hund 2017; Lopez 2009). Women's alignment with these well-worn topics is often rewarded by commercial stakeholders as algorithmic promotion calcifies existing market conventions (Bishop 2018).

Like print and broadcast media before them, social media platforms shape the experiences of their users as they conflate gender-coded sociality with consumerism. Reviving Smythe's (1977) thesis, media scholar Campbell (2011) argues that internet users are understood above all as "commodity audiences." Marketers are thus eager to exploit what he calls "the labor of devotion," a notion which captures gender-coded assumptions that "men loyally consume their favorite brands whereas women actively promote their favorite brands to other women." Discourses about feminized labor and consumerism have also been reified by the sprawling field of platform-facilitated domestic entrepreneurship. Today's digitally enabled multilevel marketing schemes have been preceded by homeworking independent contractors including "Avon ladies" (Manko 1997) and online craft platforms such as Etsy (Luckman 2013). Such efforts are small-scale, often part-time, and situated in the private sphere; the forms of reproductive labor required to sustain them are augmented by the affective labors compelled by platforms themselves. Yet, crucially, these social and cultural drives to gendered, laborious forms of entrepreneurship are also deeply imbricated with consumer culture (Banet-Weiser 2017; Duffy 2017; Duffy and Pruchniewska 2017).

The construction of—and distribution to—gendered markets are central to the logics of marketing intermediaries and stakeholders and therefore to the social media platforms with which they work (Bivens 2017; Cheney-Lippold 2011). To facilitate commercial partnerships, platforms fracture audience recommendations along gendered silos; for example, researchers have argued that the music streaming platform Spotify algorithmically recommends "related artists" by race and gender, demonstrating how technology and gender are "co-constituting" (Werner 2020, 79). Reflecting on this example can demonstrate the material consequences for uneven algorithmic recommendations—Spotify's related artists feature reifies and extends the overrepresentation of White men in many musical genres (Eriksson and Johansson 2017). TikTok has similarly been charged with basing content recommendation on "feedback loops," meaning the application consistently promotes popular app users who are aesthetically and generically similar (Strapagiel 2020). Findings such as this are significant for two reasons. Firstly, they highlight how little we know about the practical functions of the applications and platforms that organize media distribution. Secondly, they demonstrate how pervasive and embedded inequalities in media industries continue to be, betraying platforms' promises of democratization.

Conclusion and Directions for Future Research

Despite claims made by techno-enthusiasts and marketing prognosticators about our forward march into a post-gender digital society, constructions of gender lie at the heart of the social media economy. Gender (as it intersects with a wider spectrum of identities) thus remains both a productive analytical concept for digital sociologists as well as an organizational schema that is ripe for critical inquiry—and political intervention. In this chapter, we have explored how gendered notions, particularly the oft-denigrated notion of "women's work," abound on social media; such constructions underpin various communicative expressions, from consumer products shilled via Facebook groups to the affective currency that drives activity on TikTok, YouTube, and the like (Jarrett 2017; Shepherd 2014). Much like the wider category of feminized labor, such work is less a demographic reality (after all, men are active participants in the social media landscape, too) than a critique of how certain cultures and praxis are socially and/or economically devalued within contemporary capitalist economies.

In this piece, we raise several key tensions that are at the heart of the feminization of social media labor. Firstly, platforms force vulnerable communities to strategically labor in order to counter platform governance—to share resources, communicate, and raise awareness. The anxiety stemming from obscured or confusing decision-making processes means that this labor is highly affective (Ahmed 2004; Hillis, Paasonen, and Petit 2015). Secondly, it is relevant that platform governance maps onto the historical surveillance of the behavior of (often young) women in ways that do not serve them—and may even cause harm (Nakamura 2015). In a similar vein to public life offline, these women are sidelined from cultural and subcultural spaces and ushered into private and domestic ones (McRobbie and Garber 2000; Gill 2019). Mapping onto larger economies of visibility (Banet-Weiser 2018), we can see that some young women benefit from platforms' mandate to be visible; many others, meanwhile, are identified as at risk and consequently surveilled and punished.

By calling attention to the careers of social media influencers, entrepreneurs, and editors/managers, we have highlighted several mechanisms of the devaluation of women's work, including the requirements for emotional labor and affective performance, the demand to be flexible, and the compulsion to participate in the consumer marketplace. Our selection of cases to identify feminized labor subjectivities is admittedly purposeful: Through their occupations as experts in platform negotiation, influencers and entrepreneurs make illuminating case studies for the gendered mandate to perform social media labor. Yet, in closing, it seems important to consider how everyday social media users also negotiate social media platforms to undertake a spectrum of activities, such as memory work on behalf of friends and family (Humphreys 2018), the coordination of events, and the provision of access to news and information. So, while the nascent career of social media content production is a fruitful starting point to examine how platforms underscore and impel gendered labor, we see many everyday users, entrepreneurs, and professionals work to counter the power imbalance that is sustained by the activities undertaken across a sprawling social media ecology.

The experiences and strategies of those challenging highly gendered platformized labor provide urgent areas for future inquiry (see Ticona and Mateescu 2018). Even when platform mandates are successfully challenged, countering platforms' uneven power structures requires considerable investments of time and labor. To take one example, the ongoing moderation of sex workers' and performer's social media accounts is particularly cruel, as the affected users often engage enthusiastically with platforms' mandate for self-branding. Indeed, sex workers, performers, and fitness instructors work with the platform in a manner entirely compatible with the platforms' call for content production and self-promotion. As we have pointed out, feminized platform workers are emotional laborers *par excellence*. This work is ultimately bound by narrowly defined standards for commercial femininity and underpinned by calls to be "brand safe," authentic, and respectable (Bishop 2021). Platforms are affective ecologies of uncertainty; the moderation of female sexuality is broadly applied under the vague guise of inappropriate content (Gerrard, 2018). In line with this, cultural hashtags such as #femalefitness are heavily policed, obscuring content from pole dancing fitness instructors, dancers, and carnival performers, while hashtags such as #malefitness and #malemodel remain unaffected (Are, 2021). Reflecting on the political implications and inequalities is essential as the decisions that platforms make create labor for women and shape user participation and representation more broadly.

References

Abidin, Crystal. 2016. "Visibility Labor: Engaging with Influencers' Fashion Brands and #OOTD Advertorial Campaigns on Instagram." *Media International Australia* 161, no. 1: 86–100.

Acker, Joan. 1990. "Hierarchies, jobs, bodies: A theory of gendered organizations." *Gender & Society* 4.2: 139–158.

Adkins, Lisa. 2001. "Cultural feminization:" Money, sex and power" for women." *Signs: Journal of Women in Culture and Society* 26, no. 3: 669–695.

Ahmed, Sara. 2004. "Affective Economies." *Social Text* 22, no. 2: 117–139.

Amnesty International. 2018. "Troll Patrol Findings." Troll Patrol Report. https://decoders.amnesty.org/projects/troll-patrol/findings#what_did_we_find_container.

Andrews, Kylie. 2016. "Don't Tell Them I Can Type: Negotiating Women's Work in Production in the Post-War ABC." *Media International Australia* 161, no. 1: 28–37.

Are, C. (2021). The Shadowban Cycle: an autoethnography of pole dancing, nudity and censorship on Instagram. *Feminist Media Studies*, 1–18.

Arndt, M., and B. Bigelow. 2005. "Professionalizing and Masculinizing a Female Occupation: The Reconceptualization of Hospital Administration in the Early 1900s." *Administrative Science Quarterly* 50, no. 2: 233–261. Accessed April 4, 2021. http://www.jstor.org/stable/30037192.

Balaji, Murali. 2009. "Why Do Good Girls Have to Be Bad? The Cultural Industry's Production of the Other and the Complexities of Agency." *Popular Communication* 7, no. 4: 225–236.

Banet-Weiser, Sarah. 2017. " 'I'm Beautiful the Way I Am': Empowerment, Beauty, and Aesthetic Labor." In *Aesthetic Labor*, edited by A. S. Elias, Rosalind Gill, and C. Scharff, 265–282. London: Palgrave Macmillan.

Banet-Weiser, Sarah. 2018. *Empowered: Popular feminism and popular misogyny*. Durham, NC: Duke University Press.

Banks, Miranda. 2018. "Production Studies." *Feminist Media Histories* 4, no. 2: 157–161.

Baym, Nancy K. 2018. *Playing to the Crowd: Musicians, Audiences, and the Intimate Work of Connection*. New York University Press.

Baym, Nancy K. 2015. *Personal connections in the digital age*. John Wiley & Sons.

Bielby, William T., and James N. Baron. 1986. "Men and Women at Work: Sex Segregation and Statistical Discrimination." *American Journal of Sociology* 91, no. 4: 759–799.

Bishop, Sophie. 2018. "Fetishisation of the 'Offline' in Feminist Media Research." *Feminist Media Studies* 18, no. 1: 143–147. https://doi.org/10.1080/14680777.2018.1407120.

Bishop, Sophie. 2019. "Managing Visibility on YouTube through Algorithmic Gossip." *New Media & Society* 21, no. 11–12: 2589–2606. https://doi.org/10.1177/1461444819854731.

Bishop, Sophie. 2020. "Algorithmic Experts: Selling Algorithmic Lore on YouTube." *Social Media + Society* 6, no. 1: 2056305119897323.

Bishop, S. 2021. Influencer Management Tools: Algorithmic Cultures, Brand Safety, and Bias. *Social Media+ Society* 7, no. 1: 20563051211003066.

Bivens, Rena. 2017. "The Gender Binary Will not Be Deprogrammed: Ten Years of Coding Gender on Facebook." *New Media & Society* 19, no. 6: 880–898. https://doi.org/10.1177/1461444815621527.

Bivens, Rena & Haimson, Oliver. 2016. Baking gender into social media design: How platforms shape categories for users and advertisers. *Social Media+ Society* 2, no. 4: 2056305116672486.

Blakley, J. 2010. "Social Media and the End of Gender." TEDWomen Talk. https://www.ted.com/talks/johanna_blakley_social_media_and_the_end_of_gender.

Bridges, Lauren E. 2018. Flexible as freedom? The dynamics of creative industry work and the case study of the editor in publishing. *New Media & Society* 20, no. 4: 1303–1319.

Bucher, Taina. 2018. "Cleavage-Control: Stories of Algorithmic Culture and Power in the Case of the YouTube 'Reply Girls.' " In *A Networked Self and Platforms, Stories, Connections*, edited by Zizi Papacharissi, 141–159. New York and London: Routledge.

Bucher, Taina, and Anne Helmond. 2017. "The Affordances of Social Media Platforms." In *The SAGE Handbook of Social Media*, edited by Jean Burgess, Alice Marwick, and Thomas Poell, 233–253. London: Sage.

Campbell, John Edward. 2011. "It Takes an iVillage: Gender, Labor, and Community in the Age of Television–Internet Convergence." *International Journal of Communication* 5: 492–510.

Carah, Nicholas, and Daniel Angus. 2018. "Algorithmic Brand Culture: Participatory Labor, Machine Learning and Branding on Social Media." *Media, Culture & Society* 40, no. 2: 178–194.

Cheney-Lippold, John. 2011. A new algorithmic identity: Soft biopolitics and the modulation of control. *Theory, Culture & Society* 28, no. 6: 164–181.

Cirucci, Angela. 2018. A new women's work: Digital interactions, gender, and social network sites. *International Journal of Communication*, 12, 23:), 2948–2970.

Cohen, Philip N., and Matt L. Huffman. 2003. "Individuals, jobs, and labor markets: The Devaluation of Women's Work." *American Sociological Review*, 443–463.

Cook, Jessalyn. 2019. "Instagram's Shadow Ban on Vaguely 'Inappropriate' Content Is Plainly Sexist." HuffPost UK, April 30. https://www.huffpost.com/entry/instagram-shadow-ban-sexist_n_5cc72935e4b0537911491a4f.

Cotter, Kelley. 2018. "Playing the Visibility Game: How Digital Influencers and Algorithms Negotiate Influence on Instagram." *New Media & Society* 21, no. 4: 895–913. https://doi.org/10.1177/1461444818815684.

Coventry, Barbara Thomas. 2004. "On the Sidelines: Sex and Racial Segregation in Television Sports Broadcasting." *Sociology of Sport Journal* 21, no. 3: 322–341.

Craig, David, and Stuart Cunningham. 2019. *Social Media Entertainment: The New Intersection of Hollywood and Silicon Valley*. New York: New York University Press.

Daniels. Arlene K. 1987. "Invisible work." *Social problems* 34, no. 5: 403–415.

Deighton, Katie. 2020, April 13. "Young, Shafted and Black: Is Anything Being Done to Close the Influencer Ethnicity Pay Gap?" The Drum, April 13. https://www.thedrum.com/news/2020/04/13/young-shafted-and-black-anything-being-done-close-the-influencer-ethnicity-pay-gap.

deWinter, J., C. A. Kocurek, and S. Vie. 2017. "Managing Community Managers: Social Labor, Feminized Skills, and Professionalization." *Communication Design Quarterly Review* 4, no. 4: 36–45.

Duffy, Brooke Erin. 2017. *(Not) Getting Paid to Do What You Love: Gender, Social Media, and Aspirational Work*. New Haven, CT: Yale University Press.

Duffy, Brooke Erin, and Emily Hund. 2015. " 'Having It All' on Social Media: Entrepreneurial Femininity and Self-Branding among Fashion Bloggers." *Social Media + Society* 1, no. 2: 2056305115604337.

Duffy, Brooke Erin, and Urszula Pruchniewska. 2017. "Gender and Self-Enterprise in the Social Media Age: A Digital Double Bind." *Information, Communication & Society* 20, no. 6: 843–859.

Duffy, Brooke Erin, and Becca Schwartz. 2018. "Digital 'Women's Work?' Job Recruitment Ads and the Feminization of Social Media Employment." *New Media & Society* 20, no. 8: 2972–2989.

Duffy, Brooke Erin, and Emily Hund. 2019. Gendered visibility on social media: Navigating Instagram's authenticity bind. *International Journal of Communication*, 13, 20.

Duffy, Mignon. 2007. Doing the dirty work: Gender, race, and reproductive labor in historical perspective. *Gender & Society*, 21(3), 313–336.

Edwards, S. B., and Duchess Harris. 2017. *Hidden Human Computers: The Black Women of NASA*. Minneapolis, MN: ABDO.

Entwistle, Joanne, and Elizabeth Wissinger. 2006. "Keeping up Appearances: Aesthetic Labour in the Fashion Modelling Industries of London and New York." *The Sociological Review* 54, no. 4: 774–794. https://doi.org/10.1111/j.1467-954X.2006.00671.x.

Erigha, Maryann. 2019. *The Hollywood Jim Crow: The Racial Politics of the Movie Industry*. New York: New York University Press.

Eriksson, M., and A. Johansson. 2017. "Tracking Gendered Streams." *Culture Unbound: Journal of Current Cultural Research* 9, no. 2: 163–183. https://doi.org/10.3384/cu.2000.1525.1792163.

Facebook (2021) Business Success Stories *Facebook* https://www.facebook.com/business/success retrieved 09/07/2021

Federici, S. (2002). Reproduction et lutte féministe dans la nouvelle division internationale du travail. *Cahiers genre et développement* 3: 45–69.

Fernandez, C. 2019. "Is This the End of Gendered Media?" Business of Fashion, November 15. https://www.businessoffashion.com/articles/professional/is-this-the-end-of-gendered-media.

Fish, J. N., L. B. McInroy, M. S. Paceley, N. D. Williams, S. Henderson, D. S. Levine, et al. 2020. " 'I'm Kinda Stuck at Home with Unsupportive Parents Right Now': LGBTQ Youths' Experiences with COVID-19 and the Importance of Online Support." *Journal of Adolescent Health* 67, no. 3: 450–452.

García-Rapp, F. 2017. " 'Come Join and Let's BOND': Authenticity and Legitimacy Building on YouTube's Beauty Community." *Journal of Media Practice* 18, no. 2–3: 120–137. https://doi.org/10.1080/14682753.2017.1374693.

Gerrard, Ysabel. 2018. "Beyond the Hashtag: Circumventing Content Moderation on Social Media." *New Media & Society* 20, no. 12: 4492–4511. https://doi.org/10.1177/1461444818776611.

Gerrard, Ysabel, and Helen Thornham. 2020. "Content moderation: Social media's sexist assemblages." *New Media & Society* 22, no. 7: 1266–1286.

Gill, Rosalind. 2002. Cool, creative and egalitarian? Exploring gender in project-based new media work in Euro. Information, communication & society, 5(1), 70–89.

Gill, R. (2019). Surveillance is a feminist issue. In *The Routledge Handbook of Contemporary Feminism*, 148–161. Routledge.

Gillespie, Tarleton. 2018. *Custodians of the Internet: Platforms, Content Moderation, and the Hidden Decisions That Shape Social Media*. Yale University Press.

Glatt, Z. Forthcoming. "'We're all told not to put our eggs in one basket': Uncertainty, precarity and cross-platform labor in the online video influencer industry. *International Journal of Communication*.

Goldhaber, Michael J. 1997. The attention economy and the net. *First Monday* 2, no. 4. https://doi.org/10.5210/fm.v2i4.519

Hern, Alex. 2019. "TikTok's Local Moderation Guidelines Ban Pro LGBT Content." *The Guardian*, September 26. https://www.theguardian.com/technology/2019/sep/26/tiktoks-local-moderation-guidelines-ban-pro-lgbt-content.

Hesmondhalgh, David, and Sarah Baker. 2015. "Sex, Gender and Work Segregation in the Cultural Industries." *Sociological Review* 63: 23–36.

Hicks, Marie. 2017. *Programmed Inequality: How Britain Discarded Women Technologists and Lost Its Edge in Computing*. Cambridge, MA: MIT Press.

Hill, Erin. 2016. *Never Done: A History of Women's Work in Media Production*. New Brunswick, NJ: Rutgers University Press.

Hillis, K., S. Paasonen, and M. Petit, eds. 2015. *Networked Affect*. Cambridge, MA: MIT Press.

Hine, C. 2000. *Virtual Ethnography*. London: Sage.

Hochschild, Arlie R. (1983) 2012. *The Managed Heart: Commercialization of Human Feeling*. Berkeley: University of California Press.

Homant, E., and K. Sender. 2019. "Queer Immaterial Labor in Beauty Videos by LGBTQ-Identified YouTubers." *International Journal of Communication* 13, 19: 5386–5404

Humphreys, Lee. 2018. *The Qualified Self: Social Media and the Accounting of Everyday Life*. Cambridge, MA: MIT Press.

Hund, Emily. 2017. "Measured Beauty: Exploring the Aesthetics of Instagram's Fashion Influencers." In *Proceedings of the 8th International Conference on Social Media & Society*, 1–5. New York: ACM. https://doi.org/10.1145/3097286.3097330.

Hund, Emily, and Lee McGuigan. 2019. "A shoppable life: Performance, selfhood, and influence in the social media storefront." *Communication Culture & Critique* 12, no. 1: 18–35.

Hunt, Elle. 2017. "LGBTQ Community Anger over YouTube Restrictions." *The Guardian*, March 19. https://www.theguardian.com/technology/2017/mar/20/lgbt-community-anger-over-youtube-restrictions-which-make-their-videos-invisible.

Instagram. 2020. "New Instagram Features for Small Business Support (COVID-19)." Instagram for Business. https://business.instagram.com/blog/supporting-small-businesses-on-instagram?locale=en_GB.

Jarrett, Kylie. 2017. *Feminism, Labor and Digital Media: The Digital Housewife*. London and New York: Routledge.

Kerr, Aphra, and J. D. Kelleher. 2015. "The Recruitment of Passion and Community in the Service of Capital: Community Managers in the Digital Games Industry." *Critical Studies in Media Communication* 32, no. 3: 177–192.

Kiefer, H. 2020. "YouTube Star Shane Dawson Apologizes for Blackface, 'All the Racism I Put onto the Internet.'" *Vulture*, June 28. https://www.vulture.com/2020/06/youtuber-shane-dawson-apologizes-for-blackface-racist-jokes.html.

Lawson, Caitlin E. 2020. "Skin Deep: Callout Strategies, Influencers, and Racism in the Online Beauty Community." *New Media & Society* 23, no. 3: 596–612. https://doi.org/10.1177/1461444820904697.

Levinson, Alana Hope. 2015. "The Pink Ghetto of Social Media." *Medium*, July 16, https://medium.com/matter/the-pink-ghetto-of-social-media-39bf7f2fdbe1.

Light, Judith S. 1999. "When Computers Were Women." *Technology and Culture* 40, no. 3: 455–483.

Lopez, Lori K. 2009. "The Radical Act of 'Mommy Blogging': Redefining Motherhood through the Blogosphere." *New Media & Society* 11, no. 5: 729–747. https://doi.org/10.1177/1461444809105349.

Luckman, Susan. 2013. "The Aura of the Analogue in a Digital Age: Women's Crafts, Creative Markets and Home-Based Labor after Etsy." *Cultural Studies Review* 19, no. 1: 249–270.

Manko, K. L. 1997. " 'Now You Are in Business for Yourself ': The Independent Contractors of the California Perfume Company, 1886–1938." *Business and Economic History* 26, no. 1: 5–26.

Marwick, Alice E. 2013. *Status Update: Celebrity, Publicity, and Branding in the Social Media Age*. New Haven, CT: Yale University Press.

Martinez, Marta. 2020. "The Social Media Managers Are Not Okay". Medium, November 9. https://onezero.medium.com/the-social-media-managers-are-not-ok-74bc3d748149

Massanari, Adrienne. 2017. "#Gamergate and the Fappening: How Reddit's Algorithm, Governance, and Culture Support Toxic Technocultures." *New Media & Society* 19, no. 3: 329–346.

Massanari, Adrienne L. 2018. "Rethinking Research Ethics, Power, and the Risk of Visibility in the Era of the 'Alt-Right' Gaze." *Social Media + Society* 4, no. 2: 205630511876830. https://doi.org/10.1177/2056305118768302.

Mayer, Vicki. 2013. "To Communicate Is Human; to Chat Is Female: The Feminization of US Media Work." In *The Routledge Companion to Media & Gender*, edited by Cynthia Carter, Linda Steiner, and Lisa McLaughlin, 69–78. London and New York: Routledge.

Mears, Ashley. 2014. "Aesthetic Labor for the sociologies of Work, Gender, and Beauty." *Sociology Compass* 8, no. 12: 1330–1343.

Meehan, Eileen. 2012. "Gendering the Commodity Audience. Critical Media Research, Feminism, and Political Economy." In *Sex & Money. Feminism and Political Economy in the Media*, edited by Eileen Meehan and Ellen Riordan, 209–222. Minneapolis, MN: University of Minnesota Press.

McRobbie, Angela, and J. Garber. 2000. "Girls and Subcultures." In *Feminism and Youth Culture*. 2nd ed. London: Palgrave Macmillan.

Morgan, G., and P. Nelligan. 2015. "Labile Labor—Gender, Flexibility and Creative Work." *Sociological Review* 63: 66–83.

Murthy, D., and S. Sharma. 2019. "Visualizing YouTube's Comment Space: Online Hostility as a Networked Phenomena." *New Media & Society* 21, no. 1: 191–213. https://doi.org/10.1177/1461444818792393.

Myers West, Sarah. 2018. "Censored, Suspended, Shadowbanned: User Interpretations of Content Moderation on Social Media Platforms." *New Media & Society* 20, no. 11: 4366–4383. https://doi.org/10.1177/1461444818773059.

Nakamura, Lisa. 2015. "The Unwanted Labor of Social Media: Women of Colour Call Out Culture as Venture Community Management." *New Formations* 86: 106–112.

Nieborg, D. B., and T. Poell. 2018. "The Platformization of Cultural Production: Theorizing the Contingent Cultural Commodity." *New Media & Society* 20, no. 11: 4275–4292. https://doi.org/10.1177/1461444818769694.

Noble, Safiya U. 2018. *Algorithms of Oppression: How Search Engines Reinforce Racism*. New York: New York University Press.

O'Meara, Victoria. 2019. "Weapons of the Chic: Instagram Influencer Engagement Pods as Practices of Resistance to Instagram Platform Labor." *Social Media + Society* 5, no. 4: 2056305119879671.

Ouellette, L., and J. Wilson. 2011. "Women's Work: Affective Labor and Convergence Culture." *Cultural Studies* 25, no. 4–5: 548–565.

Petre, C., B. E. Duffy, and E. Hund. 2019. " 'Gaming the System': Platform Paternalism and the Politics of Algorithmic Visibility." *Social Media + Society* 5, no. 4: 2056305119879995. https://doi.org/10.1177/2056305119879995.

Postigo, Hector. 2009. "America Online volunteers: Lessons from an early co-production community." *International Journal of Cultural Studies* 12 (5), 451–469.

Roberts, Sarah T. 2019. *Behind the Screen: Content Moderation in the Shadows of Social Media*. New Haven, CT: Yale University Press.

Sender, Katherine. 2018. The gay market is dead, long live the gay market: From identity to algorithm in predicting consumer behavior. Advertising & Society Quarterly, 18(4). 10.1353/asr.2018.0001

Shepherd, Tamara. 2014. "Gendering the Commodity Audience in Social Media." In *The Routledge Companion to Media and Gender*, edited by Cynthia Carter, Linda Steiner, and Lisa McLaughlin, 175–185. London and New York: Routledge.

Smythe, Dallas W. 1977. "Communications: Blindspot of Western Marxism." *Canadian Journal of Political and Social Theory* 1, no. 3: 1–27.

Sobande, F., A. Fearfull, and D. Brownlie. 2019. "Resisting Media Marginalisation: Black Women's Digital Content and Collectivity." *Consumption Markets & Culture* 23, no. 5: 413–428. https://doi.org/10.1080/10253866.2019.1571491.

Sobieraj, Sarah. 2018. "Bitch, Slut, Skank, Cunt: Patterned Resistance to Women's Visibility in Digital Publics." *Information, Communication & Society* 21, no. 11: 1700–1714.

Sobieraj, Sarah. 2020. *Credible Threat: Attacks against Women Online and the Future of Democracy*. New York: Oxford University Press.

Steiner, Linda. 2012. "Failed Theories: Explaining Gender Difference in Journalism." *Review of Communication* 12, no. 3: 201–223.

Strapagiel, Lauren. 2020. "This Researcher's Observation Shows the Uncomfortable Bias of TikTok's Algorithm." BuzzFeed News, February 26. https://www.buzzfeednews.com/article/laurenstrapagiel/tiktok-algorithim-racial-bias.

Stuart, Forrest. 2020. *Ballad of the Bullet: Gangs, Drill Music, and the Power of Online Infamy*. Princeton, NJ: Princeton University Press.

Terranova, Tiziana. 2000. "Free Labor: Producing Culture for the Digital Economy." *Social Text* 18, no. 2: 33–58.

Ticona, Julia, and Alexandra Mateescu. 2018. "Trusted Strangers: Carework Platforms' Cultural Entrepreneurship in the On-Demand Economy." *New Media & Society* 20, no. 11: 4384–4404.

Tiidenberg, Katrin. 2019. "Playground in Memoriam: Missing the Pleasures of NSFW Tumblr." *Porn Studies* 6, no. 3: 363–371. https://doi.org/10.1080/23268743.2019.1667048.

Turkle, Sherry. 1999. "Cyberspace and Identity." *Contemporary Sociology* 28, no. 6: 643–648.

Umoh, Ruth. 2020. "Black Women Were Among The Fastest-Growing Entrepreneurs—Then Covid Arrived." Forbes, October 26. https://www.forbes.com/sites/ruthumoh/2020/10/26/black-women-were-among-the-fastest-growing-entrepreneurs-then-covid-arrived/?sh=185cf5e96e01

Webster, Judith. 2014. *Shaping Women's Work: Gender, Employment and Information Technology*. London: Routledge.

Weeks, Kathi. 2011. *The Problem with Work: Feminism, Marxism, Antiwork Politics, and Postwork Imaginaries*. Durham, NC: Duke University Press.

Werner, A. 2020. "Organizing Music, Organizing Gender: Algorithmic Culture and Spotify Recommendations." *Popular Communication* 18, no. 1: 78–90. https://www.tandfonline.com/doi/full/10.1080/15405702.2020.1715980.

CHAPTER 24

ELECTRONIC WASTE AND ENVIRONMENTAL JUSTICE

DAVID N. PELLOW

Electronic waste (e-waste) is one of the fastest-growing waste streams in the world, growing at a rate of 41.8 million tons per year (Baldè et al. 2015, 8). This includes computers, office electronic equipment, entertainment device electronics, cell phones, televisions, refrigerators, washing machines, and much more. Perhaps the most iconic form of e-waste is the personal computer. In 2008, the global ownership of computers passed the 1 billion mark, and there are an average of 300 million computers thrown away each year. Projected estimates are that by 2030 Global South nations will discard twice that number as the volume of e-waste is expected to grow exponentially (Sthiannopkao and Wong 2013).

Recycling has emerged as one response to this crisis, although the US Environmental Protection Agency estimates that only 15–20% of e-waste is recycled, with the remainder destined for landfills and incinerators (Bansal et al. 2016). Even when individuals, companies, communities, and nations recycle, such practices carry considerable risk of environmental and occupational health threats since e-waste often contains a range of hazardous chemical substances, including arsenic, cadmium, lead, phosphorus, and mercury (Gosney 2009). Such substances pose significant threats to the health and well-being of e-waste recycling workers (Asante et al. 2012), including major organ damage, lead poisoning, respiratory infections, infertility, and endocrine failure. In their study of e-waste recycling workers in the United Kingdom, Stowell and Warren (2018) develop the concept of "embodied inhabitation" to demonstrate how the considerable physical suffering of these laborers blurs the boundaries between human (workers) and nonhuman (e-waste) and yet is frequently unacknowledged by the institutions they work for as they experience myriad pressures to uphold a veneer of a "safe system of work." Specifically, Stowell and Warren reveal how discourses concerning the skill, commitment, and working-class gender identities (specifically related to masculinities) serve to normalize the suffering of e-waste workers who otherwise could receive support from management and/or the state to provide a healthier occupational environment.

The work of e-waste recycling is difficult and dangerous. For example, the process of dismantling used electronics parts involves several steps:

> circuit boards are cooked in woks over open charcoal fires to melt the lead solder, releasing toxic lead fumes . . . . Wires are stripped by hand or burned in open piles to melt the plastics to get the copper and other metals inside . . . . Plastic casings are burned, creating dioxins and furans—which are extremely hazardous to human health.
>
> (Frey 2012, 82)

Stepping back in the commodity chain well before the process of e-waste recycling, we find that the production and manufacture of computers themselves requires an enormous amount of ecological materials and results in great environmental harm. For example, the manufacture of a single computer and monitor can require 530 pounds of fossil fuels, 48 pounds of various chemicals, and 3,000 pounds of water. After a computer is disposed of, its recycling can release a spectrum of toxins into the air, land, and water, including halogenated dioxins and furans (Bansal et al. 2016).

This chapter highlights the human and environmental health risks associated with electronics recycling, with a particular emphasis on the ways in which the e-waste trade reinforces and intersects with concerns around environmental justice. In the next section, I consider several theoretical perspectives that facilitate a productive framing of the myriad challenges concerning e-waste management.

Environmental Injustice as Slow Violence in a Global Racialized Context

E-waste is a global problem, and, as with other forms of pollution, e-waste trading and dumping patterns have historically followed the "path of least resistance"—resulting in trafficking these hazards to lower-wealth regions and countries—a matter of global environmental injustice. This trade is authorized and facilitated by corporations and governments that accept e-waste as a means of job creation and revenue generation, particularly in parts of the world where millions of residents are in dire financial straits. These hazardous materials are shipped to lower-income regions of the world, oftentimes because Global South nations generally have lax regulatory enforcement regimes in place and governments and communities are frequently seeking sources of revenue to address poverty. As one study noted, given that a quarter of India's population lives below the international poverty line of $1.25/day, when an informal recycler can make $2–5/day selling e-waste up the recycling chain, there is a strong incentive to view e-waste as a commodity first and to relegate environmental health concerns to a lower priority (Mahesh 2011). In this section, I offer several theoretical perspectives that are useful for understanding and framing the global challenge of e-waste pollution.

Environmental racism is the unequal protection against environmental risks experienced by people of color, which is exacerbated by their systematic exclusion from environmental decisions affecting their communities (Bullard 2000; Mohai, Pellow, and Roberts 2009; Taylor 2016). This includes communities overburdened with pollution from a range of industrial and technological sources, such as incinerators, landfills, fossil fuel and chemical companies, pesticides, automobile emissions from interstate highways, and, of course, climate change. It is a social phenomenon that condemns individuals and communities viewed as expendable to higher rates of morbidity and mortality, a "group-differentiated vulnerability to premature death" (Gilmore 2007, 247). Environmental racism is a subset of a much larger problem, *environmental injustice*, a term used to describe what happens when *any* marginalized population (e.g., not only people of color but also low-income populations, immigrants, women, etc.) suffers a disproportionately high burden of environmental harm and is excluded from environmental decisions affecting their communities.

A number of theoretical perspectives have been brought to bear on the challenge of environmental injustice. For example, Rob Nixon's (2011) concept of "slow violence" is useful for understanding how industrial toxins affect human bodies and harm ecosystems in ways that frequently are not covered in the spectacle-driven corporate media because these destructive impacts often unfold over long periods of time and are more difficult to convey in simple discursive narratives or in visual representations. But since these environmental effects are the result of decisions made by corporate and/or governmental leaders who often have full knowledge of the consequences, it is appropriate to describe such consequences as forms of institutional violence. Articulating environmental injustices as violence is important because it is a recognition that many present-day examples of this phenomenon are built on a foundation of centuries of oppression and dispossession experienced by Indigenous peoples and communities of color, in the broader context of racial capitalism, settler colonialism, and chattel slavery (Agyeman et al. 2016; Whyte 2018). Viewed through this complex lens, environmental injustices are built into the structure of many societies, reflecting the increasingly common view that there can be no climate justice or environmental justice without racial justice (Sze 2020).

Still other scholars are linking environmental justice studies with other frameworks like world-systems theory. World-systems theory is premised on the idea that the historical and contemporary dynamics of global capitalism reveal that nations are interlinked in a network of relationships that generally benefit wealthier (core) countries at the expense of poorer (periphery) countries and that this exploitative association has served to strengthen and sustain social inequalities over the centuries (Wallerstein 2011). Closely related to this body of work is the growing literature on ecologically unequal exchange, which posits that in the global economy core nations gain disproportionate access to and *externalize* the costs of capital accumulation onto nations in the Global South, with a particular emphasis on ecological processes and outcomes (Jorgenson and Clark 2009). Examples include the fact that many Global North nations and industries extract energy and other ecological wealth from the Global South and pay less than market value for it, which leads to a decline in environmental utilization opportunities in those lower-wealth nations (Rice 2007, 1369–1392).

Environmental justice scholars have recently noted that much of world-systems scholarship has done an admirable job of theorizing global social class inequalities but has paid insufficient attention to global racial inequalities. Murphy and Schroering (2020) note that the capitalist world system is deeply rooted in and shaped by racial dynamics. In fact, this is the primary contribution of the work of scholars studying racial capitalism (Robinson 1983). Environmental justice scholars have now taken that framework to underscore that one cannot fully grasp the importance of a world-systems perspective without recognizing the ways in which racism, capitalism, and ecological destruction are intimately entangled (Fenelon and Alford 2020; Pulido 2017). One particularly productive theoretical terrain on which to achieve these linkages is around the idea of the "plantationocene" (Haraway 2015), which is a framework that centers the ubiquitous presence and power of exploitative industrial agriculture around the globe throughout the last half-millennium. The plantationocene is a way of rethinking the concept of the Anthropocene in ways that move beyond the limited viewpoint that humanity is universally and equally responsible for contributing to our global ecological and climate crises and, instead, foregrounds the role of White supremacy as an organizing principle of both markets and states that inheres quite graphically and consequentially in the centuries-old practice of maintaining dominance over the bodies of people of color and nonhuman species via plantation economies around the globe. As Murphy and Schroering (2020, 409) write, "Ultimately, what is at stake here is whether we are able and willing to apprehend the ecological changes wrought by nearly 500 years of the plantation as *not* just a matter of global capitalist expansion and integration . . . but also racial and colonial assimilation into a world-economic order that institutes a global hierarchy of human and more-than-human life with direct consequence to the Earth system."

There has emerged a debate within the field of environmental justice studies concerning the importance of governmental action in efforts to advance environmental justice and sustainability. While the vast majority of the literature embraces the goal of targeting state actors to pass legislation that will presumably be protective of vulnerable populations and ecosystems (Bullard 2000; Taylor 2016), a growing body of research is openly questioning the wisdom of this approach (Harrison 2019; Pellow 2017; Pulido 2017). The latter group of scholars points to the decades-long history of uneven enforcement actions by government agencies that allow industry to heavily pollute in communities of color with near impunity and the continued dismissal of claims of civil rights violations by those communities as strong evidence that the environmental justice movement cannot place much faith in the state for ensuring the protection of vulnerable populations.

This section lays a theoretical foundation for a deeper understanding of e-waste production, management, and pollution as a space of environmental justice struggle that reflects forms of institutional and slow violence in a global context. E-waste workers are not simply victims, however, since they exercise agency at the micro, meso, and macro scales in order to make ends meet and by attempting to improve working conditions on a daily basis. But they are engaged in a highly asymmetrical battle with powerful stakeholders in industry and governments, who operate within a series of global networks to generate revenue for individual elites, companies, and state actors. Thus, a world-systems analysis is useful for understanding how e-waste flows reflect or challenge inequalities among and within rich and poor nations. The concept of the plantationocene can be creatively deployed here as well, not only to further understand global systems of agriculture but, more broadly, to deepen our grasp of global systems of industrial extractive activity that rely on the exploitation of racialized human labor and ecosystems. Finally, there remains an open question as to whether workers and residents in e-waste processing and recycling zones around the world can or should rely on governments to secure their protection as the evidence suggests a highly uneven record of regulatory enforcement.

E-Waste as an Environmental Justice Issue

Historically, tons of e-waste have been exported every year from wealthy Global North nations to lower-income Global South nations. Specifically, when not disposed of locally, an estimated 50%–80% of e-waste was being shipped from the Global North to the Global South in the 1980s and early 1990s (Sthiannopkao and Wong 2013). Because this traffic of waste is hazardous to human and environmental health and because it flowed from affluent to lower-wealth countries, it constituted a clear case of environmental injustice (Pellow 2007) and reflected the long-standing ways in which wealthier, core nations benefit from the routine functioning of the global economy at the expense of poorer nations in the world system (Wallerstein 2011).

Moreover, studies reveal that much of the riskiest labor involving e-waste recycling is done by vulnerable populations, including migrant workers, women, ethnic minorities, and children in various nations. This is part of the much broader problem of hazardous working conditions throughout much of the electronics commodity chain. For example, there have been numerous studies revealing that workers in semiconductor plants are exposed to hundreds of harmful chemicals (LaDou 1986) and that electronics workers in corporations or in the informal e-waste sector in India, China, Europe, Scotland, Taiwan, Japan, Thailand, the United States, and Mexico have faced significant industrial chemical threats for decades (Chang, Chiu, and Tu 2006; Foran and Sonnenfeld 2006; McCourt 2006; Pandita 2006; Rocha 2006; Watterson 2006). Another study (Zhang

2020, 14) reveals how these populations and the risks associated with e-waste work intersect in the city of Guiyu, China:

> Migrant workers work without any effective protection against air pollution and contaminated water. One of the most typical jobs in the industry is melting the circuit boards to get the metal parts. Workers sit directly in front of the stove with only a small fan above their heads. Both the air and water waste in these workshops have been proven to contain toxic heavy metals and organic compounds that can cause irreversible harm to their health (Brigden, Labunska, Santillo, & Allsopp, 2005). The horrible working environment has given various illnesses to the workers. Qiu et al.'s (2005) study shows that the prevalence of illnesses such as headache/vertigo and tetter/itch among migrant workers in e-waste workplaces is much higher than among workers in other workplaces.

Research reveals that child labor is quite routine in the informal e-waste recycling sector, thus elevating their risks of exposure and illness (International Labour Organization 2014, 2015). This phenomenon continues to this day, as one scholar writes, "Hiring child labor in Guiyu is very normal" (Zhang 2020, 118). Women's vulnerability to lower wages and greater occupational health exposures in e-waste zones like Guiyu, China, is common. Studies have shown that rates of spontaneous abortions in Guiyu are significantly higher than in other communities in China (Wu et al. 2012). In more recent work, Zhang (2020) finds that migrant women workers in the e-waste zones of Guiyu, China, continue to face environmental health hazards in the workplace and in their homes (which are often the same site). And in India, women of the Dalit caste are at the lowest rung of the e-waste recycling hierarchy. This means they are generally well outside of the purview of regulators, they tend to use low-tech tools for their work, and they are usually required to do the most dangerous work, which includes the use of acid baths for e-waste processing (Wong et al. 2007). Of the 14 hazardous chemicals generally found in e-waste recycling stations, more than half are documented as having negative effects on women's reproductive and endocrine systems (Frazzoli et al. 2010), and e-waste work has been documented to harm women's fertility, as well as their morbidity and mortality (McAllister, Magee, and Hale 2014). One might ask why anyone would willingly subject themselves to such risk. A sociological perspective is useful in that regard because many women workers in this sector choose this occupation precisely because it can deliver sufficient wages to support a family and because it offers flexible work hours that allow for women to look after their children (Huysman 1994).

As if polluted workplaces were not enough, research demonstrates that many migrant workers in the e-waste business face pollution inside their homes as well, with copper, lead, and polychlorinated biphenyls (PCBs) found in their living spaces at levels much higher than the homes of non-e-waste workers—the result of exposure via contaminated clothing brought into their residences (Brigden et al. 2005; Wang et al. 2016). Thus, while the environmental threats and risks associated with e-waste production certainly reflect the dominant concern of environmental justice studies of racialized populations facing these hazards, we also find that gender and age intersect with race and nationality to place women, children, and migrants at greater risk than other groups in many circumstances.

New Directions and Debates in E-Waste Scholarship

Earlier, the primary environmental justice concerns with respect to e-waste were focused on the fact that much of the waste was being produced in affluent Global North nations like the United States, Canada, and those in Europe and being shipped to lower-income Global South nations—what appeared to be a clear case of global environmental injustice and racism. The changing dynamics of the e-waste trade have resulted in increasing volumes of that waste being produced from *within* Global South nations such as India, China, and South Africa—countries that are among the leading producers and destinations for these discards. In a major study that challenges the long-standing claim that flows of e-waste primarily move from Global North to Global South nations, Lepawsky (2015) quantified and mapped the e-waste trade that, at its peak in 1996, showed that 35% of the global volume of e-waste was flowing from Global North to Global South. By 2012, however, that portion of the trade accounted for less than 1% of the global volume. Even though much of the trade volume is not tracked because it is illegal, these figures suggest a dramatic change in the flow of e-waste. Moreover, this recent empirical research reveals that the majority of e-waste is actually traded intraregionally rather than interregionally (Lepawsky and McNabb 2010). But even within that intraregional and interregional trade, we find that it tends to flow from wealthier communities to poorer communities, thus reinforcing the environmental justice thesis. However, research demonstrates that, in many cases, the majority of electronic materials arrive in functioning order and can be reused for some time afterward. Moreover, the North–South flow of e-waste traffic is, in some other cases, actually reversed as poorer nations are exporting waste to wealthier nations where machines and parts can be refurbished, with that portion of the trade constituting 7–12% per year (Lepawsky 2015). Thus, we are forced to rethink the Global North to Global South environmental injustice narrative of the e-waste trade and examine how it has become ever more complex, while still paying attention to the ways in which both new and old inequalities are produced and reinforced by the trade.

Importantly, the claim of environmental injustice is not just about the volume of waste dumped or traded or the scale at which it occurs (i.e., Global North to South) but rather about the conditions and relationships under which those practices are produced. That is, environmental injustice is about disproportionate harm but also about the ways in which that harm reflects and reinforces unequal relations and networks. So even if the vast majority of e-waste is no longer flowing from Global North to South, we find that the conditions under which those materials are trafficked and processed still reflect highly uneven and unjust relationships, even and especially within regions, within nations, and within cities. In that sense, the e-waste flows around the world remain a form of *global* environmental injustice because all around the planet we find that the populations hosting and processing these materials are lower on the social hierarchies of those communities. But scale also matters very much in environmental justice research, and we find that at all scales—local, regional, national, and global—e-waste remains an environmental justice challenge, again, because the people who are tasked with the actual labor of e-waste recycling tend to be low-income and from marginalized populations. It should be noted that what is also missed here is the fact that the vast majority of e-waste actually ends up in domestic landfills and garbage dumps because most people do not send their used electronics to a certified dealer or recycler. As noted earlier, in the United States only 15–20% of e-waste is recycled. In that regard, the e-waste problem remains a massive environmental justice challenge because garbage dumps, landfills, and incinerators in many nations tend to be located in proximity to low-income and minority communities (Bullard 2000; Pellow 2007). This is a fact that the e-waste scholarship has unfortunately overlooked almost entirely.

In their research on the e-waste recycling sector in Agbogbloshie, Ghana, Akese and Little (2018) argue that while this may be an example of transnational environmental injustice (meaning a result of waste being imported across national borders into Ghana), one cannot begin to understand this problem without centering the many layers of local, historical, and colonial/postcolonial context that produced the conditions that gave rise to environmental injustice in the first place. Thus, writing against a universalist framework of environmental injustice, they propose the term "situated e-waste justice"—a contextualized framing of environmental justice that recognizes the specific local conditions that allow for and enable the production of toxicity and violence in a given community. The situated e-waste justice framing enables these authors to note that while much of the e-waste that ends up in Agbogbloshie is toxic, the workers and residents in this area face a much broader range of other hazards that exacerbate and exceed the e-waste problem. For example, a large percentage of e-waste workers there are migrants who have been displaced by declining agricultural opportunities and intertribal conflicts in northern Ghana and who are routinely subjected to police raids, forced evictions, housing demolitions, and other forms of state-ethnic violence, as well as flooding and fires in a landscape where the government is opposed to their presence and the local environmental conditions are precarious. Furthermore, the Agbogbloshie community in which these migrants live and work is also the site of a long-standing dispute between the government and Indigenous communities, wherein the former has repeatedly neglected the latter in terms of land, infrastructure, and housing support. Thus, there is a clear need for a "situated e-waste justice" frame in order to fully comprehend the roots of these crises and for any possibility of developing transformative solutions, meaning that we cannot expect to grasp the complexities involved in environmental justice struggles around e-waste if we isolate the e-waste issue from the larger historical, social, political, and economic contexts in which it exists. Akese and Little's research also reveals that environmental justice studies can benefit from taking seriously a world-systems perspective that offers clues as to how colonial histories and inequalities can shape the postcolonial present, which unfolds over many years as a case of "slow violence"

(Nixon 2011). Indeed, the multiple layers of inequality and conflict in the Agbogbloshie case also signal the importance of paying closer attention to racism against within-country migrants and Indigenous peoples. As Fevrier's (2020) study of this region finds, racism against migrants from northern Ghana runs deep and profoundly shapes their life chances in the struggles against environmental racism in that nation.

In a study of the changing geographies of the global e-waste trade, Lepawsky and McNabb (2010) challenge the assumption in much of the literature that this process follows a linear pattern of production, consumption, and disposal. In other words, there is a view that each of these parts of the cycle is distinct from the others and that once e-waste is disposed of, it stays in that location as a final resting place. Instead, they find that much of that waste is broken down, repurposed, and reintegrated into a spectrum of "new" consumer and industrial products, including lead used to make children's jewelry. In their comparative study of the e-waste industry in Bangladesh and Canada, Lepawsky and Mather (2011, 242–243) write,

> We flew to Dhaka, spent four months tracking what we thought was e-waste, but we couldn't find any. . . . Almost everything had value. Every object. Every component. Every material. They were all being bought and sold, assembled, disassembled and reassembled . . . . They also dwindled into their constituent materials—plastics, glass, metals . . . . Then they were sold. Money changed hands. Materials moved. We expected we would end up in dumpsites, in piles of waste. Instead, we wound up in production sites.

Toward that end, geographer Julia Corwin (2018) argues that the term "e-waste" fails to fully capture this fact, so she argues that we should refer to these materials as part of the "used electronics economy" and the "reuse and repair industry." Corwin's ethnographic fieldwork in New Delhi, India, repeatedly yielded this observation and, by comparison, an unflattering view of US consumer culture with respect to electronics. She writes,

> After many visits to electronics repair shops in New Delhi, India, I became accustomed to seeing things get fixed. The ease and regularity with which everyday things in Delhi are repaired always struck my American self as exceptional, and I regularly commented to repairers that this rarely happens in the US—that in fact, repair was so uncommon and cost-prohibitive that it was often cheaper to buy a new device. Repairers and scrapers in Delhi were rarely surprised; an electronics scrap-dealer named Anuj was the first of several people to inform me that America was a "use and throw desh," or "use and throw nation."
>
> (Corwin 2018, 15)

Corwin and other scholars forcefully argue that the electronics recycling trade is indeed a powerful source of economic value and product creation. They are working to address the generally overlooked matter of the positive financial potential of e-waste recycling on the economies of Global South nations (Widmer et al. 2005). They have a point. As one study of electronics recycling in Guiyu, China, noted, nearly 80% of the families in the town have members employed in that sector or who rely on the industry in some fashion (Greenpeace and Anthropology Department of Sun Yat-sen University 2003, 4). Furthermore, local political officials encourage the growth of the industry precisely because it is an engine of job creation (Zhang 2020). Zhang (2020) reveals that an overlooked yet significant reason for the persistence of the e-waste industry in Guiyu, China, is the dominant influence of the patrilineal clan system, which has developed a coincidence of interest with the industry through job creation and family bonds. In 2005, the electronics recycling industry generated nearly 1 billion yuan, which was fully 90% of the value of Guiyu's entire industrial output (Yang 2006).

However, even though there may be clear economic benefits derived from the e-waste trade for local communities, they are generally short term and have to be weighed against the long-term negative environmental health consequences of such activities. In other words, while it is certainly important not to overlook the positive financial dimensions of the electronics recycling industry, it would be extremely ill-advised to ignore the vastly unhealthy, risky, and environmentally harmful nature of this sector. As one study argues, just 3% of e-waste in Delhi is processed through formal channels, which means that the vast majority of the material is managed through informal networks that are unregulated and therefore less safe. More specifically, some 25,000 people work in that city's informal e-waste economy, processing 50,000 tons of materials each year (Kumar and Shah 2014). And while that labor most certainly provides a significant livelihood advancement for many of these workers, "in the absence of basic protective measures and access to formal disposal channels, the rights of these workers go unacknowledged" (McAllister, Magee, and Hale 2014, 174).

Ye Zhang (2020, 2), a Chinese social scientist who did extensive fieldwork in Guiyu, China, puts it plainly, while also citing other Chinese scholars on this subject:

> While the growth of e-waste industry has improved the earning potential of the local people, it has also brought with it serious environmental problems. The river water in Guiyu is foul-smelling, black, and acidic. The groundwater is highly polluted and no longer drinkable, with drinking water now having to be transported from other nearby places. Chemical fumes hang heavy in the air and can be smelt as soon as people enter the town. The soil has also been proved to be highly polluted with dangerous chemicals and the planted crops are contaminated
>
> (Hao, Yi, Wu, Lu, & Fang, 2015; Yin et al. 2018).

The scholarly narrative that seeks to emphasize the positive dimensions of the electronics recycling trade runs the risk of ignoring the possibilities of transformative, environmentally just, and equitable futures that are not limited to working within a fundamentally toxic economic system. That is, these studies limit themselves and their subjects to the world as it is, rather than considering radical alternatives. Relatedly, these narratives generally lack a depth of engagement with grassroots social movements seeking to bring about foundational change in communities where electronic recycling is occurring. This is in contrast to the type of engagement that we see in other scholarship that is explicitly activist or change-oriented (see Smith, Sonnenfeld, and Pellow 2006). We now turn our attention to that subject matter.

Grassroots Social Movements Respond

The study of social movements and social change has long been a core area of sociological scholarship because social scientists find that collective action and agency are important phenomena across societies and throughout history (McCarthy and Zald 1977; Morris 2000). In this brief section, I highlight some of the most significant developments in the evolution of collective action against environmental injustices within the e-waste industry. Social movements have responded to concerns within communities where these materials are dumped or processed, in order to achieve improvements in living and working conditions for laborers and residents.

While there has been plenty of protest by social movements mobilizing against the e-waste trade, perhaps the most fascinating aspect of this dynamic is the fact that some of the first and most important research on e-waste was conducted and produced by activist groups. Consider the numerous high-profile reports and books published by the Basel Action Network (2002a, 2002b, 2005), Greenpeace International (2005, 2008), Toxics Link India (2003, 2004, 2007a, 2007b, 2007c), the International Campaign for Responsible Technology (Smith, Sonnenfeld, and Pellow 2006), the Computer TakeBack Campaign, and the Silicon Valley Toxics Coalition (Dayaneni and Doucette 2005; Silicon Valley Toxics Coalition 2001). Much of this work focuses on the path of e-waste shipments from Europe and North America to Global South nations like China, India, and Nigeria. These reports feature in-depth examinations of the labor and environmental conditions under which e-waste is recycled, including the toxicological effects of the materials handled on the workers' bodies, as well as the nearby water and soil quality. The occupational hazards associated with e-waste recycling are documented in great detail. This body of research extends earlier scholarship by scientists concerning the deeply and inherently toxic nature of the electronics industry (Ladou 1984, 1985, 1986; Ladou and Lovegrove 2008). In the infamous case of the town of Guiyu, China, Deng et al. (2006) document that airborne polycyclic aromatic hydrocarbons and other heavy metals are present at levels between 100 and 600 times that of other Asian cities. In that same town, Li et al. (2008) found significant correlations between pregnant women's employment in the e-waste sector and neonatal lead toxicity, which has negative impacts on neurological health. Xing et al. (2009) found that in Guiyu the toxins from the e-waste industry are contributing to the bioaccumulation of PCBs in the bodies of residents, including in human breast milk, the direct result of exposure through fume inhalation and the consumption of fish caught in nearby water sources.

While the most visible social movement organizations in the space of e-waste struggles have been transnational environmental nongovernmental organizations

(NGOs), there are numerous examples of local organizations pushing to improve the livelihoods of e-waste workers and their families. For example, in Agbogbloshie, Ghana, many residents have resisted government evictions and home demolitions by rebuilding their residences (Amuzu 2018). More broadly, a number of civil society groups have assisted e-waste workers and residents in building solidarity and exchange networks with residents and activists in Nairobi, Kenya's, Kibera neighborhood (reportedly the largest slum in all of Africa) in order to amplify their resistance against forced evictions by state agents (Amoako 2016).

Akese and Little (2018) note that sometimes NGOs—particularly international NGOs—fail to achieve their goals of improving environmental conditions in e-waste recycling zones because they often ignore the importance of local context and histories. For example, in 2014, a "solutions-based NGO" called Pure Earth installed a number of automated wire-stripping machines in the e-waste scrap market in Agbogbloshie, Ghana. The aim was to provide a readily available alternative to the common—and highly polluting—practice of burning the wires to access the economically valuable copper wiring within. Unfortunately, this well-meaning effort has yet to pay off, and e-waste workers still burn the wires on a regular basis. As Akese and Little (2018, 81) argue, "While there are myriad reasons for continued burning, for most workers, immediate livelihood needs, housing needs, and the right to the city are more crucial than the potential long-term health risks posed by harmful e-waste practices . . . demolitions and evictions are not uncommon within the community." This is a particularly powerful indictment of the theme of "solutions-driven" or "solutions-based" environmentalism that has taken hold across much of the NGO, policy, and academic landscape recently. As the situation in Agbogbloshie indicates, any solution to an "environmental" problem that relies on approaches that ignore local cultural, social, political, and economic conditions that shape the realities for people and their ecosystems will often fall short. Social movements and NGOs that build trust and relationships with local leaders and residents may be more likely to develop solutions that work for people in those particular contexts.

These social movements have been effective at moving the electronics industry in productive directions with respect to sustainability practices. As one study documents, several environmental justice networks focused on e-waste struggles around the globe succeeded in pushing major computer corporations (such as Dell, Apple, Hewlett-Packard, and Compaq), numerous US states, and the European Union to reduce the quantity of toxic chemicals used to produce computers, agree to take back and recycle electronics at the end of life, ensure that those materials are not exported to other nations, and ensure that they are not recycled by imprisoned persons (a previously common practice in the United States) (Smith, Sonnenfeld, and Pellow 2006). The Clean Production Electronics Network is a multistakeholder group of grassroots organizations and computer corporations that formed in 2016 to find collective solutions to the problems of environmental threats in the industry. In 2020, the network announced a new initiative to monitor and reduce worker exposure to harmful chemicals throughout the supply chain (Chemical Watch 2020). If successful, this campaign will likely result in lower health risks and hazards for e-waste workers as well.

The work of grassroots organizations, NGOs, and social movements in relation to e-waste is of great importance for three reasons. First, these groups make visible and legible the "slow violence" of e-waste pollution by capturing it in worker testimonials and graphic photos that are more effectively digestible and relatable to mass publics. Second, they reveal the ways in which the world system continues to support ecologically unequal exchange via the maximization of wealth and privilege for elites within and across nations, while contributing to the suffering and exploitation of marginalized populations around the globe. And third, these forms of resistance underscore that while many communities are facing environmental injustices and environmental racism from e-waste pollution, they are also engaged in agentic maneuvers, collective efforts to improve their working conditions. Even so, moving industry practices toward greater sustainability can be limited, if not reinforced, by policy changes and new legislation. That is the focus of the next section.

Policymaking and Legislation

The preceding discussion concerning social movements' impacts on the electronics industry is intended to demonstrate how these NGO networks have affected the trajectory of this sector and produced important gains that shape outcomes for workers and communities where e-waste dumping and recycling occur. In this section, we consider a different scale of activity by relevant stakeholders—policy makers—because changes within particular companies or even across the electronics sector may be short-lived if not backed up by legislation and reinforced by regulation. This discussion reflects the debate I referenced earlier among environmental justice scholars with respect to the value of demanding and embracing governmental action to protect vulnerable communities and ecosystems, with one group generally embracing a pro-governmental regulatory approach (Bullard 2000; Taylor 2016) and the other insisting that social movements look elsewhere for protection (Pellow 2017; Pulido 2017).

The strengthening of environmental regulations in Global North nations during the 1970s and 1980s raised the cost of domestic hazardous waste management, treatment, and disposal. These new regulations created a financial incentive for companies to dump their waste abroad, which was an unintended and unfortunate consequence of successful environmental movement mobilization around pollution control in wealthy nations (Pellow 2007). One response was the development of the Basel Convention on the Control of Transboundary Movements of Hazardous Wastes—an international treaty governing the trade and dumping of hazardous wastes globally. The treaty came into force in 1992 and prohibits waste trade between parties to the convention and nonparties unless the countries have a separate waste trade agreement in place. A number of additional and problematic loopholes were built into the treaty, including the allowance for the export of hazardous waste if it was destined for reuse or recovery via recycling. The problem with that clause is that nations could claim they intended to recycle but then simply dump the waste. In 1995, a coalition of 77 Global South nations, environmental organizations, and European countries succeeded in passing the Basel Ban, which ended the export of hazardous waste from rich Organisation for Economic Co-operation and Development (OECD) nations to poor non-OECD nations, even for recycling.

At the international level, the most progressive state action yet is in the European Union. The European Union passed two major policy initiatives, known as the Directive on Waste from Electrical and Electronic Equipment (WEEE) and the Restriction on Hazardous Substances. These polices require electronics producers to take back products at the end of life and reduce the use of toxics in production (with a ban on heavy metals and flame retardants). These measures are also intended to encourage the reuse and recycling of electronic products instead of dumping them into landfills or exporting them. Moreover, they are aimed at encouraging industries to embrace ecological design that facilitates easy recovery of these products at the end of their (first) consumer life.

There are numerous other initiatives that have emerged to address the international and global challenges of e-waste production, consumption, recycling, and dumping. In 2007, Solving the E-waste Problem was launched by the Institute for the Advanced Study of Sustainability at the United Nations University in Bonn, Germany, as an effort to gather comprehensive data on e-waste in order to promote global solutions through goal-setting and communication among key stakeholders. The participants in this effort include NGOs, industry, government, and academia. Similarly, the Global E-Sustainability Initiative brings together businesses, industry associations, and NGOs to, in part, develop solutions to the e-waste problem (Ilankoon et al. 2018).

Despite these efforts, what is most concerning for scholars and advocates is that none of these policy initiatives—including the WEEE directive—addresses the *roots* of the e-waste problem. Unless the economic imperative of infinite growth itself is challenged, the social and environmental ills that activists bemoan will likely worsen. Given that e-waste of all sorts is increasing in volume globally, it has become clear that we cannot recycle our way out of this dilemma. A perverse effect of the WEEE directive is that as more material is collected for recycling, it may create a greater demand to *export* e-waste illegally to other nations for dirty recycling. This is exactly what happened with bans on e-waste in landfills—to encourage e-waste recycling—in the United States.

As noted, attempts to create solutions to the myriad challenges of environmental injustice without taking into account a range of social, political, cultural, and economic factors will likely be limited, if not counterproductive. For example, McAllister, Magee, and Hale (2014) argue that "technological solutions" intended to address the challenge of global climate change—such as solar power and electric car batteries—will undoubtedly exacerbate the problems of e-waste trafficking because those products will eventually be added to the rapidly growing stream of e-waste materials, which will have particularly negative impacts on women, who tend to do the most dangerous e-waste recycling labor. The Intergovernmental Panel on Climate Change (2011) estimates that by the year 2040 100% of solar panels currently in use will be entering the waste stream.

Furthermore, by the early 2020s, an estimated half a million electric car batteries are expected to enter the waste stream (Kanter 2011). The materials and components associated with wind energy, nanotech, and hydropower are also similarly expected to result in e-waste at the end of their (first) life (McAllister, Magee, and Hale 2014).

The evolution of policy initiatives to address the e-waste crisis reflects the fact that this is a rapidly changing environmental and social problem that is complex in its drivers and effects. The unfortunate reality is that few, if any, of these initiatives are aimed at addressing the problems associated with environmental injustices impacting affected communities. This is precisely why some scholars have argued that relying on governmental or multilateral organizations and initiatives is counterproductive and that exerting grassroots pressure on all major institutions is likely to be more effective at countering the "slow violence" of e-waste dumping and processing in a world system that continues to externalize the costs of the global electronics commodity chain on poor and racialized communities.

Conclusion

This chapter considers the evolution of research on the global movement and trade in used electronics or e-waste. The primary focus is on the degree to which e-waste trading and processing reflects concerns over environmental justice. I examine a number of theoretical perspectives that emerge from or intersect with the environmental justice literature, including the concept of "slow violence," ecologically unequal exchange, and world-systems theory. I also consider the emerging debate within the field concerning the embrace or rejection of the state as an arbiter of justice. The case of e-waste trading and recycling is a powerful illustration of "slow violence" precisely because it tends to produce harm to human bodies and ecosystems over time, rather than in an instant. That fact makes it challenging to document and mobilize around. E-waste zones are also evidence of the ways in which ecologically unequal exchange and world-systems theory are quite relevant for the study of environmental conflict because e-waste is a global phenomenon that tends to reflect the ways in which wealthier communities benefit from global trade at the expense of poor communities and their local environments.

The majority of the scholarship on this topic has traditionally framed the global e-waste trade as a clear case of environmental injustice or environmental racism because so much of these materials have been shipped from wealthy to poorer nations, particularly nations where the majority of the population is non-White. But more recent data reveal that those earlier trends and assumptions have changed as most of the used electronics volume is traded within and among wealthier nations. However, the scholars who have taken this trend to signal an end to concerns over environmental injustice may have acted in haste. As I argue, there remain key indicators that e-waste continues to harm marginalized populations and ecosystems around the world at all geographic scales, and scholars must pay closer attention to those dynamics. This includes the fact that whether e-waste is produced and remains in the Global North or the Global South, it is usually processed by vulnerable populations and that the overwhelming majority of e-waste is not recycled and, instead, sent to landfills, incinerators, and garbage dumps that tend to be located in low-income neighborhoods and communities of color (Bansal et al. 2016). Moreover, claims by some scholars that e-waste recycling adds much needed value to local economies are well grounded but should not ignore the continued evidence of harms to human and environmental health that are integral to that sector.

Future research should pursue a closer examination of the multidimensional character of environmental (in)justice dynamics associated with e-waste at the local, regional, national, and transnational scales. The concept of "situated e-waste justice" offers much to be unpacked as the local context and layered histories of communities where e-waste is being processed shape the nature and intensity of the socioenvironmental impacts and opportunities for workers, residents, and other stakeholders. Finally, while a number of social movements and policy leaders have pushed governments and industry to improve outcomes for human and environmental health, they have not pushed nearly hard enough. There is a clear need for imaginative and transformative thinking and action that asks difficult questions not only about the social and environmental consequences of e-waste trading and processing but, more deeply and importantly, about how we might address the troubling imperative of infinite growth in capitalist societies. How might the lenses of racial capitalism and degrowth be effective tools for scholars and activists imagining how to transform debates and practices concerning e-waste in the future?

References

Agyeman, Julian, David Schlosberg, Luke Craven, and Caitlin Mathews. 2016. "Trends and Directions in Environmental Justice Research." *Annual Review of Environment and Resources* 41: 321–340.

Akese, Grace, and Peter Little. 2018. "Electronic waste and the environmental justice challenge in Agbogbloshie." *Environmental Justice* 11, no. 2: 77–83.

Amoako, Clifford. 2016. "Brutal Presence or Convenient Absence: The Role of the State in the Politics of Flooding in Informal Accra, Ghana." *Geoforum* 77: 5–16.

Amuzu, David. 2018. "Environmental Injustice of Informal E-Waste Recycling in Agbogbloshie-Accra: Urban Political Ecology Perspective." *Local Environment* 23, no. 6: 603–618.

Asante, Kwadwo Ansong, Tetsuro Agusa, Charles Augustus Biney, William Atuobi Agyekum, Mohammed Bello, Masanari Otsuka, Takaaki Itai, Shin Takahashi, and Shinsuke Tanabe. 2012. "Multi-Trace Element Levels and Arsenic Speciation in Urine of E-Waste Recycling Workers in Agbogbloshie, Accra in Ghana." *Science of the Total Environment* 424: 63–73.

Baldè, C. P., F. Wang, R. Kuehr, and J. Huisman. 2015. *The Global E-Waste Monitor 2014—Quantities, Flows and Resources*. Bonn: United Nations University, IAS-SCYCLE.

Bansal, Satyam, Harsh Chaudhary, Prashant Singh, and Pratibha Singh. 2016. "Socio-economic and Environmental Impact of Electronic Waste." *Integrated Research Advances* 3, no. 1: 9–12.

Basel Action Network. 2002a. *Exporting Harm: The High-Tech Trashing of Asia*. Seattle, WA: Basel Action Network.

Basel Action Network. 2002b. *Exporting Harm: The High-Tech Trashing of Asia, the Canadian Story*. Seattle, WA: Basel Action Network.

Basel Action Network. 2005. *The Digital Dump: Exporting Re-use and Abuse to Africa*. Seattle, WA: Basel Action Network.

Brigden, K., I. Labunska, D. Santillo, and M. Allsopp. 2005. *Recycling of Electronic Waste in China and India: Workplace and Environmental Contamination*. Amsterdam: Greenpeace International.

Bullard, Robert D. 2000. *Dumping in Dixie: Race, Class, and Environmental Quality*. Boulder, CO: Westview Press.

Chang, Shenglin, Hua-Mei Chiu, and Wen-Ling Tu. 2006. "Breaking the Silicone Silence: Voicing Health and Environmental Impacts within Taiwan's Hsinchu Science Park." In *Challenging the Chip: Labor Rights and Environmental Justice in the Global Electronics Industry*, edited by Ted Smith, David A. Sonnenfeld, and David N. Pellow, 170–180. Philadelphia: Temple University Press.

Chemical Watch. 2020. "US Electronics Network to Start Worker Exposure Programme." International Campaign for Responsible Technology, July 9. https://icrt.co/current-news/.

Corwin, Julia. 2018. " 'Nothing Is Useless in Nature': Delhi's Repair Economies and Value Creation in an Electronics 'Waste'. Sector." *Environment and Planning A: Economy and Space* 50, no. 1: 14–30.

Dayaneni, Gopal, and John Doucette. 2005. *System Error—Toxic Tech Poisoning People and Planet*. San Jose, CA: Silicon Valley Toxics Coalition.

Deng, W. J., P. K. K. Louie, W. K. Liu, X. H. Bi, J. M. Fu, and M. H. Wong. 2006. "Atmospheric Levels and Cytotoxicity of PAHs and Heavy Metals in TSP and $PM_{2.5}$ at an Electronic Waste Recycling Site in Southeast China." *Atmospheric Environment* 40, no. 36: 6945–6955.

Fenelon, James, and Jennifer Alford. 2020. "Envisioning Indigenous Models for Social and Ecological Change in the Anthropocene." *Journal of World-Systems Research* 26, no. 2: 372–399.

Fevrier, Kesha. 2020. "Race and Waste: The Politics of Electronic Waste Recycling and Scrap Metal Recovery in Agbogbloshie, Accra, Ghana." PhD diss., York University.

Foran, Tira, and David Sonnenfeld. 2006. "Corporate Social Responsibility in Thailand's Electronics Industry." In *Challenging the Chip: Labor Rights and Environmental Justice in the Global Electronics Industry*, edited by Ted Smith, David A. Sonnenfeld, and David N. Pellow, 70–82. Philadelphia: Temple University Press.

Frazzoli, Chiara, Orish Ebere Orisakwe, Roberto Dragone, and Alberto Mantovani. 2010. "Diagnostic Health Risk Assessment of Electronic Waste on the General Population in Developing Countries' Scenarios." *Environmental Impact Assessment Review* 30, no. 6: 388–399.

Frey, R. Scott. 2012. "The E-Waste Stream in the World-System." *Journal of Globalization Studies* 3, no. 1: 79–94.

Gilmore, R. W. 2007. *Golden Gulag: Prisons, Surplus, Crisis, and Opposition in Globalizing California*. Oakland: University of California Press.

Gosney, M. 2009. "Introduction and Overview." In *Electronic Waste Management: Design, Analysis and Application*, edited by Ronald E. Hester and Roy M. Harrison, 1–37. Cambridge: Royal Society of Chemistry.

Greenpeace International. 2005. *Recycling of Electronic Wastes in China & India: Workplace & Environmental Contamination*. Amsterdam: Greenpeace International.

Greenpeace International. 2008. *Toxic Tech: Not in Our Backyard*. Amsterdam: Greenpeace International.

Greenpeace and Anthropology Department of Sun Yat-sen University. 2003. *Anthropological Report on E-Waste Disassemble Industry in Guiyu, Shantou. The Main Report*. Amsterdam: Greenpeace International. [In Chinese].

Hao, Di, Ru-Han Yi, Yu Wu, Yun-feng Lu, and Chuang-li Fang. 2015. "Pollution Characteristics and Exposure Risk Assessment of Polybrominated Diphenyl Ethers in Different Types Agricultural Soils in Guiyu Area." *Journal of Agro-Environment Science* 34, no. 5: 882–890.

Haraway, Donna. 2015. "Anthropocene, Capitalocene, Plantationocene, Chthulucene: Making Kin." *Environmental Humanities* 6: 159–165.

Harrison, Jill Lindsey. 2019. *From the Inside Out: The Fight for Environmental Justice within Government Agencies*. Cambridge, MA: MIT Press.

Huysman, M. 1994. "Waste Picking as a Survival Strategy for Women in Indian Cities." *Environment and Urbanization* 6, no. 2: 155–174.

Ilankoon, I. M. S. K., Yousef Ghorbani, Meng Nan Chong, Gamini Herath, Thandazile Moyo, and Jochen Petersen. 2018. "E-Waste in the International Context—A Review of Trade Flows, Regulations, Hazards, Waste Management Strategies and Technologies for Value Recovery." *Waste Management* 82: 258–275.

Intergovernmental Panel on Climate Change. 2011. *Special Report on Renewable Energy Sources and Climate Change Mitigation*. Cambridge: Cambridge University Press.

International Labour Organization. 2014. "Tackling Informality in E-Waste Management: The Potential of Cooperative Enterprises in the Management of E-Waste." Working Paper, International Labour Organization, Geneva. https://www.ilo.org/sector/Resources/publications/WCMS_315228/lang--en/index.htm.

International Labour Organization. 2015. *The Labour, Human Health and Environmental Dimensions of E-Waste Management in China in the Management of E-Waste*. Geneva: International Labour Organization. https://www.ilo.org/beijing/what-we-do/publications/WCMS_375174/lang--en/index.htm.

Jorgenson, Andrew K., and Brett Clark. 2009. "The Economy, Military, and Ecologically Unequal Exchange Relationships in Comparative Perspective: A Panel Study of the Ecological Footprints of Nations, 1975–2000." *Social Problems* 56, no. 4: 621–646.

Kanter, James. 2011. "Fancy Batteries in Electric Cars Pose Recycling Challenges." *New York Times*, August 30.

Kumar, Rashmi, and Dahyalal J. Shah. 2014. "Review: Current Status of Recycling of Waste Printed Circuit Boards in India." *Journal of Environmental Protection* 5, no. 1: 9–16.

LaDou, Joe. 1984. "The Not-so-Clean Business of Making Chips." *Technology Review* 87, no. 4: 22–36.

LaDou, Joe. 1985. "Water Contamination in the Silicon Valley." *Journal of Occupational and Environmental Medicine* 27, no. 4: 304.

LaDou, Joe. 1986. "Health Issues in the Microelectronics Industry." *Occupational Medicine-State of the Art Reviews* 1, no. 1: 1–11.

LaDou, Joe, and Sandra Lovegrove. 2008. "Export of Electronics Equipment Waste." *International Journal of Occupational and Environmental Health* 14: 1–10.

Lepawsky, Josh. 2015. "The Changing Geography of Global Trade in Electronic Discards: Time to Rethink the E-Waste Problem." *Geographical Journal* 181, no. 2: 147–159.

Lepawsky, J., and Charles Mather. 2011. "From Beginnings and Endings to Boundaries and Edges: Rethinking Circulation and Exchange through Electronic Waste." *Area* 43, no. 2: 242–249.

Lepawsky, Josh, and Chris McNabb. 2010. "Mapping International Flows of Electronic Waste." *Canadian Geographer* 54, no. 2: 177–195.

Li, Yan, Xijin Xu, Kusheng Wu, Gangjian Chen, Junxiao Liu, Songjian Chen, Chengwu Gu, Bao Zhang, Liangkai Zheng, Minghao Zheng, and Xia Huo. 2008. "Monitoring of Lead Load and Its Effect on Neonatal Behavioral Neurological Assessment Scores in Guiyu, an Electronic Waste Recycling Town in China." *Journal of Environmental Monitoring* 10, no. 10: 1233–1238.

Mahesh, Priti. 2011. "Passing the Poisonous Parcel." *Our Planet* (April): 16–19.

McAllister, Lucy, Amanda Magee, and Benjamin Hale. 2014. "Women, E-Waste, and Technological Solutions to Climate Change." *Health and Human Rights Journal* 1, no. 16: 166–178.

McCarthy, John, and Mayer Zald. 1977. "Resource Mobilization and Social Movements: A Partial Theory." *American Journal of Sociology* 82, no. 6: 1212–1241.

McCourt, James. 2006. "Worker Health and National Semiconductor, Greenock (Scotland): Freedom to Kill?" In *Challenging the Chip: Labor Rights and Environmental Justice in the Global Electronics Industry*, edited by Ted Smith, David A. Sonnenfeld, and David N. Pellow, 139–149. Philadelphia, PA: Temple University Press.

Mohai, Paul, David Naguib Pellow, and J. Timmons Roberts. 2009. "Environmental Justice." *Annual Review of Environment and Resources* 34: 405–430.

Morris, Aldon. 2000. "Reflections on Social Movement Theory: Criticisms and Proposals." *Contemporary Sociology* 29, no. 3: 445–454.

Murphy, Michael Warren, and Caitlin Schroering. 2020. "Refiguring the Plantationocene: Racial Capitalism, World-Systems Analysis, and Global Socioecological Transformation." *Journal of World-Systems Research* 26, no. 2: 400–415.

Nixon, Rob. 2011. *Slow Violence and the Environmentalism of the Poor*. Cambridge, MA: Harvard University Press.

Pandita, Sanjiv. 2006. "Electronics Workers in India." In *Challenging the Chip: Labor Rights and Environmental Justice in the Global Electronics Industry*, edited by Ted Smith, David A. Sonnenfeld, and David N. Pellow, 83–95. Philadelphia, PA: Temple University Press.

Pellow, David N. 2007. *Resisting Global Toxics: Transnational Movements for Environmental Justice*. Cambridge, MA: MIT Press.

Pellow, David N. 2017. *What is Critical Environmental Justice?* Polity Press.

Pulido, Laura. 2017. "Geographies of Race and Ethnicity II: Environmental Racism, Racial Capitalism, and State-Sanctioned Violence." *Progress in Human Geography* 41, no. 4: 524–533.

Qiu, B., L. Peng, X. J. Xu, X. Lin, X. Hong, H. Guo, and X. Huo. 2005. "Investigation of the Health of Electronic Waste Treatment Workers." *Journal of Environment and Health* 22, no. 6: 419–421.

Rice, James. 2007. "Ecological Unequal Exchange: International Trade and Uneven Utilization of Environmental Space in the World System." *Social Forces* 85, no. 3: 1369–1392.

Robinson, C. 1983. *Black Marxism: The Making of the Black Radical Tradition*. Chapel Hill: University of North Carolina Press.

Rocha, Raquel E. Partida. 2006. "Labor Rights and Occupational Health in Jalisco's Electronics Industry (Mexico)." In *Challenging the Chip: Labor Rights and Environmental Justice in the Global Electronics Industry*, edited by Ted Smith, David A. Sonnenfeld, and David N. Pellow, 161–169. Philadelphia, PA: Temple University Press.

Silicon Valley Toxics Coalition. 2001. *Poison PCs and Toxic TVs: California's Biggest Environmental Crisis That You've Never Heard of.* San Jose, CA: Silicon Valley Toxics Coalition.

Smith, Ted, David A. Sonnenfeld, and David N. Pellow. 2006. *Challenging the Chip: Labor Rights and Environmental Justice in the Global Electronics Industry.* Philadelphia, PA: Temple University Press.

Sthiannopkao, Suthipong, and Ming Hung Wong. 2013. "Handling E-Waste in Developed and Developing Countries: Initiatives, Practices and Consequences." *Science of the Total Environment* 463–464: 1147–1153.

Stowell, Alison F., and Samantha Warren. 2018. "The Institutionalization of Suffering: Embodied Inhabitation and the Maintenance of Health and Safety in E-Waste Recycling." *Organization Studies* 39, no. 5–6: 785–809.

Sze, Julie. 2020. *Environmental Justice in a Moment of Danger.* Berkeley: University of California Press.

Taylor, Dorceta. 2016. *Toxic Communities: Environmental Racism, Industrial Pollution, and Residential Mobility.* New York: New York University Press.

Toxics Link India. 2003. *Scrapping the High-Tech Myth: Computer Waste in India.* New Delhi: Toxic Link India.

Toxics Link India. 2004. *E-Waste in Chennai: Time Is Running Out.* Chennai: Toxic Link India.

Toxics Link India. 2007a. *E-Waste: Flooding the City of Joy.* New Delhi: Toxic Link India.

Toxics Link India. 2007b. *Into the Future: Managing E-Waste for Protecting Lives and Livelihoods.* New Delhi: Toxic Link India.

Toxics Link India. 2007c. *Mumbai: Choking on E-Waste.* New Delhi: Toxic Link India.

Wallerstein, Immanuel. 2011. *The Modern World-System I: Capitalist Agriculture and the Origins of the European World-Economy in the Sixteenth Century.* Berkeley: University of California Press.

Wang, Yalin, Jinxing Hu, Wei Lin, Ning Wang, Cheng Li, Peng Luo, Muhammad Zaffar Hashmi et al. 2016. "Health Risk Assessment of Migrant Workers' Exposure to Polychlorinated Biphenyls in Air and Dust in an E-Waste Recycling Area in China: Indication for a New Wealth Gap in Environmental Rights." *Environment International* 87: 33–41.

Watterson, Andrew. 2006. "Out of the Shadows and into the Gloom? Worker and Community Health in and around Central and Eastern Europe's Semiconductor Plants." In *Challenging the Chip: Labor Rights and Environmental Justice in the Global Electronics Industry*, edited by Ted Smith, David A. Sonnenfeld, and David N. Pellow, 96–106. Philadelphia, PA: Temple University Press.

Whyte, Kyle Powys. 2018. "Settler Colonialism, Ecology, and Environmental Injustice." *Environment and Society* 9, no. 1: 125–144.

Widmer, Rolf, Heidi Oswald-Krapf, Deepali Sinha-Khetriwal, Max Schnellmann, and Heinz Böni. 2005. "Global Perspectives on E-Waste." *Environmental Impact Assessment Review* 25: 436–458.

Wong, M. H., S. C. Wu, W. J. Deng, X. Z. Yu, Q. Luo, A. O. W. Leung, C. S. C. Wong, W. J. Luksemburg, and A. S. Wong. 2007. "Export of Toxic Chemicals—A Review of the Case of Uncontrolled Electronic-Waste Recycling." *Environmental Pollution* 149, no. 2: 131–140.

Wu, Kusheng, Xijin Xu, Lin Peng, Junxiao Liu, Yongyong Guo, and Xia Huo. 2012. "Association between Maternal Exposure to Perfluorooctanoic Acid (PFOA) from Electronic Waste Recycling and Neonatal Health Outcomes." *Environment International* 48: 1–8.

Xing, Guan Hua, Janet Kit Yan Chan, Anna Oi Wah Leung, Sheng Chun Wu, and M. H. Wong. 2009. "Environmental Impact and Human Exposure to PCBs in Guiyu, an Electronic Waste Recycling Site in China." *Environment International* 35, no. 1: 76–82.

Yang, Y. S. 2006. "Guiyu Town in Shantou, Guangdong: The Town of E-Waste Goes on a Win–Win Road." *Renmin Wang*, February 20. [In Chinese]. http://politics.people.com.cn/GB/1026/4120686.html.

Yin, Y. M., W. T. Zhao, T. Huang, S. G. Cheng, Z. L. Zhao, and C. C. Yu. 2018. "Distribution Characteristics and Health Risk Assessment of Heavy Metals in a Soil–Rice System in an E-Waste Dismantling Area." *Environmental Science* 39, no. 2: 916–926.

Zhang, Ye. 2020. "An Intersectional Analysis of Social and Environmental Injustice Experienced by Migrant Women Workers in China: The Case of Guiyu." PhD diss., Australian Catholic University.

CHAPTER 25

DIGITAL WAR

Mediatized Conflicts in Sociological Perspective

OLGA BOICHAK

On an August night in 2014, Halyna[1] jumped at the sound of a caravan of ambulances making its way past her high-rise apartment complex in Dnipro, Ukraine. She remembered scrolling through a battlefront update on Facebook earlier that day, and it clicked—those must be the heavily wounded Ukrainian soldiers from Ilovaysk on their way to the Mechnikov Hospital. For the first time that night, Halyna felt the distance between her peaceful civilian lifeworld and the active military battlefront of the Russian–Ukrainian war disappear. Once the high-pitched sirens had faded into the distance, she put her sleepy toddlers to bed, packed a bag full of food and hygiene supplies, and went straight to the Mechnikov Hospital to see if they needed a hand there. For the next few years, Halyna coordinated large-scale volunteering initiatives in her region: taking care of the wounded soldiers and civilians, facilitating transfers of the fallen service members home, and delivering humanitarian aid to the internally displaced persons from the occupied territories. During her numerous trips to the battlefronts, she constantly used her smartphone to check news, post updates, and connect with others near and far who, like her, were looking for ways to get involved. Present-day digital media shape individual and public perceptions of wartime realities, whereby emergent actors, narratives, events, and identities, as well as larger social institutions such as states, get drawn and encapsulated into digitally mediated environments. As our everyday experiences become increasingly saturated with media and communication technologies, the contexts of our use of these technologies collapse, creating intimate connections between life at home and places of violent conflict (Ford and Hoskins 2020).

Halyna's lived experiences of war in the digital age might be unique; yet, interlinked with those of numerous others, they constitute an integral part of social reality at the backdrop of armed conflicts. In a time where "every battle seems personal, but every conflict is global" (Singer and Brooking 2018, 22), digital technologies[2] do not simply offer new capabilities in conducting military operations: Extending the battlefronts into the realms of communication and perception, they reconstitute the social conditions shaping people's relationship to wars. Blurring the boundaries between military and civilian actors, physical and virtual battlefronts, weapons and witnesses, digital media afford unprecedented opportunities for involvement and remote participation in wars. In this context, sociologists are uniquely positioned to make sense of these emerging participatory patterns in military conflicts, attending to the higher-order social transformations that challenge and transform our understanding of armed conflicts.

So, how can we study digital wars sociologically, without resorting to concept fetishism and technologically deterministic views? Following C. Wright Mills, how can we go beyond "abstracted empiricism" (1959, 51–55) in making sense of the contemporary moment in the history of warfare and the role of digital media therein? New conditions of conduct of wars, predicated upon digital technologies of communicative power—from social media to radar and military weaponry—call for new languages and methods for understanding the emerging modes of social reality (Orr 2006). Bringing these languages and methods together, this chapter proceeds in three parts: first, I put sociological traditions of studying wars in a dialogue with media studies literature, demonstrating how an understanding of digital media can inform social theory around contemporary conflicts; next, I conceptualize digital war as a field of inquiry, mapping its emerging themes, objects of analysis, and interdisciplinary connections; I conclude with an epistemological framework for making sense of emerging participatory patterns and their significance both for the participants as well as for the larger institutions on behalf of which wars are fought. It is my hope that this chapter will serve as another link between the somewhat disparate fields of military sociology and sociology of media, connecting the two strands of sociological inquiry around the matters of public participation in military conflicts.

Sociological Perspectives on War and Media

Studying wars has traditionally been relegated to political science, international relations, and history (Heinecken 2015; Ender and Gibson 2005). However, in light of the ubiquity and pervasiveness of armed conflicts around the world, for the past few decades sociologists have attended to the conduct, causes, and consequences of wars, with a systematic empirical focus on wartime mobilization, militarisms, and the role of narratives in framing and remembering armed conflicts, as well as the institutional capacity of states at war (Garnett 1988; Segal and Burk 2012; Wimmer 2014). Founded in 1978, the Peace, War, and Social Conflict section of the American Sociological Association (2020) became one of the first academic communities dedicated to the development and application of sociological theories and approaches to the study of war and peace. The International Sociological Association, founded under the auspices of UNESCO in the aftermath of World War II (Platt 1998), established the Research Committee on Armed

Forces and Conflict Resolution shortly thereafter in 1983, joining academic and military practitioners around studying military institutions, civil–military relations, terrorism, and insurgencies (International Sociological Association 2020).

The "founding fathers" of sociology—Marx, Weber, and Durkheim—each engaged with war and social conflict in their work. Marx saw war as "capitalism by other means,"[3] whereby revolutionary changes in the social order might be accompanied by a confrontation with the state's military (Heinecken 2015). Weber ([1905] 2002) equally engaged with the modern state's monopoly on violence through bureaucratic institutions and their effects on society. Unlike the former two, Durkheim's interest ([1912] 1995) was in social cohesion and the breakdown of social fabric that takes place during violent conflicts. Drawing on these intellectual foundations, sociologists have been studying war across three focal points: the relationship between the state and its military, the military establishment and civil–military relations, and people's experiences of wars and their effects on society at large (Lang 1972; Segal and Burk 2012).

Military sociology is only beginning to investigate the role of digital media in military conflicts, predominantly attending to cybersecurity and the use of digital media in an asymmetric/irregular warfare paradigm, otherwise known as "hybrid" war (Erol and Oguz 2015; McCuen 2008; Schroefl and Kaufman 2014; Caforio and Nuciari 2018). In this strand of literature, hybrid/asymmetric war is defined in juxtaposition to older, "conventional" kinds of warfare; this concept is used by military professionals and in peacekeeping missions around the world to highlight the role of information and communication technologies, specifically mobile and locative media[4] and other many-to-many communication systems, in contemporary military conflicts (Caforio 2018). Other strands of military sociology examine militarisms and the meaning-making processes happening around armed conflicts, as well as processes and dynamics within military institutions and the society at large (Segal and Burk 2012). While digital media are mentioned in this context, researchers adopt a more socially deterministic stance by looking at them as communication tools, with less attention to the various modes of public participation and relation to wars, as well as the broader social transformations happening at the battlefields that have suddenly gone "paperless" (Ford and Hoskins 2020).

Sociologists of media and culture have been the first to attend to the dynamics of mediatized conflicts. Thompson linked mediated interactions in distant contexts to the battlefield logics of the Vietnam War, theorizing on the active role of media in orchestrating the flow of wartime events through controlling the flow of images (1995, 109–118). The very fact that this chapter appears in the *Oxford Handbook of Sociology and Digital Media* situates the studies of digital war among critical issues related to digital media and society, highlighting an emerging set of relationships between users of digital media and the larger ecosystems in which military conflicts are encapsulated. Yet to this point, there has been a dearth of research on digital war in top-ranked sociology journals—with the notable exception of *Media, War & Conflict*, a peer-reviewed interdisciplinary journal dedicated specifically to the studies of media–military relations, which includes sociological research. Another prominent interdisciplinary venue is the

Digital War journal, which publishes sociological work that illuminates the social, cultural, and political significance of digital war as an emerging interdisciplinary field of inquiry.

A comprehensive review of sociological traditions of studying wars identified four themes in which sociologists have significantly advanced understanding of wars (Wimmer 2014): (1) long-term historical and social processes at the backdrop of wars (e.g., Mann 2012; Tilly 1995, 2001); (2) tracing the relationship between political legitimacy, national identity, and wars (e.g., Wimmer 2013); (3) advanced understanding of causes and outcomes of wars from an organizational perspective of a modern state (e.g., Davis and Pereira 2003; Giddens 1987); and (4) foregrounding the shifting configurations of power in military conflicts (Thompson 1995). This section summarizes the key takeaways from sociological research in social processes at the backdrop of wars, including the role of frames, genres, and visuals in constructing state legitimacy and its contestation.

Historical and Social Processes as the Backdrop of Wars

Sociologists are uniquely positioned to attend to various nonstate actors and collectives that co-constitute discursive framings of wars and contentious political issues (Dromi 2020; Merrin 2018; Ridolfo and Hart-Davidson 2019; Schradie 2019). This strand of inquiry has been influenced by systems thinking and views wars as complex yet contingent social and political phenomena. Here, sociologists have attended to the rhythms, temporalities, and logics of social, political, and ideological transformations and contemplated long-term developments and broader social patterns in military conflicts around the world (e.g., Mann 2012; Tilly 1995, 2001). Approaches in political sociology that attend to wars through analysis of historically situated institutions, practices, and understandings (e.g., Melucci 1996; Tilly 2001) have ongoing analytical utility to the studies of digital war. Specifically, phenomenological approaches to individual and collective identities and attention to fluid networked actors (as opposed to fixed social categories) and their shifting repertoires have been profoundly influential in understanding the communicative construction of social actors in the digital age (Bakardjieva 2015; Bennett and Segerberg 2012; Kavada 2016; Milan 2015).

Scholars of war and peace have also attended to historical developments in peace activism and how various groups and identities engage with peace discourses in anti-militarism movements. Particularly in the United States, peace movements have been found to critique and question dominant understandings of security and nationalism and construct alternative epistemologies to combat widespread public resistance in times of war (Woehrle, Coy, and Maney 2008). Leitz and Meyer (2017) explored the relationship between gender and war and analyzed tensions resulting from minority groups' involvement in institutional politics, especially within feminist organizing and activism. They found that women have historically rallied around gender equality and social justice issues, which often included efforts to end U.S. involvement in wars and domestic militarism. This body of literature highlights the significance of public participation in generating alternative frames, narratives, and imaginaries of military conflicts in order to shift the hegemonic discourses of war and the subsequent policy decisions.

Frames, Narratives, and Genres of Collective Participation/Response to Wars

Sociologists have significantly advanced our understandings of state legitimacy, national identity, and cultural frames in the context of international and domestic wars, as well as their role in modern nation-state formations, which presents a departure from realist international relations approaches (Wimmer 2014). Tracing the relationship between political legitimacy and wars, Wimmer (2013) foregrounds the conflict dynamics that occur when these principles are subject to shifts, as well as theorizes on the ways in which nationalist imaginaries may affect the outcomes of interstate and civil wars. *Networked publics*—groups of citizens who strategically use digital technology to propagate their ideas among wider audiences (Baym and boyd 2012)—may help establish state legitimacy by using online spaces to craft and circulate unifying national narratives (Harvey and Leurs 2018; Woehrle, Coy, and Maney 2008). Opening a new array of opportunities for identity formation on the basis of platform affordances of interactivity and anonymity, digital media may be used to articulate a new vision of national identity, conferring state legitimacy in a fragile state (Boichak and Jackson 2020). Importantly, participation in the online public sphere is shaped by various forms of inequality and exclusion — from various levels of digital divide to marginalization of minority groups — which in turn leads to the emergence of various alternative networked counterpublics that circulate oppositional discursive interpretations of their goals and identities (Harvey and Leurs 2018; Woehrle, Coy, and Maney 2008). While these discourses usually aim to undermine state legitimacy to the detriment of geopolitical outcomes of wars, there have also been instances in which digitally networked publics were able to successfully prevent an encroaching military occupation (Boichak and Jackson 2020).

Narratives and Imaginaries

Representing an existential threat to a nation, a civilization, or a way of life, wars lead to intense social and cultural production aimed at containing (and, in many ways, interpreting) the military violence (Keller 2001). Sociologists have attended to the cultural logics of wars (Smith 2005), as well as investigated beliefs and values that drive humanitarian and postconflict reconstruction efforts (Dromi 2020). Smith (2005) foregrounds the significance of narratives used to justify military involvement from the perspective of genre. In this context, narratives are understood as stories which we construct and circulate as part of our sense-making practice. Unlike binary codes, narratives presume social phenomena to be a sequence of events, rather than a form of categorical recognition based on similarity or difference (Smith 2005, 18). Moreover, narratives not only encompass facts but also attend to what might have been, serving as both a normative and a phenomenological hermeneutic frame for understanding social reality (Smith 2005, 18). Narratives are a constitutive part of social imaginaries—values, norms, symbols, and cognitive frameworks that are constituted through people's social experiences and shape their understanding of events and their role in them (Anderson 2006).

Attending to the major characters and plot points, Smith differentiates narratives according to their mimesis/significance: from low-mimetic, mundane narratives, in which the social stakes are low, to moderate-mimetic genres, where heroes and villains have clear social stakes that develop either along an ascending (romance) or a descending (tragedy) theme, to highest-mimetic genre, which presents as an apocalyptic narrative where both the social stakes as well as the moral polarization between the good and the evil are extreme. The analytical utility of this approach to a sociological reading of cultural texts has increased in the digital age and can be successfully applied to understanding platform-mediated narratives of activism and social solidarity, including those around military involvement (Boichak and McKernan 2020; Jacobs and Smith 1997).

Visuals

Another strand of literature took a visual turn to examine image testimonies and their affective economies in military conflicts (Adelman 2018; Schankweiler, Straub, and Wendl 2018). This interest is well justified since photography turned war into a matter of popular culture: Photography was the first medium that collapsed contexts, providing the opportunity to strategically deliver information or frame an argument, thus affording different audiences an opportunity to perceive information through their own reference frames and cultural schemas (Vaidhyanathan 2018). As such, photographs lack explanatory power, letting the seer add their own hermeneutics. Through these features, photography introduced profound changes to not only how the wars were being represented but also, consequently, how they were being fought and how they were being remembered; scenic battles could be subsequently embedded in various narratives depicting the conflict. Unlike photographs that presented neatly selected and sliced stills, television introduced a relentless flow of images, many of which represented real-time temporalities (Hoskins and O'Loughlin 2010). The 24-hour news cycle had a profound impact on foreign policy through public perceptions of national security, what scholars described as the "CNN effect" (Matheson and Allan 2009). Drone warfare also deserves a mention in this context as it transformed the fields of perception beyond the cinematic toward nonhuman vision that brings remote death, subsequently reshaping the intersections between human life and technological power (Richardson 2018).

Memory Studies

Memory studies took a connective turn in sociological work within this theme of inquiry by exploring memories as a link between individual experiences and collective past and futures (Hoskins 2016). This work is of paramount importance to the field of digital war, whereby digital media are used not only for documenting battlefront events for the subsequent legitimization of wars—they also constitute past and future memories (Hoskins and O'Loughlin 2010). In the words of Derrida, "what is no longer archived in the same way is no longer lived in the same way" (1998, 18); and it is the very act of archivization that produces as much as records events, bringing them into existence and shaping their relationship with the future (Derrida 1998). Historically, we were able to learn about wars from military archives which contained data that was recorded, structured, and stored by the military establishment. We need to attend to these changes in the context of the wider changes in society, interrogating how radical transformations in data-saturated memory-making and archival practices will allow researchers to look back and study violent conflicts and affect their futures, considering what other actors and entities might be able to benefit from the data and to what ends (Ford and Hoskins 2020).

Bounding the (Battle)Field: Toward an Epistemological Framework

Mediatization, characterized by a deepening interrelationship between digital media and society, engenders higher-order processes of societal transformation: People's interactions are not simply mediated by digital technologies, but this technology-based interdependence has predicated a shift in the nature of social relations (Couldry and Hepp 2017; Lundby 2014). Digitally mediated interactions have become enfolded and embedded within the social world in a process known as "deep mediatization," characterized by rapid technological advancement, on the one hand, and an increasing human reliance on technology, on the other (Couldry and Hepp 2017; Hjarvard 2008). Processes of deep mediatization have unsettled the structural conditions of the inception, execution, and, consequently, outcomes of military conflicts around the world. With most of war-related events and our knowledge about them being mediatized, contemporary social theory needs to consider the higher-order structural changes in which imaginaries, representations, and witnessing of digitally mediated events serve to justify military campaigns and resistance toward them.

Digital media have turned into an important arena for the shaping and contestation of geopolitical outcomes, which requires a new epistemological framework for understanding wars in the digital age. How can sociology contribute to understanding the changing nature of social relations at the backdrop of digital wars fought around the world? The immediacy with which information can be amplified and the various framings and vantage points with which it is diffused, as well as the very low costs associated with reaching broad and diverse transnational publics, afford unprecedented opportunities for public participation and engagement with mediatized conflicts. Having mapped the emerging field of digital war within the sociological discipline with its respective connections to other fields, I proceed to exploring its participatory dimensions through the prism of Meyrowitz's media metaphors: conduits, languages, and environments (Eskjær, Hjarvard, and Mortensen 2015; Meyrowitz 1993). Just like imaginaries, metaphors are sense-making constructs that carry not only aesthetic but also epistemological significance (Meyrowitz 1993).

Conduits

To understand digital media as conduits means to examine their capacity to deliver various kinds of content. Information has historically played an important role in the conduct and outcomes of wars. Witness testimony, in which an individual's authentic proximity to events is digitally mediated through multimodal composition—text, images, and video footage—drives attention and affect economies, affording anyone the ability to participate in the acts of information sharing and memorialization surrounding wars (Richardson 2018).

In Raqqa, Syria, 17 citizens organized into a reporting collective to document the destruction of their city, becoming the primary source of information for their fellow citizens and the international press, who could not report from the ground at the time (Singer and Brooking 2018). Ten members of this community were later caught and executed by ISIS; many of these murders were also live-streamed (Singer and Brooking 2018). In a similar act of resistance to their city's occupation, 20 activists in Mariupol, Ukraine, ran an informal news agency to gather intelligence on separatist activity and crowdfund supplies for the Ukrainian army stationed outside the city limits. The activists were successful in countering separatism in their city—after 3 months of occupation rule, Mariupol was liberated, which further contributed to the growth and scope of activities among the activist communities (Boichak and Jackson 2020).

These two stories share a common feature: the use of digital media as conduits of participation in armed conflicts. Importantly, social media are not the only locative media used for these purposes. Private mobile telephony has been an important means of communication and coordination in the zone of the Ukrainian conflict: Soldiers and civilians reported frequent use of smartphones for entertainment, keeping in touch with friends and family, posting battlefront updates on social media, and requesting help from volunteer organizations (Shklovski and Wulf 2018). This connectivity, which enabled posting crucial battlefront updates and personal experiences of a military conflict, afforded the soldiers an ability to mobilize civilian supporters for humanitarian activism (Boichak 2017; 2019). Yet, these digitally mediated, networked spaces may also attract nefarious actors attempting to influence the development and perception of information on these conduits: Imposters, scammers, trolls, and automated accounts (bots) may resort to coordinated campaigns attempting to debase or delegitimize the claims made by war participants.

Behavioral data and metadata emerge as another by-product of mediatization. Information is not only diffused as it passes through digital media; it is also made a subject of algorithmic surveillance, which brings forward a momentous shift from the military–industrial complex of modernity to the data–industrial complex of postmodernity. This relationship between mediatized information and surveillance shapes trajectories of military conflicts by immersing the networked publics into a diffused flow of battle-front events, while also subjecting them to surveillance. "Death by metadata," in which a target whose identity remains unknown is killed in a drone strike on the basis of their digital footprint, highlights the entanglements between technologies of perception, mediation, and affective witnessing into a deadly manifestation of algorithmic power (Pugliese 2016; Richardson 2018). Algorithmic structuring of reality, which operates preemptively, not only alters the ways in which wars are fought—it also penetrates the lifeworld of individuals, erasing the distinction between witnessing and weaponry, "war" and "domesticity" (Massumi 2009; Richardson 2018). It is important to remember that the "back end" of these conduits might be just as important in the shaping and contestation of geopolitical outcomes as their user interface.

Languages

This metaphor primarily depicts the genres, framings, and affordances of each medium when it comes to participation in wars. As mediatization collapses temporal and spatial contexts, state and nonstate actors may resort to digital media to create conflicting framings and representations of military conflicts. Scholars of war posit that the formal, Clausewitzian[5] definition of war is still relevant—wars still involve an armed contestation of existing power relationships between institutions, at least one of which acts on behalf of a state (Eskjær, Hjarvard, and Mortensen 2015). It is the involvement of state-like actors in the conflict, in combination with a threshold of a thousand battle deaths, that defines war and sets it apart from other forms of mass violence and atrocities, such as riots or genocide (Wimmer 2014). By this logic, digital war is by no means a new *type* of war—rather, it can be characterized by a changing set of patterns and dynamics that accompany the use of digital media therein (Merrin 2018). In this sense, the "Clausewitzian war" becomes one among the many possibilities of achieving political ends by the conflict parties (Ford and Hoskins 2020).

As "languages," digital media become central in shaping representations of political violence, arbitrating the distinction between military and nonmilitary activities. We can see this very clearly in the Crimean example, comparing the Crimean War (1853–1856) to the annexation of Crimea that happened a century and a half later (2014). The Crimean War was a spectacle: a beautifully scripted mass-mediated event that derived its representations through the medium of photography, which, starting from the nineteenth century, had a significant impact on framing battlefront updates (Keller 2001). *The Valley of the Shadow of Death* remains among the most iconic wartime images of all time that has left a lasting imprint on our collective memory. In contrast, photographs from the annexation of Crimea—effectively the most significant breach of another state's territorial integrity since World War II—were deliberately ambiguous and obscure, depicting uniformed men with no insignia wandering around Crimea's capital city of Simferopol (Boichak 2020). Even the discursive framings of Russia's land grab suggested its nonmilitary nature, obscuring the beginning of a military conflict.

The "languages" metaphor also calls attention to the diversity of digitally mediated ways in which technologies are used in wars. In this context, crowds and crowdsourcing platforms are a particularly interesting avenue of exploring digitally mediated participation. As in this chapter's opening vignette, battlefront updates may elicit strong emotional responses among those in networked publics. This might lead to new frames and meanings being ascribed to war events as they circulate online and mobilize the networked publics for various pro-social behaviors, such as web sleuthing to collect evidence or humanitarian activism (Boulianne, Minaker, and Haney 2018). Understanding digital media as "languages" of participation in conflicts also warrants an investigation into the critical digital literacies on the part of the digital media users. Literature in cultural rhetoric and composition is a useful resource in understanding the processes of the weaponization of various forms of media in support of armed conflicts around the world (Sullivan 2017; Ridolfo and Hart-Davidson 2019).

Environments

Present-day mediatized environments elide traditional distinctions between privacy and publicness, personal communication and mass media, audience and producers, citizens and diasporas, as well as lead to the emergence of new forms of digital communication among the networked actors. Through their involvement in mediatized conflicts, publics co-structure and co-constitute power relations in their attempt to influence the geopolitical outcomes of contemporary wars. Ford and Hoskins (2020) call this emerging war ecology "radical war," foregrounding the relationships between perception, knowledge, and action in digitally mediated environments, with attention to various actors that get involved in this process.

Affording digital spaces for grassroots storytelling and activism, digital media not only complicate the notion of publicness in mediatized environments but also challenge the territorial boundaries of such publicness (Milan 2015). With this media metaphor (environments), Meyrowitz encourages analyzing the media itself, searching for "the ways in which the differences in media make a difference" (1993, 61). What does the distinction between "interstate" and "intrastate" military conflicts mean in the digital age, when there are unprecedented affordances for public participation in both types of conflict from anywhere around the world? This is where the concept of *transglocalization* provides a useful angle into understanding how digital media reconfigure the spatial and geographical dimensions of such participation. Borrowing from diaspora studies, transglocalization captures the dynamic state of networked formations that mobilize around issues of local, global, and transnational significance (Kok and Rogers 2016). While all battlefronts in a conflict are distinctively local, the networks that reconstitute power relations also operate nationally and transnationally, simultaneously, and with or without mutual awareness of each other's actions. This concept foregrounds diasporas and other networked actors who might not be co-present in the same geographical spaces in which the conflict is occurring but nonetheless make attempts to influence its outcomes (Boichak 2019; Gamlen 2019).

Studying new media ecologies also involves attention to the ways in which the emergence of each new medium alters the contexts of human participation in wars and reconfigures the existing relationships among stakeholders in this process (Meyrowitz 1993; Ford and Hoskins 2020). For example, the quick adoption of Facebook in countries such as Myanmar and Ethiopia, and its exclusive use for internet access, has directly contributed to fueling genocide, which resulted in mass atrocities, violence, and displacement (Ford and Hoskins 2020). These local histories of technological development and shaping of war are in stark contrast with those in the West, whereby citizens have been using social media for some time along with other means of accessing the internet. This speaks to the fact that media ecologies are unique and should be studied within their local contexts of use and that mapping participatory ecologies should involve not only finding the continuities and similarities across time and space but also paying attention to these local contexts and discontinuities in the use of digital media for participation in wars (Ford and Hoskins 2020).

Choosing Your Battles: Researching Participation in Digital Wars

Digital war is an emerging field of inquiry, in which scholars seek to comprehend the shifts introduced by the advancement and use of various digital media to the ways that contemporary wars are fought, represented, understood, and remembered. At the same time, digital war is an elusive concept that invokes imaginaries of clean, bloodless, and fully virtual battles happening somewhere on a computer screen. These imaginaries are as harmful as they are misleading, detracting from the casualties and suffering of those whose social reality has been transformed by an armed conflict. Even if the battles are being simulated, waged, and/or broadcast online, death and devastation remain harrowing constants—a stark contrast to the sanitized imaginaries of virtuality and immateriality promoted by the military–industrial–media–entertainment networks through our screens (Der Derian 2009).

This chapter's contribution to understanding digital media and society lies in presenting an extensive review of the existing sociological literature in the field of digital war, providing intellectual foundations for future research in this emerging field. I began by summarizing two key themes of sociological research in war and media: (1) tracing long-term historical and social processes at the backdrop of wars and (2) analyzing frames, narratives, and genres of collective participation/response to wars; drawing attention to visuals and memory studies; and mapping their connections to media studies and security studies literature. Drawing on mediatization framework, I then proceeded to analyze how digital media serve as conduits, languages, and environments affording public participation in wars. Assuming that technological interconnectedness will only deepen in the next years, sociological readings of the role of digital media in the construction of contemporary conflicts will have increasing analytical utility. In the words of Deleuze, "There is no need to fear or hope, but only to look for new weapons" (1992, 4).

So, how does one choose one's battles in this field of digital war going forward? What kinds of digital literacies do we need as academics, digital media users, and citizens for researching and participating in digital wars; and how can they inform present-day sociological theory and methods? Hoskins and O'Loughlin (2010) acknowledge the absence of a coherent research paradigm in the field of digital war due to the ever-shifting nature of its objects of analysis and identify two challenges of studying mediatized conflicts. First, observing media effects while being fully embedded in media ecology makes capturing experiences of war at best problematic: "as well as the modalities of what we analyse, we need to think about the modalities of our own analysis" (p. 187). This speaks to the "environments" metaphor, in which we need to carefully examine the role emerging technologies might play in those media ecologies, the "anatomy" of those technologies (front- and back-end), and the layers of datafied representations that are being produced through their use. Second, studying media as embedded in social practices, rather than examining the content, structure, and agencies on each medium separately, poses a challenge because of *mediality*, which links abstract mediated representations to discursive media practices rooted in the everyday: for us, for our research participants, and for the discursively constituted others out there. In this sense, quoting Matthew Moore, war can best be understood as a continuation of society by other means (Ford and Hoskins 2020), which circles us back to this chapter's opening vignette. How can we use sociological imagination to make sense of armed conflicts when we are already being made part of them?

A researcher's positionality and relationship with the object of analysis define key epistemological assumptions about the project (Donovan 2018). In ethnographic research, militant ethnographic epistemology involves producing knowledge not only about but also for the participants (Haraway 1988). To study mediatized conflicts, the researcher has to not only be immersed in the field but also become its participant. Due to the despatialized nature of digital field sites, even remote data collection, whether in ethnographic or computational modes of research, poses a series of ethical challenges in the study of military conflicts (Käihkö 2018). The ease with which researchers of digital war can access their field sites makes us permanently involved in these mediatized conflicts, which bears a series of epistemological and methodological implications on the research we produce. This understanding lies at the center of the notion of a research assemblage (Fox and Alldred 2015): from this standpoint, this chapter itself can be seen as a heterogeneous object constituted by theories, research methods and tools, entities and events of interest, the researcher, as well as contextual elements: academic culture and disciplinary requirements surrounding social inquiry, ethics, physical spaces of knowledge production, as well as human and technological resources that the inquiry involves and entails. As mediatization continues to blur the boundaries between public and private, soldiers and citizens, witnesses and weapons, development of situated, reflexive, and contextually nuanced methods of studying digital war can provide insights into the fluid nature of contemporary battlefronts, with the caveat of remaining permanently immersed therein.

Notes

1. Names have been changed throughout the chapter to protect the privacy of war participants.
2. For the purpose of the chapter, *digital media* may be defined as a combination of devices and technologies that afford numerical, discrete representation of information and/or computational capacities associated with it—therefore, it is not the digital "format" of the information per se that distinguishes the new media from the old but, rather, the computability that enables alternative means of knowledge production, which could not have been applied to analog data (Manovich 1999).
3. This might be an oversimplification of Marx's positions on conflict, but it makes sense in light of the Clausewitzian understanding of wars, so let's consider this statement as a boundary object for the purpose of this chapter.
4. Locative media encompass mobile information and communication technologies that foster geospatial awareness and interactions between participants, including the ability to track, map, annotate, search for, and communicate information about the location of self and objects. Examples of mobile locative media include social media, GPS navigators, and augmented reality games such as Pokemon Go (Hjorth et al. 2020).
5. This refers to Clausewitz's idea of war being an extension of the state's strategic interests, or "politics by other means," in which military forces serve as instruments of state power (Ford and Hoskins 2020).

References

Adelman, Rebecca A. 2018. *Figuring Violence: Affective Investments in Perpetual War*. New York: Fordham University Press.

American Sociological Association. 2020. Peace, war, and social conflict. https://www.asanet.org/communities/sections/sites/peace-war-and-social-conflict.

Anderson, Benedict. 2006. *Imagined Communities: Reflections on the Origin and Spread of Nationalism*. London: Verso.

Bakardjieva, Maria. 2015. "Do Clouds Have Politics? Collective Actors in Social Media Land." *Information, Communication & Society* 18, no. 8: 983–990.

Baym, Nancy K., and danah boyd. 2012. "Socially Mediated Publicness: An Introduction." *Journal of Broadcasting & Electronic Media* 56, no. 3: 320–329.

Bennett, W. Lance, and Alexandra Segerberg. 2012. "The Logic of Connective Action." *Information, Communication & Society* 15, no. 5: 739–768. https://doi.org/10.1080/1369118X.2012.670661.

Boichak, Olga. 2017. "Battlefront Volunteers: Mapping and Deconstructing Civilian Resilience Networks in Ukraine." Proceedings of the 8th International Conference on Social Media & Society, Toronto, ON, Canada, July, 3:1–3:10. https://doi.org/10.1145/3097286.3097289.

Boichak, Olga. 2019. "Mobilizing Diasporas: Understanding Transnational Relief Efforts in the Age of Social Media." Proceedings of the 52nd Annual Hawai'i International Conference on System Sciences (HICSS-52), Grand Wailea, HI, January 8–11. http://hdl.handle.net/10125/59716.

Boichak, Olga. 2020. "Mitigating Diffused Security Risks in Australia's North: A Case for Digital Inclusion." *The Strategist: Australian Strategic Policy Institute* (blog), September 30. https://www.aspistrategist.org.au/mitigating-diffused-security-risks-in-australias-north-a-case-for-digital-inclusion/.

Boichak, Olga, and Sam Jackson. 2020. "From National Identity to State Legitimacy: Mobilizing Digitally Networked Publics in Eastern Ukraine." *Media, War & Conflict* 13, no. 3: 258–279.

Boichak, Olga, and Brian McKernan. 2020. "'Those Who Craft the Victory': Narrating Geopolitics within the Mundane." Proceedings of the 70th Annual International Communication Association Conference, May 20–26.

Boulianne, Shelley, Joanne Minaker, and Timothy. J. Haney. 2018. "Does Compassion Go Viral? Social Media, Caring, and the Fort McMurray Wildfire." *Information, Communication & Society* 21, no. 5: 697–711. https://doi.org/10.1080/1369118X.2018.1428651.

Caforio, Giuseppe. 2018. "The Sociology of the Military and Asymmetric Warfare." In *Handbook of the Sociology of the Military*, 2nd ed., edited by G. Caforio and M. Nuciari, 497–522. Cham, Switzerland: Springer International Publishing.

Caforio, Giuseppe, and Marina Nuciari, eds. 2018. *Handbook of the Sociology of the Military*. 2nd ed. Cham, Switzerland: Springer International Publishing.

Couldry, Nick, and Andreas Hepp. 2017. *The Mediated Construction of Reality*. Cambridge: Polity Press.

Davis, D., and Anthony W. Pereira, eds. 2003. *Irregular Armed Forces and Their Role in Politics and State Formation*. Cambridge: Cambridge University Press.

Deleuze, Gilles. 1992. "Postscript on the Societies of Control." *October* 59, 3–7.

Der Derian, James. 2009. *Virtuous War: Mapping the Military–Industrial–Media–Entertainment Network* (2nd ed.). New York and London: Routledge.

Derrida, Jacques. 1998. *Archive Fever: A Freudian Impression*. Translated by E. Prenowitz. Chicago: University of Chicago Press.

Donovan, Joan. 2018. "Toward a Militant Ethnography of Infrastructure: Cybercartographies of Order, Scale, and Scope across the Occupy Movement." *Journal of Contemporary Ethnography* 48, no. 4: 482–509. https://doi.org/10.1177/0891241618792311.

Dromi, Shai M. 2020. *Above the Fray: The Red Cross and the Making of the Humanitarian NGO Sector*. Chicago: University of Chicago Press.

Durkheim, Emile. (1912) 1995. *The Elementary Forms of Religious Life*. Translated by Karen E. Fields. New York: Free Press.

Ender, Morten. G., and Ariel A. Gibson. 2005. "Invisible Institution: The Military, War and Peace in Pre-9/11 Introductory Sociology Textbooks." *Journal of Political and Military Sociology* 33, no. 2: 249–266.

Erol, Mehmet Seyfettin, and Safak Oguz. 2015. "Hibrit Savas Çalismalari ve Kirim'daki Rusya Örnegi" [Hybrid warfare studies and Russia's example in Crimea] *Gazi Akademik Bakis Dergisi* 9, no. 17: 261–277.

Eskjær, Mikkel Fugl, Stig Hjarvard, and Mette Mortensen, eds. 2015. *The Dynamics of Mediatized Conflicts*. New York: Peter Lang.

Ford, Matthew, and Andrew Hoskins. 2020. "Radical War." *Information Innovation @ UTS* (audio podcast), hosted by M. Moore, November 3. https://infoinnouts.podbean.com/e/war/.

Fox, Nick J., and Pam Alldred. 2015. "New Materialist Social Inquiry: Designs, Methods and the Research-Assemblage." *International Journal of Social Research Methodology* 18, no. 4: 399–414. https://doi.org/10.1080/13645579.2014.921458.

Gamlen, Alan 2019. *Human Geopolitics: States, Emigrants, and the Rise of Diaspora Institutions*. Oxford: Oxford University Press.

Garnett, Richard A. 1988. "The Study of War in American Sociology: An Analysis of Selected Journals, 1936 to 1984." *American Sociologist* 19, no. 3: 270–282. https://doi.org/10.1007/BF02691985.

Giddens, Anthony. 1987. *The Nation-State and Violence*. Berkeley: University of California Press.

Haraway, Donna. 1988. "Situated Knowledges: The Science Question in Feminism and the Privilege of Partial Perspective." *Feminist Studies* 14, no. 3: 575–599. https://doi.org/10.2307/3178066.

Harvey, Alison, and Koen Leurs. 2018. "Networked (In)Justice: An Introduction to the #AoIR17 Special Issue." Special issue, *Information, Communication & Society* 21, no. 6: 793–801. https://doi.org/10.1080/1369118X.2018.1438493.

Heinecken, Lindy. 2015. "The Military, War, and Society: The Need for Critical Sociological Engagement." *Scientia Militaria, South African Journal of Military Studies* 43, no. 1: 1–16.

Hjarvard, Stig. 2008. "The Mediatization of Society. A Theory of the Media as Agents of Social and Cultural Change." *Nordicom Review* 29, no. 2: 105–134.

Hjorth, Larissa, Kana Ohashi, Jolynna Sinanan, HeatherHorst, Sarah Pink, Fumitoshi Kato, et al. 2020. *Digital Media Practices in Households: Kinship through Data*. Amsterdam: Amsterdam University Press.

Hoskins, Andrew. 2016. "Memory Ecologies." *Memory Studies* 9, no. 3: 348–357.

Hoskins, Andrew., and Ben O'Loughlin. 2010. *War and Media: The Emergence of Diffused War*. Cambridge: Polity.

International Sociological Association. 2020. "RC01 Armed Forces and Conflict Resolution." https://www.isa-sociology.org/en/research-networks/research-committees/rc01-armed-forces-and-conflict-resolution/.

Jacobs, Ronald N., and Philip Smith. 1997. "Romance, Irony, and Solidarity." *Sociological Theory* 15, no. 1: 60–80. https://www.jstor.org/stable/202135.

Käihkö, Ilmari. 2018. "Conflict Chatnography: Instant Messaging Apps, Social Media and Conflict Ethnography in Ukraine." *Ethnography* 21, no. 1: 71–91. https://doi.org/10.1177/1466138118781640.

Kavada, Anastasia. 2016. "Social Movements and Political Agency in the Digital Age: A Communication Approach." *Media and Communication; Lisbon*, 4, no. 4. http://dx.doi.org/10.17645/mac.v4i4.691.

Keller, Ulrich. 2001. *The Ultimate Spectacle: A Visual History of the Crimean War*. Philadelphia, PA: Gordon and Breach.

Kok, Saskia, and Richard Rogers. 2016. "Rethinking Migration in the Digital Age: Transglocalization and the Somali Diaspora." *Global Networks* 17, no. 1: 23–46. https://doi.org/10.1111/glob.12127.

Lang, Kurt. 1972. *Military Institutions and the Sociology of War*. Beverly Hills, CA: Sage Publications.

Leitz, Lisa A., and David S. Meyer. 2017. "Gendered Activism and Outcomes: Women in the Peace Movement." In *The Oxford Handbook of Women's Social Movement Activism*, edited by H. J. McCannon, V. Taylor, J. Reger, and R. L. Einwohner, 708–728. New York: Oxford University Press.

Lundby, Knut., ed. 2014. *Mediatization of Communication*. Berlin: De Gruyter Mouton.

Mann, Michael. 2012. *A History of Power from the Beginning to AD 1760*. Vol. 1, *The Sources of Social Power*. 2nd ed. Cambridge: Cambridge University Press.

Manovich, Lev. 1999. "New Media: A User's Guide." http://manovich.net/content/04-projects/026-new-media-a-user-s-guide/23_article_1999.pdf.

Massumi, Brian. 2009. "National Enterprise Emergency: Steps toward an Ecology of Powers." *Theory, Culture & Society* 26, no. 6: 153–185. https://doi.org/10.1177/0263276409347696.

Matheson, Donald, and Stuart Allan. 2009. *Digital War Reporting*. Cambridge: Polity.

McCuen, John J. 2008. "Hybrid Wars." *Military Review; Fort Leavenworth* 88, no. 2: 107–113. http://search.proquest.com/docview/225305596?pq-origsite=summon&.

Melucci, Alberto. 1996. *Challenging Codes: Collective Action in the Information Age*. Cambridge: Cambridge University Press.

Merrin, William. 2018. *Digital War: A Critical Introduction*. London and New York: Routledge.

Meyrowitz, Joshua. 1993. "Images of Media: Hidden Ferment—and Harmony—in the Field." *Journal of Communication* 43, no. 3: 55–66. https://doi.org/10.1111/j.1460-2466.1993.tb01276.x.

Milan, Stefania. 2015. "From Social Movements to Cloud Protesting: The Evolution of Collective Identity." *Information, Communication & Society* 18, no. 8: 887–900. https://doi.org/10.1080/1369118X.2015.1043135.

Mills, C. Wright. 1959. "The Promise." In *The Sociological Imagination*. New York: Oxford University Press.

Orr, Jackie. 2006. *Panic Diaries: A Genealogy of Panic Disorder*. Durham, NC: Duke University Press.

Platt, Jennifer. 1998. *A Brief History of the ISA: 1948–1997*. Madrid: International Sociological Association. https://www.isa-sociology.org/uploads/files/histoy-of-isa-1948-1997.pdf.

Pugliese, Joseph. 2016. "Death by Metadata: The Bioinformationalisation of Life and the Transliteration of Algorithms to Flesh." In *Security, Race, Biopower: Essays on Technology and Corporeality*, edited by H. Randell-Moon and R. Tippet, 3–20. London: Palgrave Macmillan. https://doi.org/10.1057/978-1-137-55408-6_1.

Richardson, Michael. 2018. "Drone's-Eye View: Affective Witnessing and Technicities of Perception." In *Image Testimonies: Witnessing in Times of Social Media*, edited by K. Schankweiler, V. Straub, and T. Wendl, 72–86. New York and London: Routledge.

Ridolfo, Jim, and William Hart-Davidson, eds. 2019. *Rhet Ops: Rhetoric and Information Warfare*. Pittsburgh, PA: University of Pittsburgh Press.

Schankweiler, Kerstin, Verena Straub, and Tobias Wendl, eds. 2018. *Image Testimonies: Witnessing in Times of Social Media*. New York and London: Routledge.

Schradie, Jen 2019. *The Revolution That Wasn't: How Digital Activism Favors Conservatives*. Cambridge, MA: Harvard University Press.

Schroefl, Josef, and Stuart J. Kaufman. 2014. "Hybrid Actors, Tactical Variety: Rethinking Asymmetric and Hybrid War." *Studies in Conflict & Terrorism* 37, no. 10: 862–880. https://doi.org/10.1080/1057610X.2014.941435.

Shklovski, Irina, and Volker Wulf. 2018. "The Use of Private Mobile Phones at War: Accounts from the Donbas Conflict". Proceedings of the 2018 CHI Conference on Human Factors in Computing Systems, New York, NY, USA: 386:1–386:13. https://doi.org/10.1145/3173574.3173960.

Segal, David R., and James Burk, eds. 2012. *Military Sociology*. Thousand Oaks, CA: Sage Publications.

Singer, P. W., and Emerson Brooking. 2018. *LikeWar: The Weaponization of Social Media*. New York: Houghton Mifflin Harcourt.

Smith, Philip. 2005. *Why War? The Cultural Logic of Iraq, the Gulf War, and Suez*. Chicago: University of Chicago Press.

Sullivan, Ben. 2017. Bellingcat Wants Your Help to Debunk Fake News. Motherboard, March 7. https://motherboard.vice.com/en_us/article/78qbqy/bellingcat-wants-your-help-to-debunk-fake-news.

Thompson, John B. 1995. *The Media and Modernity: A Social Theory of the Media*. Stanford, CA: Stanford University Press.

Tilly, Charles. 1995. "To Explain Political Processes." *American Journal of Sociology* 100, no. 6: 1594–1610. https://www.jstor.org/stable/2782682.

Tilly, Charles. 2001. "Historical Analysis of Political Processes." In *Handbook of Sociological Theory*, edited by J. H. Turner, 567–588. New York: Springer. https://doi.org/10.1007/0-387-36274-6_26.

Vaidhyanathan, Siva. 2018. *Antisocial Media: How Facebook Disconnects Us and Undermines Democracy*. New York: Oxford University Press.

Weber, Max. (1905) 2002. *The Protestant Ethic and the Spirit of Capitalism*. Translated by Talcott Parsons. New York: Routledge.

Wimmer, Andreas. 2013. *Waves of War: Nationalism, State Formation, and Ethnic Exclusion in the Modern World*. Cambridge: Cambridge University Press.

Wimmer, Andreas. 2014. "War." *Annual Review of Sociology* 40, 173–197. https://doi.org/10.1146/annurev-soc-071913-043416.

Woehrle, Lynne M., Patrick G. Coy, and Gregory M. Maney. 2008. *Contesting Patriotism: Culture, Power, and Strategy in the Peace Movement*. Lanham, MD: Rowman & Littlefield.

CHAPTER 26

MASCULINITY, EVERYDAY RACISM, AND GAMING

STEPHANIE M. ORTIZ

THE literature on video games and gaming spans multiple disciplines and covers a wide range of issues. A significant portion of this work is centered on reading representations of race, gender, and sexuality in video games and assessing the impact of these representations (Gray and Leonard 2018; Gray, Voorhees, and Vossen 2018; Nakamura 2012; Brock 2011). Related, researchers have examined gaming spaces as sites where players form communities, enact violence toward other players, and resist oppressions (Gray and Leonard 2018; Gray, Voorhees, and Vossen 2018; Nakamura 2013, 2017; Ortiz 2019a; Cote 2017, 2020; Fox and Tang 2014, 2017). Gendered and racialized interactions that occur while gaming have an impact on participants, in addition to the ways those from marginalized groups are represented. As Gray, Buyukozturk, and Hill (2017) persuasively demonstrated, violence in gaming includes a symbolic dimension in the form of hate speech and harassment of marginalized players. Symbolic violence is a concept that attends to how social control is achieved through coercive, non-physical methods. Words, actions, and images that negate the worth and humanity of marginalized groups are forms of symbolic violence because they function to maintain a dominant group's power (Thapar-Björkert, Samelius, and Sanghera 2016). It is therefore necessary to move beyond content analysis and consider the structural implications of harassment. Sociology provides ways to explore how this racialized and gendered violence within the social world of gamers sustains racism and sexism as systems more broadly.

Racist and sexist harassment is a defining characteristic of what the literature refers to as the "toxicity" of gaming culture (Cote 2017, 2020; Gray 2012b, 2014, 2016; Massanari 2017; Ortiz 2019a, 2019b). This toxicity manifests as sexism through representations of women (Ivory 2006) and the harassment of women gamers (Condis 2018; Cote 2017, 2020). Likewise, racism within gaming has been noted in the racist representations of people of color (Brock 2011; Daniels and LaLone 2012; Leonard 2006; Nakamura 2013) and the harassment of gamers of color, where Whites enact symbolic violence to reassert their domination (Gray, Buyukozturk, and Hill 2017; Gray 2012a; Ortiz 2019b).

Notably, Cote (2017, 2020) and Gray (2020) have placed these literatures into conversation, exploring how women of color experience compounded forms of discrimination and develop strategies to resist this mistreatment.

This chapter builds on that foundation. I begin with a brief overview of how sociologists conceptualize masculinity and racism. I then show that the present study of masculinity and racism in gaming inadvertently downplays the role of race *and* gender in shaping forms of domination and resistance in gaming. I offer two analytic shifts to address this issue. First, I center Whiteness in the examination of masculinity, exploring how emotions, manhood acts, and peer socialization contribute to everyday racism in gaming. Second, I broaden the study of experiences of racism in gaming through an analysis of masculinity as a set of practices used as resistance against racism.

Sociological Literature on Masculinities and Racism

Rather than see gender as an innate, fixed, and stable category, sociologists understand gender as a social construct, shaped by political, economic, and historical processes (Pascoe and Bridges 2016). This runs counter to the ideology of gender essentialism, which is the notion that gender is a dichotomous social category and a biological trait. Gender essentialism purports that there are only two genders and that each gender has distinct inclinations, emotions, attitudes, and behaviors (Fausto-Sterling 2000). The belief in distinct and innate gender categories is used to explain away inequalities. If there are differences in occupational mobility, health outcomes, and sexual assault victimization between men and women, gender essentialism focuses our attention to supposedly immutable gender traits, which, we are told, create those differences. Gender essentialism as an ideology thereby legitimizes sexism by suggesting that unequal outcomes and domination are natural. But gender as a social construct reorients our focus to the values assigned to particular behaviors and how traits, attitudes, and practices become linked to those understood to be women and those understood to be men. In doing so, this approach questions the legitimacy of gender inequality. That is, if gender is the basis of these differences and gender is instead created through policy, interactions, and cultural norms, then there is nothing normal, natural, or just about these arrangements.

Another important aspect of the social construction of gender is that it is performed and achieved through everyday actions (West and Zimmerman 1987). While gender certainly involves roles—or bundles of social expectations for "how to be" a man or woman—gender is *enacted* through actions. The effort and actions that construct gender in everyday interactions ultimately reaffirm the "natural" differences those very actions created—for example, when parents provide fighting video games to their son and then perceive their son's enjoyment of fighting as evidence that their son is a boy who enjoys "boy's games." Similarly, discouraging the use of (or not providing access to) games considered to be "for girls" shapes what they perceive as their son's "natural" preference.

Broadly, *masculinity* refers to the "practices, behaviors, attitudes, sexualities, emotions, positions, bodies, organizations, institutions, and all manner of expectations culturally associated with (though not limited to) people understood to be male" (Pascoe and Bridges 2016, 4). *Hegemonic masculinity* describes a form of masculinity that upholds gender domination and legitimates the subordination of women. It is the "currently most honored way of being a man" in a given society (Connell and Messerschmidt 2005) and represents an ideal most men will never be able to achieve, be it due to their race, sexuality, religion, body shape/size, personality traits, emotional expressiveness, or even leisure preferences. Men are assessed by these ideals and may police each other for deviating from hegemonic ideals. Hegemonic masculinity exists in relation to *subordinate masculinities*, which fall short because of their deviant behaviors, attributes, or abilities. For instance, men of color, queer men, Muslim men, and, as I will describe in this chapter, White gamers can occupy subordinate masculinities.

While the concept of hegemonic masculinity was created to account for power and domination within the gender order, Collins (2002) reminds us that the domination of women and of men who occupy subordinate masculinities is also an issue of racism, capitalism, and heteronormativity. Hegemonic masculinity in the United States is not raceless; rather, it idealizes, rewards, and reproduces Whiteness (Chou, Lee, and Ho 2012), though not all White men have equal access to material and symbolic rewards. White men and men of color activate differential power relations in relation to women but also in relation to each other (Collins 2002). For example, controlling images of men of color defines hegemonic masculinity in opposition to White men. Men of color are represented as buffoons, thugs, rapists, savages, and dangerous foreigners who operate in relation to the hegemonic ideal of Whiteness, defining everything White men are *not* (Golash-Boza 2016). Thus, the oppressive actions of White men and the experiences of oppression of men of color in gaming must be understood not solely as issues of gender but also as issues of racism. It is this point that the next section explores within the gaming literature.

As this chapter will also make the case that White masculinity and racism are interconnected in gaming, a brief discussion of racism is also appropriate here. Sociologists conceptualize racism as systemic, with a structural component in addition to ideological and attitudinal ones (Essed 1991; Jung 2015; Bonilla-Silva 1997; Feagin 2006; Golash-Boza 2016). This means social, political, economic, cultural, and psychological rewards are allocated—though not exclusively—along racial lines (Bonilla-Silva 2021). To be sure, ideologies do heavy lifting in justifying and obscuring the structural nature and enduring character of this system. In fact, many sociologists show that racism has a cultural, hegemonic dimension that organizes symbols and meanings, reifying and naturalizing structural inequalities (Collins 2002; Omi and Winant 2014; Feagin 2020; Doane 2017). However, differences in outcomes among groups cannot exclusively be explained by attitudes or ideologies. A definition of racism as merely ideological might encourage scholars to conceptualize racism in gaming as rooted in White gamer's attitudes toward people of color. But racism in gaming is not just an issue of Whites believing themselves to be superior or Whites feeling hatred toward people of color. These attitudes and belief systems become institutionalized in structures and reproduced through everyday actions.

Masculinity and Gaming: Whiteness by any Other Name

Many scholars studying masculinity in gaming undertake a social constructionist perspective, focusing on the practices which constitute masculinities in specific contexts. Recall that this constructionist perspective challenges gender essentialism, which would posit that "man" is a fixed category determined by biology or evolution. The social constructionist perspective examines how what we label as "man" has been created as such through social processes across time. What it means to be a man changes depending on the historical period, region, and social context, such as work, the family, sports, and religious spaces. Studies exploring men and masculinity in gaming from this perspective take interest in issues such as violent behavior and aggression, men's attitudes toward women, the way they form community with other men, and how masculinities are constructed through interactions in online social spaces (Buyukozturk 2021; Ging 2019; Fox and Tang 2014, 2017; Todd 2015).

Across the research, geek masculinity has emerged as key to understanding gaming culture. Geek masculinity is a dominant form of masculinity in gaming spaces. Ging (2019) argues that participation in geek masculinity involves a simultaneous distancing from hegemonic masculinity and frequent engagement in racist and sexist practices, such as doxxing and harassment. That is, geeks may be subordinate to jocks, but in online spaces, White men build community and dignity through both nontoxic practices (e.g., bonding over games, breaking conventional rules) and the establishment and reinforcement of hierarchical distinctions between themselves and men of color.

Despite these revelations about the connections between masculinity and race online, game researchers rarely address Whiteness. This has created a seemingly colorblind body of work that purports to be representative of all men who play video games. Researchers primarily sample White individuals, but Whiteness as a sociopolitical category that co-constructs hegemonic masculinity is not a concern. This is an oversight. In contrast, sociologists have argued that gender relations and the gender order are themselves organized by class, race, and sexuality. That is, while hegemonic masculinity provides a cultural definition of what it means to be a man, scholars can overlook how this definition is racialized as White (Chou, Lee, and Ho 2012). In the context of gaming, White masculinity includes the imperative to enact racism against men of color; even if some individual White men do not engage in this behavior, they recognize their ability to engage if they so choose (Ortiz, 2021a).

Some scholars have focused on more benign and pro-social practices of (White) male gamers, such as cheating in the game, caring about competition, resisting authority, developing a specialized knowledge, and bonding with other men over a love of a game (DiSalvo 2017; Frostling-Henningsson 2009; Sanford and Madill 2006; Trepte, Reinecke, and Juechems 2012). Maloney, Roberts, and Graham (2019) note that while scholars acknowledge the existence of gamers who do *not* engage in toxic racist and sexist behavior, most gloss over them as exceptions. They argue that inclusive masculinity, such as the way men's attitudes and practices can delegitimize homophobia and domination of women, has been overlooked. Inclusive masculinity can be esteemed and valued by peers, without being reliant on the subordination of women or gay men (Anderson 2008). For Maloney, Roberts, and Graham, ignoring the possibility of inclusive masculinities in gaming essentializes an entire subculture as toxic. To gain a fuller picture of how masculinity is constructed in r/gaming, a subreddit about gaming, these collaborators sought to bring out the contradictions and capture the less sensational aspects of the gaming community, such as those discourses that signal openness and inclusion. In the r/gaming community, they observed contestations around the discourses and practices of what it means to be a man in gaming. That is, some participant comments suggest a base for pro-equality stances within gaming, which the authors argue signal a process of positive social change.

These findings should not be downplayed, but studying practices of domination does not necessarily essentialize gaming culture. Uncovering the mechanisms that discourage inclusivity is a critical piece to the complex puzzle of how everyday people challenge domination in the face of repression. For instance, men of color have been discussed as bystanders to women's harassment, and they report remaining silent in response, out of self-preservation (Ortiz 2019b). Understanding the possibilities of anti-racist and feminist interventions among White men requires understanding these perceived social costs and structural barriers which impede rigorous and widespread inclusive practices. Indeed, scholars have highlighted how inclusionary practices can and do exist alongside exclusionary practices. These exclusionary practices have come to define what scholars, journalists, and marginalized gamers understand as a toxic gaming culture (Massanari 2017; Salter and Blodgett 2017; Gray, Buyukozturk, and Hill 2017; Ortiz 2019a). This culture is bound to collective practices, behaviors, and attitudes which provide the rationale for misogyny and racism (Ortiz 2019a).

White male gaming practices within this culture are dynamic and complex (DiSalvo 2017). Gaming is a site where young White men can develop conceptualizations of, and refine, what it means to be a man. DiSalvo's respondents were hesitant to admit that they engaged in trash talk because they saw it as negative, but they also recognized these exchanges as central to being a man in gaming. DiSalvo concluded that White male gamers' choosing distinct genres and playing among themselves are self-regulating acts that reinforce these gamers' own "culture" (p. 171). While trash talk is not always racist or sexist, it has emerged as a form of gaming capital for White men to be able to harass marginalized gamers during gameplay (Consalvo 2007; Nakamura 2012; Ortiz 2019b). Gaming capital is an offshoot of the sociological concept of *cultural capital*, which refers to the cultural knowledge, competencies, skills, and assets that we can acquire to gain the advantage in social reproduction. One requires a particular knowledge to participate in a culture, and different knowledge and skills in turn provide different access to symbolic and material rewards (Bourdieu 1986). What it means to be a White man in gaming is related to the symbolic rewards that gaming capital (in the form of racist trash talk and maintaining toxic environments) provides. A study of masculinity in gaming must therefore grapple with Whiteness because racism, as I will show next, is endemic to gaming.

Everyday Racism and Gaming: A Shift from Racist Representations to Interactions

As Daniels (2013) points out, studies of race on the internet have predominantly undertaken a racial formation perspective, focusing on how race is created and transformed through racial projects. *Racial projects* are sociohistorical processes that assign meaning to racial categories and link those meaning-laden categories to social structures and the distribution of resources. Racial categories, like gender categories, are not fixed or stable; rather, they are socially constructed through negotiations between and across social actors. That is, racial projects involve actions, interpretations, and representations by everyday people and by the state, all of which imbue race with particular meanings. For example, a police officer racially profiling a Black citizen, stop-and-frisk policies, and a teenager wearing a #BLM T-shirt all draw upon and reproduce race. Under this framework, video games can be racist racial projects. As Leonard (2006, 3) states,

> Video games are not just games, or sites of stereotypes, but a space to engage American discourses, ideologies, and racial dynamics... video games offer interpretations, representations and explanations of black athleticism, female sexuality, and inner city America. They provide cues as to reality and explanations for its organization.

Video games "keep it real," employing representations to construct worlds that players can believe in (Leonard 2006), and, as such, produce images and storylines which ultimately reassert Whiteness as superior (Brock 2011; Daniels and LaLone 2012). These games provide a "virtual museum of culture," where the assumed White gamer can experience, through "performances" of, for instance, Black masculinity, an urban landscape (Miller 2008). Games can also prompt dominance and aggression toward others players (Tang and Fox 2016). Yet representations of people of color are only one dimension of racism in gaming; there is a vibrant literature documenting racist violence toward gamers of color through trash-talking. Led by Kishonna Gray, whose groundbreaking studies and theoretical innovations explore the experiences of racism in gaming among people of color, this literature marks an important shift. Reorienting the focus from the representations of people of color and the psychological predictors of aggression, Gray (2012a, 2012b, 2014, 2020) demonstrates that games are not merely imaginary worlds through which gamers confront and navigate neutral representations; they are very important social settings through which Whites target, harass, and harm people of color. Gray's body of work also highlights how people of color navigate and resist this overt racism.

While overt racism has been conceptualized as prejudice and microaggressions within the literature (Glaser and Kahn 2005; Williams et al. 2019; Senter and Ling 2017), I would argue that the framework of everyday racism is a more effective lens. While everyday racism can be similar to microaggressions in certain contexts, the two are conceptually distinct (Bourabain and Verhaeghe 2021). As Domínguez and Embrick (2020) explain, the formulation of microaggressions by Pierce and of everyday racism by Essed bear some similarities; both concepts were developed by studying the subjective lived experiences of Black people, and both consider the cumulative effects of daily race-based violence. Microaggressions deal with events in everyday life, such as racist insults, invalidations, and assaults. Part of the negative cognitive and emotional implications of microaggressions is in the energy and effort expelled in anticipating and determining *if* events constituted identity-based mistreatment. Overt racism in the form of hate speech online requires no cognitive energy to determine *if* the event was about one's race (Ortiz 2021b). While overt racism online is interpreted as stressful and emotionally harmful by victims (Eschmann 2020; Ortiz 2021b; Sobieraj 2020), the stress itself does not emerge from the appraisal process. This is why everyday racism is more appropriate in the case of racist trash talk in gaming.

Everyday racism refers to the forms of racism that are recurrent, repetitive, and familiar; these are forms of racism that people find mundane and describe as "just the way it is." Structural theorists tell us racisms are fluid (Bonilla-Silva 1997; Jung 2015). It follows that the lived experiences of racism would not be constant across time and space, either in specific social settings or by region. Thus, the particular contours of everyday racism depend on the racial ideologies and political and social context at any given point in time. Importantly, everyday racism exposes how recurrent and familiar practices enact the rules and procedures of the racial structure, all of which come to be understood by racial actors as normal. The analytic focus of everyday racism is not necessarily on the stress that it causes but, rather, on *how* the routines and interactions that people take for granted activate and reproduce the racial order on the macro-level. This is because, for Essed (1991), an exploration of the everyday is at the same time an analysis of racism as a system, a system that comprises the ligatures of our everyday world.

An everyday racism framework tells us how racism is reproduced and sustained in ways amplified by the particular features of the online gaming setting, as well as in other social domains (Ortiz 2019b). In the context of gaming, vicarious and firsthand racism via trash talk constitute everyday racism. This overt racism is a form of everyday racism not merely because of its frequency but because it is *understood as* a normal, expected part of social life (Gray 2012a, 2012b, 2014, 2020; Ortiz 2019a, 2020). Gamers of color expect to hear and witness harassment, they anticipate being victimized, they understand these arrangements as normal, and these experiences align with their treatment in other social domains (Passmore and Mandryk 2020; Ortiz 2019a). In the next section, I will suggest that if scholars want to understand how racism is produced in the everyday social context of gaming, the practices of White masculinity should be of concern.

White Masculinity and the Perpetuation of Everyday Racism

One of the issues in using masculinities to understand toxic gaming culture is fixating on the attitudes and practices of individual men, in searching for exceptions or for exemplars of hegemonic masculinity in gaming. Studies examining if and how individual White male gamers occupy hegemonic masculinity should not overlook the fact that White male gamers have created the conditions of gaming culture in which racist and sexist harassment occur (Bulut 2021; Ortiz 2019b). Understanding Whiteness as organizing the contexts of and interactions within gaming shifts the present focus on attitudes and practices toward a structural approach. This is not to suggest that sociologists do not study practices and attitudes of people. A sociological study does so in service of understanding how cultures are constructed, how resources are distributed, and how power is defended and contested, all of which are bound to both Whiteness and masculinity as inherently hierarchical identities.

In the existing literature, the connections between racism and masculinity are often implied but not explicitly explored. The gender and racial order are upheld by actions and ideologies that support domination. Not all White male gamers enact racism through overt means, but they all have the ability to do so by virtue of technological cultures and their positionality which justifies racism online as normal (Ortiz 2021a). Studies of hegemonic masculinity have been critiqued for not attending to the everyday routines and practices that legitimize it. One important site of these practices is the game development studio. Bulut's (2021) fieldwork in a predominantly White male game development studio demonstrates that White masculinity is central to the reproduction of the racist representations that have been critiqued. The study shows that White masculinity emerges as a desire to find pleasure in the Other and becomes structurally enacted in game design. Developers and designers, most of whom are White, downplay how gaming spaces provide new opportunities for racism, instead framing their designs in color-blind terms such as "escapism" and a "general freedom to do what you want." In this way, White masculinity denies its position of power while simultaneously being central to the development of games and gaming culture (Bulut 2021). Bulut's study makes an important contribution to the study of how White masculinities are re-created, performed, and rewarded in gaming because it points out how those processes are linked to the perpetuation of racism. Racism is a key aspect of the construction of hegemonic masculinity in gaming, and this hegemonic masculinity in turn provides White gamers tools to practice their domination while gaming. Possible avenues for future research in this area can draw from sociological studies that link racism to White masculinity through emotions and compensatory manhood acts. Scholars may also explore the key role of peer socialization in shaping and disciplining masculinities to model the hegemonic and racist mold.

Studies of trolling have made a connection between emotions and racism. Indeed, Cook, Schaafsma, and Antheunis (2017) show that male, self-identified trolls in gaming named personal enjoyment, pleasure, and thrill-seeking as key motivations to trolling (which included verbal comments, flaming, and trash-talking). As I show elsewhere, targets and self-identified trolls both understand trolling as involving repeated, collective acts of blatant sexism and racism (Ortiz 2020). Thus, the pleasure involved in harming others through trolling (Buckels, Trapnell, and Paulhus 2014), especially through the symbolic violence of racist hate speech while gaming, warrants a closer examination of emotions. The relationship among emotions, racism, and masculinity that has been explored in other arenas is relevant to video game spaces. For example, Cabrera's (2014) work on White masculinity on college campuses accounts for how White men feel about racism. Emotions such as anger, anxiety, and apathy shape White men's inclinations to discriminate and provide the means to discursively situate themselves as true victims of racism. Notably, White students who attended a university that was *not* predominantly White were enraged at affirmative action programs, which did not even exist at their institution. These students also noted exhaustion from encountering multiculturalism in the spaces they deemed their own. Cabrera further suggested that the competitive environment of the university provided Whites an effective cover to frame students of color as threatening to their social positions. At the same time, White male students also framed students of color as playing the victim and as irrational for their views on race and racism, which we see in gaming spaces. Cabrera's work highlights the emotional dimensions of racism that might otherwise be linked to contextual factors of video games such as competition. The competitive nature of gameplay may provide some explanation for trash talk (Yip, Schweitzer, and Nurmohamed 2018; Ortiz 2019b). However, the reason this trash talk relies on *racist* insults, as opposed to just insulting gamers' skills, can be further understood by also acknowledging the emotional consequences of the perceived harm to White men's social positions. That is, when White men interpret the presence of people of color and inclusivity efforts as "infringing" on their "fundamental freedoms" (Cabrera 2014), emotions such as anger become a key aspect of the overarching White racial frame under which racism is enacted.

In addition to highlighting the emotional dimensions of racism, sociologists account for the centrality of symbolic violence to White masculinity. Boys and men learn to signify, perform, and affirm masculinity through "manhood acts" (Schrock and Schwalbe 2009). Compensatory manhood acts are modified practices men undertake when they cannot reach the ideal of hegemonic masculinity. Sumerau (2020) argues that the threat of and ability to use violence are central to White masculinity because violence is intertwined with compensatory manhood acts. Research on compensatory manhood acts has focused on trans men, men of color, queer men, working-class men, and men working in lower-status job. Combining autoethnography and in-depth interviews with class-advantaged White, cisgender, heterosexual men, Sumerau finds that although violence is seen as something "other" men use to compensate for their lack of power, even men approximating the hegemonic ideal encounter scenarios where they must negotiate violence. While some scholars see hegemonic masculinity and toxic masculinity as conceptually distinct (i.e., some characteristics of hegemonic masculinity are not toxic), Sumerau shows how even pro-social yearnings involve a proclivity for violence. White men find ways to excuse, justify, and enact violence by situating themselves as different from "other men," whose violence is framed as intentional. Sumerau's participants understand violence as something men are supposed to practice but not something they are responsible for addressing. In White men's racism, defense of racist practices, and insistence that racism is "just the way it is" and not their responsibility (Ortiz 2021b), we can see racism in gaming as a core strategy through which male gamers signify their manhood.

Recognizing racism in gaming as related to White masculinity also opens a line of sociological research into the role of gaming in peer socialization of racial violence. Scholars have done similar research on peer socialization and homophobia (Pascoe 2013), racism (Kimmel 2007), and bullying more broadly (Thornberg 2018) among White boys. A socialization framework complements the psychological approach that dominates the literature. Psychological explorations search for racism and sexism as sets of gamer attitudes, implying that outcomes of identity-based harassment can be predicted by such attitudes. Solutions focus on education and remediating prejudice and hatred. However, racism and sexism are not simply individual attributes. They also involve cultural elements, shape the relations of people, and are embedded in technologies. Peer socialization focuses on the broader processes and patterns that contribute to the reproduction of discriminatory and oppressive behaviors. This framework introduces new questions: How are young White boys socialized by peers to participate in and excuse racist and sexist harassment? What are the social rewards and consequences for engaging in these behaviors? How do these material and symbolic rewards shape boys' and men's relationships to one another and marginalized men within gaming?

If peer socialization involves discipline and punishment for deviant masculinities, much socialization among White boys and teens likely involves symbolic violence toward people of color, racial ignorance, and color-blind racism because targeting people of color is normalized and yet predicated upon willful rejection and denial of racism and its persistence (Kimmel 2007; Mueller 2020; Bonilla-Silva 2017). I do not argue here that we focus on individual White boys and men to locate "where" racism resides or to what extent they are "racist." Indeed, the figure of "the racist" has been a great distraction in understanding how systemic racism persists through the *collective actions* of social actors (Bonilla-Silva 2021). Exploring the attitudes and personality traits of White male gamers yields important psychological insights useful for predicting behavior (Fox and Tang 2014). These efforts might also be paired with peer socialization, which can tell us how those attitudes are shaped, encouraged, and rewarded within gaming culture by other White men and, importantly, how inclusive masculinity might emerge in spite of these phenomena.

Masculinity as a Tool: Surviving Everyday Racism

There is not enough research on men of color in gaming, and there is a startling lack of attention to Asian American, Indigenous, and Latino men in particular. Within news media, popular culture, and much of the scholarly literature, Black and Latino masculinities have been demonized as more violent, more homophobic, and more aggressive than White masculinity; Asian masculinities have been feminized; and Indigenous masculinities are framed as lawless threats to coloniality (Collins 2002; Ferber 2007; Eng 2001; Hurtado and Sinha 2016; Innes and Anderson 2015). Even the research on racist trash-talking toward men of color in gaming tends to focus on their victimization, without acknowledging the gendered aspect of this racism. Focusing exclusively on racism misses the role that masculinity plays in framing men of color as deviant, dangerous, and subordinate.

Black masculinity in gaming is beginning to attract scholarly attention (Brock 2020; Chan and Gray 2021; DiSalvo and Bruckman 2010; Gray 2020; Guins 2006). Research suggests that Black male gamers are not necessarily chasing or trying to consume White hegemonic masculinity; instead, Black men use their masculinity for collective uplift, standing up to toxic cultures (Chan and Gray 2021; Gray 2020). Of course, analyzing race and gender requires nuance and an understanding that group social positions are complex and often contradictory (Anthias 2012). Because groups may be positioned as both oppressed and oppressors depending on the context (Collins and Bilge 2016), scholars need to hold both realities at the same time. Men of color are victims of racism in gaming, even as they may participate in or act as bystanders to sexist and homophobic trash talk. In these tangled matrices are questions of how these relations are managed by men of color and how those strategies challenge and sometimes uphold the toxicity.

Passmore and Mandryk (2020) provide a typology of responses to trash talk as a starting point for thinking about the race- and gender-based strategies people develop to navigate discrimination online. The study not only synthesizes previous findings but, more importantly, breaks down the strategies by race and gender group. While "enduring/ignoring" trash talk was the most reported strategy, often as the initial one people used, respondents also reported drawing from a large array of strategies. These strategies ranged from modifying their digital selves to cognitive reframing of the incidents to confronting and calling out their discriminator. Seeking social support was found to be a last-resort strategy, particularly for Latino, Black, and Asian men. Emotional social support can buffer some of the mental health consequences of discrimination (Jackson 2018), and it can also provide resources to groups to boost their self-concept (Williams and Wiggins 2010).

Outside of gaming, Davis' (2019) study of social support among Black women found that collective uplift was a significant outcome of emotional support. Validating the experiences of everyday discrimination and recentering those experiences as collective (as opposed to merely individual events) help Black women affirm and love themselves as Black women. That is, while emotional support and validation of everyday discrimination focus on sustaining individual Black women, this support also translates to conversations of racism and sexism *as systemic and intersecting issues* and the need to actively resist these structures. With regard to gaming spaces, Cote (2017) outlines the strategies that women use to navigate trash talk and mentions *social coping*, which is the mobilization of emotional support and advice from trusted others. Women gamers adopt social coping by choosing to play with friends and avoiding strangers (Cote 2017; Gray 2012b).

The ways men seek and maintain such relations of social support are tied to their ability to draw from intimate relationships with family, friends, and community members (Bowleg et al. 2013; Choi et al. 2011). However, indicators of social support in offline social domains do not necessarily capture the ways people support one another in the gaming context. For example, my interviews (Ortiz 2019a) suggest that men of color who have been victims of racist trash talk find little social support from non-gamers. Family members in particular trivialized racist trash-talking because it occurred while gaming. Men of color nevertheless noted warning new players of the emotional risks of online gaming because they recognized the negative emotional implications of this abuse. This care work, however, is an emotional tightrope. Risking ridicule from other gamers who demanded men of color not express sadness or anger in response to racist trash talk, they also risked ridicule for checking in on another player who was harmed. This might explain why social support was seen as a last-resort strategy for men of color (Passmore and Mandryk 2020), but more research is needed in this area. How do they offer emotional support and advice that validate others' experiences of racism in gaming? One way to explore this question is to focus on the deep connections men of color form with one another.

Connections with other men have been examined for the extent to which those relationships uphold and reinforce hegemonic masculinity. Bird's (1996) study of homosociality concluded that nonsexual attractions between men reproduce gender relations. Men learned key social lessons through their relationships with other men, such as emotional detachment, competition, and sexual objectification of women. These criteria for how to be a man persist despite many men's own personal dissatisfaction with gender relations and despite their desire to subvert the emotional, social, and physical expectations of their masculinity. But for men of color, nonsexual relationships with men are not exclusively tied to producing the hegemonic ideal. In fact, friendships with other men of color can be an important source of love and emotional support (Oware

2011; Way 2011; Way et al. 2014; Rogers and Way 2019), especially in the face of racism. The exceptional work of Niobe Way shows that men desire deep, intimate friendships with each other but find it difficult to find and maintain these relationships because of cultural ideals of men as stoic and uncaring. For men of color, close friendships in adolescence can provide a site to resist dominant racist ideologies of themselves as bound to stereotypical and harmful depictions. As these adolescents reach high school, the social pressure to avoid behavior that could be read as feminine becomes overwhelming (Pascoe 2013; Rogers and Way 2019).

The research on friendships in gaming suggests the capacity for close, intimate friendships to re-emerge. For example, boys were more likely than girls to rate the social aspects of gaming, such as feeling less lonely, having people to compete with, and making new friends as motivators for playing video games (Olson 2010). Adult men are also more likely to report making close friends through gaming than adult women (Cole and Griffiths 2007). Men have also reported discussing sensitive issues with their gamer friends (Cole and Griffiths 2007; Ortiz 2019b). Thus, how men of color develop close friendships with each other through gaming and fulfill the human need of deep connection and intimacy, while also buffering the everyday racism they experience more broadly, can help sociologists understand how masculinity for men of color is a tool for uplift.

Conclusion

Navigating a society where hegemonic masculinity and White supremacy are woven into the social fabric, the oppressive practices and resistance strategies of men in gaming can reveal new insights into how structural inequality becomes resisted and reproduced. Sociologists interested in race and gender as axes of oppression can learn more about how these inequalities persist by examining masculinity and everyday racism in online gaming. Using tools from the sociological study of gender and race can help scholars develop new questions about how broader social processes shape the lives of gamers.

In service of this agenda, I argued that future research should take seriously the ways White masculinity reproduces everyday racism in gaming. Scholars could study the relationship between White male gamers' emotions, gender, and discriminatory practices; the role of violence as a compensatory manhood act in gaming; and the role of peer socialization in the toxic practices of gaming culture. Debating whether or not White male gamers occupy hegemonic masculinity or a subordinate masculinity should not distract researchers from a fuller exploration of Whiteness in this context. Domination is complex; oppression does not follow a simple, additive formula (Collins and Bilge 2016). That is, White men do not always reap every benefit of their status in all social situations. It is possible for White men to be victimized on the basis of other identities. At the same time, it is also possible that White male gamers also oppress others in these settings. This should create new questions: How does White male gamers' domination of other men contribute to their group position? How does their racial oppression of others distract from or obscure their knowledge of their own subordination? What is more, how does witnessing racism against gamers of color contribute to White male gamers' critical consciousness or willingness to identify and seek out anti-racist interventions? How do White male gamers challenge racism among other White gamers? How do White men who occupy positions of power (leaders in guilds, senior developers) or high status (such as streamers) within the gaming community shape the norms around masculinity and racism?

Future researchers would also be well served by further exploring how masculinity may provide sources of resistance to everyday racism. I highlighted how close friendships among men of color can be a coping strategy for managing racism via social support. How do men of color validate and empower each other within gaming? Considering the important role of the family in socialization, how do family members contribute to resistance strategies in gaming for men of color? How are men of color carving out spaces where racism is not tolerated? Alternatively, how do anti-Blackness, xenophobia, and Islamophobia among men of color who are gamers create deeper divisions? We also need research on the barriers to men of color's interventions and support for women victims of racism and sexism in gaming. This is because whether they are bystanders or actively harassing women, when they are present, these actions contribute to the oppression of women in gaming. My interviews with men of color found that they do not necessarily understand the raced *and* gendered nature of online harassment; overhearing Black women being referred to as "roaches," for example, was labeled as a racist attack, and rape threats were described as exclusively gendered (Ortiz 2019b; Ortiz 2021a). What factors contribute to how men of color conceptualize and respond to gendered racism against women of color in these contexts?

Studying masculinity and racism together is key to understanding how structural inequality is enacted and maintained. I have discussed how studying masculinity and racism as interactional and structural—as opposed to merely sets of attitudes and predispositions held by individuals—allows scholars to account for how inequality in gaming culture persists. Racism in gaming is central to the construction of White masculinities, whether individual gamers seek to reach the hegemonic ideal or not. For men of color, their masculinities are central to how they would cope with racism in gaming, including the ways men affirm and uplift each other. Paired with cultural studies' critical readings of games, communication's discourse analyses, and psychology's exploration of attitudes, these suggestions for future research can help scholars more deeply analyze barriers to inclusive practices, especially among key demographics.

References

Anderson, Eric. 2008. "Inclusive Masculinity in a Fraternal Setting." *Men and Masculinities* 10, no. 5: 604–620. https://doi.org/10.1177%2F1097184X06291907.

Anthias, Floya. 2012. "Intersectional What? Social Divisions, Intersectionality and Levels of Analysis." *Ethnicities* 13, no. 1: 3–19. https://doi.org/10.1177%2F1468796812463547.

Bird, Sharon R. 1996. "Welcome to the Men's Club: Homosociality and the Maintenance of Hegemonic Masculinity." *Gender & Society* 10, no. 2: 120–132.

Bonilla-Silva, Eduardo. 1997. "Rethinking Racism: Toward a Structural Interpretation." *American Sociological Review* 62, no. 3: 465–480.

Bonilla-Silva, Eduardo. 2017. *Racism Without Racists: Color-Blind Racism and the Persistence of Racial Inequality in America*. 5th ed. Lanham, MD: Rowman & Littlefield.

Bonilla-Silva, Eduardo. 2021. "What Makes Systemic Racism Systemic?" *Sociological Inquiry* 91, no. 3: 513–533. https://doi.org/10.1111/soin.12420.

Bourabain, Dounia, and Pieter-Paul Verhaeghe. 2021. "Everyday Racism in Social Science Research." *Du Bois Review: Social Science Research on Race*. Published ahead of print April 29, 2021. https://doi.org/10.1017/S1742058X21000102.

Bourdieu, Pierre. 1986. "The Forms of Capital." In *Handbook of Theory and Research for the Sociology of Education*, edited by J. G. Richardson, 241–258. New York: Greenwood.

Bowleg, Lisa, Gary J. Burkholder, Jenné S. Massie, Rahab Wahome, Michelle Teti, David J. Malebranche, et al. 2013. "Racial Discrimination, Social Support, and Sexual HIV Risk among Black Heterosexual Men." *AIDS and Behavior* 17, no. 1: 407–418. https://doi.org/10.1007/s10461-012-0179-0.

Brock, André. 2011. "'When Keeping It Real Goes Wrong': Resident Evil 5, Racial Representation, and Gamers." *Games and Culture* 6, no. 5: 429–452. https://doi.org/10.1177%2F1555412011402676.

Brock, Andre. 2020. *Distributed Blackness: African American Cybercultures*. New York: New York University Press.

Buckels, Erin E., Paul D. Trapnell, and Delroy L. Paulhus. 2014. "Trolls Just Want to Have Fun." *Personality and Individual Differences* 67: 97–102. http://dx.doi.org/10.1016/j.paid.2014.01.016.

Bulut, Ergin. 2021. "White Masculinity, Creative Desires, and Production Ideology in Video Game Development." *Games and Culture* 16, no. 3: 329–341. https://doi.org/10.1177%2F1555412020939873.

Buyukozturk, Bertan. 2021. "Reproducing the Gaming Gender Hierarchy." *Symbolic Interaction*. Published ahead of print April 21, 2021. https://doi.org/10.1002/symb.553.

Cabrera, Nolan L. 2014. "'But I'm Oppressed Too': White Male College Students Framing Racial Emotions as Facts and Recreating Racism." *International Journal of Qualitative Studies in Education* 27, no. 6: 768–784. https://doi.org/10.1080/09518398.2014.901574.

Chan, Brian, and Kishonna Gray. 2021. "Microstreaming, Microcelebrity, and Marginalized Masculinity: Pathways to Visibility and Self-Definition for Black Men in Gaming." *Women's Studies in Communication* 43, no. 4: 354–362. https://doi.org/10.1080/07491409.2020.1833634.

Choi, Kyung-Hee, Chong-suk Han, Jay Paul, and George Ayala. 2011. "Managing Racism and Homophobia: Strategies for Managing Racism and Homophobia." *AIDS Education and Prevention* 23, no. 2: 145–158.

Chou, Rosalind S., Kristen Lee, and Simon Ho. 2012. "The White Habitus and Hegemonic Masculinity at the Elite Southern University." *Sociation Today* 10, no. 2, 1–27.

Cole, Helena, and Mark D. Griffiths. 2007. "Social Interactions in Massively Multiplayer Online Role-Playing Gamers." *Cyberpsychology and Behavior* 10, no. 4: 575–583. https://doi.org/10.1089/cpb.2007.9988.

Collins, Patricia Hill. 2002. *Black Feminist Thought: Knowledge, Consciousness, and the Politics of Empowerment*. New York and London: Routledge.

Collins, Patricia Hill, and Sirma Bilge. 2016. *Intersectionality*. Cambridge: Polity Press.

Condis, Megan. 2018. *Gaming Masculinity: Trolls, Fake Geeks, and the Gendered Battle for Online Culture*. Iowa City: University of Iowa Press.

Connell, R. W., and James W. Messerschmidt. 2005. "Hegemonic Masculinity: Rethinking the Concept." *Gender & Society* 19, no. 6: 829–859. https://doi.org/10.1177%2F0891243205278639.

Consalvo, Mia. 2007. *Cheating: Gaining Advantage in Videogames*. Cambridge, MA: MIT Press.

Cook, Christine, Juliette Schaafsma, and Marjolijn Antheunis. 2017. "Under the Bridge: An in-Depth Examination of Online Trolling in the Gaming Context." *New Media and Society* 20, no. 9: 3323–3340. http://doi.org/10.1177/1461444817748578.

Cote, Amanda C. 2017. "'I Can Defend Myself': Women's Strategies for Coping with Harassment while Gaming Online." *Games and Culture* 12, no. 2: 136–155. https://doi.org/10.1177%2F1555412015587603.

Cote, Amanda. 2020. *Gaming Sexism: Gender and Identity in the Era of Casual Video Games*. New York: New York University Press.

Daniels, Jessie. 2013. "Race and Racism in Internet Studies: A Review and Critique." *New Media & Society* 15, no. 5: 695–719. https://doi.org/10.1177%2F1461444812462849.

Daniels, Jesse, and Nick LaLone. 2012. "Racism in Video Gaming." In *Social Exclusion, Power, and Video Game Play: New Research in Digital Media and Technology*, edited by David G. Embrick, Talmadge J. Wright, and Andras Lukacs, 83–97. Lanham, MD: Lexington Books.

Davis, Shardé M. 2019. "When Sistahs Support Sistahs: A Process of Supportive Communication about Racial Microaggressions among Black Women." *Communication Monographs* 86, no. 2: 133–157. https://doi.org/10.1080/03637751.2018.1548769.

DiSalvo, Betsy. 2017. "Gaming Masculinity: Constructing Masculinity with Video Games." In *Diversifying Barbie and Mortal Kombat: Intersectional Perspectives and Inclusive Designs in Gaming*, edited by Gabriela Richard, Brendesha M. Tynes, and Yasmin B. Kafai. 3rd ed., 156–176. Pittsburgh, PA: ETC Press.

DiSalvo, Betsy, and Amy Bruckman. 2010. "Race and Gender in Play Practices: Young African American Males." In *Proceedings of the Fifth International Conference on the Foundations of Digital Games*, 56–63. New York: Association for Computing Machinery.

Doane, Ashley Woody. 2017. "Beyond Color-Blindness: (Re)Theorizing Racial Ideology." *Sociological Perspectives* 60, no. 5: 975–991. https://doi.org/10.1177%2F0731121417719697.

Domínguez, Silvia, and David G. Embrick. 2020. "Racial Microaggressions: Bridging Psychology and Sociology and Future Research Considerations." *Sociology Compass* 14, no. 8: e12803. https://doi.org/10.1111/soc4.12803.

Eng, David L. 2001. *Racial Castration: Managing Masculinity in Asian America*. Durham, NC: Duke University Press.

Eschmann, Rob. 2020 "Unmasking Racism: Students of Color and Expressions of Racism in Online Spaces." *Social Problems* 67, no. 3: 418–436.

Essed, Philomena. 1991. *Understanding Everyday Racism: An Interdisciplinary Theory*. Newbury Park, CA: Sage.

Fausto-Sterling, Anne. 2000. *Myths of Gender: Biological Theories about Women and Men*. New York: Basic Books.

Feagin, Joe. 2006. *Systemic Racism: A Theory of Oppression*. New York and London: Routledge.

Feagin, Joe. 2020. *The White Racial Frame: Centuries of Racial Framing and Counter-Framing*. New York and London: Routledge.

Ferber, Abby L. 2007. "The Construction of Black Masculinity: White Supremacy Now and Then." *Journal of Sport and Social Issues* 31, no. 1: 11–24. https://doi.org/10.1177%2F0193723506296829.

Fox, Jesse, and Wai Yen Tang. 2014. "Sexism in Online Video Games: The Role of Conformity to Masculine Norms and Social Dominance Orientation." *Computers in Human Behavior* 33: 314–320. https://doi.org/10.1016/j.chb.2013.07.014.

Fox, Jesse, and Wai Yen Tang. 2017. "Women's Experiences with General and Sexual Harassment in Online Video Games: Rumination, Organizational Responsiveness, Withdrawal, and Coping Strategies." *New Media and Society* 19, no. 8: 1290–1307. https://doi.org/10.1177%2F1461444816635778.

Frostling-Henningsson, Maria. 2009. "First-Person Shooter Games as a Way of Connecting to People: 'Brothers in Blood.'" *Cyberpsychology & Behavior* 12, no. 5: 557–562. https://doi.org/10.1089/cpb.2008.0345.

Ging, Debbie. 2019. "Alphas, Betas, and Incels: Theorizing the Masculinities of the Manosphere." *Men and Masculinities* 22, no. 4: 638–657. https://doi.org/10.1177%2F1097184X17706401.

Glaser, Jack, and Kahn, Kimberly B. 2005. "Prejudice, Discrimination, and the Internet." In *The Social Net: Understanding Human Behavior in Cyberspace*, edited by Y. Amichai-Hamburger, 247–274. Oxford, UK: Oxford University Press.

Golash-Boza, Tanya. 2016. "A Critical and Comprehensive Sociological Theory of Race and Racism." *Sociology of Race and Ethnicity* 2, no. 2: 129–141. https://doi.org/10.1177%2F2332649216632242.

Gray, Kishonna L. 2012a. "Deviant Bodies, Stigmatized Identities, and Racist Acts: Examining the Experiences of African-American Gamers in Xbox Live." *New Review of Hypermedia and Multimedia* 18, no. 4: 261–276. https://doi.org/10.1080/13614568.2012.746740.

Gray, Kishonna L. 2012b. "Intersecting Oppressions and Online Communities: Examining the Experiences of Women of Color in Xbox Live." *Information Communication and Society* 15, no. 3: 411–428. https://doi.org/10.1080/1369118X.2011.642401.

Gray, Kishonna L. 2014. *Race, Gender, and Deviance in Xbox Live: Theoretical Perspectives from the Virtual Margins*. London and New York: Routledge.

Gray, Kishonna L. 2016. " 'They're Just too Urban': Black Gamers Streaming on Twitch." In *Digital Sociologies*, edited by Jessie Daniels, Karen Gregory, and Tressie McMillan Cottom, 355–368. Bristol, UK: Policy Press.

Gray, Kishonna L. 2020. *Intersectional Tech: Black Users in Digital Gaming*. Baton Rouge: Louisiana State University Press.

Gray, Kishonna L., Bertan Buyukozturk, and Zachary G. Hill. 2017. "Blurring the Boundaries: Using Gamergate to Examine 'Real' and Symbolic Violence against Women in Contemporary Gaming Culture." *Sociology Compass* 11, no. 3: e12458.

Gray, Kishonna L., and David Leonard, eds. 2018. *Woke Gaming: Digital Challenges to Oppression and Social Justice*. Seattle: University of Washington Press.

Gray, Kishonna L., Gerald Voorhees, and Emma Vossen, eds. 2018. *Feminism in Play*. Cham, Switzerland: Springer International.

Guins, Raiford. 2006. "May I Invade Your Space? Black Technocultural Production, Ephemera, and Video Game Culture." In *Afrogeeks: Beyond the Digital Divide*, edited by Anna Everett and Amber J. Wallace, 113–138. Santa Barbara: Center for Black Studies Research, University of California Santa Barbara.

Hurtado, Adia, and Mrinal Sinha. 2016. *Beyond Machismo: Intersectional Latino Masculinities*. Austin: University of Texas Press.

Innes, Robert Alexander, and Kim Anderson. 2015. *Indigenous Men and Masculinities: Legacies, Identities, Regeneration*. Winnipeg, Canada: University of Manitoba Press.

Ivory, James D. 2006. "Still a Man's Game: Gender Representation in Online Reviews of Video Games." *Mass Communication and Society* 9, no. 1: 103–114. https://doi.org/10.1207/s153278 25mcs0901_6.

Jackson, Brandon A. 2018. "Beyond the Cool Pose: Black Men and Emotion Management Strategies." *Sociology Compass* 12, no. 4: e12569. https://doi.org/10.1111/soc4.12569.

Jung, Moon-Kie. 2015. *Beneath the Surface of White Supremacy: Denaturalizing US Racisms Past and Present*. Stanford, CA: Stanford University Press.

Kimmel, Michael. 2007. "Racism as Adolescent Male Rite of Passage: Ex-Nazis in Scandinavia." *Journal of Contemporary Ethnography* 36, no. 2: 202–218. https://doi.org/10.1177%2F08912 41606298825.

Leonard, David J. 2006. "Not a Hater, Just Keepin' It Real: The Importance of Race- and Gender-Based Game Studies." *Games and Culture* 1, no. 1: 83–88.

Maloney, Marcus, Steven Roberts, and Timothy Graham. 2019. *Gender, Masculinity and Video Gaming: Analysing Reddit's r/Gaming Community*. Cham, Switzerland: Springer International Publishing.

Massanari, Adrienne. 2017. "#Gamergate and the Fappening: How Reddit's Algorithm, Governance, and Culture Support Toxic Technocultures." *New Media and Society* 19, no. 3: 329–346. https://doi.org/10.1177%2F1461444815608807.

Miller, Kiri. 2008. "Grove Street Grimm: 'Grand Theft Auto' and Digital Folklore." *Source: The Journal of American Folklore* 121, no. 481: 255–285. https://doi.org/10.2307/20487609.

Mueller, Jennifer C. 2020. "Racial Ideology or Racial Ignorance? An Alternative Theory of Racial Cognition." *Sociological Theory* 38, no. 2: 142–169. https://doi.org/10.1177%2F07352 75120926197.

Nakamura, Lisa. 2012. "Queer Female of Color: The Highest Difficulty Setting There Is? Gaming Rhetoric as Gender Capital." *Ada: A Journal of Gender, New Media, and Technology* no. 1: 1–13. http://dx.doi.org/10.7264/N37P8W9V.

Nakamura, Lisa. 2013. " 'It's a Nigger in Here! Kill the Nigger!' User-Generated Media Campaigns against Racism, Sexism, and Homophobia in Digital Games." In *The International Encyclopedia of Media Studies*, edited by Kelly Gates, 6:1–15. Hoboken, NJ: Wiley-Blackwell. https://lnaka mur.files.wordpress.com/2013/04/nakamura-encyclopedia-of-media-studies-media-futu res.pdf.

Nakamura, Lisa. 2017. "Social Justice Warfare: Feminism and Anti-Racist Activism in Video Game Culture." In *Diversifying Barbie and Mortal Kombat: Intersectional Perspectives and Inclusive Designs in Gaming*, edited by Yasmin B. Kafai, Gabriela T. Richard, and Brandesha M. Tynes. Pittsburgh, PA: ETC Press.

Olson, Cheryl K. 2010. "Children's Motivations for Video Game Play in the Context of Normal Development." *Review of General Psychology* 14, no. 2: 180–187. https://doi.org/10.1037%2Fa 0018984.

Omi, Michael, and Howard Winant. 2014. *Racial Formation in the United States*. New York and London: Routledge.

Ortiz, Stephanie M. 2019a. " 'You Can Say I Got Desensitized to It': How Men of Color Cope with Everyday Racism in Online Gaming." *Sociological Perspectives* 62, no. 4: 572–588. https://doi.org/10.1177%2F0731121419837588.

Ortiz, Stephanie M. 2019b. "The Meanings of Racist and Sexist Trash Talk for Men of Color: A Cultural Sociological Approach to Studying Gaming Culture." *New Media and Society* 21, no. 4: 879–894. https://doi.org/10.1177%2F1461444818814252.

Ortiz, Stephanie M. 2020. "Trolling as a Collective Form of Harassment: An Inductive Study of How Online Users Understand Trolling." *Social Media+ Society* 6, no. 2: 2056305120928512.

Ortiz, Stephanie M. 2021a. "Call-In, Call-Out, Care, and Cool Rationality: How Young Adults Respond to Racism and Sexism Online." *Social Problems* https://doi.org/10.1093/socpro/spab060.

Ortiz, Stephanie M. 2021b. "Racists Without Racism? From Colourblind to Entitlement Racism Online." *Ethnic and Racial Studies* 44, no. 14: 2637–2657.

Oware, Matthew. 2011. "Brotherly Love: Homosociality and Black Masculinity in Gangsta Rap Music." *Journal of African American Studies* 15, no. 1: 22–39. https://doi.org/10.1007/s12111-010-9123-4.

Pascoe, C. J. 2013. "Notes on a Sociology of Bullying: Young Men's Homophobia as Gender Socialization." *QED: A Journal in GLBTQ Worldmaking* 2013: 87–104. https://doi.org/10.14321/qed.0087.

Pascoe, C. J., and Tristan Bridges. 2016. *Exploring Masculinties: Identity, Inequality, Continuity, and Change.* New York: Oxford University Press.

Passmore, Cale J., and Regan L. Mandryk. 2020. "A Taxonomy of Coping Strategies and Discriminatory Stressors in Digital Gaming." *Frontiers in Computer Science* 2: 40. https://doi.org/10.3389/fcomp.2020.00040.

Rogers, Leoandra Onnie, and Niobe Way. 2019. "Reimagining Social and Emotional Development: Accommodation and Resistance to Dominant Ideologies in the Identities and Friendships of Boys of Color." *Human Development* 61, no. 6: 311–331. https://doi.org/10.1159/000493378.

Salter, Anastasia, and Bridget Blodgett. 2017. *Toxic Geek Masculinity in Media: Sexism, Trolling, and Identity Policing.* Cham, Switzerland: Springer International.

Sanford, Kathy, and Leanna Madill. 2006. "Resistance through Video Game Play: It's a Boy Thing." *Canadian Journal of Education* 29, no. 1: 287–306. https://www.jstor.org/stable/20054157.

Senter, Mary S., and David A. Ling. 2017. ""It's Almost Like They Were Happier When You Were Down": Microaggressions and Overt Hostility Against Native Americans in a Community with Gaming." *Sociological Inquiry* 87, no. 2: 256–281.

Schrock, Douglas, and Michael Schwalbe. 2009. "Men, Masculinity, and Manhood Acts." *Source: Annual Review of Sociology* 35: 277–295. https://doi.org/10.1146/annurev-soc-070308-115933.

Sobieraj, Sarah. 2020. *Credible Threat: Attacks against Women Online and the Future of Democracy.* Oxford University Press.

Sumerau, J. E. 2020. *Violent Manhood.* Lanham, MD: Rowman & Littlefield.

Tang, Wai Yen, and Jesse Fox. 2016. "Men's Harassment Behavior in Online Video Games: Personality Traits and Game Factors." *Aggressive Behavior* 42, no. 6: 513–521.

Thapar-Björkert, Suruchi, Lotta Samelius, and Gurchathen S. Sanghera. 2016. "Exploring Symbolic Violence in the Everyday: Misrecognition, Condescension, Consent and Complicity." *Feminist Review* 112: 144–162.

Thornberg, Robert. 2018. "School Bullying and Fitting into the Peer Landscape: A Grounded Theory Field Study." *British Journal of Sociology of Education* 39, no. 1: 144–158. https://doi.org/10.1080/01425692.2017.1330680.

Todd, Cherie. 2015. "Commentary: GamerGate and Resistance to the Diversification of Gaming Culture." *Women's Studies Journal* 29, no. 1: 64–67. www.wsanz.org.nz/.

Trepte, Sabine, Leonard Reinecke, and Keno Juechems. 2012. "The Social Side of Gaming: How Playing Online Computer Games Creates Online and Offline Social Support." *Computers in Human Behavior* 28, no. 3: 832–839. https://doi.org/10.1016/j.chb.2011.12.003.

Way, Niobe. 2011. *Deep Secrets*. Cambridge, MA: Harvard University Press.

Way, Niobe, Jessica Cressen, Samuel Bodian, Justin Preston, Joseph Nelson, and Diane Hughes. 2014. " 'It Might Be Nice to Be a Girl... Then You Wouldn't Have to Be Emotionless': Boys' Resistance to Norms of Masculinity during Adolescence." *Psychology of Men and Masculinity* 15, no. 3: 241–252. https://psycnet.apa.org/doi/10.1037/a0037262.

West, Candace, and Don H. Zimmerman. 1987. "Doing Gender." *Gender & Society* 1, no. 2: 125–151. http://journals.sagepub.com/doi/pdf/10.1177/0891243287001002002.

Williams, Apryl A., Zaida Bryant, and Christopher Carvell. 2019. "Uncompensated Emotional Labor, Racial Battle Fatigue, and (in) Civility in Digital Spaces." *Sociology Compass* 13, no. 2: 1–12.

Williams, Carmen Braun, and Marsha I. Wiggins. 2010. "Womanist Spirituality as a Response to the Racism–Sexism Double Bind in African American Women." *Counseling and Values* 54, no. 2: 175–186. https://doi.org/10.1002/j.2161-007X.2010.tb00015.x.

Yip, Jeremy A., Maurice E. Schweitzer, and Samir Nurmohamed. 2018. "Trash-Talking: Competitive Incivility Motivates Rivalry, Performance, and Unethical Behavior." *Organizational Behavior and Human Decision Processes* 144: 125–144. http://dx.doi.org/10.1016/j.obhdp.2017.06.002.

CHAPTER 27

SOCIOECONOMIC INEQUALITIES AND DIGITAL SKILLS

MATÍAS DODEL

Socioeconomic and demographic structural inequalities based on age, gender, income, and educational disparities affect how we interact with technology. They also play a key role in how technology impacts our lives and can further amplify existing disparities (Robinson et al. 2015; Van Dijk 2005, 2). Structural inequalities influence the societal distribution of different levels of digital assets such as the possession of digital goods and services, as well as the way in which we behave online (Van Dijk 2005, 4). While early studies focused on the availability of technological commodities, there is a growing consensus that digital skills, not internet access or usage, are the key mediators of socioeconomic disparities' effect over internet use (Büchi et al. 2017; Dodel and Mesch 2019; Helsper and Enyon 2013; Van Dijk 2005, 2).

In this chapter, we conceptualize digital skills as facets of human capital, or the "knowledge and skills embodied in people and accumulated through schooling, training and experience that are useful in the production of goods, services and further knowledge" (De la Fuente and Ciccone 2002, 7). Digital skills do not refer exclusively to "button knowledge," meaning technical computational abilities or the understanding and knowledge of how to navigate on a digital program, device, or website. They also involve online safety, promoting more efficient uses of and the understanding of the digital medium, a critical and context-aware use of technologies, and the ability to perform more cognitively intensive tasks in a digitally mediated world (Eshet-Alkali and Amichai-Hamburger 2004; Buckingham 2015; van Laar et al. 2020). Understood this way, lack of digital skills reduces the scope of positive tangible outcomes of internet use such as jobs and income, education, psychological well-being, online safety and privacy, children's rights, use of governmental services, political participation, and the accumulation of social capital, among other things (Van Deursen et al. 2017). In other words, digital skills have already become a necessary part of the package of assets required to capitalize on the opportunities arising in the economy, the state, and the community (Kaztman 2010). Consequently, if digital skills–related disparities are not addressed, an increase in socioeconomic inequality is expected.

In this chapter we examine what we know and what we don't know about digital skills. We start by discussing what digital skills are and how are they conceptualized. Then, we discuss their role in shaping—and being shaped by—socioeconomic inequalities and how they mediate the impact of structural disparities in tangible outcomes of internet use. Finally, we discuss present challenges for the study of the intersections between digital skills and inequality, how future research could avoid some of the methodological pitfalls of the past, and how to improve public policies in the area.

What Are Digital Skills?

Being digitally "competent" has become a key issue in the debates regarding the core assets of citizenship in a knowledge society (van Laar et al. 2017). Whereas there is virtually no debate about the relevance of digital competency, there is less agreement on how to label and study it (van Laar et al. 2017). This is problematic for a comprehensive understanding of the phenomenon as disagreement relating to naming results in fragmented literatures and policy interventions related to digital competence.

The "competences" and "skills" constructs associated with both economic competitiveness and social cohesion arose substantially earlier than the widespread use of the internet (Payne 2017). While different in scope and definition, the two are sometimes used interchangeably. Indeed, non-English translations make the two constructs difficult to distinguish from one another (Ananiadou and Claro 2009). Similarly, Eshet-Alkali and Amichai-Hamburger (2004) argue that "digital literacies" is a new term for digital skills, whereas Monestier (2019) claims the same regarding the concepts of digital literacies and digital citizenship, making all of them virtually synonyms.

We advocate for the use of the term "digital skills" in the broad sense, making it interchangeable with "digital competence," "literacy," and even "citizenship." Digital skills, as argued, are more comprehensive than "button knowledge." For example, digital skills are a facet of human capital, which includes critical and context-aware use of technologies (De la Fuente and Ciccone 2002, 7), becoming part of the assets necessary to capitalize on the opportunities available to participate fully in contemporary societies (Buckingham 2015; Eshet-Alkali and Amichai-Hamburger 2004; Kaztman 2010; Van Deursen and Van Dijk 2010b; van Laar et al. 2020).

Whereas defining digital skills is somewhat complex, understanding what they are *not* is easier. Scholars agree that no one is digitally savvy just by "having access" to the internet or by spending a lot of time online (Dodel 2015; Van Deursen et al. 2017; Van Dijk 2005). This is not to say these phenomena are not related, just that digital access, usage, and skills correspond to different levels of digital divides (Van Deursen and Van Dijk 2019). Hence, what is the place of digital skills within the conceptualization of digital inequality?

Several theoretical models regard the socioeconomic antecedents and consequences of digital technologies as a sequential and somewhat hierarchical process (Dodel 2015; Van Deursen and Van Dijk 2019; Van Dijk 2005). In other words, we can think of digital inequalities as a pyramid in which both assets and disadvantages accumulate sequentially. The wider the base levels, the greater the potential for the next ones, digital skills being a structural part of this sequential phenomenon (Dodel 2015).

Scholars maintain that socioeconomic disparities affect the frequency and quality of access to digital technologies as well as motivation to connect to the internet. Differences in this material access to technology build on top of structural inequalities, conditioning the frequency and diversity of internet use, as well as the level of digital skills. In other words, digital skills are not to be confused with access to digital devices, the latter being a direct antecedent of the former. Finally, both usage and skills affect the engagement with information and communication technologies (ICTs) and how it impacts people's welfare and well-being, which are also described as the tangible outcomes of internet use (Van Deursen et al. 2017).

How Are Digital Skills Conceptualized?

Scholars have devised various frameworks for examining digital skills. In general, they share the idea that digital skills are a multidimensional construct with several subdimensions that are sequential in nature (Van Deursen and Van Dijk 2016). Scholarly empirical works in this vein predate even the first attempts to specify the construct theoretically (i.e., see Hargittai 2002). One of the earliest versions of this conceptualization is Eshet-Alkalai and Amichai-Hamburger's (2004) model. Their work emphasizes the involvement of the complex cognitive, motor, emotional, and sociological skills required to navigate digital environments effectively. Specifically, their digital literacy framework is composed of five types of digital skills: (1) understanding the information in graphical displays; (2) the reproduction or creation of new digital content based on preexisting materials; (3) the evaluation of the quality and veracity of information; (4) branching, or issues relating to hypertextual navigation; and (5) the understanding of the internet's codes of etiquette (Eshet-Alkali and Amichai-Hamburger 2004; Van Deursen and Van Dijk 2010a).

Van Dijk (2005)'s digital skills conceptualization, while similar to Eshet-Alkalai and Amichai-Hamburger's (2004) in terms of the types of skills, innovated by proposing and testing the multidimensional and sequential nature of digital skills and integrating the construct into a broader model of socioeconomic and digital inequalities (Van Deursen et al. 2017). This framework was further improved by Van Dijk and other colleagues in what is now also known as the internet skills framework (i.e., Van Deursen et al. 2017; Van Deursen and Van Dijk 2010a, 2010b; van Laar et al. 2017). Van Dijk's original formulation (Van Deursen et al. 2017) divides digital skills into two broad types: medium-related and content-related (Van Deursen and Van Dijk 2016). Medium-related skills include button knowledge (or "operational skills"), as well as the understanding of how the medium operates (sometimes called "formal" or "navigational" skills or, even more broadly, "informational," encompassing even skills related to fact-checking). Content-related skills, on the other hand, include the creation and modification of digital content (sometimes involving consideration of copyright issues), social skills linked to the socioemotional aspects of social media and information-sharing, and the more complex notion of "strategic internet skills" (Van Deursen and Van Dijk 2010b; Van Deursen, Helsper, and Eynon 2014). Again, most depictions of the model assume a sequential nature. They propose and empirically validate that content-related skills depend on medium-related skills (Van Deursen and Van Dijk 2010b; Van Deursen et al. 2017; van Laar et al. 2019).

Finally, the sequential conceptualization of digital skills also relates to their links with traditional literacies as digital skills depend on existing skills and knowledge. When traditional literacy is insufficient, we cannot expect the adequate development of digital skills (Van Deursen and Van Dijk 2016). Nonetheless, not every type of digital skill is equally dependent on traditional literacies. Button knowledge, which uses audiovisual cues to interact with users, requires only very basic reading skills and can be less dependent on written literacy. Nonetheless, the development of formal or info-navigational skills is severely impeded if people lack sufficient reading comprehension and written literacy (Van Deursen and Van Dijk 2016).

Digital Skills and Inequalities: The Evidence

There is a growing consensus that digital skills should be put at the center of the rich-get-richer phenomenon in the digital world (Robinson et al. 2015; Van Deursen, Van Dijk, and Peters 2011; van Laar et al. 2020). More refined understandings of digital inequalities tend to agree that variations in the possession of digital skills are one of the most important factors in terms of how socioeconomic disparities translate into tangible outcomes of internet use (Van Deursen, Van Dijk, and Peters 2011). In other words, digital skills appear to be the key mediators of the effects of socioeconomic status on digital engagement and its outcomes (Dodel and Mesch 2019; Van Deursen et al. 2017).

Disparities between and within Nations

These disparities are present both between nations and within them, the latter being more prominent. Nonetheless, three key findings emerge from all cross-national digital skills studies. First, there is a divide between nations, in line with the stratification hypothesis (Van Dijk 2005): the more developed the economy, the higher the levels of digital skills tend to be (International Telecommunication Union 2018). This is true even between countries in economically developed regions such as the European Union (Eurostat 2020). Second, in no country does the majority of the population have high levels of digital skills (i.e., Fraillon et al. 2019; International Telecommunication Union 2018). In fact, a significant proportion of citizens have insufficient digital skills, meaning they do not have enough digital skills to fully participate in contemporary society and the economy (i.e., Vuorikari et al. [2016] for the European Union and International Telecommunication Union [2018] for 52 countries worldwide). This is as true for children as it is for adults, as both the last waves of the EU Kids Online surveys (Smahel et al. 2020) and International Computer and Information Literacy Study (ICILS) (Fraillon et al. 2019) show. For example, 18% of the 8th-graders assessed in the ICILS did not have a functional working knowledge of digital technologies and were unlikely to be able to create digital information products without guidance (Fraillon et al. 2019). Third, the differences *between* countries pale in comparison to the differences *within* countries (Eurostat 2020; Smahel et al. 2020). In other words, without negating country-level effects, socioeconomic inequalities within countries, not between them, are the main drivers of differences in digital skills.

Antecedents of Digital Skills

Among the potential antecedents of digital skills, we will focus on what Van Dijk (2005, 13) argues are the most important categorical inequalities determining digital disparities: age, gender, and socioeconomic status, particularly educational attainments. Among the latter we include disparities based on race, ethnicity, and sensory disabilities. Finally, we also discuss a fourth cluster of antecedents contemplated by the internet skills framework: the impact of previous levels of digital inequalities on digital skills.

Age or Generation? Beyond the "Digital Native" Debate

It is commonly believed that young people are digitally savvier than older people, to the point of considering them universally skilled or "natives" in terms of digital languages. However, this belief is not supported by much of the empirical evidence (Helsper and Eynon 2010). While, on average, young people tend to have higher global levels of digital skills (see Hargittai 2002; Eurostat 2020), there are several caveats. First, multidimensional measurements show that age is positively correlated with some, but not all, types of digital skills (i.e., Eshet-Alkali and Amichai-Hamburger 2004; Smahel et al. 2020; Van Deursen and Van Dijk 2016). Both Eshet-Alkali and Amichai-Hamburger's (2004) and Van Deursen, van Dijk and Peters (2011) observational studies found that seniors tend to have less technical or medium-related skills but surpass younger generations in terms of substantive skills such as strategic and content-related ones (Van Deursen and Van Dijk 2015). Nonetheless, Van Deursen and Van Dijk (2016) found that the sequential and conditional nature of digital skills made medium-related skills such as button knowledge and informational skills hinder the global effect of content-related ones such as social and critical skills in older populations.

Second, there are substantial inequalities in the levels of digital skills within younger and older groups of individuals (i.e., Fraillon et al. 2019; Smahel et al. 2020). As Helsper and Eynon (2010) argue, age is only one among several key factors that stratify digital skills. In some cases, gender and, in even more cases, education are more important than age in explaining "digital native-ness" (Helper and Eynon 2010). Cross-national studies showing large variations in digital savviness within countries and even in the same grade or age group provide further evidence for this contention (Fraillon et al. 2019). Promoting assumptions about young people as digital natives, all of whom are astute in the ways of the online world, ignores the complexity and diversity of ICT use, as well as the role that socioeconomic status plays in their determination (Helsper and Eynon 2010).

Additionally, the evidence suggests that the relationship between age and digital skills is not completely linear (i.e., a quadratic function), even in childhood. Studies such as Kids Online show a consistent gap in the acquisition of digital skills between younger and older children, particularly regarding the assessment of the reliability of online information (Livingstone, Winther, and Hussein 2019; Smahel et al. 2020). Such findings are to be expected as traditional literacies are required for some types of digital skills to be developed (Van Deursen and Van Dijk 2016).

Nonetheless, even if the idea of digital natives can be counterproductive, there may be some truth behind it in terms of the timing of the training in digital skills and its efficacy. Apella, Rofman, and Rovner (2020) argued that whereas different types of skills can be learned at almost any age, the learning is more efficient at particular stages of life, mainly childhood, adolescence, and early adulthood. Hurwitz and Schmitt's (2020) longitudinal study adds evidence about the timing effect: Digital skills acquired during early childhood can positively impact academic performance in late childhood (at least in terms of parents' perceptions).

Gender-Based Disparities

In contrast to the effect of age, gender-based digital inequalities are subtle and complex. Digital skill inequalities based on gender were signaled since the beginning of the study of the phenomenon and are expected to persist even if digital access and usage divides are diminishing (Martínez-Cantos 2017; Van Deursen, Van Dijk, and Peters 2011). Nonetheless, gender affects *perceptions* about digital competence more than the competence itself (Hargittai and Shafer 2006; Van Deursen, Van Dijk, and Peters 2011). Hargittai and Shafer's (2006) seminal work addressed gender biases in self-perceived abilities compared to actual observed skills. Their findings show that, at the same level of observed skills, women are much more likely to evaluate their skills as lower than men. Stereotyped gender roles regarding technology, such as differences in anxiety toward technology and work- and education-related stereotypes of the role of women in ICT, may lay behind this phenomenon (Martínez-Cantos 2017; Van Deursen and Van Dijk 2015).

Nevertheless, some evidence also signals that specific differences in digital competence based on gender do exist. The International Telecommunication Union (2018) shows that countries with higher levels of gender inequality (as a whole) tend to have higher levels of gender inequalities relating to basic and, specifically, standard digital skills. Relating to children and adolescents in Europe, whereas gender differences in skills are small, in some countries there is still a visible gap between boys and girls in relation to info-navigational skills (Smahel et al. 2020).

Similarly, Martínez-Cantos (2017) studied gender-based disparities in self-assessed digital skills within the European Union between 2007 and 2014. The author found higher percentages of digital skills for men than women across every skill indicator and all years (differences were relatively stable across the seven measured years), but disparities were subtler for internet-related skills (compared to computer ones), and the greatest differences in favor of men related to more complex and less extended digital skills.

Van Dijk (2005, 11–12) argues that, far from deriving from differences in individual attributes, gender disparities are based on social inequality mechanisms: Gender differences in the appropriation of technology start developing at early stages in life, when toys and technical devices receive gendered treatment. These differences are reinforced throughout life. The ICILS 2018 findings provide ample support for Van Dijk's hypothesis and perhaps signal the reinforcing role played by formal education in forming these stereotypes. Even if the two types of digital skills measured by the ICILS are strongly correlated, girls demonstrate consistently higher levels of general ICT-related and information literacy, whereas boys exhibit more specialized or technical ICT knowledge (Fraillon et al. 2019). This result is consistent with the literature's current belief regarding gendered patterns of ICT use and attitudes toward technology and their impacts in actual digital competence.

Socioeconomic Status

Researchers have established that a plethora of individual and socioeconomic background–related attributes such as social class, income levels, and work-related disparities are some of the most consistent predictors of digital skills (Fraillon et al. 2019; Van Deursen and Van Dijk 2010b). In a number of studies, students and employed individuals, particularly those in high-paying occupations, demonstrated higher levels of most types of digital skills than their counterparts (International Telecommunication Union 2018; Van Deursen and Van Dijk 2010b; Van Deursen, Helsper, and Eynon 2014). Fraillon et al. (2019) added that even *expectations* regarding educational outcomes are consistent and positive predictors of digital literacy.

Education

There is a consensus that education-based inequalities are the strongest factors in disparities in digital skills (International Telecommunication Union 2018; Van Deursen, Van Dijk, and Peters 2011; Van Ingen and Matzat 2017). Moreover, educational attainment is the only predictor of digital skills which positively correlate with all types and levels of skills across several studies, particularly for individuals with a tertiary education (i.e., International Telecommunication Union 2018; Van Deursen and Van Dijk 2015). Van Deursen and Van Dijk (2010b) argued that this happens because digital skills and educational attainment are strongly related to similar cognitive resources. As previously described, traditional literacies, which tend to be developed in formal educational settings, are a precondition for developing and using digital skills (Van Deursen and Van Dijk 2016).

While we are not diminishing the role of informal education, we do maintain that inequalities in digital skills tend to arise when their development is left to incidental learning (Fraillon et al. 2019). For example, Eynon and Geniets (2016) found that the informal contexts frequented by digitally excluded youth are poorly resourced and insufficient to foster digital skills. Similarly, the ICILS (Fraillon et al. 2019) findings indicate the need to strengthen the role of formal schooling in the development of digital literacy.

Even though most scholars and cross-national studies agree on the role of formal education in the development of digital skills, there is less evidence on how these competences are learned and the best ways to teach them (Fraillon et al. 2019; Jara and Claro 2012). The Programme for International Student Assessment's (PISA's) 2009 findings showed that ICT engagement in school is less related to the development of digital skills and digital reading than engagement at home, even for leisure activities (OECD 2014). This outcome signals the need to consider and support children developing their skills through their own interests but also the need to reconsider how and for what purposes ICTs are used in schools (OECD 2014).

Finally, it is important to stress that inequalities in educational systems also affect children's development of digital skills through the capabilities and attitudes of their teachers regarding digital technologies. For example, teachers' perceptions about the usefulness of digital skills for their students' future jobs mediate how much they foster their development in class (Rafalow 2018). Moreover, the ICILS demonstrates that teachers' self-efficacy, ICT-related collaboration, and positive perceptions of pedagogical ICT use are the strongest predictors of their emphasizing digital competence in class, a factor that is strongly correlated with students' skills (Fraillon et al. 2019).

Vulnerable Social Groups: Disparities Based on Race, Ethnicity, and Sensory Disabilities

Race, ethnicity, and socioeconomic status create major divisions in society. While we were not able to find studies assessing the specific effects of race, ethnicity, and sensory disabilities on digital skills, there are several studies of their effect on global digital inequalities. For example, Mesch and Talmud (2011) found that race- and ethnicity-based differences in ICT access in Israel are generally related to the stratification of occupations and education in a two-step process. First, they hinder access and exposure to technology directly. This lack of exposure to the internet contributes to the development of negative attitudes toward ICTs, which, in turn, reduce the odds of access to and engagement with ICTs.

Pointing to similar mechanisms, Rafalow (2018) presented an even clearer picture of how inequalities in race and ethnicity intersect with socioeconomic stratification in the shaping of the social value of digital skills. Rafalow studied the disparities in how California teachers in the United States treated and valued similar digital skills learned outside school settings, based on race- and social class–based perceptions regarding the labor market potential of their students. Rafalow argued that even if the digital skills children learned through play could be useful for their education, only the teachers serving mostly rich and White children considered them important and fostered their development in class. In contrast, teachers serving predominantly Latino students in working-class schools considered these skills irrelevant for their future working-class jobs and, consequently, failed to develop them in class.

Socioeconomic inequalities also intersect with other factors such as sensory disabilities. As with race or ethnicity, these groups have less access to ICTs and digital skills, but these differences tend to disappear after controlling for socioeconomic status (see Dobransky and Hargittai [2016] for the United States). However, we maintain that for this group there is another type of barrier: the non-universal design of devices, systems, and applications. For example, Van Deursen, Helsper, and Eynon (2014) found that people with sensory disabilities differ in a statistically significant manner from those without such disabilities in their digital skills but only in terms of the skills related to the operation of the devices.

Internet Access as a Direct Antecedent of Digital Skills

Access to ICTs precedes the development of digital skills and is correlated with several aspects of internet usage (Fraillon et al. 2019; Van Deursen and Van Dijk 2019). For example, the ICILS 2018 showed that in most countries students' daily use of ICTs, having a computer at home, and experience in the use of digital devices have consistent and statistically significant effects on their digital skills (Fraillon et al. 2019). Based on Latin American Kids Online data, Cabello, Claro, and Dodel (2020) found that ubiquitous access to the internet through a variety of devices predicts higher levels of digital skills, even after controlling for all other socioeconomic factors.

Other national examples show similar patterns. For example, in the United States Hargittai (2002) found that time spent online and years since starting using the internet enable users to develop their digital savviness through experience. Dodel and Mesch (2018) showed that internet seniority is a strong and statistically significant predictor of digital security skills for the Israeli population. Van Deursen and Van Dijk (2019) found that in The Netherlands peripheral diversity is related to the level of internet skills.

Not having the resources to use the internet whenever and wherever individuals want forces them to use it only at fixed locales with severe time limitations for engagements, leaving them less time to practice and develop their skills (van Deursen and Van Dijk 2010b). Eynon and Geniets (2016) corroborate this hypothesis in their study of digitally disengaged and socioeconomically disadvantaged youth: These young people expressed not being able to understand the strategic potential of the internet for them as what they could do online was narrowed by the sporadic access they had in places like schools and libraries.

Moreover, scholars have already alerted us to the drawbacks of having second-tier types of internet access, in terms of both the diversity of engagements it allows and the development of digital skills (see de Araujo and Reinhard 2019; Van Deursen and Van Dijk 2019). While it is true that mobile devices have brought the internet to places where it was previously inaccessible, a phenomenon known as "mobile leapfrogging," they are not equal to more powerful and capable digital devices such as personal computers and laptops (de Araujo and Reinhard 2019). For example, in 2016, 42% of all Brazilian internet users were mobile-only users but with important inequalities according to social class: Only 23% of those in the upper classes fell into this category compared to 71% in the lower socioeconomic ones (de Araujo and Reinhard 2019). De Araujo and Reinhard (2019) found that mobile-only users have substantially lower levels of all types of digital skills than multi-device users, even after controlling for other socioeconomic factors.

Consequences of Digital Skills

The potential impact of digital skills in contemporary life is broad and diverse. The International Telecommunication Union (2018), based on the DiSTO project works (Van Deursen et al. 2017), argues that digital skills are important for seven key dimensions: employment (both for seeking jobs and during employment to adjust to changing work environments) and economic, educational, political, civic, social, and creative leisure participation.

We will organize the presentation in three core clusters: educational and occupational outcomes, subjective well-being and capital-enhancing consequences of internet use, and online safety and privacy.

Educational and Occupational Outcomes

Scholars and policy makers agree on the increasing demand for digital skills in the labor market, both present and future (Van Deursen and Van Dijk 2016). Moreover, the stratified distribution of digital skills combined with the demand for a high level of these skills in better-paying jobs with better working conditions further stratify the outcomes of twenty-first-century citizens (OECD 2014; Schleicher 2019).

ICT adoption and skill-biased technological change are intensifying job polarization[1] and increasing the fears of technological unemployment (Apella, Rofman, and Rovner 2020; Dodel and Mesch 2020). Even if evidence signals that the historic effects of technology as a whole on employment are positive (Mokyr, Vickers, and Ziebarth 2015), job polarization is on the rise. Those with digital skills are expected to be employed in better occupations, whereas the less savvy will be pushed by automation out of mid-level and clerical jobs toward jobs in the service industries or face the prospect of being unemployable (Apella, Rofman, and Rovner 2020; Dodel and Mesch 2020; OECD 2014).

Subjective Well-Being and Capital-Enhancing Consequences of Internet Use

Whereas no study claims that digital skills by themselves are positive for people's well-being, digital skills correlate with a series of capital-enhancing consequences of internet use. For example, Hofer et al. (2019) found that digital skills increase the strength of the links between online information-seeking behaviors and subjective well-being in older Swiss adults. Using a representative sample of the Swiss population, Büchi, Festic, and Latzer (2019) reported that digital coping skills, such as being able to choose the people, times, and digital applications relevant for individual goals, both reduce the perception of digital overuse and increase subjective levels of well-being.

Based on a random sample of citizens of the Belgian city of Ghent, Courtois and Verdegem (2016) studied the effects of digital inequalities on a number of positive outcomes of internet use. They found that content-related digital skills such as evaluating the reliability of information or achieving positive online social interactions are the strongest predictors (both total and direct) of positive outcomes such as finding a job or joining a cultural organization, across clusters of individuals with different levels of social support. Using a large sample of individuals living in The Netherlands, Van Ingen and Matzat (2017) reported that digital skills predict an individual's mobilization of resources when coping with negative life events. Individuals with high levels of digital skills were far more likely to engage in activities such as asking for help or advice online than those with low levels.

Compared to offline-only exchanges, the use of the internet to interact with the government can also be considered a capital-enhancing consequence of internet use in terms of the reduction of time and money spent to effectively conduct the desired task (Dodel and Aguirre 2018). Ebbers, Jansen, and van Deursen (2016), for instance, studied channel preferences for e-government interactions in The Netherlands and their relationship to digital skills. They did not find a statistically significant effect of skills on digital channel preference but found a strong impact on satisfaction within those interactions when they occurred online. They suggest that this inequality is of concern as it creates a skills-based divide in citizens' satisfaction with governmental services. Dodel and Aguirre (2018) examined how socioeconomic and digital attributes affect the chances of engaging with the government electronically for three different stages of e-government development in Uruguay. They found that digital skills are the strongest and most stable predictor across three levels of assessed activities: searching for information about government services; downloading files, forms, and receipts; and online payment of government services.

Online Safety and Privacy

Livingstone and Helsper (2010) argue that online engagement should not be seen in terms of opposites—full of opportunity or laden with risk—since it is often both. For example, Cabello-Hutt, Cabello, and Claro (2018) studied the determinants of both online opportunities and risk among Brazilian youth and found that digital skills are a direct predictor of online opportunities such as using the internet for school work, video calling, and writing a blog. Nonetheless, they also found that online opportunities are the strongest predictor of online risks such as meeting anyone face to face first met online, receiving or posting sexual messages of any kind, and acting in a hurtful or nasty way to someone on the internet. Thus, digital skills also indirectly increase the risks experienced online.

In other words, regarding the effects of digital skills on children's safety, findings provide evidence for both positive and negative effects (Sonck and de Haan 2014). The positive effect relates to the improvements in children's ability to safely navigate the online world. However, skilled children tend to perceive themselves as more capable of navigating riskier settings, thus exposing them to more risks. Sonck and de Haan (2014), based on the life-course perspective, propose that the latter is also linked to some skilled adolescents using their digital competence to better challenge the boundaries of behavior and seeking risk as part of their identity experimentation.

Parents' digital competence may also correlate with their children's competence online. Based on data from eight European countries, Livingstone et al. (2017) studied how parents of 6- to 14-year-olds mediate the internet usage of their children in order to maximize their opportunities and minimize their risks. Parents who regard themselves as less digitally skilled are more likely to use restrictive strategies, whereas those who see themselves as more digitally savvy are more likely to use enabling strategies (Livingstone et al. 2017).

Finally, a number of studies have provided statistical evidence that the integration of digital skills as an independent variable is critical to the understanding of cyber-safety and cyber-privacy behaviors in developed economies (Dodel and Mesch [2018, 2019] in Israel; Büchi, Just, and Latzer [2017] in Switzerland; and Park [2013] and Litt and Hargittai [2014] in the United States). In other words, by having adequate digital competences to engage in cyber-safety, individuals can avoid and cope with cyber victimization or privacy breaches, reducing the odds of negative outcomes in their life. Dodel, Kaiser, and Mesch (2020) replicated these findings in a developing economy (Uruguay), validating Dodel and Mesch (2019)'s theoretical model in the Global South. Digital skills, particularly operational ones, were deemed the main antecedent of cyber-safety behavior and the key mediator of the effect of other socioeconomic and demographic determinants (Dodel, Kaiser, and Mesch 2020).

Conclusion: The Future of the Study of Digital Skills and Inequality

In this chapter we defined, conceptualized, categorized, and discussed the antecedents and consequences of digital skills. We summarized empirical and theoretical evidence signaling that digital skills (or competences or literacies or citizenships) have become critical for employability and people's well-being. This scenario is not expected to diminish in the foreseeable future and probably will intensify as the twenty-first century progresses.

In terms of conceptualization, we described that digital skills are a multidimensional and sequential phenomenon, going from medium-related skills, such as button knowledge or informational digital skills, toward content-related ones, such as social content creations or critical digital skills. Ideally, digital skills should be assessed sequentially, even being dependent on more traditional literacies.

In terms of digital skills' role within socioeconomic and digital inequalities, there is an intrinsic link between them. Not only are socioeconomic and demographic attributes the key determinants of digital skills but also digital skills are the key mediator of their effects on the tangible outcomes of internet use.

Whereas there exist digital skills–based disparities between countries replicating traditional inequalities between developed and developing economies, these differences pale compared to those within countries. Age, gender, and socioeconomic status are the key antecedents of digital skills, where the role of education is particularly strong. Additionally, the material access to and the quality and quantity of internet and digital devices available to individuals are also strong determinants of digital skills.

On the effects side, digital skills have consistent and strong consequences on a variety of critical outcomes such as educational and occupational outcomes, psychological well-being, capital-enhancing consequences of internet use, and online safety and privacy. Whereas most of these effects are positive, higher digital skill levels have been linked to higher levels of both online risks and benefits in children and adolescents.

What can we expect in the near future regarding the study of digital skills? In the first place, future research should avoid some of the methodological pitfalls of the past. Not all existent digital skills–measurement strategies are equal in terms of reliability, construct validity, or external validity; and not every method is equally suited for all research problems.

Proxy methods-based studies, which use theoretically proxime concepts of digital skills, such as internet access, ICT use, or even global literacy rates, to provide a proxy measures of digital competence, were present in the literature. Nonetheless, we argue that they are expected to disappear rapidly. Such was the case of the International Telecommunication Union's digital skills dimension within the ICT Development Index, which used literacy rates as a proxy for digital skills, which was recently updated for a self-assessment approach (International Telecommunication Union 2018, 2020).

Self-assessment methods such as the internet skills scale are currently the most developed and extended methods to measure digital skills (International Telecommunication Union 2018; Van Deursen, Helsper, and Eynon 2016). Whereas there are more sophisticated measurement alternatives, we don't expect this approach to develop in the short term as this is currently the better alternative in terms of cost and money when concerns about societal inequalities in skills distribution require the use of large samples and survey-based designs (Van Deursen and Van Dijk 2010a). Moreover, the key drawbacks of the method, being the biases in the self-evaluation process, can—and should—be reduced by very low-tech techniques such as proper cognitive interviewing, questionnaire pretesting, and posterior psychometric validations (Van Deursen, Helsper, and Eynon 2016); something we argue should be mandatory for any future measurements of this kind.

We also expect more nuanced approaches such as performance-based measurements to become more widespread (i.e., the ICILS; Fraillon et al. 2019). Generally comprised of standardized tests designed to assess in-real-time digital competences in simulated digital settings, they can be applied at massive scale by using nationally representative random samples. Nonetheless, they are currently costly to develop and thus, to our knowledge, were only ever conducted within school settings, in conjunction with governments and educational institutions, such as the ICILS (Fraillon et al. 2019) or PISA's digital reading assessment (Schleicher 2019).

Nonetheless, it is not farfetched to imagine a close future where performance-based tests mutate into easy-to-install apps which could measure on-device and in-real-time digital competence for wider populations at significantly lower costs. This will also collaborate with the continuous updating of scales and frameworks, which tend to run slightly behind technological innovations. Device-agnostic frameworks and the improvement of the measurement of more complex critical digital skills could become additional reasonable and achievable short-term goals under this scenario. Finally, longitudinal studies with better skill measurements are a must, more so to understand how digital skills are developed, particularly in educational and work settings.

On a different matter, we also strongly recommend that digital equality scholars and policy makers not be seduced into thinking that accessing the internet only through mobile phones is sufficient for the development of people's digital skill levels. As we developed in this chapter, there is growing evidence that the diversity and quality of access to digital devices and the internet are also critical determinants of digital skills.

Finally, from a national development and economic perspective, governments should be interested not only in current digital skill levels but also in present and future needs and trends and the ways in which the gaps between actual and desired digital levels can be closed (International Telecommunication Union 2020). In this sense, while there is a consensus about the importance of digital skills and several initiatives are currently being developed worldwide, much less is known about which types of policies work to foster and democratize them (Pawluczuk 2020). Some domain-specific examples of successful initiatives in fields such as information literacy exist and could guide future research. For example, Guess et al. (2020) found that simple and scalable interventions can reduce the perceived accuracy of false news content.

Nonetheless, critics signal that current digital skills policies tend to focus too much on button knowledge and instrumental skills for the labor market over social and critical ones (Monestier 2019; Pawluczuk 2020). Moreover, critics also argue that the formal educational setting in which they tend to be exclusively based is problematic on two fronts. On the one hand, the focus on formal education over lifelong learning hinders the effects of the policies for adult and older populations. This is particularly critical for workers who need to update their digital skills as part of labor reconversion processes caused by job polarization and the consequences of automation (Dodel and Mesch 2020). On the other hand, given that teachers tend to see themselves as less digitally skilled than their students, they do not completely understand the centrality of their role in terms of teaching information and critical skills and guiding their students' first online experiences (Van Deursen and Van Dijk 2015).

In sum, along with more evidence of the complex ways in which socioeconomic inequalities and digital skills are intertwined and how new technological innovations will stack up with these, we are also in need of better evidence on how to create successful interventions to reduce digital skills–based disparities. These policies should be more comprehensive in terms of the types of digital skills they expect to foster and broader in scope and reach to encompass more varied and vulnerable populations which cannot be reached from schools or institutional settings.

Note

1. "Job polarization" refers to a change in the composition of the employment force as a consequence of technological change. Whereas the phenomenon is not new, in the second decade of the twenty-first century it was intensified due to advances in automation and computerization affecting all kinds of routine jobs. What the term implies is that employment will polarize, increasing the proportion of highly skilled, non-routine, cognitive jobs; decreasing the share of typically middle-class manual and non-manual routine jobs which require medium levels of skills; and increasing the share of low-skilled jobs (Dodel and Mesch 2020).

References

Ananiadou, Katerina, and Magdalean Claro. 2009. "21st Century Skills and Competences for New Millennium Learners in OECD Countries." *OECD Education Working Papers* 41. OECD Publishing, Paris.

Apella, Ignacio, Rafael Rofman, and Helena Rovner. 2020. *Skills and the Labor Market in a New Era: Managing the Impacts of Population Aging and Technological Change in Uruguay.* International Development in Focus. Washington, DC: World Bank.

Büchi, Moritz, Noemi Festic, and Michael Latzer. 2019. "Digital Overuse and Subjective Well-Being in a Digitized Society." *Social Media + Society* 5, no. 4: 2056305119886031.

Büchi, Moritz, Natascha Just, and Michael Latzer. 2017. "Caring Is not Enough: The Importance of Internet Skills for Online Privacy Protection." *Information, Communication & Society* 20, no. 8: 1261–1278.

Buckingham, David. 2015. "Defining Digital Literacy—What Do Young People Need to Know about Digital Media?" *Nordic Journal of Digital Literacy* 10: 21–35.

Cabello, Patricio, Magdalena Claro, and Matías Dodel. 2020. "Modalidades de acceso material a internet y su relación con las habilidades y prácticas digitales" [Modalities in material access to the internet and their links with digital skills and practices]. In *Infancia y adolescencia en la era digital: un informe comparativo de los estudios de kids online del Brasil, Chile, Costa*

Rica y el Uruguay [Childhood and adolescence in the digital era: A comparative report on kids online in Brazil, Chile, Costa Rica and Uruguay], edited by Daniela Trucco and Amalia Palma, 41–54. Documentos de Proyectos (LC/TS.2020/18). Santiago, Chile: Comisión Económica para América Latina y el Caribe (CEPAL).

Cabello-Hutt, Tania, Patricio Cabello, and Magdalena Claro. 2018. "Online Opportunities and Risks for Children and Adolescents: The Role of Digital Skills, Age, Gender and Parental Mediation in Brazil." *New Media & Society* 20, no. 7: 2411–2431.

Courtois, Cédric, and Pieter Verdegem. 2016. "With a Little Help from My Friends: An Analysis of the Role of Social Support in Digital Inequalities." *New Media & Society* 18, no. 8: 1508–1527.

de Araujo, Marcel Henrique, and Nicolau Reinhard. 2019. "Substituting Computers for Mobile Phones? An Analysis of the Effect of Device Divide on Digital Skills in Brazil." In *Electronic Participation. ePart 2019*, edited by P. Panagiotopoulos, 142–154. Cham, Switzerland: Springer.

De la Fuente, Angel, and Antonio Ciccone. 2002. *Human Capital in a Global and Knowledge Based Economy. Final Report*. Luxembourg: Office for Official Publications of the European Communities.

Dobransky, Kerry, and Eszter Hargittai. 2016. "Unrealized Potential: Exploring the Digital Disability Divide." *Poetics* 58: 18–28.

Dodel, Matías. 2015. "An Analytical Framework to Incorporate ICT as an Independent Variable." In *Impact of Information Society Research in the Global South*, edited by Arul Chib, Julian May, and Roxana Barrantes, 125–144. Singapore: Springer.

Dodel, Matías, and Florencia Aguirre. 2018. "Digital Inequalities' Impact on Progressive Stages of e-Government Development." In *Proceedings of the 11th International Conference on Theory and Practice of Electronic Governance*, edited by Atreyi Kankanhalli, Adegboyega Ojo, and Delfina Soares, 459–463. New York: ACM Press.

Dodel, Matías, Daniela Kaiser, and Gustavo Mesch. 2020. "Determinants of Cyber-Safety Behaviors in a Developing Economy: The Role of Socioeconomic Inequalities, Digital Skills and Perception of Cyber-Threats." *First Monday* 20, no. 7. https://firstmonday.org/ojs/index.php/fm/article/download/10830/9558.

Dodel, Matías, and Gustavo Mesch. 2018. "Inequality in Digital Skills and the Adoption of Online Safety Behaviors." *Information, Communication & Society* 21, no. 5: 712–728.

Dodel, Matías, and Gustavo Mesch. 2019. "An Integrated Model for Assessing Cyber-Safety Behaviors: How Cognitive, Socioeconomic and Digital Determinants Affect Diverse Safety Practices." *Computers & Security* 86: 75–91.

Dodel, Matías, and Gustavo S. Mesch. 2020. "Perceptions about the Impact of Automation in the Workplace." *Information, Communication & Society* 23, no. 5: 665–680.

Ebbers, Wolfgang E., Marloes G. M. Jansen, and Alexander J. A. M. van Deursen. 2016. "Impact of the Digital Divide on e-Government: Expanding from Channel Choice to Channel Usage." *Government Information Quarterly* 33, no. 4: 685–692.

Eshet-Alkali, Yoram, and Yair Amichai-Hamburger. 2004. "Experiments in Digital Literacy." *CyberPsychology & Behavior* 7, no. 4: 421–429.

Eurostat. 2020. "Individuals' Level of Digital Skills." Last updated April 15, 2020. https://appsso.eurostat.ec.europa.eu/nui/show.do?dataset=isoc_sk_dskl_i&lang=en

Eynon, Rebecca, and Anne Geniets. 2016. "The Digital Skills Paradox: How Do Digitally Excluded Youth Develop Skills to Use the Internet?" *Learning, Media and Technology* 41, no. 3: 463–479.

Fraillon, Julian, John Ainley, Wolfram Schulz, Tim Friedman, and Daniel Duckworth, eds. 2019. *Preparing for Life in a Digital World: The IEA International Computer and Information Literacy Study 2018 International Report*. Cham, Switzerland: Springer.

Guess, A. M., Lerner, M., Lyons, B., Montgomery, J. M., Nyhan, B., Reifler, J., & Sircar, N. (2020). A digital media literacy intervention increases discernment between mainstream and false news in the United States and India. *Proceedings of the National Academy of Sciences*, 117, no. 27: 15536–15545. https://doi.org/10.1073/pnas.1920498117

Hargittai, Eszter. 2002. "Second-Level Digital Divide: Differences in People's Online Skills." *First Monday* 7, no. 4. https://doi.org/10.5210/fm.v7i4.942

Hargittai, Eszter, and Steven Shafer. 2006. "Differences in Actual and Perceived Online Skills: The Role of Gender." *Social Science Quarterly* 87, no. 2: 432–448.

Helsper, Ellen Johanna, and Rebecca Eynon. 2010. "Digital Natives: Where Is the Evidence?" *British Educational Research Journal* 36, no. 3: 503–520.

Helsper, Ellen, and Rebecca Eynon. 2013. "Distinct Skill Pathways to Digital Engagement." *European Journal of Communication* 28, no. 6. https://doi.org/10.1177/0267323113499113

Hofer, Matthias, Eszter Hargittai, Moritz Büchi, and Alexander Seifert. 2019. "Older Adults' Online Information Seeking and Subjective Well-Being: The Moderating Role of Internet Skills." *International Journal of Communication* 13: 4426–4443.

Hurwitz, Lisa B., and Kelly L. Schmitt. 2020. "Can Children Benefit from Early Internet Exposure? Short- and Long-Term Links between Internet Use, Digital Skill, and Academic Performance." *Computers & Education* 146: 103750.

International Telecommunication Union. 2018. *Measuring the Information Society Report*. Vol. 1. Geneva: International Telecommunication Union.

International Telecommunication Union. 2020. *Digital Skills Assessment Guidebook*. Geneva: International Telecommunication Union. Accessed June 26, 2020. https://academy.itu.int/sites/default/files/media2/file/D-PHCB-CAP_BLD.04-2020-PDF-E_02%20June%202020.pdf

Jara, Ignacio, and Magdalena Claro. 2012. "La política de TIC para escuelas en Chile (red enlaces): Evaluación de habilidades digitales." *Campus Virtuales* 1, no. 1: 79–91.

Kaztman, Rubén. 2010. Impacto social de la incorporación de las nuevas tecnologías de información y comunicación en el sistema educativo [ICTs incorporation into educational system's social impact]. Serie Políticas Sociales [Social policy series] 166. Santiago de Chile: ECLAC. https://repositorio.cepal.org/bitstream/handle/11362/6171/lcl3254.pdf

Litt, Eden, and Eszter Hargittai. 2014. "A Bumpy Ride on the Information Superhighway: Exploring Turbulence Online." *Computers in Human Behavior* 36: 520–529.

Livingstone, Sonia, and Ellen Helsper. 2010. "Balancing Opportunities and Risks in Teenagers' Use of the Internet: The Role of Online Skills and Internet Self-Efficacy." *New Media & Society* 12, no. 2: 309–329.

Livingstone, Sonia, Kjartan Ólafsson, Ellen J. Helsper, Francisco Lupiáñez-Villanueva, Giuseppe A. Veltri, and Frans Folkvord. 2017. "Maximizing Opportunities and Minimizing Risks for Children Online: The Role of Digital Skills in Emerging Strategies of Parental Mediation." *Journal of Communication* 67, no. 1: 82–105.

Livingstone, Sonia, Daniel Kardefelt Winther, and Marium Hussein. 2019. *Global Kids Online Comparative Report*. Innocenti Research Report. Florence, Italy: UNICEF.

Martínez-Cantos, José Luis. 2017. "Digital Skills Gaps: A Pending Subject for Gender Digital Inclusion in the European Union." *European Journal of Communication* 32, no. 5: 419–438.

Mesch, Gustavo S., and Ilan Talmud. 2011. "Ethnic Differences in Internet Access: The Role of Occupation and Exposure." *Information, Communication & Society* 14, no. 4: 445–471.

Mokyr, Joel, Chris Vickers, and Nicolas L. Ziebarth. 2015. "The History of Technological Anxiety and the Future of Economic Growth: Is This Time Different?" *Journal of Economic Perspectives* 29, no. 3: 31–50.

Monestier, S. M. 2019. "The Council of Europe Digital Citizenship Education Project. Analysis of Its Human Rights and Multi-Stakeholder Governance Approach." University of Oslo, Master's thesis.

OECD (2014), "Skills and Jobs in the Internet Economy", *OECD Digital Economy Papers*, No. 242. Paris: OECD Publishing. https://doi.org/10.1787/5jxvbrjm9bns-en.

Park, Yong Jin. 2013. "Offline Status, Online Status: Reproduction of Social Categories in Personal Information Skill and Knowledge." *Social Science Computer Review*, 31, no. 6: 680–702. http://doi.org/10.1177/0894439313485202

Pawluczuk, Alicja. 2020. "Digital Youth Inclusion and the Big Data Divide: Examining the Scottish Perspective." *Internet Policy Review* 9, no. 2. doi:10.14763/2020.2.1480

Payne, Jonathan. 2017. "The Changing Meaning of Skill: Still Contested, Still Important." In *The Oxford Handbook of Skills and Training*, edited by Chris Warhurst, Ken Mayhew, David Finegold, and John Buchanan, 54–71. Oxford: Oxford University Press.

Rafalow, Matthew H. 2018. "Disciplining Play: Digital Youth Culture as Capital at School." *American Journal of Sociology* 123, no. 5: 1416–1452.

Robinson, Laura, Shelia R. Cotten, Hiroshi Ono, Anabel Quan-Haase, Gustavo Mesch, Wenhong Chen, Jeremy Schulz, Timothy M. Hale, and Michael J. Stern. 2015. "Digital Inequalities and Why They Matter." *Information, Communication & Society* 18, no. 5: 569–582. https://doi.org/10.1080/1369118X.2015.1012532

Schleicher, Andreas. 2019. *PISA 2018: Insights and Interpretations*. Paris: OECD Publishing.

Smahel, David, Hana Machackova, Giovanna Mascheroni, Lenka Dedkova, Elisabeth Staksrud, Kjartan Ólafsson, Sonia Livingstone, and Uwe Hasebrink. 2020. *EU Kids Online 2020: Survey Results from 19 Countries*. EU Kids Online. doi: 10.21953/lse.47fdeqj01ofo

Sonck, Nathalie, and Jos de Haan. 2014. "Safety by Literacy? Rethinking the Role of Digital Skills in Improving Online Safety." In *Minding Minors Wandering the Web: Regulating Online Child Safety*, edited by Simone van der Hof, Bibi van den Berg, and Bart Schermer, 89–104. Information Technology and Law Series 24. The Hague, Netherlands: T.M.C. Asser Press.

Van Deursen, Alexander J. A. M., Ellen Johanna Helsper, and Rebecca Eynon. 2014. *Measuring Digital Skills. From Digital Skills to Tangible Outcomes Project Report*. https://www.lse.ac.uk/media-and-communications/assets/documents/research/projects/disto/Measuring-Digital-Skills.pdf

Van Deursen, Alexander J. A. M., Ellen J. Helsper, and Rebecca Eynon. 2016. "Development and Validation of the Internet Skills Scale (ISS)." *Information, Communication & Society* 19, no. 6: 804–823.

Van Deursen, Alexander, Ellen Helsper, Rebecca Eynon, and Jan Van Dijk. 2017. "The Compoundness and Sequentiality of Digital Inequality." *International Journal of Communication* 11: 452–473.

Van Deursen, A. J. A. M., and J. A. G. M. Van Dijk. 2010a. "Measuring Internet Skills." *International Journal of Human–Computer Interaction* 26, no. 10: 891–916.

Van Deursen, Alexander, and Jan Van Dijk. 2010b. "Internet Skills and the Digital Divide." *New Media & Society* 13, no. 6: 893–911.

Van Deursen, Alexander J. A. M., and Jan A. G. M. Van Dijk. 2015. "Internet Skill Levels Increase, but Gaps Widen: A Longitudinal Cross-Sectional Analysis (2010–2013) among the Dutch Population." *Information, Communication & Society* 18, no. 7: 782–797. doi: 10.1080/1369118X.2014.994544

Van Deursen, A. J. A. M., and J. A. G. M. Van Dijk. 2016. "Modeling Traditional Literacy, Internet Skills and Internet Usage: An Empirical Study." *Interacting with Computers* 28, no. 1: 13–26.

Van Deursen, Alexander J. A. M., and Jan A. G. M. Van Dijk. 2019. "The First-Level Digital Divide Shifts from Inequalities in Physical Access to Inequalities in Material Access." *New Media & Society* 21, no. 2: 354–375.

Van Deursen, Alexander J. A. M., Jan A. G. M. Van Dijk, and Oscar Peters. 2011. "Rethinking Internet Skills. The Contribution of Gender, Age, Education, Internet Experience, and Hours Online to Medium- and Content-Related Internet Skills." *Poetics* 39: 125–144.

Van Dijk, Jan A. G. M. 2005. *The Deepening Divide: Inequality in the Information Society.* Thousand Oaks, CA: Sage Publications.

van Ingen, Erik, and Uwe Matzat. 2017. "Inequality in Mobilizing Online Help after a Negative Life Event: The Role of Education, Digital Skills, and Capital-Enhancing Internet Use." *Information, Communication & Society* 21, no. 4: 481–498.

van Laar, Ester, Alexander J. A. M. van Deursen, Jan A. G. M. Van Dijk, and Jos de Haan. 2017. "The Relation between 21st-Century Skills and Digital Skills: A Systematic Literature Review." *Computers in Human Behavior* 72: 577–588.

van Laar, Ester, Alexander J. A. M. van Deursen, Jan A. G. M. Van Dijk, and Jos de Haan. 2019. "The Sequential and Conditional Nature of 21st-Century Digital Skills." *International Journal of Communication* 13: 3462–3487.

van Laar, Ester, Alexander J. A. M. van Deursen, Jan A. G. M. Van Dijk, and Jos de Haan. 2020. "Determinants of 21st-Century Skills and 21st-Century Digital Skills for Workers: A Systematic Literature Review." *SAGE Open* 10, no. 1: 2158244019900176.

Vuorikari, Riina, Yves Punie, Stephanie Carretero Gomez, and Godelieve Van Den Brande. 2016. *DigComp 2.0: The Digital Competence Framework for Citizens. Update Phase 1: The Conceptual Reference Model.* JRC101254. Luxembourg: Publications Office of the European Union.

CHAPTER 28

THE DIGITAL PRODUCTION GAP IN THE ALGORITHMIC ERA

JEN SCHRADIE AND LIAM BEKIRSKY

FAKE news takes work just like journalism but without the integrity and the reporting. Still, even with disinformation, people have to think of a story idea; write it up to make it accessible to a targeted audience; design the layout in an appealing way; attach a photo, graphic, or at least a clever headline that will drive traffic using search engine optimization; figure out where and when to place it amid an array of other articles and ads; and disseminate it through provocative social media posts. Much more behind-the-scenes labor must happen for fake news to go viral, not the least of which is building up an audience that is shocked enough to want to share it.

This digital production of disinformation stands in stark contrast to the more idealistic possibilities put forth at the dawn of the social media era. We have come a long way since the wide-eyed first decade of the 2000s, when the idea of citizen journalism was a bright light at the end of a narrowing dark tunnel of brutal cuts to newsroom staff by fewer and fewer locally owned media outlets in favor of mega news corporations that had gone public (Benkler 2006; Jenkins 2006). The idea was that networked individuals (Rainie and Wellman 2012) could break free from the chains of bureaucratic news and media institutions and produce their own content online, creating a more diverse marketplace of ideas.

At the same time, though, a small group of activists, policymakers, and scholars was sounding the alarm on a digital divide around who could access this treasure trove of information (Dimaggio et al. 2004; Hargittai 2003). But what was missing from much of this initial digital divide analysis was who was on the producer end of this content firehose. With the concept of a *digital production gap*, Schradie (2011) theorized this distinction between production and consumption in analyzing digital inequalities, building on scholars who had suggested that online participation was not as egalitarian as the internet optimists would have had us believe (boyd 2009; Correa 2010; Hindman 2009).

A key mechanism of the digital production gap that Schradie (2011) articulated was controlling the digital means of production. This was a reference to a concept developed by Karl Marx, whose analysis refers to the transformation of the economy from an agrarian to an industrial society, in which those controlling the means of production were those who controlled land, labor, raw materials, factories, machines, and other capital materials. In turn, as scholars want to understand content producers whether a *New York Times* columnist or a WeChat poster, it is essential to analyze all the factors that go into controlling that means of digital production to understand any constraints on doing so, including power relations. Nonetheless, in the early 2010s, most of the methodological focus was on the individual as a unit of analysis, identifying who was more likely to produce online content according to certain demographics (Schradie 2011; Hargittai and Walejko 2008; Correa 2010). So, an individual having use of digital devices at work and at home and being able implicitly to "control" them meant having an educational level commensurate with the necessary information and communications technology skills and an income level to afford a connected computer, for example.

Social class, often defined with these variables of income or education, remains one of the most reliable predictors of digital content production. While production gaps based on social class, as well as gender, race, ethnicity, and disability, are and remain critical factors on their own, not simply in relation to class, this chapter focuses on social class as an analytical lens while also highlighting intersections. Nonetheless, this social stratification approach—which categorizes people by various socioeconomic factors—is not sufficient to explain the production gap. Yes, it is important to own a gadget or master a skill, but it is also a question of who ultimately pulls the digital strings. Indeed, the most prolific producers online are not individuals or citizen groups but corporations and states which have an ever increasing monopoly over the means of production (Schradie 2015b).

Since the early days of the web, technology has exponentially transformed what it means to be a digital producer in terms of inequalities, from algorithms and artificial intelligence (AI) to platform labor and surveillance, with the seat of power largely centered around Silicon Valley, though corporate rivals in China and elsewhere have emerged as forces to be reckoned with. Nonetheless, comparable and comparative research on content production using GAFAM (Google, Apple, Facebook, Amazon, and Microsoft) and BATX (Baidu, Alibaba, Tencent, and Xiaomi) across different countries has not kept up with the growing digital production inequalities across these corporate platforms, nor has it kept up with the exponential growth of data worldwide. We argue that it is essential to understand digital production inequalities in the context of these platform-driven technologies making who does and who does not control these digital means of production even more critical. It, Key to understanding the digital production gap is this question of power, and power relations, not simply demographic variables. Even someone with an advanced degree and an array of digital devices is no match for the power of GAFAM or BATX, as well as governments and elites which all coalesce around the hegemony of digital production. While viral online photos, videos, and other posts by everyday people certainly are common with online content production, from Black Lives Matter tweets to K-Pop fans on TikTok, in the long term, they are drowned out by people with more power.

Thus, research and analysis need to incorporate questions of who controls the digital means of production for more robust theories, models, and studies of digital inequality in general, and of digital production in particular. While the concept of controlling the digital means of production in relation to the online production gap was a key theoretical advancement, technological advancements and, more importantly, a tightening of the corporate control over them throughout the 2010s have shown that this concept is even more critical today. We are no closer to controlling the means of production than when the concept of the digital production gap was introduced. In fact, this gap has only gotten wider and deeper.

The Changing Ecosystem of Digital Content Production

To understand this transformation of digital production, it is useful to take a step back and first examine the trajectory of online content production and its resulting inequalities. Then, we will trace how the content lens is a necessary though insufficient way of theorizing the digital production gap.

Early Digital Content Production

Producing content is not new to the digital era. From the early printing press to mimeograph machines, as well as the telegraph and fax machines, people with the means to do so have been able to communicate their personal and political stories and news. And like today, corporations and states dominated these modes of communication. While the digital era certainly changed communication production, it especially transformed the distribution end of that content to enable a much broader, more efficient, and targeted reach (Rainie and Wellman 2012). In fact, this transformation is a key element of the myths around the democratization of online content.

Outside of the foundational military and university uses, early internet content generally fell into two areas—one was text content, in the form of online newsgroups, email, and even some gaming. Initially, throughout the 1980s, these text-based-only tools were often used through known social, community, or workplace networks (Turner 2006). This communication was often written by individuals to other individuals (one-to-one). Newsgroups, such as Usenet based in the U.S. or chat services on the Minitel in France, had the early social media characteristic of "one-to-many," with groups formed around common interests ranging from politics to gardening. An early scholar of social differences with regard to this content was Marc A. Smith, who found that just a small fraction of people was more likely to dominate the Usenet space. Although he did not analyze the socioeconomic background of posters, from available diffusion curves of internet access at the time, people with higher incomes and education levels were most likely to be using these services at that point (Smith 1999; Van Dijk and Hacker 2003). However, it was only a small pool of early adopters, mostly university-educated, who were even participating in these groups to begin with.

The other area of content was the growth of websites, which started to accelerate rapidly in the early 1990s. Dot-coms—startups centered in Silicon Valley—began to dominate the internet by registering website names hand over fist. But individuals could still register a domain name, whether as a .com or a .org, and develop their own website with basic graphics and lots of text. While courses on coding using html technology—the coding needed to put up a website and related content—proliferated, these producers were often limited to a small group of elite adopters. Eventually, software tools from companies like Adobe became available, but the learning curve and time it took to learn were still high. At the same time, though, the web was open, in the sense that users could create content on a website, and, as part of the semantic web, that content would match with what was being searched through early search engines. But as a proportion of the total population, content producers remained a niche group (Schradie 2015b). Barbrook and Cameron (1995) famously described a "virtual class" of entrepreneurs, software developers, engineers, communication specialists, and others, who they went on to describe as "Rich white Californians."

Nonetheless, in the late 1990s, advancements in software and interest in being able to distribute one's ideas and thoughts to the broader digital public inspired a new form of content creation: blogs. While blogs may now seem retro, "blogging" was a new word at the time that was a mashup of "web" and "log." With software like Live Journal, Blogger, and Word Press, blogging was in theory easily available, though, as Hindman (2009) pointed out and Schradie (2012) later confirmed for the United States, it tilted toward those with university education—people who had the skills, resources, and time to blog, not to mention the influence to build a following.

It was not until the early 2000s, when social media platforms emerged, that an increasing number of everyday people with a computer, an internet connection, and some know-how could share information online in text and graphic form without having to host their own website. Newsgroups of just text were and are still an important part of the social media landscape, but images and text in shorter bursts became the norm on newer integrated platforms, from Friendster and Myspace to Twitter and Facebook. These new platforms built on previous ones as Twitter was initially described as a "micro-blogging platform" and Facebook was pitched as one's own website—both of which became available to the general public in 2006 when *Time* magazine named "You" the person of the year for creating online content. While research on content production inequality was still rare, danah boyd (2007, 2009) compared American teenagers' perceptions of social media usage based on the social class and race of their users, with Myspace perceived to be associated with lower socioeconomic as well as

Latinx and Black users in the United States, whereas Facebook was perceived as a platform for wealthier, predominantly white users.

By this time, however, another piece of technology was transforming how people could use the internet to express themselves both visually and verbally—with video. The compression rates for video sharing had improved dramatically, making it practical to both upload and download video—if one had the right tools and internet speed. YouTube quickly spread worldwide—with early do it yourself (DIY) sensations like the lip-syncing and dancing of the Back Street Boys from China, which went viral on the platform in 2006 (ewo 2005).

The digital public sphere, and the utopianism that surrounded it, seemed to be in full swing across a range of content production activities, whether for entertainment or politics. But the question remained: Who was contributing to this new online town square, and who was not? This interactive web was not just an assemblage of static websites; it was dubbed "Web 2.0" for its participatory potential. Rather than a one-to-many form of content distribution, it was many-to-many. Digital creation was seen as something that was now accessible to more people and possible for wider participation (Jenkins 2006; Benkler 2006).

Nonetheless, very little research existed by this point on how representative this online space was. Some scholars had paved the way by examining individual platforms or uses (boyd 2009; Correa 2010; Hindman 2009). But if the internet was supposed to be more egalitarian and participatory than offline communication methods, who was that "You," the person of the year for creating online content? Whose voices were and were not online in these spaces? Schradie (2011, 2012, 2013, 2015a) set out to answer this question more broadly. With American survey data across 9 years between 2000 and 2008, she examined how much people reported creating content across 10 online production activities, from websites and blogs to videos and photos, as well as older newsgroups and newer social media sites. Digital consumption—or basic access to online information—divides still prevailed then, as they do now. But even among people online, social class differences persisted across all 10 production activities. People with a university education were much more likely to create online content than those with a high school degree. As the article title explained, "The Digital Production Gap: The Digital Divide and Web 2.0 Collide" (Schradie 2011).

But social class never operates on its own and has important intersections with race, ethnicity, and gender vis-à-vis digital production (which also do not depend on class to be significant both empirically and normatively). For instance, racial and ethnic gaps that persist in consumption and access seem to be reversed in production, at least in the United States (Correa and Jeong 2011; Schradie 2012). In terms of social media content creation, after controlling for social class, in the United States, Black, Asian, and Latinx university students report a higher share of content creation than white students, even when controlling for other factors (Correa and Jeong 2011). A greater share of Black Americans are active on Twitter, relative to their proportion among educated young adults in the United States (Hargittai 2015). There is also a gendered digital production gap, based on parsimonious though binary distinctions. While people who identify as women were more likely than men to consume online content, men were more likely to produce it in the public sphere. Interestingly, this inequality gap was greater for women from higher education levels compared to similar-status men than it was for women with lower education levels (Schradie 2015a). Sobieraj (2018) later unpacked some of the mechanisms behind this gender gap, such as the harassment that women face when posting in public spaces.

Technology has changed in fast-paced internet time since first theorizing the digital production gap in 2011, with 72% of Americans using at least one social media platform (Pew Research Center 2019). Longitudinal studies have noted increases in social media postings across all age groups (Bechmann 2019), with a large and consistent gap in participation over time favoring those with the highest education over the lowest education (Koiranen et al. 2019). Yet class differences persist, especially if one thinks back to Smith's (1999) early Usenet research. The question that remains is not only who is posting the most but also whose voice is most likely to be heard.

This representation remains a key area of concern in the context of digital production inequality, given that journalists, policymakers, and politicians are increasingly turning to online content to measure what matters in society, from Medium and Wikipedia posts to protest tweets and Weibo videos (Treem et al. 2016; Hindman 2009). While all content is worthy of analysis and is part of the digital public sphere, it is political information online that is often vital to the digital democracy that was supposed to be a hallmark of the internet era (Benkler 2006; Jenkins 2006; Castells 2009; Dahlberg 2007). And scholars have repeatedly found inequalities in political production activities online more generally (Oser and Bouliannne 2020), as well as with digital activism (Schradie 2019). An increasingly common way to measure online content production is through hashtags, particularly through Twitter. Nonetheless, with poor and working-class people not only less likely to be online but also less likely to be creating this type of online content, using hashtags is an extremely difficult way to assess the digital production gap.

Regardless, questions of social class and digital production have centered on a linear mathematical equation of how representative the digital public sphere pie has been. Have poor and working-class people been less likely to be online? Have they been less likely to create content for this online treasure trove? This became even more important with talk around big data, which has been critiqued by scholars for its lack of representativeness when looking at social media and digital production (Hargittai 2015; Schradie 2017), or what was later coined "big dick data" (D'Ignazio and Klein 2020), making it even more of a race in which the marginalized could never keep up. The stepped-up use of algorithms, particularly in digital distribution, has changed this formula. It is no longer a matter of linear addition but of exponential equations.

Digital Content Production Inequalities in the Algorithmic Era

While this question of the digital *content* production gap still matters as digital practices evolve, the period since 2010 has brought a greater understanding of *why* controlling the digital means of production has become even more critical. The broader utopianism of digital production began to wane as the rise of darker views of the internet began to permeate the public's consciousness—from sexist content around gamergate to emerging cries of bots and hacks into electoral political information (Woolley and Howard 2018; Massanari 2017). Underneath this dystopianism view is a growing ecosystem of digital consumption and production such that inequality is no longer just a series of points on diffusion S-curves (Rogers 2010) measuring over time if and how more people were posting online and often showing the poor and working-class far behind. Instead, with both technological advancements as well as a greater understanding of how the internet works measuring the volume of production in relation to class inequality metrics has been a necessary though insufficient way of understanding the digital production gap. While pure stratification analysis is important in terms of who is producing (and consuming) online content, it is not enough to explain production inequalities. And the stakes have never been higher. It is also not enough just to be concerned that marginalized voices have been increasingly drowned out in ever-growing data troves dominated by elites. The game changed with an increasing concentration of power and the impact of algorithms.

One of the major differences now is that an increasing amount of this production is being centralized on digital platforms, including big tech social media and content platforms like YouTube, and subject to the algorithms of Google and other search engines. The increase of mobile technologies has made the creation of software based on open-source code increasingly difficult, given that access to the internet is now almost entirely facilitated by applications. These apps and closed-off systems have been likened to "walled gardens" (Lutz 2019; Paterson 2012) and "black boxes" (Pasquale 2015), offering users very little control over their means of production and coming with more and more surveillance. While one can upload videos and photos on the fly, consistent and sophisticated digital production requires more than convenience. Smartphone technologies have amplified this loss of control since the affordances for digital production using smartphone technologies are different from those of personal computer–based internet access. While smartphones are more convenient and financially accessible, laptops and desktops are more optimal for many forms of production, thanks in part to a keyboard and larger display, as well as access to files. While sociodemographic differences have a greater influence when explaining differences in digital production activities than access to varoius devices, having use of a computer does increase the likelihood of undertaking certain "capital-enhancing activities" (Pearce and Rice 2013).

Of course, algorithms are not new. In simple terms, an algorithm is a mathematical equation—equations that were used for the early web, as well. And even when Google launched in 1998, questions were swirling around its "black box" that determined what showed up in searches. Even in the late 1990s, it was Google's secretive algorithm that controlled if and how your html-coded website about a DIY bat house fighting mosquitoes showed up in the first 10 hits of a Google search. It is simplistic, though true, to say that Google controls that algorithm. Yet the capitalist business model of who pays to promote this search system is also critical. The person who had the coding capacity then to even develop that bat house website has even less power now in getting it higher up on a page rank. What dominates search is a combination of advertisements and search engine optimization that is less and less about the topic and more and more about who can pay to promote the post, much like what leads to a larger audience on other platforms like Twitter or TikTok. The black box that is a search engine's page and feed rank algorithm means that all forms of digital content are dependent on the platform in order for them to be seen—which depends on the author's understanding of how that search engine works, as well as the resources and power they have to intervene. Thus, both the creation and publishing of content, as well as its search and display, are increasingly closed (i.e., less open), with the means of production concentrated in the hands of a small number of companies, leaving users in the dark.

What do these algorithms do for the average producer? Some scholars, like Noble (2018), have argued that these algorithms actually reinforce structural inequalities, rather than disrupt them. One of the ways by which algorithms do this is through a lack of transparency for most platforms' users. The sorting mechanisms that algorithms drive, building on big data, are likely to be understood only by those who build them. Nonetheless, even the coders in a company may work on one small section of the platform, leaving the overall algorithm in corporate control, with many users unaware of algorithms at all. A recent study carried out in the United Kingdom by the Oxford Internet Institute (2020) found that while 47% of Brits believe they have a good understanding of AI, many underestimate its importance in their daily lives, with only 26% believing that they use AI tools and services daily. Another study, of Norway's population, found that only 13% of those surveyed indicated having high or very high awareness of algorithms, with age, education, and gender all identified as key factors in this gap (Gran, Booth, and Bucher forthcoming). The researchers even suggest that algorithm awareness could constitute a new digital divide. While it is critical to document divides like these, it is even more important to situate them within the broader concept of the digital means of content production—affecting not only what one produces but in turn what one views.

On Facebook, this can mean using the right words, several pictures (instead of just one), and posting at the right time of day to achieve "maximum reach" (Bucher 2017) or even paying to promote your post so that it gets seen by more people. On YouTube, the most common videos are "vlogs, followed by gaming videos, sketches, and tutorials" (Ferchaud et al. 2018), which has evolved significantly since the platform's inception in 2006 and the days of amateur cat videos. YouTube and TikTok have even given rise to a whole new generation of digital content producers: YouTubers and TikTokers. These influencers share everything about their lives, building bonds with their users through so-called authenticity and realism (Ferchaud et al. 2018); and their increasingly performative videos are tied to their ever-increasing funding from the platform as a reward for their viral content. Driven to the top of the YouTube watch list, for example, by the platform's algorithms, which they themselves work to game through provocative (and even click-bait) language in their titles, these high–production value videos rake in increasing numbers of clicks and subscriptions; and the cycle continues. And this mechanical decision-making is far from neutral. The algorithm creates a hierarchy of visibility driven by the demands of advertisers that overwhelmingly discriminates in favor of creators overwhelmingly hailing from the middle and upper middle classes (Bishop

2018), who have the know-how, the ability, and the means to game the system. The algorithm works to the benefit of these advertisers, which means that content producers—far from fully in control of their means of production—are beholden to this algorithm which determines their visibility.

But it is essential to clarify that the users who are most adept at manipulating these algorithms are not individuals who have more or fewer attributes but are institutions, corporations, and states. For instance, some social movement groups, on both the left and the right, have dedicated staff members to monitor and track what types of messaging works for their membership and target audience (Karpf 2016; Schradie 2019). Certainly, corporations are well known for using not only algorithms but also data gleaned from the public's digital traces to target advertising. Even news outlets doing solid investigative journalism, not just so-called fake news sites, use search engine optimization for headlines and other keywords in their stories to get the greatest reach. And, of course, governments harness the power of algorithms to flood social media feeds with information, such as the well-known Russian use of bots (Woolley and Howard 2018). The goal for all these outlets is to get their story heard by a broader group of people, be it in the name of journalism, advertising, or propaganda.

So poor and working-class people now face a double exclusion with digital content production. They are less likely to produce online content than their middle- to upper-class counterparts, but they, like all individuals, also face an increasingly uphill battle to be heard even when they do create online content. Not only did a fair representation of voices not become a reality, but algorithmic capitalism has also amplified corporate voices.

Nonetheless, algorithms drive not just search and social media feeds. They are also the engine of AI that not only makes marginalized voices less visible online but also misrepresents them, like the designation of content produced for YouTube by creators with regional accents as unrecognizable by closed caption text matching (Bishop 2018). So, content by and about them is often distorted. Like big data and algorithms, AI is a Silicon Valley term that has taken on a life of its own—pun intended. AI uses information from an algorithm that it repeats exponentially for automatic decision-making behavior—from driverless cars and robots to what you see on your Instagram feed. This area of technological automation targets the poor and working class. Just because the term may denote a sterile space that seems to be devoid of bias, like algorithms, it is intentionally designed—but not by or for the poor.

Despite flippant arguments that algorithms are not inherently biased because they are mathematical equations, the writers of these algorithms certainly are. They are not representative of the general population, especially the working class and people of color. This perpetuated myth of "technologically mediated neutrality," as well as that of meritocracy, has operated in sync with a consolidation of technology and power which codifies class, racial, and gender markers of white male supremacy (Noble and Roberts 2019). The example that Noble (2018) explains in her book is how Google searches for "Black girls" tend to show pornographic and racist images. While the intent of the production of these algorithms is not necessarily classist or racist, their effect is ultimately the reproduction and perpetuation of systemic racism (Benjamin 2020). Findings such as these, however, are not new to the digital era. Other forms of media have done the same type of racialized and class profiling historically. For instance, Kendall (2005) documented similar findings about poor people in predigital media, often characterizing them as either victims without agency or cheaters. Yet the digital era ramps up these distortions, arguably widening the content gap rather than coming close to eliminating it.

And while we often focus on what the algorithms powering AI make visible, algorithms can also make certain types of content produced by marginalized and racialized people invisible, according to Benjamin (2020), who gives many examples of how the design of AI technologies themselves, such as web cameras, can literally make it more difficult for Black people to be recognized. Class intersects with race here, with people of color disproportionately excluded from the algorithmic training and coding process. This exclusion can lead to the coding of racialized stereotypes and the stigmatizing of people of color in terms of where they live, what they do, and who they interact with. The outcomes of this "neutral" process are significant: When people of color do become visible, they are subjected to surveillance (Benjamin 2020).

At the same time, we cannot assume that widespread visibility of digital production is a goal of all content creators, like it may be with YouTubers, TikTokers, tweeters, bloggers, and many others. Some want limited visibility, yet finding and ensuring privacy in these online spaces take time and savvy. LGBTQ youth, for example, may produce content in certain spaces where they can safely ask questions and post content without fear of being "outed" (Hawkins and Watson 2017). Others may be fine with public visibility in theory, though the ultimate goal is rather to stay within one's chosen silo. For example, some use Black Twitter to build and strengthen community through digital production, acting and reacting "with one another rather than with an imagined audience" (Clark 2015). White nationalist movement online communities are a different form of quasi-public discussion and content production that seeks to limit visibility; members look for "safe spaces" because they are concerned about monitoring by investigators or regulators (Caren, Jowers, and Gaby 2012). Some American conservatives, for example, left Facebook for Parler or other social platforms where they believe they are more free to post as they please (Bond 2020). In theory, groups can regulate their privacy settings online, but the algorithmic power of these platforms continues to steer people into such online groups in the first place to better monetize these preferences.

A Theoretical Framework for Controlling the Means of Digital Content Production

Rather than just assessing digital production inequalities or evaluating the more complex algorithmic and corporate systems that shape it, however, we also need to put them in a broader theoretical perspective to understand the mechanisms behind them.

Some scholars have theorized production very openly, by calling it "participation" in a utopian sense (Jenkins 2006) or by arguing that pure production is impossible because of the blurriness between consumption and production in the online world and that, furthermore, online and offline distinctions are difficult to make at all (Ritzer and Jurgenson 2010). This may be easy to say for people who have regular and consistent access to digital technologies, whatever their personal production environments—someone may like a tweet and a nanosecond later compose a lengthy post on Medium while simultaneously checking email, eating lunch, and rocking a baby. But because most people do not fully control the production or the distribution of their content, even in this scenario where one may not have child care or may have other constraints, a vast array of factors must be taken into account to theorize production itself.

When Schradie (2011) conceptualized digital production as distinct from consumption of content, she found that a key mechanism of class-based production gaps was controlling the digital means of production. At that time, a key element was continuous and unlimited internet access at home and at work with computers. It was more than just answering the question, Do you have access to a computer or an internet connection? With the advent and the increasing use of "smart" mobile devices, this is no less important since controlling the means of production is not limited to having a usable device that has the functionalities necessary for a vast array of content production. While a mobile smart phone with a camera may be great for Instagram posting, imagine having to do all your work on it or having a laptop but one which must be shared with others. Or perhaps you cannot afford an unlimited data plan so rely on locations with Wi-Fi, to which you may or may not have stable access at home. Countless other factors feed into being able to control the means of digital content production—and feed into the broader conception of digital production in the algorithmic era. Nonetheless, even someone with an arsenal of tech tools still pales in comparison to corporate and other institutions that dominate digital production. But to situate these mechanisms, it is useful to unpack several theories that can inform the digital means of production.

One digital inequality theoretical framework that scholars use is the three levels of the digital divide. The first level is broadly concerned with inequalities of access to digital devices and infrastructure; the second with inequalities of skills, uses, and an assortment of digital practices; the third with inequalities in outcomes based on digital technology use (van Deursen and Helsper 2015). The first level targets what constituted the bulk of the early digital divide literature starting in the late 1990s—the binary question of whether people had basic access to a computer or the internet. This favored research into consumption of content on the internet, especially for Web 1.0. The proportion of households without access in countries of the Organisation for Economic Co-operation and Development has shrunk to about 10% on average, with G7 countries ranging from about 20% of households in the United States to just 4% in the United Kingdom in 2019 (Organisation for Economic Co-operation and Development 2020). This slice of the population is not only overwhelmingly poor but is also even larger when the measurement of these rates is scrutinized. The 90% access rate does not distinguish between types of access and generally includes everything from high-speed access through a

MacBook to occasional, low-speed, old gadget use. As a result, it is vital not to minimize the importance of access. The COVID-19 pandemic has thrust this basic digital divide question (back) into the public discourse. With remote and online work forced upon the education system and labor market, digital inequalities at the most basic level have been laid bare. But pandemics notwithstanding, having high-quality and consistent access is still critical to any type of digital production and a necessary step that is oft forgotten or overlooked. The first-level divide is what the digital production gap had counterposed as the ability to consume, rather than produce, online content. So, in many ways, it was production's necessary twin.

But the nature of the second-level digital divide is murkier, with researchers often throwing anything into this box that does not fit into the first level of access or what we will see as the third level of outcomes. Rather than different uses or production activities, it is often categorized as analyzing users more in-depth, looking at the factors that lead to usage, for instance (Scheerder, van Deursen, and van Dijk 2017). The scholarship on the second digital divide is focused primarily on use more generally and the skills to make that use effective. Predating this theory is the work that drove its conceptualization. Scholars such as DiMaggio and Hargittai (Dimaggio et al. 2004) argued that inequalities were not limited to a binary question of computers or not or internet or not but rather that there were a range of inequalities not only across different users' sociodemographic traits but also in their skills, confidence levels, and other key factors. And indeed, all these digital inequalities feed into digital production inequalities.

Nonetheless, the second-level digital divide is not the only theoretical framework that sheds light on digital production. Shaw and Hargittai (2018) conceptualized a pipeline of online participation, which acknowledges that the process of producing is not independent from other forms of digital engagement but requires several steps before production can take place. The authors suggest that their model can be applied in different contexts for online production activities including contributing to Wikipedia (their case study), discussion forums for news media sites, and posting on social media. Shaw and Hargittai (2018) argue that studies too often focus uniquely on the output of the productive process, which ignores the relatively large pool of potential contributors or producers and how that pool slowly shrinks with all of the steps involved in needing to produce online content. Internet users can only make contributions to a site once they have heard of the site, then visited the site, and then know that it is possible to contribute to it. The results of Shaw and Hargittai's study also highlight the importance of internet experiences and skills, as well as socioeconomic and demographic factors when trying to study digital production. In effect, then, the pipeline framework is more useful in conceptualizing digital content production gaps because it broadens the lens from the overly general second-level divide, for which the main limitation is that it undertheorizes digital production.

But what of the third level of the digital divide? Scheerder, van Deursen, and van Dijk (2017) suggest that digital inequality research has mostly identified socioeconomic and sociodemographic determinants of internet use which are disconnected from outcomes. Van Deursen and Helsper (2015) argue for the existence of a third-level divide: Individuals with higher socioeconomic status can generate a greater offline return from their digital engagement than their counterparts with lower socioeconomic status. While some scholars had already been looking at the outcomes of inequalities in digital use, whether for economic or political outcomes (Dimaggio et al. 2004), this third level is still a useful concept.

Even still, focusing uniquely on identifying socioeconomic and sociodemographic factors assumes and is built on the premise that internet platforms and search engines are neutral. As internet activity is increasingly concentrated in corporate-controlled platforms, as opposed to the browser-centered public web (Paterson 2012), the technologies themselves also contribute to the disparity of outcomes that are identified in the third-level divide. The influence of the platform is even more important when considering the outcomes of digital production, which is left out from, or at least not specified in, the digital divide framework.

On the one hand, none of the theories that address Silicon Valley control look at digital production inequality in particular, especially when seeking to understand the exact mechanism behind the differences in outcomes once digital production inequality has been documented. On the other hand, by consistently treating socioeconomic and sociodemographic factors as the primary determinants of digital engagement, some scholars make the fundamental assumption that the influence of these factors is the main path toward a more democratic public sphere. However, a few theories can give insight into this theoretical weakness. One approach is the argument around data colonialism (Couldry and Mejias 2019), which compares the control of one's data to theories of body and land ownership. Another theoretical thrust is one that has tackled a Marxist approach to the means of production, highlighting the role of social media giants like Facebook in fully developing and maintaining the platform that constitutes the means of production (Fuchs and Sevignani 2013). Unlike approaches based only on a stratification analysis, both of these frameworks situate production inequality within broader power structures that significantly reduce individual users' control of and agency over the means of production. Another argument pays more attention to context around digital inequalities more broadly (Helsper 2017), building on relative deprivation theory, which assigns a greater role to the social and temporal context of the user or creator when considering digital inequalities and does not assume that factors like social class have a consistent effect on digital production. Finally, a theory of class power (Schradie 2020) outlines how a combination of individual, organizational, and contextual constraints works to limit online content production among the working class.

But it is imperative that any theory around the digital means of production be grounded in empirical data, ideally marrying the stratification and power relations approach (Schradie 2020). While individual sociodemographic measures are essential for isolating and establishing a baseline for who is producing content, they remain insufficient for explaining some of the contextual means of production factors for an individual's online production activity that may be as important for explaining the production gap. These factors include not only the corporate-controlled platforms and algorithm-driven production contexts in which production is taking place but also social class *relations*, which are broader than demographic *variables*.

Among the scholarship that uses empirical data, digital divide research remains an important foundation for looking at different types of inequalities around digital production. Yet, what we need is a more direct theoretical framework that addresses power—which is the essential ingredient for who controls the digital means of production: those with more power in society. While this includes individuals with more resources, corporations with more resources, and states with more resources, it is ultimately about more than resources. It is also about being able to wield hegemonic power This control over the means of production is crucial for understanding the disparity in outcomes that digital divide scholars have sought to address, which means research cannot focus purely on stratification analysis with a narrow focus on socioeconomic status. When digital inequality analyses are only individualized and not relational, they may overlook these important power imbalances, which are mechanisms of digital inequalities and require class to be viewed as an analytic category, not just a descriptive one (Schradie 2020). And the question of power plays an even greater role in producing online content than just accessing it.

CONCLUSION

Since new media pundits trumpeted the arrival of a utopian era of online participation and creation, the digital means of production have become more apparent as online content creation is increasingly concentrated on a limited number of powerful, closed platforms. GAFAM and BATX have done more than simply create forums for digital engagement; they increasingly control all aspects of the means of production from content creation tools to algorithms that determine what is seen and how. And none of this will disappear by giving someone a laptop or encouraging people to "just post more." As these platforms became increasingly susceptible to bots and fake news, our view of digital production has taken a turn for the dystopian as users increasingly find themselves losing control over the means of production. This trend has magnified existing socioeconomic and racial inequalities on a massive scale, and the outcomes of the digital production gap are now more serious than ever with these technologies in society. Who and what controls the algorithmic means of production has become a central inequality question around digital production. At the same time, the early web was never an egalitarian space, so reforming tech companies is not a simple fix to address the digital production gap.

Increasingly, as we have seen, this "who" is not "you" but rather ruling digital elites, governments, and corporations that have amassed control over these means of production while bringing about the resulting inequalities. The myth of meritocracy plays an important role in the tech industry's justification of the inequitable wealth distribution within the tech realm (Noble and Roberts 2019; Benjamin 2020). This myth is part of a broader discourse of Silicon Valley ideology (Schradie 2015b), built around the neoliberal principles of free markets, freedom from the state, and free labor. As we have discussed, these principles are themselves built into the social media tools and platforms that have ingrained themselves in the digital production practices of the everyday population.

To meet these threats, digital production inequality scholarship must evolve with the changing and increasingly algorithm-driven contexts and environments of production which have serious implications for socioeconomic outcomes. We need dynamic models to understand digital production—not linear ones. Stratification analysis (for the operationalization of social class) is no longer sufficient to explain the digital production gap in this new environment. Current theoretical frameworks have been useful for analyzing the increasing complexity of digital inequalities, but they do not quite capture the growing power of algorithms and closed-source platforms or the broader control by a digital ruling class of elites, corporations, and states. This new framework or model should focus on the primacy of controlling the digital means of production. This framing can connect scholarship on digital production with a rich, emerging scholarship on digital and platform labor, as well as surveillance and AI.

Another crucial limitation of much of the research on digital production inequalities is a lack of comparable data across different countries. Much of the English-language scholarship, using national samples from the United Kingdom or the United States, for example, has not been in conversation with research from other countries. Certainly, scholarship exists on online participation in non-English-speaking countries, such as Denmark (Bechmann 2019) and Finland (Ertiö, Kukkonen, and Räsänen 2020; Koiranen et al. 2019). However, more studies are needed comparatively in, on, and with the Global South as well as the Chinese digital ecosystems to better understand how political, platform, and cultural contexts can shape digital production inequalities. This is especially important when considering variations in digital production versus consumption across and even within countries and when seeking to understand the mechanisms of the production gap, from basic access metrics to contextual power differences. Along with a greater exploration of inter- and intranational differences, more qualitative and mixed-methods research is necessary to unpack these mechanisms and their influence on people's digital production practices. Finally, research on the type and quality of the content is essential to understand the impact of these differences.

So why does it matter? Certainly, more people are posting online content than produced television or radio programs of the past, but with the firehose of online information, the question remains as to whose voices dominate. Digital technology was supposed to overcome the media dominance of the elite with a broader array of voices. But most marginalized communities never got a fair shot. While scholars have been focused on inequalities of access or skills, the wider means of production have been increasingly concentrating in the hands of a small group of the digital ruling class. As a result, analyses of the digital divide in general, and online content production in particular, must incorporate both measures and processes of what the *means* of production actually are beyond simply production tools or the sociodemographics of the people who use them. The corporations and states designing the algorithms certainly are.

References

Barbrook, Richard, and Andy Cameron. 1995. "The Californian Ideology." *Mute Magazine*, September 1. https://www.metamute.org/editorial/articles/californian-ideology.

Bechmann, Anja. 2019. "Inequality in Posting Behaviour over Time: A Study of Danish Facebook Users." *Nordicom Review* 36, no. 2: 31–49. https://doi.org/10.2478/nor-2019-0012.

Benjamin, Ruha. 2020. "Race after Technology: Abolitionist Tools for the New Jim Code." *Social Forces* 98, no. 4: 1–3. https://doi.org/10.1093/SF/SOZ162.

Benkler, Yochai. 2006. *The Wealth of Networks: How Social Production Transforms Markets and Freedom*. New Haven, CT: Yale University Press.

Bishop, Sophie. 2018. "Anxiety, Panic and Self-Optimization." *Convergence: The International Journal of Research into New Media Technologies* 24, no. 1: 69–84. https://doi.org/10.1177/1354856517736978.

Bond, Shannon. 2020. "Conservatives Flock to Mercer-Funded Parler, Claim Censorship on Facebook and Twitter." *Weekend Edition Sunday*, National Public Radio, November 14.

boyd, danah. 2007. "Viewing American Class Divisions through Facebook and MySpace." (blog), June 24, 2007. https://www.danah.org/papers/essays/ClassDivisions.html.

boyd, danah. 2009. "Implications of User Choice: The Cultural Logic of My Space or Facebook?" *Interactions* 16, no. 6: 33–36. https://doi.org/10.1145/1620693.1620701.

Bucher, Taina. 2017. "The Algorithmic Imaginary: Exploring the Ordinary Affects of Facebook Algorithms." *Information Communication and Society* 20, no. 1: 30–44. https://doi.org/10.1080/1369118X.2016.1154086.

Caren, Neal, Kay Jowers, and Sarah Gaby. 2012. "A Social Movement Online Community: Stormfront and the White Nationalist Movement." *Research in Social Movements, Conflicts and Change* 33: 163–193. https://doi.org/10.1108/S0163-786X(2012)0000033010.

Castells, Manuel. 2009. *The Rise of the Network Society*. Vol. 1, 2nd ed. Chichester, UK: John Wiley & Sons. https://doi.org/10.1002/9781444319514.

Clark, Meredith. 2015. "Black Twitter: Building Connection through Cultural Conversation." In *Hashtag Publics: The Power and Politics of Discursive Networks*, edited by Nathan Rambukkana, 205–218. New York: Peter Lang. https://www.peterlang.com/view/9781454192015/chapter15.xhtml.

Correa, Teresa. 2010. "The Participation Divide among 'Online Experts': Experience, Skills and Psychological Factors as Predictors of College Students' Web Content Creation." *Journal of Computer-Mediated Communication* 16, no. 1: 71–92. https://doi.org/10.1111/j.1083-6101.2010.01532.x.

Correa, Teresa, and Sun Ho Jeong. 2011. "Race and Online Content Creation: Why Minorities Are Actively Participating in the Web." *Information, Communication & Society* 14, no. 5: 638–659. https://doi.org/10.1080/1369118X.2010.514355.

Couldry, Nick, and Ulises A. Mejias. 2019. "Data Colonialism: Rethinking Big Data's Relation to the Contemporary Subject." *Television & New Media* 20, no. 4: 336–349. https://doi.org/10.1177/1527476418796632.

Dahlberg, Lincoln. 2007. "The Internet, Deliberative Democracy, and Power: Radicalizing the Public Sphere." *International Journal of Media & Cultural Politics* 3, no. 1: 47–64. https://doi.org/10.1386/macp.3.1.47_1.

D'Ignazio, Catherine, and Lauren Klein. 2020. *Data Feminism*. Cambridge, MA: MIT Press. https://mitpress.mit.edu/books/data-feminism.

Dimaggio, Paul, Eszter Hargittai, Coral Celeste, and Steven Shafer. 2004. "Digital Inequality: From Unequal Access to Differentiated Use." In *Social Inequality*, edited by Kathryn Neckerman, 355–400. New York: Russell Sage Foundation. https://www.scholars.northwestern.edu/en/publications/digital-inequality-from-unequal-access-to-differentiated-use.

Ertiö, Titiana, Iida Kukkonen, and Pekka Räsänen. 2020. "Social Media Activities in Finland: A Population-Level Comparison." *Convergence: The International Journal of Research into New Media Technologies* 26, no. 1: 193–209. https://doi.org/10.1177/1354856518780463.

ewo 2005. Chinese Backstreet Boys – That Way. Available at: https://youtu.be/N2rZxCrb7iU.

Ferchaud, Arienne, Jenna Grzeslo, Stephanie Orme, and Jared LaGroue. 2018. "Parasocial Attributes and YouTube Personalities: Exploring Content Trends across the Most Subscribed YouTube Channels." *Computers in Human Behavior* 80: 88–96. https://doi.org/10.1016/j.chb.2017.10.041.

Fuchs, Christian, and Sebastian Sevignani. 2013. "What Is Digital Labour? What Is Digital Work? What's Their Difference? And Why Do These Questions Matter for Understanding Social Media?" *TripleC* 11, no. 2: 237–293. https://doi.org/10.31269/triplec.v11i2.461.

Gran, Anne-Britt, Peter Booth, and Taina Bucher. Forthcoming. "To Be or Not to Be Algorithm Aware: A Question of a New Digital Divide?" *Information, Communication & Society*. Published ahead of print March 9, 2020. https://doi.org/10.1080/1369118X.2020.1736124.

Hargittai, Eszter. 2003. "The Digital Divide and What to Do about It." In *New Economy Handbook*, edited by Derek C. Jones, 821–839. New York: Elsevier Science. http://www.webuse.org/webuse.org/pdf/Hargittai-DigitalDivideWhatToDo2007.pdf.

Hargittai, Eszter. 2015. "Is Bigger Always Better? Potential Biases of Big Data Derived from Social Network Sites." *Annals of the American Academy of Political and Social Science* 659, no. 1: 63–76. https://doi.org/10.1177/0002716215570866.

Hargittai, Eszter, and Gina Walejko. 2008. "The Participation Divide: Content Creation and Sharing in the Digital Age." *Information, Communication & Society* 11, no. 2: 239–256. https://doi.org/10.1080/13691180801946150.

Hawkins, Blake, and Ryan J. Watson. 2017. "LGBT Cyberspaces: A Need for a Holistic Investigation." *Children's Geographies* 15, no. 1: 122–128. https://doi.org/10.1080/14733285.2016.1216877.

Helsper, Ellen Johanna. 2017. "A Socio-Digital Ecology Approach to Understanding Digital Inequalities among Young People." *Journal of Children and Media* 11, no. 2: 256–260. https://doi.org/10.1080/17482798.2017.1306370.

Hindman, Matthew. 2009. *The Myth of Digital Democracy*. Princeton, NJ: Princeton University Press.

Jenkins, Henry. 2006. *Convergence Culture: Where Old and New Media Collide*. New York: New York University Press.

Karpf, David. 2016. *Analytic Activism: Digital Listening and the New Political Strategy*. New York: Oxford University Press. https://www.oxfordscholarship.com/view/10.1093/acprof:oso/9780190266127.001.0001/acprof-9780190266127.

Kendall, Diana Elizabeth. 2005. *Framing Class: Media Representations of Wealth and Poverty in America*. Lanham, MD: Rowman & Littlefield. https://books.google.ca/books/about/Framing_Class.html?id=eumcjBKyVloC&redir_esc=y.

Koiranen, Ilkka, Teo Keipi, Aki Koivula, and Pekka Räsänen. 2019. "Changing Patterns of Social Media Use? A Population-Level Study of Finland." *Universal Access in the Information Society* 19, no. 3: 603–617. https://doi.org/10.1007/s10209-019-00654-1.

Lutz, Christoph. 2019. "Digital Inequalities in the Age of Artificial Intelligence and Big Data." *Human Behavior and Emerging Technologies* 1, no. 2: 141–148. https://doi.org/10.1002/hbe2.140.

Massanari, Adrienne. 2017. "#Gamergate and the Fappening: How Reddit's Algorithm, Governance, and Culture Support Toxic Technocultures." *New Media & Society* 19, no. 3: 329–346. https://doi.org/10.1177/1461444815608807.

Noble, Safiya Umoja. 2018. *Algorithms of Oppression*. New York: New York University Press. https://doi.org/10.2307/j.ctt1pwt9w5.

Noble, Safiya Umoja, and Sarah Roberts. 2019. "Technological Elites, the Meritocracy, and Post-Racial Myths in Silicon Valley." In *Racism Postrace*, edited by Roopali Mukherjee, Sarah Banet-Weiser, and Herman Gray, 113–134. Durham, NC: Duke University Press.

Organisation for Economic Co-operation and Development. 2020. "Information and Communication Technology (ICT)." https://doi.org/10.1787/69c2b997-en.

Oser, Jennifer, and Shelley Boulianne. 2020. "Reinforcement Effects between Digital Media Use and Political Participation: A Meta-Analysis of Repeated-Wave Panel Data." *Public Opinion Quarterly* 84, no. S1: 355–365. https://doi.org/10.1093/poq/nfaa017.

Oxford Internet Institute. 2020. "Majority of Brits Underestimate Use of Artificial Intelligence in Their Everyday Lives but Recognise Wider Benefits for Society." Oxford Internet Institute, March 25. https://www.oii.ox.ac.uk/news/releases/new-survey-finds-majority-of-brits-underestimate-use-of-artificial-intelligence-in-their-everyday-lives-but-recognise-wider-benefits-for-society/.

Pasquale, Frank. 2015. *The Black Box Society*. Cambridge, MA: Harvard University Press. https://www.hup.harvard.edu/catalog.php?isbn=9780674970847.

Paterson, Nancy. 2012. "Walled Gardens: The New Shape of the Public Internet." In *iConference '12: Proceedings of the 2012 iConference*, 97–104. New York: ACM Press. https://doi.org/10.1145/2132176.2132189.

Pearce, Katy E., and Ronald E. Rice. 2013. "Digital Divides from Access to Activities: Comparing Mobile and Personal Computer Internet Users." *Journal of Communication* 63, no. 4: 721–744. https://doi.org/10.1111/jcom.12045.

Pew Research Center. 2019. "Demographics of Social Media Users and Adoption in the United States." June 12. https://www.pewresearch.org/internet/fact-sheet/social-media/.

Rainie, Lee, and Barry Wellman. 2012. *Networked: The New Social Operating System*. Cambridge, MA: MIT Press.

Ritzer, George, and Nathan Jurgenson. 2010. "Production, Consumption, Prosumption: The Nature of Capitalism in the Age of the Digital 'Prosumer.'" *Journal of Consumer Culture* 10, no. 1: 13–36. https://doi.org/10.1177/1469540509354673.

Rogers, Everett M. 2010. *Diffusion of Innovations*. 4th ed. New York: Simon & Schuster. https://www.simonandschuster.co.uk/books/Diffusion-of-Innovations-4th-Edition/Everett-M-Rogers/9781451602470.

Scheerder, Anique, Alexander van Deursen, and Jan van Dijk. 2017. "Determinants of Internet Skills, Uses and Outcomes. A Systematic Review of the Second- and Third-Level Digital Divide." *Telematics and Informatics* 34, no. 8: 1607–1624. https://doi.org/10.1016/j.tele.2017.07.007.

Schradie, Jen. 2011. "The Digital Production Gap: The Digital Divide and Web 2.0 Collide." *Poetics* 39, no. 2: 145–168. https://doi.org/10.1016/j.poetic.2011.02.003.

Schradie, Jen. 2012. "The Trend of Class, Race, and Ethnicity in Social Media Inequality." *Information, Communication & Society* 15, no. 4: 555–571. https://doi.org/10.1080/1369118X.2012.665939.

Schradie, Jen. 2013. "The Digital Production Gap in Great Britain." *Information, Communication & Society* 16, no. 6: 989–998. https://doi.org/10.1080/1369118X.2013.799305.

Schradie, Jen. 2015a. "The Gendered Digital Production Gap: Inequalities of Affluence." In *Communication and Information Technologies Annual*. Vol. 9, Studies in Media and Communications, 185–213. Bingley, UK: Emerald Group. https://doi.org/10.1108/s2050-206020150000009008.

Schradie, Jen. 2015b. "Silicon Valley Ideology and Class Inequality: A Virtual Poll Tax on Digital Politics." In *Handbook of Digital Politics*, edited by Stephen Coleman and Deen Freelon, 67–84. Cheltenham, UK: Edward Elgar. https://doi.org/10.4337/9781782548768.00012.

Schradie, Jen. 2017. "Big Data Is Too Small: Research Implications of Class Inequality for Online Data Collection." In *Media and Class: TV, Film and Digital Culture*, edited by June Deery and Andrea Press, 200–213. New York and London: Routledge.

Schradie, Jen. 2019. *The Revolution That Wasn't: How Digital Activism Favors Conservatives*. Cambridge, MA: Harvard University Press.

Schradie, Jen. 2020. "The Great Equalizer Reproduces Inequality: How the Digital Divide Is a Class Power Divide." *Political Power and Social Theory* 37: 81–100.

Shaw, Aaron, and Eszter Hargittai. 2018. "The Pipeline of Online Participation Inequalities: The Case of Wikipedia Editing." *Journal of Communication* 68, no. 1: 143–168. https://doi.org/10.1093/joc/jqx003.

Smith, Marc A. 1999. "Invisible Crowds in Cyberspace: Mapping the Social Structure of the Usenet." In *Communities in Cyberspace*, edited by Marc A. Smith and Peter Kollock, 195–219. New York and London: Routledge.

Sobieraj, Sarah. 2018. "Bitch, Slut, Skank, Cunt: Patterned Resistance to Women's Visibility in Digital Publics." *Information Communication and Society* 21, no. 11: 1700–1714. https://doi.org/10.1080/1369118X.2017.1348535.

Treem, Jeffrey W., Stephanie L. Dailey, Casey S. Pierce, and Diana Biffl. 2016. "What We Are Talking about When We Talk about Social Media: A Framework for Study." *Sociology Compass* 10, no. 9: 768–784. https://doi.org/10.1111/soc4.12404.

Turner, Fred. 2006. *From Counterculture to Cyberculture: Stewart Brand, the Whole Earth Network, and the Rise of Digital Utopianism*. Chicago: University of Chicago Press. https://press.uchicago.edu/ucp/books/book/chicago/F/bo3773600.html.

van Deursen, Alexander J. A. M., and Ellen J. Helsper. 2015. "The Third-Level Digital Divide: Who Benefits Most from Being Online?" In *Communication and Information Technologies Annual*. Vol. 10, Studies in Media and Communications, 29–52. Bingley, UK: Emerald Group. https://doi.org/10.1108/s2050-20602015000010002.

Van Dijk, Jan, and Kenneth Hacker. 2003. "The Digital Divide as a Complex and Dynamic Phenomenon." *Information Society* 19, no. 4: 315–326. https://doi.org/10.1080/01972240309487.

Woolley, Samuel C., and Philip N. Howard. 2018. *Computational Propaganda: Political Parties, Politicians, and Political Manipulation on Social Media*. New York: Oxford University Press. https://www.oxfordscholarship.com/view/10.1093/oso/9780190931407.001.0001/oso-9780190931407.

PART VI

DIGITAL MEDIA, POWER, AND POLITICS

CHAPTER 29

DETECT, DOCUMENT, AND DEBUNK

Studying Media Manipulation and Disinformation

GABRIELLE LIM AND JOAN DONOVAN

FOLLOWING Russia's attempted interference in the 2016 US presidential election, concerns over "fake news," disinformation, or covert influence operations carried out over social media rapt the attention of journalists, politicians, and scholars. From hoaxes to hyperbolic rhetoric to outright fabrications, groups as disparate as state agencies and pranksters continue to develop, refine, and deploy tactics that take advantage of our networked and participatory media ecosystem with the goal of influencing public discourse (Bradshaw and Howard 2019; Corpus Ong and Tapsell 2020). Social media have been called a "threat to democracy" (Kavanagh and Rich 2018; Prier 2017; Snegovaya 2015) and a "national security risk" (Morris 2019), while academics and politicians frequently claim that media are being "weaponized" (Bosetta 2018; Howard 2018; Nadler, Crain, and Donovan 2018) for malicious purposes.

Many of these fears are warranted. Yet, despite the profuse press coverage; interest from the public sector, private sector, and academia; and millions in funding, consensus on the effects and effectiveness of disinformation and influence operations has yet to be reached, let alone the best strategies to counter them. What does it mean when a headline claims that almost 50% of a conversation online is fueled by bots (Allyn 2020)? How should we take allegations by government intelligence agencies that China, Iran, and Russia are engaged in influence operations (Bell 2020)? What does it mean when Facebook takes down accounts for "coordinated inauthentic behavior" (Acker and Donovan 2019; Douek 2020)? Moreover, the topic of "fake news" and disinformation has become increasingly politicized and used by many to discredit opponents. Because disinformation impacts so many professional sectors, studying disinformation can be overwhelming and confusing without the application of theory and methods of detection.

This chapter therefore tries to demystify some of these questions—to explain the drivers, facilitators, and implications of digital influence operations and how scholars can better study them, communicate their risks, and, just as importantly, assess the claims made by others. And while influence operations, covert media manipulation, propaganda, and disinformation are not new concepts, the pervasiveness of social media, large-scale data collection, and our increasingly networked media ecosystem have necessitated new ways of studying these phenomena as well as new questions.

The field of internet studies is still nascent, and while research has been both multi- and interdisciplinary, it has not coalesced in a way that makes a literature review delineated by discipline useful. Indeed, even within disciplines, there are seemingly siloed clusters of researchers. As such, this chapter will be broken down into the technical and social variables involved in media manipulation, research methods, their observable effects on society, and proposed means of mitigation, with a conclusion on future research.

A note on definitions and terminology:

There are a lot of terms used within the study of disinformation and media manipulation, and we use several of them throughout the chapter. *Misinformation* refers to false information that is shared unknowingly, whereas *disinformation* is false information shared with the intent to deceive its audience, often for political ends. *Propaganda*, another related category, generally refers to information that is intended to persuade or promote a specific agenda, including both false and accurate information. It can further be delineated as *black propaganda*, which is deceptive in nature, or *white propaganda*, which is open and transparent (Jowett and O'Donnell 2015).

On occasion, the terms "information warfare," "influence operations," and "information operations" may also be used to refer to propaganda or disinformation; however, note that these terms also encompass actions beyond audience persuasion and media; examples include hacking a database or malware. For a more complete list of terminology, Caroline Jack (2017) provides a useful explainer of the various terms associated with modern disinformation and media manipulation. Martin Libicki (2017) also offers a comprehensive analysis of the growing range of tactics under the umbrella of information warfare. In general, researchers avoid the term "fake news" due to its highly politicized nature (Caplan, Donovan, and Hanson 2018) and multiple definitions (Wardle 2017). The big exception to this convention is when researchers are quoting or citing a source who employs the term (e.g., Malaysia's now repealed 2018 Anti-Fake News Act).

For the purposes of this chapter, we use the term "media manipulation" to broadly encompass the wide swath of phenomena described in this section. We define *media manipulation* as the sociotechnical process whereby motivated actors leverage specific conditions or features within an information ecosystem in an attempt to generate public attention and influence public discourse through deceptive, creative, or unfair means (Media Manipulation Casebook 2020a). Campaigns or operations that engage in media manipulation may use several tactics, such as memes, viral videos, forged documents, or leaked information, and may include disinformation, propaganda, or misleading content. Although broadening the inclusion of phenomena adds complexity, it is necessary for a high-level understanding of how information flows in a digitally networked information ecosystem. This allows us to expand the literature surveyed and draw connections between different but related cases.

Crucially, political partisanship and political hyperbole do not necessarily constitute media manipulation. Instead, researchers must look for attempts to cover identity, obscure the source of information, trick journalists or other influential individuals into responding, or use algorithmic means to artificially boost attention to a topic. Studies of media manipulation and disinformation should therefore begin from a single question: *Where is the lie?* Is it in the promotion of content using false identities? Is it in the underlying manipulation of algorithms to reach unsuspecting audiences? Is it the reuse of content in a new context? Even in situations where a specific claim is true, researchers must be attentive to the networks and context of distribution that may harbor deception.

Sociotechnical Approaches to Studying Media Manipulation and Disinformation

Modern-day online media manipulation is ultimately a *sociotechnical* phenomenon. By that we mean it takes advantage of social and technical conditions that on their own may not pose a threat but when combined enable motivated actors to carry out networked influence operations. Contemporary online media manipulation and disinformation, being primarily disseminated over complex integrated and technical systems, therefore require one to consider both the social and technical variables to explain specific outcomes. As Star (1999) points out in her research on infrastructure, it is the study of "boring things," like user interfaces, account management protocols, and terms of service agreements, that leads to greater appreciation of how nonhuman actants structure human–machine networks and information flows. Nonhuman actors such as software, algorithms, and digital interfaces play an important role in how media manipulation campaigns are carried out. However, social conditions that facilitate or drive humans to interact with these systems also need to be considered.

Studies of media manipulation and disinformation campaigns can therefore draw from and can be situated within the fields of political communication, the sociology of social movements, science and technology studies, and infrastructure studies (Benkler, Faris, and Roberts 2018; Acker and Beaton 2017; Krafft and Donovan 2020; Donovan 2018, 2019a; McAdam 1983; Monterde and Postill 2014; Friedberg and Donovan 2019). Sociologists often look at the ways groups come together to bring about social change through analysis of the resources available to changemakers and the political opportunities afforded in each time period. For example, when studying how the civil rights movement coordinated to carry out lunch counter sit-ins or bus boycotts, McAdam (1983) shows that the group's adoption of new tactics is not arbitrary.

Likewise, McAdam's insights about tactical innovation are useful for understanding how motivated interest groups will utilize the technology available to them in any given era to their advantage. Countering tactical innovation requires institutions and other authorities to come up with a proportional response, which often creates lag and a first mover advantage for those who can adapt quickly. According to Monterde and Postill (2014), when movements adopt and utilize communication technologies, particular social media through apps on a mobile phone, they incorporate different forms of media and mobility into their repertoire of action. Approaching the study of media manipulation and disinformation through these frameworks can act as a guide for assessing how similar technologies, when used by different groups, can provide an advantage for manipulators who are quick to adjust tactics to evade detection.

In practice, the use of methods like situational analysis and social worlds theory, as Clarke and Star (2008) describe, requires understanding the technical features of a system (e.g., trending algorithms, share buttons, commenting privileges, ad microtargeting, and more) as well as the social, political, and cultural features (e.g., political wedge issues, long-standing interpersonal animosities, racism, sexism, homophobia and transphobia, geopolitical rivalries, insurgent groups, user behavior, and so on). For example, scholars such as Gioe, Goodman, and Wanless (2019) emphasize the need for cybersecurity practitioners to focus on not just the technical aspect of security but why humans are vulnerable sites for attack. In exploring a novel approach to security in networked systems, Goerzen, Watkins, and Lim (2019) have proposed "sociotechnical security" as a framework for understanding how such systems affect the safety and well-being of communities. Other studies grounded in actor network theory include research on the social shaping of technology (Paris and Donovan 2019) and infrastructural studies (Nadler, Crain, and Donovan 2018), where both humans and nonhuman elements are considered to be actors. At the Harvard Kennedy School's Shorenstein Center on Media, Politics, and Public Policy, the Media Manipulation Casebook categorizes its case studies along technical and social vulnerabilities, while using process tracing to determine how media manipulation and disinformation campaigns are formed and how they adapt to mitigation attempts (Donovan 2020a; Media Manipulation Casebook 2020b).

Research Methods

As a result of the need to consider both the social and technical formations, the study of media manipulation has taken on a wide variety of research methods across multiple disciplines, where academic scholars are finding their footing in critical internet studies (Livingstone 2005; Ess and Consalvo 2011). From ethnography to data science to mixed-methods approaches grounded in interdisciplinary collaboration, the study of media manipulation has proved fruitful for creative research design and novel methodology. Furthermore, because of the changing landscape of the information ecosystem and the actors, motivations, and narratives involved, the methods used to detect and study media manipulation are constantly evolving. As media manipulators learn to circumvent detection, new means of detection are required.

Computational and quantitative methods have proven useful in helping to grapple with large data sets, determining the scale of campaigns, and detecting the spread of specific content and anomalous behavior. For example, the Internet Research Agency's Twitter data set contains 10 million Tweets and more than 2 million pieces of audiovisual content. Research methods include generating network graphs (Benkler, Faris, and Roberts 2018; Stewart, Arif, and Starbird 2018); the use of machine learning and natural language processing (NLP) to detect similarities, differences, or other specific characteristics in text (Torabi Asr and Taboada 2019; Oshikawa, Qian, and Wang 2020; Feldman et al. 2019); image recognition and tracing (Zannettou et al. 2018); and audio/video manipulation detection (Lyu 2020). For example, computational journalist Jeff Kao (2017), using NLP, detected over a million fake comments when investigating suspicious activity during the Federal Communication Commission's open comment period on net neutrality.

Often, computational methods are used to detect "bots," automated accounts, and their spread across the internet and specific platforms (Gorwa and Guilbeault 2018). Numerous studies rely on Twitter's API (application programming interface) to detect statistically anomalous behavior (Abrahams and Lim 2020; Jones 2019); but this method is not always replicable or reliable as access to data through platform APIs is changing, and there is a long-standing criticism that social media companies do not provide enough data to draw significant conclusions (Acker and Donovan 2019). Scholarly debates about causation versus correlation are instructive here as it may very well be the case that data-centric studies of disinformation are more descriptive of group activity than conclusive in establishing how disinformation impacts society (Donovan 2020b).

On the qualitative side, there is a wide variety of research methods including ethnography, process tracing, discourse analysis, content analysis, and grounded theory. Investigative digital ethnography, for example, integrates methods from journalism with cultural anthropology to analyze campaigns across platforms and the web (Friedberg 2020). Using this approach, Friedberg lays out how researchers can set up a computing environment, using a dedicated browser and new social media accounts, that takes advantage of recommendation algorithms' tendency to surface similar content containing misinformation. Elsewhere, Gabrielle Lim (2020a), in tracing the securitization of "fake news" in Malaysia, utilizes content and discourse analysis to draw out the narratives used to justify the Anti-Fake News Act, which criminalized the sharing and creation of "fake news." Crystal Abidin's (2020) analysis of how "meme factories" in Singapore and Malaysia shifted in response to COVID-19 uses an ethnographic approach, which includes interviews with creators of memes, while Brandy Collins-Dexter's (2020) analysis of COVID-related conspiracies and disinformation among Black communities uses multisite digital ethnography.

Due to the sociotechnical nature of media manipulation and the range of tactics and platforms used by campaign operators, mixed-methods approaches are therefore commonplace. The Media Manipulation Casebook, for example, takes a mixed-methods approach to detecting influence operations, employing content analysis and data science to trace case studies using a life cycle framework (The Media Manipulation Casebook 2020b). Joan Donovan and Brian Friedberg (2019) have also used investigative ethnographic methods along with discourse analysis and process tracing to identify novel strategies and tactics among right-leaning online communities. Integrating more methods into the mix, a report published by the University of Toronto's Citizen Lab used open-source intelligence techniques, discourse analysis, content analysis, and anomalous Twitter account behavior to identify a network of ostensibly pro-Iran personas peddling spoofed websites containing falsehoods (Lim et al. 2019). The Oxford Internet Institute has also published numerous studies, including a multicountry analysis of disinformation and social media manipulation (Bradshaw and Howard 2019), which uses a variety of methods from content analysis of news reporting on disinformation to country-specific literature reviews to expert consultations with domain knowledge. Investigative journalists and scholars have also come together to further the field, as exemplified by the most recent *Verification Handbook*, which details the wide variety of methods available for internet investigations (Silverman 2020).

In addition, some researchers analyze the design of social media platforms and the web to uncover how misinformation campaigns circulate across platforms and the web. Specifically, studies that assess online advertising business models and the technical infrastructure behind advertising technology provide ways of incorporating broader sociological insights about politics, economics, and culture (Nadler, Crain, and Donovan 2018; Noble 2018; Braun, Coakley, and West 2019). For example, Kim et al. (2018) used a custom web extension to document advertisements on Facebook during the US election in 2016. Their research reveals that some political advertising conducted by various actors, including Russia, targeted Facebook users in battleground states. In addition to revealing the tactics and vulnerabilities of media manipulation, research like this supports the case for transparency regulation in online advertising and content moderation.

Ultimately, a sociotechnical approach to understanding media manipulation necessitates a wide variety of research methods to help quantify and qualify not just the scope and scale but the context, motivations, outcomes, and implications of media manipulation and disinformation campaigns.

Identifying Actors, Motivations, and Impacts of Media Manipulation Campaigns

Because of the pervasiveness of social media, the relatively low barriers to entry, and the way they have been institutionalized by governments (Busemeyer and Thelen 2020), media manipulation is not exclusive to any one actor or groups of actors and may be utilized by both state and nonstate actors. Furthermore, the lines between the two are not clear-cut. First, attribution is difficult. For example, pro-CCP (Chinese Communist Party) activity is often pejoratively accused of being the work of a bot or "wumao" (individuals paid by the CCP to disseminate propaganda), but evidence is not always conclusive. Second, operations, factions, and movements birthed on the internet sometimes find community online before moving offline, where disinformation can mobilize protests (Donovan 2020c). Most notably, the fast growth of the conspiratorial QAnon community (a *Guardian* investigation found there were more than 3 million Facebook followers who support QAnon [Wong 2020]) has resulted in not only a number of congressional and senatorial nominees who openly support it but also mild support from President Trump himself (Liptak 2020). As such, operations are not always clearly defined as state versus nonstate, and the ability of operations to draw in genuine followers both on- and offline further complicates the question of who is behind a media manipulation event.

With those caveats in mind, however, we will delineate between foreign (operations targeting audiences in another country) and domestic (operations targeting audiences within the same country) media manipulation for the purposes of this chapter. Though it is a large generalization to split research into these two camps, doing so will help break down the largest strands of contemporary research in this field for further analysis.

Foreign Operations and Great Power Politics

Despite the fact that media manipulation and disinformation existed well before 2016, their resurgence as a popular topic of study can very likely be attributed to the 2016 US presidential election. Following Donald Trump's successful presidential campaign, it was revealed that the Russian-based Internet Research Agency (IRA) had been engaging in a years-long multicampaign operation aimed at stoking distrust in the government and animosity between different communities within the US. The metrics were astounding, with over 30 million users having shared IRA content on Facebook and Instagram between 2015 and 2017 (Howard et al. 2018).

In response, a federal jury indicted the IRA and 13 other Russian nationals for alleged election tampering (Department of Justice 2018). However, even with data on engagement, it remains unclear whether the IRA had any effect in swinging the 2016 election. David Karpf (2019) has pointed out the difficulties in measuring "direct effectiveness," while other studies have found limited or negligible effects (McCombie, Uhlmann, and Morrison 2020; Bail et al. 2020). And as pointed out by Thomas Rid (2020), the bulk of their activity was engaged in audience-building unrelated to the election. In addition, people consume information from a variety of sources. Benkler, Faris, and Roberts' (2018) analysis of the 2016 information ecosystem, for example, found that instead of Russian disinformation, the asymmetric media structure of the United States had a far more detrimental effect on Americans' news consumption.

Of course, foreign influence operations are not limited to the United States, nor are they a recent phenomenon. In a report by Bradshaw and Howard (2019), Facebook and Twitter had attributed seven countries for engaging in foreign operations: China, Venezuela, Saudi Arabia, Russia, Pakistan, Iran, and India. One of the most notable cases of foreign-targeted operations is the lead-up to and following the annexation of Crimea by Russia, where pro-Kremlin propaganda and disinformation were widely documented (Helmus 2018). Operations are also not targeted to a single country. For example, an ostensibly Iran-linked operation targeted several countries by spoofing established news organizations in the United States, the United Kingdom, Switzerland, Saudi Arabia, and Israel (Lim et al. 2019).

Impact of Foreign Operations

Overall, there is a lack of consensus on the effectiveness of foreign-targeted influence operations, whether measured by shifts in public opinion or foreign policy changes. While some claim that influence operations and media manipulation can act as force multipliers for insurgents and create a more welcoming population for an invading force (Perry 2015), others counter that their effects are minimal and do not serve any strategic usefulness. For example, while it is well known that China engages in influence operations and disinformation targeted at Taiwan (Monaco 2017), its effectiveness at swaying voters appears to be negligible as pro-democracy incumbent Tsai Ing-wen won a second term by a large margin (Sudworth 2020).

A deep dive by investigative journalist Alexei Kovalev (2020) also found that Chinese Russian-language operations are largely ineffective and generate little interest. Similarly, Alexander Lanoszka (2018), in examining Russian campaigns targeting the Baltics, argues that disinformation is ineffective at changing foreign policy preferences and that the threat of disinformation is exaggerated. A comprehensive overview of influence operations by China and Russia by Rand also found that there is no conclusive evidence about the impact of hostile disinformation campaigns (Mazarr et al. 2019). These findings are similar to analyses of influence operations from the Cold War (Walton 2019; Rid 2020).

That being said, while media manipulation on its own may not be a reliably effective strategy for achieving geopolitical aims, there are still effects which can be harmful or at least undesirable. It can tie up scarce resources among civil society, journalists, and politicians, who must then spend time debunking the falsehoods or engaging in counterspeech. Depending on the country and volume of disinformation, the effects will vary. For example, although persistent Chinese operations targeted at Taiwanese audiences appear to be ineffective, Taiwan has spent considerable resources mobilizing civil society, the private sector, and the public sector to counter cross-straits information operations (Huang 2020; Wallis et al. 2020; Monaco, Smith, and Studdart 2020). Russian influence operations in Europe have harassed Finnish journalists and researchers for reporting on and debunking pro-Kremlin falsehoods, leading to self-censorship and fears for their safety (Aro 2016). In the Middle East, the work of Andrew Leber and Alexei Abrahams (2019) on the 2017 Gulf crisis discovered strong evidence of Saudi and

Emirati state-linked activity that engaged in not only direct intervention and the mass production of online statements via automated "bot" accounts on Twitter but offline coercion or co-optation of existing social media "influencers."

Domestic Operations, Insurgent Groups, and State Control

Research focused on the domestic side of media manipulation—that is, influence operations that are attributed to or targeting domestic groups—is wide-ranging in terms of the actors, activities, and narratives studied. Campaign operators and participants range from pranksters to conspiracists, extremists, political parties, and activists to state-sponsored groups. To further complicate matters, the groups often interact with one another, form alliances, and are co-opted by political parties, pundits, or popular online personalities (Lewis and Marwick 2017). And like foreign-targeted operations, attribution is often difficult as savvy media manipulators will often lay the blame elsewhere (Daniels 2018).

That being said, recent research tries to delineate between state and nonstate operations. The former refers to activity sponsored, funded, linked to, in support of, or conducted by the state or a ruling political party, while the latter refers to activity conducted by opposition groups, activists, influencers, and extremists (organized or loosely affiliated). However, the line often gets blurred as politicians welcome and/or encourage online crowds to click, like, and share manipulated materials and disinformation campaigns, creating a feedback loop between political elites and the online groups (Parker 2020; Corpus Ong and Cabañes 2018).

State-Linked Operations

In countries characterized as illiberal or having authoritarian regimes, particular attention has been paid to state-sponsored operations, activity which includes propaganda, targeted harassment and defamation, "cybertroopers," censorship, and surveillance (Deibert 2015; MacKinnon 2012). Where once social media was hailed as an equalizing force, detailed case studies from around the world illustrate how ruling regimes are able to artificially amplify content, game engagement metrics, manufacture inauthentic grassroots support (Jones 2019), and dominate online spaces with propaganda, disinformation, and harassment (Abrahams 2019). In a 2019 survey of 70 countries, Bradshaw and Howard (2019) found evidence of organized social media manipulation campaigns being used to suppress human rights, discredit political opponents, and drown out political dissent in 26 states. What's more, individuals living in illiberal or authoritarian regimes must contend not just with media manipulation but with other forms of information control, such as internet service provider–level blocking, client-side content blocking, state ownership of media, and the criminalization of certain content (Donovan 2019b; Palfrey and Zittrain 2008). The lack of free speech and press freedom, combined with disinformation and other influence operations, creates a particularly difficult environment for free expression to thrive (Corpus Ong 2021).

Digging deeper, in the Philippines, Ong and Cabañes (2018) detail the highly professionalized industry behind political media manipulation and how state-sponsored trolling contributes to not only the silencing of voices but the consolidation of revisionist historical narratives. In Mexico, Suárez-Serrato et al. (2016) found that automated "bot" activity on Twitter repeatedly interfered with a protest movement by spamming #YaMeCanse, the most active protest hashtag in the history of Twitter in Mexico. Protestors, subsequently, used iterations of the hashtag by appending numbers (e.g., #YaMeCanse2). The persistence of the bot activity resulted in 25 versions of the hashtag as protest organizers moved away from ones that had become overly polluted. China, in addition to censoring politically sensitive content (Ruan et al. 2020; Roberts 2020; MacKinnon 2011), has a long history of engaging in domestically targeted influence operations and other narrative-shaping attempts (Repnikova and Fang 2018, 2019).

Nonstate Operations

Research on nonstate activities, on the other hand, has primarily focused on extremist groups, such as White supremacists and far-right agitators and, more recently, conspiracists (e.g., QAnon and anti-vaccination groups). Beginning in the mid 2010s, much focus was placed on ISIS (or Daesh, as it is known in Arabic-speaking countries), whose use of social media allowed the terrorist-designated group to recruit people to its cause and amplify its propaganda and exploits (Farwell 2014; Benigni, Joseph, and Carley 2017). However, as with foreign influence operations, the radicalizing effects of such content are still debated, and as Conway (2017) points out, there is much more that can be done to understand the impact of radicalization in online communities.

At the same time, research into the online and offline activities of White supremacist groups, ethno-nationalist influencers, and other far-right individuals and organizations has grown as these groups have become increasingly networked (Donovan, Lewis, and Friedberg 2018; Daniels 2018). More recently, anti-institutional and anti-government groups have also taken advantage of the networked information ecosystem to espouse violence, government overthrow, and hate speech. Take for example, the anti-government and online subculture where members use the term "Boogaloo" to identify each other online (Evans and Wilson 2020). Individuals who identify with this group have carried out serious violence, which eventually led Facebook and Discord to ban the group and accounts linked to the keyword (Owen 2020). These groups, also known as "networked factions" (Media Manipulation Casebook 2020c; Reid 2019), are able to coordinate, gain supporters, wage "memetic warfare," and in some cases bait journalists and investigators with false information during periods of crisis (Donovan and Friedberg 2019).

Impact of Domestic Operations

Although there are some similarities between domestic and foreign-targeted operations, there are some notable differences, at least in terms of current scholarship. From the study of far-right groups and reactionary subcultures, there is evidence that they are sometimes able to *mainstream the extreme*, by moving what otherwise would have been obscure or fringe content into the popular press and political discourse (Donovan and Friedberg 2019; Phillips 2018; Lewis 2018). In India, for example, investigative journalist Soma Basu (2019) found that in over 140 pro–Bharatiya Janata Party, the ruling party in India, WhatsApp groups, 23.84% of messages shared were Islamophobic, highly inflammatory, and shared with the intent to create hatred and division between Hindus and Muslims. In a similar vein, targeted harassment campaigns have also been documented around the world, with some cases involving *doxing* (unauthorized release of personal information, such as a home address or phone number), phishing and spyware attempts, defamation, and death and rape threats (Monaco and Nyst 2018). The result of such personal attacks may lead to self-censorship and a wider chilling effect, especially for women and minoritized groups (Amnesty International 2018; Franks 2019).

In addition, domestic operations over time are likely to drain civil society and journalists of already scarce resources as they must spend time debunking, fact-checking, and countering false and defamatory speech and, in some cases, engaging in the mental and emotional turmoil of constant harassment. Philippine president Rodrigo Duterte, for example, has routinely attacked opposition candidates and critics with false allegations, which not only creates a massive drain on resources for his targets but has resulted in journalists fearing for their physical safety (Stevenson 2018).

Accountability and Mitigation

While there is general agreement that something needs to be done about the potentially harmful effects of disinformation and media manipulation, the specifics of what actions to take are far less clear. Current proposed and enacted measures run the gamut from imprisonment for sharing false information to labeling misleading content. As a result, there is a patchwork of regulations, legislation, policies, and approaches rendering the governance of global internet companies uneven and opaque (Donovan 2019b; de La Chapelle and Fehlinger 2016). Furthermore, media manipulation overlaps with other concerning issues, such as surveillance, data collection, privacy, freedom of expression, abuse of power, and antitrust—all of which will have effects, unintended or otherwise, on how networked communication is conducted and the broader information ecosystem itself (Deibert and Rohozinski 2008; Lim 2020b; Corpus Ong 2021).

Proponents of fact-checking and media literacy often claim that equipping individuals with truthful knowledge and the ability to discern fact from fiction will reduce belief in disinformation and dubious content. However, the effectiveness of these programs is contested and often underresourced (Caplan, Donovan, and Hanson 2018; Bulger and Davison 2018). For example, a study on the consistency of fact-checks given across three popular fact-checking sites shows substantial differences in answers that would limit the usefulness of fact-checking as a tool for citizens attempting to discern the truth (Marietta, Barker, and Bowser 2015). However, with health misinformation, a recent meta-analysis found that there are positive impacts with regard to fact-checking (Walter et al. forthcoming) and that attempts to correct for health misinformation appear more successful than for political misinformation (Walter and Murphy 2018).

Incremental changes to content moderation by technology companies in the United States have also occurred (Roberts 2019). Recent examples include labeling misleading content; publishing transparency reports of "coordinated inauthentic behavior," a vague term coined by Facebook to refer to deceptive activity (Acker and Donovan 2019); and redirecting users to more credible and authoritative content (Skopeliti and John 2020). However, like fact-checking and media literacy, the effectiveness of these measures is still up for debate. Labeling misleading or false content, for example, may backfire as it may imply that anything without a label is true (Pennycook et al. 2020), while banning users or removing content may simply shift those users and the content to other platforms (Krafft and Donovan 2020; Donovan, Lewis, and Friedberg 2018). Social media companies have also created policies against the malicious use of so-called deep fakes, images and video generated using artificial intelligence (Paris and Donovan 2019). Deep fakes have been used by manipulators to prevent researchers from discovering imposter accounts by using reverse image search, a debunking technique that uncovers fake accounts using repurposed images mined from the open web.

Outside of the United States, attempts by technology companies have had mixed results. China, for example, has typically forced its content policies onto private companies, which are then responsible for carrying out the content moderation. The results, however, are undue censorship as companies are incentivized to overcorrect lest they run afoul of the CCP's directives (Ruan et al. 2020). In countries where there is local legislation that criminalizes false information, content removals and arrests have been common. In Singapore, for example, the Protection from Online Falsehoods and Manipulation Act has resulted in Facebook labeling content the government deems to be false—an act that has been roundly criticized by rights groups and opposition politicians (Reporters Without Borders 2019; Au-Yong 2019).

Furthermore, any countermeasures are at risk of infringing on civil and human rights (United Nations Office of the High Commission of Human Rights 2017). Already, illiberal and authoritarian-leaning governments have used disinformation as a pretense to crack down on dissent (Beiser 2018; Lim 2020a). In Egypt, for example, arrests and intimidation of regime critics and other forms of digital expression are justified as safeguarding national security from "false information" (Open Technology Fund 2019). Even within established democracies, the fear of "foreign speech" has likewise raised concerns over potential infringements on freedom of expression and the further balkanization of the internet (Lim 2020b). Debates about the kinds and types of regulation for content governance are shifting, as outlined by Bowers and Zittrain (2020), where social media platforms are increasingly outsourcing content moderation to companies that are ill-equipped to understand regional contexts (Roberts 2020) but have the effect of releasing the company from liabilities for harassment, incitement, and hate.

With regard to regulation within the United States, pressure has been mounting from politicians, civil society, and researchers. However, there is no agreement on the best course of action. Proposals include algorithmic accountability and transparency, which allows the public to scrutinize how an algorithm makes a decision (Diakopoulos 2016) and updating campaign financing regulations for the social media age (Nadler, Crain, and Donovan 2018). Others, like Phil Howard (2020), advocate for increasing the individual's agency over their own data and breaking the concentration of data held by private actors. From a high-level perspective, Ron Deibert (2020), in his book *Reset* advocates for a more principled approach, providing a framework based on republicanism and restraint. This guiding framework would, ideally, create friction in our information ecosystem while reining in corporate and state power and, in doing so, "reclaim the internet for civil society" (Deibert 2020).

Beyond tech regulation and policy, others stress the need to deal with the reasons why people may be drawn to less credible or skewed sources. Alexei Abrahams and Gabrielle Lim (forthcoming), for example, argue the need to "redress" the sociopolitical grievances that may feed the demand for dubious content, as opposed to simply "repressing" the problematic information, while Johan Farkas and Jannick Schou (2019) argue that the decline in Western democracy predates social media by decades, and as such, simply reinstating truth (however subjective that may be) is not enough.

With regard to countering foreign operations specifically, governments around the world have proposed and enacted a number of measures. The Global Engagement Center, housed in the US State Department, for example, has received increased funding to research and root out propaganda, disinformation, and other covert information operations from US rivals, such as Russia, Iran, and China (Groll and Gramer 2019). Likewise, the North Atlantic Treaty Organization (NATO) has established the NATO Strategic Communications Centre of Excellence, which is tasked with countering Russian disinformation (StratCom n.d.). Many more nations, such as Singapore, France, Nigeria, and Canada, have also proposed or enacted new laws in the name of countering disinformation (Lim, Friedberg, and Donovan 2020; Funke and Flamini 2019). However, civil society organizations and human rights defenders are critical of "anti–fake news" initiatives due to their censorship-enabling capabilities and ulterior motives (e.g. to silence voices critical of the government).

Although there has been a rise in countermeasures, it is unclear how effective any of them are at either reducing the spread and consumption of disinformation or limiting their (disputed) effects. Research into mitigation is still nascent, although some steps have been made in recent years. Maria Hellman and Charlotte Wagnsson (2017), for example, offer an analytical framework that can be used to distinguish between and assess different governmental strategies for European states countering Russian information operations. Case studies of Taiwan and Sweden often point to the success of their "whole of society" approaches. Sweden, for example, has prioritized securing election infrastructure, encouraged high-level interagency coordination, coordination with the traditional media, improving media literacy, and a high-profile fact-checking collaboration between five of its largest media outlets (Cederberg 2018). Meanwhile, Taiwan has prioritized civic tech initiatives, coordination with civil society, increased government transparency and communication, and creative counterspeech (Mchangama and Parello-Plesner 2020). While some strides have been made, Herbert Lin and Jaclyn Kerr (forthcoming) argue that democracies are not particularly well suited to defend against influence operations and that current efforts are insufficient.

Future Research

Future research on media manipulation and disinformation must take a broad approach to understanding and addressing how society shapes technology and in turn how technology shapes our cultures and politics. Bruno Latour (1990), a French sociologist, wrote, "Technology is society made durable," which means that society is enacted and reproduced through the technology we develop and distribute. Therefore, researchers of media manipulation and disinformation cannot eschew or sideline the role relations of power such as racism, sexism, religious intolerance, and other forms of discrimination play in technological change.

Alongside incorporating power relations, future research must address declining trust in journalism and politics through the lens of technology and internet studies. Communication infrastructure and how societies use, access, and distribute information matter greatly for how other institutions like politics, journalism, education, and the economy function. Since the invention of radio, communication technology has been an especially important site of social contestation, where those who control the flows of information are able to influence politics, economics, science, and the press. In the age of disinformation, a panoply of voices may enjoy the ability to use social media, but those with the most financial resources and network power have managed to harness this technology to serve their own ends. Research that interrogates and uncovers networks of actors that routinely spread disinformation to reach their political goals and/or gain profit will be crucial for improving mitigation overall.

Methodologically, this transdisciplinary field would benefit from standardized access to social media data, along with transparent and mandatory disclosures of online advertising coupled with logs of content takedowns by technology companies. Often, when studying influence operations, researchers are left with a partial window into the worlds of manipulators, which makes assessing the impacts of these campaigns difficult. While some researchers have sought out relationships with social media companies in order to gain access to data, this contravenes the values of basic science and threatens the integrity of their study results, especially if technology companies are in a position to stop publication or disrupt funding (Abdalla and Abdalla 2021). The Harvard Kennedy School's *Misinformation Review* organized a call for social media data from numerous researchers across the world to address the many issues that threaten to stall scientific advances in this field (Pasquetto et al. 2020).

Beyond accessing data, studying bots, and uncovering sock-puppet accounts, possible lines of sociological and anthropological inquiry include in-depth and longitudinal studies of racialized disinformation (i.e., media manipulation campaigns that use race as a wedge issue or impersonate different races/ethnicities). Studies that address the maligned motivations of campaign operators who use this strategy cut across a number of potential methods, including quantitative study data from campaigns that impersonate social movements, such as the Russian IRA (Freelon et al. 2020).

Overall, the presence and persistence of media manipulation campaigns risks contributing to public distrust of news, tech companies, and government especially, as research from Pew Research Center (2020) and Gallup have noted (2020). Therefore, research that takes a whole-of-society approach to media manipulation and disinformation would lead to findings that could support internet and communication policy and the factors that reduce trust in these sectors. A whole-of-society approach would address how unchecked, unmoderated, and unmanaged misinformation impacts other professional sectors and would seek solutions outside of technological tweaks to design. For example, researchers could quantify the impact of disinformation on the field of journalism by looking at the volume of debunks that were written to counter specific misinformation events, like the international conspiratorial claim that COVID-19 is a bioweapon or more niche misinformation that anarchists started the California wildfires in 2020. Further, researchers could use the burden-of-disease framework to study how medical misinformation harms public health.

Lastly, because the internet is a global technology, media manipulation and disinformation are global fields of research. Distilling the tactics used by manipulators to disrupt, disguise, and deceive provides a comparative framework for analyzing what is possible, not what is inevitable. Too often, technological determinism shapes how some conceptualize innovation, where they falsely believe technological change is an organic process that occurs outside of politics and the economy. Instead, studies of media manipulation and disinformation should invert the proposition that society is downstream of technology. More precisely, researchers must seek out how the design and use of technology are dependent upon the ways powerful people—be they state actors, foreign agents, marketers, ideological groups, corporations, far-right groups, and so on—leverage the openness and scale of the internet to reach their own political and economic ends. Future research would do well to seek out how technology reveals as much as it conceals about the agency of humans in producing social change.

References

Abdalla, Mohamed, and Moustafa Abdalla. 2021. "The Grey Hoodie Project: Big Tobacco, Big Tech, and the Threat on Academic Integrity." Cornell University. http://arxiv.org/abs/2009.13676.

Abidin, Crystal. 2020. "Meme Factory Cultures and Content Pivoting in Singapore and Malaysia during COVID-19." *Harvard Kennedy School Misinformation Review* 1, no. 3. https://doi.org/10.37016/mr-2020-031.

Abrahams, Alexei. 2019. "Regional Authoritarians Target the Twittersphere." *Middle East Report* 292, no. 3. https://merip.org/2019/12/regional-authoritarians-target-the-twittersphere/.

Abrahams, Alexei, and Gabrielle Lim. Forthcoming. "Hierarchy over Diversity: Influence and Disinformation on Twitter." In *Cyber-Threats to Canadian Democracy*, edited by Holly Ann Garnett and Michael Pal. Montreal: McGill-Queen's University Press.

Abrahams, Alexei, and Gabrielle Lim. 2020. "Repress/Redress: What the 'War on Terror' Can Teach Us about Fighting Misinformation." *Harvard Kennedy School Misinformation Review* 1, no. 5. https://doi.org/10.37016/mr-2020-032.

Acker, Amelia, and Brian Beaton. 2017. "How Do You Turn a Mobile Device into a Political Tool?" *Proceedings of the 50th Hawaii International Conference on System Sciences*. https://doi.org/10.24251/HICSS.2017.281.

Acker, Amelia, and Joan Donovan. 2019. "Data Craft: A Theory/Methods Package for Critical Internet Studies." *Information, Communication & Society* 22, no. 11: 1590–1609. https://doi.org/10.1080/1369118X.2019.1645194.

Allyn, Bobby. 2020. "Researchers: Nearly Half of Accounts Tweeting about Coronavirus Are Likely Bots." *NPR*, May 20. https://www.npr.org/sections/coronavirus-live-updates/2020/05/20/859814085/researchers-nearly-half-of-accounts-tweeting-about-coronavirus-are-likely-bots.

Amnesty International. 2018. "Toxic Twitter—The Silencing Effect." https://www.amnesty.org/en/latest/research/2018/03/online-violence-against-women-chapter-5/.

Aro, Jessikka. 2016. "The Cyberspace War: Propaganda and Trolling as Warfare Tools." *European View* 15, no. 1: 121–132. https://doi.org/10.1007/s12290-016-0395-5.

Au-Yong, Rachel. 2019. "Parliament: Workers' Party Opposes Proposed Law on Fake News, Says Pritam Singh." *The Straits Times*, May 7. https://www.straitstimes.com/politics/parliament-workers-party-opposes-proposed-law-on-fake-news-pritam-singh.

Bail, Christopher A., Brian Guay, Emily Maloney, Aidan Combs, D. Sunshine Hillygus, Friedolin Merhout, et al. 2020. "Assessing the Russian Internet Research Agency's Impact on the Political Attitudes and Behaviors of American Twitter Users in Late 2017." *Proceedings of the National Academy of Sciences* 117, no. 1: 243–250. https://doi.org/10.1073/pnas.1906420116.

Basu, Soma. 2019. "Manufacturing Islamophobia on WhatsApp in India." *The Diplomat*, May 10. https://thediplomat.com/2019/05/manufacturing-islamophobia-on-whatsapp-in-india/.

Beiser, Elana. 2018. "Hundreds of Journalists Jailed Globally Becomes the New Normal." *Committee to Protect Journalists* (blog), December 13, 2018. https://cpj.org/reports/2018/12/journalists-jailed-imprisoned-turkey-china-egypt-saudi-arabia/.

Bell, Stewart. 2020. "CSIS Accuses Russia, China and Iran of Spreading COVID-19 Disinformation." *Global News*, December 3. https://globalnews.ca/news/7494689/csis-accuses-russia-china-iran-coronavirus-covid-19-disinformation/.

Benigni, Matthew C., Kenneth Joseph, and Kathleen M. Carley. 2017. "Online Extremism and the Communities That Sustain It: Detecting the ISIS Supporting Community on Twitter." *PLoS ONE* 12, no. 12: e0181405. https://doi.org/10.1371/journal.pone.0181405.

Benkler, Yochai, Robert Faris, and Hal Roberts. 2018. *Network Propaganda: Manipulation, Disinformation, and Radicalization in American Politics. Network Propaganda*. New York:

Oxford University Press. https://oxford.universitypressscholarship.com/view/10.1093/oso/9780190923624.001.0001/oso-9780190923624.

Bosetta, M. (2018). "The Weaponization of Social Media: Spear Phishing and Cyberattacks on Democracy." *Journal of International Affairs*, September 20. https://jia.sipa.columbia.edu/weaponization-social-media-spear-phishing-and-cyberattacks-democracy.

Bowers, John, and Jonathan Zittrain. 2020. "Answering Impossible Questions: Content Governance in an Age of Disinformation." *Harvard Kennedy School Misinformation Review* 1, no. 1. https://doi.org/10.37016/mr-2020-005.

Bradshaw, Samantha, and Philip N. Howard. 2019. "The Global Disinformation Order: 2019 Global Inventory of Organised Social Media Manipulation." Working Paper 2019.3, Project on Computational Propaganda, Oxford. https://demtech.oii.ox.ac.uk/research/posts/the-global-disinformation-order-2019-global-inventory-of-organised-social-media-manipulation/

Braun, Joshua A., John D. Coakley, and Emily West. 2019. "Activism, Advertising, and Far-Right Media: The Case of Sleeping Giants." *Media and Communication* 7, no. 4: 68–79. https://doi.org/10.17645/mac.v7i4.2280.

Bulger, Monica, and Patrick Davison. 2018. *The Promises, Challenges, and Futures of Media Literacy*. New York: Data and Society Research Institute. https://datasociety.net/library/the-promises-challenges-and-futures-of-media-literacy/.

Busemeyer, Marius R., and Kathleen Thelen. 2020. "Institutional Sources of Business Power." *World Politics* 72, no. 3: 448–480. https://doi.org/10.1017/S004388712000009X.

Caplan, Robyn, Joan Donovan, and Lauren Hanson. 2018. *Dead Reckoning: Navigating Content Moderation after Fake News*. New York: Data and Society Research Institute. https://datasociety.net/library/dead-reckoning/.

Cederberg, Gabriel. 2018. *Catching Swedish Phish: How Sweden Is Protecting Its 2018 Elections*. Cambridge, MA: Harvard Belfer Center. https://www.belfercenter.org/publication/catching-swedish-phish-how-sweden-protecting-its-2018-elections.

Clarke, Adele, and Susan Star. 2008. "The Social Worlds Framework: A Theory/Methods Package." In *The Handbook of Science and Technology Studies*, 113–137. Cambridge, MA: MIT Press.

Collins-Dexter, Brandi. 2020. "Canaries in the Coalmine: COVID-19 Misinformation and Black Communities." Harvard Shorenstein Center, Cambridge, MA. https://doi.org/10.37016/TASC-2020-01.

Conway, Maura. 2017. "Determining the Role of the Internet in Violent Extremism and Terrorism: Six Suggestions for Progressing Research." *Studies in Conflict & Terrorism* 40, no. 1: 77–98. https://doi.org/10.1080/1057610X.2016.1157408.

Corpus Ong, Jonathan. 2021. "Southeast Asia's Disinformation Crisis: Where the State Is the Biggest Bad Actor and Regulation Is a Bad Word." Items, Social Science Research Council. January 12. https://items.ssrc.org/disinformation-democracy-and-conflict-prevention/southeast-asias-disinformation-crisis-where-the-state-is-the-biggest-bad-actor-and-regulation-is-a-bad-word/.

Corpus Ong, Jonathan, and Jason Vincent Cabañes. 2018. *Architects of Networked Disinformation: Behind the Scenes of Troll Accounts and Fake News Production in the Philippines*. Leeds, UK, and Manila, Philippines: Newton Tech4Dev Network. https://doi.org/10.7275/2cq4-5396.

Corpus Ong, Jonathan, and Ross Tapsell. 2020. *Mitigating Disinformation in Southeast Asian Elections: Lessons from Indonesia, Philippines and Thailand*. Riga, Latvia: NATO Strategic

Communications Centre of Excellence. https://www.stratcomcoe.org/mitigating-disinformation-southeast-asian-elections.

Daniels, Jessie. 2018. "The Algorithmic Rise of the 'Alt-Right.'" *Contexts* 17, no. 1: 60–65. https://doi.org/10.1177/1536504218766547.

Deibert, Ronald. 2015. "Authoritarianism Goes Global: Cyberspace Under Siege." *Journal of Democracy* 26, no. 3: 64–78. https://doi.org/10.1353/jod.2015.0051.

Deibert, Ronald. 2020. *Reset—Reclaiming the Internet for Civil Society*. Toronto: House of Anansi Press. https://houseofanansi.com/products/reset.

Deibert, Ronald, and Rafal Rohozinski. 2008. "Good for Liberty, Bad for Security? Global Civil Society and the Securitization of the Internet." In *Access Denied: The Practice and Policy of Global Internet Filtering*, edited by Ronald Deibert, John Palfrey, Rafal Rohozinski, and Jonathan Zittrain, 123–149. Cambridge, MA: MIT Press. https://doi.org/10.7551/mitpress/7617.003.0009.

de La Chapelle, Bertrand, and Paul Fehlinger. 2016. "Jurisdiction on the Internet: From Legal Arms Race to Transnational Cooperation." GCIG Paper 28, Centre for International Governance Innovation and Chatham House, Waterloo, ON, Canada. https://www.cigionline.org/publications/jurisdiction-internet-legal-arms-race-transnational-cooperation.

Department of Justice. 2018. "Grand Jury Indicts Thirteen Russian Individuals and Three Russian Companies for Scheme to Interfere in the United States Political System." February 16. https://www.justice.gov/opa/pr/grand-jury-indicts-thirteen-russian-individuals-and-three-russian-companies-scheme-interfere.

Diakopoulos, Nicholas. 2016. "Accountability in Algorithmic Decision Making." *Communications of the ACM* 59, no. 2: 56–62. https://doi.org/10.1145/2844110.

Donovan, Joan. 2018. "After the #Keyword: Eliciting, Sustaining, and Coordinating Participation Across the Occupy Movement." *Social Media + Society* 4, no. 1. https://doi.org/10.1177/2056305117750720.

Donovan, Joan. 2019a. "Toward a Militant Ethnography of Infrastructure: Cybercartographies of Order, Scale, and Scope across the Occupy Movement." *Journal of Contemporary Ethnography* 48, no. 4: 482–509. https://doi.org/10.1177/0891241618792311.

Donovan, Joan. 2019b. "Navigating the Tech Stack: When, Where and How Should We Moderate Content?" Centre for International Governance Innovation. October 28. https://www.cigionline.org/articles/navigating-tech-stack-when-where-and-how-should-we-moderate-content.

Donovan, Joan. 2020a. "The Lifecycle of Media Manipulation." In *Verification Handbook for Disinformation and Media Manipulation*, edited by Craig Silverman. Maastricht, The Netherlands: European Journalism Centre. https://datajournalism.com/read/handbook/verification-3/investigating-disinformation-and-media-manipulation/the-lifecycle-of-media-manipulation.

Donovan, Joan. 2020b. "Redesigning Consent: Big Data, Bigger Risks." *Harvard Kennedy School Misinformation Review* 1, no. 1. https://doi.org/10.37016/mr-2020-006.

Donovan, Joan. 2020c. "Protest Misinformation Is Riding on the Success of Pandemic Hoaxes." *MIT Technology Review*, June 10. https://www.technologyreview.com/2020/06/10/1002934/protest-propaganda-is-riding-on-the-success-of-pandemic-hoaxes/.

Donovan, Joan, and Brian Friedberg. 2019. *Source Hacking: Media Manipulation in Practice*. New York: Data and Society Research Institute. https://datasociety.net/library/source-hacking-media-manipulation-in-practice/.

Donovan, Joan, Becca Lewis, and Brian Friedberg. 2018. "Parallel Ports. Sociotechnical Change from the Alt-Right to Alt-Tech." In *Post-Digital Cultures of the Far Right*, edited by Maik Fielitz and Nick Thurston, 49–66. Bielefeld, Germany: transcript Verlag. https://doi.org/10.14361/9783839446706-004.

Douek, Evelyn. 2020. "What Does "Coordinated Inauthentic Behavior" Actually Mean?" *Slate*, July 2. https://slate.com/technology/2020/07/coordinated-inauthentic-behavior-facebook-twitter.html.

Ess, Charles, and Mia Consalvo. 2011. "Introduction: What Is 'Internet Studies'?" In *The Handbook of Internet Studies*, edited by Mia Consalvo and Charles Ess, 1–8. Chichester, UK: John Wiley & Sons. https://doi.org/10.1002/9781444314861.ch.

Evans, Robert, and Jason Wilson. 2020. "The Boogaloo Movement Is Not What You Think." *Bellingcat*, May 27. https://www.bellingcat.com/news/2020/05/27/the-boogaloo-movement-is-not-what-you-think/.

Farkas, Johan, and Jannick Schou. 2019. *Post-Truth, Fake News and Democracy: Mapping the Politics of Falsehood*. London and New York: Routledge. https://www.routledge.com/Post-Truth-Fake-News-and-Democracy-Mapping-the-Politics-of-Falsehood/Farkas-Schou/p/book/9780367322175.

Farwell, James P. 2014. "The Media Strategy of ISIS." *Survival* 56, no. 6: 49–55. https://doi.org/10.1080/00396338.2014.985436.

Feldman, Anna, Giovanni Da San Martino, Alberto Barrón-Cedeño, Chris Brew, Chris Leberknight, and Preslav Nakov, eds. 2019. *Proceedings of the Second Workshop on Natural Language Processing for Internet Freedom: Censorship, Disinformation, and Propaganda*. Hong Kong, China: Association for Computational Linguistics. https://www.aclweb.org/anthology/D19-5000.

Franks, Mary Anne. 2019. "The Free Speech Black Hole: Can the Internet Escape the Gravitational Pull of the First Amendment?" Knight First Amendment Institute, Columbia University, New York. August 21. https://knightcolumbia.org/content/the-free-speech-black-hole-can-the-internet-escape-the-gravitational-pull-of-the-first-amendment.

Freelon, Deen, Michael Bossetta, Chris Wells, Josephine Lukito, Yiping Xia, and Kirsten Adams. 2020. "Black Trolls Matter: Racial and Ideological Asymmetries in Social Media Disinformation." *Social Science Computer Review*. https://doi.org/10.1177/0894439320914853.

Friedberg, Brian. 2020. "Investigative Digital Ethnography: Methods for Environmental Modeling." Media Manipulation Casebook, October 17. https://mediamanipulation.org/research/investigative-digital-ethnography-methods-environmental-modeling.

Friedberg, Brian, and Joan Donovan. 2019. "On the Internet, Nobody Knows You're a Bot: Pseudoanonymous Influence Operations and Networked Social Movements." *Journal of Design and Science* 6. https://doi.org/10.21428/7808da6b.45957184.

Funke, Daniel, and Daniela Flamini. 2019. "A Guide to Anti-Misinformation Actions around the World." Poynter, August 13. https://www.poynter.org/ifcn/anti-misinformation-actions/.

Gallup. 2020. *Techlash? America's Growing Concern with Major Technology Companies*. Miami, FL: Knight Foundation. https://knightfoundation.org/wp-content/uploads/2020/03/Gallup-Knight-Report-Techlash-Americas-Growing-Concern-with-Major-Tech-Companies-Final.pdf.

Gioe, David V., Michael S. Goodman, and Alicia Wanless. 2019. "Rebalancing Cybersecurity Imperatives: Patching the Social Layer." *Journal of Cyber Policy* 4, no. 1: 117–137. https://doi.org/10.1080/23738871.2019.1604780.

Goerzen, Matt, Elizabeth Anne Watkins, and Gabrielle Lim. 2019. "Entanglements and Exploits: Sociotechnical Security as an Analytic Framework." In *9th USENIX Workshop on Free and Open Communications on the Internet*, Santa Clara, CA. https://www.usenix.org/conference/foci19/presentation/goerzen.

Gorwa, Robert, and Douglas Guilbeault. 2018. "Unpacking the Social Media Bot: A Typology to Guide Research and Policy." *Policy & Internet* 12, no. 2: 225–248. https://doi.org/10.1002/poi3.184.

Groll, Elias, and Robbie Gramer. 2019. "With New Appointment, State Department Ramps up War against Foreign Propaganda." *Foreign Policy*, February 7. https://foreignpolicy.com/2019/02/07/with-new-appointment-state-department-ramps-up-war-against-foreign-propaganda/.

Hellman, Maria, and Charlotte Wagnsson. 2017. "How Can European States Respond to Russian Information Warfare? An Analytical Framework." *European Security* 26, no. 2: 153–170. https://doi.org/10.1080/09662839.2017.1294162.

Helmus, Todd C. 2018. *Russian Social Media Influence: Understanding Russian Propaganda in Eastern Europe*. Research Report RR-2237-OSD. Santa Monica, CA: RAND Corporation.

Howard, Philip N. 2018. "How Political Campaigns Weaponize Social Media Bots." *IEEE Spectrum*, October 18. https://spectrum.ieee.org/computing/software/how-political-campaigns-weaponize-social-media-bots.

Howard, Philip N. 2020. "The Science and Technology of Lie Machines." In *Lie Machines*, 1–28. New Haven, CT: Yale University Press. https://yalebooks.yale.edu/book/9780300250206/lie-machines.

Howard, Philip N., Bharath Ganesh, Dimitra Liotsiou, John Kelly, and Camille François. 2018. "The IRA and Political Polarization in the United States." Working Paper 2018.2. Project on Computational Propaganda, Oxford. https://demtech.oii.ox.ac.uk/wp-content/uploads/sites/93/2018/12/The-IRA-Social-Media-and-Political-Polarization.pdf.

Huang, Aaron. 2020. *Combatting and Defeating Chinese Propaganda and Disinformation: A Case Study of Taiwan's 2020 Elections*. Cambridge, MA: Harvard Belfer Center. https://www.belfercenter.org/publication/combatting-and-defeating-chinese-propaganda-and-disinformation-case-study-taiwans-2020.

Jack, Caroline. 2017. *Lexicon of Lies: Terms for Problematic Information*. New York: Data and Society Research Institute. https://datasociety.net/library/lexicon-of-lies/.

Jones, Marc Owen. 2019. "The Gulf Information War| Propaganda, Fake News, and Fake Trends: The Weaponization of Twitter Bots in the Gulf Crisis." *International Journal of Communication* 13: 27. https://ijoc.org/index.php/ijoc/article/view/8994.

Jowett, Garth S., and Victoria O'Donnell. 2015. *Propaganda and Persuasion*. 6th ed. Thousand Oaks, CA: SAGE Publications.

Kao, Jeff. 2017. "More than a Million Pro-Repeal Net Neutrality Comments Were Likely Faked." Hackernoon, November 22. https://hackernoon.com/more-than-a-million-pro-repeal-net-neutrality-comments-were-likely-faked-e9f0e3ed36a6.

Karpf, David. 2019. "On Digital Disinformation and Democratic Myths." MediaWell, Social Science Research Council, December 10. https://mediawell.ssrc.org/expert-reflections/on-digital-disinformation-and-democratic-myths/.

Kavanagh, Jennifer, and Michael D. Rich. 2018. *Truth Decay: A Threat to Policymaking and Democracy*. Santa Monica, CA: RAND Corporation.

Kim, Young Mie, Jordan Hsu, David Neiman, Colin Kou, Levi Bankston, Soo Yun Kim, et al. 2018. "The Stealth Media? Groups and Targets behind Divisive Issue Campaigns on

Facebook." *Political Communication* 35, no. 4: 515–541. https://doi.org/10.1080/10584609.2018.1476425.

Kovalev, Alexey. 2020. "It's so Hard to Find Good Help: Chinese Broadcasters Are Making Inroads in Russia, but Beijing Has Stumbled Due to a Shortage of Capable Propagandists." Meduza, July 28. https://meduza.io/en/feature/2020/07/28/it-s-so-hard-to-find-good-help.

Krafft, P. M., and Joan Donovan. 2020. "Disinformation by Design: The Use of Evidence Collages and Platform Filtering in a Media Manipulation Campaign." *Political Communication* 37, no. 2: 194–214. https://doi.org/10.1080/10584609.2019.1686094.

Lanoszka, Alexander. 2018. "Disinformation in International Politics." SSRN Scholarly Paper ID 3172349. https://doi.org/10.2139/ssrn.3172349.

Latour, Bruno. 1990. "Technology Is Society Made Durable." Supplement, *Sociological Review* 38, no. S1: 103–131. https://doi.org/10.1111/j.1467-954X.1990.tb03350.x.

Leber, Andrew, and Alexei Abrahams. 2019. "A Storm of Tweets: Social Media Manipulation During the Gulf Crisis." *Review of Middle East Studies* 53, no. 2: 241–258. https://doi.org/10.1017/rms.2019.45.

Lewis, Becca. 2018. *Alternative Influence: Broadcasting the Reactionary Right on YouTube.* New York: Data and Society Research Institute. https://datasociety.net/library/alternative-influence/.

Lewis, Becca, and Alice E. Marwick. 2017. *Media Manipulation and Disinformation Online.* New York: Data and Society Research Institute. https://datasociety.net/library/media-manipulation-and-disinfo-online/.

Libicki, Martin C. 2017. "The Convergence of Information Warfare." *Strategic Studies Quarterly* 11, no. 1: 49–65. https://www.jstor.org/stable/26271590.

Lim, Gabrielle. 2020a. *Securitize/Counter-Securitize: The Life and Death of Malaysia's Anti-Fake News Act.* New York: Data and Society Research Institute. https://datasociety.net/library/securitize-counter-securitize/.

Lim, Gabrielle. 2020b. "The Risks of Exaggerating Foreign Influence Operations and Disinformation." Centre for International Governance Innovation, August 7. https://www.cigionline.org/articles/risks-exaggerating-foreign-influence-operations-and-disinformation.

Lim, Gabrielle, Brian Friedberg, and Joan Donovan. 2020. "Three Ways to Counter Authoritarian Overreach During the Coronavirus Pandemic." *Nieman Reports*, April 22. https://niemanreports.org/articles/three-ways-to-counter-authoritarian-overreach-during-the-coronavirus-pandemic/.

Lim, Gabrielle, Etienne Maynier, John Scott-Railton, Alberto Fittarelli, Ned Moran, and Ron Deibert. 2019. "Burned after Reading: Endless Mayfly's Ephemeral Disinformation Campaign." Citizen Lab, University of Toronto, May 14. https://citizenlab.ca/2019/05/burned-after-reading-endless-mayflys-ephemeral-disinformation-campaign/.

Lin, Herbert, and Jaclyn Kerr. Forthcoming. "On Cyber-Enabled Information Warfare and Information Operations." In *Oxford Handbook of Cybersecurity*. Oxford: Oxford University Press. https://papers.ssrn.com/abstract=3015680.

Liptak, Kevin. 2020. "Trump Embraces QAnon Conspiracy Because 'They Like Me.' " CNN, August 19. https://www.cnn.com/2020/08/19/politics/donald-trump-qanon/index.html.

Livingstone, Sonia. 2005. "Critical Debates in Internet Studies: Reflections on an Emerging Field." In *Mass Media and Society*, edited by James Curran and Michael Gurevitch, 9–28. London: Sage.

Lyu, Siwei. 2020. "Deepfake Detection: Current Challenges and Next Steps." *2020 IEEE International Conference on Multimedia Expo Workshops (ICMEW)*, London, July 6–10. https://doi.org/10.1109/ICMEW46912.2020.9105991.

MacKinnon, Rebecca. 2011. "Liberation Technology: China's 'Networked Authoritarianism.'" *Journal of Democracy* 22, no. 2: 32–46. https://doi.org/10.1353/jod.2011.0033.

MacKinnon, Rebecca. 2012. *Consent of the Networked*. New York: Basic Books. https://consentofthenetworked.com/about/.

Marietta, Morgan, David C. Barker, and Todd Bowser. 2015. "Fact-Checking Polarized Politics: Does the Fact-Check Industry Provide Consistent Guidance on Disputed Realities?" *The Forum* 13, no. 4: 577–596. https://doi.org/10.1515/for-2015-0040.

Mazarr, Michael J., Abigail Casey, Alyssa Demus, Scott W. Harold, Luke J. Matthews, Nathan Beauchamp-Mustafaga, et al. 2019. *Hostile Social Manipulation: Present Realities and Emerging Trends*. Santa Monica, CA: Rand Corporation. https://doi.org/10.7249/RR2713.

McAdam, Doug. 1983. "Tactical Innovation and the Pace of Insurgency." *American Sociological Review* 48, no. 6: 735–754. https://doi.org/10.2307/2095322.

McCombie, Stephen, Allon J. Uhlmann, and Sarah Morrison. 2020. "The US 2016 Presidential Election & Russia's Troll Farms." *Intelligence and National Security* 35, no. 1: 95–114. https://doi.org/10.1080/02684527.2019.1673940.

Mchangama, Jacob, and Jonas Parello-Plesner. 2020. "Taiwan's Disinformation Solution." *The American Interest* (blog), February 6. https://www.the-american-interest.com/2020/02/06/taiwans-disinformation-solution/.

Media Manipulation Casebook. 2020a. "Definitions – Media Manipulation." https://mediamanipulation.org/definitions/media-manipulation.

Media Manipulation Casebook. 2020b. "Methods." https://mediamanipulation.org/methods.

Media Manipulation Casebook. 2020c. "Definitions – Networked Faction." https://mediamanipulation.org/definitions/networked-faction.

Monaco, Nicholas J. 2017. "Computational Propaganda in Taiwan: Where Digital Democracy Meets Automated Autocracy." Working Paper 2017.2. Project on Computational Propaganda, Oxford. http://comprop.oii.ox.ac.uk/wp-content/uploads/sites/89/2017/06/Comprop-Taiwan-2.pdf.

Monaco, Nicholas, and Carly Nyst. 2018. "Government Sponsored Trolling." Institute for the Future, Palo Alto, CA. https://www.iftf.org/statesponsoredtrolling.

Monaco, Nick, Melanie Smith, and Amy Studdart. 2020. *Detecting Digital Fingerprints: Tracing Chinese Disinformation in Taiwan*. Palo Alto, CA: Institute for the Future; New York: Graphika; Washington, DC: International Republican Institute. https://www.iftf.org/fileadmin/user_upload/downloads/ourwork/Detecting_Digital_Fingerprints_-_Tracing_Chinese_Disinformation_in_Taiwan.pdf.

Monterde, Arnau, and John Postill. 2014. "Mobile Ensembles: The Uses of Mobile Phones for Social Protest by Spain's Indignados." In *The Routledge Companion to Mobile Media*, edited by Larissa Hjorth and Gerard Goggin, 453–462. New York and London: Routledge. https://doi.org/10.4324/9780203434833-54.

Morris, Chris. 2019. "U.S. Government Declares Grindr a National Security Risk," *Fortune*, March 27. https://fortune.com/2019/03/27/grindr-security-risk-sale/.

Nadler, Anthony, Matthew Crain, and Joan Donovan. 2018. *Weaponizing the Digital Influence Machine*. New York: Data and Society Research Institute. https://datasociety.net/library/weaponizing-the-digital-influence-machine/.

Noble, Safiya Umoja. 2018. *Algorithms of Oppression: How Search Engines Reinforce Racism*. New York: New York University Press. https://nyupress.org/9781479837243/algorithms-of-oppression.

Open Technology Fund. 2019. "The Rise of Digital Authoritarianism in Egypt: Digital Expression Arrests from 2011-2019". https://public.opentech.fund/documents/EgyptReport V06.pdf.

Oshikawa, Ray, Jing Qian, and William Yang Wang. 2020. "A Survey on Natural Language Processing for Fake News Detection." In *Proceedings of the 12th Conference on Language Resources and Evaluation (LREC 2020)*, 6086–6093. Paris: European Language Resources Association.

Owen, Tess. 2020. "Discord Just Shut Down the Biggest 'Boogaloo' Server for Inciting Violence." *Vice*, June 25. https://www.vice.com/en_us/article/akzkep/discord-just-shut-down-the-biggest-boogaloo-server-for-inciting-violence.

Palfrey, John, and Jonathan Zittrain. 2008. "Internet Filtering: The Politics and Mechanisms of Control." In *Access Denied: The Practice and Policy of Global Internet Filtering*, edited by Ronald Deibert, John Palfrey, Rafal Rohozinski, and Jonathan Zittrain, 29–56. Cambridge, MA: MIT Press. https://doi.org/10.7551/mitpress/7617.003.0005.

Paris, Britt, and Joan Donovan. 2019. *Deepfakes and Cheap Fakes*. New York: Data and Society Research Institute. https://datasociety.net/wp-content/uploads/2019/09/DS_Deepfakes_Cheap_FakesFinal-1.pdf.

Parker, Ashley. 2020. "Trump and Allies Ratchet up Disinformation Efforts in Late Stage of Campaign." *Washington Post*, September 6. https://www.washingtonpost.com/politics/trump-disinformation-campaign/2020/09/06/f34f080a-eeca-11ea-a21a-0fbbe90cfd8c_story.html.

Pasquetto, Irene V., Briony Swire-Thompson, Michelle A. Amazeen, Fabrício Benevenuto, Nadia M. Brashier, Robert M. Bond, et al. 2020. "Tackling Misinformation: What Researchers Could Do with Social Media Data." *Harvard Kennedy School Misinformation Review* 1, no. 8. https://doi.org/10.37016/mr-2020-49.

Pennycook, Gordon, Adam Bear, Evan T. Collins, and David G. Rand. 2020. "The Implied Truth Effect: Attaching Warnings to a Subset of Fake News Headlines Increases Perceived Accuracy of Headlines Without Warnings." *Management Science* 66, no. 11. https://doi.org/10.1287/mnsc.2019.3478.

Perry, Bret. 2015. "Non-Linear Warfare in Ukraine: The Critical Role of Information Operations and Special Operations." *Small Wars Journal*, August. https://smallwarsjournal.com/jrnl/art/non-linear-warfare-in-ukraine-the-critical-role-of-information-operations-and-special-opera.

Pew Research Center. 2020. "Americans' Views of Government: Low Trust, but Some Positive Performance Ratings." September 14. https://www.pewresearch.org/politics/2020/09/14/americans-views-of-government-low-trust-but-some-positive-performance-ratings/.

Phillips, Whitney. 2018. *The Oxygen of Amplification*. New York: Data and Society Research Institute. https://datasociety.net/library/oxygen-of-amplification/.

Prier, Jarred. 2017. "Commanding the Trend: Social Media as Information Warfare." *Strategic Studies Quarterly* 11, no. 4: 55–85.

Reid, Alastair. 2019. "7 Key Takeaways on Information Disorder from #ONA19." First Draft, September 18. https://firstdraftnews.org:443/latest/7-key-takeaways-on-information-disorder-from-ona19/.

Repnikova, Maria, and Kecheng Fang. 2018. "Authoritarian Participatory Persuasion 2.0: Netizens as Thought Work Collaborators in China." *Journal of Contemporary China* 27, no. 113: 763–779. https://doi.org/10.1080/10670564.2018.1458063.

Repnikova, Maria, and Kecheng Fang. 2019. "Digital Media Experiments in China: 'Revolutionizing' Persuasion under Xi Jinping." *China Quarterly* 239: 679–701. https://doi.org/10.1017/S0305741019000316.

Reporters Without Borders. 2019. "RSF Explains Why Singapore's Anti-Fake News Bill Is Terrible." April 8. https://rsf.org/en/news/rsf-explains-why-singapores-anti-fake-news-bill-terrible.

Rid, Thomas. 2020. *Active Measures: The Secret History of Disinformation and Political Warfare*. New York: Farrar, Straus and Giroux. https://us.macmillan.com/activemeasures/thomasrid/9780374287269.

Roberts, Margaret E. 2020. *Censored: Distraction and Diversion inside China's Great Firewall*. Princeton, NJ: Princeton University Press. https://press.princeton.edu/books/hardcover/9780691178868/censored.

Roberts, Sarah T. 2019. *Behind the Screen: Content Moderation in the Shadows of Social Media*. New Haven, CT: Yale University Press. https://yalebooks.yale.edu/book/9780300235883/behind-screen.

Ruan, Lotus, Masashi Crete-Nishihata, Jeffrey Knockel, Ruohan Xiong, and Jakub Dalek. 2020. "The Intermingling of State and Private Companies: Analysing Censorship of the 19th National Communist Party Congress on WeChat." *China Quarterly* 245: 1–30. https://doi.org/10.1017/S0305741020000491.

Silverman, Craig, ed. 2020. *Verification Handbook for Disinformation and Media Manipulation*. Maastricht, The Netherlands: European Journalism Centre. https://datajournalism.com/read/handbook/verification-3.

Snegovaya, Maria. 2015. *Putin's Information Warfare In Ukraine: Soviet Origins Of Russia's Hybrid Warfare*. Institute for the Study of War.

Skopeliti, Clea, and Bethan John. 2020. "Coronavirus: How Are the Social Media Platforms Responding to the 'Infodemic'?" First Draft, March 19. https://firstdraftnews.org:443/latest/how-social-media-platforms-are-responding-to-the-coronavirus-infodemic/.

Star, Susan Leigh. 1999. "The Ethnography of Infrastructure." *American Behavioral Scientist* 43, no. 3: 377–391. https://doi.org/10.1177/00027649921955326.

Stevenson, Alexandra. 2018. "Soldiers in Facebook's War on Fake News Are Feeling Overrun." *New York Times*. October 9. https://www.nytimes.com/2018/10/09/business/facebook-philippines-rappler-fake-news.html.

Stewart, Leo G., Ahmer Arif, and Kate Starbird. 2018. "Examining Trolls and Polarization with a Retweet Network." In *Proceedings of Misinformation and Misbehavior Mining on the Web, Marina Del Rey, CA, USA (MIS2)*. New York: ACM. https://faculty.washington.edu/kstarbi/examining-trolls-polarization.pdf.

StratCom. n.d. "About Us." Accessed September 2, 2020. https://www.stratcomcoe.org/about-us.

Suárez-Serrato, Pablo, Margaret E. Roberts, Clayton Davis, and Filippo Menczer. 2016. "On the Influence of Social Bots in Online Protests." In *Social Informatics*, edited by Emma Spiro and Yong-Yeol Ahn, 269–278. Lecture Notes in Computer Science. Cham, Switzerland: Springer International Publishing. https://doi.org/10.1007/978-3-319-47874-6_19.

Sudworth, John. 2020. "Taiwan's Tsai Wins Second Presidential Term." BBC News, January 11. https://www.bbc.com/news/world-asia-51077553.

Torabi Asr, Fatemeh, and Maite Taboada. 2019. "Big Data and Quality Data for Fake News and Misinformation Detection." *Big Data & Society* 6, no. 1. https://doi.org/10.1177/2053951719843310.

United Nations Office of the High Commission of Human Rights. 2017. "Freedom of Expression Monitors Issue Joint Declaration on 'Fake News', Disinformation and Propaganda." March 3. https://www.ohchr.org/EN/NewsEvents/Pages/DisplayNews.aspx?NewsID=21287&LangID.

Wallis, Jacob, Tom Uren, Elise Thomas, Albert Zhang, Samantha Hoffman, Alexandra Pascoe, et al. 2020. "Retweeting through the Great Firewall." Australian Strategic Policy Institute. https://www.aspi.org.au/report/retweeting-through-great-firewall.

Walter, Nathan, John J. Brooks, Camille J. Saucier, and Sapna Suresh. Forthcoming. "Evaluating the Impact of Attempts to Correct Health Misinformation on Social Media: A Meta-Analysis." *Health Communication*. Published ahead of print August 6, 2020. https://doi.org/10.1080/10410236.2020.1794553.

Walter, Nathan, and Sheila T. Murphy. 2018. "How to Unring the Bell: A Meta-Analytic Approach to Correction of Misinformation." *Communication Monographs* 85, no. 3: 423–441. https://doi.org/10.1080/03637751.2018.1467564.

Walton, Calder. 2019. "Spies, Election Meddling, and Disinformation: Past and Present." *Brown Journal of World Affairs* 26, no. 1. http://bjwa.brown.edu/26-1/spies-election-meddling-and-disinformation-past-and-present/.

Wardle, Claire. 2017. "Fake news. It's complicated." First Draft, February 16. https://firstdraftnews.org/latest/fake-news-complicated/.

Wong, Julia Carrie. 2020. "Down the Rabbit Hole: How QAnon Conspiracies Thrive on Facebook." *The Guardian*, June 25. http://www.theguardian.com/technology/2020/jun/25/qanon-facebook-conspiracy-theories-algorithm.

Zannettou, Savvas, Tristan Caulfield, Jeremy Blackburn, Emiliano De Cristofaro, Michael Sirivianos, Gianluca Stringhini, et al. 2018. "On the Origins of Memes by Means of Fringe Web Communities." In *IMC '18: Proceedings of the Internet Measurement Conference 2018*, 188–202. New York: ACM. https://doi.org/10.1145/3278532.3278550.

CHAPTER 30

GENDER, DIGITAL TOXICITY, AND POLITICAL VOICE ONLINE

SARAH SOBIERAJ

PUBLIC political discussions happen in face-to-face contexts—in community centers when participants address neighborhood issues, and in the impassioned exchanges transpiring during rallies and teach-ins, for example—but social networking sites, comment sections, chat rooms, and other participatory media have become integral venues for public exchanges about social and political issues. Their interactive features have helped users develop a complex and fluid network of rich, if imperfect, digital public spheres, reducing many barriers to participation in political discourse (Benkler 2008; Dahlberg 2001; Papacharissi 2002). Conventional media included participatory elements, such as newspaper op-ed pages and radio call-in programs (Schudson 1981, 1995; Razlogova 2011; Herbst 1995), but newer information communication technologies (ICTs) have increased the number of spaces where people engage in public discussion (Benkler 2008; boyd 2010) and the range of people who are able to contribute (Jenkins 2006; Gillmor 2006; Bruns 2008). What's more, the varied rules and norms existing across and within digital venues mean that discriminatory standards used to police acceptable styles of communication, topics of discussion, and forms of evidence are no longer sufficient to silence those who have historically been denied participation in mainstream publics (Benhabib 1996; Young 2002; Mansbridge 1990; Fraser 1990).

These expansions of the public sphere—in the number of venues, range of participants, and modes of communication—are well documented in the scholarly literature (e.g., Lee 2017; Schmitz et al. 2020; Eckert and Chadha 2013; Kuo 2018; Xing 2012; Choi and Cho 2017; Tufekci 2017). The work of communications scholars Sarah Jackson and Brooke Foucault Welles serves as one such example. Jackson and Welles combine large-scale network analysis with qualitative discourse analysis to map patterns of impact and influence in Twitter discussions of racialized police violence in the United

States (2015, 2016). Their analysis of the #myNYPD public relations hashtag, its co-optation by activists opposing police brutality, and the mainstream media attention it garnered demonstrates that the anchors, sources, and reporters shaping conventional news discourse were largely White and male, while the voices amplified online are far more diverse. These "crowdsourced elites" include people of color and White women without elite status (Jackson and Welles 2015, 948). Similarly, after Darren Wilson, a White police officer, fatally shot Michael Brown, a Black teenager, their analysis of related Twitter discussion showed that having official expertise or a position of authority is not required to shape public discourse. They write, "African-Americans, women, and young people, including several members of Michael Brown's working-class, African-American community, were particularly influential and succeeded in defining the terms of debate despite their historical exclusion from the American public sphere" (2016, 412).

It is important to note, however, that although participatory ICTs generate opportunities for the marginalized and oppressed, these tools are also often used to oppress. (Daniels 2009; Massanari 2020; Miller-Idriss 2020; Feshami 2021; Caren, Jowers, and Gaby 2012; Farkas, Schou, and Neumayer 2018; Dignam and Rohlinger 2019). And, as those from historically underrepresented groups become more influential in public discourse, their participation changes political life for those accustomed to the center. People used to being heard and taken seriously may feel unsettled by the issues raised, the views expressed, and/or the response to their input (Flood 2019; Massanari 2020; Sobieraj 2018). This destabilization of the norms governing who gets to participate and who is taken seriously has been met with resistance. Perhaps the most visible resistance has come in the form of identity-based attacks online against women, particularly women from devalued groups (e.g., based on race, religion, class, sexual orientation, national origin, and ability), those who participate in discourses previously dominated by men (e.g., science, politics, technology), and those who are openly feminist or otherwise perceived as noncompliant with traditional gender roles (Sobieraj 2018, 2020).

Many of sociology's key concerns—power, inequality, culture, oppression, identity, and resistance—are central to these transitions, but thus far, few sociologists have contributed to the burgeoning research on related phenomena. Our insights are needed. This chapter brings together key findings from this rapidly expanding empirical literature to shed light on women's use of digital publics as political spaces as well as the abuse and harassment they face in the process. Taken together, the research demonstrates that while women capitalize on digital publics as spaces to exercise their political voice and gain visibility, inequality among women persists, shaping whose ideas are centered and who experiences resistance. The scholarly literature further suggests that attackers use women's identities as weapons in an attempt to make speaking up intimidating and to devalue the contributions of those who do so. Critically, there is mounting evidence that identity-based attacks negatively impact women's participation and the broader information landscape, eroding the democratic potential of digital publics. The chapter closes by identifying areas where sociological interventions can advance the field.

Tools Women Use: Claiming Space and Building Community

It has been over 30 years since philosopher Nancy Fraser (1990) challenged the Habermasian conception of the singular public sphere, suggesting that parallel public spheres emerged alongside the bourgeois public sphere as places of resistance where the marginalized could connect, develop a shared vocabulary, and strategize about how to bring their concerns to a broader audience (proffering women's organizations in the 1800s as examples). Today, these publics form by using indexing affordances such as hashtags (e.g., Twitter and TikTok), group/community building features (e.g., Facebook and reddit), and comment sections (e.g., on blogs and vlogs).

A body of interdisciplinary research shows that a wide array of women use digital platforms to create space to discuss social and political concerns, build community, and advocate for change (Altoaimy 2018; Radsch and Khamis 2013; Jackson and Banaszczyk 2016; Crossley 2017; Williams and Gonlin 2017; Jackson, Bailey, and Welles 2018). For example, sociologist Allison Dahl Crossley's (2015, 2017) analysis of feminist activism on college campuses in the United States found that Facebook groups and blogs served as critical online feminist communities that proved vital to the expansion and development of feminist networks and supported mobilization both on- and offline. In some cases, women create digital publics to circumvent the dangers presented by face-to-face publics. For example, linguist Lama Altoaimy analyzed Arabic tweets in the debate surrounding women's right to drive in Saudi Arabia and found women challenging the religious establishment, talking openly about the victimization of women by hired drivers (something rarely discussed publicly because of cultural views relating to honor and shame), and arguing for women's independence. Altoaimy concluded, "For Saudi Arabian women, social media platforms such as Twitter provide a unique space to express opinions and highlight areas of concern in a way that they are unable to in any other public sphere" (2018, 1). In-depth interviews with avid citizen journalists using vlogs, blogs, and Facebook during the Arab Spring uprisings led to similar findings: "Several Libyan and Yemeni women said that cyberactivism empowered them to be active in a way they could not be in the physical world" (Radsch and Khamis 2013, 884). Similarly, Jackson, Bailey, and Welles (2018) find trans women using hashtags to build public space to connect where they discuss their unique experiences and concerns on Twitter, a practice that could be high-risk in physical publics due to anti-trans discrimination and violence.

The digital publics women build reflect the inequalities that exist in offline publics, including those *among* women (Nanditha 2021; Patil and Puri 2021; Daniels 2015; Onwuachi-Willig 2018; Loken 2014). One study of a US-based feminist Facebook group found that facilitators intended to build a safe space for women and nonbinary people to discuss concerns that are stifled by stigma and harassment in other contexts.

Yet, the technological and cultural context—including the lack of anonymity on Facebook and the norm that participants be conversant in feminist vocabulary—coupled with top-down decisions about membership and moderation, enhanced safety for some (e.g., cis women, women with more education) at the expense of others (Clark-Parsons 2018).

The research shows that some women respond to these inequalities by using digital publics to command space for marginalized voices *within* these new publics. For example, Jackson and Banaszcyk (2016) found that women of color on Twitter used the hashtags #YesAllWhiteWomen and #YesAllWomen to negotiate complex issues of intersectional power and privilege within a broader feminist counterpublic dominated by White women. Similarly, the #SayHerName campaign that emerged in the United States was used to make police violence against Black cisgender and transgender women visible in the context of a movement focused predominantly on the experiences of Black cisgender men (Brown et al. 2017). In another example, digital critiques of carceral feminism driven by women of color within feminist counterpublics have begun to shift political demands and social interventions related to gender-based intimidation and violence (Abdelmonem 2020; Terwiel 2020; Kim 2020; Rentschler 2017).

WOMEN, SOCIAL MEDIA, AND POLITICAL POWER

Women use the digital publics they build in a number of political capacities. Those who are devalued or ignored in other contexts often enter digital publics fighting to make their lived experiences visible. For example, survivors of sexual violence and abuse have used hashtags such as #MeToo, #NiUnaMenos, and #8M to share their stories and expose the prevalence of gender-based violence (Suk et al. 2021; Belotti, Comunello, and Corradi 2021; Mendes 2019; Keller, Mendes, and Ringrose 2018; Mondragon et al. 2021; Nuñez Puente, D'Antonio Maceiras, and Fernández Romero 2021; Lokot 2018). Women in a number of countries—Argentina, Australia, India, Ireland, Poland, South Korea, Ukraine, and the United States, to name a few—have also used personal testimonies in an effort to destigmatize abortion (Baird and Millar 2019; Ralph 2021). The fight for visibility also includes women struggling *over* (rather than *for*) representation. Pennington (2018) found Muslim women using the #Muslimwomensday hashtag to resist narrow stereotypes. Users highlighted demographic and lifestyle diversity among Muslim women through personal stories and selfies, making a pointed effort to broaden existing ideas about what it means to be a Muslim woman. In another example of negotiating stereotypes, Williams and Gonlin (2017) analyzed discourse surrounding a US television series with a Black female star and producer. Fans built a network of like-others who Tweeted as they watched, debating the accuracy and implications of the depictions of the protagonist and, through her, Black Womanhood. By cheering and challenging these representations with other fans, in front of (and often @mentioning) the show's producers and actors, the participants shaped how the series was interpreted and likely the ongoing work of its creators. Some efforts combine visibility politics and representational struggles, such as those behind the #WhyIStayed hashtag, which simultaneously sought to put a face on intimate partner violence and fight victim-blaming (Linabary, Corple, and Cooky 2020).

Fighting for visibility is not without complications. Nuñez Puente, D'Antonio Maceras, and Hernández Romero (2021) analyzed over 20,000 messages containing hashtags (#8M and #NiUnaMenos) related to gender-based violence in Spain and found that as hashtag use proliferated (leaving activist control), the content was often diluted (even by supportive sharers) and decoupled from the original sources. Similarly, activists with a UK rape crisis organization appreciated the way online networks facilitate rapid dissemination of information but lamented how easily they lost control of its meaning (Edwards, Philip, and Gerrard 2020). Ince, Rojas, and David (2017) refer to the shift in intended meaning that occurs when outsiders circulate movement content as distributed framing. At times, this is subversive "hijacking" or "spoiling," as several studies have shown (Jackson and Welles 2015; Kosenko, Winderman, and Pugh 2019); but distributed framing can also happen inadvertently, as when hashtags "drift"—becoming invoked in the context of more diverse phenomena (Booten 2016). Even when frames remain intact, visibility won via hashtags can be fleeting unless the efforts capture the attention of the mainstream (Olson 2016).

Scholars of social movements and political communication are still unpacking the relationship between on- and offline political engagement and activism (see Rohlinger, this volume), but several studies suggest that women's digital work can generate political action in other contexts (Crossley 2015; Jha 2017; Boling 2020; Olson 2016; Suk et al. 2021). Women's digital activism has prompted offline activity in a variety of cases including the #BringBackOurGirls campaign against Boko Haram and the Nigerian government, the meme-driven outcry after US Senator Elizabeth Warren "persisted" in reading aloud a letter from Coretta Scott King against the instruction of Senator Mitch McConnell, and the #WhyLoiter campaign that encouraged women in India to claim public space (Boling 2020; Olson 2016; Jha 2017).

Often, synergy between online publics and legacy media help with amplification and offline organizing. Radsch and Khamis (2013), for example, show that during the Arab Spring young female activists, citizen journalists, and bloggers leveraged social media and global news outlets to project their views beyond the region by creating content for news outreach. This was especially significant as there were few nonstate media outlets to carry the news, with the exception of Egypt. This synergy is likely to continue; research suggests that journalists turn to digital counterpublics (such as Black Twitter) for content (Freelon et al. 2018). For example, journalists in many countries, including the United States, Japan, India, and Australia, covered the #MeToo movement extensively (De Benedictis, Orgad, and Rottenberg 2019; Starkey et al. 2019).

With or without a boost from mainstream news organizations, research suggests that digital publics can transform public conversations about political and social issues. The right messaging at the right cultural moment can make an impact (Belotti, Comunello, and Corradi 2021; Olson 2016; Puente, Maceiras, and Romero 2021; Mondragon et al. 2020). One lexical analysis of Twitter discourse related to the infamous *La Manada* gang rape in Spain documents the influence of feminist discourses online. The study mapped the evolution of the discussion, including the development of diverging narratives and trolling behaviors. The authors tracked competing understandings of the rape and their shift over time and noted the way online discussion of the case brought forth several related debates that had previously been tackled almost exclusively in feminist environments. Ultimately, online discourse played an active part in influencing how the event was interpreted (Mondragon et al. 2020).

Taken together, then, participation in digital publics is crucial for women. It allows them to fight for visibility and influence vis-à-vis mainstream political discourse and within counterpublics that center the voices and concerns of more privileged women. For (some of) the most marginalized women, ICTs provide access to participation that would be dangerous in face-to-face venues. This discursive work can be quite influential in helping to build community, shape interpretations of social issues, attract the attention of news workers, and prompt offline mobilization. And yet, digital life is not open to all. Many are unable to participate because they lack access and/or face pronounced risk of social and or political sanctions (Zarkov and Davis 2018). Some with access and security confront logistical or psychological barriers (Mendes 2019). Even those with the luxury of participating may feel pressed out by resistance in the form of identity-based attacks and harassment.

The Landscape of Digital Abuse and Harassment

To illuminate the role of digital hostility in the lives of women who are overtly political, such as activists, elected officials, advocates, and journalists, I begin by reviewing the literature on digital abuse and harassment of women more generally. Please note that here I examine the research on digital hostility and hate coming from strangers—or at least those who appear to be strangers—rather than interpersonal cruelty meted out by people we know (see, e.g., Henry and Powell 2015). Please also note that while there is plenty of critical feedback and rudeness online, this review attends only to more hateful, frightening, ad hominem, and demeaning content. This includes tactics such as identity-based attacks, threats of violence, *doxxing* (the disclosure of private information without consent), hate speech, defamatory disinformation, and coordinated attacks (in which the target receives an onslaught of messages). At times this can be hard to discern, as some of the research cited here uses the term "incivility"—which many associate with impoliteness—and operationalizes it in such a way as to capture hate speech, identity-based attacks, etc.[1]

Many studies have attempted to gauge the volume of online abuse, but the available information is incomplete and unable to adequately assess its prevalence. Understandably so. Digital attacks are delivered in many formats (e.g., text, photo, video), in numerous languages, across a myriad of platforms (with little incentive for transparency), and often in password-protected spaces (e.g., direct messaging, email). These realities create research roadblocks at every turn. In their effort to review existing statistics for the United Kingdom, Vidgen, Margetts, and Harris lamented, "Appropriate statistics are difficult to find and, in many cases, are not provided with the necessary contextual information to fully interpret them. For instance, some of the big platforms share how much abusive content they have removed—but not how much content they host in total" (2019, 5). Even with unfettered access, interpretive struggles would remain; cultural and linguistic outsiders are rarely able to understand the content or context well enough to decode its meaning or to distinguish playful in-group content (e.g., culturally intimate humor) from hateful speech.

In the context of these constraints, two dominant research strategies emerge from academic and nongovernment organization–driven research. First, a number of researchers use content-analytic snapshots of publicly visible abuse from select platforms and examine a subset of digital toxicity (e.g., Islamophobic content) or the treatment of a subset of targets (e.g., political leaders) (Amnesty International 2018; Lingiardi et al. 2020; Sobieraj and Merchant forthcoming). Second, there are a number of survey-based approaches that ask respondents, most often from North America, Europe, or Australia, to self-report experiences with related content (Vogels 2021; Hawdon, Oksanen, and Räsänen 2017; Pacheco and Melhuish 2018; Kantar Media 2018). Even cumulatively, this data does little to paint a complete picture. The most comprehensive data comes from a team organized by Google research, which used surveys to measure online abuse experiences in 22 countries.[2] Of their respondents, 48% report having personally experienced some form of online abuse, and 25% report having personally experienced at least one form of "severe" online abuse (such as being physically threatened or impersonated) (Thomas et al. 2021, 8). Because the measures encompass a broad array of digital abuse, not only that from strangers, even these comparative data are less than ideal for assessing the question at hand.

While the big picture remains elusive, the extant literature offers many insights into the characteristics of digital hate and harassment. Most notably, it indicates that our social locations shape who is attacked who does the attacking. Lashing out online is often framed as an individual proclivity linked to mood, morality, or personality; but perpetrators are more likely to be male (Akhtar and Morrison 2019; Sest and March 2017; Henry, Flynn, and Powell 2019). What's more, online hostility can be linked to digital micro-publics organized around and supportive of misogyny, homophobia, and racialized resentment (Banet-Weiser and Miltner 2016; Bratich and Banet-Weiser 2019; Lumsden 2019; Marwick and Caplan 2018; Marwick and Lewis 2015; Massanari 2017; Jones, Trott, and Wright 2020), as well as White male rage (Ortiz 2020; Lamerichs et al. 2018; Holt, Freilich, and Chermak 2020; Daniels 2009). Some women lob digital attacks at other women but not in the way that men do (Levey 2018).

In terms of who is targeted, there is evidence that those from racial and ethnic minority groups receive a disproportionate amount of abuse (Vidgen, Margetts, and Harris 2019; Gardiner 2018; Pacheco and Melhuish 2018; Gray 2014), as do those from sexual and gender minorities (Pacheco and Melhuish 2018; Vogels 2021; Haslop, O'Rourke, and Southern 2021; Thomas et al. 2021), and religious minority groups (Luqiu and Yang 2020; Zannettou et al. 2020). Recent research also indicates that people with disabilities are targeted (Vidgen, Margetts, and Harris 2019). But the largest body of empirical work focuses on attacks against women online. Women are more likely than men to experience severe and sustained digital hostility (Broadband Commission for Digital Development Working Group on Broadband and Gender 2015; Citron 2009a, 2014; Henry, Flynn, and Powell 2019; Gardiner 2018; Duggan 2014; Special Rapporteur on Violence against Women 2018). Where counterfindings exist, a closer look often provides context. For example, Nadim and Fladmoe's (2021, 250) analysis of two waves of TNS Gallup Norway survey data (from 2013 and 2016) concluded that more men than women have experienced online harassment. However, the 2013 survey asked whether people had received "unpleasant or patronizing comments," which are more akin to incivility than to digital hate. Meanwhile, the 2016 survey asked about experiences with "hate speech in social media." The authors note that in the Norwegian context "hate speech" connotes pronounced negativity, rather than identity-based attacks as it does in most North American and European contexts, and may have shaped the results.

Attending to "just gender," however, misses the full story (Hackworth 2018). The interlocking systems of inequality and power—intersectional oppression (Crenshaw 1989)—that exist offline are reflected in the landscape of digital abuse. Women disadvantaged along multiple axes of inequality—race, religion, class, sexual orientation, and so on—endure more extensive and complex forms of hostility (Gray 2014; Femlee, Rodis, and Francisco 2018; Francisco and Felmlee 2021; Sobieraj 2020; Dhrodia 2018). The abuse may even be more damaging. My in-depth interviews with women who received digital attacks suggest that the hate directed at women of color is often more difficult to deflect than that received by White women. This is, in part, because the attacks regularly draw on deeply entrenched racial and ethnic stereotypes, lending them an air of manufactured plausibility. In this way, the option to ignore online attacks as a coping strategy is more readily available to White women, especially those with class-based markers of respectability (e.g., a high-status career) (Sobieraj 2020, 92–98). This propensity to incorporate existing stereotypes into the abuse speaks to another pattern: the way the identities of those under fire are weaponized.

IDENTITY-BASED ATTACKS AGAINST WOMEN ONLINE

Attacks against women online often intimate that their very identities make them unacceptable participants in public debate; Rather than taking issue with women's ideas or actions, attributes such as race, gender, ethnicity, religion, sexual orientation, and class often form the central basis for condemnation (Sobieraj 2020). The content flung at women includes, for example, threats of sexual violence, gendered epithets (e.g., "cunt"), gender-linked stereotypes (e.g., women as overly emotional), belittling tropes (e.g., the nagging shrew), unsolicited and demeaning commentary on physical appearance and/or presumed sexual behavior, and pornographic images altered to objectify and demean the target (e.g., Dhrodia 2018; Jane 2014a, 2014b; Levey 2018; Pain and Chen 2019; Vera-Gray 2017; Citron 2014; Sills et al. 2016; Sobieraj 2020). The implication is that the target is a woman and, therefore, has no value or that she is the *kind* of woman (e.g., a whore, a ditz, "unfuckable") who has no value (Sobieraj 2018, 2020).

For women outside the dominant group, the venom is pointedly intersectional; in addition to gender-linked toxicity, these women are confronted with abuse linked to their other devalued statuses (e.g., racialized, ableist, etc.), as well as abuse that encapsulates multiple axes of oppression (Sobieraj 2020; Femlee, Rodis, and Francisco 2018; Wagner 2020; Kuperberg 2021; Dhrodia 2018). In one study, Femlee, Rodis, and Francisco (2018) found that tweets containing the word "bitch," which were directed at Black, Asian, and Latinx women, included pronounced patterns of racialized misogyny that served to reinforce negative racial and gender stereotypes. For example, attacks lobbed at Asian women were exoticizing, were sexualizing, and invoked stereotypes of submissiveness. Similarly, Wagner (2020) found that "gendertrolling" of Canadian women doing political work was replete with racism, homophobia, and anti-Muslim hate when directed at people from those groups.

The emphasis on identity lends digital attacks a peculiar generic quality; Emma Jane has described this lingua franca—in "horror and humor" (2018b, 663)—as "rapeglish":

> An emerging yet increasingly dominant online dialect whose signal characteristic is graphic and sexually violent imagery. Often accompanied by: accusations that female recipients are overweight, unattractive, and acceptably promiscuous; all-caps demands for intimate images; and strident denials that there is any misogyny on the internet whatsoever.
>
> (Jane 2017)

Emma Jane collaborated with Nicole Vincent (2017) to build the Random Rape Threat Generator (RRTG). The RRTG website illustrates the formulaic nature of the abuse by allowing visitors to press "play," which prompts a computer program to shuffle and remix excerpts from actual threats of sexual violence (from Jane's research archive) into a fresh, new rape threat. The data included in the generator does not, unfortunately, reflect the intersectional attacks just described, but the point remains: RRTGs *could* be constructed with the content from abuse directed at Black women, Muslim women, etc.; and its repetitive attributes would be apparent.

This rubberstamp quality, I have argued elsewhere, is a critical clue to understanding attacks against women online. It tells us that although a given identity-based attack might look and feel deeply personal, the rage is structural; it reflects hostility toward the speaker as a *kind* of person, more than as a *particular* person. The rape threats, racism, ableism, and anti-Muslim sentiment are part of the struggle to control who will be allowed to hold sway in public discourse, something that ICTs have made less certain. Recognizing this as patterned resistance to inclusion illuminates the uneven distribution of abuse established in the empirical literature, by helping explain why attackers are so vicious to destabilizers: women from historically devalued groups (e.g., women of color, trans women), women speaking in or about male-dominated arenas (e.g., science, technology, politics, sports), and women perceived as feminist or otherwise noncompliant to traditional gender norms (e.g., those in positions of power, those unashamed of enjoying sex). These women are seen as threatening and/or as being particularly out of line when they lay claim to space or ask to be heard (Sobieraj 2018, 2019, 2020). This makes sense given the history of trolling, which emerged "as a form of boundary maintenance that served to distinguish communities of self-identified online insiders ... and to drive outsiders away from their spaces" (Graham 2019, 2029).

What Does This Mean for Women in the Political Arena?

Activists and politicians use social media to speak directly to the public, build supporters' enthusiasm, shape public opinion, influence the agenda, organize supporters, and mobilize donors and voters (Earl et al. 2013; Karpf 2012, 2016; Kreiss 2012; Stromer-Galley 2019; Tromble 2018; Tufekci 2017). But women's political voice and visibility come with disproportionate risk (Akhtar and Morrison 2019; Collignon and Rüdig 2020; Gardiner 2018; Mendes, Ringrose, and Keller 2018; Oates et al. 2019; Rossini, Stromer-Galley, and Zhang 2021; Sobieraj 2019; Sobieraj and Merchant forthcoming). Collignon and Rüdig (2020) used the Representative Audit of Britain to examine the intimidation and harassment of parliamentary candidates and office holders in the United Kingdom. They found that women are harassed and threatened on- and offline more than men and that the most frequent abuse comes via social media. The situation is most dire for young, higher-profile candidates. Rheault, Rayment, and Muslan (2019) also noted the price of female visibility. They predicted the incivility (broadly defined to include extreme incivility such as threats and hate speech) of over 2 million tweets directed at politicians in Canada and the United States. They found that while female politicians with little visibility fare well relative to men, those who are more visible are more heavily targeted than their male counterparts. An artificial intelligence analysis of Twitter conversations about Democratic primary candidates in the US 2020 presidential election found that the dominant narratives about the top three female candidates focused on their character and were "overwhelmingly negative," while those for the top two male candidates were positive and not about their personal qualities (Oates et al. 2019, 13). In keeping with research on digital attacks more generally, the burden is unevenly distributed among women. The Inter-Parliamentary Union's mixed-method study of digital sexism, harassment, and violence against 55 female parliamentarians from around the world (18 African, 15 European, 10 Asian-Pacific, 8 North, Central, and South American, 4 Arab) identified pronounced misogyny delivered via social media and found the abuse to be particularly severe against women who are young, members of a minority group, and/or members of an opposition party (Inter-Parliamentary Union 2016).

As with digital hostility more broadly, attacks against politically vocal women weaponize their identities. Esposito and Zollo (2021, 62–68) conducted a multi-method analysis of the 75 most viewed YouTube videos (and their 113,084 threaded comments) appearing in search queries linked to the names of the five most targeted female members of Parliament (MP) in the United Kingdom (as determined by Amnesty International). They found gender to be central, with extensive body and appearance shaming, gender stereotyping, attempts to disqualify often in the context of appearance-related commentary ("Jess Philips: tits bigger than her brain"), moral attacks (especially on the grounds of promiscuity), and threats of violence (often sexual in nature). Indian women's rights activist and politician Kavita Krishnan described her experiences in an interview: "These trolls ... they are going after me regularly, routinely, for my skin color, for my looks, telling me I'm not worth raping, what kind of torture and rape I should be subjected to, telling me what kind of men I should be sleeping with ... and on and on and on" (Mackintosh and Gupta 2021). Similarly, interviews with female journalists from five countries found that when journalists engage with their audiences online (as their employers often require), they are inundated with "sexist comments that criticize, attack, marginalize, stereotype, or threaten them based on their gender or sexuality. Often, criticism of their work is framed as misogynistic attacks and, sometimes, even involves [threats of] sexual violence" (Chen et al. 2020, 878). Many high-profile women in politics have had attackers try to discredit and humiliate them by circulating falsified nude and/or sexualized images as part of abuse campaigns, including Rwandan activist and former presidential candidate Diane Shima Rwigara, Ukrainian MP Svitlana Zalishchuk, former president of Croatia Kolinda Grabar-Kitarovic, Swedish climate activist Greta Thunberg, former parliamentary candidate Intidhar Jassim of Iraq, and US Representative Alexandria Ocasio-Cortez (Busari and Idowu 2017; Goldberg 2021; Ohlheiser 2019; Tarawnah 2020). When examined, the backlash tends to be intersectional in nature. In her work on Muslim and Jewish politicians, Kuperberg (2021) noted that multiply marginalized politicians contend with both sexist and racist treatment, which attempts to "render women incompetent using racist disloyalty tropes as well as to render women invisible by invalidating their testimonies of abuse" (p. 100). Similarly, Jankowicz et al. (2021) note that social media narratives about female politicians include an abundance of abusive racist and transphobic content. Such identity-focused attacks against women in the political arena have been found in numerous countries, including Chile, Germany, India, Japan, Pakistan, Taiwan, South Africa, Spain, the United States, and Zimbabwe (Ahmad, Hafeez, and Shahbaz 2020; Barboni and Brooks 2018; Chen et al. 2020; Fuchs and Schäfer 2020; Mertens et al. 2019; Mondragon et al. 2021; Ncube and Yemurai 2020; Southern and Harmer 2019).

Although most scholarship notes the disproportionate amount of online abuse directed at political women and its perseveration on their identities, Tromble and Koole (2020) offer a counterfinding. Their comparative, mixed-method analysis of tweets directed at members of the lower houses of Parliament and Congress in the Netherlands, the United Kingdom, and the United States found that while women received less "attention" on Twitter (roughly 25% fewer @mentions), there was no statistically significant difference in the tone of tweets directed at male versus female politicians. What's more, they find that "there do not appear to be any significant patterns that distinguish the types of negative messages targeting men and women across all three countries, and the number of explicitly sexist remarks directed at women is remarkably low" (p. 193). Given the way their data departs from other research, it would be worthwhile to replicate the research and/or to investigate rival explanations—for example, whether hostility directed at politicians on Twitter has become more gendered since the data was collected in 2013. There is some indication that online social media abuse of political figures transformed since 2010. Akhtar and Morrison (2019) surveyed 181 UK MPs about their experiences with online social media abuse and found that 100% of respondents, regardless of gender, reported some form of abuse (defamatory, racial, sexual, religious, or politically grounded), a striking 10-fold increase since 2010. Perhaps the substance of the hostility has changed in addition to its volume.

The Costs of Identity-Based Attacks against Women Online

Many women who have been targeted report psychological, economic, professional, political, and emotional effects (Barak 2005; Bates 2017; Citron 2014; Jane 2018a; Sobieraj 2020; Vakhitova et al. 2021; Vera-Gray 2017). Feminist activist and author Caroline Criado-Perez, who faced an onslaught of misogynistic abuse and threats after campaigning to diversify representation on Bank of England banknotes, reflected on her experience:

> The impact of all this on my life has been dramatic. When it was at its height I struggled to eat, to sleep, to work. I lost about half a stone in a matter of days. I was exhausted and weighed down by carrying these vivid images, this tidal wave of hate around with me wherever I went . . . . The psychological fall-out is still unravelling. I feel like I'm walking around like a timer about to explode; I'm functioning at just under boiling point—and it takes so little to make me cry—or to make me scream.
>
> (Criado-Perez 2013)

She is one of many politically vocal women who have been forced to leave their homes in order to feel safe. In rare cases, women even have been murdered in the wake of online attacks, such as UK MP Jo Cox in 2016 and Brazilian human rights activist Marielle Franco in 2018.

On- and offline abuse are intricately connected strands in a matrix of fear and risk that women navigate. This matrix is defined by the threat of male violence, sexual intimidation, and humiliation (e.g., street harassment, sexual harassment in the workplace, intimate partner violence) (Lewis, Rowe, and Wiper 2017; Vera-Gray 2017). Although digital hate has distinctive attributes (Brown 2018; Femlee, Rodis, and Francisco 2018; Kilvington 2021; Suler 2004), there are important parallels between on- and offline hostility. Lewis, Rowe, and Wiper (2017) argue that both are better understood as ongoing rather than isolated acts, cumulative in nature (many low-level incidents compounding into something greater), sexually degrading, public, part of homosocial bonding, normalized, and trivialized by law enforcement. Further, the prevalence of male physical violence against women gives digital abuse a backbone, magnifying its impact, by making the potential for escalation feel ever-present (Amnesty International 2018; Citron 2014; Stevens and Fraser 2018).

This matrix helps explain why digital abuse ultimately constrains how women use digital public spaces, much as the threat of rape, sexual harassment at work, and street harassment constrain women's use of physical publics. In response to environmental threats, women strategize about how to minimize the risk of sexual intimidation, humiliation, and violence. In physical spaces this may mean ensuring they have someone to walk home with at night, navigating around certain city blocks or construction sites as they commute, or deciding against going for a run or hike in the woods (Bedera and Nordmeyer 2015; Clark 2015; Kash 2019; Valentine 1989). In the digital arena, many women become analogously vigilant about what they do and say online. Some stop writing or speaking about controversial issues, moderate their tone, begin to reserve their ideas for password-protected venues, take participation and social media "breaks" to get away from the abuse, and, in some cases, "opt" out altogether (Citron 2014; Filipovic 2007; Franks 2011; Mantilla 2015; Sobieraj 2020; Olson and LaPoe 2017; Lenhart et al. 2016). Pasricha (2016) found that of the women in India she studied, 28% of those who experienced online abuse made an intentional decision to reduce their online presence. Another common approach is to publish but limit engagement with the public by shutting down comments or ignoring inquiries (Chen et al. 2020; Barker and Jurasz 2019; Sobieraj 2020).

Harassing those from marginalized groups out of public political discourse limits individual freedoms, but because digital hostility is patterned, it also comes with society-level costs. Robust democracies are built on political discourse in which people—including those of lower status—raise and discuss even controversial topics (e.g., immigration, abortion, religion, race), sharing their experiences, insights, and opinions without fear. Given the uneven distribution of hostility, those who self-censor, retreat into digital enclaves, or flee entirely are apt to be women, particularly those from racial, ethnic, and religious minority groups as well as those with other "unpopular" identities such as those who are LGBTQ+, poor, or differently abled. Said another way, retaliation against destabilizers means that the most underrepresented voices and perspectives—arguably those that are most needed—are likely to be the first pushed out (Sobieraj 2020). Patterned silence creates epistemological gaps reminiscent of pre-digital contexts in which participation was profoundly exclusionary and hierarchical. The fear of backlash not only shapes the commentary of individual activists, pundits, advocates, and politicians but also constrains journalists, which means that even traditional contributions to the political information environment are affected as writers limit the stories they pitch, the conclusions they draw, and the sources they include (Chen et al. 2020). Combined, we are left with errors of emphasis and omission that reduce the breadth of information available to the public as they form opinions and make choices (both politically and personally) and when those in positions of influence evaluate pressing needs in their communities and assess or create public policies (Sobieraj 2019, 2020).

Information integrity is further undermined by attacks against women online because they often trade freely in disinformation (Oates et al. 2019; Jankowicz et al. 2021; Sobieraj 2019). According to Judson et al. (2020), gendered disinformation involves "the weaponisation of rumour and stereotypes: with false, misleading or hateful narratives told, often in abusive language, in order to achieve a political impact" (p. 11). For example, one conspiracy theory suggested that US Vice President Kalama Harris was a trans woman (often referring to her as a "tranny") and that her male-to-female transition was intended to hide her "true" identity. The disinformation claimed she was born Kamal Aroush, a Libyan man from Benghazi. The "evidence" that circulated (on Gab, YouTube, via Blogs, etc.) included two images of Harris side by side, one of which had been digitally altered to look like a man. Another "smoking gun" included medical illustrations of male versus female skulls juxtaposed with images of Harris' head that "proved" she could not have been born female (Derecha 2020; Fringe Culture 2020; Jankowicz et al. 2021). Sometimes these false claims are state-aligned, as Judson et al. (2020) illustrate in their report on gendered disinformation in Poland and the Philippines; and at times they are given credence by political figures who amplify unsubstantiated claims via conventional media, as when Vox leader Santiago Abascal of Spain repeated false claims about female politicians who participated in the 8M protest on International Women's Day (Sessa 2020). But regardless of how gendered disinformation circulates, those affected must manage the fallout. Even seemingly wild accusations can pull elected officials, advocates, and activists away from their primary responsibilities to contend with reputation management, answer questions posed by journalists, or work to correct the record. This is not to suggest that disinformation is simply a personal inconvenience or distraction; disinformation undermines public trust in elected officials, experts, and journalists, while simultaneously polluting the information environment. This is significant. Elections are only legitimate if voters have sufficient information to make decisions on their own behalf, and if the public loses faith in those who run, they may not feel comfortable voting at all.

The literature on hate speech and hate crime tells us that onlookers who see themselves reflected in the hostility are also harmed by the attacks (Gelber and McNamara 2016; Perry and Alvi 2012; Pickles 2020). Gelber and McNamara (2016) conducted interviews with 101 members of Indigenous and minority ethnic communities in Australia regarding their experiences with racist hate speech and found, among other things, that it mattered little whether they had personally been attacked. The authors write, "The interviewees' own accounts of what they considered to be hate speech incidents, and their reporting of incidents concerning family and community members, blurred the distinction between whether they had personally been targeted or knew others who had. Their reports spoke strongly to the view that this was not an important differentiation to them" (p. 327). Perry and Alvi (2012) explain that this is because public acts of hate speak to many audiences: the victim (who is punished for their identity or the way it is expressed), other members of the victim's community (who are reminded that they are also outsiders and vulnerable), the broader community (for whom the distinction between insiders and outsiders is reinscribed), and the attacker's peers (who are reminded that they are insiders and superior to outsiders). Their research finds that "violence directed toward another within [a shared] identifiable target group yields strikingly similar patterns of emotional and behavioral responses among vicarious victims. They, too, note a complex syndrome of reactions, including shock, anger, fear/vulnerability, inferiority, and a sense of the normativity of violence" (p. 57).

The normalization of digital hate—the perception that it is a tedious, if inevitable, consequence of life online—creates an impression that political voice and visibility are risky endeavors (Sobieraj 2020). One likely consequence, given the uneven distribution of toxicity, is that women and men from underrepresented groups may become reluctant to lead or even participate in public political discourse even if they have yet to be targeted. Semi-structured interviews with Canadians who had run for office, been identified as promising candidates, or worked with organizations from which candidates often emerge revealed that gendered abuse and harassment weighed more heavily on women, non-Whites, and LGBTQ participants. It also weighed more on the minds of aspiring candidates than those who had run or were running for office. While most participants said the abuse would not dissuade them from running for office, some indicated that they may choose to do less visible political work as a result, and five respondents—all of whom were female—explicitly said that online harassment could or has discouraged them from running (Wagner 2020). Ninety-eight percent of the participants in a British program for potential leaders said they had witnessed online abuse (specifically "sexist abuse") against women in public life, with 78% indicating it was a concern in deciding whether or not to take on a more prominent role (Campbell and Lovenduski 2016). Even those unconcerned with social justice would likely agree that cutting a pool of potential leaders by 50% is hardly a recipe for finding the most innovative, judicious, or inspiring people; but this is an especially bleak forecast for the most underrepresented, who hope not only for excellence but to recognize themselves in their representatives.

Stepping Back to Move Forward

The amount of academic research on digital abuse and harassment has exploded since 2017. Sociological insights are essential if we are to understand the broader political, cultural, and economic consequences of this normalized hostility; but there is little sociological work on this topic overall, and almost none has been published in sociology journals. One scientometric assessment of online hate research included in the Web of Science database showed computer science, education, communications, psychology, and electrical/electronic engineering to be among the top 10 fields where this work is published; sociology was not on the list (Waqas et al. 2019). Most of the sociologists whose work is featured in this review have published their relevant research in communications journals. Whether this is a function of editorial disinterest (at sociological journals) or of the authors' perceptions is unclear, but a shift in this pattern might increase the visibility of the field and prompt more sociologists to enter this important discussion. There are several junctures where such interventions would be especially valuable.

In spite of the recent increase in research on digital misogyny, we are just beginning to grasp its origins, magnitude, and impact. While patterns are emerging, it remains difficult to get a full picture. This is true even when it comes to determining the volume and distribution of abuse. Much of the existing content-analytic research on the abusive content draws on samples from short periods of time, focuses on English-speaking countries (particularly Canada, the United States, the United Kingdom, and Australia), focuses on a narrow segment of political actors (national-level legislators), and overwhelmingly draws on Twitter data. Although we know a fair amount about the *kinds* of attacks made against women, we would benefit from more studies that capture the volume, particularly in comparative ways: over time, across national contexts, and across platforms but also across gender categories and among women with different attributes in terms of race, ethnicity, religion, class, sexual orientation, age, ability, and political affinity. Large-scale descriptive, comparative studies are an essential tool in the effort to disrupt the complacency exhibited by lawmakers and platforms thus far. Their insufficient response is a topic that falls beyond the scope of this chapter but remains one of paramount importance (Barker and Jurasz 2019; Calabro 2018; Citron 2009b, 2014; Gillespie 2018; Sobieraj 2020; Suzor et al. 2019).

Sociologists are particularly well situated to improve our understanding of the impact of this toxicity because they are poised to think beyond individual psychological or economic impact. What are the cultural consequences of patterned political hostility online? How does it shape our interest in politics, our beliefs about leaders, our assessment of issues raised by activists and advocacy groups, our trust in journalists and in news as a source of information, our interest in talking with others about the issues that concern us? How does the threat of digital attack shape the way advocacy organizations, political parties, and news organizations recruit and train participants? How do employers respond to sexual harassment and identity-based discrimination directed at their employees as they work but which comes from beyond their walls? How do they respond when fear prompts those from underrepresented groups to be less visible, vocal, or interactive? In terms of public discourse, how do conversations in more heavily moderated and less heavily moderated venues vary? What differences exist in the substance of the conversation and in who participates?

There remains a particularly large gap in our understanding of the production and circulation of abusive content. The available research is predominantly small-*n* or case-study work. These studies offer critical and nuanced insight into some of the cultures where such behavior is rationalized and celebrated, but there is a dearth of complementary work that can situate these rich insights into a bigger picture. Here, researchers might take inspiration from the work done by Benkler, Faris, and Roberts (2018), which drew heavily on social network analysis to trace the spread of disinformation during the 2016 US presidential campaign. The approach they use is particularly well suited for gendered disinformation, though some kinds of identity-based attacks resist tracing (other than direct sharing/resharing) because of the boilerplate similarities called out by Jane and Vincent (n.d.). Platform cooperation would be particularly useful in helping researchers identify production patterns (e.g., coordinated attacks), bandwagon effects, and patterns in positive and negative social sanctions in response to hate-based content (e.g., shifts in follower counts, engagement numbers). Researchers with an applied orientation would also be well served by assessing the effectiveness of attacker-oriented interventions. These might include in-use design features such as upvoting/downvoting and existing platform sanctions such as temporary account suspensions or pilot-testing any number of new efforts (e.g., education programs, auto-detect pre-emptive moderation).

The research is worth doing. The same internet and communications technologies that improved access and opportunities for inclusive participation have been deployed against those who most need them. Identity-based attacks wreak havoc in women's lives, limit their involvement in public political discourse, and expand their harm by becoming a cautionary tale—a warning to those who may consider becoming involved. The hostility also erodes democratic vitality by wearing away the civil liberties that serve as the foundation of democracy, turning activism and public service into unappealing, high-risk endeavors, diminishing the stock of the knowledge that informs policy, and promoting an ill-informed electorate.

NOTES

1. See Rossini (2020) on the distinction between incivility and intolerant discourse more broadly.
2. Microsoft's Digital Civility Index, which uses surveys to measure experiences in 30 countries, covers even more territory. Unfortunately, the key question related to a battery of negative online experiences including online harassment, receiving hate speech, etc. ("Which of these has ever happened to you *or a friend or family member* online?") makes interpretation difficult.

References

Abdelmonem, Angie. 2020. "Disciplining Bystanders: (Anti)Carcerality, Ethics, and the Docile Subject in HarassMap's 'the Harasser Is a Criminal' Media Campaign in Egypt." *Feminist Media Studies*. Published ahead of print June 30, 2020. https://doi.org/10.1080/14680777.2020.1785911.

Ahmad, Ali, Muhammas Rashid Hafeez, and Muhammad Shahbaz. 2020. "'Sell-Outs, Fatsos or Whores?': Representation of Politically Active Pakistani Women on Social Media." *Pakistan Social Sciences Review* 4, no. 1: 40–50. https://doi.org/10.35484/pssr.2020(4-I)04.

Akhtar, Shazia, and Catriona M. Morrison. 2019. "The Prevalence and Impact of Online Trolling of UK Members of Parliament." *Computers in Human Behavior* 99: 322–327. https://doi.org/10.1016/j.chb.2019.05.015.

Altoaimy, Lama. 2018. "Driving Change on Twitter: A Corpus-Assisted Discourse Analysis of the Twitter Debates on the Saudi Ban on Women Driving." *Social Sciences* 7, no. 5: 81. https://doi.org/10.3390/socsci7050081.

Amnesty International. 2018. "Troll Patrol Report." https://decoders.amnesty.org/projects/troll-patrol/findings.

Baird, Barbara, and Erica Millar. 2019. "More than Stigma: Interrogating Counter Narratives of Abortion." *Sexualities* 22, no. 7–8: 1110–1126. https://doi.org/10.1177/1363460718782966.

Banet-Weiser, Sarah, and Kate M. Miltner. 2016. "#MasculinitySoFragile: Culture, Structure, and Networked Misogyny." *Feminist Media Studies* 16, no. 1: 171–174. https://doi.org/10.1080/14680777.2016.1120490.

Barak, Azy. 2005. "Sexual Harassment on the Internet." *Social Science Computer Review* 23, no. 1: 77–92.

Barboni, Eve, and Nicola Brooks. 2018. *(Anti)Social Media: The Benefits and Pitfalls of Digital for Female Politicians*. London: Atalanta. https://static1.squarespace.com/static/595411f346c3c48fe75fd39c/t/5aa6fa310d9297a484994204/1520892494037/%28Anti%29Social_Media_Report-FINAL2-lowres.pdf.

Barker, Kim, and Olga Jurasz. 2019. "Online Misogyny: A Challenge for Digital Feminism?" *Journal of International Affairs* 72, no. 2: 95–114.

Bates, Samantha. 2017. "Revenge Porn and Mental Health: A Qualitative Analysis of the Mental Health Effects of Revenge Porn on Female Survivors." *Feminist Criminology* 12, no. 1: 22–42.

Bedera, Nicole, and Kristjane Nordmeyer. 2015. "'Never Go out Alone': An Analysis of College Rape Prevention Tips." *Sexuality & Culture* 19, no. 3: 533–542. https://doi.org/10.1007/s12119-015-9274-5.

Belotti, Francesca, Francesca Comunello, and Consuelo Corradi. 2021. "Feminicidio and #NiUnaMenos: An Analysis of Twitter Conversations during the First 3 Years of the Argentinean Movement." *Violence Against Women*, 27, no. 8: 1035–1063. https://doi.org/10.1177/1077801220921947.

Benhabib, Seyla. 1996. "Toward a Deliberative Model of Democratic Legitimacy." In *Democracy and Difference: Contesting the Boundaries of the Political*, edited by Seyla Benhabib, 67–94. Princeton, NJ: Princeton University Press.

Benkler, Yochai. 2008. *The Wealth of Networks: How Social Production Transforms Markets and Freedom*. New Haven, CT: Yale University Press.

Benkler, Yochai, Rob Faris, and Hal Roberts. 2018. *Network Propaganda: Manipulation, Disinformation, and Radicalization in American Politics*. New York: Oxford University Press.

Boling, Kelli S. 2020. "#ShePersisted, Mitch: A Memetic Critical Discourse Analysis on an Attempted Instagram Feminist Revolution." *Feminist Media Studies* 20, no. 7: 966–982. https://doi.org/10.1080/14680777.2019.1620821.

Booten, Kyle. 2016. "Hashtag Drift: Tracing the Evolving Uses of Political Hashtags over Time." In *Proceedings of the 2016 CHI Conference on Human Factors in Computing Systems*, 2401–5. CHI '16. New York: Association for Computing Machinery. https://doi.org/10.1145/2858036.2858398.

boyd, danah. 2010. "Social Network Sites as Networked Publics: Affordances, Dynamics, and Implication." In *A Networked Self: Identity, Community, and Culture on Social Network Sites*, edited by Zizi Papacharissi, 39–57. New York and London: Routledge.

Bratich, Jack, and Sarah Banet-Weiser. 2019. "From Pick-Up Artists to Incels: Con(Fidence) Games, Networked Misogyny, and the Failure of Neoliberalism." *International Journal of Communication*, 13, 5003–5028.

Broadband Commission for Digital Development Working Group on Broadband and Gender. 2015. "Cyber Violence against Women and Girls: A Worldwide Wake-up Call." Discussion Paper. United Nations, New York. https://www.broadbandcommission.org/publication/cyber-violence-against-women/.

Brown, Alexander. 2018. "What Is so Special about Online (as Compared to Offline) Hate Speech?" *Ethnicities* 18, no. 3: 297–326. https://doi.org/10.1177/1468796817709846.

Brown, Melissa, Rashawn Ray, Ed Summers, and Neil Fraistat. 2017. "#SayHerName: A Case Study of Intersectional Social Media Activism." *Ethnic and Racial Studies* 40, no. 11: 1831–1846. https://doi.org/10.1080/01419870.2017.1334934.

Bruns, Axel. 2008. *Blogs, Wikipedia, Second Life, and Beyond: From Production to Produsage*. New York: Peter Lang.

Busari, Stephanie, and Torera Idowu. 2017. "Fake Nude Photos Were Used to 'Silence Me', Disqualified Rwandan Candidate Says." CNN, August 5. https://www.cnn.com/2017/08/04/africa/rwanda-election-nude-photos-candidate/index.html.

Calabro, Svana. 2018. "From the Message Board to the Front Door: Addressing the Offline Consequences of Race- and Gender-Based Doxxing and Swatting Notes." *Suffolk University Law Review* 51, no. 1: 55–76.

Campbell, Rosie, and Joni Lovenduski. 2016. "Footprints in the Sand: Five Years of the Fabian Women's Network Mentoring and Political Education Programme." Fabian Society. https://www.fabians.org.uk/wp-content/uploads/2016/01/FootstepsInTheSand_lo.pdf.

Caren, Neal, Kay Jowers, and Sarah Gaby. 2012. "A Social Movement Online Community: Stormfront and the White Nationalist Movement." In *Media, Movements, and Political Change*, edited by Jennifer Earl and Deana A. Rohlinger, 163–193. Research in Social Movements, Conflicts and Change 33. Bingley, UK: Emerald Group. https://doi.org/10.1108/S0163-786X(2012)0000033010.

Chen, Gina Masullo, Paromita Pain, Victoria Y. Chen, Madlin Mekelburg, Nina Springer, and Franziska Troger. 2020. " 'You Really Have to Have a Thick Skin': A Cross-Cultural Perspective on How Online Harassment Influences Female Journalists." *Journalism* 21, no. 7: 877–895. https://doi.org/10.1177/1464884918768500.

Choi, Su Young, and Younghan Cho. 2017. "Generating Counter-Public Spheres through Social Media: Two Social Movements in Neoliberalised South Korea." *Javnost—The Public* 24, no. 1: 15–33. https://doi.org/10.1080/13183222.2017.1267155.

Citron, Danielle Keats. 2009a. "Cyber Civil Rights." *Boston University Law Review* 89: 61–125.

Citron, Danielle Keats. 2009b. "Law's Expressive Value in Combating Cyber Gender Harassment." *Michigan Law Review* 108, no. 3: 373–416.

Citron, Danielle Keats. 2014. *Hate Crimes in Cyberspace*. Cambridge, MA: Harvard University Press.

Clark, Sheryl. 2015. "Running into Trouble: Constructions of Danger and Risk in Girls' Access to Outdoor Space and Physical Activity." *Sport, Education and Society* 20, no. 8: 1012–1028.

Clark-Parsons, Rosemary. 2018. "Building a Digital Girl Army: The Cultivation of Feminist Safe Spaces Online." *New Media & Society* 20, no. 6: 2125–2144. https://doi.org/10.1177/1461444817731919.

Collignon, Sofia, and Wolfgang Rüdig. 2020. "Harassment and Intimidation of Parliamentary Candidates in the United Kingdom." *The Political Quarterly* 91, no. 2: 422–429. https://doi.org/10.1111/1467-923X.12855.

Crenshaw, Kimberle. 1989. "Demarginalizing the Intersection of Race and Sex: A Black Feminist Critique of Antidiscrimination Doctrine, Feminist Theory and Antiracist Politics." *University of Chicago Legal Forum* 1989, no. 1: 139–168.

Criado-Perez, Caroline. 2013. "Caroline Criado-Perez's Speech on Cyber-Harassment at the Women's Aid Conference." *New Statesman*, September 4. https://www.newstatesman.com/internet/2013/09/caroline-criado-perezs-speech-cyber-harassment-womens-aid-conference.

Crossley, Alison Dahl. 2015. "Facebook Feminism: Social Media, Blogs, and New Technologies of Contemporary U.S. Feminism." *Mobilization: An International Quarterly* 20, no. 2: 253–268. https://doi.org/10.17813/1086-671X-20-2-253.

Crossley, Alison Dahl. 2017. *Finding Feminism: Millennial Activists and the Unfinished Gender*

Dahlberg, Lincoln. 2001. "The Internet and Democratic Discourse: Exploring the Prospects of Online Deliberative Forums Extending the Public Sphere." *Information, Communication & Society* 4, no. 4: 615–633.

Daniels, Jessie. 2009. *Cyber Racism: White Supremacy Online and the New Attack on Civil Rights*. Lanham, MD: Rowman & Littlefield. https://rowman.com/ISBN/9780742561571.

Daniels, Jessie. 2015. "The Trouble with White Feminism: Whiteness, Digital Feminism and the Intersectional Internet." SSRN Scholarly Paper ID 2569369. Social Science Research Network. https://doi.org/10.2139/ssrn.2569369.

De Benedictis, Sara, Shani Orgad, and Catherine Rottenberg. 2019. "#MeToo, Popular Feminism and the News: A Content Analysis of UK Newspaper Coverage." *European Journal of Cultural Studies* 22, no. 5–6: 718–738. https://doi.org/10.1177/1367549419856831.

Derecha, Jerry. 2020. "More Cringy Woke Posturing from Mr. Kamal Aroush Harris." YouTube video, 0:59. https://www.youtube.com/watch?v=EztS-ssy5WI.

Dhrodia, Azmina. 2018. "#ToxicTwitter: Violence and Abuse against Women Online." Amnesty International. https://www.amnesty.org/en/documents/act30/8070/2018/en/

Dignam, Pierce Alexander, and Deana A. Rohlinger. 2019. "Misogynistic Men Online: How the Red Pill Helped Elect Trump." *Signs: Journal of Women in Culture and Society* 44, no. 3: 589–612. https://doi.org/10.1086/701155.

Duggan, Maeve. 2014. "Online Harassment." Pew Research Center, October 22. https://www.pewresearch.org/internet/2014/10/22/online-harassment/.

Earl, Jennifer, Heather McKee Hurwitz, Analicia Mejia Mesinas, Margaret Tolan, and Ashley Arlotti. 2013. "This Protest Will Be Tweeted." *Information, Communication & Society* 16, no. 4: 459–478. https://doi.org/10.1080/1369118X.2013.777756.

Eckert, Stine, and Kalyani Chadha. 2013. "Muslim Bloggers in Germany: An Emerging Counterpublic." *Media, Culture & Society* 35, no. 8: 926–942. https://doi.org/10.1177/0163443713501930.

Edwards, Lee, Fiona Philip, and Ysabel Gerrard. 2020. "Communicating Feminist Politics? The Double-Edged Sword of Using Social Media in a Feminist Organisation." *Feminist Media Studies* 20, no. 5: 605–622. https://doi.org/10.1080/14680777.2019.1599036.

Esposito, Eleonora, and Sole Alba Zollo. 2021. " 'How Dare You Call Her a Pig, I Know Several Pigs Who Would Be Upset If They Knew': A Multimodal Critical Discursive Approach to Online Misogyny against UK MPs on YouTube." *Journal of Language Aggression and Conflict* 9, no. 1: 47–75. https://doi.org/10.1075/jlac.00053.esp.

Farkas, Johan, Jannick Schou, and Christina Neumayer. 2018. "Cloaked Facebook Pages: Exploring Fake Islamist Propaganda in Social Media." *New Media & Society* 20, no. 5: 1850–1867. https://doi.org/10.1177/1461444817707759.

Femlee, Diane, Paulina Inara Rodis, and Sara Chari Francisco. 2018. "What a B!Tch!: Cyber Aggression toward Women of Color." In *Gender and the Media: Women's Places*, edited by Marcia Texler Segal and Vasilikie Demos, 105–123. Advances in Gender Research 26. Bingley, UK: Emerald Publishing. https://par.nsf.gov/servlets/purl/10081964.

Feshami, Kevan A. 2021. " 'We Act as One Lest We Perish Alone': A Case Study in Mediated White Nationalist Activism." *Communication, Culture and Critique* 14, no. 1: 52–69. https://doi.org/10.1093/ccc/tcaa001.

Filipovic, Jill. 2007. "Blogging While Female: How Internet Misogyny Parallels Real-World Harassment Responding to Internet Harassment." *Yale Journal of Law and Feminism* 19, no. 1: 295–304.

Flood, Michael. 2019. "Men and #MeToo: Mapping Men's Responses to Anti-Violence Advocacy." In *#MeToo and the Politics of Social Change*, edited by Bianca Fileborn and Rachel Loney-Howes, 285–300. Cham, Switzerland: Springer International Publishing. https://doi.org/10.1007/978-3-030-15213-0_18.

Francisco, Sara C., and Diane H. Felmlee. 2021. "What Did You Call Me? An Analysis of Online Harassment towards Black and Latinx Women." *Race and Social Problems*. https://doi.org/10.1007/s12552-021-09330-7.

Franks, Mary Anne. 2011. "Sexual Harassment 2.0 Special Feature: Cyberlaw." *Maryland Law Review* 71, no. 3: 655–704.

Fraser, Nancy. 1990. "Rethinking the Public Sphere: A Contribution to the Critique of Actually Existing Democracy." *Social Text* 25/26: 56–80.

Freelon, Deen, Lori Lopez, Meredith D. Clark, and Sarah J. Jackson. 2018. "How Black Twitter and Other Social Media Communities Interact with Mainstream News." SocArXiv, August 5. https://doi.org/10.31235/osf.io/nhsd9.

Fringe Culture. 2020. "Kamalas [sic] Harris Is a Man Named Kamal Aroush." *Fringe Culture: News You're Embarrassed to Admit Is True* (blog). October 22. https://fringeculture.home.blog/2020/10/22/kamalas-harris-is-a-man-named-kamal-aroush-osama-bin-ladin-is-cia-operative-named-tim-osman-who-barack-obama-is-either-related-to-or-actually-is-osman-our-world-is-just-one-big-elaborate-ongoing-jo/.

Fuchs, Tamara, and Fabian Schäfer. 2020. "Normalizing Misogyny: Hate Speech and Verbal Abuse of Female Politicians on Japanese Twitter." *Japan Forum*. https://doi.org/10.1080/09555803.2019.1687564.

Gardiner, Becky. 2018. " 'It's a Terrible Way to Go to Work': What 70 Million Readers' Comments on the Guardian Revealed about Hostility to Women and Minorities Online." *Feminist Media Studies* 18, no. 4: 592–608. https://doi.org/10.1080/14680777.2018.1447334.

Gelber, Katharine, and Luke McNamara. 2016. "Evidencing the Harms of Hate Speech." *Social Identities* 22, no. 3: 324–341. https://doi.org/10.1080/13504630.2015.1128810.

Gillespie, Tarleton. 2018. *Custodians of the Internet: Platforms, Content Moderation, and the Hidden Decisions That Shape Social Media*. New Haven, CT: Yale University Press.

Gillmor, Dan. 2006. *We the Media: Grassroots Journalism by the People, for the People*. Sebastopol, CA: O'Reilly Media.

Goldberg, Emma. 2021. "Fake Nudes and Real Threats: How Online Abuse Holds Back Women in Politics." *New York Times*, June 4. https://www.nytimes.com/2021/06/03/us/disinformation-online-attacks-female-politicians.html.

Graham, Elyse. 2019. "Boundary Maintenance and the Origins of Trolling." *New Media & Society* 21, no. 9: 2029–2047. https://doi.org/10.1177/1461444819837561.

Gray, Kishonna L. 2014. *Race, Gender, and Deviance in Xbox Live: Theoretical Perspectives from the Virtual Margins*. London and New York: Routledge.

Hackworth, Lucy. 2018. "Limitations of 'Just Gender': The Need for an Intersectional Reframing of Online Harassment Discourse and Research." In *Mediating Misogyny: Gender, Technology, and Harassment*, edited by Jacqueline Ryan Vickery and Tracy Everbach, 51–70. Cham, Switzerland: Springer International Publishing. https://doi.org/10.1007/978-3-319-72917-6_3.

Haslop, Craig, Fiona O'Rourke, and Rosalynd Southern. 2021. "#NoSnowflakes: The Toleration of Harassment and an Emergent Gender-Related Digital Divide, in a UK Student Online Culture." *Convergence*. Published ahead of print March 11, 2021. https://doi.org/10.1177/13548565521989270.

Hawdon, James, Atte Oksanen, and Pekka Räsänen. 2017. "Exposure to Online Hate in Four Nations: A Cross-National Consideration." *Deviant Behavior* 38, no. 3: 254–266. https://doi.org/10.1080/01639625.2016.1196985.

Henry, Nicola, Asher Flynn, and Anastasia Powell. 2019. "Image-Based Sexual Abuse: Victims and Perpetrators." *Trends and Issues in Crime and Criminal Justice* no. 572: 1–19. https://search.informit.org/doi/abs/10.3316/INFORMIT.336740761394777.

Henry, Nicola, and Anastasia Powell. 2015. "Embodied Harms: Gender, Shame, and Technology-Facilitated Sexual Violence." *Violence Against Women* 21, no. 6: 758–779. https://doi.org/10.1177/1077801215576581.

Herbst, Susan. 1995. "On Electronic Public Space: Talk Shows in Theoretical Perspective." *Political Communication* 12, no. 3: 263–274. https://doi.org/10.1080/10584609.1995.9963073.

Holt, Thomas J., Joshua D. Freilich, and Steven M. Chermak. 2020. "Examining the Online Expression of Ideology among Far-Right Extremist Forum Users." *Terrorism and Political Violence*. https://doi.org/10.1080/09546553.2019.1701446.

Ince, Jelani, Fabio Rojas, and Clayton A. Davis. 2017. "The Social Media Response to Black Lives Matter: How Twitter Users Interact with Black Lives Matter through Hashtag Use." *Ethnic and Racial Studies* 40, no. 11: 1814–1830. https://doi.org/10.1080/01419870.2017.1334931.

Inter-Parliamentary Union. 2016. "Sexism, Harassment and Violence against Women Parliamentarians." Issue Brief. https://www.ipu.org/resources/publications/issue-briefs/2016-10/sexism-harassment-and-violence-against-women-parliamentarians.

Jackson, Sarah J., Moya Bailey, and Brooke Foucault Welles. 2018. "#GirlsLikeUs: Trans Advocacy and Community Building Online." *New Media & Society* 20, no. 5: 1868–1888. https://doi.org/10.1177/1461444817709276.

Jackson, Sarah J., and Sonia Banaszczyk. 2016. "Digital Standpoints: Debating Gendered Violence and Racial Exclusions in the Feminist Counterpublic." *Journal of Communication Inquiry* 40, no. 4: 391–407. https://doi.org/10.1177/0196859916667731.

Jackson, Sarah J., and Brooke Foucault Welles. 2016. "#Ferguson Is Everywhere: Initiators in Emerging Counterpublic Networks." *Information, Communication & Society* 19, no. 3: 397–418. https://doi.org/10.1080/1369118X.2015.1106571.

Jackson, Sarah J., and Brooke Welles. 2015. "Hijacking #myNYPD: Social Media Dissent and Networked Counterpublics: Hijacking #myNYPD." *Journal of Communication* 65, no. 6: 932–952. https://doi.org/10.1111/jcom.12185.

Jane, Emma A. 2014a. " 'Back to the Kitchen, Cunt': Speaking the Unspeakable about Online Misogyny." *Continuum* 28, no. 4: 558–570. https://doi.org/10.1080/10304312.2014.924479.

Jane, Emma A. 2014b. " 'Your a Ugly, Whorish, Slut.' " *Feminist Media Studies* 14, no. 4: 531–546. https://doi.org/10.1080/14680777.2012.741073.

Jane, Emma A. 2017. "Rapeglish: A Definition." Random Rape Threat Generator. https://rapethreatgenerator.com/?page_id=202.

Jane, Emma A. 2018a. "Gendered Cyberhate as Workplace Harassment and Economic Vandalism." *Feminist Media Studies* 18, no. 4: 575–591. https://doi.org/10.1080/14680777.2018.1447344.

Jane, Emma A. 2018b. "Systemic Misogyny Exposed: Translating Rapeglish from the Manosphere with a Random Rape Threat Generator." *International Journal of Cultural Studies* 21, no. 6: 661–680. https://doi.org/10.1177/1367877917734042.

Jane, Emma A., and Nicole Vincent. n.d. "Random Rape Threat Generator." https://www.rapeglish.com/RRTG.html.

Jankowicz, Nina, Jillian Hunchak, Alexandra Pavliuc, Celia Davies, Shannon Pierson, and Zoë Kaufmann. 2021. *Malign Creativity: How Gender, Sex, and Lies Are Weaponized against Women Online*. Washington, DC: Wilson Center. https://www.wilsoncenter.org/publication/malign-creativity-how-gender-sex-and-lies-are-weaponized-against-women-online.

Jenkins, Henry. 2006. *Convergence Culture*. New York: New York University Press. https://www.degruyter.com/document/doi/10.18574/9780814743683/html.

Jha, Sonora. 2017. "Gathering Online, Loitering Offline: Hashtag Activism and the Claim for Public Space by Women in India through the #WhyLoiter Campaign." In *New Feminisms in South Asia*, edited by Sonora Jha and Alka Kurian, 61–84. New York and London: Routledge.

Jones, Callum, Verity Trott, and Scott Wright. 2020. "Sluts and Soyboys: MGTOW and the Production of Misogynistic Online Harassment." *New Media & Society* 22, no. 10: 1903–1921. https://doi.org/10.1177/1461444819887141.

Judson, Ellen, Asli Atay, Alex Krasodomski-Jones, Rose Lasko-Skinner, and Josh Smith. 2020. *Engendering Hate: The Contours of State-Aligned Gendered Disinformation Online*. New York: Demos.

Kantar Media. 2018. *Internet Users' Experience of Harm Online: Summary of Survey Research*. London: Ofcom and Information Commissioner's Office. https://www.ofcom.org.uk/__data/assets/pdf_file/0018/120852/Internet-harm-research-2018-report.pdf.

Karpf, David. 2012. *The MoveOn Effect: The Unexpected Transformation of American Political Advocacy*. New York: Oxford University Press.

Karpf, David. 2016. *Analytic Activism: Digital Listening and the New Political Strategy*. New York: Oxford University Press.

Kash, Gwen. 2019. "Always on the Defensive: The Effects of Transit Sexual Assault on Travel Behavior and Experience in Colombia and Bolivia." *Journal of Transport & Health* 13: 234–246. https://doi.org/10.1016/j.jth.2019.04.004.

Keller, Jessalynn, Kaitlynn Mendes, and Jessica Ringrose. 2018. "Speaking 'Unspeakable Things': Documenting Digital Feminist Responses to Rape Culture." *Journal of Gender Studies* 27, no. 1: 22–36. https://doi.org/10.1080/09589236.2016.1211511.

Kilvington, Daniel. 2021. "The Virtual Stages of Hate: Using Goffman's Work to Conceptualise the Motivations for Online Hate." *Media, Culture & Society* 43, no. 2: 256–272. https://doi.org/10.1177/0163443720972318.

Kim, Mimi E. 2020. "The Carceral Creep: Gender-Based Violence, Race, and the Expansion of the Punitive State, 1973–1983." *Social Problems* 67, no. 2: 251–269. https://doi.org/10.1093/socpro/spz013.

Kosenko, Kami, Emily Winderman, and Abigail Pugh. 2019. "The Hijacked Hashtag: The Constitutive Features of Abortion Stigma in the #ShoutYourAbortion Twitter Campaign." *International Journal of Communication* 13: 1–21.

Kreiss, Daniel. 2012. *Taking Our Country Back: The Crafting of Networked Politics from Howard Dean to Barack Obama*. New York: Oxford University Press.

Kuo, Rachel. 2018. "Racial Justice Activist Hashtags: Counterpublics and Discourse Circulation." *New Media & Society* 20, no. 2: 495–514. https://doi.org/10.1177/1461444816663485.

Kuperberg, Rebecca. 2021. "Incongruous and Illegitimate: Antisemitic and Islamophobic Semiotic Violence against Women in Politics in the United Kingdom." *Journal of Language Aggression and Conflict* 9, no. 1: 100–126. https://doi.org/10.1075/jlac.00055.kup.

Lamerichs, Micolle, Dennis Ngiuen, Mari Carmen Puerta Melguizo, Radmila Radojevic, and Anna Lange-Böhmer. 2018. "Elite Male Bodies: The Circulation of Alt-Right Memes and the Framing of Politicians on Social Media." *Participations: Journal of Audience and Reception Studies* 15, no. 1: 180–206.

Lee, Latoya A. 2017. "Black Twitter: A Response to Bias in Mainstream Media." *Social Sciences* 6, no. 1: 26. https://doi.org/10.3390/socsci6010026.

Lenhart, Amanda, Michele Ybarra, Kathryn Zickhur, and Myeshia Price-Feeney. 2016. *Online Harassment, Digital Abuse, and Cyberstalking in America*. New York: Data & Society Research Institute. https://www.datasociety.net/pubs/oh/Online_Harassment_2016.pdf.

Levey, Tania G. 2018. *Sexual Harassment Online: Shaming and Silencing Women in the Digital Age*. Boulder, CO: Lynne Rienner.

Lewis, Ruth, Michael Rowe, and Clare Wiper. 2017. "Online Abuse of Feminists as an Emerging Form of Violence against Women and Girls." *British Journal of Criminology* 57, no. 6: 1462–1481. https://doi.org/10.1093/bjc/azw073.

Linabary, Jasmine R., Danielle J. Corple, and Cheryl Cooky. 2020. "Feminist Activism in Digital Space: Postfeminist Contradictions in #WhyIStayed." *New Media & Society* 22, no. 10: 1827–1848. https://doi.org/10.1177/1461444819884635.

Lingiardi, Vittorio, Nicola Carone, Giovanni Semeraro, Cataldo Musto, Marilisa D'Amico, and Silvia Brena. 2020. "Mapping Twitter Hate Speech towards Social and Sexual Minorities: A Lexicon-Based Approach to Semantic Content Analysis." *Behaviour & Information Technology* 39, no. 7: 711–721. https://doi.org/10.1080/0144929X.2019.1607903.

Loken, Meredith. 2014. "#BringBackOurGirls and the Invisibility of Imperialism." *Feminist Media Studies* 14, no. 6: 1100–1101. https://doi.org/10.1080/14680777.2014.975442.

Lokot, Tetyana. 2018. "#IAmNotAfraidToSayIt: Stories of Sexual Violence as Everyday Political Speech on Facebook." *Information, Communication & Society* 21, no. 6: 802–817. https://doi.org/10.1080/1369118X.2018.1430161.

Lumsden, Karen. 2019. " 'I Want to Kill You in Front of Your Children' Is Not a Threat. It's an Expression of a Desire: Discourses of Online Abuse, Trolling and Violence on r/MensRights. In *Online Othering: Exploring Digital Violence and Discrimination on the Web*, edited by Karen Lumsden and Emily Harmer, 91–115. Palgrave Studies in Cybercrime and Cybersecurity. Cham, Switzerland: Springer International Publishing. https://doi.org/10.1007/978-3-030-12633-9_4.

Luqiu, Luwei Rose, and Fan Yang. 2020. "Anti-Muslim Sentiment on Social Media in China and Chinese Muslims' Reactions to Hatred and Misunderstanding." *Chinese Journal of Communication* 13, no. 3: 258–274. https://doi.org/10.1080/17544750.2019.1699841.

Mackintosh, Eliza, and Vijay Gupta. 2021. "Troll Armies, 'Deepfake' Porn Videos and Violent Threats. How Twitter Became so Toxic for India's Women Politicians." CNN. https://www.cnn.com/2020/01/22/india/india-women-politicians-trolling-amnesty-asequals-intl/index.html.

Mansbridge, Jane. 1990. "Self-Interest in Political Life." *Political Theory* 18, no. 1: 132–153.

Mantilla, Karla. 2015. *Gendertrolling: How Misogyny Went Viral*. Santa Barbara, CA: Praeger.

Marwick, Alice, and Robyn Caplan. 2018. "Drinking Male Tears: Language, the Manosphere, and Networked Harassment." *Feminist Media Studies* 18, no. 4: 543–559. https://doi.org/10.1080/14680777.2018.1450568.

Marwick, Alice, and Rebecca Lewis. 2015. *Media Manipulation and Disinformation Online*. New York: Data & Society Research Institute. http://www.chinhnghia.com/DataAndSociety_MediaManipulationAndDisinformationOnline.pdf.

Massanari, Adrienne. 2017. "#Gamergate and the Fappening: How Reddit's Algorithm, Governance, and Culture Support Toxic Technocultures." *New Media & Society* 19, no. 3: 329–346. https://doi.org/10.1177/1461444815608807.

Massanari, Adrienne. 2020. "Reddit's Alt-Right: Toxic Masculinity, Free Speech, and/r/The_Donald." In *Fake News: Understanding Media and Misinformation in the Digital Age*, edited by Melissa Zimdars and Kembrew McLeod, 179–89. Cambridge, MA: MIT Press.

Mendes, Kaitlynn. 2019. *Digital Feminist Activism: Girls and Women Fight Back against Rape Culture*. Oxford Studies in Digital Politics. New York: Oxford University Press.

Mendes, Kaitlynn, Jessica Ringrose, and Jessalynn Keller. 2018. "#MeToo and the Promise and Pitfalls of Challenging Rape Culture through Digital Feminist Activism." *European Journal of Women's Studies* 25, no. 2: 236–246. https://doi.org/10.1177/1350506818765318.

Mertens, Armin, Franziska Pradel, Ayjeren Rozyjumayeva, and Jens Wäckerle. 2019. "As the Tweet, so the Reply? Gender Bias in Digital Communication with Politicians." In *Proceedings of the 10th ACM Conference on Web Science, WebSci '19*, 193–201. New York: Association for Computing Machinery. https://doi.org/10.1145/3292522.3326013.

Miller-Idriss, Cynthia. 2020. *Hate in the Homeland: The New Global Far Right*. Princeton, NJ: Princeton University Press.

Mondragon, Nahia Idoiaga, Naiara Berasategi Sancho, Nekane Beloki Arizti, and Maitane Belasko Txertudi. 2021. "#8M Women's Strikes in Spain: Following the Unprecedented Social Mobilization through Twitter." *Journal of Gender Studies*. Published ahead of print March 15, 2021. https://doi.org/10.1080/09589236.2021.1881461.

Mondragon, Nahia Idoiaga, Lorena Gil de Montes Echaide, Nagore Asla Alcibar, and Maider Larrañaga Eguileor. 2020. " 'La Manada' in the Digital Sphere: Coping with a Sexual Aggression Case through Twitter." *Feminist Media Studies* 20, no. 7: 926–943. https://doi.org/10.1080/14680777.2019.1643387.

Nadim, Marjan, and Audun Fladmoe. 2021. "Silencing Women? Gender and Online Harassment." *Social Science Computer Review* 39, no. 2: 245–258. https://doi.org/10.1177/0894439319865518.

Nanditha, Narayanamoorthy. 2021. "Exclusion in #MeToo India: Rethinking Inclusivity and Intersectionality in Indian Digital Feminist Movements." *Feminist Media Studies*. Published ahead of print April 13, 2021. https://doi.org/10.1080/14680777.2021.1913432.

Ncube, Gibson, and Gwatisira Yemurai. 2020. "Discrimination against Female Politicians on Social Media: An Analysis of Tweets in the Run-up to the July 2018 Harmonised Elections in Zimbabwe." In *Social Media and Elections in Africa*. Vol. 2, *Challenges and Opportunities*, edited by Martin N. Ndlela and Winston Mano, 59–76. Cham, Switzerland: Springer International Publishing. https://doi.org/10.1007/978-3-030-32682-1_4.

Nuñez Puente, Sonia, Sergio D'Antonio Maceiras, and Diana Fernández Romero. 2021. "Twitter Activism and Ethical Witnessing: Possibilities and Challenges of Feminist Politics Against Gender-Based Violence." *Social Science Computer Review* 39, no. 2: 295–311. https://doi.org/10.1177/0894439319864898.

Oates, Sarah, Olya Gurevich, Christopher Walker, and Lucina Di Meco. 2019. "Running While Female: Using AI to Track How Twitter Commentary Disadvantages Women in the 2020 U.S. Primaries." SSRN Scholarly Paper ID 3444200. Social Science Research Network. https://doi.org/10.2139/ssrn.3444200.

Ohlheiser, Abby. 2019. "A Nude-Photo Hoax Was Supposed to Silence Alexandria Ocasio-Cortez. Instead, She Turned up the Volume." *Washington Post*, January 10. https://www.washingtonpost.com/technology/2019/01/10/nude-photo-hoax-was-supposed-silence-alexandria-ocasio-cortez-instead-she-turned-up-volume/.

Olson, Candi Carter. 2016. "#BringBackOurGirls: Digital Communities Supporting Real-World Change and Influencing Mainstream Media Agendas." *Feminist Media Studies* 16, no. 5: 772–787. https://doi.org/10.1080/14680777.2016.1154887.

Olson, Candi S. Carter, and Victoria LaPoe. 2017. " 'Feminazis,' 'Libtards,' 'Snowflakes,' and 'Racists': Trolling and the Spiral of Silence Effect in Women, LGBTQIA Communities, and Disability Populations before and after the 2016 Election." *Journal of Public Interest Communications* 1, no. 2: 116. https://doi.org/10.32473/jpic.v1.i2.p116.

Onwuachi-Willig, Angela. 2018. "What About #UsToo: The Invisibility of Race in the #MeToo Movement." *Yale Law Journal Forum* 128: 105–120.

Ortiz, Stephanie M. 2020. "Trolling as a Collective Form of Harassment: An Inductive Study of How Online Users Understand Trolling." *Social Media + Society* 6, no. 2. https://doi.org/10.1177/2056305120928512.

Pacheco, Edgar, and Neil Melhuish. 2018. *Online Hate Speech: A Survey on Personal Experiences and Exposure among Adult New Zealanders*. Wellington, New Zealand: Netsafe NZ. https://www.netsafe.org.nz/wp-content/uploads/2019/11/onlinehatespeech-survey-2018.pdf.

Pain, Paromita, and Victoria Chen. 2019. "This Reporter Is so Ugly, How Can She Appear on TV?" *Journalism Practice* 13, no. 2: 140–158. https://doi.org/10.1080/17512786.2017.1423236.

Papacharissi, Zizi. 2002. "The Virtual Sphere: The Internet as a Public Sphere." *New Media & Society* 4, no. 1 (February 2002): 9–27. https://doi.org/10.1177/14614440222226244.

Pasricha, Japleen. 2016. "Cyber Violence against Women In India—A Research Report." Feminism in India, November 15. https://feminisminindia.com/2016/11/15/cyber-violence-against-women-india-report/.

Patil, Vrushali, and Jyoti Puri. 2021. "Colorblind Feminisms: Ansari-Grace and the Limits of #MeToo Counterpublics." *Signs: Journal of Women in Culture and Society* 46, no. 3: 689–713. https://doi.org/10.1086/712078.

Pennington, Rosemary. 2018. "Making Space in Social Media: #MuslimWomensDay in Twitter." *Journal of Communication Inquiry* 42, no. 3: 199–217. https://doi.org/10.1177/0196859918768797.

Perry, Barbara, and Shahid Alvi. 2012. " 'We Are All Vulnerable': The in *Terrorem Effects* of Hate Crimes." *International Review of Victimology* 18, no. 1: 57–71. https://doi.org/10.1177/0269758011422475.

Pickles, James. 2020. "Sociality of Hate: The Transmission of Victimization of LGBT+ People through Social Media." *International Review of Victimology* 27, no. 3: 311–327. https://doi.org/10.1177/0269758020971060.

Puente, Sonia Núñez, Sergio D'Antonio Maceiras, and Diana Fernández Romero. 2021. "Twitter Activism and Ethical Witnessing: Possibilities and Challenges of Feminist Politics Against Gender-Based Violence." *Social Science Computer Review* 39, no. 2: 295–311. https://doi.org/10.1177/0894439319864898.

Radsch, Courtney C., and Sahar Khamis. 2013. "In Their Own Voice: Technologically Mediated Empowerment and Transformation among Young Arab Women." *Feminist Media Studies* 13, no. 5: 881–890. https://doi.org/10.1080/14680777.2013.838378.

Ralph, David. 2021. " 'Between a Whisper and a Shout': Repealing the Eighth and Pro-Choice Irish Women's Abortion Testimonies." *Gender, Place & Culture*. Published ahead of print February 25, 2021. https://doi.org/10.1080/0966369X.2020.1860911.

Razlogova, Elena. 2011. *The Listener's Voice: Early Radio and the American Public*. Philadelphia: University of Pennsylvania Press.

Rentschler, Carrie A. 2017. "Bystander Intervention, Feminist Hashtag Activism, and the Anti-Carceral Politics of Care." *Feminist Media Studies* 17, no. 4: 565–584. https://doi.org/10.1080/14680777.2017.1326556.

Rheault, Ludovic, Erica Rayment, and Andreea Musulan. 2019. "Politicians in the Line of Fire: Incivility and the Treatment of Women on Social Media." *Research & Politics* 6, no. 1. https://doi.org/10.1177/2053168018816228.

Rossini, Patrícia. 2020. "Beyond Incivility: Understanding Patterns of Uncivil and Intolerant Discourse in Online Political Talk." *Communication Research*. https://doi.org/10.1177/0093650220921314.

Rossini, Patrícia, Jennifer Stromer-Galley, and Feifei Zhang. 2021. "Exploring the Relationship between Campaign Discourse on Facebook and the Public's Comments: A Case Study of Incivility during the 2016 US Presidential Election." *Political Studies* 69, no. 1: 89–107. https://doi.org/10.1177/0032321719890818.

Schmitz, Rachel M., Jonathan S. Coley, Christine Thomas, and Anibal Ramirez. 2020. "The Cyber Power of Marginalized Identities: Intersectional Strategies of Online LGBTQ+ Latinx Activism." *Feminist Media Studies*. https://doi.org/10.1080/14680777.2020.1786430.

Schudson, Michael. 1981. *Discovering the News: A Social History of American Newspapers*. New York: Basic Books.

Schudson, Michael. 1995. *The Power of News*. Cambridge, MA: Harvard University Press.

Sessa, Miria Giovanna. 2020. "Misogyny and Misinformation: An Analysis of Gendered Disinformation Tactics during the COVID-19 Pandemic." EU Disinfo Lab, December 4. https://www.disinfo.eu/publications/misogyny-and-misinformation:-an-analysis-of-gendered-disinformation-tactics-during-the-covid-19-pandemic/.

Sest, Natalie, and Evita March. 2017. "Constructing the Cyber-Troll: Psychopathy, Sadism, and Empathy." *Personality and Individual Differences* 119: 69–72. https://doi.org/10.1016/j.paid.2017.06.038.

Sills, Sophie, Chelsea Pickens, Karishma Beach, Lloyd Jones, Octavia Calder-Dawe, Paulette Benton-Greig, and Nicola Gavey. 2016. "Rape Culture and Social Media: Young Critics and a Feminist Counterpublic." *Feminist Media Studies* 16, no. 6: 935–951. https://doi.org/10.1080/14680777.2015.1137962.

Sobieraj, Sarah. 2018. "Bitch, Slut, Skank, Cunt: Patterned Resistance to Women's Visibility in Digital Publics." *Information, Communication & Society* 21, no. 11: 1700–1714. https://doi.org/10.1080/1369118X.2017.1348535.

Sobieraj, Sarah. 2019. "Disinformation, Democracy, and the Social Costs of Identity-Based Attacks Online." MediaWell, Social Science Research Council, October 22. https://mediawell.ssrc.org/expert-reflections/disinformation-democracy-and-the-social-costs-of-identity-based-attacks-online/.

Sobieraj, Sarah. 2020. *Credible Threat: Attacks against Women Online and the Future of Democracy*. Oxford Studies in Digital Politics. New York: Oxford University Press.

Sobieraj, Sarah, and Shaan Merchant. Forthcoming. "Gender and Race in the Digital Town Hall: Identity-Based Attacks against US Legislators on Twitter." In *Social Media and Social Order*, edited by David Herbert and Stefan Fisher-Høyrem. Berlin: De Gruyter.

Southern, Rosalynd, and Emily Harmer. 2019. "Othering Political Women: Online Misogyny, Racism and Ableism towards Women in Public Life." In *Online Othering: Exploring Digital Violence and Discrimination on the Web*, edited by Karen Lumsden and Emily Harmer, 187–210. Palgrave Studies in Cybercrime and Cybersecurity. Cham, Switzerland: Springer International Publishing. https://doi.org/10.1007/978-3-030-12633-9_8.

Special Rapporteur on Violence against Women. 2018. *Online Violence against Women and Girls from a Human Rights Perspective*. A/HRC/38/47. New York: United Nations Human Rights Commission. https://undocs.org/pdf?symbol=en/A/HRC/38/47.

Starkey, Jesse C., Amy Koerber, Miglena Sternadori, and Bethany Pitchford. 2019. "#MeToo Goes Global: Media Framing of Silence Breakers in Four National Settings." *Journal of Communication Inquiry* 43, no. 4: 437–461. https://doi.org/10.1177/0196859919865254.

Stevens, Sophie, and Erika Fraser. 2018. *Digital Harassment of Women Leaders: A Review of the Evidence*. VAWG Helpdesk Research Report 210. London: VAWG Helpdesk.

Stromer-Galley, Jennifer. 2019. *Presidential Campaigning in the Internet Age*. New York: Oxford University Press.

Suk, Jiyoun, Aman Abhishek, Yini Zhang, So Yun Ahn, Teresa Correa, Christine Garlough, and Dhavan V. Shah. 2021. "#MeToo, Networked Acknowledgment, and Connective Action: How 'Empowerment through Empathy' Launched a Social Movement." *Social Science Computer Review* 39, no. 2: 276–294. https://doi.org/10.1177/0894439319864882.

Suler, John. 2004. "The Online Disinhibition Effect." *CyberPsychology & Behavior* 7, no. 3: 321–326. https://doi.org/10.1089/1094931041291295.

Suzor, Nicolas, Molly Dragiewicz, Bridget Harris, Rosalie Gillett, Jean Burgess, and Tess Van Geelen. 2019. "Human Rights by Design: The Responsibilities of Social Media Platforms to

Address Gender-Based Violence Online." *Policy & Internet* 11, no. 1: 84–103. https://doi.org/10.1002/poi3.185.

Tarawnah, Naseem. 2020. "Sextortion, Harassment, and Deepfakes: How Digital Weapons Are Being Used to Silence Women." IFEX, March 5. https://ifex.org/sextortion-harassment-and-deepfakes-how-digital-weapons-are-being-used-to-silence-women/.

Terwiel, Anna. 2020. "What Is Carceral Feminism?" *Political Theory* 48, no. 4: 421–442. https://doi.org/10.1177/0090591719889946.

Thomas, Kurt, Devdatta Akhawe, Michael Bailey, Dan Boneh, Elie Bursztein, Sunny Consolvo, et al. 2021. "SoK: Hate, Harassment, and the Changing Landscape of Online Abuse." https://research.google/pubs/pub49786/.

Tromble, Rebekah. 2018. "Thanks for (Actually) Responding! How Citizen Demand Shapes Politicians' Interactive Practices on Twitter." *New Media & Society* 20, no. 2: 676–697. https://doi.org/10.1177/1461444816669158.

Tromble, Rebekah, and Karin Koole. 2020. "She Belongs in the Kitchen, Not in Congress? Political Engagement and Sexism on Twitter." *Journal of Applied Journalism & Media Studies* 9, no. 2: 191–214. https://doi.org/10.1386/ajms_00022_1.

Tufekci, Zeynep. 2017. *Twitter and Tear Gas: The Power and Fragility of Networked Protest*. New Haven, CT: Yale University Press.

Vakhitova, Zarina I., Clair L. Alston-Knox, Ellen Reeves, and Rob I. Mawby. 2021. "Explaining Victim Impact from Cyber Abuse: An Exploratory Mixed Methods Analysis." *Deviant Behavior*. Published ahead of print June 9, 2021. https://doi.org/10.1080/01639625.2021.1921558.

Valentine, Gill. 1989. "The Geography of Women's Fear." *Area* 21, no. 4: 385–390.

Vera-Gray, F. 2017. "'Talk about a Cunt with too Much Idle Time': Trolling Feminist Research." *Feminist Review* 115, no. 1: 61–78. https://doi.org/10.1057/s41305-017-0038-y.

Vidgen, Bertie, Helen Margetts, and Alex Harris. 2019. *How Much Online Abuse Is There? A Systematic Review of Evidence for the UK*. London: Alan Turing Institute. https://www.turing.ac.uk/sites/default/files/2019-11/online_abuse_prevalence_full_24.11.2019_-_formatted_0.pdf.

Vogels, Emily A. 2021. "The State of Online Harassment." Pew Research Center, January 13. https://www.pewresearch.org/internet/2021/01/13/the-state-of-online-harassment/#:~:text=The%20State%20of%20Online%20Harassment%20Roughly%20four-in-ten%20Americans,sexual%20harassment%20or%20stalking%20By%20Emily%20A.%20Vogels.

Wagner, Angelia. 2020. "Tolerating the Trolls? Gendered Perceptions of Online Harassment of Politicians in Canada." *Feminist Media Studies*. Published ahead of print April 8, 2020. https://doi.org/10.1080/14680777.2020.1749691.

Waqas, Ahmed, Joni Salminen, Soon-gyo Jung, Hind Almerekhi, and Bernard J. Jansen. 2019. "Mapping Online Hate: A Scientometric Analysis on Research Trends and Hotspots in Research on Online Hate." *PLoS ONE* 14, no. 9: e0222194. https://doi.org/10.1371/journal.pone.0222194.

Williams, Apryl, and Vanessa Gonlin. 2017. "I Got All My Sisters with Me (on Black Twitter): Second Screening of *How to Get Away with Murder* as a Discourse on Black Womanhood." *Information, Communication & Society* 20, no. 7: 984–1004. https://doi.org/10.1080/1369118X.2017.1303077.

Xing, Guoxin. 2012. "Online Activism and Counter-Public Spheres." *Javnost—The Public* 19, no. 2: 63–82. https://doi.org/10.1080/13183222.2012.11009085.

Young, Iris Marion. 2002. *Inclusion and Democracy*. New York: Oxford University Press.

Zannettou, Savvas, Joel Finkelstein, Barry Bradlyn, and Jeremy Blackburn. 2020. "A Quantitative Approach to Understanding Online Antisemitism." *Proceedings of the International AAAI Conference on Web and Social Media* 14, no. 1: 786–797.

Zarkov, Dubravka, and Kathy Davis. 2018. "Ambiguities and Dilemmas around #MeToo: #ForHow Long and #WhereTo?" *European Journal of Women's Studies* 25, no. 1: 3–9. https://doi.org/10.1177/1350506817749436.

CHAPTER 31

DIGITAL MEDIA IN GRASSROOTS ANTI-CORRUPTION MOBILIZATIONS

ALICE MATTONI

Corruption is a global problem that affects millions of people, and since the early 1990s, governmental and financial institutions working at the national and international levels (i.e., the US Agency for International Development, the World Bank, the United Nations) have listed corruption as one of the top priorities to be confronted globally (de Sousa, Larmour, and Hindess 2009). Among others, the Organisation for Economic Co-operation and Development (2015) estimates that corruption harms economic growth, contributes to increasing social inequalities, damages political institutions through the distortion of political decisions, diminishes citizens' trust in their governments, and plays a part in the rise of other criminal activities.

International organizations are not the only ones referring to corruption as a relevant social problem. Several activists' organizations worldwide also mobilize against corruption, organizing ad hoc campaigns and participating in anti-corruption social movements (Beverley 2014). These are usually grassroots forms of collective action in which people come together to oppose corruption in its many forms, from political to corporate corruption to the petty corruption of everyday bribes to grand corruption schemes that involve money laundering and organized crime. Of course, since corruption and the related behaviors manifest in different ways in societies, it is impossible to speak about the existence of one general type of anti-corruption movement. The protest targets and forms of anti-corruption mobilization, indeed, might change considerably.

In some cases, street protests erupt in corrupt countries to oppose the corrupted political elites that activists blame for putting their private interests before those of the public. An example of this is the protests that erupted in India in April 2011, after the anti-corruption activist Anna Hazare began a hunger strike in New Delhi (Sengupta

2012). Grassroots opposition against corruption might also be linked to mobilizations on other contentious issues. Anti-austerity protests in Spain blamed the corrupt politicians for the economic and financial crisis that hit the country in 2008 (della Porta 2017). Environmental activists in eastern Europe also bridged their concerns for constructing big infrastructures with corruption in their countries (Torsello 2012).

In other cases, collective actions against corruption do not include public street protests as a reaction to corruption scandals. Instead, they engage in more proactive collective actions that aim at increasing the accountability of those who might engage in corruption due to their positions of power. Activists' might use online petitions, as happened in Italy in 2013 when hundreds of thousands of signatures supported the campaign *Senza Corruzione ... Riparte il Futuro* to change an article of the Penal Code on vote-buying (Mattoni 2017). However, social movement organizations might decide to engage in the active monitoring of public authorities and other institutions, including corporations, to detect illicit behaviors. An example is activists who take advantage of freedom of information acts to participate in budget oversight activities (Mungiu-Pippidi 2014).

A recent systematic literature review on strategies to counter corruption in the public sector argues that social media and mobile phones are relevant to empower citizens' monitoring capacity (Inuwa, Kah, and Ononiwu 2019). Similarly, in a review of the relationship between digital media and anti-corruption strategies, Kossow (2020) casts light on the digital media platforms that enhance crowdsourcing and whistle-blowing activities from the grassroots, hence supporting upward transparency. Additionally, he points out that activists might employ digital media in the framework of broad anti-corruption movements. In this regard, amid the COVID-19 pandemic emergency, the U4 Anti-Corruption Research Centre published a report that discusses online collaboration's potential to promote social accountability, stressing that digital platforms might enhance the digital participation of citizens with a watchdog function (Mullard and Aarvik 2020). Non-academic papers on the topic also testify that there is a growing body of grassroots initiatives that employ digital media to sustain anti-corruption efforts worldwide (Chêne 2019; Adam and Fazekas 2018).

This chapter focuses on how digital media entangle grassroots anti-corruption efforts, drawing on several concrete examples from all over the world. Its overall aim is to explain how a wide range of digital media shape people's collective efforts to counter corruption and how a varied ensemble of anti-corruption initiatives appropriate, transform, and structure digital media when employed for specific anti-corruption goals.

The chapter is organized as follows. First, it discusses two leading roles that digital media might have in grassroots anti-corruption struggles, each of them linked to one specific approach to corruption. On the one hand, they are in line with a view of corruption as a principal–agent problem, hence assisting activists in enlarging the monitoring and denouncing of people's capacity concerning corruption. On the other hand, they can sustain a view of corruption as a collective action problem, hence helping activists increase public awareness on corruption to change the normative understanding of what corruption is and does to societies. Second, the chapter addresses digital media as they entangle with big data. While anti-corruption activists have always relied on data of all kinds to support their struggles, this section tackles three specific types of data-related practices (data production, data embedment, and data transformation). It also shows how they are in tune with either the collective action or the principal–agent approach to corruption. Third, the chapter discusses another, more pragmatic, and situated approach to corruption and, in its framework, addresses the potential role of digital media for anti-corruption activists, arguing for the development of comparative studies on the subject matter. Finally, conclusions revisit the previous sections, taking into consideration three main directions toward which research on anti-corruption from the grassroots and its relationship with digital media might develop soon.

The Multiple Roles of Digital Media in Grassroots Anti-Corruption Efforts

While it is impossible to have a universal interpretation of corruption, each definition of this global problem has a substantial impact on how corruption is measured and how to counter it (Andersson and Heywood 2009). This, of course, also has consequences for digital media's role in countering corruption from the grassroots. For this reason, before exploring what activists do with digital media to face corruption, this section briefly sketches the two main theoretical approaches to corruption and related anti-corruption strategies.

On the one hand, there is the principal–agent theory, whose framework developed in the 1970s and 1980s and focused on politicians and bureaucrats (Rose-Ackerman 1978). It was then further developed into a principal–client–agent model to include other types of interactions, like those between citizens and politicians (Klitgaard 1988). According to this model, there is an asymmetry of information and incentives between the elected officials (the principal), the citizens who elected them (the clients), and the public servants who provide the public services that the citizens need (the agents). The latter might have more information than the elected officials and the citizens on how the public administration works, hence using this information to serve their private interests. This might be possible not only because there is an asymmetry of information but also because there is a lack of accountability mechanisms that would allow the elected officials and the citizens to monitor what the public servants do. Scholars who employ the principal–agent theory advocate for the use of incremental reforms to curb corruption through two main mechanisms: the reduction of the agents' discretion and the increase of the principals' monitorial ability of the principals (Rose-Ackerman and Palifka 2016).

On the other hand, other scholars suggest that collective action theory is instead the lens to fully grasp how corruption develops and how it can be mitigated. According to this view, and drawing on Olson (1971), corruption emerges in societies due to free-riding: Instead of thinking about the protection of collective interests that would render societies better for all its participants, individuals might decide to focus on their interest through corrupt behaviors. In this regard, corrupt behaviors might be found among public servants and citizens and elected officials alike. Scholars who adhere to the collective action theory argue for a "big bang" approach, leading to radical, wide-ranging, and sudden transformations in the whole spectrum of policy (Rothstein 2011; Persson, Rothstein, and Teorell 2013). Furthermore, other scholars suggest focusing on normative rather than legal constraints to curb corruption and see as relevant the active role of civil society organizations and the mainstream press (Mungiu-Pippidi 2013, 2015). Overall, then, increasing the awareness of what corruption is and what it does to society might also be an excellent anti-corruption strategy to avoid free-riding behaviors.

Independently from their overall approach to corruption and anti-corruption—principal–agent versus collective action problem—scholars seem to agree on the relevance of digital media when social movement organizations embrace them (Rose-Ackerman and Palifka 2016; Rotberg 2017; Hough 2017; Mungiu-Pippidi 2015; Johnston 2014). However, it seems that digital media are not always relevant in the same way for grassroots anti-corruption efforts. Activists' use of digital media seems consistent with either the principal–agent or the collective action problem approach, each time enhancing some digital media functions and not others to counter corruption, consistently with the type of approach that the grassroots anti-corruption effort seems to imply. What follows discusses more in-depth the link between the digital media functions that activists employ as leverage when they seek to oppose corruption and the type of approach that activists seem to adhere to when devising their anti-corruption strategies.

Digital Media to Tackle Corruption as a Collective Action Problem

Activists and their grassroots organizations frequently invest their resources in campaigns whose aim is quite expressive. Indeed, through these campaigns, activists attempt to increase people's awareness of corruption, with the ultimate goal of making clear that corruption is a relevant social problem with significant consequences for societies at large. Additionally, they attempt to create shared spaces for critical discussion and the potential creation of shared anti-corruption identities. Digital media play an essential role in this type of campaign, which seems to presuppose that corruption is a collective action problem to be solved by increasing awareness of how corrupt behaviors have negative consequences for societies. As already mentioned, widespread changes at the normative—more than legal—level are considered relevant in this case, with the achievement of public awareness of corruption's adverse effects as one of the critical issues at stake. In turn, this public awareness might be developed thanks to social movement organizations (Mungiu-Pippidi 2013). Digital media, as discussed in what follows, form a crucial component of this process. However, they are so in at least two different ways.

First, existing social movement organizations employ digital media to further their anti-corruption campaigns, mobilizations, and protest events. In this case, digital media support social movement organizations' quest for visibility beyond the activists' circles that support anti-corruption campaigns. In doing so, social movement organizations employ digital media to share their concerns, spread their demands, and enlarge their mobilizations' social basis. The circulation of news across various digital media types might increase the visibility of anti-corruption initiatives well beyond legacy media like the print press, television news, and radio programs. For instance, digital media had a significant role in the Christian-led anti-corruption campaign *EXPOSED* 2013 that targeted the G20 for greater transparency in international money flows to combat bribery and tax avoidance. In this case, the movement's strong Christian motivation for justice was certainly coupled with the vast networks of faith organizations behind the campaign, mostly based in the United Kingdom and the United States, and their ability to employ websites, blogs, social media platforms, and emails to spread the message of the campaign virally across the world (Bowers-Du Toit and Forster 2015). In Italy, the anti-corruption campaign *Senza Corruzione . . . Riparte il Futuro* in 2013 targeted candidates in the general elections, asking them for a public commitment. If elected, they would focus on changing one article of the Italian penal code to broaden vote-buying crime. The social movement organization that supported the campaign, Libera, counted on the social communication company Latte Creative to develop a communication strategy at the center of digital media. The official website of the campaign, coupled with the Facebook page, was particularly relevant in spreading the news about Italy's corruption, often communicating through appealing visualizations of data on its negative consequences. In doing so, activists were also ensuring broader visibility to their campaign, expanding the number of supporters and adherents who joined them in pushing candidates to commit themselves to their primary objective (Mattoni 2017).

Second, concerned citizens come together through digital media to share their views about corruption as a relevant social problem. In this case, digital media function as spaces in which people might raise their voices against corruption, creating a shared sense of belonging that rests on the construction of shared meanings. In other words, activists employ digital media, mainly social media platforms, as a means of expression where shared critical discourses against corruption might emerge from discussions about people who gather around specific social media pages, profiles, and hashtags. For instance, this happened in Nigeria, where the mainstream media censorship is particularly marked, and people employed social media as spaces for critical voices against corruption (Jimada 2019). Beyond creating public awareness, digital media might also support the emergence of new forms of digital citizenship, opposing the grassroots anti-corruption voices that participate in social media platforms to the corrupted protest targets, as happened in Indonesia (Fauzanafi 2016).

Another telling example is the *#Rezist* mobilization in Romania. During this protests, people's use of social media was relevant to trigger a public space where participants could construct shared emotions and solidarity ties that were relevant to sustain the campaign in the short term (Aid, Lilleker, and Pekalski 2018). Digital media, on some occasions, might also be combined with more traditional media in a virtuous circle, as happened with the rise of the anti-corruption movement in Guatemala in 2015 that began with the social media hashtag *#RenunciaYa*, which got favorable mainstream media coverage and culminated with the removal from office of both the president and vice president of the country (Flores 2019).

In short, digital media—and social media platforms, more precisely—might increase public awareness of corruption in two complementary ways. When social movement organizations employ digital media to increase the visibility of their mobilizations, campaigns, and protest events, they use them as collective actors to increase the awareness of individual digital media users, like those who are on Facebook, Twitter, and Instagram. When, instead, individual digital media users gather around specific anti-corruption hashtags, they create a space for critical discussion on corruption, hence increasing awareness through the exchange of information, opinions, and beliefs on how to fight corruption. In this case, the collective actors in the shape of online communities are an outcome of this process of ongoing public discussion about corruption.

Furthermore, when concerned citizens come together through social media platforms around issues like corruption, the emerging online communities might engage in protests that go beyond the online realm and spread into the streets and squares of the cities they live in. In particular, this happens when the initial outrage that spread online can resonate with the concerns, demands, and experience of already existing social movement organizations. For instance, the Facebook page *We Are All Khaled Said* in Egypt—devoted to the brutal murder of the blogger Khaled Said on June 6, 2010, by the police—rapidly became a public space where people could discuss how to fight police brutality and the widespread corruption in the country (Abdulla et al. 2018). The Facebook page *We Are All Khaled Said* represented a relevant resource for protesters mobilized in Egypt between the end of 2010 and the beginning of 2011. Similarly, activists in Morocco employed social media as a space to develop shared meanings in the framework of the February 20 movement in 2011, which demanded an increase in social justice and aimed at pushing forward more effective anti-corruption measures (Brouwer and Bartels 2014). Along the same line, the use of Facebook in Tunisia was also relevant to sustain the so-called Jasmine Revolution, which blamed President Ben Ali and his government for widespread corruption, among other undemocratic practices (Schroeder and Redissi 2011). In this country, the social media platform is paired with the digital media skills of the social movement organizations, activists, and bloggers (Zayani 2015).

Despite many studies pointing at their potential in supporting anti-corruption from the grassroots, digital media also pose some challenges to activists. Even in cases where grassroots anti-corruption campaigns eventually develop into a more structured social movement against corruption, the heavy reliance of activists on social media and the weak ties that keep together anti-corruption communities online rendered difficult the creation of solid social movements able to attain more long-term political goals. For instance, this happened in Romania's *#Rezist* mobilizations, where the online anti-corruption community proved fragile and unable to last beyond the initial street protests (Aid, Lilleker, and Pekalski 2018). The public indignation that rises in social media platforms might also find its way elsewhere, as a recent study on two scandals concerning police corruption in Russia explains (Toepfl 2011). In this case, the Russian political powerholders could employ television news programs to effectively redirect the anger toward hostile foreign powers and low-level domestic authorities, hence deflating a potentially widespread social movement against corruption. This example casts light on at least two additional challenges that activists' employment of digital media face in their anti-corruption efforts. First, collective actors do not act in a void. Their attempts to change the normative understanding of corruption in societies through digital media might occur in rather hostile environments, where other types of collective actors work in the opposite direction. Second, digital media position themselves in broad media ecologies, where other media continue to have an essential role in shaping public opinion and political agendas.

Digital Media to Counter Corruption as a Principal–Agent Problem

Beyond the potentially ephemeral nature of many anti-corruption movements and mobilizations, activists' development and employment of digital media might also give rise to other types of practices that increase the level of transparency in societies, rendering visible otherwise hidden corrupted behaviors and their consequences. In this regard, digital media become crucial in sustaining two anti-corruption practices: people's monitoring, from the grassroots, of those who have financial, economic, and political power and people's denouncing of the wrongdoings related to corruption, either at the micro-scale of briberies or at the more macro-scale of grand corruption schemes. In both cases, activists' use of digital media is related to the conception of corruption as a principal–agent problem. Through them, indeed, the people, namely the principal, might exert some pressure on the corrupted agents. Therefore, digital media become relevant for activists because they can support the overall goal of augmenting the transparency of wrongdoings related to corruption.

A recent study on how people monitor political activities argues that digital media platforms increase transparency in several ways (Munoz and Casero-Ripollés 2017). Among other things, digital media platforms might function as aggregators of already existing information that governments and public administrations render available online in the form of open data. In this way, activists might employ open data to foster transparency in public administrations to monitor public servants, elected politicians, and the like. More specifically, open data is particularly relevant for activists who want to discover corrupt behaviors (Damm et al. 2019). Several social movement organizations employ open data as a leverage to create digital platforms that enable people to check how elected members of the parliament (MPs) behave during their mandates about specific bills and debates, also related to corruption. One of these is the platform OpenPolis in Italy, which gathers, aggregates, and then publishes in a more user-friendly mode already existing information on elected MPs' activities.

However, the presence of such digital media platforms alone cannot ensure reliable and durable monitoring. Most of the time, transparency mechanisms that empower people to control their rulers, also known as "downward transparency mechanisms" (Davies and Fumega 2014), are linked to the availability of data related to the phenomena that citizens and their governments scrutinize: Downward transparency is often dependent on the presence of regulations that allow citizens to access data, like the US Freedom of Information Act, or to the creation of open data portals, like USAspending.gov that shows how the public administration allocates the tax dollars of American citizens.

Nevertheless, existing information provided by public administrations is not the only means to increase downward transparency. Activists also create digital media platforms independently from governmental agencies: In this way, they can gather, order, and visualize information on corruption that would otherwise remain unseen. Although with changing fortunes, in the past few years, activists have attempted to exploit the potential of crowd-reporting platforms in many countries across the world to monitor corruption from below, asking citizens to report the extortion of bribes and similar, small-scale forms of bribery in countries in which this practice is widespread (Zinnbauer 2015). One of the most famous examples is I Paid a Bribe, a platform that the Janaagraha Centre for Citizenship and Democracy created in India to let people denounce, anonymously, acts of bribery. The result is a living map of the bribes paid in several public offices all over the country, with short tales about what happened and what services the bribe has requested. In short, I Paid a Bribe and similar platforms that developed across the world aim at rendering visible the magnitude of a phenomenon, paying bribes, that would be otherwise difficult to capture. The use of visuals, like maps and related infographics, allows for a rapid and yet robust understanding of what happens in the country daily, almost in real time. I Paid a Bribe casts a new light on bribes in India and renders visible something that usually is not, increasing transparency.

However, the presence of high transparency in highly corrupt countries is not necessarily positive. When people can see how widespread corruption is, indeed, they might think that this is the game they should also play since all the others around them are doing the same. Instead of triggering indignation, then, digital media used to crowdsource information about corruption might lead to a more widespread resignation, which might lead people to decide not to mobilize to address the social problem (Zinnbauer 2015; Bauhr and Grimes 2014). In other words, people might decide that the fight is not worth the effort, feeling disempowered and, actually, even ready to become part of the problem, adjusting their behavior to what they think is an environment of systemic corruption. Another aspect is the problematic link between transparency and accountability since the former does not necessarily lead to the latter. A study on Wikileaks, for instance, concluded that the leaked information needs to be fully understood, scrutinized, and interpreted before people act to make the wrongdoers accountable for their acts (Davis and Meckel 2012). When the literacy to understand the leaked documents is absent, transparency does not necessarily prompt accountability. Even more so, digital media might not be as inclusive as they might seem: There is, for instance, the risk of excluding the most vulnerable parts of the population who lack the access or the literacy to employ digital media, creating asymmetries in people's participation in social accountability mechanisms (Grandvoinnet et al. 2015).

This challenge is even more prominent when digital media substitute mechanisms of social accountability that once relied on face-to-face interactions. Once again, a compelling case comes from India, in the state of Rajasthan. There, a widespread movement to promote the transparency of the public administration was to some extent successful in shaping the agenda and gradually changing how the public administration interacts with people, increasing the accountability of public officials as well as recognizing the right of people to be heard by the government (Agrawal and Nair 2018). However, once the practice of live hearings, also known as *Jan Sunwai*, became digital, it reshaped the very meaning of people's participation in social accountability. At the same time, this digitalization process created inequalities between those able to go online and those who cannot do this, either for lack of material resources or for lack of digital media literacy (Agrawal and Nair 2018). In short, the literature claims that digital media might foster transparency, but people should embrace them and include them daily. Therefore, the open question is not so much whether digital media are suitable for implementing transparency and reducing corruption. Instead, what is crucial to understand is why specific digital media platforms are successful in including people, and potential users in particular, in all its stages, from planning to creation, from implementation to evaluation (Thomas 2009; Carr and Jago 2014).

Similarly, other studies that deal with accountability mechanisms suggest more cautious interpretations of the potential digital media have in supporting accountability. For instance, a study on water delivery supplies in rural Africa, Asia, and Latin America underlined cultural aspects like the lack of confidence that governments would respond to citizens' voices but also how digital platforms are conceived and designed and why this might be decisive (Welle, Williams, and Pearce 2016). Another investigation on initiatives to improve health systems and services in Africa and Asia claims that digital media do not promote accountability if they are not supported by other offline actions, like developing positive relationships with governmental institutions (Hrynick and Waldman 2017). Additionally, the use of digital media alone might not be enough: Desk research on digital media employed in top-down initiatives to curb corruption across the world shows that administrative reforms are also needed to render digital media effective (Grönlund 2010).

A Situated and Pragmatic Outlook on Digital Media in Grassroots Anti-Corruption Struggles

The previous section discussed how digital media entangle with anti-corruption efforts from the grassroots consistently with either the principal-agent or the collective action approach. However, these two approaches to corruption are far from mutually exclusive (Marquette and Peiffer 2015). Numerous times, real-life corruption patterns are intricate, with various types of corruption entangling one another and within the same country. Some scholars go beyond the collective action and the principal–agent approaches to corruption. They suggest that a pragmatic perspective is needed to develop ad hoc anti-corruption strategies depending on specific national contexts (della Porta and Vannucci 2012) and local understanding of corruption (Walton and Jones 2017; Torsello 2016).

More specifically, some scholars suggest looking at corruption not just as a widespread problem that societies must face but instead as an ensemble of situated practices that people engage with because they offer solutions to some problems they face in their daily lives (Marquette and Peiffer 2015). Therefore, understanding what corruption is in a specific situation is the first relevant step to crafting substantial anti-corruption measures. From this perspective, one way to tackle corruption is to intervene on the causes of such challenges instead of tackling corruption directly. Social movement organizations and the individual citizens involved in them seem to be particularly well equipped to understand what corruption means for the people who live with it day after day. It is the reason why they might also imagine and then create digitally mediated solutions that are not universal but tied to specific contexts. Indeed, these actors usually organize and mobilize people outside institutional politics, often at the margins of societies. Consequently, their perspective is precious because it considers, from a pragmatic viewpoint, the situation in which anti-corruption strategies should be developed.

However, a further reflection needs to be done, again from a situated and pragmatic perspective and looking at the digital media that these political actors might use to oppose corrupt behaviors. Like corruption, digital media should be considered situated: The situations in which activists imagine, develop, and then employ them are multiple, different from the others, and tied to various corruption scenarios. Even more than this, while we often speak about digital media as a harmonious ensemble for conciseness, when we look at how anti-corruption movements employ them, we can see how internally diversified they are. Any specific type of digital media that activists employ to struggle against corruption is involved in the broader communicative ecology of which other digital media are also part. It is not just because we live in a media-saturated world where digital media live side by side with other media types. Also, activists actively combine them: Social movements rely on multifaceted "repertoires of communication" (Mattoni 2016) from which activists select the most appropriate types of media, according to their needs and skills. Anti-corruption movements are not an exception in this regard. They, too, display high levels of communicative hybridity when it comes to digital media. It happens either because they combine several types of digital media or because they insert digital media into sophisticated communication strategies.

However, the point is not so much to establish the presence and degree of such communicative hybridity. Instead, it is a question of understanding the consequences of this for the anti-corruption movements and the activists engaged in them. To reach this objective, though, it would be necessary neither to look at the overall diffusion of internet connection across a country population nor to focus on how activists employed one type of digital media platform to oppose corruption from the grassroots. However, there still is a lot to know about how anti-corruption efforts entangle digital media in their many forms. Studies based on fieldwork are still rare, except for some works on specific platforms like Facebook (i.e., Jha and Sarangi 2017; Demirhan and Çakir-Demirhan 2017; Fauzanafi 2016) or devices like mobile phones (Zanello and Maassen 2011).

Therefore, it would be fruitful to develop a comparative approach that contrasts different anti-corruption campaigns within the same country and across different countries. One way to do this is to consider the whole repertoire of communication in which activists also include digital media: Despite some few exceptions (Bosch, Wasserman, and Chuma 2018; Mattoni 2017; Tufte 2014), scholars seldom have investigated the use of digital media for grassroots anti-corruption going beyond specific digital devices or services. Such a comparative approach should aim at developing knowledge on the mechanisms that characterize the connection between distinct forms of digital media, services, and devices and different types of corruption. This concept risks remaining empty when the corruption practices remain aggregated in an abstract whole (Heywood 2017). While activists might attempt to tackle petty corruption through online crowdsourcing platforms, they might best counter systematic political corruption through whistle-blowing websites that employ highly secure protocols. However, in both cases, the connection between the type of digital media and the type of corruption would not tell the full story. The types of collective actors are also relevant. A radical collective of techies spread across the globe working together toward an anti-corruption digital platform would foster a completely different understanding of the fight against corruption for the members of a local anti-corruption association that is employing Facebook to promote its activities. Even more, the two types of collective actors would also have different types of digital media literacy, expectations toward what digital media can do for them, and inferences of what digital media are in connection to anti-corruption. Transferring a digital media platform to counter corruption from the grassroots from one country to another, for instance, might be problematic precisely because of the different situations in which social movement organizations and individual activists experience it. This is the case, for instance, of the failed attempt to transfer I Paid a Bribe from India to China (Ang 2014).

BIG DATA AND SMALL DATA IN ANTI-CORRUPTION FROM THE GRASSROOTS

The development of a situated and pragmatic approach to the use of digital media is even more relevant when thinking about the increasingly important role that big data play in the framework of anti-corruption tactics and strategies, including those that activists conceive outside institutions. This type of data emerged from some recent interconnected technological innovations in digital media (Kitchin 2014, 98). A wide range of digital media platforms, including social media, contribute to producing big data. Although they come in many forms and shapes, they share some key features that render them different from other data types. According to Kitchin (2013, 262), big data are enormous in volume, high in velocity, diverse in variety, exhaustive in scope, fine-grained in resolution, relational in nature, and flexible. Social movement organizations engage with big data either to resist the governments' and corporations' extraction of data on what people do in their daily lives or to employ it as an additional tool in the activists' repertoire of contention to sustain their mobilizations (Milan 2018). Anti-corruption social movement organizations also enthusiastically embraced the potential of big data: Among other roles, indeed, big data might have the ability to sustain both accountability and transparency mechanisms (Taylor et al. 2014).

Truth be told, though, big data is not the first and the only type of data that activists employ in their anti-corruption campaigns. Many of them usually rely on what we might name "small data," which might not share the same features of what we usually refer to as big data while being, in any case, of great importance for the activists who manage it. One of the recurrent themes of anti-corruption mobilizations, campaigns, and initiatives is gathering and spreading information on corruption, its consequences, and how people might hinder it through their collective efforts. As such, activists need data on which to base their concerns, mobilize people, and formulate their demands. Transparency International, a leading nongovernmental organization, regularly assembles data on the perception of corruption worldwide that converges in the Perception of Corruption Index. The related report, then, annually ranks countries across the world according to their index scores. In Brazil, instead, activists created an algorithm that interrogates the expenditures of elected MPs and makes them publicly available to show whether the expenses are justified or indicate a suspicious transaction. When the algorithm, whose name is Rosie, detects unclear expenses, a bot publishes this information on Twitter, asking people to provide more information on the said payments (Mattoni 2020). In short, when activists employ data—either big or small—produced through digital platforms, they are further enriching their communicative potential. Their repertoire of communication becomes an even more complex ensemble spanning from the interaction with legacy media professionals to the development of ad hoc algorithms to track corrupt behaviors.

Seen from another perspective, anti-corruption activists, who frequently put data at the center of their mobilizations, campaigns, and initiatives, could be considered one specific type of data activism, defined as an ensemble of "sociotechnical practices of engagement with data . . . or the encounter of data and data-based narratives and tactics with collective action" (Gutiérrez and Milan 2018). While activists might use data in different ways in their mobilizations, three data-related practices seem particularly relevant to understand the role that data has for social movements in fighting corruption: data creation, data usages, and data transformation. While the first two practices seem to be more in line with a principal–agent approach to corruption, the latter is instead more in tune with a collective action approach to corruption.

Activists create data to be used in their collective actions. On some occasions, they can contribute to data production on corruption that does not yet exist, often through the development of dedicated apps. Other times, they can compile new data sets that are already available to the public or even access and unveil data that already exists but is secret. An example of this is the platform Buzon X. The grassroots organization XNet, based in Barcelona, created this secure whistle-blowing platform to gather data on potential corruption scandals from anonymous sources (Mattoni 2017). Data creation practices allow for widespread monitoring of corruption, empowering people to denounce otherwise hidden corruption behaviors. From this viewpoint, data creation practices are consistent with a principal–agent approach to corruption. They enhance the monitoring and denouncing ability of activists asking to make public otherwise confidential data through the activists' digital media platforms.

Activists, then, perform practices that imply the embedment of data into their repertoire of contention. On the one hand, they can do so to sustain some moments of their collective action. For instance, data can become a trigger for public indignation and subsequent collective actions. A telling example is the already mentioned Perception of Corruption Index that Transparency International produces each year. Far from being a simple picture of the perception of corruption across the world, the compilation and spreading of such data have a performative function. The index seeks to make people aware of what their fellow citizens think about corruption in their respective countries. With this regard, including the Perception of Corruption Index in the repertoire of contention of Transparency International might be in line with a collective action approach to corruption, when activists attempt to use it to change the overall view of corruption among the general public. However, the practice of data embedment might also be more in line with a principal–agent approach to corruption when it becomes one of the central pillars of grassroots anti-corruption efforts. An example of this is the Twitter bot that employs the data produced through the software Rosie that detects Brazilian MPs' suspicious expenses. While the software gathers and produces such data, the bot uses them to foster the widespread monitoring of its Twitter followers on any MPs who might have employed public money to sustain misbehavior related to corruption.

Finally, anti-corruption activists also perform practices related to the transformation of data. Since data often does not speak for itself, especially when it comes in relevant quantities, anti-corruption activists need to rearrange data into information that can be more accessible to the broader public, transforming the data (Milan 2018; Schrock 2016). Activists can operate simple transformations, like the common visualization of data through infographic communication, and more complex forms of remediation, according to which the data also leaves the digital realm and becomes part of other media format genres. A relevant example in this regard is the 15MParato campaign in Spain. Through the whistle-blowing platform Buzon X, activists collected a batch of thousands of emails about a corruption scandal that involved Bankia's top managers. Beyond polishing and organizing them into a public, searchable database, activists involved in the campaign also used part of the emails to write down, and then perform, a theatrical piece on the corruption scandal. In this case, data from the digital environment was transformed and then transferred into the physical space of theaters and actors' performances (Mattoni 2017). In this case, data transformation practices resonate with a collective action approach to corruption: The processing of data that would otherwise be difficult to understand at first glance allows activists to increase the public awareness of corruption.

Conclusion

This chapter presented a critical literature review of the current studies on digital media in the framework of anti-corruption problems. More specifically, it sought to establish a connection between corruption scholarship and the different ways it interprets corruption, with the flourishing research that focuses on how social movements employ digital media and the consequences. What emerges is that the theoretical framework used to explain corruption and how to counter it also resonates with how we can understand, from the sociology of media viewpoint, the role that digital media might have—and might not have—in countering corruption from the grassroots.

First, consistently with studies that frame corruption as a collective action problem, activists might employ digital media as a powerful means of expression that can create collective spaces for discussion, indignation, and the creation of movements. Second, in line with research that looks at corruption as a principal–agent problem, the chapter discussed how activists might employ digital media to enhance people's ability to monitor, denounce, and hold accountable those in power who engage in corrupted practices. These two approaches and activists' real-life usages of digital media bring to light one of the tensions that characterize contemporary social movements more generally when they embed digital media—and social media platforms in particular—into their mobilizations.

The chapter then presented a third approach to digital media study in the framework of grassroots anti-corruption efforts which look at both corruption phenomena and activists' digital media usages from a pragmatic and situated perspective. Such an approach would be able to grasp at least three broad research questions, which are also linked to the increasingly important role that big data, algorithmic automation, and machine learning have in the framework of struggles against corruption from the grassroots. Even more importantly, such an approach makes visible three directions along which research on digital media and anti-corruption from the grassroots might develop soon.

First, it would be relevant to map which types of digital media configurations activists employ and why they select some digital media, leaving others in their campaigns' background. In this way, furthermore, the use of big and small data in anti-corruption struggles would also be understood as something that combines with the activists' repertoire of communication. Indeed, data-related practices should not be considered separate from the activists' overall communication strategy. It is only looking at big and small data from this perspective that it would be possible to understand the actual influence it has on anti-corruption from the grassroots, activists' agency in such struggles and their ability to reframe their collective efforts in the light of the newest technological developments.

Second, a pragmatic and situated approach might help to explain how activists embed digital media in already existing anti-corruption practices and which practices instead emerge that were not there before as a result of digital media employment. A mutual shaping of digital media and anti-corruption practices would allow us to weigh the activists' agency vis-à-vis social media, crowdsourcing, and other digital platforms. While activists imagine, design, and create these platforms in some cases, in other cases, they use already existing ones that have been developed, often with commercial purposes, to fulfill other functions. Even more, scholars might understand how certain practices related to anti-corruption can shape, or not, how activists design or appropriate digital media.

Third, such an approach might support examining the consequences of digital media use not so much at the level of the effective reduction of corruption but rather for the anti-corruption movements themselves—in other words, to look at how activists might shift their priorities as a result of technological innovation. This would also lead to an understanding of how digital media's presence might push forward supplementary understandings of what anti-corruption from the grassroots is, what it entails, and what it means to be a good citizen opposed to corruption.

Acknowledgments

The author acknowledges that this publication has been made possible by funding from the European Research Council (ERC) under the European Union's Horizon 2020 research and innovation program, Grant agreement No. 802362 BIT-ACT).

References

Abdulla, Rasha, Thomas Poell, Bernhard Rieder, Robbert Woltering, and Liesbeth Zack. 2018. "Facebook Polls as Proto-Democratic Instruments in the Egyptian Revolution: The 'We Are All Khaled Said' Facebook Page." *Global Media and Communication* 14, no. 1: 141–160.

Adam, Isabelle, and Mihály Fazekas. 2018. "Are Emerging Technologies Helping Win the Fight against Corruption in Developing Countries?" Background Paper 21. Pathways for Prosperity Commission, Oxford.

Adi, Ana, Darren Lilleker, and Dawid Pekalski. 2018. "#Rezist 2017: Communicating Dissent in a Hypermedia Environment." *Media Research: Croatian Journal for Journalism and the Media* 24, no. 1: 69–86.

Agrawal, V., and Nair, H. 2018. "From Jan Sunwai to Rajasthan Right to Hearing Act 2012: Fostering Transparency and Accountability through Citizen Engagement." *Studies in Indian Politics* 6, no. 2: 282–296. Scopus. https://doi.org/10.1177/2321023018797537

Alonso-Muñoz, L., and Casero-Ripollés, A. 2017. "Transparency and political monitoring in the digital environment. Towards a typology of citizen-driven platforms." *Revista Latina de Comunicación Social* 72, 1351–1366. Latin America & Iberia Database; Social Science Database. https://doi.org/10.4185/RLCS-2017-1223-73en

Andersson, Staffan, and Paul M. Heywood. 2009. "The Politics of Perception: Use and Abuse of Transparency International's Approach to Measuring Corruption." *Political Studies* 57, no. 4: 746–767.

Ang, Yuen Yuen. 2014. "Authoritarian Restraints on Online Activism Revisited: Why 'I-Paid-a-Bribe' Worked in India but Failed in China." *Comparative Politics* 47, no. 1: 21–40.

Bauhr, Monika, and Marcia Grimes. 2014. "Indignation or Resignation: The Implications of Transparency for Societal Accountability." *Governance* 27, no. 2: 291–320.

Beverley, Shaazka. 2014. *Curtailing Corruption: People Power for Accountability and Justice*. Boulder, CO: Lynne Rienner.

Bosch, Tanja, Herman Wasserman, and Wallace Chuma. 2018. "South African Activists' Use of Nanomedia and Digital Media in Democratization Conflicts." *International Journal of Communication* 12: 2153–2170.

Bowers-Du Toit, Nadine, and Dion Forster. 2015. "Activating Moral Imagination: EXPOSED 2013 as a Fourth Generation Faith-Based Campaign?" *Stellenbosch Theological Journal* 1, no. 1: 19–40.

Brouwer, Lenie, and Edien Bartels. 2014. "Arab Spring in Morocco: Social Media and the 20 February Movement." *Afrika Focus* 27, no. 2: 9–22.

Carr, Indira, and Robert Jago. 2014. "Petty Corruption, Development and Information Technology as an Antidote." *Round Table* 103, no. 5: 465–482.

Chêne, Marie. 2019. "Successful Approaches to Tackle Petty Corruption." Transparency International Anti-Corruption Helpdesk. Transparency International, Berlin.

Damm, Irina A., Nikolai V. Shchedrin, Olga V. Ronzhina, Evgenii A. Akunchenko, and Andrei V. Korkhov. 2019. "Anti-Corruption Potential of Openness and Accessibility of Municipal Legal Acts." *Journal of Siberian Federal University—Humanities and Social Sciences* 12, no. 3: 378–392.

Davies, Tim, and Silvana Fumega. 2014. "Mixed Incentives: Adopting ICT Innovations for Transparency, Accountability, and Anti-Corruption." *U4 Issue* 2014: 4.

Davis, James W., and Miriam Meckel. 2012. "Political Power and the Requirements of Accountability in the Age of WikiLeaks." *Zeitschrift Für Politikwissenschaft* 22, no. 4: 463–492.

della Porta, Donatella. 2017. "Anti-Corruption from Below. Social Movements against Corruption in Late Neoliberalism." *Partecipazione e Conflitto* 10, no. 3: 661–692.

della Porta, Donatella, and Alberto Vannucci. 2012. *The Hidden Order of Corruption: An Institutional Approach*. London: Ashgate.

Demirhan, Kamil, and Derya Çakir-Demirhan. 2017. *Political Scandal, Corruption, and Legitimacy in the Age of Social Media*. Hershey, PA: IGI Global.

de Sousa, Luis, Peter Larmour, and Barry Hindess, eds. 2009. *Governments, NGOs and Anti-Corruption: The New Integrity Warriors*. London and New York: Routledge.

Fauzanafi, Muhammad Zamzam. 2016. "Searching for Digital Citizenship." *Austrian Journal of South-East Asian Studies* 9, no. 2: 289–294.

Flores, W. 2019. "Youth-Led Anti-Corruption Movement in Post-Conflict Guatemala: "Weaving the Future"?." *Ids Bulletin-Institute of Development Studies* 50, no. 3: 37–51. https://doi.org/10.19088/1968-2019.129

Grandvoinnet, H., Aslam, G., and Raha, S. 2015. *Opening the Black Box: The Contextual Drivers of Social Accountability*. World Bank Publications.

Grönlund, Åke. 2010. "Using ICT to Combat Corruption." In *Increasing Transparency and Fighting Corruption through ICT*, edited by Cecilia Strand, 7–32. Stockholm: SPIDER—The Swedish Program for ICT in Developing Regions.

Gutiérrez, Miren, and Stefania Milan. 2018. "Technopolitics in the Age of Big Data." In *Networks, Movements & Technopolitics in Latin America: Critical Analysis and Current Challenges*, edited by Francisco Sierra Caballero and Tommaso Gravante, 95–109. London: Palgrave MacMillan.

Heywood, Paul M. 2017. "Rethinking Corruption: Hocus-Pocus, Locus and Focus." *Slavonic and East European Review* 95, no. 1: 21–48.

Hough, Dan. 2017. *Analysing Corruption: An Introduction*. Newcastle upon Tyne, UK: Agenda Publishing.

Hrynick, Tabitha, and Linda Waldman. 2017. "ICT-Facilitated Accountability and Engagement in Health Systems: A Review of Making All Voices Count MHealth for Accountability Projects." Brighton, UK: Institute of Development Studies.

Inuwa, Ibrahim, Muhammadou M. O. Kah, and Chidi Ononiwu. 2019. "Understanding How the Traditional and Information Technology Anti-Corruption Strategies Intertwine to Curb Public Sector Corruption: A Systematic Literature Review." In *PACIS 2019 Proceedings*, 15. Twenty-Third Pacific Asia Conference on Information Systems, Xi'an, China.

Jha, Chandan Kumar, and Sudipta Sarangi. 2017. "Does Social Media Reduce Corruption?" Supplement C, *Information Economics and Policy* 39: 60–71.

Jimada, U. 2019. "Social Media in the Public Sphere of Accountability in Nigeria." *Global Media Journal* 17, no. 32: 1–9. Sociology Collection; Sociology Database.

Johnston, Michael. 2014. *Corruption, Contention and Reform: The Power of Deep Democratization*. Cambridge: Cambridge University Press.

Kitchin, Rob. 2013. "Big Data and Human Geography: Opportunities, Challenges and Risks." *Dialogues in Human Geography* 3, no. 3: 262–267.

Kitchin, Rob. 2014. *The Data Revolution: Big Data, Open Data, Data Infrastructures and Their Consequences*. London: Sage.

Klitgaard, Robert. 1988. *Controlling Corruption*. Oakland, CA: University of California Press.

Kossow, Niklas. 2020. "Digital Anti-Corruption: Hopes and Challenges." In *A Research Agenda for Studies of Corruption*, edited by Alina Mungiu-Pippidi and Paul Heywood, 146–157. Cheltenham, UK: Edward Elgar Publishing.

Marquette, Heather, and Caryn Peiffer. 2015. "Corruption and Collective Action." Developmental Leadership Program, Anti-Corruption Resource Centre, Bergen, Norway.

Mattoni, Alice. 2016. *Media Practices and Protest Politics: How Precarious Workers Mobilise*. London and New York: Routledge.

Mattoni, Alice. 2017. "From Data Extraction to Data Leaking. Data-Activism in Italian and Spanish Anti-Corruption Campaigns." *Partecipazione e Conflitto* 10, no. 3: 723–746.

Mattoni, Alice. 2020. "The Grounded Theory Method to Study Data-Enabled Activism against Corruption: Between Global Communicative Infrastructures and Local Activists' Experiences of Big Data." *European Journal of Communication* 35, no. 3: 265–277.

Milan, Stefania. 2018. "Data Activism as the New Frontier of Media Activism." In *Media Activism in the Digital Age*, edited by Victor W. Pickard and Guobin Yang, 151–163. London: Routledge.

Mullard, Saul, and Per Aarvik. 2020. *Supporting Civil Society during the COVID-19 Pandemic.* Stockholm: U4 Anti-Corruption Resource Centre, Chr. Michelsen Institute.

Mungiu-Pippidi, Alina. 2013. "Controlling Corruption through Collective Action." *Journal of Democracy* 24, no. 1: 101–115.

Mungiu-Pippidi, Alina. 2014. *Quantitative Report on Causes of Performance and Stagnation in the Global Fight against Corruption.* Anticorrp WP3 Report. Berlin: Hertie School of Governance.

Mungiu-Pippidi, Alina. 2015. *The Quest for Good Governance.* Cambridge: Cambridge University Press.

Olson, Mancur. 1971. *The Logic of Collective Action: Public Goods and the Theory of Groups.* Cambridge, MA: Harvard University Press.

Organisation for Economic Co-operation and Development. 2015. *Consequences of Corruption at the Sector Level and Implications for Economic Growth and Development.* Paris: OECD Publishing.

Persson, Anna, Bo Rothstein, and Jan Teorell. 2013. "Why Anticorruption Reforms Fail—Systemic Corruption as a Collective Action Problem." *Governance* 26, no. 3: 449–471.

Rose-Ackerman, Susan. 1978. *Corruption: A Study in Political Economy.* New York: Academic Press.

Rose-Ackerman, Susan, and Bonnie J. Palifka. 2016. *Corruption and Government: Causes, Consequences, and Reform.* 2nd ed. Cambridge: Cambridge University Press.

Rotberg, Robert I. 2017. *The Corruption Cure: How Citizens and Leaders Can Combat Graft.* Princeton, NJ: Princeton University Press.

Rothstein, Bo. 2011. "Anti-Corruption: The Indirect 'Big Bang' Approach." *Review of International Political Economy* 18, no. 2: 228–250.

Schroeder, Peter J., and Hamadi Redissi. 2011. "Ben Ali's Fall." *Journal of Democracy* 22, no. 3: 5–19.

Schrock, Andrew R. 2016. "Civic Hacking as Data Activism and Advocacy: A History from Publicity to Open Government Data." *New Media & Society* 18, no. 4: 581–599.

Sengupta, Mitu. 2012. "Anna Hazare and the Idea of Gandhi." *Journal of Asian Studies* 71, no. 3: 593–601.

Taylor, Linnet, Josh Cowls, Ralph Schroeder, and Eric T. Meyer. 2014. "Big Data and Positive Change in the Developing World." *Policy and Internet* 6, no. 4: 418–444.

Thomas, Pradip. 2009. "*Bhoomi, Gyan Ganga,* e-Governance and the Right to Information: ICTs and Development in India." *Telematics and Informatics* 26, no. 1: 20–31.

Toepfl, Florian. 2011. "Managing Public Outrage: Power, Scandal, and New Media in Contemporary Russia." *New Media & Society* 13, no. 8: 1301–1319.

Torsello, Davide. 2012. *The New Environmentalism? Civil Society and Corruption in the Enlarged EU.* Farnham, UK: Ashgate.

Torsello, Davide. 2016. *Corruption in Public Administration: An Ethnographic Approach.* Cheltenham, UK: Edward Elgar Publishing.

Tufte, Thomas. 2014. "Civil Society Sphericules: Emerging Communication Platforms for Civic Engagement in Tanzania." *Ethnography* 15, no. 1: 32–50.

Walton, Grant, and Ainsley Jones. 2017. "The Geographies of Collective Action, Principal-Agent Theory and Potential Corruption in Papua New Guinea." Development Policy Centre Discussion Paper 58. Australian National University, Canberra.

Welle, Katharina, Jennifer Williams, and Joseph Pearce. 2016. "ICTs Help Citizens Voice Concerns over Water—Or Do They?" *IDS Bulletin* 47, no. 1: 41–54.

Zanello, Giacomo, and Paul Maassen. 2011. "Strengthening Citizen Agency and Accountability through ICT: An Extrapolation for Eastern Africa." *Public Management Review* 13, no. 3: 363–382.

Zayani, Mohamed. 2015. *Networked Publics and Digital Contention: The Politics of Everyday Life in Tunisia.* Oxford: Oxford University Press.

Zinnbauer, Dieter. 2015. "Crowdsourced Corruption Reporting: What Petrified Forests, Street Music, Bath Towels, and the Taxman Can Tell Us about the Prospects for Its Future." *Policy & Internet* 7, no. 1: 1–24.

CHAPTER 32

DIGITAL YOUTH POLITICS

JENNIFER EARL, SAM SCOVILL, AND ELLIOT RAMO

THERE has been considerable debate about youth engagement in politics in the last several decades.[1] The early 2000s featured significant concern about youth political disengagement (e.g., Delli Carpini 2000; but see contributions to Delli Carpini 2019), including that digital media usage would worsen disengagement. Other scholars responded by showing that youth are quite politically engaged (e.g., Cohen et al. 2012) but that their primary forms of engagement differ from those of earlier generations (Zukin et al. 2006; Dalton 2008). Instead of engaging almost exclusively in institutional party politics, young people are often engaged in activism, political consumption, and participatory politics (i.e., sharing, remixing, and producing political messages).

Digital media have been central to discussions of each of these forms of engagement. Broadly, digital and social media use could worsen disengagement (e.g., distracting young people with endless on-demand entertainment; see Theocharis and Quintelier [2014] and Delli Carpini [2014]) or support engagement (e.g., through offering pathways to engagement that youth otherwise lack through family, friends, or formal institutions). It might also compensate for existing social inequalities or amplify them.

In this chapter, we bring together various literatures (e.g., elections, social movement studies, internet studies) and disciplines (e.g., sociology, political science, communication) to argue that there is more evidence in favor of youth engagement, that digital and social media have facilitated engagement, and that digital and social media use helps make youth political engagement more inclusive. We review research across five forms of political engagement in making these claims but begin by discussing the history of and context for debates about youth (dis)engagement.

Academic and Public Panics over Youth Disengagement

Research on youth political engagement increased in response to an academic and public panic over youth political disengagement in the late 1990s. While Putnam (2000) was seen as the chief proponent of this panic, others joined in (Rahn and Transue 1998; Easterlin and Crimmins 1991; Mann 1999; Wilkins 2000), leaving researchers, private foundations, and the public worried that youth were woefully politically (e.g., voting) and civically (i.e., individual and collective action to improve one's community, e.g., volunteering) disengaged. Delli Carpini (2000) opined that the evidence for youth disengagement "seems endless" (p. 343), illustrating his point by citing abundant research on disengagement.

Scholarship quickly challenged this panic from two directions. First, some researchers claimed that if youth were disengaged, they may not be responsible for the crisis (Bessant 2004). The ugliness of contemporary politics made avoidance rational (Bennett 2008). A lack of youth outreach (Elliott, Earl, and Maher 2017) and/or ageism when youth become involved (Taft 2015; Gordon 2009) could also lead to disengagement.

Second, research found that youth were not disengaged but that the form of their engagement was changing (Zukin et al. 2006). Dahlgren (2000, 2005), for instance, claimed that young people had turned toward civic engagement, while Dalton (2008) argued that youth had different views of citizenship that led them to protest more but vote less. Bennett (2008) and collaborators (Bennett, Wells, and Freelon 2011) argued for a similar shift, labeling it "actualizing citizenship." Research documenting high levels of youth engagement in volunteering (Shea and Harris 2006) and/or community engagement (Zukin et al. 2006) supported claims about shifting forms of engagement, as did research showing significant participation in more individualistic forms of activism, including political consumption (Kahne, Lee, and Feezell 2013; Fisher 2012).

Crisis-minded researchers saw positive indicators of youth engagement as likely short-lived, brought on by particular candidates or popular social issues. But recent surveys continue to find youth engagement. For instance, a US survey found that only 26% of American youth had not engaged in campaigns and/or electioneering, protest, volunteering, or participatory politics (Elliott and Earl 2019). Across nine European nations, people under 35 were more likely to engage in unconventional activities, especially online activism, although they voted less often than others (Grasso 2018). Harris, Wyn, and Younes (2010) find that even when "ordinary" young people were disillusioned with electoral politics, many still care about social and political issues, engaging in practices like recycling and donating money.

Youth Deficit Model and Digital Media

After research in the early 2000s revealed that the United States was not likely teetering on the edge of an actual youth disengagement crisis, panic dissolved into a tacit but pervasive embrace of the "youth deficit model." Whether reflected in popular criticism of Greta Thunberg, the Parkland survivors, or other young public advocates, many adults implicitly and explicitly argue that youth are not "fit" or "ready" to be active. Referred to as the "youth deficit model," this view sees youth as undersocialized political actors who cannot be effective without adult tutelage: "Despite notably contradictory empirical evidence, youth ... are perceived to be ... less engaged than adults ... treated as incomplete members of society who have to be taught how to correctly engage with politics," and assumed to be politically disinterested (Earl, Maher, and Elliott 2017, 3).

These deficit assumptions are often deeply ingrained in political organizations (Gordon 2009; Gordon and Taft 2011; Taft 2010), which, as discussed more in the section on protest later in the chapter, tend to either ignore youth (implicitly positioning youth as "little adults who lack distinct political interests and concerns from adults"; Earl, Maher, and Elliott [2017, 3]) or assume that youth don't have the capacity or skills to act without adults. For instance, parent–teacher associations were originally created to speak for youth in schools and elsewhere (Skocpol and Fiorina 2004) since youth were assumed to be incapable of speaking for themselves.

Similar to the turn-of-the-century "crisis" in youth political engagement, contemporary research contradicts the deficit model, showing that young people are active in creating their own political identities (Yates and Youniss 1999). Youth are not miniaturized adults but instead hold unique views, have distinct priorities, and may consider different solutions (Earl 2018). Moreover, the political identities youth develop in adolescence influence their future political engagement (Middaugh, Clark, and Ballard 2017). Conversations with family and friends may inform youth political development and engagement, but youth are still at the center of their own development (Elliott, Earl, and Maher 2017). Success in mobilizing youth likely requires focusing on young people's strengths, identities, and interests (Youniss et al. 2002), not their assumed deficits.

Despite the evidence against the deficit model, it drives many public conversations about youth. Across newspapers in nine European countries between 2010 and 2016, Giugni and Grasso (2020) show that youth are depoliticized in coverage; youth are depicted "as actors who do not have political aims" and "where they are addressed politically, it is in negative terms" (p. 591). When the media does cover youth political engagement, it tends to focus on protest engagement (Bosi, Lavizzari, and Voli 2020). Other research shows that coverage of youth political engagement reflects broader inequalities, such that young women (Smith and Holecz 2020) and youth in poverty (Terren, Clua Infante, and Ferran-Ferrer 2020) tend to be covered less. It is important to understand contemporary research on youth political engagement against this highly skeptical history about youth, however discredited. In this review, we push past the deficit model and examine more deeply how digital and social media use affects youth political interest and knowledge, campaign and election engagement, protest participation, political consumption, and participatory politics.

Digital Media and Youth Engagement

The implications of increasing digital and social media usage among youth (Perrin 2015) quickly became part of the debates about their (dis)engagement. Fear of a youth disengagement crisis and the youth deficit model paired well with the fear that young people would get lost in digital entertainment and dislodged from face-to-face networks that support political involvement, forestalling political interest and engagement. Scholars arguing against youth disengagement also examined digital media usage, positing that new visions of citizenship were helped along by new media use (Dahlgren 2005). Thus, whether and how digital and social media use hinders or helps youth political engagement quickly became an important topic of study.

As was true for both the disengagement panic and the deficit model, the lack of empirical support for a digital-tools-lead-to-disengagement panic is clear. Research has largely found that digital and social media supports youth engagement—often in ways that reduce inequality. Indeed, in the most authoritative meta-analysis to date, Boulianne and Theocharis (2020) review 106 survey-based studies and find that the relationship between digital media use and political engagement for youth is overwhelmingly positive.

In addition to context and overall findings, three important takeaways from this discussion inform the rest of this review. First, despite clear overall trends, digital media use may impact various forms of political participation differently.[2] Thus, the rest of this chapter is a review of five different forms of political activity and their relationship to youth and digital and social media.

Second, the way people, including young people, use new media likely matters for its impacts on political engagement (Ekström and Östman 2015). For instance, while politically disinterested youth may become exposed to political news through social networking sites, leading to growing political interest (Boulianne 2019), and while youth may be pulled into offline political engagement by their interest-driven online activity (Kahne and Bowyer 2018), many non-political uses of new media will not result in civic and political engagement (Boulianne and Theocharis 2020). In other words, not all new media usage is the same. Where research allows, our review reflects on different ways youth use digital and social media for each category of political activity.

Third, research on new media and politics brought new concerns to the study of youth engagement. Importantly, there has been concern about the impacts of preexisting socioeconomic and other inequalities on digital political engagement (Schlozman, Verba, and Brady 2010; Schradie 2018), despite newer modeling that has failed to confirm this (Elliott and Earl 2018a). This debate has crossed over into work on youth engagement, asking whether digital and social media use is making youth political participation more or less unequal. While not uncontested, work in this area shows that digital and social media may help young people overcome other inequalities. For instance, in a three-country study, Xenos, Vromen, and Loader (2014) argue that social media drives political engagement so strongly that it can overcome other stratifying influences: "if one were seeking an efficient single indicator of political engagement among young people . . . social media use would appear to be as good as, or better than, SES [socio-economic status]" (p. 163).

More recent survey research draws similar conclusions:

> Young people of color are the biggest consumers of new, online forms of political media . . . young people from socioeconomically disadvantaged households are more likely to get their political information from new online media sources . . . it's not true that the rich are getting richer online . . . rather, that those with more limited resources use digital media to learn, to speak out, and to amplify their voices.
>
> (Luttig and Cohen 2016)

In the sections below, we discuss specific research on new media and inequality pertaining to the section's form of political engagement.

Political Interest and Knowledge, Young People, and Digital Media

Noteworthy precursors to political engagement include factors like civic and political knowledge, political interest, and a sense of self-efficacy. There is a substantial literature on the positive relationship between digital media use and political knowledge (Xenos and Moy 2007; Kenski and Stroud 2006) and interest (Boulianne 2011) in adult populations. However, less research has examined these questions for youth.

What research does exist suggests that findings are at least similar for youth (McAllister 2016). First, new media use can help politically disinterested youth through unanticipated news exposure. Boulianne (2019) argues that social network sites "generate political interest and expand participation" by exposing politically disengaged ties to political content. While traditional media mobilize older citizens, social media use increases both political interest and offline participation in young people. Politically interested youth consume so much political information online that optimistic researchers suggest "social media may function as a leveler of generational differences in political participation" (Holt et al. 2013, 20). While traditional news consumption may promote institutional political participation for youth, online news consumption is associated with non-institutional political engagement, although this may be tied to changing models of citizenship as well (Shehata, Ekström, and Olsson 2016).

Civic awareness, often generated through the consumption of news media, is also foundational to political participation. Boulianne's (2016) study of boycotting, signing petitions, and voting finds that online news consumption builds civic awareness but that raised awareness does not necessarily translate into action. Other research, though, finds that media literacy programs in schools build civic and political skills and yield subsequent political participation (Kahne and Bowyer 2019).

A new consideration in research on political knowledge involves false information dynamics. Although the threat of mistaking false information as real is an online risk for politically active youth (Kahne, Middaugh, and Allen 2014), false information may be a greater threat to elders (Benkler, Faris, and Roberts 2018). During the 2016 US election cycle, people over 65 shared almost seven times the amount of "fake news" as the youngest age group (Guess, Nagler, and Tucker 2019). While there is public discussion on the need for youth civic education on false information, the demographics of avid consumers and spreaders of false information are not youthful. Likewise, research on polarization suggests that, despite significant digital media use by youth, older Americans are becoming far more polarized than younger Americans (Boxell, Gentzkow, and Shapiro 2017). This is consequential since polarization can be both a consequence and a driver of misinformation consumption (Earl et al. forthcoming).

In terms of equity, the impact of digital and social media usage on political interest and knowledge is somewhat unequal. Boulianne (2016) finds that girls are less likely to consume news online and scored lower on civic awareness. In terms of racial and ethnic inequalities, digital media and the hyper-surveillant state politicize youth of color earlier (Cohen 2006). The relatively voracious political new media consumption of disadvantaged youth may increase political knowledge, interest, and efficacy and translate into greater political activity (Luttig and Cohen 2016). If it does, new media may support more equitable development of political interest and knowledge, which could lead to greater political participation.

ELECTIONS, YOUNG PEOPLE, AND DIGITAL MEDIA

Young voter turnout declined in the latter part of the twentieth century but appears to be rebounding, with each new election offering more data. That said, young voters in the United States still turn out less often than successively older voting cohorts (Jacobson 2020). Younger voter turnout (ages 18–29) declined in the United States from about 50% in 1972 to about 35% in 2000 (Shea and Harris 2006). Data from the American National Election Study between 1950 and 1980 shows that approximately 30% of young people under the age of 25 reported being "very interested" in political campaigns; by 2000, this figured dropped to 6% (Shea and Harris 2006), fueling the participation panic discussed at the beginning of this chapter.

Digital spaces designed to increase youth voting (e.g., Rock the Vote) were consequential in the 2002 and 2004 US election cycles. A study of the content and features of such campaign and voting sites revealed that non-campaign-affiliated websites were more actively engaged in appealing to young voters than traditional campaign websites. Candidate websites were not tailored to young voters with accessible language, age-specific appeals, consumable policy bites, or interactive features (Xenos and Bennett 2007). Campaign websites were also found to have struggled with interactivity, shared control, and coproduction that young people want (Xenos and Foot 2008).

The 2004 US presidential election saw 51% of youth voters turn out, with digital media again playing a role in the turnaround. Howard Dean's campaign integrated bottom-up communication from digital platforms with top-down communication from the campaign (Bennett 2008). Young voters read news, talked with others, and thought about the election at higher than anticipated levels (Xenos and Foot 2008).

While general voter turnout remained approximately the same during the 2008 election, digital media usage helped cultivate youth voting (Garcia-Castañon, Rank, and Barreto 2011), with voting rates for those under the age of 30 rising more than three times faster than those for voters over the age of 30 (Fisher 2012). The Obama campaign used digital technologies to enhance and support, rather than replace, face-to-face contact and drew on diverse tactics (e.g., summer internships, organizing fellowships) to recruit and mobilize youth (Fisher 2012).

The 2012 and 2016 US presidential elections saw slightly lower but still significant young voter participation compared to 2008; in contrast, the 2018 US midterms saw record young voter participation. Research also shows that the youth vote is leaning more democratic over time (Center for Information and Research on Civic Learning and Engagement 2020).

Other countries have also observed strong youth voting recently. Britain has experienced a rise in the number of young people voting and becoming party members (Pickard 2018). These recent trends suggest the promise and importance of supporting youth voting through new media engagement, whether through wearable devices, text messaging, social media, or other platforms, mirroring the growing engagement effects for digital media seen more broadly across time (Boulianne 2020).

Some elected officials have tried to cultivate momentum after elections using digital tools. After the 2008 election, the Obama campaign transformed into Organizing for America, blending social movement activism and electoral campaigns (Fisher 2012). Likewise, when Britain's Jeremy Corbyn became the Labour Party leader, he established a grassroots network, Momentum, that heavily relied on young people to organize, participate in, and inform others about events, particularly through digitally spreading the organization's messages (Pickard 2018).

Where inequality is concerned, Boulianne (2016) finds that the indirect effects of online news on voting behaviors may help address participation inequalities between youth voters and their elders by increasing civic awareness among youth. Likewise, first-time voters who are digital natives can be successfully mobilized to vote using digital and social media (Ohme 2019). Digital media may also support youth of color in voting.

For instance, despite facing signficiant barriers, Black youth continue to participate in and exceed White youth participation rates in voting (Rogowski and Cohen 2015). In 2008, turnout by young Black voters in the United States exceeded that of any other same-aged racial and ethnic group (Lopez and Taylor 2009). These trends reflect the significant digital and social media campaigns aimed at mobilizing Black and Latinx youth in 2008 and 2012 (Rogowski and Cohen 2015).

Protest, Young People, and Digital Media

Young people in the United States and globally have been critical to protest across the history of social movements (see Earl, Maher, and Elliott [2017] for a review of youth activism more broadly). As Schmidt (2020) writes, "Teens have been gassed and hit with rubber bullets at protests.... They keep coming back." Young people have played pivotal roles in Black Lives Matter, climate activism, Occupy Wall Street, efforts to defeat the Stop Online Piracy Act, and a wide variety of causes through Change.org (Cohen et al. 2012), among others. European youth have protested austerity programs, Russian youth have mocked Putin's authority, and young people in Hong Kong have fought to limit mainland Chinese power. Across these cases, young people have used digital and social media "to organize independently of elites and elite institutions" (Cohen et al. 2012), although at times they have worked through existing organizations and parties.

Digital media use by youth can facilitate offline action and/or allow for protest in, and through, digital spaces. While many of these kinds of actions—whether street demonstrations facilitated online or online petitions—are well known, many young people also include memes and agitprop (i.e., propaganda often in the form of art or literature) in their activism. "Cultural jamming," for instance, involves attempts to reclaim public space from corporate mass media and television culture (Jenkins 2017). But young activists have also been engaged in hacktivism, distributed denial of service attacks, and trolling (Bessant 2018). White supremacists have used digital media to recruit youth toward right-wing ideologies via online discussion forums, livestreaming services (e.g., Twitch), and online games (Condis 2019).

Given that many young people are now so-called digital natives, one of the central questions has been whether digital media usage has changed how social movement recruitment and micro-mobilization operate.[3] Maher and Earl (2017, 2019) have argued that, for many young people, recruitment is similar but with more modes of communication: friends, family (i.e., their social networks), schools, and clubs (i.e., their organizational networks) mix digital media and face-to-face encounters to encourage engagement.

For young people who lack traditional supports for activism, digital media can provide a meaningful on-ramp for engagement (Maher and Earl 2019). This is true across the ideological spectrum, including far right and racist youth movements (Bessant 2018). While digital activism may be consequential in its own right (Earl 2016), Boulianne and Theocharis (2020) show that online political engagement can encourage offline political engagement too, which is consistent with early claims by Theocharis (2011).[4] This is true even though young people are rarely the explicit target of invitations to act online (Elliott and Earl 2019).

Moreover, online spaces that may not have been developed with the intention of mobilizing young people can nonetheless play a pivitol role in engaging youth activism. For example, young people can be mobilized through online games or bulletin board systems (Beyer 2014). Websites like 4chan and Hong Kong Golden have played a notable, yet largely undocumented, role in the Umbrella Movement (Watts 2018). Young people can also be mobilized through fan activism (see Maher in this volume for a detailed review), which is often cultivated online and skews younger (Earl and Kimport 2009; Earl and Schussman 2008).

Social movement organizations (SMOs) continue to play a role in mobilizing young people but seem troubled in their interactions with youth, whether engaging digital media or not. SMOs have long been difficult spaces for many youth (Gordon 2009; Gordon and Taft 2011); digital engagement is no different. Most SMOs don't successfully digitally facilitate youth engagement (Elliott and Earl 2018b, 2019), failing in basic ways to include or invite youth participation (Elliott, Earl, and Maher 2017). In summarizing the approaches SMOs could more usefully employ to engage young people in movements, Earl argues, "Rather than simply trying to 'stand with youth' by opposing policies that might have long and dangerous legacies, we must also consider how to stand with youth by recognizing their concerns and needs as potentially distinct from adults, by thoughtfully using digital and social media, and by working side by side with youth" (2018, 17). Some older organizations have tried to appeal to young people through the creation of chapters for high school and college students (e.g., Planned Parenthood's Generation Action), but this will be more successful if decision-making is driven by young people, not the 'parent' organization.

In terms of inequality, whether the digital divide exacerbates existing inequalities in social movements or helps mitigate them has been debated. While not focused exclusively on youth, Elliott and Earl (2018a) test both first-level (i.e., access) and second-level (i.e., the ability to use technologies) digital divides on online protest participation, finding minimal effects. There is reason to believe that the same would hold for youth given that digital media provide pathways to activism for those who don't enjoy other supports (Maher and Earl 2019). Also, young people from minority groups are quite active in online political campaigns (Bonilla and Rosa 2015), including notable online and offline activism among Black youth facilitated by digital media. Police and vigilante shootings of Black youth and adults (e.g., Michael Brown, Tamir Rice, Renisha McBride, Aiyana Jones) have provoked large-scale protests and calls for change (Allen and Cohen 2015). Going forward, we are confident that when research on the massive mobilizations seen in the United States and around the world in 2020 is complete, Black, Indigenous, people of color youth will be at the center, using digital media to press their causes.

Political Consumption, Young People, and Digital Media

"Political consumerism" describes "actions by people who make choices among producers and products with the goal of changing objectionable institutional market practices" (Micheletti 2003, 2), such as boycotts and preferential buying called "buycotts." Political consumption is a non-traditional, informal, lifestyle-oriented channel of participation associated with digital media and civic engagement (Dalton 2008) that can be engaged in either individually or collectively, although it is often self-directed (Earl, Copeland, and Bimber 2017). In the United States and Europe, research has found that political consumption is popular among young people (Ward 2008; Ward and de Vreese 2011; Dutra de Barcellos, Teixeira, and Venturini 2014). This has led some to argue that it is important to expand the definition of political participation in order to see political consumption not as a way "out" of political engagement but as one form of young people's increased political expression and involvement (Soler-i-Martí 2015).

While we agree that political consumption is an important form of political engagement, a recent meta-analysis suggests that the relationship to age is uncertain at best (Copeland and Boulianne 2020). There is substantial global variation, with youth in some countries involved far less in political consumption (Barbosa et al. 2014). Thus, while youth may engage in political consumption with some frequency, they are not necessarily more likely to engage in it compared to other age groups.

Also, the relationship between political consumption and digital media is more assumed than established. Many studies associate political consumption with youth and digital media, but few examine the extent to which digital media use is uniquely impactful, even if respondents report finding information that informs political consumption decisions online (Earl, Copeland, and Bimber 2017). Exceptions include Xenos, Vromen, and Loader (2014), who find a positive and statistically significant relationship between social media use and both individualized political activities (e.g., raising money, buy-/boycotting) and collective political activities (e.g., joining political groups).

That said, political consumption is also a form of engagement that is inclusive. Studying 12- to 17-year-olds, Harp et al. (2010) find that Black youth are more likely to participate in political consumerism and a variety of other forms of online and offline political engagement than their same-aged White peers. These particular findings reflect a broader trend of political consumerism being a tool used by women and racial and ethnic minorities to create change (Jenkins 2012a).

Participatory Politics, Young People, and Digital Media

"Participatory politics" is a newer term for action that includes "interactive, peer-based acts through which individuals and groups seek to exert both voice and influence on issues of public concern" that are "not guided by deference to elites or formal institutions" (Cohen et al. 2012, 6). According to Soep (2014), participatory politics include a variety of activities: circulation (i.e., sharing of information), dialogue and feedback (e.g., blog comments), production of content (e.g., making a video), investigation (i.e., pursuit of information beyond established sources), and mobilization (e.g., voting or protest participation). Online memes about "pepper spray cop," a University of California at Davis police officer who used pepper spray against a group of students engaged in Occupy Wall Street, are good illustratons of participatory politics. Online activists used software like Photoshop to place the police officer into unrelated photographs, still photos from films, and classical paintings. These images became iconic to the Occupy movement and demonstrate the importance of both critical thinking and media skills in promoting and defending causes in the digital age (Jenkins 2012b).

Work by Herrera (2012) shows how Egyptian youth activists became revolutionaries by interacting with online media such as popular music, games, Hollywood movies, and information-sharing on social networking sites. Hope and Matthews (2018, 174) explain the ways that young Muslims influence the discourse around radicalization and terrorism in online spaces using humor. Mundt, Ross, and Burnett (2018) interviewed Black Lives Matter activists and found that the most important use of social media was "providing activists with the ability to control their own narrative" (p. 9), which allowed the movement to scale-up, build coalitions, and recruit new participants. These meaning-making activities are important not only to activism but also to politics broadly.

The MacArthur-funded Research Network on Youth and Participatory Politics fielded a nationally representative survey of 3,000 people between the ages of 15 and 25 years, oversampling Black, Latinx, and Asian American youth. The study confirmed the importance of participatory politics and found that interest-driven online activities lay "a foundation for engagement in participatory politics through the development of 'digital social capital' " (Cohen et al. 2012, ix). The survey also showed that 41% of young people engage in at least one form of participatory politics, which is approximately equal to the 44% of young people who reported engaging in other political acts like voting (Cohen et al. 2012).

In a panel survey, youth who increased their political engagement the most were those who discussed politics on social media. These respondents included people of color and individuals with low socioeconomic resources (Luttig and Cohen 2016). This may be because the norms and skills young people learn through social media and other forms of online engagement transfer to their involvement in the political realm (Allen and Cohen 2015). Some research suggests that participatory politics supplements institutional political engagement (Shrestova and Jenkins 2016), and other work shows it is more independent of such engagement (Hirzalla and van Zoonen 2011); but this may reflect country-level differences as opposed to inherent relationships between different kinds of activities.

One challenge facing those engaged in participatory politics is conflict—especially online (Middaugh, Bowyer, and Kahne 2017). Online spaces offer opportunities for civic expression, but they also open up space for negative interactions (Weinstein, Rundle, and James 2015). One approach young people employ to manage this risk is to adopt different strategies for online civic expression, such as using some platforms for political speech but avoiding such speech in other online spaces (Weinstein 2014). Many young people also engage online to educate and persuade others and have developed strategies to deal with conflict such as sharing links to information or acknowledging others' point of view (James et al. 2016). Just as other areas of political engagement include pressures against engagement (e.g., voter suppression, repression of social movements), youth and other participatory politics participants may need support to manage the conflict they encounter as they engage.

Participatory politics is inclusive, allowing participation and access, particularly for youth of color, that institutional politics has not (Allen and Cohen 2015). Undocumented youth are increasingly using social media to "come out" as undocumented, leveraging tools like live video streaming to engage in a form of political resistance (Jenkins 2012b). Like activism, participatory politics creates new pathways to political engagement for those who lack traditional pathways such as having politically involved parents, staying up to date with current events, volunteering, and participating in extracurricular activities (Jenkins 2012b). Luttig and Cohen (2016) find that while individuals with more resources have been shown to be more likely to engage in more traditional political activities, the same is not true for participatory politics.

Conclusion

Overall, youth engagement does not appear to be in the dire straits that many feared in the late 1990s and early 2000s. Despite facing existential challenges like climate change and persistent racism as well as participation challenges caused by unwelcoming organizations and seemingly poisoned political environments, youth are engaging. Digital and social media have become entrenched in many young people's lives and, as such, part of their political lives. Fortunately, the evidence suggests that technology use is facilitating youth engagement across the board—helping them build political and civic knowledge and identities, participate in institutional politics, protest, consume with social conscience, and engage broadly with politics and culture through participatory politics. Young people are also learning to handle the risks and challenges they face on digital and social media and, in some cases (e.g., polarization and fake news), are handling it better than their elders. Also, digital and social media seem to be more of a compensatory technology in the political lives of youth, helping equalize the knowledge and action playing field.

There are also a number of useful online resources that can help drive youth engagement even further. For instance, the Digital Civics Toolkit (www.digitalcivicstoolkit.org) is a collection of evidence-based exercises for helping young people develop civic and political skills. While focused on the classroom, other initiatives are not; for instance, YR Media, formerly Youth Radio, helps young people build investigative and reporting skills as well as marketable media production and editing skills. In campaigns and elections, Tufts University's Center for Information and Research on Civic Learning and Engagement has long been a leader in tracking and promoting youth engagement in democratic institutions. The Informing Activists Project offers a growing set of videos by social movement scholars addressing practical strategic and tactical questions that young activists—whether organizers, participants, or young people interested in perhaps becoming active—may want to ask themselves, walking young people through what social movement research says on the topic in short videos. Harvard's "10 Questions for Young Changemakers" (https://yppactionframe.fas.harvard.edu/home) site focuses young people on 10 evidence-based questions that they may want to ask themselves as they engage and try to engage others in participatory politics. These online resources are the tip of the iceberg, representing evidence-based interventions. Many more resources exist on digital and social media, underscoring one of the many reasons that digital and social media usage is so important to youth engagement and to the equitability of that engagement.

There are also important frontiers for future research. First, age is only one axis of identity and inequality. It is important for future research to build on work on intersectionality to better understand how dynamics differ when researchers consider intersecting identities and axes of inequality. For instance, Terriquez (2015) finds that online spaces were critical for DREAMers who used those spaces in order to come out as undocumented and as queer, but many social movements and SMOs have been slow to embrace intersectional youth identities (Elliott, Earl, and Maher 2017). Future research on digitally facilitated political participation should further consider intersectional identities. Second, as platforms proliferate, it may be useful for research to consider whether they substantially differ in the opportunities they facilitate for youth political engagement of different forms. For instance, do Twitter, Facebook, TikTok, YouTube, Discord, GroupMe, and other platforms differ substantially in their overall level, form, organization of youth engagement, or the equality of that engagement?

Notes

1. Researchers vary in their definition of youth. Most include up through college-aged young people (early 20s). Research on voting frequently uses age 25, with some researchers

considering people under 30 or 35. Research on how the public defines youth is similarly variable; for many, it pushes into the upper 20s.
2. While some mean electoral participation when they use the term "political participation," we use it broadly to include institutional, non-institutional, individualized (e.g., political consumption), and "expressive" (e.g., participatory politics) forms of participation. We do not include civic activity such as community volunteering.
3. Researchers have also been interested in youth activist identities. While vital to continuing engagement, activist identities do not automatically develop from participation. In fact, many young people who engage in activism don't see themselves as activists (Maher, Johnstonbaugh, and Earl 2020). Digital media can play a formative role in the adoption of more general political identities among youth (Kahne, Lee, and Feezell 2013) and may support alternative political identities that lead to activist engagement (Dahlgren and Olsson 2007).
4. We acknowledge that drawing the boundaries between online and offline activism is difficult, particularly for youth, given pervasive use of digital and social media (Maher and Earl 2019). Many "offline" engagements were facilitated through social and digital media. The work on digital activism we reference tends to focus on more fully online forms of participation (e.g., online petitioning).

REFERENCES

Allen, Danielle, and Cathy Cohen. 2015. "The New Civil Rights Movement Doesn't Need an MLK." *Washington Post*, April 10. https://www.washingtonpost.com/opinions/the-new-civil-rights-movement/2015/04/10/e43d2caa-d8bb-11e4-ba28-f2a685dc7f89_story.html.

Barbosa, Livia, Fátima Portilho, John Wilkinson, and Veranise Dubeux. 2014. "Trust, Participation and Political Consumerism among Brazilian Youth." *Journal of Cleaner Production* 63: 93–101.

Benkler, Yochai, Rob Faris, and Hal Roberts. 2018. *Network Propaganda: Manipulation, Disinformation, and Radicalization in American Politics*. New York: Oxford University Press.

Bennett, W. Lance. 2008. "Changing Citizenship in the Digital Age." In *Civic Life Online: Learning How Digital Media Can Engage Youth*, edited by W. Lance Bennett, 1–24. Cambridge, MA: MIT Press.

Bennett, W. Lance, Chris Wells, and Deen Freelon. 2011. "Communicating Civic Engagement: Contrasting Models of Citizenship in the Youth Web Sphere." *Journal of Communication* 61, no. 5: 835–856.

Bessant, Judith. 2004. "Mixed Messages: Youth Participation and Democratic Practice." *Australian Journal of Political Science* 39, no. 2: 387–404. doi: 10.1080/1036114042000238573

Bessant, Judith. 2018. "Right-Wing Populism and Young 'Stormers': Conflict in Democratic Politics." In *Young People Re-Generating Politics in Times of Crises*, edited by Sarah Pickard and Judith Bessant, 139–159. Palgrave Studies in Young People and Politics. Cham, Switzerland: Springer Nature.

Beyer, Jessica L. 2014. *Expect Us: Online Communities and Political Mobilization*. New York: Oxford University Press.

Bonilla, Yarimar, and Jonathan Rosa. 2015. "#Ferguson: Digital Protest, Hashtag Ethnography, and the Racial Politics of Social Media in the United States." *American Ethnologist* 42, no. 1: 4–17.

Bosi, Lorenzo, Anna Lavizzari, and Stefania Voli. 2020. "Representation of Youth in the Public Debate in Greece, Italy, and Spain: Does the Political Leaning of Newspapers Have Any Effect?" *American Behavioral Scientist* 64, no. 5: 620–637.

Boulianne, Shelley. 2011. "Stimulating or Reinforcing Political Interest: Using Panel Data to Examine Reciprocal Effects between News Media and Political Interest." *Political Communication* 28, no. 2: 147–162.

Boulianne, Shelley. 2016. "Online News, Civic Awareness, and Engagement in Civic and Political Life." *New Media & Society* 18, no. 9: 1840–1856.

Boulianne, Shelley. 2019. "Transforming the Disengaged: Social Media and Youth in Canada." In *What's Trending in Canadian Politics? Understanding Transformations in Power, Media, and the Public Sphere*, edited by Mireille Lalancette, Vincent Raynauld, and Erin Crandall, 86–105. Vancouver, Canada: University of British Columbia Press.

Boulianne, Shelley. 2020. "Twenty Years of Digital Media Effects on Civic and Political Participation." *Communication Research* 47, no. 7: 947–966.

Boulianne, Shelley, and Yannis Theocharis. 2020. "Young People, Digital Media, and Engagement: A Meta-Analysis of Research." *Social Science Computer Review* 38, no. 2: 111–127.

Boxell, Levi, Matthew Gentzkow, and Jesse M. Shapiro. 2017. "Greater Internet Use Is not Associated with Faster Growth in Political Polarization among US Demographic Groups." *Proceedings of the National Academy of Sciences of the United States of America* 114, no. 40: 10612–10617.

Center for Information and Research on Civic Learning and Engagement. 2020. "Broadening Youth Voting." Accessed September 6, 2020. https://circle.tufts.edu/our-research/broadening-youth-voting#youth-voting-in-recent-elections.

Cohen, Cathy. 2006. "African American Youth: Broadening Our Understanding of Politics, Civic Engagement and Activism." Social Science Research Council. Accessed April 30, 2020. http://ya.ssrc.org/african/.

Cohen, Cathy J., Joseph Kahne, Benjamin Bowyer, Ellen Middaugh, and Jon Rogowski. 2012. *Participatory Politics: New Media and Youth Political Action*. Chicago: MacArthur.

Condis, Megan. 2019. "Hateful Games: Why White Supremacist Recruiters Target Gamers and How to Stop Them." In *Digital Ethics: Rhetoric and Responsibility in Online Aggression*, edited by Jessica Reyman and Erika M. Sparby, 143–159. New York and London: Routledge.

Copeland, Lauren, and Shelley Boulianne. 2020. "Political Consumerism: A Meta-analysis." *International Political Science Review*. Published ahead of print March 4, 2020. https://doi.org/10.1177%2F0192512120905048.

Dahlgren, Peter. 2000. "The Internet and the Democratization of Civic Culture." *Political Communication* 17, no. 4: 335–340.

Dahlgren, Peter. 2005. "The Internet, Public Spheres, and Political Communication: Dispersion and Deliberation." *Political Communication* 22, no. 2: 147–162.

Dahlgren, Peter, and Tobias Olsson. 2007. "Young Activists, Political Horizons and the Internet: Adapting the Net to One's Purposes." In *Young Citizens in the Digital Age: Political Engagement, Young People and New Media*, edited by Brian D. Loader, 68–81. New York and London: Routledge.

Dalton, Russell J. 2008. *The Good Citizen: How a Younger Generation Is Reshaping American Politics*. Washington, DC: CQ Press.

Delli Carpini, Michael X. 2000. "Gen.com: Youth, Civic Engagement, and the New Information Environment." *Political Communication* 17, no. 4: 341–349.

Delli Carpini, Michael X. 2014. "The Political Effects of Entertainment Media." In *Oxford Handbook of Political Communication*, edited by Kate Kenski and Kathleen Hall Jamieson, 851–870. Oxford: Oxford University Press.

Delli Carpini, Michael X., ed. 2019. *Digital Media and Democratic Futures*. Philadelphia: University of Pennsylvania Press.

Dutra de Barcellos, Marcia, Caio Mascarello Teixeira, and Jonas Cardona Venturini. 2014. "Personal Values Associated with Political Consumption: An Exploratory Study with University Students in Brazil." *International Journal of Consumer Studies* 38, no. 2: 207–216.

Earl, Jennifer. 2016. "Protest Online: Theorizing the Consequences of Online Engagement." In *The Consequences of Social Movements*, edited by Lorenzo Bosi, Marco Giugni, and Katrin Uba, 363–400. Cambridge: Cambridge University Press.

Earl, Jennifer. 2018. "Youth Protest's New Tools and Old Concerns." *Contexts* 17, no. 2: 15–17.

Earl, Jennifer, Lauren Copeland, and Bruce Bimber. 2017. "Routing around Organizations: Self-Directed Political Consumption." *Mobilization* 22, no. 2: 131–153.

Earl, Jennifer, Rina James, Elliot Ramo, and Sam Scovill. Forthcoming. "Protest, Activism, and False Information." In *Routledge Companion to Media Misinformation & Populism*, edited by Howard Tumber and Silvio Waisbord. New York and London: Routledge.

Earl, Jennifer, and Katrina Kimport. 2009. "Movement Societies and Digital Protest: Fan Activism and Other Nonpolitical Protest Online." *Sociological Theory* 27, no. 3: 220–243.

Earl, Jennifer, Thomas V. Maher, and Thomas Elliott. 2017. "Youth, Activism, and Social Movements." *Sociological Compass* 11, no. 4: e12465.

Earl, Jennifer, and Alan Schussman. 2008. "Contesting Cultural Control: Youth Culture and Online Petitioning." In *Digital Media and Civic Engagement*, edited by W. Lance Bennett, 71–95. Cambridge, MA: MIT Press.

Easterlin, Richard A., and Eileen M. Crimmins. 1991. "Private Materialism, Personal Self-Fulfillment, Family Life, and Public Interest: The Nature, Effects, and Causes of Recent Changes in the Values of American Youth." *Public Opinion Quarterly* 55, no. 4: 499–533.

Ekström, Mats, and Johan Östman. 2015. "Information, Interaction, and Creative Production: The Effects of Three Forms of Internet Use on Youth Democratic Engagement." *Communication Research* 42, no. 6: 796–818.

Elliott, Thomas, and Jennifer Earl. 2018a. "Online Protest Participation and the Digital Divide: Modeling the Effect of the Digital Divide on Online Petition-Signing." *New Media & Society* 20, no. 2: 698–719.

Elliott, Thomas, and Jennifer Earl. 2018b. "Organizing the Next Generation: Youth Engagement with Activism Inside and Outside of Organizations." *Social Media & Society* 4, no. 1: 1–14.

Elliott, Thomas, and Jennifer Earl. 2019. "Kids These Days: Supply and Demand for Youth Online Political Engagement." In *Digital Media and Democratic Futures*, edited by Michael X. Delli Carpini, 69–100. Philadelphia: University of Pennsylvania Press.

Elliott, Thomas, Jennifer Earl, and Thomas V. Maher. 2017. "Recruiting Inclusiveness: Intersectionality, Social Movements, and Youth Online." *Research in Social Movements, Conflicts, and Change* 41: 279–311.

Fisher, Dana R. 2012. "Youth Political Participation: Bridging Activism and Electoral Politics." *Annual Review of Sociology* 38, no. 1: 119–137.

Garcia-Castañon, Marcela, Alison D. Rank, and Matt A. Barreto. 2011. "Plugged In or Tuned Out? Youth, Race, and Internet Usage in the 2008 Election." *Journal of Political Marketing* 10, no. 1–2: 115–138.

Giugni, Marco, and Maria Grasso. 2020. "Talking about Youth: The Depoliticization of Young People in the Public Domain." *American Behavioral Scientist* 64, no. 5: 591–607.

Gordon, Hava Rachel. 2009. *We Fight to Win: Inequality and the Politics of Youth Activism*. New Brunswick, NJ: Rutgers University Press.

Gordon, Hava R., and Jessica K. Taft. 2011. "Rethinking Youth Political Socialization Teenage Activists Talk Back." *Youth & Society* 43, no. 4: 1499–1527.

Grasso, Maria. 2018. "Young People's Political Participation in Europe in Times of Crisis." In *Young People Re-Generating Politics in Times of Crises*, edited by Sarah Pickard and Judith Bessant, 179–196. Palgrave Studies in Young People and Politics. Cham, Switzerland: Springer Nature.

Guess, Andrew, Jonathan Nagler, and Joshua Tucker. 2019. "Less than You Think: Prevalence and Predictors of Fake News Dissemination on Facebook." *Science Advances* 5, no. 1: eaau4586. https://advances.sciencemag.org/content/5/1/eaau4586.

Harp, Dustin, Ingrid Bachmann, Tania Cantrell Rosas-Moreno, and Jaime Loke. 2010. "Wave of Hope: African American Youth Use Media and Engage More Civically, Politically Than Whites." *Howard Journal of Communications* 21, no. 3: 224–246.

Harris, Anita, Johanna Wyn, and Salem Younes. 2010. "Beyond Apathetic or Activist Youth: 'Ordinary' Young People and Contemporary Forms of Participation." *Young* 18, no. 1: 9–32.

Herrera, Linda. 2012. "Youth and Citizenship in the Digital Age: A View from Egypt." *Harvard Educational Review* 82, no. 3: 333–352.

Hirzalla, Fadi, and Liesbet van Zoonen. 2011. "Beyond the Online/Offline Divide: How Youth's Online and Offline Civic Activities Converge." *Social Science Computer Review* 29, no. 4: 481–498.

Holt, Kristoffer, Adam Shehata, Jesper Strömbäck, and Elisabet Ljungberg. 2013. "Age and the Effects of News Media Attention and Social Media Use on Political Interest and Participation: Do Social Media Function as a Leveller?" *European Journal of Communication* 28, no. 1: 19–34.

Hope, Andrew, and Julie Matthews. 2018. " 'How Not to Be a Terrorist': Radicalisation and Young Western Muslims' Digital Discourses." In *Young People Re-Generating Politics in Times of Crises*, edited by Sarah Pickard and Judith Bessant, 161–177. Palgrave Studies in Young People and Politics. Cham, Switzerland: Springer Nature.

Jacobson, Louis. 2020. "A Closer Look at Turnout, Young Voters and a Key Bernie Sanders Strategy." Politifact. Accessed March 4, 2020. https://www.politifact.com/article/2020/mar/04/closer-look-turnout-young-voters-and-key-bernie-sa/.

James, Carrie, Daniel T. Gruner, Ashley Lee, and Margaret Rundle. 2016. "Getting into the Fray: Civic Youth, Online Dialogue, and Implications for Digital Literacy Education." *Journal of Digital and Media Literacy*. https://www.researchgate.net/publication/324728452_Getting_Into_the_Fray_Civic_Youth_Online_Dialogue_and_Implications_for_Digital_Literacy_Education

Jenkins, Henry. 2012a. " 'Cultural Acupuncture': Fan Activism and the Harry Potter Alliance." *Transformative Works and Cultures* 10: 206–229.

Jenkins, Henry. 2012b. "The New Political Commons." *Options Politiques*, November 1.

Jenkins, Henry. 2017. "From Culture Jamming to Cultural Acupuncture." In *Culture Jamming Activism and the Art of Cultural Resistance*, edited by M. Dery, M. DeLaure, and M. Fink, 133–160. New York: New York University Press.

Kahne, Joseph, and Benjamin Bowyer. 2018. "The Political Significance of Social Media Activity and Social Networks." *Political Communication* 35: 470–493.

Kahne, Joseph, and Benjamin Bowyer. 2019. "Can Media Literacy Education Increase Digital Engagement in Politics?" *Learning, Media and Technology* 44, no. 2: 211–224.

Kahne, Joseph, Nam-Jin Lee, and Jessica T. Feezell. 2013. "The Civic and Political Significance of Online Participatory Cultures among Youth Transitioning to Adulthood." *Journal of Information Technology & Politics* 10, no. 1: 1–20.

Kahne, Joseph, Ellen Middaugh, and Danielle Allen. 2014. "Youth, New Media, and the Rise of Participatory Politics." In *From Voice to Influence: Understanding Citizenship in a Digital Age*, edited by Danielle Allen and Jennifer S. Light, 35–58. Chicago: University of Chicago Press.

Kenski, Kate, and Natalie Stroud. 2006. "Connections between Internet Use and Political Efficacy, Knowledge, and Participation." *Journal of Broadcasting & Electronic Media* 50, no. 2: 173–192.

Lopez, Mark Hugo, and Paul Taylor. 2009. *Dissecting the 2008 Electorate: Most Diverse in U.S. History*. Washington, DC: Pew Research Center.

Luttig, Matthew D., and Cathy J. Cohen. 2016. "How Social Media Helps Young People—Especially Minorities and the Poor—Get Politically Engaged." *Washington Post*, September 9. https://www.washingtonpost.com/news/monkey-cage/wp/2016/09/09/how-social-media-helps-young-people-especially-minorities-and-the-poor-get-politically-engaged/.

Maher, Thomas V., and Jennifer Earl. 2017. "Pathways to Contemporary Youth Protest: The Continuing Relevance of Family, Friends, and School for Youth Micromobilization." In *Social Movements and Media*, edited by Jennifer Earl and Deana Rohlinger, 55–87. Bingley, UK: Emerald Publishing.

Maher, Thomas V., and Jennifer Earl. 2019. "Barrier or Booster? Digital Media, Social Networks, and Youth Micromobilization." *Sociological Perspectives* 62, no. 6: 865–883.

Maher, Thomas V., Morgan Johnstonbaugh, and Jennifer Earl. 2020. " 'One Size Doesn't Fit All': Connecting Views of Activism with Youth Activist Identification." *Mobilization* 25, no. 1: 27–44.

Mann, Sheilah. 1999. "What the Survey of American College Freshmen Tells Us about Their Interest in Politics and Political Science." *PS: Political Science & Politics* 32, no. 2: 263–268.

McAllister, Ian. 2016. "Internet Use, Political Knowledge, and Youth Electoral Participation in Australia." *Journal of Youth Studies* 19, no. 9: 1220–1236.

Micheletti, Michele. 2003. *Political Virtue and Shopping: Individuals, Consumerism, and Collective Action*. New York: Palgrave.

Middaugh, Ellen, Benjamin Bowyer, and Joseph Kahne. 2017. "U Suk! Participatory Media and Youth Experience with Political Discourse." *Youth & Society* 49, no. 7: 902–922.

Middaugh, Ellen, Lynn Schofield Clark, and Parissa J. Ballard. 2017. "Digital Media, Participatory Politics, and Positive Youth Development." Supplement 2, *Pediatrics* 140: S127–S131.

Mundt, Marcia, Karen Ross, and Charla M. Burnett. 2018. "Scaling Social Movements through Social Media: The Case of Black Lives Matter." *Social Media + Society* 4, no. 4: 2056305118807911.

Ohme, Jakob. 2019. "When Digital Natives Enter the Electorate: Political Social Media Use among First-Time Voters and Its Effects on Campaign Participation." *Journal of Information Technology & Politics* 16, no. 2: 119–136.

Perrin, Andrew. 2015. "Social Media Usage: 2005–2015." Pew Research Center, October 8. https://www.pewresearch.org/internet/2015/10/08/social-networking-usage-2005-2015/.

Pickard, Sarah. 2018. "Momentum and the Movementist 'Corbynistas': Young People Regenerating the Labour Party in Britain." In *Young People Re-Generating Politics in Times of*

Crises, edited by Sarah Pickard and Judith Bessant, 115–137. Palgrave Studies in Young People and Politics. Cham, Switzerland: Springer Nature.

Putnam, Robert D. 2000. *Bowling Alone: The Collapse and Revival of American Community.* New York: Simon & Schuster.

Rahn, Wendy M., and John E. Transue. 1998. "Social Trust and Value Change: The Decline of Social Capital in American Youth, 1976–1995." *Political Psychology* 19, no. 3: 545–565.

Rogowski, Jon C., and Cathy J. Cohen. 2015. *Black Millennials in America: Documenting the Experiences, Voices and Political Future of Young Black Americans.* Chicago: Black Youth Project.

Schlozman, Kay Lehman, Sidney Verba, and Henry E. Brady. 2010. "Weapon of the Strong? Participatory Inequality and the Internet." *Perspectives on Politics* 8, no. 2: 487–509.

Schmidt, Samantha. 2020. "Teens Have Been Gassed and Hit with Rubber Bullets at Protests. They Keep Coming Back." *Washington Post*, June 6. https://www.washingtonpost.com/dc-md-va/2020/06/05/teens-protests-george-floyd-tear-gas/.

Schradie, Jen. 2018. "The Digital Activism Gap: How Class and Costs Shape Online Collective Action." *Social Problems* 65, no. 1: 51–74.

Shea, Daniel M., and Rebecca Harris. 2006. "Why Bother? Because Peer-to-Peer Programs Can Mobilize Young Voters." *PS: Political Science and Politics* 39, no. 2: 341–345.

Shehata, Adam, Mats Ekström, and Tobias Olsson. 2016. "Developing Self-Actualizing and Dutiful Citizens: Testing the AC-DC Model Using Panel Data among Adolescents." *Communication Research* 43, no. 8: 1141–1169.

Shrestova, Sangita, and Henry Jenkins. 2016. "From Voice to Influence: An Introduction." In *From Voice to Influence*, edited by Danielle Allen and Jennifer S. Light, 1–18. Chicago: University of Chicago Press.

Skocpol, Theda, and Morris P. Fiorina. 2004. *Civic Engagement in American Democracy.* Washington, DC: Brookings Institution Press.

Smith, Katherine A., and Valentina Holecz. 2020. "Not Seen and Not Heard? The Representation of Young Women and Their Political Interests in the Traditional Print Public Sphere." *American Behavioral Scientist* 64, no. 5: 638–651.

Soep, Elisabeth. 2014. *Participatory Politics: Next-Generation Tactics to Remake Public Spheres.* Cambridge, MA: MIT Press.

Soler-i-Martí, Roger. 2015. "Youth Political Involvement Update: Measuring the Role of Cause-Oriented Political Interest in Young People's Activism." *Journal of Youth Studies* 18, no. 3: 396–416.

Taft, Jessica K. 2010. *Rebel Girls: Youth Activism and Social Change across the Americas.* New York: New York University Press.

Taft, Jessica K. 2015. " 'Adults Talk Too Much': Intergenerational Dialogue and Power in the Peruvian Movement of Working Children." *Childhood* 22, no. 4: 460–473.

Terren, Ludovic, Anna Clua Infante, and Núria Ferran-Ferrer. 2020. "Falling on Deaf Ears? An Analysis of Youth Political Claims in the European Mainstream Press." *American Behavioral Scientist* 64, no. 5: 608–619.

Terriquez, Veronica. 2015. "Intersectional Mobilization, Social Movement Spillover, and Queer Youth Leadership in the Immigrant Rights Movement." *Social Problems* 62, no. 3: 343–362.

Theocharis, Yannis. 2011. "The Influence of Postmaterialist Orientations on Young British People's Offline and Online Political Participation." *Representation* 47: 435–455.

Theocharis, Yannis, and Ellen Quintelier. 2014. "Stimulating Citizenship or Expanding Entertainment? The Effect of Facebook on Adolescent Participation." *New Media & Society* 18, no. 5: 817–836.

Ward, Janelle. 2008. "The Online Citizen-Consumer: Addressing Young People's Political Consumption through Technology." *Journal of Youth Studies* 11, no. 5: 513–526.

Ward, Janelle, and Claes de Vreese. 2011. "Political Consumerism, Young Citizens and the Internet." *Media, Culture and Society* 33, no. 3: 399–413.

Watts, Rob. 2018. "The Crisis of Democracy in Hong Kong: Young People's Online Politics and the Umbrella Movement." In *Young People Re-Generating Politics in Times of Crises*, edited by Sarah Pickard and Judith Bessant, 97–113. Palgrave Studies in Young People and Politics. Cham, Switzerland: Springer Nature.

Weinstein, Emily C. 2014. "The Personal Is Political on Social Media: Online Civic Expression Patterns and Pathways among Civically Engaged Youth." *International Journal of Communication* 8: 210–233.

Weinstein, Emily C., Margaret Rundle, and Carrie James. 2015. "A Hush Falls over the Crowd? Diminished Online Civic Expression among Young Civic Actors." *International Journal of Communication* 9: 84–106.

Wilkins, Karin Gwinn. 2000. "The Role of Media in Public Disengagement from Political Life." *Journal of Broadcasting & Electronic Media* 44, no. 4: 569–580.

Xenos, Michael, and W. Lance Bennett. 2007. "The Disconnection in Online Politics: The Youth Political Web Sphere and US Election Sites, 2002–2004." *Information, Communication & Society* 10, no. 4: 443–464.

Xenos, Michael, and Kirsten Foot. 2008. "Not Your Father's Internet: The Generation Gap in Online Politics." In *Civic Life Online: Learning How Digital Media Can Engage Youth*, edited by W. Lance Bennet, 51–70. Cambridge, MA: MIT Press.

Xenos, Michael, and Patricia Moy. 2007. "Direct and Differential Effects of the Internet on Political and Civic Engagement." *Journal of Communication* 57, no. 4: 704–718.

Xenos, Michael, Ariadne Vromen, and Brian D. Loader. 2014. "The Great Equalizer? Patterns of Social Media Use and Youth Political Engagement in Three Advanced Democracies." *Information, Communication & Society* 17, no. 2: 151–167.

Yates, Miranda, and James Youniss, eds. 1999. *Roots of Civic Identity: International Perspectives on Community Service and Activism in Youth*. New York: Cambridge University Press.

Youniss, James, Susan Bales, Verona Christmas-Best, Marcelo Diversi, Milbrey Mclaughlin, and Rainer Silbereisen. 2002. "Youth Civic Engagement in the Twenty-First Century." *Journal of Research on Adolescence* 12, no. 1: 121–148.

Zukin, Cliff, Scott Keeter, Molly Andolina, Krista Jenkins, and Michael X. Delli Carpini. 2006. *A New Engagement? Political Participation, Civic Life, and the Changing American Citizen*. Oxford: Oxford University Press.

CHAPTER 33

TRANSFORMATIONS IN AMERICAN POLITICAL PARTICIPATION

DEANA A. ROHLINGER

IN MAY 2020, a couple of dozen people clad in gym clothes assembled across the street from a courthouse in Clearwater, Florida. Fitness enthusiasts were angry that the city had shuttered the health clubs in response to the global pandemic. The novel coronavirus didn't seem to affect anyone they knew, and gym-goers were angry about all of the restrictions. Gym members weren't the only ones who were angry. On Mayday workers from Amazon, Whole Foods, Instacart, FedEx, Target, and Walmart engaged in a series of work stoppages to advocate for better practices and equipment to protect workers from contracting COVID-19 and to do more for employees who fell ill with the virus. Protest organizers explicitly connected the dots between racism, structural inequalities, and health. Workers, for example, accused Jeff Bezos, the owner of Amazon and Whole Foods, of building his empire on the backs of predominantly BIPOC (black, indigenous, and people of color) workers and making himself a trillionaire during the pandemic at these same workers' expense. In an opinion piece in *Street Roots*, Alli, a Whole Foods employee, writes about the top-down racism of the company and derides Bezos for using the pandemic as a photo op rather than for protecting the BIPOC communities from which he benefits. She criticizes Amazon's commitment to "fight against systemic racism and injustice" and argues that it has done the opposite:

> While workers are being deemed "essential" during a pandemic, it is very rarely followed up with any action proving they are essential (and no those thank-you commercials and Hero shirts are not what they're talking about). With having health benefits being stripped away months before COVID-19 hit, a joke of a "hazardous pay" (which got taken away much too early) and bare to minimum personal

protective equipment and safety protocols, team members are forced to work in poor conditions.

(Alli 2020)

These efforts continued throughout the summer with workers staging walkouts and caravanning from, in the case of Amazon, one distribution center to the next in states where cases were on the rise. Protests spilled into the streets later that month as Americans called for the overhaul of the criminal justice system after three unarmed Black people—Ahmaud Arbery, Breonna Taylor, and George Floyd—were killed by active and retired law enforcement officers. Throughout the summer and into the fall, citizens expressed their grievances outside of state houses and the White House, protesting everything from Trump's use of federal agents to grab citizens off the streets in Portland, Oregon, to state stay-at-home orders and local mask mandates. Americans' political engagement swelled beyond protests. The United States Election Project, which is run by Dr. Michael McDonald at the University of Florida, reported that nearly 160 million Americans had voted in the 2020 election—a record high 66.7% of eligible voters (McDonald 2020).

The election results prompted additional protests, and on January 6, 2021, Americans were reminded that some political participation is intended to undermine democratic processes and institutions. After more than a month of denying his decisive electoral loss and urging his backers to support his "Stop the Steal" campaign, Trump called his "warriors" to come to Washington, DC, for, what he tweeted, would be a "big protest." Online and at the event, however, discourse took a more ominous turn. Trump, Rudy Giuliani, Donald Trump Jr., and several Republican politicians urged the crowd to show strength and never concede the election. The angry group marched to the US Capitol, overpowered police, and seized the building. As of March 2021, the attempted insurrection has led to more than 280 arrests and another failed effort to impeach Donald Trump.

The purpose of outlining these events is threefold. First, the examples underscore that protest and voting are only two types of activities in which citizens can engage in the digital age. Political participation, which refers to the various forms of individuals' activities that are intended to alter politics or the political system more broadly (van Deth 2014), includes a vast array of actions such as signing petitions, canvassing, contributing to political organizations and causes, protesting gym closures, as well as more digitally enabled forms of expression like political consumerism and hashtag activism (Dalton 2006; Schlozman, Verba, and Brady 2010; Ward and de Vreese 2011; Dreher, McCallum, and Waller 2016). In the contemporary media system, where "new" and "old" media are bound together in a dynamic, networked space (Chadwick 2013), everything from purchasing secondhand fashion to engaging in political discussions online is a form of political participation. Likewise, in the digital age, online participation can motivate individuals to get politically involved offline (Vitak et al. 2011; Bond et al. 2012; Boulianne 2015). Bennett and Segerberg (2012), for example, found that organizations mobilizing against inequality in the wake of a worldwide economic crisis used a combination of online images, messages, and discussions as well as offline activities, including protest opportunities, to mobilize over 15 million citizens in 60 cities across Spain in 2011. Similarly, Eltantawy and Wiest (2011) found that social media proved critical in the Arab Spring revolutions. Activists, who had been debating and organizing online, were able to quickly expand their reach and mobilization capacity via platforms such as Facebook to try and pressure states to adopt democratic principles and practices. And, as of this writing, social scientists, politicians, and pundits alike are connecting the dots between the discussion of violence against the government on social media platforms such as Facebook, Twitter, Gab, and Parler and the insurrection at the US Capitol.

Second, the series of events in the introduction reminds us that citizens are not the only ones who can engage the political system using digital media. Elected officials, including the president, and corporations can use digital media to mobilize citizens to their own benefit. In the case of the attack on the US Capitol, investigative journalists tracked the origins of the "Stop the Steal" campaign to Roger Stone, a Republican operative whose prison sentence for seven felonies recently had been cut short by a Trump commutation. The "Stop the Steal" campaign first emerged during the 2016 primaries, claiming that moderate Republicans like Jeb Bush and Mitt Romney were trying to "steal" the nomination from Trump. The slogan briefly emerged again during the 2018 Florida recount for Senate and governor but really gained traction in 2020. Immediately after Trump's electoral loss, established political organizations such as the Conservative Political Action Conference and the Republican National Committee joined forces with more conspiratorial figures such as Ali Alexander (aka Ali Akbar) to mobilize Trump supporters to contribute money to the "Stop the Steal" campaign. Not only did these mobilization efforts result in the attack on the Capitol, but they also raised more than $200 million in funds—much of which went to Trump's leadership political action committee, Save America.

Third, the examples underscore the fact that the causes and consequences of political participation can be difficult to unpack in the digital age. For example, it is increasingly difficult to assess the motivations and intents of individuals' participation on- and offline. Some of the individuals went to Washington, DC, on January 6, 2021, in order to express support for Donald Trump, whom they erroneously believed had been robbed of a second term. Others, however, went with the intent to seize the Capitol and the legislators in it. Likewise, it can be difficult to assess who benefits from political participation. The events of January 6 underscore the fact that digital media efforts not only have the power to mobilize but also can benefit politicians and political action groups more than they do the citizens protesting in the streets.

The purpose of this chapter is to offer a critical review of the sociological literature on political participation and, in doing so, to underscore the importance of power dynamics to understanding political engagement. I argue that the academic focus on social movements, the organizations that animate them, and the conditions under which they emerge and decline made it difficult for sociologists to incorporate digital media into their theorizing. A key problem in this regard is that sociologists have not done a good job of accounting for the ability of individuals and small groups to use technologies to advocate for political change. One way for sociologists to rebalance their theoretical and empirical efforts is to think more critically about the relationship between structure and agency and how this might (dis)empower individuals and groups in the digital age. I illustrate the utility of this approach by, first, outlining how power and digital media interact and affect whether and how an individual gets politically involved and, then, discussing how the relationship between power and digital media shapes the form a group takes as well as its influence in political processes. I conclude the chapter by discussing directions for future research.

POWER AND PARTICIPATION

Sociologists studying participation generally are interested in understanding the conditions under which average citizens challenge political elites and political institutions. Early theorizing, for instance, emphasized the centrality of negative emotions and mental states, such as frustration and alienation, to political participation, particularly in social movements, and to political violence (Lipset 1960; Toch 1965; Kornhauser 1959). Scholars accounted for the emergence of negative emotions and mental states in a number of ways. Social scientists writing after the Great Depression argued that frustration was a result of absolute deprivation, such as a sharp economic decline, that affected individuals' quality of life. Because individuals typically cannot act collectively against the source of their deprivation and resulting frustration (e.g., the abstract factors leading to economic decline and the inability of individuals to purchase necessities), negative emotions are redirected toward safe and available objects. During this time frame, White Americans took their frustration out on Black Americans, who were beaten and lynched at increased numbers (Dollard et al. 1939). Although sociologists have moved away from understanding emotion as a solely negative motivation for participation (Jasper 2011; Flam and King 2005; Gould 2009), current research continues to find links between economic decline and large-scale, anti-government demonstrations and riots (Caren, Gaby, and Herrold 2016).

Most contemporary theorizing in sociology on political participation focuses on social movements and specifically considers when or why citizens organize and challenge political institutions (Rohlinger and Gentile 2017). In the United States, sociologists typically focus on organizations as the drivers of change and, then, try to elucidate when political systems might be more vulnerable to movement pressure. For decades, a subset of sociologists have focused empirical attention on identifying the conditions that help explain when and why citizens join movements (Kitschelt 1986; Meyer and Staggenborg 1996; Meyer and Minkoff 2004; McAdam 1999; Tarrow 2011). These scholars found that conditions such as the opening of new avenues for participation, political realignment within the polity, the election of influential allies, visible conflicts among elites, and a decline in state capacity or desire to repress citizen dissent signal that a political system is vulnerable to external challenges and that movement groups have an "opportunity" to effect change (Tarrow 1998b; Meyer 2004). More recent theoretical innovations try to explain a fuller range of collective action (e.g., social movements and revolutions) by identifying mechanisms and processes that occur across a wider range of "contentious politics" (McAdam, Tarrow, and Tilly 2001).

The emphasis on organizations, conditions, and processes meant that sociologists often focused on the outcomes of social movements (Amenta et al. 2010). This shaped how sociologists approached the study of mass media, with scholars predominantly focusing on how movements were covered in the news as well as the strategies movement groups used to attract media attention (McCarthy, McPhail, and Smith 1996; Smith et al. 2001; Gamson and Wolfsfeld 1993; Ryan 1991). In other words, the narrow focus on news media outcomes ultimately made it difficult for sociologists to incorporate digital technology into their theorizing (Rohlinger 2015). In fact, some sociologists were fairly dismissive of new technology as a social force, labeling technology as just another resource activists could use to build networks and further their political goals (Tarrow 1998a; Diani 2000). In 2011, however, Jennifer Earl and Katrina Kimport pushed back on conceptualizing information communication technologies as resources, noting that digital media had distinct affordances and that, when these affordances were fully exploited, they fundamentally changed the logic of collective action. Among other critical observations, Earl and Kimport noted that individuals or small groups, rather than formalized movement organizations, could be the locus of change because digital media allowed them to quickly express their grievances, when and where they choose. In other words, digital media made organizing more individualized and more global, which broadened the range of grievances around which individuals could organize and expanded protest targets beyond political actors (Earl and Kimport 2011). This challenge to extant theory paved the way for other scholars to think more critically about when and how individuals get involved in social movements, whether or not they stay involved in movements over time, and the extent to which digital media potentially altered core movement processes such as cultivating collective identities (Rohlinger and Bunnage 2015, 2017, 2018; Crossley 2015; Ackland and O'Neil 2011).

Sociologists, however, have a long way to go before they better understand how digital media facilitate—and potentially hinder—political participation more generally. The most glaring problem with current theorizing relative to political participation in the digital age is that sociologists do not spend enough time thinking about the relationship between structure and agency and how this might (dis)empower individuals and some groups. Structure—in this case, platform structure, algorithms, and moderation policies—reinforces inequality and can disempower segments of the citizenry (Noble 2018; Gillespie 2018; Beer 2009; Stjernfelt and Lauritzen 2020; Benjamin 2019). For example, Benjamin (2019) traces how the internet's history is entrenched in racist practices as well as how computer code provides an overarching technological narrative with racism at its roots. Similarly, Gillespie (2018) highlights how moderation policies and inconsistent enforcement practices can silence the political voices of the populace, including those of women, people of color, and LGBTQ+ individuals seeking to connect online. In other words, the structure of the digital world and the relative social power of those navigating it affect how they engage politically (Schradie 2019). This point has not been lost on all sociologists. In a 2019 symposium on political communication and social movements, the contributing sociologists universally commented on the fact that movement scholars had a very flat understanding of the audiences of movement messages and noted that they almost never considered how audiences actively decide what to consume, believe, and act on (Earl 2019; Rohlinger 2019b; Sobieraj 2019).

Individual Participation: Opting Out, Free Spaces, and Public Places

Social location, which reflects the many intersections of individual experiences related to, among other factors, race, ethnicity, gender, class, age, ability, religion, sexual orientation, education, and geographic location, affects how much power and influence an individual has in a society. In the United States, White, upper-class, heterosexual, highly educated men have more power than White women and people of color with similar characteristics (Connell 1995; Schrock and Schwalbe 2009). This relative social power can affect who participates in digital spaces and how. Individuals with less social power might decide not to engage in political talk or political behavior because they fear how those with more social power might respond. Alternatively, those with less social power might seek out "free spaces" online where they can discuss their ideas and experiences and organize outside the view of more dominant groups (Sobieraj 2020; Evans and Boyte 1986). In contrast, those with more social power typically have few fears of speaking out or of getting politically engaged in public ways. This is in part because those with social power created and manage the digital spaces in which others engage (Benjamin 2019). This section briefly discusses how social power, which varies by social location, affects individual participation.

There are at least two reasons individuals might not become politically engaged in the digital age; both are related to social location. First, individuals may have limited access to digital media or limited digital skills. Scholars have long found that technological inequities affect who is able to go online (Anderson et al. 1995; Schement 2001). Not surprisingly, the college-educated, the wealthy, Whites, and urban dwellers all have more access to the internet (DiMaggio et al. 2001) and, correspondingly, more choices regarding whether (and when) to get politically engaged. Similarly, digital skills are not equally distributed across a population. Factors such as parental education, experiences with technology, and the use of technology in the classroom all affect how comfortable individuals feel about using digital media in their daily lives (Hargittai 2010; Aagaard 2017; Goode 2010). Second, and related, individuals with less social power may be wary of the consequences associated with online political participation and decide not to risk it. In her book, Sarah Sobieraj (2020), who interviewed 52 women who had been abused online by strangers, finds that harassment and threats cause women to censor their speech online in some cases and abandon digital public spaces in others.

Other individuals with more limited social power may get involved online but choose "free spaces" where they are likely to encounter like-minded or similarly situated individuals. For example, the Queer Sisters, a women's group in Hong Kong, created a bulletin board in 1999 to allow women identifying as lesbian or queer to foster a sense of belonging online (Nip 2004). This trend also emerges among individuals holding extreme political points of view. White supremacist groups have long used online spaces to cultivate a collective identity and organize outside the view of the mainstream (Futrell and Simi 2004; Adams and Roscigno 2005). There is evidence that groups can cultivate relatively free spaces on public platforms as well. Apryl Williams and Vanessa Gonlin (2017) find that Black women use the show *How to Get Away with Murder* to discuss Black womanhood on Twitter. Likewise, people of color use the hashtag #BlackTwitter to create a virtual forum so that they can discuss everyday racial discrimination and challenge racial bias publicly (Lee-Won, White, and Potocki 2018; Graham and Smith 2016). While these public conversations put participants at more risk for trolling from others, typically individuals representing more powerful social groups (Phillips 2015), research suggests that these efforts provide a critical counterpublic that pushes back against subordinated statuses (Jackson and Foucault Welles 2016; Graham and Smith 2016; Freelon, McIlwain, and Clark 2018).

Those individuals with greater degrees of social power are rarely concerned with negative consequences associated with political participation on- or offline and can, consequently, leverage the advantages of digital media in potentially productive and potentially destructive ways (Van Laer and Van Aelst 2010). In their analysis of the strategic voting movement in 2000, for instance, Earl and Schussman found that entrepreneurial individuals who also had internet access, high levels of education, and a fair number of digital skills were able to create virtual spaces that linked voters together and enabled voters in "safe" states to swap their votes with individuals in more competitive states. The goal of these sites was to keep individuals living in competitive states such as Florida from "wasting" their vote on a third-party candidate. An individual in safe states pledged to vote for the third-party candidate if an individual in a competitive state promised to vote for the Democratic or Republican candidate (Earl and Schussman 2003, 2004). Of course, the digital political engagement of individuals with social power does not always advance democratic processes. For instance, trolling and doxing are typically activities in which individuals with social power engage and which are intended to silence the voices of the less powerful (Sobieraj 2020). More concerning, platforms and legal institutions rarely hold those with social power accountable for their bad behavior. For example, when it was revealed that New Hampshire lawmaker Robert Fisher created a misogynistic forum on reddit called the Red Pill, his colleagues voted against disciplinary action. Fisher resigned only because of public outrage—and intense protest—over his founding of the forum (Dignam and Rohlinger 2019).

Group Participation: From Grassroots to Astroturf

Individuals do not have to politically engage alone. In order to increase their relative influence on politicians and political processes, individuals may choose to get involved with a group that mobilizes around the issues about which they care (McCarthy and Zald 1977). Political influence, however, is not equally distributed across groups. A group's power is affected by its resources and capacity, which, to some extent, reflect its membership. Groups that require membership dues to support their lobbying and media efforts often represent a wealthier demographic than those groups that rely on volunteers and donations alone. Not surprisingly, groups that represent individuals with social power often have more voice and influence in political processes (Schradie 2019). The effects of social power on politics, for instance, played out visibly during the Obama administration. The National Rifle Association, whose membership is at least half White (Parker et al. 2017), effectively staved off the passage of federal gun control laws and deregulated gun ownership in the states, despite Obama's push for gun regulation (Reich and Barth 2017). Similarly, groups that are comprised of or represent individuals with social power rarely fear state repression. In an analysis of more than 15,000 protest events in the United States between 1960 and 1990, Davenport, Soule, and Armstrong (2011) find that protests involving African Americans are more likely than White protest events to draw a police presence during most years. Moreover, once at the protests, police are more likely to use force or violence against protestors (Davenport, Soule, and Armstrong 2011).

Group power and relative influence are also affected by financial and human resources. Advocating for policy change requires time, energy, money, and, more often than not, expertise and political connections (Staggenborg 1988). Compare the relative effectiveness of the Tea Party movement to the Occupy Wall Street movement. While both movements were a response to the Great Recession, only the Tea Party movement attracted professional and corporate financial backing (Skocpol and Williamson 2012; Van Dyke and Meyer 2014). This infusion of financial and human resources was critical to helping the Tea Party movement consolidate power with states and shift the makeup of Congress over time (Rohlinger, Bunnage, and Klein 2014; Rohlinger and Bunnage 2015; Williamson, Skocpol, and Coggin 2011). The social power of a group's constituents as well as the resources and capacity it has are often, but not always, related. Here, I discuss three types of groups—grassroots organizations, social movement organizations, and astroturf organizations—and outline how they vary in terms of their resources, capacity, and constituency; I then discuss what these differences mean in terms of how they use digital media to involve supporters and affect political change.

Grassroots organizations, which are also sometimes referred to as "informal movement" groups, are primarily comprised of citizen volunteers, who are interested in effecting change in their communities via local or state political processes (Staggenborg

1988; Tarrow 2011). In other words, grassroots groups "grow" from the ground up, and their local strength enables activists to effectively organize, pressure politicians, and effect political change. While grassroots organizations may use digital media to connect with one another and share information regarding their strategies, tactics, and events (Costanza-Chock 2012; Tremayne 2014), they primarily focus on solving local problems (Lichterman 1996). The Occupy Wall Street, 15-M, and Black Lives Matter movements are all examples of grassroots efforts where local groups use digital media to organize, network, share information, and, ultimately, pressure elected officials to address local concerns (Gaby and Caren 2012; Juris 2012; Mercea 2012; Micó and Casero-Ripollés 2014; Freelon, McIlwain, and Clark 2018). Supporters of the Occupy Wall Street movement, for instance, mobilized around the slogan "We are the 99%" but focused their energies on very different local problems. In New York, activists founded alternative banks for community use. Meanwhile, in Denver, activists protested mass home foreclosures (Gitlin 2012; Castells 2012).

However, social power can influence the effectiveness of a grassroots organization. NIMBY (not in my backyard) groups, for instance, often are comprised of affluent, digitally savvy residents of an area who oppose the placement of human facilities such as homeless shelters, power plants, and landfills near their homes. NIMBY groups have a great track record of getting what they want, which means that undesirable facilities ultimately are located in poorer neighborhoods (Gibson 2005; Gerrard 1994). Grassroots groups comprised of working-class citizens with limited internet access and limited digital skills, in contrast, cannot rely on digital media to organize and often have less time, less energy, and fewer financial resources to dedicate to activism. This influenced both the relative effectiveness of the group as well as how individuals felt about their activism (Schradie 2018, 2019).

Grassroots organizations are particularly effective at framing political debates and getting out the vote in the digital age. Stated differently, grassroots efforts often are better at garnering recognition for causes than they are at effecting policy change (Gamson 1990). Citizens take to the streets in protest and amplify their messages via digital media (Earl and Kimport 2011). These messages rebound across the media landscape as they are picked up and rehashed by pundits and news outlets alike. The Tea Party movement, the Occupy Wall Street movement, and the Black Lives Matter movement are all good examples in this regard insofar as they forced politicians on both sides of the aisle to discuss the size and function of the federal government, economic inequality, and institutional racism, respectively. Grassroots Tea Party groups organizing online, for instance, got a boost from pundits such as Sean Hannity, conservative outlets such as Fox News, and mainstream outlets like *USA Today*—all of which amplified citizens' calls for smaller government and less government spending. Politicians took note, and some of those who didn't heed the call found themselves unemployed after the next election cycle (Berry and Sobieraj 2014). Similarly, opinion leaders on the misogynistic subreddit The Red Pill urged forum users to recognize that American men were at a political crossroads and that they needed to rally behind Donald Trump. In fact, forum leaders insisted that users who did not support and vote for Trump were "imposters" and "beta males" (read, not real men) hired by Hillary Clinton to sabotage a potential Trump presidency (Dignam and Rohlinger 2019).

Social movement organizations, in contrast, rely on paid professionals and primarily use institutional channels, such as lobbying, to influence party platforms and policy processes (Diani and McAdam 2003). Unlike grassroots organizations, social movement groups typically are hierarchically structured with a clear division of labor and identifiable leaders, who are often elected by members who pay yearly membership dues. In other words, social movement organizations depend on dues, donors, and grants to fund their day-to-day expenses, including their professional media campaigns (McCarthy and Zald 1977). Professionalized organizations such as the Sierra Club and the Humane Society are very popular in the United States. In fact, David Meyer and Sidney Tarrow (1998) argue that we live in a "social movement society," where countless professional groups represent the interests and issues of the upper-middle and upper classes in the United States and beyond.

While these groups have the professional expertise to be politically effective, many long-established movement groups struggle to make good use of digital media, particularly on the left. While more research is needed on differences between conservative and liberal movements' use of digital media, the small extant literature suggests that liberals and conservatives understand the value of technologies relative to organization and mobilization differently. Conservatives regard digital media as a way to spread "the truth" to a broader public and mobilize converts to action. Liberals, in contrast, use digital media to share information, which has implications for mobilization, but often regard movement-building as something that requires face-to-face interaction (Schradie 2018, 2019). It will be interesting to see if a global pandemic shifts how liberal organizations think about digital media relative to their political projects.

These different orientations affect how professional groups on the right and left use digital media to effect political change. Conservative groups have invested in online platforms and content and use websites, newsletters, reports, as well as social media to share information and get supporters politically engaged (Schradie 2019; Rohlinger and Brown 2013). Groups on the left, however, are more likely to treat their web pages and social media accounts as brochures and do little more than try and sell their issues and campaigns to visitors (Earl et al. 2010; Schradie 2019). Although this requires more empirical examination, it seems to have influenced the course of movements on the left. For example, established feminist groups such as the National Organization for Women were slow to use digital media as a way to interact with their constituents. Consequently, feminists, and young feminists in particular, have formed networks, communities, and organizations online and outside of established movement organizations (Rohlinger 2015; Reger 2012; Crossley 2015).

Of course, digital media also have led to the emergence of a broad range of hybrid organizations, some of which make communication and mobilizing support around discrete campaigns their core function (Heaney and Rojas 2014; Flanagin, Stohl, and Bimber 2006). For example, the progressive "big tent" organization MoveOn mobilizes people and money around elections and issues that its surveyed members have indicated are their priorities such as voter rights and healthcare. The group sends individuals emails regarding the issues in which they expressed support and asks for small donations and delineated participation (Karpf 2012; Rohlinger and Bunnage 2015).

Social movement organizations that make good use of digital media can effectively reframe issues and move people from their armchairs to the streets (Fisher et al. 2005). More important, digital media can help broaden both how groups think about where political engagement can occur as well as who they target in their change efforts. Fans of pop culture juggernauts such as *Star Wars*, *Game of Thrones*, and *Harry Potter*, for instance, can form online communities that provide a foundation for political action (see Maher chapter in this volume). Similarly, digital media make it easier for groups to raise awareness about—and to target—corporate practices. People for the Ethical Treatment of Animals (PETA) has a long history of using technology to raise awareness and, more importantly, create content and spaces tailored to different target audiences. For example, the organization has different websites for kids, high school and college students, and constituents over 50 years old. Similarly, PETA often creates new websites and games to raise awareness about corporate practices. The group went after Kentucky Fried Chicken for its treatment of chickens at factory farms and slaughterhouses. The campaign featured the website "Kentucky Fried Cruelty," where the group housed a video exposing the abuse, celebrity endorsements, campaign news, the game Super Chick Sisters (based on Super Mario Brothers), and a donation tab (Rohlinger 2019a).

Finally, astroturf organizations are "synthetic" grassroots groups, meaning that they look like a citizen-run organization but, in fact, are funded by wealthy individuals, companies, political action committees, or even governments to support particular sets of interests. Like the fake grass after which they are named, astroturf groups try to simulate grassroots organizations, including their use of digital media. Astroturf organizations are best understood as public relations campaigns that sometimes incentivize participation (e.g., pay individuals to publicly engage on the group's behalf). Working Families for Walmart is a good example in this regard. The organization, which was funded by Walmart and created by a public relations firm, opposed union-funded groups that were critical of the company's business practices, including substandard wages and healthcare benefits. The group was exposed as an astroturf organization when it was discovered that employees of the public relations firm were fabricating blog posts in which they pretended to be a couple traveling the country in an RV and staying in Walmart parking lots (McNutt and Boland 2007; Walker 2014). More recently, the Associated Press reported that protests over stay-at-home orders in states across the country may have looked like grassroots efforts but, in fact, were backed by Republicans and organized by conservative groups including FreedomWorks and Americans for Prosperity (Burnett and Slodysko 2020).

Astroturf groups have a lot of resources at their disposal and, consequently, can use a variety of tactics to promote their ideas via digital media. However, the sociological literature on astroturfing and its effects on political participation is quite sparse. We know, for example, that astroturf groups can "piggyback" on the events of grassroots groups and use their resources to take over movement messages online and absorb their supporters in the "real" and "virtual" worlds. This happened in the Tea Party movement. In Florida, for instance, grassroots activists mobilized citizens across the state to influence local and state elections. Once this hard work was done, Americans for Prosperity, a Koch brothers–funded group, began bussing supporters to the state capital to support the newly elected Rick Scott, who championed Tea Party movement issues. The group then formed an expensive, members-only Tea Party caucus in the state, where Democrats and Republicans alike sought the audience of the reformed movement in order to garner support for prospective legislation (Rohlinger, Bunnage, and Klein 2014). As the "Stop the Steal" example discussed at the outset of the chapter suggests, astroturf organizations and their effects on political participation are ripe for research.

Conclusion

When it comes to understanding political participation in the digital age, sociology has largely fallen behind other disciplines, primarily communications and political science, that have made communication and digital media central to their understanding of political engagement. However, sociology can certainly make up ground. A key advantage sociology has relative to other disciplines is its focus on power and the relational dynamics between structure and agency. This particular focus offers sociologists the tools and a theoretical tradition to locate individuals and groups within a larger social system and clearly identify factors that advantage some individuals and groups over others. Sociologists such as Jen Schradie (2019) are doing some of this work already. In her book, Schradie argues that access to digital devices, skills, empowerment, and time, which varies by class, accounts for how individual activists use digital media to agitate around labor issues. Sociologists should continue to develop frameworks that account for individual participation on- and offline. We cannot understand how political participation is truly transformed by digital media until we recognize and name the technological gaps that exist by social location as well as workarounds that individuals use to bridge digital divides.

More generally, sociologists need to think about how power flows within (and across) social and political systems. The existing literature and the Capitol siege make clear that grassroots efforts are vulnerable to co-optation by more powerful individuals and groups. Ideas and groups that have a small but virulent base on the periphery of politics can (and do) cross over into the mainstream. This is clear not only in the "Stop the Steal" campaign but also in other efforts such as attempts to legislate protections for conservatives on college campuses. What began as an effort by one man to prove that professors discriminated against conservative students nearly 20 years ago is now a regular talking point of Republican politicians. Likewise, numerous states have considered or passed legislation protecting conservatives on college campuses (Rohlinger and Brown 2013). Getting politicians and more powerful groups to rally around a cause is not always intentional. As mentioned, not all Tea Party groups wanted to be absorbed by Americans for Prosperity and sidelined after working so hard to get their preferred candidates elected. Cases such as these are likely to be instructive insofar as they illuminate the factors that facilitate grassroots takeovers.

Focusing on how power flows will also illuminate how groups of various types work together for their own purposes. The "Stop the Steal" campaign is potentially instructive in this regard because the president, politicians, a political party, and extremist grassroots organizations seem, in varying degrees, to have coordinated their efforts to raise money and/or to disrupt the democratic status quo. This certainly will not be the last time that we see odd bedfellows using digital media to frame debates and mobilize citizens to action. The question is whether sociologists will think more deeply about our system and its democratic possibilities.

References

Aagaard, Jesper. 2017. "Breaking Down Barriers: The Ambivalent Nature of Technologies in the Classroom." *New Media & Society* 19, no. 7: 1127–1143. doi: 10.1177/1461444816631505.

Ackland, Robert, and Mathieu O'Neil. 2011. "Online Collective Identity: The Case of the Environmental Movement." *Social Networks* 33, no. 3: 177–190.

Adams, Josh, and Vincent J. Roscigno. 2005. "White Supremacists, Oppositional Culture and the World Wide Web." *Social Forces* 84, no. 2: 759–778. doi: 10.1353/sof.2006.0001.

Alli. 2020. "I Work at Whole Foods, and I Am Calling Out Its Hypocrisy." *Street Roots*, July 3. www.streetroots.org/news/2020/07/03/opinion-i-work-whole-foods-and-i-am-calling-out-its-hypocrisy.

Amenta, Edwin, Neal Caren, Elizabeth Chiarello, and Yang Su. 2010. "The Political Consequences of Social Movements." *Annual Review of Sociology* 36: 287–307.

Anderson, Robert H., Christopher Kedzie, Tora K. Bikson, Brent R. Keltner, Sally Ann Law, Constantijn Panis, et al. 1995. *Universal Access to E-Mail: Feasibility and Societal Implications.* Santa Monica, CA: RAND Corporation.

Beer, David. 2009. "Power through the Algorithm? Participatory Web Cultures and the Technological Unconscious." *New Media & Society* 11, no. 6: 985–1002. doi: 10.1177/1461444809336551.

Benjamin, Ruha. 2019. *Race after Technology: Abolitionist Tools for the New Jim Code.* New York: Polity.

Bennett, Lance, and Alexandra Segerberg. 2012. "The Logic of Connective Action." *Information, Communication & Society* 15, no. 5: 739-76

Berry, Jeffrey, and Sarah Sobieraj. 2014. *The Outrage Industry: Political Opinion Media and the New Incivility*. New York: Oxford University Press.

Bond, Robert M., Christopher J. Fariss, Jason J. Jones, Adam D. I. Kramer, Cameron Marlow, Jaime E. Settle, et al. 2012. "A 61-Million-Person Experiment in Social Influence and Political Mobilization." *Nature* 489, no. 7415: 295–298. doi: 10.1038/nature11421.

Boulianne, Shelley. 2015. "Social Media Use and Participation: A Meta-Analysis of Current Research." *Information, Communication & Society* 18, no. 5: 524–538. doi: 10.1080/1369118X.2015.1008542.

Burnett, Sara, and Brian Slodysko. 2020. "Pro-Trump Protesters Push Back on Stay-At-Home Orders." *Associated Press*, April 17. https://apnews.com/article/mi-state-wire-tx-state-wire-va-state-wire-texas-virus-outbreak-ea4c17f541c7c63fac52941a6f43b885.

Caren, Neal, Sarah Gaby, and Catherine Herrold. 2016. "Economic Breakdown and Collective Action." *Social Problems* 64, no. 1: 133–155. doi: 10.1093/socpro/spw030.

Castells, Manuel. 2012. *Networks of Outrage and Hope: Social Movements in the Internet Age.* Malden, MA: Polity Press.

Chadwick, Andrew. 2013. *The Hybrid Media System: Politics and Power, Oxford Studies in Digital Politics.* New York: Oxford University Press.

Connell, R. W. 1995. *Masculinities.* Cambridge: Polity.

Costanza-Chock, Sasha. 2012. "Mic Check! Media Cultures and the Occupy Movement." *Social Movement Studies* 11, no. 3–4: 375–385.

Crossley, Alison Dahl. 2015. "Facebook Feminism: Social Media, Blogs, and New Technologies of Contemporary U.S. Feminism." *Mobilization: An International Quarterly* 20, no. 2: 253–268. doi: 10.17813/1086-671X-20-2-253.

Dalton, Russell. 2006. *Citizen Politics: Public Opinion and Political Parties in Advanced Industrial Democracies.* 4th ed. Washington, DC: CQ Press.

Davenport, Christian, Sarah A. Soule, and David A. Armstrong. 2011. "Protesting While Black?: The Differential Policing of American Activism, 1960 to 1990." *American Sociological Review* 76, no. 1: 152–178. doi: 10.1177/0003122410395370.

Diani, Mario. 2000. "Social Movement Networks Virtual and Real." *Information, Communication & Society* 3, no. 3: 386–401.

Diani, Mario, and Doug McAdam, eds. 2003. *Social Movements and Networks: Relational Approaches to Collective Action.* New York: Oxford University Press.

Dignam, Pierce, and Deana Rohlinger. 2019. "Misogynistic Men Online: How the Red Pill Helped Elect Donald Trump." *Signs* 44, no. 3: 589–612.

DiMaggio, Paul, Eszter Hargittai, W. Russell Neuman, and John Robinson. 2001. "Social Implications of the Internet." *Annual Review of Sociology* 27: 307–336.

Dollard, John, Neal Miller, Leonard Doob, O. H. Mowrer, and Robert Sears. 1939. *Frustration and Aggression.* New Haven, CT: Yale University Press.

Dreher, Tanja, Kerry McCallum, and Lisa Waller. 2016. "Indigenous Voices and Mediatized Policy-making in the Digital Age." *Information, Communication & Society* 19, no. 1: 23–39. doi: 10.1080/1369118X.2015.1093534.

Earl, Jennifer. 2019. "Symposium on Political Communication and Social Movements: Audience, Persuasion, and Influence." *Information, Communication & Society* 22, no. 5: 754–766. doi: 10.1080/1369118X.2019.1568519.

Earl, Jennifer, and Katrina Kimport. 2011. *Digitally Enabled Social Change: Activism in the Internet Age.* Cambridge, MA: MIT Press.

Earl, Jennifer, Katrina Kimport, Greg Prieto, Carly Rush, and Kimberly Reynoso. 2010. "Changing the World One Webpage at a Time: Conceptualizing and Explaining 'Internet Activism.'" *Mobilization* 15, no. 4: 425–446.

Earl, Jennifer, and Alan Schussman. 2003. "The New Site of Activism: On-Line Organizations, Movement Entrepreneurs, and the Changing Locations of Social Movement Decision Making." *Research in Social Movements, Conflicts and Change* 24: 155–187.

Earl, Jennifer, and Alan Schussman. 2004. "From Barricades to Firewalls? Strategic Voting and Social Movement Leadership in the Internet Age." *Sociological Inquiry* 74, no. 4: 439–463.

Eltantawy, Nahed, and Julie Wiest. 2011. "The Arab Spring| Social Media in the Egyptian Revolution: Reconsidering Resource Mobilization Theory." *International Journal of Communication* 5: 1207–1224.

Evans, Sara, and Harry Boyte. 1986. *Free Spaces: The Sources of Democratic Change in America.* New York: Harper & Row.

Fisher, Dana, Kevin Stanley, David Berman, and Gina Neff. 2005. "How Do Organizations Matter? Mobilization and Support for Participants at Five Globalization Protests." *Social Problems* 52, no. 1: 102–121.

Flam, Helena, and Debra King. 2005. *Emotions and Social Movements*. New York: Routledge.

Flanagin, Andrew, Cynthia Stohl, and Bruce Bimber. 2006. "Modeling the Structure of Collective Action." *Communication Monographs* 73, no. 1: 29–54.

Freelon, Deen, Charlton McIlwain, and Meredith Clark. 2018. "Quantifying the Power and Consequences of Social Media Protest." *New Media & Society* 20, no. 3: 990–1011. doi: 10.1177/1461444816676646.

Futrell, Robert, and Pete Simi. 2004. "Free Spaces, Collective Identity, and the Persistence of U.S. White Power Activism." *Social Problems* 51, no. 1: 16–42.

Gaby, Sarah, and Neal Caren. 2012. "Occupy Online: How Cute Old Men and Malcolm X Recruited 400,000 US Users to OWS on Facebook." *Social Movement Studies* 11, no. 3-4: 367–374. doi: 10.1080/14742837.2012.708858.

Gamson, William. 1990. *The Strategy of Social Protest*. 2nd ed. Homewood, IL: Dorsey Press.

Gamson, William, and Gadi Wolfsfeld. 1993. "Movement and Media as Interacting Systems." *Annals of the American Academy of Political and Social Science* 578: 104–125.

Gerrard, Michael. 1994. "The Victims of NIMBY." *Fordham Urban Law Journal* 21, no. 3/4: 495–522.

Gibson, Timothy A. 2005. "NIMBY and the Civic Good." *City & Community* 4, no. 4: 381–401. doi: 10.1111/j.1540-6040.2005.00144.x.

Gillespie, Tarleton. 2018. *Custodians of the Internet: Platforms, Content Moderation and the Hidden Decisions that Shape Social Media*. New Haven, CT: Yale University Press.

Gitlin, Todd. 2012. *Occupy Nation: The Roots, the Spirit, and the Promise of Occupy Wall Street*. New York: It Publishers.

Goode, Joanna. 2010. "The Digital Identity Divide: How Technology Knowledge Impacts College Students." *New Media & Society* 12, no. 3: 497–513. doi: 10.1177/1461444809343560.

Gould, Deborah. 2009. *Moving Politics: Emotion and ACT UP's Fight against AIDS*. Chicago: University of Chicago Press.

Graham, Roderick, and 'Shawn Smith. 2016. "The Content of Our #Characters:Black Twitter as Counterpublic." *Sociology of Race and Ethnicity* 2, no. 4: 433–449. doi: 10.1177/2332649216639067.

Hargittai, Eszter. 2010. "Digital Na(t)ives? Variation in Internet Skills and Uses among Members of the 'Net Generation.' " *Sociological Inquiry* 80, no. 1: 92–113. doi: 10.1111/j.1475-682X.2009.00317.x.

Heaney, Michael T., and Fabio Rojas. 2014. "Hybrid Activism: Social Movement Mobilization in a Multimovement Environment." *American Journal of Sociology* 119, no. 4: 1047–1103. doi: 10.1086/674897.

Jackson, Sarah J., and Brooke Foucault Welles. 2016. "#Ferguson Is Everywhere: Initiators in Emerging Counterpublic Networks." *Information, Communication & Society* 19, no. 3: 397–418. doi: 10.1080/1369118X.2015.1106571.

Jasper, James. 2011. "Emotions and Social Movements: Twenty Years of Theory and Research." *Annual Review of Sociology* 37: 285–303.

Juris, Jeffrey S. 2012. "Reflections on #Occupy Everywhere: Social Media, Public Space, and Emerging Logics of Aggregation." *American Ethnologist* 39, no. 2: 259–279. doi: 10.1111/j.1548-1425.2012.01362.x.

Karpf, David. 2012. *The MoveOn Effect: The Unexpected Transformation of American Political Advocacy*. Oxford: Oxford University Press.

Kitschelt, Herbert. 1986. "Political Opportunity Structures and Political Protest: Anti-Nuclear Movements in Four Democracies." *Journal of Political Science* 16, no. 1: 57–85.

Kornhauser, William. 1959. *The Politics of Mass Society*. New York: Free Press.

Lee-Won, Roselyn J., Tiffany N. White, and Bridget Potocki. 2018. "The Black Catalyst to Tweet: The Role of Discrimination Experience, Group Identification, and Racial Agency in Black Americans' Instrumental Use of Twitter." *Information, Communication & Society* 21, no. 8: 1097–1115. doi: 10.1080/1369118X.2017.1301516.

Lichterman, Paul. 1996. *The Search for Political Community: American Activists Reinventing Commitment Cambridge University Press*. Cambridge: Cambridge University Press.

Lipset, Seymour Martin. 1960. *Political Man: The Social Bases of Politics*. Baltimore, MD: Johns Hopkins University Press.

McAdam, Doug. 1999. *Political Process and Development of Black Insurgency, 1930–1970*. Chicago: University of Chicago Press.

McAdam, Doug, Sidney Tarrow, and Charles Tilly. 2001. *Dynamics of Contention*. New York: Cambridge University Press.

McCarthy, John, Clark McPhail, and Jackie Smith. 1996. "Images of Protest: Dimensions of Selection Bias in Media Coverage of Washington Demonstrations, 1982 and 1991." *American Sociological Review* 61: 478–499.

McCarthy, John, and Mayer Zald. 1977. "Resource Mobilization and Social Movements: A Partial Theory." *American Journal of Sociology* 82, no. 6: 1212–1241.

McDonald, Michael. 2020. "United States Election Project: 2020 November General Election Turnout Rates." Last updated December 7, 2020. http://www.electproject.org/2020g.

McNutt, John, and Katherine Boland. 2007. "Astro Turf, Technology and the Future of Community Mobilization: Implications for Nonprofit Theory." *Journal of Sociology and Social Welfare* 34, no. 3: 165–178.

Mercea, Dan. 2012. "Digital Prefigurative Participation: The Entwinement of Online Communication and Offline Participation in Protest Events." *New Media & Society* 14, no. 1: 153–169.

Meyer, David. 2004. "Protest and Political Opportunities." *Annual Review of Sociology* 30: 125–145.

Meyer, David, and Debra Minkoff. 2004. "Conceptualizing Political Opportunities." *Social Forces* 82, no. 4: 1457–1892.

Meyer, David, and Sidney Tarrow. 1998. *The Social Movement Society: Contentious Politics for a New Century*. New York: Rowman and Littlefield Publishers, Inc.

Meyer, David S., and Suzanne Staggenborg. 1996. "Movements, Countermovements, and the Structure of Political Opportunity." *American Journal of Sociology* 101, no. 6: 1628–1660.

Micó, Josep-Lluís, and Andreu Casero-Ripollés. 2014. "Political Activism Online: Organization and Media Relations in the Case of 15M in Spain." *Information, Communication & Society* 17, no. 7: 858–871. doi: 10.1080/1369118X.2013.830634.

Nip, Joyce. 2004. "The Queer Sisters and Its Electronic Bulletin Board: A Study of the Internet for Social Movement Mobilization." *Information, Communication & Society* 7, no. 1: 23–49.

Noble, Safiya Umoja. 2018. *Algorithms of Oppression: How Search Engines Reinforce Racism*. New York: New York University Press.

Parker, Kim, Juliana Menasce Horowitz, Ruth Igielnik, J. Baxter Olphant, and Anna Brown. 2017. "The Demographics of Gun Ownership." In *America's Complex Relationship with Guns*. Washington, DC: Pew Research Center.

Phillips, Whitney. 2015. *This Is Why We Can't Have Nice Things: Mapping the Relationship between Online Trolling and Mainstream Culture*. Cambridge, MA: MIT Press.

Reger, Jo. 2012. *Everywhere & Nowhere: Contemporary Feminism in the United States*. New York: Oxford University Press.

Reich, Gary, and Jay Barth. 2017. "Planting in Fertile Soil: The National Rifle Association and State Firearms Legislation." *Social Science Quarterly* 98, no. 2: 485–499. doi: https://doi.org/10.1111/ssqu.12423.

Rohlinger, Deana. 2015. *Abortion Politics, Mass Media, and Social Movements in America*. New York: Cambridge University Press.

Rohlinger, Deana. 2019a. *New Media and Society*. New York: New York University Press.

Rohlinger, Deana A. 2019b. "Symposium on Political Communication and Social Movements: Ships Passing in the Night." *Information, Communication & Society* 22, no. 5: 724–738. doi: 10.1080/1369118X.2019.1568514.

Rohlinger, Deana, and Jordan Brown. 2013. "Mass Media and Institutional Change: Organizational Reputation, Strategy, and Outcomes in the Academic Freedom Movement." *Mobilization: The International Quarterly Review of Social Movement Research* 18, no. 1: 41–64.

Rohlinger, Deana, and Leslie Bunnage. 2015. "Connecting People to Politics over Time? Internet Communication Technology and Activist Persistence in MoveOn and the Tea Party Movement." *Information, Communication & Society* 18, no. 5: 539–552.

Rohlinger, Deana, and Leslie Bunnage. 2017. "Did the Tea Party Movement Fuel the Trump-Train? The Role of Social Media in Activist Persistence and Political Change in the 21st Century." *Social Media + Society* 3, no. 2: 2056305117706786. doi: 10.1177/2056305117706786.

Rohlinger, Deana, and Leslie Bunnage. 2018. "Collective Identity in the Digital Age: Thin and Thick Identities in MoveOn.Org and the Tea Party Movement." *Mobilization: An International Quarterly* 23, no. 2: 135–157.

Rohlinger, Deana, Leslie Bunnage, and Jesse Klein. 2014. "Virtual Power Plays: Social Movements, ICT, and Party Politics." In *The Internet and Democracy: Voters, Candidates, Parties and Social Movements*, edited by Bernard Groffman, Alex Trechsel, and Mark Franklin, 83–109. New York: Springer.

Rohlinger, Deana, and Hailey Gentile. 2017. "Sociological Perspectives on Social Movements." In *Springer Handbook of Social Movements across Disciplines*, edited by Conny Roggeband and Bert Klanderman, 2–32. New York: Springer.

Ryan, Charlotte. 1991. *Prime Time Activism: Media Strategies for Grassroots Organizing*. Boston: South End Press.

Schement, Jorge Reina. 2001. "Of Gaps by Which Democracy We Measure." In *The Digital Divide: Facing a Crisis or Creating a Myth?*, edited by Benjamin M. Compaine, 303–308. Cambridge, MA: MIT Press.

Schlozman, Kay Lehman, Sidney Verba, and Henry E. Brady. 2010. "Weapon of the Strong? Participatory Inequality and the Internet." *Perspectives on Politics* 8, no. 2: 487–509.

Schradie, Jen. 2018. "The Digital Activism Gap: How Class and Costs Shape Online Collective Action." *Social Problems* 65, no. 1: 51–74. doi: 10.1093/socpro/spx042.

Schradie, Jen. 2019. *The Revolution that Wasn't: How Digital Activism Favors Conservatives*. Cambridge, MA: Harvard University Press.

Schrock, Douglas, and Michael Schwalbe. 2009. "Men, Masculinity, and Manhood Acts." *Annual Review of Sociology* 35, no. 1: 277–295. doi: 10.1146/annurev-soc-070308-115933.

Skocpol, Theda, and Vanessa Williamson. 2012. *The Tea Party and the Remaking of Republican Conservatism*. New York: Oxford University Press.

Smith, Jackie, John McCarthy, Clark McPhail, and Boguslaw Augustyn. 2001. "From Protest to Agenda Building: Description Bias in Media Coverage of Protest Events in Washington, D.C." *Social Forces* 79, no. 4: 1397–1423.

Sobieraj, Sarah. 2019. "Audiences in Social Context: Bridging the Divides between Political Communications and Social Movements Scholarship." *Information, Communication & Society* 22, no. 5: 739–746. doi: 10.1080/1369118X.2019.1568517.

Sobieraj, Sarah. 2020. *Credible Threat: Attacks against Women Online and the Future of Democracy*. New York: Oxford University Press.

Staggenborg, Suzanne. 1988. "The Consequences of Professionalization and Formalization in the Pro-Choice Movement." *American Sociological Review* 53, no. 4: 585–606.

Stjernfelt, Frederik, and Anne Mette Lauritzen. 2020. "Facebook and Google as Offices of Censorship." In *Your Post Has Been Removed: Tech Giants and Freedom of Speech*, 139–172. Cham, Switzerland: Springer International Publishing.

Tarrow, Sidney. 1998a. "Fishnets, Internets and Catnets: Globalization and Transnational Collective Action." In *Challenging Authority: The Historical Study of Contentious Politics*, edited by Michael Hanagan, Leslie Page Moch, and Wayne te Brake, 228–244. Minneapolis: University of Minnesota Press.

Tarrow, Sidney. 1998b. *Power in Movement: Social Movements and Contentious Politics*. 2nd ed. New York: Cambridge University Press.

Tarrow, Sidney. 2011. *Power in Movement: Social Movements and Contentious Politics*. 3rd ed. New York: Cambridge University Press.

Toch, Hans. 1965. *The Social Psychology of Social Movements*. Indianapolis, IN: Bobbs-Merrill.

Tremayne, Mark. 2014. "Anatomy of Protest in the Digital Era: A Network Analysis of Twitter and Occupy Wall Street." *Social Movement Studies* 13, no. 1: 110–126.

van Deth, Jan W. 2014. "A Conceptual Map of Political Participation." *Acta Politica* 49, no. 3: 349–367. doi: 10.1057/ap.2014.6.

Van Dyke, Nella, and David S. Meyer, eds. 2014. *Understanding the Tea Party Movement*. Farnham, UK, and Burlington, VT: Ashgate.

Van Laer, Jeroen, and Peter Van Aelst. 2010. "Internet and Social Movement Action Repertoires." *Information, Communication & Society* 13, no. 8: 1146–1171. doi: 10.1080/13691181003628307.

Vitak, Jessica, Paul Zube, Andrew Smock, Caleb Carr, Nicole Ellison, and Cliff Lampe. 2011. "It's Complicated: Facebook Users' Political Participation in the 2008 Election." *Cyberpsychology, Behavior, and Social Networking* 14, no. 3: 107–114. doi: 10.1089/cyber.2009.0226.

Walker, Edward T. 2014. *Grassroots for Hire: Public Affairs Consultants in American Democracy*. Cambridge: Cambridge University Press.

Ward, Janelle, and Claes de Vreese. 2011. "Political Consumerism, Young Citizens and the Internet." *Media, Culture & Society* 33, no. 3: 399–413. doi: 10.1177/0163443710394900.

Williams, Apryl, and Vanessa Gonlin. 2017. "I Got All My Sisters with Me (on Black Twitter): Second Screening of How to Get Away with Murder as a Discourse on Black Womanhood." *Information, Communication & Society* 20, no. 7: 984–1004.

Williamson, Vanessa, Theda Skocpol, and John Coggin. 2011. "The Tea Party and the Remaking of Republican Conservatism." *Perspectives on Politics* 9, no. 1: 25–43.

Index

Note: Tables are indicated by *t* following the page number

Abascal, Santiago, 627
AbolishBigData 2009 movement, 83
abstracted empiricism, 512
acceleration society, 13, 16
acquaintance society, 372
AddHealth data, 255
affect and technology, 63–66
affective labor, 322, 370, 470, 473–476, 479, 481
affective news, 62, 67–68, 71
affective publics, 62, 64, 68–72
Afrofuturistic reimagining, 330
The Age of Surveillance Capitalism (Zuboff), 202
agenda-building in digital media, 127
aging support and digital technology, 150–151
Ajana, Btihaj, 324
Alexander, Ali, 685
algorithms
　digital production gap inequalities, 572–576
　EdgeRank algorithms, 49
　importance of, 36–37
　navigating platforms' algorithmic structures, 479
　platform management of, 183
　recommender systems and, 51
Alibaba platform, 30
alterity principle, 343
alternative imaginaries of datafication, 82–83
alternative spirituality, 162
Amazon, 184, 199, 231, 683–684
ambient journalism, 126
American Civil Liberties Union, 250
American National Election Study, 668
American Sociological Association, 512–513

Amnesty International, 477
Anonymous, 420, 421, 425–429
Ansari, Aziz, 243
anti-corruption. *See* grassroots anti-corruption mobilizations
anti-fake news, 601
anti-militarism movements, 514
anti-Muslim sentiment, 622–623
anti-rape technology, 329
anti-unionism, 186
apolitical fandoms, 406
Apple App Store, 197, 199, 210
Apple Classrooms of Tomorrow program, 100
application programming interface (API), 593
Arab Spring, 418, 428, 685
Arbery, Ahmaud, 684
artificial intelligence (AI)
　algorithms and, 575–576
　Big data and, 76, 83
　digital production gap and, 568
　digital religion and, 168
　identity confirmation, 249
　IoT and, 220
　media manipulation and, 600
aspirational labor, 323
Astroturf groups, 693–694
Atmos (Aō Air 2020), 316
audience engagement on Twitter, 126
augmented reality (AR), 210, 305, 523n4
Australian Digital Inclusion Index, 150
autoethnography, 537
autonomy in wearable technology, 328
awareness system with newsfeeds, 126

Baby Boomers, 296
Ballad of the Bullet (Stuart), 446
Bannon, Steve, 432
Basel Action Network, 500
Basel Convention on the Control of Transboundary Movements of Hazardous Wastes, 502
BATX (Baidu, Alibaba, Tencent, and Xiaomi), 568, 580
beauty apps, 206
Bedi, Sonu, 248
behavioural futures markets, 224
Benjamin, Ruha, 329–330
Benson, Rodney, 121–122
Berger, Peter, 27, 161, 172
Berson, Josh, 321
Besecke, Kelly, 167
Bezos, Jeff, 683
Bharatiya Janata Party, 599
biopolitical dimensions of apps, 206
Bivens, Rena, 329
Black Lives Matter movement, 69, 250, 418, 475, 533, 569, 670, 691
Black masculinity, 533, 538
black propaganda, defined, 590
blended families, 139
bloc recruitment, 407
bloggers/blogging, 122, 164, 254, 323, 368, 480, 570, 616, 649, 693
body-positive activists, 254–255
Boko Haram, 618
botnet, 425, 435n2
boundary object, 420
Bourdieu, Pierre, 121–122
brand unsafe designation, 476
Breed, Warren, 120
bribery activism, 651
#BringBackOurGirls, 618
Brown, Dan, 165
Brown, Michael, 615
Buddhism, 162, 164
Bulman, George, 100
Bumble, 257
Bush, Jeb, 685
busyness culture, 10, 19, 20–21
button knowledge, 548, 549
Buzon X platform, 656

Californian counterculture, 168
call-out culture, 474
Calvard, Thomas, 324–325
campaign for respect, 447
Campbell, Heidi, 162–163
Cant, Callum, 183
captology system, 51
Care.com, 183–184
career and technical education (CTE), 103–104
CARROT suite of apps, 210
Castells, Manuel, 13–15
casual gamer, 382, 384–387, 391n2
celebrification on Twitter, 124
Center for Information and Research on Civic Learning and Engagement, 675
Change.org, 670
child labor, 495
China, e-waste industry, 495, 499
China Internet Network Information Center, 367
Chinese Communist Party (CCP), 595, 600
Christianity, 161–167
chronographies of power, 14
Chronos, 20
chronoscopic time, 12–13
Church of England, 165
Church of Scientology, 421, 423, 426–427
citizen journalism, 125, 126, 459, 567, 616, 618
citizen scoring schemes, 77
civic engagement, 48, 62, 83, 664, 672
Clark, Lynn Schofield, 165
clock time, 10, 14, 20
cloudwork, 184–185
CNN effect, 516
code of the tweet, 452
code-switching strategies, 453
cognitive frames in frame theory, 98
collective action
    affective publics and, 65–66
    against corruption, 647–650
    political participation as, 687
    theory of, 647
    trolls and hacktivists, 421, 426
    against White masculinity, 537
collective identity, 45, 355n2 420, 424, 443, 514, 687, 689
collectivities, 31, 35

colonialism, 77, 79, 349, 492. *See also* data colonialism
color-blind racism, 537
commercial content moderation, 47
commodity audience, 479–480
community-based moderation, 46–47
community governance, 48
compensatory manhood acts, 536–537
Computable Bodies: Instrumented Life and the Human Somatic Niche (Berson), 321
Computer TakeBack Campaign, 500
computer technology, 159, 168
confirmation bias, 49
Confucianism, 364
connective action, 66, 72, 419
connective ambition, 452
Conservative Political Action Conference, 685
conspiracy theories, 593, 603, 627
consumptive curation, 41, 49
contemporary speed theory, 12–15
content moderation, 45–48, 53, 471, 594, 600
content-related skills, 551, 553, 558, 560
content sharing, 199
context collapse, defined, 43
coordinated inauthentic behavior, 589, 600
Corbyn, Jeremy, 669
core-periphery network, 280
coronavirus pandemic. *See* COVID-19 global pandemic
corporate-controlled platforms, 579–580
corruption. *See* grassroots anti-corruption mobilizations
Corwin, Julia, 498
cosplay, 400, 403
Cottom, Tressie McMillan, 318
Couldry, Nick, 325–326
counter culture, 169
counter data action, 77
counter imaginaries, 82–83
COVID-19 global pandemic
    anti-corruption mobilization, 645
    app development and use during, 201, 203–204
    conspiracies and disinformation about, 593, 603
    datafication and, 78, 81, 85
    digital divide and, 292–293, 578

education during, 112
Foucauldian perspective on response, 206–207
negotiation frame and, 98
online dating during, 247, 257
online learning during, 109–111
political participation, 683–686
sense of time during, 22
technology and social distancing, 138–139
Cox, Jo, 626
Cramer, Kathlyn, 69
Criado-Perez, Caroline, 329, 625–626
Crimean war, 519–520
criminalization of POCs, 454
critical feminist thinking, 85
critical race theory, 85
critical technical practice, 84
crowd sourcing, 184
Cuban, Larry, 99–100, 101–102
Cult of the Dead Cow, 428
cultural acupuncture, 406
cultural capital, 403, 532–533
cultural dimension of data, 78
cultural jamming, 670
cultural labor, 322–323
curation
    content moderation, 45–48
    curatorial matrix, 40, 41–43
    defined, 40
    identity curation, 43–45
    introduction to, 40–41
    of news and information, 48–50
    recommender systems, 50–53
    summary of, 53–54
curatorial code, 41, 42
curatorial matrix, 40, 41–43
cyberian counter culture, 169
cyberqueer spaces, 341, 343
cybersex, 272
cyberspace, 169–170, 342, 350
cybertroopers, 597

Daniels, Jessie, 318
data
    AddHealth data, 255
    at the center, 80
    counter data action, 77

data (*cont.*)
   cultural dimension of, 78
   digital pornography collection, 276–279
   grassroots anti-corruption mobilizations, 654–657
   importance of, 36–37
   infrastructures of, 50, 77–79, 81–82, 81*t*, 84–85, 86*t*
   at the margins, 80
   material dimension of, 81–82
   ownership of wearable technology, 318
   seemlessness of production, 40
   structural dimension of, 78
   symbolic dimension of, 78
data activism, 83–84
Data 4 Black Lives, 83
data colonialism, 224, 325–326, 579
Data Feminism (D'Ignazio, Klein), 328
data incontinence, 227
data journalism, 84
data politics, 84, 320
data poverty, 78–79
data protection laws (DPLs), 226, 234
data resistance, 77
datafication/datafied society
   of everyday life, 324
   fundamental aspects of, 80–84, 81*t*
   infrastructure of data, 81–82
   introduction to, 33, 76–78
   marginalized persons and, 78–80
   meaning-making in, 82–83
   reclaiming agency in, 83–84
   surveillance and, 202
   understanding data at the margins, 84–86, 86*t*
dataveillance, 81, 202–204, 206, 223
dating apps and websites
   discrimination and exclusion, 248–250
   examples of, 244*t*
   introduction to, 143, 200, 241–242
   market for, 242–247
   politics and, 250–251
   research trends, 247–256
   summary of, 256–257
   underrepresented populations, 251–256
dating online, 143–145, 247, 257
Dating4Disabled, 255

deceleration, period of, 22
decoloniality, 78–79, 84–85, 86*t*
deep mediatization, 28, 33–34, 517
Deibert, Ron, 601
Deleuze, Gilles, 208
Deliveroo, 183
demand-side response (DSR), 231
democracy and technology, 61–63
democratization, 226, 272, 569
deviant masculinities, 537
Dewey, John, 103–104
digital advertising, 125
digital basics learning, 106
Digital Civics Toolkit, 675
digital competence, 549, 553–555, 559–561
digital cruising, 243, 346–347
digital divide, 99, 100, 292–294, 446, 578
digital dualism, 2, 343–344
digital hostility, 619, 621, 624, 626
digital inequality, 44, 293, 444, 446–448, 458–459
Digital Labour and Karl Marx (Fuchs), 202
digital literacies, 44, 520, 522, 549, 550, 554–555
digital materiality, 10, 21
digital native debate, 552–553
digital politics. *See* youth engagement in digital media politics
digital pornography
   data considerations, 276–279
   defined, 271
   introduction to, 269–271
   overview of, 271–273
   sociological research approach, 280–282
   summary of, 282–283
   as technical and commercial artifact, 273–276
digital production gap
   algorithmic inequalities, 572–576
   controlling means of, 576–580
   ecosystem of, 569–576
   introduction to, 567–569
   summary of, 580–581
digital religion
   digital media text, 165–168
   digital technologies of, 168–170
   introduction to, 159–160
   post-secular society, 160–162

spread of religion and, 162–165
    summary of, 170–172
digital sex work, 477
digital skills
    antecedents of, 552–557
    conceptualization of, 550–551
    consequences of, 557–559
    defined, 549–550
    digital native debate, 552–553
    education-based inequalities, 554–555
    educational and occupational outcomes, 557
    future research studies, 559–562
    gender-based disparities, 553–554
    global disparities in, 551–552
    inequalities in, 551–557
    introduction to, 446, 548–549
    online safety and privacy, 558–559
    socioeconomic status, 554
    subjective well-being and, 558
    vulnerable social groups and, 555–556
digital sociology, 1, 5, 270–273, 280–282
digital surveillance
    of children, 148–149
    concerns in wearable technology, 326–328
    surveillance-as-service, 224
    surveillance capitalism, 129, 202
    surveillant assemblage, 81, 327
digital war
    collective participation and responses, 515
    conduits of, 518–519
    environments of, 520–521
    historical and social processes, 514–515
    introduction to, 5, 511–512
    language metaphor in, 519–520
    mediatization framework, 517–521
    memory studies, 517
    narratives and imaginaries, 515–516
    participation research, 521–523
    sociological perspectives on, 512–517
    visual examination of, 516
Digital War journal, 514
digitalization
    inequalities with, 652
    mediatization and, 33–34
    of religion, 160, 162, 170–172
    of society, 291

    of streetlife, 445–446, 453
    view of time and, 9, 12–13, 19
digitized humanitarian initiatives, 202
D'Ignazio, Catherine, 328
Dijck, Jose van, 324
direct access, 32–33
direct-to-consumer communications, 50
disability-centric dating sites, 255
Discovering the News (Schudson), 121
discrimination in dating apps, 248–250
disenchantment of the world, 159–160
disinformation. *See* media manipulation and disinformation
distributed denial of service (DDOS) attacks, 425, 428
DIY (do-it-yourself) pornography, 272
"Do Artifacts Have Politics?" (Winner), 111
domestic labor, 141, 221, 230–232
Douyin, 368
doxing/doxxing, 425, 427, 531, 599, 619, 689
DREAMers, 675
drone warfare, 516
Du Bois, W.E.B., 103
Durkheim, Émile, 161, 513

e-movements, 419
e-waste (electronic waste)
    as environmental justice issue, 494–497
    environmental racism and, 491–494
    grassroot social movements and, 500–502
    introduction to, 4, 490–491
    new research directions, 496–500
    policymaking and legislation, 502–504
    summary of, 504–505
Earl, Jennifer, 687
EdgeRank algorithms, 49
educational technology and inequality
    digital skills, 554–555
    frame theory and, 98–99
    impact frame and, 98, 99–102
    introduction to, 97–98
    negotiation frame and, 102–111
    summary of, 111–113
Educational Testing Services, 100
eHarmony.com, 241
el buen vivir (good living), 83
elections and youth engagement, 668–670

Electronic Disturbance Theater, 428
emancipatory communication practices, 84
emotional labor, 183, 470, 474–476, 482
empty signifiers, 71–72
Engels, Friedrich, 201
environmental injustice, 491–498, 503–504
environmental racism, 492–494, 498, 502, 504
environmental rationality, 82
Escobar, Arturo, 86
esotericism, 162
EU Kids Online surveys, 552
everyday life and technology, 221–222
everyday racism, 529, 533–541
exclusion in dating apps, 248–250
EXPOSED campaign, 648

face concerns *(cha xu ge ju)*, 364
face/facework in Chinese society
    deciding when to give, 369
    defined, 362, 363
    impression management, 368
    on internet, 365–367
    introduction to, 3, 362–363
    methodology of, 371–372
    overview of, 364–365
    renqing, in, 364–365, 370–371
    risks and challenges, 366
    self-presentation and, 363, 365–366, 368–369
    on social media, 367–371
    as universal social phenomenon, 363–364
face negotiation theory (FNT), 363–364, 366
face-to-face (FTF) interactions, 366, 368, 371
Facebook
    anti-corruption hashtags, 648–649
    identity performance on, 44
    labeling false content, 600
    LGBTQ+ use of, 342
    Messenger app, 199
    Millennial use of, 295
    political messages on, 405
    popularity of, 199
    queer African migrant groups, 345
    as shaper of political landscape, 48–49
    social relations through, 30–31
    South Korean users, 366
    streetlife impact by, 451

fact-checking tools, 599–600, 601
Fairlie, Robert, 100
fake news, 567, 575, 580, 589–590, 593, 668
false information, 590, 598–600, 668
family, defined, 139–140
Family Education Rights and Privacy Act, 111
family life and technology
    digital media and, 141–142
    historical and modern definitions, 139–140
    intergenerational support and aging, 150–151
    introduction to, 138–139
    life course examples, 142–151
    parenting impact, 146–149
    partnering impact, 143–146
    transforming family practices through, 151–153
fan object, 394–409, 409n1
fans/fandom
    community element, 399–400
    consumption element, 397–398, 399
    defined, 394–395
    emotional connection with, 401–402
    engagement element, 398–399
    fan, defined, 395–397
    fan activism and, 406–409
    as ideal type, 397–402
    identity and, 400–401
    inequality and, 402–404
    knowledge element, 398
    participatory politics and, 404–405
Fast Company, 316
fat authenticity, 254
Federal Communication Commission (FCC), 593
feminism/feminist approach to digital media, 206, 280, 420, 430, 692. *See also* women's use of digital publics as political spaces
Feminist Data Set (Sinders), 85
feminized social media labor
    emotional and affective performances, 473–476
    features of, 473–481
    flexibility of, 478–479
    future research directions, 481–483
    gendered consumer economies, 479–481
    introduction to, 469–471

visibility politics, 475, 476–478
women's work and, 470, 471–473
Fernandez, Chantal, 469
field theory, 121–122
15MParato campaign, 656
Fighting Online Sex Traffic Act (2018), 477
figurations of collectivities, 35
Fischer, Robert, 689
floating signifier, 71
Floyd, George, 684
Forbes, 316, 330
formal skills, 551
Foucault, Michel, 204–207
4chan, 3, 417, 420–425, 671
fourth Industrial Revolution, 322
frame conflicts, 420
Franco, Marielle, 626
free labor, 320, 322–323, 325, 581
free markets, 179, 581
free porn, 274–275
free spaces online, 688–689
Free Time (Rose), 23
free trade, 179
freedom to choose identity, 380
frictionless homogeneity, 234–235
From Satori to Silicon Valley (Roszak), 169
Fuchs, C., 202–204

GAFAM (Google, Apple, Facebook, Amazon, and Microsoft), 568, 580
game apps, 199
Gamergate, 384, 403, 418, 420–421, 429–432
Games Done Quick, 405
GameStop, 434
gamification strategies, 199–200
gaming/gaming culture. *See* identity in video game culture; masculinity and racist interactions in gaming
Gamson, William, 29
gangs/gang activity, 446, 452, 456
gatekeeping role of the press, 127
gaymers, 386
geek masculinity, 531
gender differences, 17, 553–554. *See also* women's use of digital publics as political spaces
gender-linked toxicity, 622
gendered consumer economies, 479–481

gendertrolling, 622
General Data Protection Regulation, 226
geo-locative dating/ hook-up apps, 349
geographically tethered work, 183–184
geolocation apps, 204, 211, 242–243
ghost work, 47
Gidaris, Constantine, 325
Giddons, Anthony, 29, 144–145
gig economy
    defined, 178
    future of research, 187–188
    platform work and, 181–187
    sociological dimensions of, 181–188
    work and labor changes, 178–181
gig workers, 2, 182, 185, 203
Giuliani, Rudy, 684
glamour labor, 323
Global North
    app developers, 203, 206
    datafication and, 86
    dating apps, 249
    e-waste in, 493–494, 496, 502, 505
    hook-up apps, 347–348
    internet of things, 219, 223
    work and labor changes, 178–180
global racial inequalities, 493
Global South
    app developers, 203
    big data and, 76, 79–80
    dating apps, 249
    e-waste in, 490–491, 493–494, 496, 505
    work and labor changes, 179–180
Gmail app, 199
Gonzo pornography, 273–274
Google, 49–50, 169, 229, 573
Google Maps app, 199, 211
Google Play, 197
Grabar-Kitarovic, Kolinda, 624
grassroot social movements, 500–502, 690–692
grassroots anti-corruption mobilizations
    Big data and small data in, 654–657
    collective action for, 647–650
    digital media role in, 646–652
    introduction to, 4, 644–646
    principal-agent theory, 646, 650–652
    struggles with, 652–654
    summary of, 657–658

grassroots organizations, 83, 501–502, 647, 690–695
grassroots storytelling, 520
Gray, Kishonna, 534
Great Depression, 686
great power politics, 595–597
Great Recession, 690
Greenpeace International, 500
Gregory, Karen, 318, 323–324
Grindr app, 243, 250, 251, 256, 346–349
group-face, 364
group political participation, 690–694
grrrl gamers, 386
guanxi network, 364

Habermas, Jürgen, 61, 63, 162
hacktivists. *See* trolls and hacktivists
Hadden, Jeffrey, 161
Harari, Yuval Noah, 159
Haraway, Donna, 320
hard technology, 169
hardcore gamer, 381–384, 391n2
hardcore pornography, 274
Harris, Kamala, 627
Harry Potter Alliance, 407, 408
Hartley, John, 64
Harvey, David, 179
Hasinoff, Amy, 329
hate speech
    as digital hostility, 619, 621
    in gaming culture, 528, 534, 536
    online spread of, 63
    as racists, 628
    by White supremacist, 598
Hazare, Anna, 644–645
health-related self-care, 205
hegemonic masculinity, 530, 531, 537
Hermida, Alfred, 126
hidden workers, 474
high-speed society, 10–12
Hinduism, 165, 166–167
HIV/AIDS, 348
Hjarvard, Stig, 163
Hogan, Bernie, 43
homelessness, 449, 452, 454
Homo Deus (Harari), 159
homophobia, 341, 532, 537, 592, 620, 622

Hong Kong Golden, 671
hook-up culture, 143, 347–348
Hoover, Stewart, 163
Horrocks, Peter, 124
How to Get Away with Murder (TV show), 689
human-app health assemblage, 209
Hustler magazine, 273, 280–281
hybridity, defined, 125
hyper-real testaments of religion, 172
hyperconnectivity, 19–20

I Paid a Bribe platform, 651
ICT Development Index, 560
identity
    collective identity, 420
    curation of, 43–45
    defined, 378–380
    in fandom/fan activism, 400–401
    floating forms of, 387–390
    fragmented forms of, 384–387
    marginalized identities, 45
    self-identity, 31, 379
    social relations and, 30–31
    solid forms of, 381–384
identity-based attacks, 619, 621–623, 625–628
identity-based harassment, 537
identity in video game culture
    casual gamer, 382, 384–387, 391n2
    defined, 378–380
    gaming and, 380–390
    hardcore gamer, 381–384, 391n2
    introduction to, 378
    summary of, 390–391
    volatile gamer, 387–390
identity performance, 41, 44
identity work, 339–340, 342, 345, 353–354, 474
imagined communities, 31, 410n8 453
impact frame, 98, 99–102, 106–108
inappropriate/ d others, 380
inclusive masculinity, 532, 538
India
    anti-corruption activism, 651–652
    e-waste industry, 495, 498–499
individual political participation, 688–689
individualization of media consumption, 149
Industrial Revolution, 201
industrialisation of the home, 230

inequality. *See also* educational technology and inequality
  algorithmic inequalities, 572–576
  digital inequalities, 44, 293, 444, 446–448, 458–459
  in fandom/fan activism, 402–404
  fans/fandom and, 402–404
  global racial inequalities, 493
  social inequality, 3, 4, 103, 144, 297, 492, 644, 663
  socioeconomic inequality, 446
  in streetlife, 444, 446–448, 458–459
influence operations, 589–598, 602
information and communication technologies (ICTs)
  accelerating speed of, 13
  digital skills and, 554–555
  everyday life and technology, 222
  future trends in sociology of, 128–130
  introduction to, 2
  marginalized women and, 619
  political-economic constraints with, 122
  quality time impact, 19
  shift in gatekeeping roles, 127
  work-family boundaries, 16–19
information and communication technologies (ICTs), use by older adults
  advancing research on, 302–306
  challenges with use, 306
  defined, 293–294
  digital divide and, 292–294
  impact of use, 298–301
  introduction to, 291–293
  in long-term care facilities, 296–297, 302–303
  measures and data, 303–304
  missing target groups in, 302–303
  new areas of use, 304–305
  overview of, 294–296
  physical health outcomes, 300–301
  predictive factors in use, 297–298
  psychosocial impact of, 299–300
  social exclusion through, 301–302
  summary of, 306–307
information ecosystem, 50, 590–595, 598–601
information management, 221, 225–228
information operations, 590, 596, 601
information privacy, 327
information warfare, 590
Infowars, 434
infrastructure of data, 81–82
ingratiation strategies, 368
Instagram
  anti-corruption hashtags, 649
  fandom on, 399
  LGBTQ+ people's experiences, 350
  popularity of, 199
  racism on, 477
  social relations through, 31
  Support Small Businesses sticker, 475
instantaneous time, 9, 12
Institute for the Advanced Study of Sustainability, 503
intensive motherhood, 146
Inter-Parliamentary Union, 624
intergenerational support and digital technology, 150–151
Intergovernmental Panel on Climate Change, 503
International Campaign for Responsible Technology, 500
International Computer and Information Literacy Study (ICILS), 552, 554, 555, 561
International Labour Organization, 180
International Telecommunication Union, 554, 560
Internet & American Life Project, 109
internet of things (IoT)
  control and, 228–229
  domestic labor, 230–232
  everyday life and technology, 221–222
  frictionless homogeneity, 234–235
  information management, 225–228
  introduction to, 219–221
  political economy and, 224–225
  resistance and, 232–233
  smart home imaginary, 223–233
  world folding, 234
Internet Relay Chat (IRC) channels, 427
Internet Research Agency (IRA), 593, 595
interracial relationships, 249–250
intersectionality and streetlife, 458
intimate partner surveillance, 145, 149
investigative journalism, 575, 594, 685

invisible religion, 162, 167
Invisible Women: Data Bias in a World Designed for Men (Criado-Perez), 329
involuntary celibates, 251
IoT. *See* internet of things
irreligious power, 168
Islam, 161, 162, 165, 166, 252

Jackson, Sarah, 614–615
Jan Sunwai, 652
Janaagraha Centre for Citizenship and Democracy, 651
Jane, Emma, 622
Jenkins, Henry, 404
Jim Crow segregation, 472
job polarization, 557, 562, 562n1
Jobs, Steve, 322
journalistic significance of Twitter
  impact of, 126–128
  introduction to, 118–119
  professional journalists and, 122–125
  sociology of journalism before Twitter, 119–122
Judaism, 162–163, 165, 166

K-Pop fans, 407, 408, 569
Kalanick, Travis, 183
Kelly, Kevin, 170
Kentucky Fried Chicken, 693
Kids Online, 553, 556
Kimport, Katrina, 687
King, Rodney, 121
Kjoni, Eron, 430
Klein, Lauren F., 328
Kovalev, Alexei, 596
Krishnan, Kavita, 624
Ku Klux Klan, 428
Kurzweil, Ray, 169

La Manada gang rape, 619
labile laborers, 478
labor changes and gig economy, 178–181
labor force racialization, 23
labor time, 10–11, 21
Laclau, Ernesto, 70–71
landline telephone, 141
Latour, Bruno, 602

Latte Creative, 648
learned cultural creations, 421
Leary, Timothy, 169
leisure revolution, 13
Lenski, Gerhard, 161
Lévi-Strauss, Claude, 71
LGBTQ+ persons/communities
  acronym use, defined, 355n1
  background and history, 341–342
  closets and outings, 350–353
  community and connection through, 342–345
  dating apps, 249, 251–254
  as digital content producers, 576
  fandom communities, 403
  in gaming community, 384, 386
  homophobia and, 341, 532, 537, 592, 620, 622
  identity-based attacks, 626
  identity curation of youth, 45
  introduction to, 3, 339–341
  navigating platforms' algorithmic structures, 479
  rights of marriage and parenting, 139–140
  same-sex couples/parents, 139
  sex, romance and dating, 346–350
  transphobia, 253, 341, 346, 592, 624
liberal bias complaints in media, 121
lifeworlds, 61, 511, 519
live streaming, 368
Livejournal, 350
locative media, 518, 523n4
long-distance parenting, 147
long-term care facilities (LTCFs), 296–297, 302–303
Luckmann, Thomas, 27
ludification strategies, 199–200
lulz, defined, 424
Lupton, Deborah, 319–320

Make America Great Again movement, 71
Manheim, Ernest, 29
marginalized identities, 45
marginalized persons
  Chinese facework and, 370
  data and, 78–80
  dating apps and, 245, 348
  race-based marginalization, 473

streetlife and, 455
    underrepresented populations in dating apps, 251–256
    undocumented migrants, 78, 674–675
Marx, Karl, 201, 513, 568
masculinity and racist interactions in gaming
    Black masculinity, 538
    everyday racism, 529, 534–540
    introduction to, 528–529
    masculinity, defined, 530
    representations and interactions, 533–535
    sociological perspective on, 529–531
    summary of, 540–541
    White masculinity, 530, 531–533, 535–538
mass shootings, 256–257
Match.com, 241, 251
material dimension of data, 81–82
materialist phenomenology, 36–37
McConnell, Mitch, 618
McDonald, Michael, 684
McFall, Liz, 325
Media, War & Conflict journal, 513
media effects, 99, 101, 108, 522
media generations, 29
media manipulation and disinformation
    accountability and manipulation of, 599
    definitions and terminology of, 590–591
    domestic operations, 597–599
    foreign operations, 595–597
    future research on, 602–603
    identifying actors and groups, 594–599
    introduction to, 589–591
    nonstate operations, 598
    research methods, 592–594
    sociotechnical approaches to, 591–592
    state-linked operations, 597–598
Media Manipulation Casebook, 594
mediatization framework of digital war, 517–521
mediatization of religion, 163
Medicaid, 255
medium-related skills, 551
Mejias, Ulises, 325–326
memes, 164, 407, 421, 428, 432–434, 593, 673
memetic warfare, 598
memory studies on digital war, 517
messaging apps, 199

#MeToo, 617
metric culture, 324, 326
Metric Culture: Ontologies of Self-Tracking Practices (Ajana), 324
Meyer, Birgit, 164
micro-blogging platform, 367, 570
micro-labor platforms, 47
micro-nudge, 321
microaggressions, 534
microwork, 184–185
migrant workers, 180, 494–495
military-industrial complex, 168
Millennials, 295
Mills, C. Wright, 512
MindGeek, 274–276, 279, 281–282
misinformation, defined, 590
Misinformation Review journal, 602
misogyny, 341, 620, 622, 629, 689
mixed-weight relationships, 255
mobile apps. *See also* specific mobile apps
    economy and use patterns, 198–201
    Foucault, Michel and, 204–207
    introduction to, 197–198
    political economy approach, 201–204
    sociomaterial perspectives, 207–212
mobile leapfrogging, 557
Modern Romance (Ansari), 243, 247
Momentum network, 669
mommy blogs, 480
monetization processes, 322–323
Moody, Kim, 187
Moor, Liz, 325
Moors, Annelies, 164
moral economy, 228
Moravec, Hans, 169
Morgan, David, 140, 166
Mormons, 163
MoveOn, 692–693
Moyer-Lee, Jason, 186
Mubarak, Hosni, 69
Muslims, 166–167
#Muslimwomensday, 617
#myNYPD, 615
MySpace, 342, 350, 570–571

Nafus, Dawn, 320
Nakamura, Lisa, 383, 473

nation-state formations, 515
National Assessment of Educational Progress, 100
National Center for Educational Statistics, 101
National Education Association, 101
National Organization for Women, 692
National Rifle Association, 690
natural language processing (NLP), 593
navigational skills, 551
Neff, Gina, 320, 329
negotiation frame in educational technology
    benefits of, 108–109
    contemporary negotiations, 105–108
    historical negotiations, 103–104
    introduction to, 102–103
    online learning during global pandemic, 109–111
    summary of, 111–113
neoliberalism, 179–180, 366
neonatal lead toxicity from e-waste, 500
nerd theology, 170
net locality, 445
Netflix, 29, 199, 275
network-based moderation, 46
network time, 9, 12–13
networked curation, 41–42, 45–46, 50
networked framing, 64–66
networked gatekeeping, 64–66
networked publics, 447, 515
networked racialized hostility, 477
New Age, 162, 164
Next-Generation Affiliate Tracking Software (NATS), 274
NIMBY (not in my backyard) groups, 691
Nintendo Power magazine, 382–383
Nissenbaum, Helen, 327
#NiUnaMenos, 617
Noble, David, 168
Noble, Sofiya, 330
nongovernmental organizations (NGOs), 500–502
North Atlantic Treaty Organization (NATO), 601

Obama, Barack, 429, 669
occupational segregation, 472
Occupy movement, 69

Occupy Wall Street, 428, 670, 690–691
Öffentlichkeit, defined, 63
OkCupid, 243, 246, 250
On Populist Reason (Laclau), 70–71
online dating, 143–145, 247, 257
online face/facework, 365–367
online learning during global pandemic, 109–111
online safety and privacy, 558–559
ontological friction, 226, 227
OpenPolis, 650–651
optimisation culture, 19–21
Organisation for Economic Co-operation and Development (OECD), 503, 577, 644
organized religion, 161
overseas foreign workers, 147–148
Oxford Internet Institute, 574

paganism, 162
PageRank system, 49
Palmer, Keke, 473
parenting impact from technology, 146–149
Park, Robert, 119
participatory culture, 166, 167, 171, 426, 432
participatory politics, 404–405, 673–674
partnering impact from technology, 143–146
Partridge, Christopher, 165
pay-to-click monetization schemes, 274–275
PC culture, 420
Penthouse magazine, 273
People for the Ethical Treatment of Animals (PETA), 693
people of color (POC), 341, 355n2 454
A People's History of Computing in the United States (Rankin), 109
Perception of Corruption Index, 656
personal computers, 169
Pew Research Center, 109, 200–201, 246, 295, 603
phenomenological sociology, 27–28
The Philosophy of Money (Simmel), 11
phreaking, defined, 435n3
pink ghetto, 474
PlanetOut, 344
Planned Parenthood, 250
platform collectivities, 31
platform work

cloudwork, 184–185
defined, 181
geographically tethered work, 183–184
in gig economy, 181–187
implications of, 185–187
labor and surveillance, 568
playbour, 322
Playboy magazine, 273, 280–281
Pokémon GO, 209
police violence, 459, 614–615
political economy
consumerism, 672
internet of things and, 224–225
mobile apps and, 201–204
of pornography, 269–270
political participation
by groups, 690–694
by individuals, 688–689
introduction to, 683–686
power and, 686–688
summary of, 694–695
politics. *See also* women's use of digital publics as political spaces; youth engagement in digital media politics
biopolitical dimensions of apps, 206
communication technologies and, 62
data politics, 84, 320
dating apps and websites, 250–251
fandom/fan activism in, 404–405
great power politics, 595–597
participatory politics, 673–674
trolls and hacktivists impact on, 418–421
visibility politics, 475, 476–478
polychlorinated biphenyls (PCBs), 495, 500
polycyclic aromatic hydrocarbons, 500
polymedia environments, 148
Poole, Christopher, 423
populism, 70–72
porn wars, 271–272
PornHub.com, 274–275
pornography. *See* digital pornography
post-secular society, 160–162
post-traditional spirituality, 162
precarious work, 180–181
pregnancy apps, 206
prejudice in gaming culture, 534
premediation, 66–67, 72

principal-agent theory, 646, 650–652
privacy concerns
with digital media, 148–149
digital skills and, 558–559
information privacy, 327
online safety and privacy, 558–559
in wearable technology, 326–328
problematic content assessments, 477
productive curation, 41, 45, 51, 52
professional journalists and Twitter, 122–125
progressive spirituality, 162
project-based work, 184
propaganda, defined, 590
Protection from Online Falsehoods and Manipulation Act, 600
protest culture, 665, 670–672, 683–684
protest tweets, 572
Protestant church, 163
public sphere and technology
affect and, 63–66
affective news, 67–68
affective publics, 62, 68–72
introduction to, 61–62
populism and, 70–72
solidarity and distance, 62–63
summary of, 72
Pure Earth, 501
pure relationship, defined, 144
push marketing, 274–275, 281

QQ Zone, 367
Quantified: Biosensing Technologies in Everyday Life (Nafus), 321
quantified self (QS) movement, 205, 319–322
quantitative philosophy of time, 11, 20
quasi-acquaintance society, 372
queer African migrant Facebook groups, 345
queer people of color (POC), 341

race
datafication and, 85
in fandom communities, 403–404
streetlife and, 445–446, 453–454
wearable technology and, 329–331
race-based marginalization, 473
racial fetishization, 248–249, 348
racial projects, 533

racialization, 152, 252, 458
racism. *See also* masculinity and racist interactions in gaming
   anti-Muslim sentiment, 622–623
   color-blind racism, 537
   in entertainment industry, 472–473
   environmental racism, 492–494, 498, 502, 504
   everyday racism, 529, 533–541
   global racial inequalities, 493
   networked racialized hostility, 477
   police violence, 614–615
   sexual racism, 248–250, 252, 348–349
   on social media, 477
   systemic racism, 537, 575, 683
Radde-Antweiler, Kerstin, 165
radical war, 520
Raelian movement, 169
raid tactics, 424–425
Random Rape Threat Generator (RRTG), 622
Rankin, Joy Lisi, 109
rapeglish, 622
re-figuration adjustment, 35
recommender systems, 50–53
recursivity, defined, 35–36
Red Pill, 689
Reddit, 44, 251, 344, 405
redpilling, defined, 433
RedTube.com, 274
The Religion of Technology (Noble), 168
religious-social shaping, 162–163
renqing, in facework, 364–365, 370–371
Renren, 369
#RenunciaYa, 649
Reply Girls, 478–479
Republican National Committee, 685
Research Network on Youth and Participatory Politics, 673
Reset (Deibert), 601
Restriction on Hazardous Substances, 503
#Rezist mobilization, 648–650
rich white Californians, 570
The Rise of the Network Society (Castells), 13–14
Roberts, Sarah T., 330
Rodríguez, Clemencia, 80
Roman Catholic church, 163, 164–165

Romney, Mitt, 685
root mean square error (RMSE), 51
Rose, Nikolas, 324
Roszak, Theodore, 169
Russian disinformation campaigns, 595
Rwigara, Diane Shima, 624

Said, Khaled, 649
same-sex couples/parents, 139
Save America, 685
Schneier, Bruce, 326
Schudson, Michael, 121
Schüll, Natasha Dow, 321
Schütz, Alfred, 29
Schwartz, Barry, 243
Schwartz, Becca, 329
science and technology studies (STS), 9–10, 15, 17, 23n1
Scientology, 169
Scruff app, 346
search engines, 48–50, 274–275, 570, 573, 579
Second Life, 342
Second Life (Radde-Antweiler), 165
secularization, 160–162, 170–171
self and identity theories, 43–45
self-branding, 124, 323–324, 366, 482
self-employment, 185–186
self-identity, 31, 379
self-knowledge, 51, 54n2 323, 328
self-optimization, 20, 317, 321, 324
self-organizing networks, 420
self-perception, 293, 388
self-presentation and facework, 363, 365–366, 368–369
self-representation, 340, 351, 353
self-tracking apps/devices, 21, 84, 205, 211, 317–325, 328
Self-Tracking (Neff, Nafus), 320
self-worth, 31
sensation-seeking behavior, 279
sensitizing concept, 33–34
Senza Corruzione . . . Riparte il Futuro campaign, 648
settler colonialism, 492
settler violence, 349
sex tourism, 249
sex work/workers, 249, 477, 482

sexism in gaming culture, 528–529, 541
sexting, 245
sexual racism, 248–250, 252, 348–349
sexual scripts theory, 278
sharing economy, 185
Shelby, Renee Marie, 329
Silent Generation, 295, 296
Silicon Valley ideology, 581
Silicon Valley Toxics Coalition, 500
Simmel, Georg, 11–12
Sinders, Caroline, 85
Skype, 138, 148, 203
Slack, Andrew, 407
sleep-tracking apps, 211
slow violence, 492, 502
smart grid demand-side response (DSR) trial, 231
smart home imaginary, 223–233
Smith, Marc A., 570
Smythe, Dallas, 479–480
SnapChat, 44, 199
Snedden, David, 103–104
Sobieraj, Sarah, 688–689
social construction of reality
    consequences of mediated life, 28–29
    deep mediatization, 28, 33–34
    figurational approach to, 34–36
    introduction to, 27–28
    materialist phenomenology of, 36–37
    social relations and, 30–33
The Social Construction of Reality (Berger, Luckmann), 27
social coping, 539
Social Credit System in China, 77
social engagement, 49, 297, 300
social exclusion, 77, 292–293, 301–302
social friction, 221, 235
social imaginaries, 82–83, 516
social inequality, 3, 103, 144, 297, 492, 644, 663
social media. *See also* feminized social media labor; specific social media platforms
    apps for, 199
    content moderation on, 45
    face/facework on, 367–371
    identity curation on, 43
    news storytelling on, 67–68
    racism on, 477
    use by law enforcement, 454
    women's use of digital publics, 617–619
social movement organizations (SMOs), 655, 671
social movements
    Astroturf groups, 693–694
    fan activism and, 406
    grassroot e-waste movements, 500–502
    political participation by, 690–694
    trolls and hacktivists, 419
    women and political power, 617–619
social network sites (SNSs), 451, 453
social practice theory (SPT), 220
social support, 293, 296, 300, 306, 451, 538–541, 558
sociotechnical media manipulation and disinformation, 591–592
solidarity and distance, 62–63
South Park (TV show), 164
speed theory, 9–10, 12–15
spiritual imagination, 160, 169
spiritual power of technology, 170
spiritual revolution, 162
spiritual seekers, 162, 171
Spotify, 481
Srnicek, Nick, 181
standard employment relationship, 178–179, 185
Starr, Paul, 121
status labor, 323
STEM framework, 104
stigmatization, 252, 386
Stone, Roger, 685
Stop Online Piracy Act, 670
"Stop the Steal" campaign, 684, 685, 694
storytelling online, 64–65, 447
Stout, Daniel, 163
stranger society, 372
Strategic Communications Centre of Excellence (NATO), 601
strategic internet skills, 551
Strava athletic tracking app, 209
streetlife
    background on urban poor, 444
    defined, 443
    digital inequality and, 444, 446–448, 458–459
    digitalization of, 445–446, 453

streetlife (*cont.*)
  emerging research on, 448–455
  future research directions, 457–459
  intersectionality and, 458
  introduction to, 443–444
  police violence and, 459
  research and ethics, 455–457
  technology access, 448–450
  technology outcomes, 453–455
  technology use, 450–452
structural dimension of data, 78
subjective well-being, 557, 558
subordinate masculinities, 530
Super Chick Sisters game, 693
Supplemental Security Income (SSI), 255
Support Small Businesses sticker, 475
surveillance-as-service, 224
surveillance capitalism, 129, 202
surveillant assemblage, 81, 327
swatting, defined, 422
symbolic capital, 364
symbolic dimension of data, 78
symbolic interactionism, 365, 447
systemic racism, 537, 575, 683

Taylor, Breonna, 684
Tea Party, 690, 691, 694
Teachers and Machines: The Classroom Use of Technology since 1920 (Cuban), 99–100
techno-cultural tropes, 170
techno-spirituality, 169, 170
technofeminism, 329
technological determinism, 9, 15, 17
technology use in schools, 3
technophiles, 169, 329
telephone history, 141–142
tempo of modernity, 10–12
temporal contours of family development, 32
temporary work in public sector, 179
text-based-only tools, 348, 569
thing-power, 208–209
3AM theory of sexual media socialization, 278–279
Thunberg, Greta, 624, 665
TikTok
  digital content producers on, 574
  everyday people on, 569
  fandom on, 400
  identity performance on, 44
  political messages on, 407
  popularity of, 199
  self-presentation on, 368
  social relations through, 31
time and technology
  boundaries of, 16–19
  contemporary speed theory, 12–15
  introduction to, 9–10
  optimisation culture, 19–21
  sociotechnical practice of, 15–16
  summary of, 21–22
  tempo of modernity, 10–12
Time magazine, 169, 570
time-management apps, 20–21
Time & Society, 21
timeless time, 9, 12, 14
Tinder, 145, 245, 253–254, 349–350
Todas Gamers, 387
Tönnies, Ferdinand, 119
toxic masculinity, 537
Toxics Link India, 500
traditional news outlets, 50
transglocalization, 520–521
transnational families, 139, 151
transparency activism, 651
Transparency International, 656
transphobia, 253, 341, 346, 592, 624
trolls and hacktivists
  Anonymous and, 420, 421, 425–429
  everyday racism and, 536
  4chan and, 3, 417, 420–425
  future research, 434–435
  Gamergate and, 384, 403, 418, 420–421, 429–432
  introduction to, 246, 417–418
  political mobilization online, 418–421
  US presidential election and, 432–434
Trump, Donald, 123, 251, 407, 420, 595, 684, 685, 691–692
Trump, Donald, Jr., 684
Tumblr, 44, 342, 344–345, 353, 404, 477
Turner, Hal, 424
Twitch, 44
Twitter. *See also* journalistic significance of Twitter

Anonymous use of, 427–428
anti-corruption hashtags, 649
application programming interface, 593
audience engagement on, 126
Black Americans, 571
code of the tweet, 452
dating apps and, 255
fandom on, 399, 400
Gamergate and, 430
gang activity on, 456
identity performance on, 44
media manipulation on, 594, 596
political messages on, 405, 407
protest tweets, 572
social relations through, 30, 31
US presidential elections and, 623

U4 Anti-Corruption Research Centre, 645
Uber, 183
underrepresented populations in dating apps, 251–256
undocumented migrants, 78, 674–675
United Kingdom's Brexit referendum, 129
United States Election Project, 684
Upwork, 184–185
urban poor, 443–444, 446–459
US Capitol riots (2021), 685
US Communications Decency Act (1996), 435
US Freedom of Information Act, 651
US presidential election (2004), 669
US presidential election (2012), 669
US presidential election (2016), 432–434, 669
US presidential election (2020), 623
usage gaps, 457
Usenet, 569, 572

Vandaele, Kurt, 187
video sharing, 368, 571
video streaming, 199, 201, 674
virtual class of entrepreneurs, 570
virtual meetings, 22
virtual reality (VR), 159, 170–171, 292, 305
visibility labor, 323, 478
visibility politics, 475, 476–478
vital materialism, 208, 209
volatile gamer, 387–390
vote-buying, 645

Wagner, Rachel, 166
Wajcman, Judy, 329
WallStreetBets, 434–435
Warren, Elizabeth, 618
Washington, Booker T., 103
Waste from Electrical and Electronic Equipment (WEEE), 503
We Are All Khaled Said in Egypt, 649
wearable technology
    introduction to, 3, 316–319
    privacy and surveillance concerns, 326–328
    quantified self (QS) movement, 319–322
    race and, 329–331
    women and, 328–329
    work and, 322–326
Web of Science database, 629
Weber, Max, 119, 159–160, 168, 170, 513
WebMD, 200
WeChat, 30, 347, 363, 367–371, 568
Weibo, 363, 367, 572
Welles, Brooke Foucault, 614–615
Wenglinsky, Harold, 100–101
Western civilization, 11
WhatsApp, 140, 187
White masculinity, 530, 531–533, 535–538
white propaganda, defined, 590
White supremacists/supremacy, 424, 493, 598, 670, 689
Whole Foods, 683
#WhyIStayed, 618
#WhyLoiter, 618
WikiLeaks, 428, 434
Wilson, Brian, 160
Wilson, Darren, 615
Winner, Langdon, 111
witness testimony in digital war, 518–519
wizard activist, 408
women and wearable technology, 328–329
women's use of digital publics as political spaces
    abuse and harassment, 619–621
    future research on, 629–630
    identity-based attacks, 619, 621–623, 625–628
    introduction to, 614–615
    social media power, 617–619
    tools used, 616–617
    women in politics, 623–625

women's work, 4, 17, 470, 471–473
work and wearable technology, 322–326
work changes and gig economy, 178–181
work-family boundaries, 16–19
work-related apps, 199
working mothers, 139
world folding, 234
World of Warcraft, 406–407
world-systems theory, 492–493

X-rated movies, 277
xenophobia, 433, 541
XNet, 656

Ye Zhang, 499
YouPorn.com, 274–275
youth deficit model, 665–666
youth disengagement concerns, 664–667
youth engagement in digital media politics
    concern over youth disengagement, 664–667
    elections and, 668–670
    introduction to, 663
    overview of, 666–667
    participatory politics, 673–674
    political consumerism and, 672
    political interest and knowledge, 667–668
    protests and, 670–672
    summary of, 674–675
    youth deficit model, 665–666
YouTube
    Anonymous use of, 427–428
    digital content producers on, 574
    fandom on, 399, 405
    gang activity on, 456
    popularity of, 199
    racism on, 477
    Reply Girls, 478–479
YR Media, 675

Zalishchuk, Svitlana, 624
ziji ren (in-group persons), 369
Zoom meetings, 22, 84, 138, 148, 203
Zuboff, Shoshana, 202
Zuckerberg, Mark, 48